Visit us at

www.syngress.com

Syngress is committed to publishing high-quality books for IT Professionals and delivering those books in media and formats that fit the demands of our customers. We are also committed to extending the utility of the book you purchase via additional materials available from our Web site.

SOLUTIONS WEB SITE

To register your book, visit www.syngress.com/solutions. Once registered, you can access our solutions@syngress.com Web pages. There you may find an assortment of valueadded features such as free e-books related to the topic of this book, URLs of related Web sites, FAQs from the book, corrections, and any updates from the author(s).

ULTIMATE CDs

Our Ultimate CD product line offers our readers budget-conscious compilations of some of our best-selling backlist titles in Adobe PDF form. These CDs are the perfect way to extend your reference library on key topics pertaining to your area of expertise, including Cisco Engineering, Microsoft Windows System Administration, CyberCrime Investigation, Open Source Security, and Firewall Configuration, to name a few.

DOWNLOADABLE E-BOOKS

For readers who can't wait for hard copy, we offer most of our titles in downloadable Adobe PDF form. These e-books are often available weeks before hard copies, and are priced affordably.

SYNGRESS OUTLET

Our outlet store at syngress.com features overstocked, out-of-print, or slightly hurt books at significant savings.

SITE LICENSING

Syngress has a well-established program for site licensing our e-books onto servers in corporations, educational institutions, and large organizations. Contact us at sales@syngress.com for more information.

CUSTOM PUBLISHING

Many organizations welcome the ability to combine parts of multiple Syngress books, as well as their own content, into a single volume for their own internal use. Contact us at sales@syngress.com for more information.

SYNGRESS®

The Best Damn Exchange, SQL and IIS Book Period

Conrad H. Agramont Jr.
Timothy Blum
Kevvie Fowler
Raymond Arthur Gabriel
Twan Grotenhuis

K. Brian Kelley
Matt Shepherd
Robert McLaws
Henrik Walther
Gene Whitley

KEY	SERIAL NUMBER
001	HJIRTCV764
002	PO9873D5FG
003	829KM8NJH2
004	BAL923457U
005	CVPLQ6WQ23
006	VBP965T5T5
007	HJJJ863WD3E
008	2987GVTWMK
009	629MP5SDJT
010	IMWQ295T6T

PUBLISHED BY
Syngress Publishing, Inc.
Elsevier, Inc.
30 Corporate Drive
Burlington, MA 01803

The Best Damn Exchange, SQL and IIS Book Period

Printed and bound by CPI Group (UK) Ltd, Croydon, CR0 4YY

ISBN 13: 978-1-59749-219-5

Publisher: Amorette Pedersen
Acquisitions Editor: Andrew Williams
Project Manager: Greg deZarn-O'Hare

Page Layout and Art: SPi
Copy Editor: Mike McGee, Darlene Bordwell,
    and Judy Eby

For information on rights, translations, and bulk sales, contact Matt Pedersen, Commercial Sales Director and Rights, at Syngress Publishing; email m.pedersen@elsevier.com.

Technical Editors

Rodney Buike (MCSE) is an IT Pro Advisor with Microsoft Canada. As an IT Pro Advisor, Rodney spends his day helping IT professionals in Canada with issues and challenges they face in their environment and careers. He also advocates for a stronger community presence and shares knowledge through blogging, podcasts, and in-person events.

Rodney's specialties include Exchange Server, virtualization, and core infrastructure technologies on the Windows platform. Rodney worked as a LAN administrator, system engineer, and consultant and has acted as a reviewer on many popular technical books. Rodney is also the founder and principal content provider for Thelazyadmin.com and a former author for MSExchange.org.

Rodney enjoys all his personal and professional activities and is up-front about the support he gets from his family and especially his wife, Lisa. Without her support, what he does would not be possible.

Kirk Vigil (MCSE, MCSA), coauthor of *MCSA/MSCE Exam 70-291: Implementing, Managing, and Maintaining a Windows Server 2003 Network Infrastructure* and How *to Cheat at Managing Windows Server Update Services* is a senior systems consultant for NetBank, Inc. in Columbia, SC. He has worked in the IT integration industry for over 13 years, specializing in Microsoft messaging and network operating system infrastructures. He has worked with Microsoft Exchange since its inception and continues to focus on its advancements with the current release of Exchange 2007 as well as its integration with the Windows Server line of products.

Kirk holds a bachelor's degree from the University of South Carolina. He also works as an independent consultant for a privately owned integration company, lending technical direction to local business practices. He is a contributing author to *Microsoft Certified Professional Magazine*. Kirk would first like to thank God, for without Him nothing is possible. Kirk would also like to thank his beautiful girlfriend, Kimberley Paige, for her continued and loving support as Kirk's takes on more "bookwork" as she likes to call it. She is irreplaceable and loved very much. Kirk thanks his family for their unconditional love and support. Lastly, Kirk is grateful to the owners, editors, and writers of Syngress/Elsevier Publishing for the opportunity to continue working with them as a technical writer/editor.

Robert J. Shimonski (MCSE) is an Entrepreneur and best-selling author and editor of hundreds of published books and thousands of magazine and industry articles. Rob consults within today's most challenging business and technology environments and brings frontline industry knowledge to the reader in every page he writes. Rob is always on top of the latest trends and reporting the state of the business and technology industry from a real-world perspective. As of the writing of this book, Rob is currently on assignment testing and developing secure Vista images and designing a Longhorn upgrade for a large global firm.

Mark Horninger (A+, Net+, Security+, MCSE+I, MCSD, MCAD, MCDBA, MCTS, MCITP, MCPD) is president and founder of Haverford Consultants Inc. (www.haverford-consultants.com), located in the suburbs of Philadelphia, PA. He develops custom applications and system engineering solutions, specializing primarily in Microsoft .Net Technology and Microsoft SQL Server. He was a contributing author to *Configuring and Troubleshooting Windows XP Professional; MCSA/MCSE Exam 70-292 Study Guide & DVD Training System: Managing and Maintaining a Windows Server 2003 Environment for an MCSA Certified on Windows 2000; and Designing SQL Server 2000 Databases for .NET Enterprise Servers*, all of which were published by Syngress, an imprint of Elsevier Inc. Mark is also an adjunct professor teaching Web design at Kaplan University.

Mark has over 15 years of computer consulting experience and has passed 50+ Microsoft Certification Exams.

He lives with his wife, Debbie, and son, Robby, in the Philadelphia area. Mark would like to thank his wife, Debbie, for her infinite patience, love, and support during this project.

Chris Adams is a Program Manager for Microsoft Corp. Focused heavily on "customer experience," Chris spends his time working closely with customers to ensure that their voices are heard for current and shipped products. He spends most of his time focusing on building and reviewing technical content for IIS, working with IIS most valuable professionals (MVPs), and spearheading new and exciting programs to best reach customers for the IIS team. Chris has owned such things as www.iis.net, the IIS Webcast Series, and the IIS Diagnostics Tools releases while at Microsoft. Chris was formally a Microsoft Product Support Services (PSS) engineer, technical lead, and supportability lead for the IIS product and has deep technical experience in the use and functionality of IIS 4.0, 5.0, 5.1, 6.0, and 7.0. Chris is currently Microsoft certified as an MCP, MCSA, and MCSE.

Contributing Authors

Conrad H. Agramont Jr. is a Partner Technology Specialist with Microsoft, where he focuses on technical readiness for Microsoft Infrastructure Partners focusing on the small to midmarket enterprises. Conrad was previously the Senior Architect for a Microsoft Gold Partner, where he was responsible for product planning, software architecture, and technical evangelism, focusing on service providers worldwide. He was also a Program Manager at Microsoft, driving hosting scenarios and architecting components for the Microsoft Provisioning System, Microsoft Solutions for Hosted Messaging and Collaboration, and Windows-Based Hosting 3.0. Conrad has more than 10 years of experience working in the Microsoft automation and hosting space, speaking at public events, and publishing articles in magazines. He is also an active blogger, focusing on many Microsoft-related topics. His blog can be found at http://agramont.net/

Timothy Blum (MCDBA, MCTS, MCITP) is the senior database administrator at HighPoint Solutions, LLC, which provides business and technology solutions to the pharmaceutical and life sciences industry. He currently provides senior-level strategic and technical consulting to HighPoint Solutions' clients in the northeast region of the U.S. His specialties include Microsoft SQL Server design and implementation, Integration Services, Data Transformation Services, Analysis Services, business intelligence architecture and design, and database tuning. During his 15 years working in the IT industry, Timothy has held positions as a senior SQL Server database administrator, PICK database administrator, Oracle database developer, and a C++, VB, ASP, and UNIX Business Basic programmer for companies such as CEI Network, DDS Ltd, and ECC Management Services.

Kevvie Fowler is the manager of managed security services at Emergis Inc., where he is responsible for the delivery of specialized security and incident response services. Kevvie has more than 10 years of professional information security and IT experience within development, database, and host/network platforms. In 2007, Kevvie was a featured presenter at the Black Hat USA security conference, where he presented his ground-breaking research on SQL Server database forensics. Kevvie is a GIAC Gold Certified Forensic Analyst, and he holds several other certifications, including CISSP, MCTS, MCSD, MCDBA, and MCSE.

Raymond Arthur Gabriel (MCSD, MCAD, MCSD .Net) formed a consulting practice, Integrated MicroSystems Design Corp. (www.imicrodev. net), in 1989 to provide technical consulting services as an application architect and solution developer. He has 20 years of experience in IT, including full life-cycle experience with multitier Windows and Web application development.

Raymond holds an associate's degree in electronic engineering from the Cleveland Institute of Electronics and is a member of the IEEE. He currently resides in Chester County, PA, with his wife, Sharon, whose support is an eternal source of great encouragement.

Twan Grotenhuis (MCT, MCSE NT4, 2000 and 2003, MCSE+messaging 2000 and 2003, MCSE+security 2000 and 2003, CCNA) is a consultant with Sylis Netherlands. He currently provides strategic and technical consulting to several customers of Sylis in the Netherlands. His specialties include Microsoft Exchange and ISA architecture, design, implementation, troubleshooting, and optimization. Twan has been involved in several major Exchange implementation and migration projects where designing the new messaging infrastructure was his main focus.

K. Brian Kelley (MCSE, GSEC, Security+) is a systems architect for AgFirst Farm Credit Bank. At AgFirst he provides infrastructure and security guidance with respect to Windows-based technologies, including Active Directory, Internet Information Server, and Microsoft SQL Server. Brian, author of *Start to Finish Guide to SQL Server Performance Monitoring*, is a regular columnist and blogger at SQLServerCentral.com, where he focuses primarily on SQL Server security. He is also a frequent contributor to *SQL Server Standard Magazine*. Brian's background includes stints with BellSouth as a systems administrator and with the United States Air Force as a communications/computer systems officer in a multitude of IT-related roles.

Brian holds bachelor's degrees from The Citadel, the Military College of South Carolina, and is a member of the Professional Association of SQL Server (PASS), the SQL Server Worldwide Users Group, the Information Systems Audit and Control Association (ISACA), and the Association for Computing Machinery. He is also active in the Midlands PASS chapter, an official PASS chapter for South Carolina. Brian currently resides in Columbia, SC, with his family.

Matt Shepherd (CISSP, MCSE, MCDBA, GCFW, CEH) is a consultant in the Security and Privacy Division at Project Performance Corporation of McLean, VA. Matt uses his experience as a network administrator, IT manager, and security architect to deliver high-quality solutions for Project Performance Corporation's clients in the public and private sector. Matt holds bachelor's degrees from St. Mary's College of Maryland, and he is currently working on his master's of science in information assurance.

Robert McLaws is a technology writer from Mesa, AZ. He currently resides in northern Phoenix, where he works as a contract software consultant. He started a Web site called LonghornBlogs.com in October 2003. The site, now called Windows-Now (www.windows-now.com/default.aspx), has received several awards, including *PC Magazine's* Top 100 Sites of 2004 and CMP Media's Top 10 Tech Blogs of 2005.

Henrik Walther (Exchange MVP, MCSE Messaging/Security) is a senior consultant working for Interprise Consulting A/S (a Microsoft Gold Partner) based in Copenhagen, Denmark. Henrik has more than 14 years of experience in the IT business, where he primarily works with Microsoft Exchange, ISA Server, MOM, IIS, clustering, Active Directory, and virtual server technologies.

In addition to his job as a senior consultant, Henrik runs the Danish Web site Exchange-faq.dk. He is also the primary content creator, forums moderator, and newsletter editor at the leading Microsoft Exchange site, MSExchange.org. Henrik is the author of *CYA: Securing Exchange Server 2003 & Outlook Web Access* (Syngress Publishing), and he has been a reviewer on several other messaging books (including another Exchange 2007 book).

Gene Whitley (MBA, MCSE, MCSA) is the President of SiGR Solutions (www.sigrsolutions.com), a systems integrator and value-added reseller in Charlotte, NC. He entered into the systems integration and value-added reseller industry in 1995, and in 2005, he started his own company, SiGR Solutions, which provides services and product procurement for businesses of all sizes, including Fortune 1000 companies.

Gene started his IT career in 1992 with Microsoft, earning his MCP in 1993 and MCSE in 1994. He has been the lead consultant and project manager on numerous Active Directory and Exchange migration projects for companies throughout the U.S. When not working, he spends his time with his wife and best friend, Samantha. Gene holds an MBA from Winthrop University and a BSBA in Management Information Systems from the University of North Carolina at Charlotte.

Contents

Chapter 1

Introducing Exchange Server 2007

Solutions in this chapter:

- What Is Exchange Server 2007?
- Exchange 2007 Themes
- Architectural Goals with Exchange Server 2007
- Role-based Deployment and Server Roles
- New Management Approach
- High Availability (HA) Improvements
- Exchange Server 2007 Services
- Exchange Server Permissions
- 64-Bit Support Only
- Active Directory-based Routing Topology
- De-emphasized Features
- Discontinued Features

☑ Summary

Introduction

This chapter gives a basic understanding of what Exchange Server 2007 is as well as an overview of the new features and improvements included in the product. Exchange Server 2007 now uses a role-based approach, which makes it much simpler to deploy different server roles to match the topology of your organization. In addition, Exchange Server 2007 has moved to being a true 64-bit application. Exchange Server 2007 also takes advantage of Windows PowerShell, making it possible to do complex tasks in a simple and automated way using scripts. Most complicated tasks that used to consist of several hundred lines of code can now typically be done with one line of code using the EMS.

Finally, this chapter lists the features that have been de-emphasized and discontinued in this version of Exchange Server 2007.

What Is Exchange Server 2007?

Exchange Server 2007 is Microsoft's new version of the industry's leading server software for e-mail, calendaring, and unified messaging. Exchange Server 2007 is considered the biggest upgrade in the history of the Exchange Product group. It has been totally reengineered, and most of the code has been completely rewritten. In addition, Exchange Server 2007 is the first released Microsoft product to take advantage of the new Windows PowerShell (formerly known as Monad) called the EMS. The "2007" indicates the close alignment of this release with the Microsoft Office 2007 wave of products, which together deliver a best-in-class enterprise messaging and collaboration solution.

Exchange 2007 Themes

In 2003, the Exchange Product group came up with three Exchange themes aimed at reflecting the different types of Exchange situations. Since their introduction, the themes have stayed constant, having played an important role during the development of Exchange Server 2007. Following is an overview of all three themes.

IT Pro Situation

The *IT Pro Situation* theme focuses on making sure that Information Technology (IT) professionals get what they need. The Exchange product team knows that e-mail is mission-critical, and that without it, there will be a loss of productivity and revenue. They also know that current systems are too complex and expensive, and that many of the day-to-day tasks would be better suited to scripted automation rather than tedious manual configuration. With Exchange Server 2007, the Exchange product team was able to give us this control.

Info Worker Situation

The *Info Worker Situation* theme focuses on availability. IT professionals need access to e-mail, voicemail, and faxes. Today, people are mobile and require access to all kinds of messaging data. With Exchange Server 2007, the Exchange Product team can make things easier for IT professionals.

Organizationwide Situation

The *Organizationwide Situation* theme focuses on security and control throughout the organization's messaging environment. Today, e-mail needs to be secure. Filtering out spam and removing viruses in order to provide a clean message stream needs to be a core design goal for any messaging system. The Exchange Product group began their road to e-mail security using Exchange Server 2003 Service Pack 2, which greatly improved overall security by introducing Sender ID filtering and version 2 of the SmartScreen-based Intelligent Message Filter (IMF). With Exchange Server 2007, security has improved. Another requirement is that the messaging environment conform to legal and corporate-wide policies, requiring us to journal, archive, and search through large amounts of messages. Luckily, these requirements have also been improved upon and have been added to Exchange Server 2007.

Architectural Goals with Exchange Server 2007

When the Exchange Product group developed Exchange Server 2007 they had four main architectural goals:

- **Simplicity**   Deliver a product with a simple and intuitive user interface
- **Flexibility**   Make the product flexible, especially regarding deployment and management
- **Trustworthiness**   Secure all communication by default (OWA uses secure sockets layer [SSL], Hub Transport Server uses Transport Layer Security [TLS], and so forth)

Scalability

Scalability is achievable by using 64-bit code (reduced input/output [I/O], more data in address space, and so forth). The Exchange Server 2007 Product group delivered these goals. Many are of the opinion that too many management tasks must be accomplished by running the respective *cmdlets* in the EMS. Many of the management tasks missing from the Exchange Management Console (EMC) user interface will be added into the release of Exchange Server 2007 Service Pack 1.

Role-Based Deployment and Server Roles

Unlike previous versions of Exchange, Exchange Server 2007 is easy to deploy. Although you could dedicate an Exchange 2000 or 2003 server as either a front-end, back-end, or bridgehead server, you always had to install all of the Exchange binaries and services even if they were not required. Although it was possible to disable some of the Exchange Services that weren't required, this monolithic approach forced you to use valuable resources, disk space and/or Exchange components you didn't necessarily need to install.

This has all changed with Exchange Server 2007, which has a great new role-based setup wizard, allowing you the ability to deploy individual server roles (see Figure 1.1).

Figure 1.1 Exchange Server 2007 Setup Wizard

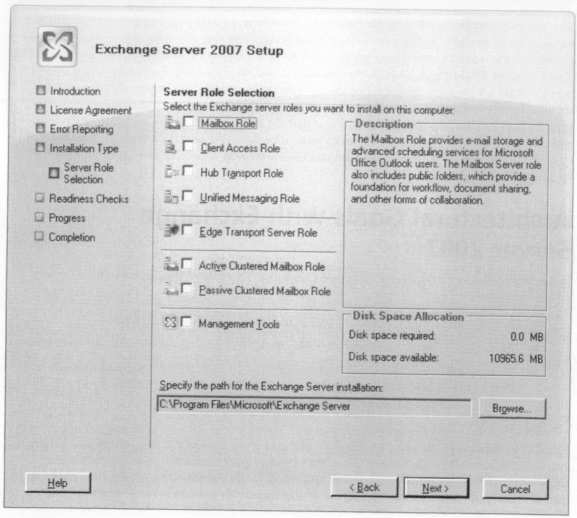

Based on the new server role-based approach, you can now select what server role(s) you want to install on a given server, thus deploying Exchange Server 2007 in a more flexible way. Exchange Server 2007 provides five distinct server roles that include specific features and functionality, thereby providing the messaging functionality you want.

NOTE

A server role is a unit that logically groups the required features and components that are required to perform a specific function in your messaging environment.

The server roles are as follows: Client Access Server, Hub Transport, Mailbox, Unified Messaging, and Edge Transport. All server roles except the Edge Transport server can be installed on the same physical server (typical scenario for a small organization), or distributed across multiple servers (typical for large organizations). It depends on your organizational requirements and sometimes on your budget.

The following sections give a short overview of each server role included in Exchange Server 2007.

Mailbox Server Role

The Exchange 2007 *Mailbox Server role* hosts mailbox databases where user and resource mailboxes are stored. This server role hosts the Public Folder database, used by organizations for the sharing of documents, calendar, contact, and task data, as well as for archiving distribution lists. As you will see in chapter 3, a legacy Outlook client (that is Outlook 2003 and earlier) requires a public folder database in order to connect to Exchange Server 2007.

In addition to hosting mailbox and public folder databases, the Mailbox Server also provides rich calendaring functionality, resource management, and offline address book downloads. The Mailbox Server role also provides services that calculate e-mail address policies (called recipient policies in Exchange Server 2000 and 2003) as well as address lists for recipients. Lastly, this server role enforces managed folders.

The Exchange Product group also improved the high availability (HA) and recovery features for the mailbox Server. Exchange Server 2007 includes a new continuous replication mechanism that can be used with both non-clustered and clustered mailbox Servers. Using Structured Query Language (SQL) technology, the new continuous replication feature uses log file shipping. Log file replay makes it possible to replicate any changes done in the active databases to a passive copy. When speaking about non-clustered mailbox Servers, this feature is more specifically known as Local Continuous Replication (LCR), making it possible to switch to the passive copy of the database using a manual switch. The continuous replication feature combined with Windows clustering is known as Cluster Continuous Replication (CCR) and provides automatic failover to the passive database should the active database fail or shutdown unexpectedly.

Client Access Server Role

The *Client Access Server (CAS) role* replaces the front-end. This means that the CAS provides mailbox access for all types of Exchange clients, with the exception of Outlook MAPI clients. In a nutshell, the CAS accepts clients accessing their mailbox using Post Office Protocol version 3 (POP3), Internet Messaging Access Protocol 4 (IMAP4), Outlook AnyWhere (formerly known as Remote Procedure Call [RPC over HTTP], Outlook Web Access (OWA) and Exchange ActiveSync (EAS).

> **NOTE**
>
> The Outlook Mobile Access (OMA component is no longer a part of the Exchange Server product.

In addition to providing client access, the CAS is also responsible for providing access to the Offline Address Book (if using a Web-based distribution method), the Autodiscover service, and the Availability service.

The Availability service is a new Web-based service providing access to the Offline Address Book (OAB) and free information (housed in a public folder). In addition, Out Of Office (OOF) messages and several Unified Messaging features such as Play on phone are accessed using this service.

The Autodiscover service makes is easier to configure Outlook 2007 and Exchange ActiveSync clients, as end users only need to provide their e-mail address and password in order to configure an Outlook or EAS profile. If Outlook 2007 is configured on a workstation part of the Active Directory domain, you don't need to provide any information; instead you simply click **Next** a couple of times and the Outlook profile is created, using the cached credentials of the current logged on user. (For more information about the Client Access Server role, see Chapter 5).

Hub Transport Server Role

The *Hub Transport Server* role is deployed inside your organization's Active Directory. This server role handles all internal mail flow and is also responsible for applying transport rules as well as journaling policies to the respective messages flowing through your organization. In addition, the Hub Transport Server delivers messages to the recipient mailboxes stored on the Mailbox Server. Messages sent from one user to another user that have their respective mailboxes stored on the same Mailbox server, use the Hub Transport Server in order to deliver a message. This means that a Hub Transport Server must be deployed in each Active Directory site that contains a Mailbox Server.

NOTE

Message routing in Exchange Server 2007 is no longer based on Exchange routing groups and routing groups are no longer part of the Exchange product. Instead, Exchange Server 2007 uses your Active Directory site topology.

A Hub Transport Server is typically only used for internal mail flow; however, this depends on whether you have deployed an Edge Transport server as the Internet-facing Simple Mail Transfer Protocol (SMTP) server in your demilitarized zone (DMZ). If you use an Edge Transport Server, all inbound and outbound e-mail will pass through the Edge Transport Server. If you don't want to deploy an Edge Transport Server, you can let the Hub Transport Server act as the Internet-facing SMTP server in your organization, although this isn't recommended. (For more information about the Hub Transport Server role, see Chapter 6).

Unified Messaging Server Role

The *Unified Messaging Server role* is new to the Exchange product line. This server role combines voice messaging, fax, and e-mail into one single unified inbox, making it possible to access all of this information from a host of client solutions: Outlook 2007, Outlook Web Access 2007, Windows Mobile 5.0, and so forth.

Unified Messaging gives your end-users features like the following:

Auto Attendant

An *auto attendant* is a set of voice prompts that gives external users access to the Exchange 2007 Unified Messaging system. An auto attendant lets the user use either the telephone keypad or speech inputs to navigate the menu structure, place a call to a user, or locate a user and then place a call to that user. An auto attendant gives the administrator the ability to:

- Create a customizable set of menus for external users.

- Define informational greetings, business hours greetings, and non-business hours greetings.

- Define holiday schedules.

- Describe how to search the organization's directory.

- Describe how to connect to a user's extension so external callers can call a user by specifying their extension.

- Describe how to search the organization's directory so external callers can search the organization's directory and call a specific user.

- Enable external users to call the operator.

Call Answering

Call answering includes answering an incoming call on behalf of a user, playing their personal greeting, recording a message, and submitting it for delivery to their inbox as an e-mail message.

Fax Receiving

Fax receiving is the process of submitting a fax message for delivery to the Inbox.

Subscriber Access

The subscriber access feature enables dial-in access for company users. Company users or subscribers who are dialing into the Unified Messaging system can access their mailbox using Outlook Voice Access. Subscribers who use Outlook Voice Access can access the Unified Messaging system by using the telephone keypad or voice inputs. By using a telephone, a subscriber or user can:

- Access voicemail.

- Listen, forward, or reply to e-mail messages.

- Listen to calendar information.

- Access or dial contacts stored in the global address list or a personal contact list.

- Accept or cancel meeting requests.

- Set a voicemail Out-of-Office message.

- Set user security preferences and personal options.

The Unified Messaging Server role integrates Exchange Server 2007 with your organization's existing telephony network and brings the features found in Unified Messaging to the core of the Exchange Server product line. (For more information about the new Unified Messaging role, see Chapter 11).

Edge Transport Server Role

The Exchange Product Group developed the Edge Transport Server to give enterprises powerful out-of-the-box protection against spam without needing to invest in a third-party solution. The messaging hygiene features in the *Edge Transport Server role* are agent-based and consist of multiple filters that are frequently updated.

Although the primary role of the Edge Transport Server is to route mail and perform message hygiene, it also includes features that allow you to rewrite SMTP addresses, configure transport rules, enable journaling, and associate company disclaimers.

The Edge Transport Server can also be used to set up a business-to-business domain security relationship, thereby reducing management overhead that might otherwise be required to provide domain security between two business partners. Domain security enables message-level encryption and digital signatures, and ad hoc business-to-business and partner-to-partner message security.

The Edge Transport Server uses Active Directory Application Mode (ADAM) to store the required Active Directory data, including Accepted Domains, Recipients, Safe Senders, Send Connectors, and a Hub Transport Server list (used to generate dynamic connectors so that they don't have to be created manually). The Active Directory data is replicated to the Edge Transport Server using an EdgeSync service that runs on the Hub Transport Server on the internal network. Since the EdgeSync service uses Lightweight Directory Access Protocol (LDAP) for replication, you only need to open two additional ports (besides port 25 used for SMTP) for Edge Server to internal Hub Transport Server communication (default ports 50389 and 50636, respectively). (For more information about the Edge Transport Server role, see Chapter 7).

New Management Approach

Exchange Server 2007 will make your job as Exchange administrators much easier and more effective than in previous versions of Exchange.

EMC Console

The Exchange Management Console (EMC) is one of the most notable additions to Exchange Server 2007. The EMC is a complete rewrite of the Exchange System Manager user interface navigation tree. The Exchange Product group needed to organize the eight levels of tree navigation in Exchange Server 2003, so they developed the console with the goal of making it simple, intuitive, and more organized, using less nesting in hopes of reducing the learning curve, and effectively organizing all actions while maintaining strict consistency. In order to accomplish this goal, the Exchange Product group developed a new graphical user interface (GUI) using MMC 3.0, and divided the EMC into four different work areas: *Console* tree, *Work* pane, *Result* pane, and *Action* pane (see Figure 1.2). In addition, the Console tree is divided into four different work centers, making navigation much easier. Lastly, the entire console is built on top of the Windows PowerShell, making all user interface commands visible in shell *cmdlets* for noting and future scripting.

Figure 1.2 Exchange Server 2007 Work Centers

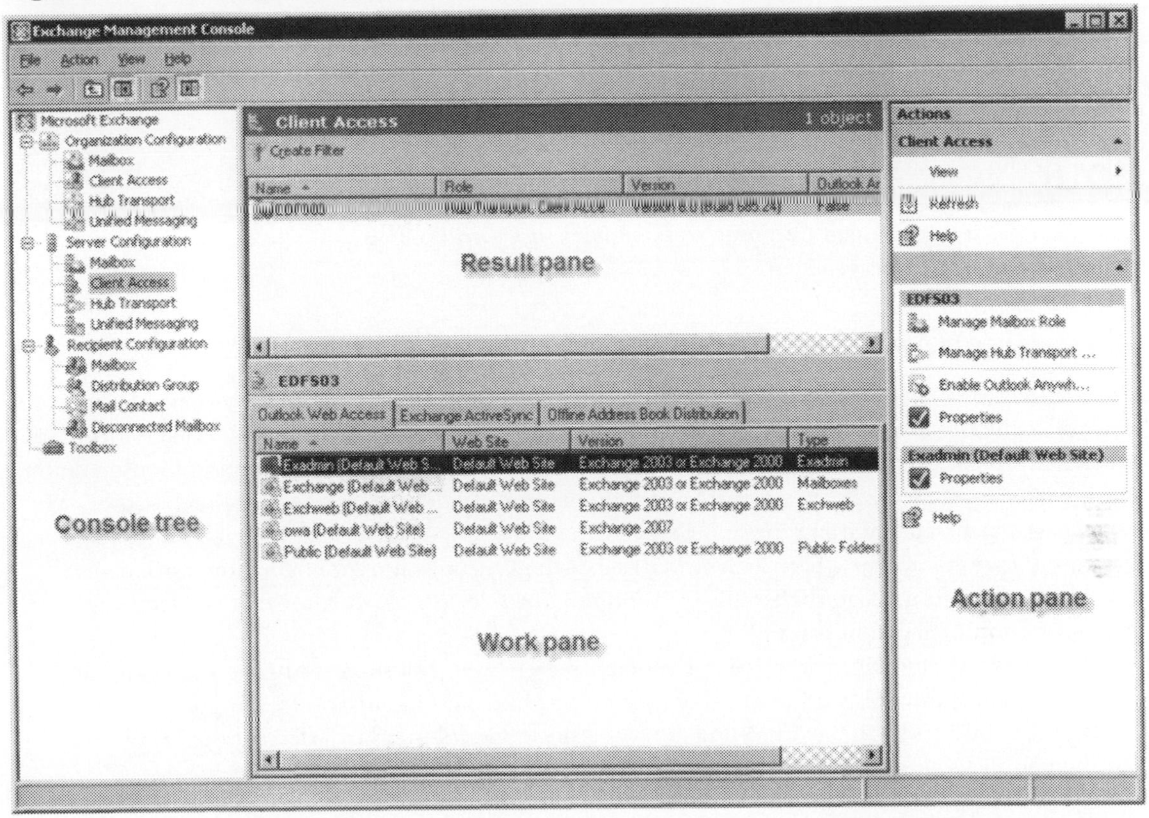

The following are short descriptions of each of the work panes available in the Exchange 2007 Management Console.

Console Tree

The purpose of the *Console tree* (located on the left side of the EMC) is to organize nodes based on the types of server roles that have been deployed in the Exchange Server 2007 organization.

Work Pane

The *Work* pane (located on the bottom of the EMC) is designed to display objects based on the server role subnode selected beneath the Server Configuration work center.

Result Pane

The *Result* pane (located on the top of the EMC) contains various configuration tabs that display the different objects available based on the selected work center node or subnode in the Console tree.

Action Pane

The *Action* pane (located on the right side of the EMC) lists the various actions that are available for a selected object. The Action pane is an MMC 3.0 feature that can be hidden if you want to use context menus (i.e., right-click menus).

Four New Work Centers

The Console tree is divided into four work centers, that directly map the type of data you need to manage in your organization.

Organization Configuration Work Station

The *Organization Configuration* work center contains any global or systemwide configuration data and settings in the organization. This is where you find features such as E-mail Address Policies (formerly Recipient Policies), Address Lists, Accepted Domains, and so forth). The Organization Configuration work center is categorized by server role, as configuration data can be both *server-level* based or *organizationally* based. By using this approach, it's easy for the Exchange Administrator to discover the configuration data for a particular server role. If the Organization Configuration work center is selected, you can manage the Exchange Administrator roles (formerly known as the Exchange Administration Delegation Wizard).

The *Server Configuration* work center contains server-level data such as Storage Group, Mailbox databases, client protocols, and receive connectors. Just like the Organization Configuration work center, the subnodes in this work center are based on server roles. When selecting the Server Configuration work center node, you get an overview of the Exchange 2007 Servers in your Exchange organization, where you can see the server name, the build version, and which server roles are installed on each Exchange server.

The *Recipient Configuration* work center node is used for recipient management. Here is where you see various recipient type nodes such as mailboxes, distribution groups, mail contacts, and disconnected mailboxes.

NOTE

With Exchange Server 2007, mail-enabled objects are no longer managed via the Active Directory Users and Computers snap-in; instead, they have to be managed via the EMC or the Exchange Management Shell (EMS) (See Chapter 3.)

The *Toolbox* work center can be considered a central repository for different Exchange tools that will help you diagnose and troubleshoot Exchange-related issues, in addition to giving you best practice recommendations in terms of properly configuring and optimizing the servers in your organization. As shown in Figure 1.3, tools such as the Best Practices Analyzer, Database

Recovery Management, Database Troubleshooter, Mail Flow Troubleshooter, and a Performance Troubleshooter can be found here. In addition, the Toolbox center is also the place to track messages using the Message Tracking Queue Viewer, and to track performance using the Performance Monitor.

Figure 1.3 Exchange Toolbox Work Center

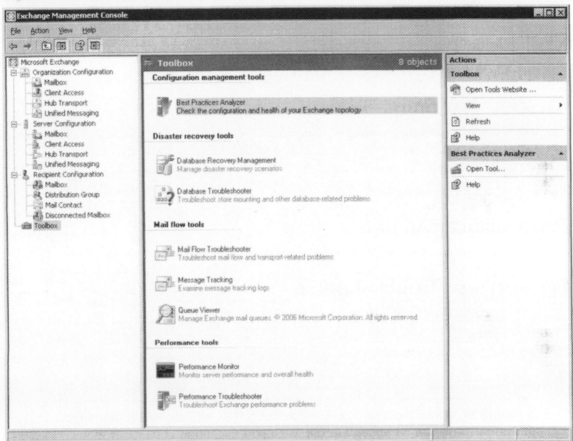

The following sections are short descriptions of each administrator tool available in the Toolbox work center.

Exchange Server Best Practices Analyzer

The Exchange Server Best Practices Analyzer (ExBPA) is a tool that is used for checking the configuration and health of the Exchange server topology. Every time you run the tool it checks for updated eXtensible Markup Language (XML) files as best practices for Exchange Server are reviewed and updated.

Database Recovery Management

This tool is used to manage disaster recovery scenarios. It can help reduce recovery time and streamline the recovery process after database problems occuur on production servers running Microsoft Exchange Server.

Database Troubleshooter

This tool is used to help troubleshoot store mounting and other database-related problems.

Mail Flow Troubleshooter

This tool is used for troubleshooting mail flow and transport-related problems.

Message Tracking

This tool is used for examining message tracking logs.

Queue Viewer

This tool is used for managing Exchange mail queues.

Performance Monitor

This tool is used for monitoring server performance and overall health.

Performance Troubleshooter

This tool is used for troubleshooting server performance problems.

NOTE

A cool thing about the Toolbox work center is that it's extensible; meaning additional tools can be added via the Microsoft Exchange Eeb site. It would have been cooler if 3rd party tools could have been added to the Toolbox center as well, but unfortunately it's limited to Microsoft's own Exchange tools.

New Wizards

The Exchange Product Group also included some new wizards in an effort to get rid of the older Exchange System Manager internally (see Figure 1.4).

Figure 1.4 Exchange 2007 Wizard

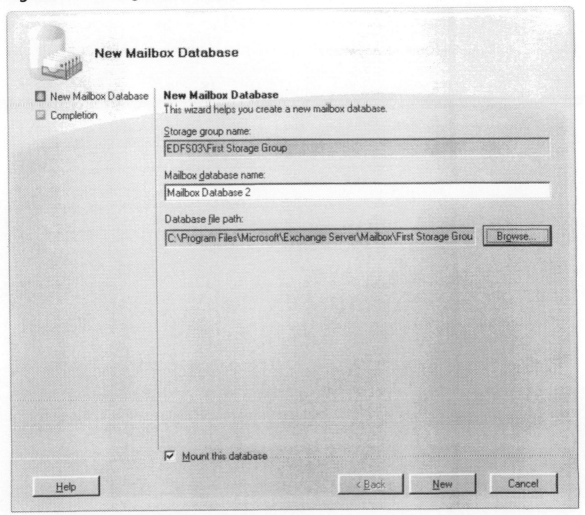

Exposed *CMDlet* Code

The EMC is built on top of the Windows PowerShell engine (formerly known as Monad), which ultimately means that the GUI wizards are just executing shell *cmdlets* in the background. Each executed wizard task in the user interface exposes the actual *cmdlet* code when the wizard has completed (see Figure 1.5). The cool thing about this is the fact that you can copy the exposed code to your computers clipboard, paste it to a text editor such as Notepad, edit it, and save it as a PS1script and/or paste it direct into the EMS to execute immediately.

Figure 1.5 Exposed *CMDlet* Code

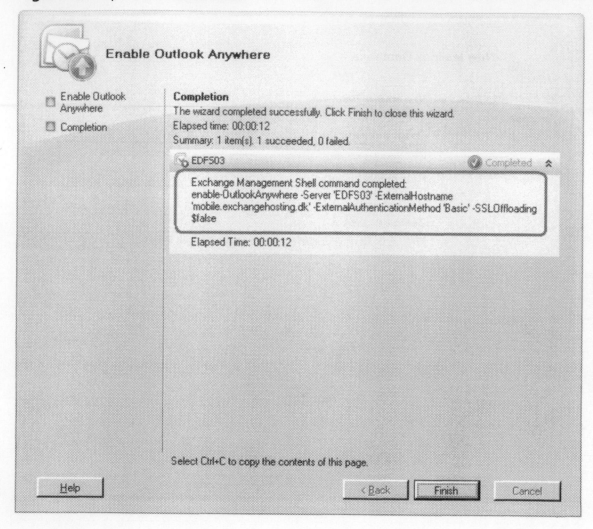

Here is the *cmdlet*, including the necessary parameters for enabling Outlook Anywhere:

```
enable-OutlookAnywhere –Server:'EDFS03' –ExternalHostname:'mobile.exchangehosting.dk' –
ExternalAuthenticationMethods:'Basic' –SSLOffloading:'$false'
```

EMS

The Exchange Product Group included an EMS (see Figure 1.6) in order to make the Exchange Administrator's job easier. The new EMS is based on Windows PowerShell (formerly known as Monad). By using this new shell you can accomplish all of the tasks available in the EMC. The shell is there to make it easier to do bulk and/or repetitive administrative tasks.

Figure 1.6 EMS

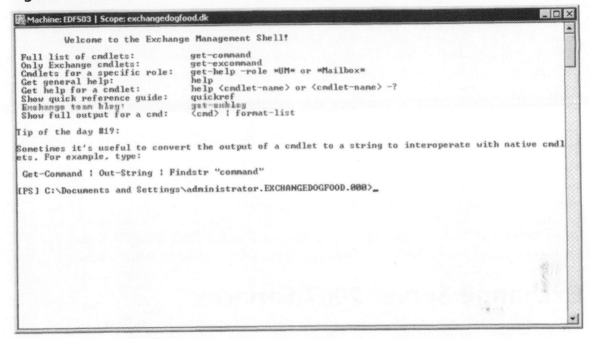

Tip

To get up to speed with the new EMS, I recommend you study the following two Microsoft PDF files, which give you a pretty good primer on use and functionality:
Introduction to the Exchange Management Shell: www.microsoft.com/downloads/details.aspx?familyid=1dc0f61b-d30f-44a2-882e-12ddd4ee09d2&displaylang=en
Exchange Management Shell Quick Reference: www.microsoft.com/downloads/details.aspx?familyid=01A441B9-4099-4C0F-B8E0-0831D4A2CA86&displaylang=en

HA Improvements

The availability requirements for messaging and collaboration servers have increased drastically over the years, catapulting these servers to be amongst the most mission-critical servers in the datacenter. Several recent reports have concluded that e-mail is more important to end users than their phones. So, it's in your best interest as the Exchange Administrator to achieve as high an uptime as possible. Each of these facts played an important role when the Exchange Product Group developed Exchange Server 2007, so it should come as no surprise that HA and disaster recovery was of utmost concern, and the reason behind the many improvements and new functionality in the Exchange Server 2007 product. Most especially is the new continuous replication functionality, which uses log file shipping and replay to keep a second copy of a Mailbox database in sync with the production database.

LCR

LCR is a solution that uses the new continuous replication technology introduced in Exchange Server 2007. LCR is a new functionality that uses built-in asynchronous log shipping and log replay technology to create and maintain a replica of a storage group on a second set of disks that are connected to the same server as the production storage group. The interesting thing about LCR is that it only requires one Exchange Server 2007 with the Mailbox Server role installed. However, it does require that there only be one viable database in each storage group.

CCR

The most interesting new feature when it comes to HA is the CCR solution, which, like LCR, uses the new Exchange Server 2007 continuous replication technology. CCR is a clustered solution that eliminates the single point of failure that exists in traditional Exchange cluster setups. This is done by maintaining a copy of the database on the active node; in the event of a database corruption, this allows both services and databases to fail over to the passive node. CCR can only be deployed in a two-node active/passive cluster. (LCR and CCR are covered in more detail in Chapter 8).

Exchange Server 2007 Services

The services used by the different Exchange Server 2007 roles are either completely new services or services that have changed since Exchange 2003. Table 1.1 lists each of the Exchange Server 2007 services along with a short description.

Table 1.1 Exchange Server 2007 Services

Service	Description
Exchange Active Directory Topology Service	This service provides Active Directory topology information to Exchange services. If this service is stopped, most Exchange services cannot start.
Microsoft Exchange ADAM	This service provides the ADAM directory service function to the Edge Transport Server.
Microsoft Exchange Credential Service	This service manages the credentials that the Hub Transport Server uses to authenticate to ADAM for a subscribed Edge Transport Server.
Microsoft Exchange EdgeSync	This service provides data replication and synchronization between Active Directory and ADAM for a subscribed Edge Transport Server.
Microsoft Exchange File Distribution	This service provides file distribution services.
Microsoft Exchange IMAP4	This service provides IMAP4 services to clients. If this service is stopped, clients cannot connect to the computer using the IMAP4 protocol.

Table 1.1 Continued

Service	Description
Microsoft Exchange Information Store	The Microsoft Exchange Information Store service manages the Microsoft Exchange Information Store. This includes mailbox stores and public folder stores. If this service is stopped, mailbox stores and public folder stores on this computer are unavailable. If this service is disabled, any services that explicitly depend on it will not start.
Microsoft Exchange Mailbox Assistants	This service performs background processing of mailboxes in the Exchange store.
Microsoft Exchange Mail Submission Service	This service submits messages from the Mailbox server to the Hub Transport Servers.
Microsoft Exchange Monitoring	Microsoft Exchange Monitoring enables applications to call the Exchange diagnostic *cmdlets*.
Microsoft Exchange POP3	This service provides POP3 services to clients. If this service is stopped, clients cannot connect to this computer using the POP3 protocol.
Microsoft Exchange Replication Service	The Microsoft Exchange Replication Service provides replication functionality used by Local Continuous Backup (Replication) and CCR.
Microsoft Exchange Search Indexer	Microsoft Exchange Search Indexer drives indexing of mailbox content. This improves the performance of the content search.
Microsoft Exchange Service Host	Microsoft Exchange Service Host provides a host for several Microsoft Exchange services.
Microsoft Exchange Speech Engine	Microsoft Exchange Speech Engine provides speech processing services for Microsoft Exchange. If this service is stopped, speech recognition services will not be available to Unified Messaging clients.
Microsoft Exchange System Attendant	Microsoft Exchange System Attendant provides monitoring, maintenance, and Active Directory lookup services (e.g., monitoring of services and connectors, defragmenting the Exchange Store, and forwarding the Active Directory lookups to a global catalog server). If this service is stopped, monitoring, maintenance, and lookup services are unavailable. If this service is disabled, any services that explicitly depend on it will not start.
Microsoft Exchange Transport Log Search	This service provides remote search capability for Microsoft Exchange Transport log files.

Continued

Table 1.1 Continued

Service	Description
Microsoft Exchange Transport Service	This service provides the SMTP to Exchange 2007 transport servers.
Microsoft Exchange Unified Messaging	This service enables Microsoft Exchange Unified Messaging features. This enables voice and fax messages to be stored in Microsoft Exchange and gives users telephone access to e-mail, voicemail, calendar, contacts, or an automated attendant. If this service is stopped, users will not be able use the Unified Messaging features.
Microsoft Search (Exchange)	Microsoft Search (Exchange) quickly creates full-text indexes on content and properties of structured data to enable fast linguistic searches on this data.

Exchange Server Permissions

In previous versions of Exchange, administrative groups were administrative boundaries that contained servers and other objects. Although these administrative groups could be used to segregate administration within your organization, they were far from flexible and thus have been discontinued in Exchange Server 2007. Instead, you can now delegate permissions from the organization down to the server. No matter whether your organization uses a centralized or decentralized administrative model, you can delegate permissions to more closely match that model and easily adapt to new models as your organization changes.

All permissions in an Exchange Server 2007 organization are configured by assigning administrative access roles to Active Directory users or groups. As can be seen in Figure 1.7, four different Exchange administrator roles exist in Exchange Server 2007.

The following is a brief description of each role:

Exchange Organization Administrators Group

The Exchange Organization Administrators Group role provides administrators with full access to all Exchange properties and objects in the Exchange organization.

Exchange Recipient Administrators Group

The Exchange Recipient Administrators Group role has permissions to modify any Exchange property on an Active Directory user, contact, group, dynamic distribution list, or public folder object.

Exchange Server Administrators

The Exchange Server Administrators role has access to only local server Exchange configuration data, either in the Active Directory or on the physical computer on which Exchange Server 2007

Figure 1.7 Adding an Exchange Administrator to an Administrator Role

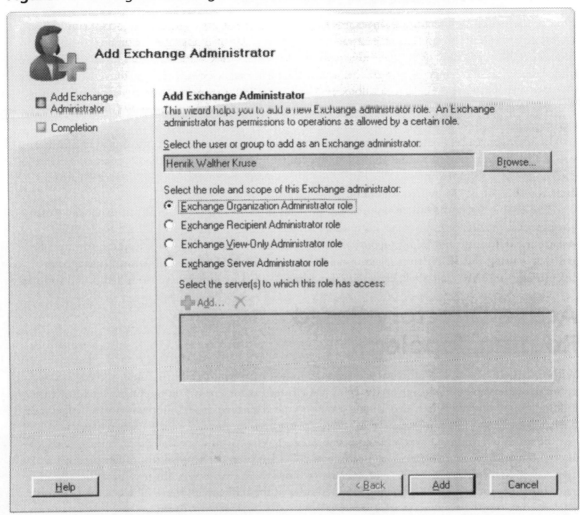

is installed. Users who are members of the Exchange Server Administrators role have permission to administer a particular server, but do not have permission to perform operations that have global impact in the Exchange organization.

Exchange View-Only Administrators Group

The Exchange View-Only Administrators Group role has read-only access to the entire Exchange organization tree in the Active Directory configuration container, and read-only access to all of the Windows domain containers that have Exchange recipients.

64-Bit Support Only

One of the major architectural changes in the Exchange Server 2007 product is the shift to a true 64-bit environment. As you might be aware, previous versions of Exchange did support 64-bit processors, however they didn't take advantage of them since they were still only 32-bit applications under the hood. Exchange Server 2007 is a true 64-bit messaging platform, and thus gives significant database scalability creating larger mailbox and/or public folder stores in your environment. This is possible due to the fact that 64-bit processing allows you to store much more data in memory, causing a lot less I/O load on the disks.

In addition, there is support for much larger mailboxes (+2GB). The move to 64-bit also means you are no longer limited to the 4 GB memory limitation of Exchange 2003 in your servers. Exchange 2007 supports up to eight TB of memory, but at the time of this writing, the hardware limit is 64 GB of RAM, which should be sufficient.

The 64-bit Support Only heading is not 100 percent true, since a 32-bit version actually exists; however it is meant for evaluation and testing purposes only. The 32-bit version is a *time bombed* version in addition to not being supported in a production. There's only one exception to this rule, and that is using the 32-bit versions to install the Management Console and perform management tasks (using the EMC and Shell, extending the Active Directory and Schema with Setup, and so forth.)

Active Directory-Based Routing Topology

With Exchange Server 2007, the way messages are routed between the Hub Transport servers (known as *Bridgehead* servers in Exchange Server 2003) has changed considerably. You no longer need to set up routing group connectors between routing groups in the Exchange organization when you design your Exchange topology. The routing group functionality has been removed from the Exchange product (see the list of discontinued features later in this chapter). Why has this flexible way of routing messages throughout an Exchange organization been removed? It has been determined that routing groups actually have several drawbacks, one being long stretches of time where two servers disagree about a connection state, in many situations causing routing loops. Another is the difficulty in tracking why a message took a given route at a given point in time, because the link state table for the Exchange topology was never persistent and/or logged. Lastly, the routing groups and routing group connector concept forced Exchange administrators to recreate and mimic the underlying network, which can be a time-consuming task.

So, how do you set up your routing topology in Exchange Server 2007? You don't! Exchange Server 2007 is a site-aware application, meaning that it can determine its own Active Directory site membership and the Active Directory site membership of other servers by querying Active Directory. Instead of using its own routing group topology, Exchange uses the AD directory service site topology to determine how messages are transported in the organization. This means that the Hub Transport servers in your Exchange organization retrieve information from Active Directory in order to determine how messages should be routed between servers. You need to deploy a Hub Transport server in each site containing a Mailbox server, meaning when user A in one site sends a message to user B in another site, the Mailbox server contacts the Hub Transport server in its own site, and then routes the message to the Hub Transport server in user B's site, ultimately delivering the message to the mailbox server hosting user B's mailbox.

De-emphasized Features

The following legacy Exchange features have been de-emphasized in Exchange Server 2007. What does that mean? It means that these features are still included in the Exchange product, but they're not prioritized anymore, and will most likely disappear in the next Exchange release after Exchange Server 2007 (currently codenamed E14).

- Public Folders
- Proxy Address Generators
- CDO 1.21
- MAPI32
- CDOEX (CDO 3.0)
- Exchange WebDAV extensions
- ExOLEDB
- Store Events
- Streaming backup APIs
- Exchange Server Virus Scanning API (VSAPI)

Discontinued Features

Because of the major architectural changes in Exchange Server 2007, several of the features and components included in previous versions of Exchange have been discontinued in Exchange Server 2007. Discontinued features are features that for some reason or other didn't make it into Exchange Server 2007, either because they were replaced by other new features or because the Exchange Product team no longer thought it made sense to keep supporting them in Exchange Server 2007. Below is a comprehensive list of features that didn't make it into Exchange Server 2007.

Architecture Features

Several architectural related features were removed or replaced in Exchange Server 2007.

- Routing Groups
- Administrative Groups
- Link State Routing
- Routing Objects
- IMF (replaced by Content Filter which can be considered IMF v3)
- Network Attached Storage (NAS)
- Exchange installable File System (ExIFS)
- Event Service

Recipient-related Features

- Exchange extensions in Active Directory Users and Computers MMC snap-in
- Microsoft Exchange Server Mailbox Merge Wizard (ExMerge)
- Recipient Update Service (RUS)

Mobile Features

- Outlook Mobile Access (OMA)
- Outlook Mobile Access Browse
- Always-Up-To-Date version 1 (AUTD v1)
- S/MIME (will be back when Exchange 2007 SP1 releases)

Outlook Web Access Features

- S/MIME Control component (will be back when Exchange 2007 SP1 releases)
- Rules, Notes, Post Forms, Monthly Calendar view
- Custom Forms
- Editing personal distribution lists
- URL commands except for free/busy, galfind, navbar and contents
- Public folder access
- Exchange Web forms

Public Folder Features

- Public Folder Management via GUI (but will be back when Exchange 2007 SP1 releases)
- Non-MAPI top-level hierarchies in a public folder store
- Public folder access using NNTP
- Public folder access using IMAP4

Protocol Features

- Network News Transfer Protocol (NNTP)
- Management of POP3/IMAP4 via GUI (Will most likely be back when Exchange 2007 SP1 releases)
- X.400 Message Transfer Agent (MTA)
- SMTP Virtual Server Instances

Connector Features

- Connector for Novell GroupWise and migration tools
- Connector for Lotus Notes (an Exchange 2007 version is under development)

HA Features

- Active/Active (A/A) clustering

Exchange 5.5-related Features

- Installing Exchange 5.5. into an Exchange 2007 organization
- Support for Exchange 5.5 in same forest as Exchange 2007
- Installing Exchange 2007 into an organization containing Exchange 5.5 servers (mixed mode)
- Active Directory Connector (ADC)
- Site Replication Service (SRS)

APIs and Development Features

- Transport Event hooks
- Workflow Designer (included in Exchange 2003 SDK)
- CDO for Workflow (on Exchange 2003 media)
- CDOEXM
- Exchange WMI classes
- MAPI Client on Exchange Server

Tools and Management Features

- Monitoring and Status Node
- Message Tracking Center Node and tracking mechanism
- Mailbox Recovery Center
- Mailbox Management Service
- Clean Mailbox tool
- Migration Wizard
- ExProfRe
- Inter-Organization Replication tool (InterORG)

Summary

Exchange Server 2007 is a huge product packed with many completely new features, as well as improvements to existing features from Exchange 2003. This chapter took a brief look at some of the more interesting new features such as the EMC and the EMS, as well as the new HA improvements. This chapter discussed the fact that Exchange 2007 is the first 64-bit version of Exchange ever released, and listed all the features that have been de-emphasized or even discontinued in Exchange Server 2007.

Chapter 2

Installing Exchange Server 2007

Solutions in this chapter:

- Exchange 2007 Server Editions and CAL Types
- Exchange 2007 Prerequisites
- Installing Exchange 2007 Using the Setup Wizard
- Installing Exchange 2007 Using Unattended Setup
- Verifying the Installation of Exchange Server 2007
- Licensing an Exchange 2007 Server
- Finalizing Deployment of Exchange Server 2007
- Adding and Removing Exchange 2007 Server Roles
- Uninstalling Exchange Server 2007

☑ Summary

☑ Solutions Fast Track

☑ Frequently Asked Questions

Introduction

In this chapter, we will go through the requirements of Exchange 2007. We'll look at what's required in terms of hardware and software, in addition to the Active Directory forest in which Exchange Server 2007 is to be installed. We'll then see, step by step, how you install Exchange 2007 Server into a clean Active Directory forest (that is, a forest that doesn't contain an Exchange organization or has had the schema extended with the Exchange attributes). We'll also take a brief look at the new Finalizing Deployment and End-to-End Scenario pages. Finally, you'll get an understanding of how you add and remove Exchange 2007 server roles on an existing Exchange 2007 server as well as how to remove an Exchange 2007 server from your organization.

This chapter does not cover transitions, coexistence, and other interoperability with Exchange 2000, 2003, and foreign messaging systems; it simply goes through the procedures of installing Exchange Server 2007 in a clean Active Directory environment. It also does not cover complex Exchange organizations distributed across multiple physical locations involving multiple Active Directory forests. The intention of the chapter is to get you started with the product.

Coexistence and Exchange 2007 transitions are covered in Chapter 10.

Exchange 2007 Server Editions and CAL Types

As is the case with previous versions of Exchange, Exchange Server 2007 exists in two different editions: a Standard Edition and an Enterprise Edition.

Standard Edition

Like previous Standard Editions of Exchange, Exchange 2007 Standard Edition has been designed to meet the messaging and collaboration requirements of small to medium-sized corporations and is aimed at meeting specific messaging server roles, such as branch offices. The Standard Edition has:

- Support for five storage groups
- Support for five databases
- No database storage limit
- Local Continuous Replication (LCR)

NOTE

Now that we are accustomed to referring to the EDB databases as Mailbox and Public Folder "Stores", the Exchange Product group thought they should be changed back to Mailbox and Public Folder "Databases", as they were prior to and including Exchange 5.5.

Enterprise Edition

So what extra benefits will you get out of deploying an Exchange 2007 Enterprise edition in your environment? The Enterprise edition of Exchange Server 2007 has been designed for large enterprise corporations. The Enterprise edition has support for:

- 50 Storage Groups
- 50 databases
- No database storage limit
- Local Continuous Replication (LCR)
- Exchange 2007 Clustering
    - Single Copy Clusters (SCC) using MSCS
    - Cluster Continuous Replication (CCR) using MSCS

Exchange Server 2007 Client Access Licensing

Exchange 2003 and earlier versions offered only one type of Exchange Client Access License (CAL), but with Exchange 2007 we now have two types: a Standard CAL and an Enterprise CAL.

Standard CAL

In addition to the features of Exchange 2003 CAL, the Exchange 2007 Standard CAL provides us with the following:

- Org-wide policy management
- Cross–org mailbox search
- Continuous Replication Technologies
- Mail-flow rules
- Server roles

Enterprise CAL

In addition to the features of Exchange 2007 Standard CAL, the Enterprise CAL provides us with the following:

- Unified messaging
- Per user journaling
- Exchange Hosted Services Filtering
- Forefront Security for Exchange Server (Microsoft's antivirus product, formerly known as Antigen)

NOTE

Before you get too involved in planning the budget for a transition to Exchange 2007 in your organization, you should be aware of one very important thing. Many of you who have Exchange 2003 deployed in your organizations might very well be aware of the fact that each Exchange 2003 CAL included the right to install Outlook 2003 on the devices for which these CALs were obtained. You probably think this hasn't changed a bit with Exchange 2007 CALs. Think again, because Exchange Server 2007 Standard or Enterprise does not include the right to install Outlook on devices for which CALs are obtained! This means that your organization might have to wait to make the transition to Exchange 2007 until you're ready to deploy Office 2007 as well. To read more about this Exchange 2007 CAL change, visit www.microsoftvolumelicensing.com/userights/ProductPage.aspx?pid=111.

Exchange 2007 Prerequisites

Before you begin installing Exchange Server 2007, you should make sure that the computer on which you are installing the product meets the recommended hardware and software requirements. In addition, you should make sure that the Active Directory domain in which you are installing Exchange Server 2007 is configured with the correct functional level. The minimum Windows Active Directory functional level for Exchange 2007 is Windows 2000 native mode. If you are installing Exchange Server 2007 into an existing Exchange organization, it is also important to note that the organization should be running in native mode; however, since the purpose of this chapter is to show you how to install Exchange Server 2007 into a clean Active Directory forest, you really don't need to worry about this now.

IMPORTANT

The Exchange Server 2007 32-bit evaluation version is meant to be used in a test environment only and should never be used in a production environment, because it is not supported by Microsoft. The only Exchange Server 2007 component you may use in a production environment is the Exchange 2007 Management Tools (more specifically, the Exchange Management Console, the Exchange Management Shell, the Exchange Help file, and the Exchange Best Practices Analyzer tool). These can be installed on a 32-bit machine running either Windows 2003 Server with Service Pack 1 (SP1) or Windows XP Professional with Service Pack 2 (SP2).

Although the hardware and software requirements are the same, this chapter does not cover how to install an Exchange server into an existing Exchange organization. It also does not go into detail on how you transition from Exchange 5.5, 2000, or 2003 to Exchange 2007. Instead, these topics are covered in Chapter 10.

Hardware Requirements

The hardware requirements for a production Exchange 2007 server are described in the following sections.

Processor

Exchange Server 2007 exists in both 32- and 64-bit versions, but only the 64-bit version is supported in a production environment. This means that the server hardware on which you plan to install Exchange Server 2007 must have one of the following 64-bit processor types installed:

- x64 architecture-based processor that supports Intel Extended Memory 64 Technology (Intel EM64T)
- x64 architecture-based computer with AMD 64-bit processor that supports AMD64 platform

Note that the Intel Itanium IA64 processor is not listed, since it is not supported by Exchange Server 2007.

NOTE

If you are planning to use Exchange Server 2007 for either testing or evaluation purposes, you can use the 32-bit evaluation version. This simply requires an Intel Pentium or compatible 800 megahertz (MHz) or faster 32-bit processor. The Exchange 2007 Evaluation version can be downloaded from www.microsoft.com/exchange.

Memory

The memory requirements for a 64-bit Exchange 2007 server that is to be deployed in a production environment are 2 gigabytes (GB) of RAM per server. However, bear in mind that those are the minimum requirements. The recommend requirements are:

- 2GB of RAM per server plus approximately 5 megabytes (MB) of RAM per user mailbox located on the respective server
- A paging file equivalent to the amount of server memory plus 10MB

Also be aware that it's recommended to add additional memory if you're planning to use more than four storage groups (approximately 2GB per three storage groups).

Disk Space

Disk space requirements are as follows:

- At least 1.2GB of disk space on the drive on which Exchange Server 2007 is to be installed
- 200MB or more of disk space on the system drive

When installing the Unified Messaging role on a server, you will also need to allocate an additional 500MB for each Unified Messaging language pack that is installed.

Drives

A DVD drive isn't really a requirement, because you can install Exchange 2007 from an attached network drive or even a mounted ISO file.

Software Requirements

In addition to the hardware requirements, Exchange Server 2007 has some software requirements that need to be fulfilled before you can begin your install.

Operating System

When planning to install Exchange Server 2007 in a production environment, you will need Microsoft Windows Server 2003 64-bit version with Service Pack 1 or Windows Server 2003 R2 64-bit version.

Both Standard and Enterprise Editions are supported by the 64-bit version of Exchange Server 2007, but bear in mind that the Enterprise Edition is required if you are planning on deploying an Exchange 2007 cluster. (This goes for both Single Copy Clusters and Cluster Continuous Replication setups.)

If you plan on installing the Exchange 2007 32-bit version (for testing or evaluation purposes), you would need to install the 32-bit version of Microsoft Windows Server 2003 SP1 or Windows Server 2003 R2.

SOME INDEPENDENT ADVICE

Since Exchange 2007 can be installed on a server running either Windows Server 2003 R2 or Windows Server 2003 SP1 or higher, those of you who deal with Windows 2003 Small Business Server (SBS) are probably wondering whether Exchange 2007 will be supported in the current edition of SBS. Unfortunately, the answer is no. You will have to wait for the next major release of SBS, which will be based on the Windows Longhorn server. Even worse, the next version of SBS won't be released for approximately six to 12 months after Windows Longhorn server hits the streets.

File Format

All disk partitions must be formatted with the NTFS file system (that's right, FAT is, fortunately, not supported). This means that all disk partitions holding any files or data in the following list should be formatted using NFTS:

- System partition
- Partition storing Exchange Server binaries

- Partitions containing transaction log files
- Partitions containing database files
- Partitions containing other Exchange Server files

Software Required

The following software is required for any of the five different Exchange 2007 server roles. Server roles were previously discussed in detail in Chapter 1.

- Microsoft .NET Framework Version 2.0
- Microsoft Management Console (MMC) 3.0 (bear in mind that MMC 3.0 is installed by default when you use Windows Server 2003 R2)
- Windows PowerShell V1.0
- HotFix for Windows x64 (KB904639)

NOTE

If you haven't installed .NET Framework 2.0, the MMC 3.0 snap-in, or Windows PowerShell when you launch the Exchange Server 2007 installation program, you will be provided with links to each respective piece of software so that you can install each separately.

Required Windows Components

Depending on the Exchange 2007 server roles you plan to install, different Windows components are required before doing so. This section lists each role as well as the required Windows components.

Mailbox Server

The following components are required for the Mailbox server:

- Enable network COM+ access
- Internet Information Services
- World Wide Web Service

Client Access Server

The following components are required for the Client Access server:

- World Wide Web Service

- Remote procedure call (RPC) over Hypertext Transfer Protocol (HTTP) Proxy Windows networking component (required only if you are deploying clients that will use the Outlook Anywhere functionality, previously called RPC over HTTP)

- ASP.NET v2.0

In addition, if you're planning to use OWA 2007 in your organization where you have non-English domain controllers, it's important you install the hotfix mentioned in MS KB article 919166; otherwise you'll experience issues in looking up recipients in the GAL using OWA 2007.

Hub Transport Server

No additional Windows components are required by the Hub Transport server; however, you must make sure that the SMTP and NNTP services are *not* installed.

Edge Transport Server

The following components are required for the Edge Transport server:

- ADAM

- Like the Hub Transport role, SMTP and NNTP must *not* be installed

---

NOTE

ADAM is an included Windows component of Windows Server 2003 R2. However, to install ADAM on a Windows 2003 server with SP1 or higher, you will need to download the ADAM installation package separately. You can download ADAM by clicking Active Directory Application Mode in the Downloads section of the following link: www.microsoft.com/windowsserver2003/adam.

As you might recall, Exchange Server 2000 and 2003 made extended use of the Windows Server 2000 or 2003 SMTP and NNTP protocol stacks, requiring that they be installed components (both subcomponents of IIS) prior to installing the Exchange Server product itself. Both the Hub Transport server and the Edge Transport server require NNTP *not* be installed, because it is one of the features that are not supported in Exchange Server 2007. Thus, you need to make sure this component isn't installed on the server, because the Exchange Server 2007 Readiness Check will fail if it is. In addition, because Exchange Server 2007 no longer uses the Windows Server SMTP protocol stack but instead uses its own, you also need to make sure that the Windows Server SMTP component isn't installed on the server. As with NNTP, the Exchange Server 2007 Readiness Check will fail if the SMTP component is found on the server.

NOTE

The SMTP engine included in Exchange Server 2007 has been written from the ground up using managed code within the Exchange Product group itself and not the Windows Server group. The Windows Server Group was responsible for the SMTP component of IIS, which was used by the Microsoft Exchange Transport service (MSExchangeTransport.exe) in both Exchange 2000 and 2003.

Unified Messaging Server

The following components are required for the Unified Messaging server:

- Microsoft Speech service (if Exchange 2007 setup doesn't find this component, it will install it automatically)

- Microsoft Windows Media Encoder (the x64 edition can be downloaded from http://go.microsoft.com/fwlink/?LinkId=67406)

- Microsoft Windows Media Audio Voice Codec (can be downloaded from http://support.microsoft.com/kb/917312)

- Microsoft Core XML Services (MSXML) 6.0 (can be downloaded from http://go.microsoft.com/fwlink/?linkid=70796)

Server Requirements

As is the case with Exchange Server 2000 and 2003, Exchange Server 2007 relies on and is heavily integrated with Active Directory. So, before you install Exchange Server 2007 on a server, it is mandatory that the server be part of an Active Directory forest. The only exception to this rule is the Edge Transport Server role, which should instead be installed in a workgroup in your perimeter network. The server on which you plan to install Exchange 2007 should also be configured with a static IP address; in addition, you should verify that the DNS server settings are configured to point at the respective DNS servers in the particular Active Directory forest (see Figure 2.1).

Active Directory Requirements

First, you want to make sure any domain controllers and global catalog servers in the Active Directory domain in which you're planning to install the Exchange 2007 server are running Windows Server 2003 SP1 or Windows Server 2003 R2. In addition, you need to set the Active Directory Domain functional level to at least Windows 2000 Native or Windows Server 2003 because these modes are required by the new Exchange 2007 Server Universal Groups.

Figure 2.1 Configuring TCP/IP Settings

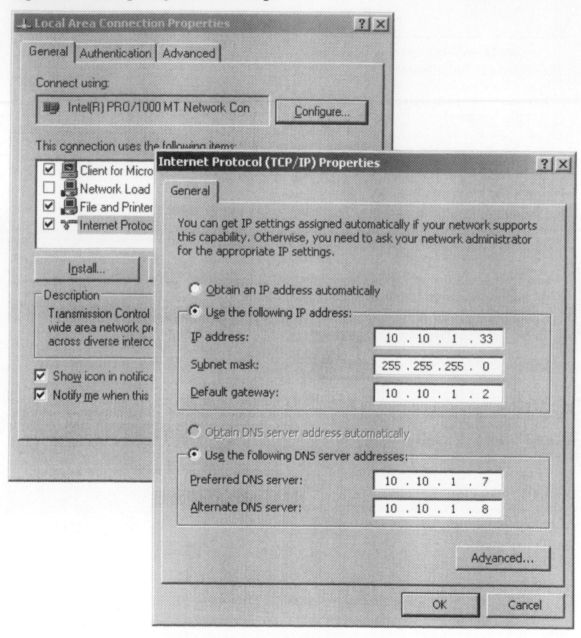

To change the Active Directory functional level, you need to perform the following steps:

1.   Log on to a Domain Controller in the respective Active Directory Domain.

2. Click **Start | All Programs | Administrative Tools** and then click **Active Directory Users and Computers**.

3. When the Microsoft Management Console (MMC) snap-in has launched, right-click the **Active Directory** domain in the left pane, then click **Raise Domain Functional Level** in the context menu, as shown in Figure 2.2.

Figure 2.2 Raising the Domain Functional Level

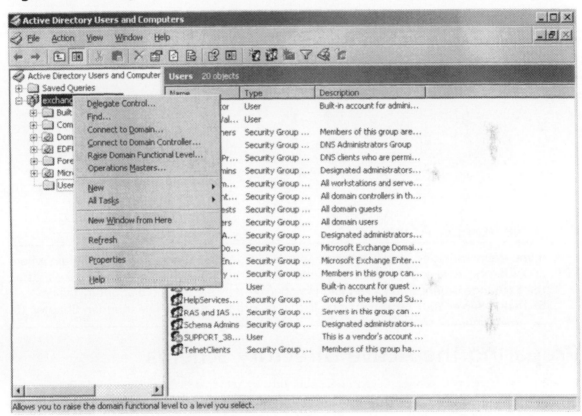

4. Now select **Windows 2000 native** or **Windows Server 2003** in the domain functional level drop-down menu and click **Raise** (Figure 2.3).

Figure 2.3 Available Domain Functional Levels

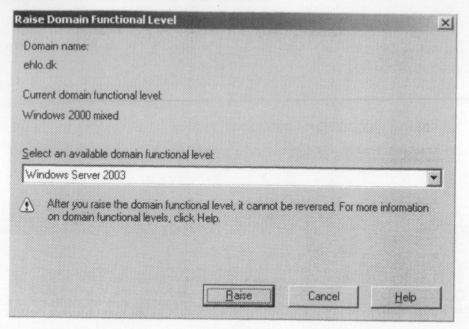

If you are planning to install Exchange Server 2007 into an Active Directory domain where an Exchange 2000 or 2003 organization already exists, you also need to make sure that the Exchange organization is running in native mode. This and more about installing Exchange Server 2007 into an existing Exchange organization can be found in Chapter 10.

Preparing the Active Directory Schema

Now that we have been through the hardware and software required by Exchange Server 2007, let's take a look at what we need to prepare before we can install an Exchange 2007 server into a clean Active Directory domain.

The first step is to prepare your Active Directory schema for the new Exchange 2007 attributes by extending it using the *Setup /PrepareSchema* command-line switch. Exchange Server 2007 adds many new attributes and classes to the Active Directory schema (even more than Exchange Server 2003 did!) and makes additional modifications to the existing classes and attributes.

To be able to run the *Setup /PrepareSchema* switch, you must be logged on with an account that is a member of both the Schema Admins and the Enterprise Admins Active Directory groups. In addition, you must run this command from a machine that belongs to the respective Active Directory domain and is located in the same Active Directory site as the server holding the Schema Master role. The *Setup /PrepareSchema* command will connect to the server holding the Schema Master role and import the required LDAP Data Interchange Format (LDIF) files containing all the new Exchange 2007 specific classes and attributes.

NOTE

It is recommended that you run the *Setup /PrepareSchema* command-line switch on your Domain Schema Master server itself.

To prepare the schema, perform the following steps:

1. Log on to the server from where you want to run the command, with an account that is a member of both the **Schema Admins** and **Enterprise Admins** groups.

2. Now click **Start | Run** and type **cmd.exe,** followed by pressing **Enter** or clicking **OK.**

3. In the Command Prompt window, navigate to the folder in which the Exchange 2007 server setup files are located (for example, **CD C:Exchange Server 2007 RTM – 64-bit**).

4. Type **Setup /PrepareSchema** and press **Enter** (see Figure 2.4).

Figure 2.4 Running Setup with the *PrepareSchema* Switch

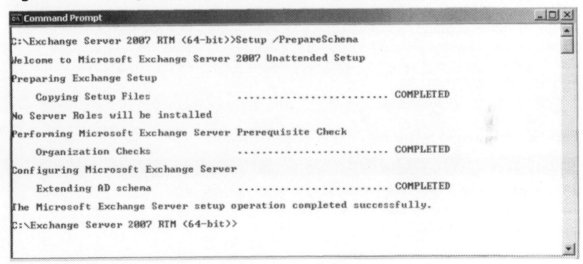

```
C:\Exchange Server 2007 RTM (64-bit)>Setup /PrepareSchema
Welcome to Microsoft Exchange Server 2007 Unattended Setup
Preparing Exchange Setup
    Copying Setup Files            ..................... COMPLETED
No Server Roles will be installed
Performing Microsoft Exchange Server Prerequisite Check
    Organization Checks            ..................... COMPLETED
Configuring Microsoft Exchange Server
    Extending AD schema            ..................... COMPLETED
The Microsoft Exchange Server setup operation completed successfully.
C:\Exchange Server 2007 RTM (64-bit)>
```

Since *Setup /PrepareSchema* needs to be run in the site holding the Schema Master, some of you might question what to do if you need to prepare the Active Directory schema in a site that doesn't have any 64-bit servers installed yet. You really don't have to worry about this, since you can just run this command using the 32-bit version of Exchange Server 2007. "What? Are you telling me to run *Setup /PrepareSchema* using the unsupported 32-bit version in a production environment?" we hear some of you grumble. To answer that question, yes. As a matter of fact, the 32-bit version of Exchange is supported in a production environment in terms of Exchange 2007 administration, which includes extending the AD.

NOTE

You do not necessarily need to run the *Setup /PrepareSchema* command prior to running the *Setup /PrepareAD* command, which is covered next. When *Setup / PrepareSchema* hasn't been run prior to running the *Setup /PrepareAD*, the *Setup / PrepareSchema* command will be run as part of the *Setup /PrepareAD* command. So, why would you want to run the *Setup /PrepareSchema* command before *Setup / PrepareAD*? Well, in most scenarios you would jump right to the *Setup /PrepareAD*, the exception being those environments using a split permission model, where different individuals might administer the Exchange Organization over the Active Directory forest.

Preparing the Active Directory

The next command you need to run is the *Setup /PrepareAD* command, which will prepare the current domain, configure global Exchange objects in Active Directory, and create the Exchange Universal Security Groups (USGs) in the root domain. To run this command you need to use an account that is a member of the Enterprise Admins group. (If you install Exchange 2007 into an existing Exchange organization, it also needs to be a member of the Exchange Admins group.) Next, go through the same steps you performed when you extended the schema, but replace *Setup / PrepareSchema* with *Setup /PrepareAD /ON:*<organizational name> (see Figure 2.5, where we use EHLO as the organization name).

Figure 2.5 Running Setup with the *PrepareAD* Switch

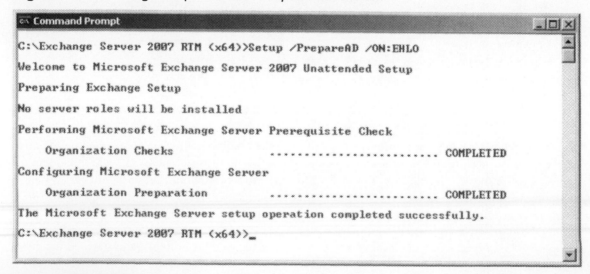

```
Command Prompt                                                        _ □ ×

C:\Exchange Server 2007 RTM (x64)>Setup /PrepareAD /ON:EHLO

Welcome to Microsoft Exchange Server 2007 Unattended Setup

Preparing Exchange Setup

No server roles will be installed

Performing Microsoft Exchange Server Prerequisite Check

    Organization Checks            ........................ COMPLETED

Configuring Microsoft Exchange Server

    Organization Preparation       ........................ COMPLETED

The Microsoft Exchange Server setup operation completed successfully.

C:\Exchange Server 2007 RTM (x64)>_
```

If you are running the *Setup /PrepareSchema* and */PrepareAD* commands in an organization with a large Active Directory topology, the replication time could take quite a while. If you want to keep an eye on the replication process, you might want to use the Active Directory Replication Monitor tool (replmon.exe), which is part of the Microsoft Windows Server 2003 Support Tools Setup package. You can install the Support Tools directly off the Windows Server 2003 CD media by navigating to the **Support | Tools** folder and simply double-clicking the **SUPTOOLS.MSI** file. In the Windows Server Support Tools Setup Wizard, click **Next**, accept the EULA, and click **Next** two more times. Click **Install Now** and finally click **Finish**. When the Support Tools have been installed, you can launch Replmon by clicking **Start | Run**, typing **ReplMon.exe**, and clicking **OK**.

To verify that *Setup /PrepareAD* ran successfully, you can open the Active Directory Users and Computers snap-in and confirm that a new Organizational Unit (OU) called Microsoft Exchange Security Groups now exists and that the following Exchange Universal Security Groups (USGs) exist beneath it:

- Exchange Organization Administrators

- Exchange Recipient Administrators

- Exchange View-Only Administrators

- Exchange Servers

- Exchange2003Interop

Preparing Any Additional Active Directory Domains in a Forest

If you're dealing with an Active Directory forest consisting of multiple Active Directory domains, you would also need to prepare those domains for Exchange 2007. You can do this by running any of the following commands (see Figure 2.6):

- *Setup /PrepareDomain* from the domain in question

- *Setup /PrepareDomain:*<FQDN of the additional domain you want to prepare> from any domain using the correct credentials

- *Setup /PrepareAllDomains* to prepare any and all domains in which you haven't run *Setup / PrepareSchema or Setup /PrepareAD*

Figure 2.6 Running Setup With the *PrepareDomain* Switch

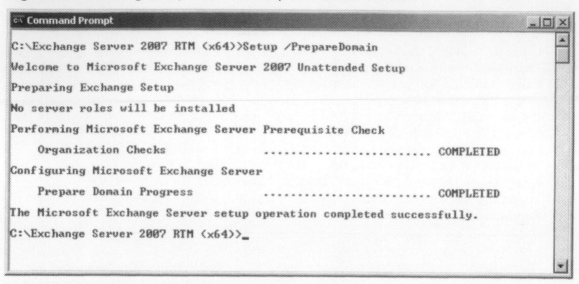

Installing Exchange 2007 Using the Setup Wizard

Because of the heavily improved and role-based setup wizard, installing Exchange 2007 is much easier than installing previous versions of Exchange. Because the Exchange 2007 Setup Wizard is role based, you can either select to install a typical Exchange Server installation, which will install the Hub Transport, Client Access, and Mailbox Server roles on the same server (which is what you typically want to do in an Exchange organization that will consist of one Exchange 2007 Server only), or you can do a custom Exchange Server installation, which lets you choose the server roles that should be installed on the respective servers. You would typically choose to do a custom Exchange Server installation in a large Exchange organization where you want to separate the various Exchange 2007 Server roles among different servers. Those of you who are dealing with large Exchange organizations probably have dedicated Exchange front-end servers, bridgehead servers, and back-end servers (Mailbox and/or Public Folder Servers) in place already. Because the Exchange 2007 Setup Wizard is role based, you have the option of selecting the server roles to be deployed on each server, and you can thereby design an Exchange topology matching your needs.

NOTE

Another benefit of a role-based approach is that Exchange 2007 Setup only installs the Exchange files and services necessary for the server role you deploy. This means that the respective servers won't waste disk space and resources on unnecessary files and services, as previous versions of Exchange did.

When all the mentioned hardware, software, and Active Directory requirements have been met, you can finally install Exchange Server 2007. You can do so using the GUI-based Exchange 2007 Setup Wizard or using unattended Setup (which gives you the option of creating command-line scripts for unattended installations using batch files). First, let's go through how installation is accomplished using the Exchange 2007 Setup Wizard.

After inserting the Exchange Server 2007 media in the DVD drive on the server or mapping to a share where the Exchange Server 2007 binary files are held, you can launch the installation by double-clicking the **Setup.exe** file (see Figure 2.7).

SOME INDEPENDENT ADVICE

As most of you know, although it's generally avoided, you could install Exchange 2000 and 2003 on a server that also acted as domain controller. You might ask if Microsoft included support for this in Exchange Server 2007, since it was so widely discouraged in previous releases. It is again a supported as an install on a domain controller, but Microsoft strongly recommends against it for security, performance, and availability reasons. The only situation where it would be okay to have Exchange 2007 installed on a server acting as a domain controller would be one in which you were dealing with a Small Business Server (SBS).

Figure 2.7 Running Exchange 2007 Setup

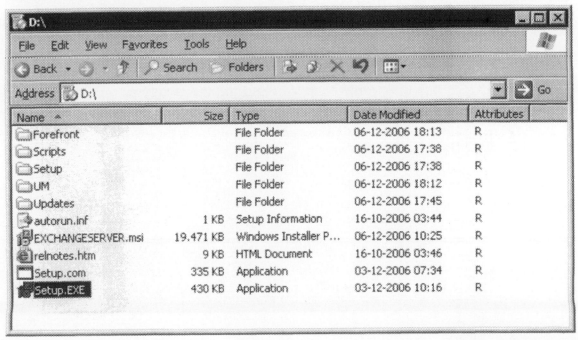

The Exchange 2007 Bootstrapper (a.k.a. the splash screen) will now appear and show you whether the required software has been properly installed on the server. As mentioned earlier in this chapter, you need to install .NET Framework 2.0, Microsoft Management Console (MMC) 3.0, and Windows PowerShell 1.0 before you can install Exchange Server 2007. If all three components have been properly installed, each link will be grayed out, allowing you to continue the installation process with step 4, installing Microsoft Exchange. If this is not the case, as in Figure 2.9, which shows we're missing the PowerShell component, you must click the link for each missing component in each step to download and install the needed Exchange 2007 prerequisites. (Since we used Windows Server 2003 R2 in our test environment, MMC 3.0 was already installed).

If you use Windows Server 2003 R2, we recommend that you install the .NET Framework 2.0 component via **Control Panel | Add or Remove Programs | Add/Remove Windows Components** because this is a standard Windows component included in the Windows Server 2003 R2 edition (see Figure 2.8).

Figure 2.8 Adding the Microsoft .NET Framework 2.0 Component

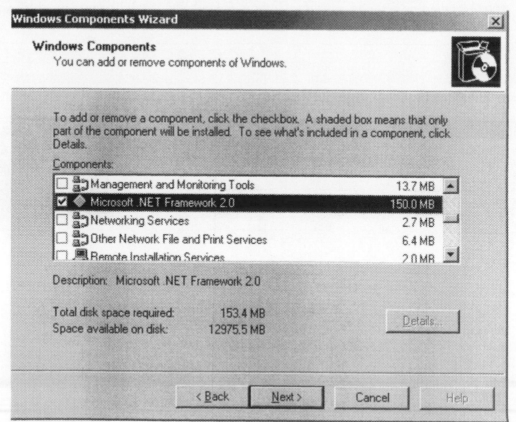

When all prerequisites are met, click **Step 4: Install Microsoft Exchange** (see Figure 2.9).

Figure 2.9 Exchange 2007 Setup Splash Screen

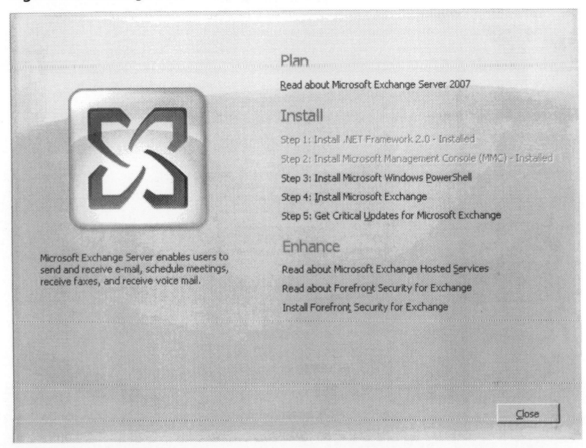

Setup will copy the necessary files and soon after begin initializing. After initialization completes, you will be taken to the first step in the Installation Wizard, the Introduction page. Click **Next** (see Figure 2.10).

Next you will be presented with and need to accept the terms of the end-user license agreement (EULA). We know that reading the license agreement is not among the most exciting things in the world, but you should at least spend a couple of minutes skimming through it. When you have done so, select **I accept the terms in the license agreement**, and then click **Next**.

You now have the option of enabling error reporting, and we highly recommend you do so to help improve the quality, reliability, and performance of the Exchange Server 2007 product. Microsoft is very serious about every single error report it collects, and since all of us are interested in seeing the best messaging and collaboration product getting better and better, why not enable error reporting?

NOTE

Microsoft does not collect any personal information such as e-mail address, so you
have nothing to worry about in terms of your privacy.

Figure 2.10 Exchange Server 2007 Setup Wizard Introductory Page

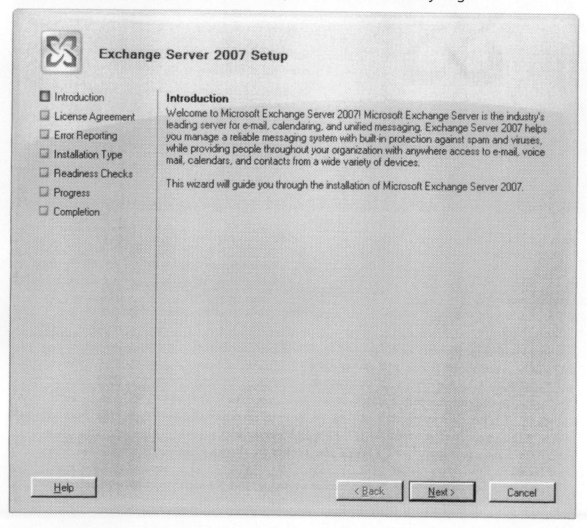

When you have enabled (or for some reason disabled) error reporting, you can click **Next** (see Figure 2.11).

Figure 2.11 The Error Reporting Page

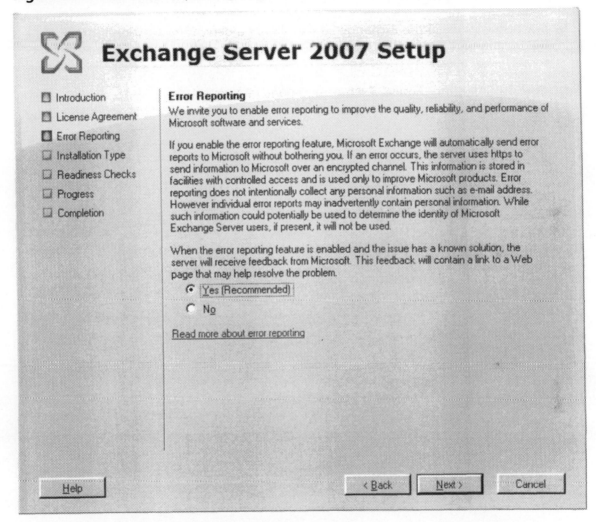

We have now reached the step where we need to choose the kind of Exchange roles we want to install and run. For the purpose of this chapter, we will do a Typical Exchange Server Installation, which installs the Hub Transport, Client Access, and Mailbox server roles. The Exchange Management Tools (Exchange Management Console and Shell) will, of course, also be installed when we choose this installation type.

Click **Typical Exchange Server Installation** and then **Next**, as shown in Figure 2.12.

NOTE

You have the option of specifying the path to which the Exchange Server files should be installed. The default path is C:\Program Files\Microsoft\Exchange Server, but best practice is to install the Exchange Server files on a dedicated partition instead of on the System partition.

Figure 2.12 Selecting Typical Exchange Server Installation

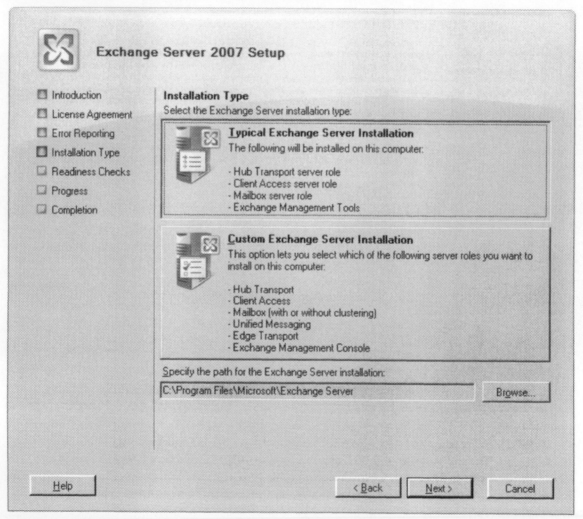

If you plan to deploy either a single Exchange 2007 server role or one including the Unified Messaging server or Edge Transport server roles, you should choose the **Custom Exchange Server Installation** type, which allows you to choose the specific roles you require in your environment. In addition, if you want to deploy a clustered mailbox server or perhaps only install one or two server roles on a given server, you also need to choose the custom installation type. When choosing a **Custom Exchange Server Installation** type, you'll see a screen similar to the one shown in Figure 2.13.

Figure 2.13 Selecting Custom Exchange Server Installation

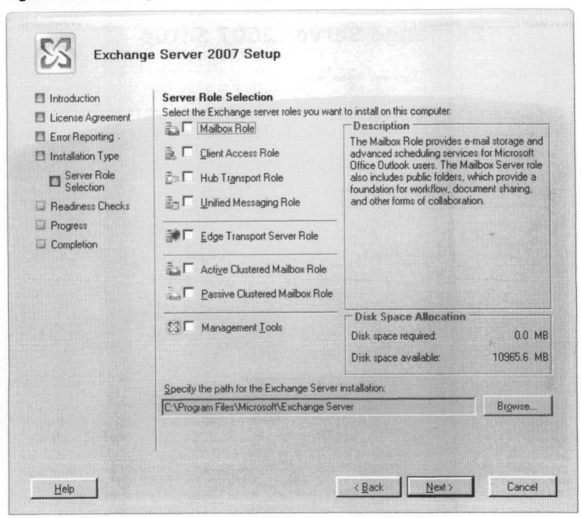

NOTE

Although this chapter focuses on just the Typical Exchange Server Installation type, fear not—we will also go through to the deployment steps for both an Edge Transport server role as well as a clustered mailbox server (both Clustered Continuous Replication and Single Copy Cluster setups) in Chapters 7 and 8.

Since we are installing this server into a new Exchange organization, we will now be asked to enter the name of the new Exchange organization (see Figure 2.14).

Figure 2.14 Specifying the Name for the New Exchange 2007 Organization

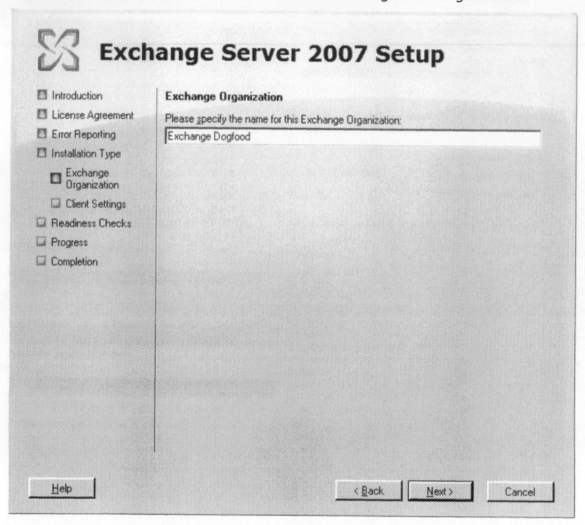

When clicking **Next**, we'll be taken to the **Client Settings** page, where we need to specify whether there are any legacy clients (that is, Outlook 2003 and earlier) still in use in our organization. If this is the case, we need to select **Yes**, creating and mounting a Public Folder database on the server, because legacy Outlook clients use Public folders to retrieve free/busy calendar information. If you only have Outlook 2007 clients in the organization, you can safely select **No**, removing the need to create a Public Folder database on your Exchange 2007 server. The reason behind this is the ability for the Outlook 2007 client to use the new Exchange 2007 Web-based availability service (discussed more in Chapter 5) to retrieve free/busy information for other users.

NOTE

If you select No and enter into a scenario where Outlook 2003 and earlier clients are introduced into your environment at a later time, you can always go back and manually create a Public Folder database to house the Free/Busy calendaring information of these legacy clients.

Click **Yes** or **No**, depending on your scenario, then click **Next** (see Figure 2.15).

Figure 2.15 Specifying Whether Outlook 2003 or Earlier Is Used in the Organization

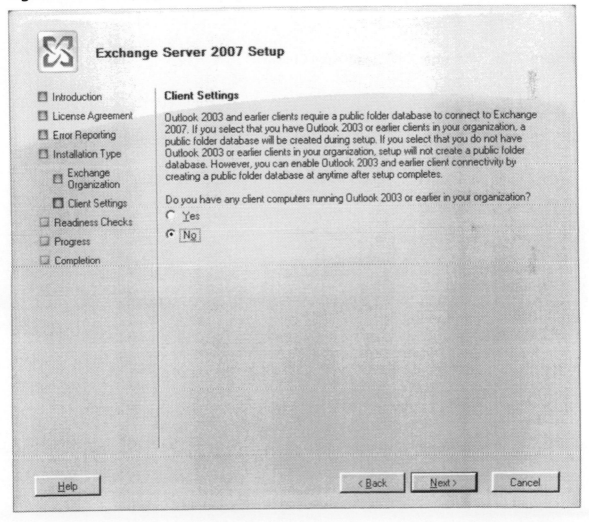

Next, the Exchange 2007 Installation Wizard will perform a readiness check to see whether the server itself, as well as the Active Directory forest, fulfils the prerequisites for the selected server roles.

NOTE

When the Exchange Server 2007 Setup Wizard checks whether Exchange is ready to be installed on the particular server, it uses the engine from the Exchange Best Practices Analyzer (ExBPA) tool to perform the necessary checks. Actually, the first thing that the Setup wizard will do is to download the latest version of the prereq.xml file from Microsoft.com (similar to when ExBPA download updates) so that the most up-to-date prerequisites information is always used.

If the prerequisite check for each server role completes without any errors or important warnings, we can click **Install** (see Figure 2.16), preparing the organization (if that is not already done), copying the necessary Exchange files, and installing each Exchange 2007 server role.

Figure 2.16 Exchange 2007 Readiness Check

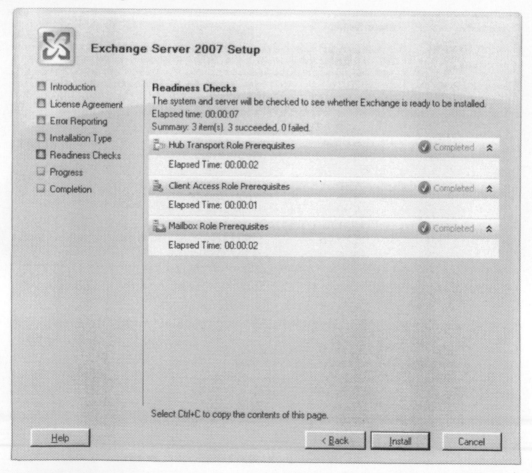

If you install the 32-bit version of Exchange or if a component required by Exchange Server 2007 hasn't been installed on the server, the particular server role check will give you a warning or fail, as shown in Figure 2.17. The cool thing about the checks is that we are given information about what causes the check to fail, and in most cases we're given a Recommend Action link that provides much more detail about what is actually causing the check to fail.

Figure 2.17 Readiness Check Failed

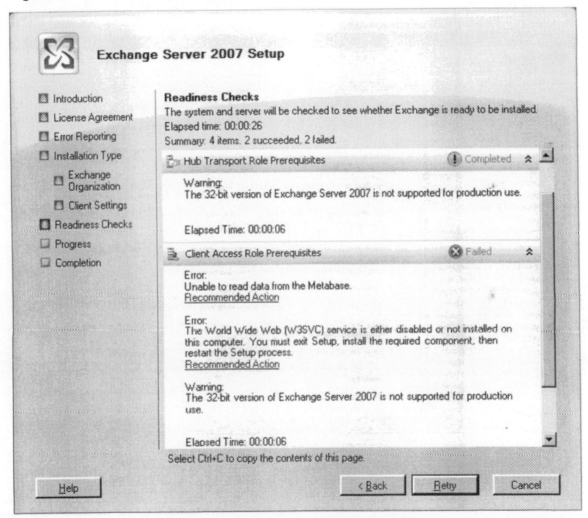

Clicking the link brings us to the **Microsoft Exchange Server Analyzer Articles** on the Microsoft TechNet Web site (see Figure 2.18). Depending on which components need to be installed before the Readiness Checks can complete successfully, it determines whether you can simply click the **Retry** button after the component has been installed. In most cases this will work, but with some components, such as the World Wide Web Service (W3SVC), it is required that you exit the Setup Wizard and run it again from the beginning.

Figure 2.18 Microsoft Exchange Server Analyzer Articles

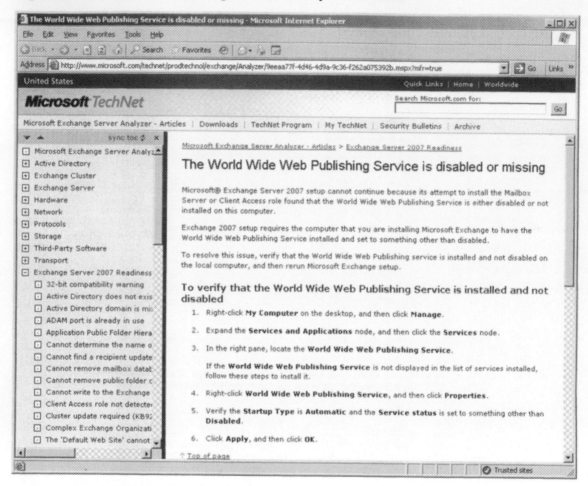

When the installation process has completed, we can click **Finish** to exit the Exchange 2007 Installation Wizard. Note that you can launch the Exchange Management Console automatically after clicking **Finish**, so you can immediately begin finalizing your installation (see Figure 2.19).

Figure 2.19 Exchange Server 2007 Setup Completed

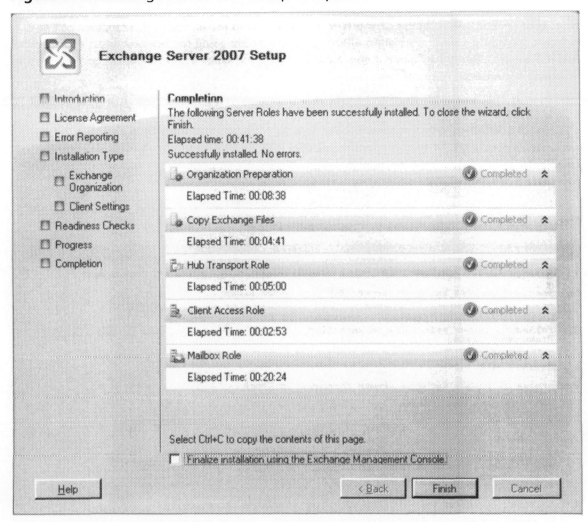

Installing Exchange 2007 Using Unattended Setup

Now that we have been through a typical installation of Exchange Server 2007 using the Setup Wizard, let's take a look at how you do a typical installation of Exchange Server 2007 using an unattended setup. This is done via the command prompt, and as in the case when doing a GUI installation, you need to insert the Exchange Server 2007 media in the DVD drive on the server, or map to a share containing the necessary Exchange Server 2007 binaries. Navigate to the DVD or mapped drive by typing **CD** *<letter of DVD drive>*:. You can install Exchange Server 2007 in unattended mode using Setup.exe. Setup.exe supports many different parameters and switches, so to whet your appetite, we recommend you type **Setup.exe /?** to list all available parameters and switches, providing a short description of each. Because we are going to do a basic installation into an Active Directory forest that does not contain any existing Exchange organization, we need to use the following command:

```
Setup.exe /mode:Install /roles:HT,CA,MB,MT /on:EHLO
```

First the command tells Setup.exe that we want to install one or more server roles with the */mode:Install* parameter. We then specify the roles we want to install using the */roles:<roles>* parameter. Finally, we specify the name of the new Exchange organization with the */on:<Exchange organization>* parameter (see Figure 2.20).

Figure 2.20 Running Setup in Unattended Mode

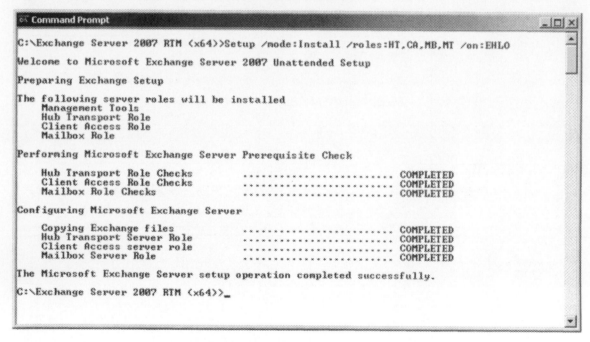

NOTE

If you have any legacy Outlook clients (Outlook 2003 and earlier versions) in your environment, you should also add */EnableLegacyOutlook* to the command. */EnableLegacyOutlook* makes sure that a Public Folder database is created on the Exchange 2007 server, which is necessary for the sharing of Free/Busy calendar information using the legacy Outlook client.

As with the Setup Wizard, Exchange 2007 unattended setup will do a set of prerequisite checks. If these are successful, setup will continue, copying the necessary Exchange files and finally installing the specified Exchange 2007 server roles.

Verifying the Installation of Exchange Server 2007

After Exchange Server 2007 has been installed, we recommend that you verify that the installation completed without any serious warnings or errors. If you didn't encounter any errors during installation, there's a good chance everything is in perfect shape, but you won't know for sure until you have checked the Windows event logs and the Exchange 2007 setup logs as well as doing a visual verification that each selected role has been installed. Start by examining both the application logs and the system logs for any warnings or errors related to the Exchange Server 2007 setup. If any are found, you can trace the problem using the provided information in the event URL, TechNet, or the troubleshooting section of the Exchange setup guide. If everything looks good, move on and verify that no errors have been logged in the ExchangeSetup.log and ExchangeSetup. msilog, both located in the ExchangeSetupLogs folder located in the root of the system drive (typically C:).

In addition, you should check that all the respective Exchange 2007 services have been configured to start automatically and are indeed started (see Figure 2.21).

Figure 2.21 A List of Exchange 2007 Services

Name	Description	Status
Microsoft Exchange Active Directory Topology	Provides AD topology information to Exchange services. If this service is stopped, most Exchange services ar...	Started
Microsoft Exchange EdgeSync	The Exchange EdgeSync Service.	Started
Microsoft Exchange File Distribution	Microsoft Exchange File Distribution Service.	Started
Microsoft Exchange Hygiene Update	The Exchange Hygiene Update Service.	Started
Microsoft Exchange IMAP4	Provides Internet Message Access Protocol (IMAP4) Services to clients. If this service is stopped, clients are u...	
Microsoft Exchange Information Store	Manages the Microsoft Exchange Information Store. This includes mailbox stores and public folder stores. If t...	Started
Microsoft Exchange Mail Submission Service	Submits messages from the Mailbox server to the Hub Transport servers.	Started
Microsoft Exchange Mailbox Assistants	Performs background processing of mailboxes in the Exchange store.	Started
Microsoft Exchange Monitoring	Allows applications to call the Exchange diagnostic cmdlets.	
Microsoft Exchange POP3	Provides Post Office Protocol version 3 (POP3) Services to clients. If this service is stopped, clients are unable...	
Microsoft Exchange Replication Service	The Exchange Replication Service provides replication functionality used by Local Continuous Replication and ...	Started
Microsoft Exchange Search Indexer	Drives indexing of mailbox content, which improves the performance of content search.	Started
Microsoft Exchange Service Host	Provides a host for several Microsoft Exchange services	Started
Microsoft Exchange System Attendant	Provides monitoring, maintenance, and Active Directory lookup services, for example, monitoring of services ...	Started
Microsoft Exchange Transport	The Microsoft Exchange Transport Edge Service.	Started
Microsoft Exchange Transport Log Search	Provides remote search capability for Microsoft Exchange Transport log files.	Started

If a service that has been configured to start automatically is in a stopped state, try to start it. If you're unsuccessful, check the related error in the application log.

TIP

If the installation of Exchange 2007 completes the installation of one or more server roles but then fails at another one, you don't need to reinstall the server roles that were already installed. Instead, the Exchange 2007 Setup Wizard will start in maintenance mode the next time you launch it, and from there you can simply tick the server roles that failed the first time.

To complete your installation, it's a good idea to run the Exchange Best Practices Analyzer tool, now integrated into the Exchange Management Console (EMC) and found under the Toolbox node, as shown in Figure 2.22.

Figure 2.22 Opening the Best Practices Analyzer

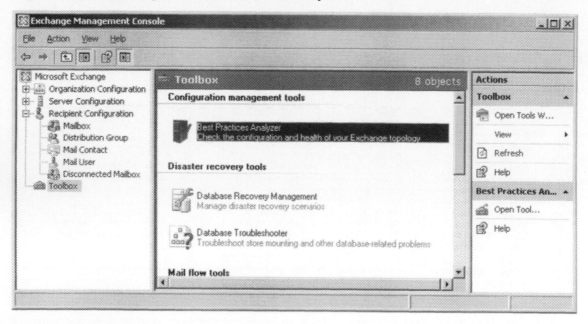

Licensing an Exchange 2007 Server

Unlike Exchange Server 2000 and 2003, you have to license Exchange Server 2007. By default, Exchange Server 2007 has a built-in time bomb (120 days), as you will notice the first time you launch the Exchange Management Console, when you will be presented with a dialog box similar to the one shown in Figure 2.23.

Figure 2.23 The License Warning

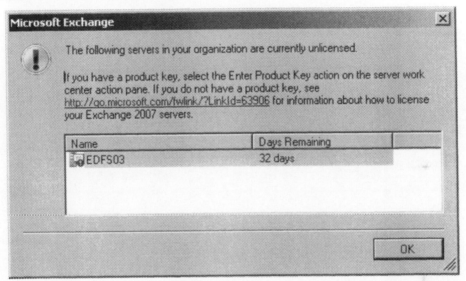

If you purchased and have a Standard or Enterprise product key ready, now is a good time to license your Exchange 2007 server.

NOTE

You will not be able to license a 32-bit version of Exchange Server 2007 because this version is meant for testing and other evaluation purposes.

To license an Exchange Server 2007 server, you will need to perform the following steps:

1. Open the Exchange Management Console, then select the **Server Configuration** work center node.

2. You will be presented with a list of Exchange 2007 servers in your Exchange organization in the work pane. Select the server you want to license and click **Enter Product Key** in the Actions pane on the right (see Figure 2.24).

Figure 2.24 Selecting the Exchange 2007 Servers That Are to Be Licensed

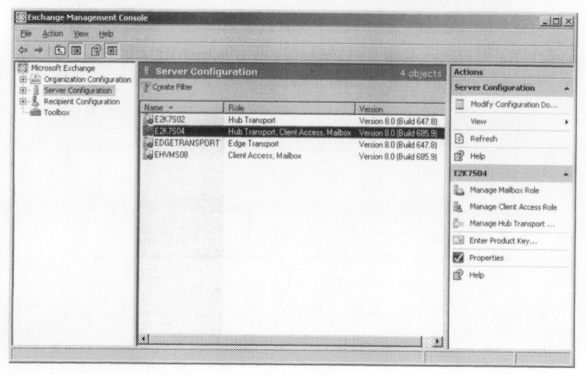

3. In the **Enter Product Key Wizard**, enter your product key license and click **Enter** (see Figure 2.25).

Figure 2.25 Entering the Product Key

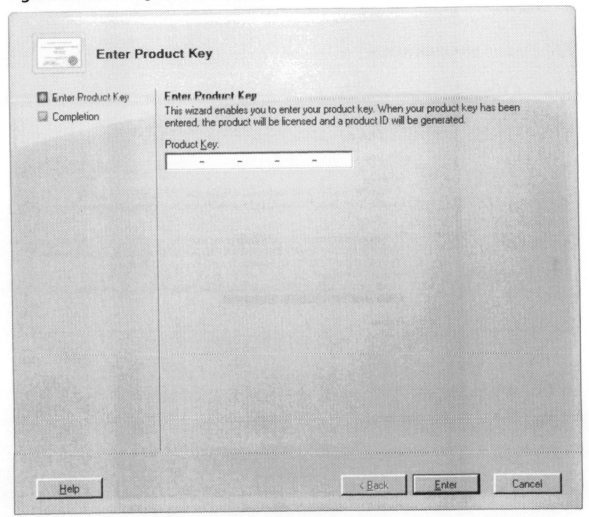

4. On the **Completion page**, click **Finish** (see Figure 2.26).

NOTE

If you're licensing an Exchange 2007 Enterprise Server with the Mailbox server role installed, you need to restart the Microsoft Exchange Information Store service for the change to be reflected in the EMC.

Figure 2.26 Exchange 2007 Server Successfully Licensed

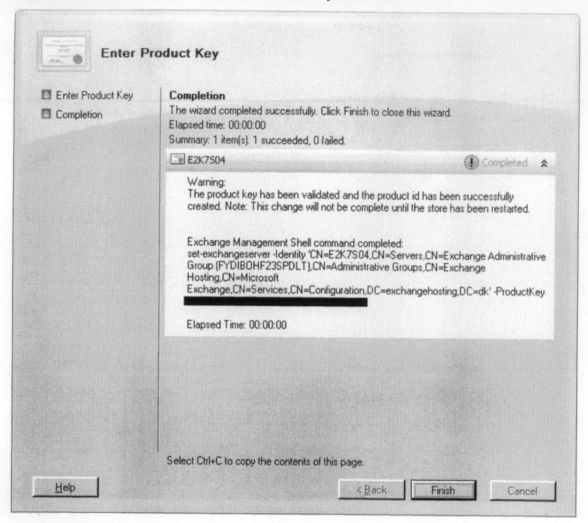

To verify that an Exchange 2007 Server has been properly licensed, you can open the Properties page for the respective server. If the server is licensed, you'll see a Product ID number under the General tab, as shown in Figure 2.27. If it isn't licensed, it will show *Unlicensed* instead of a product ID number.

Figure 2.27 The Properties Page for a Licensed Exchange 2007 Server

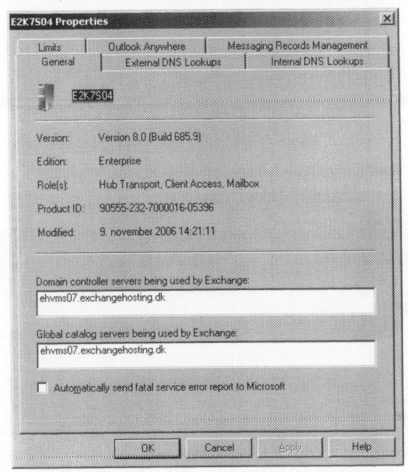

NOTE

You can also license an Exchange 2007 server using the Exchange Management Shell. To do so, run the following command: *Set-ExchangeServer –Identity* Servername – *ProductKey* <product key that consists of 25 digits>.

Finalizing Deployment of Exchange Server 2007

When you launch the Exchange Management Console for the first time, the Microsoft Exchange node will be selected. Under this node you'll find two new tabs: Finalize Deployment and End-to-End Scenario. The Finalize Deployment tab provides a list of recommended tasks you should perform (depending on the server roles installed on the server) to finalize the deployment of your Exchange 2007 server (see Figure 2.28).

Figure 2.28 The Finalize Deployment Tab

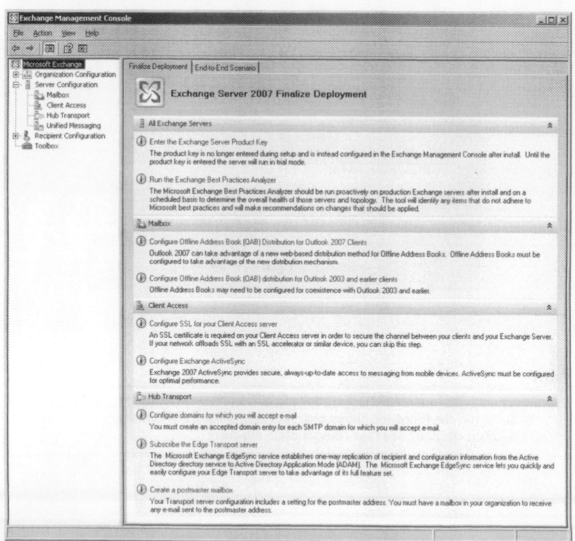

The tasks listed under this tab are applied to features that are enabled by default and need additional configuration. We highly recommend that you follow each task carefully so as not to overlook anything. However, don't rely 100 percent on this list; these are just Microsoft's attempt to show you the most basic configuration settings. Your environment could require additional configuration forethought and planning.

The End-to-End Scenario tab (see Figure 2.29) provides a list of tasks that are optional, but it's a good idea to review and complete them anyway.

Figure 2.29 The End-to-End Tab

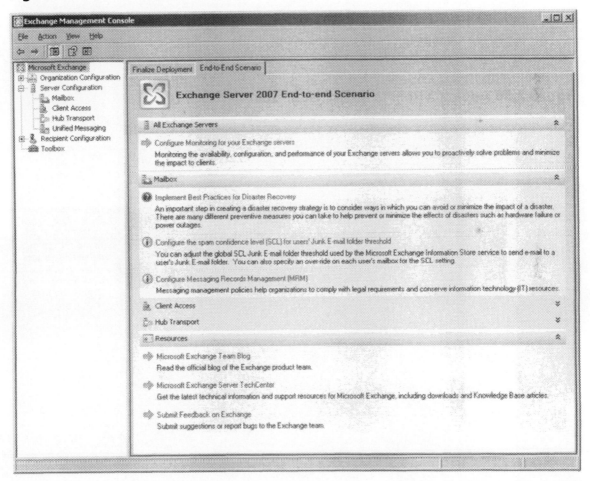

Adding and Removing Exchange 2007 Server Roles

After you have installed one or more Exchange 2007 server roles on a server, you have the option of adding roles later as required. This can be done using the GUI or command-line interface (CLI). Adding a server role using the GUI is done by following these steps:

1. Log on to the respective server with an account that has Exchange Organization Administrator rights.

2. Open the **Control Panel**.

3. Click **Add or Remove Programs**.

4. Select **Microsoft Exchange Server 2007**.

5. Click the **Change** button (see Figure 2.30).

Figure 2.30 Adding a Role to an Exchange 2007 Server

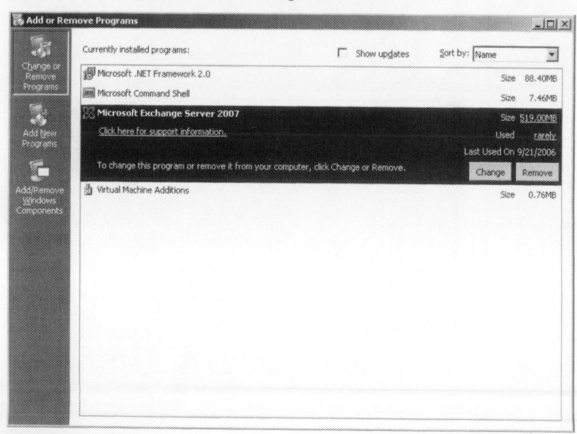

6. In the **Exchange Server 2007 Setup Wizard**, click **Next** (see Figure 2.31).

Figure 2.31 Exchange Server 2007 Setup in Maintenance Mode

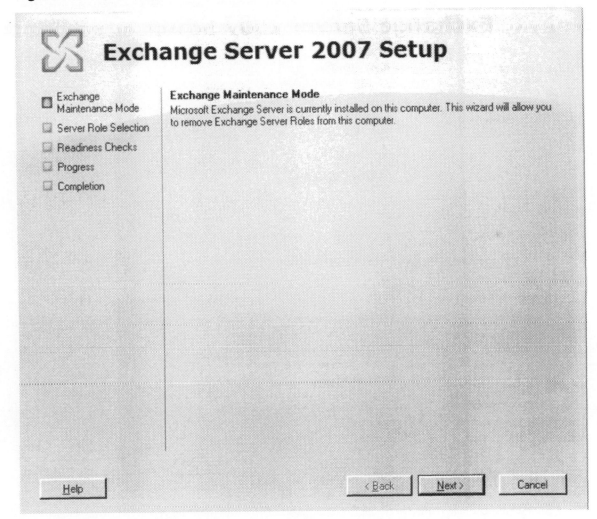

7. Now tick the roles you want to install on the server, then click **Next** (see Figure 2.32).

Figure 2.32 Selecting the Server Role to Be Added to the Exchange 2007 Server

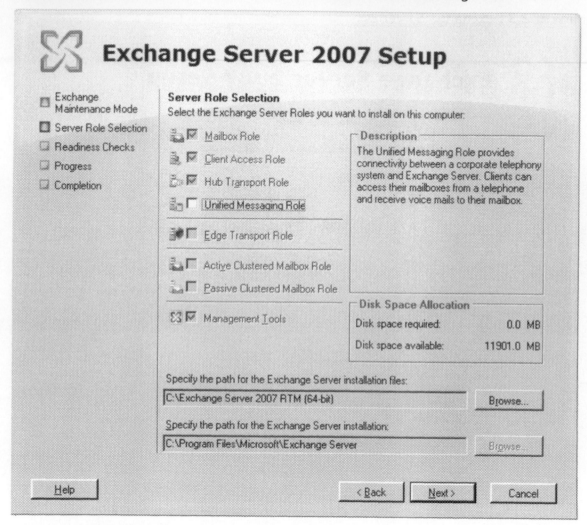

8. When the Exchange Server 2007 Setup Wizard has installed the respective roles, click **Finish**.

To add one or more roles via the CLI, you need to use ExSetup.exe and not Setup.exe, as you might have thought. ExSetup.exe can be found in the C:\Program Files\Microsoft\Exchange Server\ Bin folder. To add a role, perform the following steps:

1. Log on to the respective server using an account that has Exchange Organization Administrator rights.

2. Click **Start | Run**, type **CMD.exe** and click **OK**.

3. Now change to the Exchange Bin folder by typing **CD C:\Program Files\Microsoft\ Exchange Server\Bin** and press **Enter**.

4. Type **ExSetup.exe /mode:Install /roles:**<*roles to be installed*> as shown in Figure 2.33 (where we add the Hub Transport server role to an existing Exchange 2007 server) and press **Enter**.

Figure 2.33 Adding a Server Role Using Unattended Setup

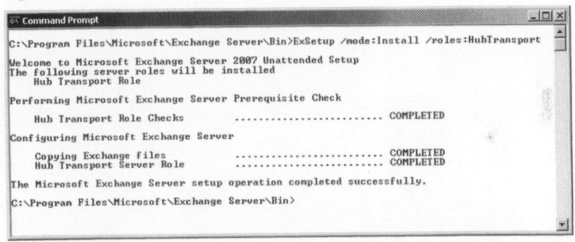

The process of removing a role from an Exchange 2007 server is very similar to that of adding a server role. To remove one or more roles from an existing Exchange 2007 server, do the following.

1. Log on to the respective server with an account that has Exchange Organization Administrator rights.

2. Open the **Control Panel**.

3. Click **Add or Remove Programs**.

4. Select **Microsoft Exchange Server 2007**.

5. Click the **Remove** button.

6. In the **Exchange Server 2007 Setup Wizard**, click **Next** (see Figure 2.34).

Figure 2.34 Exchange Server 2007 in Maintenance Mode

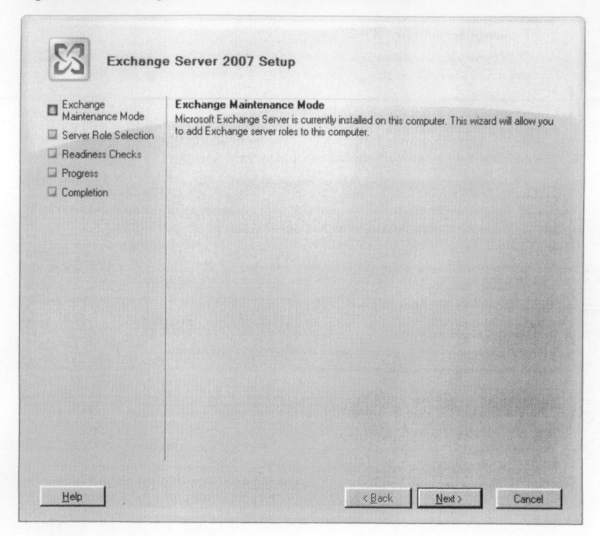

7. Clear the check boxes for the roles you want to remove and click **Next** (see Figure 2.35).

Figure 2.35 Removing an Exchange 2007 Server Role

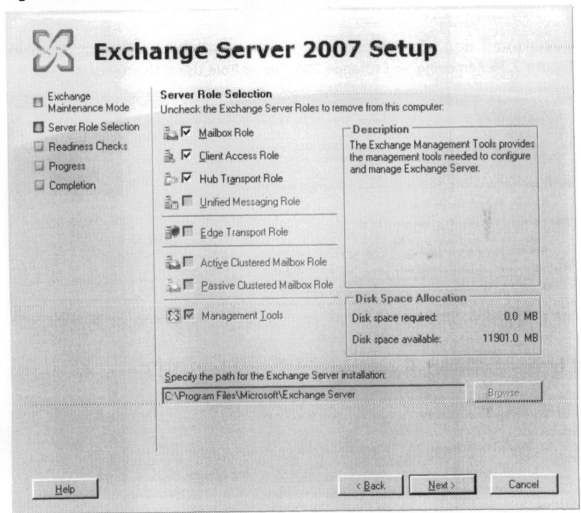

8. Let the readiness check complete, then click **Uninstall**. When the Exchange Server 2007 Setup Wizard has uninstalled the respective server roles, click **Finish**.

To remove one or more roles using the CLI, you must again use ExSetup.exe by performing the following steps:

1. Log on to the respective server using an account that has Exchange Organization Administrator rights.

2. Click **Start | Run**, type **CMD.exe** and click **OK**.

3. Now change to the Exchange Bin folder by typing **CD C:\Program Files\Microsoft\Exchange Server\Bin** and press **Enter**.

4. Type **ExSetup.exe /mode:Uninstall /roles:<*roles to be installed*>**, as shown in Figure 2.36.

Figure 2.36 Removing an Exchange 2007 Server Role Using Unattended Setup

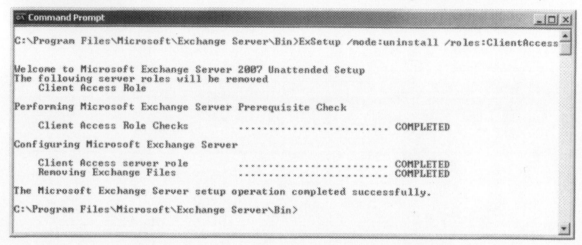

Uninstalling Exchange Server 2007

There might be situations in which you want to completely remove an Exchange 2007 server from your Exchange organization. This can be done using either the Exchange 2007 Installation Wizard or Setup.com.

Uninstalling Exchange 2007 using the Installation Wizard is done the following way:

1. Log on to the respective server with an account that belongs to the Enterprise Admins group.

2. Open the **Control Panel**.

3. Click **Add or Remove Programs**.

4. Select **Microsoft Exchange Server 2007**.

5. Click the **Remove** button.

6. Now clear the check box for each server role, including **Management Tools**, and click **Next**.

7. When the Readiness check has completed, click **Uninstall**.

> **NOTE**
>
> To remove the Mailbox server role, you'll need to make sure no mailboxes exist in the Mailbox database(s) on the respective server. In addition, if you have any Public Folder databases on the server, you'll need to move any existing offline address books to a Public Folder database on another server. Also, keep in mind that you will need to manually delete any EDB and transaction log files after you have uninstalled Exchange, because this is not done via the Exchange Server 2007 Setup Wizard.

Uninstalling Exchange Server 2007 using the CLI can be done the following way:

1. Log on to the respective server using an account that belongs to the Enterprise Admins group.

2. Click **Start | Run**, type **CMD.exe** and click **OK**.

3. Now change to the Exchange Bin folder by typing **CD C:\Program Files\Microsoft\ Exchange Server\Bin** and press **Enter**.

4. Type **ExSetup.exe /mode:Uninstall**.

Removing all server roles from an Exchange 2007 server will also remove any installation files as well as the Exchange server object and all its child objects from the Active Directory forest.

Summary

In this chapter we focused on the hardware, software, and system requirements for an Exchange Server 2007 installation. We went through how you prepare a greenfield Active Directory forest (that is, an Active Directory forest without an existing Exchange organization) for an Exchange 2007 Server deployment. We also took a step-by-step walk through the process of installing a typical Exchange 2007 server into an Active Directory forest using both the GUI and the CLI. We touched on how to properly license an Exchange 2007 server and introduced the new Finalize Deployment and End-to-End Scenario task lists. Finally, we took a look at how you can add and remove Exchange 2007 server roles from an existing Exchange 2007 server with multiple server roles already installed, as well as how to completely uninstall Exchange 2007 from a server and ultimately from the Active Directory forest.

Solutions Fast Track

Exchange 2007 Server Editions and CAL Types

☑ As is the case with previous versions of Exchange, Exchange Server 2007 exists in two different editions: a Standard Edition and an Enterprise Edition.

☑ Exchange 2003 and earlier versions offered only one type of Exchange CAL, but with Exchange 2007 we now have two types: a Standard CAL and an Enterprise CAL.

☑ Before you get too involved in planning the budget for a transition to Exchange 2007 in your organization, you should be aware of one very important thing. Many of you who have Exchange 2003 deployed in your organization could very well be aware of the fact that each Exchange 2003 Client Access License (CAL) included the right to install Outlook 2003 on the devices for which these CALs were obtained. You probably think that this hasn't changed in regard to Exchange 2007 CALs. Think again because Exchange Server 2007 Standard or Enterprise does not include the right to install Outlook on devices for which CALs are obtained!

Exchange 2007 Prerequisites

☑ It's important that you examine the system hardware, software, and Active Directory requirements before you begin installing Exchange 2007 into a production environment.

☑ You'll need an x64 architecture-based processor that supports Intel Extended Memory 64 Technology (Intel EM64T) and an AMD 64-bit processor that supports the AMD64 platform, but bear in mind that the Intel Itanium IA64 processor isn't supported by Exchange Server 2007.

☑ The minimum Windows Active Directory functional level for Exchange 2007 is Windows 2000 native mode. If you are installing Exchange Server 2007 into an existing Exchange organization, it is also important to note that the organization should be running in native mode.

☑ Exchange Server 2007 exists in 32-bit and 64-bit versions; however, the 32-bit version is not supported in a production environment and is meant to be used for evaluation and testing purposes only. If you install the 32-bit version of Exchange 2007 in a production environment and experience an issue, you will not be able to get any support from Microsoft Support Services. There is one exception to the rule, though: The 32-bit version of the Exchange 2007 Management Tools (more specifically, the Exchange Management Console, the Exchange Management Shell, the Exchange Help file, and the Exchange Best Practices Analyzer tool) are supported for management tasks in a production environment.

☑ As most of you might recall, Exchange Server 2000 and 2003 made extended use of the Windows Server 2000 or 2003 SMTP and NNTP services, requiring that they be installed components (both subcomponents of IIS) prior to installing the Exchange Server product itself. Both the Hub Transport server and the Edge Transport server requires that both these services aren't installed, because NNTP support has been dropped in Exchange 2007 and Exchange 2007 now has its own SMTP service.

Installing Exchange 2007 Using the Setup Wizard

☑ Because of the heavily improved and role-based Setup Wizard, installing Exchange 2007 is much easier than was the case with previous versions of Exchange. Because the Exchange 2007 Setup Wizard is role based, you can either select to install a typical Exchange Server installation, which will install the Hub Transport, Client Access, and Mailbox Server roles on the same server (which is what you typically want to do in an Exchange organization that will consist of one Exchange 2007 Server only), or you can do a custom Exchange Server installation, which lets you choose the server roles that should be installed on the respective server. You would typically choose to do a custom Exchange Server installation in a large Exchange organization where you want to separate the various Exchange 2007 Server roles among different servers.

☑ A benefit of a role-based approach is that Exchange 2007 Setup installs only the Exchange files and services necessarily for the server role you deploy. This means that the respective server won't waste disk space and resources on unnecessary files and services the way previous versions of Exchange did.

☑ A typical Exchange Server 2007 installation will install the Hub Transport, Client Access, and Mailbox server roles and the Management Tools (more specifically, the Exchange Management Console, the Exchange Management Shell, the Exchange Help file, and the Exchange Best Practices Analyzer tool) on a server.

Installing Exchange 2007 Using Unattended Setup

☑ Setup.com supports many different parameters and switches that will let you install Exchange Server 2007 using unattended setup. To whet your appetite, we recommend that you type **Setup.exe /?** to list all available parameters and switches, providing a short description of each.

Verifying the Installation of Exchange Server 2007

☑ After Exchange Server 2007 has been installed, we recommend that you verify that the installation completed without any serious warnings or errors. If you didn't encounter any problems during installation of Exchange Server 2007, there's a good chance everything is fine, but you won't know for sure until you have checked the Windows Event logs and the Exchange 2007 setup logs as well as do a visual verification that each selected role has been installed.

☑ If the installation of Exchange 2007 completes the installation of one or more server roles but then fails at another one, you don't need to reinstall the server roles that were already installed. Instead, the Exchange 2007 Setup Wizard will start in maintenance mode the next time you launch it, and from there you can simply tick the server roles that failed the first time.

Licensing an Exchange 2007 Server

☑ Unlike Exchange Server 2000 and 2003, you have to license Exchange Server 2007. By default, Exchange Server 2007 has a built-in time bomb (120 days), as you will notice the first time you launch the Exchange Management Console.

☑ You will not be able to license a 32-bit version of Exchange Server 2007, since this version is meant for testing and other evaluation purposes.

☑ If you're licensing an Exchange 2007 Enterprise Server with the Mailbox server role installed, you need to restart the Microsoft Exchange Information Store service for the change to be reflected in the EMC.

Finalizing Deployment of Exchange Server 2007

☑ When you launch the Exchange Management Console for the first time, the Microsoft Exchange node will be selected. Under this node you'll find two new tabs: Finalize Deployment and End-to-End Scenario. The Finalize Deployment tab provides a list of recommended tasks you should perform (depending on the server roles installed on the server) to finalize the deployment of your Exchange 2007 server.

☑ The tasks listed on the Finalize Deployment tab are applied to features that are enabled by default and that need additional configuration. We highly recommend you follow each task carefully so as not to overlook anything, but don't rely 100 percent on this list, since these are just Microsoft's attempt to show you the most basic configuration settings.

☑ The End-to-End Scenario tab provides a list of tasks that are optional, but it's a good idea to review and complete them anyway.

Adding and Removing Exchange 2007 Server Roles

☑ All Exchange 2007 server roles can be installed on a single server (except the Edge Transport server role, which must be installed on its own hardware in the perimeter network). So, if you're a small organization, you do not need to invest in more than one piece of hardware for your Exchange server. Bear in mind, however, that if you plan to cluster the mailbox server role, the mailbox server must run on its own hardware.

☑ You can add and remove Exchange server roles from an Exchange 2007 server as required using the Windows Control Panel's Add or Remove Programs function or the ExSetup.exe CLI.

Uninstalling Exchange Server 2007

☑ There might be situations in which you want to completely remove an Exchange 2007 server from your Exchange organization. This can be done using either the Exchange 2007 Installation Wizard or Setup.com.

☑ Removing all server roles from an Exchange 2007 server will also remove any installation files as well as the Exchange server object and all its child objects from the Active Directory forest.

Frequently Asked Questions

Q: Which processors (CPUs) are supported by Exchange Server 2007?

A: This depends on whether we're speaking of the 32-bit version or the 64-bit version. The 32-bit version supports any Intel Pentium or compatible 800MHz or faster 32-bit processor. The 64-bit version supports Intel Extended Memory 64 Technology (Intel EM64T) and AMD 64-bit processor that supports AMD64 platform, but bear in mind that the Intel Itanium IA64 processor isn't supported by the 64-bit version of Exchange 2007.

Q: What are the memory requirements of the Exchange Server 2007 64-bit version?

A: The minimum requirements are 2GB RAM, but it's recommended that you install 2GB per server plus 5MB of RAM per mailbox. The more RAM, the better, since the 64-bit architecture allows Exchange 2007 to store much more data in the address space compared to previous versions of Exchange, which only existed in 32-bit versions. If we're talking about an Exchange 2007 Mailbox Server with more than four storage groups, it's recommended you install 2GB RAM per three storage groups (if you have between five and eight storage groups, you should install 4GB; if you have between nine and 12, you should install 6GB, and so on).

Q: Is it supported to use the 32-bit version of Exchange 2007 in a production environment?

A: No! Only the 64-bit version should be used in a production environment. The 32-bit version is meant to be used for evaluation and testing purposes. There is one exception to the rule, though: The 32-bit version of the Exchange 2007 Management Tools (more specifically, the Exchange Management Console, the Exchange Management Shell, the Exchange Help file, and the Exchange Best Practices Analyzer tool) is supported for management tasks in a production environment.

Q: Which operating systems does Exchange 2007 support?

A: You must install Exchange 2007 on a server running Windows Server 2003 with SP1 or Windows Server 2003 R2. Both the Standard and Enterprise Editions of these operating systems are supported, but bear in mind that you need to install the Enterprise Edition if you plan to use clustering features such as Cluster Continuous Replication (CCR) or Single Copy Clusters (SCC).

Q: I remember that Exchange 2000 and 2003 required the SMTP and NNTP Windows components to be installed before Exchange could be installed. Is this also the case with Exchange 2007?

A: No, this has changed with Exchange 2007. Exchange 2007 requires that you install neither the SMTP nor NNTP Windows components. The reason is that Exchange 2007 now includes its own SMTP service, which has been built from the ground up using managed code. The NNTP feature has been dropped in Exchange 2007.

Q: Should the Active Directory Forest and Domain(s) still be prepared using *ForestPrep* and *DomainPrep*, as was the case in Exchange 2000 and 2003?

A: The Active Directory forest as well as any domains should be prepared for Exchange 2007, but the *ForestPrep* and *DomainPrep* switches don't exist any longer. Instead you must use *PrepareSchema* and *PrepareDomain* or *PrepareAD* (which will run both *PrepareSchema* and *PrepareDomain*). But note that it's not mandatory that you run these switches before you start installing Exchange 2007, since they will be run automatically during the installation, if you have the appropriate permissions.

Q: Can I install Exchange 2007 in a Windows 2000 Active Directory?

A: No. Exchange 2007 can only be installed in a Windows 2003 Active Directory. In addition, each domain controller must be running Windows Server 2003 with SP1 applied.

Q: To what forest-level mode must the Active Directory be set to be able to install Exchange 2007?

A: The forest-level mode should be set to Windows 2000 Native mode or Windows 2003 Native mode.

Q: I heard that Exchange 2007 must be licensed with a product key. Could you confirm whether this is correct?

A: You heard right. Each Exchange 2007 server in an Exchange organization must be properly licensed using a 25-digit product key, which can be found on the DVD case or can be requested via the TechNet or MSDN sites. An unlicensed version of Exchange 2007 will expire after 120 days.

Chapter 3

Managing Recipients in Exchange 2007

Solutions in this chapter:

- **Managing Recipients Using the Exchange 2007 Management Console**

- **Managing Recipients in a Coexistence Environment**

- **Granting Access and/or *SendAs* Permissions to a Mailbox**

- **Creating a Custom Recipient Management Console**

- **Recipient Filtering in Exchange 2007**

☑ Summary

☑ Solutions Fast Track

☑ Frequently Asked Questions

Introduction

One of the things that have changed drastically in Exchange Server 2007 is the way in which you manage recipients. As most of us are aware, recipients were managed via Active Directory Users and Computers (ADUC) MMC snap-in in the Exchange 2000 and 2003 environments, but with Exchange 2007, the recipient management tasks have been integrated back into the Exchange Management Console and removed from ADUC, as was the case in Exchange versions prior to Exchange Server 2000. In addition to performing the recipient tasks using the Exchange Management Console, you also have the option of using the Exchange Management Shell, which is perfectly suited for performing bulk user changes using *one-liners* (single-line commands).

So, why did the Exchange Product group choose to move away from extending and using the ADUC MMC snap-in to manage recipients in Exchange 2007? There are several reasons. For one, the team wanted to attack the cost of managing recipient users by introducing automation. This automation has been introduced via PowerShell CMDlets, which, as mentioned, really shine when it comes to bulk user changes. For another, they wanted to truly support the split-permissions model, making it possible for an Exchange Administrator to do any relevant Exchange tasks from within a single console: the Exchange Management Console (EMC). Another goal was to simplify the management of the Global Address List (GAL) and recipient types from within the EMC. This goal was accomplished because only the objects and attributes that pertain to Exchange are shown in this console. Finally, the Exchange Product group wanted to have *explicit* recipient types instead of *implicit* ones. Exchange 2007 has a total of 14 different explicit recipient types, each with its own individual icon and recipient type details, lowering the overall administrative burden.

We'll be honest and say that there's been a lot of hype on the Internet about whether moving the management of recipients to the EMC was a good idea or not. During the Exchange 2007 Technology Adoption Program (TAP) and the Rapid Deployment Program (RDP), many Exchange Administrators, as well as independent consultants, expressed their opinion about this move. The majority of them think it's a bad decision, primarily because it leads to huge retraining costs (for help desk staff and others), and it means you suddenly have to administer users using two different consoles, the ADUC and the EMC. We think that the overall concern is valid, but at the same time we understand the Exchange Product group's decision to make the move. Since the group has no intention of changing this post-RTM, we'll have to live with it.

After reading this chapter, you will have a good understanding of what has changed since Exchange Server 2003. You will also be provided with step-by-step instructions on how you perform recipient management tasks using primarily the EMC but also some CMDlets in the Exchange Management Shell (EMS). In addition, we'll talk about how you should manage recipients when your systems are coexisting with an Exchange 2000 environment (where Exchange 2007 coexists with Exchange 2000 and/or 2003), how you create a custom recipient management console, and how to use recipient filters.

Managing Recipients Using the Exchange 2007 Management Console

As mentioned in the introduction to this chapter, the management of recipients in Exchange Server 2007 as well as their Exchange-related properties has been moved back into the EMC in addition to the EMS, both of which are based on Windows PowerShell. This means that all management of Exchange recipient objects should be modified from within the EMC or EMS, not using the ADUC snap-in.

In this first section of the chapter, we'll take a look at how you manage recipients using the EMC. Recipient management for all types of recipients, such as user mailboxes, mail-enabled contacts, and users and distribution groups, is done under the Recipient Configuration work center node, shown as selected in Figure 3.1. As you can see, we have four recipient type subnodes beneath this work center. In order, we have a Mailbox, Distribution Group, Mail Contact, and a Disconnected Mailbox node.

Figure 3.1 Recipient Work Center Node in the Exchange Management Console

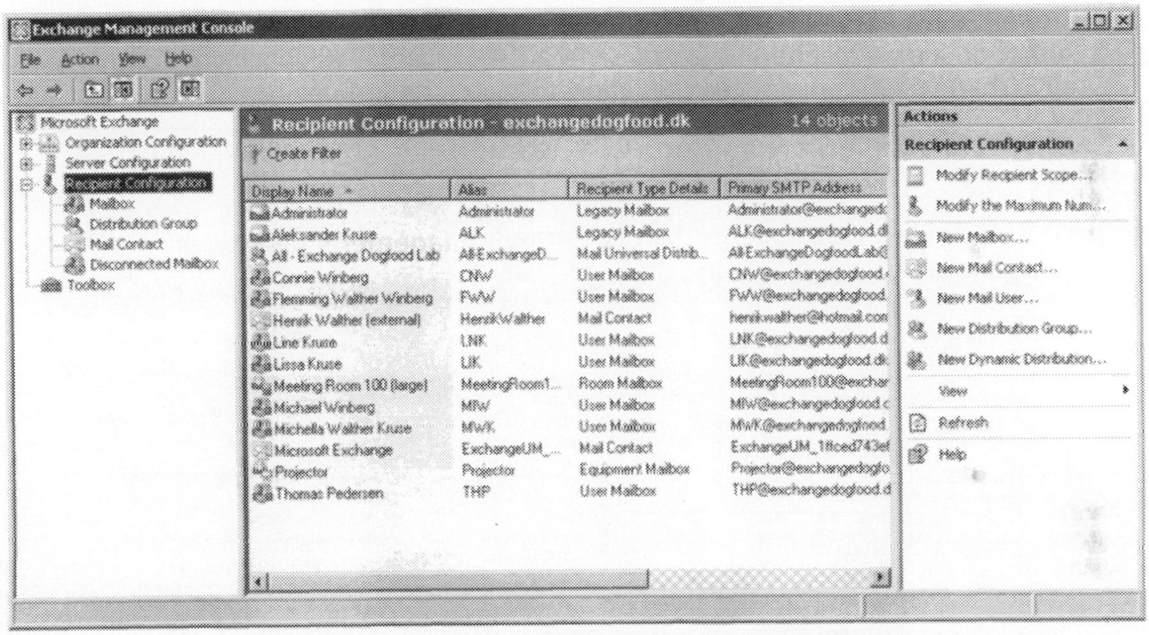

Also notice that when the Recipient Configuration work center node is selected, all types of recipient objects are listed in the Results pane, with the exception of disconnected mailboxes, since these aren't physically located in the Active Directory. If you take a closer look at the screenshot in Figure 3.1, you can also see that each type of recipient object has its own individual icon as well as recipient type description, due to the fact that they now are explicit and not implicit, as was the case in Exchange Server 2003. This is a nice addition because it makes it so much easier to differentiate the recipient types in Exchange 2007.

If you take a look at the tasks provided in the Action pane, you can see that it's possible to create any recipient type without having to specifically select the corresponding recipient type subnode beneath the Recipient Configuration work center node. If you select a recipient type subnode instead, you'll only see a list of the recipient types specific for that subnode. Furthermore, the available tasks in the Action pane are specific only to that particular recipient type.

Managing Mailboxes

All right, let's start by taking a look at the Mailboxes subnode, shown in Figure 3.2, which displays all mailbox user objects. *Mailbox user objects* are objects that have been mailbox enabled. Note that not only mail user objects created in Exchange 2007 are displayed, but also legacy (Exchange 2000 and 2003) mailbox user objects. You cannot see it in Figure 3.2, but there's also a *Server and Organizational Unit* column, which, as implied by the names, tells us the name of the mailbox server on which the mailbox is located and in which Active Directory OU the user object resides.

NOTE

Although legacy mailboxes are exposed via the Exchange Management Console, not all Exchange 2007-specific features apply to these types of mailboxes.

Figure 3.2 Mailbox Subnode in the Exchange Management Console

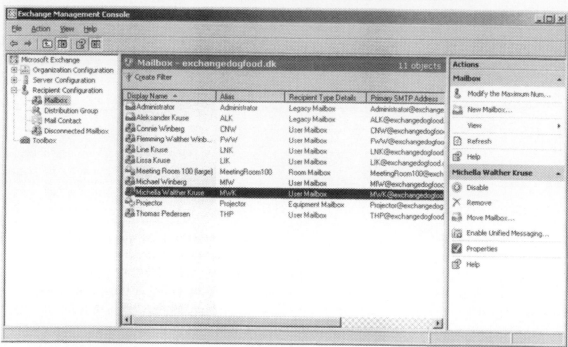

When we look at mailbox user objects, we see that five explicit mailbox recipient types exist in Exchange 2007. Four of these are listed in Figure 3.3, which is a screenshot of the first page you're presented with when you launch the **New Mailbox** Wizard.

Figure 3.3 New Mailbox Wizard Introduction Page

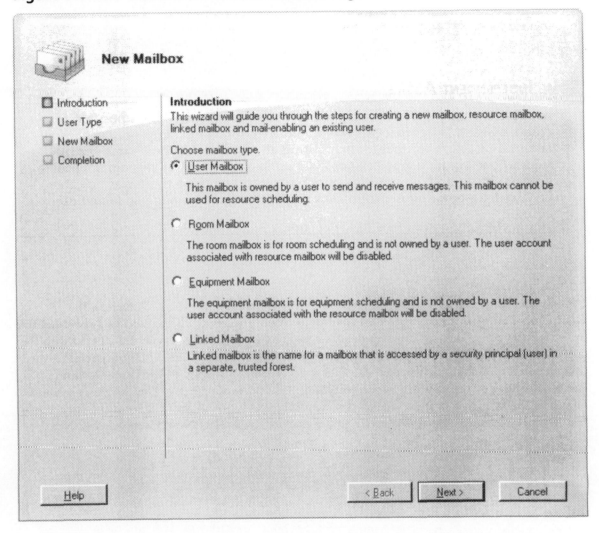

We have *user mailboxes*, which are the type of mailbox you create when mailbox-enabling an ordinary end user. We have *room mailboxes* (a.k.a. resource mailboxes), which are used for room scheduling. Note that this type of mailbox isn't owned by a user and that the associated user account is in a disabled state after creation. We also have *equipment mailboxes*, which are similar to room mailboxes except that they are used for equipment-scheduling purposes, such as booking an overhead projector. Then we have *linked mailboxes*, which are a special type of mailbox that can be used to link to a user account in a separate trusted forest. Finally, we have *shared mailboxes*, which aren't included in the EMC but instead need to be managed via the EMS using the New-Mailbox CMDlet (you need to use the *–Shared* parameter). A shared mailbox is a type of mailbox that multiple users can log onto. It's not associated with a user account that can be used to log onto the Active Directory but is instead associated with a disabled user account, as in the case of room and equipment mailboxes.

SOME INDEPENDENT ADVICE

Because Exchange 2007 uses explicit mailbox recipient types, it's possible to create a search filter that lists all room mailboxes, for example, or perhaps all legacy mailboxes, for that matter. Listing all resource mailboxes in the ADUC snap-in back in Exchange 2000 or 2003 using a search filter was not a trivial process; it required you to use custom attributes because there was no other way to differentiate resource mailboxes from ordinary mailbox-enabled user accounts.

Creating a User Mailbox

Let's go through the steps necessary to create a user mailbox using the EMC. With either the **Recipient Configuration** work center node or the **Mailbox** subnode selected, click **New Mailbox** in the **Action** pane. This will bring up the New Mailbox Wizard, and you will be presented with the page shown back in Figure 3.3. Select **User Mailbox** and click **Next**. On the **User Type** page, you have the option of choosing whether you want to create a new mailbox–enabled user account in Active Directory or whether you want to mailbox-enable an existing Active Directory user account. Choosing the latter will bring up a GUI picker containing a list of all Active Directory user accounts that do not have an associated mailbox. In this example we will select **New User** and click **Next** (see Figure 3.4).

NOTE

To be able to create a new mailbox (also known as creating a new mailbox-enabled user), the account you're logged on with must have the appropriate permissions in Active Directory, in addition to having the Exchange Recipient Administrator permission. Membership in the Account Operators group should be sufficient. If you want to create a new mailbox for an existing user (also known as mailbox-enabling an existing user), you only need Exchange Recipient Administrator permissions.

Figure 3.4 Selecting the User Type

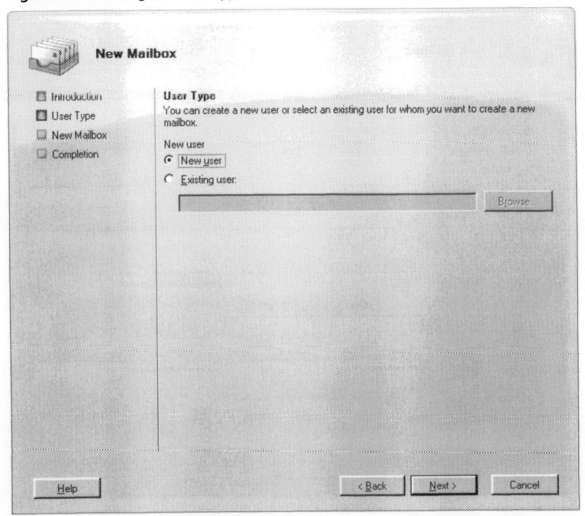

On the User Information page, select the Organizational unit in which you want the user object to be created by clicking the **Browse** button. Enter the name and account information and click **Next** (see Figure 3.5).

As you can see in Figure 3.5, you can specify that the user must change his password at the next logon, just as you could when provisioning Exchange 2000/2003 users in ADUC.

Figure 3.5 Entering User Name and Account Information

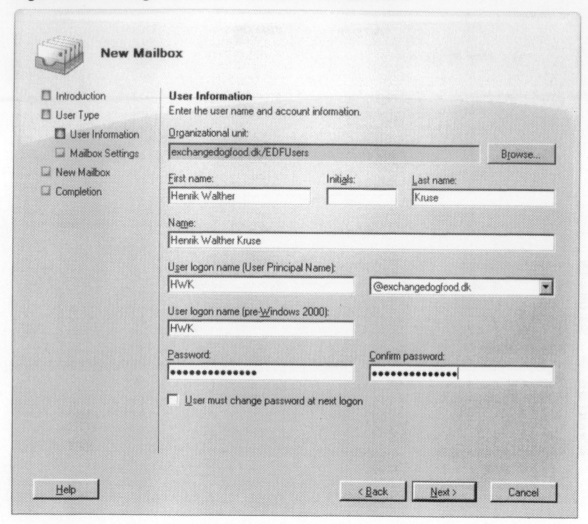

On the Mailbox Settings page, you can specify the Exchange 2007 Mailbox Server Storage group as well as the Mailbox database in which the mailbox for the user should be created (see Figure 3.6). On this page you also have the option of applying any required managed folder mailbox and Exchange ActiveSync mailbox policies. (These are discussed in more detail in Chapter 5.) When you're ready, click **Next** once again.

As you can see in the bottom of the Mail Settings page, you need an Exchange Enterprise Client Access License (CAL) to take advantage of the messaging records management features of Exchange 2007. (Exchange licensing and client CALS were discussed earlier in Chapter 2.)

Figure 3.6 Choosing the Server, Storage Group, and Mailbox Database for the Mailbox

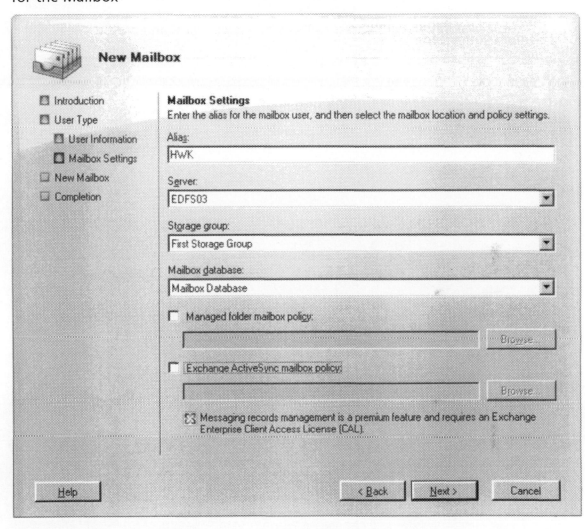

On the New Mailbox page, you can see a configuration summary of the mailbox-enabled user account that will be created. Click **New**, and then click **Finish** on the **Completion** page (see Figure 3.7).

SOME INDEPENDENT ADVICE

As is the case with all wizards in the Exchange 2007 Management Console, the Completion page shown in Figure 3.7 will provide you with the CMDlet and any parameters that will be used to create the mailbox-enabled user account. This CMDlet can be copied to the clipboard by pressing **Ctrl + C**, so you can use it for creating mailbox-enabled user accounts directly via the EMS in the future. A good idea is to paste the code into Notepad or another text editor so that you can change parameters, such as the name, alias, and organization unit, to meet your needs.

Figure 3.7 The New Mailbox Completion Page

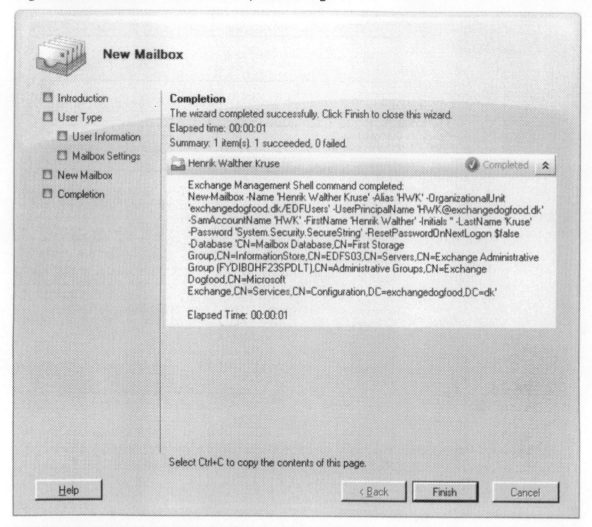

These are all the steps required to create a mailbox-enabled user. This process wasn't harmful at all, was it?

If you want to create a user mailbox using the EMS, you need to use the *New-Mailbox* or *Set-Mailbox* CMDlets, depending on whether you want to create a new mailbox-enabled user or mailbox-enable an existing user account. To get a list of all the available parameters for these two CMDlets, you can open the EMS and type **Get–Help New–Mailbox** and **Get–Help Set–Mailbox**, respectively.

Manipulating Mailboxes in Exchange 2007

Once we have created a user mailbox, we can manipulate it in several ways by highlighting it in the Results pane and then choose the action we want to perform in the Action pane.

As you can see in Figure 3.8, we can disable the mailbox, meaning all of the Exchange attributes are removed from the respective Active Directory user account.

Figure 3.8 Set of Actions for a User Mailbox in the Actions Pane

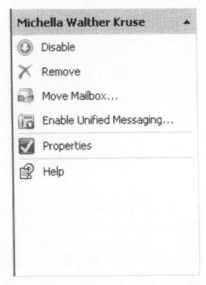

Although the account will no longer be mailbox enabled, the mailbox can still be found under the Disconnected Mailbox subnode. From there, it can be reconnected to the same or any other nonmailbox-enabled user account, until the default 30-day deleted mailbox retention policy for Exchange 2007 databases kicks in and purges the mailbox. (We'll take a closer look at reconnecting mailboxes later in this chapter.) When you try to disable a mailbox, you'll first receive the warning message shown in Figure 3.9.

Figure 3.9 The Warning Received When You're Disabling a Mailbox

Another option is to remove the mailbox, which not only removes the mailbox but also deletes the associated user account in Active Directory—so think twice before you click Yes to the warning message shown in Figure 3.10. Exchange 2007 beta 2 builds and earlier didn't even include a warning message about this action, which led to a few frustrated Exchange consultants who participated in the Exchange 2007 Rapid Deployment Program (RDP), a program where selected customers deployed Exchange 2007 beta 2 in a production environment.

Figure 3.10 Warning Received When You're Removing a Mailbox

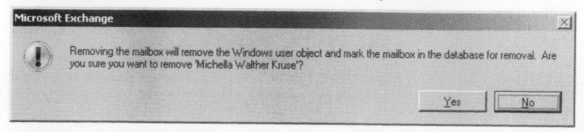

NOTE

Unless you have delivered mail to a mail-enabled user object, selecting either the Disable or the Remove Action pane action will *not* place that mailbox in the Disconnected Mailbox subnode. The reason behind this is simply that the mailbox is created only when it receives its first piece of mail, so there is no mailbox to disconnect.

To disable or remove a user mailbox using the EMS, you need to use the *Disable-Mailbox* and *Remove-Mailbox* CMDlets, respectively. So if, for example, you wanted to disable the mailbox for a user named Michella Kruse Walther with a UPN of MWK, you would need to run the following command:

```
Disable-Mailbox -Identity MWK
```

followed by pressing **Enter**. This will bring you a command-line warning message similar to the one shown in Figure 3.9. Click **Y** for Yes.

Likewise, removing the user mailbox for the same user would be done by running the following command:

```
Remove-Mailbox -Identity MWK
```

followed by pressing **Enter**. This will bring you a command-line warning message similar to the one shown in Figure 3.10. Click **Y** for Yes.

Moving a Mailbox

We can also move a mailbox to another server, storage group, and mailbox database; we do this by clicking the **Move Mailbox** link in the Action pane, bringing up the Move Mailbox Wizard Introduction page, shown in Figure 3.11. Here we specify the server, storage group, and mailbox database the respective mailbox should be moved to. When you have done so, click **Next**

Figure 3.11 The Move Mailbox Wizard Introduction Page

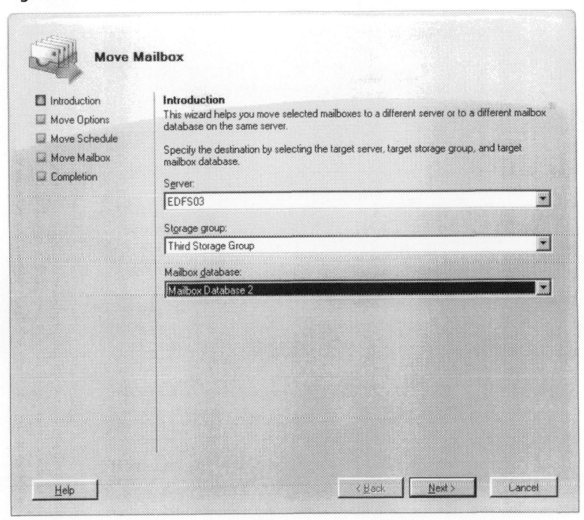

On the Move Options page, we can specify how the mailboxes that contain corrupted messages should be managed. We can configure the Move Mailbox Wizard to skip any mailboxes containing one or more corrupted messages or simply let it skip corrupted messages (Figure 3.12). If we select the latter, we have even more granular control and can specify the maximum number of messages to skip before the mailbox move should be cancelled. In this example, we choose **Skip** the mailbox and click **Next**.

Figure 3.12 Move Mailbox Wizard Options

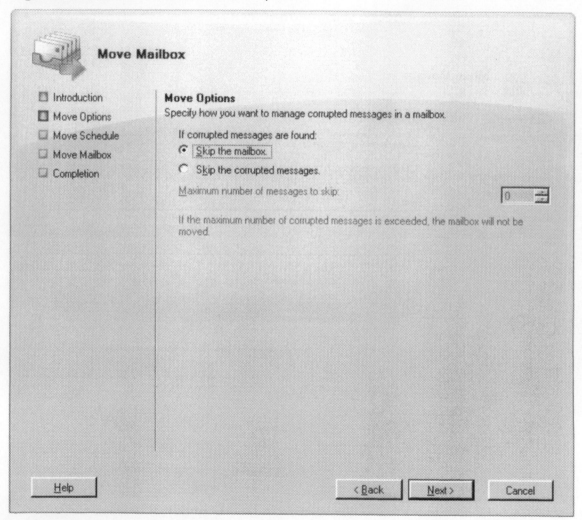

We're now taken to the Move Schedule page shown in Figure 3.13, where we can specify when the mailbox move should occur as well as the maximum length of time the move should run before it should be cancelled. The idea behind the Move Mailbox Schedule option is to allow you to schedule the mailbox moves to occur during nonworking hours. In this example, we select **Immediately** and click **Next**.

Figure 3.13 The Move Mailbox Wizard Schedule Page

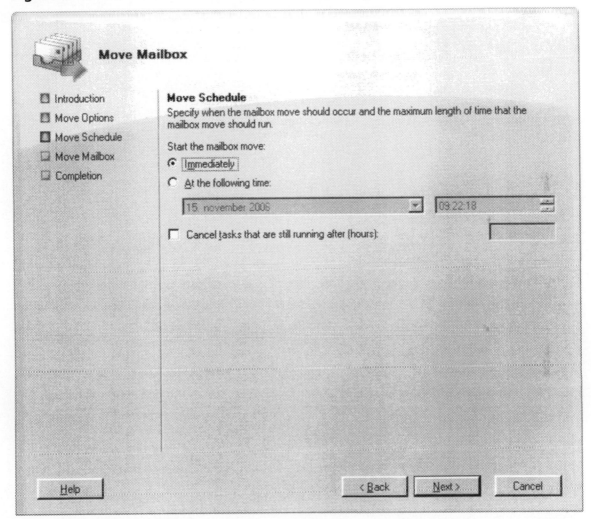

Next we are taken to the Move Mailbox page (see Figure 3.14), where we can verify that the parameters for the mailbox move are correct before the actual move takes place. When you're ready, click **Move**.

Figure 3.14 The Move Mailbox Wizard Summary Page

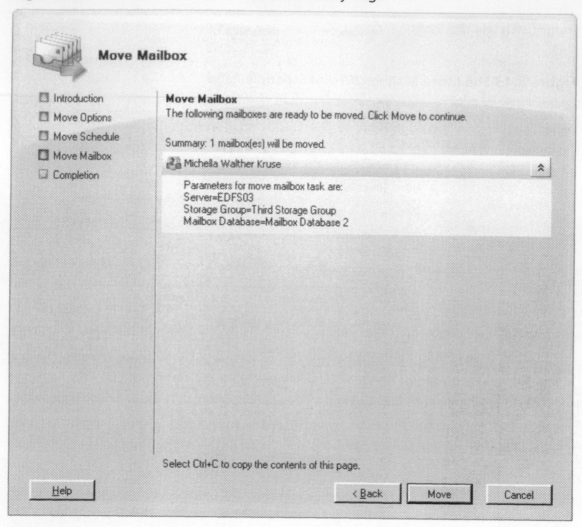

Depending on the size of the mailbox, you will need to have a little patience while the move takes place. The Move Mailbox Wizard needs to first open the source mailbox and then create a destination mailbox on the target database. Only then does it start to move the contents of the mailbox, completing its task by finally deleting the source mailbox and closing its connection. When the mailbox has been moved successfully, you'll be taken to the Completion page, where you can see the CMDlet as well as the parameters used to move the mailbox (see Figure 3.15). Click **Finish** to exit the Move Mailbox Wizard.

Figure 3.15 The Move Mailbox Wizard Completion Page

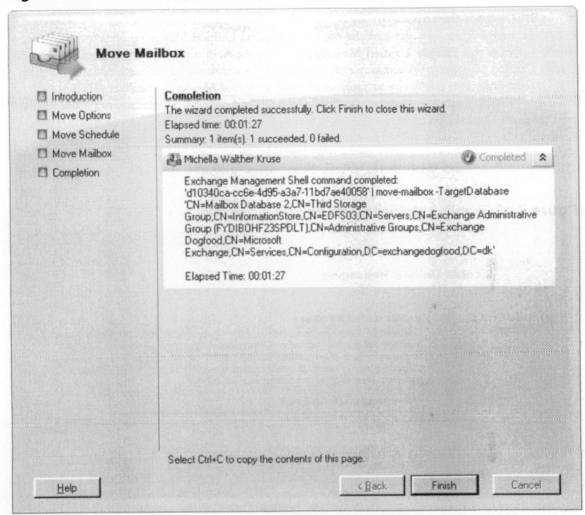

To move a mailbox using the EMS, you can use the *Move-Mailbox* CMDlet. To get a list of available parameters for this CMDlet, type **Get-Help Move-Mailbox** in the EMS.

Enabling Unified Messaging for a Mailbox

If you have installed the Unified Messaging Server role on an Exchange 2007 server in your Exchange organization, you also have the option of enabling Unified Messaging for a user mailbox. When you click the **Enable Unified Messaging** link in the Action pane, you will be faced with the Enable Unified Messaging Wizard shown in Figure 3.16. In addition to enabling Unified Messaging for a user mailbox, this is where you apply any required Unified Messaging Mailbox Policies, a mandatory setting, as well as creating a mailbox extension and personal identification number (PIN), used to access Outlook Voice Access (OVA). When you have enabled Unified Messaging for a user mailbox, an e-mail message will be sent to the respective mailbox, notifying that user that they have been enabled for unified messaging. The e-mail message will include information about the PIN as

Figure 3.16 Enabling Unified Messaging for a User Mailbox

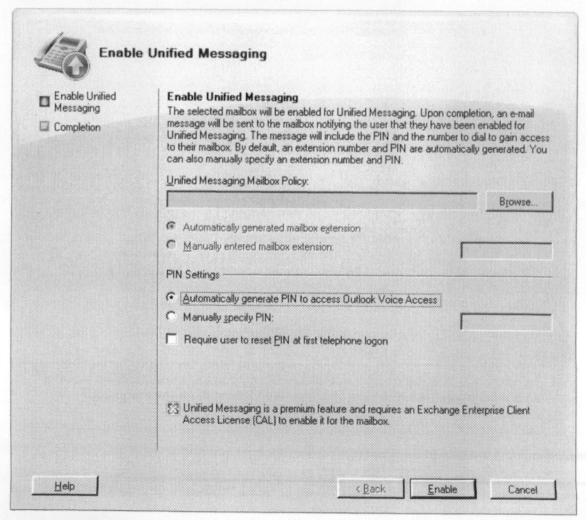

well as the number and extension the user needs to dial to gain access to the mailbox. When you're ready, click **Enable** and then click **Finish** on the Completion page.

We will talk much more about the Unified Messaging functionality in Chapter 10.

Let's now take a look at the Property page for a mailbox user object, which allows us complete control over all Exchange-related settings from within the EMC. We gain this control by selecting a user mailbox, either beneath the Recipient Configuration work center node or the Mailbox subnode, followed by clicking **Properties** in the Action pane. (Alternatively, you can right-click the user mailbox object and select **Properties** in the context menu.) The tab that will be selected by default is the General tab (see Figure 3.17).

Figure 3.17 The General Tab on the User Mailbox Property Page

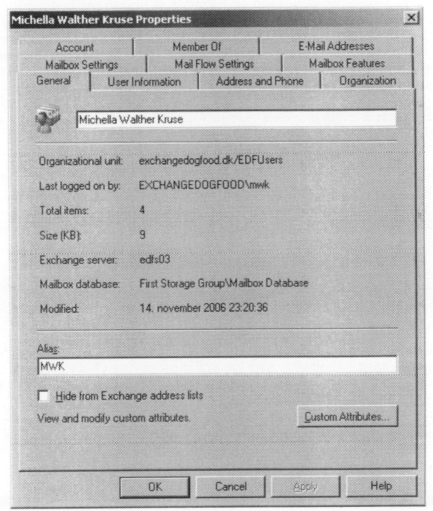

Here we have the option of changing the display name as well as the alias of the user mailbox. In addition, we can see information about which Active Directory OU the user mailbox object is located in, the last user that logged onto the mailbox, the total items and size of the mailbox, and the mailbox server, storage group and mailbox database on which the user mailbox resides. From this tab we also have the option of hiding the user mailbox from any Exchange address list. Finally, we can click the **Custom Attributes** button to specify any custom attributes that should apply to this user mailbox. Like Exchange 2000 and 2003, Exchange 2007 gives you the option of specifying up to 15 different custom attributes.

SOME INDEPENDENT ADVICE

Some of you might be wondering what custom attributes can be used for in the first place. Well, custom attributes can be used for many different purposes. For example, they can be used for personal information about your users that does not easily fit into any existing field. Examples of custom attribute fields include employee numbers, cost center, health insurance data, and Social Security information.

Bear in mind that custom attributes can also be used to create recipient conditions for dynamic distribution groups, e-mail address policies, and address lists. Exchange hosting providers especially can take advantage of custom attributes in segmenting dissimilar customer environments.

Let's move on to the User Information tab. As you will see, this is where you can find and, if required, modify user information such as first name, initials, last name, name (also known as display name), and Web page, in addition to adding special notes about the particular user account (see Figure 3.18). Any changes made here are of course also reflected in Active Directory and visible from the Property page of an Active Directory user account using the ADUC snap-in.

WARNING

Be careful about what you type in the Notes field, since any information entered here can be seen by someone looking at the properties of the respective user mailbox object on the Phone/Notes tab in the Global Address List (GAL) in Outlook.

Figure 3.18 The User Information Tab on the User Mailbox Property Page

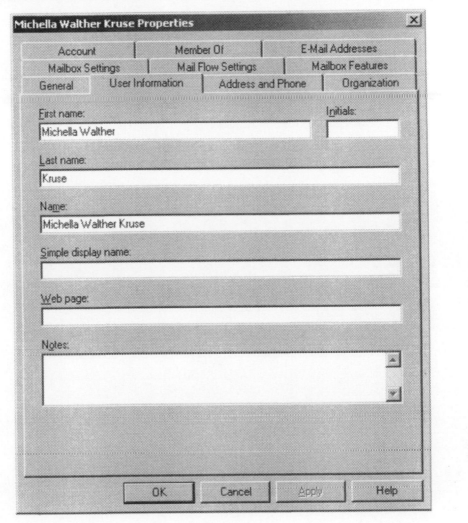

Under the Address and Phone tab, as shown in Figure 3.19, we can find and, if required, modify user information such as street address, city, state/province, ZIP/postal code, country/region, and phone and pager numbers (for the few people who still use a pager).

Figure 3.19 The Address and Phone Tab on the User Mailbox Property Page

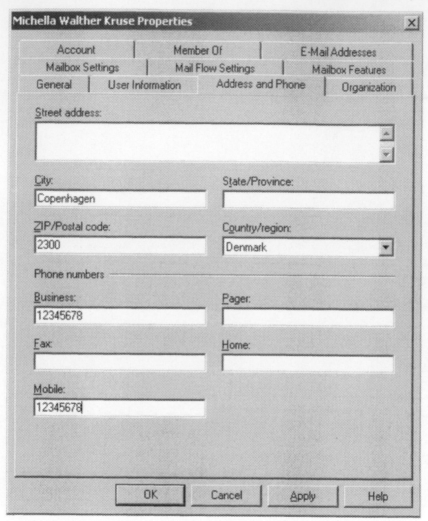

Under the Organization tab (see Figure 3.20), we have the option of entering user information such as title, company, department, and office as well as specifying the user's manager.

Figure 3.20 The Organization Tab on the User Mailbox Property Page

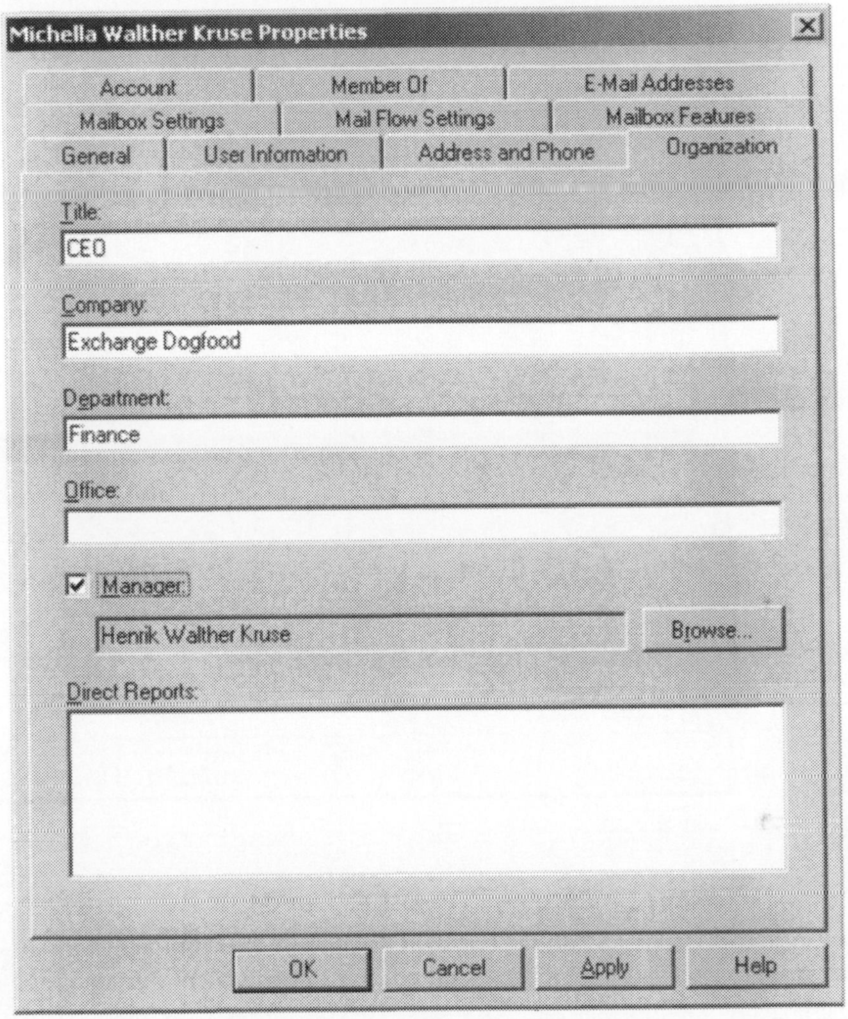

By specifying the manager for each of the recipients in your organization, you can create a virtual organization chart, accessed by looking at the Property page of the user mailbox object in the GAL in Outlook 2007, shown in Figure 3.21.

The Direct Reports field lists mailbox user's accounts and/or contacts that are managed by the respective recipient. Note that the user account Direct Report field is populated automatically when a recipient is designated as a manager for another recipient.

Figure 3.21 A Virtual Organization Chart in Outlook 2007

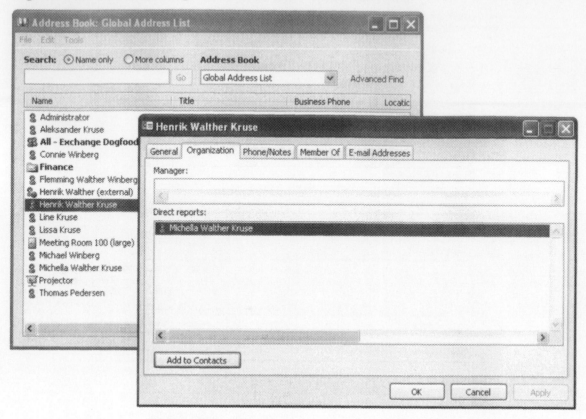

Let's move on to the Mailbox Settings tab shown in Figure 3.22. From here we can apply Managed folder mailbox policies (used for messaging records management purposes) and configure per-user level storage quotas. In addition, we can set deleted items' retention time, which by default uses the mailbox database defaults of 14 days.

We'll cover how you create and apply managed folder mailbox policies in Chapter 4.

Figure 3.22 Storage Quotas for a User Mailbox

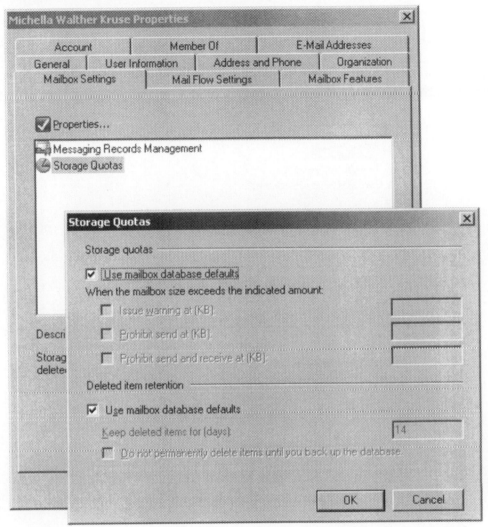

NOTE

The Messaging Records Management feature in Exchange 2007 is considered a premium feature and requires an Exchange Enterprise Client Access License (CAL).

Under the Mail Flow Settings tab, we can choose to manage delivery options, message size restrictions, and message delivery restrictions, as shown in Figure 3.23.

Figure 3.23 The Mail Flow Settings Tab for a User Mailbox

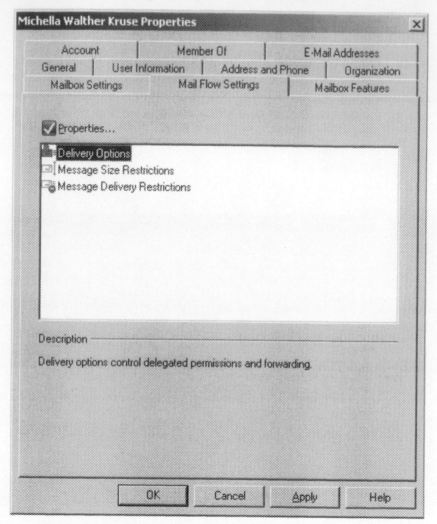

Let's take a look at the Properties for Delivery Options (see Figure 3.24). Highlight **Delivery Options** and then click **Properties**. Here we can grant send-on-behalf permissions to other user mailbox objects in the organization. We can also enable forwarding so that all mail received by the respective mailbox is forwarded to another specified user mailbox. We can even configure the forwarding feature so that the message is delivered to both the originally destined mailbox as well as the configured forwarder user mailbox. Finally, we have the option of setting a recipient limit, used to set the maximum number of recipients the user mailbox is allowed to send in a given e-mail message.

Figure 3.24 Delivery Options for a User Mailbox

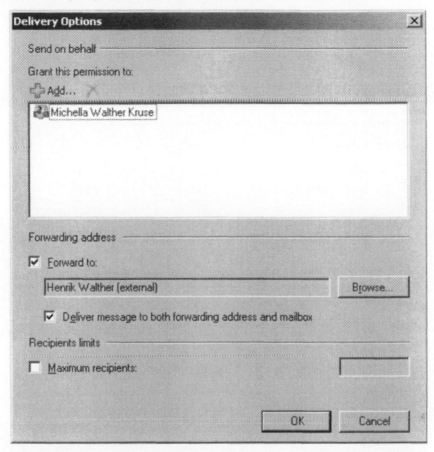

Click **OK** and then click the **Properties** button for **Message Size Restrictions** (see Figure 3.25). Here we can set the maximum receive and send message size (in KB) for the user mailbox.

Figure 3.25 Setting Message Size Restrictions for a User Mailbox

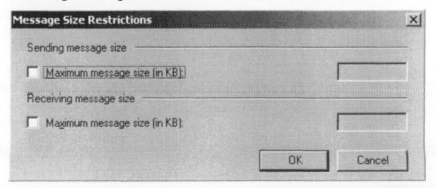

Click **OK** and then click the **Properties** for **Message Delivery Restrictions** (see Figure 3.26). Here we can specify who may send messages to the respective user mailbox, require that all senders are authenticated (preventing anonymous users from sending to the user mailbox), and finally, create a list of senders that should be rejected from sending to this user.

Figure 3.26 Message Delivery Settings for a User Mailbox

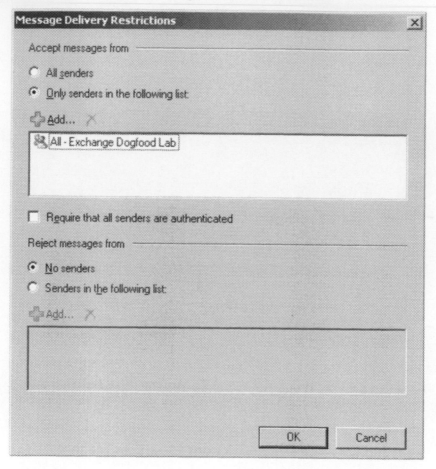

Click **OK** to get back to the property page, then click the **Mailbox Features** tab, shown in Figure 3.27.

This tab allows you to control client access to Outlook Web Access (OWA), Exchange ActiveSync (EAS), Unified Messaging (UM), and Outlook MAPI. In addition to being able to enable or disable access from all these client access methods, you also have the ability to apply an Exchange ActiveSync policy to the user mailbox account by clicking the **Properties** of **Exchange ActiveSync**.

In Chapter 5 we'll show how you create Exchange ActiveSync policies as well as how to apply them to user mailbox accounts throughout your Exchange organization.

If you have enabled Unified Messaging for the user mailbox object, you can also configure UM features by clicking **Properties** of **Unified Messaging**. However, that topic is covered in Chapter 10 and so won't be covered here.

Figure 3.27 The Mailbox Features Tab for a User Mailbox

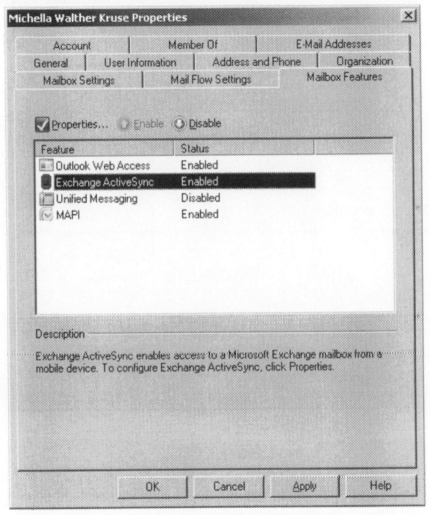

The next tab is the Account tab (see Figure 3.28). There's not much to say about the options available here, since most of you should recognize them from the ADUC snap-in. This is where you can find and modify the user principal name (UPN), the UPN domain, and the user logon name (pre-Windows 2000). Finally, you have the option of specifying that the user must change his or her password at next logon.

Figure 3.28 The Account Tab for a User Mailbox

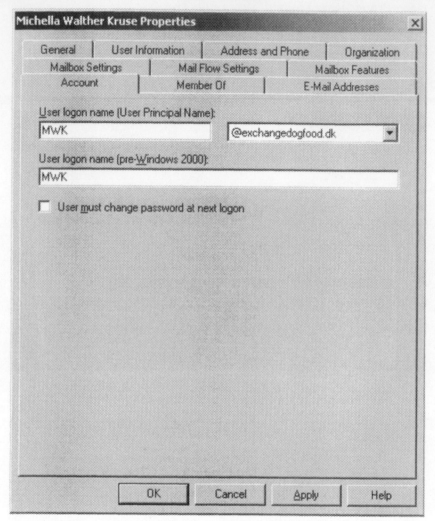

The Member Of tab should not need any explanation, so let's quickly move on to the E-Mail Addresses tab (see Figure 3.29). This is where you can see which e-mail addresses are currently stamped on the user mailbox object. You can change as well as add e-mail addresses from here. Just bear in mind that you'll need to untick **Automatically update e-mail addresses based on e-mail address policy** if you want to manually control which addresses applied as e-mail address policies have the ability to overwrite changes applied here.

We'll talk a lot more about e-mail address policies in Chapter 6.

Figure 3.29 The E-Mail Addresses Tab for a User Mailbox

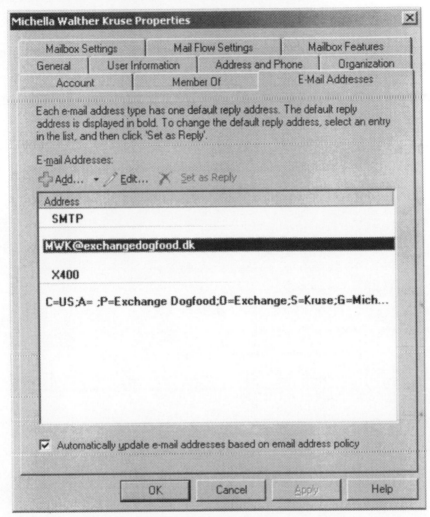

All right, we have just been through all the tabs available for a user mailbox object. Was it as boring as you had thought it would be?

Creating a Room or Equipment Mailbox

Creating a room or equipment mailbox is a very similar process to creating an ordinary user mailbox, so we'll not go through each page in the New Mailbox Wizard again. Instead, let's look at the **User Information** page, where you enter the information about the resource mailbox (see Figure 3.30). As you can see, we have a specific OU called Meeting Rooms set up specifically for housing room mailboxes.

NOTE

You cannot create OUs from within the EMC; instead, you need to do so using the ADUC snap-in.

Figure 3.30 Creating a New Room Mailbox

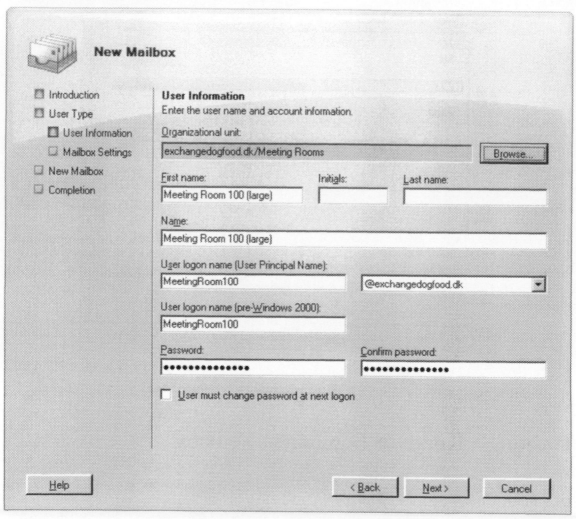

When the meeting room or equipment mailbox has been created, you can manipulate and modify it the exact same way you can with a user mailbox because it is nothing more than a user mailbox with a disabled account association. Again, there's no reason to take you through all the tabs on the property page again.

Some of you might be wondering how a room or equipment mailbox is differentiated from an ordinary user mailbox. The only difference (other than the disabled account object association) is that a room mailbox is created with a *–Room* parameter, and an equipment mailbox is created with an *–Equipment* parameter. These mailboxes are also explicit, using their own icon and recipient type details.

NOTE

Room and equipment mailboxes can be included in meeting requests and be configured to automatically process incoming requests.

Creating a Linked Mailbox

A *linked mailbox* is a mailbox that needs to be associated with a user account belonging to another trusted forest. Linked mailboxes are typically used when we choose to use the Exchange resource forest model, where Exchange 2007 is deployed in its own separate Active Directory forest (done to centralize Exchange in a single forest).

Although Figure 3.31 implies that you link the mailbox directly to a user account in another trusted forest, this isn't the case. You still need to create a user account in the Exchange resource forest, because an Exchange 2007 mailbox requires that you have an associated account in the same Active Directory forest in which Exchange 2007 is deployed. This was no different than Associated External Accounts in Exchange 2000 and 2003.

NOTE

The Exchange 2007 resource forest model is considered a complex design and should only be used by large organizations that really need to deploy Exchange 2007 in its own Active Directory forest.

Figure 3.31 Creating a Linked Mailbox

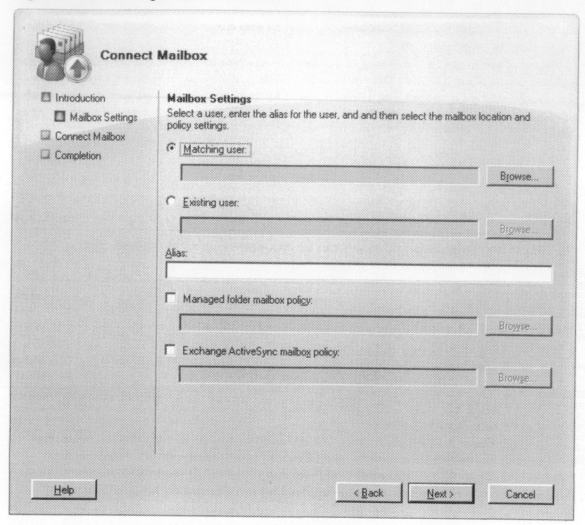

Managing Distribution Groups

As is the case with Exchange 2000 and 2003, Exchange 2007 has two types of distribution groups: *mail-enabled distribution groups*, which are used strictly for distributing messages, and *mail-enabled security groups*, which are used to assign permissions to users as well as to distribute messages. In addition, the query-based distribution group introduced in Exchange 2003 has made its way into Exchange 2007, albeit with a new name and a few changes. These groups are now called *dynamic distribution groups* and, as the name implies, are still dynamic in nature and based on a set of configured criteria. More about them later.

Distribution groups can contain other distribution groups, user mailboxes (mailbox-enabled users), and mail contacts (mail-enabled contacts). You can get a list of the mail-enabled distribution groups in your organization by selecting the **Distribution Group** subnode beneath the Recipient Configuration work center node, as shown in Figure 3.32. This is also the place where you create new groups as well as modify any existing ones.

Just like user mailbox objects, distribution groups are explicit in Exchange 2007, meaning that each type of group is differentiated using an individual icon as well as a *recipient type details* description, as you can see in Figure 3.32. As you can also see in this figure, we have four different explicit group types:

- Mail Universal Distribution groups

- Mail Universal Security groups

- Dynamic Distribution groups

- Mail Non-Universal groups

  - Domain Local groups

  - Global groups

WARNING

Although pre-existing Mail Non-Universal groups are shown under the Distribution Group subnode in the figure, you should be aware that the administration of these group types is limited. Actually, it's recommended that you do not use these types of groups for distributing messages in Exchange 2007.

Another word of warning when you are creating groups in ADU&C snap-in console: Any group created as a Distribution Global group will not be available when you're trying to mail-enable that group via the EMC. Groups created in the ADUC MMC snap-in must be Universal Distribution groups if they are later to be mail-enabled using the EMC.

Figure 3.32 Listing Distribution Group Types Under the Distribution Group Subnode

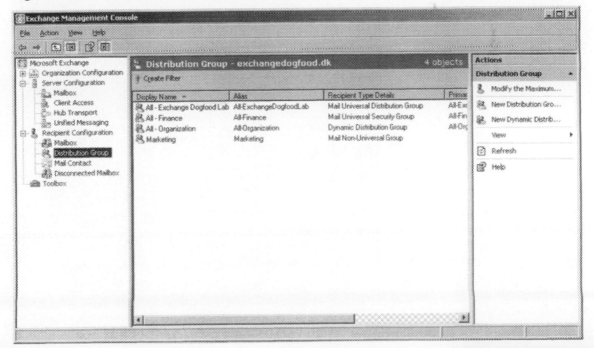

Some Independent Advice

You may ask, "What should I use in my organization—mail-enabled security groups or ordinary mail-enabled distribution groups?" That's a really good question, and here is something to consider: Choosing mail-enabled security groups will give you the option of using the group as both a distribution group as well as using it to assign permissions to user account objects in your Active Directory forest. This means that using mail-enabled security groups will lower the number of groups in your organization, thereby lowering the amount of maintenance required. Be careful using mail-enabled security groups; you could accidentally assign too many permissions to the wrong users! Double check the membership of the distribution list before assigning it to a resource's ACL.

When highlighting a group under the Distribution Group subnode, you get a set of actions that can be performed on it in the Action pane. When highlighting a Mail Universal Security group, for example, we get the set of actions shown in Figure 3.33. We can disable the group, removing all Exchange-related properties from the group; remove it (which physically removes the group object from Active Directory!); or access the Properties page for the group by choosing the Properties action.

If we had highlighted a Dynamic Distribution group, we would not have had the option to disable it, but only to remove it.

Figure 3.33 Actions for a Mail Universal Security Group in the Actions Pane

Highlighting a Mail Non-Universal group will also give us the option of converting it to a Universal group, as shown in Figure 3.34. We highly recommend you do this.

Figure 3.34 Actions for a Mail Non-Universal Group in the Actions Pane

Let's access the Properties page for a Mail Universal Distribution group. The first tab we're presented with is the General tab (see Figure 3.35), where we can change the name and alias of the group as well as view or modify any specified custom attributes.

We also have the option of changing the group name under the Group Information tab. We can also specify the person (AD user account) that manages the respective group by selecting the **Managed By** option, clicking **Browse**, and choosing an account in AD. The person specified here will also be shown as the Owner when users user the GAL to open the Properties page of the group from within Outlook. On a side note, this person has the option of receiving delivery reports when messages are sent to the group, which is configurable on the Advanced tab. Finally, we have a Notes field, where we can enter administrative notes about the group. Again, as with user notes, bear in mind that end users will be able to see these notes from their Outlook clients when accessing them in the GAL.

The Members tab should not need any further explanation; it is simply the place where you add and/or remove members from the group. The Member Of tab lists any distribution groups that include this group on its member list. Note that you cannot use this tab to add the selected group to other distribution groups! The E-Mail Addresses tab is the place where you can see all the e-mail addresses for the group as well as modify or add new e-mail addresses. By default, the e-mail addresses are stamped on the distribution group by the e-mail address policy in the Exchange organization; however, you have the option of disabling this behavior and instead administering these lists manually by deselecting the option **Automatically update e-mail addresses based on recipient policy**.

Figure 3.35 The General Tab for a Distribution Group

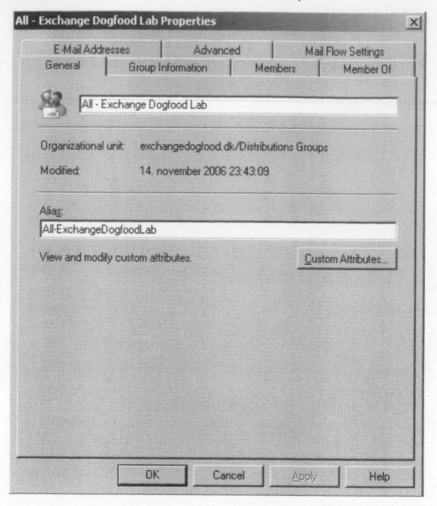

On the Advanced tab, shown in Figure 3.36, we can specify a simple display name, used if the original display name of the group contains Unicode characters and you have third-party applications that don't support Unicode. In addition, you can define an expansion server, used to expand group membership. When a message is sent to a distribution group, Exchange must access the membership list to deliver the message to each member of the group. When dealing with large distribution groups, this can be a very resource-intensive task, thus giving a reason to define a particular hub transport server role as your expansion server.

Figure 3.36 The Advanced Tab

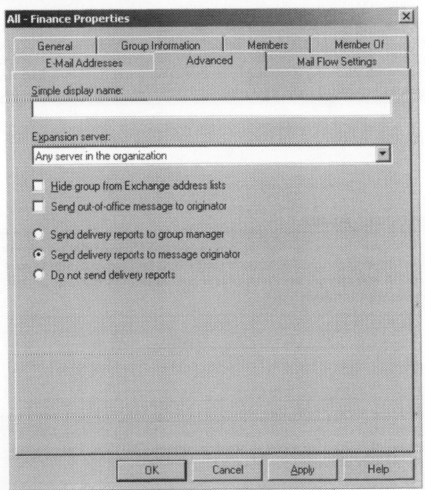

SOME INDEPENDENT ADVICE

If you specify an expansion server for a particular distribution group, you should always make sure it's well documented because the group will then depend on this specified server to deliver messages. This means that if you someday find out you want to replace your existing hub transport server with a new one, and that particular hub transport server has been explicitly assigned as an expansion server for one or more distribution groups, those groups will no longer be able to deliver messages to the respective members.

Under the Advanced tab, you also have the option of hiding the group from the Exchange Global Address Lists (GAL) and specify that any out-of-office messages should be sent to the originator (the sender of the message) instead of the group. Lastly, you have the option of specifying whether delivery reports should be sent or not. If you choose to have them sent, you can select whether they should be sent to the message originator or the group manager specified under the Group Information tab. Note that if you decide to send delivery reports to the group manager, a group manager *must* be selected under the Group Information Managed By field or you will receive a warning message telling you to do so.

The last tab is Mail Flow Settings, where you can configure the maximum group receiving size in KB as well as defining who should be allowed to send messages to the group.

SOME INDEPENDENT ADVICE

Larger "All User" based distribution groups should always have a limited number of allowed senders defined because these groups tend to encompass your entire organization and can get you in trouble if everyday messages can be delivered to everyone in your company.

NOTE

When accessed via the Exchange Management Console, the property pages are identical for Mail Universal Distribution groups and Mail Universal Security groups, so there's no reason to go through the tabs under the Properties page of a Mail Universal Security group.

Creating a New Distribution Group

To create a new distribution group, click the **New Distribution Group** link in the Action pane, bringing up the New Distribution Group Wizard shown in Figure 3.37. The first page is the Introduction page, where you need to specify whether you want to create a new distribution group or mail-enable an existing security group. If you choose to mail-enable an existing group, click the **Browse** button and you will be presented with a GUI picker, where all security groups that haven't been mail-enabled will be listed. For the purposes of this example, we'll select **New group**, then click **Next**.

Figure 3.37 The Introduction Page in the New Distribution Group Wizard

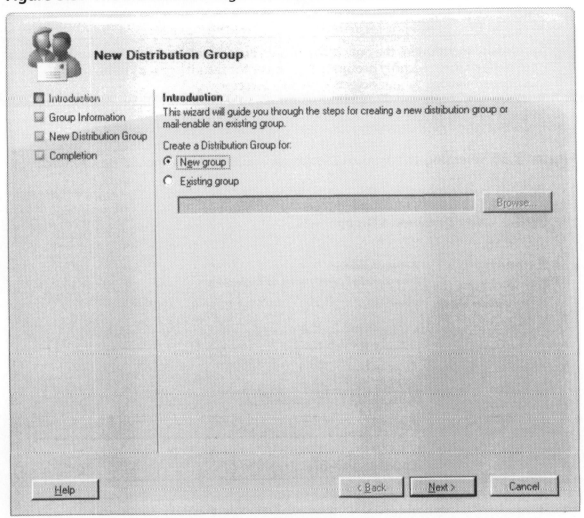

On the Group Information page shown in Figure 3.38, we'll have to specify whether we want to create a new mail-enabled distribution group or a mail-enabled security group. We'll then need to specify the OU in which the group should be created in Active Directory and finally give it an appropriate name and alias. The alias is automatically filled in and duplicated with whatever you used for a name; however, it can still be changed without altering the name.

NOTE

As already mentioned, the only difference between mail-enabled distribution groups and mail-enabled security groups is the ability for security groups to be used to assign permissions to user objects in Active Directory.

Figure 3.38 Selecting the Type of Distribution Group That Should Be Created

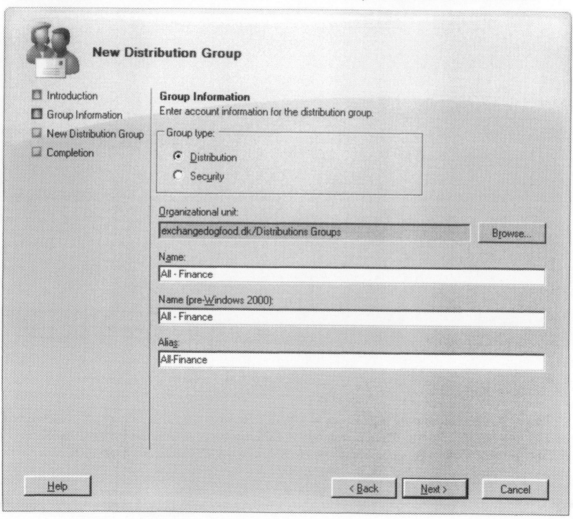

Let's click **Next**, which will bring us to the New Distribution Group page, where you should verify the information in the Configuration Summary pane. Once it's verified, click **New** and finally click **Finish**.

To create or modify existing distribution groups via the EMS, use the *New-DistributionGroup* and *Set-DistributionGroup* CMDlets. An example of creating a distribution group might look like the following:

```
New-DistributionGroup -Name "New Group" -OrganizationalUnit
syngress.local/users -SamAccountName "New-Group" -Type security
```

Creating a New Dynamic Distribution Group

Dynamic distribution groups, which were known as query-based distribution groups in Exchange 2003, provide the same type of functionality as ordinary distribution groups, but instead of manually adding members to the group's membership list, you can use a set of filters and conditions that you predefine when creating the group to derive its membership. When a message is set to a dynamic distribution group, Exchange queries the Active Directory for recipients matching the specified filters and conditions. The primary advantage of using dynamic distribution groups over ordinary distribution groups is that dynamic groups lower the administrative burden, since you don't have to maintain any distribution group membership lists. If we should mention any disadvantage of using dynamic distribution groups, it is that this type of group puts more load on the Global Catalog servers in your Active Directory forest. This is based on the fact that each time a message is sent to a dynamic distribution group, Exchange will have to query them based on the criteria defined in the group.

You create a new dynamic distribution group by clicking **New Dynamic Distribution Group** in the Action pane under the **Distribution Group** subnode of the Recipient Configuration work center node.

This will bring up the **New Dynamic Distribution Group Wizard** shown in Figure 3.39. Here you specify the OU in which the group should be created and give the group a meaningful name. When you have done so, click **Next**.

Figure 3.39 Naming a New Distribution Group

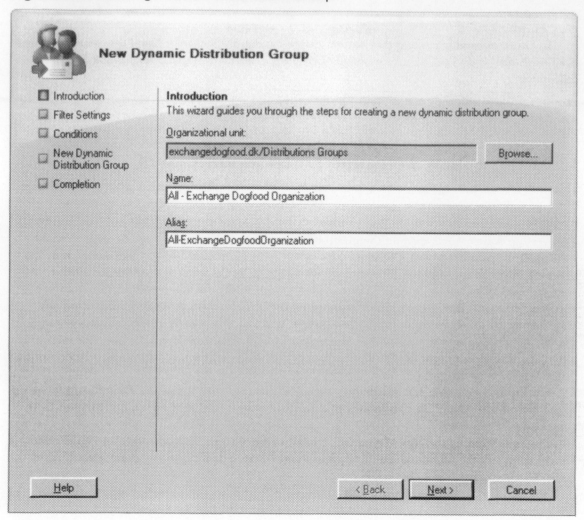

The next page is the Filter Settings page (see Figure 3.40) where you will need to specify the recipient container the filter should be applied to. Clicking the **Browse** button will bring up a GUI picker where you can choose an individual OU or even the whole Active Directory domain, for that matter. On this page you also have the option of specifying the type of recipients that should be included in your filter. For example, this could be **All recipient types** or just **Users with Exchange mailboxes**. When you have made your choices, click **Next**.

Figure 3.40 Selecting Filter Settings for a New Dynamic Distribution Group

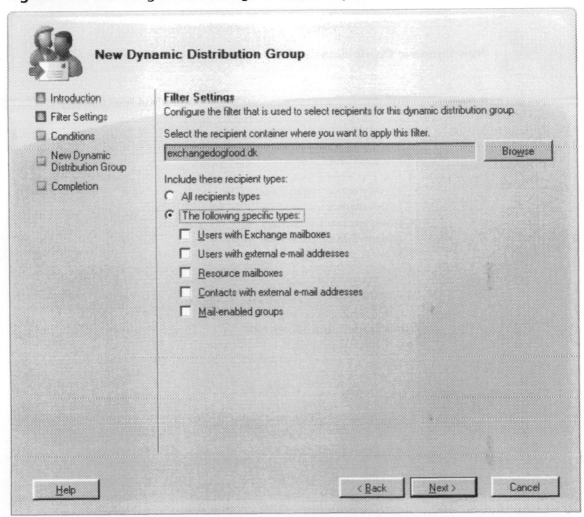

We have now reached the most interesting of all pages in the wizard, where we actually select and define the conditions that should be used by the group. As you can see in Figure 3.41, we can select conditions such as **Recipient is in a State or Province**, **Recipient is in a Department**, or **Recipient is in a company** as well as any of the 15 custom attributes that you might have defined on your mailbox-enabled user objects, so there should be plenty of possibilities. For the purposes of our example, we have selected **Recipient is in a Company** and edited the condition so that all recipients in a company called Exchange Dogfood will receive the messages sent to the respective dynamic distribution group. When you have selected the required conditions, you can click the **Preview** button in the lower-right corner to display all recipients who meet your criteria and whether they are the correct recipients you intended for the group. When you're ready, click **Next**, **New**, and finally **Finish**.

Figure 3.41 Choosing Conditions for a New Dynamic Distribution Group

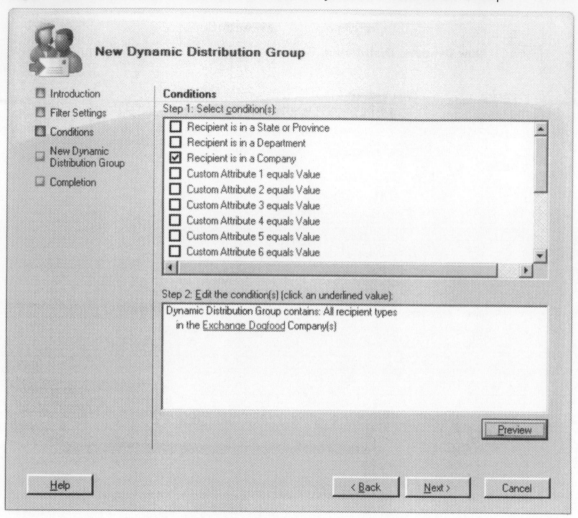

Since most of the Properties pages for a dynamic distribution group are more or less identical to that of an ordinary distribution group, we will not cover them here, with the exception of two tabs, which we want to quickly show you. The Filter and Conditions tabs are where you change the filter and condition behavior for a dynamic distribution group. As you can see in Figure 3.42, the Filter tab is where you can change the recipient container and the recipient types used by the group.

Figure 3.42 The Filter Tab

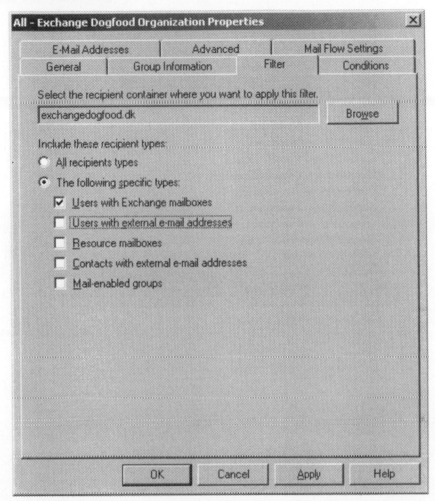

Under the Conditions tab, shown in Figure 3.43, you can change the conditions that should be used to define your group, as well as use the **Preview** button to list all users meeting your conditions.

To create or modify existing dynamic distribution groups via the EMS, use the *New-DynamicDistributionGroup* and *Set-DynamicDistributionGroup* CMDlets.

Figure 3.43 The Conditions Tab

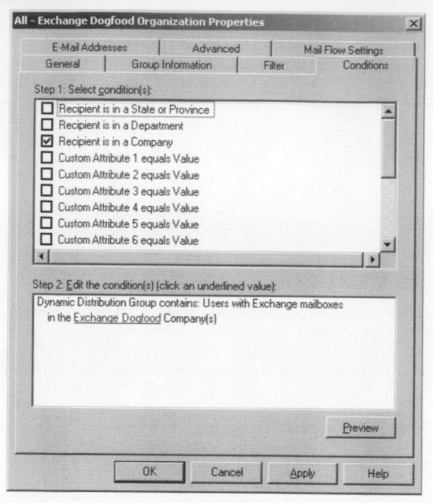

SOME INDEPENDENT ADVICE

So, what do you do if you want to use conditions other than those available in the New Dynamic Distribution Group Wizard? Is this even possible? As a matter of fact, it is, but only by using the *New-DynamicDistributionGroup* CMDlet in the EMS. You should also bear in mind that any conditions and filters other than those provided in the GUI must be *managed* using the EMS. If, for example, you wanted to create a custom recipient filter that included all recipients in an OU called *EDFUsers*, with a mailbox located on a server called EDFS03, you would need to run the following command:

```
New-DynamicDistributionGroup -Name "EDFS03 - Mailbox Users"
-OrganizationalUnit EDFSUsers -RecipientFilter "((RecipientType
-eq 'UserMailbox' -and ServerName -eq 'EDFS03') -and -not(Name
-like 'SystemMailbox{*')))"
```

When viewing the Filter tab on the Properties page of a dynamic distribution group, created using a custom filter, you will see something similar to the display in Figure 3.44, showing the complete recipient filter.

Managing Mail Contacts and Mail Users

We manage mail contacts (mail-enabled contacts) and mail users (mail-enabled users) under the Mailbox Contact subnode beneath the Recipient Configuration work center node. So, what is a mail contact? Most of you should know what it is, since this type of object has existed since Exchange 2000 was released to manufacturing. For those of you who would like a refresher, a mail contact is an AD object without security principals as well as a mailbox. Because this object doesn't have any security principals, it cannot be used to log onto the network and/or be used in an ACL to assign access to a resource. The purpose of this object is simply to represent an external recipient (using a name and an external SMTP address) in the Exchange address lists. This could be customer or a consultant, for example.

A mail user (mail-enabled user) is an object that does have an account in Active Directory as well as an *external* e-mail address associated with it, but this type of recipient does not have an Exchange mailbox in the organization. A mail user is also listed in the Exchange address lists. The only difference between a mail contact and a mail user is that a mail user can log onto the Active Directory and can be used in an ACL to gain access to domain resources. Mail users are typically used for contract employees who are on site for a period of time and require access to the network but want to use their own mailbox (for example, a mailbox in another Exchange organization that they access using OWA or Outlook Anywhere) or simply use a messaging system other than Exchange.

Figure 3.44 The Filter Tab on the Properties Page When a Filter Has Been Created Through the Exchange Management Shell

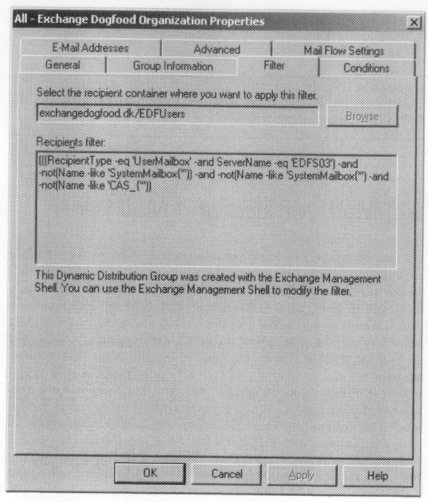

As you can see in Figure 3.45, these recipient types are also explicit and therefore differentiated, using their own icon and recipient type details.

Figure 3.45 Mailbox Contact Subnode in the Exchange Management Console

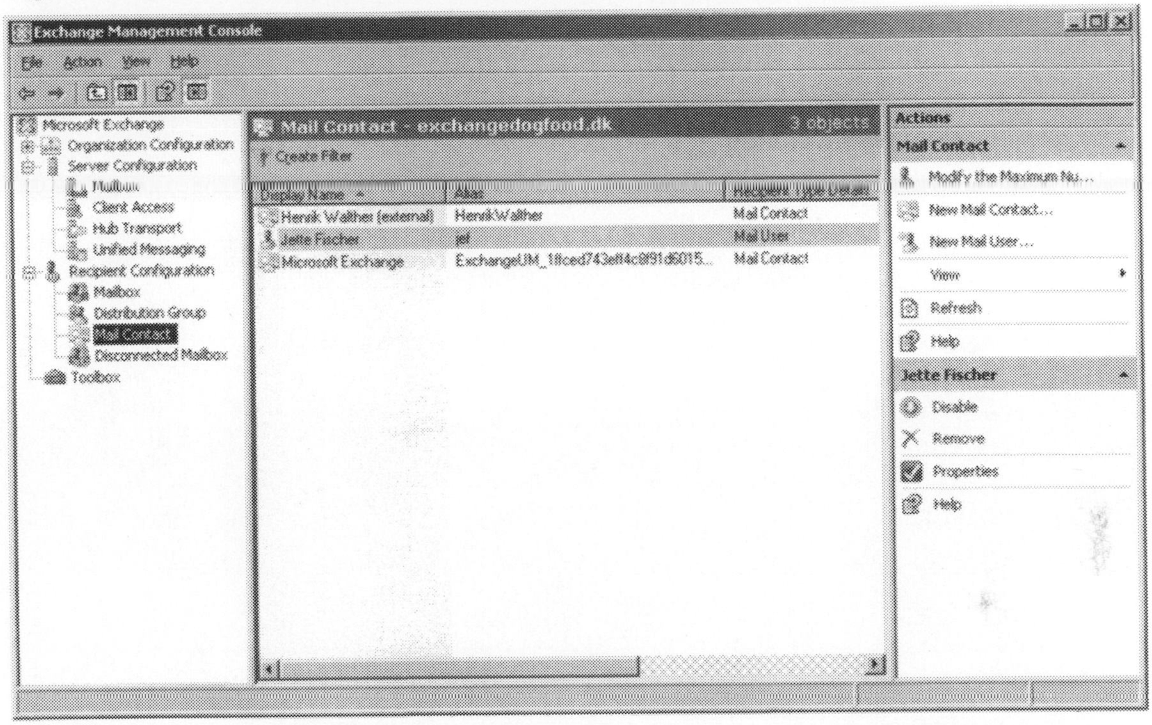

When highlighting an existing mail contact or mail user, we can either disable or remove the Mail object and/or access its Properties page. As is also the case with a user mailbox, disabling a mail contact or a mail user will remove the Exchange properties from the object, whereas removing a mail contact or mail user will instead delete the object entirely in Active Directory, so be careful when using the Remove action.

Creating a Mail Contact

To create mail contacts, you need to click the **New Mail Contact** link in the Action pane under the **Mail Contact** subnode. This will bring up the **New Mail Contact Wizard** shown in Figure 3.46. Here we need to select whether we want to create a new mail contact or want to mail-enable an existing contact. If you select **Existing contact** you can click the **Browse** button, bringing up a GUI picker and listing all contacts that haven't been mail-enabled. In this example, we'll select **New Contact** and click **Next**.

Figure 3.46 Choosing Whether to Create a New Mail-Enabled Contact or Mail-Enabling an Existing Contact

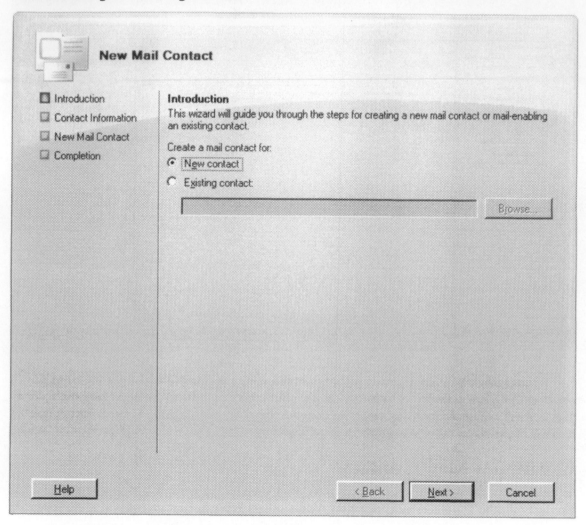

On the Contact Information page shown in Figure 3.47, we'll need to enter the account information that is required to either create a mail contact or mail-enable a contact. We'll need to provide things such as name and alias as well as add the external e-mail address we want to associate with the Mail Contact object. When you have done so, click **Next**, and then click **New** on the **Summary** page, and finally click **Finish**.

Figure 3.47 Creating a New Mail Contact

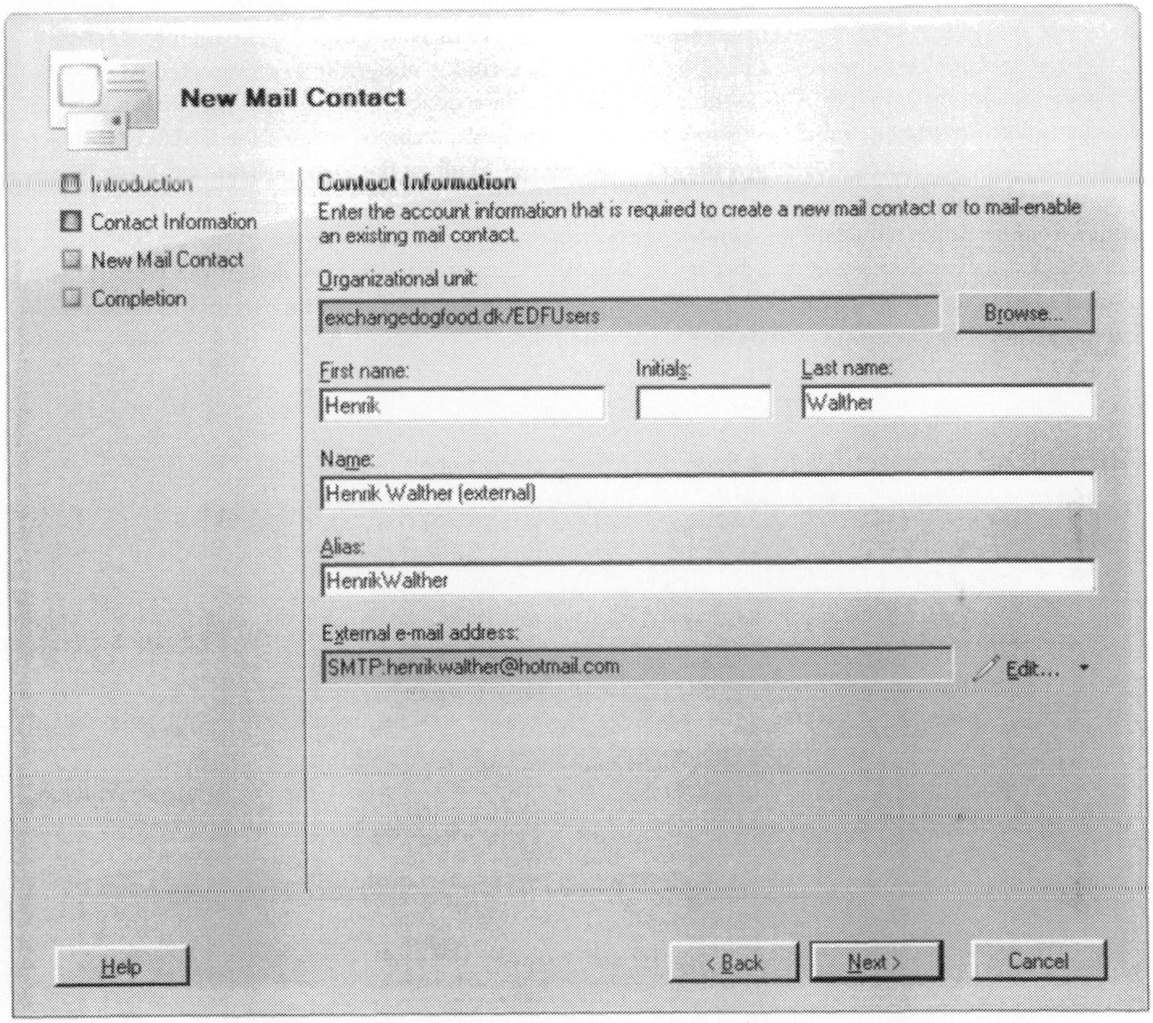

The process of creating a mail user is almost identical to creating a mail contact, the only exception being the need to specify the user account information during creation.

To create a new mail-enabled contact via the EMS, use the *New-MailContact* CMDlet. To modify this type of recipient, use the *Set-MailContact* CMDlet. To create a new mail-enabled user via the EMS, use the *New-MailUser* CMDlet. To modify this type of recipient, use the *Set-MailUser* CMDlet.

Managing Disconnected Mailboxes

When you either disable or remove a mailbox, that mailbox will be *marked* for deletion but will not be automatically deleted. Instead, it will be kept in the respective Mailbox database for the number of days specified on the Mailbox database Properties page (under the Limits tab), called **Keep deleted mailboxes for**, more commonly referred to as *mailbox retention*. Like Exchange 2000 and 2003, Exchange 2007 will, by default, keep deleted mailboxes for 30 days before they are purged (permanently deleted).

After you disable or remove a mailbox, you can then find it under the Disconnected Mailbox subnode, as shown in Figure 3.48. If the mailboxes you have disabled or removed are within the last 30-day retention period and do not show up under this node, chances are that the EMC is connected to another mailbox server other than the one hosting the Mailbox database on which the mailboxes originally resided. As you can see in the top of the Results pane, the EMC informs us which mailbox server the Disconnected Mailbox subnode is connected to. As you also can see in Figure 3.48, you can connect to another mailbox server by clicking the **Connect to Server** link in the Action pane, then clicking the **Browse** button to bring up a GUI picker where all mailbox servers in your Exchange 2007 organization will be listed.

Figure 3.48 Connecting to a Specific Mailbox Server

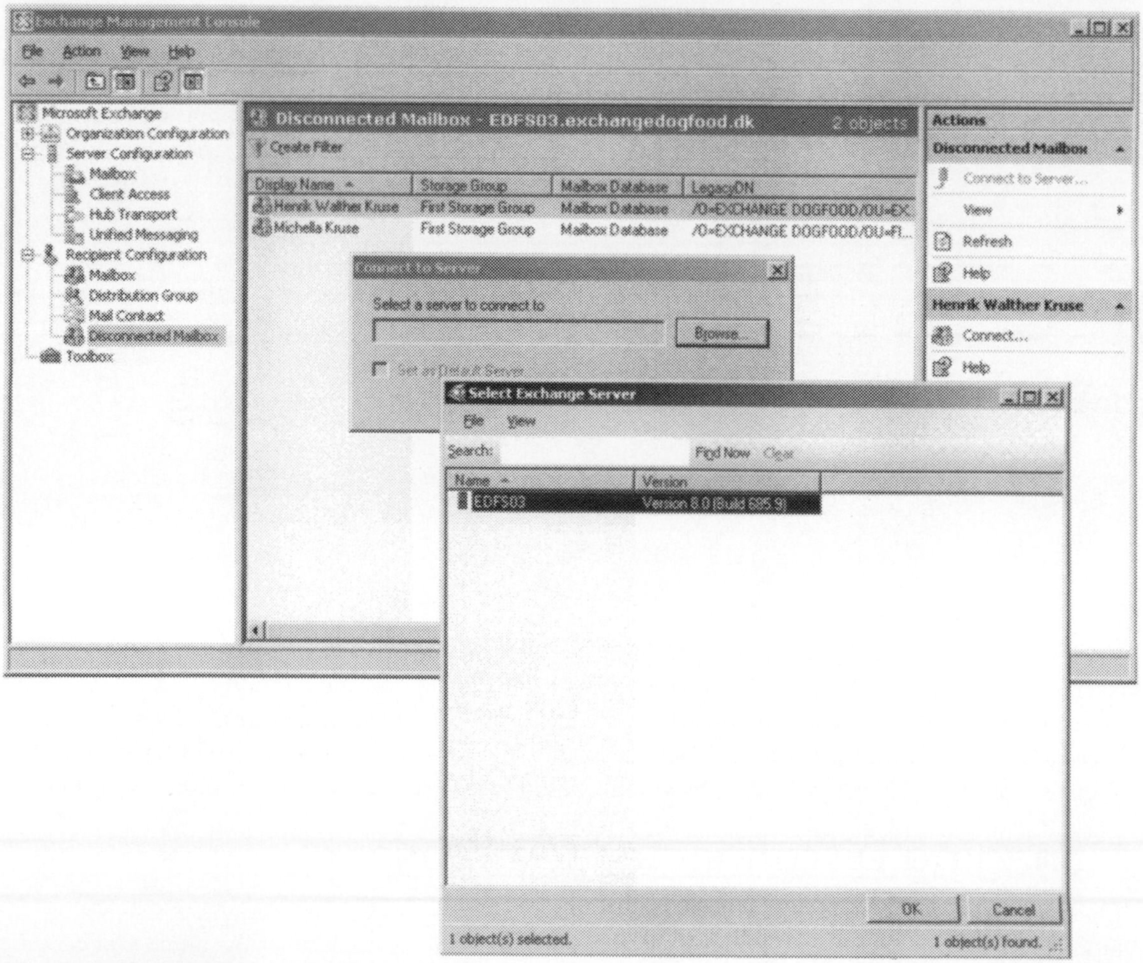

When you're connected to the correct mailbox server, you can reconnect a disconnected mailbox by highlighting the **Mailbox** object and clicking the **Connect** link in the Action pane. This brings up the Connect Mailbox Wizard Introduction page, shown in Figure 3.49. Here you can specify the type of mailbox the disconnected mailbox should be reconnected to. When you have selected a mailbox type, click **Next**.

Figure 3.49 Selecting the Mailbox Type to Which the Mailbox Will Be Connected

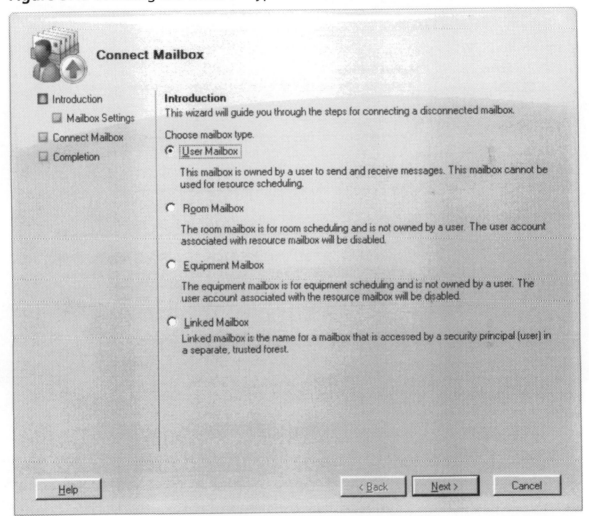

On the Mailbox Settings page, we select a user, enter the alias for the user, and, if required, select any Managed folder or Exchange ActiveSync mailbox policy settings.

As you can see in Figure 3.50, we can either connect the mailbox to a user using the **Matching user** or **Existing user** option. If we select the **Matching user** option, Exchange will search and try to locate a user matching that of the disconnected mailbox within the Active Directory forest. If you would rather pick an existing user manually, you should select **Existing user**. When you have made your choices, click **Next**, then **Connect**, and finally **Finish**.

Figure 3.50 Connecting a Disconnected Mailbox

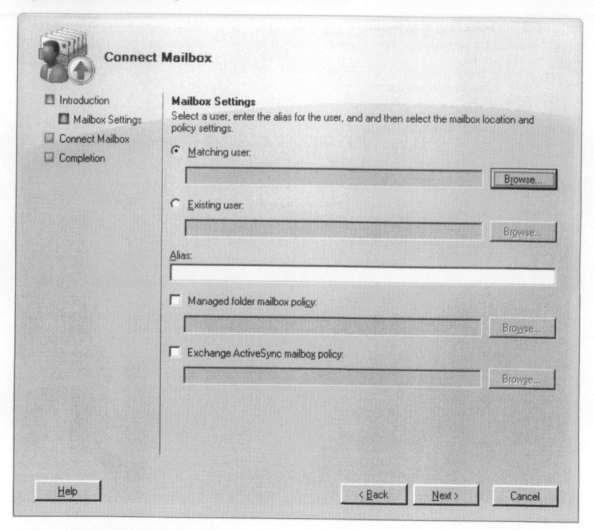

Okay, so what if you don't want the mailbox to be disconnected but would rather permanently delete a user mailbox right away? Well, in this particular scenario, you need to switch to the EMS because there's no way to do so via the GUI. More specifically, you need to run the *Remove-Mailbox* command with the *Permanent* parameter. So, for example, if you were to delete the AD user account and the mailbox for a user with a UPN named *LIK* in an Active Directory domain called *exchangedogfood.dk*, you would need to run the following command:

```
Remove-Mailbox -Identity exchangedogfoodlik -Permanent $true
```

You will then get the warning message shown in Figure 3.51. Type **Y** to confirm you want to do it, and then press **Enter**.

Figure 3.51 Permanently Removing a User Mailbox

Notice that the warning message says *Will remove the Windows user object and will remove the mailbox from the database*, unlike the warning message back in Figure 3.10, which says *Will remove the Windows user object and mark the mailbox in the database for removal.*

Some Independent Advice

So how do you delete a mailbox that has already has been disconnected? This is a little trickier! To do so, you first need to retrieve the mailbox GUID of the disconnected mailbox using the *Get-MailboxStatistics* CMDlet. However, it's not enough to simply run this CMDlet, since it won't list disconnected mailboxes. To delete the disconnected mailbox for a user with a display name of Line Kruse, you instead need to type **$Temp = Get-MailboxStatistics | Where {$_.DisplayName -eq 'Line Kruse'}** followed by pressing **Enter**. Then you need to run a command similar to the following: **Remove-Mailbox –Database "edfs03mailbox database 2" –StoreMailboxIdentity $Temp.MailboxGuid** followed by pressing **Enter**. You will then get the warning message shown in Figure 3.52. Click **Y** for Yes, and press **Enter**.

The disconnected mailbox has now been deleted from the specified mailbox database.

Figure 3.52 Deleting a Disconnected Mailbox

Managing Recipients in an Exchange Coexistence Environment

During a transition from Exchange 2000/2003 to Exchange 2007, deploying Exchange 2007 Server into your existing Exchange organization can take a long time, depending on the size of your existing setup and organizational layout.

Managing Exchange 2000/2003 and 2007 Mailbox–Enabled User Objects in a Coexistence Environment

Which tool (the ADUC snap-in or EMC) should you use to manage mailbox-enabled user objects within a coexistence environment? The choice is actually pretty straightforward; just follow the set of guidelines laid out in Table 3.1.

Table 3.1 Tools to Manage Exchange 2000/2003 and 2007 Mailboxes in a Coexistence Environment

Administrative Task	ADUC Snap-in	EMC/EMS
Create Exchange 2007 Mailbox-enabled users		X
Create Exchange 2000/2003 Mailbox-enabled users	X	
Manage Exchange 2007 Mailbox-enabled users		X
Manage Exchange 2000/2003 Mailbox-enabled users	X	X
Remove Exchange 2007 Mailbox-enabled users		X
Remove Exchange 2000/2003 Mailbox-enabled users	X	X
Move Exchange 2007 Mailbox-enabled users		X
Move Exchange 2000/2003 Mailbox-enabled users	X	X

> **W**ARNING
>
> Although you have the option of managing Exchange 2007 Mailbox and
> Mail-enabled users using the ADUC snap-in, it isn't supported and will result
> in Exchange 2007 mailboxes that might not be fully functional. In addition,
> you should opt to use the Exchange 2007 tools to move Exchange 2000/2003
> user mailboxes.

Managing Exchange 2000/2003 and 2007 Mail-Enabled Objects in a Coexistence Environment

Unlike mailbox-enabled user objects, you can administer mail-enabled objects (contacts, distribution groups, and the like) using your tool of choice, since these types of objects aren't tied to a specific server version. Best practice, however, is to manage these objects from either the Exchange 2007 EMC or EMS. There's only one mail-enabled object that you *must* manage from the EMC or EMS at all times, and that is dynamic distribution groups. This is based on the fact that this type of object uses the new Exchange 2007 OPATH format for its recipient filter and cannot be managed under the older Exchange tools.

The Recipient Update Service in a Coexistence Environment

The infamous Recipient Update Service (RUS), which most of us know from Exchange 2000 and 2003, is no longer part of the Exchange 2007 product. RUS was responsible for stamping e-mail addresses, in addition to address list membership along with a few other things, but it didn't always work as expected and was very difficult to troubleshoot when it acted up. With Exchange 2007, the RUS (and thereby the asynchronous behavior used to provision objects) has been replaced by a new synchronous process, the *EmailAddressPolicy* CMDlet, used to stamp the e-mail address onto objects immediately! Yes, you no longer have to wait for several minutes to see e-mail addresses on your objects, as was often the case with the antiquated RUS. We'll talk more about this new task in Chapter 6.

There's one important detail to keep in mind about the RUS when you're working in a coexistence environment. You will need to continue using the Exchange 2003 System Manager to provision a RUS for each domain that contains Exchange Recipients; note that this is also the case even when you're provisioning domains with pure Exchange 2007 recipients in them!

Granting Access and/or *SendAs* Permissions to a Mailbox

In some situations, one or more users might need to be granted permissions to access another user's mailbox. This could be a temporary access—for example, during vacations, maternity leave, or for other reasons—where one or more users need to take over the work of the user who will be absent. It could also be a more permanent access, where, for example, a secretary needs to access her boss's mailbox. Another reason could be that all users in a particular department (such as a helpdesk) need a shared mailbox.

You cannot grant permissions to a mailbox using the EMC. Instead, you need to use the EMS for this task—more specifically, the *Add-MailboxPermission* CMDlet, which has been created for granting permissions to a mailbox. To, for example, grant full access permissions to a mailbox, you would need to use the following command:

```
Add-MailboxPermission "respective mailbox" -User "user to have permissions"
-AccessRights: FullAccess
```

To learn more about the *Add-MailboxPermission* CMDlet and any available parameters and syntaxes, you can type **Get-Help Add-MailboxPermission** in the EMS.

There might also be times where you need to grant *SendAs* permission to a mailbox for another user. To do this you can use the *Add-ADPermission* CMDlet or the ADUC MMC snap-in. To do so using the *Add-ADPermission* CMDlet, you should run the following command:

```
Add-ADPermission -Identity "respective mailbox" -User "user to have permissions"
-ExtendedRights: SendAs
```

To grant *SendAs* permissions to a user via the ADUC MMC snap-in, perform the following steps:

1. On a domain controller in the Active Directory, click **Start | Run**, type **dsa.msc** and then press **Enter**.

2. In the menu, click **View**, then **Advanced Features**.

3. Drill down to and open the Properties page for the AD user object to which you want to grant another user *SendAs* permissions.

4. Now click the **Security** tab.

5. Click **Add** and select the AD user object that should be granted *SendAs* permission, then click **OK**.

6. Now select the added user in the **Group or user names** box, then check **Allow** for the *SendAs* permission in the permissions list, as shown in Figure 3.53.

Figure 3.53 The Security Tab on the AD User Object Properties Page

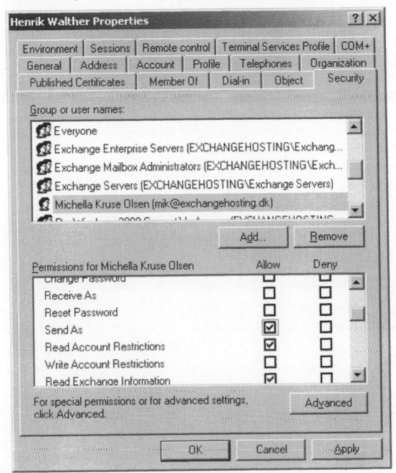

7. Click **OK** and close the ADUC MMC snap-in.

Creating a Custom Recipient Management Console

Depending on the organization, there could be times when you want to create an Exchange 2007 EMC that shows only the Recipient Configuration work center node. This is especially true in situations where you have a helpdesk that is used to having a customized ADUC console snap-in that provided the respective organizational units (OUs) holding the Exchange user objects they were to administer. After the transition to Exchange 2007, it would be a little too drastic to let the helpdesk staff have the full-blown EMC at their disposal, right? To create a custom EMC exposing only the Recipient Configuration work center node, you will first need to click **Start**, then type **MMC.exe**, followed by pressing **Enter**. This will bring up an empty MMC console, as shown in Figure 3.54. Click **File** in the menu, then click **Add/Remove Snap-in**.

Figure 3.54 An Empty MMC Console

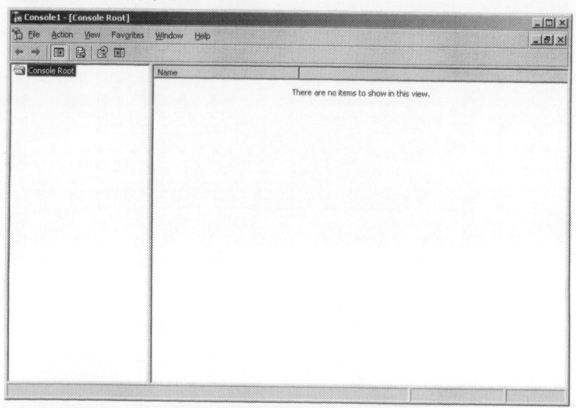

In the **Add/Remove Snap-in** window, click **Add**, then scroll down and select the **Exchange Server 2007** snap-in, as shown in Figure 3.55. Click **Add** again, then click **Close** and finally **OK**.

Figure 3.55 Selecting the Exchange Server 2007 Snap-in

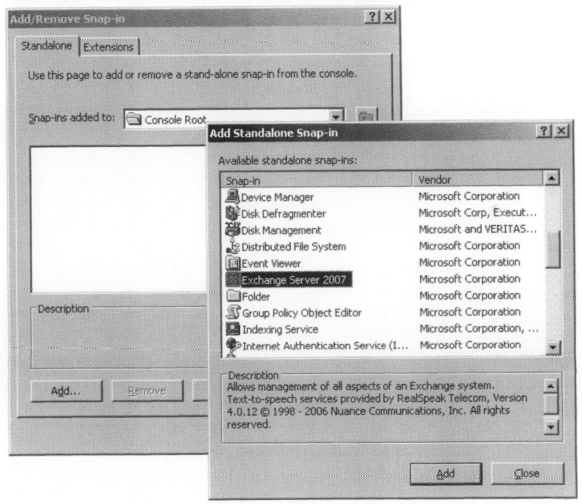

Expand the **Microsoft Exchange** tree and right-click the **Recipient Configuration** work center node, selecting **New Window from Here** in the context menu, as shown in Figure 3.56.

Figure 3.56 Choosing New Window from Here in the Context Menu

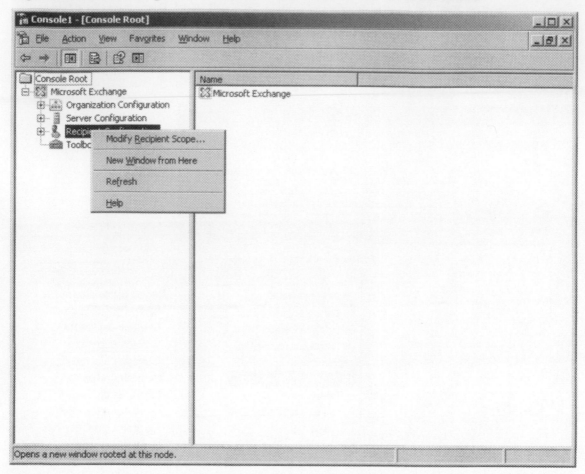

We now have a basic Exchange 2007 Recipient Management snap-in, as you can see in Figure 3.57, but honestly, we can't keep it this simple, right? We need to make it more functional.

Figure 3.57 A Standard Custom Exchange 2007 Recipient Management Console

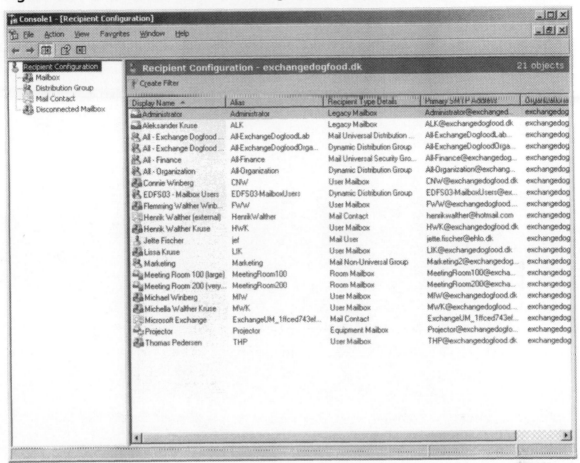

The first thing you want to do is to enable the Action pane in addition to removing the Standard menus and Standard toolbar, since these aren't required by Exchange 2007. To do so, click **View | Customize** and deselect **Standard menus (Action and View)** and **Standard toolbar**. Lastly, select **Action pane**, and click **OK** (see Figure 3.58).

Figure 3.58 Customizing the View for the Exchange 2007 Recipient Management Console

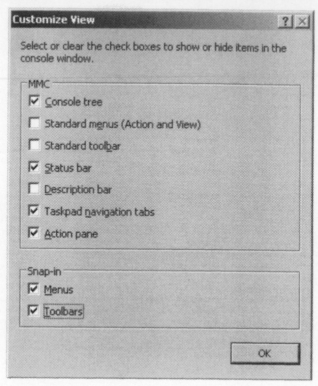

Let's spiff up the console a little more before we save it. To do so, click **File | Options**; in the **Options** window, replace *Console1* with the text **Exchange 2007 Recipient Management**. Now click the **Change Icon** button and navigate to the **Bin** directory under the *C:Program FilesMicrosoftExchange Server* folder. Here you can select the **ExSetupUI.exe** file, click **Open**, and you have the option of choosing the Exchange 2007 icon shown in Figure 3.59. Do so and click **Apply**.

Now select **User mode – limited access, single window** in the **Console mode** drop-down menu, as shown in Figure 3.60. Finally, deselect the **Allow the user to customize views** option, and click **OK**.

Figure 3.59 Choosing the Exchange 2007 Icon for the Console

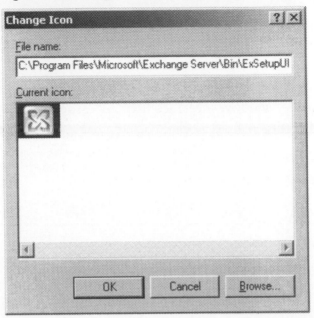

Figure 3.60 Custom Exchange 2007 Recipient Management Console Options

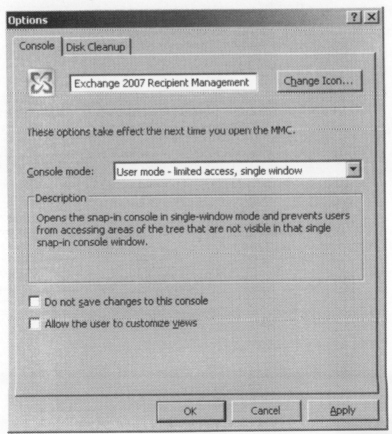

You can now save the console by clicking **File | Save As**. Save the console as **Exchange 2007 Recipient Management Console.msc** and answer **Yes** to the message shown in Figure 3.61.

Figure 3.61 The Single-Window Interface MMC Message

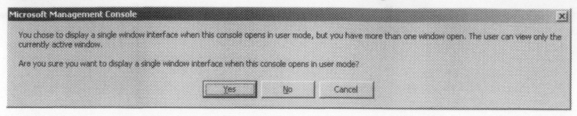

Now close the console and reopen it from where it was saved. It should now look similar to the one shown in Figure 3.62.

Figure 3.62 The Custom Recipient Management Console

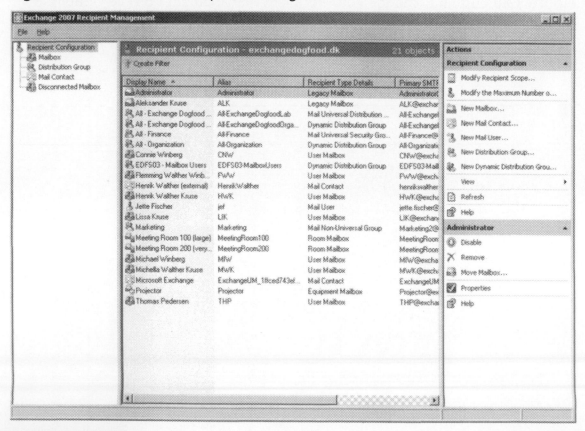

Now that looks much better.

You can also create isolated Management Consoles for the Organization Configuration, Server Configuration, and Toolbox work center nodes. You can do this by following the same steps but opening a new console window by right-clicking the respective work center node. If you have both the Exchange 2007 Tools and the Windows AdminPak installed on a server or workstation, you can even create a single console with access to both the ADUC snap-in and the Exchange 2007 Management Console, as shown in Figure 3.63.

Figure 3.63 A Custom User Management Console

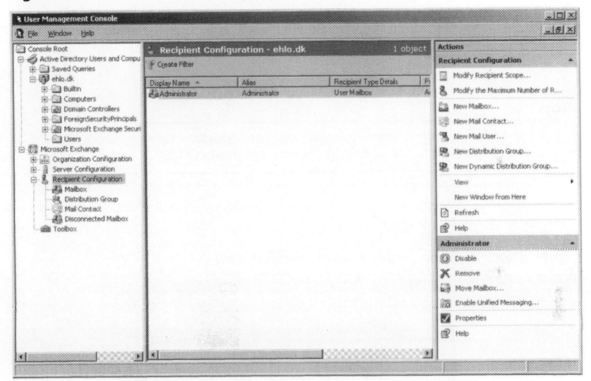

Recipient Filtering in Exchange 2007

If you have already deployed and/or are planning to deploy Exchange 2007 in an organization consisting of several thousand recipients, you can quickly lose the administrative overview. This is where recipient filtering comes into the picture. By creating a filter using either the EMC or the EMS, you will be able to find the recipient or set of recipients you're looking for in a matter of seconds.

Creating a recipient filter is done by selecting the Recipient Configuration work center node or the particular recipient subnode. Let's, for example, select the **Mailbox** subnode. Here we will create a filter by clicking the **Create Filter** button located in the top-left corner of the **Result** pane, as shown in Figure 3.64.

Figure 3.64 The Create Filter Button in the Exchange Management Console

After we have clicked **Create Filter**, we need to specify the type of property we want to filter on, selecting from among 35 available property types such as Alias, Company, Custom Attributes, E-mail Addresses, Recipient Type Details, Server, and Unified Messaging Mailbox Policy. Let's try to create a filter based on the **Recipient Type Details** property, setting it to the **Equals** comparison operator and finally choosing a value it should filter on. In this example we'll choose **Legacy Mailbox** and click **Apply Filter**. We could have also selected User Mailbox, Linked Mailbox, Shared Mailbox, Room Mailbox, or Equipment Mailbox, depending on our preference.

NOTE

A total of six different comparison operators are available: Contains, Does Not Contain, Does Not Equal, Ends With, Equals, and Starts With.

As you can see in Figure 3.65, any legacy mailboxes (mailboxes on an Exchange 2000 or 2003 server) are listed in the Result pane.

Figure 3.65 Displaying Legacy Mailbox Filtered View

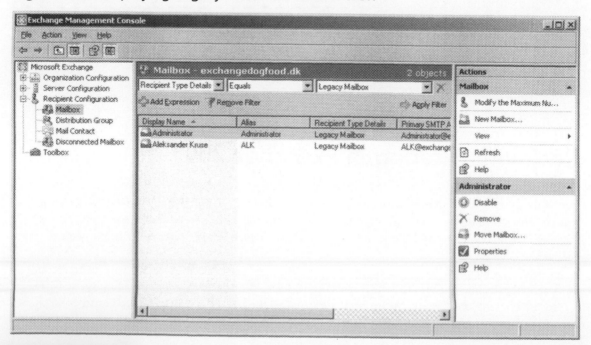

Note that you can add expressions by clicking the **Add Expression** button. You can even remove separate expressions by clicking the red cross icon to the right of the particular filter. You can also remove the complete filter by clicking **Remove Filter**.

SOME INDEPENDENT ADVICE

The work center node or subnode you select has a direct impact on the operators that will be available in the filter you create. In addition, depending on the properties and the type of comparison operators you choose, you will have a different set of values to choose from. Some combinations even allow you to type the value yourself instead of having to choose from a drop-down box.

If you would rather perform recipient filtering using the EMS, you can do so with the *Get-Mailbox –filter* command.

Summary

In this chapter we focused on how recipients are managed in Exchange 2007. First we had a look at how the different recipient type objects are managed using the Exchange Management Console (EMC), then we went through how we should deal with recipients in a coexistence environment.

We also examined, step by step, how to create a custom MMC that contains the Exchange 2007 Recipients work center, which can be used, for example, by the helpdesk staff in your organization. Finally, we took a look at the options available when we use the new recipient filtering features in Exchange 2007.

Solutions Fast Track

Managing Recipients Using the Exchange 2007 Management Console

☑ Management of recipients in Exchange Server 2007, as well as their Exchange-related properties, has been moved back into the Exchange Management Console (EMC) in addition to the Exchange Management Shell (EMS), both of which are based on Windows PowerShell. This means that all management of Exchange recipient objects should be modified from within the EMC or EMS, not using the ADUC snap-in.

☑ We have four recipient type subnodes beneath the Recipient Configuration work center. In order, we have a Mailbox, a Distribution Group, a Mail Contact, and a Disconnected Mailbox node.

☑ Each type of recipient object has its own individual icon as well as recipient type description due to the fact that they now are explicit and not implicit, as was the case in Exchange Server 2003. This is a nice addition because it makes it so much easier to differentiate the recipient types in Exchange 2007.

☑ Although legacy mailboxes are exposed via the EMC, not all Exchange 2007-specific features apply to these types of mailboxes.

☑ Because Exchange 2007 uses explicit mailbox recipient types, it's possible to create a search filter that lists all room mailboxes, for example, or perhaps all legacy mailboxes, for that matter. Listing all resource mailboxes in the ADUC snap-in back in Exchange 2000 or 2003 using a search filter was not a trivial process; it required you to use custom attributes because there was no other way to differentiate resource mailboxes from ordinary mailbox-enabled user accounts.

☑ The Exchange 2007 Move Mailbox Wizard is the tool you should use to move legacy mailboxes from Exchange 2000 or 2003 Server to an Exchange 2007 Mailbox Server.

☑ As is the case with Exchange 2000 and 2003, there are two types of Distribution Groups in Exchange 2007: mail-enabled distribution groups, which are used strictly for distributing messages, and mail-enabled security groups, which are used both to assign permissions to users as well as to distribute messages. In addition, the query-based distribution group introduced in Exchange 2003 has also made its way into Exchange 2007, albeit with a new name and a few changes.

☑ Dynamic distribution groups, which were known as query-based distribution groups in Exchange 2003, provide the same type of functionality as ordinary distribution groups, but instead of manually adding members to the group's membership list, you can use a set of filters and conditions that you predefine when creating the group to derive its membership.

☑ We manage mail contacts (mail-enabled contacts) and mail users (mail-enabled users) under the Mailbox Contact subnode beneath the Recipient Configuration work center node.

☑ When you either disable or remove a mailbox, that mailbox will be marked for deletion but will not be automatically deleted. Instead, it will be kept in the respective mailbox database for the number of days specified on the mailbox database Properties page (under the Limits tab), called "Keep deleted mailboxes for," more commonly referred to as *mailbox retention*. Like Exchange 2000 and 2003, Exchange 2007 will, by default, keep deleted mailboxes for 30 days before they are purged (permanently deleted).

Managing Recipients in a Coexistence Environment

☑ During a transition from Exchange 2000/2003 to Exchange 2007, deploying Exchange 2007 server into your existing Exchange organization can take a long time, depending on the size of your existing setup and organizational layout. This means that you might have to manage mail-enabled users from both the EMC and the ADUC MMC snap-in for a period of time.

☑ Although you have the option of managing Exchange 2007 mailbox and mail-enabled users using the ADUC snap-in, it isn't supported and will result in Exchange 2007 mailboxes that might not be fully functional. In addition, you should opt to use the Exchange 2007 tools for moving Exchange 2000/2003 user mailboxes.

☑ The infamous Recipient Update Service (RUS), which most of us know from Exchange 2000 and 2003, is no longer part of the Exchange 2007 product. RUS was responsible for stamping e-mail addresses, in addition to address list membership along with a few other things, but didn't always work as expected and was very difficult to troubleshoot when it acted up. With Exchange 2007, the RUS (and thereby the asynchronous behavior used to provision objects) has been replaced by a new synchronous process, the *EmailAddressPolicy* CMDlet, used to stamp the e-mail address onto objects immediately.

Granting Access and/or *SendAs* Permissions to a Mailbox

☑ In some situations, one or more users might need to be granted permissions to access another user's mailbox. This could be a more temporary access during vacations, maternity leave, or other reasons, where one or more users need to take over the work of the user who will be absent. It could also be a more permanent access, where a secretary needs to access her boss's mailbox, for example. Another reason could be that all users in a particular department (such as a helpdesk) need a shared mailbox.

Creating a Custom Recipient Management Console

☑ Depending on the organization, at times you might want to create an Exchange 2007 Management Console that shows only the Recipient Configuration work center node. This is especially true in situations where you have a helpdesk that is used to having a customized ADUC console snap-in that provides the respective OUs holding the Exchange user objects they were to administer.

☑ You can create isolated Management Consoles for the Organization Configuration, Server Configuration, and Toolbox work center nodes. You can do this by following the same steps but opening a new console window by right-clicking the respective work center node. If you have both the Exchange 2007 Tools and the Windows AdminPak installed on a server or workstation, you can even create a single console with access to both the ADUC snap-in and the Exchange 2007 Management Console.

Recipient Filtering in Exchange 2007

☑ If you have already deployed and/or are planning to deploy Exchange 2007 in an organization consisting of several thousand recipients, you can quickly lose the administrative overview. This is where recipient filtering comes into the picture. By creating a filter using either the EMC or the EMS, you will be able to find the recipient or set of recipients you're looking for in a matter of seconds.

☑ Creating a recipient filter is done by selecting the Recipient Configuration work center node or the particular recipient subnode.

Frequently Asked Questions

Q: Can I manage legacy mailboxes (Exchange 2000/2003 mailboxes) using the Exchange Management Console or the Exchange Management Shell?

A: Yes, this is supported, but bear in mind that although legacy mailboxes are exposed via the EMC and the EMS, not all Exchange 2007-specific features apply to these types of mailboxes. However, as soon as a legacy mailbox has been moved to an Exchange 2007 Mailbox Server, the mailbox will have the same feature set as a mailbox created directly on an Exchange 2007 Mailbox Server. Note that managing Exchange 2007 mailboxes using the ADUC MMC snap-in is not supported.

Q: Is it necessary to create the Active Directory user object in the ADUC MMC snap-in before I can create a mailbox using the Exchange 2007 Management Console?

A: No, this is not necessary. When you create a new mailbox in the EMC using the New Mailbox Wizard, you'll have the option of creating an Active Directory user object as well. You can even specify in which OU it should be created.

Q: I've heard that Exchange 2007 has several different recipient type objects. What's that all about?

A: You heard true. Exchange 2007 has a total of 14 different explicit recipient types, all having their own individual icon and recipient type details, which lowers the overall administrative burden. For example, you can create a recipient filter that, say, lists all room mailboxes much more easily than was true back in Exchange 2000/2003 without using a custom attribute field or the like.

Q: Do the new room and equipment mailboxes require an Active Directory User object in the Active Directory, as was the case with a resource/group mailbox in Exchange 2000/2003?

A: Yes. Even though Exchange 2007 includes dedicated room and equipment mailboxes, which aren't logged on to, an Active Directory User object in Active Directory is still required. But keep in mind that the User object that gets created when you create either a room or equipment mailbox will be disabled by default.

Q: What's the difference between disabling and removing a mailbox in Exchange 2007?

A: Disabling a mailbox removes all Exchange attributes from the Active Directory user account, which means that the user account no longer will be mailbox-enabled. The User object will remain in Active Directory, though. Although disabling a mailbox will remove the mailbox from the respective account, the mailbox won't be permanently deleted. By default, it can be found under the Disconnected Mailbox subnode for 30 up to 30 days after the mailbox was disabled. The mailbox can, at any time during this period, be reconnected to another User object from here. Removing a mailbox will not only mark the Exchange data for deletion, but the associated user object will also be deleted from the Active Directory. However, because of the default deleted mailbox retention settings, the mailbox can be reconnected to another user object within 30 days.

Q: Once I've moved a legacy mailbox (Exchange 2000/2003 mailbox) to an Exchange 2007 server, can I then moved it back to an Exchange 2000/2007 server if I need to, for some reason?

A: Yes, this is supported. Mailboxes can be moved both ways. But bear in mind that you'll lose any Exchange 2007-specific features, such as Unified Messaging, once you do so.

Q: How many mailboxes can I move at a time when I'm using the Exchange 2007 Move Mailbox Wizard? I remember that the Exchange 2003 version of the Move Mailbox Wizard could process four mailboxes at the same time.

A: It's correct that the Exchange 2003 Move Mailbox Wizard was limited to processing four mailboxes at the same time, but actually it was possible to run four threads at a time, meaning that you (of course, depending on your hardware) could move 16 mailboxes at the same time. This hasn't changed with Exchange 2007, so the same limitations apply to the Exchange 2007 Move Mailbox Wizard.

Chapter 4

Managing the Exchange 2007 Mailbox Server Role

Solutions in this chapter:

- **Managing the Exchange 2007 Mailbox Server**
- **Exchange 2007 Storage Groups**
- **Exchange 2007 Mailbox Databases**
- **Exchange 2007 Public Folder Databases**
- **Managing Organizationwide Mailbox Server Configuration Settings**

☑ **Summary**

☑ **Solutions Fast Track**

☑ **Frequently Asked Questions**

Introduction

The Exchange 2007 Mailbox Server role is, without surprise, the one hosting mailbox database in which the user's mailboxes are stored. This is also the server role that hosts Public Folder databases, which contain the Public Folders organizations use for sharing documents, calendars, contacts, and tasks as well as for archiving distribution lists. As you saw in Chapter 2, where we went through a typical installation of Exchange Server 2007, a legacy Outlook client (that is, Outlook 2003 and earlier) requires a Public Folder database to connect to Exchange Server 2007.

In addition to being the server that hosts mailbox and Public Folder databases, the mailbox server also provides rich calendaring functionality, resource management, and offline address book downloads. The Mailbox Server role also provides services that calculate e-mail address policies (called *recipient policies* in Exchange Server 2000 and 2003) as well as address lists for recipients. Finally, this server role enforces managed folders.

NOTE

If all end users use Outlook 2007 and you don't use Public Folders for sharing documents, calendars, contacts, and tasks as well as for archiving distribution lists, you don't need to create a Public Folder database on your Exchange 2007 Server(s). The reason is that Outlook 2007, in addition to MAPI, uses Web services for accessing things such as free/busy information, out-of-office (OOF) messages, offline address books (OABs), and the like. Since it's the Exchange 2007 Client Access Server roles that are responsible for these Web services, we won't cover them in this chapter (see Chapter 5 instead).

After reading this chapter, you will have gained a good understanding of how you manage the Mailbox Server roles feature set, both in terms of the Mailbox Server level as well as organizationwide.

Managing the Exchange 2007 Mailbox Server

The mailbox server holds the Exchange Store, which provides a single repository for managing multiple types of unstructured information in one infrastructure. The store hasn't changed much since Exchange Server 2003 but has been further improved and, of course, contains multiple new features. The Exchange Store is still made up of multiple interacting logical components, where the primary three still are storage groups, mailbox databases (formerly known as mailbox stores), and Public Folder databases (formerly known as Public Folder stores).

NOTE

Back in Exchange 2000 and 2003, the databases containing either mailboxes or Public Folders were known as mailbox stores and Public Folder stores, respectively, but with Exchange Server 2007 they are now referred to as *mailbox databases* and *Public Folder databases*.

The Exchange Product Group had several design goals related to mailbox server storage design. One of the goals was to allow an average user to have a considerably larger mailbox (2GB and larger) than was the case in Exchange 2003, where the norm was approximately 100MB to 300MB. Another design goal was to reduce the I/O (to lower the demand from the storage subsystem), done by taking advantage of 64–bit hardware, which gives us the opportunity to use much more memory than was the case in previous Exchange versions. Because Exchange Server 2007 can take advantage of more memory, a larger chunk of each user's mailbox can be stored in the memory, which reduces disk I/O.

In Figure 4.1 you see a screenshot of the Exchange Management Console (EMC) with the Mailbox node selected. As you can see, this particular server holds several storage groups, mailbox databases, and a single Public Folder database.

Figure 4.1 The Mailbox Subnode in the Server Configuration Work Center

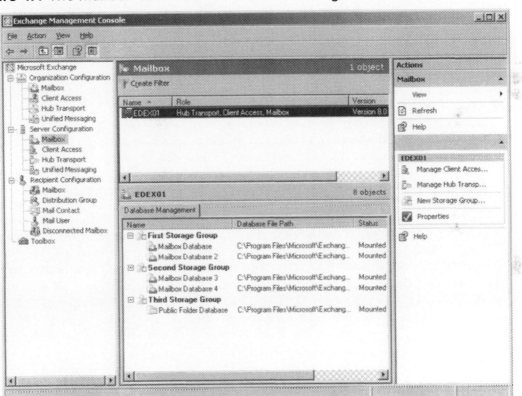

In the following sections, we'll go through how you manage and configure storage groups, mailbox databases, and Public Folder databases.

Exchange 2007 Storage Groups

A *storage group* is a grouping of mailbox and/or Public Folder databases that shares a single backup schedule and a single set of transaction log files. Storage groups are managed using their separate server processes; the idea behind splitting up databases in storage groups is primarily to reduce the overhead that results from multiple sets of transaction log files.

As most of you'll recall, Exchange Server 2003 Standard Edition supported one storage group and two stores—one mailbox and one Public Folder store (when excluding the Recovery Storage Group, of course). Exchange Server 2003 Enterprise Edition supported a total of four storage groups, each containing a maximum of five store databases. The limit of a database in Exchange Server 2003 Standard Edition was 16GB (although raised to 75GB when Exchange 2003 Service Pack 2 was applied). There was no limit on a database in Exchange Server 2003 Enterprise Edition; well, actually, there was a 16 terabyte limit, but this limit was caused by hardware.

As we explained in Chapter 2, Exchange Server 2007 comes in two flavors: a Standard Edition and an Enterprise Edition, just like previous versions of Exchange. The mailbox server in Exchange Server 2007 Standard Edition supports a total of five storage groups and five databases. Unlike Exchange 2003 and previous versions of Exchange, there's no longer a database storage limit in the Standard Edition.

The mailbox server in the Exchange 2007 Enterprise Edition supports up to 50 storage groups and a maximum of 50 databases per server. Exchange 2007 allows you to create up to five databases in each storage group, as is the case with Exchange 2003, but best practice is to create one database per storage group. So, why should you have a one-to-one relationship between storage groups and databases? That's primarily because you'll be up and running a lot faster when dealing with disaster recovery scenarios and the like.

As was the case with Exchange 2003, it's still okay to keep all storage groups on the same spindles, but in terms of performance, it's better to keep them separated—although that would be quite unrealistic for most organizations that were using, for example, 30 storage groups!

Local and Cluster Continuous Replication

Exchange Server 2007 finally has native support for continuous replication, which is a functionality that will make it possible to keep a second copy of a database held in a particular storage group. The second copy of a database will be updated using log file shipping and log file replay. The idea with keeping a second copy of a database is, of course, to get up and running in a couple of minutes by being able to switch to the second database with just a couple of mouse clicks (or CMDlets), should the original database crash or get corrupted. Having a second constantly updated copy of a database also means you don't have to perform a full backup of the database as often as you used to. With local continuous replication or cluster continuous replication deployed, you could, for example, take a weekly backup instead of a daily one, which is the typical backup schedule.

The new continuous replication functionality can be enabled for storage groups on a single Exchange 2007 mailbox server (known as *local continuous replication*), and it can also be used with an Exchange 2007 mailbox cluster (known as a *clustered continuous replication setup*). We won't dive into the details of how you enable, configure, and manage this functionality in this chapter; we cover them in depth in Chapter 8.

Creating a New Storage Group

Let's take a look at how you create a new storage group in Exchange Server 2007:

1. Open the Exchange Management Console and expand the **Server Configuration** work center node, then select the **Mailbox** subnode.

2. Now click **New Storage Group** in the **Action pane**.

3. The **New Storage Group Wizard** shown in Figure 4.2 will appear. Here you'll need to provide a name for the new storage group as well as specify the location for the transaction log files and the system files. Do so by clicking the **Browse** buttons, then click **New**.

> **NOTE**
>
> You also have the option of enabling local continuous replication for the storage group by putting a check mark in the **Enable Continuous Replication for this storage group** box. If you don't do so while creating the storage group, you can easily do so later.

Figure 4.2 Creating a New Storage Group

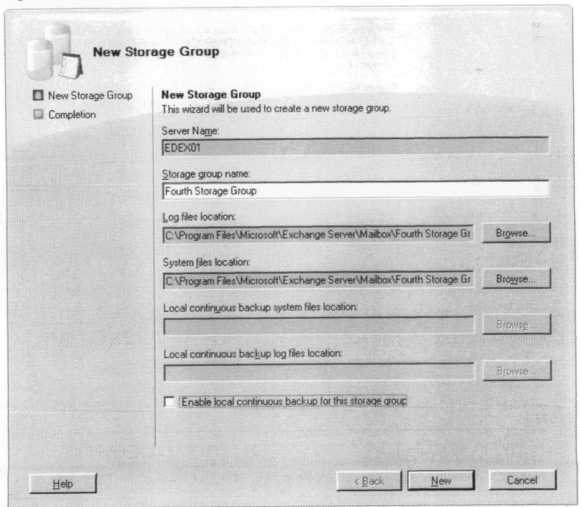

4. On the **Completion** page, you can see whether or not the storage group was created successfully, as well as the CMDlet code required to create the storage group using the Exchange Management Shell (EMS). Click **Finish** to exit the wizard (see Figure 4.3).

Figure 4.3 Creation of New Storage Group Completed Successfully

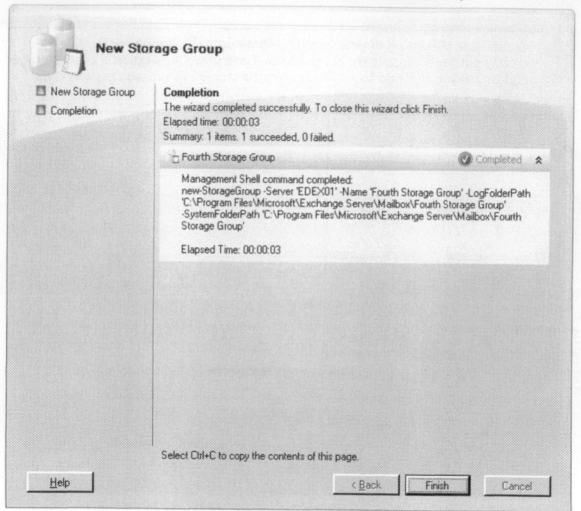

NOTE

As you can see in Figure 4.3, you can also create a new storage group via the EMS using the *New-StorageGroup* cmdlet. For additional information about the *New-StorageGroup* cmdlet, type **Get-Help New-StorageGroup** in the EMS.

Now let's try to open the Properties page for a storage group so that we can see what can be configured here (see Figure 4.4). It looks as though not much can be configured from here; actually, you can only change the name of the respective storage group as well as enable or disable circular logging. Most of us know circular logging, but for the few readers who don't, this is a feature that, when enabled, will allow Exchange to overwrite the transaction log files. This will reduce disk space used by the log files and is a best practice when you, for example, move a large group of mailboxes from one storage group to another. But under normal circumstances, you should keep this feature disabled; enabling it will limit your capability of restoring all data in a database doing a disaster recovery. Here's the reason that this is so: As we already mentioned, enabling the feature will allow Exchange to overwrite the log files every time a new file is generated. This means that you'll only be able to restore data up to the last full backup of a database, and if you do this, say, each night and the database crashes and is corrupted in the afternoon, you'll want be able to restore any data generated in the database between the last full backup and the time of the disaster. So, we repeat: Unless you know what you're doing, keep this feature disabled.

Figure 4.4 The Properties Page of a Storage Group

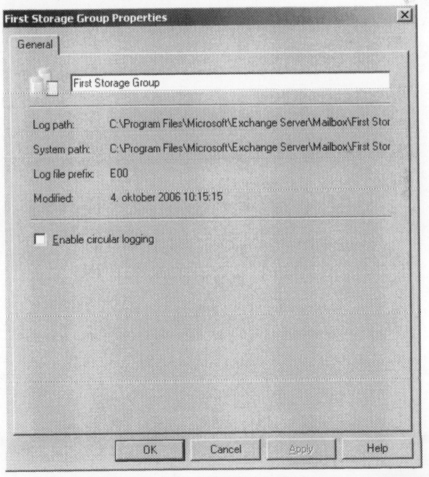

Moving a Storage Group

At times you might need to move a given storage group from one location to another. To do so you need to perform the following steps:

1. In the Exchange Management Console, click the **Server Configuration** work center node, then select the **Mailbox Server** subnode.

2. Now click the **storage group** you want to move and select **Move Storage Group** in the **Action pane**. Alternatively, you can right-click the respective **storage group** and select **Move Storage Group** from the context menu.

3. In the **Move Storage Files Wizard**, click the **Browse** button and specify the new location for the log and system files, then click **Move** (see Figure 4.5).

Figure 4.5 Moving a Storage Group

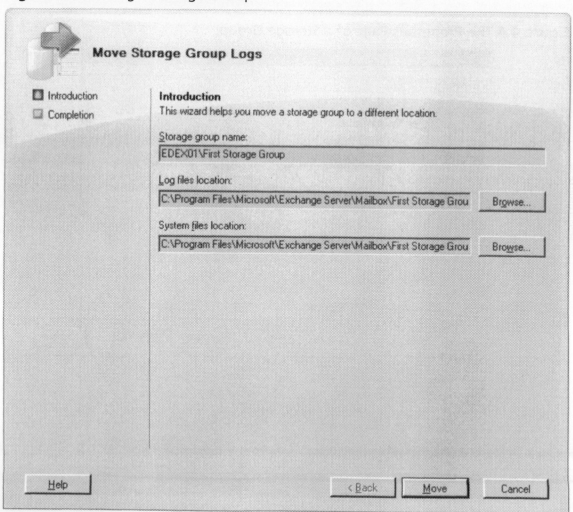

Removing a Storage Group

Removing a storage group is perhaps the simplest task of all, but bear in mind that you'll need to delete any mailbox and/or Public Folder databases contained in the storage group before you do so. When you're ready, perform the following steps:

1. In the Exchange Management Console, click the **Server Configuration** work center node, then select the **Mailbox Server** subnode.

2. Now click the **storage group** you want to delete and select **Remove** in the **Action pane**. Alternatively, you can right-click the respective **storage group** and select **Remove** from the context menu.

3. You'll now be asked whether you're sure that you want to remove the storage group. Click **Yes**.

4. When the storage group has been removed, you will get a warning stating that you need to manually remove the Storage Group folder and any log files beneath it (see Figure 4.6). click **OK**.

Figure 4.6 Storage Group Removal Warning

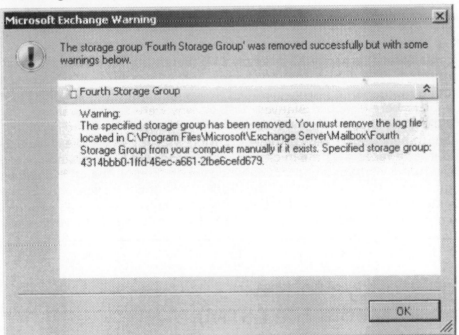

NOTE

If you want to remove a storage group using the EMS, you can do so using the *Remove-StorageGroup* CMDlet. To get a list of the available parameters, type **Get-Help Remove-StorageGroup** in the EMS.

Managing Exchange 2007 Mailbox Databases

As is the case with previous versions of Exchange, databases in Exchange Server 2007 are still based on the Extensible Storage Engine (ESE). The purpose of ESE is to provide an interface to the underlying database structure, which is responsible for managing changes made to the database (more specifically, the .EDB file). To do so, ESE uses transaction log files so that a database is kept in a reliable state. It does so by writing any changes made to a database (for example, via an Outlook MAPI client) first to one or more transaction log files and only thereafter to the database itself.

SOME INDEPENDENT ADVICE

During the early development stages of Exchange Server 2007 (which, back then, was code-named Exchange 12 or simply E12) there were serious plans about moving away from the ESE (which, formerly known as the Joint Engine Technology, or JET, is nothing more than a heavily modified Access database) to a new SQL database. These plans were dropped relatively fast. So, why were the plans about moving to a SQL database dropped in the first place? The decision was based on many factors, but the primary reason was customers. Staying with JET would mean that customers would not be faced with the migration work associated with moving to a new store, which is perhaps a good thing when you look at all the other architectural changes that have been made to the product. Will the next version of Exchange (code-named E14) use a SQL database? We don't know, but there's a good chance ESE won't be replaced with SQL before E15 (yes, that's right, the version *after* E14!).

Saying Goodbye to the Streaming Media File (.STM)

In Exchange Server 2000 and 2003 a database is made up of 2 files: an .EDB file and an .STM file. The purpose of the streaming file (.STM) is, as many of you might be aware, to house raw Internet content message streams as defined in Request for Comment (RFC) 822. Since the .EDB file isn't very suitable for storing raw Internet content message streams, the idea of introducing the .STM file was understandable, but with Exchange Server 2007 the .STM file has been removed, together with the Exchange Installable File System (ExIFS). The reasoning behind this decision was to reduce the overall I/O footprint for Exchange Server 2007.

What about Support for Single-Instance Storage?

As is the case with previous versions of Exchange, Exchange Server 2007 maintains single-instance storage (SIS) of messages. That means that if a message is sent to one recipient and it is copied to 20 other recipients residing in the same mailbox store, Exchange Server 2007 maintains only one copy of the message in its database. Exchange Server 2007 will instead create pointers to the message, and these pointers will link both the original recipient and the 20 additional recipients to the original message. If the original recipient and the 20 additional recipients are moved to another mailbox store, only one copy of the message is maintained in the new mailbox store. Since SIS hasn't changed since Exchange Server 2003, we won't go into this technology in depth but instead refer you to MS KB article 175481 (http://support.microsoft.com/kb/175481) if you want to learn more.

New Size for Transaction Log Files

Another improvement regarding storage changes in Exchange Server 2007 is that the transaction log files now are 1MB instead of 5MB, as was the case in previous version of Exchange. What's the reason behind this decision? In previous versions of Exchange, if a crash destroyed the last few log files that hadn't yet been committed to the database, you would need to restore or repair the database to have it mounted again. Exchange Server 2007 introduces a new feature called *lost log resilience*, or LLR for short, which will hold the last few log files in memory until the database is shut down. This means that you'll never have a case where part of log file 5, for example, has been written to the database, but part of log file 4 hasn't. The benefit of this feature is that if you don't mind losing the last few log files, you can tell Exchange to simply throw away the data and mount the database.

The reason that the log files have been reduced to 1MB is to reduce LLR exposure. Now if you lose the last log, it costs up to 1MB of the most recent data instead of 5MB.

Another improvement worth mentioning in regard to transaction log files in Exchange Server 2007 is that the log file sequence numbers now can go above 1 million. As some of you might be aware, previous versions of Exchange had a limit of 1 million, so if a database had been running long enough to generate a million logs, you had to shut it down and start over from log #1 ("resetting the log sequence"). This would happen every few years, for most databases. With the smaller log sizes and the increasing number of messages passing through most databases, the Exchange Product group decided that 4 billion would be a better maximum log number.

NOTE

It's a best practice to separate database and transaction log files on different disk spindles. This makes it easier to recover your data if there's a disk failure and provides the best overall performance (by optimizing disk I/O).

Creating a New Mailbox Database

Creating a new mailbox database is straightforward; you do so by performing the following steps:

1. In the EMC, click the **Server Configuration** work center node, and then select the **Mailbox Server** subnode.

2. Now select the **storage group** in which you want to create the new mailbox database.

3. Select **New Mailbox Database** in the **Action pane**. Alternatively, you can right-click the respective **mailbox database** and select **New Mailbox Database** from the context menu.

4. Name the new mailbox database and specify the location where you want the .EDB file to be created, then click **New** (see Figure 4.7).

Figure 4.7 Creating a New Mailbox Database

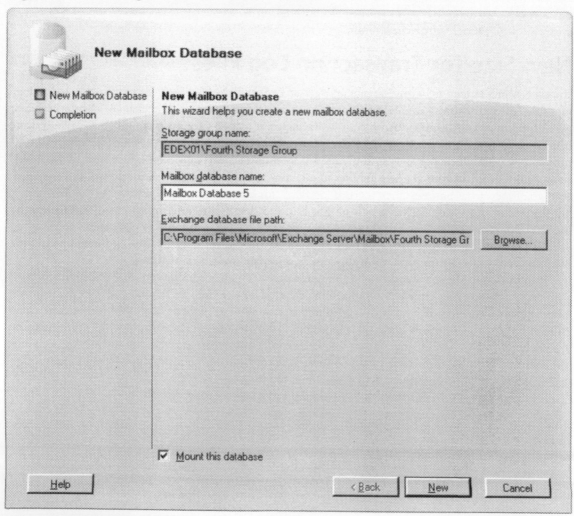

5. On the **Completion** page, click **Finish** to create (and, if selected in the previous screen) mount the new mailbox database (see Figure 4.8).

Figure 4.8 The New Mailbox Database Completion Page

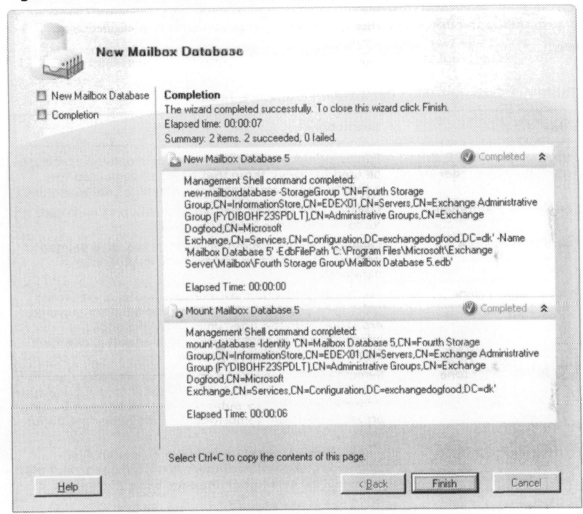

As shown in Figure 4.8, you can also create a new mailbox database using the *New-MailboxDatabase* CMDlet. To get a list of available parameters, type **Get-Help New-MailboxDatabase**.

Now that we have created a new mailbox database, let's take a look at the Properties page for such a database. We do so by selecting the database and clicking **Properties** in the Action pane.

The first tab is General. Here we can rename the mailbox database as well as see information such as database copy path (only available when local continuous replication has been enabled for the storage group containing the particular database), last full backup, and status (mounted or dismounted) as well as the last time a modification was made. In addition, you have the option of enabling Journal Recipient, used to specify the mailbox that should receive a copy of all messages sent to and from mailboxes in a particular mailbox database. We'll talk much more about journaling in Chapter 6.

As is the case with Exchange Server 2003, we also have the option of specifying the maintenance schedule, which is the time where the Exchange maintenance tasks will run. The Exchange maintenance tasks are a series of operations that are performed to ensure logical consistency in a database.

If you're planning to have multiple storage groups with each separate set of databases on a single Exchange 2007 mailbox server, it's recommended that you configure the maintenance schedule for each database so that they don't overlap. In addition, this schedule should be configured so that it doesn't conflict with your backup schedule.

The Exchange database maintenance tasks consist of 10 operations, which are listed in Table 4.1.

Table 4.1 Exchange 2007 Database Maintenance Tasks

Tasks	Description
Purge mailbox and Public Folder database indexes	Purges indices that the client creates in database tables to be used for views; those that have not been used for a specified time are cleaned up when this subtask occurs.
Tombstone maintenance	Compacts the deleted message information that is used for local and Public Folder replication.
Dumpster cleanup	Cleans up any messages that have passed their deleted item retention date on mailbox and Public Folder databases.
Public Folder expiry	Expired messages that are in Public folders and that are older than a specified time value. The setup for message expiration is on the Age Limits tab in the public information store container in the Microsoft Exchange Server Administrator program.
Age folder tombstone	Removes folder tombstone entries that are older than a specified time (the default is 180 days). Folder tombstone information is used by public folder replication. The aging prevents the folder tombstone list from growing without limits.
Folder conflict cleanup	Cleans up any conflicts on messages that have been modified by two different users at the same time and that have resulted in the given message being in conflict.
Update server versions	Updates the version information as necessary for any Public Folder databases that contain a replica of a system configuration folder.
Secure folders cleanup	Checks secure folders to ensure that no message has a reference count of zero, indicating no folder currently has a reference to the particular message.
Site folder check	Used by Public Folder databases to ensure that no duplicate site folders exist.
Deleted mailbox cleanup	Checks Active Directory to determine whether there are any deleted mailboxes. The information store performs an Active Directory lookup for each user in the MDB.

On the General tab (see Figure 4.9), you also have the option of configuring the database not to mount during startup and enable the **This database can be overwritten by a restore** option, which is used when you need to restore a database from backup. Nothing has changed here compared with Exchange Server 2003.

Figure 4.9 The General Tab on the Properties Page for a Mailbox Database

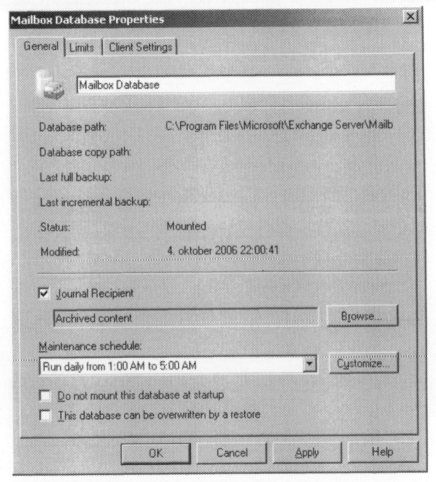

Let's move on to the Limits tab (see Figure 4.10). As is also the case with Exchange Server 2003, we here have the option of configuring the storage limit for the mailboxes in the particular mailbox database. Note that the options "Issue warning at (KB)," "Prohibit send at (KB)," and "Prohibit send and receive at (KB)" in Exchange Server 2007 are by default set drastically higher (around 2GB) than was the case in Exchange Server 2003. Again, this is to take advantage of the Exchange 2007 64-bit architecture.

On this tab you also have the option of changing the warning message interval and the deletion settings. Note that the "Keep deleted items for (days)" and "Keep Deleted mailboxes for (days)" options have other default settings than was the case in Exchange Server 2003. The end user can now retrieve items from the dumpster 14 days back, and any deleted mailboxes will not be purged before approximately a month passes, meaning that the reason for restoring a database to retrieve data in a deleted mailbox will be reduced even further.

Figure 4.10 The Limits Tab on the Properties Page for a Mailbox Database

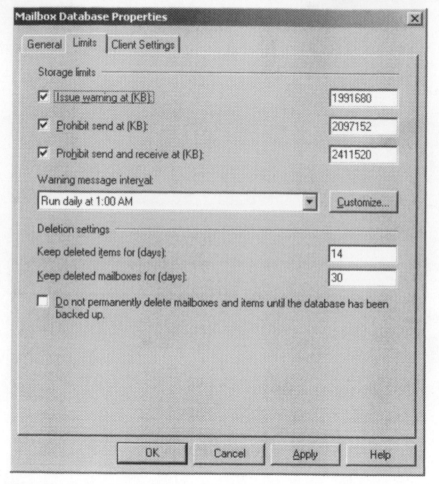

Now it's time to take a look at what's hiding under the Client Settings tab. As you can see in Figure 4.11, this is the place where you can specify the public folder database as well as the offline address book (OAB) that should be the default for mailboxes in the particular mailbox database.

NOTE

The OAB is an address book that Outlook 2003 and 2007 download to the local computer (client). With the OAB file held locally on the client, it doesn't need to have access to Active Directory to browse and look up recipients in the GAL. Outlook 2003 and 2007 also use the OAB when working in cached mode, which means that it can take up to 24 hours before newly created mailbox-enabled recipients can be looked up by clients working in cached mode. OAB files can still be distributed using Public Folders (used by legacy clients such as Outlook 98, 2000, and 2003), but in Exchange 2007, OAB distribution is Web based.

Figure 4.11 The Client Settings Tab on the Properties Page for a Mailbox Database

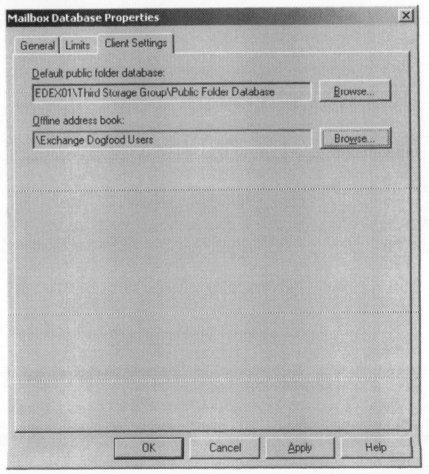

Exchange 2007 Public Folder Databases

Public Folders are still supported in Exchange Server 2007, but bear in mind that they have been deemphasized, which means that there's a good chance they won't be included in the next version of Exchange (currently code-named E14). With this in mind, it's a good idea to start thinking about migrating to another solution, such as SharePoint.

NOTE

Even though Public Folders have been deemphasized in Exchange Server 2007, Microsoft will support them until the end of 2016, so most of you should have sufficient time available to migrate Public Folder data to another solution, such as SharePoint.

A Public Folder database is a database used to store Public Folders. The data contained in a Public Folder can be accessed by any mailbox-enabled users as long as they have the appropriate permissions. The Public Folders in the Public Folder database can exist as single copies or multiple copies (also referred to as *replicas*). Using replicas, you can configure Public Folders to be synchronized between specified servers so that they always are up to date, no matter which mailbox server a given client is connected to. Since a Public Folder isn't replicated automatically, you must configure which Public Folder database should contain a replica of any given Public Folder.

Because Public Folders are widely used by organizations for sharing documents, calendars, contacts, and tasks and for archiving distribution lists, one would think that you could administer these folders from within the EMC, but unfortunately the administration tasks you can do from within the EMC are extremely limited. So, if you need to do tasks other than create, delete, and move Public Folder databases as well as configure limits and the like, you will, depending on the specific task, need to do so using the EMS, an Outlook client, or System Manager on an Exchange 2003 Server that's still part of the Exchange organization. The following step-by-step instructions tell you how to perform the most common tasks regarding administration of Public Folders.

Creating a New Public Folder Database

Creating a new Public Folder database is just as straightforward as creating a mailbox database. It is done by performing the following steps:

1. In the Exchange Management Console, click the **Server Configuration** work center node, then select the **Mailbox Server** subnode.

2. Now click the **storage group** in which you want to create the database, then select **New Public Folder Database** in the **Action pane**. Alternatively, you can right-click the respective **storage group** and select **New Public Folder Database** from the context menu.

3. In the **New Public Folder Database Wizard**, enter a name for the database, then click the **Browse** button and specify the location for the .EDB file.

4. Finally, click **New** (see Figure 4.12).

Figure 4.12 Creating a New Public Folder Database

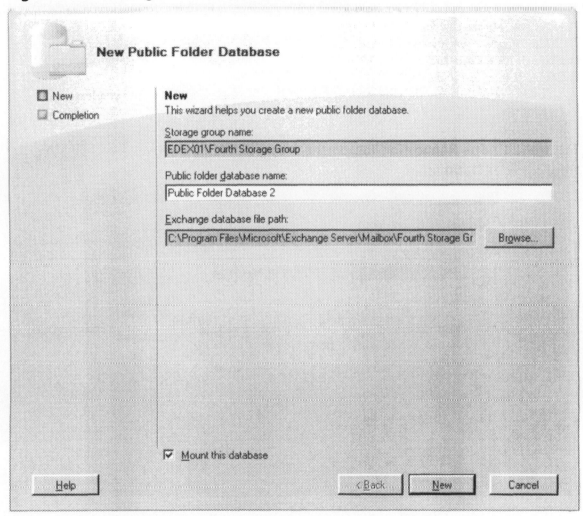

Now that we have created a new Public Folder database, let's take a look at the Properties page for the database.

The General tab is almost identical to that of a mailbox database, so let's move on and click the **Replication** tab. As you can see in Figure 4.13, you can specify the Public Folder database replication interval, the replication interval for "Always Run" (in minutes), and the replication message size limit. The replication intervals used to configure the interval at which replication of Public Folders or content may occur and the Replication interval for "Always Run" (minutes) is used to define what "always run" means (by default, it's 15 minutes).

The "Replication message size limit (KB)" setting is used to specify the size of a replication message. If it's set to a large value, smaller messages can be aggregated into a single replication messages as high as the defined value.

Unless you have a specific reason for changing these settings, we recommend you leave the defaults intact.

Figure 4.13 The Replication Tab on the Properties Page of a Public Folder Database

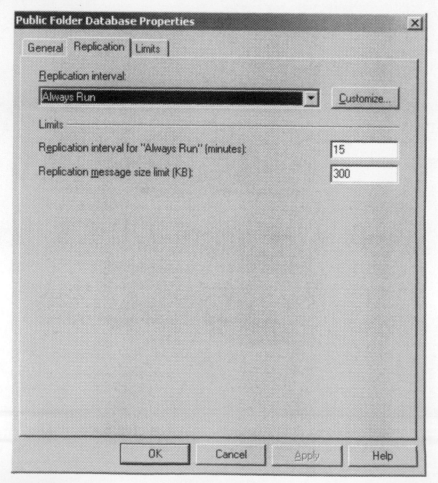

Let's take a look at what's hiding under the Limits tab. As you can see in Figure 4.14, this is the place where we configure the storage limits for a Public Folder database. As is the case with the default storage limits for a mailbox database, the Public Folder database limits are set much higher than was the case in previous Exchange versions. When the database is approximately 2GB in size, a warning will be generated, and when it's over 2GB, end users will be prohibited from posting messages to a Public Folder in the Public Folder database. The maximum item size is approximately 10MB.

Note that the "Keep deleted items for (days)" option is configured to 14 days, just as is the case for a mailbox database—again, a much higher setting than in previous versions of Exchange.

Note that you also have the option of setting an age limit for the Public Folders that exists in the particular Public Folder database.

Figure 4.14 The Public Folder Database Properties Page

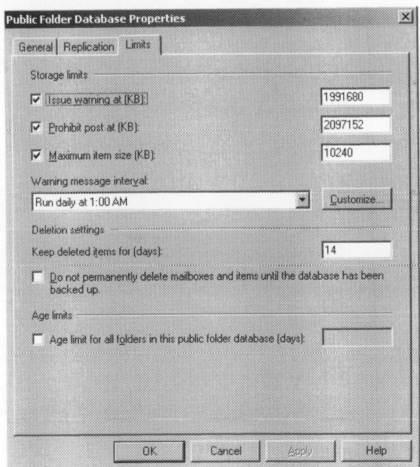

These settings can also be set using either CMDlets or the Exchange 2003 System Manager.

Creating a Public Folder

You can create a Public Folder using the EMS, an Outlook MAPI client, or the System Manager on an Exchange 2003 Server that still exists in the Exchange organization.

Creating a public folder using the EMS is done using the *New-PublicFolder* CMDlet. So, if for example we wanted to create a new Public Folder named *Finance*, we would need to type the following command in the EMS:

```
New-PublicFolder -Name Finance
```

followed by pressing **Enter** (see Figure 4.15).

Figure 4.15 Creating a New Public Folder Via the Exchange Management Shell

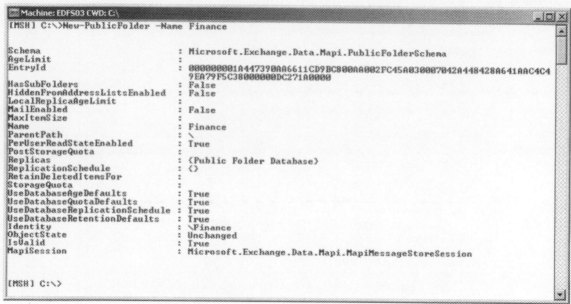

If you still have an Exchange 2003 Server in your Exchange organization, you can also create new Public Folders using the System Manager by following these steps:

1. On the respective Exchange 2003 server, open the System Manager by clicking **Start** | **All Programs** | **Microsoft Exchange** | **Exchange System Manager**.

2. Drill down to and expand the **Folders** node.

3. Depending on whether you want to create a top-level folder or a child node, right-click the **Public Folders** or the top-level folder in which you want to create the new Public Folder, then choose **New | Public Folder** in the context menu (see Figure 4.16).

Figure 4.16 Selecting a Public Folder Store in the Exchange 2003 System Manager

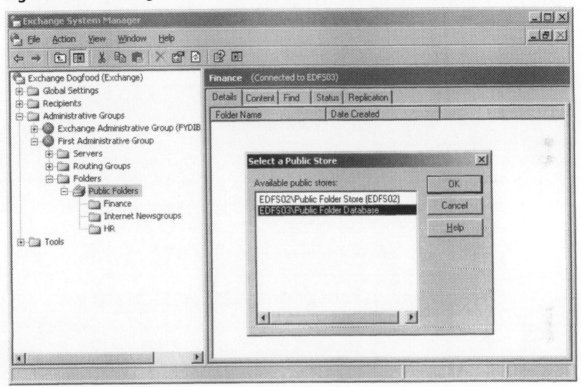

4. Give the new Public Folder a name, then click **OK** (see Figure 4.17).

Figure 4.17 The General Tab on the Properties Page of a Public Folder

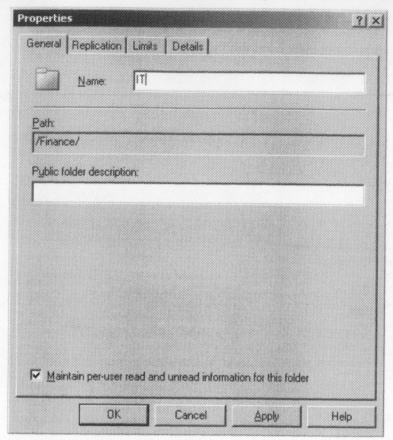

Finally, you create Public Folders using an Outlook MAPI client, although this requires your user account got the appropriate permissions to do so. You do so by using the following steps:

1. Open an Outlook MAPI client (in this case, Outlook 2007).

2. If it's not already selected, click the yellow **Folder List** icon in the lower-left corner.

3. Expand **Public Folders | All Public Folders**.

4. Depending on whether you want to create a top-level or a child-level folder, right-click either **All Public Folders** or the top-level folder in which you want to create the Public Folder.

5. In the context menu, select **New Folder**.

6. In the **Create New Folder** window, type a name for the new folder and specify the type of data the Public Folder should be used for, then click **OK** (see Figure 4.18).

Figure 4.18 Creating a New Public Folder Using Outlook 2007

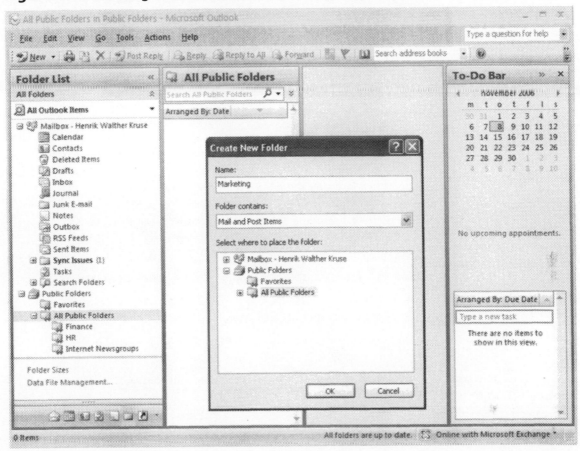

If you later want to remove a Public Folder, you can do so using the *Remove-PublicFolder* cmdlet, the Exchange 2003 System Manager, or an Outlook MAPI client.

NOTE

To get a list of the Public Folders that exist in the Public Folder hierarchy, use the *Get-PublicfolderStatistics* CMDlet.

Administering Public Folder Permission Settings

As is the case with previous versions of Exchange, Exchange Server 2007 allows you to configure Public Folder client permissions as well as administrative rights. Client permissions are used to grant user accounts access to a Public Folder, and you can do so using a preconfigured set of permissions, or you can set up custom permissions. Administrative rights are used to specify users or groups that should be allowed to use the EMS or Exchange 2003 System Manager or to change the replication limits as well as other settings for a Public Folder.

You can configure client permission settings for a Public Folder using the EMS, the Exchange 2003 System Manager, or an Outlook MAPI client.

To give or remove client permissions using the EMS, you'll need to use the *Add-PublicFolder-ClientPermission* and/or *Remove-PublicFolderClientPermission* CMDlets. So, to give a user account named *HEW* belonging to a domain named *Exchangedogfood.dk* permissions to create items in a Public Folder called *Finance* on a server called *EDFS03*, we would need to use the following command:

```
Add-PublicFolderClientPermission -Identity \"Finance" -User HEW -AccessRights
CreateItems -Server "EDSF03"
```

To remove this permission again, you would need to type:

```
Remove-PublicFolderClientPermission -Identity \"Finance" -User
HEW -AccessRights CreateItems -Server "EDSF03"
```

The available parameters for the *Add-PublicFolderClientPermission* and *Remove-PublicFolderClientPermission* CMDlets are listed in Table 4.2.

Table 4.2 Public Folder Client Permission Parameters

Parameter	Description
AccessRights	This parameter is used to specify the rights you want to add to the Public Folder (such as *CreateItems* or *DeleteOwnedItems*).
DomainController	This parameter is used to specify the domain controller to use to write this configuration change to Active Directory. You need to use the FQDN of the DC to be used. *Note:* This parameter is optional.
Identity	This parameter is used to specify a unique identifier (name) for the Public Folder.
User	This parameter is used to specify the UPN, domain/user, or alias of the user that should be granted rights to the public folder.
Server	This parameter is used to specify the server on which the selected operations should be performed.

In addition, as is also the case with previous versions of Exchange, you can use the Exchange 2003 System Manager (if you still have an Exchange 2003 server in your Exchange organization) or an Outlook MAPI client to set client permissions on a Public Folder.

To set client permissions on a Public Folder using the Exchange 2003 System Manager, use the following steps:

1. On the respective Exchange 2003 server, open the System Manager by clicking **Start | All Programs | Microsoft Exchange | Exchange System Manager**.

2. Drill down to the **Folders** and expand the **Public Folders** node.

3. Now right-click the **Public Folder** for which you want to add or remove client permissions, then select **Properties**.

4. Click the **Permissions** tab, as shown in Figure 4.19.

Figure 4.19 The Permissions Tab on the Properties Page of a Public Folder in Exchange 2003 System Manager

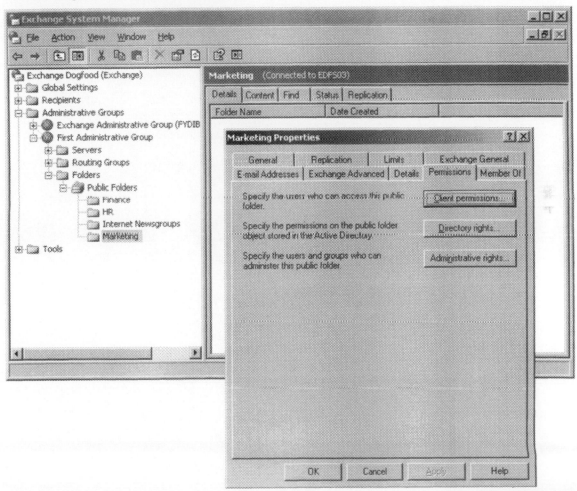

5. Click the **Client Permissions** button. Here you can see each user that already has been granted permissions on the Public Folder.

6. Click **Add** and add the respective user(s) to the client permission list, then click **OK**.

7. Now select the user(s) you just added, then grant the type of permission you want the user to have by using the **Roles** drop-down box or by ticking the different permissions individually (see Figure 4.20).

Figure 4.20 Public Folder Client Permissions

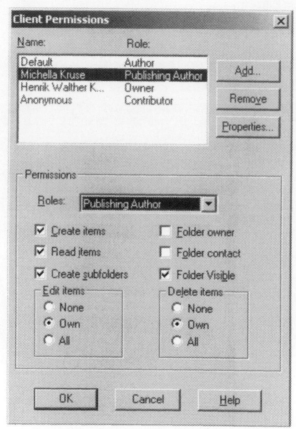

8. Click **OK** twice and close the Exchange 2003 System Manager.

SOME INDEPENDENT ADVICE

If you have a large Public Folder hierarchy and on a relatively frequent basis you need to grant user permissions to the Public Folders in the hierarchy, we recommend you use the Manage Public Folder Settings Wizard, which was introduced in Exchange Server 2003 SP2. This wizard (see Figure 4.21) makes it a breeze to grant user permissions to the folders in your Public Folder hierarchy, but it can also be used to modify replica lists and more.

Figure 4.21 The Manage Public Folder Settings Wizard

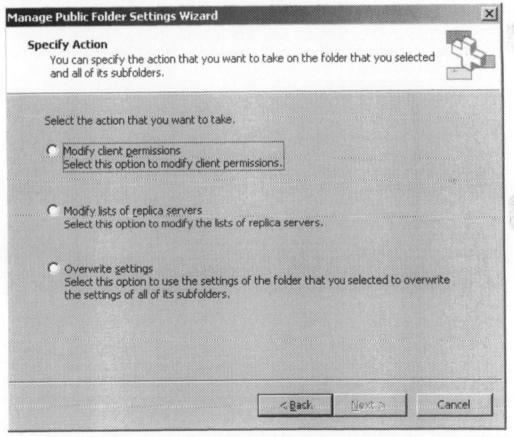

You launch the Manage Public Folder Settings Wizard by right-clicking a top Public Folder, then selecting **Manage Settings** in the context menu. You can read more about this wizard in one of our articles for MSExchange.org at www.msexchange.org/tutorials/Public-Folder-Improvements-Exchange-2003-Service-Pack-2.html.

Adding client permissions using an Outlook MAPI client is done using the following steps:

1. Open the Outlook MAPI client (in this case Outlook 2007).

2. If it's not already selected, click the yellow **Folder List** icon in the lower-left corner.

3. Expand **Public Folders | All Public Folders**.

4. Right-click the respective **Public Folder** and select **Change Sharing Permissions** in the context menu.

> **NOTE**
>
> If you don't have the option of choosing **Change Sharing Permissions** in the context menu, your user account most likely doesn't have administrative permissions for that particular Public Folder.

5. Under the **Permissions** tab, click **Add** and add the respective user(s), then click **OK** (see Figure 4.22).

6. Now grant the user(s) the required permissions, either by using the **Permission Level** drop-down box or by ticking the permissions individually.

7. Finally, click **OK**.

To add or remove Public Folder Administrative permissions, you can use the *Add-PublicFolderAdministrativePermission* and *Remove-PublicFolderAdministrativePermission* CMDlets.

To give a user account named *HEW* belonging to a domain named *Exchangedogfood.dk* permissions to modify the ACL for a Public Folder called *Finance* on a server called *EDFS03*, we would need to use the following command:

```
Add-PublicFolderAdministrativePermission -Identity \"Finance"
-User HEW -AccessRights ModifyPublicFolderACL -Server "EDSF03"
```

To remove this permission, again you would need to type:

```
Remove-PublicFolderAdministrativePermission -Identity \"Finance"
-User HEW -ModifyPublicFolderACL ModifyPublicFolderACL -Server "EDSF03"
```

Figure 4.22 The Permissions Tab on the Properties Page of a Public Folder in Outlook 2007

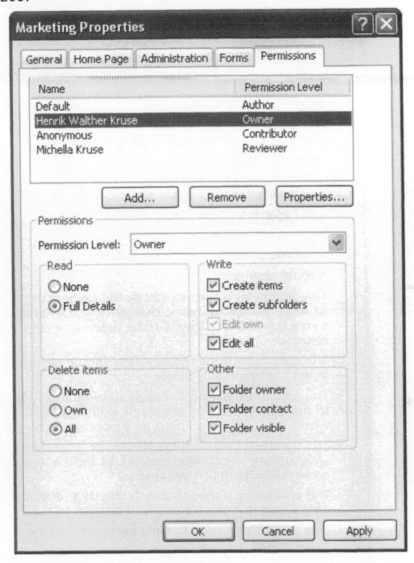

Table 4.3 lists the parameters that are relevant to the *PublicFolderAdministrativePermission* and *Remove-PublicFolderAdministrativePermission* CMDlets.

Table 4.3 Public Folder Administrative Permission Parameters

Parameter	Description
AccessRights	This parameter is used to specify the rights to be added. Available values are:
	None
	ModifyPublicFolderACL
	ModifyPublicFolderAdminACL
	ModifyPublicFolderDeletedItemRetention
	ModifyPublicFolderExpiry
	ModifyPublicFolderQuotas
	ModifyPublicFolderReplicaList
	AdministerInformationStore
	ViewInformationStore
	AllStoreRights
	AllExtendedRights
DomainController	This parameter is used to specify the domain controller to use to write this configuration change to Active Directory. You need to use the FQDN of the DC to be used. *Note:* This parameter is optional.
Identity	This parameter is used to specify a unique identifier (name) for the Public Folder.
Instance	This parameter is used to enable passing an entire object to the command to be processed; primarily used in scripts where an entire object must be passed to the command.
Owner	This parameter specifies the NT Owner access control list (ACL) on the object. Available values are the user principal name (UPN), domain/user, or alias.
User	This parameter is used to specify the UPN, domain/user, or alias of the user that should be granted rights to the Public Folder.
Deny	This parameter is used to deny permission to the respective Public Folder.
InheritanceType	This parameter is used to specify the type of inheritance. Available values are:
	None
	All
	Descendents
	SelfAndChildren
	Children
Server	This parameter is used to specify the server on which the selected operations should be performed.

As is also the case with the user permissions, you can configure administrative permissions using the Exchange 2003 System Manager. You do so by following these steps:

1. On the respective Exchange 2003 Server, open the System Manager by clicking **Start** | **All Programs** | **Microsoft Exchange** | **Exchange System Manager**.

2. Drill down to the **Folders** and expand the **Public Folders** node.

3. Now right-click the Public Folder for which you want to add or remove administrative permissions, then select **Properties**.

4. Click the **Permissions** tab.

5. Click the **Administrative Rights** button. Here you can see each user that has already been granted permissions to administer the Public Folder.

6. Click **Add** and add the respective user(s) to the administrative permission list (see Figure 4.23), then click **OK**.

Figure 4.23 Administrative Rights on a Public Folder

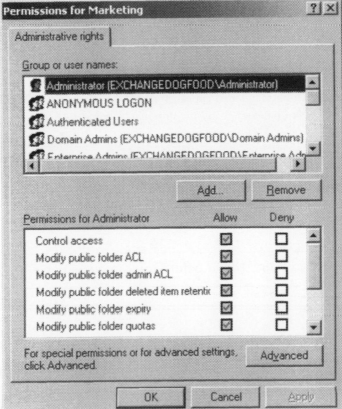

7. Now select the **user(s)** you just added, then grant the type of administrative permission you want the user to have. You do so by ticking the respective permission boxes under **Permissions for Administrator**.

8. Finally, click **OK** and exit the Exchange 2003 System Manager.

Managing Public Folder Replica Settings

Another feature missing in the Exchange 2007 Management Console is the option of configuring Public Folder replication settings. This also has to be done using either the EMS or an Exchange 2003 server that's still part of your Exchange organization.

To stop or resume Public Folder replication, you can use the *Stop-PublicFolderReplication* and *Resume-PublicFolderReplication* CMDlets, respectively.

To add Public Folder databases to or remove them from a replica list, you'll need to use the an Exchange 2003 System Manager.

Mail-Enabling a Public Folder

You might run into situations where you want to mail-enable a Public Folder—perhaps you'll want your users to be able to send messages to the folder in addition to posting messages. Because Public Folders by default are not mail-enabled, you need to mail-enable them using either the *Enable-MailPublicFolder* CMDlet or an Exchange 2003 System Manager. To mail-enable the Finance Public Folder we created earlier using the *Enable-MailPublicFolder* CMDlet, we would need to type:

```
Enable-MailPublicFolder -Identity "\Finance" followed by Enter
```

If you don't want the Public Folder to appear in the GAL, you would need to include the *HiddenFromAddressListsEnabled* parameter, and the command would look like the following:

```
Enable-MailPublicFolder -Identity "\Finance" -HiddenFromAddressListsEnabled
```

followed by pressing **Enter**.

NOTE

You need to create a Public Folder before you can mail-enable it.

To get a list of the mail-enabled Public Folders in your organization, you can use the *Get-MailPublicFolder* CMDlet. To get information for a specific mail-enabled Public Folder, type **Get-MailPublicFolder –Identity <public_folder>**.

If you don't specify an SMTP address when you mail-enable a Public Folder, it will use the name of the Public Folder. So, if the Public Folder is called *Finance* and the domain is *Exchangedogfood.dk*, the address will be *finance@exchangedogfood.dk*. If you want to use another primary SMTP address, you need to set it using the *Set-MailPublicFolder* CMDlet. The command would then be:

```
Set-MailPublicFolder -Identity "\Finance" -PrimarySmtpAddress:
economy@exchangedogfood.dk
```

followed by pressing **Enter**.

Many other *Set-MailPublicFolder* CMDlet parameters are available. We won't go into details on each of them, but instead we list each of them with a short description in Table 4.4.

Table 4.4 Parameters Available for a Mail-Enabled Public Folder

Parameter	Description
AcceptMessagesOnlyFrom	Accept messages only if sent by the specified recipients.
AcceptMessagesOnlyFrom-DLMembers	Accepts messages sent to the DL only if sent by DL members.
Alias	Used to specify the alias (mail nickname) of the Public Folder. If not specified, it is stamped as the Public Folder Name. The string must comply with RFC 2821 requirements for valid "local part" SMTP addresses.
Contacts	Specifies the contacts for the Public Folder.
CustomAttribute (1–15)	Used to specify a custom attribute.
DeliverToMailboxAndForward	Specifies whether or not e-mail will be sent to a forwarding address.
DisplayName	Specifies the display name of the Public Folder Proxy Object.
DomainController	Specifies which DC to connect to.
EmailAddresses	Proxy addresses. Example: user@exchangedogfood.dk.
EmailAddressPolicyEnabled	Used to have a recipient policy applied to the Public Folder.
ForwardingAddress	Delivery options: Sets the forwarding address for the folder.
GrantSendOnBehalfTo	Distinguished name of other mailboxes that can send on behalf of this folder.
HiddenFromAddressLists-Enabled	Specifies whether or not the mailbox is viewable from address lists.
Instance	This is an actual ADObject instance that is piped to and consumed by the task.

Continued

Table 4.4 Continued

Parameter	Description
MaxReceiveSize	This parameter specifies the maximum size of e-mail messages that can be received, from 1KB to 2,097,151KB. If not specified, there is no limit.
MaxSendSize	This parameter specifies the maximum size of e-mail messages that can be sent, from 1KB to 2,097,151KB. If not specified, there is no limit.
Name	Used to specify the name of the Public Folder.
PrimarySmtpAddress	Used to specify the primary SMTP address to be used by the Public Folder.
PublicFolderType	Used to specify the type of Public Folder.
RejectMessagesFrom	Used to specify SMTP addresses that should not be allowed to send messages to the Public Folder.
RejectMessagesFrom-DLMembers	Used to specify distribution lists that should not be allowed to send to this Public Folder.
RequireSenderAuthentication-Enabled	Specifies whether or not senders must be authenticated.
SimpleDisplayName	Used to specify a simple (a.k.a. friendly) display name.
WindowsEmailAddress	An e-mail address in the format *E-mailAddress@exchangedogfood.dk*.

NOTE

If you want to remove the mail attributes from a mail-enabled public folder, use the *Disable-MailPublicFolder* CMDlet.

To mail-enable a Public Folder using an Exchange 2003 System Manager, perform the following steps:

1. On the respective Exchange 2003 Server open the System Manager by clicking **Start | All Programs | Microsoft Exchange | Exchange System Manager**.

2. Drill down to the **Folders** and expand the **Public Folders** node.

3. Now right-click the **Public Folder** you want to mail-enable, then select **Properties**.

4. Select the **E-mail Addresses** tab (see Figure 4.24).

Figure 4.24 The E-mail Addresses Tab on the Properties Page for a Public Folder

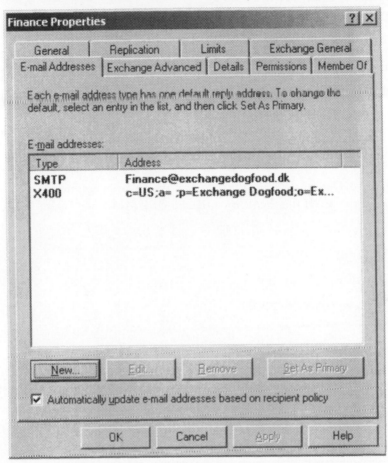

5. Click the **New** button, then click **SMTP Address**.

6. Type the SMTP address you want to assign to the Public Folder, then click **OK** twice and exit the **Exchange 2003 System Manager**.

NOTE

Features such as delivery restriction, Send on behalf etc. can of course also be configured via the Exchange 2003 System Manager, you do so under the **Exchange General** tab.

Moving a Mailbox or Public Folder Database

Moving either a mailbox or Public Folder database is very similar to moving a storage group. You do so by performing the following steps:

1. In the Exchange Management Console, click the **Server Configuration** work center node, then select the **Mailbox Server** subnode.

2. Now click the **mailbox** or **Public Folder database** you want to move and select **Move Database Files** in the **Action pane**. Alternatively, you can right-click the respective **mailbox** or **Public folder database** and select **Move Database Files** from the context menu.

3. In the **Move Database Files Wizard**, click the **Browse** button and specify the new location of the .EDB file, then click **OK** and click **Move** (see Figure 4.25).

Figure 4.25 Moving a Database

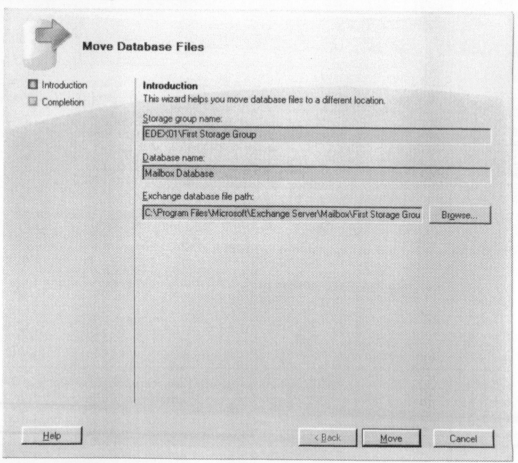

Removing a Mailbox or Public Folder Database

You might come across situations where you need to remove either a mailbox or Public folder database. You do so by performing the following steps:

1. In the Exchange Management Console, click the **Server Configuration** work center node, then select the **Mailbox Server** subnode.

2. Now click the **mailbox** or **Public Folder database** you want to remove and select **Remove** in the **Action pane**. Alternatively, you can right-click the respective **mailbox** or **Public Folder database** and select **Remove** from the context menu.

3. You will now be warned that the database file (.EDB file) needs to be removed manually. Click **OK** (see Figure 4.26).

Figure 4.26 Database Removal Warning

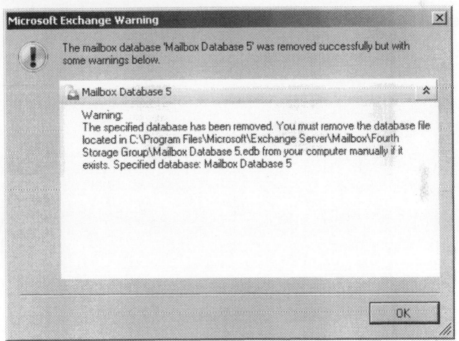

NOTE

To remove a mailbox or Public Folder database via the EMS, you can use the *Remove-MailboxDatabase* and *Remove-PublicFolderDatabase* CMDlets, respectively.

Managing Organizationwide Mailbox Server Configuration Settings

In addition to the features and functionality available at the mailbox server level, Exchange Server 2007 also has a feature set that is organizationwide. In this section we'll take a look at the feature set that can be applied to the entire Exchange Server 2007 organization.

If it's not already open, open the EMC and click the **Mailbox** node under the **Organization Configuration** work center in the navigation tree in the left side of the MMC console. This will bring us to a screen similar to the one shown in Figure 4.27.

Figure 4.27 The Address Lists Tab on the Organization Configuration Mailbox Node

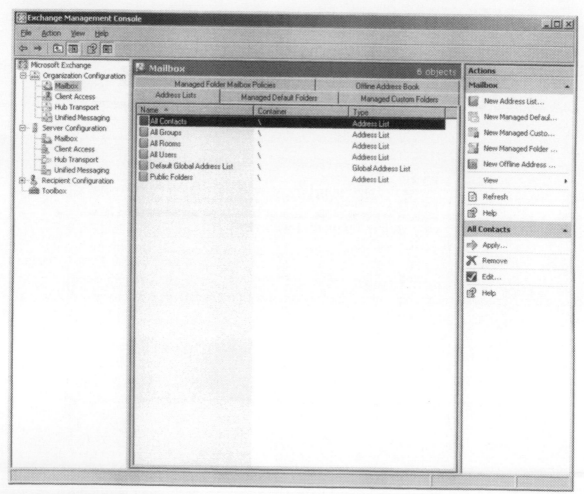

As you can see, a total of six tabs are available under the Mailbox node. We will go through each of them in the following sections.

Address Lists

The first tab is the Address Lists tab, on which all the default created address lists are listed. The purpose of address lists is to help you organize the different types of recipients within your Exchange organization so that they are listed in a meaningful way when your end users look up recipients in their mail clients. As you can see, we have an All Contacts list, which contains all mail contact objects within Active Directory. We have an All Groups list, which contains all distribution group objects. Then we have an All Rooms list, which is a type of list that didn't exist in Exchange Server 2000 or 2003, and there's a simple explanation why it is so. As you saw in Chapter 3 Exchange Server 2007 introduces a new type of mailbox, a so-called room mailbox, which basically is a mailbox that is used for room scheduling and not owned by a user. The All Rooms list contains all room mailboxes.

> **NOTE**
>
> There are two types of resource mailbox in Exchange Server 2007. One of them is the room mailbox; the other is the equipment mailbox (which is used to schedule equipment such as projectors and the like). Only the room mailboxes are listed in the All Rooms address list.

We also have an All Users list, which, as its name indicates, lists all mailbox user objects (including room and equipment mailboxes as well as linked, shared, and legacy mailboxes) within Active Directory. As in previous versions of Exchange, there is also a Default Global Address List (also known as the GAL), which lists all recipients within the Exchange organization. Finally, we have a Public Folders list, which surprisingly enough lists all Public Folders in the organization, if you have any.

Although the default address lists might be sufficient for some, they are far from enough for large organizations that have an Active Directory forest with multiple Active Directory domains. If this is the case, you might want to create additional address lists, which is done by following these steps:

1. Select the **Mailbox** subnode under the **Organization Configuration** work center node in the navigation tree to the left, then click **New Address List** in the **Action pane**. Alternatively, right-click the **Mailbox** subnode or somewhere in the white space in the **Work pane**.

2. Type a name for the new address list, then choose the container in which you want to create the address list (a backslash [\] creates it as a top address list), but you can also create it as a subaddress list to an existing one. Now specify the type of recipients that should be included in the address list. In this example, we choose **All recipient types**. When you have decided which one should be included, click **Next** (see Figure 4.28).

Figure 4.28 Creating a New Address List

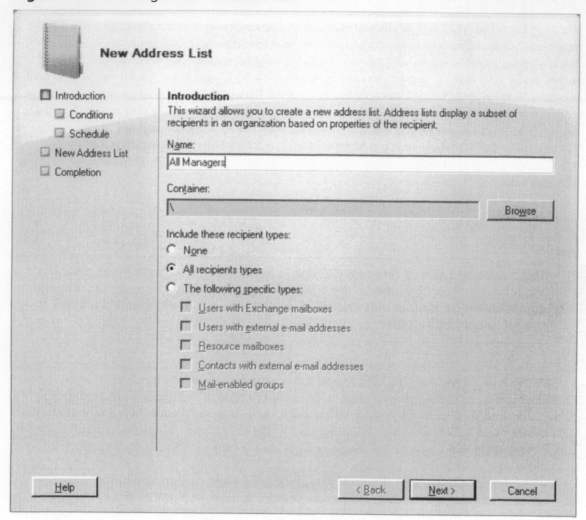

3. We now have the option of selecting the conditions we want to associate with the new address list (see Figure 4.29). For the purposes of this example, we chose **Recipient is in a Department**. In **Step 2**, click the blue **specified** link.

Figure 4.29 Specifying the Conditions for the New Address List

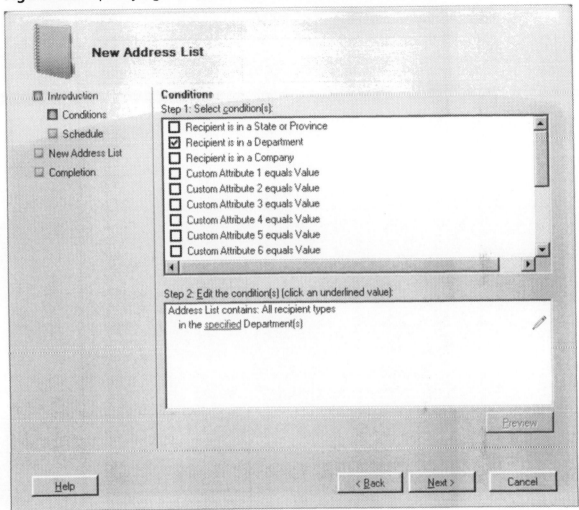

4. Type the name the **Department** field of the recipients you want to have listed in the address list. In this example, we want to list all recipients belonging to the management department. Click **Add** to add department(s) to the list (see Figure 4.30), then click **OK**.

Figure 4.30 Specifying the Department

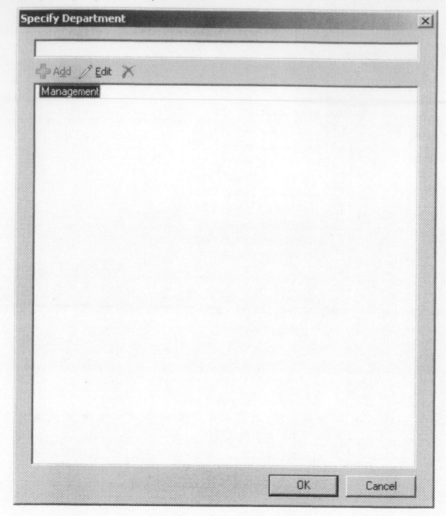

5. Now click the **Preview** button to verify that the respective recipients are listed as in Figure 4.31, and then click **OK** again.

NOTE

You can also create an address list based on a custom recipient filter (also called an *OPath filter*), but doing so is only possible using the EMS. Once you've created an address list using a custom recipient filter, you can also only manage it via the

EMS. To create an address list using a custom recipient filter, you need to use the following command: New-AddressList –Name <String> -RecipientFilter <String>.

For examples as well as a further explanation, see the Exchange 2007 Help File or type **Get-Help New-AddressList** in the EMS.

Figure 4.31 Address List Preview

6. We now have the option of specifying when the address list should be applied and the maximum length of time it is permitted to run. In this example, we will apply it immediately, but you could also schedule it to be applied sometime in the future. Click **Next** when you have decided when to apply the address list (see Figure 4.32).

Figure 4.32 Specifying When the Address List Should Be Applied

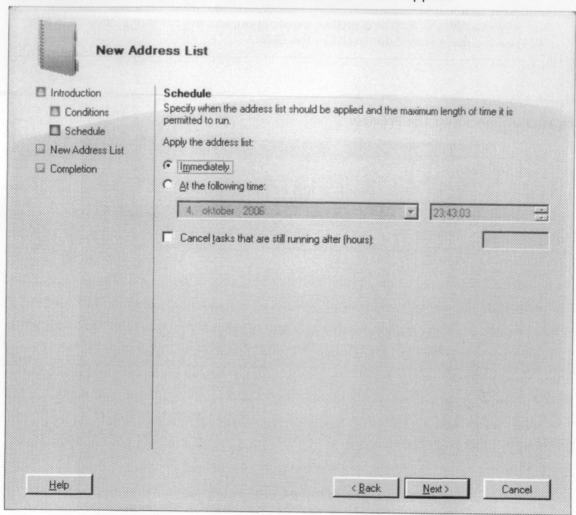

7. You now will see a **Configuration Summary**. Here you can see the type of recipients that will be included in the address list, and you can also see the recipient filter. If everything looks good, click **New** to create and apply the list see (Figure 4.33).

Figure 4.33 The New Address List Summary Page

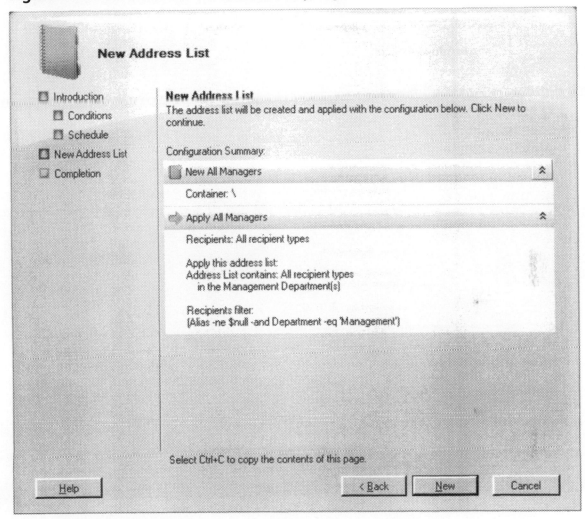

8. After a few seconds, the **New Address List Wizard** will have completed successfully, and you can then click **Finish** (see Figure 4.34).

Figure 4.34 The New Address List Completion Page

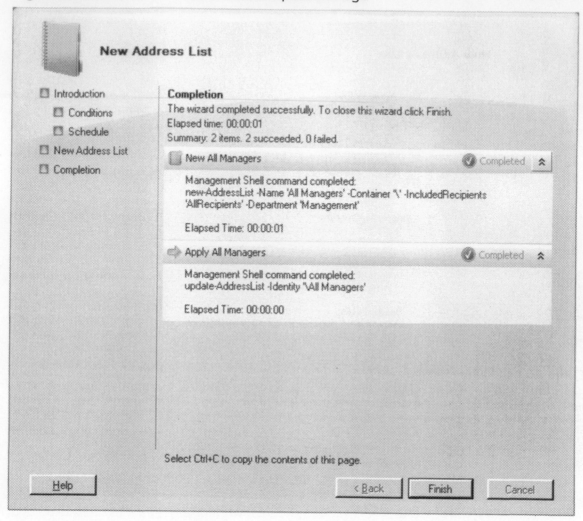

The address list has now been created as well as applied (unless you chose to schedule it), and you should be able to see it immediately in any mail client that is connected to the Exchange 2007 server. In Figure 4.35, we can see the list address list we just created via the OWA 2007 client.

Figure 4.35 Viewing the Address List Using OWA 2007

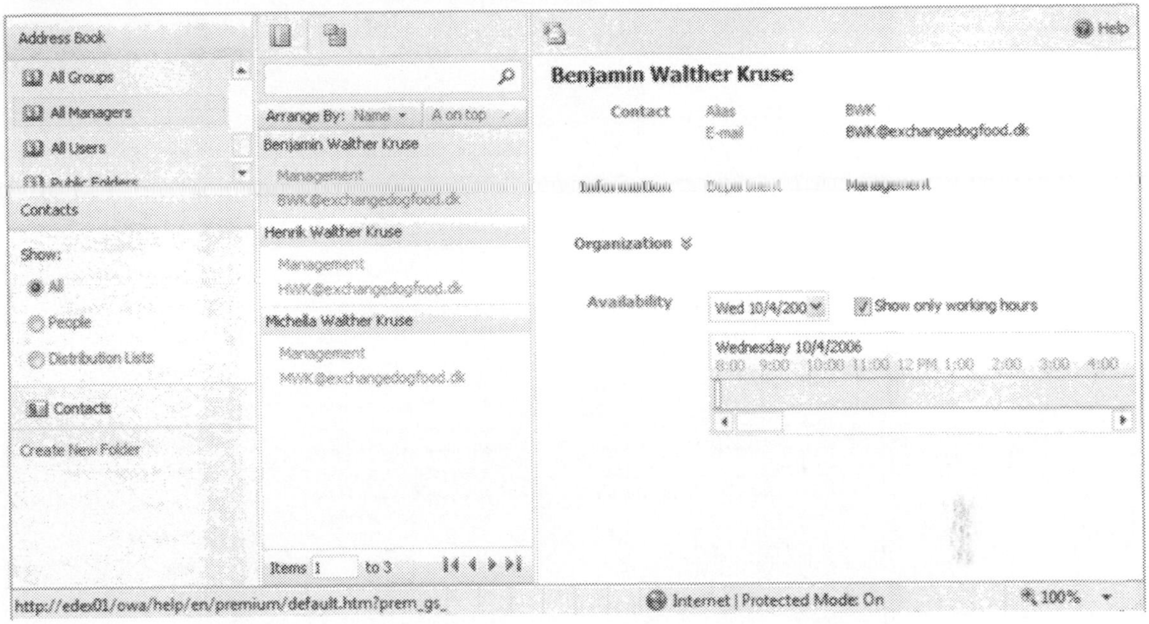

Any address list you create can also be edited later. You do this by selecting the respective **address list**, then clicking **Edit** in the **Action pane**. Alternatively, you can right-click the **address list** and select **Edit** in the context menu. You can also reapply or remove an address list using this method.

To create an address list using the EMS, you need to use the *New-AddressList* CMDlet. For a description of this CMDlet as well the available parameters, type **Get-Help New-AddressList** in the EMS.

Managed Default Folders

Under the Managed Default Folders tab (see Figure 4.36), we can manage the default mailbox folders (such as Inbox, Calendar, and Sent Items) by applying managed content settings to a specific folder or, if needed, the entire mailbox. For example, we would be able to apply a managed content setting to a default folder such as the Inbox so that particular types of items in this folder (and any subfolders) are either deleted or moved to another folder after, say, 15 days. If the items are deleted, we can even enable journaling (also called *archiving*) for the items, if required.

Figure 4.36 The Managed Default Folders Tab

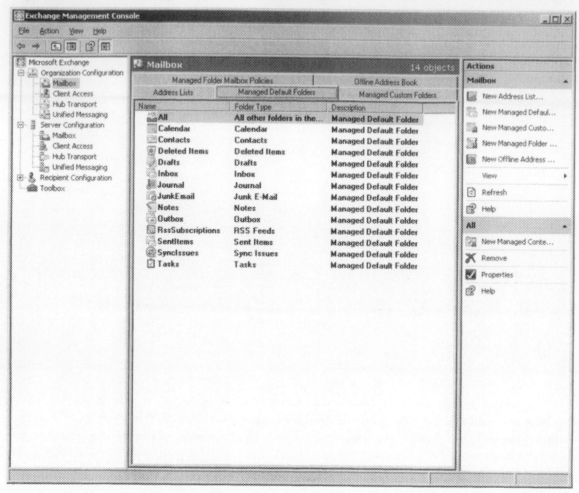

Since this is a new feature in Exchange that can be a bit difficult to understand, let's look at an example:

1. To apply managed content settings to a specific default folder, select the appropriate **default folder**, then click **New Managed Content Settings** in the **Action pane**. Alternatively, you can right-click **default folder**, then click **New Managed Content Settings** in the context menu.

2. In the **New Managed Content Settings Wizard**, type a name for the managed content settings (see Figure 4.37). This is merely the name that will be displayed in the EMC.

Figure 4.37 The New Managed Content Settings Introduction Page

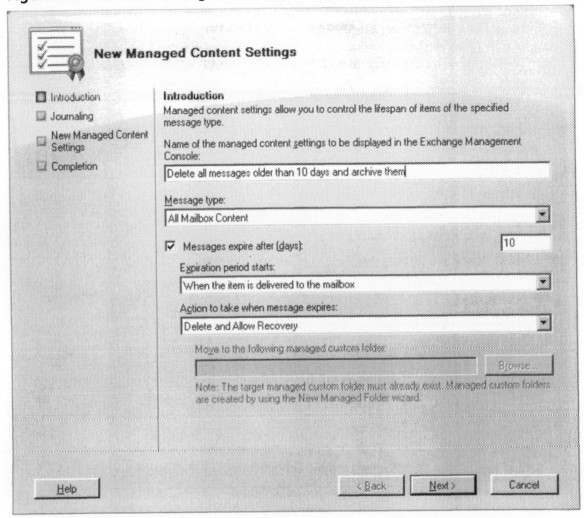

3. Select the type of messages these settings should apply to, then tick **Messages expire after (days)** and specify the number of days after which the messages will expire.

4. Now you need to select when the expiration period starts. Here you can choose between **When the item is delivered to the mailbox** and **When the item is moved to the folder**.

5. Finally, you need to decide what action should be taken when the message or item expires. Here you can choose among **Delete and Allow Recovery**, **Mark as Past Retention Limit**, **Move to a Managed Custom Folder**, **Move to the Deleted Items Folder**, and **Permanently Delete**. If you choose the action **Move to a Managed Custom Folder**, you also need to specify the managed custom folder by clicking the **Browse** button. (Note that the managed custom folder must already exist!)

6. Now click **Next**.

7. We now have the option of enabling journaling by putting a check mark in **Forward copies to:** and selecting a mailbox that should be used for journaling. In addition, we can assign a label to the copy of the respective message or item as well as select the appropriate message format (**Exchange MAPI Message FORMAT – TNEF** or **Outlook Message Format *.MSG**).

8. When you're done, click **Next** (see Figure 4.38).

Figure 4.38 Configuring Journaling Settings

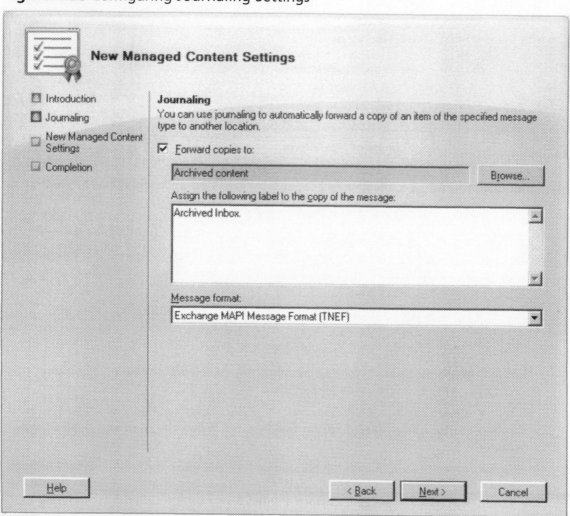

9. We're now taken to the Configuration Summary page, where you can verify that everything has been configured as required. If this is the case, you can click **New** (see Figure 4.39) so that the Managed Content Settings are created.

Figure 4.39 The New Managed Content Settings Summary Page

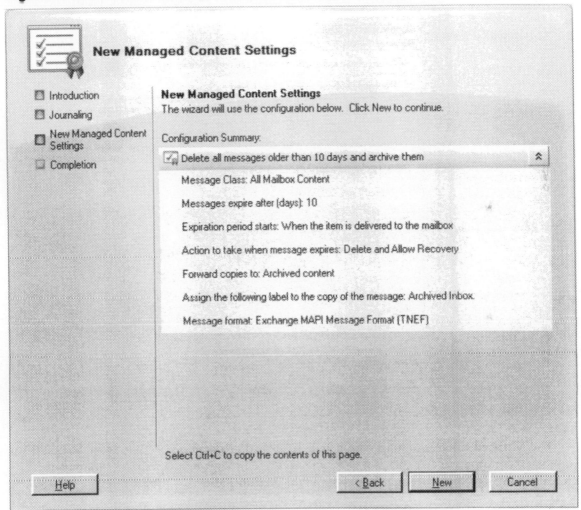

10. If the wizard completes successfully, we'll get a screen like the one shown in Figure 4.40, and we can click **Finish** to exit the wizard.

Figure 4.40 The New Managed Content Settings Completion Page

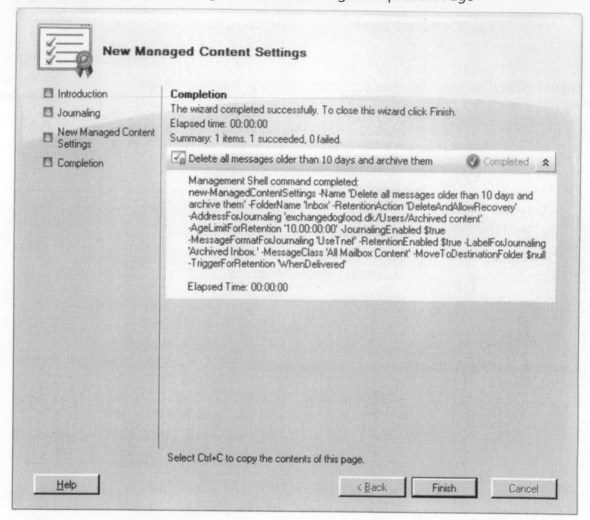

The Managed Content Settings have now been applied to a managed default folder. Should you for some reason want to change it later, you can do so by clicking the respective **Managed Content Settings**, then selecting **Properties** in the **Action pane**.

SOME INDEPENDENT ADVICE

By taking Properties of a managed default folder, you can type a comment that should be displayed when the respective folder is viewed in Outlook.

Although it's not required, in addition to the default managed folders that are created automatically when Exchange Server 2007 is installed, you can create additional default managed folders. Typically you would want to create managed custom folders (which we cover next), but in some situations it would make sense to create an additional instance of one or more default managed folders. Let's say, for example, that some users should have items in their inboxes deleted after 30 days, but others require items to be left in their mailboxes for one year. In this case you would need to created two managed content settings, with different names for the inbox, and then apply them to the users, depending on their message retention needs, using managed folder mailbox policies (which we will cover later in this chapter).

If you want to apply managed content settings to default folders using the EMS, you will need to use the *New-ManagedContentSettings* CMDlet with the respective parameters. For details on how to do this, open the EMS and type **Get-Help New-ManagedContentSettings**.

Managed Custom Folders

Under the Managed Customer Folders tab, we can create custom folders that are used for messaging records management. Custom folders differ from default folders in that they do not show up in a mailbox by default.

As you can see in Figure 4.41, no custom folders exist after an installation of Exchange Server 2007. Instead, you must add them manually as required.

Figure 4.41 The Managed Custom Folders Tab

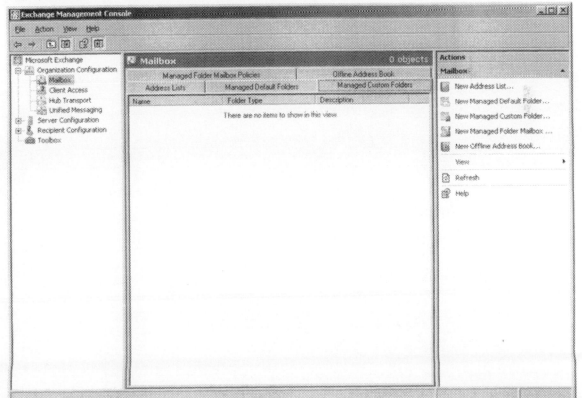

Let's try to create a custom folder. To do so, perform the following steps:

1. If you haven't already done so, click the **Managed Custom Folders** tab.

2. Click **New Managed Custom Folder** in the **Action pane**.

3. In the **New Managed Custom Folder Wizard**, type a name for the new custom folder.

4. Type the name you want the folder to have when viewed in an Outlook client.

5. Specify the storage limit in KB for the custom folder and any subfolders.

6. If you want to display a comment when the custom folder is viewed in Outlook, you can type one as well.

7. Now click **New** (see Figure 4.42).

Figure 4.42 The New Managed Custom Folder Wizard

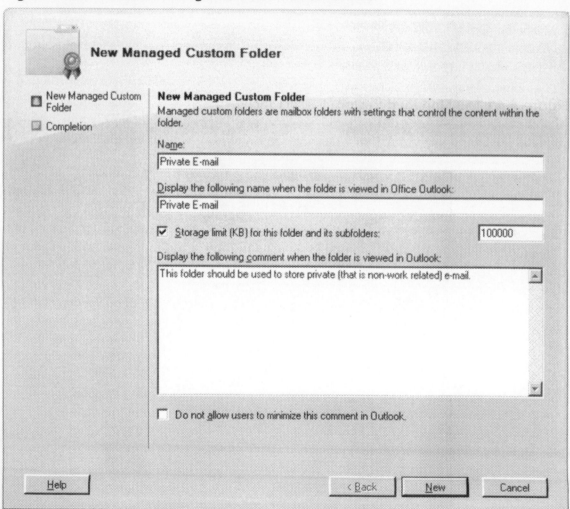

8. On the **Completion** page, click **Finish** (see Figure 4.43).

Figure 4.43 The New Managed Custom Folder Wizard Completion Page

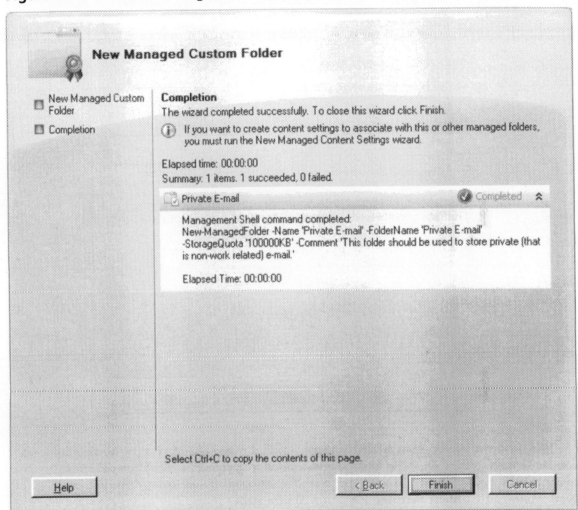

When the managed custom folder has been created, you can always modify it by selecting it in the **Work pane**, then clicking **Properties** in the **Action pane**. This way you can change one or more of the specified settings (see Figure 4.44), if you should require to do so.

Figure 4.44 The Properties Page of a Managed Custom Folder

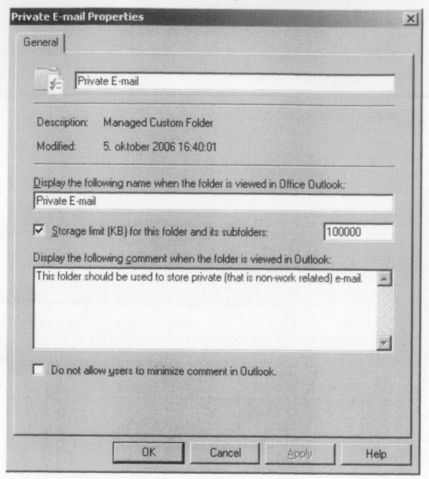

When the managed custom folder has been created, it would also make sense to apply managed content settings to the folder. This procedure is identical to applying managed content settings to a managed default folder: You select the respective managed custom folder, then click the **New Managed Content Settings** link in the **Action pane**.

Managed Folder Mailbox Policies

When we have created a set of Managed Default Folders and Managed Custom Folders, they would need to be linked with one or more Managed Folder Mailbox Policies, so that they the managed folders can be applied to the recipients within the organization. In the following we will go through how you create a Managed Folder Mailbox Policy.

1. Click the **Managed Folder Mailbox Policies** tab.

2. Click **New Managed Folder Mailbox Policy** in the **Action pane**.

3. In the **New Managed Folder Mailbox Policy Wizard** (see Figure 4.45), type a name for the new managed folder mailbox policy.

4. Click **Add** to specify the managed folders that you want to link to this policy.

Figure 4.45 The New Managed Folder Mailbox Policy Wizard

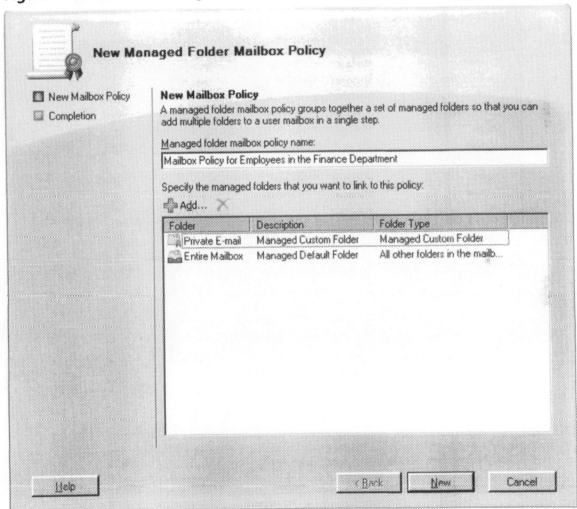

5. Now select the managed folders you want to link to the new managed folder mailbox policy, then click **OK** (Figure 4.46).

Figure 4.46 Selecting the Managed Folder That Should Be Linked With the Policy

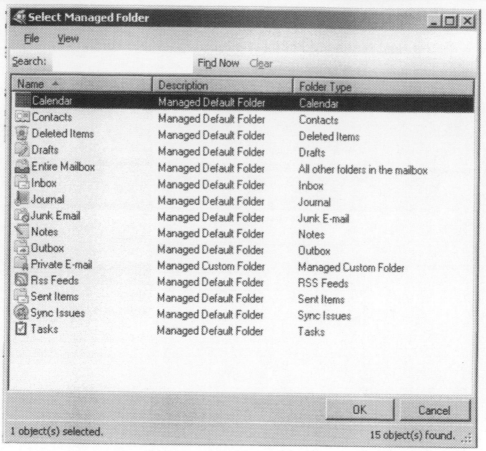

6. Click **New**, then click **Finish** (see Figure 4.47).

Figure 4.47 The New Managed Folder Mailbox Policy Wizard Completion Page

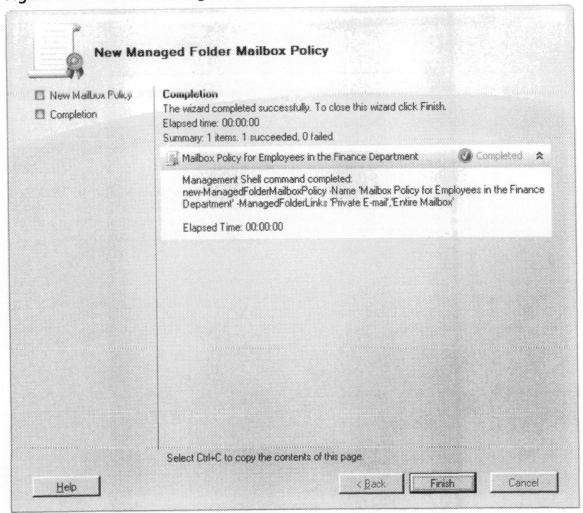

When you have created a managed folder mailbox policy, you can always add and remove managed folders from it by select the respective policy under the **Managed Folder Mailbox Policy** tab, then clicking **Properties** in the **Action pane**. This will bring you to the screen shown in Figure 4.48.

NOTE

If you want to create a new managed folder mailbox policy using the EMC, you can do so with the *New-ManagedFolderMailboxPolicy* CMDlet. For details about the necessary parameters, type **Get-Help New-ManagedFolderMailboxPolicy**.

Figure 4.48 The Properties Page for the Mailbox Policy

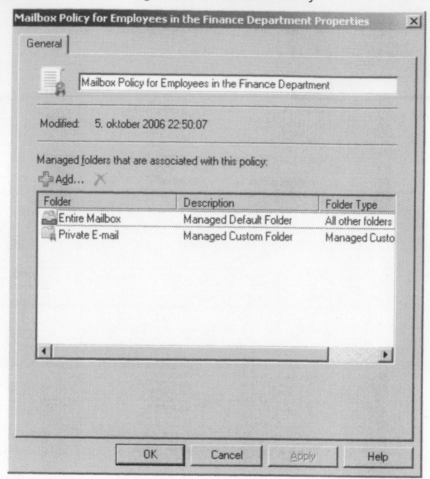

Now we have created a couple of managed folders and linked them to a policy, but we're not quite finished yet. For a managed folder to show up in a recipient mailbox, we need to do two more things. First, we need to apply the policy to a recipient mailbox. To do so, perform the following steps:

1. In the Exchange Management Console, click the **Mailbox** subnode under the **Recipient Configuration** work center node.

2. Take **Properties** for the mailbox for which you want to apply the policy.

3. Now click the **Mailbox Settings** tab (Figure 4.49).

Figure 4.49 The Mailbox Settings Tab

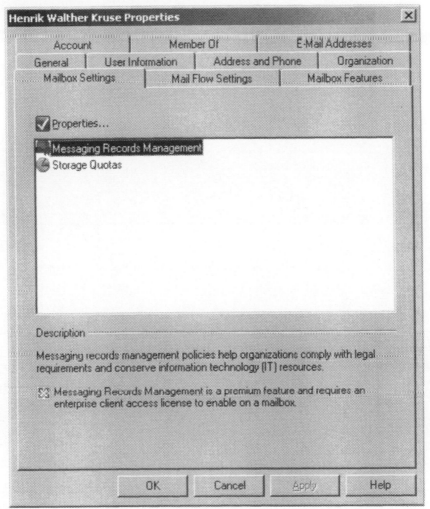

4. Select **Messaging Records Management,** then click the **Properties** button.

5. Tick **Managed folder mailbox policy,** then click **Browse** (see Figure 4.50).

Figure 4.50 Messaging Records Management

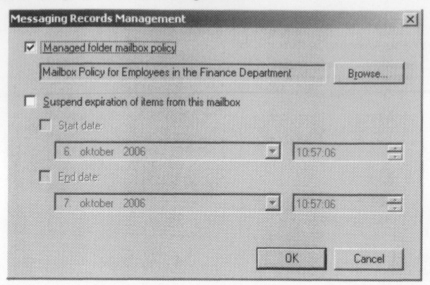

As shown in Figure 4.50, it's possible to suspend expiration of items from a mailbox for a specified period. This could be a good idea.

6. Select the respective **managed folder mailbox policy**, then click **OK** three times (see Figure 4.51).

The final thing we need to do is to schedule the messaging records management enforcement process to run at a specified time.

Figure 4.51 Selecting the Managed Folder Mailbox Policy

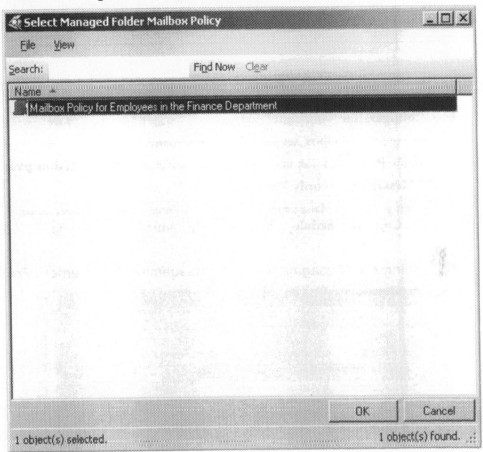

SOME INDEPENDENT ADVICE

The messaging records management enforcement process is disabled by default. This means that although you have applied a managed folder mailbox policy to one or more recipients, the respective managed folders will not show up in the user's client (Outlook 2007 or OWA 2007) until the process has run at least one time.

Depending your organization's legal needs with regard to messaging records resource management, this could be every 24th hour, or if your legal needs are more relaxed, perhaps once a week.

The messaging records management enforcement process is actually a managed folder assistant, or more precisely, an Exchange mailbox assistant, that's responsible for creating the managed folders in your user mailboxes as well as applying the configured managed content settings to them throughout your organization. One managed folder assistant exists for each mailbox server deployed in your organization. When the managed folder assistant begins, it will process all mailboxes on the given mailbox server. If it doesn't finish processing all the mailboxes in the scheduled time, it will start where it left off the next time it's scheduled to run.

To enable the managed folder assistant, you need to perform the following steps:

1. In the Exchange Management Console, click the **Mailbox** subnode under the **Server Configuration** work center node.

2. Select the respective **Mailbox server** in the **Result pane**.

3. Now click the **Properties** link under the mailbox server name in the **Action pane**.

4. Click the **Messaging Records Management** tab.

5. The Messaging Records Management Enforcement Process is set to **Never Run**. Change that to **Use Custom Schedule**, then click the **Customize** button (see Figure 4.52).

Figure 4.52 Starting the Messaging Records Management Enforcement Process

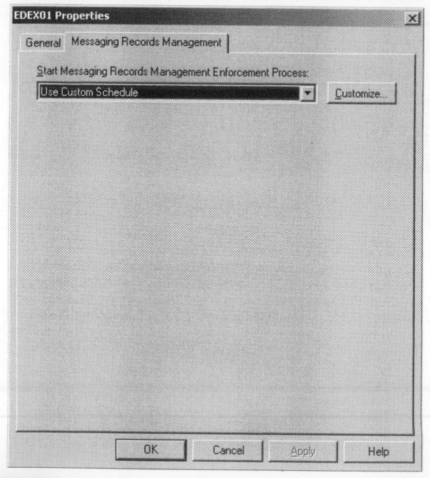

6. In the schedule, specify the times and days when the managed folder assistant should run. In Figure 4.53, we set it to run for one hour at midnight every day.

Figure 4.53 Specifying the Schedule

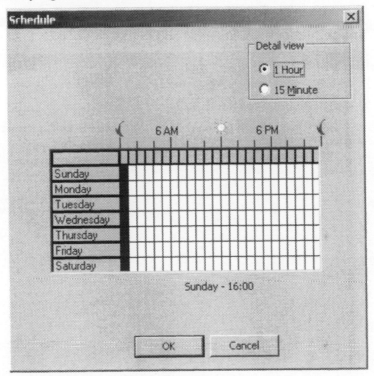

7. Click **OK** twice to return to the EMC.

To configure the schedule using the EMS, you need to run the *Set-MailboxServer* CMDlet with the *ManagedFolderAssistantSchedule* parameter. For detailed syntax and parameter information, type **Get-Help Set-MailboxServer** in the EMS.

Bear in mind that even though the managed mailbox assistant has been scheduled to run for one hour, it doesn't mean it will do so. If the assistant has processed all mailboxes in under one hour, it will stop.

Now that you have scheduled the mailbox folder assistant, the managed folders you have linked to a policy that has been applied to a set of mailboxes will appear after the managed folder assistant has run. But what if you want to force a newly created managed folder to appear in the mailboxes, before the schedule runs? Don't worry; you can use the *Start-ManagedFolderAssistant* CMDlet in the EMS to process all mailboxes immediately. But think twice before doing so, because the managed folder assistant can be a resource-intensive process for the mailbox server and the network in general.

When the managed folder assistant has run, the managed folders will appear in the mail client (Outlook 2007 and Outlook 2007), as shown in Figure 4.54.

Figure 4.54 Managed Folders in Outlook 2007

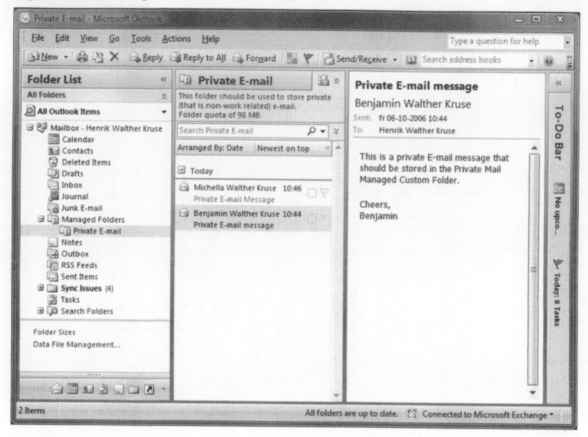

Here we see the Private e-mail folder we created earlier in this chapter. Notice the comment we specified as well as the configured quota for this managed folder.

Offline Address Books

We have reached the last tab under the Mailbox subnode, which is the Offline Address Book tab (see Figure 4.55). As you might have guessed, this is where we can view a list of the offline address books in the Exchange organization.

The OAB functionality has change radically in Exchange Server 2007, so before we dive into the configuration settings for OABs, a little introduction to the new behavior of this type of address book is in order. Exchange Server 2007 introduces a completely new distribution mechanism for OABs,

Figure 4.55 The Offline Address Book Tab

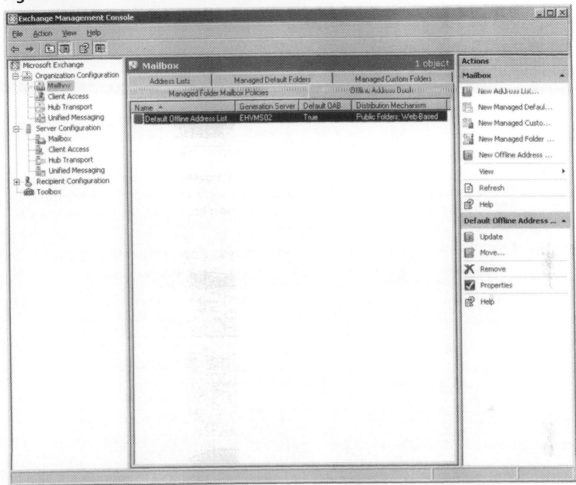

a mechanism that isn't based on Public Folders, as was the case with Exchange Server 2000 and 2003. OABs in Exchange Server 2007 use HTTP(S) and the Background Intelligent Transfer Service (BITS), which provides us with several benefits, such as support for more concurrent clients, even more reduced bandwidth usage, and finally, much better control over the distribution points. (We'll bet that any of you have had your issues with OABs!) To use the new distribution mechanism, it's required that the clients run Outlook 2007, but there's still support for legacy clients (Outlook 2003 and earlier), since you can choose to have both a Public Folder and a Web-based distribution point. (In Exchange Server 2007, OABs are located on the Client Access Server in the site.) The OAB mechanism depends on the following components:

- **OABGen Service**   This is the service that is running on the OAB Generation server (Exchange 2007 Server with the Mailbox server role installed) in order for the OABs to be created.

- **Exchange File Distribution Service** This runs on a CAS server and is the service responsible for getting the OAB content from the Exchange 2007 Mailbox server (OABGen server).

- **OAB Virtual Directory** This is an IIS virtual directory on the Client Access Server (CAS). This is where the clients download the OABs from.

- **Autodiscover Service** This service also runs on a CAS server and is the one that makes sure the correct OAB URL is returned to Outlook clients.

When you install an Exchange Server 2007, one OAB is created by default. Let's take a look at the settings configured for the default OAB. To do so, perform the following steps:

1. Select the OAB in the **Work pane**, then click the **Properties** link in the **Action pane**. Alternatively, right-click the **OAB** to bring up its context menu, and select **Properties**. As you can see in Figure 4.56, this OAB has been scheduled for updates at 5:00 A.M. each day.

Figure 4.56 The General Tab on the Offline Address Book Properties Page

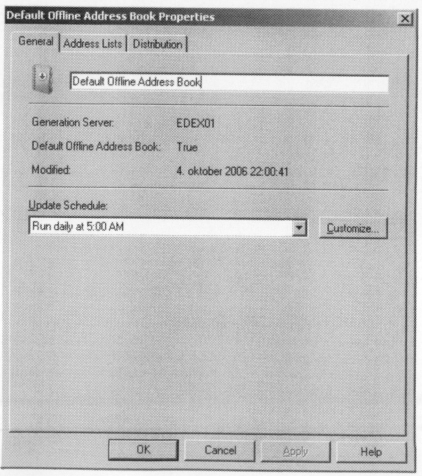

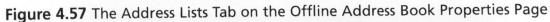

2. Click the **Address Lists** tab. As we can see in Figure 4.57, the default OAB includes the default GAL, which is all mail-enabled objects.

Figure 4.57 The Address Lists Tab on the Offline Address Book Properties Page

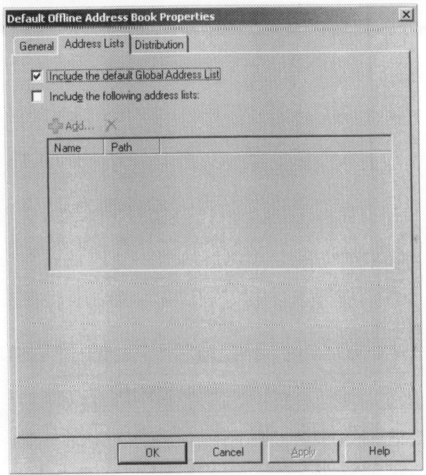

3. Now click the **Distribution** tab. As you can see in Figure 4.58, this is the place where you specify the type of Outlook clients OAB should support. By default, only Outlook 2003 SP2 and later are supported. This is also the place where you enable the type of distribution point you want to provide to the clients. When you're installing Exchange Server 2007 into an Active Directory forest that doesn't contain an Exchange 2000 or 2003 organization and you select **No** when the Exchange Server 2007 Installation Wizard asks whether you've got any Outlook 2003 or earlier clients in your organization, only the Web-based distribution point will be enabled. If you answer **Yes** to this question, the Installation Wizard will create and mount a Public Folder database on the Exchange 2007 server as well as enable the Public Folder distribution mechanism.

Figure 4.58 The Distribution Tab on the Offline Address Book Properties Page

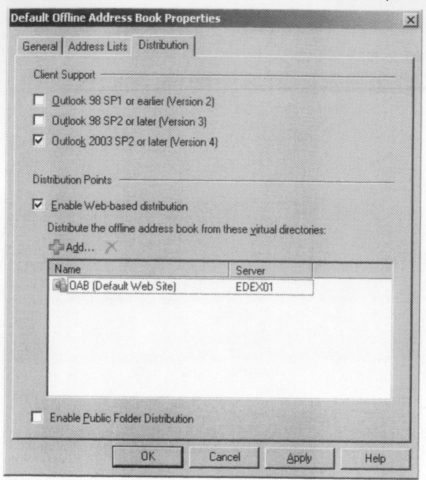

4. Click **OK** to exit the Properties for the Default OAB.

Creating a New Offline Address Book

Now that you have seen the default settings configured for the default OAB, let's try to create a new OAB. We do this the following way:

> **NOTE**
>
> The default OAB should be sufficient for most organizations, but using multiple OABs is common practice in environments where there's a need to isolate users from each other based on country, organization, or the like. Multiple OABs are especially commonly used by Exchange hosting providers that host multiple customers (domains) in their Exchange environments.

1. Click **New Offline Address Book** in the **Action pane**.

2. In the **New Offline Address Book Wizard** that appears, type a name for the OAB (see Figure 4.59).

Figure 4.59 Creating a New Offline Address Book

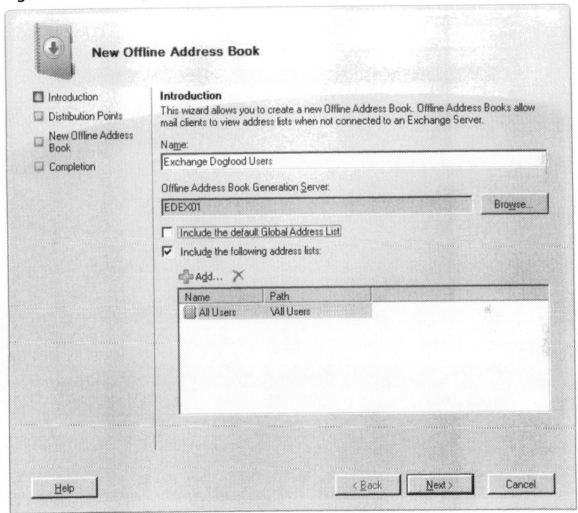

3. Click the **Browse** button to specify the mailbox server that should be the OAB generation server for this OAB, select the respective **server**, and click **OK** (see Figure 4.60).

Figure 4.60 Selecting the Mailbox Server

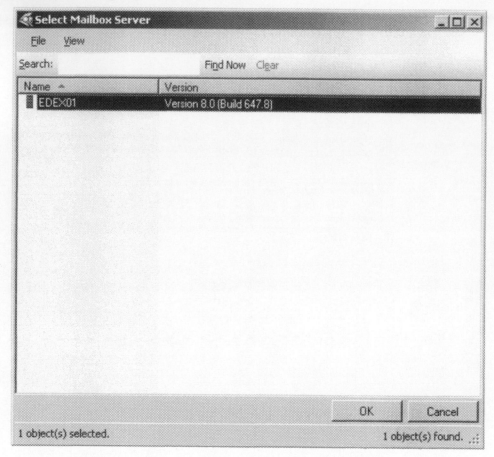

4. Now click the **Add** button, select the server address lists that should be included in the OAB, and click **Next**.

5. Choose whether you want to enable Web-based distribution or Public Folder distribution or both. If you enable Web-based distribution, you also need to select the OAB virtual directory in which this OAB should be stored (see Figure 4.61).

Figure 4.61 Specifying the Type of Distribution Point to Use

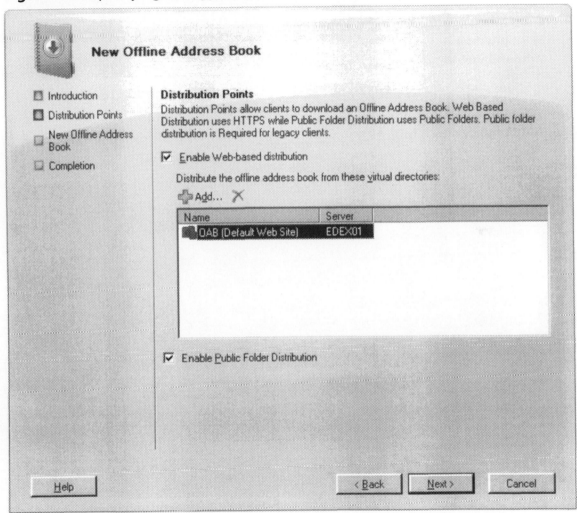

6. Click **Next**, then click **New** on the Configuration Summary page (see Figure 4.62).

Figure 4.62 The New Offline Address Book Wizard Summary Page

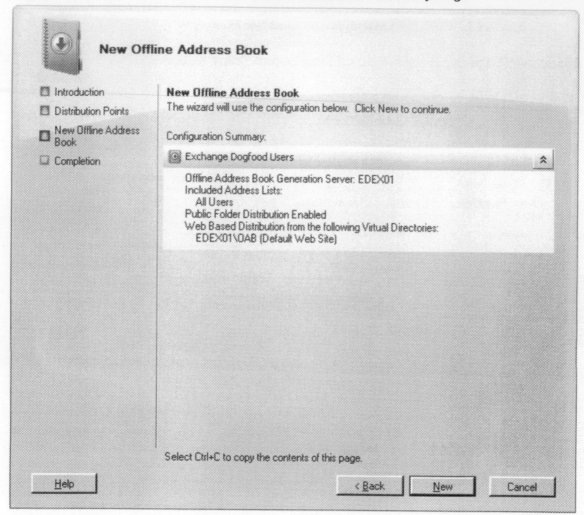

7. On the completion page click **Finish**.

When you have multiple OABs on a mailbox server, you can select the one that should be the default (via the Action pane or associated context menu).

Since OABs relating to Outlook 2007 are downloaded using a Web-based distribution method, you also have the option of specifying the internal URL (which refers to the URL from which Outlook clients inside the corporate network can access the virtual directory) as well as the external URL (which refers to the URL from which Outlook clients outside the corporate network can access the directory) to the OAB Web site. This is not configured under the Mailbox node but by taking the Properties page of OAB (the default Web site), which can be found under the Server Configuration work center, where you select the Client Access Server node (see Figure 4.63).

Figure 4.63 The URLs Tab of the Properties Page for OAB (Default Web Site)

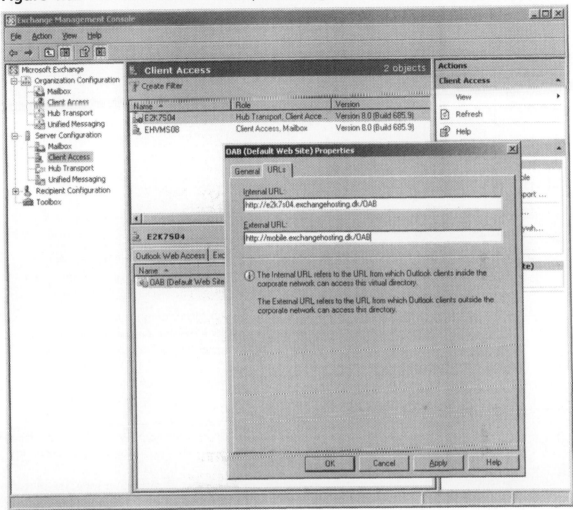

TIP

When it comes to detailed information about OABs, one of the best resources on the Internet is a blog run by Dave Goldman. Dave works as an Exchange Escalation Engineer (EE) for Microsoft in North Carolina and is, among other things, the guy behind the OABInteg tool, which is used to troubleshoot OAB issues. You can visit Dave's blog at http://blogs.msdn.com/dgoldman.

If you want to create a new OAB using the EMS, you can do so with the *New-OfflineAddressBook* CMDlet. For details about the necessary parameters, type **Get-Help New-OfflineAddressBook**.

Summary

In this chapter, we had a look at the feature set that can be configured on an Exchange 2007 server with the Mailbox Server role installed. As you have seen throughout the chapter, many tasks can be performed on this server role. We didn't cover every single task, but we primarily concentrated on how you deal with storage groups, mail and Public Folder databases, and administering Public Folders in Exchange 2007. In addition, we had a quick look at each of the organizationwide settings available on this server, but most of them were relatively superficial.

Solutions Fast Track

Managing the Exchange 2007 Mailbox Server

☑ The Exchange Store hasn't changed much since Exchange Server 2003 but has been further improved and of course contains multiple new features.

☑ Back in Exchange 2000 and 2003, the databases containing either mailboxes or Public Folders were known as *mailbox stores* and *Public Folder stores*, respectively, but with Exchange Server 2007 they are now referred to as *mailbox databases* and *Public Folder databases*.

☑ 64-bit hardware gives us the opportunity to use much more memory than was the case in previous Exchange versions. Because Exchange Server 2007 can take advantage of more memory, it means that a larger chunk of each user's mailbox can be stored in memory, which reduces disk I/O.

Exchange 2007 Storage Groups

☑ The Mailbox server in the Exchange 2007 Enterprise Edition supports up to 50 storage groups and a maximum of 50 databases per server. Exchange 2007 allows you to create up to five databases in each storage group, as was the case with Exchange 2003, but best practice is to create one database per storage group. The Standard Edition supports up to five databases in a single storage group.

☑ As is the case with Exchange 2003, it's still okay to keep all storage groups on the same spindles, but in terms of performance, it's better to keep them separated, although this would be quite unrealistic for most organizations that were using, for example, 30 storage groups!

☑ Exchange Server 2007 finally has native support for continuous replication, which is a functionality that will make it possible to keep a second copy of a database held in a particular storage group. The second copy of a database will be updated using log file shipping and log file replay. The idea of keeping a second copy of a database is, of course, to get up and running in a couple of minutes by being able to switch to the second database using a few mouse clicks (or CMDlets), should the original database crash or become corrupted.

Exchange 2007 Mailbox Databases

☑ As is the case with previous versions of Exchange, databases in Exchange Server 2007 are still based on the Extensible Storage Engine (ESE). The purpose of ESE is to provide an interface to the underlying database structure, which is responsible for managing changes made to the database (more specifically the .EDB file).

☑ With Exchange Server 2007, there's no longer a database limit for the Standard Edition.

☑ In Exchange Server 2000 and 2003, a database was made up of two files: an .EDB file and an .STM file. The purpose of the streaming file (.STM) is, as many of you might be aware, to house raw Internet content message streams as defined in Request for Comment (RFC) 822. The .STM has been removed from Exchange Server 2007.

☑ The default limit for mailboxes in Exchange Server 2007 is 2GB.

☑ As was the case with previous versions of Exchange, Exchange Server 2007 maintains single-instance storage of messages.

Exchange 2007 Public Folder Databases

☑ The default limit for Public Folders in Exchange Server 2007 is 2GB.

☑ Public Folders are still supported in Exchange Server 2007, but they have been deemphasized. This means that there's a chance Public Folders won't be included in the next version of Exchange (currently code-named E14), but Microsoft will support Public Folders until the end of 2016.

☑ The Public Folders tasks you can perform through the EMC are extremely limited, which means that you need to do most of these tasks via either the EMS or the System Manager on an Exchange 2003 server that still is part of the Exchange organization.

Managing Organizationwide Mailbox Server Configuration Settings

☑ The purpose of address lists is to help you organize the different types of recipients within your Exchange organization so that they are listed in a meaningful way when your end users look up recipients in their mail clients.

☑ Using the Managed Default Folders feature, we can manage the default mailbox folders (such as Inbox, Calendar, and Sent Items) by applying managed content settings to a specific folder or, if needed, the entire mailbox. For example, we would be able to apply managed content settings to a default folder such as the Inbox so that particular types of items in this folder (and any subfolders) are either deleted or moved to another folder after, say, 15 days.

☑ Messaging records management is a premium feature that requires an Exchange 2007 Enterprise CAL to enable on a mailbox.

☑ Exchange Server 2007 introduces a completely new distribution mechanism for OABs, a mechanism that isn't based on Public Folders, as was the case with Exchange Server 2000 and 2003. OABs in Exchange Server 2007 use HTTP(S) and the Background Intelligent Transfer Service (BITS), which provides us with several benefits, such as support for more concurrent clients, even more reduced bandwidth usage, and finally, much better control over the distribution points.

Frequently Asked Questions

Q: Wasn't Exchange Server 2007 supposed to use SQL instead of ESE as the database repository?

A: During the early development phases of Exchange Server 2007, this was the plan, but it was changed rather quickly. We'll not see SQL as the database repository until E15 (the Exchange version after E14!).

Q: You mentioned that 2GB is the default limit for mailboxes in Exchange Server 2007. Won't that put quite an I/O load on the disk spindles holding the mailbox databases?

A: No, actually, this isn't the case, since Exchange Server 2007 is 64-bit, which means that much more address space can be allocated in memory and will result in reduced I/O load on the disk spindles holding the mailbox databases.

Q: I really miss being able to manage Public Folders using the Exchange 2007 Management Console (EMC). Is there a chance that Public Folder management will be implemented in the EMC GUI sometime in the future?

A: Yes, if the Exchange Product Group receives sufficient customer feedback on this issue, this will be implemented in a post-RTM version. If we're lucky, it's already in Exchange 2007 Service Pack 1.

Q: After reading this chapter, I can see that Public Folders still are supported in Exchange Server 2007, but what will happen to Public Folders in future versions of the Exchange product?

A: Although Public Folders are supported in Exchange Server 2007, bear in mind that they have been deemphasized and will be dropped in a future version of Exchange (most likely E15, which is the version after E14), but since Microsoft has committed to support Public Folders until the end of 2016, there should be plenty of time for migrating your Public Folder data to a SharePoint-based or similar solution.

Q: Is it possible to get logon statistics for the users connecting to the mailbox and Public Folder databases on my Exchange 2007 Mailbox Servers?

A: Yes, you can use the *Get-LogonStatistics* CMDlet for this purpose. Running this CMDlet in the EMS will give you information about things such as the number of open attachments, folders, and messages as well as number of messaging operations, progress operations, table operations, transfer operations, total operations, and successful RPC calls. Finally, you can retrieve information such as latency, client version, client IP address, and access and logon times. To get the full list of information, type **Get-LogonStatistics | FL**.

Chapter 5

Managing the Client Access Server

Solutions in this chapter:

- Managing the Exchange 2007 Client Access Server
- The AutoDiscover Service
- The Availability Service
- Client Access Servers and the SSL Certificate Dilemma
- Managing Outlook Anywhere
- Managing Outlook Web Access 2007
- Managing Exchange ActiveSync
- Managing POP3/IMAP4

☑ Summary

☑ Solutions Fast Track

☑ Frequently Asked Questions

Introduction

The Client Access Server (CAS) replaces the front-end server we all know from Exchange 2000 and 2003 and adds some additional functionality. The CAS provides mailbox access for all types of Exchange clients except Outlook MAPI clients, which, as most of you are aware, connect directly to the Mailbox Server on which the respective mailbox is stored. This means the CAS manages access for any user who opens their mailbox using Outlook Anywhere (formerly known as RPC over HTTP), Outlook Web Access (OWA), Exchange ActiveSync (EAS), POP3, and last but not least, IMAP4.

In addition to providing client access, the CAS is responsible for supplying access to things such as automatic profile configuration, free/busy information, Out of Office (OOF) messages, the Offline Address Book (OAB), as well as Unified Messaging (UM), but only for Outlook 2007 and Outlook Web Access 2007. Only these two client versions can take advantage of the new Web-based Exchange services known as the AutoDiscover and Availability services. Legacy clients such as Outlook 2003 and earlier cannot use these two new Exchange Web services.

After reading this chapter, you should have a good understanding of how you can manage the feature set on the CAS, at both the server level and organizationwide.

Managing the Exchange 2007 Client Access Server

The Client Access Server should always be deployed on a domain-member server on the internal network, and not in the DMZ, which many thought was a security best practice for front-end servers in Exchange 2000 and 2003. This is true for several reasons: one is the fact that CAS servers communicate with mailbox servers using RPC traffic, and to make this work, it required several open ports into your network via your intranet firewall. This is not a best practice since it makes it easier for an intruder to gain access to your Active Directory (especially since it is RPC-specific ports that must be opened!). In addition, a member server has too many access rights to domain-member servers on the internal network, and thus does not justify deployment in your DMZ.

Alternatively, it is highly recommended to publish the CAS using an Internet Security and Acceleration (ISA) Server (ISA Server 2006 is preferred) in your perimeter network. This makes it possible to have your users pre-authenticated on the ISA Server before actually reaching the internal network.

A typical CAS scenario following security best practices is shown in Figure 5.1.

Figure 5.1 A Typical Client Access Server Scenario

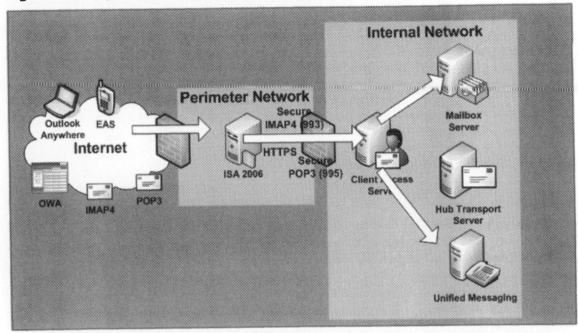

If you plan to split your Exchange 2007 Server roles onto different servers, bear in mind that the CAS is the first server role you should deploy. In addition, at least one CAS is required in each site a Mailbox Server has been deployed.

The AutoDiscover Service

Several features in Exchange Server 2007 are based on Exchange Web services. One of these services is known as the AutoDiscover service. As most of you are aware, few end-users know how to configure an Outlook profile; this is where the AutoDiscover service shines by simplifying Outlook client deployment through creation of an automatic connection between the Exchange Server and Outlook 2007 clients. No longer are special scripts, complex user intervention, or tools such as the Custom Installation Wizard from the Office Resource Kit needed. Before Outlook 2007 and Exchange Server 2007, information such as the name of the Exchange server and the user account and password were all required when configuring an Outlook profile. With the advent of the AutoDiscover service, all you need to enter is the e-mail address and password and the AutoDiscover service will do the rest, automatically discovering and configuring the client's home mailbox server information. Entering a username and password, however, is only required when you are configuring clients not logged on to the Active Directory domain. If you're configuring an Outlook 2007 profile on a machine logged on to the Active Directory domain, AutoDiscover will fetch the domain information from the account you are logged on with, meaning you only have to click Next a few times to configure your Outlook 2007 profile.

Other features provided via the AutoDiscover service are the Offline Address Books (OABs), Unified Messaging (UM) information, and Outlook Anywhere settings.

As similar services did in previous versions of Outlook and Exchange, the AutoDiscover service will automatically update an Outlook profile should a user's respective mailbox be moved to another server in the organization.

NOTE

You can read more about the new AutoDiscover Service, and how to configure Outlook 2007 using this Exchange Web service in the following article, which is located at MSExchange.org: http://www.msexchange.org/tutorials/Uncovering-New-Outlook-2007-Discover-Service.html.

It's not only Outlook 2007 that can take advantage of the new Web-based AutoDiscover services, but Windows mobile devices running the next versions of Windows Mobile (codenamed Crossbow [5.2] and Photon [6.0], and at the time of this writing, still in beta) can also be provisioned automatically using this service.

When the Client Access Server role is installed on an Exchange 2007 Server, a virtual IIS directory named AutoDiscover is created under the Default Web Site, as shown in Figure 5.2.

Figure 5.2 AutoDiscover Virtual Directory in IIS Manager

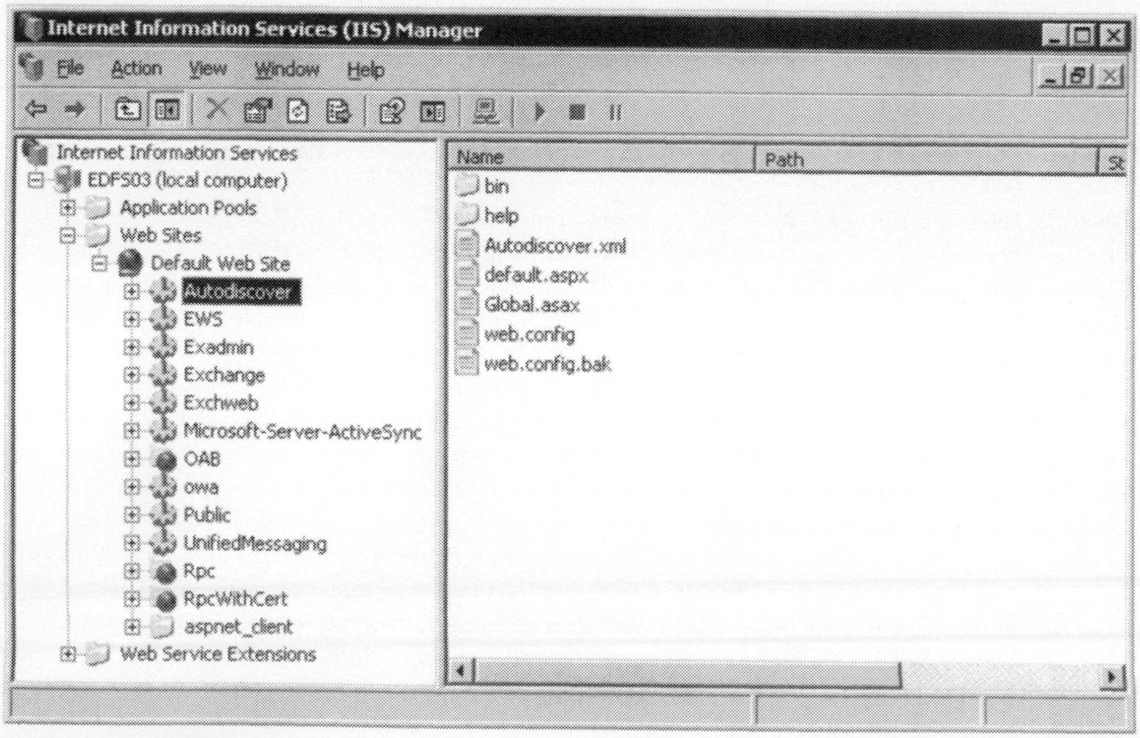

When you open an Outlook 2007 client, this is the virtual directory it connects to in order to download any necessary information.

In addition to this virtual directory, a new object named the service connection point (SCP) is also created in Active Directory. The SCP object contains the authoritative list of AutoDiscover service URLs in the forest, and can be updated using the *Set-ClientAccessServer* cmdlet.

Figure 5.3 illustrates what happens when Outlook 2007 connects to an Exchange 2007 server.

Figure 5.3 The AutoDiscover Service Process from an Internal Outlook Client

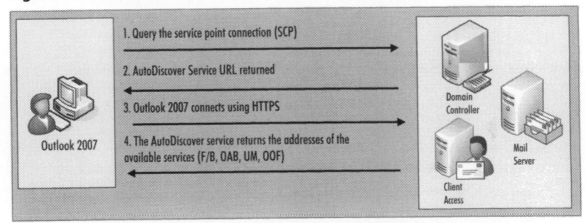

To see the URLs to each of these services in Outlook, hold down the **Ctrl** key and right-click your Outlook icon in the Systray. Choose **Test E-mail AutoConfiguration** in the context menu. In the **Test E-mail AutoConfiguration** window, enter your e-mail address and password and make sure you only have **Use AutoDiscover** ticked. Then, click **Test**. Outlook will now test each of the services provided by the AutoDiscover service and list the URLs it finds, as well as list any issues or errors for each.

The Availability Service

Just like the AutoDiscover service, the Availability service is an Exchange Web service, which is installed by default when deploying the Client Access Server role on an Exchange 2007 server. The purpose of the Availability service is to provide secure, consistent, and up-to-date (that is, data in real time!) free/busy data to clients using this service. Since only Outlook 2007 and OWA 2007 can take advantage of this new service, legacy clients, (Outlook 2003 and earlier, as well as OWA 2003), still depend on a Public Folder database, containing the SCHEDULE+ FREE/BUSY system folder. Since only Outlook 2007 and OWA 2007 can use the Availability service to obtain free/busy information, it's important that Exchange 2007 be able to interact with legacy systems, too. Table 5.1 shows how free/busy data is obtained based on which front-end client version is used compared to the version of Exchange Server the back-end source and target mailboxes resides.

Table 5.1 Free/Busy Retrieval Methods

Client	Source Mailbox	Target Mailbox	Free/Busy Retrieval
Outlook 2007	Exchange 2007	Exchange 2007	The Availability service will read the free/busy info directly from the calendar in the target mailbox.
Outlook 2007	Exchange 2007	Exchange 2003	The Availability service will make an HTTP connection to the /Public virtual directory of the Exchange 2003 mailbox.
Outlook 2003	Exchange 2007	Exchange 2007	Free/busy info will be published in source Public Folders.
Outlook 2003	Exchange 2007	Exchange 2003	Free/busy info will be published in source Public Folders.
Outlook Web Access 2007	Exchange 2007	Exchange 2007	OWA 2007 will call the Availability service API, which reads the free/busy info from the target mailbox.
Outlook Web Access 2007	Exchange 2007	Exchange 2003	OWA 2007 will call the Availability service API, and then make an HTTP connection to the /Public virtual directory of the Exchange 2003 mailbox.
Any	Exchange 2003	Exchange 2007	Free/busy info is published in source Public Folders.

Outlook 2007 discovers the Availability Service URL using the AutoDiscover service. Actually, the AutoDiscover service is to Outlook what DNS is to a Web browser, acting like a DNS Web Service for Outlook. It is used to find various services like the Availability service, and the UM and OAB services. It simply tells Outlook 2007 where to go to locate the various Web services required: UM, OAB, and Availability.

You should be aware of many aspects when configuring the Availability service. I recommend you check out the Availability Service FAQ over at the Exchange 2007 Wiki, found at www.exchangeninjas.com/AvailabilityServiceFAQ.

Client Access Servers and the SSL Certificate Dilemma

In previous versions of Exchange, you simply issued a request for an SSL certificate, and when received, assigned this certificate to the Default Web Site in the IIS Manager. That was basically it. Exchange 2007, however, is a different beast, especially when it comes to securing client connectivity to the CAS using SSL certificates.

You may have noticed that a default self-signed SSL certificate is assigned to the Default Web Site during the installation of the Exchange 2007 CAS role. If you take a closer look at this certificate, you'll notice it contains multiple *subject alternative names* (Figure 5.4).

Figure 5.4 SSL Certificate with Subject Alternative DNS Names

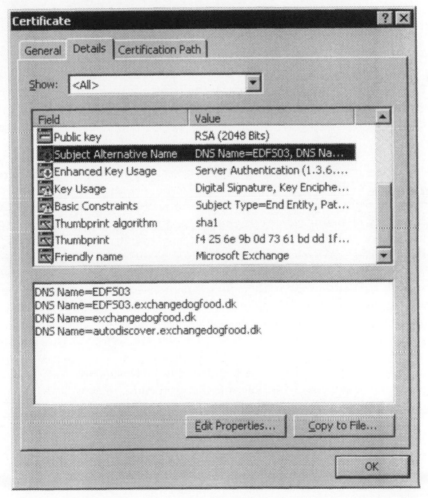

I hear some of you grumbling, "So, what is that all about?" Well, instead of having to require multiple certificates, maintain the configuration of multiple IP addresses, IIS Web sites for each IP port, and a certificate combination, you can create a single certificate that enables clients to successfully connect to each host name using SSL and subject alternative names. You see, in order to support Outlook Anywhere, OWA, Exchange ActiveSync (EAS) and especially the new Web-based AutoDiscover service, which requires a common name of *autodiscover.domain.com*, you must use an SSL certificate containing subject alternative names.

Since the default SSL certificate is self-signed and, therefore by default, untrusted by clients, and because Outlook Anywhere and Exchange ActiveSync require a trusted SSL certificate, we have to replace this certificate with an SSL certificate issued by a trusted third-party provider. Unfortunately, only a few SSL certificate providers can issue an SSL certificate containing one or more subject alternative names. To make matters worse, these providers charge something like $600 per year for such a certificate.

NOTE

At the time of this writing, only Entrust.com, GeoTrust.com, and VeriSign offered these types of SSL certificates. Hopefully this will change as more and more organizations begin to deploy Exchange 2007.

If you don't assign an SSL certificate with additional subject alternative names, where one of these matches the hostname of the Exchange 2007 CAS, internal Outlook 2007 clients will generate certificate security warnings since the SSL certificate won't match the name used to configure these clients. Notice, however, that Outlook 2007 won't generate a warning if the self-signed untrusted default SSL certificate assigned to the Default Web Site. This is by design. When the Exchange 2007 CAS role is installed, the setup wizard creates an Active Directory service discovery record, and if the Outlook 2007 client can see that record (meaning they are on the internal network), it ignores the trust warning. It uses the service discovery record as the trust (assuming someone that can write that to the Active Directory can be trusted regarding the URL for the CAS), rather than checking that it trusts the issuer of the cert. The idea behind this is that while you are on the intranet, Exchange is secure out of the box, using SSL and ignoring any prompts.

So why not just leave the self-signed SSL certificate on the Default Web Site? Well, because then Outlook Anywhere and Exchange ActiveSync wouldn't work, since these two features require the common name on the SSL certificate to match the external URL used to access the CAS, so the certificate will be trusted by the client. In addition, OWA 2007 would generate a security warning when a user connects to his mailbox using OWA 2007.

"Okay," you say, "fair enough, but what do I do if my organization can't afford to throw $600 towards an SSL certificate each year?" Well, in that case, the solution would be to use multiple Web sites. Besides the Default Web Site (which you should leave in its default state with the self-signed untrusted SSL certificate assigned), we would need two additional Web sites.

- One for Exchange ActiveSync (EAS), OWA, and Outlook Anywhere

- One for the AutoDiscover service

In order to configure this type of setup, you must do the following:

First, add two additional virtual IP addresses to the NIC on your Exchange 2007 CAS, as shown in Figure 5.5.

Figure 5.5 Additional Virtual IP Addresses

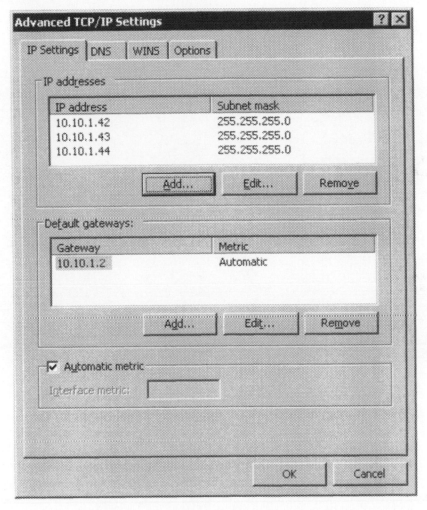

Now assign a specific IP address to the Default Web Site, as shown in Figure 5.6.

Figure 5.6 Assigning a Specific IP Address to the Default Web Site

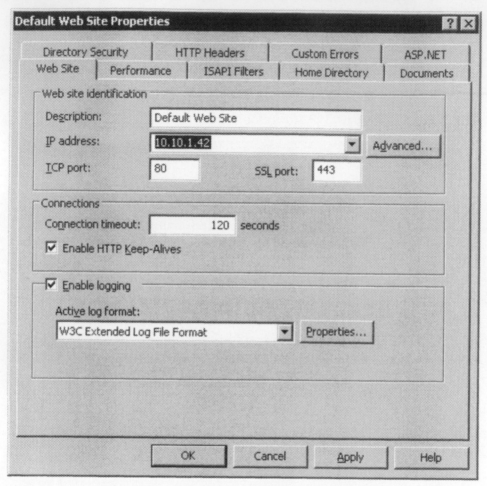

Create two new Web sites using IIS Manager, and call them something like **Clients** and **AutoDiscover**. When creating the Web sites, use the default settings and specify the same path as the one configured in the Default Web Site (C:\InetPub\wwwroot). Make sure to also select *Read and Run Scripts (such as ASP)* only.

When the Web sites have been properly created, we can create the required virtual directories using the Exchange Management Shell. To create the OWA and Exchange ActiveSync directories, enter the following commands, bearing in mind that the *—WebSiteName* value is case sensitive:

```
New-OWAVirtualDirectory -OwaVersion: Exchange2007 -Name "owa" -WebSiteName
"Clients"

New-ActiveSyncVirtualDirectory -WebSiteName "Clients"

New-AutodiscoverVirtualDirectory -WebSiteName AutoDiscover -
BasicAuthentication:$true -WindowsAuthentication:$true
```

If you still have Exchange 2000 or 2003 back-end servers in your organization and these are accessed via the CAS, you also need to create the legacy OWA virtual directories. You do so using the following commands:

```
New-OwaVirtualDirectory -OwaVersion: "Exchange2003or2000" -Name "Exchange" -WebSite
"Clients" -VirtualDirectoryType: Mailboxes

New-OwaVirtualDirectory -OwaVersion: "Exchange2003or2000" -Name "Public" -WebSite
"Clients" -VirtualDirectoryType: PublicFolders

New-OwaVirtualDirectory -OwaVersion: "Exchange2003or2000" -Name "Exadmin" -WebSite
"Clients" -VirtualDirectoryType: Exadmin

New-OwaVirtualDirectory -OwaVersion: "Exchange2003or2000" -Name "ExchWeb" -WebSite
"Clients" -VirtualDirectoryType: ExchWeb
```

The last virtual directory we must create is the /Rpc and /RpcWithCerts virtual directories used by Outlook Anywhere. These directories cannot be created using the Exchange Management Shell, thus we must create them from a file. To do so, we first save both of the directories to a file. This is done by right-clicking the directory name and choosing **All Tasks | Save Configuration to a File** in the context menu. Type a name for the file and click **OK** to save it as an XML file. Now, right-click the new Clients Web site, select **New | Virtual Directory (from file)**. Next, specify the location to the XML file storing the virtual directory configuration settings, open it, click **Read File**, highlight the location name, and click **OK** to create the new virtual directory as shown in Figure 5.7.

Figure 5.7 Importing the Virtual Directory from the XML File

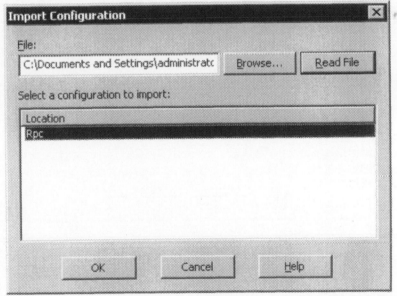

NOTE

The Rpc and RpcWithCerts virtual directories are created under the Default Web Site when you add the RPC over HTTP Proxy component. Instructions on how this is done are included in the next section.

When all Web sites and virtual directories have been created, your IIS Manager should look similar to Figure 5.8.

Figure 5.8 Web Sites in IIS Manager

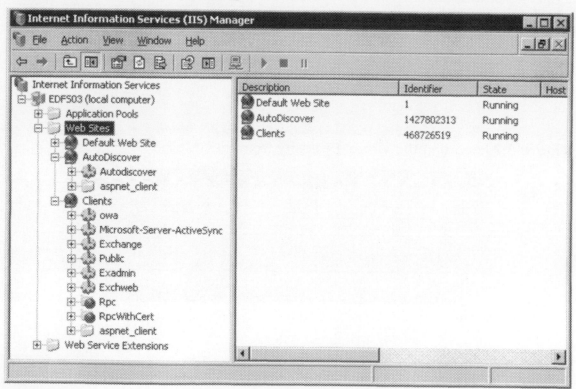

Now you just need to assign an SSL certificate to each Web site. You should leave the self-signed SSL certificate assigned to the Default Web Site and assign a traditional third-party SSL certificate to the Clients and AutoDiscover Web sites, respectively. The name specified in the common name field of the SSL certificate, which will be assigned to the AutoDiscover Web site, should be autodiscover.domain.com. The common name for the Clients Web site can be anything you like (such as mobile.domain.com)

Instructions on how you request and then assign an SSL certificate to a Web site is covered in the following section.

Managing Outlook Anywhere

Outlook Anywhere makes it possible for your end users to remotely access their mailbox from the Internet using their full Outlook client. Those of you with Exchange 2003 experience most likely know the technology behind the Outlook Anywhere feature already since Outlook Anywhere is just an improved version of RPC over HTTP.

The technology behind Outlook Anywhere is basically the same as in Exchange 2003. It still works by encapsulating the RPC-based MAPI traffic inside an HTTPS session, which is then ultimately directed toward the server running the RPC over HTTP proxy component on your internal network, giving you the same functionality when using the Outlook client from a machine on your internal network. When the HTTPS packets reach the RPC over HTTP proxy server, all of the RPC MAPI traffic protocols are removed from the HTTPS packets and forwarded to the respective Mailbox server. This means that by using RPC over HTTP, your end-users no longer have to use a virtual private network (VPN) connection to connect to their respective Exchange mailboxes using their favoritte, *fatter*, Outlook client.

The first necessary step when deploying Outlook Anywhere is the valid installation of a Secure Sockets Layer (SSL) certificate from a trusted Certificate Authority (CA), one your clients trust by default.

SOME INDEPENDENT ADVICE

Security best practice is to publish Outlook Anywhere using a reverse proxy such as an ISA 2006 Server in your perimeter network (aka DMZ or screened subnet). By using ISA Server 2006 in the perimeter network to route RPC over HTTP requests and positioning the Client Access Server on the internal network, you only need to open port 443 on the intranet firewall in order for you Outlook clients to communicate with the Mailbox server.

Installing a Third-Party SSL Certificate

To issue a request for an SSL certificate, you can use the IIS Manager, a method most of us are already familiar with. I have included the required steps for those who need a refresher.

1. Log on to the Exchange 2007 Server on which the Client Access Server role is installed.

2. Click **Start** | **All Programs** | **Administrative Tools** and select **Internet Information Services (IIS) Manager.**

3. Expand *<Server name>* (*local computer*) | **Web Sites**, and then open the **Property** page for the **Default Web Site**.

4. Click the **Directory Security** tab, as shown in Figure 5.9.

Figure 5.9 The Directory Security Tab of the Default Web Site in the IIS Manager

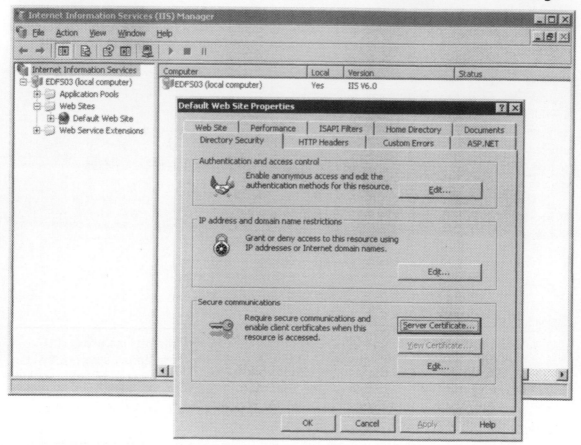

5. Click **Server Certificate**, and then click **Next**.

6. Select **Create a new certificate**, as shown in Figure 5.10, and then click **Next**.

Figure 5.10 Selecting to Create a New Certificate

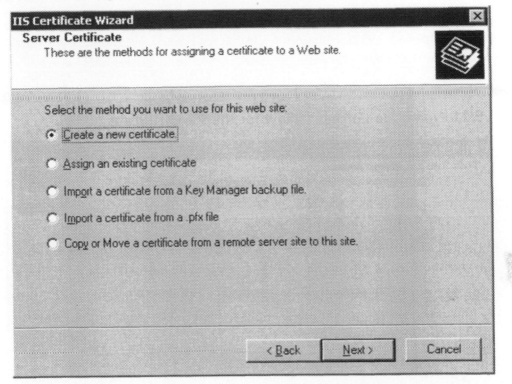

As mentioned earlier in this chapter, during setup Exchange 2007 installs an SSL certificate on the default Web site by default. If you haven't removed this certificate yet, do so now before you proceed with the next steps.

7. Since we're preparing a certificate request for a third-party SSL certificate, select **Prepare the request now, but send it later** and click **Next**.

8. Type a name (such as **SSL Client Access to Exchange**) for the new certificate, one that's easy to refer to and remember. Leave the bit length at 1024 and click **Next**.

9. Enter the **organization** and **organizational unit name**, and then click **Next**.

10.   We have now reached the most important step in the IIS Certificate Wizard, where we have to enter the common name for the Default Web Site. This common name *must* match the name of the URL through which we access the Client Access Server from a client on the Internet. The common name is usually *mail.domain.com*, *mobile.domain.com*, or *owa.domain.com*. When you have entered the common name, click **Next** (Figure 5.11).

Figure 5.11 Typing the Common Name for the SSL Certificate

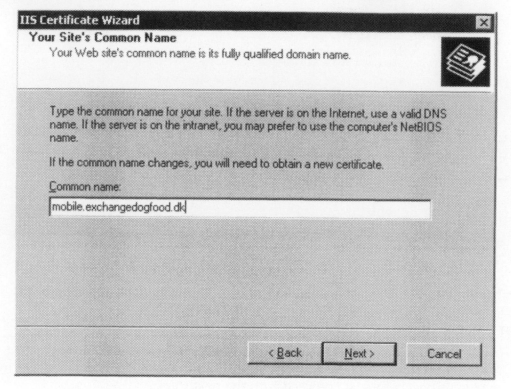

> **NOTE**
>
> It is very important you enter the correct common name since it cannot be changed once you have received your SSL certificate from your third-party provider.

11. Now enter the respective geographical information and click **Next**.

12. Specify the path and file name to save the certificate request, and then click **Next.**

13. Verify that the information in the request is correct (especially the Issued To information), then click **Next** and finally **Finish**, exiting the IIS Certificate Wizard.

SOME INDEPENDENT ADVICE

You can also issue a request for an SSL certificate using the *New-ExchangeCertificate* cmdlet in the Exchange Management Shell. In order to request a certificate using this cmdlet, type:

New-ExchangeCertificate –GenerateRequest –FriendlyName "SSL Client Access to Exchange" –DomainName mobile.exchangedogfood.dk -path c:\certreq.txt

If you're going to issue a request for an SSL certificate with additional DNS names in the Subject Alternative Name property, you actually need to use the *New-ExchangeCertificate* cmdlet. For more information, see the Exchange 2007 Documentation at http://technet.microsoft.com/en-us/library/aa995942.aspx.

Okay, now that I have a pending certificate request, what certificate authority provider should I use? Well, if you want a good and extremely cheap SSL certificate, trusted by 99 percent of all browsers as well as all Windows Mobile 5.0 devices on the market, I can highly recommend GoDaddy (www.godaddy.com). Unfortunately, they don't support adding additional DNS names in the Subject Alternative Name property, however. Here you can get an SSL certificate for a mere $20 per year. I don't think you'll find it much cheaper anywhere else.

When you have decided on which certificate authority provider you want to use, you'll need to send the certreq.txt file to them. I won't go into detail on how this is accomplished since this process is different from provider to provider, and because each provider typically has very detailed information about how you do this.

When you have received the SSL certificate from the certificate provider, you need to perform the following steps:

1. Log on to the Exchange 2007 Server on which the Client Access Server role is installed.

2. Click **Start** | **All Programs** | **Administrative Tools** and select **Internet Information Services (IIS) Manager**.

3. Expand *<Server name> (local computer)* | **Web Sites**, and then open the **Property** page for the Default Web Site.

4. Click the **Directory Security** tab and select the **Server Certificate** button.

5. Select **Process the pending request and install the certificate**, as shown in Figure 5.12, and then click **Next**.

Figure 5.12 Processing the Pending Request

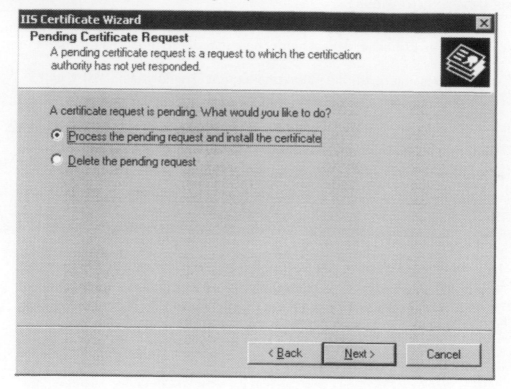

6. Specify the path to the certificate file or the file containing the Certificate Authority response, and then click **Next**.

7. Specify the SSL port that should be used (443), click **Next** and then **Finish** to exit the IIS Certificate Wizard.

8. Now that we have installed the SSL certificate we can enable SSL on the Default Web Site. This is done by clicking the **Edit** button shown back in Figure 5.9, and then checking the option button **Require secure channel (SSL)**, as shown in Figure 5.13.

9. Click **OK** twice and exit the IIS Manager.

Figure 5.13 Enabling SSL on the Default Web Site

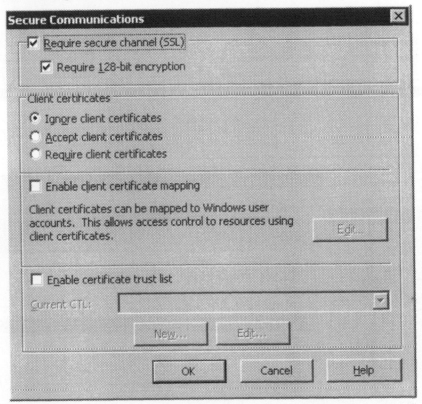

Adding the RPC over HTTP Proxy Component

Next, we need to install the RPC over HTTP Proxy component on the Exchange 2007 Server on which the Client Access Server role has been installed. Since this is a standard Windows 2003 Server component, you install it using the following steps:

1. Log on to the respective Client Access Server.

2. Click **Start** | **Control Panel**, and then open **Add or Remove Programs**.

3. Click **Add/Remove Windows Components**.

4. Select **Network Services** and then click the **Details** button.

5. Check **RPC over HTTP Proxy**, as shown in Figure 5.14.

6. Click **Ok** | **Next** and let the installation complete.

Figure 5.14 Installing the RPC over HTTP Proxy Component

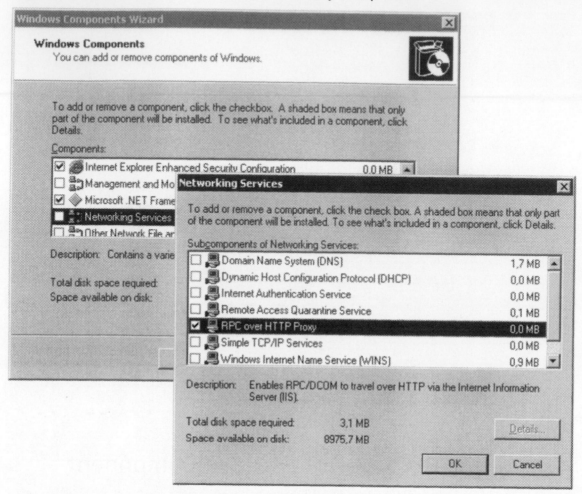

Enabling Outlook Anywhere

With the SSL certificate in place and the RPC over HTTP Proxy component installed, we can move on and enable Outlook Anywhere. In order to do so, perform the following steps:

1. Open the **Exchange Management Console**, then expand the **Server Configuration** work center and select **Client Access**.

2. Click the **Enable Outlook Anywhere** link in the Action pane.

3. In the Outlook Anywhere wizard that appears, type the *external host name* for your Exchange organization, as shown in Figure 5.15.

Figure 5.15 Enabling Outlook Anywhere

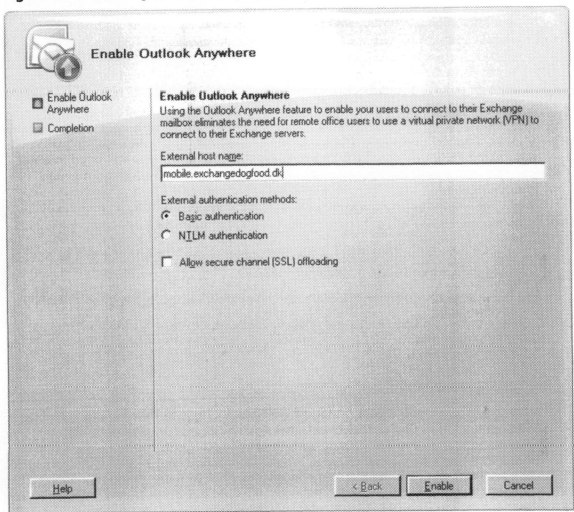

4. Select the type of external authentication method you want to use for Outlook clients accessing their mailbox over the Internet. You can select Basic or NTLM authentication, but it is recommended you select NTLM authentication, especially if you have a firewall such as an ISA 2006 Server, which supports this authentication method.

Some Independent Advice

So, why is it I should choose NTLM over Basic authentication when enabling Outlook Anywhere? Well, because if you choose Basic authentication, you will need to enter your password each time Outlook is opened, even when you're located on your internal network.

5. You have the option of allowing secure channel (SSL) offloading, which should be selected if you have a device that can handle this capability.

6. When you have made your selections, click the **Enable** button and then select **Finish** to exit the wizard.

Some Independent Advice

If for some reason you would rather enable Outlook Anywhere using the Exchange Management Shell, you can do so with the *Enable-OutlookAnywhere* cmdlet. In order to enable Outlook Anywhere with the same settings as those configured in Figure 5.15, you would need to type: Enable-OutlookAnywhere –Server <servername> -ExternalHostname "mobile.exchangedogfood.dk" –ExternalAuthenticationMethod "NTLM" –SSLOffloading $False

Configuring the Outlook Client

In this section, we'll go through the needed steps required to configure an Outlook 2007 client to be able to take advantage of Outlook Anywhere.

To configure an Outlook 2007 client for Outlook Anywhere access, perform the following steps:

1. Open the respective Outlook client (Outlook 2003 or 2007), and then click **Tools | Account Settings**.

2. Double-click the **E-mail** profile, and then select **More Settings**.

3. Choose the **Connection** tab and check **Connect to Microsoft Exchange using HTTP** (as shown in Figure 5.16), and then click **Exchange Proxy Settings…**

Figure 5.16 Enabling Outlook Anywhere in Outlook 2007

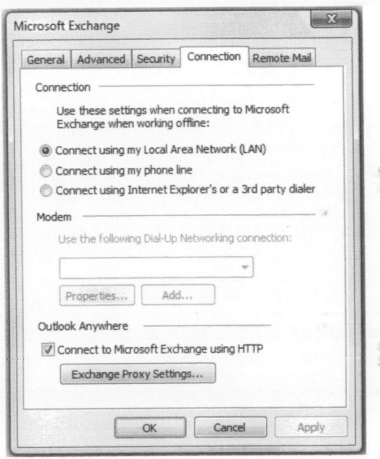

4. Enable and fill out each field as shown in Figure 5.17. Make sure you select NTLM Authentication if that's the method you use in the publishing rule on your ISA server. Click **OK** twice, then select **Next**, **Finish**, and **Close** to exit Outlook Account Settings.

Figure 5.17 Configuring the Exchange Proxy Settings

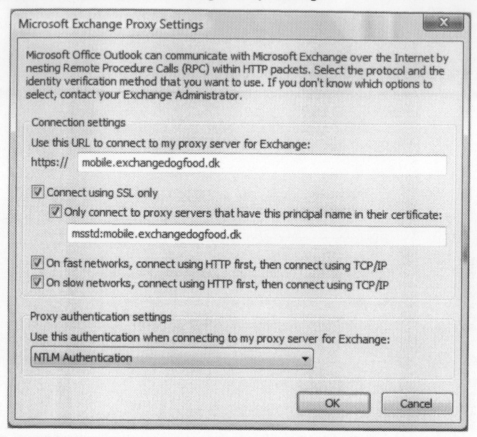

The next time the respective end user is away from the office, they will be able to connect to the Exchange Server using their Outlook client.

Managing Outlook Web Access 2007

During the development of Exchange Server 2007, one of the goals for the Exchange Product group was to make the best Web mail client in the world even better. This task resulted in Outlook Web Access (OWA) 2007 having to be completely rewritten in managed code in order to make it scale even better, and to make it easier to add new features to the UI in the future. Speaking of the UI, one thing you'll notice immediately is that it has been completely redesigned. The number of clicks required to get tasks done has been drastically reduced. Actions and responses are now in place, meaning they are opened in the same browser window instead of in separate multiple dialogs or property sheets. All pop-up notifications have been removed so there are no concerns of being blocked by pop-up blockers. In addition, the drag-and-drop functionality and right-click context menus have been vastly improved. Additionally, OWA 2007 supports 47 different languages!

Finally, unlike OWA 2003, which did all the UI rendering on the back-end server, OWA 2007 now does all the UI rendering on the CAS, thereby significantly reducing the load on the Mailbox server.

Configuring Outlook Web Access Server-Side

After having installed the CAS role on a server, you can manage most of the OWA-related features directly from within the Exchange Management Console, more specifically under the Client Access node located beneath the Server Configuration work center.

As you can see in the Work pane, when selecting one of the CAS servers in the Result pane, Outlook Web Access 2007 displays all of the virtual directories listed in Table 5.2. Notice all of them but one (owa) are legacy OWA virtual directories, only used when accessing mailboxes and/or Public Folders stored on a legacy Exchange Server (Exchange 2000 or 2003).

Table 5.2 Exchange 2007 and Legacy Exchange Virtual OWA Directories

Virtual Directory	Version	Description
Exadmin	Exchange 2000, 2003	The /Exadmin virtual directory is used when administering Public Folders via the Exchange 2000 or 2003 System Manager.
Exchange	Exchange 2000, 2003	The /Exchange virtual directory is used by OWA when accessing mailboxes on legacy Exchange Servers (Exchange 2000 or Exchange 2003).
ExchWeb	Exchange 2000, 2003	The /ExchWeb virtual directory is used by the /Exchange virtual directory for accessing mailboxes on legacy Exchange Servers (Exchange 2000 or Exchange 2003).
owa	Exchange 2007	The /owa virtual directory is used by Outlook Web Access when accessing mailboxes on Exchange 2007 mailbox servers.

Continued

Table 5.2 Continued

Virtual Directory	Version	Description
Public	Exchange 2000, 2003	This virtual directory is used to access public folders by using the Outlook Web Access application for mailboxes located on computers running Exchange 2007, Exchange Server 2003, or Exchange 2000 Server. Only public folders on servers that are running Exchange 2003 or Exchange 2000 will be available through Outlook Web Access.

NOTE

With Exchange Server 2007, you can longer access Public Folders using the OWA 2007 interface.

Because the /owa virtual directory (vdir) is the only vdir used when accessing a user mailbox stored on an Exchange 2007 Mailbox Server, this is also the vdir under which you configure most of the OWA-related functionally (I say most since some settings must still be configured using the IIS Manager).

Let's take a closer look at the configuration options available on the Property page of the owa virtual directory.

The first tab, which is the General tab shown in Figure 5.18, shows us information such as the name of the CAS, the Web site to which the owa vdir belongs, as well as the Exchange version and the last time the vdir was modified. In addition, this is where we can specify the Internal and External URL used to access OWA (the internal URL will always be pre-entered).

Figure 5.18 The General Tab on the OWA Property Page

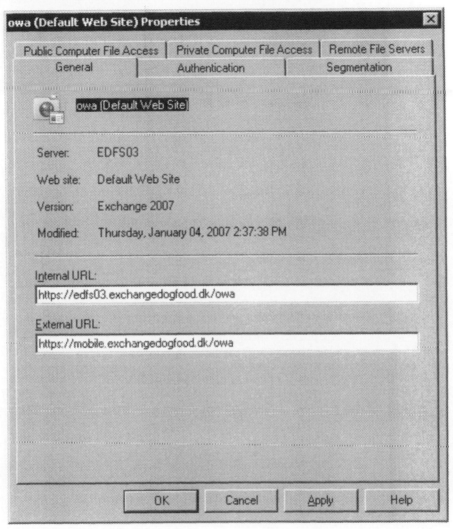

Moving on to the **Authentication** tab (Figure 5.19), here we have the option of specifying the authentication method used to authenticate OWA users. Notice forms-based authentication is enabled by default, unlike OWA 2003 where you had to enable this feature manually. If for some reason you don't want to have forms-based authentication enabled, you can choose to switch to basic by clicking **Use one or more standard authentication methods**. One reason you might want to do this is because you have an ISA Server 2006 deployed in your perimeter network and you are using it to pre-authenticate user logons, thus enabling **Basic authentication** instead.

Figure 5.19 The Authentication Tab on the OWA Property Page

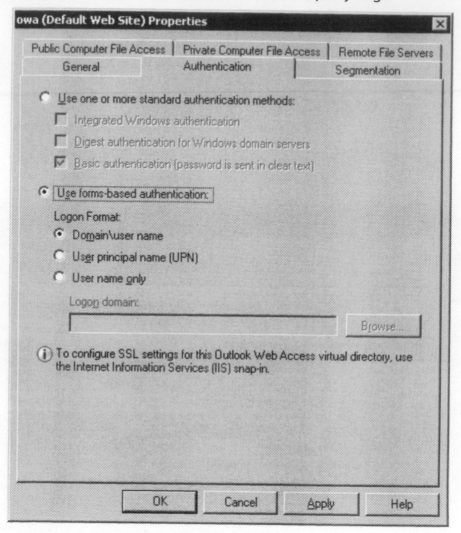

Before we move on, I want to bring your attention to the sentence in the bottom on the Authentication window pane, which says that in order to configure SSL settings for the Outlook Web Access virtual directory, you should use the IIS Manager. Since the SSL certificate that is installed on the Default Web Site is a self-signed untrusted SSL certificate, there will come a day where you want to replace it with an SSL certificate from a third-party certificate provider (I showed you how this was done in the previous section in this chapter).

Now click the **Segmentation** tab shown in Figure 5.20. In previous versions of Exchange, segmentation was very complex to configure, because you had to do so directly in the Registry (at least until the Exchange 2003 Outlook Web Administration tool was released). With Exchange Server 2007 it couldn't be easier. You simply select the feature you want to disable, click the

Disable button and that's it. You don't even have to do an *IISRESET /noforce* afterwards. Most impressively, there is no need to log off and back on since the change is applied immediately!

Figure 5.20 The Segmentation Tab on the OWA Property Page

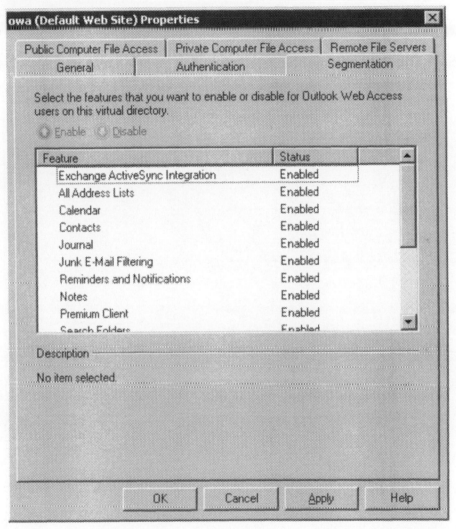

www.syngress.com

> **TIP**
>
> If you want to turn off an OWA feature for one or more users, you can do so using the *Set-CASMailbox* cmdlet. For example, we can turn off the calendar for a user with the following command:
>
> Set-CASMailbox <user> -OWACalendarEnabled: $False

The next tab is the Public Computer File Access tab, shown in Figure 5.21. Here we can enable and disable direct file access. Direct file access is a feature that makes it possible for your users to open any file that is available through OWA. This is not only file attachments, but also files located in Windows SharePoint Services document libraries and/or on Windows file server shares.

Figure 5.21 The Public Computer File Access Tab on the OWA Property Page

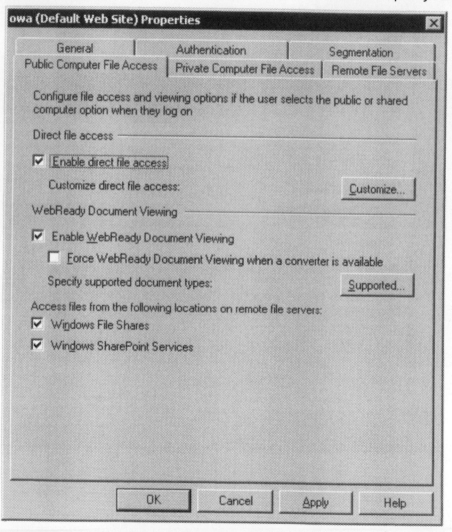

When you have enabled the direct file access feature, click the **Customize** button. Here you can specify which types of files users can access without having to save them first. You can do this by clicking the **Allow** button under *Always Allow* (Figure 5.22) and then adding or removing file types from the list as necessary.

Figure 5.22 Direct File Access Settings

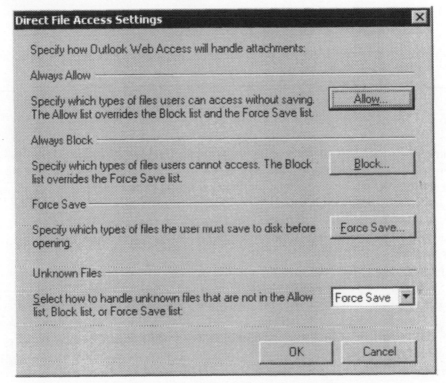

For more comprehensive coverage of the configuration options of the Direct file access feature, you might want to read the following article of mine at the MSExchange.org site: http://www.msexchange.org/tutorials/Drilldown-OWA-Direct-File-Access-Exchange-Server-2007-Part1.html.

Under the Block list button, you can specify any file types your users should not be allowed to access via OWA. The Force Save list is used to specify file types your users must save to disk before they can be opened. The last option, called Unknown Files, is used to specify how unknown file types that haven't been specified in the Allow list, Block list, or Force Save list should be handled. Here you can select between Force Save, Allow, and Block.

> **NOTE**
>
> The Allow list overrides the Block list and the Force Save list, so choose wisely when adding/removing file types from the Allow list.

Let's click OK in order to get back to the main Public Computer File Access tab. The next option here is called **WebReady Document Viewing**. When this option is enabled (the default setting), the file types specified can be viewed simply by using Internet Explorer (Exchange renders the specified file types into HTML), instead of opening the actual file type's locally associated application, such as Word, Excel, PowerPoint, and so on. This is a great feature when using a public Internet kiosk, for example, which may not have the required application installed.

Note that you can configure to mandate this feature, such that WebReady Document Viewing is forced, even when a converter is available.

Lastly, we can specify whether our OWA users should be able to access files from internal Windows File Shares or Windows SharePoint Services. OWA 2007 has a document access feature built into the UI, making it possible for users to access documents on any of these types of servers. I suggest you read the following article at MSExchange.org: http://www.msexchange.org/tutorials/Drilldown-OWA-Direct-File-Access-Exchange-Server-2007-Part2.html.

Let's skip the next tab, the Private Computer File Access tab, since the configurable options are identical to the ones we just went through. The reason why there's a private and public computer file access tab is because you have the option of further locking down access from a public computer, such as an Internet kiosk. These are directly related to the OWA forms–based logon options: "This is a public or shared computer" and "This is a private computer."

This brings us to the last Remote File Servers tab. As you can see in Figure 5.23, this tab is used to specify remote file server access. OWA accesses only internal Windows file share and Windows SharePoint Services document libraries. In addition, a file name can be specified by using a fully qualified domain name (FQDN) that is internal, or that is included in the list of sites to be treated as internal.

Figure 5.23 The Remote File Servers Tab on the OWA Property Page

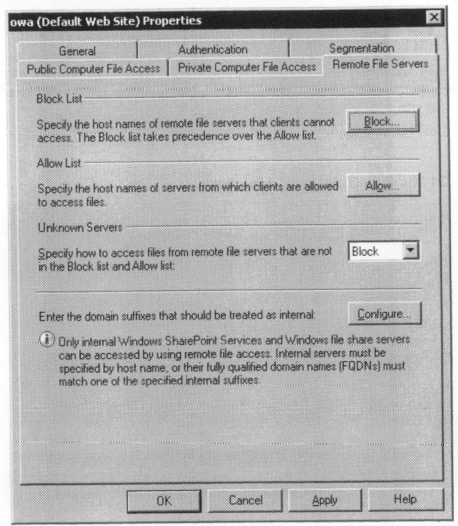

You can also specify how to access files from unknown remote file servers, not in the **Block** or **Allow** lists. Here, you can choose either Allow or Block.

The very last configuration option to cover is related to which domain suffixes should be treated as internal Web sites. This is done by clicking the **Configure** button and then entering the domain suffix for sites whose FQDN names should be treated as internal.

Outlook Web Access Client-Side Features

The first thing you'll notice when you log on to your mailbox using OWA 2007 is the new and improved logon page shown in Figure 5.24. Here you can specify whether you're logging on from a public/shared computer or a private computer, as was also the case in OWA 2003. You should select public or shared computer if you're logging on to your mailbox from an Internet kiosk or a shared computer at a customer site, and so on. If this is the case, also make sure you log off correctly, closing all browser windows when you have finished checking your e-mail.

Figure 5.24 The New OWA 2007 Logon Page

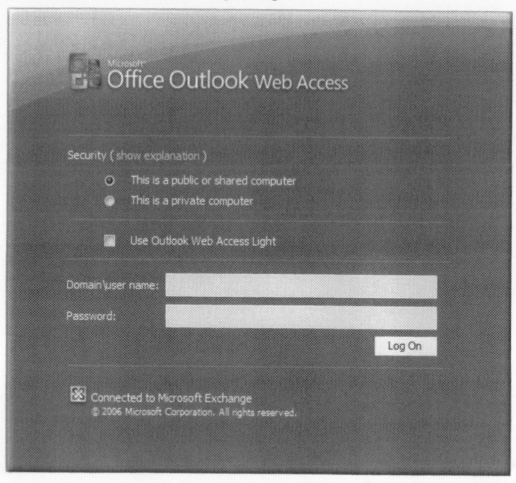

If you are logging on from one of your own private computers, you can safely select. This is a private computer. Doing so will allow you a longer period of inactivity before the session expires, as well as grant you access to features that have been configured for private computer logons only.

NOTE

The OWA 2007 logon page will remember your "private" selection and the username you entered on trusted machines, meaning you only have to enter your password the next time you log on from a trusted machine.

Finally, you have the option of checking Use Outlook Web Access Light. OWA Light is the solution for all browsers and operating systems other than IE6 or IE7 on a Windows platform. So if you're a Firefox, Mac, or even a Linux user, this Web mail client is for you. Simply put, if you like to use off-brand browsers, something else other than IE6+, use OWA light. Although OWA 2007 Light should be considered a light version of the rich OWA 2007 Web mail client, I can assure you it's better than most of the other Web mail clients on the market. Actually, it's very impressive!

NOTE

For more information on the OWA 2007 Light Web mail client, I recommend you check out the following post on the MS Exchange team blog: http://msexchangeteam. com/archive/2006/09/13/428901.aspx.

If this is your first time accessing your mailbox using OWA 2007, after you have entered your username (by default you need to use domainusername) and password, and clicked the **Log On** button, you'll be presented with the screen shown in Figure 5.25. On this screen, you can check **Use the blind and low vision experience** if required, as well as choose the primary language for your OWA 2007 GUI. Lastly, you can change your time zone if desired. When ready, click **OK**.

Figure 5.25 The OWA 2007 Logon Settings Page

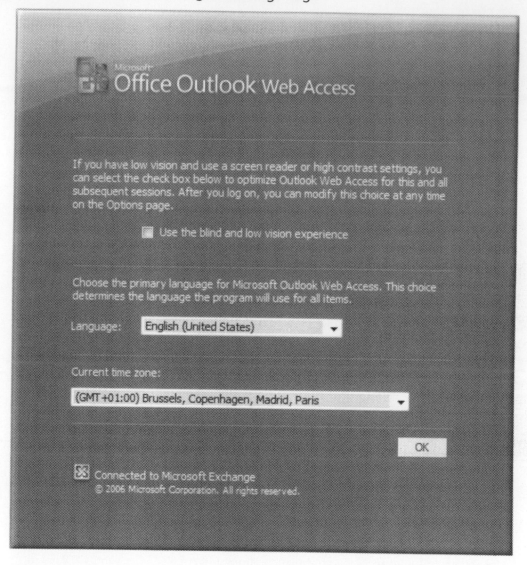

Your mailbox will now be opened. As you can see in Figure 5.26, the OWA 2007 UI is totally different from OWA 2000 and 2003; it's much crisper.

Figure 5.26 The New OWA 2007 UI

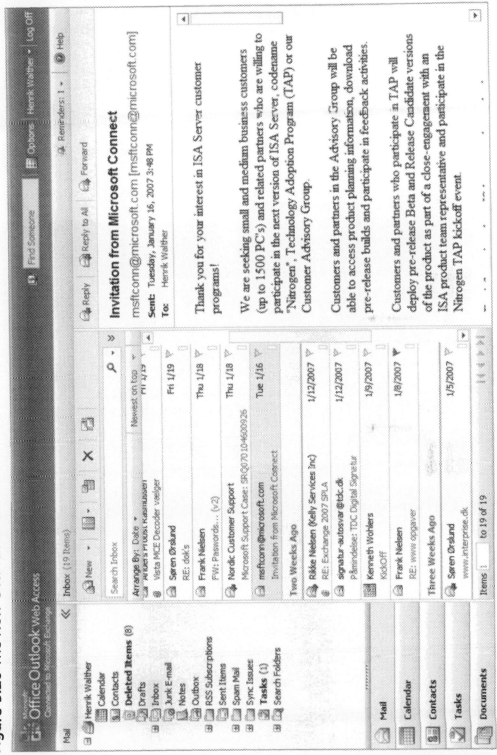

In the following, you will find some of my personal favorite features in OWA 2007. To be honest, some of these would have been quite hard to find, no matter how intensively you explored the OWA UI.

Mailbox Limit Notification

When you're nearing the quota of your mailbox, you'll get a notification. In addition, you'll always be able to see your mailbox limit, as well as the current size of your mailbox, by simply holding the cursor over the mailbox in the top left corner, as shown in Figure 5.27.

Figure 5.27 Mailbox Limit Notification

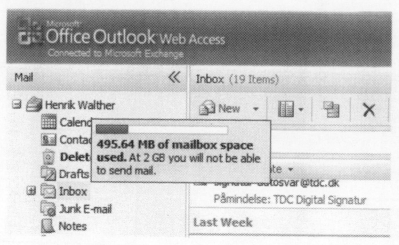

Open Other Mailbox

A feature that was requested by many in OWA 2003 was the option of opening an additional mailbox using OWA. Although OWA 2007 includes this feature, making it possible to enter the name of a user's mailbox and then open it as shown in Figure 5.28, the mailbox will be opened in a separate browser window. Although many would like the option of being able to open an additional mailbox in the same OWA session, this is definitely a step in the right direction.

Figure 5.28 Opening Another Mailbox

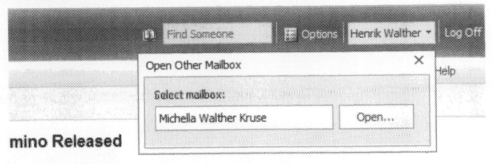

View Message Header

Finally, it's possible to see the message header for an e-mail message using OWA 2007! In order to do so, open the respective message and click the envelope icon to the left of the printer icon in the toolbar, shown in Figure 5.29.

Figure 5.29 Message Header in OWA 2007

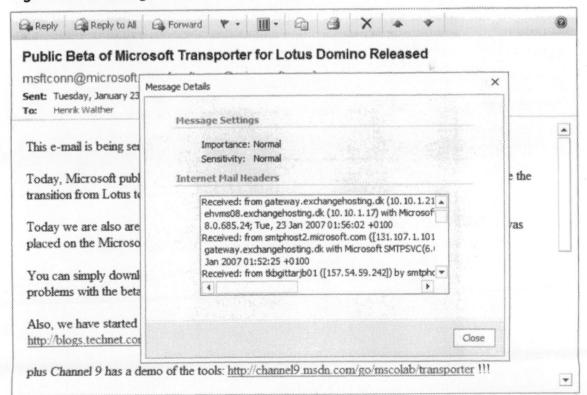

Creating Multiple Calendars

With OWA 2007, you can now create multiple calendars in your mailbox. For example, you can create both a work and a private calendar, as shown in Figure 5.30.

Figure 5.30 Multiple Calendars in OWA 2007

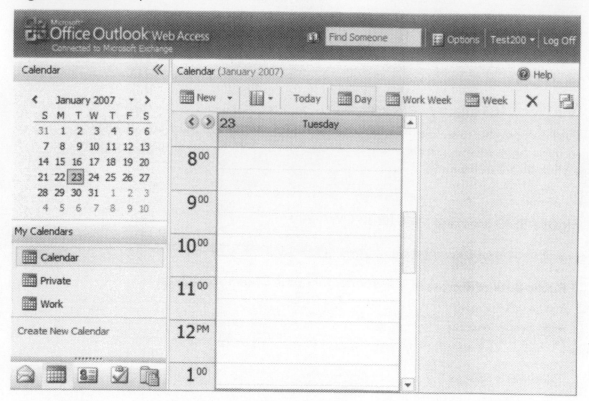

Meeting and Appointment Reminders

Reminders are now integrated into OWA 2007 and are viewable by clicking the reminders drop-down box in the folder title area, as shown in Figure 5.31.

Figure 5.31 Reminders in OWA 2007

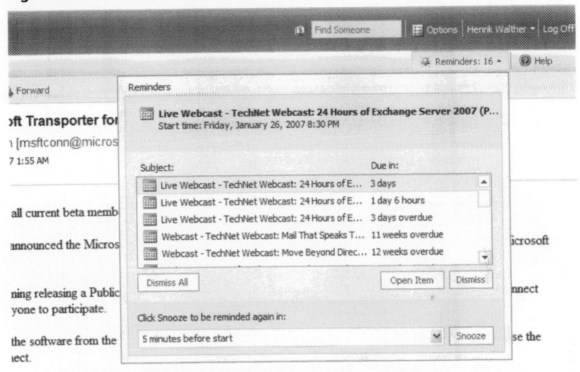

Change Password Option

The change password option is now integrated directly in the OWA 2007 UI (Figure 5.32), meaning you no longer need to mess with configuring this feature in IIS Manager. It simply just works. As in previous versions of Exchange, this feature can be found on the OWA options page.

Figure 5.32 The Change Password Option in OWA 2007

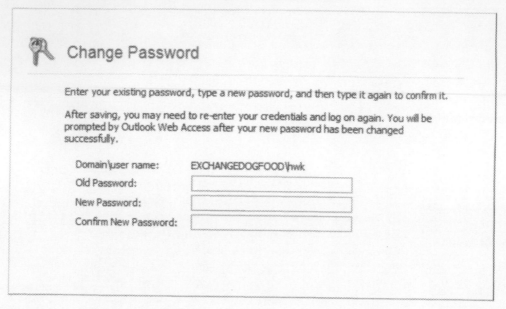

Direct Link Access

Another new feature in OWA 2007 is the new direct link access feature (Figure 5.33), which allows OWA users to access documents located in a share on a file server or documents on a SharePoint Server.

Figure 5.33 Direct Link Access

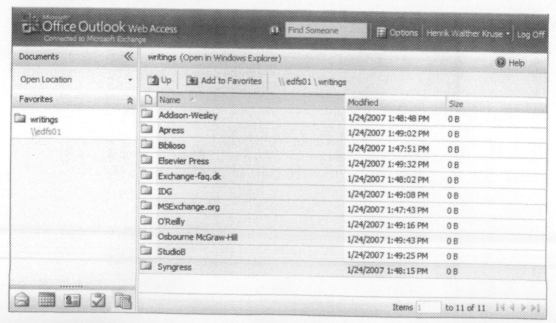

For more information on this feature, you can refer to the following article on MSExchange.org: http://www.msexchange.org/tutorials/Drilldown-OWA-Direct-File-Access-Exchange-Server-2007-Part2.html.

Compose Messages in HTML

OWA 2007 now supports HTML as a message formatting tool, which means you're no longer bound to those boring plain text messages. You can now create great looking messages from directly within OWA 2007.

Junk E-Mail Lists

You can now add senders to your Safe Senders, Blocked Senders, and Safe Recipients lists by right-clicking on the respective message and selecting Junk E-mail. These lists can be viewed via the OWA options page. Note that the Junk Mail feature is not turned on by default and must be enabled.

Improved Signature Editor

The signature editor in OWA 2007 is also light years better than the one included in OWA 2003. Now you can actually create great looking signatures just like in Outlook. The signature shown in Figure 5.34 is my signature at work.

Figure 5.34 The Rich Signature Editor in OWA 2007

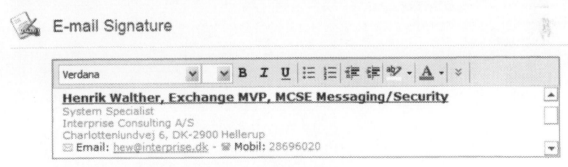

WebReady Document Viewing Feature (Open as Webpage)

Another nice addition to OWA 2007 is the new WebReady Document Viewing feature, which lets you tell Exchange to render certain types of file types into HTML if you don't have the right application installed locally. Exchange 2007 will ship with support for transcoding the following file types by default: DOC, DOT, RTF, WBK, WIZ, XLS, XLK, PPT, PPS, POT, PWS, and PDF. The transcoding engine has a pluggable architecture so the Exchange Product group can add support for new file types in future service packs if necessary. To use the WebReady Document Viewing feature, click the **Open as Web Page** link to the right of the respective attachment shown in Figure 5.35.

Figure 5.35 WebReady Document Viewing

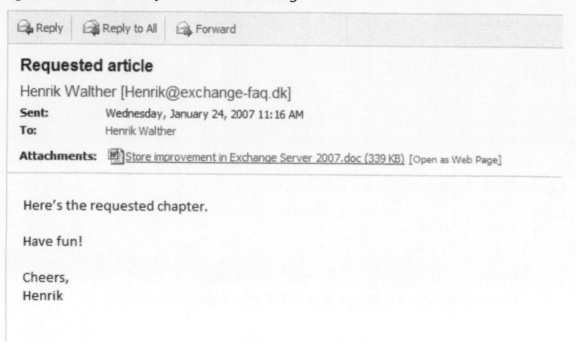

This will render the document file into HTML, and after a few seconds you'll be able to read it directly in the browser window, as shown in Figure 5.36. Now that is pretty impressive, right?

Figure 5.36 An HTML Rendered Word Document

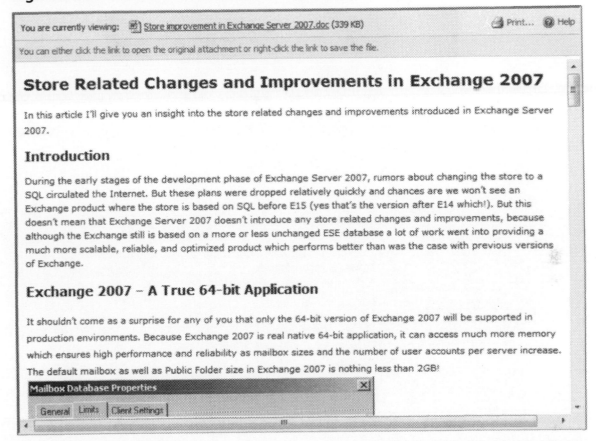

Mark All as Read

A small, and personally very useful feature not in OWA 2003, was the option to mark all items in a specific folder as read when using the Outlook client. With OWA 2007, this feature has finally made its way into the UI, as shown in Figure 5.37.

Figure 5.37 Mark All Messages in a Folder as Read

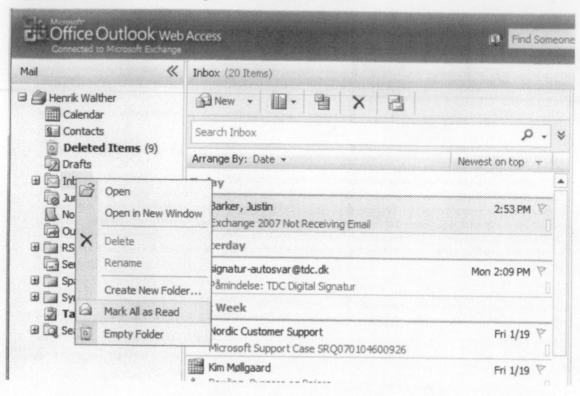

All right, I better stop here! Be sure to explore the new OWA 2007 UI intensely since there are lots of great features buried within.

Simplifying the URL to Outlook Web Access

As was possible with previous versions of Exchange, you can simplify the URL to OWA in order to provide an even easier experience for your end users. As mentioned earlier in this section, the default URL to OWA 2007 is https://server.domain.com/owa. Although your users have to type fewer characters compared to previous versions of OWA, why not skip the /owa part and just use https://server.domain.com? Possibly because it may be more complicated to configure than it is a benefit to end users, I hear some of you grumbling. Actually, however, this is extremely easy to configure. Simply perform the following steps:

1. Log on to the server upon which the Client Access Server role has been installed.

2. Open the IIS Manager by clicking **Start** | **All Programs** | **Administrative Tools** | **Internet Information Services (IIS) Manager**.

3. In the IIS Manager, expand **Server (local computer)** | **Web Sites**, and then right-click the **Default Web Site** and select **Properties**.

4. Click the **Home Directory** tab, as shown in Figure 5.38.

Figure 5.38 Specifying Redirection URL

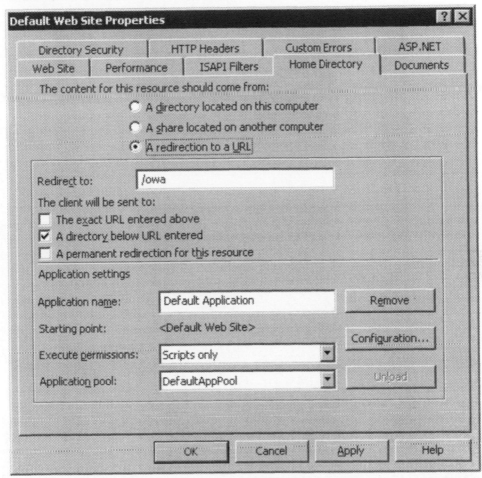

5.   Select **A redirection to a URL**, and then type **/owa** in the **Redirect to:** field.

6.   Check **A directory below URL entered**.

7.   Click **OK** and exit the IIS Manager.

You can now tell your end users they can access the Web mail client using https://mail.domain. com, or whatever URL you use to access OWA from the Internet.

Although the preceding solution should be sufficient for most end users, several of you may have end users who don't understand they must type https instead of http before the actual URL. Most of them probably don't know the difference between a secure and a nonsecure site. In order to eliminate frustrations for the end user, you can configure OWA in such a way that they simply need to type http://mail.domain.com to be redirected to the proper OWA URL. In order to both simplify the OWA URL as well as redirect from HTTP to HTTPS, you must create a custom HTML page. In order to do so, perform the following steps:

1. Create the HTML page. You can do so in a Notepad document. Enter the HTML code shown in Figure 5.39.

Figure 5.39 Code Snippet Used for Redirection

2. Save it as **SSL_OWA.HTM** (remember to select **All Files** in **Save As type**: drop-down box).

3. Open the IIS Manager by clicking **Start** | **All Programs** | **Administrative Tools** | **Internet Information Services (IIS) Manager**.

4. In the IIS Manager, expand **Server (local computer)** | **Web Sites**, and then right-click the **Default Web Site** and select **Properties**.

5. Click the **Home Directory** tab and select **A redirection to a URL**.

6. In the **Redirect to:** field, type **/owa** and then check **A directory below URL entered**.

7. Click the **Custom Errors** tab.

8. In the HTTP Error table, select **403;4**, as shown in Figure 5.40.

Figure 5.40 Modifying the 403-4 Custom Error Message File

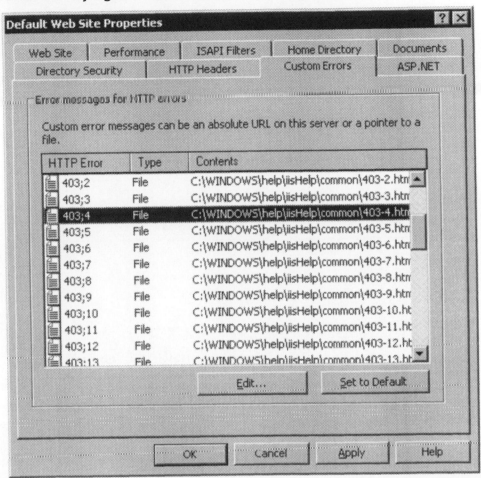

9.   Click **Edit** and then point to the **SSL_OWA.HTM** file you saved earlier, as shown in Figure 5.41.

Figure 5.41 Specifying the New HTM File

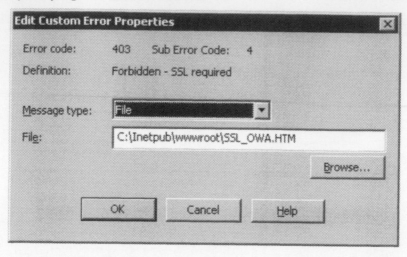

10.   Click **OK** twice and exit the IIS Manager.

11.   Open a **Command Prompt** windows and type **IISRESET /noforce** in order to apply the changes.

Your end users should now be able to access OWA using http://mail.domain.com or whatever the URL is to OWA in your environment.

Managing Exchange ActiveSync

One of the features that have really been improved upon in Exchange Server 2007 is, without doubt, the Exchange ActiveSync communication protocol. Exchange Server ActiveSync is still based on the DirectPush technology, (sometimes also referred to as AUTD v2) introduced first in Exchange Server 2003 SP2, improving the mobile messaging experience for your users by providing close to real-time over-the-air access to your e-mail messages, schedules, contacts, tasks lists, and other Exchange server mailbox data. Actually, DirectPush is the only method available when synchronizing your mailbox using Exchange ActiveSync (EAS) in Exchange Server 2007, and is thus enabled by default. That means AUTD v1, based on text messaging (SMS), has officially been dropped. But who would miss it? I seriously doubt anyone, as AUTD wasn't very widely used, especially since very few mobile carriers (especially in Europe) supported this method.

To refresh your memory, I thought it would be a good idea to include Figure 5.42, showing you how DirectPush works behind the scenes.

Figure 5.42 DirectPush behind the Scenes

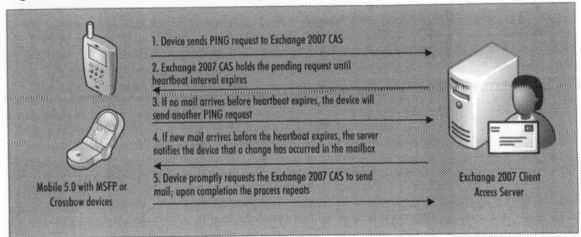

DirectPush works by keeping an HTTPS connection alive between a mobile device and the Exchange 2007 CAS server. Because DirectPush uses long-standing HTTPS requests, it's important that both your mobile carrier and your firewall are configured with a time-out value from the default to 15 to 30 minutes. If a short time-out value is configured, it will cause the device to initiate a new HTTPS request much more frequently, which not only shortens battery life on your device, but is also more costly since more data will be transferred.

TIP

If you use an ISA 2004 or 2006 firewall in your organization, Microsoft KB article 905013 (http://support.microsoft.com/kb/905013) describes the steps necessary in order to configure the firewall to support long-standing HTTPS requests.

So what about the current Windows mobile devices on the market today? Are they supported by Exchange Server 2007? Yes, all devices with Exchange ActiveSync will be able to synchronize with an Exchange 2007 mailbox. If you don't have a Windows mobile 5.0 device with the Messaging and Security Feature Pack (MSFP) installed, a part of the Adaptation Kit Update V2 (AKU2) ROM, you can use a third-party solution such as RoadSync from DataViz (http://www.dataviz.com) to sync with Exchange 2007. Currently, the Exchange ActiveSync protocol is licensed by the following companies:

- Nokia
- Sony Ericsson

- Motorola
- Symbian
- Palm
- DataViz

For more information about mobile device support in Exchange Server 2007, see www.microsoft.com/exchange/evaluation/features/owa_mobile.mspx.

Okay, enough talk about DirectPush. Let's take a look at the other new or enhanced mobile features included with Exchange Server 2007:

- **Support for HTML messages**   Messages can now be viewed in HTML format, which means you now can read messages containing HTML code, tables, and so on (just as with most newsletters). Replies to an HTML-formatted e-mail message will not disrupt formatting either, keeping HTML e-mail threads intact. In the past, the mobile device converted the message to plain text. This was also true when you replied to or forwarded the HTML formatted message.

- **Support for follow-up flags**   Exchange Server 2007 supports using quick flags from a mobile device running Crossbow, the codename for the next release of Windows mobile (in beta at the time of this writing). This means that quick flags set from a Crossbow device will be synchronized to the mailbox, and be visible in both Outlook and OWA, too. The same is true the other way.

- **Support for fast message retrieval**   Fetching the body of an e-mail message has been improved further. You no longer need to select **Mark for download** or click **Get the rest of this message** since this will happen automatically in the background. Note also that this feature requires the new Crossbow version of Windows Mobile.

- **Meeting attendee information**   You can now synchronize information about attendee availability to your mobile device; pretty much the same as you do in Outlook now. You can forward or reply to a meeting request, as well as see the acceptance status of attendees. In addition, you can even see GAL information for each attendee.

- **Enhanced Exchange Search**   With the enhanced Exchange search feature, you can now search your whole mailbox, instead of just the messages cached locally on the mobile device. The search feature supports rich/query filters, meaning you can search for messages using the *test*, *data*, *from*, *to*, *flags*, *categories*, *attachments*, *importance*, and *restricted to* specific fields. The number of items returned can be constrained and/or paged through. Lastly, the search is lightning fast since it's only initiated from the device and is physically executed on the server. Note that this feature requires Crossbow on the mobile device.

- **Windows SharePoint Services and Universal Naming Convention (UNC) document access**   Just as with OWA 2007, you can access documents stored on either a file server (UNC shares) or a SharePoint server. You can even forward a large document without downloading it to the mobile device first! Note that this feature requires Crossbow on the mobile device.

- **Reset PIN/Password**   With Exchange Server 2007, you can require that a device password be entered on a mobile device after a period of inactivity. If this device password should be forgotten at a later time, it's possible to unlock the device by using a device recovery password. Note that this feature requires Crossbow on the mobile device.

- **Enhanced device security through password policies**   With Exchange Server 2007, you can enhance the security of a Windows mobile device by configuring additional password requirement settings, such as password history tracking, password expiration, and by prohibiting the use of passwords that are too simple (password complexity). We take a closer look at these features later in this section. Note that this feature requires Crossbow on the mobile device.

- **AutoDiscover for over the air (OTA) provisioning**   Exchange 2007 ActiveSync supports the new Web-based AutoDiscover service, which we talked about earlier in this section. Support for AutoDiscover simplifies provisioning since you only need to specify your e-mail address and password when configuring the mobile device for Exchange ActiveSync. Note that this feature requires Crossbow on the mobile device.

- **Support for Out of Office configuration**   Like with Outlook 2007 and OWA 2007, you can set Out of Office (OOF) messages directly from your mobile device. The OOF messages are saved directly to the Exchange 2007 server so an OOF message set on a mobile device can be seen in Outlook and OWA as well. Note that this feature requires Crossbow on the mobile device.

I bet you agree this is a pretty comprehensive list of new features and improvements. Unfortunately, there are also a few features that didn't make it into the RTM version of Exchange Server 2007. The following is a list of those features:

- **Information Rights Management (IRM)**   Originally, the plan was to include IRM support for mobile devices in the RTM version of Exchange Server 2007, but because of some stability issues in rare situations this feature was removed just before its release.

- **Outlook Mobile Access (OMA)**   OMA has been dropped completely and will therefore not be included in an Exchange 2007 SP. I'm certain only a very few of us will miss this, shall I say, slightly clumsy Web-based mobile device Web mail client.

- **Support for S/MIME**   As with OWA 2007, unfortunately the RTM version of Exchange Server 2007 doesn't support S/MIME. This is not because the feature has been dropped, but due to the fact that the Exchange Product group simply didn't have the time to finish it before its release. I am sure many of us would not have had any issues waiting a few more months for the RTM version if S/MIME for OWA 2007 and Windows mobile devices were included.

Configuring the Exchange ActiveSync Virtual Directory

As with Exchange Server 2003, Exchange ActiveSync is still accessed using the Microsoft-Server-ActiveSync virtual directory, which by default is located under the Default Web Site in IIS Manager, as can be seen in Figure 5.43.

Figure 5.43 Microsoft Server ActiveSync Virtual Directory in IIS Manager

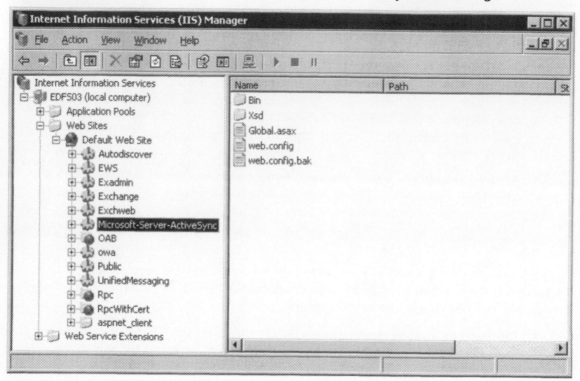

The IIS Manager is still the tool used to configure settings such as authentication methods, IP addresses, and domain name restrictions, as well as secure channel (SSL). However, with the EAS virtual directory related settings, you can control many directly from within the Exchange Management Console.

TIP

All Microsoft-Server-ActiveSync virtual directory–related settings, with the exception of SSL which must be configured using the IIS Manager, can also be configured using the Exchange Management Shell. You do so using the *Set-ActiveSyncVirtualDirectory* cmdlet. You can view the properties of the virtual directory using the *Get-ActiveSyncVirtualDirectory* cmdlet.

If we expand the Server Configuration work center node and click the Client Access subnode, we'll get a list of the CAS servers in our Exchange 2007 organization. Select a CAS, and then click the Exchange ActiveSync tab in the Work pane. Open the Property page for the Microsoft-Server-ActiveSync virtual directory. On the General tab, you can find information such as the name of the CAS, the Web site to which the virtual directory belongs, whether SSL is enabled or not, and when the virtual directory was last modified (see Figure 5.44). In addition, we have the option of specifying the internal and external URL used to access the CAS using Exchange ActiveSync. The internal URL is configured by default, but the external URL must be entered manually. The external URL is used by the AutoDiscover service when a mobile device supporting AutoDiscover tries to connect to the CAS using only the e-mail address and password.

Figure 5.44 The Properties Page of the Microsoft Server ActiveSync Virtual Directory in EMC

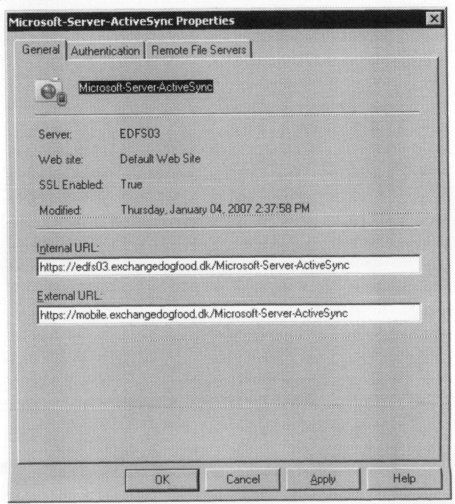

NOTE

Windows Mobile 5.0 and earlier don't support the AutoDiscover service, only the next version of Windows mobile, codenamed Crossbow and currently in beta, supports this feature.

Let's move on to the **Authentication** tab (Figure 5.45). Here we have the option of enabling **Basic authentication (password sent in clear text)**, typically the authentication method used by Exchange ActiveSync clients. In addition, we can specify how the CAS should handle client certificates.

Figure 5.45 The Authentication Tab on the Microsoft Server ActiveSync Properties Page

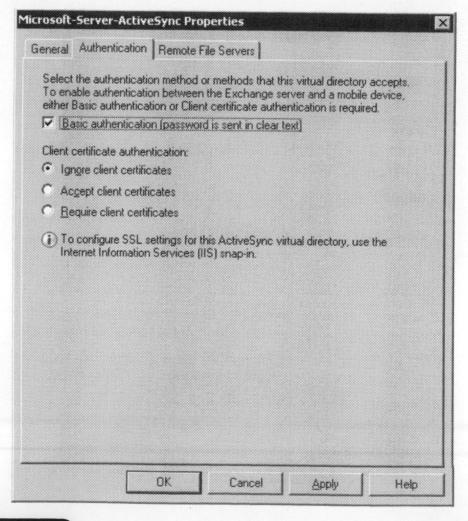

Finally, we have a **Remote File Servers** tab. We won't go through the available options here since they are identical to those covered in the Outlook Web Access section in this chapter and simply allow the access of files on remote file shares or SharePoint servers.

TIP

Windows mobile 5.0 and earlier devices cannot take advantage of the direct link access feature, which allows you to access documents in a share on a file server, or documents located on a SharePoint Server. Only the next version of Windows mobile, codenamed Crossbow and currently in beta at the time of this writing, supports the direct link access feature.

Configuring ActiveSync Policies

As many of us remember, Exchange Server 2003 SP2 introduced a set of device security settings that allowed us to push out a policy to mobile devices accessing the Exchange 2003 Server using Exchange ActiveSync. We had the option of *enforcing passwords on the devices, setting the minimum password length, setting the inactivity timeout, setting a device to be remotely wiped after x number of failed logon attempts, setting how often the device security settings should be pushed out to the devices*, and more. One problem with the device security settings feature in Exchange Server 2003 SP2 was its limitation to one global policy, which applied to all users, unless they were explicitly added to an exception list, excluding them from all security policy. With Exchange Server 2007, it is now possible to create multiple Exchange ActiveSync policies, giving you much more control of your mobile deployment.

In the following example, I'll show you step by step how an Exchange ActiveSync policy is created.

1. Open the **Exchange Management Console**, and then expand the **Organization Configuration** work center node.

2. Click the **Client Access** subnode, and then select **New Exchange ActiveSync Mailbox Policy** in the Action pane.

3. In the **New Exchange ActiveSync Mailbox Policy**, enter a name for your policy and then check and configure the options that should be applied to the user mailboxes to which this policy is assigned, as shown in Figure 5.46.

Figure 5.46 Creating a New Exchange ActiveSync Mailbox Policy

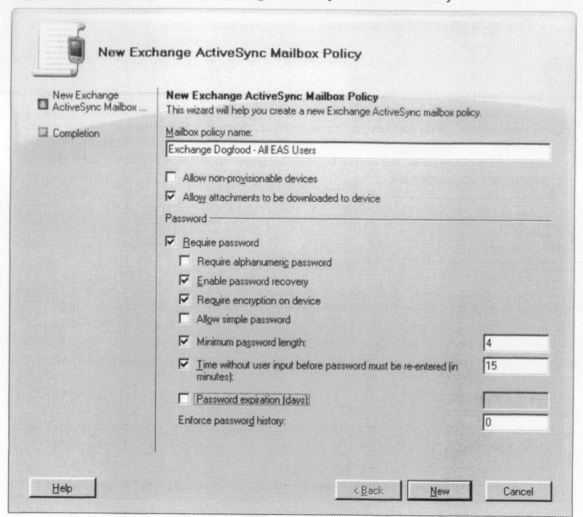

NOTE

If you have experience with configuring the device security settings in Exchange 2003 SP2, the options listed in Figure 5.46 should be familiar, with the exception of four. The four new options are **Enable password recovery, Require encryption on device, Password expiration (days)**, and **Enforce password history**. The first option, **Enable password recovery**, will store a user's password on the Exchange Server so it's possible to retrieve a lost device password should the user forget it. A lost password can be retrieved by the IT staff using the Exchange Management Console or the Exchange Management Shell, but a user can also retrieve it himself via the Mobile Device page in OWA 2007. The second option, **Require encryption on device**, will encrypt the data on the storage card in a device, but keep in mind this option is only supported with devices running the next version of Windows mobile, codenamed "Crossbow." The third option, **Password expiration (days)**, allows us to specify after how many days a device password should stay active before expiring. The fourth option, **Enforce password history**, makes it possible to enforce password history so users must use a completely new password when it has expired.

4. When ready, click **New**, and then **Finish** on the following page.

TIP

If you would rather create an Exchange ActiveSync policy using the Exchange Management Shell, you can do so using the *New-ActiveSyncMailboxPolicy* cmdlet. For example, the policy configured in Figure 5.46 could be created using the Exchange Management Shell by typing:

New-ActiveSyncMailboxPolicy –Name "Exchange Dogfood – All EAS Users" –AllowNonProvisionableDevices $false –DevicePasswordEnabled $true –AlphanumericDevicePasswordRequired $false –MaxInactivityTimeDeviceLock "00:15:00" –MinDevicePasswordLengh "4" –PasswordRecoveryEnabled $true –DeviceEncryptionEnabled $true –AttachmentsEnabled $true –AllowSimpleDevicePass word $false –DevicePasswordExpiration "unlimited" –DevicePasswordHistory "0"

After you have configured an Exchange ActiveSync Mailbox Policy, you can always change it later if required. You can do this by selecting the respective policy in the Result pane, and then clicking the Properties link in the Action pane. This will bring you to a screen similar to the one shown in Figures 5.47 and 5.48.

Figure 5.47 The General Tab on the Properties Page of an Exchange ActiveSync Mailbox Policy

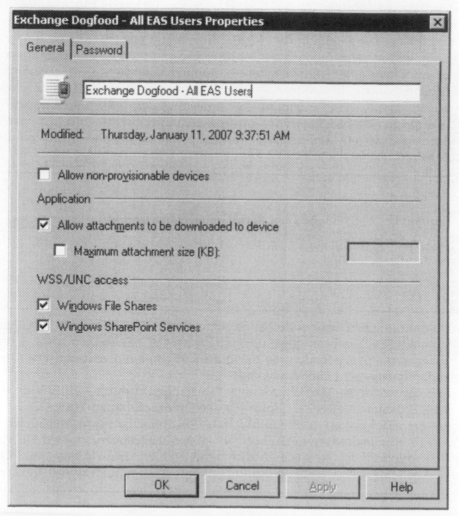

Figure 5.48 The Password Tab on the Properties Page of an Exchange ActiveSync Mailbox Policy

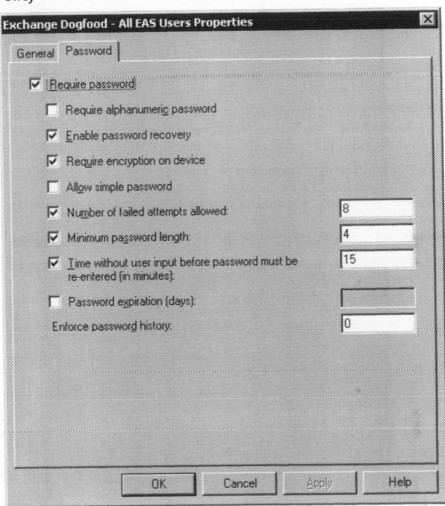

Assigning an Exchange ActiveSync Policy to a User

So how do we assign an Exchange ActiveSync (EAS) policy to one or more users once it's created? This can be done using either the Exchange Management Console or the Exchange Management Shell. To assign an EAS policy to a user, perform the following steps:

1. Open the **Excha.nge Management Console**, and then expand the **Recipient Configuration** work center node.

2. Select the **Mailbox** subnode and highlight the *user mailbox* to which you want to assign the EAS policy.

3. Click **Properties** in the **Action pane**.

4. Click the **Mailbox Features** tab, as shown in Figure 5.49.

Figure 5.49 Enabling/Disabling Exchange ActiveSync on a Per User Basis

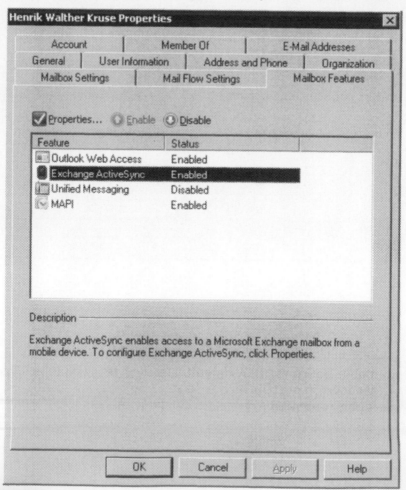

5. Select **Exchange ActiveSync**, and then click the **Properties** button.

6. Check **Apply an Exchange ActiveSync mailbox policy**, and then click **Browse**, as shown in Figure 5.50.

Figure 5.50 Assigning an Exchange ActiveSync Mailbox Policy to a User Mailbox

7. In the **Select ActiveSync Mailbox Policy** window (Figure 5.51), choose the respective EAS mailbox policy and then click **OK** three times.

Figure 5.51 Selecting an Exchange ActiveSync Mailbox Policy

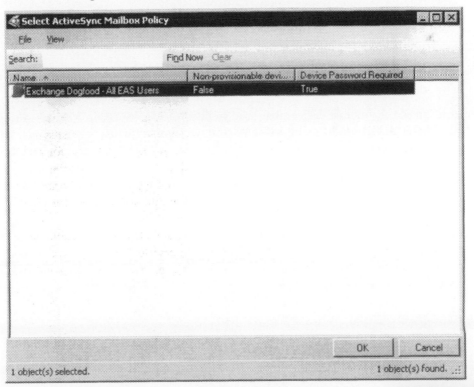

TIP

To assign an EAS mailbox policy to a mailbox using the Exchange Management Shell, use the *Set-CASMailbox* cmdlet. For example, if you want to assign an EAS mailbox policy named *Exchange Dogfood – All EAS users* to a user alias called HWK, type the following command:

Set-CASMailbox HWK –ActiveSyncMailboxPolicy "Exchangedogfood – All EAS Users"

Managing Mobile Devices

Now that we have finished our mobile deployment, how do we go about managing the mobile devices in our organization? Well, unlike Exchange Server 2003 SP2, which required you to download a separate Web administration tool (called the Mobile Administration Web tool) that among other things allowed you to delete device partnerships and remote wipe stolen or lost devices from a central location, these features and more are an integral part of the Exchange Management Console.

To manage the mobile device(s) for a specific user, you must perform the following steps:

1. Open the **Exchange Management Console**.
2. Expand the **Recipient Configuration** work center and click **Mailbox**.
3. Select the *user mailbox* for which you want to manage a mobile device.
4. Click **Manage Mobile Device**.
5. The Manage Mobile Device wizard now appears (Figure 5.52).

Here you can see the mobile devices that have an established partnership with the respective user mailbox. Under **Additional device information**, you can see when the first synchronization occurred, when the last device wipe command was issued, the acknowledge time for the device wipe, when the device was last updated with a policy, as well as the last ping heartbeat in seconds (this should be between 15 and 30 minutes, depending on how keep alive sessions have been configured with your mobile service provider and on your firewall). Finally, you can see the recovery password here (if enabled by policy).

Under Action, you have the option of either removing (a.k.a., deleting) a mobile device partnership, as well as performing a remote wipe of a mobile device. Performing a remote wipe of a mobile device will delete any data held in memory as well as on the storage card. In other words, the device will be reset to its factory defaults.

Figure 5.52 Managing Mobile Devices

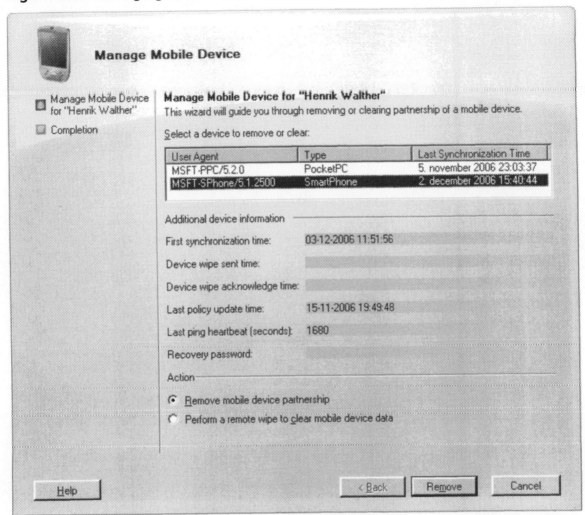

> **NOTE**
>
> Removing a mobile device partnership will not delete any data on the mobile device.

In order to reduce the load on IT staff (primarily the Helpdesk), the Exchange Product group also implemented these mobile device management features into OWA 2007. This means users can manage their own devices, as shown in Figure 5.53.

Figure 5.53 Managing Mobile Devices in OWA 2007

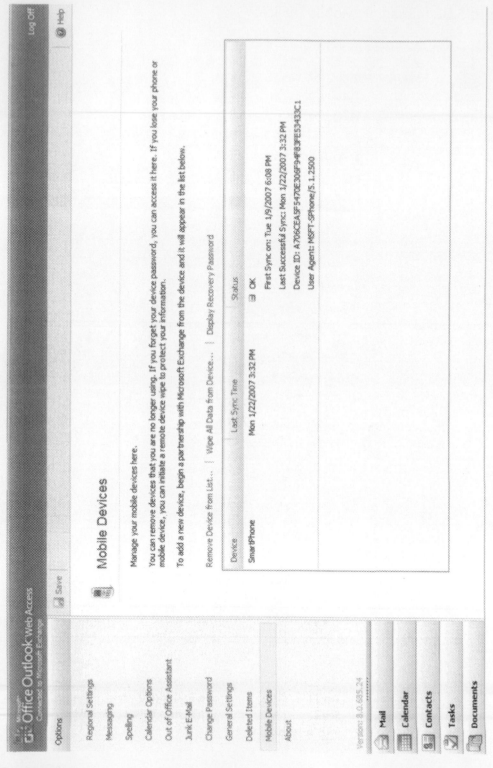

TIP

To remove a mobile device partnership or remote wipe a mobile device using the Exchange Management Shell, you must use the *Remove-ActiveSyncDevice and ClearActiveSyncDevice* cmdlets, respectively. For further details on how to do this, type *Get-Help Remove-ActiveSyncDevice* and/or *Get-Help ClearActiveSyncDevice* in the Exchange Management Shell.

Managing POP3/IMAP4

Like its predecessors, Exchange Server 2007 also supports the Post Office Protocol version 3 (POP3) and Internet Message Access Protocol version 4 (IMAP4) clients; however, since these client protocols aren't that popular anymore (especially now that we have Outlook Anywhere, a superb Web mail client and EAS), the POP3 and IMAP4 protocols are disabled by default.

Both the POP3 and IMAP4 protocols have been rewritten from the ground up in managed code, and are no longer dependent on the IIS component. Instead, they run as a separate Windows Service.

Because the Exchange Product group focused on rewriting the POP3 and IMAP4 protocols in managed code, and because of the general time pressure that lay over their heads during the development of the Exchange Server 2007 product, they unfortunately didn't have time to build a GUI to administer these protocols. This means that you cannot use the Exchange Management Console to configure or manage the POP3 and IMAP4 protocols. Instead, this must be done using the respective cmdlets in the Exchange Management Shell.

NOTE

If the Exchange Product group receives sufficient feedback from customers requiring a GUI for managing the POP3 and IMAP4 protocols, we can expect one to be included in Exchange Server 2007 Service Pack 1.

Other things worth noting about the POP3 and IMAP4 services in Exchange Server 2007 is that we are limited to only one POP3 or IMAP4 service per server, and the same SSL certificate must be used for all POP3 and IMAP4 connections to the respective Client Access Server. In addition, Public Folder access through an IMAP4 client is no longer supported. Also, bear in mind that IPSec isn't supported when you have an ISA Server deployed between clients and the Exchange server.

Okay, enough focus on what's missing with the POP3 and IMAP4 protocols. After all, there are a few new improvements. Support for TLS encryptions has been added, Kerberos authentication is now supported, and, finally, the search feature for both POP3 and IMAP4 clients has been heavily improved.

Enabling the POP3 and IMAP4 Services

As mentioned earlier, both the POP3 and IMAP4 services are disabled by default. If you decide to use one or both of these services, the first thing you must do is enable them and set them to an Automatic service startup type using the Services MMC snap-in. You can do this by clicking **Start | Run** and typing **Services.msc**, which brings up the Services snap-in (shown in Figure 5.54).

Figure 5.54 Starting the POP3 and IMAP4 Services in the Services Snap-in

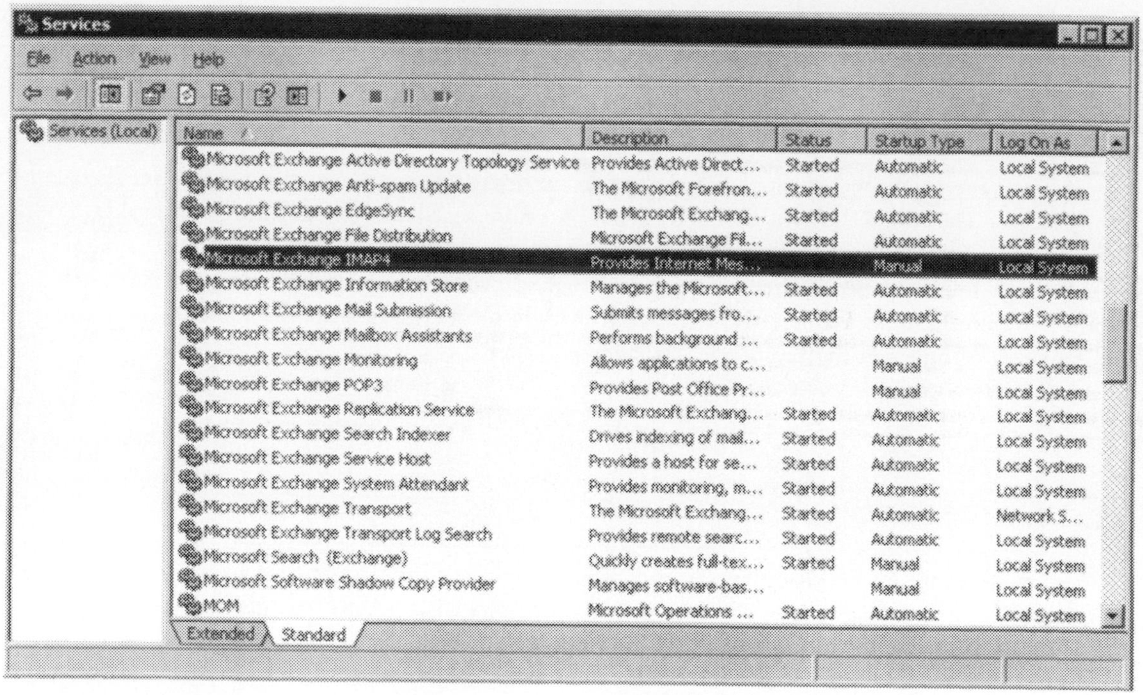

Then drill down and open the property page for **Microsoft Exchange POP3**, as shown in Figure 5.55. Select **Automatic** in the **Startup type** drop-down menu, and then click **Start**.

Figure 5.55 Setting the Service to Automatic Startup

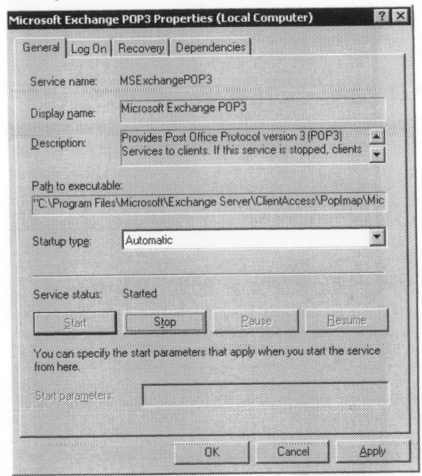

Repeat these steps for the **Microsoft Exchange IMAP4** service, if needed.

NOTE

You can also enable the POP3 and IMAP4 services using the *Set-Service* and *Start-Service* cmdlets in the Exchange Management Shell. To set the services to start automatically, use the ***Set-Service MSExchangePOP3*** and ***Set-Service MSExchangeIMAP4*** cmdlet options, respectively. Next, you can start the services by typing ***Start-Service MSExchangePOP3*** and ***Start-Service MSExchangeIMAP4***.

When you have enabled the POP3 or IMAP4 service, you can verify functionality by making a telnet call to the Client Access Server on port 110 or 143, respectively. To do so, open a Command Prompt window and type: Telnet <server> 110 or Telnet <server> 143, and press Enter. You will then get the POP3 or IMAP4 banner, as shown in Figure 5.56.

Figure 5.56 Verifying the Service Is Running

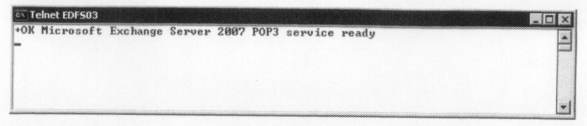

Configuring the POP3 or IMAP4 Services

In order to configure more specific settings for the POP3 or IMAP4 services, you must use the *Set-PopSettings* and *Set-ImapSettings* cmdlets. We won't dive further into the parameters available with these commands, but instead will briefly mention that you can configure features such as *maximum connections, connection timeouts, banner to displayed, login method*, and so on.

To see a full list of each parameter available, as well as their descriptions, type either Get-Help Set-PopSettings or Get-Help Set-ImapSettings, depending on which service you want to configure further.

Limiting Access to the POP3 and IMAP4 Service

When the POP3 and IMAP4 services have been started, all mailbox-enabled users can access their mailbox using one of these two services. Since there might be situations where you want to lock down access to these two services to a specific set of users (for example, in a shared hosting environment), I thought it would be a good idea to show you how to set access these services on a per-user basis.

To enable or disable access to POP3, use the following cmdlets:

```
Set-CASMailbox <user mailbox> -ImapEnabled $true
```

```
Set-CASMailbox <user mailbox> -ImapEnabled $false
```

To enable or disable access to IMAP4, use the following cmdlets:

```
Set-CASMailbox <user mailbox> -PopEnabled $true
```

```
Set-CASMailbox <user mailbox> -PopEnabled $false
```

If you need to enable or disable one of these services for thousands of users, you could make use of piping. Let's say you wanted to enable IMAP4 access to all users with a mailbox on a particular Exchange 2007 Server, you could type:

```
Get-Mailbox <servername> | Set-CASMailbox -ImapEnabled $true
```

Of course this is just a simple command to show you how powerful the Exchange Management Shell is when it comes to bulk-enabling a feature for a set of users.

Summary

In this chapter, we had a look inside the services that are provided by, and can be configured for, an Exchange 2007 Server with the Client Access Server role installed. As you have seen throughout the chapter, many tasks can be performed on this server role. The CAS role is the one responsible for providing access to the AutoDiscover and Availability Services, used by features such as free/busy information, Unified Messaging, Out of Office messages, and Offline Address Books, as well as providing auto-profile settings to Outlook 2007 clients. Since the CAS replaces the earlier front-end server we know from Exchange 2000 and 2003, this server role is also responsible for proxying Internet clients such as Outlook Anywhere (formerly known as RPC over HTTP), Exchange ActiveSync devices, Outlook Web Access (OWA), and, finally, POP3 and IMAP4 to the Mailbox servers in the organization.

Solutions Fast Track

Managing the Exchange 2007 Client Access Server

☑ The Client Access Server role replaces the front-end server we know from Exchange 2000 and 2003, and adds some additional functionality.

☑ The Client Access Server is also responsible for providing access to the Offline Address Book (OAB), but only for Outlook 2007 clients—Outlook 2007 being the only client version that can take advantage of the new Web-based distribution method.

☑ The AutoDiscover service and the Availability service are two new Web-based services that provide functionalities such as automated profile configuration, free/busy time, meeting suggestions, and Out of Office (OOF) messages.http://blogs.msdn.com/mca/rss.xml. Another Web-based service on the CAS is the Unified Messaging (UM) service, which provides automatic UM settings in Outlook 2007.

☑ The Client Access Server should always be deployed on a domain-member server, on the internal network, and not in the DMZ (which many thought was a security best practice for Exchange 2000 or 2003 front-end servers).

The AutoDiscover Service

☑ The AutoDiscover service simplifies Outlook client deployment by creating an automatic connection between Exchange Server and Outlook 2007 clients without the need for using special scripts, complex user intervention, or tools such as the Custom Installation Wizard from the Office Resource Kit.

☑ If you're configuring an Outlook 2007 profile on a machine logged on to the Active Directory, AutoDiscover will fetch the domain account information from the logged-on user credentials, meaning you only have to click Next a few times and that's it.

☑ When the Client Access Server role is installed on an Exchange 2007 Server, a virtual IIS directory named AutoDiscover is created under the Default Web Site.

☑ When installing the CAS, a new object named the *service connection point (SCP)* is also created in Active Directory. The SCP object contains the authoritative list of AutoDiscover service URLs in the forest, and can be updated using the *Set-ClientAccessServer* cmdlet.

The Availability Service

☑ The purpose of the Availability service is to provide secure, consistent, and up-to-date (that is, data in real time!) free/busy data to clients using this service. Since only Outlook 2007 and OWA 2007 can take advantage of this new service, legacy clients such as Outlook 2003 and earlier, as well as OWA 2003, still depend on a Public Folder database containing the SCHEDULE+ FREE/BUSY system folder.

☑ Since only Outlook 2007 and OWA 2007 can use the Availability service to obtain free/busy information, it's important that Exchange 2007 can interact with legacy systems, too.

☑ Outlook 2007 discovers the Availability Service URL using the AutoDiscover service. Actually, the AutoDiscover service is like a DNS Web Service for Outlook, since it's used to find various services like Availability Service, UM, and OAB. It simply tells Outlook 2007 where to go when searching for these Web services.

Client Access Servers and the SSL Certificate Dilemma

☑ In previous versions of Exchange, you simply issued a request for an SSL certificate, and when received, assigned this certificate to the Default Web Site in the IIS Manager. But in Exchange 2007, it is a different beast when it comes to securing client connectivity to the CAS using SSL certificates.

☑ A default self-signed SSL certificate is assigned to the Default Web Site during the installation of the Exchange 2007 CAS role. If you take a closer look at this certificate, you'll notice that it contains *multiple subject alternative names*.

☑ An SSL certificate that supports additional *subject alternative names* typically costs in the range of $600 per year.

Managing Outlook Anywhere

☑ Outlook Anywhere makes it possible for your end users to remotely access their mailbox from the Internet using their full Outlook client. Those of you with Exchange 2003 experience most likely know the technology behind the Outlook Anywhere feature already since Outlook Anywhere is just an improved version of RPC over HTTP.

☑ The technology behind Outlook Anywhere is basically the same as in Exchange 2003 since it still works by encapsulating the RPC-based MAPI traffic inside an HTTPS session, which then is directed toward the server running the RPC over HTTP proxy component on your internal network. This gives you the same functionality as you get by using the

Outlook client from a machine on your internal network. When the HTTPS packets reach the RPC over HTTP proxy server, all the RPC MAPI traffic is removed from the HTTPS packets and forwarded to the respective Mailbox server.

☑ In order to use Outlook Anywhere, you must install a valid Secure Sockets Layer (SSL) certificate from a trusted Certificate Authority (CA) that the clients trust by default.

Managing Outlook Web Access 2007

☑ During the development of Exchange Server 2007, one of the goals for the Exchange Product group was to make the best Web mail client in the world even better. In order to do this, Outlook Web Access (OWA) 2007 was completely rewritten in managed code to make it scale even better and make it easier to add new features to the GUI in the future. Speaking about the GUI, one thing you'll notice immediately is that the interface has been completely redesigned.

☑ OWA 2007 supports 47 different languages in total!

☑ Forms-based authentication is enabled by default, unlike OWA 2003 where you had to enable this feature manually.

☑ We can specify whether our OWA users should be able to access files from internal Windows File Shares or Windows SharePoint Services. OWA 2007 has a document access feature built right into the UI, which makes it possible for the users to access documents on any of these types of servers.

☑ OWA Light is the solution for all browsers and operating systems other than IE6 or IE7 on a Windows platform. So if you're a Firefox, Mac, or even a Linux user, or simply just a user of something other than IE6+, this Web mail client is for you.

☑ The new URL for OWA 2007 is https://mobile.domain.com/owa.

☑ Just as with previous versions of Exchange, you can simplify the URL to OWA in order to provide an even better experience for your end users.

Managing Exchange ActiveSync

☑ One of the features that has really been improved in Exchange Server 2007 is, without a doubt, the Exchange ActiveSync communication protocol. Exchange Server ActiveSync is still based on the DirectPush technology (sometimes also referred to as AUTD v2) that was introduced in Exchange Server 2003 SP2. This improves the mobile messaging experience for your users by providing close to real-time over-the-air access to your e-mail messages, schedules, contacts, tasks lists, and other Exchange server mailbox data.

☑ DirectPush is the only method you can use when synchronizing your mailbox using Exchange ActiveSync (EAS) in Exchange Server 2007, and is therefore enabled by default. That means AUTD v1, which was based on text messaging (SMS), has been dropped.

☑ DirectPush works by keeping an HTTPS connection alive between a mobile device and the Exchange 2007 CAS server. Because DirectPush uses long-standing HTTPS requests, it's important that both your mobile carrier and your firewall are configured with a time-out value from the default to between 15 and 30 minutes. If a short time-out value is configured, it will cause the device to initiate a new HTTPS request much more frequently, which not only shortens battery life on your device, but becomes more expensive since more data will be transferred.

☑ With Exchange Server 2007, it's possible to create multiple Exchange ActiveSync policies, giving you much more control of your mobile deployment.

Managing POP3/IMAP4

☑ Like its predecessors, Exchange Server 2007 also supports the Post Office Protocol version 3 (POP3) and Internet Message Access Protocol version 4 (IMAP4) clients, but since these client types aren't that popular anymore (especially with the evolution of Outlook Anywhere, a superb Web mail client and EAS), they are disabled by default.

☑ Both the POP3 and IMAP4 protocols have been rewritten from the ground up in managed code, and are no longer dependant on the IIS component. Instead, they run as a separate Windows Service.

☑ Other things worth noting about POP3 and IMAP4 services in Exchange Server 2007, is the fact that we are limited to one POP3 or IMAP4 service per server, and the same SSL certificate must be used for all POP3 and IMAP4 connections to the respective Client Access Server.

☑ When the POP3 and IMAP4 services have been started, all mailbox-enabled users can access their mailbox using one of these two services. Since there might be situations where you want to lock down access to these two services to a specific set of users (for example, in a shared hosting environment), you can use the Exchange Management Shell cmdlets *Set-PopSettings* and *Set-ImapSettings* to enable or disable specific users individually.

Frequently Asked Questions

Q: Can the CAS be used to proxy requests to Exchange 2000 or 2003 back-end servers?

A: Yes, the CAS is capable of proxying requests to both Exchange 2000 and 2003 back-end servers.

Q: If I deploy a CAS in my legacy Exchange organization, will I get the OWA 2007 UI when logging on to OWA?

A: No. As is also the case with previous versions of Exchange, you will always get the UI of the back-end server. So, in this case you'll get the OWA 2003 UI.

Q: How can I configure the /owa virtual directory using the Exchange Management Shell?

A: You can use the *Set-OwaVirtualDirectory* cmdlet to configure OWA-related settings via the Exchange Management Shell. For example, in order to enable forms-based authentication for the /owa virtual directory, you would need to run the following command: *Set-OwaVirtualDirectory -Identity "owa (default Web site)" -FormsAuthentication:$true*. For more information about available parameters, type **Get-Help Set-OwaVirtualDirectory** in the Exchange Management Shell.

Q: I've noticed an SSL certificate is installed on the Default Web Site, by default. Would you recommend I replace it?

A: Yes, if you plan on using all of the Mobile Exchange 2007 features, OWA, ActiveSync, and Outlook Anywhere since they require the *subject alternative name* in the SSL cert to match what is configured on the client for accessibility from the Internet.

Q: Can I assign an Exchange 2007 ActiveSync Mailbox Policy to a legacy (Exchange 2000 or 2003) Exchange mailbox?

A: No. You can only assign Exchange 2007 ActiveSync Mailbox policies to mailboxes stored on Exchange 2007 Mailbox Servers.

Q: Does CAS support clustering?

A: No, only Exchange 2007 Mailbox servers can be clustered (using Single Copy Cluster or Cluster Continuous Replication), but you can use NLB to load balance CAS roles—either using Windows NLB or some sort of hardware solution.

Q: Where does the UI rendering for OWA 2007 take place?

A: Unlike OWA 2003, which did all the UI rendering on the back-end server, OWA 2007 now does all the UI rendering on the CAS and thereby significantly reduces the load on the Mailbox server.

Q: I can't seem to find the place where you manage the POP3 and IMAP4 services in the Exchange Management Console?

A: That is because there is no UI for these services. You must configure these two services using the Exchange Management Shell since the Exchange Product group didn't add management tasks for the services to the EMC. Expect these services to be added to the UI in Exchange 2007 Service Pack 1.

Chapter 6

Managing the Hub Transport Server Role

Solutions in this chapter:

- **Message Transport and Routing Architecture in Exchange 2007**

- **Managing the Hub Transport Server**

- **Managing Message Size and Recipient Limits**

- **Message Tracking with Exchange Server 2007**

- **Using the Exchange 2007 Queue Viewer**

- **Introduction to the Exchange Mail Flow Troubleshooter Tool**

- **Configuring the Hub Transport Server as an Internet-facing Transport Server**

☑ **Summary**

☑ **Solutions Fast Track**

☑ **Frequently Asked Questions**

Introduction

The Exchange 2007 Hub Transport server role should be installed on a domain-member server, and should always be deployed on your internal network, not in the perimeter network as some might. The Hub Transport server replaces the bridgehead server we know from Exchange 2000 and 2003, and therefore takes care of all the internal mail flow in the organization. All internal messages will pass through the Hub Transport server, even if the sender and recipient mailbox are located in the same AD site—heck, even if they're on the same Mailbox server!

In addition to being responsible for all mail flow inside the organization, the Hub Transport server has a set of transport agents that lets us configure rules and settings that can then be applied as messages pass through the server. The Hub Transport server also allows us to create messaging policies and rule settings that match the specific regulations and compliance requirements in the organization.

Since the Hub Transport server typically sends and receives Internet messages through an Edge Transport server in the perimeter network, it doesn't have any anti-spam agents installed, and doesn't allow inbound messages from unauthenticated (untrusted) e-mail servers on the Internet—at least not in its default state. Since not all organizations can, nor will, deploy an Edge Transport server in their perimeter network, I'll show you how you can configure the Hub Transport server to be the Internet-facing transport server in your organization.

Message Transport and Routing Architecture in Exchange 2007

A lot has changed in regards to transport and routing architecture in Exchange Server 2007. First, Exchange no longer uses the SMTP protocol stack included with Internet Information Services (IIS), as was the case with previous versions of the product. Instead, the Exchange Product group has rewritten the SMTP transport stack in managed code, resulting in a much more stable and secure protocol stack. For example, the new transport stack runs as the Network Service account and uses several new mechanisms that reduce the risks associated with Denial-of-Service attacks and other security issues. The new SMTP transport stack is now known as the Microsoft Exchange Transport service (MSExchangeTransport.exe), and because it's no longer dependent on IIS, it is not located within the IIS Manager anymore. As a matter of fact, you don't even install IIS on the Hub Transport server unless it's combined with the Mailbox or Client Access server role on the same hardware.

You no longer need to set up routing group connectors between routing groups in the Exchange organization when you design your Exchange topology, as there is no such functionality built into the Exchange 2007 product. "Why has this flexible way of routing messages throughout an Exchange organization been removed?" I hear some of you grumble. Well, routing groups actually have several drawbacks, including long stretches of time where two servers disagree about a connection state, possibly causing routing loops. Another drawback is that when tracking a message, it can be quite confusing when trying to determine why a message took a given route at a given point in time, because the link state table for the Exchange topology was never persistent or logged. Lastly, the routing groups and routing group connector concept forced Exchange administrators to re-create and mimic the underlying network, which can be quite a time-consuming and even redundant task.

So how do you set up your routing topology in Exchange Server 2007? Well, you don't! Exchange Server 2007 is a site-aware application, which means it can determine its own Active Directory site membership and the Active Directory site membership of other servers by querying Active Directory. So, instead of using its own routing group topology, Exchange makes use of the AD directory service site topology to determine how messages are transported in the organization. This means that the Hub Transport servers in your Exchange organization retrieve information from Active Directory in order to determine how messages should be routed between servers. You need to deploy a Hub Transport server in each site that contains a Mailbox server, such that when user A in one site sends a message to user B in another site, the Mailbox server contacts the Hub Transport server in its own site, and then routes the message to the Hub Transport server in user B's site, ultimately delivering the message to the mailbox server hosting user B's mailbox.

NOTE

All Hub Transport servers use secure SMTP when exchanging messages internally in the organization. They use the industry standard SMTP Transport Layer Security (TLS) so that all traffic between the Hub Transport servers are authenticated and encrypted. This removes the capability for internal snooping. In addition, all RPC communication between Hub Transport and Mailbox servers is encrypted.

I've tried to illustrate how messages are routed in a basic Exchange 2007 organization in Figure 6.1. Notice that the Mailbox and Hub Transport servers use RPC as the basis of communication, but that two Hub Transport servers speak SMTP when exchanging messages.

Figure 6.1 Path for Message Sent from a User in One AD Site to a User in Another AD Site

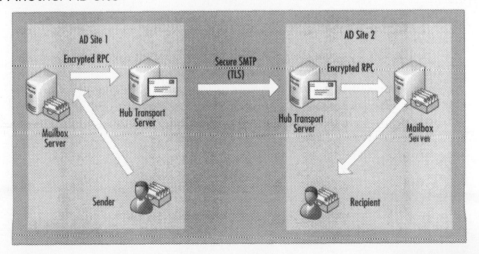

NOTE

When multiple paths exist to a specific AD site, a Hub Transport server will use deterministic algorithms to choose one of the available paths. Since one of the paths will always be chosen, the algorithms are deterministic. To read more about AD site and connector selection algorithms used by routing, see the following blog post on the MS Exchange Team blog: http://msexchangeteam.com/archive/2006/09/15/428920.aspx

When a Hub Transport server in an AD site establishes an SMTP connection to a Hub Transport server in another AD site, in order to deliver a message, it makes use of round-robin load balancing mechanisms. This means that if the first Hub Transport server contacted doesn't respond to a connection, it will try to establish an SMTP connection to the next Hub Transport server in the AD site. This makes Hub Transport servers are fault-tolerant out of the box.

Since routing is determined from Active Directory sites, the Exchange link state update functionality, used in previous versions of Exchange, has been discontinued. The link state functionality of old was used by each routing group master to update and keep their link state tables current, propagating this information back to the other Exchange Servers in the organization. The use of Active Directory sites in Exchange 2007 creates a more deterministic routing topology.

Managing the Hub Transport Server

All organizationwide Hub Transport settings are stored in Active Directory. This means that any modifications or configuration settings, except receive connector specific settings, are reflected on all Hub Transport servers in the organization. In the following, we'll go through each of the tabs available under the Hub Transport subnode shown in Figure 6.2. Since it would be silly to cover the receive connectors in a section of their own, they will be included in this section as well.

Remote Domains

The first tab is the Remote Domains tab. Here, you can configure message transfer settings between Exchange 2007 and external SMTP domains. When you set up a remote domain, you can control mail flow with more precision, designate message formatting and policy, and specify acceptable character sets for messages that are sent to, and received from, the remote domain. As you can see in Figure 6.2, there's a default remote domain entry configured after installation of the Hub Transport server role. The domain address space is configured as *, which represents all external domains. This means the settings configured in the remote domain entry are applied to all outbound messages. If you have specific requirements for one or more external SMTP domain names, you can configure additional remote domain entries as necessary. I'll show you how a new remote domain entry is created later on, but first let's take a look at the settings configured for the default remote domain entry. When looking at the Properties of the Default Remote Domains entry, you are presented with the General tab, as shown in Figure 6.3.

Figure 6.2 Available Tabs under the Hub Transport Node

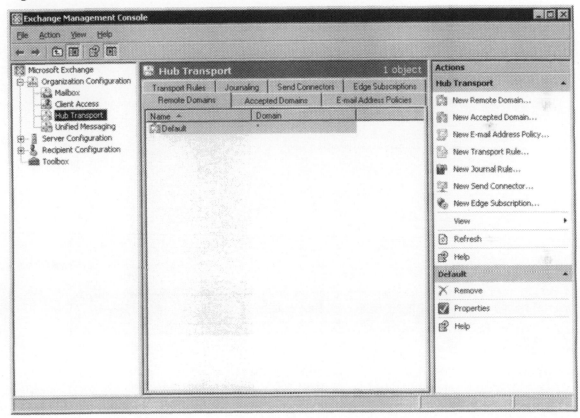

Figure 6.3 Out-of-Office Message Options

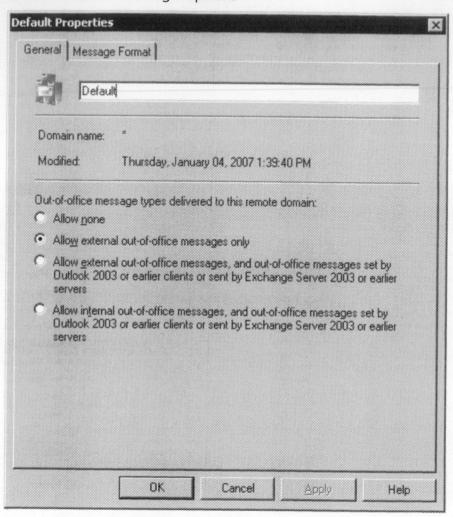

Here, we can specify how the Hub Transport server should handle out of office (OOF) messages to the specified SMTP domains in the remote domains entry. We have four options to choose from:

- **Allow none**   No out-of-office messages will be delivered to the remote domain.

- **Allow external out-of-office messages only**   Only out-of-office messages configured as external using an Outlook 2007 or OWA 2007 client, and where the respective mailbox is stored on an Exchange 2007 Mailbox server, will be delivered to the remote domain.

- **Allow external out-of-office messages, and out-of-office messages set by Outlook 2003 or earlier clients or sent by Exchange Server 2003 or earlier servers** Out-of-office messages that are configured as external with an Outlook 2007 or OWA 2007 client, and where the respective mailbox is stored on an Exchange 2007 Mailbox server, will be delivered to the remote domain. In addition, out-of-office messages set by Outlook 2003 and earlier, regardless of the server version of their mailbox store, will be delivered to the remote domain. In other words, out-of-office messages that are sent by Exchange 2003 or earlier servers, no matter what client version was used to set the out-of-office message, will be delivered to the remote domain.

- **Allow internal out-of-office messages, and out-of-office messages set by Outlook 2003 or earlier clients or sent by Exchange Server 2003 or earlier servers** Only out-of-office messages that are configured as external with an Outlook 2007 or OWA 2007 client, and where the respective mailbox is stored on an Exchange 2007 Mailbox server, will be delivered to the remote domain. In addition out-of-office messages that are set by Outlook 2003 and earlier, regardless of the server version of their mailbox store, will be delivered to the remote domain. Out-of-office messages that are sent by Exchange 2003 or earlier servers, no matter what client version was used to set the out-of-office message, will be delivered to the remote domain.

The *Allow external out-of-office messages only* option is selected by default.

Let's continue on to the next tab, the Message Format tab, shown in Figure 6.4. I bet this tab looks familiar to many of you, as it's very similar to the one we all know from Exchange 2003, although Exchange 2007 offers a few new options.

The following is a short description of each option under the Message Format tab:

- **Allow automatic replies** This option allows automatic replies to be sent to the remote domain.

- **Allow automatic forward** This option will allow automatic forwards to be sent to the remote domain.

- **Allow delivery reports** This option allows delivery reports to be sent to all recipients in any remote domain.

- **Allow non-delivery reports** This option allows NDRs to be sent to all recipients in any remote domain.

- **Display sender's name on messages** This option allows a user's display name to be visible to the recipient of the message.

- **Use message text line wrap at column** If you want to use line-wrap in message text for outgoing messages, this option should be enabled. When enabled, you must specify the line-wrap size (between 0 and 132 characters). To set the value to unlimited, leave the field blank.

Figure 6.4 Message Format Options

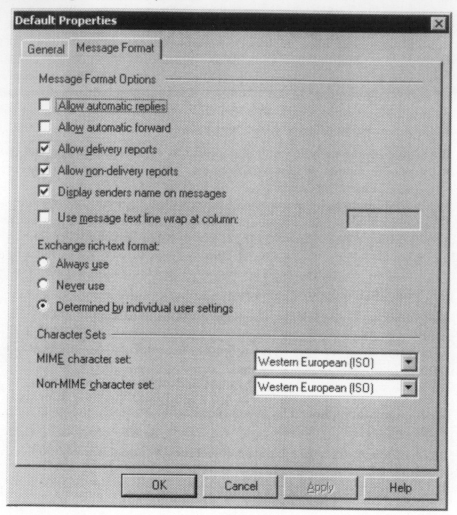

Creating a New Remote Domains Entry

To create a new Remote Domains entry, click **New Remote Domain** in the Action pane. This will launch the New Remote Domain wizard shown in Figure 6.5. Here, you simply need to enter a name for the new entry, as well as specify the external SMTP domain to which you want to apply the settings. If the domain contains subdomains, you may also want to check **Include all subdomains**. When you have entered the necessary information, click **New** and then **Finish** on the completion page.

Figure 6.5 The New Remote Domain Page

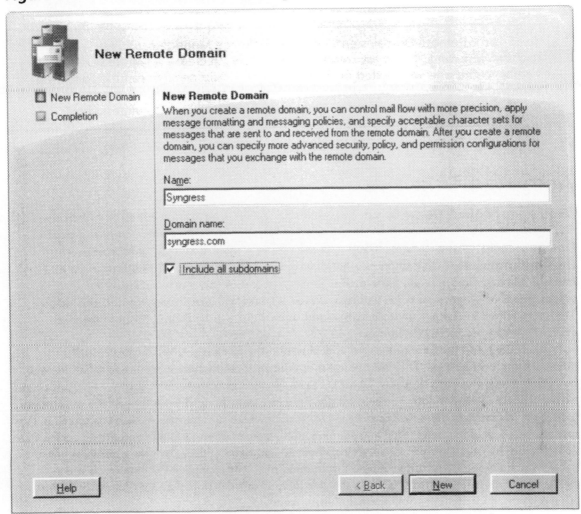

Notice that you don't specify the different settings during the creation of the Remote Domains entry. Instead, this is done by opening the Property page of the remote domain entry after the fact.

TIP

To create a Remote Domains entry via the Exchange Management Shell, you need to use the *New-RemoteDomain* cmdlet. For example, to create a remote domain entry similar to the one we created in Figure 6.5, you would need to run the following command:

New-RemoteDomain –Name "Syngress" –DomainName "*.syngress.com".

Accepted Domains

Under the **Accepted Domains** tab, we specify the SMTP domains for which our Exchange 2007 organization should either be authoritative, relay to an e-mail server in another Active Directory Forest within the organization, or relay to an e-mail server outside the respective Exchange organization. The difference between internal and external relayed domains is that internal relaying simply sends the e-mail messages directly to the e-mail server in the organization. Messages sent to an external relayed domain will first be delivered to the Edge Transport server in the perimeter network, and from there will be routed to the respective external e-mail server on the Internet.

When the first Hub Transport server is deployed in the Exchange 2007 organization, the domain name of the Active Directory Forest root domain is configured as an authoritative domain by default. Since the Hub Transport server has been installed into an Active Directory Forest named exchangedogfood.dk, this domain name is the authoritative domain for this Exchange 2007 organization by default (Figure 6.6). Since we use a split-DNS setup, where the internal and external domain names match, we don't need to do any configuration changes after the Hub Transport server has been deployed. Many organizations use an internal domain name that differs from the external domain name, which among other things is used for inbound mail. For example, it's common to use a domain.local domain internally. If this is the case in your organization, you must manually create an accepted domain matching your external domain name.

Figure 6.6 The Properties Page for an Accepted Domain

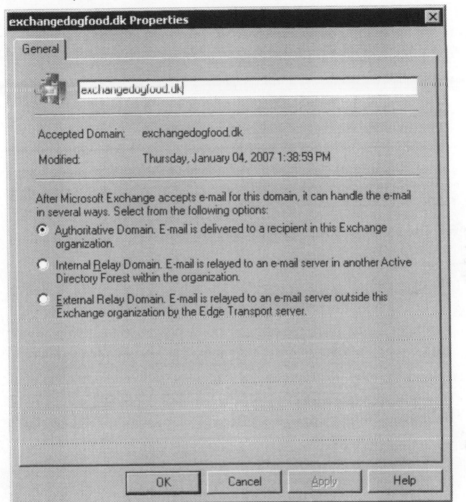

Creating a New Accepted Domain

Creating a new accepted domain is a straightforward task. You simply click **New Accepted Domain** in the Action pane. In the New Accepted Domain wizard, enter a name for the accepted domain entry and the domain for which you want to receive e-mail.

NOTE

Any accepted domain that is added under the Accepted Domains tab can be linked to an E-mail Address Policy (EAP), such that it will generate recipient e-mail addresses for the accepted domain. As a matter of fact, every EAP must link to an accepted domain, such that e-mail messages sent to e-mail addresses specified in an EAP are allowed to be routed by the Hub Transport servers in the organization. You'll see what I mean when we cover e-mail address policies next.

As we already talked about, the Hub Transport server can handle messages for a particular domain in several different ways, as shown in Figure 6.7. Choose the desired option and click New and then Finish on the next page.

Figure 6.7 The New Accepted Domain Wizard

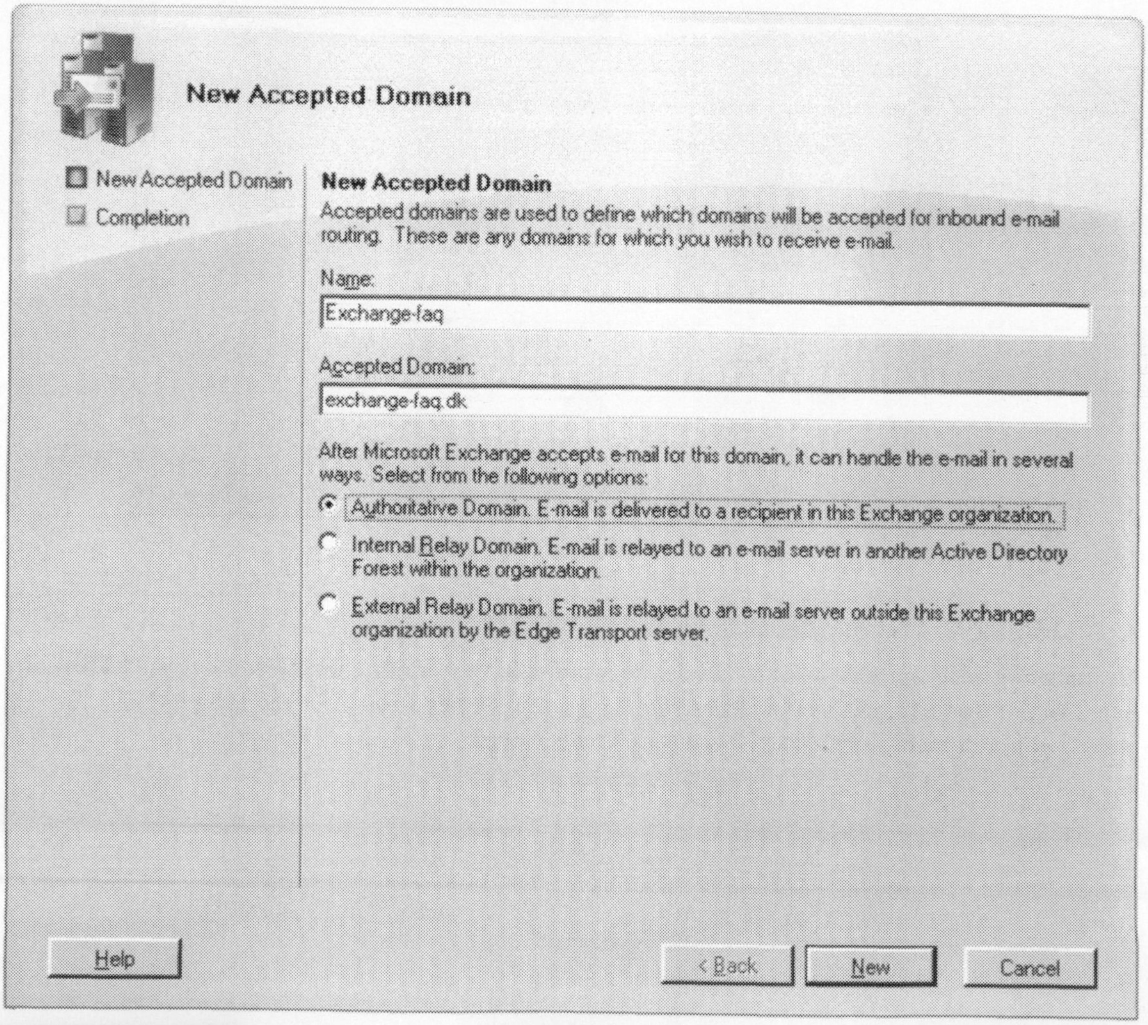

TIP

To create an accepted domain entry via the Exchange Management Shell, you need to use the *New-AcceptedDomain* cmdlet. For example, to create an accepted domain entry similar to the one we created in Figure 6.7, you would need to run the following command:

New-AcceptedDomain –Name "Exchange-faq" –DomainName "exchange-faq.dk" –DomainType "Authoritative"

E-mail Address Policies

E-mail address policies were known as recipient policies back in Exchange 2000 and 2003. Exchange address policies define the proxy addresses stamped onto recipient objects in the Exchange organization. With Exchange 2007, the recipient policies have been separated into two types: accepted domains (which we just covered) and e-mail address policies. Those of you with Exchange 2000 and/or 2003 experience know that recipient policies also controlled which SMTP namespaces were accepted by the Exchange organization. Some of you probably are wondering why these two features were separated in Exchange 2007. The Exchange Product group made this separation for three chief reasons. First, if a domain was specified for an e-mail address recipient policy but wasn't configured as the authoritative domain, the e-mail sent to the recipients with e-mail addresses defined by the policy would not be routed within the Exchange organization for this domain. Even though this is an invalid scenario, the Exchange 2000 and 2003 System Manager allowed this type of configuration. Secondly, the authoritative domain concept was hidden under the e-mail address recipient policy GUI, which wasn't very intuitive for administrators. Lastly, relay domains were controlled via the SMTP connectors GUI, allocated in a completely different location from where the authoritative domains (recipient policies) were controlled.

SOME INDEPENDENT ADVICE

This separation of accepted domain and e-mail address policies is not the only change in regards to e-mail address policies. The infamous Recipient Update Service (RUS), which most of us know from Exchange 2000 and 2003, is also no longer part of the Exchange 2007 product. RUS was responsible for stamping e-mail addresses on AD objects, in addition to address list membership, and a few other things. However, it didn't always work as expected and was very difficult to troubleshoot when it acted up. With Exchange 2007, the RUS (and thereby the asynchronous behavior used to provision objects) has been replaced by a new synchronous process (the *EmailAddressPolicy* cmdlet), which is used to stamp e-mail address onto objects immediately! Yes, you no longer have to wait for several minutes to see e-mail addresses on your objects, as was often the case with the antiquated RUS.

For a detailed explanation about the removal of RUS, see the following blog on the MS Exchange Team blog: http://msexchangeteam.com/archive/2006/10/02/429053.aspx

---

Okay, so to carve it in stone, before you begin creating a new e-mail address policy, you must first add the respective domain name under the Accepted Domains tab.

As you can see in Figure 6.8, we have several e-mail address policies in our Exchange 2007 organization, listed in prioritized order (the lower the number, the higher the priority), as was also the case in Exchange 2000 and 2003. If you want to move a particular policy up the list, highlight the policy and click Change Priority in the Action pane. You must have at least two EAPs aside from the default in order to see the Change Priority Action pane option.

Figure 6.8 A Prioritized List of the E-mail Address Policies in the Organization

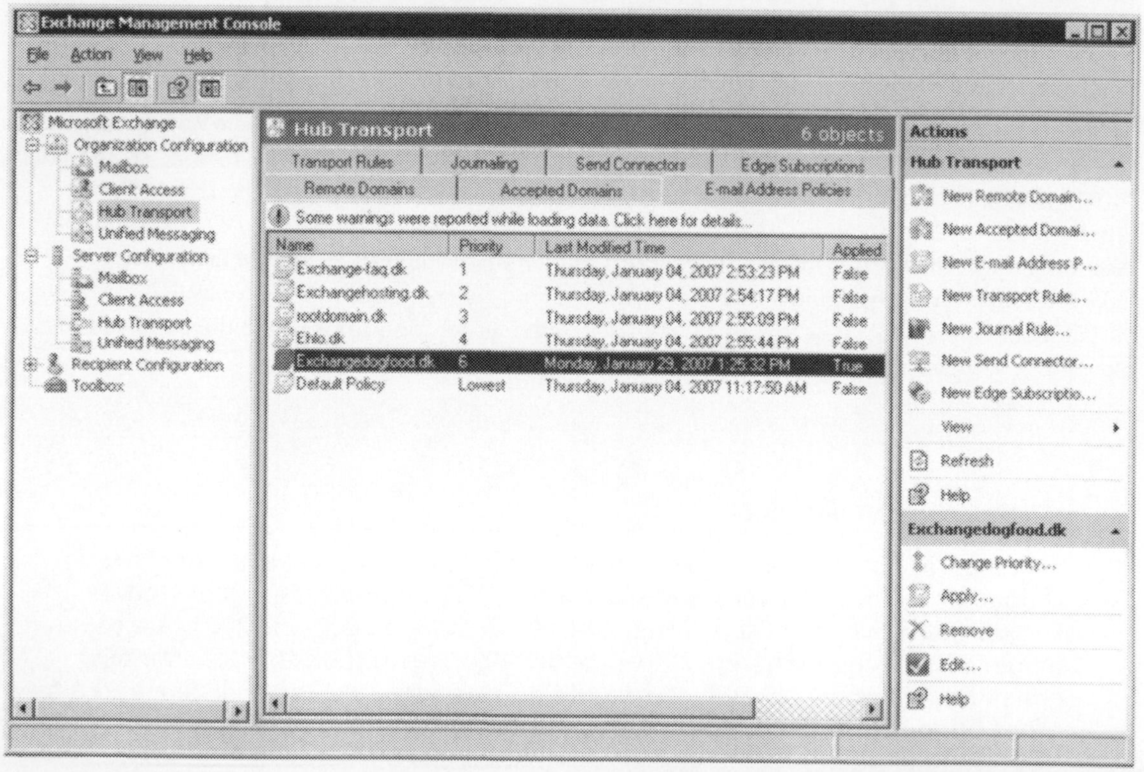

Creating a New E-mail Address Policy

Creating a new e-mail address policy is a straightforward task, although much different from Exchange 2000 and 2003. In order to do so, perform the following steps:

1. Click **New E-mail Address Policy** in the Action pane.

2. On the Introduction page of the New E-Mail Address Policy wizard, enter a *name* for the new policy, and then specify what type of recipients should be included (Figure 6.9). Afterward, click **Next**.

Figure 6.9 The New E-Mail Address Policy Window

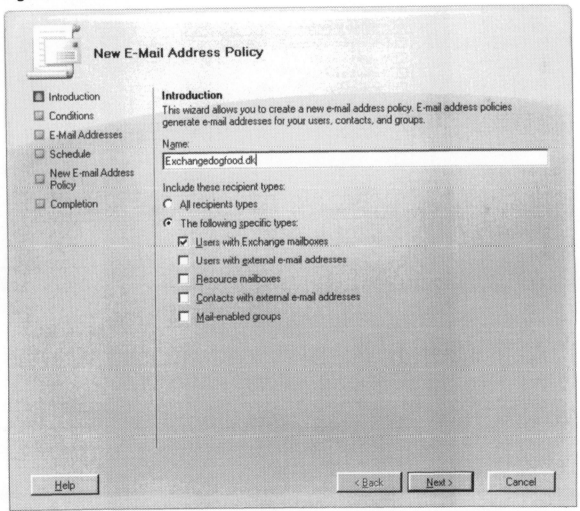

3. You can now be a bit more selective when defining your target group by using the filter
    and selecting one or more conditions, as shown in Figure 6.10. When you have configured
    any conditions you want applied to the policy, click **Next**.

Figure 6.10 The New E-Mail Address Wizard Conditions Page

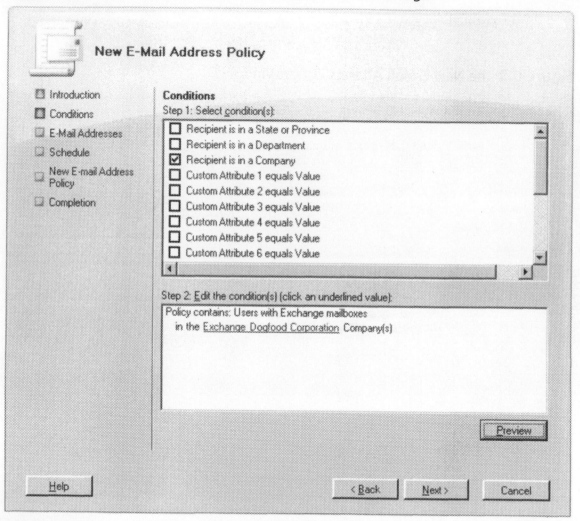

4. Click **Add** and select the **E-mail address local part** to be used to create the username portion of the e-mail address. Then, choose an e-mail domain from the **E-mail address domain** in the drop-down box, as shown in Figure 6.11. When ready, click **OK** and **Next**.

Figure 6.11 Specifying the Local Part of the E-mail Addresses and the E-mail Address Domain

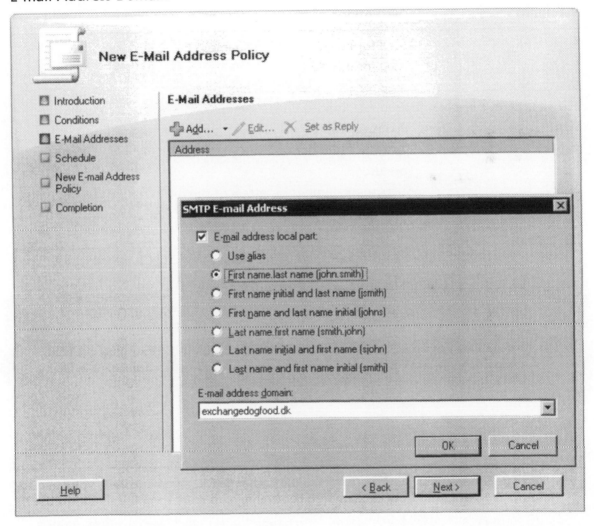

As you can see in Figure 6.11, you can choose between seven local e-mail address parts. The local part of an e-mail address is the name format appearing before the *at sign* (@). If none of the default seven local parts fit what you need to use for your e-mail address policy, you can use the variables listed in Table 6.1.

Table 6.1 Available E-Mail Address Parameters

Variable	Description
%g	Used for given name (first name)
%i	Used for middle initial
%s	Used for surname (last name)
%d	Used for display name
%m	Used for Exchange alias
%xs	Uses the x number of letters of the surname. For example, if x = 2, then the first two letters of the surname are used.
%xg	Uses the x number of letters of the given name. For example, if x = 2, then the first two letters of the given name are used.

5. On the **Schedule** page, specify when the e-mail address policy should be applied and the maximum length of time it is permitted to run (Figure 6.12). Then, click **Next**.

6. On the **Configuration Summary** page, click **New**. If you selected to apply the policy immediately, the proxy address will now be applied to all recipients matching the filter. When this task has completed, click **Finish** on the Completion page.

TIP

To create a new e-mail address policy via the Exchange Management Shell, you need to use the *New-EmailAddressPolicy* cmdlet. For example, to create a policy similar to the one we created using the GUI wizard, you would need to run the following command:
New-EmailAddressPolicy –Name "Exchangedogfood.dk" –IncludedRecipients "MailboxUsers" –ConditionalCompany "Exchange Dogfood Corporation" –Priority "Lowest" –EnabledEmailAddressTemplates "SMTP:%g.%s@exchangedogfood.dk"

Figure 6.12 The New E-Mail Address Wizard Schedule Page

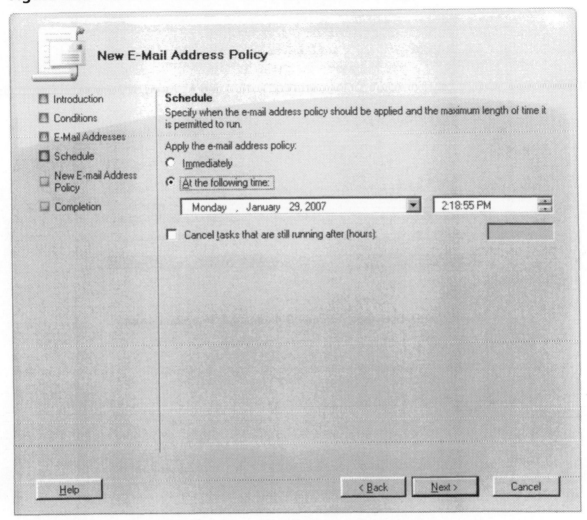

When a new E-mail address policy has been created and applied to the recipients, you can verify that the proxy address has been stamped on the respective user objects under the **E-Mail Addresses** tab on the Properties page of a recipient object, as shown in Figure 6.13.

Figure 6.13 The E-mail Addresses Tab on the User Mailbox Property Page

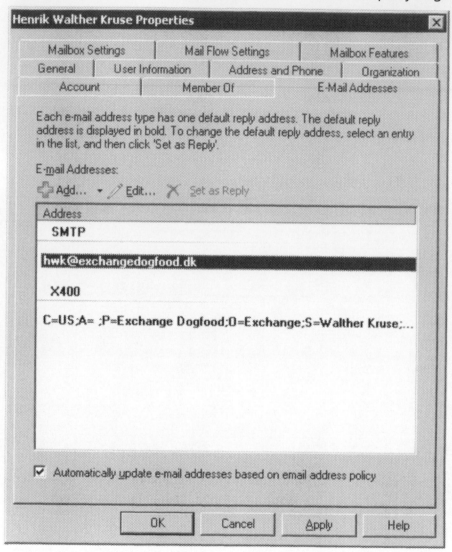

When a recipient has Automatically Update E-mail Addresses Based On Email Address Policy option enabled, all primary e-mail addresses (default reply addresses) of e-mail address types will always be set from the e-mail address policy. This means that if you edit the primary address to be a different e-mail address, it will always revert back to the one specified in the e-mail address policy.

Transport Rules

With the increasing complexity of government and industry regulations, there's a greater need for efficient management of internal message routing. Exchange 2007, or more specifically the Hub Transport Server role, now includes a new transport rules agent, providing an easy and flexible way to set rules for internal message routing and content restriction throughout the Exchange organization. We can now, for example, append disclaimers to all messages sent within the organization, or create an ethical wall between two departments or groups that exchange confidential data every day. An ethical wall can help isolate an individual or group from information to which they should not have access.

Transport rules consist of three components: conditions, exceptions, and actions. These rules can be created under the **Transport Rules** tab. I'll demonstrate to you how easy it is, for example, to append a disclaimer to all messages sent within the organization. To do so, perform the following steps:

1. Click the **Transport Rules** tab shown back in Figure 6.2.

2. Click **New Transport Rule** in the Action pane.

3. On the **Introduction** page of the New Transport Rule wizard, type **Corporate Disclaimer**, and enter a relevant *comment*, as shown in Figure 6.14.

Figure 6.14 The New Transport Rule Wizard Introduction Page

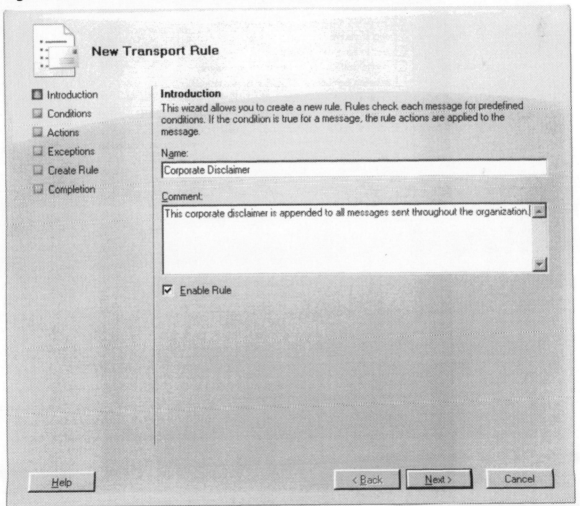

4. Click **Next**.

5. On the **Conditions** page, check **from users inside or outside the organization** (Figure 6.15), and then click **Next**.

Figure 6.15 The New Transport Rule Wizard Conditions Page

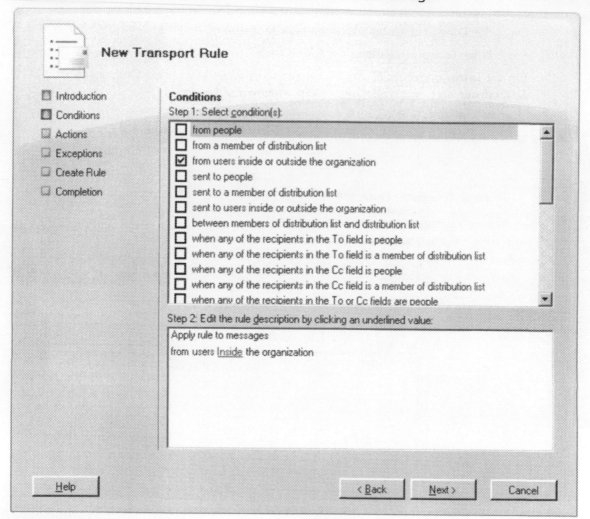

6. Now, check **append disclaimer text using font, size, color, with separator and fallback to action if unable to apply**. In Step 2, click the *disclaimer text* link shown in Figure 6.16.

Figure 6.16 The New Transport Rule Wizard Actions Page

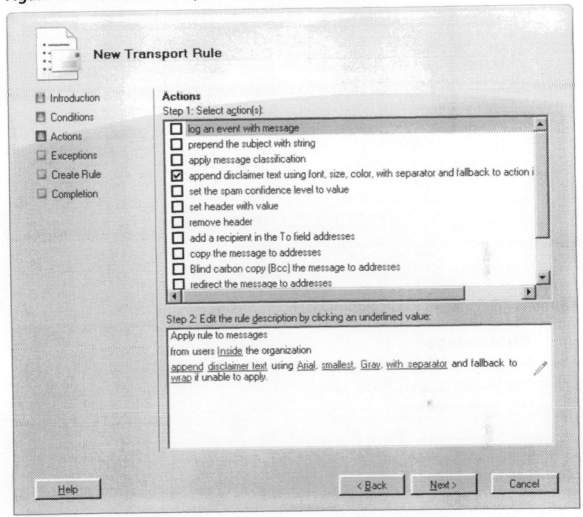

7. In the **Disclaimer text** box, type the disclaimer you want to be appended to messages inside your organization. When finished, click **OK**, as shown in Figure 6.17.

8. Click **Next**.

9. On the **Exceptions** page, click **Next**.

10. Click **New** on the **Create Rule (Configuration Summary)** page.

11. On the **Completion** page, click **Finish**.

Figure 6.17 The Specify Disclaimer Text Box

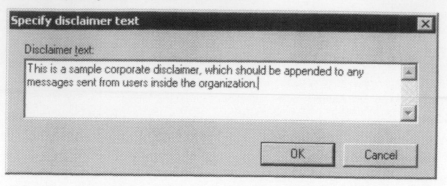

Now, any message sent from a user within the organization will have a disclaimer appended to each outgoing message, like the one shown in Figure 6.18.

Figure 6.18 A Test Message with Disclaimer Appended

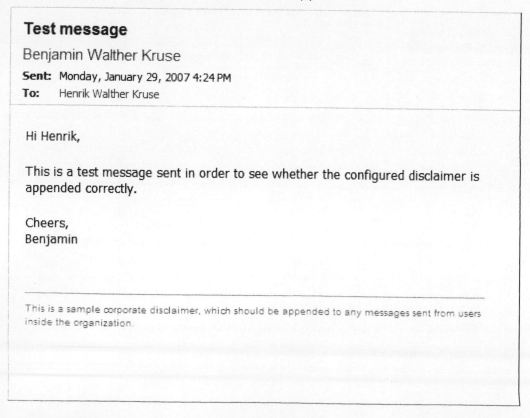

Any time after a transport rule has been created, you can modify it as required. You do this by selecting the rule and clicking **Edit Rule** in the Action pane.

TIP

To create a transport rule via the Exchange Management Shell, you need to use the *New-TransportRule* cmdlet. For example, to create a rule similar to the one we generated using the GUI wizard, you would need to run the following command:

New-TransportRule –Name "Corporate Disclaimer" –Comments "This corporate disclaimer is appended to all messages sent throughout the organization." –Conditions "Microsoft.Exchange.MessagingPolicies.Rules.Tasks.FromScopePredicate" –Actions "Microsoft.Exchange.MessagingPolicies.Rules.Tasks.ApplyDisclaimerAction" –Exceptions –Enabled $true –Priority "0"

Journaling

Exchange Server 2003 natively supported journaling on a per *mailbox store* level. This functionality is also included in Exchange Server 2007, and is known as *standard journaling*. Standard journaling allows you as an Exchange administrator to enable journaling on a *per mailbox database* level. There's not much to say about standard journaling, other than that it is enabled on the property page of a Mailbox database. It then simply works.

Although standard journaling is sufficient for some, it's too basic for most organizations today. Keeping up with increasing regulatory and compliance regulations requires a much richer archival solution. Therefore, Exchange 2007 also includes premium journaling, a Hub Transport server feature based on a new journaling agent that can be configured to match the specific needs of an organization. Premium journaling lets you create journal rules for single mailbox recipients or for entire groups within the organization.

NOTE

Premium journaling, also known as per-recipient journaling, requires an Exchange Enterprise Client Access License (CAL).

Rules can apply to inbound or outbound messages, or both. In addition, the scope can apply to global, internal or external messages. The messages can be archived to any SMTP address, meaning you are not forced to archive to an Exchange mailbox anymore, but can archive to an Exchange-hosted archive solution. You can even archive to a third-party archive solution.

In order to create a journal rule, perform the following steps:

1. With the **Journaling** tab selected, click **New Journal Rule**.

2. In the New Journal Rule wizard (Figure 6.19), enter a *descriptive name*.

Figure 6.19 The New Journal Rule Wizard

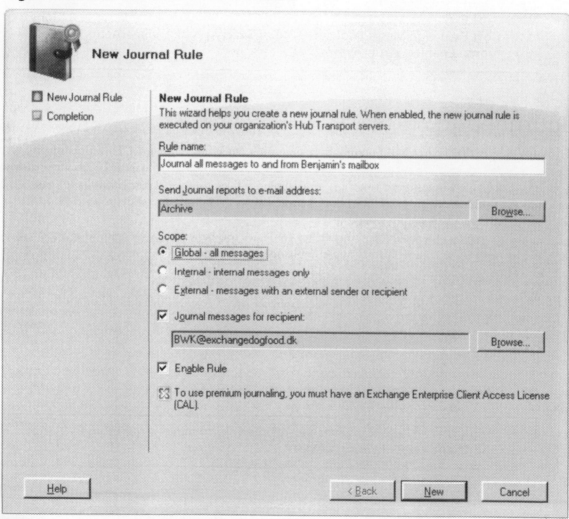

3. Click **Browse** and select the *recipient* who should receive the *journal reports*.

4. Choose the **scope** you want the journal rule to apply to.

5. If the rule should apply to a single mailbox, check **Journal message for recipient**, then click **Browse** and select the *recipient*.

6. Click **New** to create the rule. On the **Completion** page, click **Finish**.

NOTE

If you don't tick **Journal messages for recipient**, the Journal rule will archive all messages sent by all users throughout the Exchange organization.

TIP

To create a Journal rule via the Exchange Management Shell, you need to use the *New-JournalRule* cmdlet. For example, to create a rule similar to the one we generated using the GUI wizard, you would need to run the following command:
New-JournalRule –Name "Journal all messages to and from Benjamin's mailbox"
–JournalEmailAddress "exchangedogfood.dk/users/Archive" –Scope "Global"
–Enabled $True –Recipient "BWK@exchangedogfood.dk"

When the user Benjamin sends an e-mail message, a journal report will be sent to the specific Journal report e-mail address, as shown in Figure 6.20. As you can see, the journal report includes the message sent by Benjamin as an attachment, as well as information such as sender, subject, and message-ID.

Send Connectors

Send connectors are used to control how Hub Transport servers send messages using SMTP. That is, how it handles connections to other e-mail servers. This means that a Hub Transport server requires a Send connector in order to successfully deliver messages to their destination. It's important to note that an *explicit* Send connector isn't created during the installation of a Hub Transport server. However, internal Hub Transport servers use SMTP when delivering messages to each other, and although an explicit Send

Figure 6.20 A Test Journal Report Message

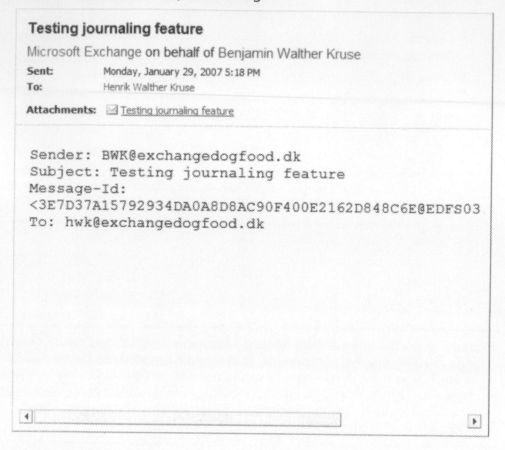

connector is not created by default, this doesn't mean that internal Hub Transport servers cannot deliver a message to another internal Hub Transport server. The reason behind this is that *implicit*, and invisible, Send connectors are automatically computed based on the Active Directory site topology, and based on the topology internal messages they are then routed between the Hub Transport servers in the organization.

Send connectors are stored in Active Directory, and when such a connector is created, their scope is global, not local like receive connectors.

If you don't have an Edge Transport server deployed in your organization's perimeter network, or if no Edge Subscription has been configured (which creates a Send connector automatically), you cannot send mail to other e-mail servers outside your organization. In this case, you must create a Send connector manually. To do so, perform the following steps:

1. Click the **Send Connectors** tab shown back in Figure 6.2.

2. Select **New Send Connector** in the Action pane.

3. The **New SMTP Send Connector** page will appear. On this **Introduction** page, enter a descriptive name (such as *To ISP* or *To Internet*) for the connector, and then select the type

of Send connector you want to create, as in the drop-down box shown in Figure 6.21. As you can see, you can choose between four different types of Send connectors:

- **Custom**   Select Custom in order to create a customized connector used to connect with other systems that are not Exchange servers.

- **Internal**   Internal Send connectors are used to send e-mail to servers in your Exchange organization. When selected, the connector will be configured to route e-mail to your internal Exchange servers as smart hosts.

- **Internet**   Internet Send connectors are used to send e-mail to the Internet. When selected, the connector will be configured to use Domain Name System (DNS) MX records to route e-mail.

Figure 6.21 Selecting the Required Send Connector Type

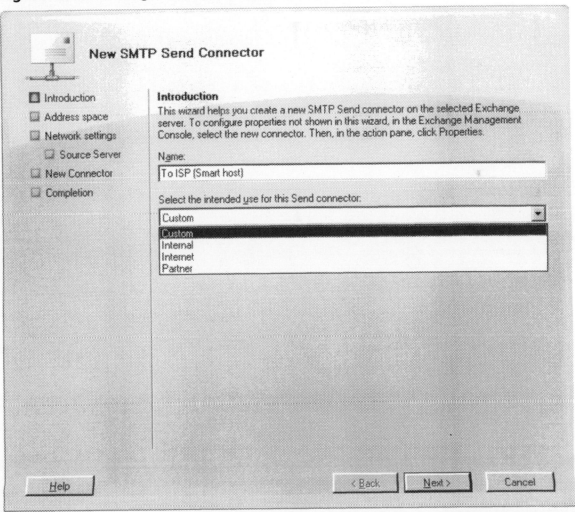

- **Partner**   Partner Send connectors are used to send e-mail to partner domains. When selected, this connector will be configured to only allow connections to servers that authenticate with Transport Layer Security (TLS) certificates for Simple Mail Transfer Protocol (SMTP) domains that are included in the list of domain-secured domains. You can add domains to this list by using the *-TLSSendDomainSecureList* parameter in the *Set-TransportConfig* command.

4. On the **Address space** page shown in Figure 6.22, enter the domain or domains to which the Send connector should route mail. If the connector should be used to route outbound mail to the Internet simply add an asterisk (*). When ready click **Next**.

Figure 6.22 Specifying the Address Space

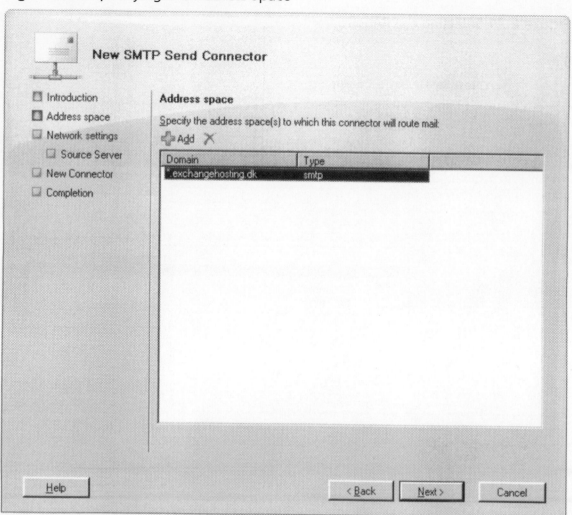

5. On the **Network Settings** page shown in Figure 6.23, specify how you want to send mail with the connector. Here, you can choose to use Domain Name System (DNS) "MX" records to route the mail automatically, or you can choose to have all mail routed to a specified smart host.

Figure 6.23 Configuring Network Settings

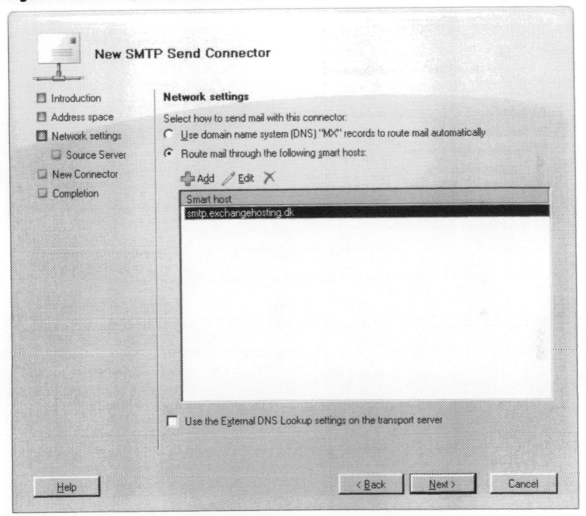

IMPORTANT

If you're a small shop using a cheap ISP that doesn't allow outbound traffic on port 25 from your DSL, you typically need to route outbound mail through a smart host located at your ISP.

6. If you elected to use a smart host in the previous step, you now need to configure the authentication method used to properly authenticate with the specified smart host. If this is a smart host located at your ISP, you typically don't need to authenticate, and can safely select **None**, as shown in Figure 6.24. Click **Next**.

Figure 6.24 Configuring the Smart Host Authentication Settings

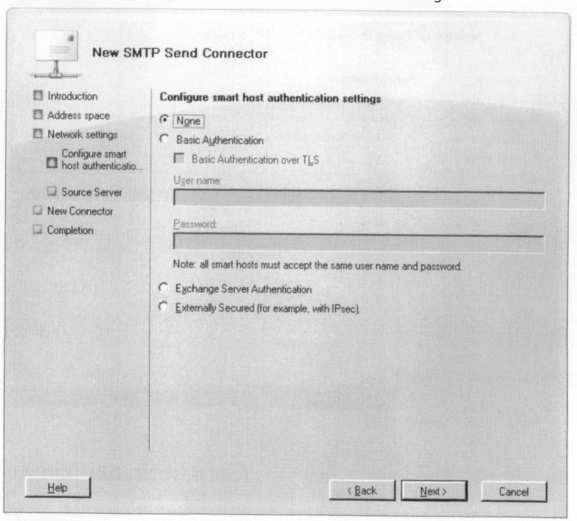

7. Now it's time to associate the connector with a Hub Transport server in the organization (Figure 6.25). The wizard will try to do this for you, but you can change the selection if required. Click **Next**.

Figure 6.25 Specifying the Source Server

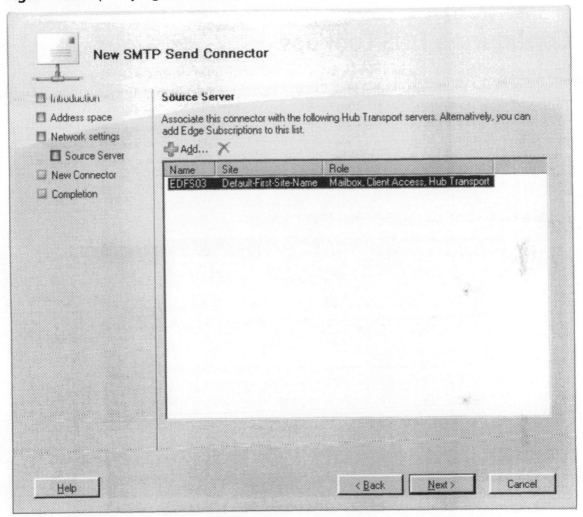

8. On the **Configuration Summary** page, make sure you configured the connector as required, and then click **Next**.

9. On the **Completion** page, click **Finish**.

TIP

To create a Send connector via the Exchange Management Shell, you must use the *New-SendConnector* cmdlet. For example, to create a Send Connector similar to the one we generated in the previous steps, run the following command:

New-SendConnector –Name 'To ISP (Smart host)' –Usage 'Internet' –AddressSpaces 'smtp:*.exchangehosting.dk;1' –DNSRoutingEnabled $true –UseExternalDNSServersEnabled $false –SourceTransportServers 'EDFS03'.

When you have created a Send connector, you can disable, enable, modify, and remove it by selecting the respective Send connector, and then choosing the required tasks in the Action pane.

Configuring DNS Lookups

You can configure a Hub Transport server to use different settings for external and internal DNS lookups. Click the **Properties** of your Hub Transport server under the **Server Configuration | Hub Transport** work center node. On the **External DNS Lookups** tab shown in Figure 6.26, specify that DNS server(s) should be used to resolve IP addresses of servers outside your organization. As you can see, you have the option of using the DNS settings configured for one of the network cards in the server, or by specifying the IP address of the DNS server(s) directly. You have the exact same options available under the Internal DNS Lookups tab. The only difference is that under this tab you specify the DNS server(s) that should be used to resolve IP addresses of servers inside your organization.

Figure 6.26 Configuring External DNS Lookups

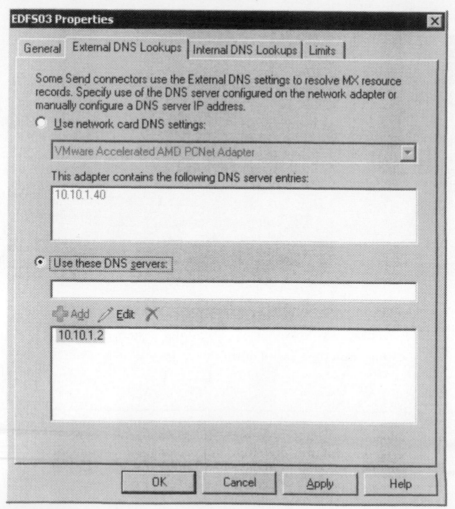

Configuring Outbound Message Limits

You can configure how the Hub Transport server should process outbound messages. This is done by opening the Property page of the respective Hub Transport server object in the Result pane. Here, you click the **Limits** tab. As you can see in Figure 6.27, you have the option of setting the retry interval—in other words, how often the Hub Transport server should try to resend an outbound message to a destination server, which for some SMTP servers don't accept the message the first time it's sent.

Figure 6.27 Configuring Outbound Message Limits

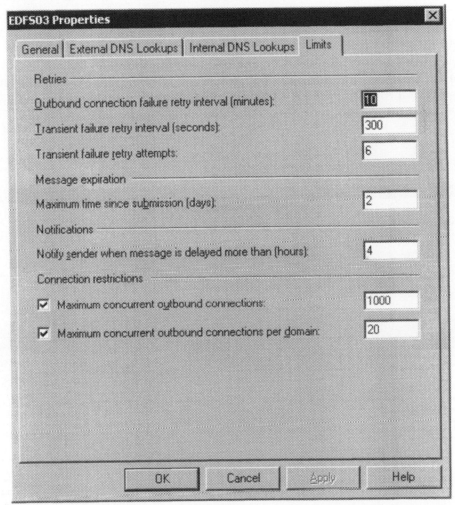

Under Message expiration, we can specify the amount of days a message held locally in a message queue as undeliverable should expire. As you can see, the default setting is 2 days, wherein the message will be removed from the message queue and a non-delivery report (NDR) will be sent to the sender of the message.

In addition, we can specify after how many hours a non–deliver report (NDR) should be generated and delivered to the sender of the message. By default, the sender will be notified every fourth hour.

Finally, we can configure connection restrictions for concurrent outbound connections and concurrent outbound connections per domain. Unless you're dealing with a very large organization, you should leave the connection restrictions at their defaults.

Typically, the default settings should be sufficient for most organizations, but if you're in a situation where you need to adjust them a little, this is the place to do it.

Receive Connectors

A *Receive connector* represents an inbound connection point for SMTP, and controls how a Hub Transport server receives messages over SMTP. No Receive connector, no inbound mail. This means that in order for a Hub Transport server to receive messages from the Internet (from e-mail clients as well as other e-mail servers), at least one Receive connector is required.

When you install the Hub Transport server role on a server, two Receive connectors are created by default. A Client <servername> and a Default <servername> receive connector, as shown in Figure 6.28. These two connectors are required in order for internal mail flow to work.

Figure 6.28 Default Receive Connectors

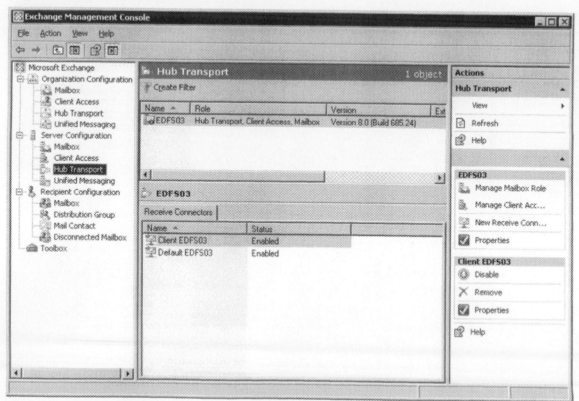

NOTE

By default, a Hub Transport server only accepts inbound messages from other Transport servers (that is, Hub Transport and Edge Transport servers) that are part of the Exchange organization, authenticated Exchange users, and internal legacy Exchange servers (Exchange 2000 and 2003). This means that e-mail servers that are external to the organization by default cannot deliver messages to a Hub Transport server. The reason behind this decision is to make Hub Transport servers secure out of the box by default. "But isn't it a little too aggressive to not allow inbound messages from the Internet?" I hear some of you grumble. Well, perhaps it is, but since the Exchange Product group is convinced that all organizations around the globe will deploy an Edge Transport server in their perimeter networks, the Exchange Product Group doesn't see this as an issue at all. Luckily, it's a rather painless process to allow untrusted e-mail servers (that is, e-mail servers not part of the Exchange organization except the Edge Transport server) to deliver messages directly to a Hub Transport server. I'll show you how in the section titled "Configuring the Hub Transport Server as an Internet-Facing SMTP Server" later in this chapter.

A Receive connector only listens for connections that match the settings configured on the respective connector. That is, connections that are received through a specific local IP address and port, and from a particular IP address range. Receive connectors are local to the Hub Transport server on which they're created. This means that a receive connector created on one Hub Transport server cannot be used by another Hub Transport server in the organization. So, by creating Receive connectors, you can control which server should receive messages from a particular IP address or IP address range. In addition, you can create custom connector properties for messages arriving from a particular IP address or IP address range. You could, for example, allow larger message sizes, more recipients per message (both of these will be covered later in this chapter) or perhaps more inbound connections.

Creating a Receive Connector

To create a Receive connector, you must perform the following steps:

1. Open the **Exchange Management Console** and select **Hub Transport** under the **Server Configuration work center node** (shown back in Figure 6.28).

2. In the Result pane, select the Hub Transport server on which you want to create the Receive connector.

3. Now click **New Receive Connector** in the Action pane.

4. The **New SMTP Receive Connector** wizard will appear. Type a *descriptive name* for the connector, and select the type of connector you want to create. As can be seen in Figure 6.29, you can select between five different Receive connector types:

    ■ **Custom** This option is used to create customized Receive connectors, which are used to connect with systems that are not Exchange servers.

- **Internet** This option is used to create a Receive connector that will receive e-mail from servers on the Internet. This connector will be configured to accept connections from anonymous users.

- **Internal** Internal Receive connectors are used to receive e-mail from servers within your Exchange organization. Note that this connector type will be configured to only accept connections from internal Exchange servers.

- **Client** Client Receive connectors are used to receive e-mail from authenticated Exchange users. This means that this connector will be configured to only accept client submissions from authenticated Exchange users.

- **Partner** Partner Receive connectors are used to receive e-mail from partner domains. This connector will be configured to only accept connections from servers

Figure 6.29 Selecting the Receive Connector Type

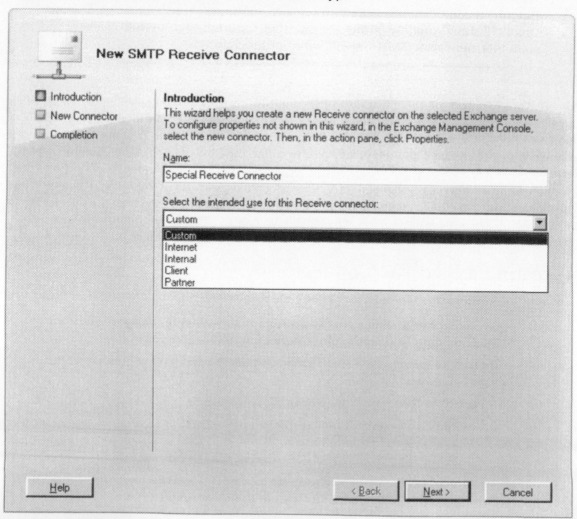

that authenticate with Transport Layer Security (TLS) certificates for SMTP domains included in the list of domain-secured domains. You can add domains to this list by using the *-TLSReceiveDomainSecureList* parameter in the *Set-TransportConfig* command.

5. When you have selected the type of connector you want to create, click **Next**.

6 As shown in Figure 6.30, you now have the option of modifying the IP address and port that should be used to receive mail. With Custom, Internet, and Partner Receive connectors, you also have the option of entering a FQDN that should be provided in response to *HELO* and *EHLO* commands. When ready, click **Next**.

7. On the **Configuration Summary** page, click **New**. On the **Completion** page, click **Finish**.

Figure 6.30 Entering the Local IP Addresses that Should Be Used to Receive Mail

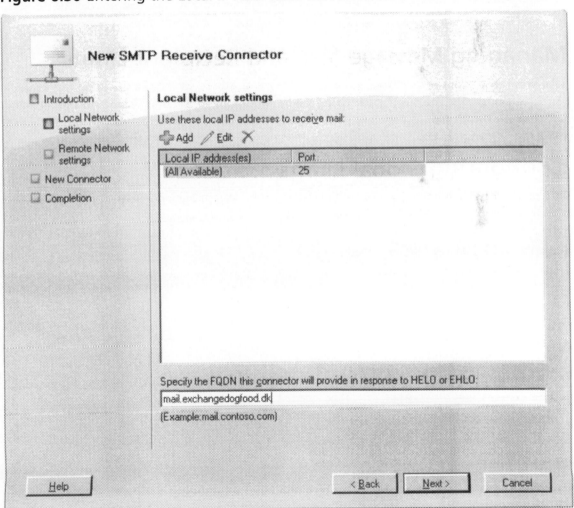

Tip

To create a Receive connector via the Exchange Management Shell, you must use the *New-ReceiveConnector* cmdlet. For example, to create a Receive Connector similar to the one we generated in the previous steps, run the following command:

New-ReceiveConnector –Name 'Special Receive Connector' –Usage 'Custom' –Bindings '0.0.0.0:25' –Fqdn 'mail.exchangedogfood.dk' –RemoteIPRanges '0.0.0.0– 255.255.255.255' –Server 'EDFS03'

At any time, you can modify an existing Receive connector as required. You do this by selecting the respective Receive connector and clicking **Properties** in the **Action** pane. In addition, any existing Receive connectors can be disabled, enabled, and removed as necessary. You do this by selecting the particular Receive connector and clicking the required task in the **Action** pane.

Managing Message Size and Recipient Limits

Like previous versions of Exchange, Exchange 2007 allows you to restrict the size of messages users can send and receive. The message size limits can be set globally in the organization on a per-server, per-connector level, and/or a per-user basis. Message size and recipient limits can only be configured using the Exchange Management Shell. In the following, I'll show you how to configure these limits.

Configuring Global Limits

By default, the global limits are set to unlimited, as can be seen in Figure 6.31.

Figure 6.31 Listing Global Limits

```
Machine: EDFS03 | Scope: exchangedogfood.dk                          _ □ ×
[PS] C:\>Get-TransportConfig | FL


ClearCategories                 : True
GenerateCopyOfDSNFor            : {5.4.8, 5.4.6, 5.4.4, 5.2.4, 5.2.0, 5.1.4}
InternalSMTPServers             : {}
JournalingReportNdrTo           : {}
MaxDumpsterSizePerStorageGroup  : 18MB
MaxDumpsterTime                 : 7.00:00:00
MaxReceiveSize                  : unlimited
MaxRecipientEnvelopeLimit       : unlimited
MaxSendSize                     : unlimited
TLSReceiveDomainSecureList      : {}
TLSSendDomainSecureList         : {}
VerifySecureSubmitEnabled       : False
VoicemailJournalingEnabled      : True
Xexch50Enabled                  : True
```

To configure new limits that apply to all Exchange 2007 Servers in the organization, you must use the following command:

```
Set-TransportConfig -MaxReceiveSize:<value> -MaxSendSize:<value>
-MaxRecipientEnvelopeLimit:<value>
```

NOTE

When you set the MaxReceiveSize or MaxSendSize, it's important to note that if you only specify a number such as 100, it defaults to kilobytes (KBs). This means that it is generally a good idea to specify the number followed by either KB or MB.

Configuring Server Limits

Since message size limits are controlled via Send and Receive connectors, you cannot configure message size limits per server. You can, however, configure the maximum number of recipients allowed per message. That is, the maximum number of recipients that can be included on a single e-mail message and submitted to the Pickup directory. By default, the maximum number of recipients is 100, which can be verified by running *Get-TransportServer | FL* in the Exchange Management Shell. To change this setting, you must use the following command:

```
Set-TransportServer -PickupDirectoryMaxRecipientsPerMessage:<value>
```

Configuring Connector Limits

By default, the default maximum message size for both Send and Receive connectors is 10 MB. You can verify this by running *Get-SendConnector | FL* and *Get-ReceiveConnector | FL*, respectively.

Send Connectors

To change the maximum message size limit on a Send connector, use the following command:

```
Set-SendConnector <name of connector> -MaxMessageSize:<value>
```

Receive Connectors

To change the maximum message size limit on a Receive connector, use the following command:

```
Set-ReceiveConnector <name of connector> -MaxMessageSize:<value>
```

NOTE

When you set the MaxMessageSize, it's important to note that if you only specify a number such as 100, it defaults to kilobytes (KBs). This means that it is generally a good idea to specify the number followed by either KB or MB.

Configuring Per-User Limits

You can also configure message size limits on a per-user level, if required. Message size limits set on a user override global limits and connector limits. The default message size limit for both sent and received messages on a user mailbox is unlimited, as can be seen by running *Get-Mailbox | FL*. In order to change this setting, run the following command:

```
Set-Mailbox -MaxReceiveSize:<value> -MaxSendSize:<value>
```

NOTE

When you set the MaxReceiveSize and MaxSendSize, it's important to note that if you only specify a number such as 100, it defaults to kilobytes (KBs). This means it's generally a good idea to specify the number followed by either KB or MB.

Message Tracking with Exchange Server 2007

When message tracking is enabled, all Simple Mail Transfer Protocol (SMTP) transport activity on all messages that transfer to and from an Exchange 2007 computer with a Hub Transport, Mailbox, or Edge Transport server role installed are recorded into a log, located by default in the C:\Program Files\Microsoft\Exchange Server\TransportRoles\Logs\MessageTracking directory. Message tracking logs can be used for message forensics, mail flow analysis, reporting, and troubleshooting.

When message tracking is enabled (which is the case by default), the maximum age for message tracking log files is 30 days. After 30 days, the oldest message tracking log files are deleted using circular logging. This is only true if the message tracking log reaches its specified maximum size (which, by default, is 10 MB), or a message tracking log file reaches its specified maximum age.

NOTE

The Message Tracking directory, which is responsible for holding the message tracking log files, has a default size limit of 250 MB.

In order to launch the Message Tracking tool, perform the following steps:

1. Open the **Exchange Management Console**.
2. Select the **Toolbox** work center node.
3. Click the **Message Tracking** icon and select **Open Tool** in the **Action** pane.

The tool will launch after a few seconds and look for any available updates. If updated, click **Go to Welcome screen** and you will be brought to the Message Tracking Parameters screen shown in Figure 6.32. Here you can check the different parameters you want to include in your search criteria. In this example, I have specified to get a list of all messages sent to me between January 1 and January 30, 2007 from a specific e-mail address. When the relevant parameters have been checked and specified, click **Next**.

Figure 6.32 The Message Tracking Parameters Page

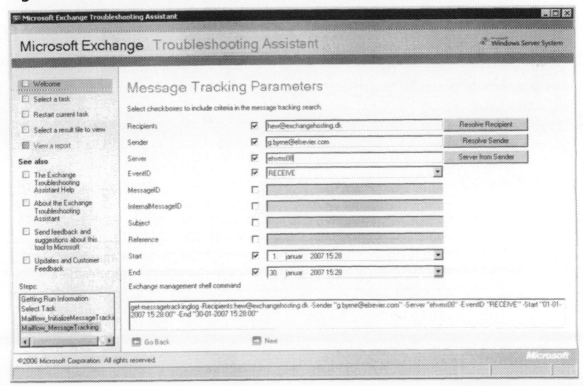

The Message Tracking tool will now search for all messages matching the search criteria specified on the previous screen, as shown in Figure 6.33. Here we get all sorts of information about the messages, and if we want to further filter our search, we can click **Next** and check or change any relevant parameters.

Figure 6.33 List of Messages Included Based on Search Criteria

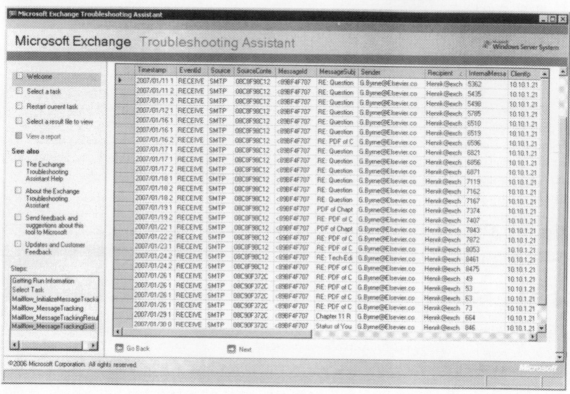

TIP

In order to use the message tracking feature to search for particular messages via the Exchange Management Shell, you can use the *Get-MessageTrackingLog* cmdlet.

Using the Exchange 2007 Queue Viewer

Typically, mail flow within the organization just simply works; however, as an Exchange administrator, one of your jobs is to regularly keep an eye on the message queues within the Exchange organization. This is where the Queue Viewer comes in. With the Queue Viewer, now an Exchange *tool*, and therefore located under the Toolbox work center node in the Exchange Management Console, you can view information about queues and examine the messages held within them.

Exchange Server 2007 uses five different types of queues, and the routing of a message determines the type of queue where a particular message is stored. In the following, I list the five different queues types:

Submission Queue

The submission queue is a persistent queue used by the categorizer in order to gather the messages that need to be resolved, routed, and processed by Transport agents. Each message received by the categorizer is a component of Exchange transport and therefore processes all inbound messages as well as determines what to do with the messages based on information about the intended recipients. All messages received by a transport server enter processing in the Submission queue. Messages are submitted through SMTP-receive, the Pickup directory, or the store driver. The categorizer retrieves messages from this queue and, among other things, determines the location of the recipient and the route to that location. After categorization, the message is moved to a delivery queue or to the unreachable queue. Each Exchange 2007 transport server has only one Submission queue. Messages that are in the Submission queue cannot be in any other queues at the same time.

Mailbox Delivery Queue

The Mailbox Delivery queues hold messages that are being delivered to a mailbox server by using encrypted Exchange RPC. Mailbox Delivery queues exist on Hub Transport servers only. The Mailbox Delivery queue holds messages that are being delivered to mailbox recipients whose mailbox data is stored on a Mailbox server not located in the same site as the Hub Transport server. More than one mailbox delivery queue can exist on a Hub Transport server. The next hop for a Mailbox Delivery queue is the distinguished name of the mailbox store.

Remote Delivery Queue

Remote Delivery queues hold messages that are being delivered to a remote server using SMTP. Remote Delivery queues can exist on both Hub Transport servers and Edge Transport servers, and more than one Remote Delivery queue can exist on each server. Each Remote Delivery queue contains messages that are being routed to recipients that have the same delivery destination. On a Hub Transport server, these destinations are outside the Active Directory site in which the Hub Transport server is located. Remote Delivery queues are dynamically created when they are required and are automatically deleted from the server when they no longer hold messages and the configurable expiration time has passed. By default, the queue is deleted three minutes after the last message has left the queue. The next hop for a Remote Delivery queue is an SMTP domain name, a smart host name or IP address, or an Active Directory site name.

Poison Message Queue

The Poison Message queue is a special queue used to isolate messages that are detected to be potentially harmful to the Exchange 2007 system after a server failure. Messages that contain errors potentially fatal to the Exchange Server system are delivered to the Poison Message queue. This queue is typically empty, and if no poison messages exist, the queue does not appear in the queue viewing interfaces. The Poison Message queue is always in a ready state. By default, all messages in this queue are suspended. The messages can be deleted if they are considered to be harmful to the system. In the event a message in the Poison Message queue is determined to be unrelated to the message itself, delivery of the message can be resumed. When delivery is resumed, the message enters the Submission queue.

Unreachable Queue

The Unreachable queue contains messages that cannot be routed to their destinations. Typically, an unreachable destination is caused by configuration changes that have modified the routing path for delivery. Regardless of the destination, all messages that have unreachable recipients reside in this queue. Each transport server can have only one Unreachable queue.

When a message is received by transport, the mail item will be created and then saved into the queue database.

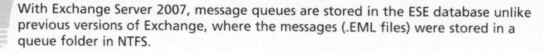

TIP

With Exchange Server 2007, message queues are stored in the ESE database unlike previous versions of Exchange, where the messages (.EML files) were stored in a queue folder in NTFS.

As mail items are saved in the queue database, they are assigned a unique identifier. If a particular mail item is routed or being sent to more than one recipient, the item can have more than one destination. Each destination represents a separate routing solution for the mail item, and each routing solution causes a routed mail item to be created. A message that is being sent to recipients in two different domains appears as two distinct messages in the delivery queues, even if only one transport mail item is in the database.

To launch the Queue Viewer, perform the following steps:

1. Open the **Exchange Management Console**.

2. Click the **Toolbox** work center node.

3. Click the **Queue Viewer** icon, and then select **Open Tool** in the **Action** pane.

If you have launched the Queue Viewer from a Hub Transport server, it will connect to the local queue by default. If you want to connect to a queue stored on another Hub Transport server, click **Connect to Server** in the **Action** pane (Figure 6.34).

Figure 6.34 The Queue Viewer Tool

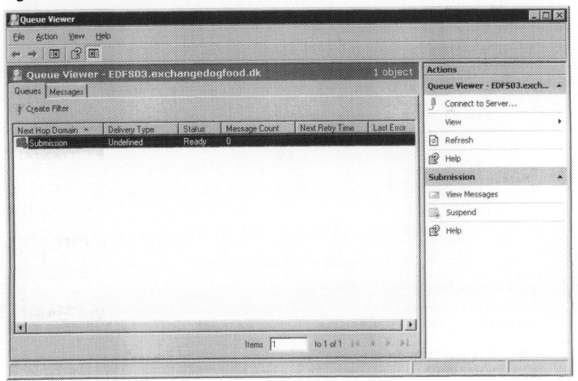

From within the Queue Viewer, you can view queues and messages, as well as suspend and resume them. In addition, you can retry a queue or message, remove a queue or message completely, or export either of them so they can be transferred to another Hub Transport server for further delivery.

TIP

To view or manipulate message queues or individual messages via the Exchange Management Shell, use the *Get-Queue* and *Get-Message* cmdlets.

Introduction to the Exchange Mail Flow Troubleshooter Tool

If you're experiencing mail flow issues in your organization, you can also give the new Exchange Mail Flow Troubleshooter a try. This diagnostic tool helps perform the following functions:

- Starting with the mail flow symptoms, it moves customers through the correct troubleshooting path.

- Provides easy access to various data sources that are required to troubleshoot problems with mail flow.

- Automatically diagnoses the retrieved data and presents an analysis of the possible root causes.

- Suggests corrective actions.

- Provide guidance to help users manually diagnose the data where and when automation is not possible.

In order to launch the Exchange Mail Flow Troubleshooter, perform the following steps:

1. Open the **Exchange Management Console**.
2. Select the **Toolbox** work center node.
3. Click the **Exchange Mail Flow Troubleshooter** icon, and then select **Open Tool** in the **Action** pane.

When the tool has been launched, it will check to see whether any updates are available on Microsoft.com, and then bring you to the welcome screen. You then need to enter an identifying label for the analysis you're about to perform, and then specify what symptoms you're seeing. As you can see in Figure 6.35, you can choose between six different symptoms, and depending on which one you select, the tool will programmatically execute a set of troubleshooting steps to identify the root cause of the mail flow issue you're experiencing. The tool automatically determines what set of data is required to troubleshoot the identified symptoms and collects configuration data, performance counters, event logs, and live tracing information from an Exchange server and other appropriate sources. The tool analyzes each subsystem to determine individual bottlenecks and component failures, and then aggregates the information to provide root cause analysis.

Figure 6.35 The Exchange Mail Flow Troubleshooter Tool

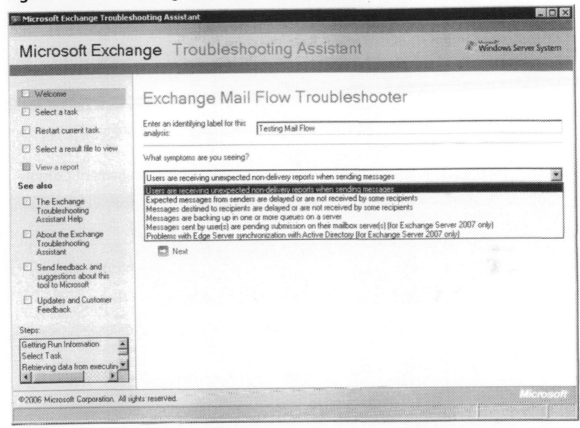

Configuring the Hub Transport Server as an Internet-Facing Transport Server

One of the design goals for Exchange 2007 was to be as secure as possible, by default, in the same way that the Hub Transport server is configured to only accept messages from internal Exchange users, Exchange servers, and legacy Exchange servers. This means that the Hub Transport server doesn't accept inbound messages sent from unauthenticated (untrusted) e-mail servers, which typically define external e-mail servers on the Internet. Instead, it expects to receive inbound messages from the Internet via an Edge Transport server in the perimeter network.

If you're an Exchange administrator in a small organization, or if you're primarily doing Exchange consulting for small shops, chances are IT budgets hinder you from deploying an Edge Transport server in the perimeter network, when transitioning to Exchange Server 2007 (especially if the environment will only consist of a single Exchange 2007 server). Luckily, it's a pretty simple process to change this behavior since you just need to allow untrusted servers to deliver messages to the Hub Transport server. This is accomplished by enabling **Anonymous users** under the **Permission Groups** tab of the **Default Receive connector.**

To get to this property page, you must do the following:

1. Open the **Exchange Management Console**.

2. Expand the **Server Configuration** work center node, and then select **Hub Transport**.

3. Highlight the respective Hub Transport server in the Result pane, as shown in Figure 6.36.

Figure 6.36 The Default Receive Connector in the Exchange Management Console

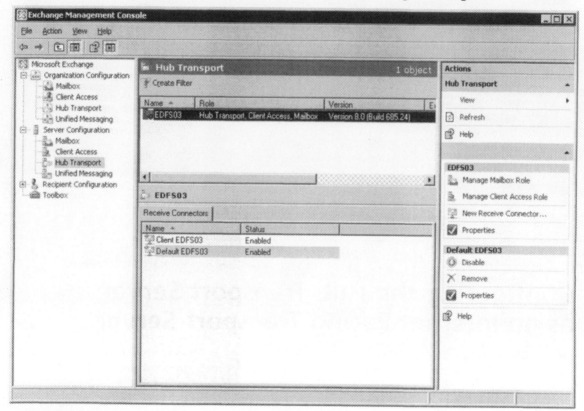

4. Open the **Properties** page of the **Default** *<servername>* **Receive Connector** in the **Work** pane.

5. Click the **Permissions Groups** tab, check **Anonymous users** and click **OK**, as shown in Figure 6.37.

Figure 6.37 The Permission Groups Tab on the Default Receive Connector
Properties Page

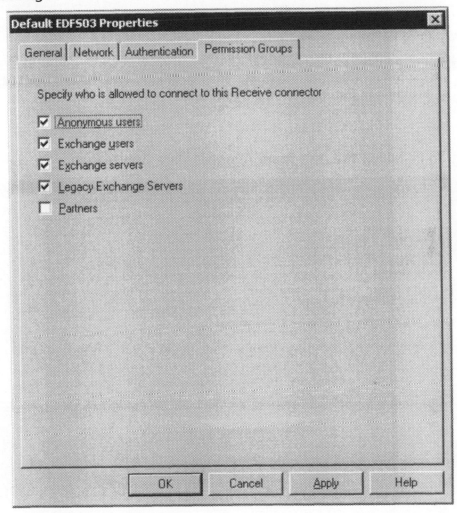

Although we haven't covered the Edge Transport server yet, this server role is also the one that
holds all the message hygiene features available in Exchange Server 2007. If you decide not to deploy
an Edge Transport server in your perimeter network, you might wonder whether it's possible to let
the Internet-facing Hub Transport server take care of filtering out spam and other unwanted e-mail
before it reaches your mailbox servers. The answer is yes it is; however, because there are not any
anti-spam filtering agents installed on a Hub Transport server by default (since the Exchange Product
group expects you to deploy an Edge Transport server in the perimeter network), you must do so

manually by running the *install-AntispamAgents.ps1* script located in the Exchange 2007 scripts folder. This can be found under C:\Program Files\Microsoft\Exchange Server. To run this script, do the following:

1. Open the **Exchange Management Shell**.
2. Type **CD "program files\microsoft\exchange server\scripts"** and press **Enter**.
3. Run the **install-AntispamAgents.ps1** script by typing **.\install-AntispamAgents.ps1**, and then pressing **Enter**, as shown in Figure 6.38.

Figure 6.38 Installing the Anti-Spam Agents on the Hub Transport Server

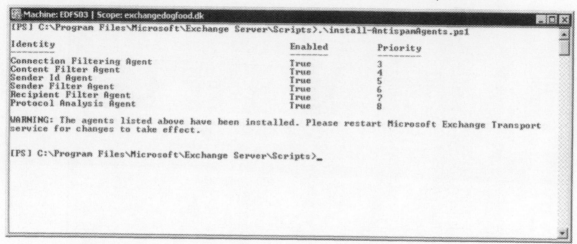

4. Restart the **Microsoft Exchange Transport** service.
5. Close and re-open the **Exchange Management Console** in order for the change to be reflected in the UI.

We now have a new Anti-spam tab under the Hub Transport node beneath the Organization Configuration work center, as shown in Figure 6.39. As you can see, all the anti-spam filtering agents normally found on an Edge Transport server are now listed here. For an explanation of each, see Chapter 7.

Figure 6.39 List of Available Anti-Spam Agents

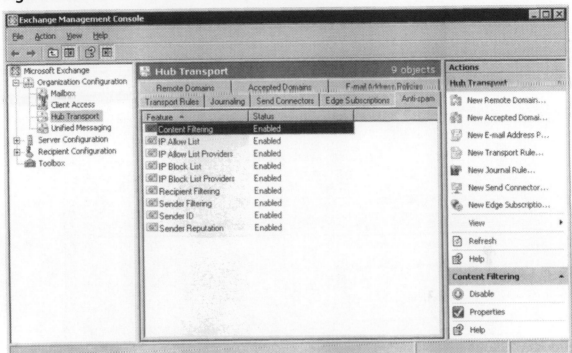

Of course, this solution allows all spam messages and other unwanted e-mail to enter your internal network before it's filtered, but most small shops should be able to live with that. If not, you might want to consider using a hygiene service such as **Exchange Hosted Services (EHS)**, which not only provides efficient anti-spam filtering, but also virus protection and other interesting services. You can read more about EHS at http://www.microsoft.com/exchange/services.

Changing the SMTP Banner

Something else you might want to do in a scenario where inbound messages are directly routed to a Hub Transport server is to change the advertised FQDN sent in *HELO/EHLO* commands in SMTP. This is done under the General tab of the Default Receive connector property page, as shown in Figure 6.40.

Figure 6.40 The General Tab on the Default Receive Connector Properties Page

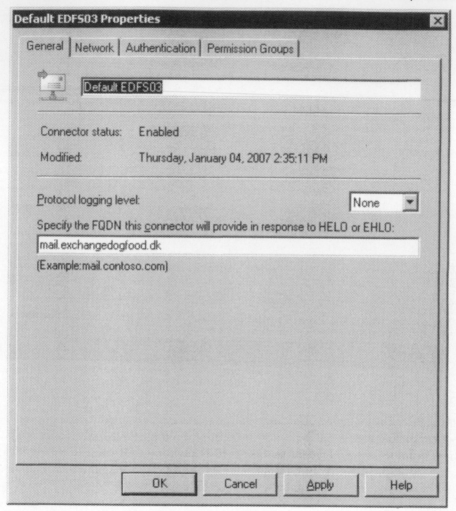

Disabling the EdgeSync Service

Since the EdgeSync service on the Hub Transport server isn't used, when you don't have an Edge Transport server deployed in your perimeter network, it's also a good idea to disable this service (Figure 6.41) in order to save a few system resources. Just by simply running and not replicating with an Edge Transport server, this service actually uses a little under 30 MB.

Figure 6.41 Disabling the EdgeSync Service

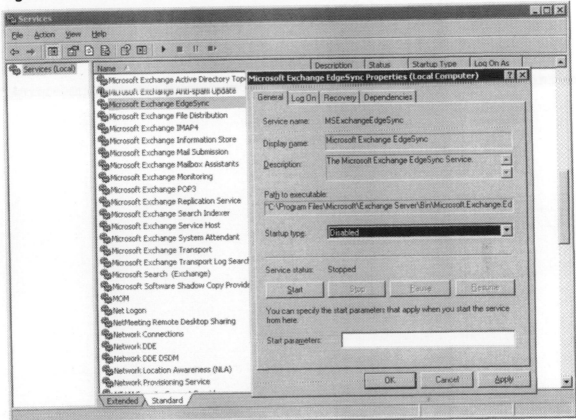

Pointing the MX Record
to the Hub Transport Server

The final thing you must do is point your domain's MX record to the Hub Transport server. This is done differently depending on your specific scenario, but typically you just need to redirect port 25 to the IP address of the Hub Transport server in your firewall. If you're publishing your messaging environment using an ISA 2006 Server, this is done under the **To** tab on the **Inbound SMTP** properties page, as shown in Figure 6.42.

Figure 6.42 Redirect Inbound Mail on an ISA 2006 Server

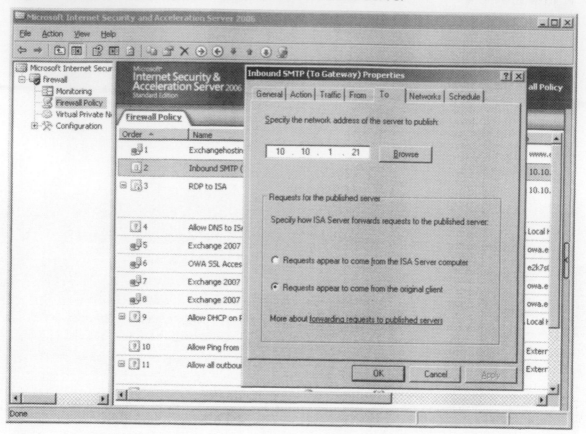

Missed Features

There are a few drawbacks in choosing to have inbound messages go directly to a Hub Transport server instead of via an Edge Transport server in your perimeter network, as best practices tell us.

Attachment Filter

Although the Hub Transport server does contain some attachment options, you won't be able to scan the incoming MIME stream for malicious attachment types, and thereby reject them at the protocol layer. However, you could get this functionality on a Hub Transport Server by installing an anti-virus product such as **Microsoft Forefront for Exchange Server**.

Address Rewrite Agent

You also won't be able to take advantage of the address rewrite functionality since the Address Rewrite agent can only be installed on an Edge Transport server. An explanation of this feature is outside the scope of this chapter. Instead, refer to Chapter 7.

Summary

In this chapter, we started out taking a brief look at the changes made in regards to message routing and architecture in Exchange Server 2007. We then went through the configuration settings available on the Hub Transport server. Next, we discussed how you can create journaling and transport rules so your organization can navigate the ever-increasing complexity of government and industry regulations and compliance demands. We also covered the purpose of Send and Receive connectors, and how to control message size limits in your organization. In addition, we took a look at the different transport server–related tools such as Message Tracking, the Queue Viewer, and the Exchange Mail Flow Troubleshooter tools. Finally, we went through the steps necessary to configure a Hub Transport server as the Internet-facing transport server in your organization.

Solutions Fast Track

Message Transport and Routing Architecture in Exchange 2007

☑ A lot has changed in regards to transport and routing architecture in Exchange Server 2007. First, Exchange no longer uses the SMTP protocol stack included with Internet Information Services (IIS), as was the case with previous versions of the product. Instead, the Exchange Product group has rewritten the SMTP transport stack in managed code, resulting in a much more stable and secure protocol stack.

☑ The new SMTP transport stack is now known as the Microsoft Exchange Transport service (MSExchangeTransport.exe), and because it's no longer dependent on IIS, it is not located within IIS Manager.

☑ With Exchange Server 2007, the Exchange routing topology is no longer based on separate Exchange routing groups. Instead Exchange 2007 takes advantage of the existing site topology in Active Directory. Because Exchange 2007 is now dependent on Active Directory sites—that is, Hub Transport servers use Active Directory sites as well as the cost assigned to the Active Directory IP site link to determine the least-cost routing path to other Hub Transport servers within the organization—all sites containing one or more Mailbox servers must also have at least one Hub Transport server.

☑ Bear in mind that Mailbox and Hub Transport servers use RPC as the basis of communication, but that two Hub Transport servers use SMTP/TLS when exchanging messages.

☑ Exchange Server 2007 is no longer dependent on Link State updates.

Managing the Hub Transport Server

☑ All organizationwide Hub Transport settings are stored in Active Directory. This means that any modifications or configuration settings, except Receive connector specific settings, are reflected on all Hub Transport servers in the organization.

☑ When you set a remote domain, you can control mail flow with more precision, specify message formatting and policy, and designate acceptable character sets for messages that are sent to, and received from, the remote domain.

☑ Under the Accepted Domains tab, we specify the SMTP domains for which our Exchange 2007 organization should either be authoritative, relay to an e-mail server in another Active Directory Forest within the organization, or relay to an e-mail server outside the respective Exchange organization.

☑ E-mail address policies were known as recipient policies back in Exchange 2000 and 2003. Exchange address policies define the proxy addresses stamped onto recipient objects in the Exchange organization.

☑ With the increasing complexity of government and industry regulations, there's a greater need for the efficient management of internal message routing. Exchange 2007, or more specifically the Hub Transport Server role, includes a new transport rules agent that provides easy and flexible ways to set rules for internal message routing and content restriction throughout the Exchange organization.

☑ Exchange Server 2007 supports both Standard and Premium journaling (the latter requires Exchange 2007 Enterprise CALs). Standard journaling is similar to the journaling functionality we had in Exchange 2003 since it's journaling per Mailbox database. Premium journaling is a Hub Transport server feature based on a new journaling agent that can be configured to match the specific needs of an organization. Premium journaling lets you create journal rules for single mailbox recipients or for entire groups within the organization.

☑ Send connectors are used to control how Hub Transport servers send messages using SMTP, and how connections are handled with other e-mail servers. This means that a Hub Transport server requires a Send connector in order to deliver messages to the next hop on the way to their destination.

☑ A Receive connector only listens for connections that match the settings configured on the respective connector—that is, connections that are received through a specific local IP address and port, and/or from a particular IP address range. Receive connectors are local to the Hub Transport server on which they're created. This means a receive connector created on one Hub Transport server cannot be used by another Hub Transport server in the organization.

Managing Message Size and Recipient Limits

☑ Like previous versions of Exchange, Exchange 2007 allows you to restrict the size of messages a user can send and receive. The message size limits can be set globally in the organization, or on a per-server, per-connector, or per-user basis. Message size and recipient limits can *only* be configured using the Exchange Management Shell.

Message Tracking with Exchange Server 2007

☑ When message tracking is enabled, the Simple Mail Transfer Protocol (SMTP) transport activity of all messages transferred to and from an Exchange 2007 computer that has the Hub Transport, Mailbox, or Edge Transport server role installed are recorded into a log that, by default, is located in the C:\Program Files\Microsoft\Exchange Server\TransportRoles\ Logs\MessageTracking directory. Message tracking logs can be used for message forensics, mail flow analysis, reporting, and troubleshooting.

☑ When message tracking is enabled (which is the case, by default), the maximum age for message tracking log files is 30 days. After 30 days, the oldest message tracking log files are deleted using circular logging.

☑ The Message Tracking directory, responsible for holding the message tracking log files, has a default size limit of 250 MB.

☑ The Message Tracking tool can be found in the Toolbox Work Center.

Using the Exchange 2007 Queue Viewer

☑ With the Queue Viewer now an Exchange *tool*, and thus located under the Toolbox work center in the Exchange Management Console, you can view information about queues and examine the messages held within them.

☑ Exchange Server 2007 uses five different types of queues, and the routing of a message determines which type of queue a particular message is stored in.

☑ With Exchange Server 2007, message queues are stored in the ESE database, unlike previous versions of Exchange where the messages (.EML files) were stored in a queue folder in NTFS.

Introduction to the Exchange Mail Flow Troubleshooter Tool

☑ If you're experiencing mail flow issues in your organization, you can also give the new Exchange Mail Flow Troubleshooter a try. It's used by starting with mail flow symptoms and slowly moving customers through the correct troubleshooting path, providing easy access to various data sources required to troubleshoot problems with mail flow. Based on the collected data, it will present an analysis of the possible root causes and then suggest corrective actions as necessary.

Configuring the Hub Transport Server as an Internet-facing Transport Server

☑ If you're an Exchange administrator in a small organization, or if you're primarily doing Exchange consulting for small shops, chances are the IT budget may hinder you from deploying an Edge Transport server in the perimeter network when transitioning to Exchange Server 2007 (especially if the environment will only consist of a single Exchange 2007 server). In this case, you can configure a Hub Transport server as the Internet-facing transport server in your organization.

☑ By default, no anti-spam filtering agents are installed on a Hub Transport server (since the Exchange Product group expects you to deploy an Edge Transport server in the perimeter network as a best practice). If you want to use the anti-spam agents on a Hub Transport server, you can install them by running the *install-AntispamAgents.ps1* script located in the Exchange 2007 \scripts folder, which can be found, by default, under C:\Program Files\ Microsoft\Exchange Server.

Frequently Asked Questions

Q: What protocol is used when two internal Hub Transport servers exchange messages?

A: Hub Transport servers use secure SMTP when exchanging messages internally. They use the industry standard SMTP Transport Layer Security (TLS), so that all traffic between the Hub Transport servers are authenticated and encrypted. This will remove the capability for internal snooping.

Q: What protocol is used when a Hub Transport server delivers a message to a mailbox on a Mailbox server?

A: When a Hub Transport server communicates with a Mailbox server, it's done using encrypted RPC. Again, this will remove the capability for internal snooping.

Q: Is there no way to make use of the Exchange 2007 anti-spam agents if I don't deploy an Edge Transport server in my organization's perimeter network?

A: Yes, you can install the anti-spam agents on a Hub Transport server by running the *install-AntispamAgents.ps1* script located in the Exchange 2007 \scripts folder, found by default under C:\Program Files\Microsoft\Exchange Server.

Q: I've deployed Exchange 2007 in my organization, but I cannot receive inbound messages from the Internet. Why?

A: One of the design goals for Exchange 2007 was to be as secure as possible, by default—for example, the Hub Transport server has been configured in such a way that it only accepts messages from internal Exchange users, Exchange servers, and legacy Exchange servers. This means that the Hub Transport server doesn't accept inbound messages sent from unauthenticated (untrusted) e-mail servers, which typically are external e-mail servers on the Internet. Instead it expects to receive inbound messages from the Internet via an Edge Transport server in the perimeter network. In order to be able to receive inbound messages from e-mail servers on the Internet, you must check to allow Anonymous users, located under the Permission Groups tab on the Default <servername> Receive connector property page.

Q: I don't see any Routing Groups in the Exchange Server 2007 Management Console?

A: Routing groups have been discontinued in Exchange 2007. Instead, Exchange 2007 takes advantage of the existing site topology in Active Directory.

Q: Since a Hub Transport server uses the SMTP protocol to exchange messages with internal transport servers and other e-mail servers on the Internet, I don't understand why I shouldn't install the Windows IIS SMTP component prior to installing the Exchange 2007 Hub Transport server role?

A: Exchange 2007 no longer uses the SMTP protocol stack included with Internet Information Services (IIS), as was the case with previous versions of the product. Instead, the Exchange Product group has rewritten the SMTP transport stack in managed code, resulting in a much more stable and secure protocol stack.

Chapter 7

Managing the Edge Transport Server

Solutions in this chapter:

- **Deploying the Edge Transport Server Role**
- **Enabling Name Resolution Lookups between the Edge Transport and Hub Transport Servers Suffix**
- **Installing the ADAM Component**
- **Verifying That the EdgeSync Service Works as Expected**
- **Manually Configuring the Required Connectors**
- **Pointing Your MX Records to the Edge Transport Server**
- **Deploying Multiple Edge Transport Servers in the Organization**

- ☑ Summary
- ☑ Solutions Fast Track
- ☑ Frequently Asked Questions

Introduction

The Exchange Product Group developed the edge transport server to give enterprises powerful out-of-the-box protection against spam without needing to go out and invest in a third-party solution. The messaging hygiene features in the Edge Transport server role are agent based and consists of multiple filters that are frequently updated.

Although the primary role of the edge transport server is to route mail and do message hygiene, it also includes features that will let you do other things, such as rewriting SMTP addresses, configuring transport rules, and enabling journaling and associated disclaimers.

After reading this chapter you will have learned what the edge transport server is all about; you will be aware of how an edge transport server is properly deployed as well as know how to configure most of the features available with this server role.

NOTE

Exchange 2007 also includes a new feature called *Domain Security,* which provides a set of functionality that offers a low-cost alternative to S/MIME or other message-level security solutions. The purpose of the Domain Security feature set is to provide administrators a way to manage secured message paths over the Internet with business partners.

Deploying the Edge Transport Server Role

The Edge Transport server role in Exchange Server 2007 is meant to be installed in your organization's perimeter network (also called a *demilitarized zone [DMZ]* or *screened subnet*). This server role supports Simple Mail Transfer Protocol (SMTP) routing (more specifically, SMTP-relay and Smart Host functionality) and provides several antispam filtering agents and support for antivirus extensibility. The edge transport server is the only server role that shouldn't be part of your Active Directory directory service forest; it should instead be installed on a stand-alone server in a workgroup as shown in Figure 7.1.

Although the Edge Transport server role is isolated from Active Directory, it's still able to communicate with the Active Directory using a collection of processes known as EdgeSync, which runs on the hub transport server. Since it is part of the Active Directory, the Hub Transport server has access to the necessary Active Directory data. The edge transport server uses Active Directory Application Mode (ADAM) to store the required Active Directory data, which is data such as accepted domains, recipients, safe senders, send connectors, and a hub transport server list (used to generate dynamic connectors so that you don't need to create them manually).

Figure 7.1 A Typical Edge Transport Server Scenario

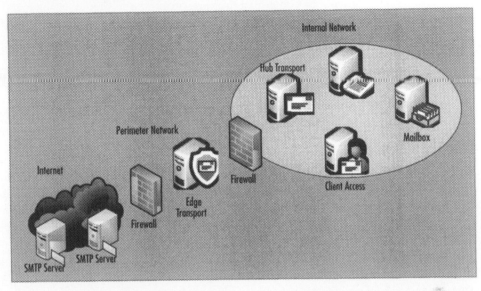

It's important to understand that the EdgeSync replication is encrypted by default and that the replication is a one-way process from Active Directory to ADAM. This means that no data is replicated from ADAM to AD.

The first time that EdgeSync replication occurs, the ADAM store is populated, and after that, data from Active Directory is replicated at fixed intervals. You can specify the intervals or use the default settings, which, for configuration data, is every hour and every fourth hour for recipient data.

Some Independent Advice

Although the Edge Transport server role has been designed to provide improved antispam and antivirus protection for an Exchange 2007 environment, you can deploy this server role in an existing Exchange 2003 organization as well. Since you install the Edge Transport server role on a stand-alone machine in the perimeter network (the DMZ or screened subnet), this is even a relatively simple task. Even though you would be able to use the Edge Transport server role as a smart host or an SMTP relay server in an Exchange 2003 environment, you will not be able to replicate configuration and recipient data from Active Directory to ADAM, because this requires an Exchange 2007 hub transport server. This doesn't hinder you from using the filtering agent that doesn't rely on the EdgeSync service. If you use the Intelligent Message Filter (IMF) only in your Exchange 2003 environment, deploying an edge transport server in the perimeter network (the DMZ or screened subnet) would make sense because it would provide an additional layer of antispam protection. You could also install ForeFront for Exchange Server 2007 on the edge transport server so that you could filter out antivirus messages as well.

The edge transport server has its own Jet database to process the delivery of inbound as well as outbound e-mail messages. When inbound e-mail messages are stored in the Jet database and are ready for delivery, the edge transport server looks up the respective recipient(s) in the ADAM store, which, as mentioned, among other things contains recipient data replicated from the Active Directory using the EdgeSync service.

In a scenario in which you have deployed multiple edge transport servers in your organization, the edge transport servers use DNS round robin (which is supported by most DNS servers today) to network and load-balance network traffic between the servers.

Prerequisites

The Exchange 2007 Edge Transport server role can be installed on either a Windows 2003 Server R2 Standard Edition or Windows 2003 Server SP1 Standard Edition. As already mentioned, it's important that you install the Edge Transport server role on a standalone machine outside the Active Directory forest, since installing this server role on a server that is member of Active Directory isn't supported, nor it would be a good idea, since doing so would introduce a major security risk.

Since the Edge Transport server should be deployed in the perimeter network (the DMZ or screened subnet), it's recommended that you use a multihomed setup, meaning that the server has two network adapters: one connected to the perimeter network and one to the internal network. This will give you the option of specifying the ports and/or services that should be allowed on each adapter. For example, we want to allow LDAP replication from only the internal network when we show you how to configure the Security Configuration Wizard (SCW) later in this chapter. But the choice is yours, really, since an edge transport server will work just fine using a single network adapter as well, albeit in a less secure way.

Creating a DNS Suffix

Before you can install the Exchange 2007 Edge Transport server role on the server, you should make sure that you have created a DNS suffix, because you cannot change the server name once the server role has been installed. In addition, the readiness check will fail if a DNS suffix cannot be located. Creating the DNS suffix is a very simple process, performed via the following steps:

1. Log onto the edge transport server with the Administrator account or another account with administrator permissions.

2. Click **Start,** right-click **My Computer,** and select **Properties** in the context menu.

3. Now click the **Computer Name** tab and then click the **Change** button (see Figure 7.2).

Figure 7.2 The Computer Name Tab

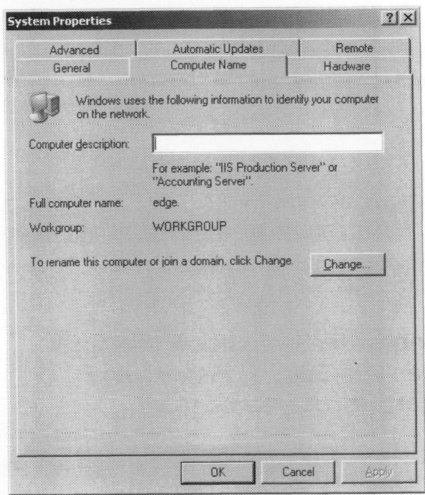

4. Click the **More** button.

5. Now enter the respective **DNS suffix** (see Figure 7.3) and then click **OK** four times.

Figure 7.3 The DNS Suffix and NetBIOS Computer Name

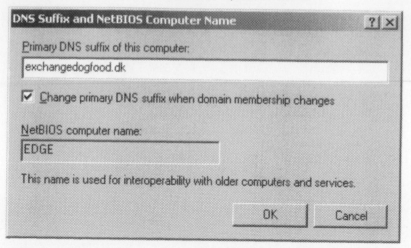

6. Click **Yes** to reboot the server so that the changes take effect.

Enabling Name Resolution Lookups between the Edge Transport and Hub Transport Servers Suffix

It's important that the edge transport server and any hub transport servers in your Exchange 2007 organization are able to see each other using name resolution. To accomplish this goal, you can create the necessary host record in a forward lookup zone on the internal DNS server used by the edge transport and hub transport servers.

NOTE

Since any Exchange 2007 hub transport server in your Exchange organization needs to be added to the Active Directory, before you can install this role only the host name of the edge transport server needs to be manually added to the respective forward lookup zone.

You do so by performing the following steps:

1. Log onto the internal DNS server used by the edge transport and hub transport servers.

2. Click **Start | Administrative Tools** and then click **DNS**.

3. In the **DNS Management snap-in**, expand the **Server** node and then **Forward Lookup Zones** (see Figure 7.4).

Figure 7.4 DNS Management MMC Snap-in

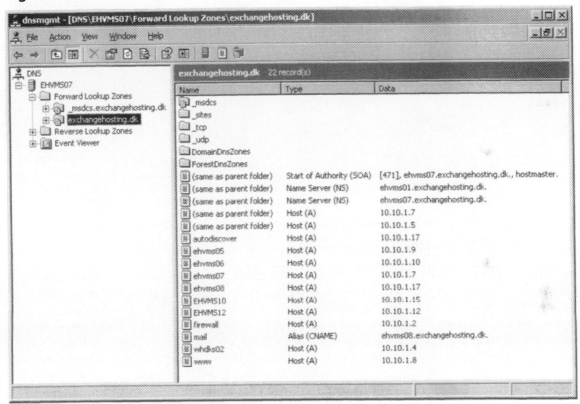

4. Now right-click the respective **Forward Lookup Zone** and select **New Host (A)** in the context menu.

5. Enter the **hostname** and **IP address** of the edge transport server and click **Add Host** (see Figure 7.5).

Figure 7.5 Creating a New Host (A) Record

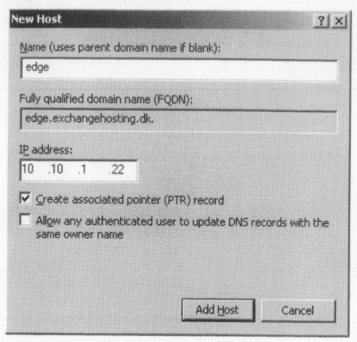

6. Close the **DNS Management snap-in** and log off the internal DNS server.

You may also choose to simply add the hostname and IP address of the edge transport server to the local hosts file on each hub transport server, and the hostname and IP address of any hub transport server to the local hosts file on the edge transport server in your Exchange organization. Although this is a perfectly supported solution, we don't recommend you use it unless you're dealing with a small shop that has maybe one edge transport server and one or perhaps two hub transport servers. If you're a messaging administrator/consultant in a large Exchange organization that contains multiple edge transport servers as well as several hub transport servers, it's far better to keep the name resolution centralized on an internal DNS server.

You add the hostname and IP address to the local hosts file on the server by performing the following steps:

1. Log onto the edge transport or hub transport server.

2. Click **Start | Run** and type **C:\windows\system32\drivers\etc** and press **Enter**.

3. Now open the **hosts** file in **Notepad**.

4. Type the **IP address** and **hostname** of the server (see Figure 7.6).

Figure 7.6 Entering the IP Address in the Hosts File

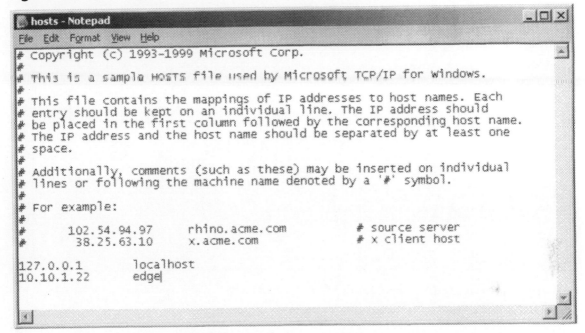

5. Save the changes and close **Notepad**.

6. Now open a **Command Prompt Window** by clicking **Start | Run** and then typing **CMD.EXE**.

7. You now need to purge and reload the remote cache name table, which is done by typing **NBTSTAT –R** followed by pressing **Enter** (see Figure 7.7).

Figure 7.7 Purging and Preloading NBT Remote Cache Name Table

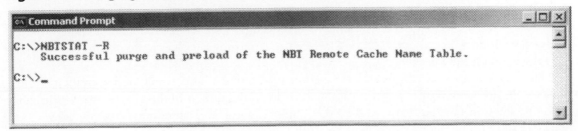

8. Verify that you can ping the respective servers using the fully qualified domain name, and make sure it's the correct IP address that's resolved (see Figure 7.8).

Figure 7.8 Pinging the Edge Transport Server

```
Command Prompt                                                    _ |□| x

C:\>ping edge.exchangehosting.dk

Pinging edge.exchangehosting.dk [10.10.1.22] with 32 bytes of data:

Reply from 10.10.1.22: bytes=32 time<1ms TTL=128
Reply from 10.10.1.22: bytes=32 time<1ms TTL=128
Reply from 10.10.1.22: bytes=32 time<1ms TTL=128
Reply from 10.10.1.22: bytes=32 time<1ms TTL=128

Ping statistics for 10.10.1.22:
    Packets: Sent = 4, Received = 4, Lost = 0 (0% loss),
Approximate round trip times in milli-seconds:
    Minimum = 0ms, Maximum = 0ms, Average = 0ms

C:\>_
```

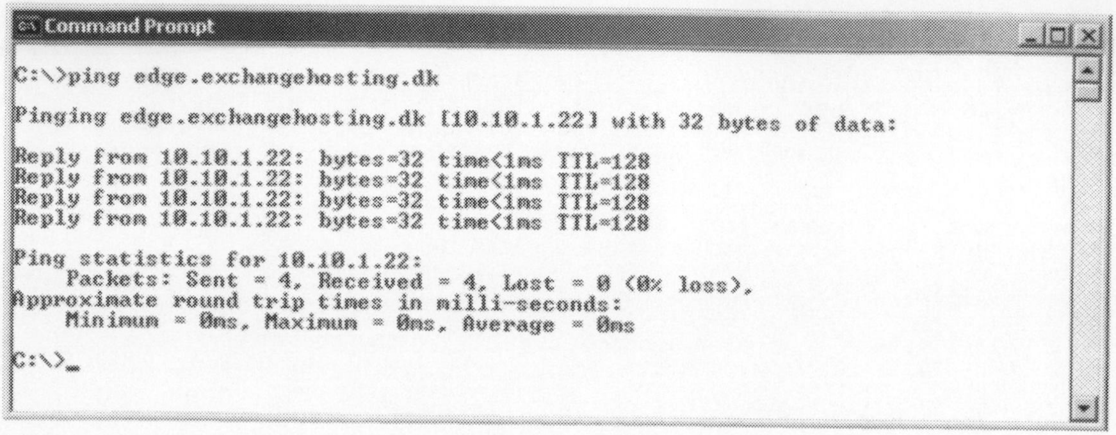

NOTE

You need to perform Steps 1 through 8 on each edge transport and hub transport server in your Exchange organization.

Configuring DNS Settings

If you choose to run the edge transport server in a multihomed setup where you have a network adapter connected to the internal network and one to the external network (perimeter network), you need to pay special attention in configuring DNS. Since the external network adapter doesn't have access to the DNS server in your Active Directory on the internal network, you should configure this network adapter to use a public DNS server (or a DNS server located in your perimeter network), so that the edge transport server can perform name resolutions, required to resolve SMTP domain names to MX or Mail Exchange records as well as route mail to the respective SMTP servers on the Internet.

The internal network adapter should be configured to use a DNS server located in the perimeter network or, alternatively, to use a hosts file. As you saw in the section of this chapter titled "Enabling Name Resolution Lookups between the Edge Transport and Hub Transport Servers," the edge transport and hub transport servers must be able to locate each other using name resolution.

As was also the case with Exchange Server 2000 and 2003, you can configure the edge transport server to use a DNS server (typically an external DNS server) for routing mail other than the DNS server specified on the external network adapter. In Exchange 2000 and 2003, this was done by taking the Properties of the default SMTP virtual server in the System Manager and then clicking the Delivery tab and finally the Advanced button. On an edge transport server, you configure the

DNS servers by taking Properties for the **Edge Transport** server object in the **Result pane**. On the **Properties** page, click the **External DNS Lookups** tab and specify the DNS server that should be used for routing mail to other SMTP servers on the Internet (see Figure 7.9).

Figure 7.9 External DNS Lookups

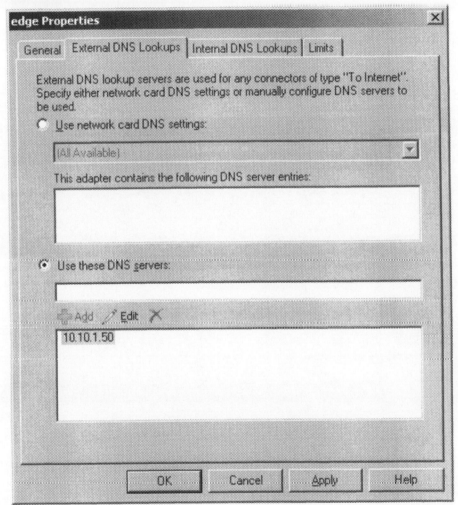

Installing the ADAM Component

Since the Edge Transport server role uses ADAM directory service as the repository for the replicated configuration and recipient data, it should come as no surprise that you'll need to install ADAM before you can install the Edge Transport server role. If you plan to install the Edge Transport server role on a Windows 2003 R2 server, you can install the component via **Add or Remove Programs** | **Add/Remove Windows Components** | **Active Directory Services**, where you need to tick **Active Directory Application Mode (ADAM)**, as shown in Figure 7.10. Next, click **OK** twice.

Figure 7.10 Adding the ADAM Component

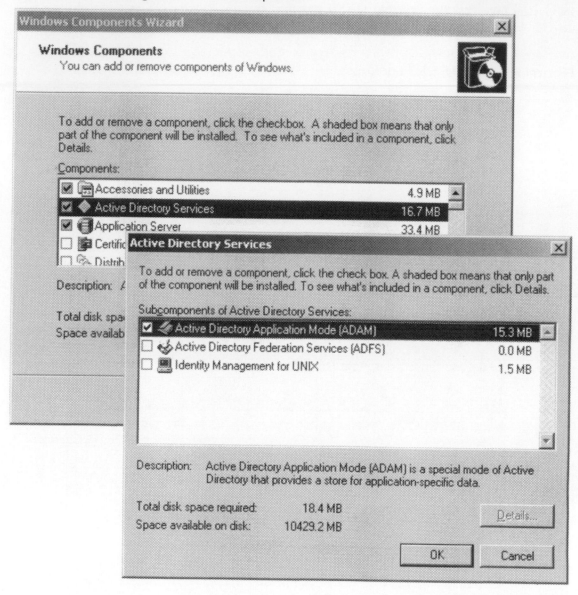

To install ADAM on a Windows 2003 server with SP1 or later will require downloading the ADAM installation package by clicking **Active Directory Application Mode** in the **Downloads** section under the following link: **www.microsoft.com/windowsserver2003/adam**.

Installing .NET Framework 2.0 and Windows PowerShell

As is the case with any other Exchange 2007 Server role, you also need to install both the .NET Framework 2.0 component as well as Windows PowerShell, which we showed you how to do in Chapter 3.

Saying Goodbye to the Windows SMTP and NNTP Protocol Stacks

As most of you might recall, Exchange Server 2000 and 2003 extended and made use of the Windows Server 2000 or 2003 SMTP and NNTP services and thus required you to install both the Windows NNTP and the SMTP components (which both are part of IIS) prior to installing the Exchange Server product itself. Since NNTP is one of the features that aren't supported in Exchange Server 2007, you need to make sure that this component isn't installed on the server. If it is, the Exchange Server 2007 readiness check will fail. In addition, because Exchange Server 2007 no longer uses the Windows Server SMTP service but instead has its own, which has been written from the ground up in managed code, you also need to make sure that the Windows Server SMTP component isn't installed on the server. As with NNTP, the Exchange Server 2007 readiness check will fail if this component is found on the server. You might ask why the Exchange Product Group replaced the Windows SMTP component with its own. Well, by doing so, the Exchange Product Group has reduced the risks that are associated with DoS attacks, eliminated the dependency on IIS, and reduced the work required to properly secure the server for deployment in the perimeter network (the DMZ or screened subnet).

Installing the Edge Transport Server Role

Now you can begin the actual installation of the Exchange 2007 Edge Transport server role. As is the case with all the other Exchange Server 2007 roles, you install this role by performing the following steps:

1. Navigate to the **Exchange Server 2007 source directory** (DVD media or the network share containing the Exchange Server 2007 binaries).

2. Double-click **Setup.exe**.

3. When the Exchange Server 2007 setup splash screen appears, click **Step 4: Install Microsoft Exchange**.

SOME INDEPENDENT ADVICE

Although we're using the Exchange Server 2007 Installation Wizard to install the Edge Transport server role, you can, as we stated in Chapter 3, also install this server role in unattended mode. To do so, you need to execute a command similar to the following: **Setup.exe /mode:Install /role: ET.**

The MMC 3.0 component will only appear as installed if you're installing Exchange Server 2007 on a Windows Server 2003 R2 edition. If you're installing the Edge Transport server role on a Windows 2003 server with SP1 or later applied, you need to download and install MMC 3.0 manually.

4. When the Exchange Server 2007 Installation Wizard has initialized, click **Next**.

5. Accept the End User License Agreement (EULA) and click **Next**.

6. You now have the option of enabling **Error Reporting** (which is recommended so that the Exchange Product Group receives information about any issues you encounter; in the end this information will give us a better product). When you have decided whether you want to enable error reporting or not, you can click **Next**.

7. Since you're going to install the Edge Transport server role, you now need to choose **Custom Exchange Server** Installation and then click **Next** (see Figure 7.11). This is also the screen where you have the option of changing the path for the Exchange Server installation (in the bottom of the screen).

Figure 7.11 The Exchange Server 2007 Setup Wizard

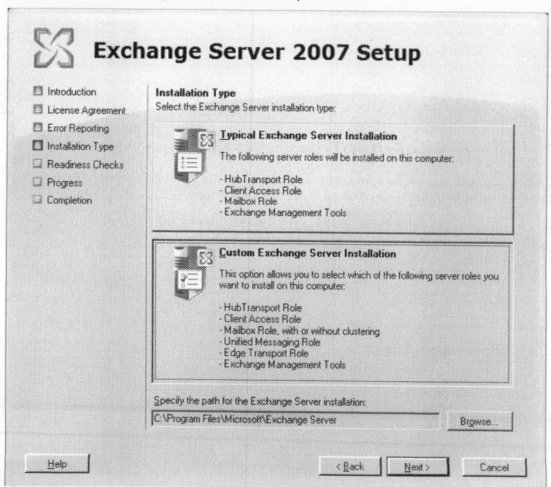

8. Tick **Edge Transport Role** (see Figure 7.12) and click **Next**.

Figure 7.12 Selecting the Edge Transport Role

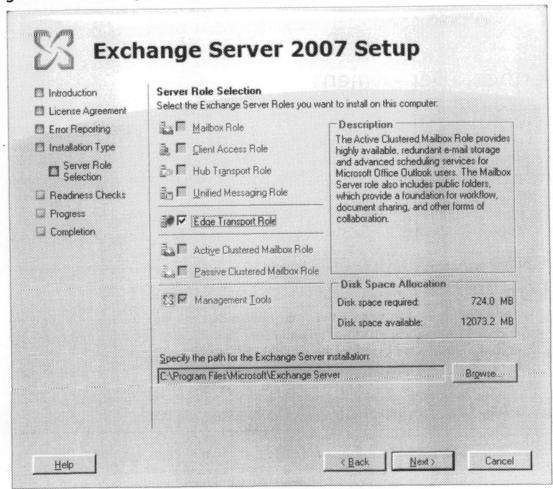

> **NOTE**
>
> Selecting the Edge Transport role automatically checks and installs the Exchange Management Tools and grays out any other server role.

9. When you have selected the **Edge Transport serve**r **role** as well as the installation path, click **Next**. If the readiness check completes without any issues, you can begin the installation by clicking the **Install** button. The Installation Wizard will now copy the required files and then begin the installation. Since the server on which the Edge Transport role exists is a standalone machine that doesn't belong to an Active Directory forest, and since this type of installation is pretty small, the installation process will complete relatively fast.

10. When the installation has completed, click **Finish**.

Verifying Deployment

Now that the Exchange 2007 Edge Transport server role has been properly installed, you're faced with several tasks that need to be completed before you're done. The first task on the list is to verify the installation and review the server setup logs. If the installation process fails or errors occur during the installation, it's a very good idea to follow the suggestions to track down the source of the problem (reviewing the setup logs, confirming that events 1003 and 1004 appear in the Application log, and checking that all required services are installed as well as operating in the correct startup mode and so on), but if the installation process completes without any issues, you can move right on to the next task on the list.

Creating and Importing an Edge Subscription File

This task is perhaps the most interesting one of them all; it's the task where you subscribe the edge transport server by establishing a one-way replication of recipient and configuration information from the Active Directory service to ADAM using the EdgeSync service (see Figure 7.13).

Figure 7.13 One-Way Replication with the EdgeSync Service

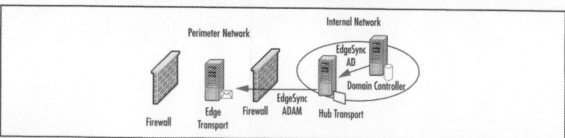

The EdgeSync service makes it a rather painless process to configure the edge transport server so that you can take advantage of its full feature set.

Some Independent Advice

Although the recommended method for establishing end-to-end mail flow between the Edge Transport server(s) and the Hub Transport servers within the Exchange organization is to create an edge subscription for the Edge Transport server, you can also do so by manually creating and configuring the Send connectors (that the EdgeSync service creates automatically). Although this will establish working end-to-end mail flow between the Edge Transport server(s) and the Hub transport server(s), you should bear in mind that you cannot use the recipient lookup feature or safe list aggregation, because these features require that the Edge Transport server has a subscription to the organization.

To configure an edge transport server subscription, you need to perform the following steps:

1. Export the edge transport server to an XML file using the *New-EdgeSubscription* CMDlet. To do so, open the Exchange Management Shell (EMS), type **New-EdgeSubscription –file "C:\EdgeSubscriptionFile.xml"** (or whatever you want to name the file; the name of the file doesn't have any impact on anything), and press **Enter**, as shown in Figure 7.14.

Note

When you run the *New-EdgeSubscription* CMDlet, an ADAM account is created as well. This account is used to secure Lightweight Directory Access Protocol (LDAP) communications during data transfer. The credentials for the account are also retrieved when you run the CMDlet

Figure 7.14 Creating a New Edge Subscription File

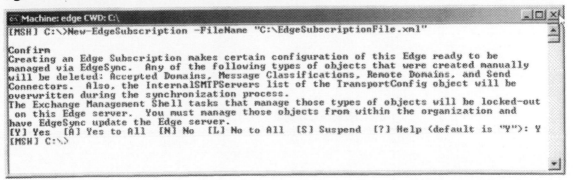

2. You now need to confirm that you really want to create an edge subscription, since this process makes certain configurations of the Edge Transport server so that it's ready to be to managed via EdgeSync. Because this is exactly what you want to do, type **Y** and then press **Enter**.

WARNING

Any accepted domains, message classifications, remote domains, and send connectors will be overwritten when you make a new edge subscription file. Also bear in mind that the Internal SMTP Servers list (a list of all internal SMTP server IP addresses or IP address ranges that should be ignored by the Sender ID and Connection filtering agents) of the *TransportConfig* object will be overwritten during the synchronization process. In addition, the Management Shell tasks that manage these types of objects will be locked out on the edge transport server, which means that you need to manage those objects from within the organization and then have the EdgeSync service update the edge transport server. When you run the *New-EdgeSubscription* CMDlet on a newly installed Edge Transport server, this information can be ignored, since you haven't configured anything manually on the server yet.

3. Since the XML file, which you can see in Figure 7.15, saved in the root of the C: drive needs to be imported on a Hub Transport server, you need to transfer the file to a Hub Transport server in the Exchange 2007 organization. You could do so by copying the file to a diskette or, perhaps even smarter, by using the Disk Drives feature in a Remote Desktop Connection client (if you have enabled Remote Desktop on the Edge Transport server and have TCP port 3389 open in the firewall between the parameter network and the internal network).

Figure 7.15 The Edge Subscription XML File

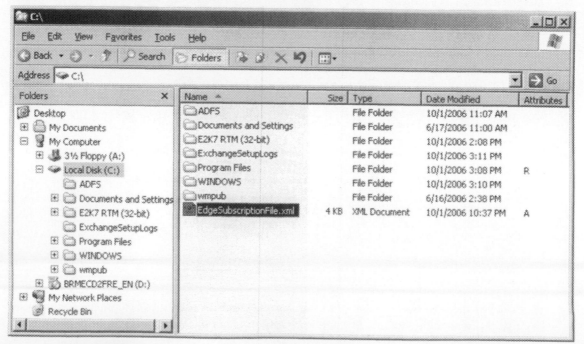

4. When the file has been transferred to a Hub Transport server, you need to import it by opening the **Exchange Management Console (EMC)**, expanding the **Organization Configuration** node, and selecting **Hub Transport**.

NOTE

To import the Edge Subscription file on a Hub Transport server, you must log on with an account that is local Administrator on the respective Hub Transport server as well as belonging to the Exchange Organization Administrators group.

5. Now click the **Edge Subscriptions** tab (see Figure 7.16).

Figure 7.16 The Edge Subscriptions Tab on the Hub Transport Server

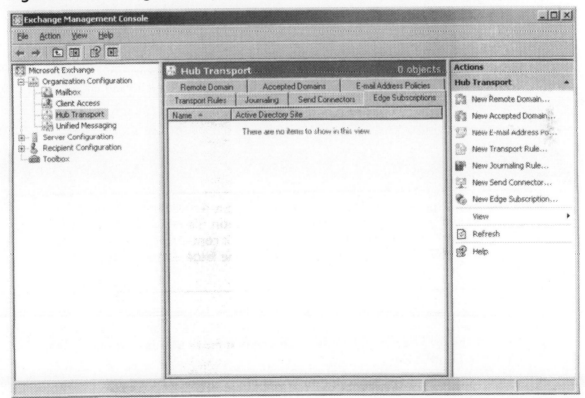

6. Since you have to create a new edge subscription, click **New Edge Subscription** in the **Action pane** (or if you prefer, right-click somewhere in the **Work pane** and select **New Edge Subscription** in the context menu).

NOTE

Importing the Edge Subscription file will establish an authenticated communication channel as well as completing the edge subscription process by beginning an initial replication. The Send connector, which is used when messages are sent to the Internet via the Edge Transport server, is created by default. In addition, the EdgeSync service will replicate the Send Connector configuration, accepted domains, remote domains, and safe sender lists as well as recipient data (SMTP address including contacts, distribution lists, and proxy addresses) from Active Directory to the ADAM store.

7. You will now be taken to the **New Edge Subscription Wizard**, where you have to specify the Active Directory site in which the Edge Transport server will become a member. If you have only one site, select **Default-First-Site-Name**. If your Exchange organization is deployed across multiple sites, click the drop-down list and choose the respective site.

NOTE

If your Active Directory topology consists of multiple Active Directory sites, it's recommended that you import the Edge Subscription file on a Hub Transport server that is located in the site that has the best network connectivity to the perimeter network (the DMZ or screened subnet) in which the Edge Transport server is deployed.

8. Now specify the location of the **Edge Subscription** file by clicking **Browse** and then **New** (see Figure 7.17).

9. Wait for the **New Edge Subscription Wizard** to complete and then click **Finish**.

Figure 7.17 Creating a New Edge Subscription

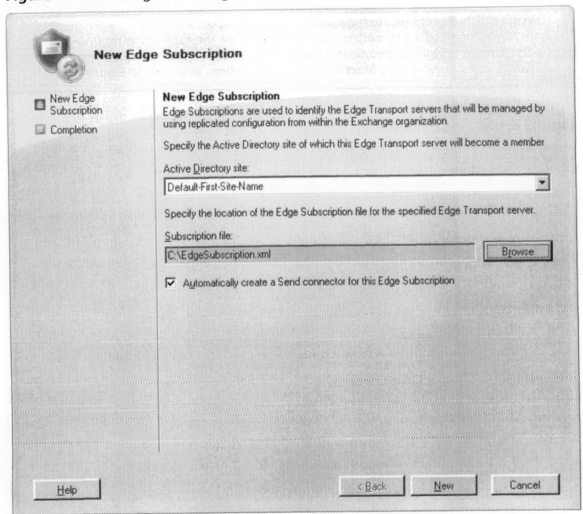

SOME INDEPENDENT ADVICE

If you instead wanted to import the Edge Subscription file using Exchange Management Shell (EMS), you could do so using the *New-EdgeSubscription –FileName: "C:\EdgeSubscriptionFile.xml" –Site: "Default-First-Site-Name"* CMDlet, as shown in Figure 7.17.

When the Edge Subscription file has been imported, it's a good security practice to delete the XML file.

Now that you have created an edge subscription, the EdgeSync service on the Hub transport server will synchronize configuration data such as each hour and recipient data every fourth hour to the Edge Transport server.

If you don't want to wait for four hours before the replication occurs, you can force the EdgeSync synchronization manually. To do so, open the EMS on a Hub Transport server and type **Start-EdgeSynchronization**, as shown in **Figure 7.18**.

Figure 7.18 Manually Starting the Edge Synchronization

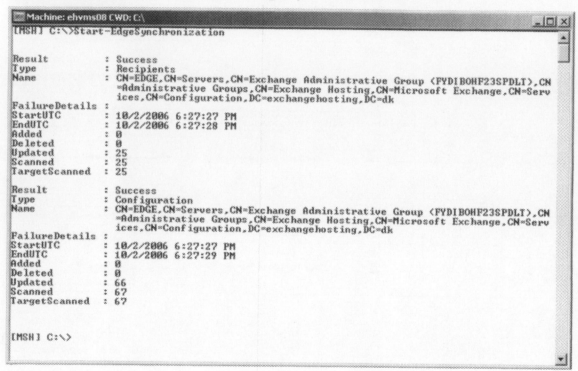

Forcing a synchronization using *Start-EdgeSynchronization* is also a very good idea if you have made bulk changes in Active Directory (perhaps added 50 new mail-enabled or mailbox-enabled users) so that these changes are replicated immediately.

NOTE

When the EdgeSync service synchronizes data from Active Directory to the ADAM store on the edge transport server, it is sent hashed to protect the synchronized data. In addition, the LDAP connection is secured by the ADAM credentials, which are stored in the Edge Subscription file.

Verifying That the EdgeSync Service Works As Expected

To see whether the Hub Transport server configuration data has propagated properly to the Edge Transport server, you should verify that a send connector has been created on the server. You do so by performing the following steps:

1. Log onto the Edge Transport server.

2. Open the **EMC**.

3. Click the **Edge Transport** node in the navigation tree in the **left pane**.

4. Now click the **Send Connectors** tab in the **Work pane** (see Figure 7.19).

Figure 7.19 The Send Connector on the Edge Transport Server

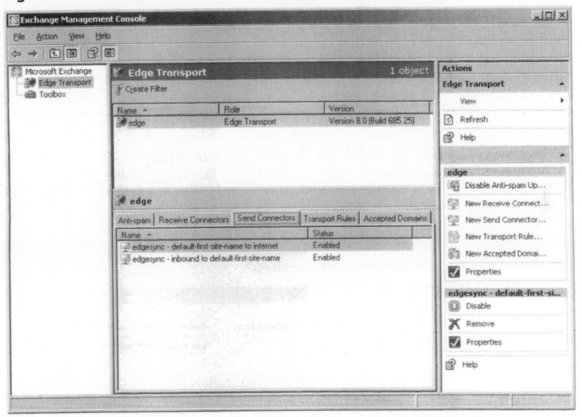

5. Verify that a **Send connector** has been created. Also make sure that each domain listed under the **Accepted Domains** tab on the **Hub Transport server** is listed when you type **Get-AcceptedDomain** in the **EMS** on the **Edge Transport server**. You should get a list similar to the one shown in Figure 7.20.

Figure 7.20 Listing the Accepted Domain

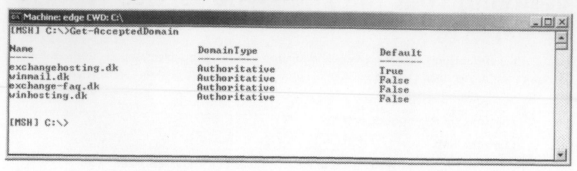

If everything is as expected, you now have a working Edge Transport server in your parameter network (your DMZ or screened subnet). Congratulations!

Creating a Postmaster Mailbox

No matter whether you plan to deploy an edge transport server in your organization or you simply will configure the hub transport server as the Internet-facing server, it's recommended that you create a postmaster mailbox. Since by now you most likely have installed a hub transport server in your organization, chances are you already have created a postmaster mailbox. But if you haven't, you need to perform the following steps:

1. On the edge transport or the hub transport server in your organization, open the **EMS** and type **Get-TransportServer**, as shown in Figure 7.21. This CMDlet will tell us the name of the transport server, whether message tracking has been enabled, and the external SMTP address used for the postmaster.

Figure 7.21 Retrieving the Postmaster Address

2. If no postmaster address is specified, you can do so by typing **Set-TransportServer –ExternalPostmasterAddress postmaster@*exchangehosting.dk*** (replace the domain name with the SMTP domain used in your organization) and pressing **Enter**.

To associate the configured external postmaster SMTP address with a specific mailbox, perform the following steps:

1. On an Exchange 2007 server in your organization, open the **EMC**, expand the **Recipient Configuration** work center node, and select the **Mailbox** subnode.

2. Now choose **Properties** for the mailbox you want to associate with the postmaster SMTP address and click the **E-mail addresses** tab.

3. Click **Add**; type **postmaster@*exchangehosting.dk*** (replacing the domain name with the SMTP domain used in your organization), as shown in Figure 7.22; and click **OK** twice.

Figure 7.22 The E-mail Addresses Tab

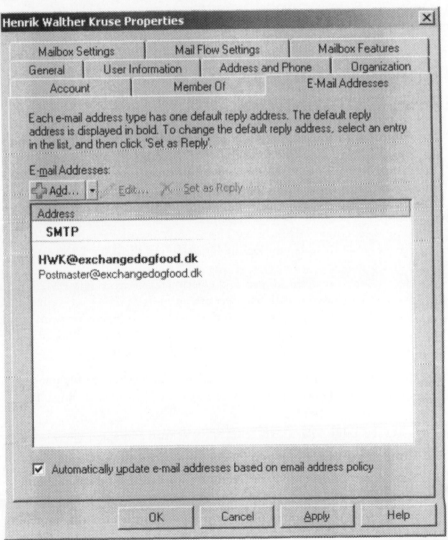

If you originally did a transition from Exchange Server 2000 or 2003, the postmaster SMTP address will most likely already be associated with the Administrator mailbox. If this is the case, you need to remove the SMTP address from this mailbox before you can associate it with another mailbox.

Some Independent Advice

The EdgeSync service supports edge subscription with only one Active Directory forest, so if your organization consists of multiple forests and you want to replicate each with your Edge Transport server(s), you will first need to synchronize the recipient addresses to one forest, which you then replicate with the edge transport server using the EdgeSync service.

Manually Configuring the Required Connectors

We assume that most organizations will create an edge subscription for the Edge Transport servers they choose to deploy in their perimeter network (DMZ or screened subnet). Since the EdgeSync service will automatically create the connector necessary to get a mail flow established to and from the Internet and to and from the Hub Transport server in the Exchange organization, no additional post-tasks are necessary regarding connectors; they will be replicated from the Hub Transport server to the Edge Transport server. But if for some reason you choose not to use an EdgeSync subscription, you'll need to create these connectors manually. The Edge Transport server will need four connectors: two receive connectors (one is created during the installation of the Edge Transport server) and two send connectors.

Since the Edge Transport server is located in the perimeter network (the DMZ or screened subnet), we assume that you have installed two network adapters in the server so that you can bind one receive connector and one send connector to the internally configured network adapter and one receive connector and one send connector to the externally configured network adapter.

To create and configure the required connectors, follow these steps:

1. Create a **Send connector** that is configured to send messages to the Internet. To do so, log on to the **Edge Transport server,** open the **EMC,** and click **Edge Transport** in the navigation tree.

2. Now select the **Edge Transport** server in the **Result pane** and then click the **Send Connectors** tab.

3. Click **New Send Connector** in the **Action pane** to launch the **New Send Connector Wizard**.

4. Give the new Send connector a name, such as **Send Connector (To Internet)**, choose **Custom** in the Intended Usage drop-down menu, and click **Next** (see Figure 7.23).

Figure 7.23 The New SMTP Send Connector Wizard

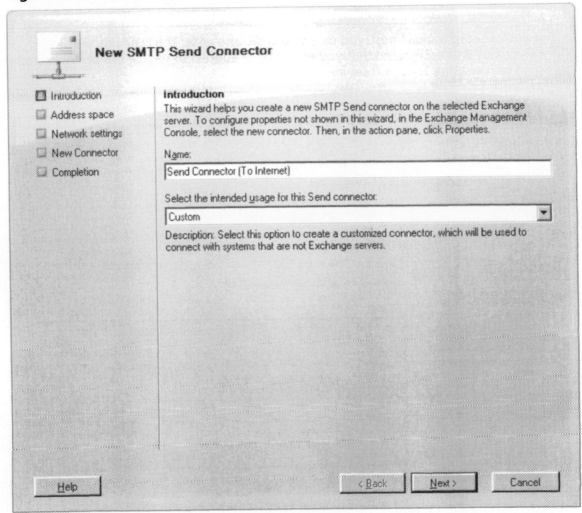

5. Now set the address space to ★, which means *all domains*, and click **Next**.

6. You now need to decide whether you want to route mail using domain name system (DNS) MX records or using a smart host. If you're required to route mail through an SMTP gateway located at your ISP or perhaps in your perimeter network (the DMZ or screened subnet), select **Smart Host** and enter the IP address of the respective SMTP server. (If you choose to use a smart host, select **None** on the **Smart host security settings** page, which will appear when you click **Next**.) Otherwise, select to route it using **DNS MX records**. On this page you also have the option of using external DNS lookup settings on the server. If you have or will create external DNS servers, enable this option and click **Next** (see Figure 7.24).

TIP

If you're using a smart host, you can, of course, also enter the FQDN of the SMTP server, but we recommend that you enter the IP address to reduce the performance load on the Edge Transport server.

Figure 7.24 The New SMTP Send Connector Network Settings

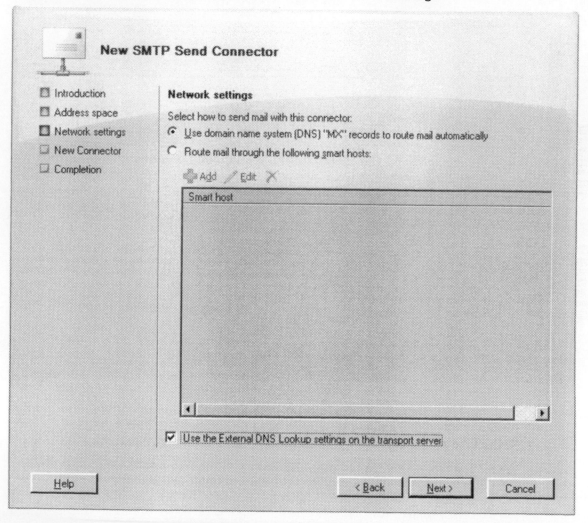

7. On the **Configuration Summary** page, click **New** and then click **Finish** on the Completion page.

   Okay, you have created the first Send connectors; now let's move quickly on to the second.

8. Once again, click **New Send Connector** in the **Action pane** to launch the New Send Connector Wizard.

9. Call the new Send connector **Send Connector** (to internal hub transport server) or something similarly meaningful and then select **Internal** in the intended usage drop-down menu. Click **Next**.

10. On the **Address Space** page, enter the **domains** that you already have added under the accepted domains tab on the Hub Transport server and click **Next** (see Figure 7.25).

Figure 7.25 The New SMTP Send Connector Address Space

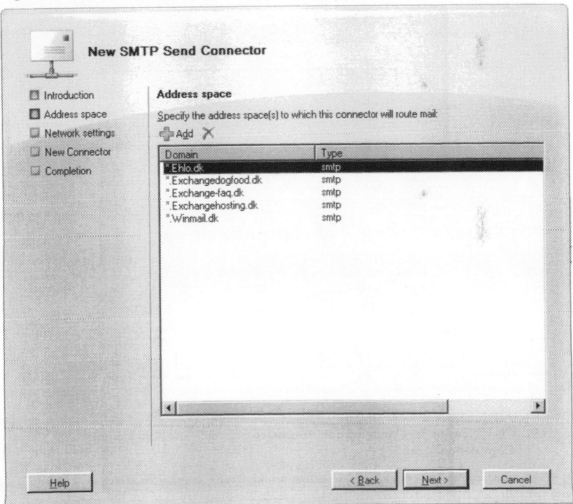

11.   Now select to route mail using a smart host. Enter the **IP address** of your hub transport server and click **Next**.

12.   On the **Smart host security settings** page, select **None** and click **Next** (see Figure 7.26).

Figure 7.26 The Smart Host Security Settings

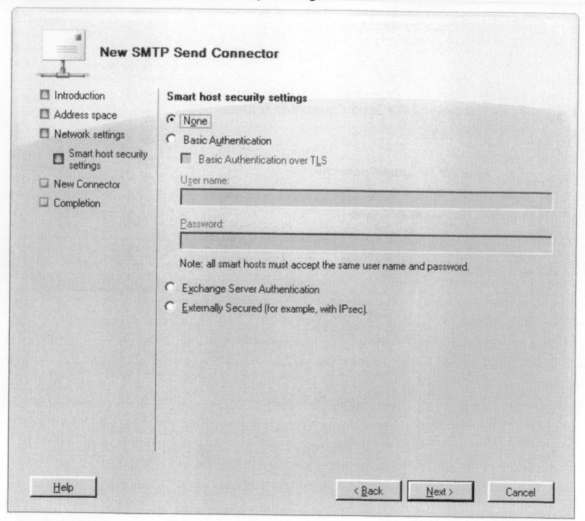

13.   Click **New** on the **Configuration Summary** page and click **Finish** on the **Completion** page.

The next thing to do is to change the settings for the Receive connector, which are created automatically when you install an Edge Transport server. You'll need to perform these steps:

1. To change the settings for this connector, click the **Receive Connectors** tab, open **Properties** for the **Default internal receive connector** *<server name>*, and click the **Network** tab.

2. Change the local IP address(es) from **(All available)** to the **IP address** configured on the Internet-facing network adapter (see Figure 7.27). Then click **OK**.

Figure 7.27 The Properties Page of the Default Internal Receive Connector

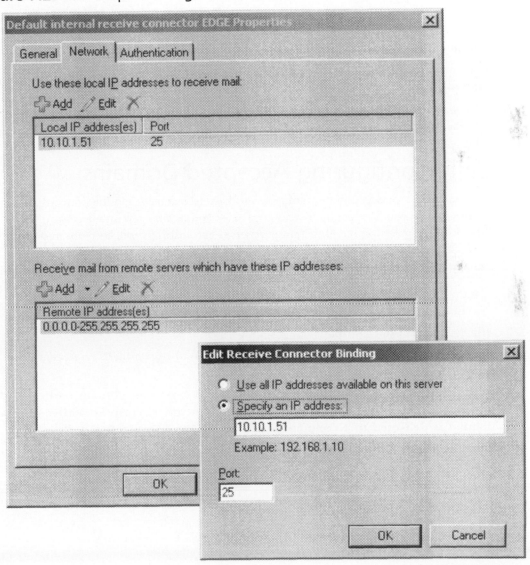

That's all you need to modify on the default receive connector. Now you can move on and create an additional Receive connector:

1. With the **Receive Connectors** tab selected, click **New Receive Connector** in the **Action pane** to launch the New Receive Connector Wizard.

2. Give the new Receive connector a name, such as **Receive Connector (from internal Hub Transport server)**; select **Internal** in the intended usage drop-down menu; and click **Next**.

3. On the **Remote Network Settings** page, enter the **IP address** of the Hub Transport server on the internal network. (Make sure you removed the default address range!) Then click **Next**.

4. On the **Configuration Summary** page, click **Finish** on the **Completion** page.

5. Now bring up the **Properties** page for the new Receive connector and then click the **Network** tab.

6. Change the **local IP address(es)** from **(All available)** to the IP address configured on the internally facing network adapter and then click **OK**.

Manually Configuring Accepted Domains

If you choose not to use an edge subscription, you also have to manually add the domains accepted by your organization. If you have configured an edge subscription, this step isn't necessary, since the accepted domains configured on the Hub Transport server automatically will be replicated to the Edge Transport server.

To manually add accepted domains to an edge transport server, perform the following steps:

1. On the Edge Transport server, open the **EMC** and click **Edge Transport** in the **Navigation tree**. Next, select the **Edge Transport server** in the **Result pane**.

2. Click the **Accepted Domains** tab.

3. Click **New Accepted Domain** in the **Action pane** to launch the New Accepted Domain Wizard.

4. Give the **new accepted domain entry** a name and type in the **domain name** for which you want to accept inbound mail. Also make sure that you select **Authoritative Domain. E-mail is delivered to a recipient in this Exchange organization** and then click **New** (see Figure 7.28).

Figure 7.28 The New Accepted Domain Wizard

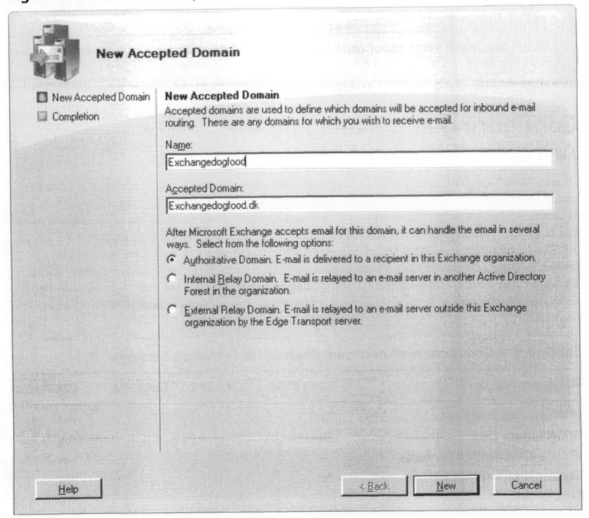

5.   On the **Completion** page, click **Finish**.

Repeat Steps 1 through 5 for each domain for which you want to accept inbound mail.

> **NOTE**
>
> We'll talk much more about configuring accepted domains on a hub transport server in Chapter 6.

Configuring and Managing the Antispam Filtering Agents

It's very likely that you have deployed an Exchange 2007 edge transport server to filter out most of the spam and other unsolicited e-mail messages sent to your organization so that they never reach the Exchange servers on your internal network. The Edge Transport server includes several antispam features that have been created to do just that. Most are features that we already know from Exchange Server 2003 and Exchange Server 2003 SP2; they have simply changed names and of course been improved further. In Table 7.1 you can see a comparison of antispam features from Exchange Server 2003 RTM, Exchange 2003 SP1, Exchange 2003 SP2, and Exchange Server 2007. It's not difficult to see that the Exchange Product Group invested significantly in improving the antispam features in the Exchange product.

Table 7.1 A Comparison of Antispam Features in Exchange Versions

Antispam Feature	E2K3 RTM	E2K3 SP1	E2K3 SP2	E2K7 RTM
IP Allow and Deny List	Yes			Yes
IP DNS Black Lists	Yes			Yes
IP Safe List (Bonded Senders)				Yes
Sender Filtering	Yes			Yes
Sender ID		No	Yes	Yes
Recipient Filtering	Yes			Yes
Content Filtering (IMF)		Yes		Yes
Content Filter Updates			Bi-weekly	Intra
Computational Puzzle Validation				Yes
Protocol Analysis Data Gathering				Yes
Protocol Analysis Sender Reputation				Yes
Open Proxy Validation				Yes
Dynamic Spam Data Update Service				Yes
Per User/OU spam Settings				Yes
Admin Quarantine Mailbox				Yes
Automatic DNS Block Lists				Yes

In addition to antispam features, the edge transport server also has full support for antivirus scanning. Surprisingly enough, the company's own ForeFront Security for Exchange server is a perfect match for the edge transport server. But the server also got full support for third-party products.

The antispam features on the Edge Transport server are known as *filtering agents*. You can see a list of these agents in Figure 7.29.

Figure 7.29 Filtering Agents on the Edge Transport Server

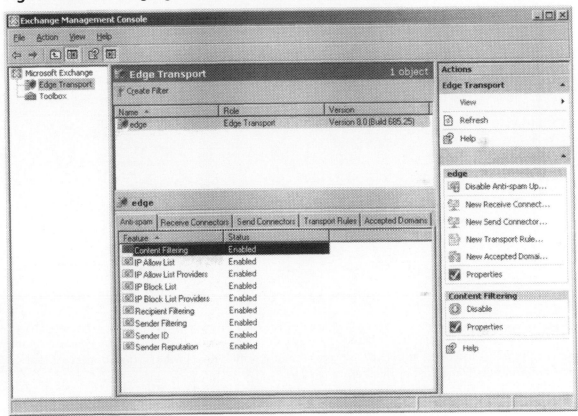

Figure 7.30 Installing the Filtering Agents on the Hub Transport Server

Hub Transport	9 objects

Remote Domain		Accepted Domains		E-mail Address Policies	
Transport Rules	Journaling	Send Connectors	Edge Subscriptions	Anti-spam

Feature ▲	Status
Content Filtering	Enabled
IP Allow List	Enabled
IP Allow List Providers	Enabled
IP Block List	Enabled
IP Block List Providers	Enabled
Recipient Filtering	Enabled
Sender Filtering	Enabled
Sender ID	Enabled
Sender Reputation	Enabled

When an SMTP session is established between an external SMTP server and the edge transport server, the filters listed in Figure 7.29 are applied in a specific order. In the next section, we'll look at the order in which the various filters are applied.

Connection Filtering

When an SMTP session is established to the Edge Transport server, the first filter applied is the Connection Filter. The Connection Filtering agent will first check whether the IP address of the external SMTP server is listed on the **IP Allow list**, which is shown in Figure 7.31.

NOTE

You can specify individual IP addresses as well as a range of IP addresses under the **Allowed Addresses** tab on the **IP Allow List** Properties page (see Figure 7.31).

Figure 7.31 The IP Allow List

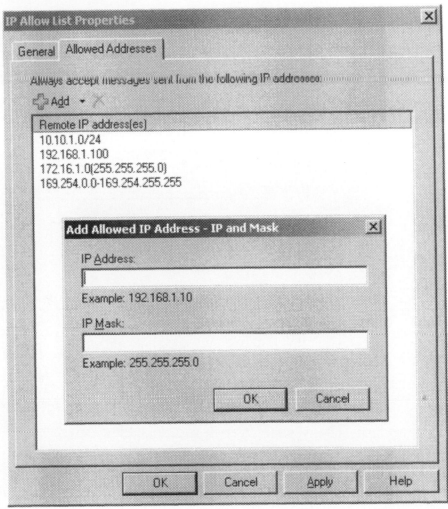

If the IP address is listed here, the SMTP server will be allowed to connect and transmit e-mail messages to the Exchange 2007 organization, but the e-mail messages will be sent to the Sender Filtering agent for further processing.

If the IP address of the SMTP server isn't listed on the IP Allow list, the Connection Filtering agent will check to see whether the server is listed on the IP Block list shown in Figure 7.32.

Figure 7.32 The IP Block List

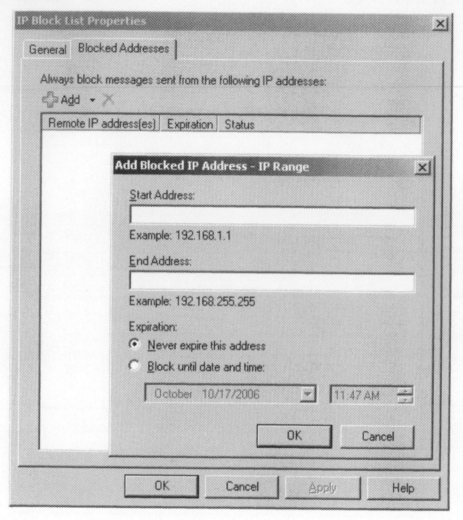

If the IP address of the SMTP server is listed on the IP Block list, connections from the server will be refused.

NOTE

A neat little improvement to the IP Address Block list is that you now can set an expiration date and time for an individual IP address or a range of IP addresses. This was not possible with Exchange Server 2003 SP2.

If the IP address of the SMTP server isn't listed on either the IP Allow list or the IP Block list, the Connection Filtering agent will check to see whether the IP address is allowed by any IP Allow list provider you have specified (see Figure 7.33).

Figure 7.33 IP Allow List Providers

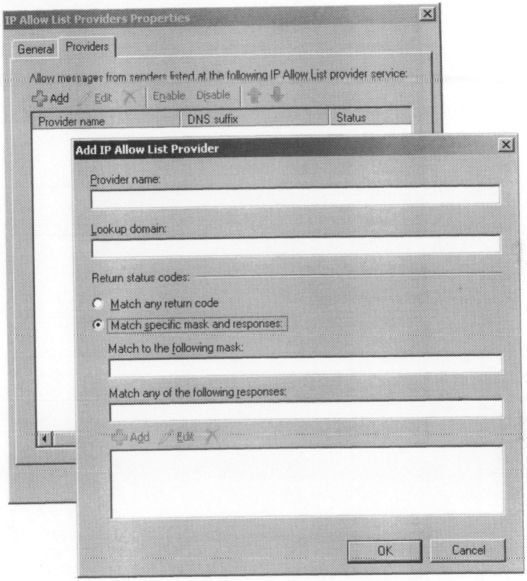

An IP Allow list provider is a provider that maintains a list of sender domains/IP addresses that you can rely on for sending legitimate e-mail messages and not spam. You can specify multiple IP Allow list providers and even specify how the providers' features should interpret the returned status.

If the SMTP server isn't listed on any of these lists, the Connection Filtering agent will do one last check before it allows the SMTP connection. It will check whether the server is listed on any real-time block lists (RBLs) you have specified under the Providers tab on the IP Block List Providers Properties page (see Figure 7.34).

Figure 7.34 Adding an IP Block List Provider

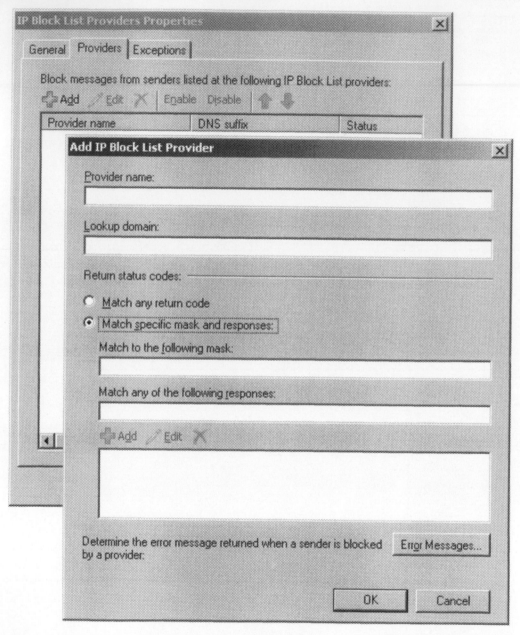

An RBL is an Internet-based service that tracks systems (and then adds those systems' IP addresses to a public list) that are known to send or suspected of sending out spam.

NOTE

You can read more about what RBLs are as well as how they work at http://en.wikipedia.org/wiki/DNSBL. In addition, you can find a list of the most popular RBLs at www.email-policy.com/Spam-black-lists.htm.

In addition to specifying IP Block list providers, you can also enter a custom error message that should be returned to the blocked SMTP server. Last but not least, there's an **Exceptions** tab where you can specify IP addresses to which e-mail messages shouldn't be blocked, regardless of the feedback from the RBL.

Sender Filtering

When the Connection Filtering agent has processed the SMTP connection, the next filtering agent involved is Sender Filtering, which will check the e-mail address of the sender against the list of e-mail addresses or domains you have specified under the **Sender Filtering Properties** page (see Figure 7.35).

The Sender Filtering agent lets you reject individual e-mail addresses, single domains, or whole blocks of domains (that is, a domain and any subdomains). When the Sender Filtering agent rejects an e-mail message, a "554 5.1.0 Sender Denied" message is returned to the sending server. The agent also lets you reject any e-mail messages that don't contain a sender.

In addition to rejecting e-mail address and/or domains specified on the Blocked Senders list on the Sender Filtering Properties page, you can also choose to stamp messages instead of rejecting them (done under the **Action** tab). When you choose this action, the metadata of the message will be updated to indicate that the message was sent by a blocked sender. The stamp will then be used when the Content Filtering agent calculates the spam confidence level (SCL) of the message.

Bear in mind that the Sender Filtering agent overrides the Outlook Safe Senders list (which we will talk about later in this section), which means that senders specified on the Block Senders list will be rejected even though they are included on a Outlook Safe Senders list.

Figure 7.35 Blocked Sender List on the Sender Filtering Properties Page

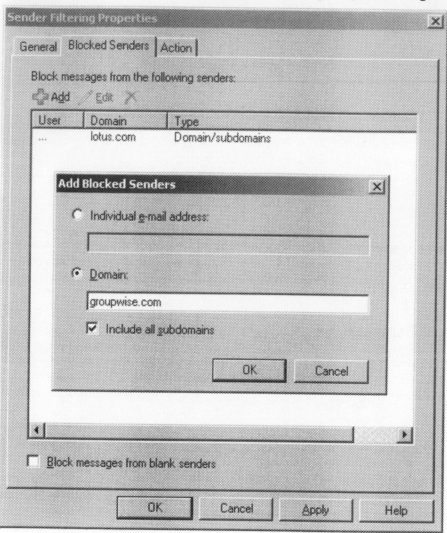

Recipient Filtering

When a message has been processed by the Sender Filtering agent and hasn't been rejected, it will be handed over to the Recipient Filtering agent. (Well, this isn't exactly true; the Connection Filtering agent will run once more, before doing so.) This will check the recipient of a given e-mail message against the Recipient Block list. As you can see in Figure 7.36, you can block recipients based on their e-mail addresses (that is, the SMTP address in the RCPT TO: field) as well as messages sent to recipients not listed in the Global Address List (GAL). The edge transport server can only check whether a recipient is in the GAL if you use EdgeSync subscription; otherwise, recipient data will not be replicated from Active Directory to ADAM.

NOTE

Any SMTP addresses entered on the Blocked Recipients list will only be blocked for senders located on the Internet. Internal users will still be able to send messages to these recipients.

Figure 7.36 The Blocked Recipients List on the Recipient Filtering Properties Page

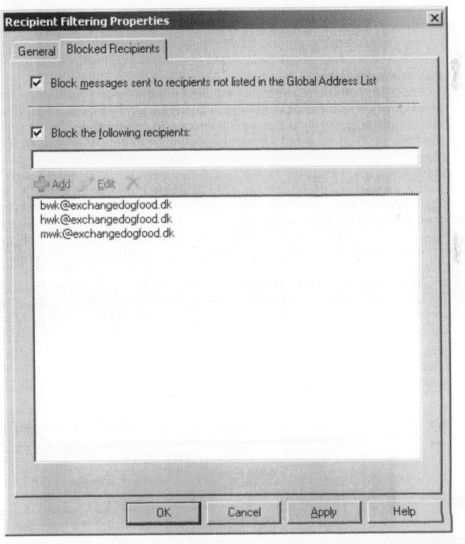

If an external sender sends an e-mail message to a recipient that is either listed on the Blocked Recipient list or not present in the GAL, a "550 5.1.1 User unknown SMTP" session error will be returned to the sending server.

It worth noting that the Recipient Filtering agent works for only domains for which the Edge Transport server is authoritative. This means that any domains for which the Edge Transport server is configured as a relay server won't be able to take advantage of Recipient Filtering. Diagrams of the Edge Transport Server with the Recipient Filtering Agent disabled and enabled are shown in Figures 7.37 and 7.38, respectively.

SOME INDEPENDENT ADVICE

As mentioned earlier in this chapter, the EdgeSync service will replicate recipient data from Active Directory to ADAM every fourth hour. With this in mind, be aware that any new recipients created on your mailbox server on the internal network won't be able to receive e-mail messages from external senders before the EdgeSync service has taken place hereafter.

The Recipient Lookup feature also includes a SMTP Tarpitting feature that helps combat *directory harvest attacks (DHAs)*. A DHA is a technique spammers use in an attempt to find valid SMTP addresses within an organization. This is typically done with the help of a special program that is capable of generating random SMTP addresses for one or more domains. For each generated SMTP address, the program also sends out a spam message to the specific address. Because the program will try to deliver a message to each generated SMTP address, an SMTP session is, of course, also established to the respective edge transport server (or whatever SMTP gateway is used in the organization). The program can therefore collect a list of valid SMTP addresses, since the SMTP session will either respond with "250 2.1.5 Recipient OK" or "550 5.1.1 User unknown," depending on whether the SMTP address is valid or not.

This is where the SMTP Tarpitting feature comes into the picture. This feature basically delays the "250 2.1.5 Recipient OK" or "550 5.1.1 User unknown" SMTP response codes during an SMTP session. By default, the SMTP Tarpitting feature on an Edge Transport server is configured to a delay of 5 seconds (but the value can be changed for each Receive connector), which should help make it more difficult for a spammer to harvest valid SMTP addresses from your domain.

Figure 7.37 The Edge Transport Server with the Recipient Filtering Agent Disabled

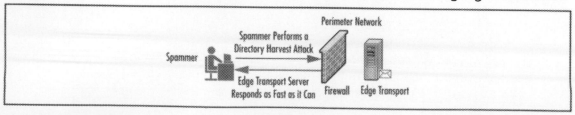

Figure 7.38 The Edge Transport Server with the Recipient Filtering Agent Enabled

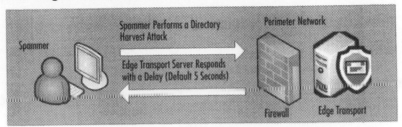

Sender ID Filtering

When an e-mail message has been processed by the Recipient Filtering agent and still hasn't been rejected, it will be handed over to the Sender ID Filtering agent.

The Sender ID is an e-mail industry initiative invented by Microsoft and a few other industry leaders. The purpose of Sender ID is to help counter spoofing (at least to make it more difficult to spoof messages), which is the number-one deceptive practice used by spammers. Sender ID works by verifying that every e-mail message indeed originates from the Internet domain from which it was sent. This is accomplished by checking the address of the server sending the mail against a registered list of servers that the domain owner has authorized to send e-mail.

If you don't have any experience with Sender ID, it can be a bit difficult to understand, so let's take a closer look at how it works.

An organization can publish a Sender Policy Framework (SPF) record on the public DNS server(s) hosting their domain. The published SPF record contains a list of the IP addresses that should be or are allowed to send out messages for a particular domain. If a particular organization has published a SPF record and someone at that organization sends a message to a recipient behind an Edge Transport server in another organization, the Edge Transport server will examine the SPF record to see whether the SMTP server that sent the message is listed there (see Figure 7.39).

Figure 7.39 How Sender ID Works Behind the Scenes

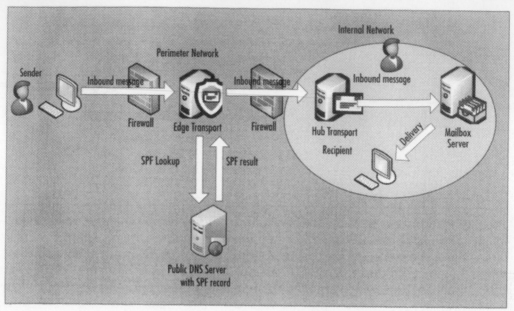

Sender ID can provide several different results and stamp them appropriately. Table 7.2 lists each of the results as well a short description and the action taken.

Table 7.2 Sender ID Results

Sender ID Result	Description	Action Taken
Neutral	Domain is neutral (makes no decision about IP address)	Stamp and Accept
Pass (+)	IP address for PRA permitted set	Stamp and Accept
Fail (-)		
- Domain doesn't exist		
- Sender isn't permitted		
- Malformed domain		
- No Purported Responsible Address (PRA) in header	IP address for PRA not permitted set	Stamp and Accept then either Delete or Reject

Table 7.2 Continued

Sender ID Result	Description	Action Taken
Soft Fail (~)	IP address for PRA not permitted set	Stamp and Accept
None	No SPF record published for the domain	Stamp and Accept
Temp Error	Transient error (could be unreachable DNS server)	Stamp and Accept
Perm Error	Possible error in record so couldn't be read correctly	Stamp and Accept

No matter what the result of the SPF check, the result will be used in the calculation process when an SCL rating is generated for a message.

> **TIP**
>
> In you want to check which IP addresses are allowed to send e-mail messages for a given domain, you can use a wizard such as the one at www.dnsstuff.com/pages/spf.htm, or open a command prompt and type **nslookup –q=TXT domain.com**. You should then be able to see the SPF record, including the list of the IP addresses allowed to send e-mail messages for this domain.

For additional information about Sender ID, visit http://en.wikipedia.org/wiki/Sender_id.

When the Sender ID Filtering agent checks whether a sending SMTP server has an appropriate purported responsible address (PRA), you can specify what action it should take for a given e-mail message that doesn't have an appropriate PRA.

You can configure it to **Reject message**, **Delete message** or **Stamp message with Sender ID result and continue processing**; the last one is the option selected by default (see Figure 7.40).

If you set Sender ID to reject the message, the message will be rejected by the Edge Transport server and an SMTP error response will be returned to the sender.

If you configure Sender ID to delete message, the message will be deleted without sending an SMTP error response to the sender. Since the message is deleted without informing the sending SMTP server, you would think that the sending SMTP server would retry sending the message, but this is not the case. The Sender ID filter has been made so cleverly that the Edge Transport server will send a fake *OK* SMTP command before deleting the message.

When you configure Sender ID to stamp messages with the Sender ID result and continue processing, the e-mail message will be stamped with information that will be used when the message is evaluated by the Content Filtering agent (which we will look at in a moment) to calculate the SCL.

Figure 7.40 The Action Tab on the Sender ID Properties Page

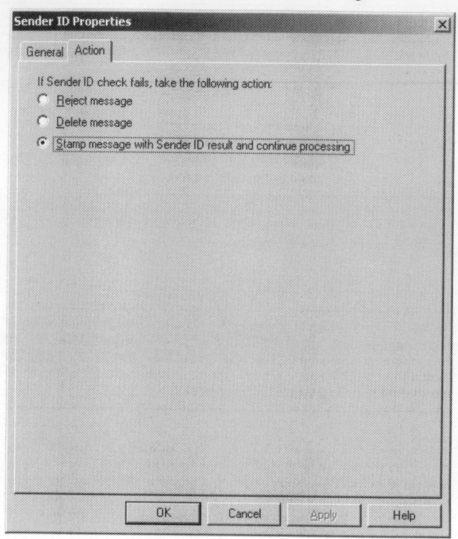

Figure 7.41 The Sender ID Framework SPF Record Wizard

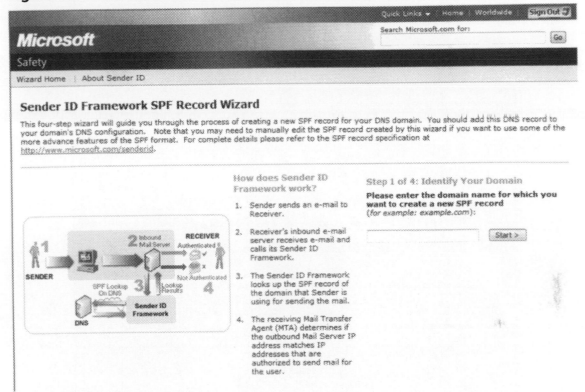

Content Filtering

The Content Filtering agent can be considered the next generation of the Intelligent Message Filter (or IMF version 3), which most of us know from Exchange Server 2003 (version 2 came with Exchange 2003 SP2). This means that the Content Filter is based on the SmartScreen technology, originally developed by Microsoft Research. When an e-mail message is received by an Edge Transport server with the Content Filtering agent enabled, it will evaluate the textual content of the messages and then assign the message an SCL rating based on the probability that the message is spam. This rating is stored as a message property called an *SCL rating*. The Content Filter is regularly updated using the Antispam Update Service (Windows Update) to ensure that it always contains the most up-to-date information when it's running. Since the Content Filter is based on the characteristics of many millions of messages (Hotmail, among others, is used to collect the necessary information about both legitimate as well as spam messages), it recognizes both legitimate messages and spam messages. The Content Filter can very precisely determine whether an inbound e-mail message is a legitimate message or spam.

The Content Filter can also, via spam signatures, analyze messages for phishing characteristics. If the message is a phishing attempt, the Content Filtering agent will stamp it with a property before delivering it to the recipient's inbox. When the message is delivered, Outlook 2007 will render it differently and warn the user that this most likely is a phishing attempt. When the message is viewed in Outlook 2007, all content will be flattened, any links will be disabled, and no images will be loaded.

Just as was the case with IMF in Exchange Server 2003, you can, with the help of the Content Filter, assign an SCL rating to the messages flowing into your organization. The Content Filter stamps the messages that it inspects with an SCL property (actually a MAPI property) with a value between 0 and 9. As you can see in Figure 7.42, depending on how a message is rated, you can delete, reject, or quarantine it to a specified mailbox.

Figure 7.42 The Action Tab on the Content Filtering Properties Page

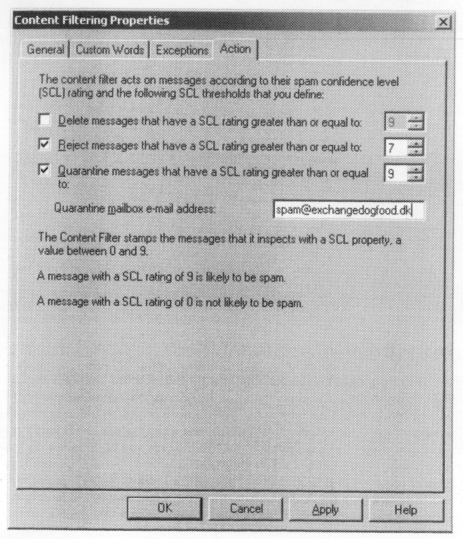

If a message equals the SCL delete threshold, the message will be deleted without notifying the sending server. If the message equals the SCL reject threshold, the message will also be deleted, but a rejection response will be returned to the sending server. If a message equals the SCL quarantine threshold, the message will be sent to the e-mail address specified in the **Quarantine mailbox e-mail address:** field. Bear in mind, though, that before a message can be quarantined, you need to create and configure a mailbox that should be used for this purpose. To do so, perform the following steps:

1. Create a new mailbox called **Quarantined Messages** or similar.

2. Depending on how many recipients as well as how many messages are received by your Exchange organization, configure a reasonable **quota** for this mailbox.

3. Set up delegation if you're going to open the mailbox as an additional mailbox under your primary mailbox account.

4. On the Edge Transport server, open the **EMS**, type **Set-ContentFilterConfig –QuarantineMailbox** *<SmtpAddress>*, and press **Enter**.

All quarantined messages will now be sent to the specified e-mail address, so be sure to check it for any false positives on a regular basis. When you find a false positive, you can resend it to the original recipient by opening the message and clicking **Resend**.

In addition, you can create a list of words and/or phrases that won't be blocked no matter the SCL rating of the particular message (the Content Filter will assign an SCL rating of 0 to messages including these words and/or phrases). You can also create a list of words and/or phrases that should be blocked no matter the SCL rating (see Figure 7.43).

Figure 7.43 The Custom Word List on the Content-Filtering Properties Page

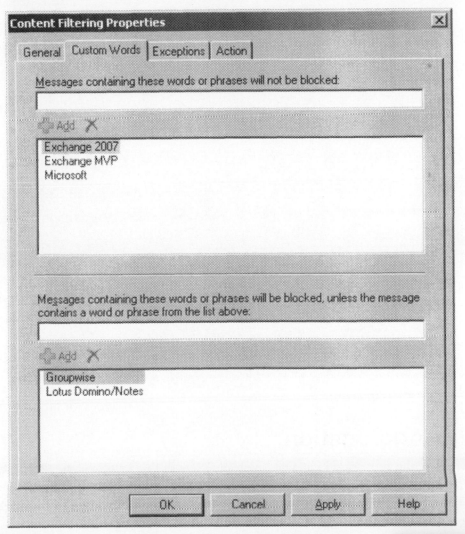

If for some reason you don't want to block any messages destined for a particular SMTP address, you can add the address to an exceptions list (see Figure 7.44).

Figure 7.44 The Exceptions List on the Content-Filtering Properties Page

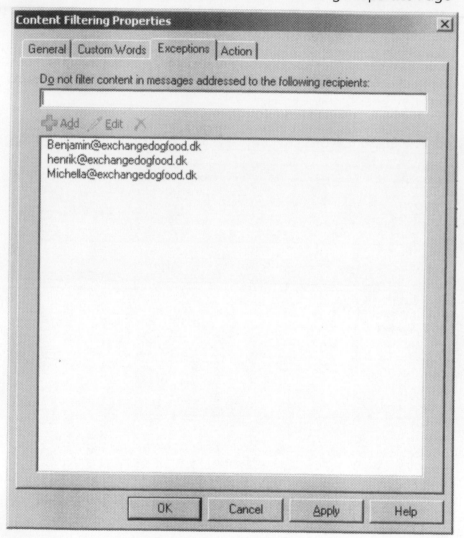

Safelist Aggregation

The content-filtering agent includes another antispam feature that isn't visible in the EMC GUI. Called *safelist aggregation*, it is a feature that basically collects data from the Safe Senders and Safe Recipients lists, which can be found under the Junk E-Mail Options in Outlook 2007 (see Figure 7.45).

Figure 7.45 The Safe Senders List in Outlook 2007

The e-mail addresses and/or domains that the end users in your Exchange organization have added to the Safe Senders and/or Safe Recipients list are stored on the respective mailbox servers on which a mailbox is located and can from here be pushed to Active Directory service, where the lists can be stored on each user object. If you use the EdgeSync service, these lists will, as part of the recipient data, be replicated from Active Directory to the ADAM store on the edge transport server.

To reduce the number of false positives on the Edge Transport server, the Content Filtering agent can, using safelist aggregation, let the e-mail addresses and domains configured on the Safe Sender list be allowed to pass through to end users' mailboxes without additional processing by the rest of the filtering agents. If you enable **Also trust e-mail from my Contacts** on the **Safe Senders** tab in Outlook 2007, shown in Figure 7.45, all Outlook contacts in user mailboxes will be allowed to pass through the filtering agents as well. Pretty neat, right?

Even though you have enabled the Content Filtering agent, you still need to enable and configure the safelist aggregation feature before you can use it. To do so, perform the following steps:

1. Log on to the Exchange 2007 server that has the Mailbox server role installed and open the **EMS**.

2. To read the Safelist collection from each user's mailbox and then hash and write it to the respective user objects in Active Directory, you will need to run the *Update-Safelist* CMDlet. When using the *Update-Safelist* CMDlet, you are expected to provide the identity for the mailbox you want to run the CMDlet on. Since you want to run the *Update-Safelist* CMDlet on all mailbox users on the mailbox server, you will need to use piping. To run *Update-Safelist* for all mailbox users, type **"get-mailbox | where {$_.RecipientType -eq [Microsoft.Exchange.Data.Directory.Recipient.RecipientType]::MailboxUser } | update-safelist"** and then press **Enter.**

3. Since the *Update-Safelist* CMDlet is a onetime-only command, you need to use the Windows Scheduler to schedule the CMDlet to run, let's say, once every 24 hours. To do so, create a batch file with the following code:

```
"C:\Program Files\Windows Powershell\v1.0\Powershell.exe" -psconsolefile
"C:\Program Files\Microsoft\Exchange Server\bin\exshell.psc1" -command
"Get-Mailbox | where {$_.RecipientType -eq [Microsoft.Exchange.Data.
Directory.Recipient.RecipientType]::MailboxUser } | Update-Safelist"
```

4. Save the batch file as **Update-Safelist.bat** or something similar. (Remember to change Notepad to all files instead of .txt files.)

5. Now schedule this batch file to be run every 24th hour (for example, at 00.00). To do this, open a command prompt window (or use the Windows Scheduler, which can be found in the Control Panel), type **AT 00.00 /every:M,T,W,Th,F,S,SU cmd /c "C:\Update-Safelist.bat"**, and press **Enter**.

6. To see whether *Update-Safelist* has updated the respective Active Directory user objects, you can check the *msExchSafeRecipientsHash* and *msExchSafeSendersHash* attributes for a couple of user objects using ADSI Edit or a similar tool. If these attributes have a value of *<Not Set>,* they haven't been updated, but if they instead have a value similar to *0xac 0xbd 0x03 0xca*, the user objects have been updated.

NOTE

To use ADSI Edit, you need to install the Windows Server 2003 Support Tools on the respective Exchange 2007 server.

To see whether safelist aggregation works as expected on the edge transport server, try to add a custom word or phrase to the Custom Words block list, which is found on the Properties page of the Content Filter. Now add the e-mail address of the private e-mail account (such as a Hotmail) to the Safe Senders list of your mailbox in Outlook 2007. Finally, send an e-mail message containing the word or phrase you added to the block list to your Exchange 2007 Mailbox user account. If the message appears in your mailbox, the safelist aggregation feature works as expected.

Outlook E-mail Postmark Validation

In addition to the safelist aggregation feature, the Content Filtering agent includes one more feature that will help reduce the number of false positives in your Exchange organization. The feature, called Outlook E-Mail Postmark Validation, is a computational proof that Outlook applies to all outbound messages to help recipient messaging systems distinguish legitimate e-mail messages from junk. With Outlook E-Mail Postmark Validation enabled, the Content Filtering agent will parse all inbound messages for a computational postmark header. If a valid as well as solved computational postmark header is present in a message, it means that the client computer that generated the message solved the computational postmark. The result of a postmark validation will be used when the overall SCL rating for an inbound message is calculated.

NOTE

If no computational postmark header exists or if the header is invalid, the SCL rating will not be changed.

On a default installation of the Edge Transport server role, the Outlook E-Mail Postmark Validation feature is enabled by default, but to verify that the feature indeed is enabled on your system, you can open the **EMC** and type **Get-ContentFilterConfig** (see Figure 7.46).

Figure 7.46 The Content Filter Configuration Settings

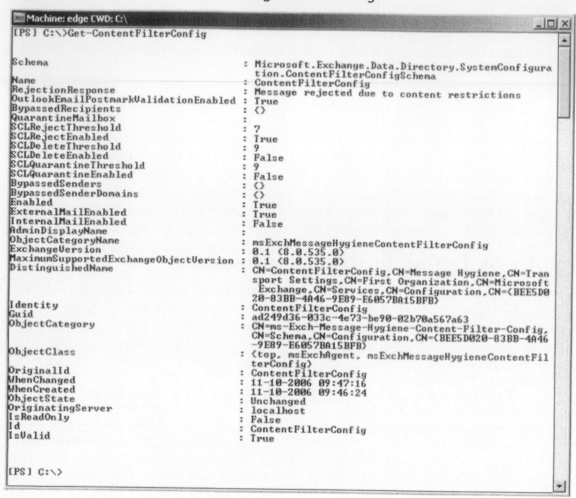

If the feature is set to **False** for some reason, you can enable it by typing **Set-ContenFilterConfig –OutlookEmailPostmarkValidationEnabled $True** and pressing **Enter**.

Attachment Filtering

As most of you are aware, Exchange Server 2003 didn't include a function that let you filter out specific attachments. Instead you had to create your own SMTP OnArrival Event Sink, use a third-party product, or strictly rely on the OWA 2003 and Outlook 2003 attachment control feature. However, since you really should filter out unwanted attachment types on an SMTP gateway in your perimeter network (the DMZ or screened subnet) before they arrive at your internal network, the last two options aren't recommend. An attachment filtering mechanism should have been a native feature in Exchange a long time ago, but finally the wait is over with the Edge Transport server in Exchange Server 2007. Let's do attachment filtering at the server level (hooray!). You now have the possibility of filtering out messages based on attachment filename, filename extension, or file MIME content type. You even have the choice of filtering out both the message and the attachment or just stripping the attachment. You can even choose to delete both the message and the attachment "silently," meaning that both will be deleted without notifying the sender of the message.

Some Independent Advice

In recent years more and more focus has been placed on deploying messaging environments, where each individual e-mail message is ether digitally signed or encrypted, or even protected using Information Rights Management (IRM). Here in Denmark where I live, the governmental institutions have an especially strong desire for protecting messages while they're in transit. If you're doing the same in your organization or are planning to do so, you should bear in mind that stripping an attachment from a digitally signed, encrypted, or IRM-protected e-mail message will invalidate the message so that it becomes unreadable. One way to solve this problem in dealing with digitally signed or encrypted messages is to put up some kind of black box that takes care of signing and encrypting the messages after the attachment filter processes them. The company I work for got such a product, which is becoming more and more popular here in Denmark.

The Attachment Filtering agent applies right after the Content Filtering agent and can be configured using the *Add-AttachmentFilterEntry* CMDlet. Unfortunately, there's no way to configure Attachment Filtering via the EMC GUI; you will have to do so using the EMS. We don't really know why this feature hasn't been included in the GUI, but our guess is that the Exchange Product team didn't have the time to integrate the feature in the GUI. If this is the case, we expect it to be included in Exchange Server 2007 Service Pack 1, but only time will tell.

Before you start to configure the Attachment Filter agent, you first need to make sure that the agent is enabled. To do so, you will need to open the EMS and type **Get-TransportAgent**. On a default installation of an Edge Transport server, this agent should be enabled by default, but if it for some reason is disabled, you can enable it by typing **Enable-TransportAgent –Identity "Attachment Filtering Agent"** and then pressing **Enter**.

Now that the agent is enabled, type **Get-AttachmentFilterEntry | FL** and press **Enter**. This will give you a list of all filename extensions and content types on which the Attachment Filtering agent can filter (see Table 7.3).

Table 7.3 Filename Extensions and Content Types

Type	Name	Identity
ContentType	Application/x-msdownload	ContentType:application/x-msdownload
ContentType	Message/partial	ContentType:message/partial
ContentType	Text/scriptlet	ContentType:text/scriptlet
ContentType	Application/prg	ContentType:application/prg
ContentType	Application/msaccess	ContentType:application/msaccess
ContentType	Text/javascript	ContentType:text/javascript
ContentType	Application/x-javascript	ContentType:application/x-javascript
ContentType	Application/javascript	ContentType:application/javascript
ContentType	x-internet-signup	ContentType:x-internet-signup
ContentType	Application/hta	ContentType:application/hta
FileName	*.wsh	FileName:*.wsh
FileName	*.wsf	FileName:*.wsf
FileName	*.wsc	FileName:*.wsc
FileName	*.vbs	FileName:*.vbs
FileName	*.vbe	FileName:*.vbe
FileName	*.vb	FileName:*.vb
FileName	*.url	FileName:*.url
FileName	*.shs	FileName:*.shs
FileName	*.shs	FileName:*.shb
FileName	*.sct	FileName:*.sct
FileName	*.scr	FileName:*.scr
FileName	*.scf	FileName:*.scf
FileName	*.reg	FileName:*.reg
FileName	*.prg	FileName:*.prg
FileName	*.prf	FileName:*.prf
FileName	*.pcd	FileName:*.pcd
FileName	*.ops	FileName:*.ops
FileName	*.mst	FileName:*.mst
FileName	*.msp	FileName:*.msp
FileName	*.msi	FileName:*.msi
FileName	*.ps11xml	FileName:*.ps11xml
FileName	*.ps11	FileName:*.ps11

Table 7.3 Continued

Type	Name	Identity
FileName	*.ps1xml	FileName:*.ps1xml
FileName	*.ps1	FileName:*.ps1
FileName	*.msc	FileName:*.msc
FileName	*.mdz	FileName:*.mdz
FileName	*.mdw	FileName:*.mdw
FileName	*.mdt	FileName:*.mdt
FileName	*.mde	FileName:*.mde
FileName	*.mdb	FileName:*.mdb
FileName	*.mda	FileName:*.mda
FileName	*.lnk	FileName:*.lnk
FileName	*.ksh	FileName:*.ksh
FileName	*.jse	FileName:*.jse
FileName	*.js	FileName:*.js
FileName	*.isp	FileName:*.isp
FileName	*.ins	FileName:*.ins
FileName	*.inf	FileName:*.inf
FileName	*.hta	FileName:*.hta
FileName	*.hlp	FileName:*.hlp
FileName	*.fxp	FileName:*.fxp
FileName	*.exe	FileName:*.exe
FileName	*.csh	FileName:*.csh
FileName	*crt	FileName:*.crt
FileName	*.cpl	FileName:*.cpl
FileName	*.com	FileName:*.com
FileName	*.cmd	FileName:*.cmd
FileName	*.chm	FileName:*.chm
FileName	*.bat	FileName:*.bat
FileName	*.bas	FileName:*.bas
FileName	*.asx	FileName:*.asx
FileName	*.app	FileName:*.app
FileName	*.adp	FileName:*.adp
FileName	*.ade	FileName:*.ade

You can add file extensions or filenames to this list using the *Add-AttachmentFilterEntry* CMDlet. For example, if you wanted to filter out zip files, you would need to run the following command: *Add-AttachmentFilterEntry -Name ★.zip -Type FileName*. If you wanted to filter out messages with a specific MIME type, such GIF files, you would need to use the command *Add-AttachmentFilterEntry -Name image/gif -Type ContentType*. If you wanted to filter out messages that contain an attachment with a specific filename, say one called *dangerous_file*, you would use the command *Add-AttachmentFilterEntry -Name dangerous_file -Type FileName*.

If you want to remove an attachment filter entry later, you do so using the *Remove-AttachmentFilterEntry* CMDlet. For example, if you wanted to remove the ZIP attachment filter entry, you would need to type *Remove-AttachmentFilterEntry −Identity filename: ★.zip*.

That's pretty simple, right?

To be able to use more advanced features such as scanning files in a ZIP file, you would need to install Forefront Security for Exchange Server (which we will talk a bit about later in this chapter) or a supported third-party product.

As mentioned, you can choose to block a whole message, including the attachment (will return a delivery status notification to the sender); strip the attachment but allow the message through (will replace the attachment with a text file explaining why the attachment was stripped); or silently delete both the message as well as the attachment (will delete both without notifying the sender).

You can also configure a custom response message that will be included in the delivery status notification, which is returned to the sender when a message and an attached file are blocked. This is done using the *Set-AttachmentFilterListConfig* CMDlet. An example could be *Set-AttachmentFilterListConfig −Action Reject -RejectResponse "This message has been rejected since the attached file type isn't allowed in this organization".*

NOTE

All attachment filter entries on an Edge Transport server use the same attachment filtering behavior—that means the same custom response message as well as action (reject, strip, or silent delete).

If you only want to strip the attachment but allow the message through, you would need to use the command *AttachmentFilterConfigList −Action Strip*. If you want to include a custom admin message in the text file that replaces the stripped attachments, you would need to use the command *AttachmentFilterConfigList −Action Strip −AdminMessage "The attachment in this message has been filtered as it's not allowed in this organization."* Finally, to silently delete both the message and the attachment, use the command *AttachmentFilterConfigList −Action SilentDelete*.

The last thing we'll mention regarding the Attachment Filtering agent is that you can exclude a list of connectors from attachment filtering, which means that attachment filtering won't be applied to messages flowing through the specified connectors. You can exclude one or more connectors using *Set-AttachmentFilterListConfig −Action Reject −ExceptionConnectors <Connector_GUID>*. To get the GUID for a receive connector, type **Get-ReceiveConnector | FL**.

If you want to see a list of the current settings for *AttachmentFilterListConfig*, type
Get-AttachmentFilterListConfig and press **Enter** (see Figure 7.47).

Figure 7.47 The Attachment Filter List Configuration Settings

For any additional information on how to configure the attachment filtering behavior using the
Set-AttachmentFilterListConfig CMDlet, see the Exchange Server 2007 Help file or type **Get-Help**
Set-AttachmentFilterListConfig in the EMS.

Sender Reputation

The Edge Transport server also includes a brand-new antispam feature called *Sender Reputation*.
The Sender Reputation agent, which is enabled by default (although only for externally received
messages), is an antispam feature that blocks inbound messages according to characteristics of the
sender. The agent actually relies on persistent data about the sender so that it can determine which
action to take on inbound messages.

The Sender Reputation agent analyses whether a sender forges the *HELO/EHLO* statement when establishing an SMTP session to the edge transport server. This is done on a per-sender basis, which makes it easier to see whether it's a spammer or a legitimate sender. A spammer typically provides many different unique *HELO/EHLO* statements in a specific time period, and they often also provide an IP address in the *HELO/EHLO* statement that doesn't match their original IP address (that is, the IP address from which the connection originated). In addition, they often try to provide a local domain name, which is the name of the organization to which the Edge Transport server belongs. In most cases the behavior of a legitimate sender is to use a different but more constant set of domains in the *HELO/EHLO* statement.

The Sender Reputation agent also performs a reverse DNS lookup when an external SMTP server establishes an SMTP session. This means that the edge transport server verifies that the IP address of the SMTP server matches the registered domain name, which the server submits in the *HELO/EHLO* command. If the IP address doesn't match the resolved domain name, there's a good chance you're dealing with a spammer.

As you already know, an inbound message is assigned an SCL rating when the Content Filter is applied. This SCL rating is also analyzed by the Sender Reputation agent. The agent calculates statistics about a sender by looking at how many messages from that sender in the past had either a low or high SCL rating.

Lastly the Sender Reputation agent is capable of performing an open proxy test against the sender's IP address. If the connection is looped back to the edge transport server through known open proxy ports and protocols—more specifically, SOCKS 4 and 5, Wingate, Telnet, Cisco, HTTP CONNECT, and HTTP POST—the sending server is considered an open proxy. As you can see in Figure 7.48, you enabled this feature on the Properties page of Sender Reputation.

NOTE

For the Edge Transport server to perform an open proxy test against an external server, keep in mind that you need to open the required outbound ports in any firewall located between the edge transport server and the Internet. The following ports are used during an open proxy test: 1080, 1081, 23, 6588, 3128, and 80. If you're using a proxy server in your organization, you also need to configure the Sender Reputation agent to use the proxy server for open proxy tests. You do this using the *Set-SenderReputationConfig –ProxyServerName* CMDlet. For details on how to configure a proxy, type **Get-Help Set-SenderReputationConfig** in the EMS or refer to the Exchange Server 2007 Help file.

Figure 7.48 The Sender Confidence Tab on the Sender Reputation Properties Page

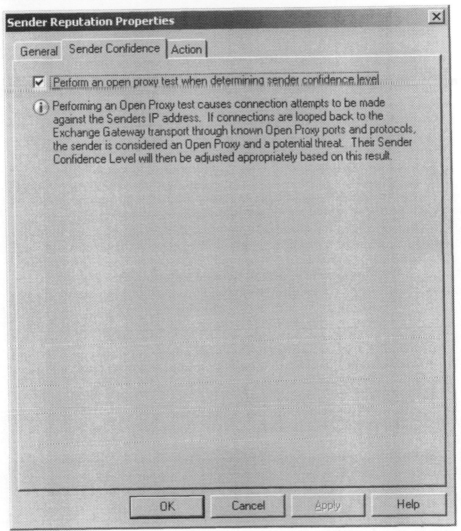

Depending on the results of these analyses and tests, the Sender Reputation agent assigns a sender reputation level (SRL) to the sender. As is the case with the SCL rating, this SRL can be a number between 0 and 9. The higher an SRL rating that is assigned to a sender, the more likely it is that the sender is a spammer. Under the Action tab, which also is found on the Sender Reputation Properties page, you can configure an SRL block threshold (see Figure 7.49), and when the threshold is exceeded, the sender is added to the IP Block list for a specified number of hours (the default is 24 hours).

Figure 7.49 The Action Tab on the Sender Reputation Properties Page

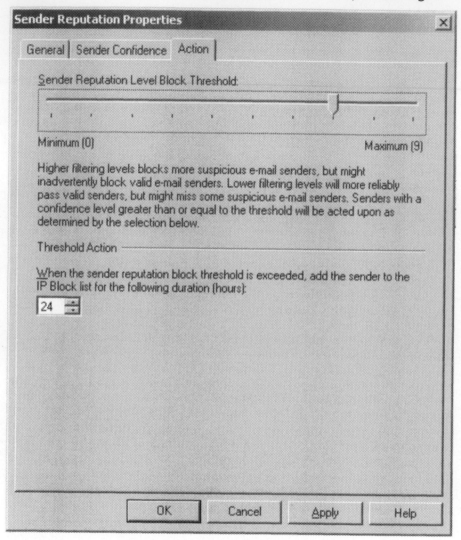

It's not in the hands of the Sender Reputation agent to decide how blocked messages are handled; this is instead controlled by the Sender Filter agent, which can be configured to block, reject, or stamp messages from blocked senders and continue processing.

NOTE

Senders that haven't yet been analyzed by Sender Reputation are assigned an SRL rating of 0. Only after the Edge Transport server has received 20 or more messages from a particular sender is an SRL calculated.

Antivirus Scanning

After a given message has been through the Attachment filter, it will be scanned by the antivirus product installed on the server, which could be ForeFront Security for Exchange Server 2007 (included in the Exchange 2007 Enterprise CAL) or a supported third-party product.

It should come as no surprise that the Edge Transport server role integrates perfectly with the ForeFront Security for Exchange Server 2007 product, but the server role also has rich support for partner antivirus providers. So you're not bound to use the ForeFront Security for Exchange Server product if you choose to deploy an edge transport server in your organization's perimeter network (DMZ or screened subnet).

Some of the third-party products that have shipped since Exchange Server 2007 was released in December 2006 are:

- Symantec
- Trend Micro
- GFI
- Kaspersky
- McAfee
- Sophos

All of these third-party providers participated in the Exchange 2007 Technology Adoption Program (TAP), so these products take full advantage of Exchange Server 2007 features.

NOTE

On February 8, 2005, Microsoft acquired the security software firm Sybari, the company behind the Exchange AntiGen product. The primary reason behind this purchase was to help enterprise customers become more secure. Since then Microsoft rebranded the AntiGen product series to ForeFront Security, which means that the old Exchange AntiGen product now is known as ForeFront Security for Exchange Server. Not only has the product name changed, but Microsoft has also been busy improving the product as well as integrating it more tightly with Exchange Server 2007; now the product is recommended as *the* antivirus solution for the edge transport server. For more information about ForeFront Security for Exchange Server, see www.microsoft.com/forefront/default.mspx.

SOME INDEPENDENT ADVICE

As some of you might be aware, in 2004 Microsoft published a document called *The Coordinated Spam Reduction Initiative* (which can be downloaded from http://tinyurl. com/yxzsc5). Even today, it's an extremely interesting document that focuses on how you can reduce the amount of spam using different filters, mechanisms, and the like. Comparing the content of the document with the features included in the Edge Transport server role, you will notice that most of them have been implemented in Exchange Server 2007.

Outlook Junk E-Mail Filtering

When a message has been through all the filtering agents, the message will finally be send to the recipient mailbox, where the Outlook Junk E-Mail Filter will take the appropriate action, depending on the SCL rating of the message. If the message has an SCL rating that is equal to or greater than the SCL Junk E-Mail folder threshold, which is specified on the Content Filtering Properties page, it will be moved to the Junk e-mail folder in the recipient's mailbox.

Securing the Edge Server Using the Windows 2003 Security Configuration Wizard (SCW)

Because the Edge Transport server is located in the perimeter network (the DMZ or subscreened network), it's much more vulnerable to potential attacks than the other Exchange 2007 server roles on the internal network. It's therefore highly recommended as well as a best practice to lock down the Edge Transport server role into as tight a state as possible.

You can lock down the Edge Transport server with the Security Configuration Wizard (SCW), a tool for reducing the attack surface of computers running Windows Server 2003 R2 or Windows 2003 server with Service Pack 1 (SP1) or higher applied. The SCW tool makes it a relatively easy and simple process to lock down the Edge Transport server, since you can do so using the SCW GUI wizard.

> **NOTE**
>
> The SCW can also be used to lock down the other Exchange 2007 server roles as well as Exchange 2003 front-end and back-end servers. Whether you want to do so depends on how aggressive the security policies are in your organization.

To lock down our Edge Transport server with the SCW, you first need to install the component. On the edge transport server, click **Start** | **Control Panel** | **Add or Remove Programs**. Now click **Add/Remove Windows Component**. Tick the **Security Configuration Wizard** component and click **Next** (see Figure 7.50). When the component has been installed successfully, click **Finish**.

Figure 7.50 Adding the Security Configuration Wizard Component

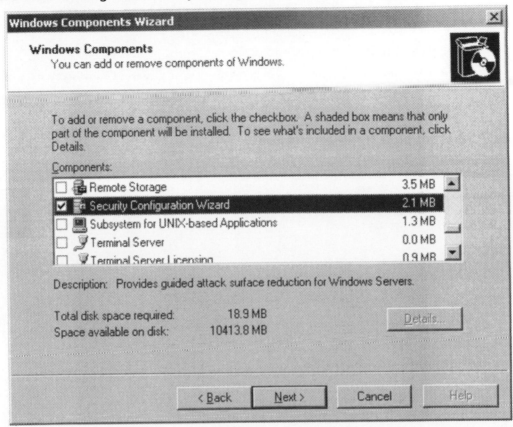

You now need to register the Exchange 2007 SCW extension file, which is located in the Scripts directory under C:Program FilesMicrosoftExchange (or whatever the path to your Exchange installation is). Since you need to do so using the *scwcmd register* command, open a command prompt window and type the following: **scwcmd register /kbname:MSExchangeEdge /kbfile: "C:\program files\ Microsoft\Exchange Server\scripts\Exchange2007.xml."** Next, press **Enter**. See Figure 7.51.

Figure 7.51 Registering the Exchange 2007 SCW Extension File

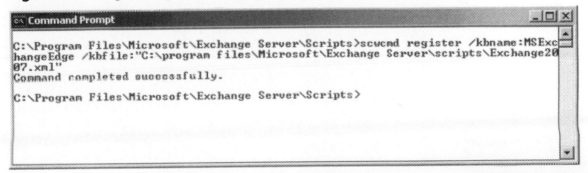

Now that the Exchange 2007 SCW extension file has been properly registered, you can launch the SCW Wizard. This is done by clicking **Start | Administrative Tools | Security Configuration Wizard**. Then follow these steps:

1. On the **Welcome to Security Configuration Wizard** page, click **Next**.

2. Since you're going to create a new security policy, select **Create a new security policy** and click **Next** (see Figure 7.52).

Figure 7.52 Creating a New Security Policy

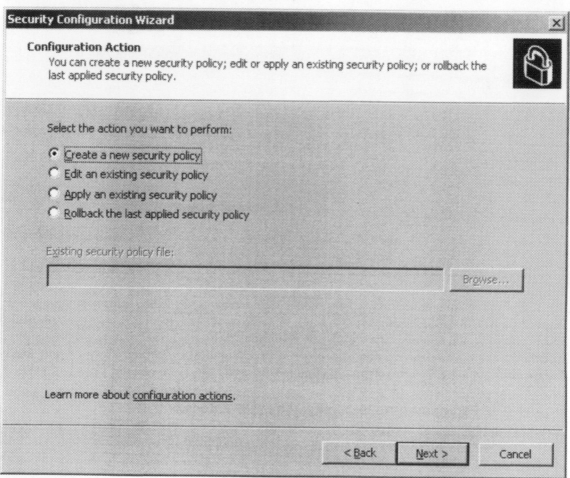

3. The NetBIOS name of the Edge Transport server will be pre-entered on the next page, and since you're going to apply the security policy to this, leave it like this and click **Next**.

4. When the security configuration database has been processed, click the **View Configuration Database** button.

If the Exchange Server 2007 SCW extension file has been properly registered, you should see an entry for the edge transport server role as well as the other Exchange 2007 server roles in the **SCW Viewer,** as shown in Figure 7.53.

Figure 7.53 SCW Viewer

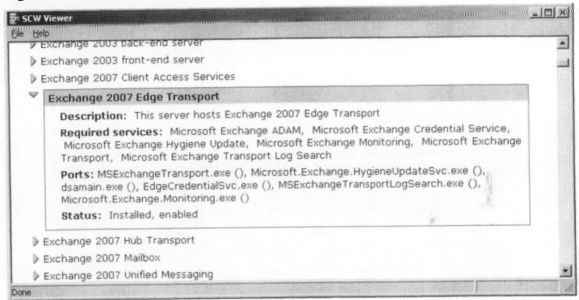

NOTE

If you don't see any entries for the Exchange 2007 server roles in the SCW Viewer, try running the SCW register command again. If it still doesn't show up, check the SCWRegistrar_log.xml file (located in the %*windir*%securitymsscwlogs directory) for any issues.

---

5. If you do see entries for the Exchange 2007 server roles in the SCW Viewer, close the viewer and click **Next**.

6. On the **Role-Based Service Configuration** page, click **Next**.

7. Now choose **Selected roles** in the drop-down box; uncheck all roles except **Exchange 2007 Edge Transport**, as shown in Figure 7.54; and click **Next**.

Figure 7.54 Selecting the Edge Transport Server Role

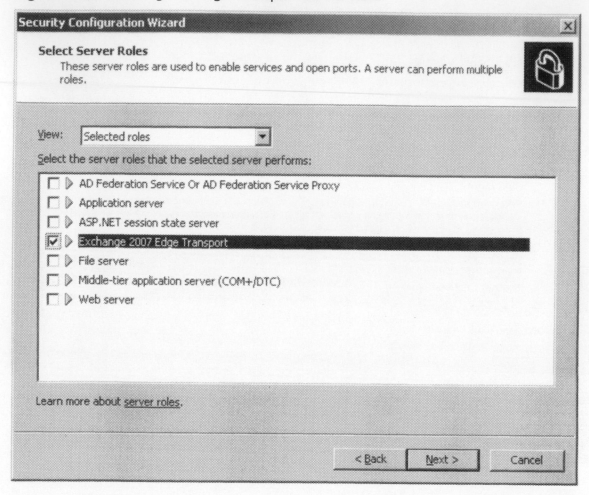

8. On the **Select Client Features** page, leave the default settings untouched (because you under normal circumstances don't need to change them, since they are configured based on the roles you chose in the beginning of the SCW). Click **Next**.

9. On the **Select Administration and Other Options** page, leave the default settings untouched. (As in Step 15, these are selected based on the role chosen in the beginning of the SCW.) Click **Next**.

10. Now you'll get a list of additional services found on the server while the SCW processed the security configuration database. When installing the edge transport server in a production environment, you should take your time and examine any services listed on this page, and then wisely decide whether they're required or not. If they're not required or you're unsure about this, I suggest that you uncheck them (you can always can enable them again, should they be required) and click Next.

11. You'll now need to decide how unspecified services (which basically are services not in the database yet) should be handled. You can choose to leave the startup mode as it is or have the service disabled. We recommend that you select **Disable the service** and then enable it manually should it be required. When you have decided how you would like unspecified services to be handled, click **Next**.

12. On the **Confirm Service Chances** page, verify that the service configuration for each service is set as expected, as shown in Figure 7.55 and click **Next**.

Figure 7.55 Confirming Service Changes

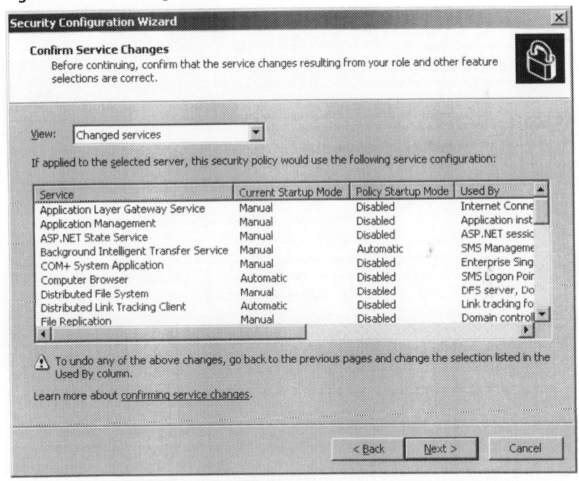

13. You have now reached the **Network Security** section of the SCW, which is where you'll configure inbound ports using the Windows firewall based on the roles and administration options selected on the previous pages. In addition, this is where you can restrict access to ports and indicate whether port traffic is signed or encrypted using IPSec. It's very important that you configure this portion correctly, since answering the questions

incorrectly might prevent the edge transport server from communication with the servers it's required to communicate with. Click **Next**.

14. On the **Open Ports and Approve Applications** page, you need to pay special attention. As you read earlier in this chapter, the Edge Transport server will need to replicate data from Active Directory to the local ADAM store at a scheduled set of intervals. Because this is done using LDAP via port 50389 and 50636, you need to add both these ports on this page. To do so, click the **Add** button shown in Figure 7.56.

Figure 7.56 Adding the Respective Ports

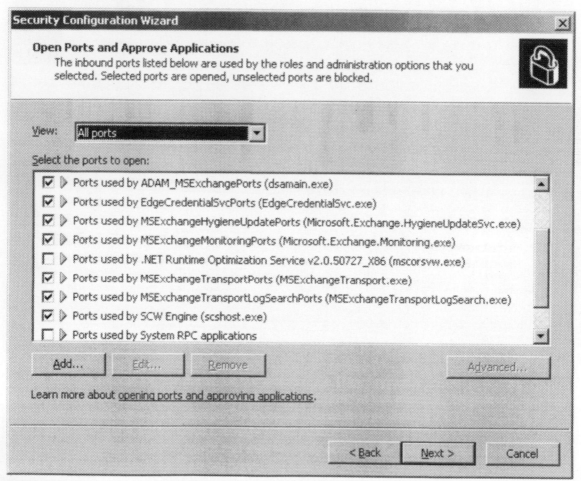

15. On the **Add Port or Application** page, enter 50389 in the port number field, check **TCP,** and click **OK** (see Figure 7.57).

16. Repeat **Step 15,** but enter port **50636** instead. Click **OK**.

Figure 7.57 Adding the LDAP Port

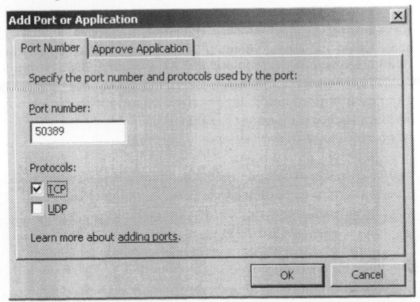

17 Select the newly added port **50389** in the list and click the **Advanced** button.

18. Click the **Local Interface Restrictions** tab and select **Over the following interfaces**. Check the network adapter connected to the internal network and click **OK**.

19. Repeat **Steps 17** and **18** for port **50636**.

20. Now click **Next** and confirm the port configuration settings. Click **Next** again.

NOTE

If you have enabled and allowed Remote Desktop connections to the Edge Transport server, we also recommend that you do Steps 17 and 18 for 3389 (Remote Desktop Protocol). This will block any connection attempts on port 3389 from external sources.

21. You have now reached the **Registry Settings** section in the SCW, and since you can skip this section, check **Skip this section** and click **Next**. Do the same on the **Audit Policy** page and click **Next**.

22. Now that you're through all the security configuration settings, it's time to save and apply the security policy. On the **Save Security Policy** page, click **Next**.

23. On the **Security Policy Filename** page, type a name for the policy and a description of the policy (this is optional). Click **Next** (see Figure 7.58).

Figure 7.58 Security Policy Filename

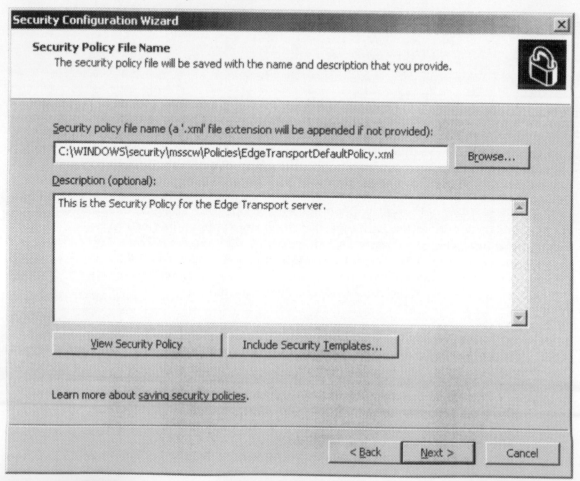

24. You will now be informed that applying this security policy to the selected server will require a reboot after the policy is applied. This is required for the configured applications or services to run properly. Click **OK,** select **Apply Now,** and click **Next** (see Figure 7.59).

Figure 7.59 Applying the Security Policy

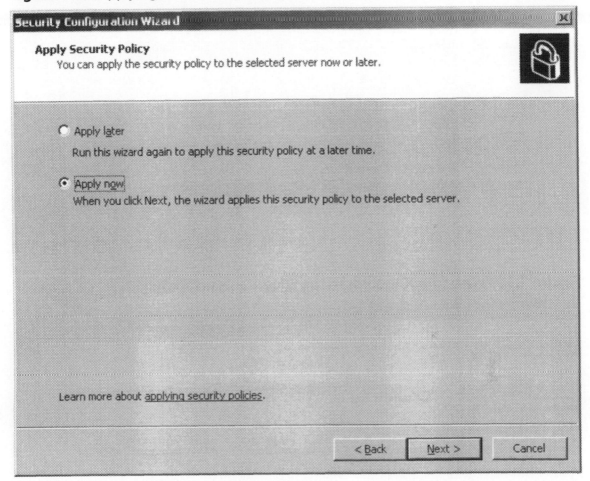

25. When the security policy has been applied, click **Next** and finally **Finish** to exit the SCW.

26. Reboot the server and verify that everything works as expected (mail flow, EdgeSync replication, Remote Desktop, and so on).

NOTE

If you're planning to deploy multiple Edge Transport servers in your perimeter network (DMZ or screened subnet), you can easily copy this Edge Transport server security policy XML file to the rest of the edge transport servers and apply it using the SCW.

Pointing Your MX Records to the Edge Transport Server

When the Edge Transport server has been fully deployed, the next step is to put it into production by routing incoming as well as outgoing messages through this server. To route incoming messages through it, you need to point the organization's MX or Mail Exchange record(s) to this server, unless you've got another Internet-facing SMTP server in front of your Edge Transport server, in which case you should just configure your Internet-facing SMTP server to forward all messages to the Edge Transport server.

To see the MX records for your domain, perform the following steps:

1. Open a **Command Prompt** window.

2. Type **Nslookup** and press **Enter**.

3. Now type **Set type=MX**.

4. Type your **SMTP domain** (such as *domain.com*) and press **Enter**.

This sequence of steps will list the MX records for your SMTP domain, similar to what is shown in Figure 7.60.

Figure 7.60 Pointing MX Records to the Edge Transport Server

```
Command Prompt - nslookup                                    _ | □ | X

C:\>nslookup
Default Server:  firewall.exchangehosting.dk
Address:  10.10.1.2

> set type=mx
> exchange-faq.dk
Server:  firewall.exchangehosting.dk
Address:  10.10.1.2

Non-authoritative answer:
exchange-faq.dk MX preference = 10, mail exchanger = mail.winhosting.dk
exchange-faq.dk MX preference = 20, mail exchanger = mxbackup.gratisdns.dk

mail.winhosting.dk        internet address = 213.185.8.11
mxbackup.gratisdns.dk     internet address = 195.140.140.55
> _
```

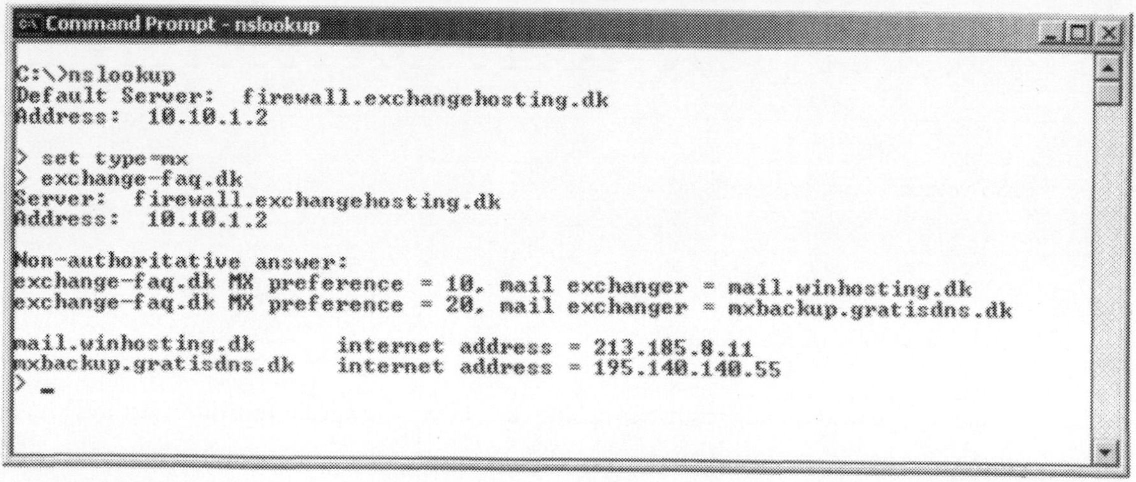

You can also use a Web-based service such as www.checkdns.net or www.dnsreport.com to retrieve your MX record information.

If you've got more than one MX record, the one with the lowest preference number is typically the one you should worry about, since any MX record with higher preference numbers are secondary MX record servers for your domain (that is, servers that will receive any messages, whereas for some reason your primary MX record doesn't respond to an *EHLO* or *HELO* command).

If you don't have an SMTP server in front of the Edge Transport server, you will need to change the MX record to point to your new server. This change will need to be done on the DNS server that hosts your SMTP domain (typically a DNS server located at your Internet service provider, or ISP).

TIP

In most cases, you make the MX record change yourself (via a Web-based administration panel), but if you are in doubt about how to make this change, ask your ISP/DNS provider to do it for you.

Depending on how your specific setup has been configured, there's also a chance that you simply need to change a rule in your ISA Server (or whatever firewall you have deployed in your organization) so that the rule points to the external IP address of the Edge Transport server.

In Chapter 12, which covers how you publish the different Exchange 2007 services and protocols through an ISA 2006 Server, we'll go through step-by-step instructions on how to publish your Exchange 2007 Server SMTP protocol, which is the same procedure for both an Edge Transport and a Hub transport server.

Deploying Multiple Edge Transport Servers in the Organization

If you're a messaging administrator or consultant working for a relatively large organization, deploying one edge transport server in the parameter network (DMZ or screened subnet) might not be sufficient. So your big question might be whether it's possible to deploy multiple Exchange 2007 edge transport servers, and if it is, how is the data in the ADAM store replicated between each edge transport server? Luckily you can answer yes to both of these questions; this section explains how to do exactly that.

You can deploy additional Edge Transport servers in your organization by cloning the configuration from the server that has already been deployed in the perimeter network. This is done by copying and exporting the configuration from an existing Edge Transport server (source server) to an XML file using the ExportEdgeConfig.ps1 script, which can be found in the Scripts directory under C:\Program Files\Microsoft\Exchange.

The ExportEdgeConfig.ps1 script exports all user-configured settings as well as data (except the EdgeSync subscription settings and the certificates that are used by the Microsoft Exchange EdgeSync service) to the XML file.

The configuration then needs to be copied and imported from the XML file to the newly installed edge transport server (target server), which is done using the ImportEdgeConfig.ps1, also found in the Scripts directory.

When you import the XML file on a new Edge Transport server using the ImportEdgeConfig. ps1, the script checks whether the configuration information and data exported from the source server are valid for the target server. If for some reason they aren't valid, the script will write the invalid setting(s) to an answer file that you can modify to specify the target server information that is used during the import configuration step.

Although you export all the configuration information except the EdgeSync subscription settings (including the configuration data in ADAM) from the source server and import it on the target server, you still must run the EdgeSync service on each Edge Transport server, since configuration data in ADAM cannot be replicated among the Edge Transport servers. This means that you need to run the EdgeSync subscription process after you have imported the cloned configuration.

When you have multiple Edge Transport servers deployed in the perimeter network, you can network and load-balance network traffic among the servers using the Domain Name System (DNS) round-robin mechanism. To use the round-robin mechanism, you need to enable the feature on the DNS server that resolves the names of the edge transport servers. When enabled, DNS uses round robin to rotate the order of resource record (RR) data returned in query answers where multiple records of the same type exist for a queried DNS domain name. This means that should one edge transport server be down, the Hub Transport server or the external SMTP server that tries to deliver an e-mail message to this Edge Transport server will retry, and then because of the rotation used by round robin, it will try to submit the e-mail message to another Edge Transport server in the perimeter network. The round-robin mechanism is enabled by default on servers running either Windows Server 2003 SP1 or later and Windows Server 2003 R2.

So to sum up, you need to perform the following steps in deploying additional Edge Transport servers in your perimeter network:

1. Install a clean edge transport server (following the guidelines in the beginning of this chapter).

2. Use the ExportEdgeConfig.ps1 script to export the source server's configuration information to an XML file. You do this by opening the **EMS**, where you navigate to **C:\Program Files\ Microsoft\Exchange Server\Scripts;** typing **.\ExportEdgeConfig.ps1 –CloneConfigData: "C:\CloneConfigData.xml"**; and then pressing **Enter** (see Figure 7.61).

Figure 7.61 Cloning an Edge Transport Server

3. Now copy the **CloneConfigData.xml** file to the **target server**.

4. Before importing the XML file, you need to validate it using the ImportEdgeConfig.ps1 script. To do so, open the **EMS**; navigate to **C:\Program Files\Microsoft\Exchange Server\Scripts**; type **.\ImportEdgeConfig.ps1 –CloneConfigData: "C:\CloneConfigData.xml" -IsImport $false -CloneConfigAnswer: "C:\CloneConfigAnswer.xml"**; and press **Enter**.

5. You will now be informed that the answer file has been created successfully. Now open the **CloneConfigAnswer.xml** file in **Notepad**, and modify any settings that are reported invalid for the target server.

6. On the target server, use the ImportEdgeConfig.ps1 script to import the XML file. To do so, open the **EMS**; navigate to **C:\Program Files\Microsoft\Exchange Server\Scripts**; type **./ImportEdgeConfig -CloneConfigData:\"C:\CloneConfigData.xml"** **-IsImport $true –CloneConfigAnswer: "C:\CloneConfigAnswer.xml"**; and press **Enter**.

You will now be informed that the import of the Edge configuration information succeeded.

The final step is to set up the EdgeSync service so that relevant configuration and recipient data are replicated from Active Directory to the ADAM store. Since we already went through these steps earlier in this chapter (in the "Creating and Importing an Edge Subscription File" section), we won't repeat them here.

The Edge Transport Rules Agent

Part of the new E-Mail Policy and Compliance feature set in Exchange Server 2007 is the edge transport rules agent, which is used to establish and enforce regulatory or corporate policies on e-mail messages sent to or received from the Internet.

Just as with the Hub Transport server, the transport rules agent on the Edge Transport server is capable of applying transport rules to messages flowing into and out of the organization, but although the transport rules agent looks very similar for both types of server roles, don't let it fool you. Although both server roles have a transport rules agent, several of the actions that are available for each server role are different. Actions such as applying message classification, appending disclaimer text, and sending bounced messages to senders with enhanced status code are all rules that are available on the Hub Transport server but not on the Edge Transport server.

For further information about the Hub Transport server-specific rules, see Chapter 6.

Table 7.4 lists all the available action properties and Table 7.5 all available property sets.

Table 7.4 Action Properties for Rules on the Edge Transport Server

Action Property	Expected Format	Description
Addresses	Array of Simple Mail Transfer Protocol (SMTP) addresses	On an Edge Transport server, *Addresses* accepts an array of SMTP addresses that are each enclosed in double quotation marks.
Classification	Single message classification object	*Classification* accepts a single message classification object. To specify a message classification object, use the

Continued

Table 7.4 Continued

Action Property	Expected Format	Description
		Get-MessageClassification command. For example, use the following command to apply the *ExCompanyInternal* message classification to an action:
$Action.Classification= (Get-Message Classification- ExCompanyInternal). Identity		
EnhancedStatusCode	Single delivery status notification (DSN) code of 5.7.1, or any value between 5.7.10 and 5.7.999	*EnhancedStatusCode* specifies the DSN code and related DSN message to display to the senders of messages that are rejected by the *RejectMessage* transport rule action. The DSN message that is associated with the specified DSN status code is displayed in the user information portion of the NDR that is displayed to the sender. The specified DSN code must be an existing default DSN code or a customized DSN status code that you can create using the *New-SystemMessage* CMDlet.
EventMessage	Single string	*EventMessage* accepts a single string that is displayed in an event log, which is added to the Application event log on the local computer.
FallBackAction	Single value with the choices of Wrap, Ignore, or Reject	
Font	Single value with the choices of *Arial*, *CourierNew*, or *Verdana*	*Font* specifies the font of the disclaimer text when the text is added to an e-mail message. The default font is *Arial*. Enclose the value in double quotation marks.
FontColor	Single value with the choices of *Black*, *Blue*, *Fuchsia*, *Gray*, *Green*,	*FontColor* specifies the color of the font of the disclaimer text when the text is added to an

Table 7.4 Continued

Action Property	Expected Format	Description
	Lime, Maroon, Navy, Olive, Purple, Red, Silver, Teal, White, or *Yellow*	e-mail message. The default color is *Gray*. Enclose the value in double quotation marks.
FontSize	Single value with the choices of *Smallest, Smaller, Normal, Larger,* or *Largest*	*FontSize* specifies the size of the font of the disclaimer text when the text is added to an e-mail message. The default size is *Smallest*. Enclose the value in double quotation marks.
HeaderValue	Single string	*HeaderValue* accepts a single string that is applied to the header specified using the *MessageHeader* action property. Enclose the string in double quotation marks.
Location	Single value with the choices of *Append* or *Prepend*	*Location* specifies where the disclaimer is inserted into the e-mail message. Append puts the disclaimer at the bottom of the e-mail message thread. Prepend puts the disclaimer at the start of the newest e-mailmessage. Enclose the value in double quotation marks.
MessageHeader	Single string	*MessageHeader* accepts a string that specifies which *Message Header* to add or modify. The string that is specified by the *HeaderValue* action property is inserted into the header that is specified by *MessageHeader*. Enclose the string in double quotation marks.
Prefix	Single string	*Prefix* accepts a string that is prepended to the subject of the e-mail message. Enclose the string in double quotation marks.
RejectReason	Single string	*RejectReason* accepts a string that is used to populate the administrator information portion of the NDR that is returned to the e-mail sender if an e-mail message is rejected. Enclose the string in double quotation marks.

Continued

Table 7.4 Continued

Action Property	Expected Format	Description
SclValue	Single integer	*SclValue* accepts a single integer from 0 to 9, which is used to configure the spam confidence level (SCL) of the e-mail message. Enclose the integer in double quotation marks.
Separator	Single value with the choices *WithSeparator* or *Without-Separator*	*Separator* specifies whether a separator is placed between the disclaimer and the e-mail message body. Enclose the value in double quotation marks.
Text	Single string	*Text* accepts a string that is used to populate the disclaimer message that is added to an e-mail message. Enclose the string in double quotation marks.

NOTE

Unlike the Hub Transport server, the Edge Transport server only allows you to specify an array of SMTP addresses. This is because the Edge Transport server doesn't have access to Active Directory, unlike the Hub Transport server, on which you can specify an array of Active Directory mailboxes, contacts, mail-enabled users, and distribution group objects.

Table 7.5 Supported Actions on the Edge Transport Server

Rule Action	Action Name	First Action Property	Additional Action Property	Rule Description
Log an event with message	*LogEvent*	*Event-Message*	Not applicable	*LogEvent* inserts an event into the Application log on the local computer.
Prepend the subject with string	*Prepend-Subject*	*Prefix*	Not applicable	*PrependSubject* prepends a string to the start of the e-mail message subject field.

Table 7.5 Continued

Rule Action	Action Name	First Action Property	Additional Action Property	Rule Description
Set the spam confidence level to value	*SetScl*	*SclValue*	Not applicable	*SetScl* configures the SCL on an e-mail message.
Set header with value	*SetHeader*	*Message-Header*	*HeaderValue*	*SetHeader* creates a new message header field or modifies an existing message header field.
Remove header	*Remove-Header*	*Message-Header*	Not applicable	*RemoveHeader* removes the specified message header field from an e-mail message.
Add a recipient in the To field addresses	AddTo-Recipient	*Addresses*	Not applicable	*AddToRecipient* adds one or more e-mail addresses to the To address list of the e-mail message. The original recipients can see the additional address.
Copy the message to addresses	*CopyTo*	Addresses	Not applicable	*CopyTo* adds one or more e-mail addresses to the carbon copy (CC) field of the e-mail message. The original recipients can see the original address.
Blind carbon copy (BCC) the message to addresses	*BlindCopyTo*	*Addresses*	Not applicable	*BlindCopyTo* adds one or more e-mail addresses to the blind carbon copy (BCC) address list of the e-mail message. The original recipients aren't notified and can't see the additional address.

Continued

Table 7.5 Continued

Rule Action	Action Name	First Action Property	Additional Action Property	Rule Description
Drop connection	*Disconnect*	*Not applicable*	Not applicable	*Disconnect* ends the connection between the sending server and the edge transport server without generating an NDR message.
Redirect the message to addresses	*Redirect-Message*	*Addresses*	Not applicable	*RedirectMessage* redirects the e-mail message to one or more e-mail addresses that are specified by the administrator. The message isn't delivered to the original recipient, and no notification is provided to the recipient or the sender.
Put message in quarantine	*Quarantine*	Not applicable	Not applicable	*Quarantine* redirects the e-mail message to the spam quarantine mailbox that is configured by using the *QuarantineMailbox* parameter on the *Set-ContentFilterConfig* CMDlet. Note: You must populate the *QuarantineMailbox* parameter with the *Set-ContentFilterConfig* CMDlet, and you need to make sure that the specified mailbox has been created. If the *QuarantineMailbox* hasn't beenpopulated and a mailbox hasn't been created, any messages sent to this mailbox will be lost and an NDA will be generated!

Table 7.5 Continued

Rule Action	Action Name	First Action Property	Additional Action Property	Rule Description
Reject the message with status code and response	*SmtpReject-Message*	*StatusCode*	*Reject-Reason*	*SmtpRejectMessage* deletes the e-mail message and sends a notification to the sender. The recipients don't receive the message or notification. This action enables you to specify a delivery status notification (DSN) code.
Silently drop the message	*Delete-Message*	Not applicable	Not applicable	*DeleteMessage* deletes the e-mail message without sending a notification to either the recipient or the sender.

Creating Transport Rule

Creating a new edge transport agent rule can be done following these steps:

1. Log on to the Edge Transport server. Open the **EMC** and click the **Edge Transport work center node** in the **navigation tree**. Now select the edge transport server in the **Result pane.** In the **Work pane**, click the **Transport Rules** tab.

2. Now click **New Transport Rule** in the **Action pane** or, alternatively, right-click in the **Work pane** and select **New Transport Rule** in the context menu.

3. This will bring up the **New Transport Rule Wizard.** The first step is to specify a name that will match the purpose of the rule. In this example you want to send all messages with

an attachment equal to or higher than 50 MB to the Quarantine mailbox. Once you have entered the name and comment (optional), click **Next**.

4. You also have the option of having the rule enabled when it's created by checking **Enable Rule** (see Figure 7.62).

Figure 7.62 The New Transport Rule Wizard

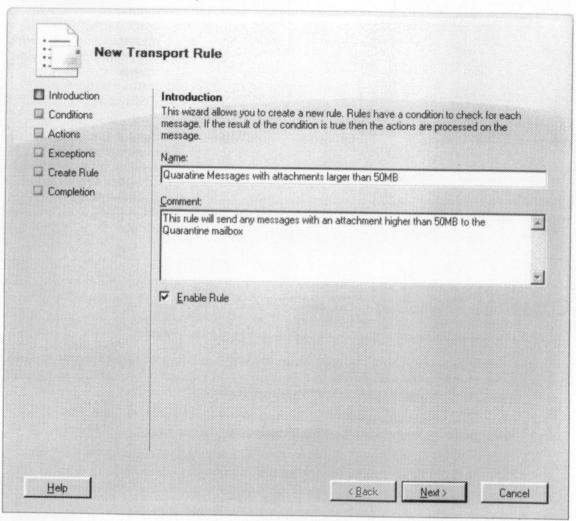

5. Next, select the condition(s) for the new rule. For the purpose of this example, you want to apply the rule to messages with an attachment equal to or larger than 50 MB, so you'll check **When the size of any attachment is greater than or equal to limit**, set the value to **50000KB,** and click **Next** (see Figure 7.63).

Figure 7.63 Transport Rule Conditions

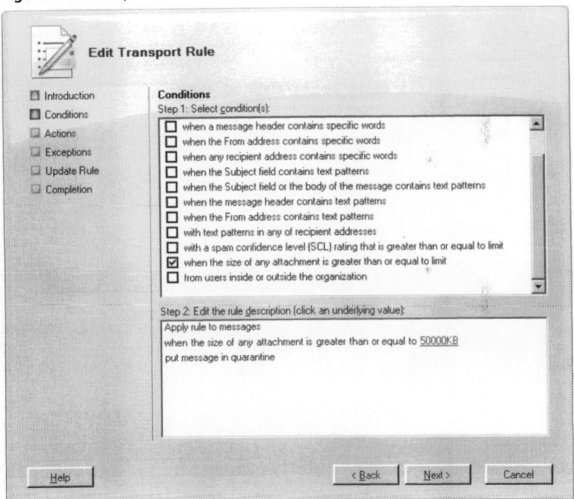

6. On the **Actions** page you can select the action(s) that should be taken for the messages matching the configured conditions. In this example, you check **Put message in quarantine** and click **Next** (see Figure 7.64).

Figure 7.64 Transport Rule Actions

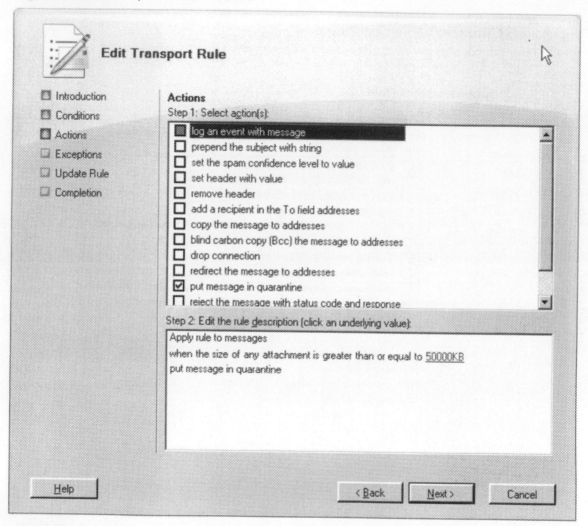

7. On the next page you have the option of specifying one or more exceptions. In this example, you won't specify any exceptions, so just click **Next** (see Figure 7.65).

Figure 7.65 Transport Rule Exceptions

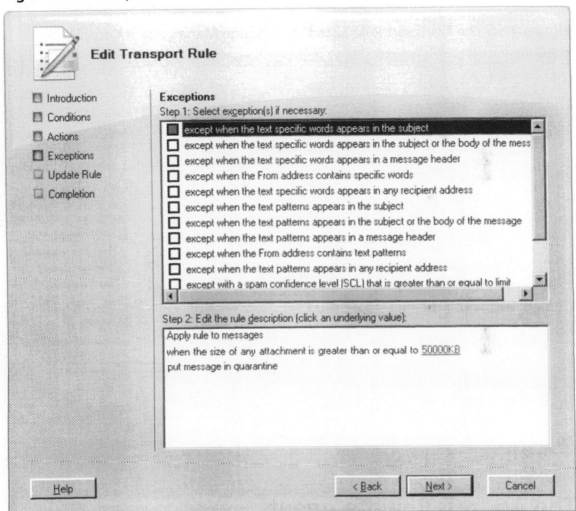

8. On the **Configuration Summary** page, click **New** to create the new rule.

9. Finally, click **Finish** to exit the New Transport Rule Wizard.

The newly created rule will now be listed in the Work pane, as shown in Figure 7.66, and you can at any time disable it or update it as required. If you have multiple rules, you can also change the priority among them.

Figure 7.66 The Transport Rule Listed in Exchange Management Console

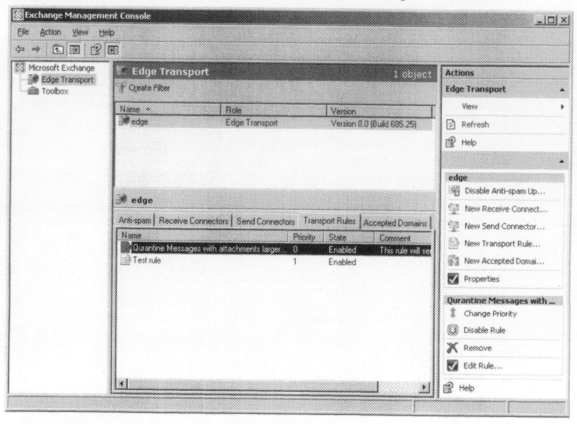

The Address Rewrite Agent

The edge transport server also has an agent, called the *address rewrite agent*, which can be configured to enable modification of the SMTP addresses on both inbound as well as outbound e-mail messages. You might want to do this if, for example, your organization consists of multiple domains (perhaps after a merger or acquisition) and should be presented with a consistent appearance of e-mail addresses to external recipients on the Internet. The address rewrite agent can also be used if the organization uses third-party vendors to, for example, provide e-mail support and/or other services. In this situation the organization's customers would expect messages to come from your domain, not from a third-party vendor. Another purpose of the address rewrite agent could be to enable routing of inbound e-mail messages from outside the Exchange 2007 organization to the internal recipients.

The address rewrite agent rewrites e-mail addresses by rewriting the SMTP headers in the e-mail messages, which flow in and out of the Edge Transport server. You can enable address rewriting on both inbound as well as outbound messages. The typical reason that you want to enable address rewriting on outbound messages is because you have multiple internal domains (for example, one root domain with multiple subdomains). With the address rewrite agent, you could then rewrite the SMTP header so that all outbound messages appear to come from the same domain instead of domain.com, subdomain1.domain.com, subdomain2.domain.com, and so on.

A reason that you would want to enable address rewriting on inbound messages could be because inbound e-mail messages would need to be routed to the intended recipients.

To create a new address rewriting entry on an edge transport server, you first need to make sure that either the address rewriting inbound agent and/or the address rewriting outbound agent is enabled. This should be the case on a newly installed edge transport server installation, but it's always a good idea to verify that this is the case. You can see whether these agents are enabled or disabled by opening the **EMS** and typing **Get-TransportAgent** (see Figure 7.67).

Figure 7.67 Checking Whether the Address Rewriting Agent Is Enabled

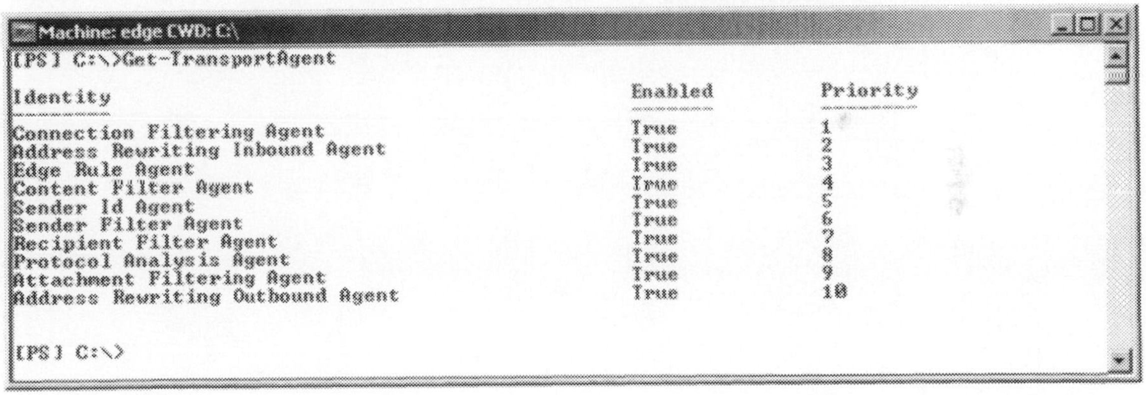

If the respective agent(s) are set to True, it means that the agent(s) is enabled. If the required agent is disabled (set to False), you will need to enable it by typing **Enable-TransportAgent –Identity "Address Rewriting Inbound Agent"** and/or **Enable-TransportAgent –Identity "Address Rewriting Outbound Agent"** depending on which agent you'll configure.

For the purpose of this book, we'll only rewrite the headers for a single SMTP address and then a single SMTP domain, but this should give you an idea how the address rewrite agent works.

To create a new address rewriting entry for a single SMTP address, you need to use the *New-AddressRewriteEntry* CMDlet. For example, say that you want to rewrite the SMTP address henrik@exchangedogfood.dk to henrik@exchange-faq.dk. To do so you would need to create an

AddressRewriteEntry using the following command: **New–AddressRewriteEntry –Name "Address rewrite entry for henrik@exchangedogfood.dk" –InternalAddress henrik@exchangedogfood.dk –ExternalAddress henrik@exchange-faq.dk** followed by pressing **Enter**.

If you wanted to create a new address rewriting entry for a single SMTP domain, you would need to use the following command: **New–AddressRewriteEntry –Name "Address rewrite entry for Exchangedogfood.dk" –InternalAddress exchangedogfood.dk –ExternalAddress exchange-faq.dk** followed by pressing **Enter**.

To read additional information about the address rewrite agent, consult the Exchange Server 2007 Help file.

Monitoring the Edge Transport Server

As is also the case with any of the other Exchange 2007 Server roles, you should make sure that you're always up to date with best practices relating to the Edge Transport server. We recommend that you run the Exchange Best Practices Analyzer tool on the box on a regular basis. In addition, you should monitor the server using Microsoft Operations Manager (MOM) 2005 or a similar product so that you can react proactively to any events or alerts generated by the Edge Transport server. MOM 2005 has its own Exchange Server 2007 Management Pack, which makes it possible to monitor activity such as messages per SCL level, total messages sent to quarantine, and rejected and/or deleted messages. You can also generate MOM reports showing you things such as hit rate for block lists, top spam-sending domain, top spam-sending IP address, and top targeted domain or individual recipient. All reports can, of course, be seen on a per-server basis.

Summary

In this chapter we focused on the Edge Transport server role included in the Exchange Server 2007 product. We went over the requirements of the server role as well as step-by-step instructions on how you deploy one or more edge transport server(s) in your perimeter network (DMZ or screened subnet). We then had a look at the available antispam filtering agents as well as how they are configured. Then we discussed how you properly secure an Edge Transport server using the Security Configuration Wizard (SCW). Lastly, we had a look at the transport rules agent and as well as the address rewriting feature, and we briefly discussed how you can and why you should monitor an edge transport server using a monitoring solution such as Microsoft Operations Manager (MOM) 2005.

Solutions Fast Track

Deploying the Edge Transport Server Role

☑ Remember that the Edge Transport server role should be isolated in the perimeter network (also called a DMZ or screened subnet), away from your Active Directory. The server role should therefore be installed in a workgroup on a standalone server.

☑ It's highly recommend that you install two network adapters in the server on which you're planning to install the Edge Transport server. One network adapter should be Internet facing; the other should be intranet facing. This way you can secure the Send and Receive connectors much more efficiently than would be the case with only a single network adapter.

☑ If your organization consists of multiple forests and you want to use the EdgeSync service in each of them, you must replicate all recipient addresses to one forest and then set up an edge subscription to that forest, because the EdgeSync service supports replication with only one forest at a time.

Enabling Name Resolution Lookups between the Edge Transport and Hub Transport Servers Suffix

☑ Bear in mind that to use several of the antispam features, you must use an edge subscription. This way, configuration as well as recipient data are replicated from Active Directory to the ADAM store using the EdgeSync service. It is possible to not use an EdgeSync subscription, but you will then not be able to use several of the antispam features on the Edge Transport server. In addition, you need to create all Send and Receive connectors manually.

☑ If you're a small shop and cannot afford to have an additional Exchange 2007 server with the Edge Transport server role deployed in your DMZ, but you still want to take advantage of the antispam filtering agents to filter out spam in your organization, you're in luck, because you have the option of installing the antispam filtering agents on an Exchange 2007 server with the Hub Transport server role installed. To do so you need to run the install-AntiSpamAgents.ps1 script located in the Exchange scripts folder (by default, located under C:\Program Files\Microsoft\Exchange Server) on the hub transport server.

☑ Since Microsoft played an important role in the invention of the Sender ID e-mail authentication technology, it's not surprising that Sender ID is supported in Exchange 2007, but some are wondering whether the DomainKeys e-mail authentication technology (which was invented by Yahoo, DomainKeys and Cisco) is supported in Exchange 2007. The answer is unfortunately not, but who knows—maybe they will implement DomainKeys support in a future service pack.

Installing the ADAM Component

☑ When you deploy an Edge Transport server in your perimeter network (DMZ or screened subnet), it's very important that you secure it properly. The best way to lock it down is to use the Security Configuration Wizard (SCW).

☑ One of the great things about using a one-way replication method from Active Directory to the Edge Transport server is that you only need to open one single inbound port in your intranet firewall, which is port 25 (SMTP). The respective LDAP port only needs to be allowed outbound.

Verifying That the EdgeSync Service Works as Expected

☑ An important step in deploying an Edge Transport server in your DMZ is to change your MX records so that they point at the new Edge Transport server. If you don't host your own public DNS server, this is typically done on the public DNS server at your ISP. If, for example, you're using an ISA server to forward SMTP traffic to a server in your DMZ, you simply need to change the respective rule so that it points to your Edge Transport server instead.

☑ You can see information about your MX records by using NSLookup, as shown in this chapter, but there are also several nice Web-based tools that can help you retrieve your MX records (and many other such things). Some of the best are dnsstuff.com and checkdns.net.

Manually Configuring the Required Connectors

☑ Unlike the other Exchange 2007 Server roles, the Edge Transport server role uses Active Directory Application Mode (ADAM) to store configuration data. For this reason, you cannot recover an Edge Transport server using the setup /m:recoverserver switch as is the case with the other server roles in your organization. However, you can back up an Edge Transport server using the ExportEdgeConfig.ps1 script contained in the Exchange scripts folder, which by default is located under C:\Program Files\Microsoft\Exchange Server. To recover or clone an Edge Transport server, you can use the ImportEdgeConfig.ps1 contained in the same folder.

☑ When you have multiple Edge Transport servers deployed in the perimeter network, you can network and load-balance network traffic among the servers using Domain Name System (DNS) round robin mechanism.

Pointing Your MX Records to the Edge Transport Server

- ☑ Part of the new E-mail Policy and Compliance feature set, in Exchange Server 2007, is the Edge Transport Rules agent, which is used to establish and enforce regulatory or corporate policies on e-mail messages sent to or received from the Internet. Just as with the Hub Transport server, the transport rules agent on the Edge Transport server is capable of applying transport rules to messages flowing into and out of the organization, but although the Transport Rules agent looks very similar for both types of server roles, don't let it fool you. Although both server roles have a transport rules agent, several of the actions that are available for each server role are different.

- ☑ Unlike the Hub Transport server, the Edge Transport server only allows you to specify an array of SMTP addresses. This is because the Edge Transport server doesn't have access to Active Directory, as does the Hub Transport server, on which you can specify an array of Active Directory mailboxes, contacts, mail-enabled users, and distribution group objects.

The Address Rewrite Agent

- ☑ If your organization consists of multiple domains (for example, after a merger or acquisition), you can use the address rewrite agent to provide a single consistent SMTP domain to the Internet.

- ☑ Address rewriting can also be used to allow third-party vendors to provide support or other e-mail-based services using your SMTP domain. Because your customers and partners expect e-mail to come from your organization, this makes sense.

Deploying Multiple Edge Transport Servers in the Organization

- ☑ If you use Microsoft Operations Manager (MOM) 2005 as the monitoring solution in your organization, you should install the Exchange 2007 MOM Management Pack and configure it to monitor the Edge Transport server(s) in your DMZ too. The Exchange 2007 MOM Management Pack can monitor your Edge Transport servers proactively as well as provide a wealth of reporting options, such as monitoring activity related to messages per SCL level, total messages sent to quarantine, and rejected and/or deleted messages. You can also generate MOM reports showing you things such as hit rate for block lists, top spam-sending domain, top spam-sending IP address, and top targeted domain or individual recipient. All reports can, of course, be seen on a per-server basis.

Frequently Asked Questions

Q: I have deployed a single Exchange 2007 server with the Hub Transport, Client Access and Mailbox Server roles in my test environment. Although I've configured our firewall to forward SMTP traffic to the Exchange 2007 server, I cannot receive any messages from the Internet.

A: This behavior is actually by design. By default, an Exchange 2007 Hub Transport server is configured so that it doesn't accept anonymous e-mail from the Internet. Instead, Microsoft recommends that you deploy an Edge Transport server in your DMZ and have any inbound as well as outbound e-mail messages routed through this server. But if you cannot afford this or for some other reason don't want to deploy an Edge Transport server, you can configure your Hub Transport server to accept e-mail by configuring the default *<servername>* Receive connector to accept anonymous e-mail from the Internet. You do so by accessing the properties for the default Receive connector, which is located under **Server Configuration | Hub Transport** in the EMC. Here you select the **Permissions Groups** tab and enable **Anonymous users**.

Q: Is there any way I can test that the provider I have specified on my Edge Transport server's IP Block list feature works as expected?

A: Yes. You can use the *Test-IPBlockListProvider* CMDlet to test a provider. You must use the following format: **Test-IPBlockListProvider –IPAddress 192.168.1.10 –Provider ProviderName**.

Q: Since message queues are stored in an ESE database for either an Edge Transport or a Hub Transport server, I was wondering if it's possible to defragment the database used to store these messages queues?

A: Yes, this is definitely possible. To defragment such a database, you must first stop the Microsoft Exchange Transport Service on the respective server. The database used to store message queues is mail.que, by default located under c:program filesexchange serverTransportRolesdataqueuemail. que. So to defragment the database, you must type **Eseutil /d c:\program files\exchange server\TransportRoles\data\queuemail.que**.

Q: Can I see the message queues on an Edge Transport server using the Exchange Management Shell?

A: Yes. At any time you can have the queue listed by running the *Get-Queue* CMDlet, which displays information about existing queues on the Edge Transport server on which it's run. If you don't specify any parameters, the command queries all queues on the local server and returns a single page of results (1000 objects).

Q: Can I use an Edge Transport server as the SMTP gateway for a legacy messaging organization such as Exchange 2000 or 2003?

A: Yes. An Edge Transport server can be deployed as an SMTP relay and smart host server for your existing Exchange messaging infrastructure. However, keep in mind that you cannot take advantage of EdgeSync and therefore cannot use several of the attractive antispam features.

Chapter 8

High Availability for Exchange 2007 Mailbox Servers

Solutions in this chapter:

- **Managing the Local Continuous Replication Feature**

- **Managing a Cluster Continuous Replication-Based Setup**

- **Managing a Single Copy Cluster-Based Setup**

☑ Summary

☑ Solutions Fast Track

☑ Frequently Asked Questions

Introduction

The availability requirements for messaging and collaboration servers have increased drastically over the years, with the result that these servers are now among the most mission-critical servers in the datacenter. Several recent reports have concluded that e-mail is more important to end users than their phones. So it's not rocket science; it's in the interests of you as the Exchange Administrator to achieve as high an uptime as possible. Each of these facts played an important role when the Exchange Product Group developed Exchange Server 2007, so it's no surprise that when speaking of high availability as well as disaster recovery, we can find many improvements as well as new functionality in the Exchange Server 2007 product.

Exchange Server 2007 includes three primary high-availability solutions relating to the Mailbox Server role, although one of these features isn't really new at all but has instead changed name and been further improved since Exchange Server 2003. We're referring to the Single Copy Cluster (SCC) functionality, which is a clustered solution that uses a single copy of a storage group on storage that is shared between the nodes in a cluster. Those of you with just a little bit of Exchange cluster experience would say that the SCC solution is similar to a traditional Exchange 2000/2003 active/passive cluster setup, and you're right.

SOME INDEPENDENT ADVICE

With Exchange Server 2007, active/active clusters are no longer supported; only active/passive clusters are supported. If you have experience deploying Exchange 2000/2003 in an active/active cluster, most likely you understand why this was dropped in Exchange 2007. An Exchange cluster configured with two active nodes has never performed as well as one would have expected, since the failover causes the remaining node to take on additional processing operations. Constraints such as number of concurrent user connections per node and average CPU load per server limits also play an important role in the reason that active/active Exchange cluster setups have never been successful.

Then we have Local Continuous Replication (LCR), which is a solution that uses the new continuous replication technology introduced in Exchange 2007. LCR is a new functionality that uses built-in asynchronous log shipping and log replay technology to create and maintain a replica of a storage group on a second set of disks that are connected to the same server as the production storage group. As mentioned, the LCR solution uses log shipping and log replay and gives you the option of switching to the passive copy of the storage group in a matter of minutes, should the database in the active storage group become corrupted and shut down for one reason or another. The interesting thing about LCR is that this solution doesn't require more than a single Exchange 2007 server with the Mailbox Server role installed.

Finally, we have the Clustered Continuous Replication (CCR) solution, which, like LCR, uses the new Exchange 2007 continuous replication technology, but as the name implies, CCR is a clustered solution that eliminates the single point of failure that exists in traditional Exchange cluster setups today. This is done by maintaining a copy of the database on the active node; in the event of a database corruption, this allows both services and databases to fail over to the passive node. CCR can only be deployed in a two-node active/passive cluster.

Managing the Local Continuous Replication Feature

In this first section of the chapter we'll take a closer look at the architecture behind the new Local Continuous Replication (LCR) feature. We'll then go through the steps necessary to enable this feature; finally, we'll look at how we can take advantage of LCR should the database in the active copy of the storage group fail.

Local Continuous Replication under the Hood

The Exchange Product group developed the Local Continuous Replication (LCR) technology to provide a native data availability solution that can be used to recover an Exchange database on an Exchange 2007 standalone server in a matter of a few minutes. In Exchange 2003 as well as previous versions, you needed to recover the lost database by restoring it from backup, which, depending on the database size, could take up to many hours. With LCR, you will be able to switch over to an exact replica (that is, a fully updated copy) of the crashed database by running a simple Exchange 2007 task.

So how does this LCR magic work? As most of us know, the database type Exchange uses is Extensible Storage Engine (ESE). ESE employs transaction log files, which means that every time a modification is made, a transaction log file is generated (instead of the change being committed directly to the database). The reason is that when the ESE database is modified, the modification won't be made directly in the physical database but instead in memory of the respective Exchange 2007 Mailbox Server. This means that should the database for some reason become corrupted or shut down, Exchange always will be able to recover the lost data (which is held in memory, remember) by using the log files.

Each log file that is generated because of a modification in the database belonging to the active copy of the storage group is replicated (copied) from the source log folder (the log folder defined for the Storage Group containing the respective database) to a target log folder associated with the passive copy of the storage group. This isn't the entire truth, because each log file is first copied to an inspector log folder located beneath the target log folder, where it is inspected to make sure it is correct. (If it isn't correct, the log file will be recopied). Finally the file is copied to the target log folder and from there replayed into the database belonging to the passive copy of the storage group.

The target log folder also contains an IgnoredLogs folder that holds any valid log files that for some reason cannot be replayed. A typical reason is that the particular log is too old. In addition, the subfolder can contain an InspectionFailed and an E00OutofDate folder. The first is a folder that holds any log files that failed inspection. When this happens, an event 2013 will be logged in the application log. The E00OutofDate folder will hold any E00.log files that are present in the target log folder when a failover occurs.

A new Exchange 2007 service called the Microsoft Exchange Replication Service will be installed on any Exchange 2007 servers with the Mailbox Server role installed. These are responsible for replicating the log files to the target log folder. As you can see, we've tried to illustrate the basic architecture of LCR in Figure 8.1.

Figure 8.1 The Basic Local Continuous Replication Architecture

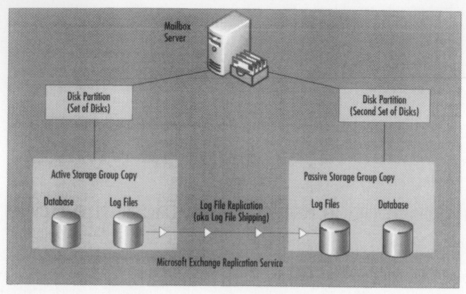

The log files that are replicated from the active copy to the passive copy of the storage group will be replayed in batches in order to provide the best performance possible.

Since LCR keeps an exact replica of the active copy of the storage group, the number of Exchange backups needed is also reduced drastically. But it's important to understand that LCR in no way eliminates traditional backups of the databases on your Exchange 2007 Mailbox servers; instead, it provides you with the option of taking weekly instead of daily backups, for example.

SOME INDEPENDENT ADVICE

Bear in mind that if you want to enable LCR for a storage group, the storage group may not contain more than one mailbox or public folder database. This is because LCR doesn't support multiple databases in the same storage group. Actually, you won't even be able to enable LCR on a storage group containing multiple databases. In addition, you cannot enable LCR for a storage group containing a Public Folder database if more than one Public Folder database exists in the organization. The reason is that LCR and Public Folder replication cannot run at the same time.

When you're partitioning the disks that should be storing the passive copies your storage groups, it is best practice to take advantage of mount points, because they will let you surpass the 26-drive-letter limitation that exists on a Windows 2003 server. If you end up in a situation where you need to switch to a passive copy of a storage group, using mount points will make the recovery process much more painless because you can quickly change drive letters and paths.

As has been the case with mailbox stores and log files in previous versions of Exchange, it's also recommended that you place the databases and log files for a passive copy of a storage group on separate disks, just as you do with active copies of storage groups.

You should, of course, also make sure that you partition the disks that are to be used for the passive copies of the storage groups, so they are at least the same size at the disks holding the active storage group copies. Finally, keep in mind that a Mailbox Server with LCR enabled will use approximately 30–40 percent more CPU and memory than a Mailbox Server on which LCR hasn't been enabled. These extra resources are primarily used by log file verification as well as log file replay.

TIP

LCR enables you to offload Volume ShadowCopy Service (VSS) backups from the active storage group to the passive storage group, which will preserve disk I/O on the disks on which the active storage group is located. This also means that you can perform restores from a passive copy of a storage group.

As you can understand, LCR is an ideal solution for small or medium-sized organizations because the functionality allows rapid recovery from database issues and requires only an extra set of disks for the database copies. LCR increases the availability of databases on an Exchange 2007 standalone server in an affordable way. For small shops that don't have a big fancy server with multiple sets of disks, it is possible to keep the LCR copy on an external USB disk.

Enabling Local Continuous Replication on a Storage Group

The LCR feature is enabled on a Storage Group level under the Mailbox subnode, located beneath the Server Configuration work center node in the left pane of the Exchange System Management Console, as shown in Figure 8.2.

1. To enable LCR for the First Storage Group, select it in the work pane, and click **Enable local continuous replication** in the Action pane.

Figure 8.2 The Local Continuous Replication Link in the Action Pane

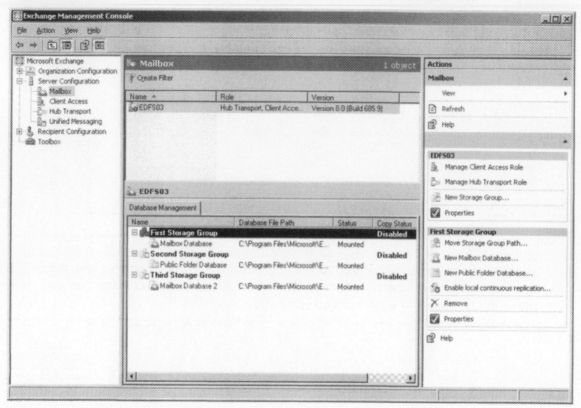

2. This will bring up the Local Continuous Replication Wizard's Introduction page, shown in Figure 8.3. As you can see, this page shows us the storage group as well as mailbox database name. Because there aren't many interactions on this page, simply click **Next**.

Figure 8.3 Enable Storage Group Local Continuous Replication

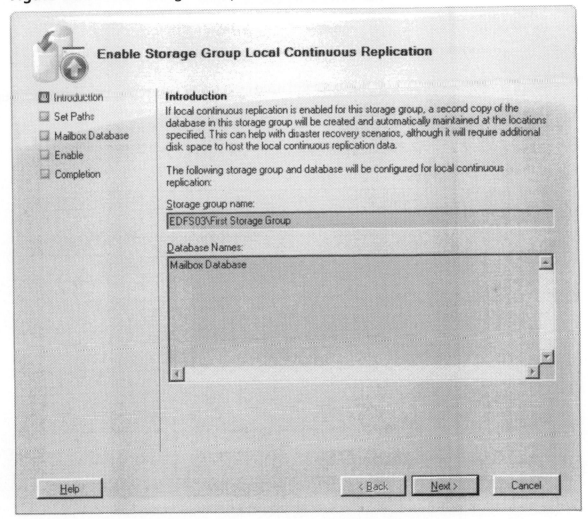

3. Now let's specify the path to the LCR files for the respective storage group (see Figure 8.4). For the purpose of this example, we're simply specifying the E: drive, which is a second set of disks on the server. When the location has been specified, we can click **Next**.

Figure 8.4 Specifying the Paths for the Replicated Log and System Files

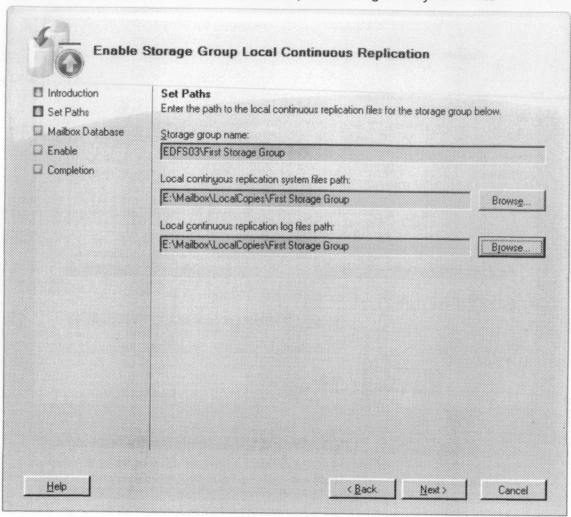

4. On the Mailbox Database page, we have to specify the path to the location of the second copy of the database, as shown in Figure 8.5. When you have done so, click **Next**.

Figure 8.5 Specifying the Path for the Database Copy

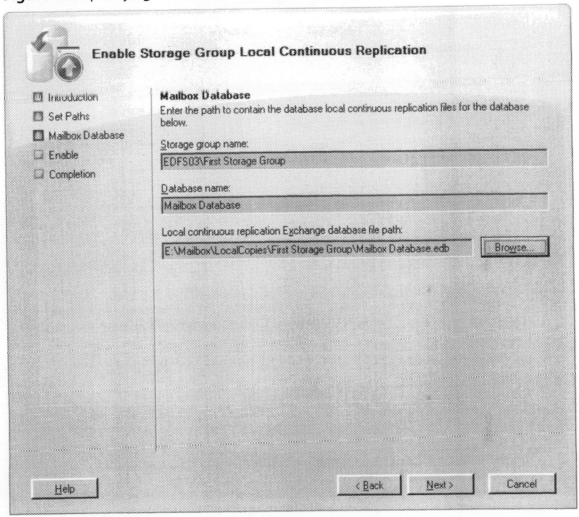

5. We have now reached the step where we enable LCR for the storage group, so let's do so by clicking **Enable** and see what happens. As shown in Figure 8.6, the Local Continuous Replication Wizard completed successfully. Click **Finish**.

Figure 8.6 The Local Continuous Replication Feature was Enabled with Success

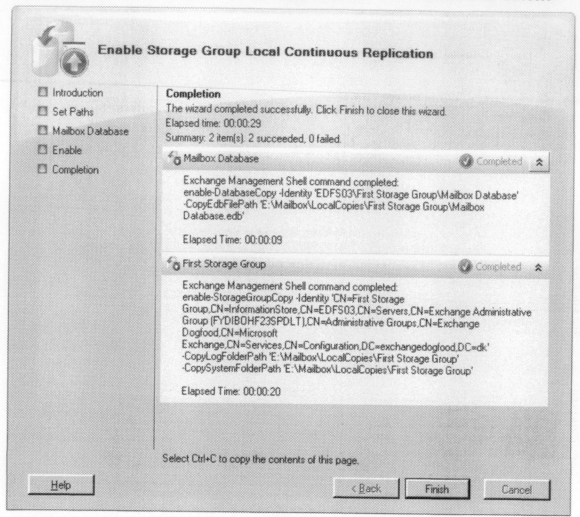

If you would rather enable LCR for a storage group via the EMS, you will have to do so using the *Enable-DatabaseCopy* and *Enable-StorageGroupCopy* CMDlets. To enable LCR for the First Storage Group, you would need to first run the following command:

```
Enable-DatabaseCopy –Identity "EDFS03\First Storage Group\Mailbox Database"
-CopyEDBFilePath:"E:\Mailbox\LocalCopies\First Storage Group\Mailbox Database.edb"
```

Then type:

```
Enable-StorageGroupCopy –Identity "EDFS03\First Storage Group"
-CopyLogFolderPath:"E:\Mailbox\LocalCopies\First Storage Group"
-CopySystemFolderPath:"E:\Mailbox\LocalCopies\First Storage Group"
```

NOTE

Even though we're dealing with a secondary copy of a production database, it's still a best practice to keep the log files and database separated on their own set of disks.

Now notice that the copy status for the First Storage Group has change to Healthy (see Figure 8.7).

Figure 8.7 The Copy Status for the Storage Group Is Healthy

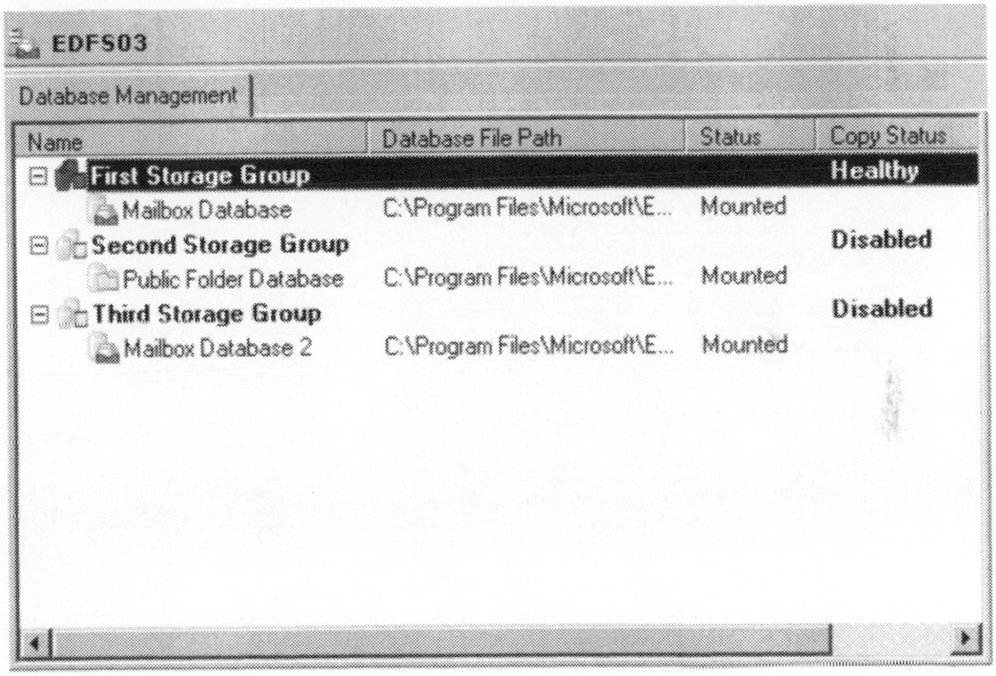

Viewing the Status for a Local Continuous Replication Copy

To view basic health and status information for an LCR copy, you can bring up the Properties page for the storage group on which LCR has been enabled. To do this, select the respective storage group and click the **Properties** link in the Action pane. On the Properties page, select the **Local continuous replication** tab, as shown in Figure 8.8. Here you can see the basic health for an LCR copy.

Figure 8.8 The LCR Status Properties Page

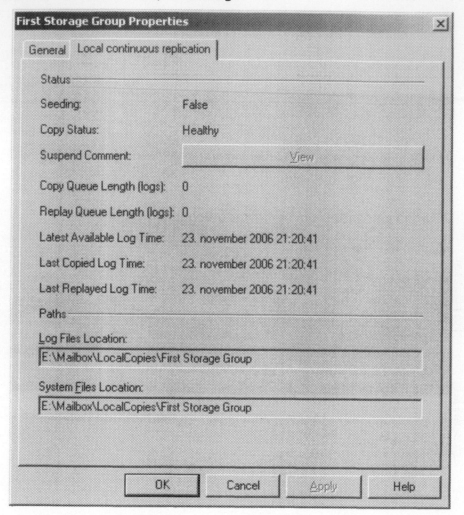

Table 8.1 lists the health and status information, with a short description of each.

Table 8.1 Local Continuous Replication Health and Status Information

Health/Status Information	Description
Seeding	Used to indicate whether seeding of the passive database occurs or not. Can have a status of True or False.
Copy Status	Used to indicate whether log file copying has started. Can have a status of Healthy, Suspended, or Broken.
Suspend Comment	Can be used to view *suspend* comment if LCR has been suspended.

Table 8.1 Continued

Health/Status Information	Description
Copy Queue Length (logs)	Used to display the number of log files that are waiting to be copied to the passive storage group's log file folder. Note that a copy is not considered complete until it has been inspected for corruption.
Replay Queue Length (logs)	Used to display the number of log files waiting to be replayed into the passive storage group's database.
Latest Available Log Time	Used to display the time stamp on the active storage group of the most recently detected new log file.
Last Copied Log Time	Used to display the time stamp on the active storage group of the last successful copy of a transaction log file.
Last Replayed Log Time	Used to display the time stamp on the passive storage group of the last successful replay of a log file.

In addition, you can see the path to the log file and system file location for the passive storage group copy.

If you want even more information about the health and status of an LCR copy, you can open the EMS and type **Get-StorageGroupCopyStatus –Identity <Storage Group> | FL**, as shown in Figure 8.9.

Figure 8.9 Retrieving LCR Status Information via the Exchange Management Shell

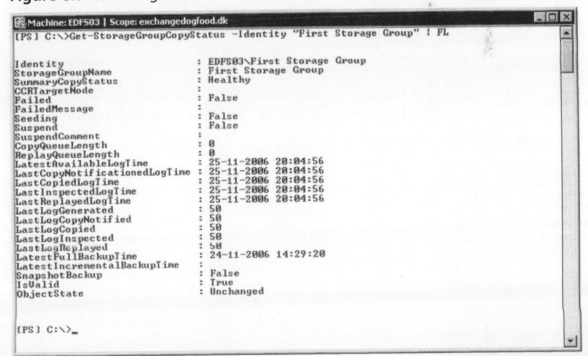

If you want to dig deeper into these topics, we recommend that you refer to the Exchange 2007 Help file.

Switching to the Passive Storage Group Copy When Disaster Strikes

When disaster strikes and the database or log files in the active copy of the storage group have become corrupted and have shut down, you have the option to recover database availability by switching to the LCR copy (the passive copy of the storage group).

You can recover from corruption of either one or more log files or the database using a variety of methods, depending on whether you use mount points or not. One method is to run the *Restore-StorageGroupCopy* CMDlet with the *ReplaceLocations* parameter, which will activate the LCR copy as the active storage group copy in one step. To activate the LCR copy as the active storage group, you first need to make sure that the active database is dismounted, which should already be the case if it's corrupted. If this is not the case, you should dismount it now. When you have done so, we're ready to run the *Restore-StorageGroupCopy* CMDlet, which in the case of this example is done for the First Storage Group. So the command to run in the EMS is:

```
Restore-StorageGroupCopy –Identity "First Storage Group" -ReplaceLocations:$true
```

An integrity check will now be passed for the log files, and if it's completed without errors, the storage group copy switch will be completed and the production paths will be updated, as shown in Figure 8.10.

Figure 8.10 Switching to the LCR Copy Using the *Restore-StorageGroupCopy* CMDlet

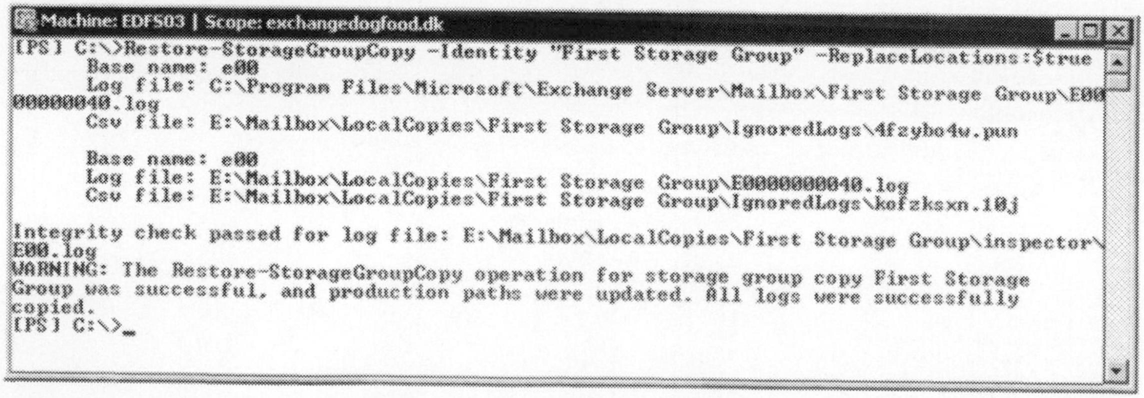

All there is to do now is to mount the database using either the EMC or the EMS. Now notice that the *Database File Path* will have changed, as shown in Figure 8.11.

Figure 8.11 Database File Path Change

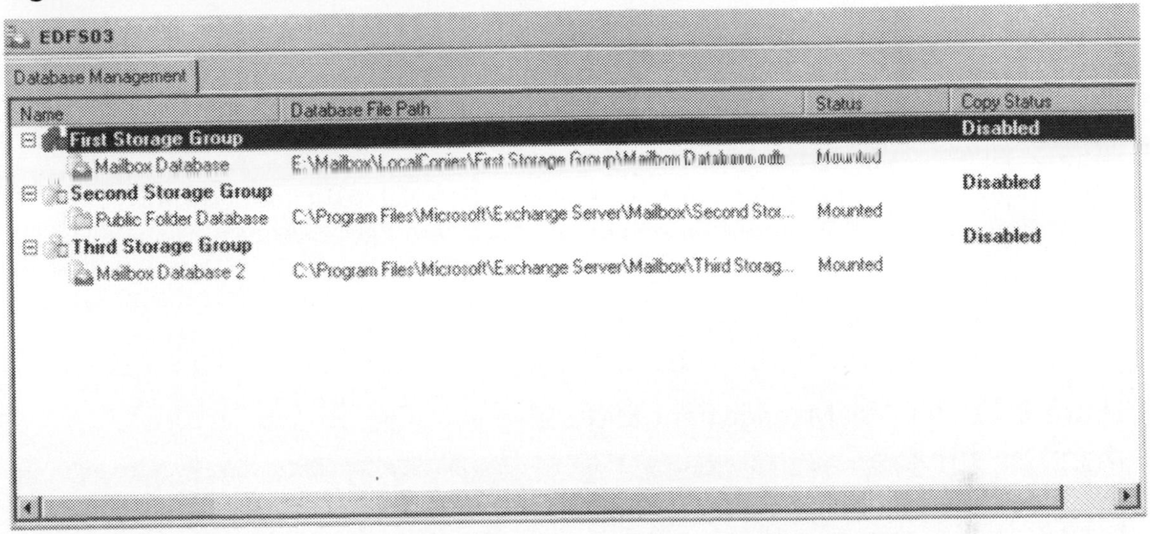

> **NOTE**
>
> When you have run the *Restore-StorageGroupCopy* CMDlet against a storage group, LCR for the respective storage group will be disabled. So remember to re-enable LCR for the particular storage group after you perform a switch to the LCR copy.

Although this method is straightforward and fully supported, Microsoft actually recommends that instead you use a method whereby you run the *Restore-StorageGroupCopy* CMDlet without the *ReplaceLocations* parameter, to activate the copy in its current location, and then either move the files manually, change drive letters, or use mount point assignments to have the copy files reflected under the respective production paths so that the production database is maintained in the expected location. Following this method means that the active storage group copy will continue to have meaningful filenames that represent that they indeed are active production copies. Why is this the preferred method? Because Microsoft believes that using the *Restore-StorageGroupCopy* CMDlet with the *ReplaceLocations* parameter could lead to future confusion in distinguishing the active copy of the data from the passive copy of the data, and to be honest, we agree. That said, we cannot see why you shouldn't use the *ReplaceLocations* parameter if you know what you're doing; just make sure that you switch back to the original disk set again.

Let's examine an example of how you would use the recommend method. First, make sure that the production database is dismounted. Then open the EMS and type **Restore-StorageGroupCopy –Identity "First Storage Group"**.

This command will activate the copy and leave the path for the production storage group intact. Now you can choose between either moving the LCR copy files to the location of the original production database manually using Windows Explorer or using Xcopy or a similar tool. Just be sure to move or delete the files in the folder you move the files to first. When the files have been moved, you simply need to mount the database again, and that's it.

The second option available when using the *Restore-StorageGroupCopy* CMDlet without the *ReplaceLocations* parameter is to change the drive letter for the partition holding the LCR copy to the drive letter used by the production storage group. This can be done using either the Disk Management MMC snap-in or the Diskpart tool.

1. To do so using the MMC snap-in, click **Start | Run** and type **Diskmgmt.msc**. This will bring up the MMC snap-in shown in Figure 8.12. Now right-click the partition holding the production storage group and its database, then select **Change drive letter and paths** in the context menu.

Figure 8.12 The Disk Management MMC Snap-in

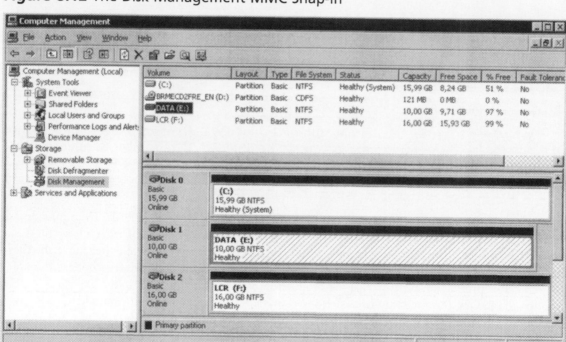

2. In the Change Drive Letter and Paths For window, click **Change**, then specify an unallocated drive letter and click **OK**, as shown in Figure 8.13.

3. Click **OK** to the confirmation message and click **OK** to close the Change Drive Letter and Paths window.

4. Now change the drive letter for the partition holding your LCR copy to the drive letter that originally was assigned the partition that holds the production storage group, which in this example is **E:**.

Figure 8.13 Specifying the Drive Letter for the Partition

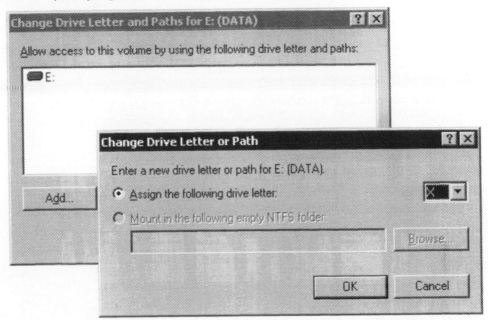

It's important that the partition for which you change the drive letter for doesn't contain any other data used by other applications. If it does, you will most likely destroy functionality for the respective applications!

When you have changed the drive letter, all there is to do is to mount the database again, but remember, the paths for the active and passive storage groups must be the same on each partition.

> **NOTE**
>
> A restart of the server might be required for you to be able to assign the E: drive to the partition holding the LCR copy.

The last option available involves the use of mount points. A *mount point* is a feature with which you can surpass the 26-drive-letter limitation that exists in Windows 2003 Server. Using volume mount points, you can graft, or mount, a target partition into a folder on another physical disk. Since volume mount points are transparent to Exchange 2007 as well as most other programs, they are pretty popular, especially in deploying Exchange 2000/2003 cluster environments.

To use mount points to switch LCR storage group copies, you must already have configured the partitions holding the storage group copies to use them. If you haven't done so, the mount point option cannot be used. In this example, the Third Storage Group's folder as well as the LCR copy for this storage group, which is called Third Storage Group, point to an NTFS volume mount point.

You can see whether a particular folder in Windows Explorer is a mount point because the icon is represented as a disk and not the normal yellow folder icon (see Figure 8.14).

Figure 8.14 The Mount Point Icon in Windows Explorer

1. As is the case with the options we have covered, the first thing you should do before switching the storage group copies using NTFS volume mount points is to make sure that the database is in a dismounted state. If this is not the case, you should dismount it manually now. The next step is to open the EMS and type **Restore-StorageGroupCopy –Identity "Third Storage Group"** (which is the storage group used in this example).

2. Next open the Disk Management MMC snap-in, right-click the partition that is used as the NTFS volume mount point by the production storage group, then select **Change Drive Letter or Paths** in the context menu. In the Change Drive Letter and Paths window, remove the existing path by highlighting it, then click the **Remove** button (see Figure 8.15).

Figure 8.15 Changing the NTFS Volume Mount Point Path

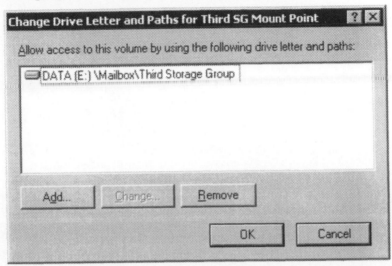

3. You now need to confirm that you want to remove the path. Click **Yes**.

4. Now remove the mount point for the partition used for the LCR copy, using the same steps. This is required to be able to use the LCR copy path as a mount point for the Production Storage Group copy.

5. We're now ready to mount the LCR copy to the Production Storage Group. We do so by right-clicking the partition that was used for the LCR copy, then choosing **Change Drive Letter or Paths** in the context menu. Now click **Add** and select **Mount** in the following empty NTFS folder. Click **Browse** and specify the path to the production storage group (see Figure 8.16). Finally, click **OK** twice and close the Disk Management MMC snap-in.

6. Now verify that the folder within Windows Explorer contains the expected data, and then mount the database again.

Is that cool or what?

Suspending Local Continuous Replication

On occasion, you might need to suspend LCR for a storage group. You need to suspend LCR, should either the active or passive storage group copy for some reason become unavailable. Suspending LCR is also necessary if you need to seed the LCR copy (seeding is covered next in this chapter). Finally, you need to suspend LCR when you're performing an integrity check on the passive copy's transaction logs and database file, which is a recommended practice now and then.

Figure 8.16 Specifying the New Path for the NTFS Volume Mount Point

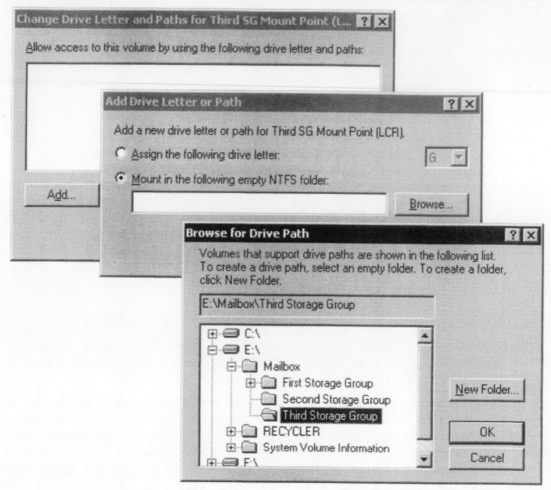

Suspending LCR means that all log file shipping as well as log file replaying is halted.

Suspending LCR is a straightforward process; it's done by selecting the respective storage group in the EMC, then clicking **Suspend Local continuous replication** in the Action pane. When you click this link, you'll need to confirm that you really want to suspend LCR. In addition, you'll have the option of specifying why LCR was suspended. This comment can be viewed by clicking the **View Comment** button on the Properties page of the storage group (shown in Figure 8.17).

Figure 8.17 Suspending Local Continuous Replication

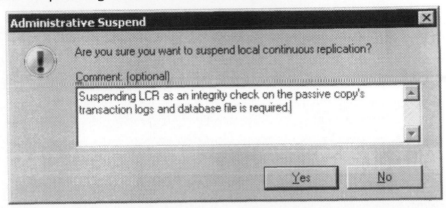

If you'd rather to suspend LCR for a storage group via the EMS, you'll need to do so using the *Suspend-StorageGroupCopy* CMDlet. To suspend LCR for the First Storage Group, where the comment shown in Figure 8.17 is specified, you should run the following command:

```
Suspend-StorageGroupCopy -Identity "First Storage Group" -SuspendComment
"Suspending LCR as an integrity check on the passive copy's transaction
logs and database file is required."
```

Again, you need to confirm that you really want to suspend LCR for the storage group. To do so, type **Y** for Yes and press **Enter**.

Resuming Local Continuous Replication

When the active or passive storage group are available again or when you have performed the integrity check or whatever type of maintenance you have completed, you need to resume LCR for the storage group. Again, this can be done via either the EMC or the EMS. To perform this task using the EMC, select the respective storage group and click **Resume local continuous replication** in the Action pane. When you do, the warning message shown in Figure 8.18 will appear. Click **Yes** and watch the Copy Status change to **Healthy** once again. Both log file shipping and log file replay have now been resumed.

Figure 8.18 Resuming Local Continuous Replication

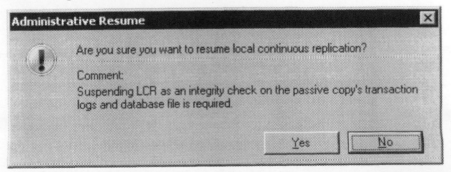

To resume LCR for a storage group via the EMS, type **Resume-StorageGroupCopy-Identity "First Storage Group"**.

Manually Seeding a Database Copy

Before we start talking about how to perform a manual seeding of a database copy, it would be a good idea to define the term *seeding* in terms of LCR. Seeding is the process whereby a database is added to a storage group copy. This can be a blank database or a copy of the database the storage group uses as the production database. When you enable LCR on a storage group using the EMC or via the EMS using the *Enable-DatabaseCopy* and *Enable-StorageGroupCopy* CMDlets, seeding normally takes place automatically. If it happens automatically, why should we even care about it, then? The answer is that there are a few situations in which manually seeding is required. The first is after you have performed an offline defragmentation of the production database belonging to the storage group for which you have enabled LCR. The second is if or when Exchange detects a corrupt log file, which the Microsoft Exchange Replication Service cannot replay into the database copy. The third is after a page scrubbing of a database on the active node in a Cluster Continuous Replication (CCR) setup occurs, and you then want to propagate these changes to the passive node in the CCR setup. Yes, you're right, the last one isn't really related to LCR but only continuous replication in clustered environments, where CCR is used. We'll talk much more about CCR later in this chapter.

Seeding a database copy manually can be done using the *Update-StorageGroupCopy* CMDlet in the EMS. Before doing so, you must suspend LCR for the respective storage group and then remove any .log, .chk, .jrs, and .edb files from the passive storage group's database copy, log files, and system files paths. To seed the database copy for the First Storage Group, you use the *Update-StorageGroupCopy* CMDlet and type **Update-StorageGroupCopy-Identity: "First Storage Group"**.

Running this command will create a temporary temp-seeding folder, and after a little while the seeding will take place, as shown in Figure 8.19.

Figure 8.19 Seeding a Mailbox Database Copy

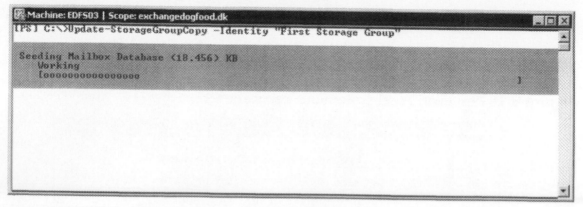

When seeding has taken place, the Microsoft Exchange Replication Service will start to replicate any .log, .chk, and .jrs files to the folder paths. When it's finished, you can resume LCR for the storage group, and you're back in business.

If you don't want to delete any .log, .chk, .jrs, and .edb files manually before running the *Update-StorageGroupCopy* CMDlet, you can tell the CMDlet to do it for you using the *DeleteExistingFiles* parameter. This method requires that you confirm the deletion of these files, as shown in Figure 8.20. The method you use is up to you, since they do the same thing.

Figure 8.20 Specifying That the *StorageGroupCopy* CMDlet Delete Any Existing Files

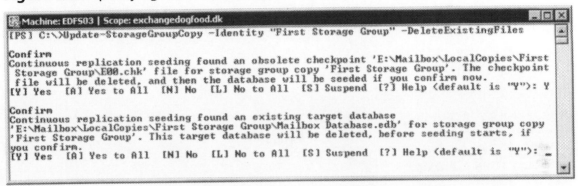

In addition, you can use the *ManualResume* parameter if you don't want replication to occur automatically on the storage group copy.

Another method available for seeding a database copy is to dismount the database in the EMC, suspend LCR for the storage group containing the database, and then copy the .edb file to the LCR copy folder using Windows Explorer. When the file has been copied, you then mount the database again using the EMC and resume LCR. Bear in mind that if you choose this method, your end users will be disconnected until the database is mounted. So unless there's a specific reason that you would use this method, we recommend that you use the *StorageGroupCopy* CMDlet.

Performing an Integrity Check of the Passive Copy Using Eseutil

It's a recommended best practice to periodically verify the integrity of the passive storage group copy to make sure neither the database copy nor any of the log files are corrupted. This is done by running a physical consistency check against both the database copy as well as the log files using Exchange Server Database Utilities (Eseutil.exe).

As mentioned earlier in this chapter, you need to suspend LCR on the storage group for which you want to verify the integrity of the passive database and log files.

To verify the physical integrity of the log files that have been replicated to the passive copy of the storage group, you'll need to open either a Command Prompt window or the EMS. In either the Command Prompt window or the EMS you should run Eseutil with the /k switch followed by the log file prefix of the storage group.

The log file prefix for a storage group can be found under the General tab of the respective storage group, as shown in Figure 8.21.

Figure 8.21 Log File Prefix

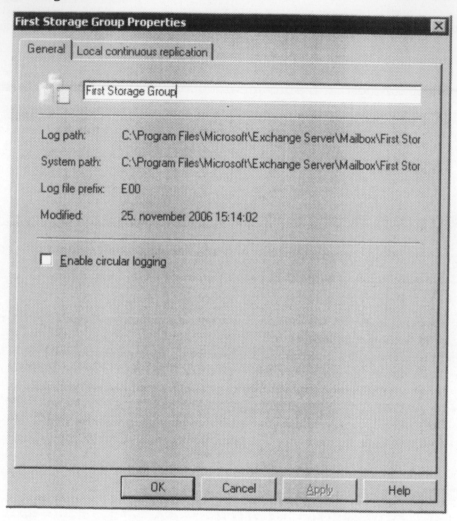

As you can see, the log file prefix for the First Storage Group typically is E00. To see the path for the log files, refer back to Figure 8.8. For the purpose of this example, the path is E:\Mailbox\LocalCopies\First Storage Group, so we'll need to type **Eseutil /k "E:\Mailbox\LocalCopies\First Storage Group\E00"**.

This will initiate checksum mode and start verifying each log file located under the specified path, as shown in Figure 8.22. If no corrupted log files are detected, the operation will complete successfully after a few seconds or minutes, depending on how many log files are contained in the respective folder.

Figure 8.22 Integrity Check of the LCR Log Files

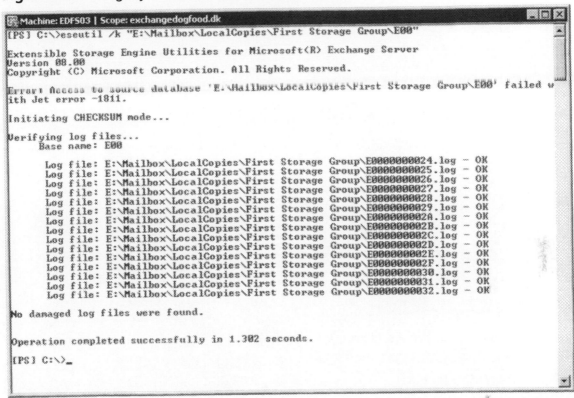

When the log files have been verified, we can move on to checking the integrity of the database copy. This is also done by running Eseutil with the /k switch but instead followed by the full path the database copy. In this example, we need to run the following command: **Eseutil /k "E:\Mailbox\LocalCopies\First Storage Group\Mailbox Database.edb"**.

Eseutil will once again initiate checksum mode and then create a temporary database so that the database copy can be checked for any errors (see Figure 8.23). Again, the time required for the integrity check depends on the size of the database.

When you have performed an integrity check of both the log files and the database copy (and hopefully Eseutil.exe hasn't found too many corrupted log files or issues with the database copy), you should make sure that LCR for the respective storage group is resumed again. Should you be so unlucky that Eseutil.exe finds one or more corrupted log files or corruption in the database copy, you need to disable LCR on the storage group, then remove the corrupted log files and/or database copy file. When the files have been removed, you can re-enable LCR, which will create a database copy and seed it as well as replicate any existing log files from the active copy of the storage group to the specified path.

Figure 8.23 Integrity Check of the LCR Database Copy

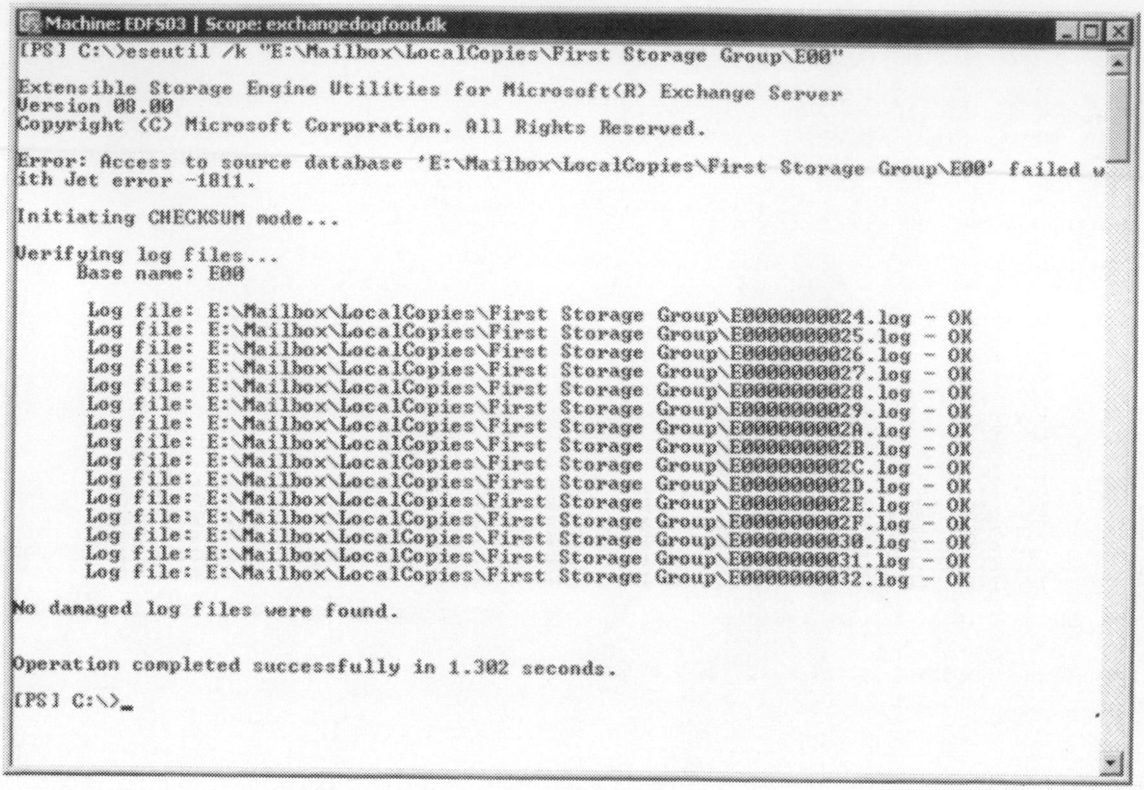

```
Machine: EDFS03 | Scope: exchangedogfood.dk                                    _□×
[PS] C:\>eseutil /k "E:\Mailbox\LocalCopies\First Storage Group\E00"

Extensible Storage Engine Utilities for Microsoft(R) Exchange Server
Version 08.00
Copyright (C) Microsoft Corporation. All Rights Reserved.

Error: Access to source database 'E:\Mailbox\LocalCopies\First Storage Group\E00' failed w
ith Jet error -1811.

Initiating CHECKSUM mode...

Verifying log files...
      Base name: E00

      Log file: E:\Mailbox\LocalCopies\First Storage Group\E0000000024.log - OK
      Log file: E:\Mailbox\LocalCopies\First Storage Group\E0000000025.log - OK
      Log file: E:\Mailbox\LocalCopies\First Storage Group\E0000000026.log - OK
      Log file: E:\Mailbox\LocalCopies\First Storage Group\E0000000027.log - OK
      Log file: E:\Mailbox\LocalCopies\First Storage Group\E0000000028.log - OK
      Log file: E:\Mailbox\LocalCopies\First Storage Group\E0000000029.log - OK
      Log file: E:\Mailbox\LocalCopies\First Storage Group\E000000002A.log - OK
      Log file: E:\Mailbox\LocalCopies\First Storage Group\E000000002B.log - OK
      Log file: E:\Mailbox\LocalCopies\First Storage Group\E000000002C.log - OK
      Log file: E:\Mailbox\LocalCopies\First Storage Group\E000000002D.log - OK
      Log file: E:\Mailbox\LocalCopies\First Storage Group\E000000002E.log - OK
      Log file: E:\Mailbox\LocalCopies\First Storage Group\E000000002F.log - OK
      Log file: E:\Mailbox\LocalCopies\First Storage Group\E0000000030.log - OK
      Log file: E:\Mailbox\LocalCopies\First Storage Group\E0000000031.log - OK
      Log file: E:\Mailbox\LocalCopies\First Storage Group\E0000000032.log - OK

No damaged log files were found.

Operation completed successfully in 1.302 seconds.

[PS] C:\>_
```

We'll bet that most of you understand the importance of during periodically integrity checks of both the log files as well as the database copy—right?

Disabling Local Continuous Replication on a Storage Group

There might come a time when you no longer want to have the LCR feature enabled for a particular storage group. Luckily, it's a painless process to disable this feature once it's enabled.

You can disable LCR for a storage group via either the EMC or the EMS. To disable LCR using the EMC, you need to select the Storage Group level under the Mailbox subnode, located beneath the Server Configuration work center node; you then click **Disable local continuous replication** in the Action pane, as shown in Figure 8.24.

Figure 8.24 Disable LCR Action Link

When we disable LCR for a storage group, we'll get the warning message shown in Figure 8.25, which tells us that LCR will be disabled for the replication database copy for the respective Storage Group. Since this is exactly what we want to do, click **Yes**.

Figure 8.25 Disabling Local Continuous Replication Confirmation

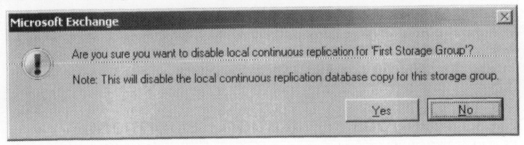

After we click Yes, believe it or not we'll get an additional warning message. This one informs us that we must delete the files (that is, the log files, EDB database, and so on) manually from the path (which in this example is E:\Mailbox\LocalCopies\First Storage Group) we specified when we originally enabled LCR (see Figure 8.26). Once you have clicked **OK** and deleted these files, LCR has been properly disabled.

Figure 8.26 Disabling Local Continuous Replication

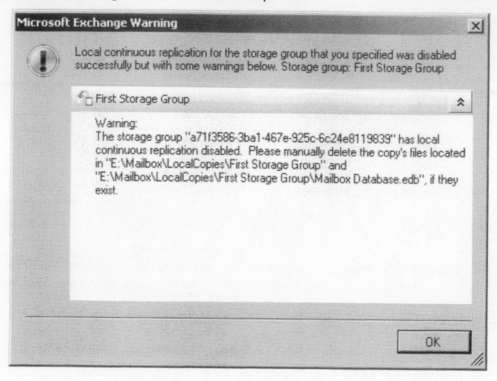

If you want to disable LCR for a Storage Group via the EMS, you need to do so using the *Disable-StorageGroupCopy* CMDlet. To disable the LCR for the First Storage Group, type **Disable–StorageGroupCopy –Identity "First Storage Group"**. When you do, you'll get the same warning message as the one shown in Figure 8.25.

Local Continuous Replication Performance Objects and Counters

When the Exchange 2007 Mailbox Server role is installed, setup adds two LCR-related performance objects to the Windows 2003 Performance Monitor. To open the Performance Monitor, either click **Start | Run** and type **Perfmon** or click **Start | Administrative Tools** and select **Performance**. This will bring up the Performance Monitor, shown in Figure 8.27.

Figure 8.27 The Performance Monitor

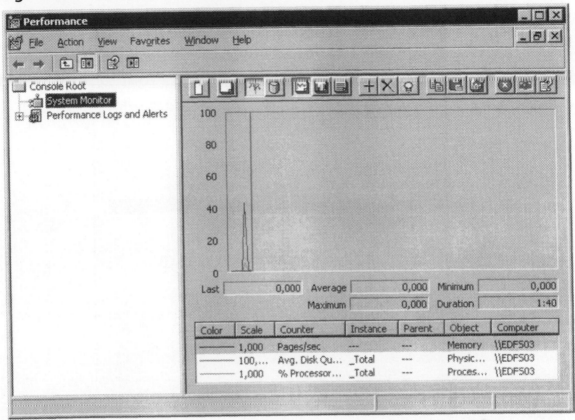

The first object is the MSExchange Replica Seeder performance object, which, as you can see in Figure 8.28, contains only one counter, called Seeding Finished %. This counter is used to show the progress of database seeding in percent. When you add this counter, you can choose which instance (in this case, the particular storage group) you want to view the database seeding for.

Figure 8.28 Continuous Replication Performance Objects

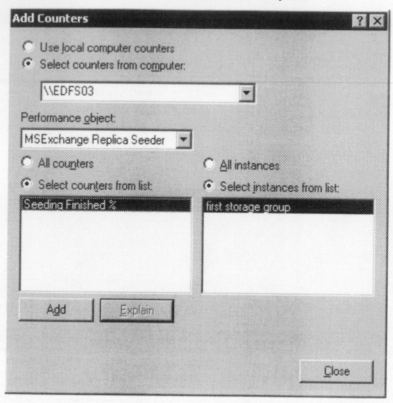

The MSExchange Replication performance object contains at least 14 different counters (see Table 8.2).

Table 8.2 Continuous Replication Performance Counters

Performance Counter	Description
Copy Queue Exceeds Mount Threshold (CCR only)	Copy Queue Exceeds Mount Threshold (CCR Only) is 1 if the copy queue length is larger than the Mount Threshold specified by the Auto Database Mount Dial. This counter is used only with CCR. It will always be 0 with LCR.
CopyGenerationNumber	Copy Generation Number is the generation of the last log file that has been copied.
CopyNotificationGenerationNumber	Copy Notification Generation Number is the generation of the last log file the copier knows about.

Table 8.2 Continued

Performance Counter	Description
CopyQueueLength	Copy Queue Length is the number of log generations waiting to be both copied and inspected successfully.
Failed	Failed is 1 if the replica instance is set to failed, otherwise 0.
InspectorGenerationNumber	Inspector Generation Number is the generation of the last log file that has been inspected.
ReplayBatchSize	Replay Batch Size is the number of log generations replayed together.
ReplayGenerationNumber	Replay Generation Number is the generation of the last log file that has been replayed successfully.
ReplayGenerationsComplete	Replay Generations Complete is the number of log generations already played in the current replay batch.
ReplayGenerationsPerMinute	Replay Generations Per Minute is the rate of replay in log generations per minute in the current replay batch.
ReplayGenerationsRemaining	Replay Generations Remaining is the number of log generations remaining to be played in the current replay batch.
ReplayNotificationGenerationNumber	The generation of the last log file that replay knows about.
ReplayQueueLength	Replay Queue Length is the number of log generations waiting to be replayed.
Suspended	Suspended is 1 if the continuous replication is suspended. When the continuous replication is suspended, logs are not copied and replayed into the passive copy.

As you can see, all these counters can be used to determine how replication for an LCR-enabled storage group have progressed, but a high-availability feature such as LCR should really be monitored using a proactive and automated monitoring solution such as Microsoft Operation Manager (MOM) with the Exchange Server 2007 Management Pack installed.

Managing a Cluster Continuous Replication-Based Setup

Exchange Server 2007 introduces another new high-availability feature called Cluster Continuous Replication (CCR). This feature takes the new Exchange Server 2007 log file shipping and replay mechanisms (known as continuous replication) and combines them with the features that are available in a more traditional two-node Windows 2003 server active/passive cluster setup. A traditional two-node active/passive cluster has its benefits but has also always had one major drawback: You still have a single point of failure when it comes to the information stores. CCR provides redundancy for both Exchange Services and the information stores.

As is the case with traditional Exchange clusters, CCR uses Windows Clustering Services to provide virtual servers (which, in Exchange 2007, are called clustered mailbox servers) and failover capabilities. CCR has one big difference from traditional clusters, though, and that is that functionality doesn't require any kind of shared storage subsystem, because each node contains a local copy of the information stores. This eliminates the dependency on SAN technology in the cluster design, which makes CCR a more cost-efficient solution because you can use a storage option such as Direct Attached Storage (DAS) or Serial Attached SCSI.

With CCR, the transaction logs generated on the active node are replicated to the information store on the passive node using log file shipping. These replicated log files are then posted into the database(s) on the passive node using the log file replay technology. This means that should the active node or a database on this node fail or for some other reason go offline, an automatic failover to the passive node will occur. When the passive node becomes the active node, the replication of log files will happen from the new active node to the passive node.

Another thing worth mentioning about CCR is that the feature supports stretched clustering (called *geoclustering*), but bear in mind that the nodes must belong to the same subnet. This means that as the cluster is stretched between the locations, the subnet must be stretched, too.

TIP

When Exchange 2007 supports Longhorn server (which will be provided via a service pack when the Longhorn product has been released), we will be able to take advantage of stretched clustering spanning multiple subnets, both on the public as well as the private network (also called the heartbeat network).

Last but not least, you can reduce the frequency of backups and restores as well as perform backups of the databases on the passive node, and thereby not impact the performance of the active node. In Figure 8.29 you can see a basic CCR scenario.

Figure 8.29 A Basic Cluster Continuous Replication Scenario

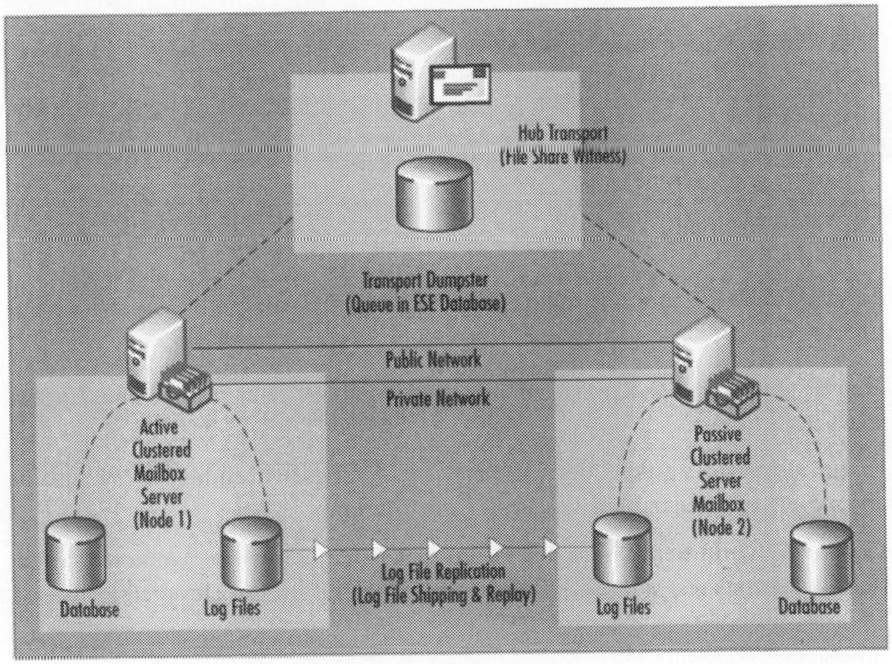

Prerequisites

To set up a CCR-based cluster, the following are required:

- A Windows 2003 Active Directory forest with at least one domain controller (raised to 2000 or 2003 forest functional level)

- Two Windows 2003 Server R2 Enterprise Editions or Windows 2003 Server SP1 Enterprise Editions

- One Windows File Share Witness, which is recommended to be an Exchange 2007 Hub Transport Server in the existing Exchange 2007 organization; note that CCR-based clusters don't use a shared quorum as traditional clusters do

- A Cluster Service Account in the Active Directory forest (we'll create this one later in this section)

You also need to apply the update mentioned in MS KB article 921181 to both servers that will act as nodes in the Exchange Server 2007 Clustered Mailbox setup. The update adds a new file share witness feature to the current Majority Node Set (MNS) quorum model. The file share witness feature lets you use a file share that is external to the cluster as an additional "vote" to determine the status of the cluster in a two-node MNS quorum cluster deployment, which is a requirement to use the CCR functionality in Exchange Server 2007.

To deploy CCR, the following hardware requirements must be met:

- Two network interface cards (NICs) installed in each node—one for the public and one for the private cluster network (the heartbeat network)

- Extra sets of disks or a DAS, SAN, or Serial SCSI solution to hold the database and transaction log files

In addition to the software and hardware requirements, you also should be aware of the following general requirements:

- When dealing with CCR environments, you must and can only use one database per storage group.

- You cannot create a public folder database in a CCR environment if you already have more than one public folder database in your organization.

- In a CCR environment, Microsoft recommends that you create no more than 30 storage groups and databases (one database per storage group) on the clustered mailbox server.

- The cluster on which Exchange 2007 is installed cannot contain Exchange Server 2000/2003 or any version of Microsoft SQL Server. Running Exchange 2007 in a cluster with any of these other applications is simply not supported.

SOME INDEPENDENT ADVICE

Some of you might wonder whether the licensing rules have changed regarding Exchange 2007 cluster setups. Unfortunately, this isn't the case; you still have to purchase an Exchange 2007 Enterprise Edition CAL for each node in your cluster (also any passive nodes). The reason is that the passive node still runs Exchange code although the node is the passive one.

Configuring the Network Interface for Each Node

When you start the servers that are to be the nodes in the cluster, begin by naming the machines EDFS07 and EDFS08 or whatever naming scheme you want to use. (These names have nothing to do with the Exchange server name that your clients will be configured to connect to later.) Now name the two network connections Public and Private (see Figure 8.30) for the external and the internal networks, respectively. Remember to do this on both nodes.

Figure 8.30 Network Connections

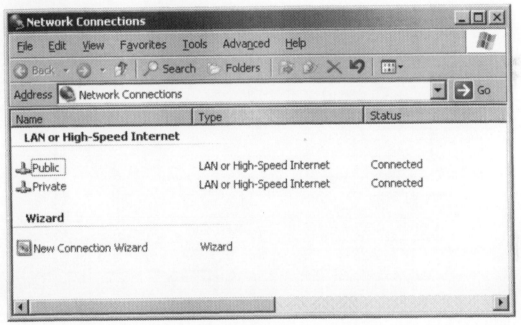

1. Click **Advanced | Advanced Settings**. If it's not already the case, make sure Public is listed first on the binding order list, then Private, and Remote Access Connections last. Also make sure that you clear the **File and Printer Sharing** check box for Microsoft Networks for the Private network connection, as shown in Figure 8.31.

Figure 8.31 Binding Order

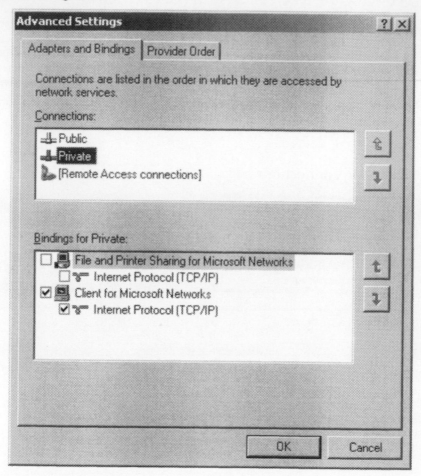

2. Now configure the **Public** network with the TCP/IP settings that should be used in your environment (see Figure 8.32).

Figure 8.32 Configuring the Public Network Interface

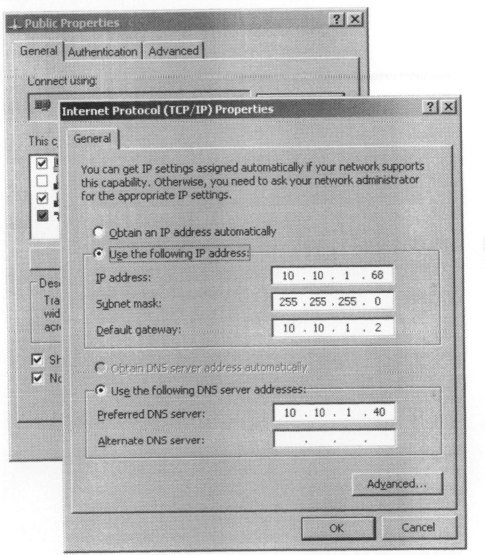

We also need to configure the Private network with an IP address and a subnet mask, as shown in Figure 8.33. Nothing else is required, since this network is used only for communication (heartbeats) between the nodes in the cluster.

Figure 8.33 Configuring the Private Network Interface

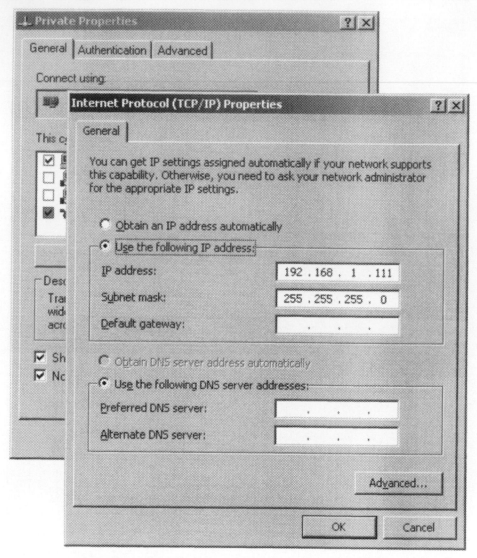

1. Click **Advanced**, then select the **DNS** tab. Here you should clear both the **Register this connection's addresses in DNS** and **Use this connection's DNS suffix** check boxes, as shown in Figure 8.34.

Figure 8.34 Configuring DNS Settings for the Private Network Interface

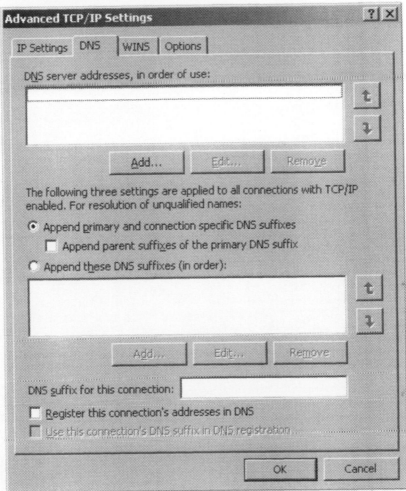

2. Click the **WINS** tab. Clear the **Enable LMHOSTS lookup** option and select **Disable NetBIOS over TCP/IP**, as shown in Figure 8.35.

3. Click **OK** three times and close the Network Connections window.

Figure 8.35 Configuring WINS Settings for the Private Network Interface

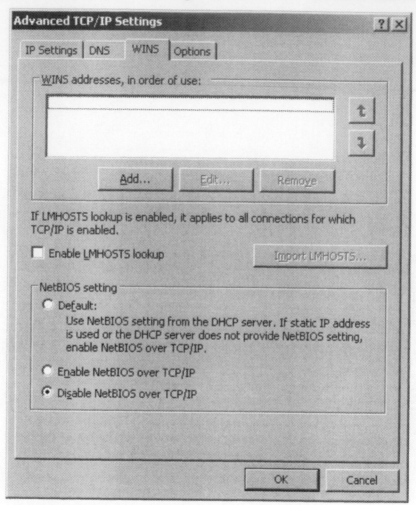

Adding the Servers to the Active Directory Domain

Since a CCR setup requires both nodes to be part of the same Active Directory domain, now would be a good time to make this the case. You can add the nodes to the domain by right-clicking **My Computer** and selecting **Properties** in the context menu. Now click the **Computer Name** tab (see Figure 8.36), then the **Change** button, and specify the domain.

Figure 8.36 Adding the Nodes to the Domain

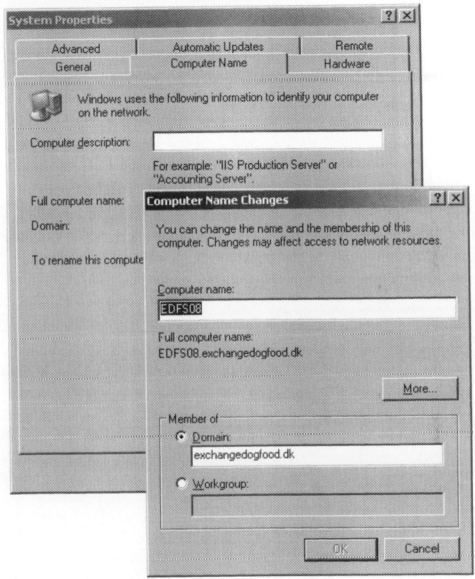

When you have added both servers to the domain as well as rebooted each, we can move on to creating the necessary cluster service account.

Creating a Cluster Service Account

Because each node belonging to the cluster needs to use the same account, we need to create a cluster service account.

The cluster service account must be a member of either the Exchange Server Administrators (ServerName) group or the Exchange Organization Administrators group. In addition, it must be a member of the local administrators group on each node in the cluster. For our purposes, we'll add it to the Exchange Organization Administrators group.

To create the cluster service account:

1. Log onto a domain controller in the respective Active Directory domain, then click **Start | Run** and type **DSA.msc** to open the Active Directory Users and Computers MMC snap-in. Now right-click the Organizational Unit (OU) in which you want the service account to be created, then choose **New | User** in the context menu. Give the account a meaningful name and user logon name (such as **Cluster Service Account** and **svc-cluster**), as shown in Figure 8.37. Now click **Next**.

Figure 8.37 Creating the Cluster Service Account

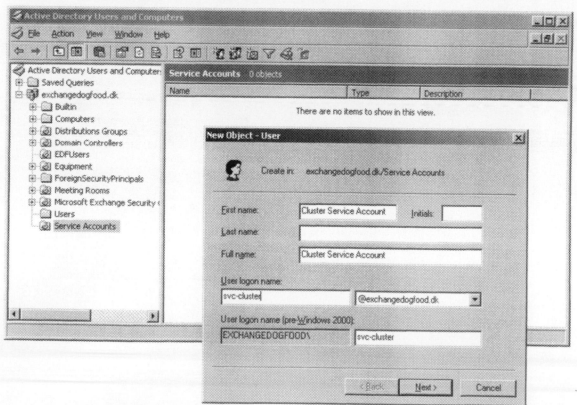

2. Give the service account a complex password and uncheck **User Must change password at next logon**, then check **Password never expires**, as shown in Figure 8.38. Click **Next**.

Figure 8.38 Specifying the Password for the Cluster Service Account

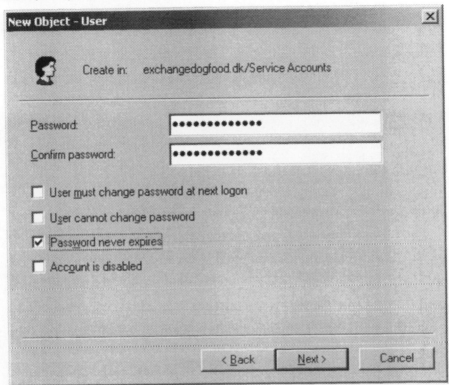

On the New User object completion page click Finish.

3. Now we need to give the new cluster service account the appropriate permissions. To do so, open the **Properties** page for the user object and select the **Member Of** tab. Make sure it's the respective Active Directory domain that's shown in the **From this location** field, then click the **Add** button and type **Exchange Organization Administrators**, as shown in Figure 8.39. Click **OK**.

Figure 8.39 Adding the Cluster Service Account to the Exchange Organization Administrators Group

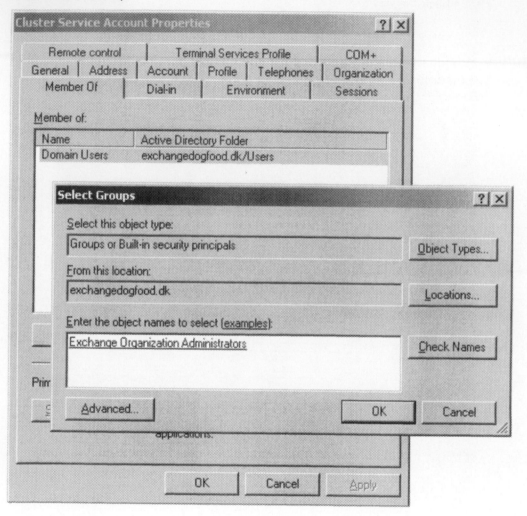

4. Now switch over to the server that will be the first node in the cluster and click **Start | Run**. Type **compmgmt.msc**. Expand **Local Users and Groups** and select the **Groups** container. Open the **Properties** page for the Administrators group object in the right pane, then click the **Add** button. Make sure that the Active Directory

domain is shown in the **From this location** field, as shown in Figure 8.40, and type **Cluster Service Account** (or whatever name you gave the account in your setup). click **Check Names** to verify that it resolves successfully. Click **OK** and close the Computer Management MMC snap-in.

Figure 8.40 Adding the Cluster Service Account to the Local Administrators Group

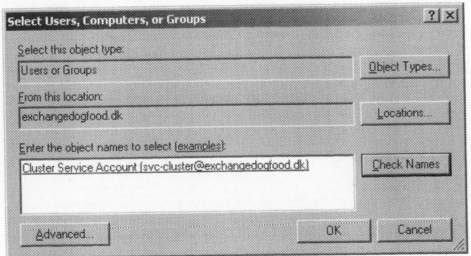

5. Repeat Steps 1–4 for the server that will be the second node in the cluster.

Creating and Configuring the Windows 2003 Server Cluster

Now that the two servers are ready to act as nodes in a Windows 2003 cluster, it's time to create the actual Windows 2003 Server Cluster. To do so:

1. Log onto EDFS07 with a domain admin account, then click **Start | Administrative Tools | Cluster Administrator**, and select **Create new cluster** in the drop-down box. Click **OK** and then click **Next**, as shown in Figure 8.41.

Figure 8.41 Creating a New Cluster

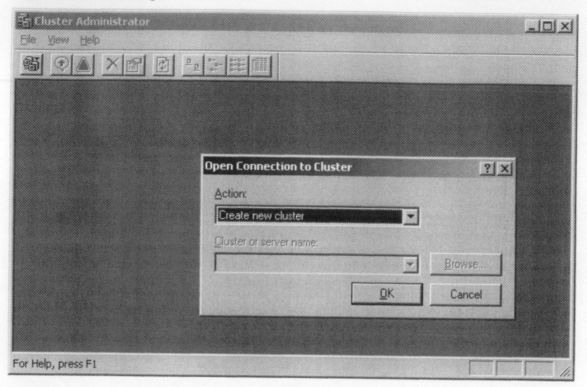

NOTE

You can also open a command prompt and type **Cluster.exe /create /wizard** to start the Cluster Wizard.

2. Now specify the domain name as well as the cluster name (the name for the Windows 2003 cluster, *not* the Exchange cluster name to which the clients will connect) as shown in Figure 8.42, then click **Next**.

Figure 8.42 Specifying the Cluster Name and Domain

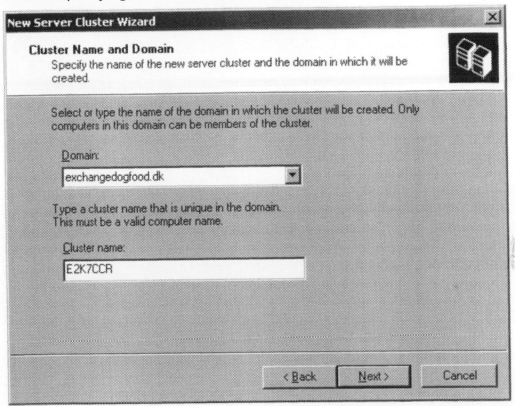

3. If it's not already entered, type the name of the Windows 2003 server that is to be the first node in the cluster (in this case, **EDFS07**), then click **Next** (see Figure 8.43).

Figure 8.43 Adding the First Cluster Node to the New Cluster

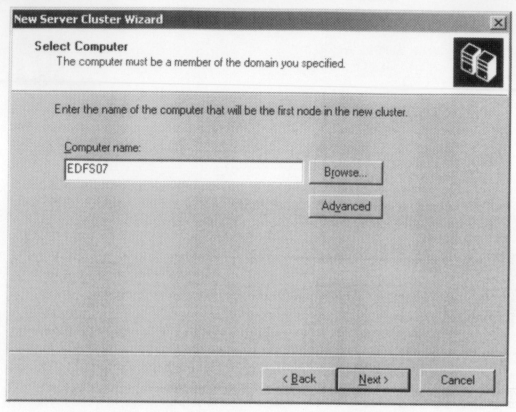

4. Let the Cluster Wizard determine the cluster configuration and click Next.

NOTE

You can ignore the two warnings shown in Figure 8.44, since the nodes in a cluster continuous replication-based mailbox server setup aren't going to share the same disk subsystem.

Figure 8.44 Analyzing Cluster Configuration

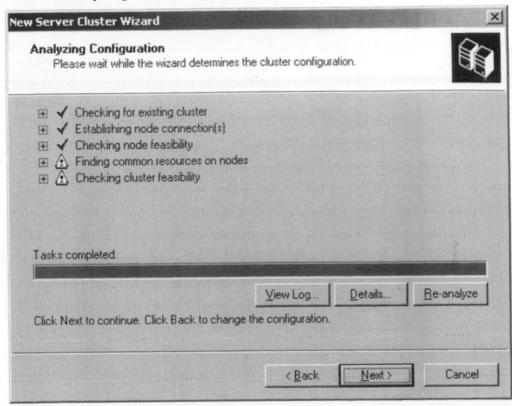

5. Now enter the IP address that the cluster management tools should use to connect to the cluster (in this case, **10.10.1.218**) and click **Next** (see Figure 8.45).

Figure 8.45 Specifying the IP Address to Which the Cluster Management Tools Should Connect

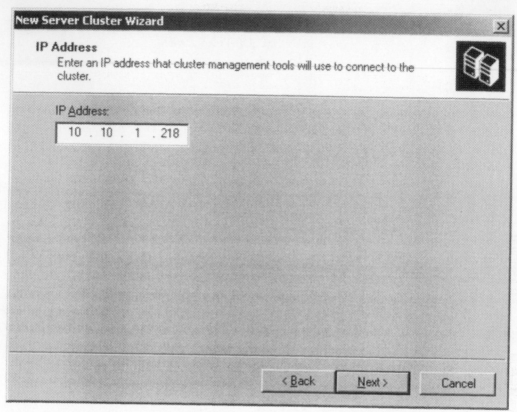

6. Enter the credentials of the cluster service account and click **Next** (see Figure 8.46).

Figure 8.46 Entering the Credentials of the Cluster Service Account

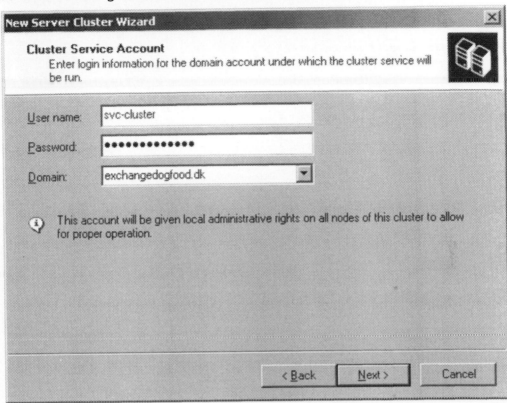

7. Now click **Quorum** and select **Majority Node Set** as the resource type, then click **OK** and **Next** (see Figures 8.47 and 8.48).

Figure 8.47 Proposed Cluster Configuration

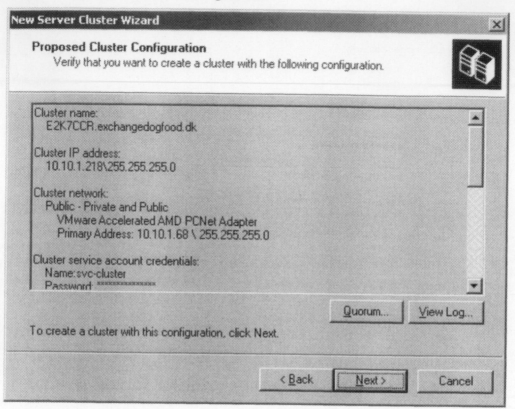

NOTE

The Majority Node Set resource type manages cluster configuration data that might or might not be on a cluster storage device. For example, the Majority Node Set resource type can manage cluster configuration data that is actually stored on multiple nodes in a cluster at the same physical location or in a geographically dispersed cluster. The Majority Node Set resource ensures that the cluster configuration data is kept consistent across the various nodes.

Figure 8.48 Setting Majority Node Set as the Resource Type

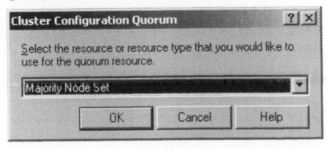

8. Now wait for the cluster to be configured, then click **Next** (see Figure 8.49).

Figure 8.49 Creating the Cluster

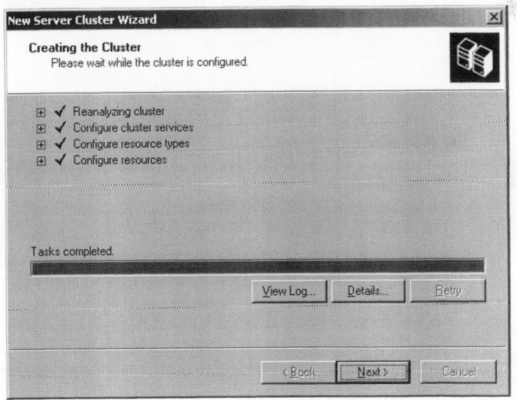

9. When the cluster has been completed successfully, you can click **Finish**.

We now have a full working Windows 2003 cluster running, but since there's only one node, it's not very fault tolerant. So let's add the second Windows 2003 server too. Do the following:

1. Right-click **EDFS07** in the left pane of the Cluster Administrator, then selecting **New | Node**, as shown in Figure 8.50.

Figure 8.50 Adding a Second Node to the Cluster

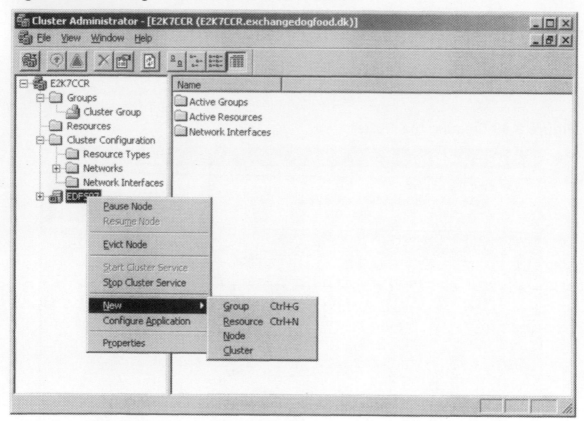

2. The Add Nodes Wizard will launch and you can click **Next**. Enter the name of the server that is going to be the second node (for the purpose of this example, **EDFS08**), then click **Next** (see Figure 8.51).

Figure 8.51 Entering the Name of the Second Node

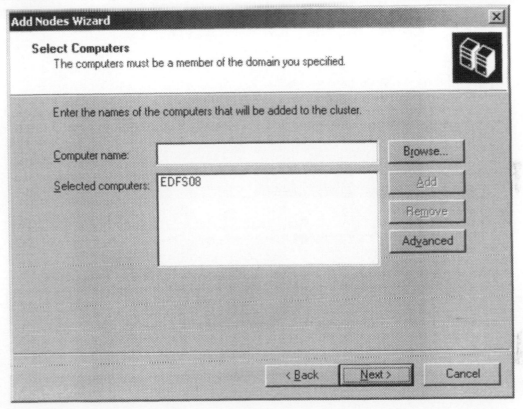

3. Again, let the Add Notes Wizard determine the cluster configuration, then click **Next** (see Figure 8.52).

Figure 8.52 Analyzing Cluster Configuration

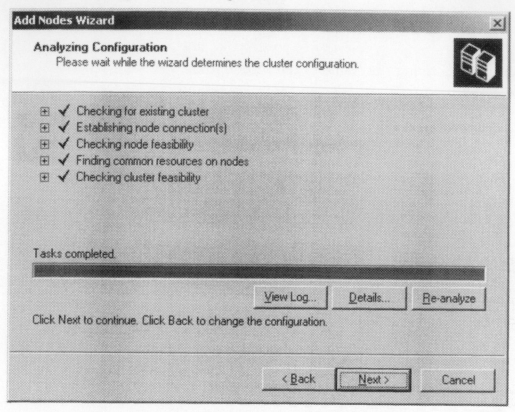

4. Enter the password for the cluster service account (in this case, **svc-cluster**, which we created earlier in the chapter), then click **Next** (see Figure 8.53).

Figure 8.53 Entering the Password for the Cluster Service Account

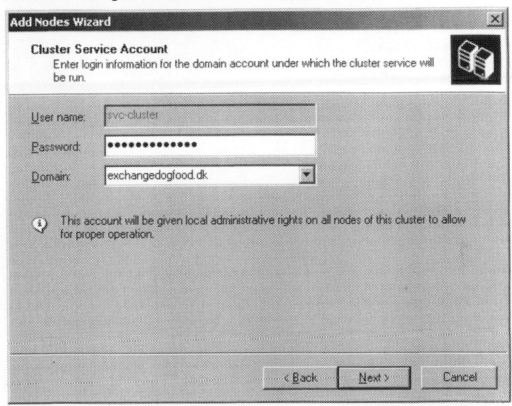

5. When you are verified, you'll want to add the second node to the cluster with the configuration shown in Figure 8.54. Click **Next**.

Figure 8.54 Proposed Cluster Configuration for Node Two

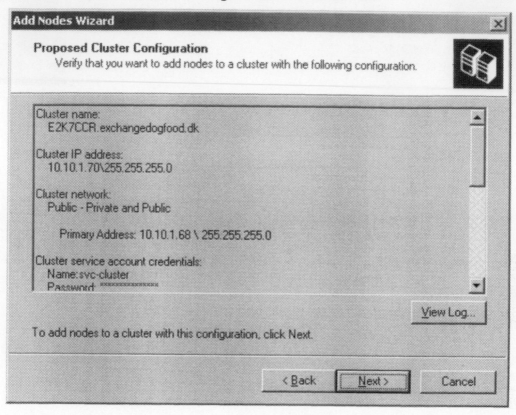

6. When the cluster has been configured properly without any errors or warnings (see Figure 8.55), click **Next**.

Figure 8.55 The Cluster Is Configured for the Second Node

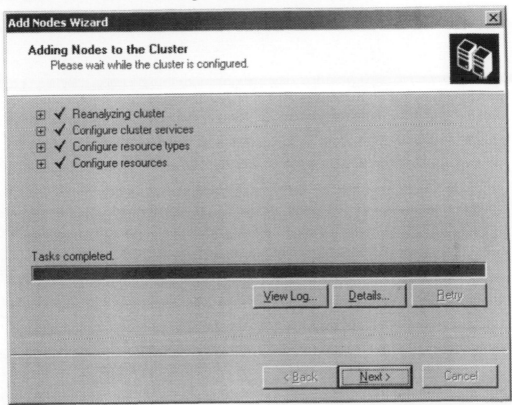

7. When the Add Notes Wizard has completed successfully, click **Finish**.

The second Windows server is now part of the cluster, as shown in Figure 8.56.

Figure 8.56 Cluster Administrator with Two Nodes

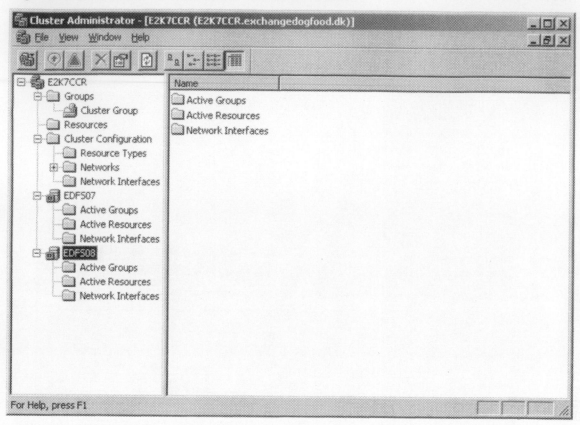

Installing the Necessary Windows Components

Before we move on to install the Exchange Server 2007 binaries, we need to make sure that the required Windows components have been installed. All types of Exchange Server 2007 installations (no matter what server role we're talking about) need the Microsoft .NET Framework 2.0 component installed.

If you have installed Windows Server 2003 Enterprise Edition with Service Pack 1 on the nodes, you need to download the Microsoft .NET Framework Version 2.0 Redistributable Package (x86) from Microsoft.com, since it's only a standard Windows component for Windows Server 2003 R2. If you're using Windows Server 2003 R2-based servers, you can install the component by clicking **Start | Control Panel | Add or Remove Programs | Add/Remove Windows Components**, checking the **Microsoft .NET Framework 2.0** check box as shown in Figure 8.57, then clicking **Next**.

Figure 8.57 Installing the Microsoft .NET Framework 2.0 Windows Component

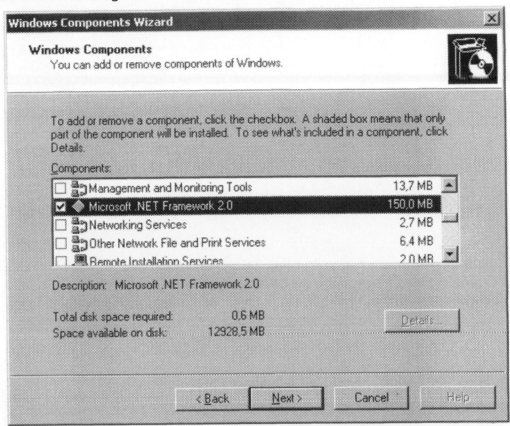

Since we're deploying a clustered mailbox server, we also need to install the following IIS 6.0 components on each node:

- Enable network COM+ access
- Internet Information Services
- World Wide Web Service

When you have done so, you can move on to configure the File Share Witness.

Configuring the Majority Node Set Quorum with File Share Witness

No doubt some of you are thinking: What the heck is a Majority Node Set quorum with File Share Witness? We can understand why; this is a completely new type of quorum model that is made available by installing the update (MS KB article 921181) mentioned in the beginning of this chapter section.

The update makes it possible to use a file share witness that is external to the cluster as an additional "vote" to determine the status of the cluster in a two-node MNS quorum cluster deployment, which is a requirement for using the CCR functionality in Exchange Server 2007.

The file share for this file share witness can be located on any type of Windows server in your environment, but best practice is to use an Exchange 2007 Hub Transport server in the Active Directory server site containing the nodes in the respective cluster. We'll also use a Hub Transport server in this example.

The first thing you need to do is to create the file share on the Hub Transport server. You can do this either via the CLI or by using the GUI. In this example we'll use the GUI:

1. Log on to the Hub Transport server with a domain admin account, then open Windows Explorer and create a new folder called **MNS_FSQ_E2K7CCR** on the C: drive or wherever you want it to be created, as shown in Figure 8.58.

NOTE

It's recommended that you use the *MNS_FSQ_clustername* naming convention when you create this folder.

Figure 8.58 The Majority Node Set File Share Quorum Folder

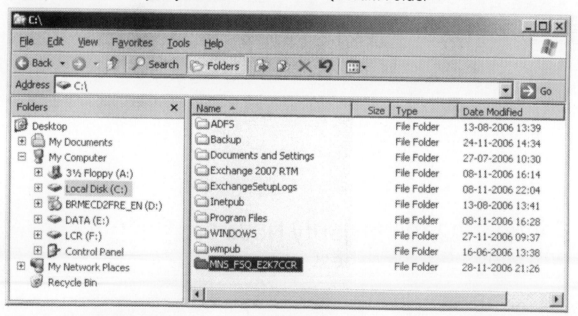

2. Now open the **Properties** page for the newly created folder and click the **Sharing** tab (see Figure 8.59).

Figure 8.59 The Majority Node Set File Share Quorum Folder Share

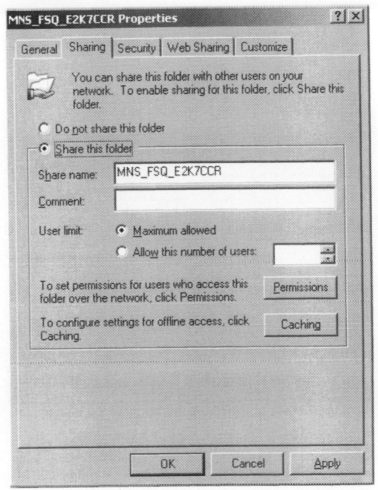

3. Click **Permissions** and configure the share permissions so that only the Cluster Service Account is allowed access to this share (see Figure 8.60).

Figure 8.60 Share Permissions for the Majority Node Set File Share Quorum Folder

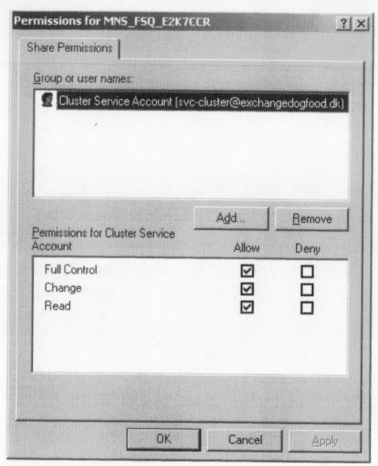

4. Click **OK**, then select the **Security** tab. Here you should give Full Control to the local administrator and the cluster service account, as shown in Figure 8.61. Make sure you clear **Allow inheritable permissions from the parent to propagate to this object and all child objects** when doing so, then click **OK** twice and log off the server.

Figure 8.61 Security Permissions to the Majority Node Set File Share
Quorum Folder

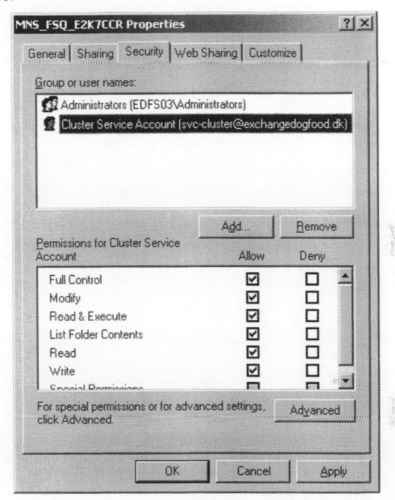

5. Back on EDFS07 or EDFS08, we now need to set the Majority Node Set Private Property attribute to point to the file share we just created. We do so by opening a command prompt, then issuing the command **Cluster res "Majority Node Set" /priv MNSFileShare=\\EDFS03\MNS_FSQ_E2K7CCR**.

NOTE

Make sure to replace the server name so that it matches the name of the Hub Transport server in your environment.

You will get a warning that all properties were stored but not all changes will take effect until the next time the resource is brought online, just as is shown in Figure 8.62.

Figure 8.62 Configuring the Majority Node Set on EDFS07

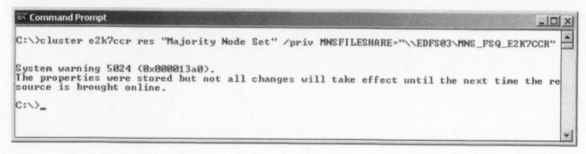

SOME INDEPENDENT ADVICE

In a couple of the CCR-based cluster deployments I've done, I have gotten an error message similar to the following when running the command *Cluster res "Majority Node Set" /priv MNSFileShare=\\EDFS03\MNS_FSQ_E2K7CCR*:

Too many command line parameters have been specified for this option.
See "CLUSTER RESOURCE /?" for correct syntax

Should you experience this error, too, you should be able to get going using the following command syntax instead:

Cluster <ClusterName> res "Majority Node Set" /priv MNSFileShare=UNCPath

6. To force all changes to take effect, we will move the cluster group from one node to the other (taking the cluster group offline and online again). Do this using the command **Cluster Group "Cluster Group" /Move**. When you have done so, you will see that the cluster group is now online on E2K7Node2, as shown in Figure 8.63.

Figure 8.63 Moving the Cluster Group from One Node to the Other

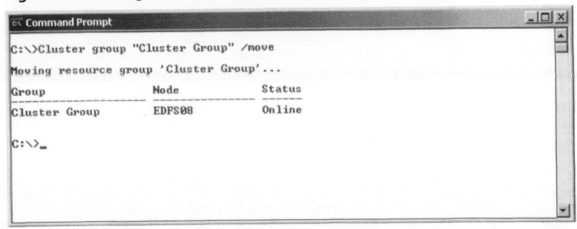

7. Now let's verify that the 7Priv property is set correctly. This can be done by issuing the command **Cluster Res "Majority Node Set" /Priv**.

As you can see in Figure 8.64, this property has been set correctly for the purposes of our example.

Figure 8.64 Verifying That the Property of *IPriv* Is Set Correctly

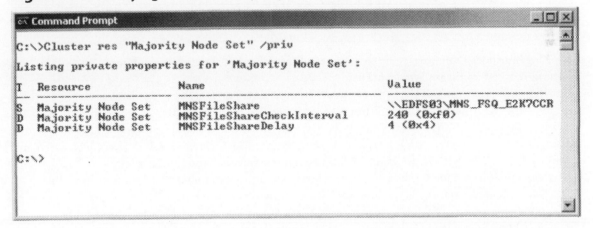

Configuring the Transport Dumpster

When deploying a CCR–based cluster in your environment, an important step is to enable the Transport Dumpster on the Hub Transport server.

The Transport Dumpster is a new feature of the Exchange 2007 Hub Transport server that can submit recently delivered mail after an unscheduled outage. For an e-mail message to be able to be retained in the Transport Dumpster, at least one of the message recipients must have his or her mailbox located on a CCR–based mailbox cluster server, because the Transport Dumpster works only with mailboxes located on a CCR–based mailbox server cluster. As mentioned earlier in this chapter, with CCR the replication of mailbox data from the active node to the passive node is *asynchronous*, which means that the passive node will always lag behind the passive node (although not by much). This means that should a failure of the active node occur, there's a chance that not all transaction log files will have been replicated to the passive node before this happens. This is where the Transport Dumpster comes into the picture. It can resubmit recently delivered mail and thereby constitute for the majority of the changes in the database(s). When a failure of the active node results in a lossy failover to the passive node, the cluster mailbox server will ask all the Hub Transport servers in the site to redeliver any lost mail.

NOTE

Should any of the messages that are being resubmitted to the cluster mailbox server be duplicates, the store is intelligent enough to discard any duplicates it finds.

The Transport Dumpster is enabled by default; you can see the default configured settings by running the *Get-TransportConfig* CMDlet.

Microsoft recommends that you configure the *MaxDumpsterSizePerStorageGroup* parameter, which specifies the maximum size of the Transport Dumpster queue for each storage group to a size that is 1.25 times the size of the maximum message that can be sent. For example, if the maximum size for messages is 10 megabytes (MB), you should configure the *MaxDumpsterSizePerStorageGroup* parameter with a value of 12.5 MB. In addition, Microsoft recommends that you configure the *MaxDumpsterTime* parameter, which specifies how long an e-mail message should remain in the Transport Dumpster queue, to a value of 07.00:00:00, which is seven days. This amount of time is sufficient to allow for an extended outage to occur without loss of e-mail. When you use the Transport Dumpster feature, additional disk space is needed on the Hub Transport server to host the Transport Dumpster queues. The amount of storage space required is roughly equal to the value of *MaxDumpsterSizePerStorageGroup* multiplied by the number of storage groups.

You use the *Set-TransportConfig* CMDlet to enable and configure the Transport Dumpster. So, for example, to configure the maximum size of the dumpster per storage group to 25 MB with a dumpster life of 10 days, you would need to run the command *Set-TransportConfig -MaxDumpsterSize PerStorageGroup 25MB -MaxDumpsterTime 10.00:00:00*.

To see the *MaxDumpsterSizePerStorageGroup* and *MaxDumpsterTime* configuration settings, you can type **Get-TransportConfig**, as shown in Figure 8.65

Figure 8.65 Transport Configuration Settings

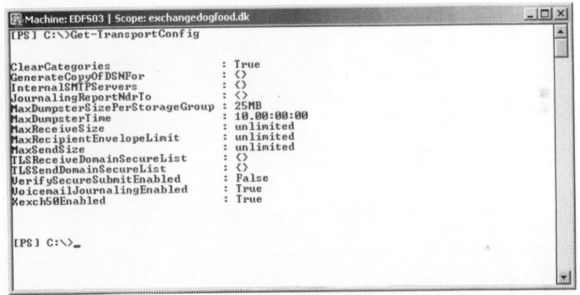

```
Machine: EDFS03 | Scope: exchangedogfood.dk                          _ □ ×
[PS] C:\>Get-TransportConfig


ClearCategories                 : True
GenerateCopyOfDSNFor            : {}
InternalSMTPServers             : {}
JournalingReportNdrTo           : {}
MaxDumpsterSizePerStorageGroup  : 25MB
MaxDumpsterTime                 : 10.00:00:00
MaxReceiveSize                  : unlimited
MaxRecipientEnvelopeLimit       : unlimited
MaxSendSize                     : unlimited
TLSReceiveDomainSecureList      : {}
TLSSendDomainSecureList         : {}
VerifySecureSubmitEnabled       : False
VoicemailJournalingEnabled      : True
Xexch50Enabled                  : True


[PS] C:\>_
```

Installing Exchange 2007 on the Active Node

It's time to install the Exchange Server 2007 binaries on each node. We'll start with EDFS07, which is the active node. To do so:

1. Double-click **Setup.exe** on the network share or the DVD media containing the Exchange 2007 setup files.

2. The Exchange Server 2007 Installation Wizard splash screen will launch, and as you can see in Figure 8.66, Step 1: Install .NET Framework 2.0, Step 2: Install Microsoft Management Console (MMC), and Step 3: Install Windows PowerShell have already been completed.

Figure 8.66 The Exchange Server 2007 Splash Screen

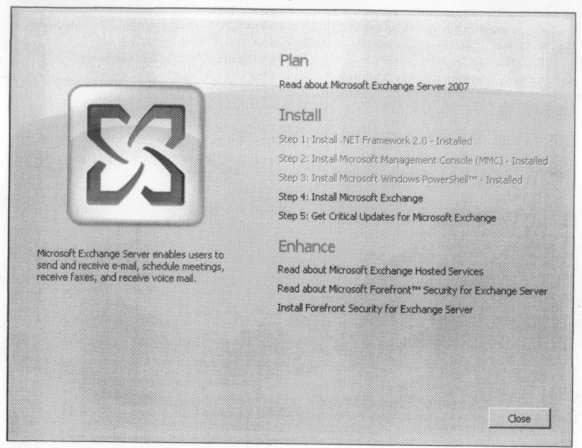

Plan

Read about Microsoft Exchange Server 2007

Install

Step 1: Install .NET Framework 2.0 - Installed

Step 2: Install Microsoft Management Console (MMC) - Installed

Step 3: Install Microsoft Windows PowerShell™ - Installed

Step 4: Install Microsoft Exchange

Step 5: Get Critical Updates for Microsoft Exchange

Enhance

Read about Microsoft Exchange Hosted Services

Read about Microsoft Forefront™ Security for Exchange Server

Install Forefront Security for Exchange Server

Microsoft Exchange Server enables users to send and receive e-mail, schedule meetings, receive faxes, and receive voice mail.

Close

NOTE

If you have installed Windows Server 2003 with Service Pack 1 on each node, you need to download Microsoft Management Console (MMC) 3.0 and install it manually (by following the link in Step 2). But since I'm using Windows 2003 R2 Servers in my environment, the MMC 3.0 is installed by default.

Click **Step 4: Install Microsoft Exchange**. Then click **Next** and accept the **License Agreement**. Click **Next** once again. Decide whether you want to enable error reporting or not (it's a good idea to enable this function, since the Exchange Product Group will receive any obscure errors you should experience in your CCR setup), then click **Next**.

3. Now select **Custom Exchange Server Installation** (see Figure 8.67) and click **Next**.

Figure 8.67 Selecting a Custom Exchange Server Installation

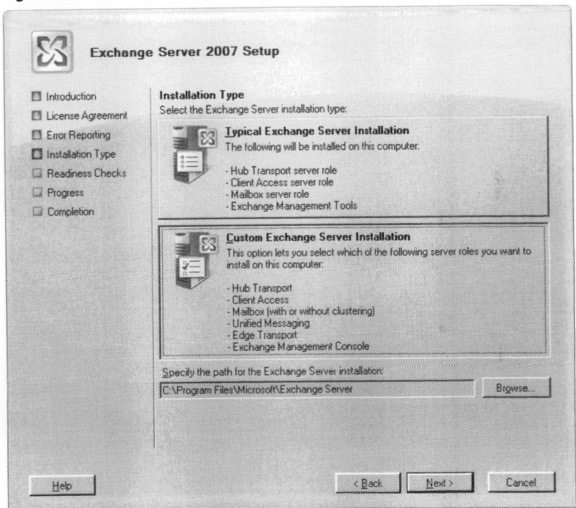

4. Check **Active Clustered Mailbox Role** as shown in Figure 8.68 and click **Next**.

Figure 8.68 Selecting to Install an Active Clustered Mailbox Role

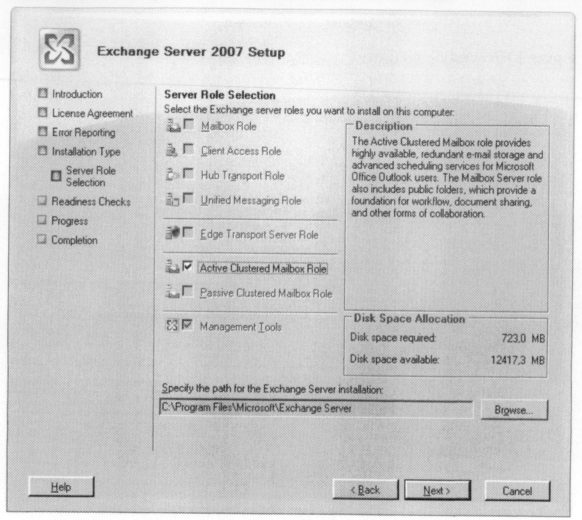

5. Now select **Cluster Continuous Replication**, then specify a name for the mailbox server (the name you want your Outlook clients to connect to) and a unique IP address on your public network. Finally, specify the path for the clustered mailbox server database files (which in the example is **E:**) or use the default path (see Figure 8.69).

   If you're installing CCR in a production environment, you should keep the transaction log files and database on separate disks, but if you're deploying CCR in a test environment, you simply use the default path.

Figure 8.69 Selecting to Install a Cluster Continuous Replication Cluster and Specifying the Name and IP Address of the Clustered Mailbox Server

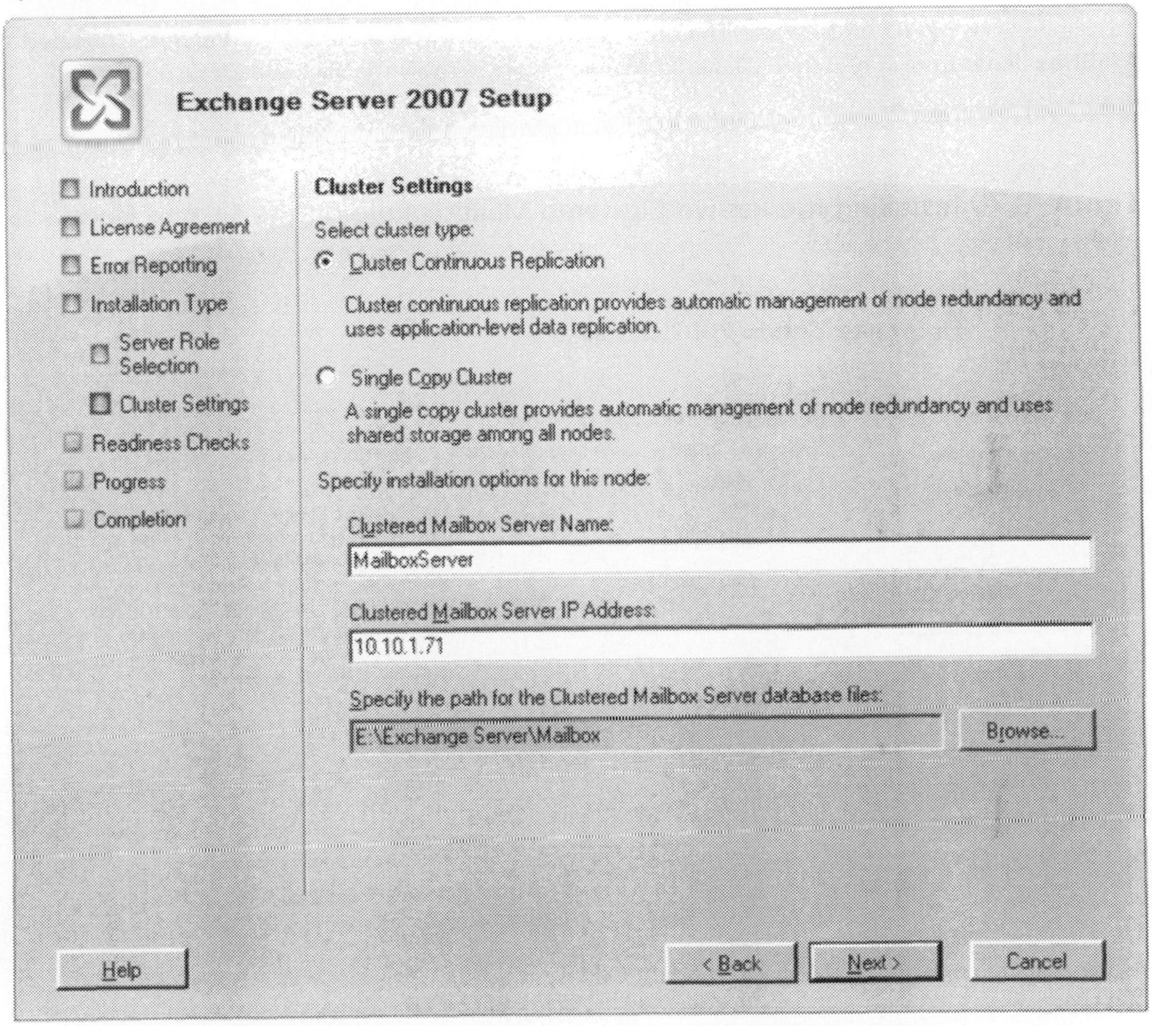

6. Let the readiness check complete, and if no issues are found, click **Next** to begin the installation.

The Exchange Server 2007 Installation Wizard will now copy the needed Exchange files, install and configure the Mailbox Role, and finally create and configure the clustered mailbox server resources locally and create the object in Active Directory. After all steps have been completed, untick **Exit Setup** and open Exchange System Manager (yes, this will be corrected in a later build), then click **Finish**. We don't want to open the EMC just yet; we'll install Exchange on the second node first.

Installing Exchange 2007 on the Passive Node

Log on to EDFS08 with a domain admin account and do the same steps as we did when installing Exchange Server 2007 on EDFS07. The only difference is that you should select **Passive Clustered Mailbox Role** instead of Active Clustered Mailbox Role, as shown in Figure 8.70.

Figure 8.70 Installing the Passive Clustered Mailbox Role on the Second Node

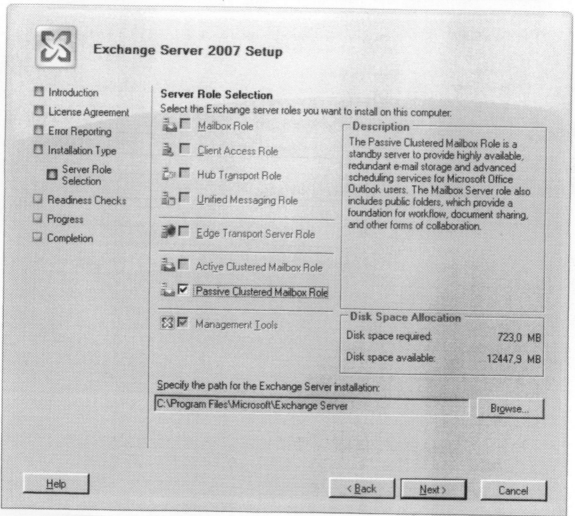

Testing the Functionality of the Clustered Mailbox Server

It's time to verify that our Exchange 2007 clustered mailbox server is working as expected. Let's first open the Cluster Administrator and check whether the respective Exchange resources have been created. If you take a look at Figure 8.71, it looks good; we have both nodes listed in the left pane and all Exchange resources have been created and are currently owned by EDFS07.

Figure 8.71 Listing All Exchange Cluster Resources in the Cluster Administrator

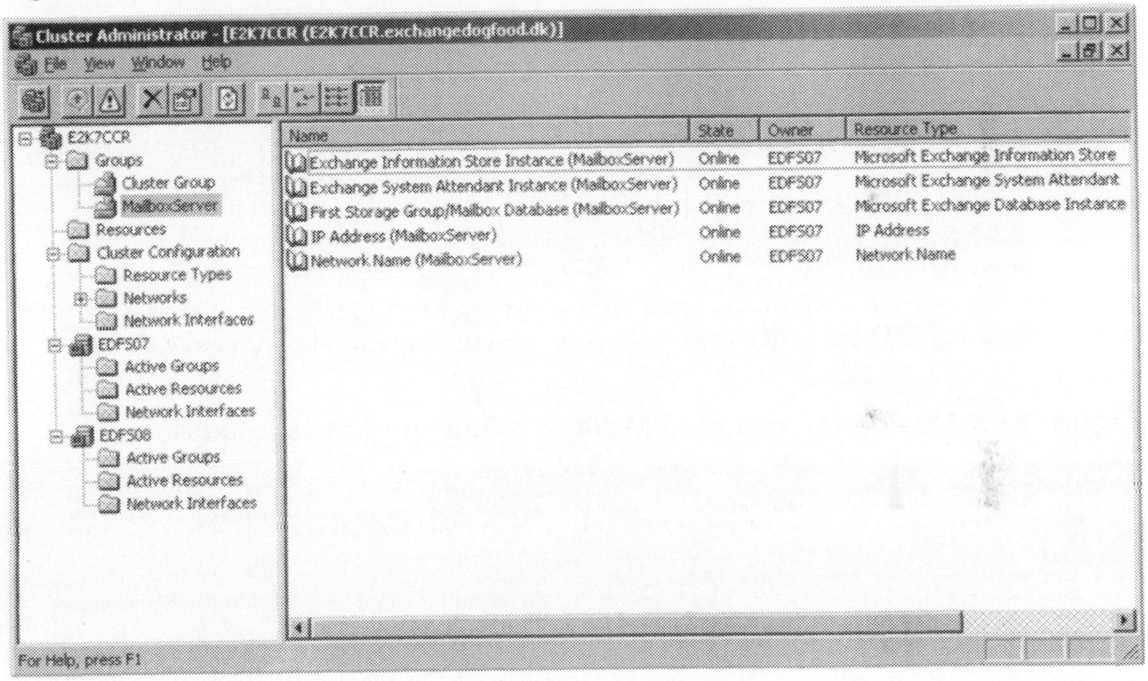

Try to open the EMS by clicking **Start | All Programs | Microsoft Exchange Server 2007 | Exchange Management Shell** on one of the nodes, then type **Get-ClusteredMailboxServerStatus –Identity MailboxServer**. As you can see in Figure 8.72, the status of the clustered mailbox server is Online, and EDFS7 is currently the active node.

Figure 8.72 Requesting the Online Status of the Clustered Mailbox Server

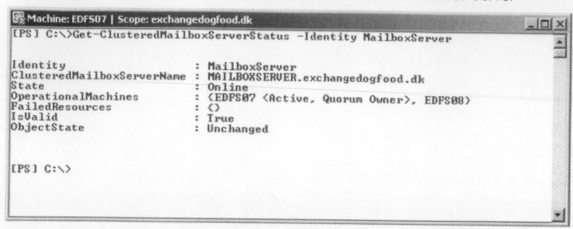

Now that we have verified that the clustered mailbox server is online, let's try to move the Exchange resources from node one to node two using the *Move-ClusteredMailboxServer* CMDlet. In the environment used in this chapter, we do so by issuing the command *Move-ClusteredMailboxServer -Identity:MailboxServer -TargetMachine:EDFS08 -MoveComment:"Verifying the Move Clustered Mailbox Server Functionality!"*

You're then asked to confirm this action. Type **Yes**, then press **Enter**. After a while the clustered mailbox resources will have been moved to the second node (EDFS08), as shown in Figure 8.73.

Figure 8.73 Moving the Clustered Mailbox Resources to the Second Node

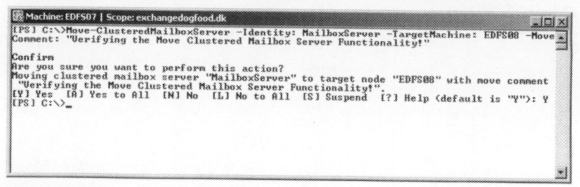

WARNING

Even though it's possible to move the cluster resource groups between nodes using the Cluster Administrator console, you should *always* do so using the *Move-ClusteredMailboxServer* CMDlet, because the Move Group task in the Cluster Administrator console isn't Exchange 2007 aware.

Viewing the Clustered Mailbox Server From Within the Exchange Management Console

Let's take a look at the clustered mailbox server in the EMC. To do so, click **Start | All Programs | Microsoft Exchange Server 2007 | Exchange Management Console**, then drill down to **Server Configuration | Mailbox** Notice that the clustered mailbox server we named MailboxServer is listed in the Results pane and that it's recognized as a cluster server, as shown in Figure 8.74.

Figure 8.74 Viewing the Clustered Mailbox Server in the Exchange Management Console

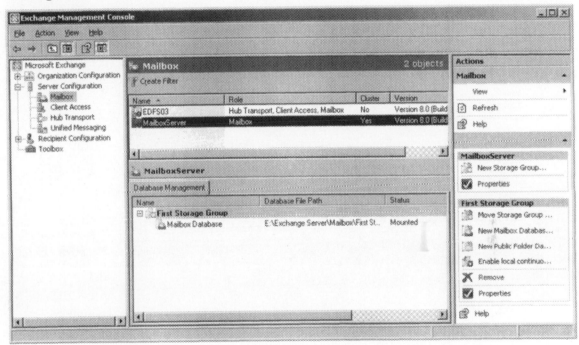

Simulating a Failover from One Node to the Other

Now let's try to simulate a failover from EDFS08 (currently the active node) to EDFS07 so that we can see what will happen from the Outlook client perspective. To switch from one node to the other, we'll issue the CMDlet we used earlier in the chapter: *Move-ClusteredMailboxServer -Identity: MailboxServer -TargetMachine:EDFS07 -MoveComment:"Simulating a failover from one node to the other, seen from the end-user perspective"*.

When a manual move or a failover occurs, the balloon shown in Figure 8.75 will appear because all services need to be stopped on EDFS07 before they can be moved and brought online on EDFS08.

Figure 8.75 Connection to the Exchange Server Has Been Lost

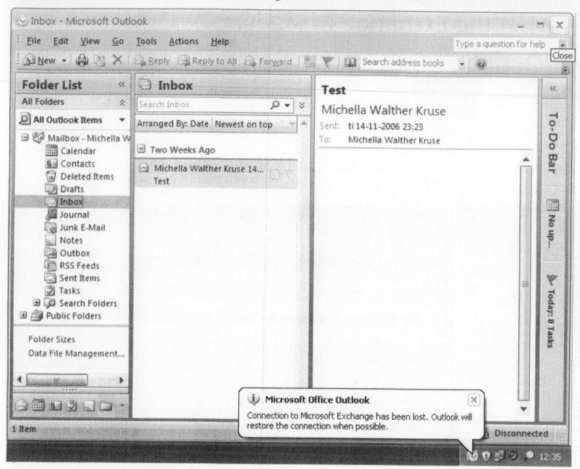

Depending on the number as well as the size of the databases in your Cluster Continuous Replication setup, this will take somewhere between 10 seconds to a couple of minutes, which shouldn't cause panic for the end users in the organization.

When EDFS08 has taken over, the end users will be notified that the connection to the Exchange Server has been restored (see Figure 8.76).

As you have seen you throughout this chapter, you benefit from several advantages when you choose to install the Exchange 2007 Mailbox Server role in a Cluster Continuous Replication setup in your organization. The primary benefit is that you no longer have a single point of failure in regard to the Mailbox/Public Folder databases. Should the database on one node crash, an automatic failover to the other node containing the secondary database will be completed. This also means that you no longer need to use a shared storage system in the CCR setup, as is the case with Exchange 2007 Single Copy Clusters as well as cluster setups in previous versions of Exchange. In addition, the two nodes in the CCR setup can even be placed in two different locations, as long as they belong to the same subnet. Not only that, the installation of the Exchange 2007 cluster has also been further

Figure 8.76 Connection to the Exchange Server Has Been Restored

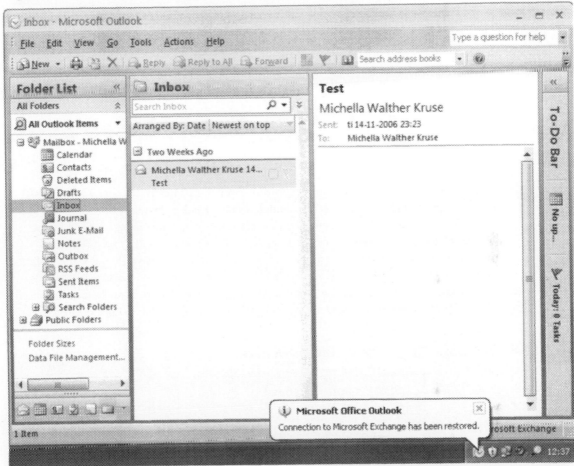

simplified over previous versions. Since the CCR setup uses log file shipping and replay to a secondary database, you also don't have to do full online backups as often as was the case in Exchange 200x and earlier versions. Last but certainly not least, the failover process has been improved in several areas now that the new file share witness model has been introduced.

Backup Choices in a CCR Setup

When you deployed a cluster with Exchange 2003, the only option available when the stores were going to be backed up was to take a backup of the stores running on the production servers. With CCR (and LCR), you have the option of taking a backup of the database copies on the passive node, thereby eliminating any heavy load on the active node, both in terms of I/O to the disk spindles as well as CPU usage.

Keep in mind, though, that you can only perform a backup on the passive node using VSS, which means that Windows Backup cannot be used for this purpose. Instead you need to use Microsoft Data Protection Manager version 2 (DPM v2) or a third-party backup application that supports VSS backups.

It's also worth mentioning that any backups performed via the passive node will be backups of the database copies, not the databases on the active node. So, you might wonder, what will happen to the transaction log files on the active node? When the backups have been performed on the passive node, all log files associated with the respective storage group on the active node will be truncated. In addition, the database header on the active node will be modified, and this will generate a log file that will be replicated to the passive node and then modify the database header on the passive node afterward.

To read more about how you back up the databases in Exchange 2007, see Chapter 10.

Managing a Single Copy Cluster-Based Setup

In addition to the CCR type of setup, Exchange 2007 supports the Single Copy Clusters (SCC) type, which, as mentioned in the beginning of the chapter, is more or less identical to the traditional active/passive clusters we know from previous versions of Exchange. This means that a SCC-based cluster only provides service failover and still has a single point of failure when it comes to the databases, unless a shared storage solution that provides redundancy in other means is used in the environment. An SCC-based cluster using a fault-tolerant SAN is just as good as a CCR-based cluster in terms of data availability, but such a solution is much more expensive than a CCR solution.

An SCC is basically a clustered mailbox server that consists of two or more servers (known as *nodes*) that share the same storage (for databases and log files). The shared storage subsystem is typically a SAN. In Figure 8.77 you can see what the architecture behind a typical SCC scenario looks like.

Figure 8.77 A Basic Single Copy Cluster Scenario

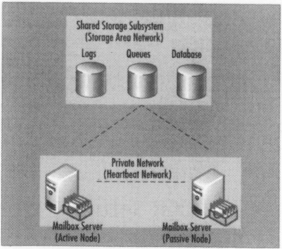

The primary benefit of an SCC is that it provides high availability of server resources because one node takes over should the active node be taken offline or fail for some reason. In addition, you can apply hotfixes, service packs, and the like to the nodes without having any downtime of your mission-critical mailbox servers. However, bear in mind that an SCC is susceptible to failure of the shared storage subsystem. This means that no matter how many nodes are part of your cluster, you'll always have a single point of failure when you're using SCC opposite a CCR-based cluster, which, as we demonstrated, provides storage group failover via the new log file shipping and replay functionality.

Since most of you don't have the necessary hardware for a cluster, before you actually decide to deploy one in your environment, we thought it would be a clever idea to show you how to install an SCC in a Virtual Server 2005 R2 environment. Pretty much all the steps in this section can be used to install the SCC on real hardware, too.

Some Independent Advice

Some of you might wonder whether standby blusters are supported in Exchange 2007, just as they were in Exchange 2003. A *standby cluster* is a Windows cluster that matches a production Exchange cluster in terms of hardware and software configuration, including Windows and Exchange versions and any updates or hotfixes that have been applied. In addition, a standby cluster has the Exchange program files installed but has not yet been configured with any Exchange Virtual Servers (EVS). Lastly, a standby cluster can only be used when all Exchange Virtual Servers on the production cluster are offline.

So, is a standby cluster supported in Exchange 2007? The answer is no, but then it's really not that useful anymore, since Exchange 2007 gives us the ability to recover an Exchange 2007 cluster using the new *Exsetup /RecoverCMS* switch (which is similar to the */DisasterRecovery* switch we know from previous versions of Exchange). Even better, the */RecoverCMS* switch can be used to recover both Exchange 2007 CCR and SCC-based cluster setups. We'll take a closer look at the */RecoverCMS* switch in Chapter 10.

Prerequisites

To follow the steps throughout this section, you need the following:

- One physical machine running Virtual Server 2005 R2. Since this product is free to download from the Microsoft Web site, getting it shouldn't be a problem. You can download Virtual Server 2005 R2 from the following link: www.microsoft.com/windowsserversystem/virtualserver/software/default.msp.

- A Windows 2003 Active Directory forest with at least one domain controller (raised to 2000 or 2003 forest functional level).

- At least one existing Exchange 2007 Hub Transport/Client Access server already installed in the aforementioned forest.

- Two virtual guests running Windows 2003 R2 or Windows 2003 SP1 Enterprise Edition with at least 512MB RAM and two virtual NICs each—one for the Public network and one for the Private network (the heartbeat network). This means that you need to create an additional virtual network on the virtual host server; None (Guest Only) is sufficient for this network.

NOTE

To install a Exchange 2007 Single Copy Cluster, you also need to install the cluster hotfix mentioned in MS KB article 898790, which at the time of this writing can be requested by contacting Microsoft Product Support Services. Microsoft is working on making it public.

Configuring the Network Settings for each Network Interface

In this example, we'll create an SCC consisting of two active/passive clusters that will be part of the same Exchange organization as the CCR-based cluster we discussed previously in this chapter. This means that you will need to install two NICs in each node (which we recommend you call *public* and *private* so that you can see what belongs to which network) and then configure the private and public interfaces for evach of the two nodes identically to the network interfaces we configured on the two nodes in the CCR-based cluster setup. The only difference would be the IP addresses, since using the same ones would result in IP conflicts, but everything from the binding order, WINS, DNS, and so on should be the same for each interface. So instead of going through all the steps again, refer back to the "Configuring the Network Interfaces for Each Node" subsection of the "Managing a Cluster Continuous Replication-Based Cluster Setup" section of this chapter.

Creating the Shared Cluster Disks

As those of you with cluster experience are aware, a Windows cluster requires a quorum cluster disk. This quorum disk is used to store cluster configuration database checkpoints and log files that help manage the cluster as well as maintain consistency. Since we're dealing with a virtual environment, we need to create this disk in the Virtual Server 2005 R2 Web console. This is done by following these steps:

1. Open the **Virtual Server Manager**, then click **Create | Fixed Size Virtual Hard Disk** under **Virtual Disks**, as shown in Figure 8.78.

Figure 8.78 Creating a Fixed-Size Virtual Hard Disk

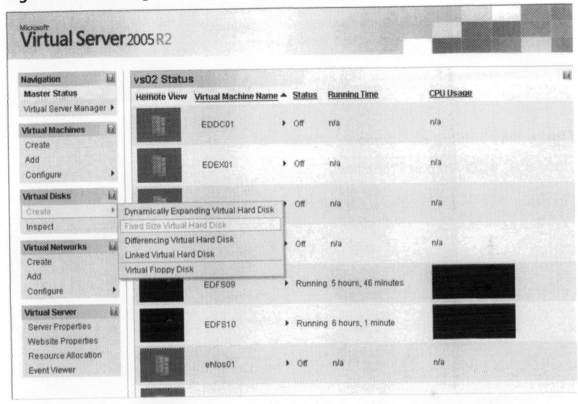

2. Place the virtual hard disk file (.VHD) in the folder containing your two virtual Windows 2003 Servers, then set the size to **500MB** (or less if you're low on disk space). Then click **Create** (see Figure 8.79).

Figure 8.79 Specifying the Virtual Hard Disk Filename and Size

Fixed Size Virtual Hard Disk

Specify the location where you want to create a fixed size virtual hard disk. You can select a location from a list of known locations or type the fully qualified path. The list of known locations includes any locations stored within the search paths or in the default configuration folder. Both settings are specified on the Search Paths page.

Location: None

Virtual hard disk file name: E:\E2K7SCC\Shared Disks\Quorum.vhd

Size: 500   Units: MB

Create

3. We now need to add the virtual quorum disk to each of the two virtual Windows 2003 Servers. Let's add it to EDFS09 first. We do this by clicking **Master Status | EDFS09 | Edit Configuration**. Since this disk needs to be shared between the nodes, we need to click **SCSI Adapters**, then **Add SCSI Adapter** (see Figure 8.80). Under the new SCSI adapter, check **Share SCSI Bus for Clustering**, then set the SCSI adapter ID to **6** (or whatever SCSI adapter ID is unused in your environment). Click **OK**.

Figure 8.80 Adding an Additional Shared SCSI Adapter

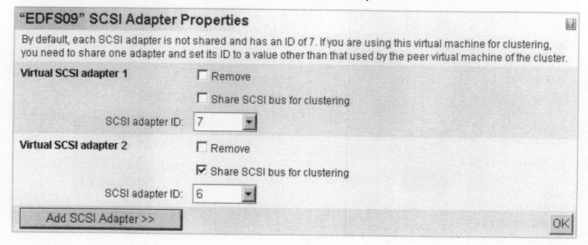

4. We now need to make the new disk visible on each node, so click **Hard disks | Add disk**, then select **SCSI 1 ID 0** in the **Attachment** drop-down menu. Finally, specify the path to the virtual Quorum disk, which in this example is **E:\E2K7SCC\Shared Disks\ Quorum.vhd**, as shown in Figure 8.81. Click **OK**.

Figure 8.81 Adding a Virtual Hard Disk

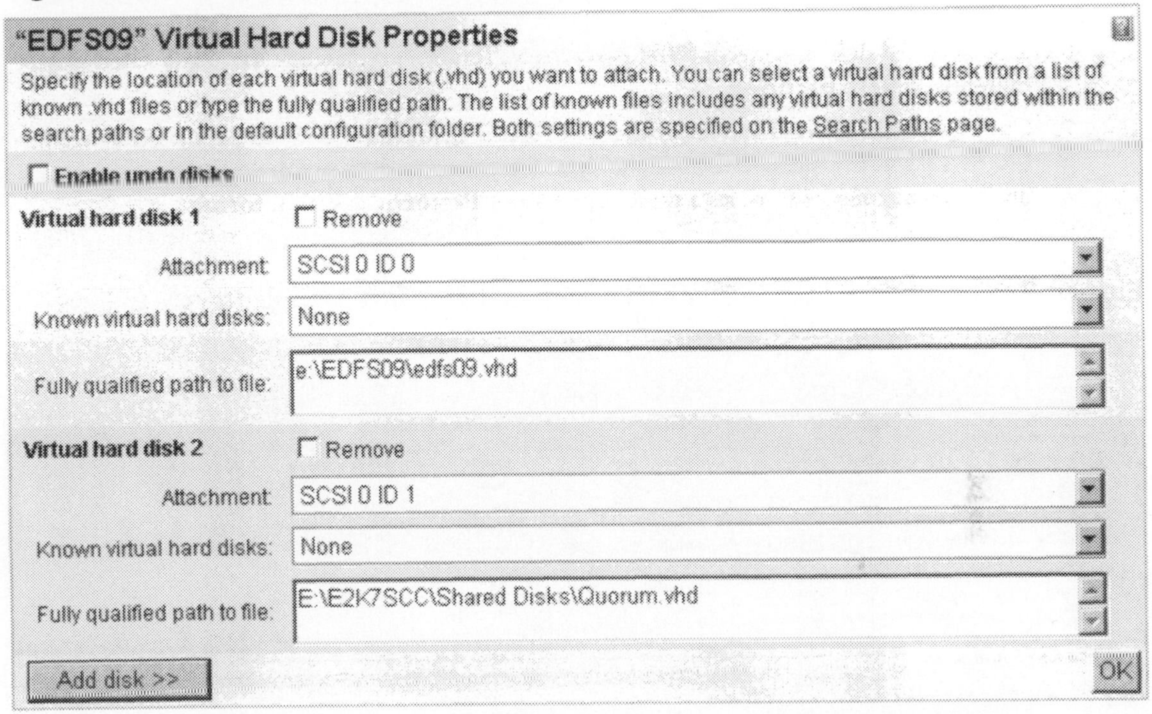

"EDFS09" Virtual Hard Disk Properties

Specify the location of each virtual hard disk (.vhd) you want to attach. You can select a virtual hard disk from a list of known .vhd files or type the fully qualified path. The list of known files includes any virtual hard disks stored within the search paths or in the default configuration folder. Both settings are specified on the Search Paths page.

☐ Enable undo disks

Virtual hard disk 1   ☐ Remove

Attachment: | SCSI 0 ID 0 |

Known virtual hard disks: | None |

Fully qualified path to file: | e:\EDFS09\edfs09.vhd |

Virtual hard disk 2   ☐ Remove

Attachment: | SCSI 0 ID 1 |

Known virtual hard disks: | None |

Fully qualified path to file: | E:\E2K7SCC\Shared Disks\Quorum.vhd |

[Add disk >>]   [OK]

SOME INDEPENDENT ADVICE

If you're installing the SCC in a Virtual Server 2005 R2 environment like I do in this example, you need to create a virtual SCSI adapter for each disks you want to share between the nodes. Since you should place the databases and log files on share disks as well, I recommend you create two additional virtual fixed sized disks more, one called Logs.vhd and one called Databases.vhd. When these have been created you need to add two additional virtual SCSI adapters on each virtual guest, and since the two disks should be shared between the nodes this should have Share SCSI bus for clustering enabled and configured with SCSI adapter ID 6 like the adapter for the quorum disk we already created. When you have done so you will be able to add the two disks under Virtual Hard Disk Properties on each node respectively.

5. We now need to partition the Quorum disk in the Disk Management console on EDFS09, so start the virtual machine, log on using a domain admin account, click **Start | Run**, and type **Compmgmt.msc**. Under **Storage**, click **Disk Management** (see Figure 8.82).

Click **Next** three times in the Initialize and Convert Disk Wizard that appears, then click **Finish**.

6. The detected disk now needs to be partitioned. To do so, right-click the unallocated space then select **New partition**.

7. Click **Next** three times and select the drive letter **Q** (for quorum), then click **Next** again. Use **NTFS** as the file system type and type **Quorum** in the Volume label field. To speed up the formatting process, it's a good idea to tick **Perform a quick format**.

Figure 8.82 Partitioning the Shared Disks and Assigning Drive Letters

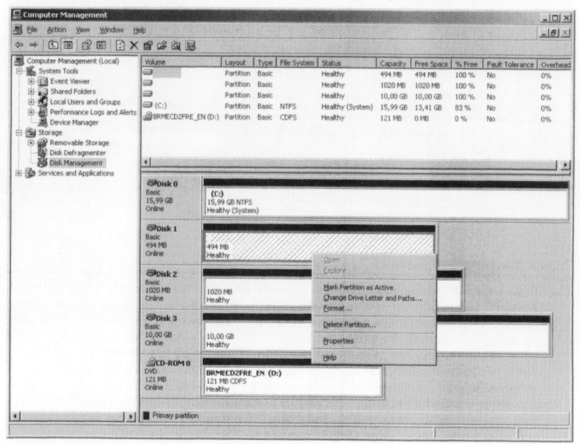

8. Now turn off EDFS09, then turn on EDFS10 and log on to the server with a domain admin account. Again, click **Start | Run** and type **Compmgmt.msc**. Under **Storage**, click **Disk Management Mark the Quorum disk (disk 1) active** and assign it the drive letter **Q** (see Figure 8.83).

Now verify that you can access the Q: drive from Windows Explorer. Also try to create a test file on each server and make sure you can see it both ways.

Figure 8.83 Allocating Drive Letters to the New Partitions on the Second Node

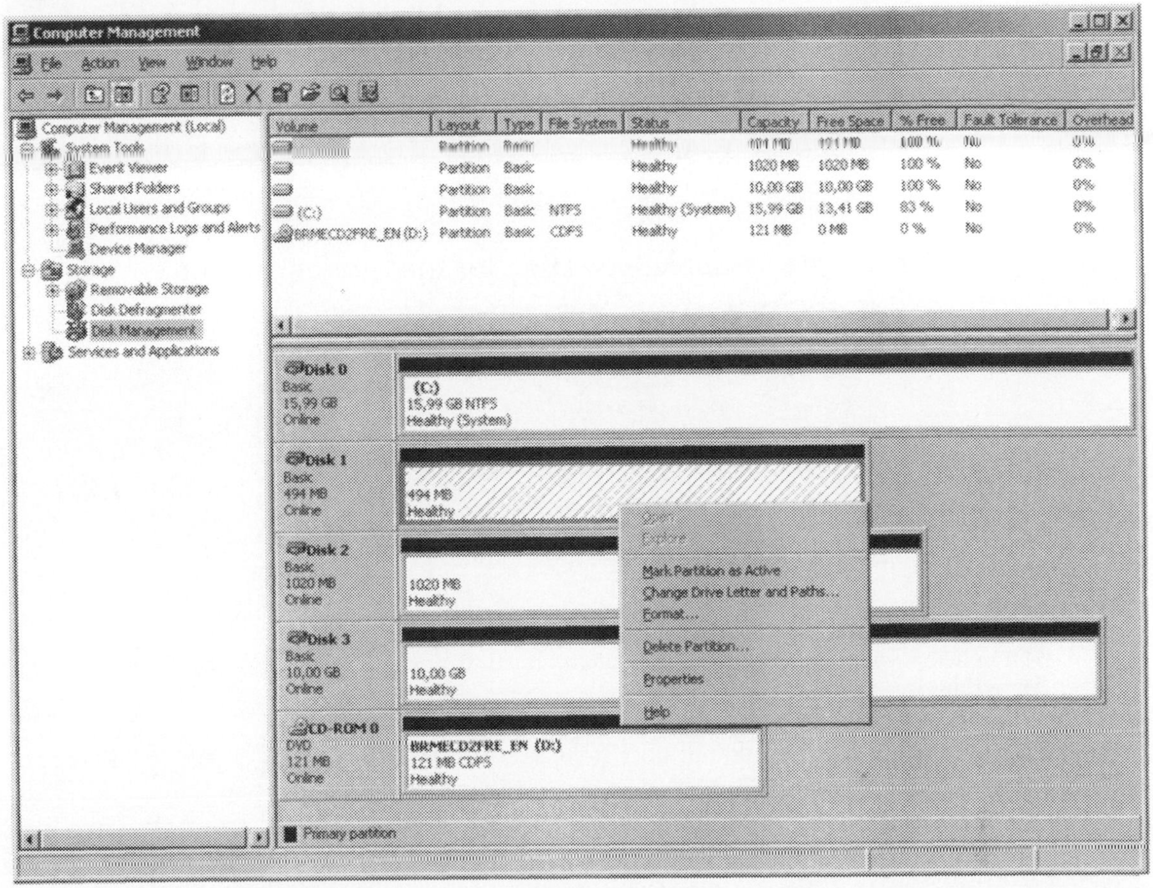

Creating the Windows Server 2003 Cluster

We have reached the point where we can create the actual Windows 2003 cluster. To do so:

1. Turn off EDFS10, then log on to EDFS09 with a domain admin account. Now click **Start | Administrative Tools | Cluster Administrator**, then select **Create new cluster** in the drop-down box and click **OK**, then click **Next**.

2. If it's not already the case, specify the domain in which the two Windows 2003 Servers are members, then type the name of the cluster (in this case, **E2K7SCC**), then click **Next**.

3. If it's not already entered, type the name of the Windows 2003 Server, which will be the first node in the cluster (in this case, **EDFS09**), then click **Next**.

4. The Cluster Wizard will now determine the cluster configuration, and after a while you should get a check mark in each checked configuration step. We can now click **Next**.

5. Now enter an IP address that cluster management tools will use to connect to the cluster and click **Next**.

6. Enter the cluster service account and password, then click **Next**.

7. You now see a screen with the proposed cluster configuration. Click the **Quorum** button and make sure that the cluster configuration quorum is set to **Disk Q**, as shown in Figure 8.84. Then click **Next**.

Figure 8.84 Selecting the Resource Type Used for the Quorum Resource

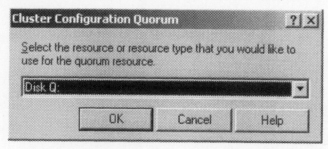

8. The cluster will now be created. Again, you need to wait for each step to complete, then click **Next | Finish**.

We have created the cluster itself, but since it consists of only one node, we'll need to add the other Windows server as well. To do so:

1. Turn on EDFS10 and log in with a domain admin account. Now click **Start | Administrative Tools | Cluster Administrator**. Select **Add nodes to cluster** in the drop-down menu, then specify the cluster name in the **Cluster or server name** box and click **OK**.

2. Click **Next** in the Add Nodes Wizard.

3. Type **EDFS10** (or whatever you named the second server), then click **Add** and click **Next**.

4. When the configuration has been analyzed, click **Next**.

5. Enter the password for the cluster service account (in this case, the administrator account), then click **Next**.

6. Verify that you want to add the node to the cluster with the configuration shown on the proposed cluster configuration page, then click **Next**.

7. After a short period, the node will be added to the cluster. If it's not, you might want to expand the respective task as well as view the log. If each task has completed successfully, click **Next | Finish** and verify that none of the nodes contains an error icon in the Cluster Administrator (see Figure 8.85).

Figure 8.85 The Cluster Administrator Will Cluster Resources Listed and Online

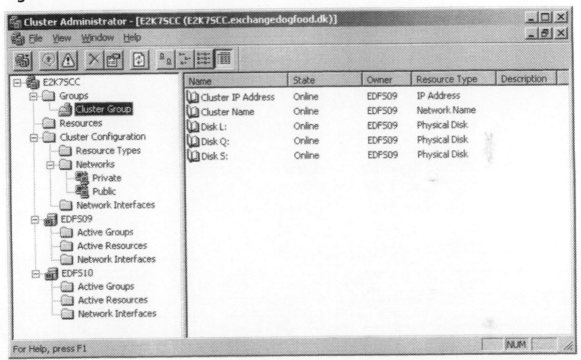

8. There's one last thing you want to do before moving on, and that is to right-click and select **Properties** for the Private network in the left pane. Since the sole purpose of the Private network is to be used for communication between the internal cluster nodes, you should select **Internal cluster communications only (private network)**, as shown in Figure 8.86, then click **OK**. Do the same for the Public network, but set it to **Client access only (public network)**.

We now have a fully operational two-node active/passive Windows cluster up and running.

Figure 8.86 Changing the Cluster Role for the Private Network

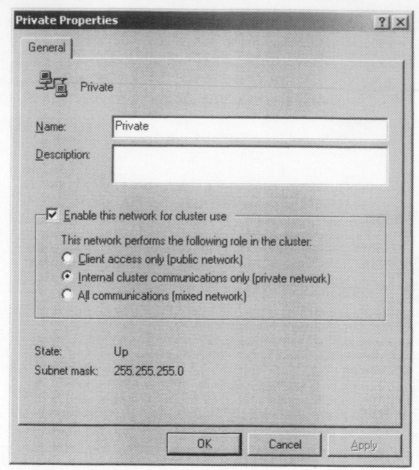

Installing the Necessary Windows Components

Before we move on and try to install the Exchange Server 2007 Beta 2 bits, we need to make sure that the required Windows components have been installed. All types of Exchange Server 2007 installations (no matter what server role we're talking about) need the Microsoft .NET Framework 2.0 component installed.

> **NOTE**
>
> If you have installed Windows Server 2003 Enterprise Edition with Service Pack 1 on the nodes, you need to download the Microsoft .NET Framework Version 2.0 Redistributable Package (x86), since it's only a standard Windows component for Windows Server 2003 R2.

Since we're installing the Mailbox Server role in the cluster, we also need to install the following IIS 6.0 components:

- Enable network COM+ access
- Internet Information Services
- World Wide Web Service

Installing Exchange Server 2007 on the Active Node

It's time to install the Exchange Server 2007 binaries on each node. Let's start with EDFS09. We'll do this using the GUI, so do the following:

1. Navigate to the network share or DVD media that contains the Exchange 207 binaries, and double-click **Setup.exe**.

2. On the Exchange 2007 Setup splash screen, click **Step 4: Install Microsoft Exchange**. Then click **Next**. Accept the **License Agreement** and then click **Next** once again. Decide whether you want to enable error reporting or not (it's a good idea to enable this functionality since the Exchange Product Group will receive any obscure errors you should experience in your cluster setup), then click **Next**.

3. Now select **Custom Exchange Server Installation**, then click **Next**.

4. Check **Active Clustered Mailbox Role** and click **Next**.

5. Now select **Single Copy Cluster**, then specify a name for the mailbox server (the name you want your Outlook clients to connect to) and a unique IP address on your public network. Finally, specify the path for the clustered mailbox server database files (the virtual shared database disk you created earlier), then click **Next** (see Figure 8.87).

Figure 8.87 Specifying the Name and IP Address of the Clustered Mailbox Server

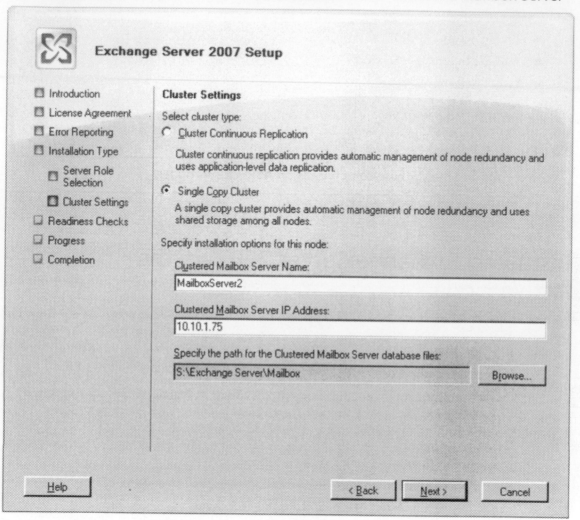

6. Let the readiness check complete, and if no issues are found, click **Next** to begin the installation.

7. The Exchange Server 2007 Installation Wizard will now copy the needed Exchange files, install and configure the Mailbox role, then create and configure the clustered mailbox server resources locally and create the object in Active Directory. When each step has been completed, clear the **Exit Setup and open Exchange System Manager** check box, then click **Finish**. We don't want to open the EMC just yet; we'll install Exchange on the second node first.

8. Log on to EDFS10 with a domain admin account and perform the same steps we did in installing Exchange Server 2007 on EDFS09. The only difference is that you should check **Passive Clustered Mailbox Role** instead of **Active Clustered Mailbox Role**.

When you have installed the Exchange Clustered Mailbox Role on the second node, we can move on to the next section, where we verify that the functionality of the clustered mailbox server works as expected.

Testing the Functionality of the Single Copy Cluster

It's time to verify that our Exchange 2007 clustered mailbox server is working as expected. Let's first open the Cluster Administrator and check whether the respective Exchange Resources have been created. If you take a look at Figure 8.88, it looks good; we have both nodes listed in the left pane and all Exchange resources have been created and are currently owned by EDFS09.

Figure 8.88 Listing All Exchange Cluster Resources in the Cluster Administrator

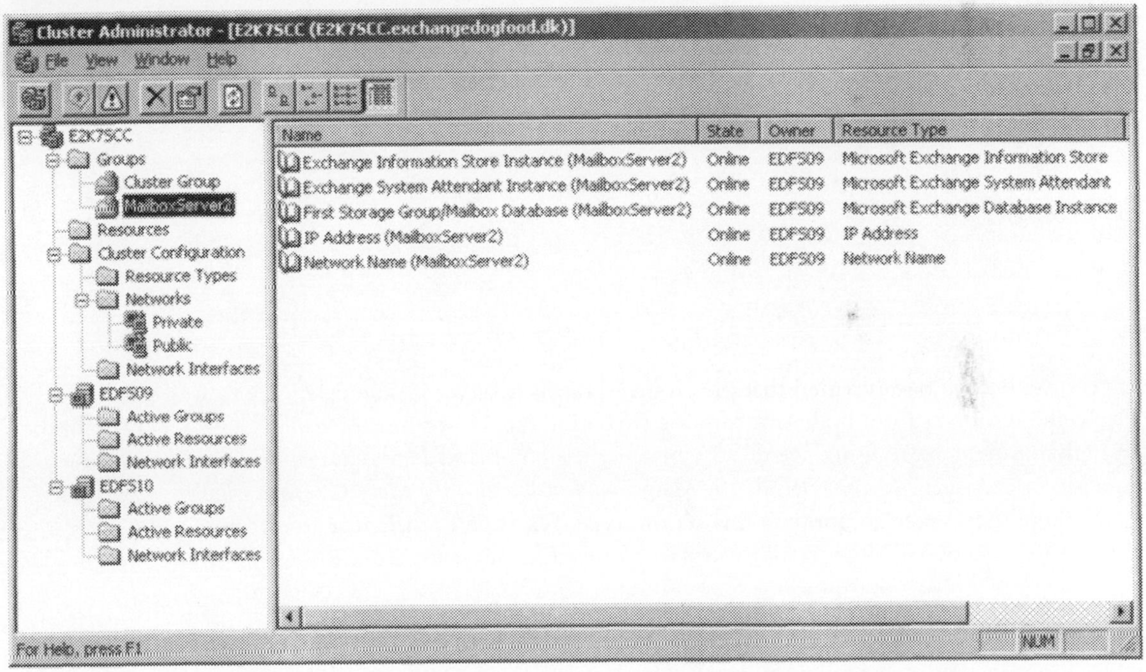

If you look closer at Figure 8.88, though, you can see that two cluster groups exist: one containing the cluster IP, name, and the shared disks, and one created by Exchange 2007 setup containing the Exchange Information Store, System Attendant, Storage Groups, and Database instances as well as the Exchange virtual server IP address and network name. WE recommend that you move all shared resources from the cluster group to the MailboxServer2 group (or whatever you called it); otherwise, you will have problems mounting the database when moving the clustered mailbox server from one node to the other (which we'll do in just a moment).

In addition, if you have assigned a shared disk specifically for the transaction log files, remember to change the path for these files. You can do so by selecting the respective storage group under **Server Configuration | Mailbox node** in the EMC, then click the **Move Storage Group** link in the Action pane. In the Move Storage Group Wizard, change the path for the log files to the **L:** drive or whatever drive you assigned them.

Now try to open the EMS by clicking **Start | All Programs | Microsoft Exchange Server 2007 | Exchange Management Shell** on one of the nodes, then type **Get-ClusteredMailboxServerStatus**. As you can see in Figure 8.89, the status of the clustered mailbox server is Online, and EDFS09 is currently the active node. This just keeps getting better and better, doesn't it?

Figure 8.89 Verifying That the Cluster Is Online

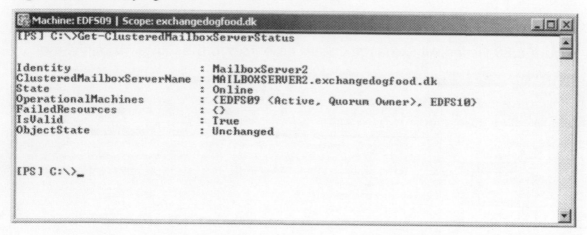

Now that we have verified that the clustered mailbox server is online, let's try to move the Exchange resources from node one to node two using the *Move-ClusteredMailboxServer* CMDlet. In the test environment we're using, we do so by issuing the command *Move-ClusteredMailboxServer -Identity: MailboxServer2 -TargetMachine:EDFS10 -MoveComment:"Testing the Move Clustered Mailbox functionality!"*.

You're then asked to confirm this action. Type **Yes**, then press **Enter** (see Figure 8.90). After a while the clustered mailbox resources will be moved to the second node.

Figure 8.90 Moving the Clustered Mailbox Resources to the Second Node

```
Machine: EDFS09 | Scope: exchangedogfood.dk                    _ □ ×
[PS] C:\>Move-ClusteredMailboxServer -Identity MailboxServer2 -TargetMachine: ED
FS09 -MoveComment:"Testing the Move Clustered Mailbox funtionality!"

Confirm
Are you sure you want to perform this action?
Moving clustered mailbox server "MailboxServer2" to target node "EDFS09" with
move comment "Testing the Move Clustered Mailbox funtionality!".
[Y] Yes  [A] Yes to All  [N] No  [L] No to All  [S] Suspend  [?] Help
(default is "Y"):Y
[PS] C:\>_
```

WARNING

Although it's possible to move the cluster resource group between the nodes using the Cluster Administrator console, you should always do so (just as is the case with CCR-based clusters) using the *Move-ClusteredMailboxServer* CMDlet because the Move Group task in the Cluster Administrator console isn't Exchange 2007 aware.

Let's also take a look at the clustered mailbox server in the EMC. To do so, click **Start | All Programs | Microsoft Exchange Server 2007 | Exchange Management Console**, then drill down to **Server Configuration | Mailbox**. Notice that the clustered mailbox server we named MailboxServer is listed in the Results pane and that it's recognized as a cluster server (see Figure 8.91). Also notice that the Mailbox Database for this server points to the S: drive, exactly as we specified during the installation of the Active Clustered Mailbox role.

Figure 8.91 Viewing the Clustered Mailbox Server in the Exchange Management Console

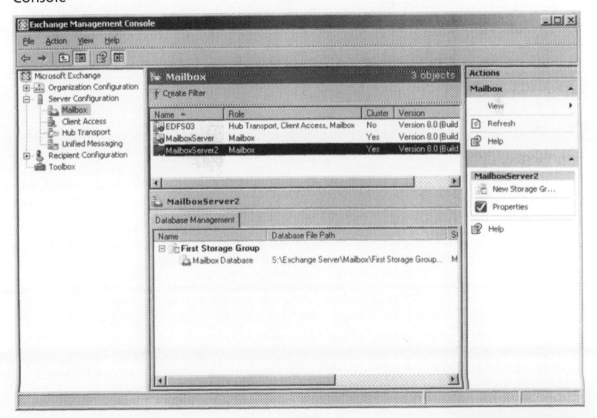

Summary

In this chapter we focused on the Mailbox server-related high-availability features included in Exchange Server 2007. First we took a look at how the Local Continuous Replication (LCR) feature works, and then we covered how it's implemented as well as managed. We then moved on to the new Cluster Continuous Replication (CCR) functionality, which makes it possible to deploy a mailbox server cluster, providing not only service availability but also database availability, which means that no single point of failure exists when using this type of cluster. We covered how to deploy a CCR-based cluster step by step as well as showed you how to manage it once deployed. Finally, we took a close look at the Single Copy Cluster (SCC) feature, which is similar to the traditional active/passive clusters we know from Exchange 2000 and 2003. We showed you the steps involved in deploying this type of cluster in a virtual server environment so that you can decide whether this is the type of cluster you want to use in your production environment.

Solutions Fast Track

Managing the Local Continuous Replication Feature

☑ The Exchange Product Group developed the Local Continuous Replication (LCR) technology to provide a native data availability solution that can be used to recover an Exchange database on an Exchange 2007 standalone server in a matter of a few minutes.

☑ Since LCR keeps an exact replica of the active copy of the storage group, the number of Exchange backups needed is also reduced drastically. But it's important to understand that LCR in no way eliminates traditional backups of the databases on your Exchange 2007 Mailbox servers; instead, it provides you with the option of taking weekly instead of daily backups, for example.

☑ As you can understand, LCR is an ideal solution for small or medium-sized organizations because the functionality allows rapid recovery from database issues and only requires an extra set of disks for the databases copies. LCR increases the availability of databases on an Exchange 2007 standalone server in an affordable way. For small shops that don't have a big fancy server with multiple sets of disks, it is possible to keep the LCR copy on an external USB disk.

☑ When disaster strikes and the database or log files in the active copy of the storage group become corrupted and shut down, you have the option of recovering database availability by switching to the LCR copy (the passive copy of the storage group).

☑ It's a recommended best practice to periodically verify the integrity of the passive storage group copy to make sure that neither the database copy nor any of the log files are corrupted. This is done by running a physical consistency check against both the database copy as well as the log files using Exchange Server Database Utilities (Eseutil.exe).

☑ When the Exchange 2007 Mailbox Server role is installed, setup adds two LCR-related performance objects to the Windows 2003 Performance Monitor.

Managing a Cluster Continuous Replication-Based Setup

☑ Exchange Server 2007 introduces a new high-availability feature called Cluster Continuous Replication (CCR). This feature combines the new Exchange Server 2007 log file shipping and replay mechanisms (known as continuous replication) with the features that are available in a more traditional two-node Windows 2003 server active/passive cluster setup.

☑ With CCR, the transaction logs generated on the active node are replicated to the information store on the passive node using log file shipping. These replicated log files are then posted into the database(s) on the passive node using the log file replay technology. This means that should the active node or a database on this node fail or for some other reason go offline, an automatic failover to the passive node will occur.

☑ A Majority Node Set (MNS) quorum with File Share Witness is a completely new type of quorum model that is made available by installing the update (MS KB article 921181) mentioned in this chapter. The update makes it possible to use a file share witness that is external to the cluster as an additional "vote" to determine the status of the cluster in a two-node MNS quorum cluster deployment, which is a requirement to use the CCR functionality in Exchange Server 2007.

☑ The Transport Dumpster is a new feature of the Exchange 2007 Hub Transport server that can submit recently delivered mail after an unscheduled outage. For an e-mail message to be able to be retained in the Transport Dumpster, at least one of the message recipients must have his or her mailbox located on a CCR-based mailbox cluster server, because the Transport Dumpster works only with mailboxes located on a CCR-based mailbox server cluster.

☑ Moving the Exchange resources from node one to node two should be done using the *Move-ClusteredMailboxServer* CMDlet. In the environment used in this chapter, we did so by issuing the cmdlet *Move-ClusteredMailboxServer -Identity:MailboxServer -TargetMachine:EDFS08 -MoveComment:"Verifying the Move Clustered Mailbox Server Functionality!"*.

☑ When we deployed a cluster with Exchange 2003, the only option available when the stores were going to be backed up was to take a backup of the stores running on the production servers. With CCR (and LCR), you have the option of taking a backup of the database copies on the passive node, thereby eliminating any heavy load on the active node related to both I/O to the disk spindles as well as CPU usage.

Managing a Single Copy Cluster-Based Setup

☑ Exchange 2007 supports the Single Copy Clusters (SCC) type, which is more or less identical to the traditional active/passive clusters we know from previous versions of Exchange. This means that a SCC-based cluster only provides service failover and still has a single point of failure when it comes to the databases, unless a shared storage solution that provides redundancy via other means is used in the environment. An SCC-based cluster using a fault-tolerant SAN is just as good as a CCR-based cluster in terms of data availability, but such a solution is much more expensive than a CCR solution.

☑ Exchange Server 2007 doesn't support active/active clusters anymore; only active/passive clusters are supported in Exchange 2007.

☑ Although it's possible to move the cluster resource group between the nodes using the Cluster Administrator console, you should always do so (as is the case with CCR-based clusters) using the *Move-ClusteredMailboxServer* CMDlet because the Move Group task in the Cluster Administrator console isn't Exchange 2007 aware.

Frequently Asked Questions

Q: Why would I want to deploy CCR instead of SCC?

A: Deploying CCR instead of SCC has several advantages. First, you no longer have a single point of failure regarding databases. Second, unlike SCC, CCR doesn't require a shared storage subsystem such as a SAN, because the nodes in a CCR don't share the same disks. Third, you have the option of spanning the CCR between two locations (although they must be on the same subnet, which means the subnet has to be stretched).

Q: You mentioned that it was possible to back up the passive copy of the databases in a CCR using a backup application with VSS support for Exchange databases. Is this also possible when we use LCR on a single Exchange 2007 box?

A: Yes, this is also supported on a single box with LCR enabled for one or more storage groups.

Q: How should I proceed when implementing storage design for a CCR-based setup?

A: To achieve storage resiliency, it is recommended that the passive copy be placed on a storage array that is completely isolated from the active copy's storage array. Isolating the arrays from one another also provides the flexibility to use a variety of storage solutions. If the storage solutions used by the active copy and the passive copy are isolated from each other, your storage solutions don't even need to be the same type or brand.

Q: Should I use an identical set of disks for the database copies in a CCR or LCR setup?

A: It's a best practice to size the active and passive storage solutions equivalently. The storage solution used by the passive copy should be sized in terms of both performance and capacity to handle the production load in the event of a failure.

Q: How many databases can I have in each storage group when I'm using either LCR or CCR?

A: You can only have one database in each storage group when you use either LCR or CCR. In addition, you cannot have more than one Public Folder database in the organization if you want to replicate a Public Folder database using continuous replication technology.

Q: Why would I want to use continuous replication technology in my Exchange environment?

A: Continuous replication provides service availability and service continuity for an Exchange 2007 mailbox server, without the cost and complexity of a shared storage cluster.

Chapter 9

Disaster Recovery with Exchange Server 2007

Solutions in this chapter:

- **Backing Up Exchange 2007 Using Windows 2003 Backup**
- **Restoring Exchange 2007 Storage Groups and Databases Using Windows 2003 Backup**
- **Repairing a Corrupt or Damaged Exchange 2007 Database Using Eseutil**
- **Recovering an Exchange 2007 Server Using the RecoverServer Switch**
- **Recovering an Exchange 2007 Cluster Using the RecoverCMS Switch**

☑ Summary

☑ Solutions Fast Track

☑ Frequently Asked Questions

Introduction

As mentioned in the previous chapter, the messaging and collaboration servers are mission critical, being perhaps the most vital servers in our datacenters today. It's therefore of the utmost importance that these servers be up and running all the time. Most service level agreements today require more than 99.99 percent uptime when it comes to the messaging and collaboration servers in the organization. In the previous chapter we showed you some of the options available to provide high availability of the Exchange 2007 Mailbox Servers. But even if you have HA solutions such as CCR-based mailbox servers available, a disaster can still strike in your environment, and if this happens, you better be prepared since downtime typically means lost productivity and revenue. In this chapter, we'll go through the steps necessary to back up the different Exchange 2007 Server roles in your organization, and, just as important, look at how you restore Exchange 2007 servers and data should it be required.

Backing Up Exchange 2007 Using Windows 2003 Backup

Frequent backups of the Exchange 2007 servers in an organization are important operational tasks that, though a bit trivial, should be taken very seriously. I can only imagine one thing worse than a complete failure of an Exchange 2007 server, and that's a complete failure of an Exchange 2007 server without any backups to restore from. In the first section of this chapter, we'll take a look at what you must back up, depending on which Exchange 2007 Server roles were deployed in your organization.

Backing Up an Exchange 2007 Mailbox Server

One of the most important things to back up regarding Exchange 2007 Mailbox Servers are the databases, which hold user mailboxes and public data. As you saw in the previous chapter, Exchange 2007 provides a new continuous replication functionality that keeps a second copy of one or more databases in a storage group in sync with the active versions of the databases using log file shipping and replay. This provides an extra level of protection for Mailbox and Public Folder databases. However, although the new functionality allows you to make less frequent backups of your databases, it doesn't eliminate the *need* for database backups. In this section, we'll show you how to perform a backup of the databases on an Exchange 2007 server.

> **NOTE**
>
> Another reason why it's crucial to conduct frequent full backups of your Exchange databases with an Exchange-aware backup application is to commit and delete any transaction log files generated since the last full backup. If these log files aren't committed, they will take up more and more space on your disks, and when there's no more disk space for the log files, the database will be dismounted.

Since Exchange 2007 databases still use ESE, you can (just as with previous versions of Exchange), back them up using the Exchange-aware native Windows 2003 backup tool. Exchange 2007 supports two different backup methods. The first is a legacy streaming backup method based on the ESE application programming interface (API), which allows you to back up one or more storage groups at the same time. However, only one backup job can run against a specific storage group. Most of us are familiar with this type of backup since it's the one we have used for ages when referring to Exchange databases. The ESE API backup method is supported by the Windows 2003 backup tool, as well as most third-party backup products.

Then we have the Volume Shadow Copy Service (VSS) backup method, which some of you may know from Exchange 2003 where it was first introduced. The interesting thing about VSS is that this method, in addition to what the legacy streaming backup method offers, can also make an online backup of the copy database when using either Local Continuous Replication or Cluster Continuous Replication in your setup. This means you can schedule the backup windows anytime you want since taking a backup of the database copy has no performance-related impact on the active database. Unfortunately, this method isn't supported by the Windows 2003 backup tool when speaking Exchange databases (only file level backups), and Microsoft doesn't offer any products capable of using VSS, at least not at the time of this writing.

NOTE

The Data Protection Manager (DPM) v2 product will support VSS backups, however. DPM is a server software application that enables disk- and tape-based data protection and recovery for file servers, servers running Microsoft Exchange, and servers running Microsoft SQL Server in an Active Directory Domain Services (AD DS) domain. DPM performs replication, synchronization, and recovery point creation to provide reliable protection and rapid recovery of data for both system administrators and end users.

Let's go through the steps necessary to back up an Exchange 2007 Mailbox and Public Folder database on an Exchange 2007 Mailbox Server. The first thing you need to do is launch the Windows 2003 backup tool, which can be done by clicking **Start | Run** and typing **NTBackup**. Now click **Switch to Advanced Mode** and then click the **Backup** tab shown in Figure 9.1.

Figure 9.1 Windows 2003 Backup Tool

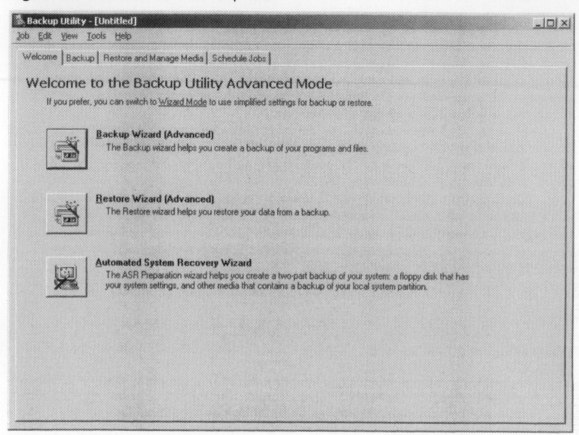

Under the **Backup** tab expand **Microsoft Exchange Server | Mailbox Server | Microsoft Information Store** and check the storage group(s) containing the **Mailbox** and **Public Folder** database (Figure 9.2). Now specify the backup media or filename you want to perform the backup to, and then click **Start Backup**.

Figure 9.2 Selecting the Storage Groups to Be Backed Up

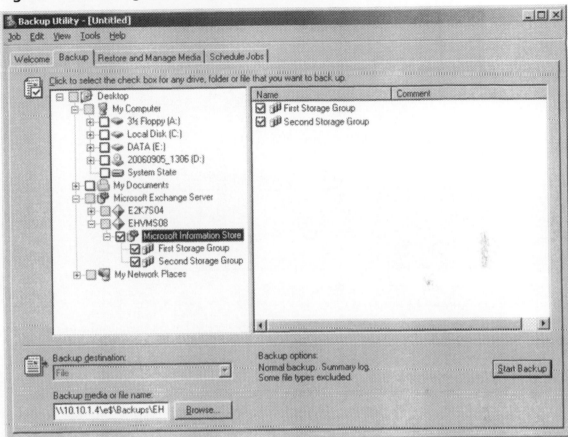

As you can see in Figure 9.3, you now have the option of entering a description for the respective backup job, as well as specify whether the backed-up data should be appended to an existing backup. In addition, you can create a scheduled backup job so it runs, let's say, every day at midnight. By clicking the **Advanced** button, you also have the option of having the backed-up data verified when the job completes.

Figure 9.3 Backup Job Information

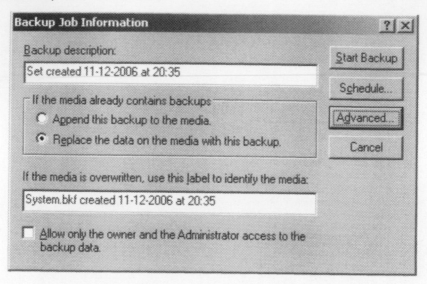

Typically, you should set up an automated backup job schedule, but for the purpose of this example we'll just choose to back up the databases once. When ready, click **Start Backup**.

When the backup job has completed, you can view a report, which will contain any warnings or errors that might occur during the backup.

That's how you back up the Mailbox and Public Folder databases, as well as commit and delete any existing transaction log files using the Windows 2003 Backup tool. Sounds simple, right?

Some of you might wonder whether there isn't anything else you need to back up on an Exchange 2007 Mailbox Server? The answer is no critical files at least since you can always recover an Exchange 2007 Mailbox Server using the *Setup /Mode:RecoverServer* command (shown later in the chapter), but it's always a good idea to back up the System State of the respective server as well.

Backing Up an Exchange 2007 Hub Transport Server

Since an Exchange 2007 Server with the Hub Transport Server role installed was designed to store all configuration data in the Active Directory configuration container, not much needs to be backed up on a server with this role installed either. But just as with the Mailbox server role, you should back up the System State.

Some of you may be wondering why I haven't mentioned anything about backing up the message queues stored in an ESE database on an Exchange 2007 Hub Transport Server… Well, there shouldn't be any need to do so since you can mount the message queues on another existing, or newly installed, Hub Transport server if required. You just need to retrieve the mail.que (which, by default, is located under C:\Program Files\Microsoft\Exchange Server\TransportRoles\data\Queue) from the failed Hub Transport server.

For step-by-step instructions on how to move a message queue from a failed Hub Transport server to another Hub Transport server in the organization, search under "Working with the Queue Database on Transport Servers" in the Exchange 2007 Documentation Help file.

One thing you might want to back up regarding an Exchange 2007 Hub Transport Server is the Message Tracking and Protocol logs which, by default, are located under C:\Program Files\ Microsoft\Exchange Server\TransportRoles\Logs. These files can be backed up using a file level backup.

As is the case with a Mailbox Server, you can recover a Hub Transport server using the *Setup/Mode:RecoverServer* command.

Backing Up an Exchange 2007 Client Access Server

When using Exchange 2007 Server with the Client Access Server role installed, there are several files you should back up. The first, and perhaps most important, to back up is the IIS Metabase, which among other things is used to store OWA Virtual Directory configuration data. You can back up the IIS configuration on a CAS using the following command:

```
get-owavirtualdirectory "owa (default web site)" | export-clixml owa.xml -depth 1
```

In order to restore the IIS configuration from the owa.xml file, you need to use a Windows PowerShell script similar to the following (save it as Restore-OWA.PS1 or use some other meaningful name):

```
$ErrorActionPreference = 'stop'
$savedprops = @(
'DirectFileAccessOnPublicComputersEnabled',
'DirectFileAccessOnPrivateComputersEnabled',
'WebReadyDocumentViewingOnPublicComputersEnabled',
'WebReadyDocumentViewingOnPrivateComputersEnabled',
'ForceWebReadyDocumentViewingFirstOnPublicComputers',
'ForceWebReadyDocumentViewingFirstOnPrivateComputers',
'RemoteDocumentsActionForUnknownServers',
'ActionForUnknownFileAndMIMETypes',
'WebReadyFileTypes',
'WebReadyMimeTypes',
'WebReadyDocumentViewingForAllSupportedTypes',
```

```
'AllowedFileTypes',
'AllowedMimeTypes',
'ForceSaveFileTypes',
'ForceSaveMimeTypes',
'BlockedFileTypes',
'BlockedMimeTypes',
'RemoteDocumentsAllowedServers',
'RemoteDocumentsBlockedServers',
'RemoteDocumentsInternalDomainSuffixList',
'LogonFormat',
'ClientAuthCleanupLevel',
'DefaultDomain',
'FormsAuthentication',
'BasicAuthentication',
'DigestAuthentication',
'WindowsAuthentication',
'GzipLevel',
'FilterWebBeaconsAndHtmlForms',
'NotificationInterval',
'DefaultTheme',
'UserContextTimeout',
'ExchwebProxyDestination',
'VirtualDirectoryType',
'RedirectToOptimalOWAServer',
'DefaultClientLanguage',
'LogonAndErrorLanguage',
'UseGB18030',
'UseISO885915',
'OutboundCharset',
'CalendarEnabled',
'ContactsEnabled',
'TasksEnabled',
'JournalEnabled',
'NotesEnabled',
'RemindersAndNotificationsEnabled',
'PremiumClientEnabled',
'SpellCheckerEnabled',
'SearchFoldersEnabled',
```

```
'SignaturesEnabled',
'ThemeSelectionEnabled',
'JunkEmailEnabled',
'UMIntegrationEnabled',
'WSSAccessOnPublicComputersEnabled',
'WSSAccessOnPrivateComputersEnabled',
'ChangePasswordEnabled',
'UNCAccessOnPublicComputersEnabled',
'UNCAccessOnPrivateComputersEnabled',
'ActiveSyncIntegrationEnabled',
'AllAddressListsEnabled',
'InternalUrl',
'ExternalUrl'
)
$vdir = import-clixml $args[0]
'Recreating "' + $vdir.name + '"' + ' owa version: ' + $vdir.owaversion
if ($vdir.owaversion -eq 'Exchange2007') {
new-owavirtualdirectory -website $vdir.website -internalurl
$vdir.internalurl -externalurl $vdir.externalurl
}
else {
new-owavirtualdirectory -website $vdir.website -owaversion $vdir.
owaversion -name $vdir.displayname -virtualdirectorytype $vdir.
virtualdirectorytype
}
$new = get-owavirtualdirectory $vdir.name
'Restoring properties'
foreach ($prop in $savedprops) {
if ($prop -eq 'ExchwebProxyDestination' -or $prop -eq
'VirtualDirectoryType') {
continue
}
$new.$prop = $vdir.$prop
}
$new | set-owavirtualdirectory
```

To restore the IIS configuration data that were saved in the owa.xml file, type **Restore-OWA. PS1 owa.xml**.

In addition to the IIS metabase, you should back up the System State and the files listed in Table 9.1.

Table 9.1 Files Needed to Restore the IIS Configuration

Data	Location
Microsoft Office Outlook Web Access Web site, and Web.config file	C:\Program Files\Microsoft\Exchange Server\ClientAccess\Owa
IMAP4 and POP3 protocol settings	C:\Program Files\Microsoft\Exchange Server\ClientAccess\
Availability service	Active Directory configuration container and file system, including the Web.config file C:\Program Files\Microsoft\Exchange Server\ClientAccess\exchweb\ews
Autodiscover	IIS metabase
Exchange ActiveSync	Active Directory configuration containerFile system, including the Web.config file in the \ ClientAccess\Sync folder IIS metabase
Outlook Web Access virtual directories	Active Directory configuration container and file system C:\Program Files\Microsoft\Exchange Server\ClientAccess\
Web services configuration	IIS metabase

Like a Mailbox or Hub Transport Server, a Client Access Server can be restored using the *Setup /Mode:RecoverServer* command.

Backing Up an Exchange 2007 Unified Messaging Server

Exchange 2007 servers with the Unified Messaging (UM) role installed store most of the configuration data in the Active Directory, which means it's very limited what you need to back up on the UM server itself.

Table 9.2 lists the files you need to back up.

Table 9.2 Files to Back Up on Unified Messaging Server

Data	Location
Custom audio prompts: Custom audio files (.wav) for UM Dial Plans and UM Auto Attendants Custom audio files (.wav) for telephone user interface (TUI) or Voice Access	C:\Program Files\Microsoft\Exchange Server\UnifiedMessaging\Prompts
Incoming calls: .eml and .wma files for each voicemail	C:\Program Files\Microsoft\Exchange Server \UnifiedMessaging\temp

In addition, you should back up the System State.

The rest of the configuration data is, as mentioned previously, stored in Active Directory, which makes it possible to restore using the *Setup /Mode:RecoverServer* command.

Backing Up an Exchange 2007 Edge Transport Server

An Exchange 2007 Server with the Edge Transport Server role installed can be restored by using a Cloned Configuration (employing the ImportEdgeConfig.ps1 script). For step-by-step instructions on how you deal with clone configuration, see Chapter 7. In addition to cloned configuration, you should back up System State as well as the Message Tracking and protocol logs, which are located in C:\Program Files\Microsoft\Exchange Server\TransportRoles\Logs. The message queues that are stored in an ESE database just like message queues on a Hub Transport server can be mounted on another Edge Transport server.

Restoring Exchange 2007 Storage Groups and Databases Using Windows 2003 Backup

So now that you have seen how to back up Mailbox and Public Folder databases, you should of course also be aware of how you restore these databases properly should you experience a database corruption or find them unusable in some other way. In this section, I'll show you how to perform a restore of a Mailbox database from the backup set we created earlier in this chapter. When you restore a Mailbox or Public Folder database from a backup set, any associated transaction log files are restored as well. It's important you understand that a restore of a Mailbox database will copy the database file (.EDB) into its original location on the disk, and thereby overwrite any existing .EDB file. In addition, any transaction log files will be copied to a temporary location, which can be specified when doing the actual restore. Upon the restore's completion (hopefully without any serious warnings or errors!), the log files will be replayed into the restored version of the database. In addition to the log files, a file called Restore.env will also be copied to the specified temporary folder. This file keeps control of which storage group the log files belong to, as well as the database paths and range of log files that have been restored.

In order to restore the aforementioned Mailbox database, we need to perform the following steps. First, open the **Exchange Management Console**, expand **Server Configuration**, and then select the **Mailbox** subnode. Now choose the respective Mailbox server in the **Result** pane, and then dismount the Mailbox database, as shown in Figure 9.4.

Figure 9.4 Dismounting the Mailbox Database

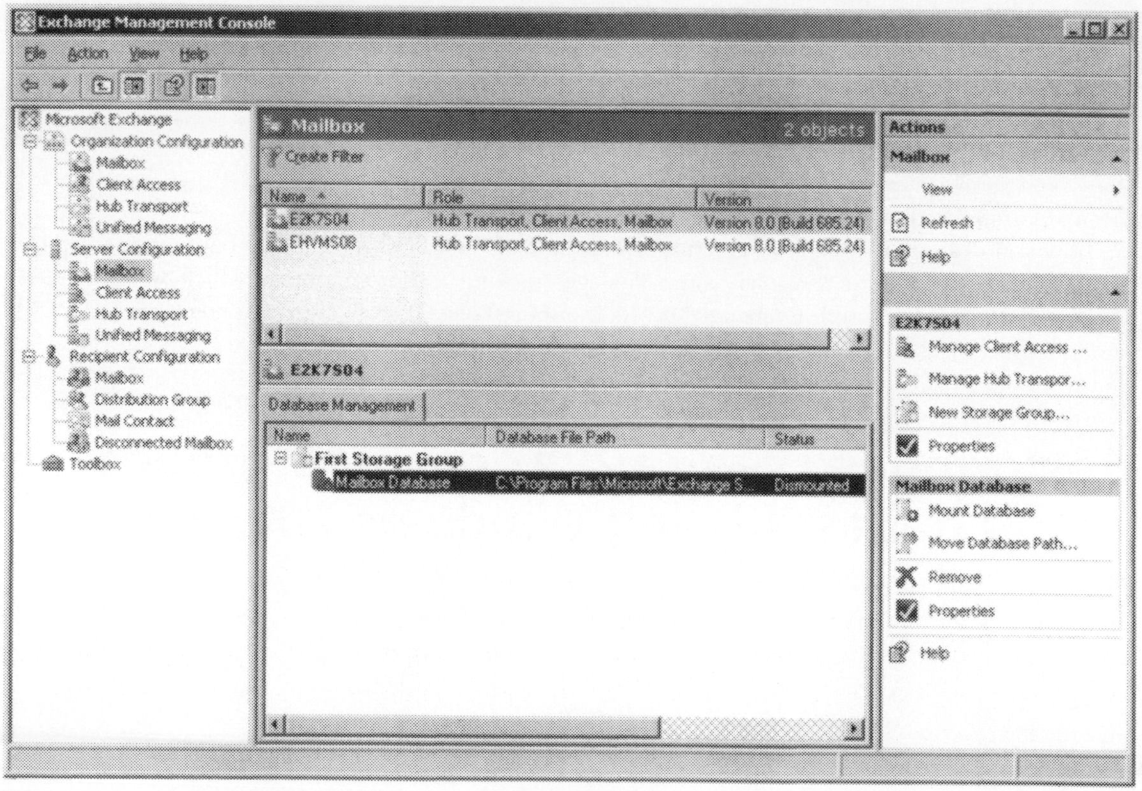

Now open the properties page for the Mailbox database. Check **This database can be overwritten by a restore** (Figure 9.5) and click **OK**.

Figure 9.5 Allowing the Mailbox Database to Be Overwritten by a Restore

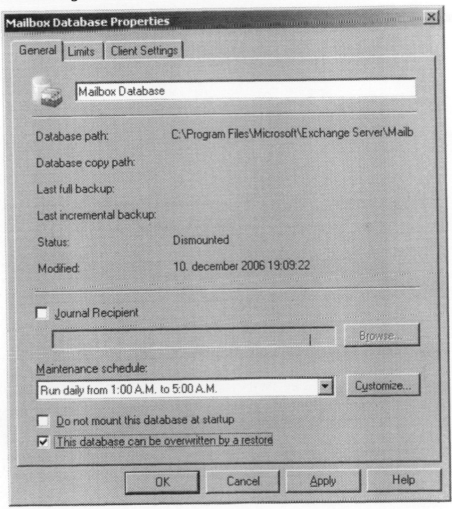

We're now ready to restore the databases using the Windows 2003 Backup tool, so let's launch this tool by clicking **Start | Run** and typing **NTBackup**, and then selecting the **Restore and Manage Media** tab. Expand the desired media item and backup set, then check the **log files** and **mailbox database**, as shown in Figure 9.6. We can then click **Start Restore**.

Figure 9.6 Restoring the First Storage Group

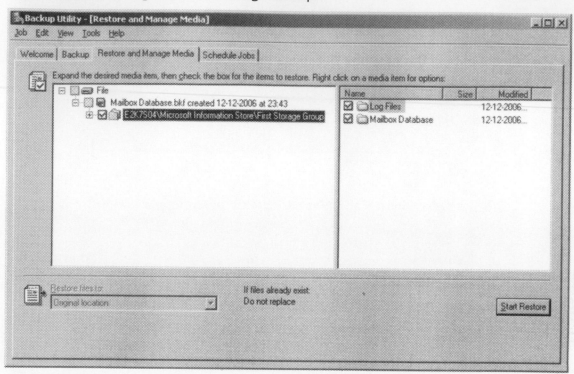

You'll be faced with a screen similar to the one shown in Figure 9.7. Here, you need to specify the server you want to restore the database to (the local server on which the Windows 2003 Backup tool is run is typically pre-entered here), and the temporary location for log and patch files. In addition, you need to specify whether the restore you're performing is the last restore set. If you select this option, all the restored log files will be replayed automatically into the database after the restore has completed. You typically want to do this if you don't have any incremental or differential backups of the database's log files you need to restore after this restore. Finally, you have the option of specifying that the database should be mounted automatically after the restore has occurred. When you have made your selections, click **OK**.

Figure 9.7 Restoring Database Store Options

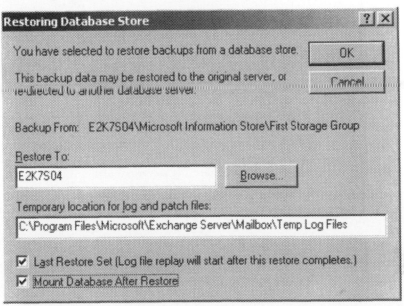

The restore will now begin. Depending on the size of the database, it will take some time to complete. Since the database in this example is under 11MB, the restore took less than a second, as you can see in Figure 9.8. When the restore has completed, you can click the **Report** button to see a detailed log of the restore process. When ready, click **Close**.

Figure 9.8 Restore Completed Successfully

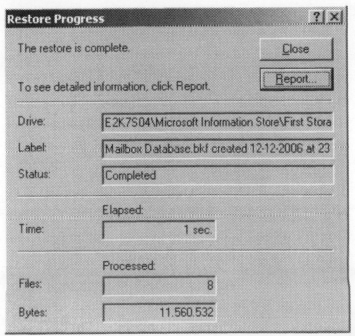

If your restore completed successfully, you can now switch back to the Exchange Management Console, where the restored Mailbox database should have been mounted automatically, and we can call the restore a success.

Repairing a Corrupt or Damaged Exchange 2007 Database Using Eseutil

There may be situations where you either don't have a proper backup set to restore a particular database from, or perhaps you found out that the database you just restored to replace a corrupt or damaged database is also corrupt or damaged. This is where Extensible Storage Engine Utilities for Microsoft Exchange Server (Eseutil) comes in. Eseutil is a command-line utility that can be used to perform a range of database tasks including repair, offline defragmentation, and integrity checks. Eseutil hasn't changed much from Exchange 2003 since Exchange still uses ESE databases when speaking Exchange 2007. This means that pretty much all of the switches and parameters available in Eseutil are the same as in previous versions. Since there are plenty of books and online documentation describing how you should approach fixing a corrupt database using Eseutil, I'll provide you with the most common Eseutil switches, as well as a few examples.

Eseutil, as in previous versions, is located in the Bin folder under your Exchange installation path, which in Exchange 2007, by default, is C:\Program Files\Microsoft\Exchange Server. However, you no longer need to run the tool from that path; you can just open a Command Prompt window and type **Eseutil**, as shown in Figure 9.9.

Figure 9.9 Eseutil Modes

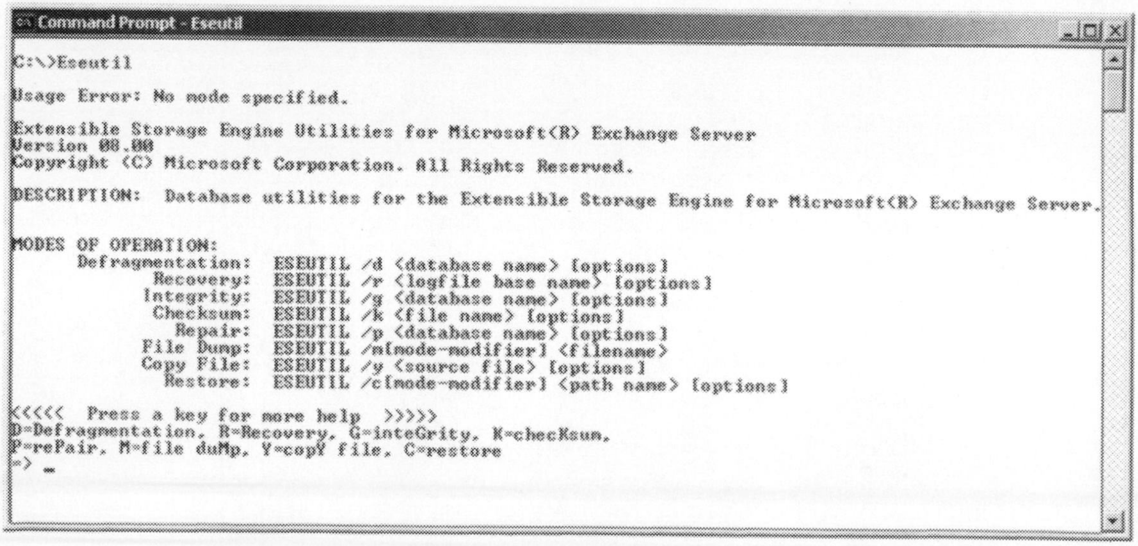

> **NOTE**
>
> You can also run Eseutil directly from the Exchange Management Shell.

Before we move on, we want to stress that it's very important you always try to restore your databases from a backup if possible, since there's a good chance you will lose some data when performing a repair of a database. The reason for this is that Eseutil often needs to discard rows from tables or even entire tables. In addition, you should have a repaired database running in your production environment only for a temporary period, which means that after you have repaired a database, you should move all mailboxes from the database to a new one. Needless to say, you should also be sure to make a copy of the database before performing a repair using Eseutil.

> **NOTE**
>
> Did you know that when a database corruption occurs, 99.9 percent of the time it's caused by the underlying hard disk drive subsystem? Yes, it's true! This means there's a pretty good chance the database corruption experienced is caused by an I/O issue on the disk set in your Exchange 2007 server. You should therefore always examine the Application and System logs, searching for any events that might indicate this to be the problem.

Eseutil /P can, in addition to the Mailbox and Public Folder databases, also be run against the ESE database-based message queues on either a Hub Transport or Edge Transport server in your Exchange 2007 organization.

To repair a corrupted or otherwise damaged database, run Eseutil with the /P switch. So, to repair a database called Mailbox Database.edb located in E:\Program Files\Microsoft\Exchange Server\Mailbox\First Storage Group, you would need to type:

```
Eseutil /P "E:\Program Files\Microsoft\Exchange Server\Mailbox\First Storage Group\
Mailbox Database.edb"
```

After pressing **Enter**, you would receive the warning message shown in Figure 9.10.

Figure 9.10 An Eseutil Repair Warning

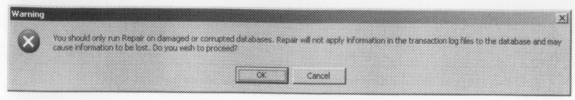

NOTE

You must have the necessary amount of free space (equal to 110 percent of the database file size) on the disk containing the database before you can run Eseutil /P and Eseutil /D.

Click **OK** to proceed, and then wait until Eseutil has repaired the database. If the database is completed successfully, it's highly recommended you perform a full backup of the database, since restoring a backup made before the repair would roll the database back to the state it was in at the time of the backup, which wouldn't be very smart.

After you have run Eseutil /P against a database, also run Eseutil /D in order to fully rebuild indexes and defragment the database. In order to run Eseutil /D against the database, type:

```
Eseutil /D "E:\Program Files\Microsoft\Exchange Server\Mailbox\First Storage Group\
Mailbox Database.edb"
```

When an offline defragmentation has been completed, there's one additional thing to do: repair the database at the application level (repair information and relationships between mailboxes, folders, items, and attachments) by running the Information Store Integrity Checker (Isinteg) utility with the *-fix* parameter. Figure 9.11 shows the parameters and syntaxes available for the Isinteg utility.

Figure 9.11 Isinteg Switches

```
C:\>isinteg
Microsoft Exchange Information Store Integrity Checker v08.00.0685.024
Copyright (c) 1986-2000 Microsoft Corp.    All rights reserved.
Usage:
  isinteg -s ServerName [-fix] [-verbose] [-l logfilename] -test testname[[, testname]...]
     -s               ServerName
     -fix             check and fix (default - check only)
     -verbose         report verbosely
     -l filename      log file name (default - .\isinteg.pri/pub)
     -t refdblocation (default - the location of the store)
     -test testname,...
        folder message aclitem mailbox(pri only) delfld acllist
        rcvfld(pri only) timedev rowcounts attach morefld ooflist(pri only)
        global searchq dlvrto replstate(pub only)
        peruser artidx(pub only) search newsfeed(pub only) dumpsterprops
        Ref count tests: msgref msgsoftref attachref acllistref aclitemref
        newsfeedref(pub only) fldrcv(pri only) fldsub dumpsterref
        Groups tests: allfoldertests allacltests
  isinteg -dump [-l logfilename] (verbose dump of store data)

C:\>_
```

If you aren't comfortable running the Eseutil and Isinteg utilities manually on your databases, you also have the option of performing a repair using a wizard–driven interface. This is where the new Disaster Recovery Management tool, a sibling of tools such as the Exchange Best Practices Analyzer Tool (ExBPA), comes into play. To invoke this tool, click the **Toolbox** work center node in the navigation tree in the **Exchange Management Console**, then open the tool by selecting it in the Result pane and clicking **Open Tool** in the **Actions** pane (Figure 9.12).

Figure 9.12 Disaster Recovery Management Tool

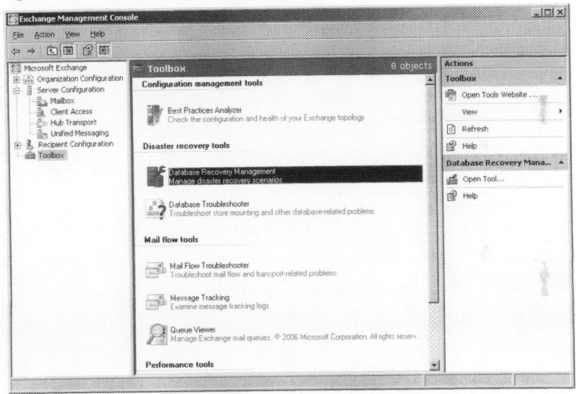

The tool will now check if there is any tool or configuration file updates available on Microsoft. com, and if so, apply them without requiring a restart. Once any updates have been applied, click the **Go to Welcome Screen** link, then enter an identifying label for the activity, and click **Next**. When the tool has connected to the Active Directory, you will be presented with the task list shown in Figure 9.13. Here, you should select the **Repair Database** task.

Figure 9.13 Exchange Troubleshooting Assistant Tasks

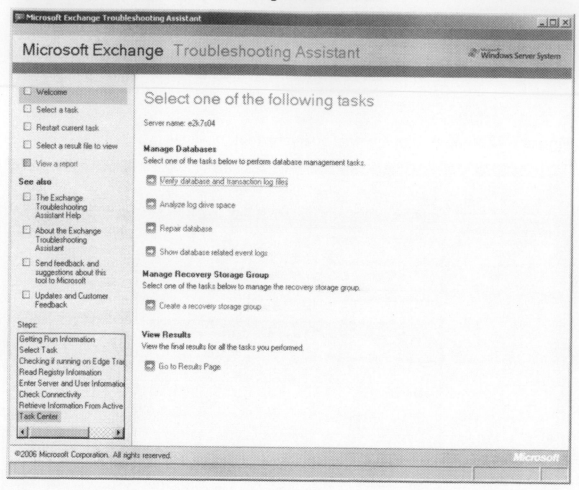

Now select the storage group that contains the database you wish to repair, click **Next**, and on the **Select Databases to Repair** page, check the respective database, as I did in Figure 9.14. Then, click **Next**.

Figure 9.14 Selecting the Database to Repair

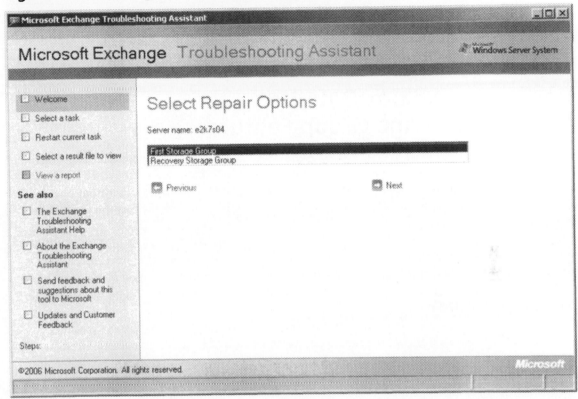

You will now need to read a repair task warning. I suggest you read it carefully. When you have done so, choose **Continue to Perform Repair Task**, and then click **OK** in the confirmation dialog box shown in Figure 9.15.

Figure 9.15 ExTRA Confirmation

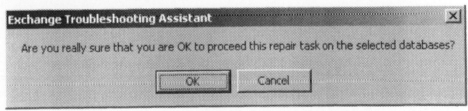

The tool will now run Eseutil /P and then Eseutil /D, followed by Isinteg –fix –test alltests against the respective database, just like we did manually earlier in this section. After a while, depending on the size of the database, you will be taken to a Report Repair Results page where you can see if the actions completed without any issues, and if not, it will show an explanation why it didn't.

Restoring Mailbox Data Using the Recovery Storage Group Feature

The Recovery Storage Group (RSG) feature, which was originally introduced back in Exchange 2003, gives you, the Exchange administrator, the option of mounting a second copy of a mailbox database (typically a mailbox database restored from backup) so you can extract data from one or more mailboxes in the respective database during working hours without affecting the production databases.

Depending on how much you have used the new Exchange 2007 Management Console (EMC), you may have noticed you can no longer create an RSG from within the EMC. With Exchange 2007, this is instead done using the new Database Recovery Management tool, which as you saw in the previous section, is found under the Exchange Toolbox work center, or by using the Exchange Management Shell (EMS).

When mounting a copy of a Mailbox database to an RSG, you can extract the data from a mailbox and then merge the data with another mailbox located in a mailbox database in a production storage group. You can also extract the data and copy it to a specific folder in another mailbox. With Exchange 2003 RTM, the data was extracted, copied, and merged with another mailbox or mailbox folder using the Microsoft Exchange Server Mailbox Merge Wizard (ExMerge) tool, but in Exchange 2003 SP1 the process was integrated into the Exchange 2003 System Manager GUI.

There are a few things you should be aware of when dealing with RSGs. First, they cannot be accessed by any protocols other than MAPI, and although they can be accessed using MAPI, this doesn't mean you can connect to a mailbox stored in a recovery database using an Outlook MAPI client. MAPI is strictly used to access mailboxes using the Exchange Troubleshooting Assistant and the respective Exchange Management Shell cmdlets. In addition, you should be aware that you still cannot use RSGs to restore Public Folder data, only mailbox data. It's also worth mentioning that even though you can create up to 50 storage groups on an Exchange 2007 Enterprise edition server, you're limited to one RSG per server. However, it's supported to add multiple mailbox databases to an RSG as long as all databases belong to the same storage group. Finally, you should note that although it's possible to add a restored mailbox database to an RSG on another Exchange 2007 server, it's important you understand that the Exchange 2007 server must belong to the same Active Directory forest.

With the preceding in mind, let's move on and see how you manage RSGs.

Managing Recovery Storage Groups Using the Exchange Troubleshooting Assistant

You can create a Recovery Storage Group (RSG) either by using the Disaster Recovery Management tool, which is based on the Microsoft Exchange Troubleshooting Assistant (ExTRA), or by running the *New-StorageGroup* cmdlet with the *–Recovery* parameter in the Exchange Management Shell.

To create the RSG using the Disaster Recovery Management tool, you should first launch it from beneath the Toolbox work center in the navigation tree of the Exchange Management Console (EMC). Let the tool check for any tool or configuration file updates available, and then click the **Go to Welcome** screen link. Enter an identifying label for this activity (such as Create RSG), and then click **Next**. In the **Tasks** list that appears, click **Create a Recovery Storage Group**, and then select the storage group you want to link with the recovery storage group, as shown in Figure 9.16. Then, click **Next** once again.

Figure 9.16 Selecting the Storage Group to Link with the RSG

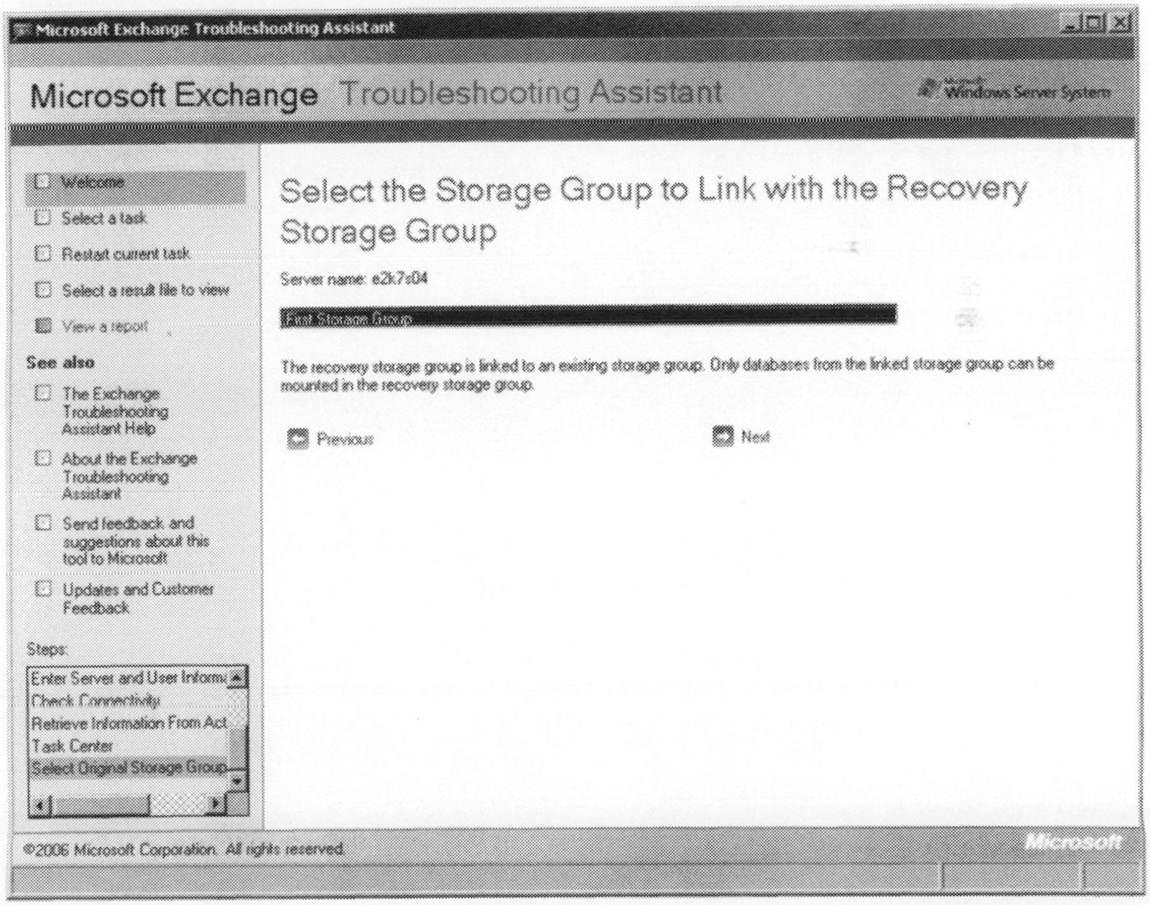

Now it's time to create the RSG, but before doing so you need to give it a name (the default name is Recovery Storage Group, which should be okay in most situations). When you have entered an appropriate name, click **Create the recovery storage group** (Figure 9.17).

Figure 9.17 Creating the RSG

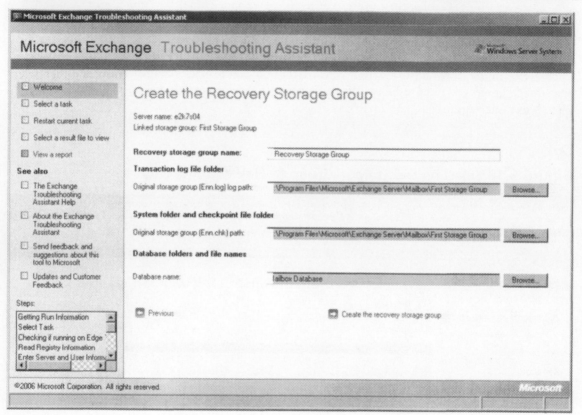

After a little while, you will be presented with a screen similar to the one in Figure 9.18, and the RSG for the respective Mailbox database has now been created.

Figure 9.18 RSG Result

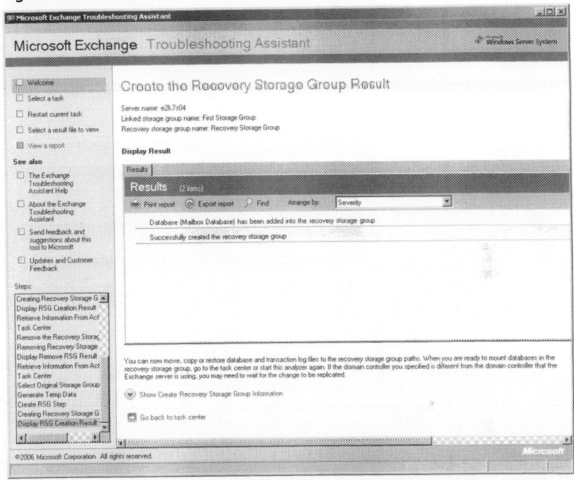

With the RSG created, we can move, copy, or restore database and transaction log files to the recovery storage group paths. To see the path for the recovery storage group log and database files, click **Show Create Recovery Storage Group Information**. By default, the path is C:\Program Files\Microsoft\Exchange Server\Mailbox\<Storage Group>\RSG*xxxxxxxxx*, as you can see in Figure 9.19. The RSG*xxxxxxxxx* folder will appear empty in Windows Explorer until you have moved, copied, or restored the database and transaction log files to it.

Figure 9.19 Storage Group and Recovery Storage Group Paths

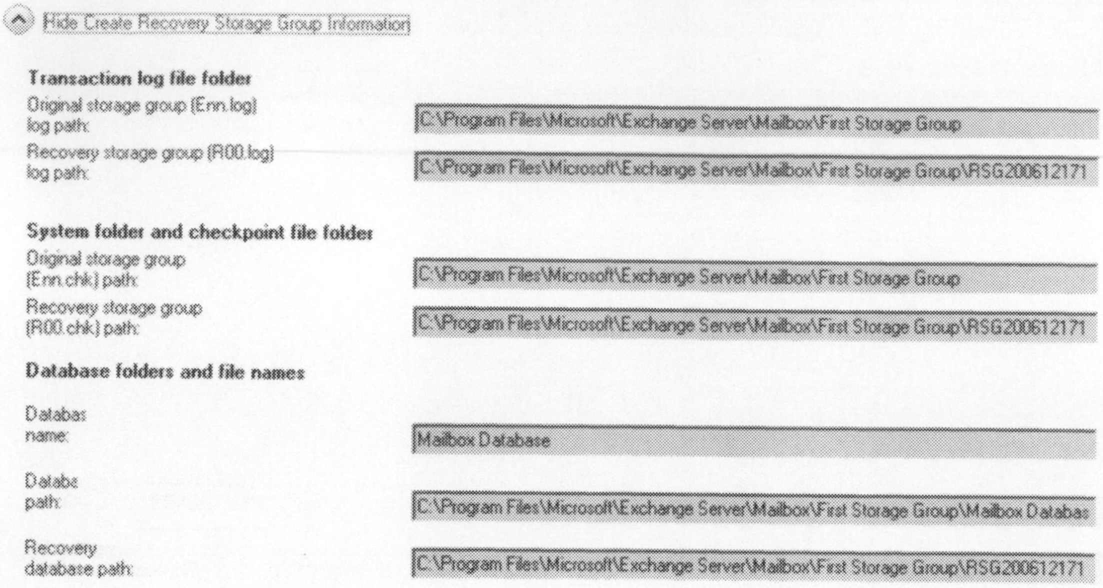

⌃ Hide Create Recovery Storage Group Information

Transaction log file folder

Original storage group (Enn.log)
log path:

> C:\Program Files\Microsoft\Exchange Server\Mailbox\First Storage Group

Recovery storage group (R00.log)
log path:

> C:\Program Files\Microsoft\Exchange Server\Mailbox\First Storage Group\RSG200612171

System folder and checkpoint file folder

Original storage group
(Enn.chk) path:

> C:\Program Files\Microsoft\Exchange Server\Mailbox\First Storage Group

Recovery storage group
(R00.chk) path:

> C:\Program Files\Microsoft\Exchange Server\Mailbox\First Storage Group\RSG200612171

Database folders and file names

Database
name:

> Mailbox Database

Database
path:

> C:\Program Files\Microsoft\Exchange Server\Mailbox\First Storage Group\Mailbox Databas

Recovery
database path:

> C:\Program Files\Microsoft\Exchange Server\Mailbox\First Storage Group\RSG200612171

For the purpose of this example, we will restore a Mailbox database from a backup using the Windows 2003 Backup tool. So let's launch the Windows 2003 Backup tool in advanced mode, and then click the **Restore and Manage Media** tab. Here we need to select the Mailbox database and log files we want to restore. When you have done so, click the **Start Restore** button.

> **NOTE**
>
> Note that the Restore Files To: Drop-Down box is set to Original Location. Also notice we cannot change this selection. But does that mean the Mailbox database currently in production will be replaced by the one we restore from backup? No, this is not the case. First, we haven't dismounted the production Mailbox database, and second, we haven't enabled the *This Database Can Be Overwritten By A Restore* option on the Mailbox database property page. Because of this, the Mailbox database will be restored to the recovery storage group we just created.

Now specify the Exchange Server to which you want to restore the respective Mailbox database, and then enter a temporary location for the log and patch files. Lastly, check **Last Restore Set** (Log File Replay will start after this restore completes) since this is the last restore set. When you are done, click **OK** and wait for the restore job to complete. Then, click the **Close** button.

The respective files have now been restored to the RSG*xxxxxxxxx* folder, as you can see in Figure 9.20.

Figure 9.20 The Restored Mailbox Database in Windows Explorer

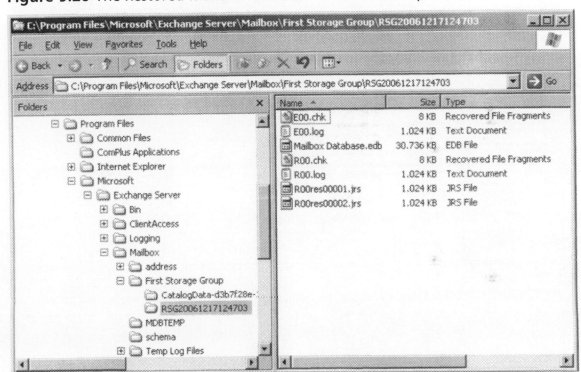

Since we didn't check the *Mount Database After Restore* option, the Mailbox database will now be in a dismounted state. With this in mind, let's switch back to the ExTRA Task Center. As shown in Figure 9.21, we now have several new recovery storage group–related tasks available. Since the Mailbox database needs to be mounted before we can extract data from it, we have to click **Mount or dismount databases in the recovery storage group.**

Figure 9.21 Selecting Mount or Dismount Databases in the Recovery Storage Group

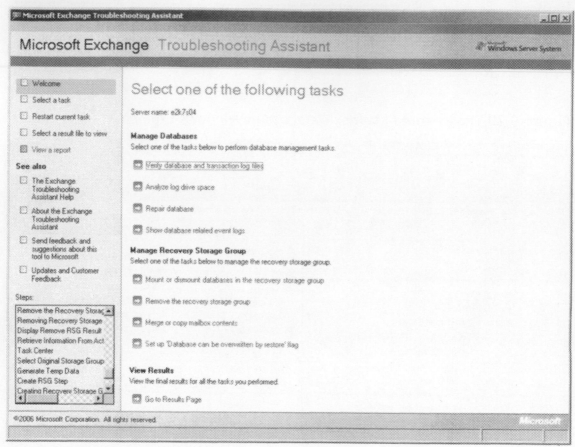

On the **Mount or Dismount Database** page, check the respective Mailbox database and click **Mount selected database** (Figure 9.22).

Figure 9.22 Mounting the Mailbox Database Using the ExTRA Tool

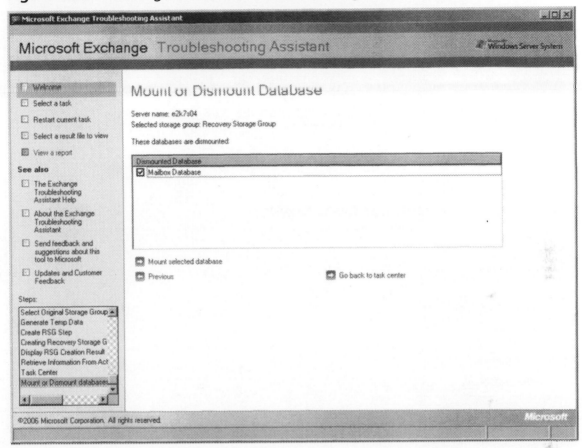

Once the Mailbox database has been mounted, click **Go back to task center**, and then select **Merge or copy mailbox content**. This will bring us to a screen similar to the one shown in Figure 9.23, here you should just make sure the Mailbox database you wish to extract data from is selected, and then click **Gather merge information**.

Figure 9.23 Selecting a Mounted Database in the Recovery Storage Group

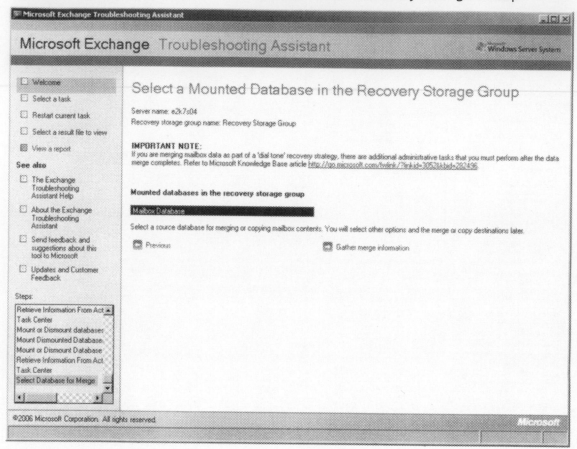

We now have the option of swapping the Mailbox database mounted to the RSG and the linked production Mailbox database (a recommended step if you're performing a dial-tone database restore) by checking Swap Database Configurations, as can be seen in Figure 9.24. Since this option will swap the two databases, both of them need to be dismounted, which will affect mail service to the end users whose mailboxes are stored in the respective database.

Figure 9.24 The Database Swap Option

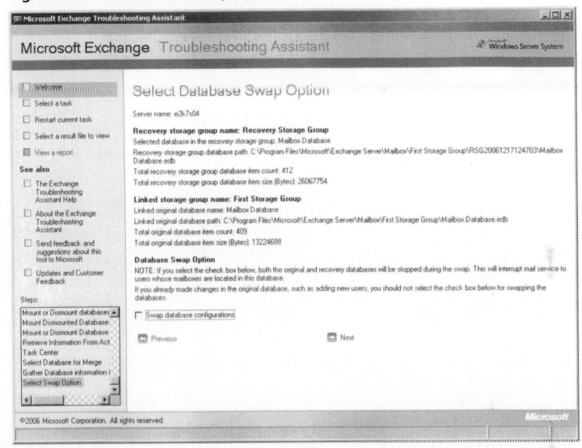

Since we aren't dealing with a dial-tone database restore in this example, just click **Next**. On the **Select Merge Options** page, click **Perform pre-merge tasks** (Figure 9.25).

Figure 9.25 Specifying Merge Options

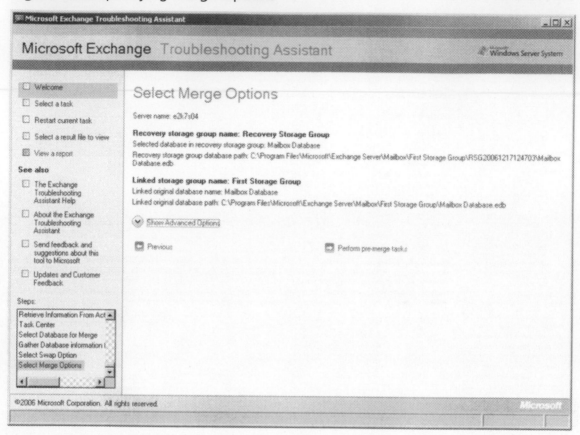

NOTE

Note that you have the option of clicking Show Advanced Options. Under the Advanced options, we can specify different match and filtering options, as well as the bad item limit. This is also the place where you specified whether all merge mailbox data should be merged to the respective mailboxes in the production Mailbox database, or whether they should be copied to a single target mailbox.

The final step is to select the mailboxes you want to merge. You do this by checking the box to the left of each user name in the list, as shown in Figure 9.26.

Figure 9.26 Selecting the Mailboxes to Merge

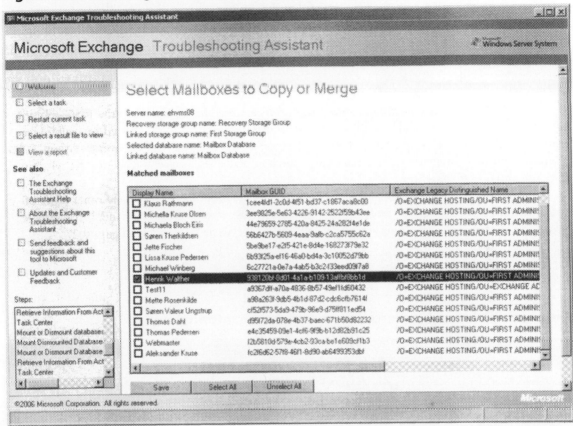

Now wait for the tool to merge the mailbox data from the Mailbox database in the recovery storage group for the selected mailbox. When the mailbox data merge has completed, you should be able to see the content deleted from the production Mailbox database. You don't even need to restart the Outlook or OWA client for the restored data to appear!

When you have merged or copied the required Mailbox data, you can use ExTRA to dismount and then remove the recovery storage group. Be sure you delete the files in the RSG*xxxxxxxxx* folder after you have removed it so the files don't take up valuable disk space.

Managing Recovery Storage Groups Using the Exchange Management Shell

As mentioned earlier in this chapter, you can also manage an RSG using the Exchange Management Shell (EMS). If you know your cmdlets, restoring mailbox data from a Mailbox database in a recovery storage group can be done a lot faster than when you're using ExTRA.

The first step is to create the RSG. In order to create an RSG via the EMS, you need to run the *New-StorageGroup* cmdlet with the *–Recovery* parameter. So, to create an RSG for the first storage group on a server named E2K7S04, type:

```
New-StorageGroup -Server E2K7S04 -LogFolderPath "E:\Program Files\Microsoft\
Exchange Server\Mailbox\First Storage Group\RSG -Name "Recovery Storage Group"
-SystemFolderPath "E:\Program Files\Microsoft\Exchange Server\Mailbox\First Storage
Group\RSG" -Recovery
```

The *LogFolderPath* and *SystemFolderPath* parameters are used to specify where the RSG-related files should be located. As you can see, we specified they should them to be restored to a subfolder called RSG under E:\Program Files\Microsoft\Exchange Server\Mailbox\First Storage Group\RSG. If you intend to do the same, please make sure there's sufficient disk space available for the Mailbox database you're restoring from backup.

To see if a respective storage group is a recovery storage group (as well as many other types of information), you can use the *Get-StorageGroup <storage group name> | FL* command. If the storage group is a recovery storage group, it will say True under Recovery, as shown in Figure 9.27

Figure 9.27 Full List of Recovery Storage Group Information

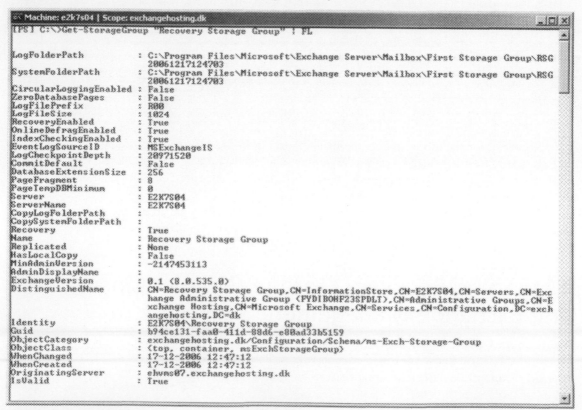

The next step is to add a recovery database (either moved, copied, or restored from backup) to the RSG, this is done by running the *New-MailboxDatabase* cmdlet with the *MailboxDatabaseToRecover* parameter. So, to add a recovery database to the recovery storage group on a server named E2KS04 with the edb file path pointing to E:\Program Files\Microsoft\Exchange Server\Mailbox\First Storage Group\RSG, type:

```
New-MailboxDatabase -MailboxDatabaseToRecover "Mailbox Database" -StorageGroup
"E2K7S04Recovery Storage Group" -EDBFilePath "E:\Program Files\Microsoft\Exchange
Server\Mailbox\First Storage Group\RSG\Mailbox Database.edb"
```

With the Mailbox Database created in the recovery storage group, we now need to configure it to allow overwrites by running the *Set-MailboxDatabase* cmdlet with the *−AllowRestore* parameter. To allow file restores for the recovery database just created, type:

```
Set-MailboxDatabase -Identity "E2K7S04\Recovery Storage Group\1Mailbox Database"
-AllowFileR
estore $true
```

Now that we have created a recovery database in the recovery storage group and allowed it to be overwritten by a file restore, it's time to restore the mailbox database version from which you want to extract and copy or merge data to the mailbox database in production. To do so, launch the Windows 2003 Backup tool and restore the respective Mailbox database version using the same steps as we did when we used the ExTRA to recover Mailbox data.

We now need to mount the restore Mailbox database using the *Mount-Database* cmdlet. In order to do so, type:

```
Mount-Database -Identity "E2K7S04\Recovery Storage Group\Mailbox Database"
```

With the Mailbox database mounted, we can now extract Mailbox data from it. For example, if you want to merge the mailbox data of an existing user in the recovery database to the production Mailbox database, you need to type:

```
Restore-Mailbox -Identity <username> -RSGDatabase "servername\RSG
name\database name"
```

In Figure 9.28, we recovered mailbox data for a user called Test User 1 on a server named E2K7S04.

Figure 9.28 Restoring Mailbox Data from a Mailbox in a Recovery Storage Group

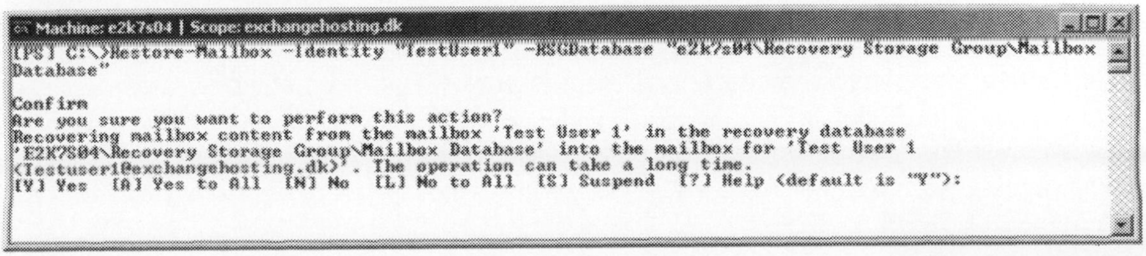

NOTE

Depending on the size of the mailbox to be recovered, this merging process can take a long time.

If you need to recover mailbox data for all users in the RSG, you would need to use the following command:

```
Get-MailboxStatistics -Database "Recovery Storage Group\Mailbox Database"
| Restore-Mailbox
```

Let's suppose the mailbox in the recovery database that you want to recover data from has in the meantime been deleted from the production Mailbox database. In this case, you have the option of recovering the mailbox data to a target folder in another mailbox by using the following command:

```
Restore-Mailbox -RSGMailbox "Test User 1" -RSGDatabase "servername\RSG name\
database name" -Identity "Test User 2" -TargetFolder "Test User 1 Recovered data"
```

Just as with recovering data using the ExTRA tool, when using the Exchange Management Shell you should remember to remove the RSG after the required data has been recovered. To do so, first run the command to remove the recovery database:

```
Remove-MailboxDatabase -Identity "E2K7S04\Recovery Storage Group\Mailbox Database"
```

Click **Yes** to the confirmation warning, and then type the following command in order to remove the RSG:

```
Remove-StorageGroup -Identity "E2K7S04\Recovery Storage Group"
```

Finally, delete the RSG folder manually using Windows Explorer.

Recovering an Exchange 2007 Server Using the RecoverServer Switch

What could be worse than facing one or more seriously corrupted Exchange 2007 mailbox databases? Yes, you guessed right: facing a completely dead Exchange 2007 Server. In this section, I'll shine some light on the steps necessary to restore an Exchange 2007 Server that has experienced a major hardware failure causing a complete loss of data. As is the case with Exchange 2000 and 2003, you can recover an Exchange 2007 Server in a fairly straightforward way. As you probably know, we could use the DisasterRecovery switch to recover a dead Exchange 2000 or 2003 Server on new hardware, but with Exchange 2007 this switch no longer exists. Instead, it has been replaced by the new RecoverServer switch, which is similar to the DisasterRecovery switch. The interesting thing about the RecoverServer switch is that it can be used to recover all types of Exchange 2007 Server roles, except the Edge Transport Server role, which uses ADAM and not the Active Directory to store configuration data.

> **NOTE**
>
> To recover a server with the Edge Transport Server role installed, you must use the cloned configuration tasks to export and import configuration information. You can read more about the cloned configuration tasks in Chapter 7.

When you run Setup with the RecoverServer switch on a new Windows 2003 Server that is configured with the same name as the one that has crashed or is permanently down for some reason, Setup will read the configuration information for the respective Exchange 2007 server from the Active Directory. In addition to applying the roles and settings stored in Active Directory, Setup will, as is the case when installing an Exchange 2007 Server role without the RecoverServer switch, install the Exchange files and services required for the respective Exchange 2007 server role(s). This means that local customizations done on the server (such as Mailbox databases, Receive connectors, custom OWA settings, SSL certificates, and so on) need to be re-created or recovered manually afterwards.

In this section, we'll go through the steps necessary to recover an Exchange 2007 server with the Hub Transport, Mailbox Server, and Client Access Server roles installed.

Restoring and Configuring the Operating System

When you have received a replacement server or replacements for the failed hardware components, it's important you configure and partition the disk sets in the new server so they are identical to the way they were configured in the failed server. When the hardware is configured according to the documentation you wrote for the failed Exchange 2007 (which you did write, right?), we can begin installing the operating system from the Windows 2003 Server 64-bit media. When Windows 2003 Server has been installed, it's important you install the Windows Components required by the Exchange Server 2007 Server roles, as well as any service packs and Windows updates that were applied on the failed server. For details about which Windows components are required for each server roles, refer back to Chapter 2.

In addition to that already mentioned, you should also make sure you name the new server with the same server name. Before doing so, however, it's important the failed Exchange 2007 server be turned off. In addition, you should add the server to the respective Active Directory domain, first resetting the computer account for the respective Exchange 2007 server. In order to reset the computer account, you must perform the following steps:

1. Log on to a domain controller or another server with the Adminpak installed in the Active Directory domain, and then open the **Active Directory Users and Computers (ADUC) MMC** snap-in.

2. In the ADUC MMC snap-in, navigate to the organizational unit (OU) containing your computer accounts (by default, the Computers OU), right-click the computer account that should be reset, and then select **Reset Account**, as shown in Figure 9.29.

Figure 9.29 Resetting the Computer Account in the ADUC MMC Snap-in

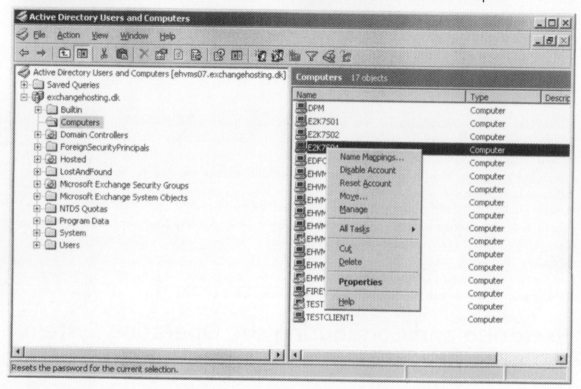

3. Click **Yes** to the warning in the dialog box that appears, and then click **OK**.

We can now join the new server to the domain without issues. Do so and perform the required reboot.

Installing Exchange 2007 Using the RecoverServer Switch

Now that Windows 2003 has been installed properly, we can move on and start installing Exchange 2007 by running Setup.exe with the RecoverServer switch. In order to do so, perform the following steps:

1. Click **Start | Run** and type **CMD**. Then, press **Enter**.

2. Change to the directory or media containing your Exchange 2007 Setup files, and then type **Setup.com /M:RecoverServer**. As can be seen in Figure 9.30, Exchange 2007 Setup will now prepare the Exchange 2007 setup, and then perform the mandatory prerequisite checks. Finally, it will begin to copy the Exchange files and then configure each Exchange 2007 Server role by reading the required configuration information from Active Directory.

Figure 9.30 Recovering an Exchange 2007 Server Using the RecoverServer Switch

NOTE

If you're recovering an Exchange 2007 server with the Hub Transport Server role installed, and this is the only Exchange 2007 server with this role installed, its recommended you run Setup.com /M:RecoverServer with the /DoNotStartTransport syntax since there's a few post-recovery steps that should be completed before this role is made active.

When the Exchange setup has completed each phase successfully, we're close to calling the server recovery a success. However, there are a few post-recovery steps that need to be finished, depending on what Exchange 2007 Server roles are installed on the server. It's obvious a recovered server with the Mailbox Server role must have the respective Mailbox database and Public Folder database restored from backup, or copied back from the disks on the old server (if possible). If the Public Folders are replicated with other Exchange 2000/2003 or 2007 servers in the Exchange organization, you don't need to restore it since an empty Public Folder database will be backfilled from the other Public folder server(s).

NOTE

If you need to restore one or more Mailbox and/or Public Folder databases to the recovered server using the Windows 2003 Backup tool, note that you must catalog the respective backup (.BKF). This is done by selecting the **Restore and Manage Media** tab, and then clicking **Tools | Catalog** a backup file in the menu.

If the Hub Transport Server role is installed on the recovered Exchange 2007 server, you may also need to restore any saved message queue databases (which in Exchange 2007 are stored in an ESE database and not in the NTFS file system as was the case with Exchange 2000 and 2003) and place them in the right folder (should be done while the Microsoft Exchange Transport service is stopped, which is why it's a good idea to run the RecoverServer switch with the /DoNotStartTransport syntax if you're recovering an Exchange 2007 server with the Hub Transport Server role installed), as well as reconfigure any Receive connectors since these are stored locally on the Hub Transport Server and not in Active Directory, as is the case with Send Connectors.

In addition, you may need to restore the Client Access Server settings (custom OWA files and/or virtual directories). Custom virtual folder settings can be restored by using the script method mentioned earlier in this chapter.

NOTE

Although it should be the most comprehensive, as well as fastest, way to recover a server using the RecoverServer switch, it's worth mentioning that it's fully supported to restore an Exchange 2007 Server by restoring the System State as well as all the Exchange installation files. Bear in mind, however, that this method requires you restore Exchange 2007 on the same hardware.

Recovering an Exchange 2007 Cluster Using the RecoverCMS Switch

To finish off this chapter, we wanted to talk a little about how you can recover an Exchange 2007 clustered mailbox server (both CCR and SCC) by using the *ExSetup.exe* command with the

RecoverCMS switch. Since we're talking about restoring a cluster, many of you may think the tasks involved are terribly complex. As a matter of fact, it's a relatively simple task. The biggest challenge is rebuilding the Windows 2003 cluster itself, which as you learned in Chapter 8, is a rather harmless process. Once you have rebuilt the Windows 2003 cluster on new hardware, you need to install the Passive Clustered Mailbox Role on one of the Windows 2003 cluster nodes, navigate to the Exchange Bin folder (which, by default, is located under C:\Program Files\Microsoft\Exchange Server\), and then run the following command:

```
ExSetup.exe /RecoverCMS /CMSName:<name of the clustered mailbox server>
/CMSIPAddress:<IP address of the clustered mailbox server>
```

When the clustered mailbox server has been recovered successfully (if the recovered clustered mailbox server is based on a CCR), you need to enable replication as replication, which, by default, will be in a suspended state after recovery using the RecoverCMS switch. In addition you must (both when recovering a CCR and SCC) start the Exchange System Attendant service manually since it will stop right after the clustered mailbox server has been recovered.

The next step is to restore the respective Mailbox and/or Public Folder databases that existed on the failed clustered mailbox server from backup, or move/copy them from their respective locations.

NOTE

If you're recovering a Single Copy Cluster (SCC) and stored the Mailbox and Public Folder databases on a storage area network (SAN), you won't need to restore the databases from backup as long as each node points to the same shared storage subsystem that the failed clustered mailbox server did.

When any required Mailbox and/or Public Folder databases have been restored, you should now install the Passive Clustered Mailbox Role on the second node (and if recovering an SCC, any additional nodes). If you recovered a clustered mailbox server that is based on SCC, we can now call the recovery of the clustered mailbox server a success, but if you use CCR, there's one final task to complete, and that is to reseed the replica and resume replication. To reseed the second copy of the database(s), you should run the following command in the Exchange Management Shell:

```
Update-StorageGroupCopy -Identity: <Servername\Name of StorageGroup>
```

When the storage group(s) have been reseeded, you can resume replication by running:

```
Resume-StorageGroupCopy -Identity:<Servername>\Name of Storage Group>
```

So, this was not as difficult as you had imagined it, right?

Restoring Mailbox Databases Using the Improved Database Portability Feature

As those of you with plenty of disaster recovery experience from Exchange 2003 might be aware, Mailbox database portability (that is mounting a Mailbox database to an alternative Exchange Server) was rather limited in this version of Exchange, actually the only options available were to mount the respective Mailbox database into a recovery storage group (RSG), into a storage group on a server with the same name as the failed server, or into the storage group on an Exchange Server in the same administrative group. Although mailbox databases were portable between Exchange 2003 servers (on the same service pack level) in the same administrative group, certain tasks were involved with this procedure. You had to rename the Mailbox databases appropriately, as well as re-link each mailbox in the database to an Active Directory user account before the mailbox could be accessible to an end user. In addition, several other issues might exist if the Mailbox database contained a System Attendant mailbox. Finally, depending on what type of third-party applications were running on the particular Exchange server, it was also best practice to reboot the server once the Mailbox database move was completed.

With Exchange 2007, the Mailbox database portability feature has been improved drastically. Now you can port and recover a Mailbox database to any server in the Exchange 2007 organization, and because of the new Autodiscover service (which we discussed in Chapter 5), all Outlook 2007 clients will be redirected to the new server automatically the first time they try to connect after the Mailbox database has been mounted on another Exchange 2007 server.

> **NOTE**
>
> Since only Outlook 2007 clients can take advantage of the new Autodiscover service introduced in Exchange 2007, any legacy clients (Outlook 2003 and earlier) won't be redirected to the new server automatically.

Some of you might wonder if Exchange 2007 (unlike Exchange 2003) allows you to port or recover a Public Folder database to another server. The answer is no. Doing so is still not supported since it will break Public Folder replication. The proper method for moving a Public Folder database to another server is to add the respective server to the Public Folder replica list.

Okay, now that you have heard how cool the new Mailbox database portability improvements in Exchange 2007 are, let's take a look at the steps needed they entail:

First, it's important you make sure the Mailbox database you wish to port or recover to another server is in a clean shutdown state. If not, you must perform a soft recovery of the database, which is done by running Eseutil /R <ENN> against it. ENN is the prefix of the storage group to which you want to commit any existing transaction log files. One method you can use to find this prefix is to open the property page of the respective storage group containing the Mailbox database you wish to port or recover to another Exchange 2007 server (see Figure 9.31).

Figure 9.31 The Transaction Log Files Prefix

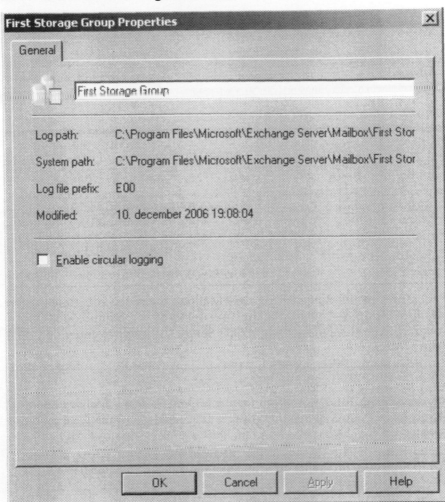

Once the Mailbox database is in a clean shutdown state, the next step is to move the Mailbox database (.EDB file, transaction log files, and Exchange Search catalog) to the system path folder of the respective storage group on the other server, and then create a new Mailbox database in the storage group using the following command:

```
New-MailboxDatabase -StorageGroup <Servername>\<Name of Storage Group> -Name <Name
of Mailbox Database>
```

In this example, you will mount a database named Mailbox database to the Third Storage Group on an Exchange 2007 Server called EHVMS08. Therefore, the command we need to run is shown in Figure 9.32.

Figure 9.32 Creating a New Mailbox Database in the Third Storage Group

Because Exchange 2007 won't create an .EDB file for a newly created Mailbox database before it's mounted for the first time, using the *New-MailboxDatabase* cmdlet to create a new Mailbox database, while the Mailbox Database.edb file is placed in the folder of the Third Storage Group will not conflict in any way. Actually, you can just move ahead and mount the ported Mailbox database.

NOTE

It's important that the name of the new Mailbox database you create using the *New-MailboxDatabase* cmdlet matches the name of the Mailbox database you ported or recovered from the old Exchange 2007 Server; otherwise, you won't be able to mount it.

To mount the Mailbox database, you can use the Mount-Database "Mailbox Database" or the Exchange Management Console. When the Mailbox database has been mounted appropriately, there's only one more task to complete, and that is to modify (re-link) the Active Directory user account objects associated with a mailbox in the Mailbox database that we ported to a new server, so they point to the correct server. This can be done by using the following command:

```
Get-Mailbox –Database "E2K7S04\Mailbox Database" | Move-Mailbox –TargetDatabase
"EHVMS08\Mailbox Database" –ConfigurationOnly: $True
```

You then must confirm that you wish to perform this operation. Type **Y** for Yes, and press **Enter**.

NOTE

If you receive an error when trying to run this command, check to make sure the Mailbox database is mounted on the old Exchange 2007 server.

Now would be a good time to access a few mailboxes (using Outlook 2007 or OWA 2007) stored in the Mailbox database we ported so you can verify the end users still have mailbox connectivity.

Summary

In this chapter, we took a look at how to properly back up the different server roles in Exchange 2007. We then went through how you restore an Exchange 2007 Server with one or more server roles installed, as well as how you can restore a corrupt Mailbox or Public Folder database using the Windows 2003 Backup tool, and if this isn't an option, how you can repair a corrupt database using Eseutil. We also had walked through how you can recover mailbox data using the improved Recovery Storage Group (RSG) feature. In addition, I showed you how it's possible to recover a failed Exchange 2007 server using the RecoverServer and RecoverCMS switches. Lastly, we talked about the improvements that have been made regarding database portability in Exchange 2007.

Solutions Fast Track

Backing Up Exchange 2007 Using Windows 2003 Backup

☑ Frequent backups of the Exchange 2007 servers in an organization are important operational tasks, which perhaps can be a bit trivial, but should be taken very seriously. I can only imagine one thing that's worse than a complete failure of an Exchange 2007 server, and that's a complete failure of an Exchange 2007 server without having any backups to restore from.

☑ One of the most important things to back up regarding Exchange 2007 Mailbox Servers are the databases that hold user mailboxes and public data.

☑ Since Exchange 2007 databases still use ESE, you can (just as with previous versions of Exchange) back them up using the Exchange-aware native Windows 2003 backup tool.

☑ Exchange 2007 supports two different backup methods. The first is a legacy streaming backup, which is a backup method based on the ESE application programming interface (API) that allows you to back up one or more storage groups at the same time. However, only one backup job can run against a specific storage group. Then we have the Volume Shadow Copy Service (VSS) backup method, which some of you may know from Exchange 2003, where it was first introduced. The interesting thing about VSS is that this method, in addition to what the legacy streaming backup method offers, can also take an online backup of the copy database when using either Local Continuous Replication or Cluster Continuous Replication in your setup.

Restoring Exchange 2007 Storage Groups and Databases Using Windows 2003 Backup

☑ It's important you understand that a restore of a Mailbox database will copy the database file (.EDB) into its original location on the disk, and thereby overwrite any existing .EDB file.

☑ Once a restore has completed, the log files will be replayed into the restored version of the database. In addition to the log files, a file called Restore.env will also be copied to the specified temporary folder, and this file is the one that keeps control of which storage group the log files belong to, as well as the database paths and range of log files that have been restored.

Repairing a Corrupt or Damaged Exchange 2007 Database Using Eseutil

☑ There may be situations where you either don't have a proper backup set to restore a particular database from, or perhaps you have found out that the database you just restored, in order to replace a corrupt or damaged database, is corrupt or damaged itself. In such situations, you have the option of repairing the database using Extensible Storage Engine Utilities for Microsoft Exchange Server (Eseutil).

☑ Eseutil hasn't changed much from Exchange 2003 since Exchange still uses ESE databases when speaking Exchange 2007. This means that pretty much all of the switches and parameters available in Eseutil are the same as in previous versions.

☑ As in previous versions, Eseutil is located in the Bin folder under your Exchange installation path, which in Exchange 2007, by default, is C:\Program Files\Microsoft\Exchange Server.

☑ When a database corruption occurs, 99.9 percent of the time it's caused by the underlying hard disk drive subsystem.

Restoring Mailbox Data Using the Recovery Storage Group Feature

☑ The Recovery Storage Group (RSG) feature, which was originally introduced back in Exchange 2003, gives you (the Exchange administrator) the option of mounting a second copy of a mailbox database (typically a mailbox database restored from backup). This way, you can extract data during work hours from one or more mailboxes in the respective database without affecting the production databases.

☑ With Exchange 2007, the RSG feature is accessed using the new Database Recovery Management tool, which is found under the Exchange Toolbox work center. You can also work with RSGs using the Exchange Management Shell (EMS).

☑ When you have merged or copied the required Mailbox data, you can use ExTRA to dismount and then remove the Recovery Storage Group. Be sure you delete the files in the RSG*xxxxxxxxx* folder again after you have removed it so the files don't take up valuable disk space.

Recovering an Exchange 2007 Server Using the RecoverServer Switch

☑ Just as with Exchange 2000 and 2003, you can recover an Exchange 2007 Server in a fairly straightforward way. As you perhaps know, we could use the DisasterRecovery switch to recover a dead Exchange 2000 or 2003 Server on new hardware, but with Exchange 2007 this switch no longer exists. Instead, it has been replaced by the new RecoverServer switch, which is similar to the DisasterRecovery switch.

☑ The RecoverServer switch can be used to recover all types of Exchange 2007 Server roles except for the Edge Transport Server role, which uses ADAM and not the Active Directory to store configuration data.

☑ If you're recovering an Exchange 2007 Server with the Hub Transport Server role installed, and this is the only Exchange 2007 Server with this role installed, it's recommended you run Setup.com /M:RecoverServer with the /DoNotStartTransport syntax since there's a few post-recovery steps that should be completed before this role is made active.

☑ When you run Setup with the RecoverServer switch on a new Windows 2003 Server that is configured with the same name as the one that has crashed or is permanently down for some reason, Setup will read the configuration information for the respective Exchange 2007 server from the Active Directory. In addition to applying the roles and settings stored in Active Directory, Setup will (just as when installing an Exchange 2007 Server role without the RecoverServer switch) install the Exchange files and services required for the respective Exchange 2007 server role(s).

Recovering an Exchange 2007 Cluster Using the RecoverCMS Switch

☑ You can recover an Exchange 2007 clustered mailbox server (both CCR and SCC) by using the *ExSetup.exe* command with the RecoverCMS switch.

☑ If you're recovering a Single Copy Cluster (SCC) and have stored the Mailbox and Public Folder databases on a storage area network (SAN), you won't need to restore the databases from backup as long as each node points to the same shared storage subsystem as the failed clustered mailbox server did.

Recovering Mailbox Databases Using the Improved Database Portability Feature

☑ With Exchange 2007, the Mailbox database portability feature has been improved drastically. Now you can port and recover a Mailbox database to any server in the Exchange 2007 organization, and because of the new Autodiscover service (which we discussed in Chapter 5), all Outlook 2007 clients will be redirected to the new server automatically the first time they try to connect after the Mailbox database has been mounted on another Exchange 2007 server.

☑ It's important that the name of the new Mailbox database you create using the *New-MailboxDatabase* cmdlet matches the name of the Mailbox database you ported or recovered from the old Exchange 2007 Server. Otherwise, you won't be able to mount it.

Frequently Asked Questions

Q: Now that we have Local Continuous Replication (LCR) and Cluster Continuous Replication (CCR), should you still take regular backups of the Exchange 2007 databases using a backup application?

A: It's important to understand that LCR and CCR aren't replacements for traditional regular backups. Instead, they are meant to serve as the primary fast recovery solution in case one or more of your production databases shuts down. But with LCR or CCR, you can change your backup schedule from daily to weekly backups.

Q: I heard you can take backups of the passive databases when using LCR or CCR, but I don't have the option of choosing the passive database in Windows 2003 Backup?

A: You're right in that LCR or CCR gives you the option of performing the backup of the passive database(s), but although the Windows 2003 Backup tool supports Volume Shadow Copy Service (VSS) backups, this is only the case when performing file-level–based backups of the databases. In order to perform a backup of the passive databases, you must use a third-party backup solution that supports VSS backups or Microsoft's Data Protection Manager version 2 (DPM v2), which at the time of this writing is still a beta product.

Q: How do you create and manage a Recovery Storage Group (RSG) in the Exchange 2007 Management Console?

A: You don't. With Exchange 2007, the RSG feature cannot be managed using the Exchange Management Console, as was the case in Exchange 2003. Instead, you must create and manage RSGs using the Database Recovery Management tool (which can be found beneath the Toolbox work center node) or the Exchange Management Shell.

Q: Is it possible to restore a Public Folder database to a Recovery Storage Group (RSG) in Exchange 2007?

A: No. Unfortunately, the RSG feature is still limited to Mailbox databases only.

Q: Can I recover all types of Exchange 2007 Server roles using the new RecoverServer switch?

A: Yes, almost. The only Exchange 2007 Server role that cannot be recovered using the RecoverServer switch is the Edge Transport server since this server doesn't belong to the Active Directory. To recover an Edge Transport server, you must instead use the cloned configuration method, which you can read more about in Chapter 7.

Chapter 10

Transitioning from Exchange 2000 or 2003 to Exchange 2007

Solutions in this chapter:

- **Preparing the Environment for a Transition to Exchange Server 2007**

- **Exchange 2003 and Exchange 2007 Coexistence**

- **Replicating Public Folders to Exchange 2007**

- **Pointing Internet Clients to the Client Access Server**

- **Moving Legacy Mailboxes to Exchange 2007**

- **Redirecting Inbound Mail to the Exchange 2007 Server**

- **Decommissioning the Legacy Exchange Server**

- ☑ **Summary**
- ☑ **Solutions Fast Track**
- ☑ **Frequently Asked Questions**

Introduction

Since only the Exchange 2007 64-bit version is supported in a production environment, and because previous versions of Exchange (2000 and 2003) exist only in 32-bit versions, an in-place upgrade from Exchange 2000 or 2003 to Exchange Server 2007 isn't a supported scenario. Instead you must do a transition from these legacy Exchange Server(s) to Exchange 2007. A *transition* is the process in which you perform an upgrade to Exchange 2007—that is, you move data from any legacy Exchange servers in your Exchange organization to new Exchange 2007 servers, after which you decommission the legacy Exchange servers. A transition should not be confused with a migration; unlike a transition, a *migration* is the process in which you move data from a non-Exchange messaging system (such as GroupWise, Lotus Notes or SendMail) to an Exchange organization, or move data from a legacy Exchange organization in an existing Active Directory Forest to an Exchange organization in a new Active Directory Forest.

In this chapter we'll look more closely at performing a transition from a legacy Exchange organization consisting of a single Exchange 2003 server to an Exchange 2007 server, which will be installed as a typical Exchange Server installation.

Preparing the Environment for a Transition to Exchange Server 2007

Before we begin deploying the Exchange 2007 Server in our legacy Exchange organization, there are several preliminary requirements that we must complete. We need to prepare the Active Directory forest, the existing Exchange organization, and the server on which we plan to install Exchange Server 2007. In the following sections, we'll go through each preliminary requirement that must be completed before we even start to think about deploying Exchange Server 2007.

Preparing the Active Directory Forest

First we must make sure that the domain controller that is the schema master in the Active Directory forest runs Windows Server 2003 with at least Service Pack 1 applied. This is also true for any Global Catalog servers in each Active Directory site in which you plan to deploy Exchange 2007. We recommend that you run Windows Server 2003 with Service Pack 1 applied on all domain controllers in the Active Directory forest, since this version supports Exchange 2007 service notifications, allows users to browse the address book in Microsoft Outlook Web Access, and provides the ability to look up distribution list membership in a more efficient manner than in Windows 2000 Server.

> **NOTE**
>
> If you have any non-English domain controllers in your Active Directory Forest, you should also be sure you apply the hotfix mentioned in MS KB article 919166 (http://support.microsoft.com/kb/919166) to the respective domain controller; otherwise you can experience issues accessing the address book when you're using OWA 2007.

Although Exchange 2007 supports 32-bit-based Global Catalog servers, you should seriously consider replacing them with 64-bit-based servers instead. An organization with 20,000 Active Directory objects or more will gain a significant increase in performance by doing so. Actually, you can expect a 64-bit Global Catalog server with 14 GBs of RAM installed to handle the workload of up to 11 32-bit Global Catalog servers. Talk about an improvement that saves you a lot of money on hardware in the long term as well as patch management!

Finally, Exchange 2007 requires that the domain functional level is set to Windows 2000 Server or Windows Server 2003. You do this by following these steps:

1. Open the Active Directory Users and Computers MMC snap-in on a domain controller in your Active Directory, then right-click the **domain** and choose **Raise Domain Functional Level** in the context menu. Now change the domain functional level to **Windows Server 2003**, as shown in Figure 10.1, then click **Raise**.

Figure 10.1 Raising the Domain Functional Level to Windows Server 2003

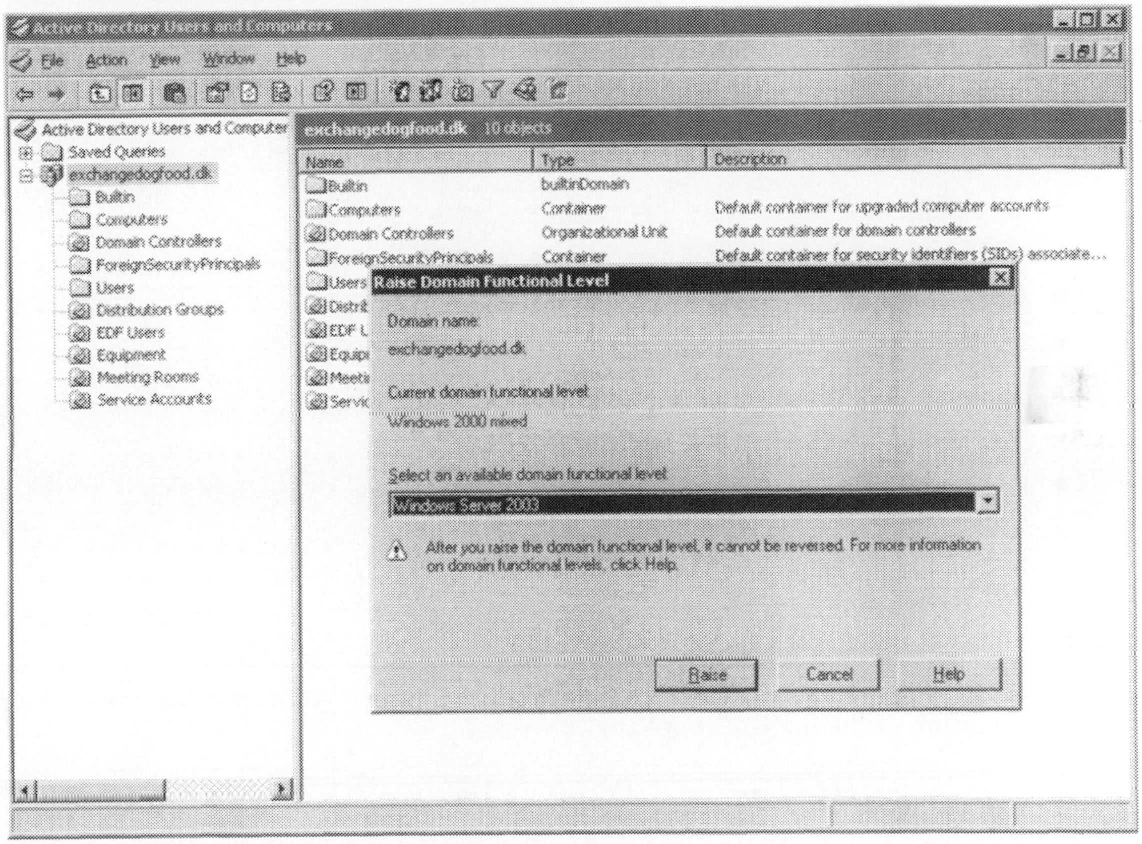

2. You will now receive an informational note similar to one shown in Figure 10.2. If you're dealing with a large topology that contains many domain controllers, you should keep this information in mind, but if you have only a couple of domain controllers deployed, you can safely ignore this information. Click **OK**.

Figure 10.2 Raise Domain Functional Level Information

Preparing the Legacy Exchange Organization

Since Exchange Server 2007 requires the legacy Exchange organization to run in native mode, we need to decommission any pre-Exchange 2000 servers (that is, Exchange 5.5 Servers and previous versions) that exist in the Exchange organization. Does this mean that you cannot do a transition directly from Exchange 5.5 to Exchange 2007 in the same Active Directory forest? Yes, that is correct! Those of you, hopefully few, who still have an Exchange 5.5 organization and want to move to Exchange 2007 must first upgrade to 2000 or 2003 and then do the transition from Exchange 2000 or 2003 to Exchange 2007.

You must also make sure that any Exchange 2000 servers in your Exchange organization run with Exchange 2000 Service Pack 3 and that any Exchange 2003 servers have Service Pack 2 applied. In addition, you should note that if you plan to keep at least one Exchange 2000 or 2003 server in the Exchange organization, the following services are unsupported by Exchange Server 2007:

- Novell GroupWise connector (Exchange 2003 Service)
- Microsoft Mobile Information Server (Exchange 2000 Service)
- Instant Messaging Service (Exchange 2000 Service)
- Exchange Chat Service (Exchange 2000 Service)
- Exchange 2000 Conferencing Server (Exchange 2000 Service)
- Key Management Service (Exchange 2000 Service)
- cc:Mail connector (Exchange 2000 Service)
- MS Mail connector (Exchange 2000 Service)

NOTE

At the time of this writing, the Exchange Product Group is working on an Exchange 2007 version of the Novell GroupWise connector.

When you're ready to switch your Exchange organization to native mode, you do so by following these steps:

1. Open the Exchange 2003 System Manager. Right-click the **Exchange Organization** node and select **Properties** in the context menu. Now click the **Change Mode** button, as shown in Figure 10.3.

Figure 10.3 Switch the Exchange Organization to Native Mode

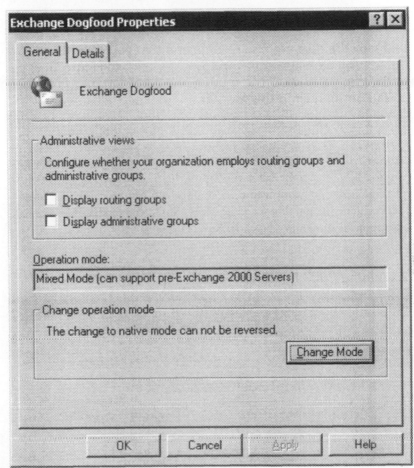

2   You will now receive a warning message similar to the one shown in Figure 10.4. Click
    Yes, click **OK**, and then close the Exchange 2003 System Manager.

Figure 10.4 Switch the Exchange Organization to Native Mode

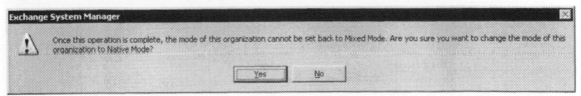

SOME INDEPENDENT ADVICE

If it's not already the case, we also recommend that you check **Display routing groups** and **Display administrative groups** (refer back to Figure 10.3) because we'll need to verify the existence of the routing and administrative groups created by Exchange 2007 Setup later in this chapter.

If you're unsure whether your environment is ready for the deployment of the first Exchange 2007 server, it's a good idea to run the latest version of the Exchange Best Practices Analyzer (ExBPA) to see if there's anything you need to do before you can proceed. The latest version of ExBPA, version 2.7, which you can download at www.exbpa.com, includes an Exchange 2007 Readiness Check option, as shown in Figure 10.5.

Figure 10.5 Exchange 2007 Readiness Check Option in ExBPA 2.7

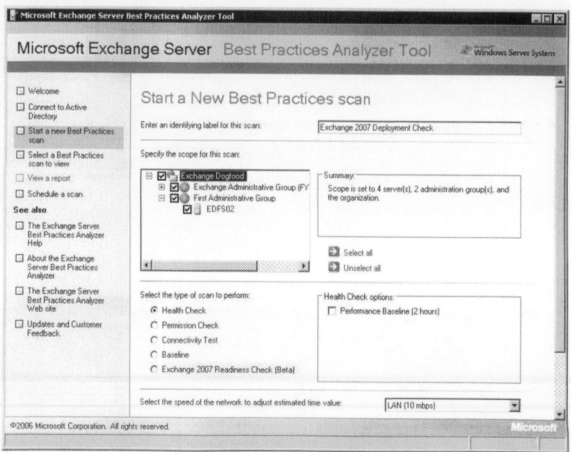

Suppressing Link State Updates

Depending on your topology, Link State updates must be suppressed on any Exchange 2000 or 2003 servers in the Exchange legacy organization when you're deploying an Exchange 2007 Server. Bear in mind, however, that this is required only if you're planning to establish more than one routing group connector in the organization.

To suppress Link State updates on any Exchange 2000 or 2003 servers in your organization:

1. Log onto the respective servers, then open the registry editor by clicking **Start | Run** and typing **regedit** followed by pressing **Enter**.

2. Now navigate to **HKEY_LOCAL_MACHINE\System\CurrentControlSet\Services\ RESvc\Parameters** and right-click on **Parameters**, then select **New | DWORD**. Type **SuppressStateChanges** as the name value for the new DWORD. Finally, double-click **SuppressStateChanges** and enable it by entering **1** in the data value field, as shown in Figure 10.6.

When the *SuppressStateChanges* key has been created, close the registry editor, then restart the Simple Mail Transfer Protocol (SMTP) service, the Microsoft Exchange Routing Engine service, and Microsoft Exchange MTA Stacks service so that the change takes effect.

Figure 10.6 Suppressing Link State Updates

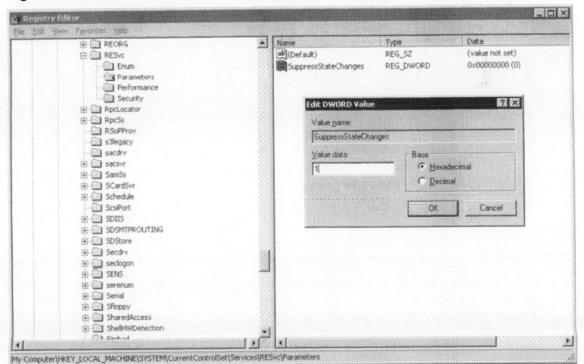

For the purpose of this explanation, we're deploying a single Exchange 2007 server into a legacy Exchange organization consisting of a single Exchange 2003 server, which means we don't need to suppress Link State updates. But as mentioned, this is a required step on all legacy Exchange servers if you're planning to establish more than one routing group connector in your Exchange organization. Keep this in mind if you're planning to move from a multiple Exchange 2000 or 2003 scenario to Exchange 2007.

Extending the Active Directory

With all prerequisites fulfilled, we can move on and prepare the Active Directory using the respective Exchange 2007 Setup.exe switches. Exchange 2007 Setup includes several switches; in this section we'll go through each of those related to preparing the Active Directory.

IMPORTANT

Each of the switches we discuss here will run automatically during the deployment of the first Exchange 2007 server in the Exchange legacy organization (if the account you're logged on with has Schema and Enterprise Admin rights!), so it's not mandatory that you run them before installing Exchange 2007. However, depending on the size as well as the topology of your environment, it might be wise to prepare the Active Directory first using these switches before you start the actual deployment process.

Prepare Legacy Exchange Permissions

The first thing we need to do in deploying an Exchange 2007 into a legacy Exchange organization is to run *Setup.com /PrepareLegacyExchangePermissions,* to grant specific Exchange permissions in the Active Directory domain(s) in which one or more Exchange 2000 or 2003 Servers exists or where Exchange 2000 or 2003 *DomainPrep* has been executed. The reason we must run *Setup.com /PrepareLegacyExchangePermissions* is that the Exchange 2003 or Exchange 2000 Recipient Update Service won't otherwise function correctly after the Active Directory schema has been updated with Exchange 2007-specific attributes.

TIP

For a detailed explanation of why *Setup.com /PrepareLegacyExchangePermissions* must be run in an Active Directory domain in which one or more Exchange 2000 or 2003 Servers exists or where Exchange 2000 or 2003 *DomainPrep* has been executed, search for "preparing legacy Exchange permissions" in the Exchange 2007 Documentation found at www.microsoft.com/technet/prodtechnol/exchange/e2k7help.

To run *Setup.com /PrepareLegacyExchangePermissions,* you must open a Command Prompt window and navigate to the directory, network share, or DVD media containing your Exchange 2007 Setup files, then simply type **Setup.com /PrepareLegacyExchangePermissions** followed by pressing **Enter**, as shown in Figure 10.7. Bear in mind that the account you're logged on with must be a member of the Enterprise Admins group.

Figure 10.7 Preparing Legacy Exchange Server Permissions

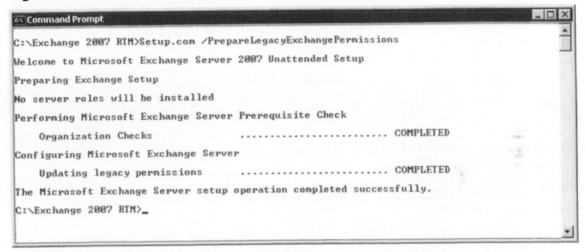

Some Independent Advice

Some of you might be in a situation where you want to prepare the Active Directory domain before you install the x64-bit version of Windows Server 2003 on a server in the Active Directory forest, and therefore you cannot run *Setup.com /PrepareLegacy-ExchangePermissions* using the 64-bit version of Exchange 2007 because you don't have any x64-bit Windows 2003 Servers deployed yet. But fear not—using the 32-bit version of Exchange 2007 to *prepare* your production Active Directory environment is fully supported. As mentioned in the introduction to this chapter, the 32-bit version of Exchange 2007 is not supported in a production environment except for management tasks, and preparing the Active Directory is considered a management task.

Prepare Schema

The next command to run to prepare the environment is *Setup.com /PrepareSchema,* which will connect to the domain controller schema master and import LDAP files to update the schema with Exchange 2007-specific attributes. To do so, open a Command Prompt window and type **Setup.com /PrepareSchema** followed by pressing **Enter**, as we did with the previous switch.

Setup will now update the schema as necessary, as shown in Figure 10.8. To run this command, the account you're logged on with must be a member of both the Enterprise and Schema Admins groups.

Figure 10.8 Running Setup.com with the *PrepareSchema* Switch

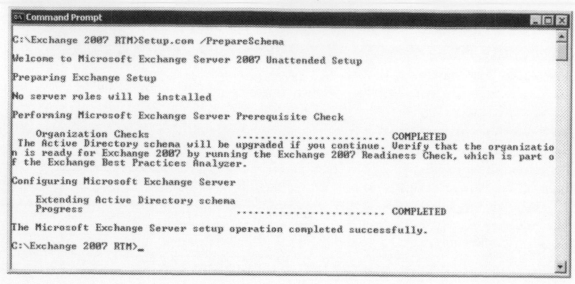

Prepare AD

The *Setup.com /PrepareAD* command is used to configure global Exchange objects in Active Directory, create the Exchange Universal Security Groups (USGs) in the root domain, and prepare the current domain. The global objects reside under the Exchange organization container. In addition, this command creates the Exchange 2007 Administrative Group, which is named Exchange Administrative Group (FYDIBOHF23SPDLT), as well as creating the Exchange 2007 Routing Group, called Exchange Routing Group (DWBGZMFD01QNBJR).

You can run the *Setup.com /PrepareAD* command before running */PrepareLegacyExchangePermissions* and */PrepareSchema,* as shown in Figure 10.9. Doing so will run the */PrepareLegacyExchangePermissions* and */PrepareSchema* commands automatically. Running this command requires you log on with an account that is a member of the Enterprise Admins group.

Figure 10.9 Running Setup.com with the *PrepareAD* Switch

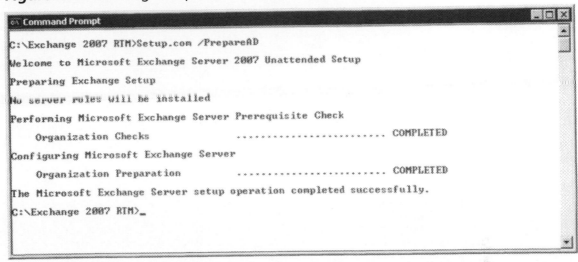

As you might be aware, Exchange 2007 doesn't use Routing Groups and Administrative Groups, as Exchange 2000 or 2003 did. Administrative Groups have been dropped completely, and message routing in Exchange 2007 is based on Active Directory sites. But for Exchange 2007 to c-exist with Exchange 2000 or 2003, Exchange must create the mentioned Administrative Group and Routing Group, which can only be viewed via an Exchange 2000 or 2003 System Manager or by using ADSI Edit, as shown in Figures 10.10 and 10.11.

Figure 10.10 Exchange 2007 Administrative and Routing Group in the Exchange 2003 System Manager

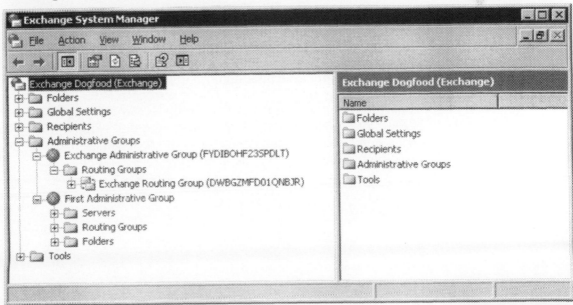

Figure 10.11 Exchange 2007 Administrative and Routing Groups in ADSI Edit

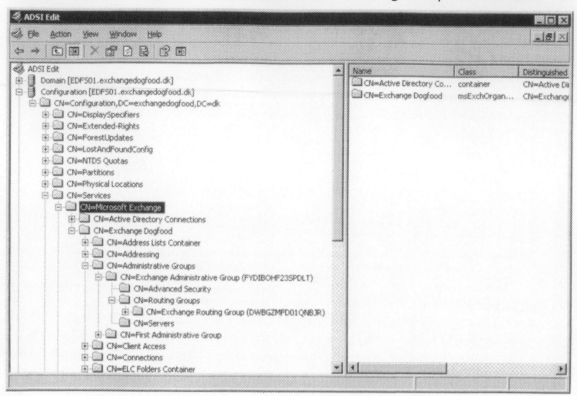

SOME INDEPENDENT ADVICE

Okay, with all these boring switches, it's time for a little fun! Did you know that although coding a product such as Exchange 2007 is a lot of hard work, the Exchange Product Group always has time for a little humor? To prove it, let's take the GUID of the Administrative Group shown in Figure 10.10 and shift each letter upward. Now do the same for the GUID of the Exchange Routing Group shown in Figure 10.11, but do it downward. Did you manage to see what it translates to? Yes, it's EXCHANGE12ROCKS!

For those who don't know, "Exchange 12" was the codename for Exchange Server 2007 until the product got a real name in April 2006.

PrepareDomain and *PrepareAllDomains*

It's also possible to prepare a local domain or all domains in the Active Directory using the *Setup.com / PrepareDomain* and *Setup.com /PrepareAllDomains,* respectively. These switches will set permissions on the Domain container for the Exchange servers, Exchange Organization Administrators, Authenticated Users, and Exchange Mailbox Administrators; create the Microsoft Exchange System Objects container if it does not exist; set permissions on this container for the Exchange servers, Exchange Organization Administrators, and Authenticated Users; and in the current domain, create a new domain global group called Exchange Install Domain Servers. In addition, it will add the Exchange Install Domain Servers group to the Exchange Servers USG in the root domain.

Like the commands we've already been through, these commands also need to be run from a Command Prompt window, as shown in Figure 10.12.

Figure 10.12 Running Setup.com with the *PrepareDomain* Switch

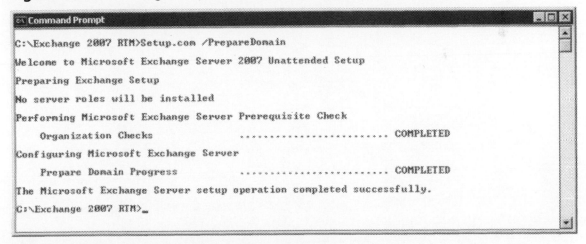

Preparing the Exchange 2007 Server

When our environment has been prepared for Exchange Server 2007, the next step is to prepare the server on which you plan to install Exchange 2007 and then begin the actual Exchange installation. Since all these steps were covered intensely in Chapter 2, we won't repeat them here, but we will quickly mention a couple of things that are different in installing Exchange 2007 into a legacy Exchange organization. During the installation, you're given the option of creating a routing group connector between the administrative group containing the legacy Exchange server(s) and the Exchange 2007 administrative group, as shown in Figure 10.13.

Figure 10.13 Preparing the Exchange 2007 Routing Group Connector

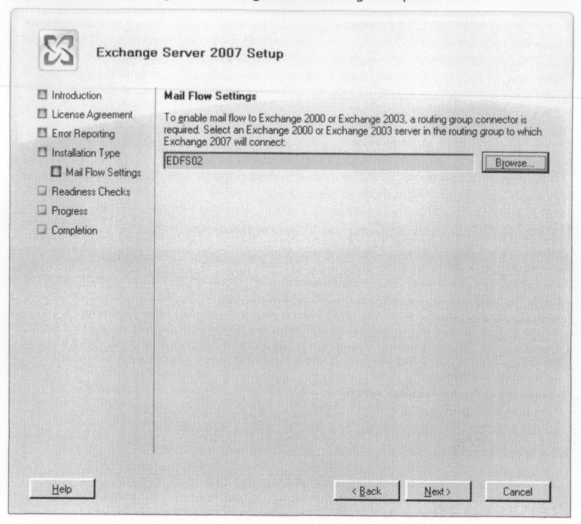

This routing group connector is created in both directions and needs to be created to establish mail flow between the servers in the legacy routing group and the Exchange 2007 routing group. In addition, the Exchange 2007 Setup Wizard won't ask you whether a Public Folder database to support legacy Outlook clients should be created but will instead do so automatically. The reason behind this behavior is probably that the Exchange Product Group took for granted that all organizations that will make a transition to Exchange 2007 still have legacy Outlook clients deployed in the organization.

When Exchange 2007 has been installed successfully, you should remember to complete the tasks listed under the Deployment tab on the Microsoft Exchange node, or at least the tasks relevant to your environment. You should also skim through the optional tasks list on the End-to-End Scenario tab. Again, refer to Chapter 2 for further information.

Exchange 2003 and Exchange 2007 Coexistence

It should come as no surprise that there are several things you should be aware of when you're dealing with a coexistence environment consisting of Exchange or 2003 and Exchange 2007. Most of the management-related tasks (creating and moving mailboxes and administering public folders) were mentioned in Chapter 3, but there are also a few things you should be aware of when it comes to organization wide or global settings.

When the first Exchange 2007 server has been deployed in the legacy Exchange organization, most of the Global Settings that originally were configured on an Exchange 2000 or 2003 server will be transferred to the Exchange 2007 Server automatically, since global Exchange settings are stored in Active Directory. This means that recipient policies, Internet Message Formats, SMTP connectors, and Exchange delegation permissions are applied to user mailboxes stored on the Exchange 2007 as well.

SOME INDEPENDENT ADVICE

Any Exchange ActiveSync (EAS) device policy settings you have enabled on an Exchange 2003 SP2 server will not be transferred to Exchange 2007. This means that you must make sure that you enable any EAS polices you created on the Exchange 2007 server for the legacy mailboxes you move to the Exchange 2007 server.

Figure 10.14 shows you the default policy originally created on our Exchange 2003 server.

Figure 10.14 The Exchange 2003 Default Policy

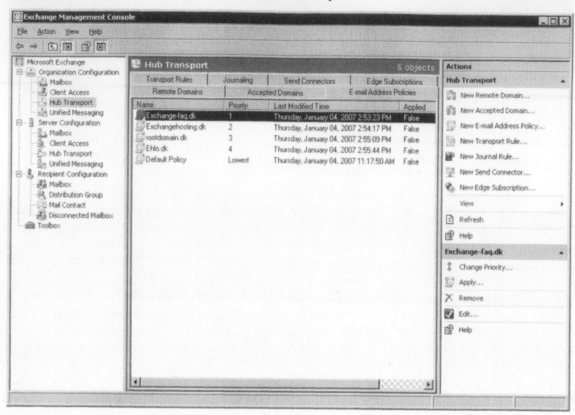

Also note that when the Exchange 2007 server has been deployed in the legacy Exchange organization, any of the organization-level settings should be managed using Exchange 2007 Management tools (EMC or EMS) during the coexistence period.

Replicating Public Folders to Exchange 2007

When you deploy an Exchange 2007 server with the Mailbox Server role installed into a legacy Exchange organization, Exchange Setup will create one Mailbox database and one Public Folder database on the server by default, as shown in Figure 10.15.

The Public Folder database is created so that you can replicate any Public Folder data stored on your legacy Exchange servers to Exchange 2007. Even if you don't use Public Folders to store data in

Figure 10.15 Exchange 2007 Mailbox and Public Folder Databases

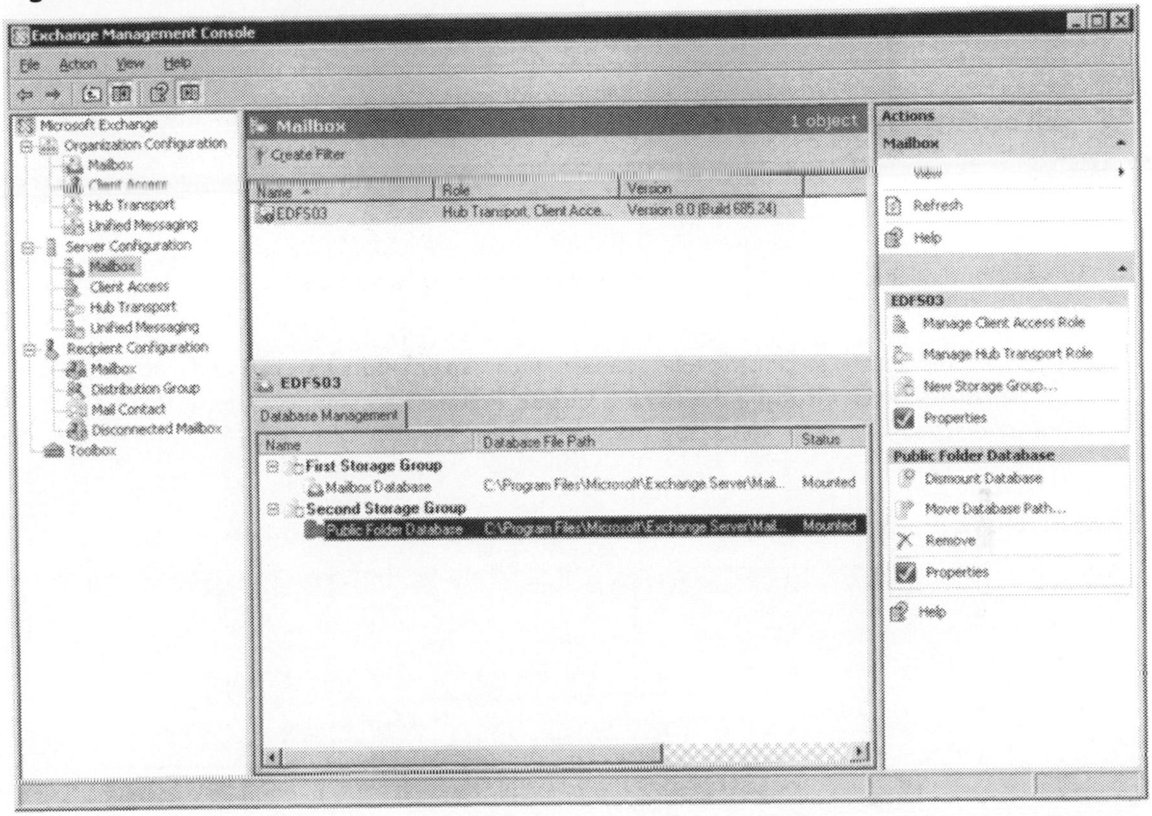

your environment, there's one other reason you might want to keep the Public Folder database mounted on your Exchange 2007 server. As you might know, Exchange 2007 no longer uses a Public Folder (or more specifically, a System Folder named SCHEDULE+ FREE BUSY in your Public Folder hierarchy) to store free/busy information for the mailbox users in the organization. Instead, free/busy information is stored directly in each user's mailbox and retrieved using a new Web-based service called the Availability service. The advantage of this new approach is that there are no longer any 15-minute delays when free/busy time for a user is updated. Instead, the update happens instantly. So why would we want to keep the Public Folder database on our Exchange 2007 server if free/busy information is retrieved using this new method? If you still have legacy Outlook clients (that is, Outlook 2003 and earlier versions) running in your organization, these clients still need to use the Public Folder method to retrieve free/busy information, since only Outlook 2007 supports the new Availability service.

If you don't use Public Folders to store data and only have Outlook 2007 clients deployed in your organization, you can safely remove the Public Folder database because you don't have anything to use it for. This also means you can skip the following steps.

Okay, let's get going with setting up a replica for the Public Folders on our Exchange 2003 server that should be replicated with the new Exchange 2007 Public Folder database. To do so, we must use either the Exchange 2003 System Manager or the EMS. For the purpose of this example, we'll use the Exchange 2003 System Manager.

NOTE

Managing Public Folders using the EMC is not possible in Exchange 2007 RTM but will be integrated into Exchange 2007 Service Pack 1.

To add the Exchange 2007 Public Folder database to the replica list on the Exchange 2003 server, do the following:

1. Open the Exchange 2003 System Manager, then expand **Administrative Groups | First Administrative Group | Folders | Public Folders,** as shown in Figure 10.16.

Figure 10.16 Public Folders in the Exchange 2003 System Manager

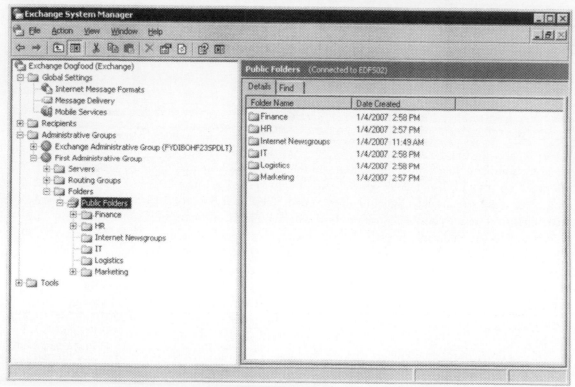

2. Now open the **Properties** page of each public folder, then click the **Replication** tab and add the **Exchange 2007 server** to the replica list, as shown in Figure 10.17.

Figure 10.17 Public Folder Replication Tab

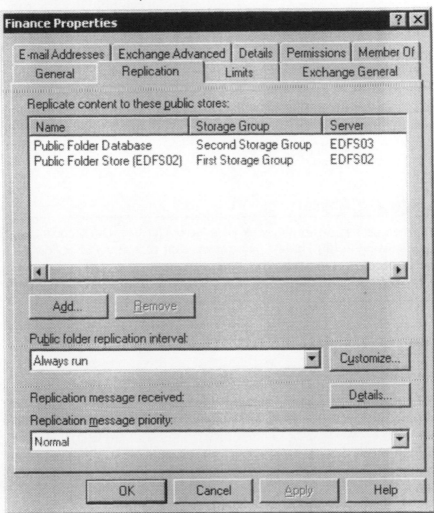

> **NOTE**
>
> Exchange 2003 Service Pack 2 introduced a new Public Folder Settings Wizard that makes it a breeze to add servers to replica lists. So if you have a lot of Public Folders in your Public Folder tree, we highly recommend that you use this wizard, which you can read more about in one of the author's article at MSExchange.org (www.msexchange.org/tutorials/Public-Folder-Improvements-Exchange-2003-Service-Pack-2.html). If you have thousands of Public Folders, you might want to use the Public Folder replica scripts located in the Exchange Scripts folder (which can be found under C:\Program Files\Microsoft\Exchange Server).

Even if you have legacy Outlook clients in your organization, you don't need to set up a replica for the SCHEDULE+ FREE BUSY or the OFFLINE ADDRESS BOOK system folder, since this will be done automatically when you deploy an Exchange 2007 server in a legacy Exchange organization.

When all Public Folders have been replicated to the Exchange 2007 server, you can remove the old Exchange 2000 or 2003 server(s) from the replica lists and then dismount the old Public Folder database. You should verify that your clients still are capable of seeing Public Folder data as well free/busy information and accessing the offline address book before you delete it, though. If this is not the case, we recommend that you wait a little longer so that you're sure the replication has occurred properly.

Some Independent Advice

Unlike previous versions of Outlook Web Access (OWA), OWA 2007 doesn't include a GUI for accessing Public Folders. This means that to access Public Folders using Internet Explorer, you must open a separate browser window and type **https://FQDN/public**. It's important that you're aware of this missing feature.

Pointing Internet Clients to the Client Access Server

Now would be a good time to point any Internet client that is OWA, EAS, or RPC over HTTP (now called Outlook AnyWhere) in your organization to the client access server running on the Exchange 2007 server. If you're using a firewall such as ISA Server (which you do, right?), this change is done at your ISA Server firewall. If for some reason you don't use an ISA Server in your DMZ but perhaps a Check Point FireWall-1 or another "firewall" such as a Cisco PIX, you should do the redirection there. If you don't have a firewall, you should make the change on the external DNS server hosting your Internet domain.

Note

If your ISA server is configured to preauthenticate your OWA users, you must change the Authentication method for the OWA virtual directory under **Server Configuration | Client Access** in the EMC to **Basic** authentication, since it's configured to use forms-based authentication by default.

So, you ask, will any users with a mailbox on my Exchange 2000 or 2003 server still be able to use OWA, Exchange ActiveSync, or Outlook AnyWhere (formerly known as RPC over HTTP) to access their mailboxes? Yes, this will work just fine, since the client access server is backward compatible and will redirect the clients to the respective legacy mailboxes on the Exchange 2000 or 2003 server.

NOTE

When you make these changes, your users will no longer be able to access their mailboxes using Outlook Mobile Access (OMA), because OMA has been discontinued in Exchange 2007.

Moving Legacy Mailboxes to Exchange 2007

Now we have reached the point at which we're going to move our legacy mailboxes from Exchange 2000 or 2003 Server to Exchange 2007. Doing so is a straightforward process and can be done using either the Move Mailbox Wizard in the EMC or the *Move-Mailbox* CMDlet in the EMS. We'll use the EMC. Do the following:

1. If it's not already open, launch the EMC, then expand the **Recipient Configuration** work center and click the **Mailbox** subnode. Now highlight all the legacy mailboxes, as shown in Figure 10.18, and then click the **Move Mailbox** task in the Action pane.

Figure 10.18 Selecting Legacy Mailboxes in the Exchange Management Console

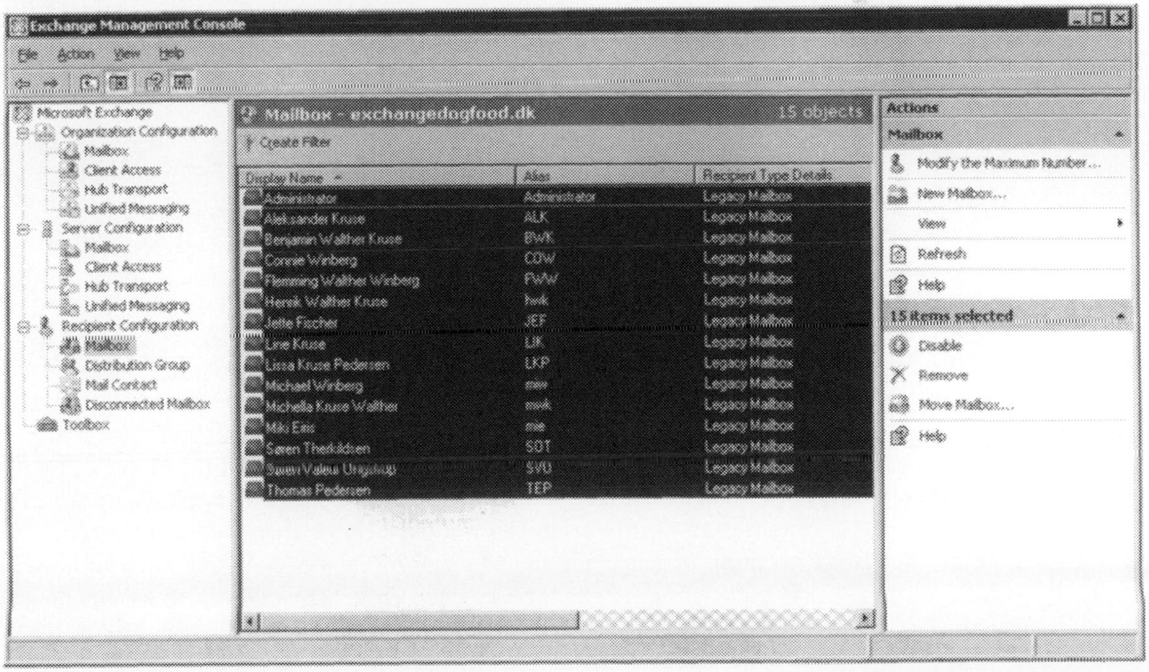

2. This will launch the Exchange 2007 Move Mailbox Wizard, where you need to specify the destination server, storage group, and mailbox database. Select the **Exchange 2007 Server** in the drop-down box (see Figure 10.19), and then click **Next**.

Figure 10.19 Specifying the Exchange 2007 Server as the Destination Server

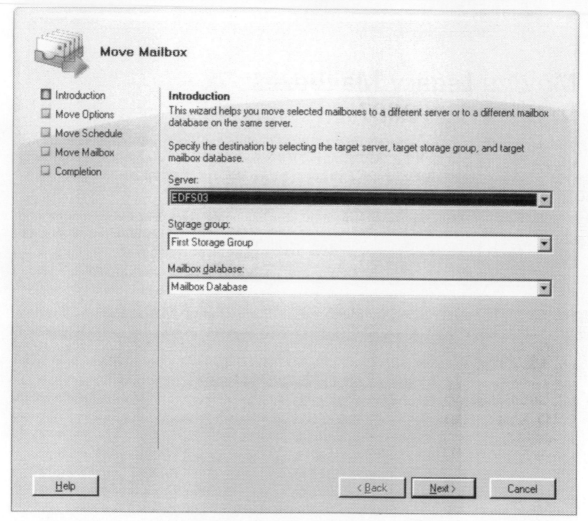

3. On the Move Option page, specify how you want to manage any corrupted messages found in a mailbox, then click **Next**. This will bring us to the Move Schedule page, where we can specify whether we want to move the mailboxes immediately or at a scheduled time. In addition, we have the option of cancelling the Move Mailbox job after X number of hours. When you have made your selections, click **Next**, then click **Move** on the Move Mailbox page to begin moving the mailboxes to the Exchange 2007 server, as shown in Figure 10.20.

Figure 10.20 The Move Mailboxes Summary Page

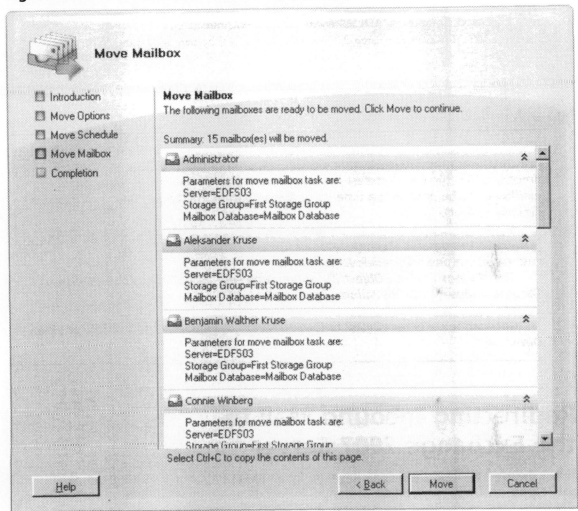

As is the case with the Move Mailbox Wizard in Exchange 2003, the Exchange 2007 Move Mailbox Wizard can move four mailboxes at a time, and only one instance of the wizard can run on a server.

4. When all the mailboxes have been moved to the Exchange 2007 server, click **Finish** to exit the Move Mailbox Wizard, and then check to make sure that mail flow between the Internet and the mailboxes on the Exchange 2007 server works as expected in both directions.

If you will be running in a coexistence environment for a period of time, it's important to understand that mailboxes stored on an Exchange 2007 server must not be managed using the Active Directory Users and Computers (ADUC) MMC snap-in but instead must be managed using the EMC or the EMS. However, Exchange 2003 mailboxes can still be managed using ADUC.

NOTE

If you want to move the mailboxes using the EMS, do so using the *Move-Mailbox* CMDlet. Using the *Move-Mailbox* CMDlet gives you a set of advanced options, among which the most interesting one is the option of specifying the number of mailboxes to be moved at a time (as you read earlier, the Move Mailbox Wizard is limited to four).

If you wanted to move all mailboxes from a legacy Exchange server named EDFS02 to the default Mailbox database on an Exchange 2007 server named EDFS03, you could use one of the below commands:

Get-Mailbox | Where-Object {$_.servername –eq "EDFS02"} | Move-Mailbox –TargetDatabase: "EDFS03Mailbox Database"

or

Get-mailbox –Server EDFS02 | Move-Mailbox –TargetDatabase "EDFS03Mailbox Database"

Redirecting Inbound Mail to the Exchange 2007 Server

When all legacy mailboxes have been moved to the Exchange 2007 server, we can point SMTP traffic (port 25/TCP) directly to the Exchange 2007 server so that inbound messages are routed directly to it. It's recommended to deploy an Edge Transport server in your perimeter network (DMZ) and let this server route inbound messages to the Exchange 2007 server on your internal network. For instructions on how to deploy an Edge Transport server, see Chapter 7.

If you don't want to deploy an Edge Transport server, you should bear in mind that you need to change the Permission Groups settings on the Default <server> receive connector under the Server Configuration work center node | Hub Transport subnode in the EMC so that Anonymous users are allowed to connect to the Exchange 2007 server, as shown in Figure 10.21. Otherwise you won't be able to receive e-mail messages from other SMTP servers on the Internet.

Figure 10.21 Permission Groups Settings on the Default Receive Connector

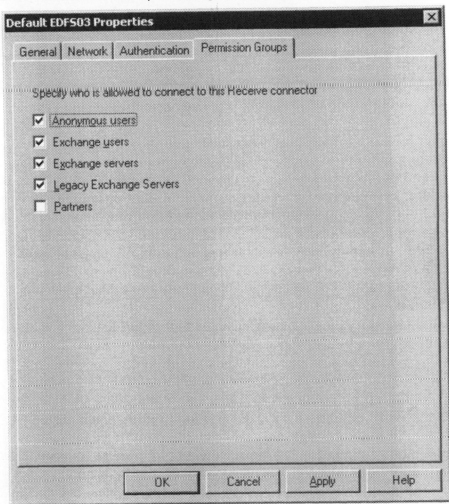

In addition, you should make sure that any Send connector on the Organization Configuration | Hub Transport | Send Connector tab is configured properly so that it can send outbound mail (using either a smart host or DNS MX), as shown in Figure 10.22.

Figure 10.22 Permission Groups Settings on the Default Receive Connector

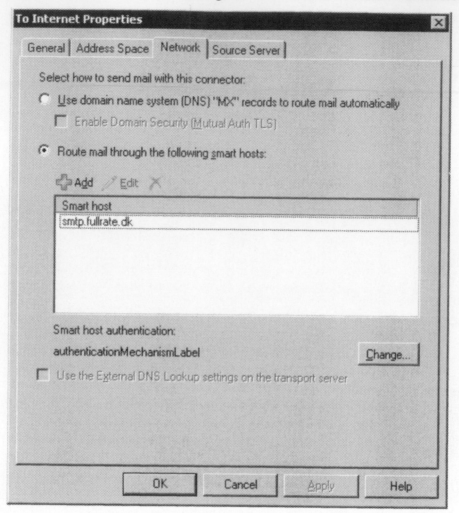

When the necessary changes have been made, we can delete the routing group connector that was set up to establish mail flow between the Exchange 2003 and 2007 routing groups. To do so:

1. Expand **Administrative Groups** | **First Administrative Group** | **Routing Groups** | **Connectors** and right-click the respective **Routing Group Connector,** then select **Delete** in the context menu, as shown in Figure 10.23.

Figure 10.23 Deleting the Routing Groups Connector

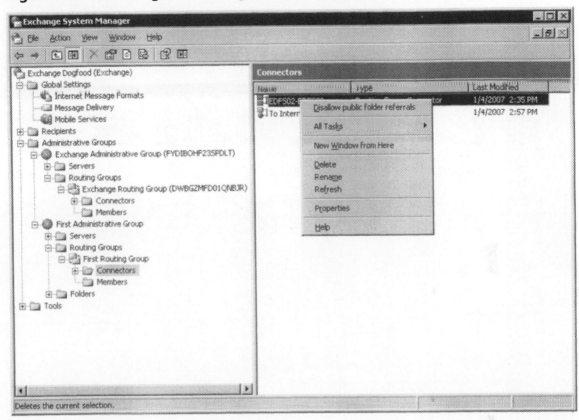

2. Since the routing group connector won't be deleted at both ends, you also need to delete it under the **Exchange Administrative Group (FYDIBOHF23SPDLT)** | **Exchange Routing Group (DWBGZMFD01QNBJR)** | **Connectors.**

Decommissioning the Legacy Exchange Server

The final step is to decommission the Exchange 2000 or 2003 server and we can consider the transition done. The Exchange 2003 server should be removed using the Exchange 2003 Setup program, which can be launched via Add or Remove Programs (see Figure 10.24).

Figure 10.24 Add or Remove Programs

Before we begin uninstalling the Exchange 2003 server, we first need to assign the Recipient Update Service (RUS) to our Exchange 2007 server. We do this not because RUS should be used (in fact, Exchange 2007 no longer uses RUS) but because the Exchange 2003 Setup program won't let us uninstall Exchange 2003 before RUS has been assigned to another server. To assign RUS to the Exchange 2007 Server:

1. Open the Exchange 2003 System Manager, then expand the **Recipients** node and select **Recipient Update Services**. Now open the **Properties** pages for both Recipient Update Service (Enterprise Configuration) and Recipient Update Service (domain), then click the **Browse** button under the **Exchange Server** text box and specify the Exchange 2007 Server instead. Click **OK** twice and close the System Manager, as shown in Figure 10.25.

Figure 10.25 Assigning the Recipient Update Service to the Exchange 2007 Server

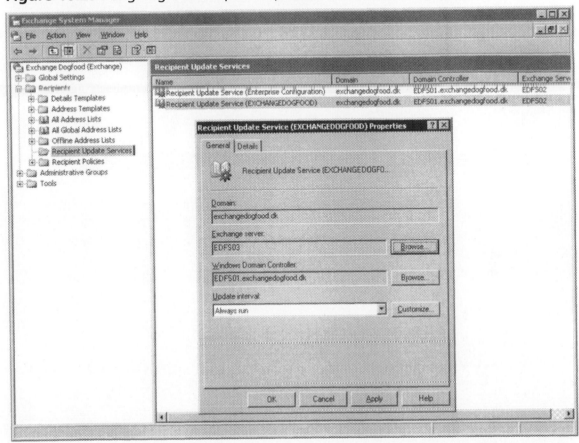

2. Now we can continue uninstalling the server, so select **Microsoft Exchange**, then click the **Change/Remove** button.

3. The Exchange 2000 or 2003 Wizard will appear. Click **Next**, then select **Remove** in the Action drop-down box, as shown in Figure 10.26. Click **Next**.

Figure 10.26 Exchange 2003 Installation Wizard Component Selection Page

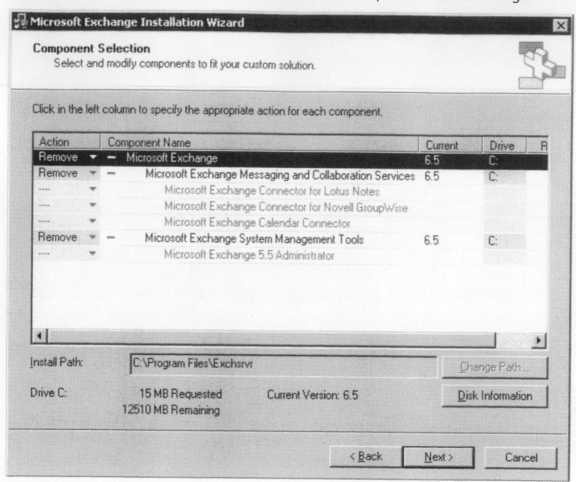

4. On the Installation Summary page, click **Next**, and wait for the Exchange 2003 uninstall process to complete (see Figure 10.27).

Figure 10.27 The Exchange 2003 Uninstall Process

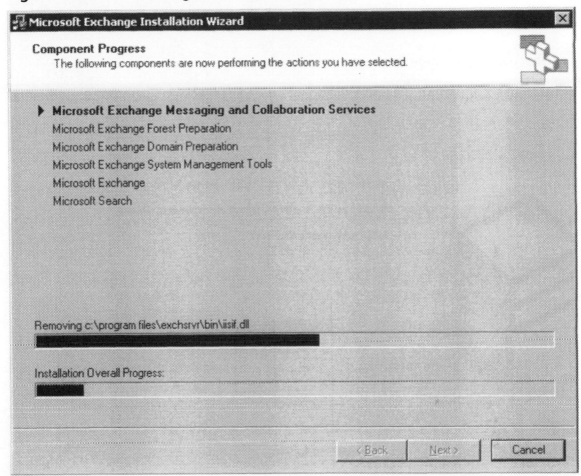

NOTE

If the Exchange 2000 Setup files aren't located on an accessible drive or network share, you will be prompted to insert the Exchange 2003 CD media during the uninstallation process.

5. When the uninstall process has completed, click **Finish** to exit the Exchange 2003 Setup Wizard (see Figure 10.28).

Figure 10.28 Exchange 2003 Successfully Uninstalled

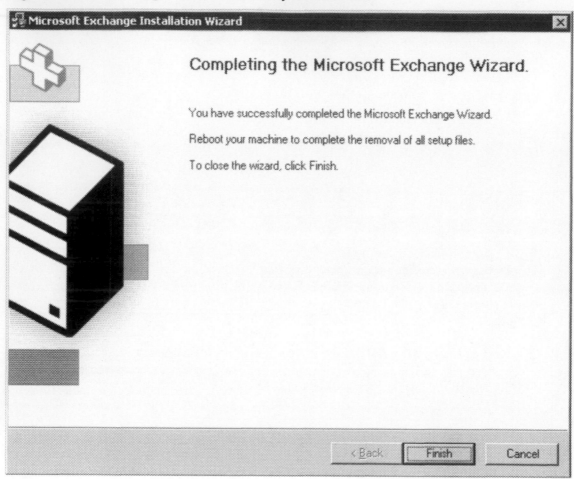

> **NOTE**
>
> If the Exchange 2003 uninstallation fails for some reason, it could be necessary to remove the Exchange 2003 server by deleting the Server object in the Exchange System Manager, or if you're unsuccessful doing this, too, then by using ADSI Edit.

Summary

As you saw throughout this chapter, making a transition from an Exchange 2000 or 2003 server to Exchange 2007 in the same Active Directory forest is a straightforward process, and since Exchange 2007 coexists just fine with legacy Exchange servers, you can do the transition at your own pace. Coexistence support is laudable, since a transition process typically happens in several phases. First, you redirect your Internet clients to the client access server (CAS), then move the legacy mailboxes to the Mailbox server, and finally, point inbound mail to the Hub Transport server.

Solutions Fast Track

Preparing the Environment for a Transition to Exchange Server 2007

☑ The domain controller that is the schema master in the Active Directory forest should run Windows Server 2003 with at least Service Pack 1 applied.

☑ Any Global Catalog servers in each Active Directory site in which you plan to deploy Exchange 2007 should run Windows Server 2003 with at least Service Pack 1 applied.

☑ For any non-English domain controllers in your Active Directory forest, apply the hotfix mentioned in MS KB article 919166 (http://support.microsoft.com/kb/919166).

☑ Exchange 2007 requires that the domain functional level is set to Windows 2000 Server or Windows Server 2003.

☑ Since Exchange Server 2007 requires that the legacy Exchange organization is running in native mode, we need to decommission any pre-Exchange 2000 servers (that is, Exchange 5.5 servers and previous versions) that exist in the Exchange organization.

☑ Depending on your topology, Link State updates must be suppressed on any Exchange 2000 or 2003 servers in the Exchange legacy organization when you're deploying an Exchange 2007 Server. Bear in mind that this is required only if you're planning to establish more than one routing group connector in the organization.

Exchange 2003 and Exchange 2007 Coexistence

☑ are several things you should be aware of in dealing with a coexistence environment consisting of Exchange or 2003 and Exchange 2007. Most of the management-related tasks (creating and moving mailboxes and administering public folders) were mentioned in Chapter 3.

☑ Most of the Global Settings that originally were configured on an Exchange 2000 or 2003 server will be transferred to the Exchange 2007 server automatically, since global

Exchange settings are stored in Active Directory. This means that recipient policies, Internet Message Formats, SMTP connectors, and Exchange delegation permissions are applied to user mailboxes stored on the Exchange 2007 as well.

☑ Any Exchange ActiveSync (EAS) device policy settings you have enabled on an Exchange 2003 SP2 server will not be transferred to Exchange 2007. This means that you must make sure that you enable any EAS polices you created on the Exchange 2007 server for the legacy mailboxes you move to the Exchange 2007 Server.

Replicating Public Folders to Exchange 2007

☑ Managing Public Folders using the EMC is not possible in Exchange 2007 RTM but will be integrated with Exchange 2007 Service Pack 1.

☑ Even if you don't use Public Folders to store data in your environment, there's one other reason that you might want to keep the Public Folder database mounted on your Exchange 2007 server. As you might know, Exchange 2007 no longer uses a Public Folder (or more specifically, a System Folder named SCHEDULE+ FREE BUSY in your Public Folder hierarchy) to store free/busy information for the mailbox users in the organization. Instead, free/busy information is stored directly in each user's mailbox and retrieved using a new Web-based service called the Availability service.

☑ If you don't use Public Folders to store data and only have Outlook 2007 clients deployed in your organization, you can safely remove the Public Folder database because you don't have anything to use it for.

☑ Unlike previous versions of Outlook Web Access (OWA), OWA 2007 doesn't include a GUI for accessing Public Folders. This means that to access Public Folders using Internet Explorer, you must open a separate browser window and type **https://FQDN/public**. It's important that you're aware of this missing feature.

Pointing Internet Clients to the Client Access Server

☑ When the CAS has been deployed, you should point any Internet client that is OWA, EAS, or RPC over HTTP (now called Outlook AnyWhere) in your organization to the client access server running on the Exchange 2007 server. If you're using a firewall such as ISA Server, this change is done at your ISA Server firewall. If for some reason you don't use ISA Server in your DMZ but perhaps a Check Point FireWall-1 or a wannabe firewall such as a Cisco PIX, you should do the redirection there.

☑ When you have pointed your Internet clients to the CAS, your users will no longer be able to access their mailboxes using Outlook Mobile Access (OMA), because OMA has been discontinued in Exchange 2007.

Moving Legacy Mailboxes to Exchange 2007

☑ Moving legacy mailboxes to an Exchange 207 Mailbox server is a straightforward process and can be done using either the Move Mailbox Wizard in the EMC or the *Move-Mailbox* CMDlet in the EMS.

☑ If you will be running in a coexistence environment for a period of time, it's important to understand that mailboxes stored on an Exchange 2007 server must not be managed using the Active Directory Users and Computers (ADUC) MMC snap-in but instead must be managed using the EMC or the EMS. However, Exchange 2003 mailboxes can still be managed using ADUC.

☑ If you want to move the mailboxes using the EMS, do so using the *Move-Mailbox* CMDlet. Using the *Move-Mailbox* CMDlet gives you a set of advanced options, among which the most interesting one is the option of specifying the number of mailboxes to be moved at a time (the Move Mailbox Wizard is limited to four).

Redirecting Inbound Mail to the Exchange 2007 Server

☑ When all legacy mailboxes have been moved to an Exchange 2007 server, we can point SMTP traffic (port 25/TCP) directly to the Exchange 2007 server so that inbound messages are routed directly to it.

☑ It's recommended to deploy an Edge Transport server in your perimeter network (DMZ) and let this server route inbound messages to the Exchange 2007 server on your internal network.

☑ If you don't want to deploy an Edge Transport server, you should bear in mind that you need to change the Permission Groups settings on the Default <server> receive connector under the Server Configuration work center node | Hub Transport subnode in the EMC so that Anonymous users are allowed to connect to the Exchange 2007 server.

Decommissioning the Exchange Legacy Server

☑ Exchange 2003 server should be removed using the Exchange 2003 Setup program.

☑ Before uninstalling the Exchange 2003 server, we first need to assign the Recipient Update Service (RUS) to our Exchange 2007 server.

☑ Before uninstalling the Exchange 2003 server, we first need to delete the routing group connector assigned to the Exchange 2003 Server.

☑ If the Exchange 2000 Setup files aren't located on an accessible drive or network share, you will be prompted to insert the Exchange 2003 CD media during the uninstall process.

☑ If the Exchange 2003 uninstallation for some reason should fail, it might be necessary to remove the Exchange 2003 server by deleting the Server object in the Exchange System Manager, or if you're unsuccessful doing this, too, then by using ADSI Edit.

Frequently Asked Questions

Q: Can I do an in-place upgrade from Exchange Server 2000 or 2003 to Exchange 2007?

A: No. An in-place upgrade from an Exchange 2000 or 2003 server to Exchange 2007 is not supported. To upgrade from any of these Exchange legacy servers to Exchange 2007, you must perform a transition, meaning that you'll deploy Exchange 2007 into the existing Exchange organization and then move Exchange data and settings to Exchange 2007.

Q: Can I do a transition from Exchange 5.5 to Exchange 2007?

A: No. A transition from Exchange 5.5 or earlier versions is not supported. To move from Exchange 5.5 to Exchange 2007, you must first upgrade to Exchange 2000 or 2003 and then move to Exchange 2007 from there.

Q: In which order should I deploy Exchange 2003 Server roles when doing a transition from Exchange 2000 or 2003 to Exchange 2007?

A: In a scenario where you will install the different Exchange 2007 Server roles on different hardware, you should first deploy the CAS, then moved on and deploy the Edge Transport server in your DMZ. After you have deployed the Edge Transport server, you can deploy the Hub Transport server and then finally the Mailbox server. If you plan to use Unified Messaging (UM) in your organization, you should deploy this server role after the Mailbox Server roles have been properly deployed.

Q: How should I decommission any legacy Exchange servers (Exchange 2000 or 2003) when I've deployed Exchange 2007 in my Exchange organization?

A: First, you should make sure that you have deleted any routing group connector assigned to the respective Exchange 2000 or 2003 server. Then you should assign RUS to the Exchange 2007 server (because an Exchange server responsible for RUS cannot be uninstalled). You can then open the Exchange 2000 or 2003 Setup program and remove each Exchange component in the Setup menu.

Q: How do I establish a mail flow between the legacy Exchange servers and Exchange 2007 server in the organization?

A: Because of the routing topology changes in Exchange 2007, you must set up a routing group connector between the legacy routing group and the Exchange 2007 routing group. You have the option of doing this during setup, but it can also be accomplished afterward using the *New-RoutingGroup* CMDlet in the EMS.

Q: When I try to uninstall an Exchange 2000 or 2003 server using the Exchange Setup program, I receive an error message and cannot proceed. How should I remove the legacy Exchange server?

A: If you have moved all mailboxes from the legacy Exchange server, deleted any routing group connectors associated with it as well as assigned RUS to another server. (If you only have one legacy Exchange server, you can assign it to an Exchange 2007 server because it isn't used in Exchange 2007.) If you still receive an error message when trying to uninstall, you have two other options. You can either delete the respective server object using the Exchange System Manager, or if this isn't possible, use ADSI Edit.

Q: Will I lose all my global Exchange settings when I've finished the transition from Exchange 2000 or 2003 to Exchange 2007?

A: No. Global Exchange settings such as recipient policies, Internet Message Formats, SMTP connectors, and Exchange delegation permissions will be transferred to the Exchange 2007 server automatically, since global Exchange settings are stored in Active Directory.

Chapter 11

Introduction to Exchange Server 2007 Unified Messaging

Solutions in this chapter:

- **What Is Exchange 2007 Unified Messaging?**
- **Exchange 2007 Unified Messaging Features**
- **The Unified Messaging Infrastructure**
- **The Unified Messaging Mailbox Policies**

☑ **Summary**

☑ **Solutions Fast Track**

☑ **Frequently Asked Questions**

Introduction

Unified Messaging is the integration of voice, fax, and e-mail messages into the user's Inbox. Exchange Server 2007 Unified Messaging connects Exchange Server with the existing telephony network infrastructure to provide access to different kinds of messages in a single location. After reading this chapter, you will have a thorough understanding of Unified Messaging and the way it is integrated into Exchange 2007. Furthermore, you will know the different Unified Messaging components and features that make up the Exchange 2007 Unified Messaging service.

Bear in mind that this chapter is an introduction to the feature set provided by the Unified Messaging server role, and not a comprehensive chapter on how to configure and integrate UM with your existing PBX infrastructure.

What Is Exchange 2007 Unified Messaging?

Unified Messaging brings voice, fax, and e-mail messages together into one mailbox that is accessible by telephone or e-mail on a computer or mobile device.

Normally, you would manage your voicemail and fax messages in a different way than you would manage your e-mail. It usually requires various clients and methods to acquire these different messages. E-mail is read on a computer with something like Outlook or a Web mail client, voicemail messages are obtained through the telephone, and fax messages come to—and are sent from—physical fax machines, or they are integrated into a messaging system through a third-party application. Besides the different access methods, the process also results in separate address lists for each of the three messaging types, making it hard to keep all of the address lists straight.

SOME INDEPENDENT ADVICE

Once you have implemented Exchange 2007, you will find Unified Messaging a valuable extra service. Calculate the costs of maintaining your current voicemail, auto attendant, and fax servers and compare it with the costs of a Unified Messaging service that probably provides more functionality than all of your current systems combined. In most cases, you will see that Unified Messaging is not only more useful, but also costs less.

To install the Unified Messaging role, there must be a mailbox server, client access server, and a Hub Transport server available. The Unified Messaging role can be installed on the same server as the other roles (except the Edge Transport server role), and can also be installed on a dedicated server.

You can select the feature in the custom installation screen, as shown in Figure 11.1.

Figure 11.1 Exchange Setup Wizard Custom Installation

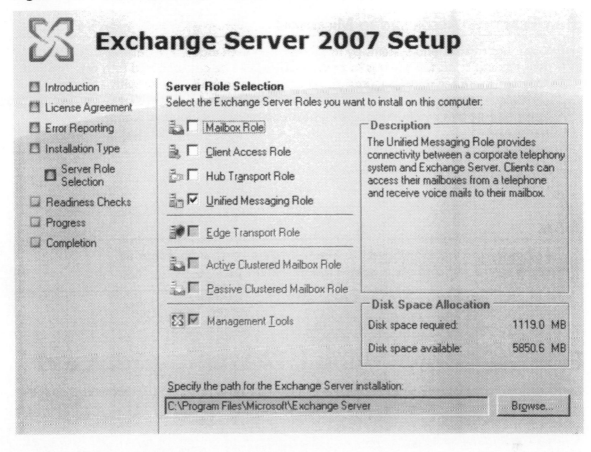

Unified Messaging brings the different message types together and provides a single point of access to these messages, resulting in a better user experience. To provide this, Exchange Server 2007 contains the following core features:

- Call answering
- Fax receiving
- Outlook Voice Access (OVA)
- Automated Attendant

These features are discussed in more detail in the next section.

Best Practices According to Microsoft

Consolidate sites and systems by implementing Exchange 2007 Unified Messaging. All voicemail and fax systems in branch offices can be consolidated into one Unified Messaging server. Replacing individual offices' voice mail systems with a single centralized system can drastically lower support and maintenance costs for the voicemail system by eliminating the most expensive component: legacy voice mail hardware.

Note

For more information, read the Unified Messaging whitepaper at www.microsoft.com/exchange/evaluation/um.mspx.

Exchange 2007 Unified Messaging Features

Exchange 2007 gives users Unified Messaging features such as call answering, fax receiving, Outlook voice access, and an Auto Attendant.

Call Answering

The Call Answering feature consists of functions to answer incoming calls on behalf of the mailbox owner, play their personal greeting, record a voicemail message, and submit the recorded voicemail message from a caller to the mailbox as an attachment to an e-mail message. The voicemail messages are attached to e-mail messages as WMA-files which can be played from within the Outlook client or on a phone by clicking the "play on phone" link in the e-mail message (see Figure 11.2). The name of the sender of the message that contains the voicemail is determined by using Caller-ID and the global address list and contacts. To set a personal greeting, the mailbox owner has to gain access to their mailbox by using a phone. The feature that provides phone access to the mailbox is called Outlook Voice Access, which will be covered later in this section. As all messages are routed through the Hub Transport server, voicemail messages are also routed through this server. This way, transport rules can be applied to these messages.

Figure 11.2 An Example Exchange Voice Mail Message

Fax Receiving

When someone sends a fax message to a recipient on the Unified Messaging system, the Unified Messaging server handles the call. Incoming fax calls are answered and routed the same way voice calls are. The only difference is the attachment. Fax messages contain a TIFF file as an attachment, which carries the fax message.

Outlook Voice Access

Outlook Voice Access (OVA) provides access to a mailbox through any telephone. To gain this access, users dial a subscriber access number that is configured in a dial plan. A dial plan is made from rules that determine how calls are routed in the Unified Messaging environment. When a call is made to the subscriber access number, the system will present a welcome message and ask the user for the pin-code to gain access to the mailbox. If authorization is successful, a series of voice commands provides ways to:

- Listen to e-mail and voice mail messages
- Reply, delete, forward, and save e-mail and voice messages
- Listen to appointments and meeting information
- Accept or decline requests
- Send an "I'll be late" message to all meeting attendees
- Reply to meeting requests by sending a spoken message to all attendees

- Cancel a meeting

- Access the global address list and their personal contacts to locate contact details or send a voice message

- Change their PIN-code, spoken name, or Voicemail greeting

Best Practices According to Microsoft

Use the Outlook 2007 client which is part of the Office 2007 suite. For Unified Messaging, the advantage of using the Outlook 2007 client with Exchange 2007 is that users can change their Unified Messaging settings from within their Outlook client.

The interaction with the Outlook Voice Access system is based on automatic speech recognition (ASR), but it is also possible to perform many actions by using Touch-Tone dialing. Unified Messaging language packs are available that allow the OVA system to speak additional languages to callers. These packs contain pre-recorded prompts like "Welcome. You are connected to Microsoft Exchange," in the selected language. They also enable text-to-speech so content can be read to the caller in the language the message was written in.

Auto Attendants are replacements for human operators. Auto Attendants can provide anonymous incoming calls with a series of voice prompts that help them locate the appropriate department or employee and place a call to that number. The Auto Attendant consists of voice prompts (WAV files) that callers get to hear instead of a human operator. This feature can also be used with Touch-Tone or speech inputs. The Auto Attendants are completely customizable so as to meet the business needs of any organization.

Some Independent Advice

Install Unified Messaging language packs for all languages in which you will receive e-mail. To provide a great user experience, make sure the text-to-speech module can read all the messages in a correct manner.

Note

Unified Messaging language packs can be downloaded at www.microsoft.com/downloads/details.
aspx?familyid=A59E41BD-5760-45EF-8299-1DC57601D9BD&displaylang=en.

The Unified Messaging Infrastructure

Because the Unified Messaging component of Exchange Server 2007 connects with telephony and fax systems, you should be familiar with basic telephony concepts and terminology.

- **Private Branch eXchange (PBX)**   A PBX is a device that acts as a switch for switching telephony calls. This device is used to provide internal telephone connections and offer access to telephone numbers through shared outside lines to make calls external to the company. Additional communication devices can be connected to a PBX besides telephones—such as fax machines, voice mail systems, and others. Calls from outside the company are transferred to the appropriate extension or forwarded by a human operator.

- **IP-PBX**   An IP-PBX is a PBX that operates with Internet Protocol (IP). This simplifies the infrastructure because telephones can be connected to the same local area network (LAN) as the computers and servers. The IP-PBX switches calls to the appropriate phone by using the IP address of the telephone. For using IP-based telephony, all telephones must support the IP protocol. A hybrid IP-PBX supports IP phones, but is also able to connect traditional analog and digital telephones.

- **Voice over Internet Protocol (VoIP)**   This technology enables the use of IP-based networks as the infrastructure for telephone calls.

- **IP or VoIP gateway**   IP/VoIP gateways are hardware devices that can be used to connect legacy PBX systems to local area networks to provide IP-based telephony services. These gateways convert the legacy protocols from the PBX to VoIP-based protocols like SIP and RTP. For an up-to-date list of supported gateways, see the link in the shortcut area of this section.

- **Dial plan**   The dial plan is a set of rules that is used by the PBX to determine which action to take when it receives a call. For example, a 0 is often used to get to the public telephone network. When the first number is not a 0, the PBX knows it will be an internal call, but then needs to know how many more numbers to wait for before taking action. Within the Unified Messaging server, the dial plan creates a link between an Exchange Server 2007 recipient's phone extension in the Active Directory and the recipient's Unified Messaging–enabled mailbox. After a dial plan is configured, a Unified Messaging server must be added to the plan. This links the dial plan and the server and enables the server to accept and handle incoming calls.

- **Hunt group**   A hunt group is a set of extensions shared by users. When a PBX receives a call for a number that is assigned to a hunt group, it searches through the connected extensions to find an available phone. Hunt groups are often used to distribute calls among members of support or sales departments. Customers call one number for the support team, and the call could be routed to any member of the team who is not currently on the phone. Within the Unified Messaging configuration, a hunt group is a logical representation of an existing PBX or IP-PBX hunt group. This provides Unified Messaging possibilities for the pilot number (shared telephone number of the hunt group).

An Exchange 2007 Unified Messaging component connects with the existing telephony infrastructure to create a Unified Messaging infrastructure. Figure 11.3 shows an example of a Unified Messaging infrastructure.

Figure 11.3 Unified Messaging Infrastructure

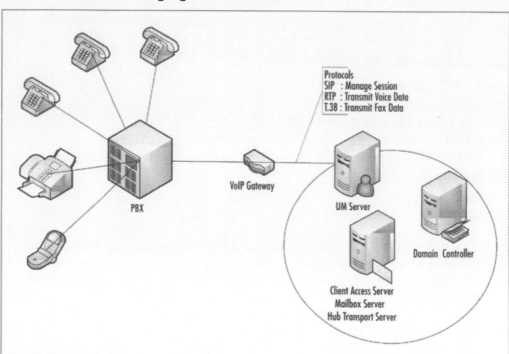

This Unified Messaging infrastructure consists of the following components:

- **PBX and connected phones**   The PBX is connected to the external telephone system using one or more lines. The telephones are directly connected to the PBX system. Incoming calls are routed by the PBX to the appropriate phone.

- **VoIP gateway**   The PBX system is attached to the VoIP gateway. The VoIP gateway, meanwhile, is connected to the PBX with a fixed number of ports; this depends on the gateway's capabilities. Whenever there's no answer or a "do not disturb" signal on a user's phone, the call is routed to the VoIP gateway with information about the destination phone number and the ID of the caller. The PBX also forwards calls made to specific telephone numbers—for example, when users call the telephone number to access the Automated Attendant services on the Unified Messaging server. When using an IP-PBX, it's not always necessary to use a VoIP or IP gateway. Figure 11.4 shows the wizard that configures the connection between the Unified Messaging server and the VoIP gateway.

- **Exchange 2007 Unified Messaging server**   The VoIP gateway is attached to the server. This Unified Messaging server takes calls from the IP gateway and handles the requests. The Unified Messaging server uses the SIP protocol and listens for requests on the default SIP port 5060 tcp. For speech processing, the server depends on the Microsoft Speech Server (MSS) component. This component is installed as part of the Unified Messaging role and runs as the MS Exchange Speech Engine service.

- **Domain controllers**   The domain controllers provide directory information, enabling the Unified Messaging server to route the incoming calls. Within the directory, all the Unified Messaging–enabled users have a phone extension number attribute. This attribute is used by the Unified Messaging server to find the appropriate user and route the message to their mailbox.

Figure 11.4 UM IP Gateway Wizard

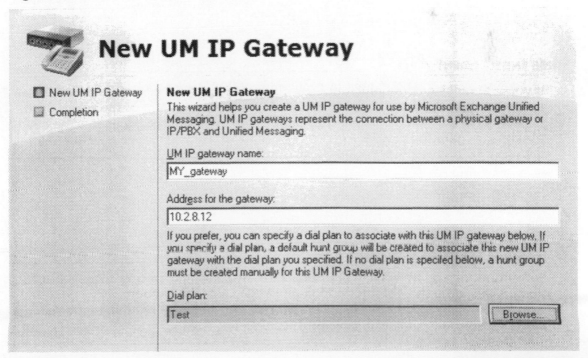

BEST PRACTICES ACCORDING TO MICROSOFT

Obtain assistance of a Unified Messaging specialist to make sure there is a smooth transition to Exchange 2007 Unified Messaging from a legacy voice mail system.

The Unified Messaging server uses three IP protocols for Unified Messaging communications:

- **(SIP) Session Initiation Protocol**   SIP is a real-time signaling protocol and is used to maintain the communication session. TLS can be used to secure the SIP traffic. Exchange Server 2007 Unified Messaging uses only SIP over tcp.

- **(RTP) Real-Time Transport Protocol**   RTP is the protocol used for the transport of voice traffic between the VoIP gateway and the Unified Messaging server. RTP provides high-quality, streaming voice connections. RTP traffic can also be secured by using TLS.

- **T.38 (Real-Time Facsimile)**   This protocol is the fax transport protocol used by the Unified Messaging server. The Unified Messaging server assumes that all incoming calls are voice, so a fax call originates as a voice call using the RTP protocol. When the Exchange Unified Messaging server detects the fax tone, the call is switched to the T.38 protocol.

SOME INDEPENDENT ADVICE

If you are thinking about replacing your current PBX, take a look at systems that can be directly connected to Exchange 2007 Unified Messaging. One of the few is Cisco Call Manager 5.x. Using a system that can be directly connected eliminates the need for an extra gateway device.

NOTE

For information on IP-PBX and PBX support to http://technet.microsoft.com/en-us/library/aa996831.aspx. For information on IP/VOIP gateway support, visit http://technet.microsoft.com/en-us/library/bb123948.aspx. To find Unified Messaging partners, go to http://directory.microsoft.com.

The Unified Messaging Mailbox Policies

When a new Exchange 2007 recipient is created, it is not UM-enabled. Once you enable a user for Unified Messaging, you can manage, modify, and configure the UM-related properties for the user. You can then view and modify UM-related settings such as the associated UM dial plan, the associated UM mailbox policy, and the extension number for the user.

UM-related settings are stored for a user in two places: the recipient's mailbox and the user's Active Directory object. When you enable a recipient for Unified Messaging, you are setting a specific property on the user's mailbox.

Using Unified Messaging mailbox policies enables you to apply and standardize Unified Messaging configuration settings for Unified Messaging–enabled users. You can create Unified Messaging mailbox policies and then add the policy to a collection of Unified Messaging–enabled mailboxes to apply a common set of policies or security settings. Unified Messaging mailbox policies are required before you can enable users for Unified Messaging.

The default Unified Messaging mailbox policy is generated when you create the first dial plan, but you can establish additional mailbox policies based on your business's needs. With a Unified Messaging mailbox policy, you can configure the following settings:

- Dial plan (required)
- Maximum greeting length
- Number of unsuccessful login attempts before the password is reset
- Minimum number of digits required in a PIN
- Number of days until a new PIN is required
- Number of previous passwords disallowed
- Restrictions on international calling

Figure 11.5 shows the General tab of a Unified Messaging mailbox policy.

Figure 11.5 A Unified Messaging Mailbox Policy

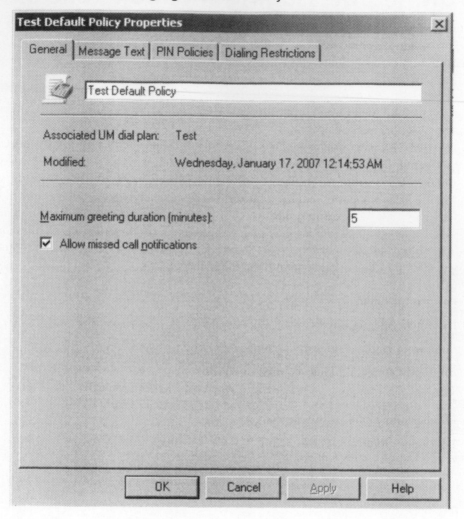

Each mailbox can be linked to only one Unified Messaging mailbox policy.

NOTE

Try to reduce the number of Unified Messaging mailbox policies to simplify administration. For more information on managing Unified Messaging mailbox policies, visit http://technet.microsoft.com/en-us/library/aa996341.aspx

When you enable a user account for Unified Messaging, you must specify a mailbox policy and an extension, and you must assign a PIN or configure the system to generate the initial PIN for the user. When the user is Unified Messaging–enabled, Exchange Server sends the user an e-mail message indicating that the user's account has been enabled; the message also contains the PIN.

BEST PRACTICES ACCORDING TO MICROSOFT

Implement strong PIN requirements for Unified Messaging users. This can be enforced by creating Unified Messaging PIN policies that require six or more digits for PINs, and increasing the level of security for your network. You can also enhance the level of security of your network by reducing the number of failed logon attempts for UM-enabled users.

Summary

This chapter focused on the Unified Messaging server (included in Exchange Server 2007) and its role. This server role provides a connection between PBX systems and the e-mail system. Installing this role requires the other Exchange roles to be installed (except for the Edge server role). Unified Messaging offers voicemail and fax messages in your mailbox and provides telephone access to that mailbox. The embedded speech recognition enables users to navigate through their mailbox by using voice commands.

Solutions Fast Track

What Is Exchange 2007 Unified Messaging?

- ☑ Unified Messaging is the combination of voice, fax, and e-mail messages.

- ☑ Unified Messaging centralizes access to different types of messages at one location.

- ☑ Unified Messaging allows users to access their mailbox through an ordinary phone.

Exchange 2007 Unified Messaging Features

- ☑ The Exchange Unified Messaging server provides a voice mail and fax system.

- ☑ The Auto Attendant provides a customizable, speech-enabled service that answers phone calls and automates dialing through directory integration, acting as a switchboard application.

- ☑ Outlook voice access lets users access their mailbox by using a phone and voice commands.

The Unified Messaging Infrastructure

- ☑ The Exchange 2007 Unified Messaging server can be connected directly to some IP-PBX systems. Other PBX systems can be connected by implementing a gateway device between the PBX and the Unified Messaging server.

- ☑ Domain controllers provide the necessary information for finding the correct mailbox for each incoming call.

- ☑ The communication used between the telephony system and the Unified Messaging server is based on standard protocols.

Frequently Asked Questions

Q: Is it possible to test the Unified Messaging service of Exchange 2007 without a PBX?

A: It is possible to try out the server by using a soft phone (telephone emulator). Instructions can be found at http://technet.microsoft.com/en-us/library/aa998254.aspx.

Q: What languages are supported by the automated speech recognition (ASR) system?

A: Currently, only English is supported.

Q: Which gateways of PBX does Exchange 2007 support?

A: Exchange 2007 currently supports VoIP gateways from Intel (PIMG and TIMG gateways) and AudioCodes (MediaPack and Mediant2000). With these gateways, it is possible to connect Exchange 2007 UM to a large range of PBX systems. The Cisco Call Manager 5.x is tested and can be connected directly to Exchange 2007 UM.

Q: How does a PBX forward WMA files to the exchange server? What format is used, and where is this configured in Exchange 2007?

A: The PBX does not create the file. The PBX forwards the call to the Unified Messaging server where it is recorded, saved as a sound file, and mailed to the appropriate mailbox. By default, the server uses wma encoding. This is configured in the dial plan on the Settings tab.

Chapter 12

Getting Started with IIS 7.0

Solutions in this chapter:

- Inside the Changes in IIS 7.0
- IIS 6.0 versus 7.0: The Delta

☑ Summary

☑ Solutions Fast Track

☑ Frequently Asked Questions

Introduction

Many variables must be taken into account when you are considering a move to IIS 7.0 and Windows "Codename: Longhorn" server. Microsoft has gone to great lengths to reduce the obstacles and make this move as seamless as possible. This chapter prepares you for the foundation of IIS 7.0 and helps you structure it in a way that is familiar. Knowledge of IIS 6.0 helps in understanding not only "how" but also "why" the product was changed. In the following chapters, you will learn the fundamentals that are necessary to move to IIS 7.0.

Inside the Changes in IIS 7.0

In this chapter we introduce the fundamentals that are accomplished using IIS 7.0 versus past versions, especially IIS 6.0. These fundamentals include:

- An introduction to the installation changes of IIS 7.0 from a very high level, and how it sets the foundation for deploying secure applications.

- Why developers like IIS 7.0. A look inside IIS 7.0's new core server.

- The configuration. Why did Microsoft start over and rebuild what already worked?

- The administration stack is more powerful than ever before. In the past, administrators had two options "out of box" to configure IIS without script—IIS Manager and AdsUtil. vbs. IIS 7.0 has a command-console utility, IIS Manager, whose areas are developer extensible.

- The most efficient diagnostics stack. Why Request Tracing is just the butter on top of the potato or ketchup on fries.

All these fundamentals are collectively necessary and revolutionary. Never in the history of Internet Information Services (IIS) has there been so many feature redesigns as there are in IIS 7.0.

IIS 7.0 improves the features for administrators and provides a friendlier environment for developers. As a continuation of Microsoft's Trustworthy Computing effort, IIS 7.0 improves security while also achieving greater efficiency, granularity, and performance.

The differences between IIS 7.0 and its predecessors are immense. The installation is more detailed than that of IIS 6.0. Administrators now have more control over the features they want to install. The ability to delegate tasks to users without granting full administrative rights allows IIS 7.0 to be easily managed without compromising security. The IIS Manager user interface is more powerful and task oriented. Command-line capabilities have also improved with the implementation of Appcmd.exe. This utility can be used for viewing and configuring objects in IIS 7.0, making it easier for administrators who need to make many changes to their system. Windows Management

Instrumentation (WMI) is friendlier than it was in version 6.0. In IIS 7.0, WMI allows access to manage multiple servers.

IIS 7.0 is modular and not so monolithic as the IIS 6.0 core was. Developers can add any functionality they like by creating their own modules and adding them to the core server. For instance, if developers do not like a certain function within IIS 7.0, they can replace it with their own by adding components that are easier to develop. The ability to do this is more convenient with the implementation of new application programming interfaces (APIs). Developers are no longer dependent on Internet Server Application Programming Interfaces (ISAPIs) and their complexity to extend server functionality. A major change in the architecture of IIS 7.0 from previous versions is that .config files now hold configuration information for the IIS instead of the metabase. The .config files also live side by side with ASP.NET settings and can be deployed with application content such as pages and images.

IIS 7.0 also has new diagnostic features. The most impressive is a feature called Failed Request Tracing (FREB), which can be enabled and used in diagnosing server request failures or delays. With FREB, you can define a failed request-tracing rule that will capture trace events for that request and log them as they occur without having to reproduce the error. Administrators no longer have to dig through large report files searching for the information they need to troubleshoot a specific failed request. FREB makes resolving request failures a lot easier.

All these changes in IIS 7.0 bring about a better platform for developers, easier management for administrators, improved server performance, and better overall security.

Installing IIS 6.0

Although more stable and secure than its predecessors, IIS 6.0 was unable to shrink its memory footprint. With previous versions of IIS, when certain features were disabled, their code remained loaded and resident in memory. For example, when an administrator installed IIS 6.0 and only chose to enable IIS Manager and Web services, code for all other features were also loaded as common files and then stored in memory. This meant that administrators would also have to be concerned about patches for all of IIS, even if a patch applied to a feature they weren't using. For administrators to remove certain features from previous versions, they had to completely uninstall IIS from the system. It was an all-or-nothing installation. While developing IIS 7.0, Microsoft felt that it had an opportunity to improve security by reducing the footprint in memory while making the platform more modular and more efficient.

After you install IIS Manager and Web services, the inetsrv directory for IIS 6.0 appears (see Figure 12.1), and the directory for IIS 7.0 appears, as shown in Figure 12.2. In examining the differences, you see that none of the subdirectories under inetsrv carry over to IIS 7.0. The only top-level subdirectories you have in IIS 7.0 are the .config files and whatever language(s) you are supporting on your server. For our purposes, we are supporting U.S. English; therefore, we have an en-US directory. All configuration changes take place in the config subdirectory, so you have only one directory to find and manage.

Figure 12.1 Simple inetsrv Directory Structure

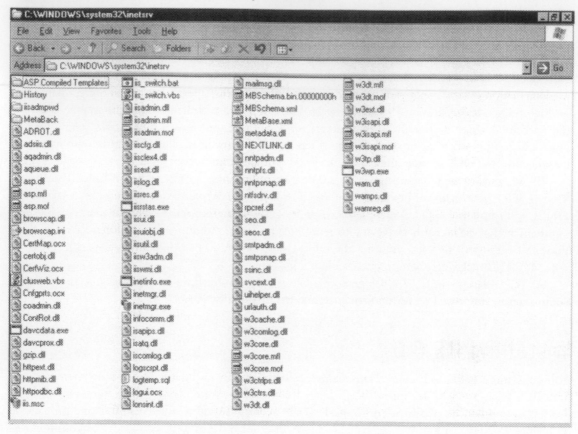

Two options can be used to install IIS 6.0, neither of which was done by default on Windows Server 2003:

- **User Interface**   Administrators could install IIS 6.0 manually via the user interface, by choosing the features they wanted.

- **Unattended Installation**   Administrators had the option of conducting unattended and automated installations of IIS 6.0.

Figure 12.2 inetsrv Directory with IIS 7.0

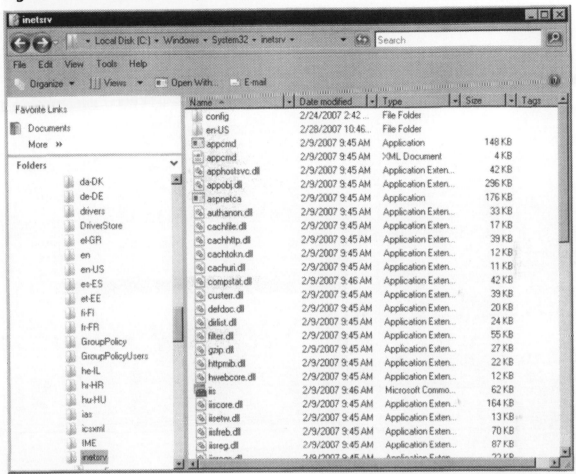

Installing IIS 6.0 via the User Interface

Although IIS 6. 0 is easy to install, learning where to install it from and getting there were difficult tasks. In the user interface of Windows Server 2003, you had to go to **Control Panel | Add or Remove Programs | Add/Remove Windows Components | Application Server**; administrators could then choose IIS and begin to enable the features they wanted. It was not very convenient or easy to find. Figure 12.3 shows the screen where IIS 6.0 selects the user interface.

Figure 12.3 IIS 6.0 Selected In User Interface

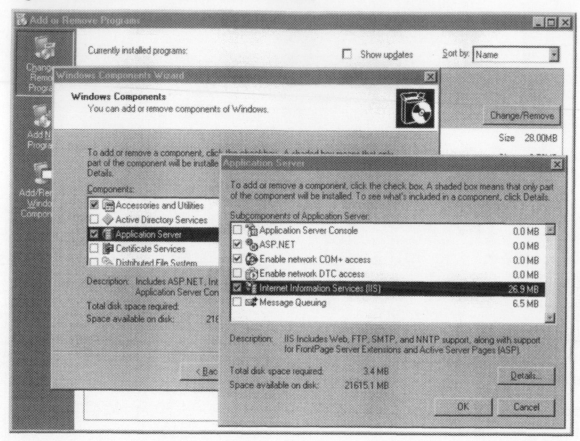

Installing IIS 6.0 Using Unattended Installation

IIS 6.0 administrators also had the option of using the unattended installation method. Information technology (IT) professionals accustomed to conducting rollouts, are familiar with the unattended installation method of previous versions of Windows. Just like Windows, IIS 6.0 unattended installations required the creation of answer files, which contain answers to questions that can be automated during the installation process. The extent and complexity of the answer file depended on when you installed IIS 6.0. Unattended installations could be accomplished at two distinct moments:

1. **Install IIS 6.0 simultaneously with the operating system**   Unattended installations could be conducted at the same time that the operating system was installed. The answer file created with standard text in this scenario can be long and complex, even for savvy veterans. Not only were administrators creating the sections for IIS, which included a Components and an optional Internet server section, they also created the sections for installing the

operating system. Using the unattended installation method required using the *Winnt32.exe* command. Following is the syntax required for the *Winn32.exe* command.

Winnt32 /unattend:AnswerFile /s:InstallSource

AnswerFile is the name of the file that contains the answers to questions that need to be automated, and *InstallSource* is the location of the installation files.

2. **Installing IIS 6.0 after the operating system is installed**   Using the *Sysocmgr.exe* tool, administrators could install IIS 6.0 and the components they wanted from a command line, with the aid of an answer text file. Similar to the answer file for unattended installation with the operating system, the answer file here also has a Components section and optional InternetServer section, but does not include all of the options for the installation of the operating system. Following is the syntax used with the *Sysocmgr.exe* tool. Figure 12.4 shows what administrators might have in their answer files.

Sysocmgr /i:%windir%\inf\sysoc.inf /u:c:\AnswerFile.txt

The */i* switch points to the path where the *sysoc.inf* file resides, which must be read by the *sysocmgr* command. The */u* switch indicates the path to the answer file.

Figure 12.4 Example Answer File

```
[Components]
Aspnet=on
iis_common=on
iis_ftp=on
iis_asp=on
iis_www=on

[InternetServer]
SvcManualStart=www,ftp
```

In this example, the Components section of the answer file would enable ASP.NET, the IIS Common files, the File Transfer Protocol (FTP), the Active Server Pages, and Web services. The InternetServer section would set both the Web and FTP service to manual instead of automatic.

BEST PRACTICES ACCORDING TO MICROSOFT

When you are creating an answer file for operating system deployment, Microsoft suggests using the Setup Manager found on the Windows Server 2003 CD. The tool is included in the *Deploy.cab* file under the \Support\Tools folder.

> **SOME INDEPENDENT ADVICE**
>
> Although using the Setup Manager is the preferred way of creating answer files, the chance of error is still there. Keep your answer files short; the longer they are the greater the chance of problems. If you are just creating an answer file to install IIS 6.0, then creating it via notepad is more efficient and examples can be found throughout the Internet.

IIS 6.0 Core Server

IIS 6.0 contains several core components that perform important functions. The following are the core components with a brief description of each:

- *HTTP.sys*   Implemented as a kernel mode driver. Used to receive requests and forwards them to the request queue, while also sending responses to the client.

- **Worker Processes (*w3wp.exe*)**   Runs as user-mode code. Uses *HTTP.sys* to receive requests and send responses. Also runs ASP.NET applications and Extensible Markup Language (XML) Web services.

- **Web Service Administration and Monitoring**   A set of features found in the Web service. Also runs in user-mode. Responsible for Hypertext Transfer Protocol (HTTP) administration and worker process management.

- *Inetinfo.exe*   Runs as a user-mode component. Hosts the IIS metabase and other services such as Simple Mail Transfer Protocol (SMTP), FTP, and Network News Transfer Protocol (NNTP).

- **IIS Metabase**   The data store containing all of the IIS configuration information. Saved as plain text and formatted in XML. (For more information about the metabase, see the section "Where the Metabase Took Us…and Fell Short.")

HTTP.sys

A kernel mode driver and part of the Transmission Control Protocol/Internet Protocol (TCP/IP) networking subsystem, *HTTP.sys*, listens for requests that want to connect to Internet Protocol (IP) addresses and port numbers used by Web sites running on IIS. It is used by IIS for handling HTTP requests, but also fulfills several other functions including caching HTTP responses in kernel mode, managing Transmission Control Protocol (TCP) connections, implementing connection limits, time-outs, queue length limits, managing bandwidth throttling, and handling text-based logging for Web services.

Worker Processes

One of the most important changes in the core of IIS 6.0 was the use of *worker processes* (*w3wp.exe*). These processes acted liked processing hosts for user-developed code. They could each host ISAPI extensions and filters, as well as Active Server Pages (ASP) applications and static content. Figure 12.5 shows the inside of a worker process (*w3wp.exe*).

With ISAPI, developers could create filters to access the core server. ISAPI filters are used to preprocess and post-process HTTP requests. ISAPI filters are driven by Web server events, not client requests. An ISAPI filter could be notified when a Read or Write event occurs and then modify the data that is to be returned to the client. ISAPI extensions are sometimes referred to as ISAPI applications, and can be called from any Web page to perform dynamic and interactive functions such as validating a form or accessing a database. ISAPI extensions and filters are written in C or C++ and are quite cumbersome to create and deploy. The deployment of ISAPI extensions and filters required server administrator rights.

By examining Figure 12.5, you see that requests can be handled by mapping them to the static file handler (default), the Common Gateway Interface (CGI) handler, or through an ISAPI extension. In Figure 12.6, requests using managed code (as shown with the solid lines) must first go through the IIS pipeline and then through an ISAPI filter before it even reaches the ASP.NET pipeline. The response (depicted as the dotted lines) then goes through the same pipeline but in reverse.

Figure 12.5 Inside a Worker Process (W3WP.EXE)

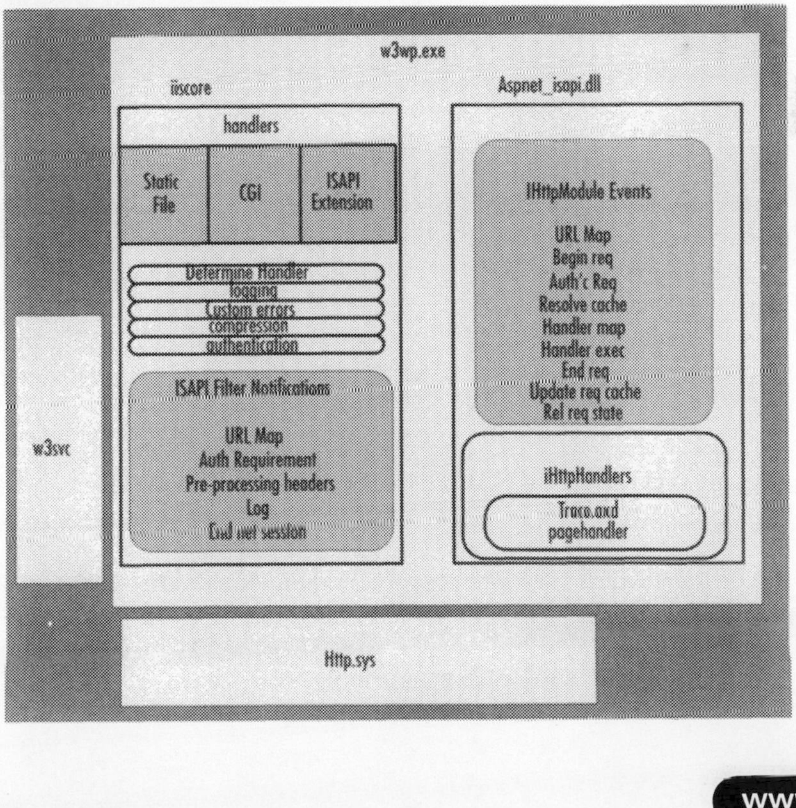

Figure 12.6 Request Going to ASP.NET Pipeline

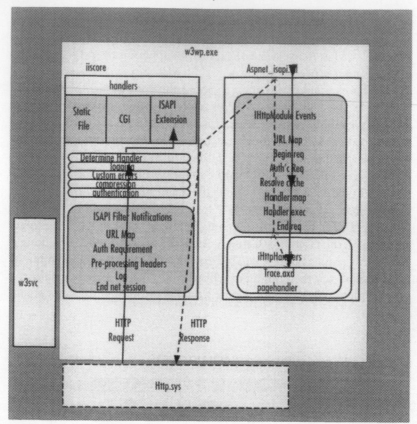

Also at issue was ISAPI deployment. In IIS 6.0 this was also cumbersome. Unfortunately, ISAPI deployment wasn't as easy as using FTP to copy the binary file to the server and have it work. To deploy ISAPI filters or extensions to the appropriate configuration for your site or application, as mentioned earlier, you had to have administrative rights on that local server and then restart the worker process that it resided in. Microsoft has resolved these issues in IIS 7.0 by making managed code a priority and allowing easier deployments of both native modules and managed code.

Web Service Administration and Monitoring

The user mode component Web Service Administration and Monitoring serves two roles in IIS:

- **HTTP Administration** By interacting with the metabase, the Web service gathers configuration data that *HTTP.sys* needs and is used to manage worker processes for application pools.

■ **Managing Worker Processes**   Managing worker processes includes starting, maintaining information, recycling, and the time to restart them.

Inetinfo.exe

A user mode component, *Inetinfo.exe* hosts the IIS metabase, FTP, SMTP, and NNTP services. It depends on the IIS Admin service to host the metabase.

Where the Metabase Took Us…and Fell Short

The metabase in IIS is a hierarchical structure used for storing configuration information. It was introduced in IIS 4.0 as a replacement for storing configuration information in the registry. The metabase was improved in IIS 6.0, first by formatting it into a text file using XML, and then by allowing it to be edited while running.

One of the metabase's shortcomings is that it is difficult to read and difficult to locate exactly what you're looking for. The old metabase supported outdated interfaces such as Admin Base Objects (ABOs). It also incorporated its own access control lists (ACLs); therefore, it does not use the existing ACLs from the file system. This made it very difficult to maintain. Putting in or extending the metabase schema was incredibly difficult. Figures 12.7 and 12.8 show both *metabase.xml* and *mbschema.xml*. Notice how difficult it would be to find something specific in either file.

Figure 12.7 IIS 6.0 Metabase

Figure 12.8 IIS 6.0 Schema

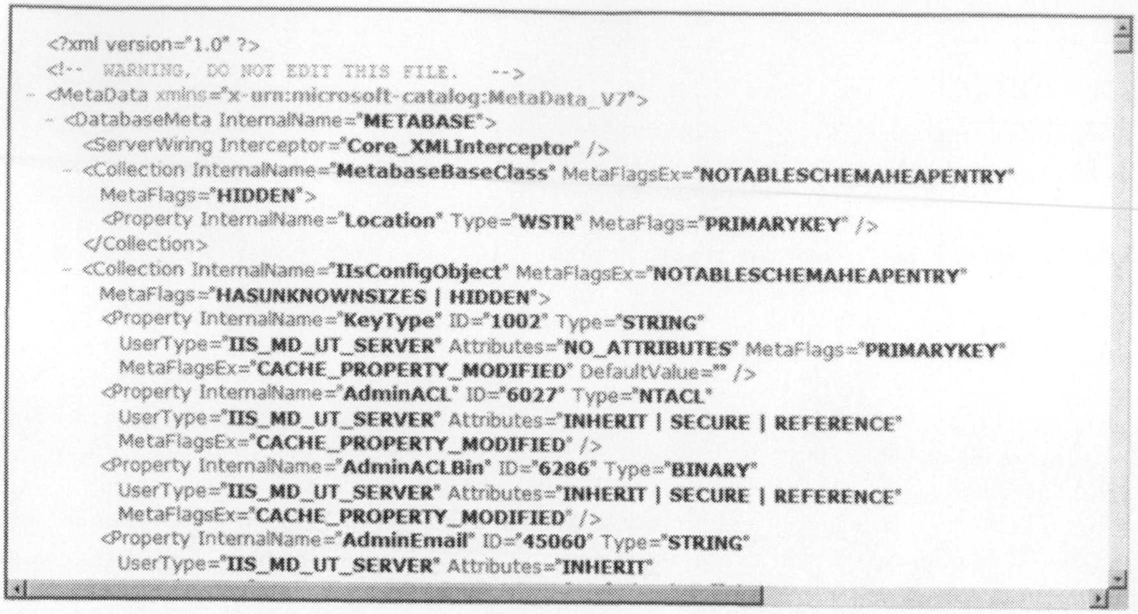

```xml
<?xml version="1.0" ?>
<!-- WARNING, DO NOT EDIT THIS FILE. -->
<MetaData xmlns="x-urn:microsoft-catalog:MetaData_V7">
  <DatabaseMeta InternalName="METABASE">
    <ServerWiring Interceptor="Core_XMLInterceptor" />
    <Collection InternalName="MetabaseBaseClass" MetaFlagsEx="NOTABLESCHEMAHEAPENTRY"
      MetaFlags="HIDDEN">
      <Property InternalName="Location" Type="WSTR" MetaFlags="PRIMARYKEY" />
    </Collection>
    <Collection InternalName="IIsConfigObject" MetaFlagsEx="NOTABLESCHEMAHEAPENTRY"
      MetaFlags="HASUNKNOWNSIZES | HIDDEN">
      <Property InternalName="KeyType" ID="1002" Type="STRING"
        UserType="IIS_MD_UT_SERVER" Attributes="NO_ATTRIBUTES" MetaFlags="PRIMARYKEY"
        MetaFlagsEx="CACHE_PROPERTY_MODIFIED" DefaultValue="" />
      <Property InternalName="AdminACL" ID="6027" Type="NTACL"
        UserType="IIS_MD_UT_SERVER" Attributes="INHERIT | SECURE | REFERENCE"
        MetaFlagsEx="CACHE_PROPERTY_MODIFIED" />
      <Property InternalName="AdminACLBin" ID="6286" Type="BINARY"
        UserType="IIS_MD_UT_SERVER" Attributes="INHERIT | SECURE | REFERENCE"
        MetaFlagsEx="CACHE_PROPERTY_MODIFIED" />
      <Property InternalName="AdminEmail" ID="45060" Type="STRING"
        UserType="IIS_MD_UT_SERVER" Attributes="INHERIT"
```

Metabase backup provided a way to ensure that restoration could take place in case of corruption or if a server crashed. Although effective, the tools used in backing up the metabase in IIS 6.0 were quite old. It was not uncommon to back up the metabase and store it remotely by creating a common batch file. Using both *xcopy.exe* and *iisback.vbs*, one could automate the backup process. To run a script to conduct the backup, a user or IIS administrator had to be a member of the local Administrators group of the computer where they were backing up the metabase. Figure 12.9 is an example of what might be in a batch file that would use both *xcopy.exe* and *iisback.vbs* to back up the metabase.

Figure 12.9 Example of Backup Batch File

```
set server=servername
set name=%date%-%server%
iisback /backup /b %name% /e %password%
xcopy %windir%\system32\inetsrv\metaback\%name%.*…
\\backupserver\share$\server%
xcopy /o /x /e /h /y /c c:\web \backupserver\share$\%server%
```

Another method of backing up the metabase in IIS 6.0 was through the IIS Manager, which would let an administrator save a copy of the metabase by right-clicking **Web Sites** and selecting **All Tasks | Save Configuration to a File.** You would then provide a filename and path for the backup. IIS 6.0 then created a machine key to encrypt some metabase parts in this file. This method then limited the backup to only being restored on the machine where it was originated. To be able to use a backup conducted in this manner on a separate machine, required the administrator to select the **Encrypt configuration using password** check box, which then substituted a password that the administrator created for the place of the machine key that was typically created. This was very easy to overlook.

Administration: A Review

IIS 6.0 administration was primarily done in the user interface with IIS Manager. Very limited in remote capabilities, administrators were required to loosen the network security settings for Distributed Component Object Model (DCOM) so that true remote administration could take place. If remote administration was required and the traffic had to go through a firewall, administrators had to open TCP 135, thereby creating another security risk.

Finally, IIS Manager dealt with administration at a high-level via category-based tabs, not task-oriented, which is more detailed, less error prone, and easier to configure. For instance, Web site security is exposed via the "Directory Security" tab as shown in Figure 12.10. This shows the lack of task-oriented security and the overall lack of organization available in IIS Manager.

Figure 12.10 Web Sites Security in IIS Manager

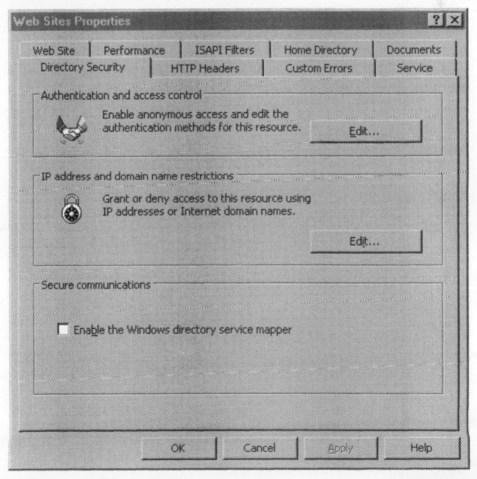

Another tool for administering IIS 6.0 was the use of *adsutil.vbs*. This utility used VBScript along with Active Directory Services Interfaces (ADSI), to modify an IIS configuration. One of the pitfalls with using *adsutil.vbs* was that first there was no ability to delegate to users, and thus you really couldn't do so without increasing security risks. *Adsutil.vbs* used old technology (ADSI); Microsoft is encouraging administrators to use WMI instead since the release of Windows Server 2003. Microsoft included eight different scripts that used WMI to help administrators manage IIS. The problem was that learning what eight different scripts did and how they made things more "simple" was counterproductive. IIS 7.0 remedies this with the implementation of *Appcmd.exe*. The following are the eight scripts that administrators needed to know:

- *iisapp.vbs*   Lists Web applications running on an IIS machine
- *iisback.vbs*   Backs up, restores, lists, and deletes IIS configurations
- *iisCnfg.vbs*   Exports and imports IIS configurations as XML file, able to copy configurations and save them to disk
- *iisext.vbs*   Enables and lists applications; adds and removes application dependencies; enables, disables, and lists Web service extensions; adds, removes, enables, disables, and lists Web service extension files
- *iisFtp.vbs*   Creates, deletes, starts, stops, and lists FTP sites, and configures Active Directory user isolation for FTP sites
- *iisFtpdr.vbs*   Creates and deletes virtual directories within FTP sites, and displays the virtual directories within a given root
- *iisvdir.vbs*   Creates and deletes virtual directories within Web sites, and displays the virtual directories within a given root
- *iisweb.vbs*   Creates, deletes, starts, stops, and lists Websites

Troubleshooting Failed Requests with IIS 6.0

Regardless of the product and the manufacturer, troubleshooting is a fact of life and a skill that improves with experience and time. IIS 6.0 improved its diagnostics capabilities from earlier versions. Still, most of the utilities used for troubleshooting were add-on tools that were not part of IIS 6.0 itself, but provided by the operating system itself or were available for download. The following is a list of tools or built-in features used for troubleshooting problems with IIS 6.0:

- *WFetch.exe*   Used for troubleshooting HTTP connections. Can display the headers in HTTP Requests and HTTP Response packets sent between a client and a server.
- **File Monitor (*FileMon.exe*)**   Used for viewing and capturing file system activity in real time.

- **Registry Monitor (*RegMon.exe*)**   Similar to File Monitor except that it is used for viewing and capturing registry activity in real time.

- **IIS Request Monitor**   Captures information about HTTP requests in IIS worker processes; good for isolating and understanding problems when worker processes become slow or unresponsive.

- **Secure Sockets Layer Diagnostic Tool (*SSL Diag*)**   Useful in identifying configuration problems in the metabase, certificates, or certificate stores when running Web sites that use SSL.

- **Authentication and Access Control Diagnostics (*authdiag.exe*)**   Provides the ability to review, test, and correct problems or issues with authentication and authorization.

- **IIS Enterprise Tracing for Windows**   New in Windows Server 2003, this tool allows you to trace HTTP requests as they move through various components in the server architecture.

- **Network Monitor**   A network tracing tool that allows you to view activity on the network.

- **System Monitor**   Formerly known as Performance Monitor in Windows 2000, this tool helps you to view and collect system performance data.

- **HRPlus**   Provides error lookup functionality.

- **Microsoft Debugging Tools for Windows**   Used in debugging and diagnosing application problems.

As can be seen, IIS 6.0 has numerous add-on tools that were quite effective in troubleshooting problems. One feature that was expanded in service pack 1 (SP1) of Windows Server 2003 was Enterprise Tracing for Windows (ETW). ETW works by implementing tracing providers used for debugging and capacity planning. It implements these providers to track HTTP requests as they move through IIS components. For instance, if an ISAPI filter causes a delay or the hanging of an HTTP request, ETW can help determine which ISAPI filter is at fault.

Conducting an ETW tracing session can be quite cumbersome. It involves everything from obtaining each provider's Globally Unique Identifier (GUID), specifying flags and levels in a text file, starting the tracing session that held numerous switches, and finally generating the tracing report. The following is an example of a command that starts up the tracing process; notice all the parameters and switches. Once the tracing report was created it was usually difficult for administrators and developers to pinpoint the cause of the failure.

logman start iis_trace –pf iis_providers.guid -ets

Basically, tracing in IIS 6.0 through ETW was difficult because it didn't provide a user interface, it was very difficult to restrict to certain extensions or paths, and it was not extensible so developers could not write custom events.

IIS 6.0 versus IIS 7.0: The Delta

IIS 6.0 was a monumental step forward for the Web platform for Windows. At the highest priority stood security, followed by reliability and scalability. With IIS 7.0, Microsoft stood true to all of these important areas and delivered a rock-solid product; however, as with any release, there is still room for improvement. The following sections help us to understand the differences between IIS 6.0 and IIS 7.0, why changes were made, and what the benefits are for customers.

The major differences between IIS 6.0 and IIS 7.0 are:

- A modular core server consisting of simplified setup and a unified pipeline for request execution

- An all new delegatable, distributable configuration system allowing non-administrators as well as non-Windows credentials access to Web server configuration

- A completely rewritten IIS Manager that is task-oriented and extensible

- An extensible WMI provider that offers native access to the new configuration as well as access via Windows PowerShell

- A single, all-inclusive, command-line utility called *AppCmd.exe* that simplifies access to configuration and state information (done in individual VBS files with IIS 6.0)

- An IIS and *ASP.NET* diagnostics engine that is extensible and allows granular access to runtime-specific information about requests

- A brand-new Failed Request Tracing feature to identify causes of request failures

Modular Core Server

The biggest change in architecture between IIS 6.0 and IIS 7.0 is the modular core server. Remember that the core server in IIS 6.0 was monolithic and its installation was all or none. In IIS 7.0 all of that changes. Figure 12.11 is a diagram of the modular core server in IIS 7.0. As mentioned earlier, the new modular core allows administrators to load only what they need. Figure 12.12 shows that modules can be completely uninstalled from the server at any time.

Figure 12.11 IIS 7.0 Modular Server Core

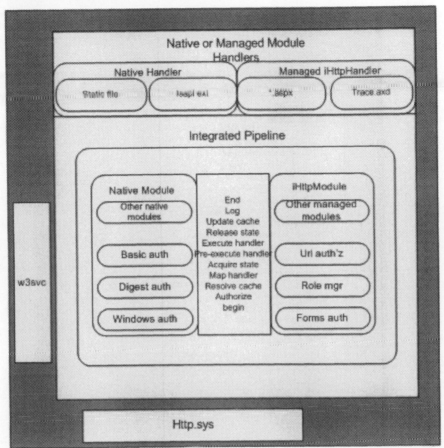

Because of the changes made to the core server in IIS 7.0, the memory footprint is smaller and the risk of loading unused code and it being available for exploitation is removed, along with achieving better performance. The ability to customize server workload will reduce its attack surface. Patching requirements are also minimized. When a patch was released in the IIS 6.0 monolithic model, the entire core was re-done and sent out. Now only those modules that require patching will receive them.

Figure 12.12 IIS 7.0 Module Selection

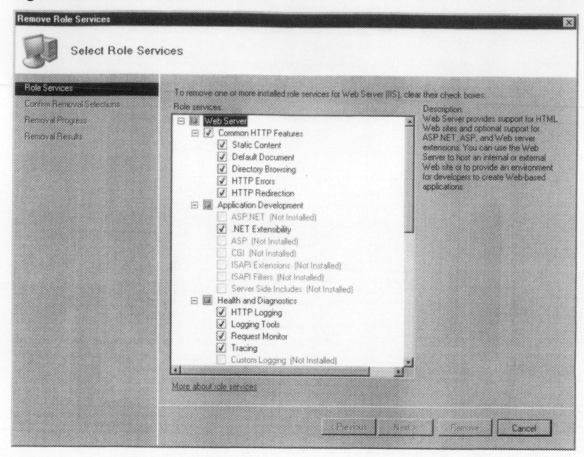

The new extensible APIs are a big improvement over the previous ISAPI model. Practically every aspect of IIS provides extensibility, thus allowing developers to tailor the server to meet their own needs, regardless of whether they use managed or native code. The new modular architecture has allowed Microsoft to eliminate duplication, and as such, IIS 7.0 has a single pipeline for all code regardless if whether it's managed or native code.

NOTE

IIS 7.0's new native API still requires users to know C\C++. Microsoft offers an additional capability by allowing a developer to use managed code to interact with the server.

Delegation: Less Is Often Better

In IIS 6.0, for a user to do any tasks on the server required administrative rights, which were a security nightmare for server administrators. Now with IIS 7.0, administrators are able to delegate tasks to users without leaving the door wide open. In IIS 7.0, administrators can delegate features in IIS Manager to Web site and Web application administrators, allowing them to manage their sites and applications remotely without having administrative access to the server.

Best Practices According to Microsoft

Microsoft recommends a strategy of starting with the minimum rights and working up. It does not recommend opening rights up completely and later locking them down. Doing so could cause applications to become unstable.

Some Independent Advice

Delegation creates a new culture in IT. When Active Directory came out, the ability to delegate administrative tasks to users was possible. For users who had administrator rights before delegation, it was considered a slap in the face. They felt as though they were no longer trusted. Although delegation is a great security tool, be prepared for the human factor, especially from those who used to have full administrative rights.

Server administrators still have complete control over what management features are delegated to application owners.

- **Feature Delegation**   The ability to configure which features of a Web site or application to delegate to Web site and application administrators. Provides the ability to delegate control of specific features to site or application administrators without having to provide them with full administrative control of the server.

- **Administrators**   This feature allows server administrators the ability to create site and application administrators. Server administrators include both the local server's administrators group and the members of the Domain Administrators group.

- **Management Service**   A management service for IIS 7.0 that enables server, site, and application administrators the ability to connect to IIS 7.0 remotely using IIS Manager. It also allows site and application administrators the ability to connect to IIS 7.0 on the server locally, when they are a member of a Windows group.

Figure 12.13 shows the Feature Delegation screen from within the new IIS Manager.

Figure 12.13 Feature Delegation in IIS Manager

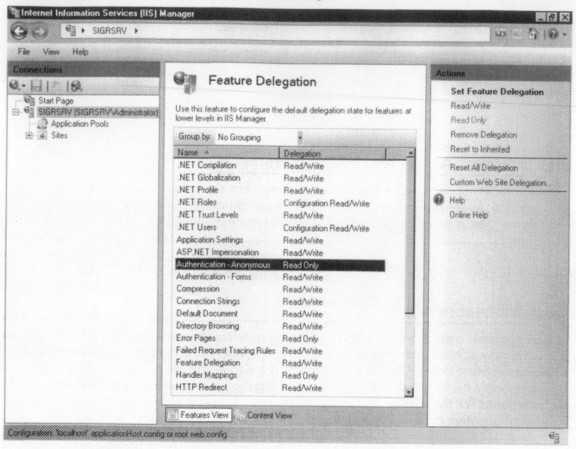

Improved User Interface for Users, Partners, and Microsoft

The interface in IIS has changed in version 7.0. It has become more task-oriented, helping administrators do exactly what they want, and not forcing them to search for the correct tab or control button. IIS Manager is extensible as is the rest of IIS 7.0. It allows you to administer most of the features in IIS 7.0 and monitor the server's operation. Administrators can manage both IIS and *ASP.NET* configuration settings, membership and user data, and runtime diagnostic information.

As seen in the previous section, the new interface can also be used to enable delegation. The new IIS Manager can remotely manage servers via Hypertext Transfer Protocol Secure sockets (HTTPS), therefore making remote management more secure friendly and not forcing IT administrators to open additional ports on firewalls. The ports for HTTPS (443), which are required for remote IIS

Manager use, are typically already opened on the firewall. IIS Manager is completely extensible, allowing the creation of custom modules that add new functionality. For example, a developer could create a diagnostics module used to view event viewer data relevant to IIS. Figure 12.14 shows the new IIS Manager interface.

Figure 12.14 IIS Manager in IIS 7.0

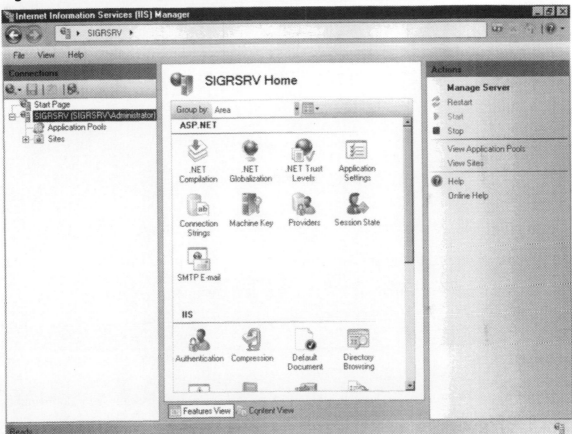

WMI with Logical Layout, Strong Support for PowerShell

IIS 7.0 includes a new WMI provider that provides access to configuration and server state information to people using VBScript, Jscript, and Windows PowerShell. Because IIS 7.0 is modularized, to take advantage of the capabilities of WMI in IIS you must enable the feature allowing you to use WMI with IIS 7.0. Figure 12.15 shows the IIS Management Scripts and Tools feature being enabled in Longhorn Server.

Figure 12.15 Enabling WMI for IIS 7.0

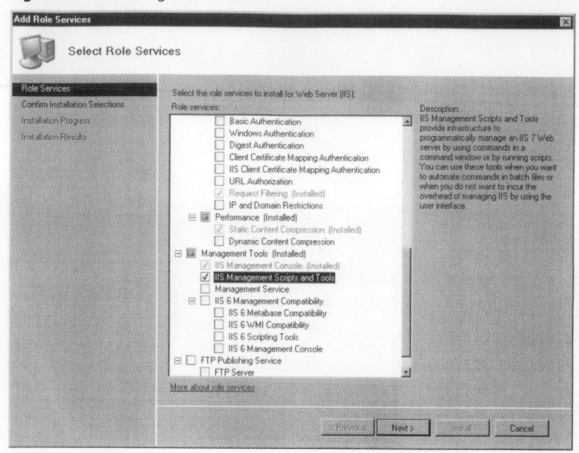

WMI is used to build scripts for Web administration, such as accessing, reading, and modifying key configuration files such as ApplicationHost.config and Web.config, the files that replaced the old metabase. Script writers have the ability to add, remove, or edit any part of the IIS 7.0 configuration. For example, WMI scripts have the ability to add modules at either the global or section level, configure custom HTTP errors, Multipurpose Internet Mail Extensions (MIME) Maps, Secure Sockets Layer (SSL) bindings, and ASP settings. WMI scripting in IIS 7.0 continues to be important for automating frequently repeated tasks, such as creating Web sites.

One can view the logical layout of WMI namespaces of IIS 7.0 by using WMI CIM studio, which can be downloaded for free at www.microsoft.com/downloads/details. aspx?FamilyID=6430f853-1120-48db-8cc5-f2abdc3ed314&DisplayLang=en.

Another way of accessing WMI is through PowerShell. PowerShell is a new command-line scripting technology created by Microsoft to provide administrators with control and automation of system administration tasks. The PowerShell script, which we will call *PowerWMI.ps1*, will retrieve information from the *Win32_Process* class and echo back the Name and WorkingSetSize for each item. The results are shown in Figure 12.16. The following is the PowerShell script.

```
$strComputer = "."
$colItems = get-wmiobject -class "Win32_Service" -namespace "root\cimv2" -
computername $strComputer
foreach ($objItem in $colItems) {
  write-host $objItem.Name, $objItem.State
}
```

Figure 12.16 Using PowerShell with WMI

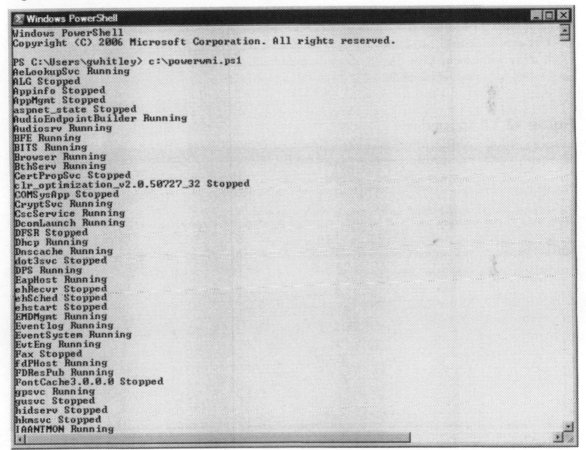

IIS 7.0 now includes a new WMI provider used to access both configuration and server state information. Developers and administrators alike can use VBScript, Jscript, and Windows PowerShell to take advantage of this. By using WMI CIM Studio, we can view the logical layout of objects and classes in a WMI namespace.

AppCmd: Swiss Army Knife for IIS Administrators and Developers

A major improvement in the administration of IIS 7.0 comes in the form of the command line utility *Appcmd.exe*. Think of the eight scripts mentioned earlier that IIS 6.0 administrators needed to know. Now think of having all of that capability tied into one command. *Appcmd.exe* provides a comprehensive set of management functionality and better support for bulk operations than the user interface. *Appcmd.exe* makes it easy to read and write configurations, access site and application pool state information, create virtual directories, and perform any other administrative task directly from the command line. Other abilities include starting and stopping sites, recycling application pools, listing the running worker processes, and examining currently executing requests. It supports linked operations like those found in Windows PowerShell, which allows multiple operations on a related set of objects to be performed together from a single command line. It's no wonder that *Appcmd.exe* is called the Swiss Army knife for IIS Administrators and Developers. Figure 12.17 shows *Appcmd.exe* performing numerous commands.

Figure 12.17 Appcmd.exe

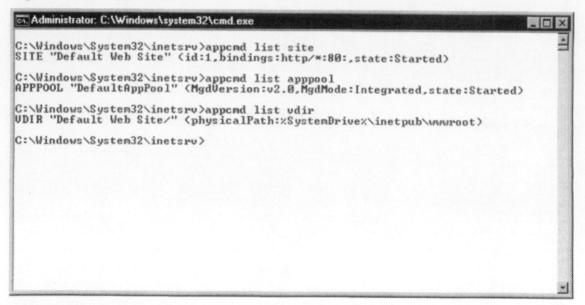

Diagnostics 101

IIS 7.0 provides new tools to help debug applications and monitor the server. The following are two new features available to both administrators and developers:

- Runtime State and Control API (RSCA)
- FREB

Runtime State and Control API (RSCA)

RSCA allows developers to see running requests on a server in real-time. This feature exposes the active state of sites and application pools and running worker processes. RSCA allows administrators to start and stop sites and recycle application pools. This capability comes in handy when investigating server issues or tuning server performance, because being able to quickly see what is going on in the system itself and controlling it while troubleshooting is powerful. To break it down, RSCA does the following:

- Provides in-process state information (current processes running, application pools process ID, currently executing requests, and AppDomains loaded)

- Real-time starting and stopping of sites

FREB

When a user informs you that there is a problem with the Web server, the first thing you do is try to reproduce the problem; however, a lot of times you can't. That's where FREB comes into play. Possibly the most anticipated feature in IIS 7.0, it does the following:

- Traces all requests through the pipeline

- Identifies requests that are stuck or failing

- Identifies time taken in each module, helping to analyze long running requests

- Provides that there be no need in reproducing the error for tracing failed requests

- Administrators can configure custom failure definitions per Universal Resource Locator (URL) based on time-taken or HTTP status and sub-status codes)

To use FREB you must create at least one failed request tracing rule where you can set the trace attributes per site or per application. This then allows you to capture an XML-formatted log of a specific problem when it occurs. As stated earlier, administrators and developers will no longer have to reproduce the problem.

FREB can also be left enabled on a server, allowing administrators and developers the ability to continuously capture trace logs for requests that have encountered a configurable failure condition, while avoiding any performance of saving trace logs. This allows you to capture information when errors occur, even if it's an intermittent problem. This eliminates the difficult task of having to conduct deep debugging of issues.

Because the tracing infrastructure is exposed to IIS modules and the server's extensible model, all components, whether they came with IIS or were developed by a third party, can emit detailed tracing information during request processing. You can even write your own modules that provide data to IIS 7.0's trace files information.

Figure 12.18 shows an example of setting up the location of where the XML-formatted log will reside after you set up FREB.

Figure 12.18 FREB Log Location

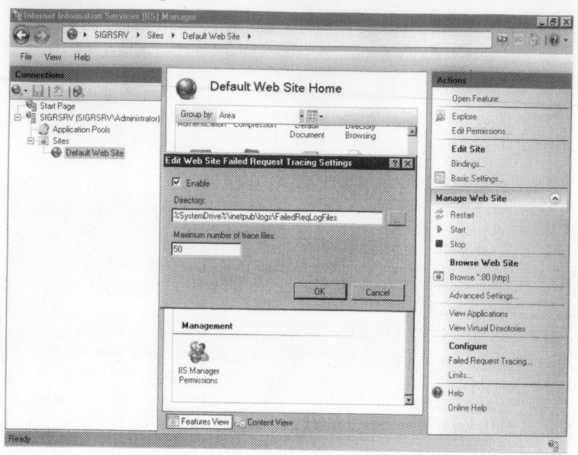

Once again, FREB is probably the most anticipated feature offered by IIS 7.0, which both developers and administrators will rely on.

Summary

Possibly the most anticipated release of IIS ever, version 7.0 rebuilt from the ground up does not disappoint. A new modular design allows administrators to load what they want without the risk of having unwanted and unused code residing in memory and creating a security concern. The new modular design also allows developers to add any functionality they wish. A new set of publicly available API's removes the reliance on ISAPI and having to know C and C++ when wanting to extend IIS. Managed code no longer has second class citizenship; it has the same access to the pipeline that native code does. WMI now provides native access to managing servers. The old metabase and its complexities have been replaced by more manageable *.config* files.

Security is improved. Server administrators can now delegate tasks to Web administrators and developers without having to provide total server administrative rights. Administrative tools are easier to use and more powerful. The new and improved IIS Manager is now task-oriented and wizard-based, thereby walking administrators through the necessary steps to achieve what they need to. IIS 7.0 now has a complete administrative command line utility in *Appcmd.exe* that can be used to view and configure objects.

Diagnostic features are now easier to use and more powerful. FREB is a feature that is able to trace all requests through the pipeline, identify stuck or failing requests, and is useful in analyzing long running scripts. FREB allows administrators to enable it, create a rule, and then never worry about having to recreate an error.

Microsoft has brought about a lot of changes to an already solid platform, and improves upon it with IIS 7.0. Both developers and administrators will benefit from its features.

Solutions Fast Track

Inside the Changes in IIS 7.0

☑ The IIS 6.0 core was monolithic and did not easily support extensions. With two pipelines present it had the possibility of producing duplication.

☑ The IIS 6.0 metabase was large and difficult to read and locate.

☑ Most diagnostic tools in IIS 6.0 were add-ons and not built into the product. These tools were difficult to use, such as ETW.

☑ FREB enables administrators and developers to trace all requests throughout the pipeline. By enabling FREB on the server, administrators and developers never have to reproduce the error.

IIS 6.0 versus 7.0: The Delta

☑ IIS 7.0 has a modular core; developers are able to add any functionality they want. Only modules that are enabled are loaded in memory, which is more efficient and more secure.

☑ Administrative delegation is available. Server administrators can now provide the access needed by Web administrators and developers without having to provide full administrative rights.

☑ IIS Manager is now more complete and robust, basically allowing any part of IIS to be managed by the user interface.

☑ Appcmd.exe provides a more comprehensive management functionality and better support for bulk operations than IIS Manager.

Frequently Asked Questions

Q: In IIS 7.0, do ISAPI filters give you any advantage over modules and managed code?

A: No. Because of the new modular core, both managed code and native code subscribe to the same events.

Q: Does IIS 7.0 run on Windows Server 2003?

A: No. IIS 7.0 will only run on certain versions of Vista and the upcoming Longhorn Server.

Q: Can I manage IIS 7.0 via the command line?

A: Yes. By using the new Appcmd.exe utility, you can manage IIS and ASP.NET

Q: I have existing ADSI and WMI scripts that work in IIS 6.0. Will they work in IIS 7.0?

A: Yes, but you must enable the IIS 6.0 Management Compatibility feature.

Q: In IIS 7.0, how do I troubleshoot hard-to-reproduce failed request issues?

A: Use FREB.

Chapter 13

Installation of IIS 7.0

Solutions in this chapter:

- Install Types Available in IIS 7.0
- Installation Features Sets
- IIS 7.0 Modules

☑ Summary

☑ Solutions Fast Track

☑ Frequently Asked Questions

Introduction

Installation procedures were completely rewritten for Windows Vista and Longhorn Server. The previous installer, SysOcMgr.exe, has been replaced by a more modular setup process. To complicate matters, IIS 7.0 is broken down into many different feature sets, each of which has independent modules associated with it. Unlike previous versions of IIS, IIS 7.0 setup will install to your system only the selected modules and nothing more. This means that modules will not be physically present on the system. For this reason, it is imperative that you understand each feature set, and the subsequent modules, to be successful at installing only the features desired and nothing more and furthermore ensure that you do not install more than is needed.

Install Types Available in IIS 7.0

Users need to understand that installation technology has been merged together for Windows Vista and Longhorn server. For IIS 7.0, it is important to evaluate the installation method that fits your environment. The following installation types are available:

- Using Vista's Add Windows Features
- Using Vista's Command-Line Package Manager (pkgmgr.exe)
- Using Windows Server's Unattended Installation (code-named "Longhorn")

IIS 7.0 is now modular, giving administrators and developers alike complete control of the features they require while minimizing the memory footprint of the Web server. Now not only are unneeded and unwanted components disabled, they aren't even installed. Previously, even if an administrator chose not to enable certain features of IIS, the modules making up those features still ran in memory, even though they didn't execute.

Setup in IIS 7.0 includes more than 40 installable features, providing administrators the ability to deploy whatever they need. Setup for both Vista and the upcoming Longhorn Server uses what is referred to as a *declarative model,* whereby each feature of the operating system defines its own set of components and dependencies. Vista and Longhorn Server benefit from a single binary base sharing a code base between them. For this reason, the dependencies are known for all features, and depending on those features chosen by the administrator, smaller service packs and patches are possible, thus reducing the time it takes to perform updates.

Since Vista and Longhorn Server use a single component setup that unifies the OS installation, services the OS, and provides installation of optional features, administrators no longer need to use sysocmgr.exe. There are various ways of installing IIS 7.0, including the following:

- Vista's Programs and Features
- Longhorn Server's Server Manager
- Command-Line Package Manager (pkgmgr.exe)
- Unattended installation

Vista's Programs and Features

In Windows Vista, operating system features such as IIS 7.0 are installed via Programs and Features in Control Panel, which replaces Add/Remove Programs in previous versions of Windows such as Windows XP. We will walk through the installation of IIS 7.0 on Windows Vista using the Programs and Features method. You must have administrator rights or the ability to use the *runas* command and provide the administrator credentials when prompted. This installation works on Vista Home Premium, Business, and Ultimate editions. In this example we will install just the default Web server for IIS 7.0:

1. In Windows Vista, click **Start | Control Panel**, as shown in Figure 13.1.

Figure 13.1 Selecting Control Panel

2.   In Classic View of Control Panel, select **Program and Features**, as shown in Figure 13.2.

Figure 13.2 Selecting Programs and Features

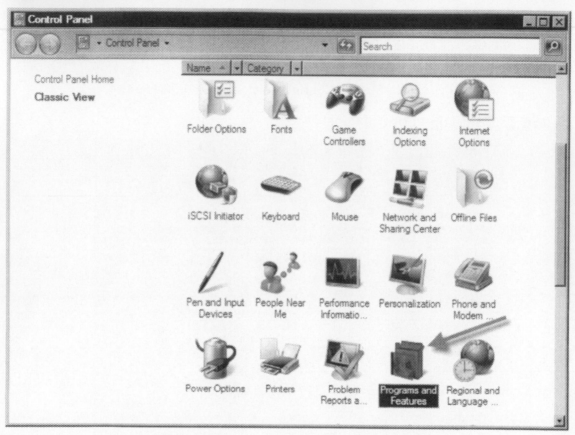

3. On the left, select **Turn Windows features on or off** (see Figure 13.3).

Figure 13.3 Selecting Turn Windows Features On or Off

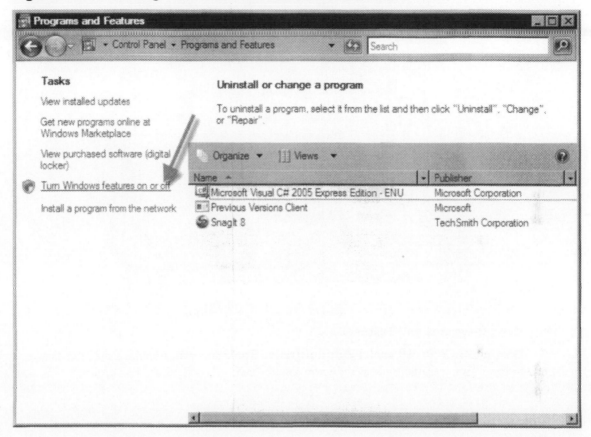

4. Now you should see the Windows Features box. Scroll down until you see Internet Information Services. Now choose **Internet Information Services**, as shown in Figure 13.4, and click **OK**.

Figure 13.4 Selecting IIS

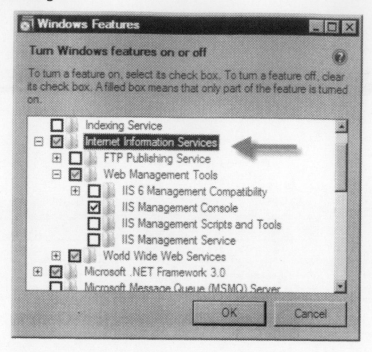

5.   Close **Programs and Features**.

6.   Now go to **Control Panel | Administrative Tools** and you should see the IIS Manager in the list of available tools, as shown in Figure 13.5.

Figure 13.5 Administrative Tools

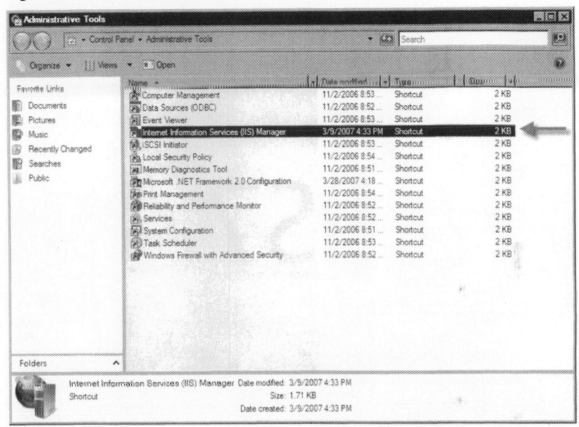

7. To test our installation, open **Internet Explorer** and go to **http://localhost**. You should
    see the screen shown in Figure 13.6.

Figure 13.6 Testing Localhost

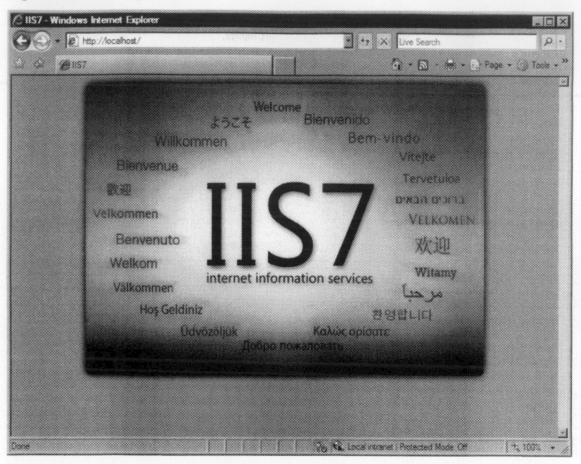

Longhorn's Server Manager

Installation using Longhorn's Server Manager provides a single interface that allows administrators to install and uninstall server roles and features. It also provides quick status on the state of installed roles and provides entry points to role management tools. To install IIS 7.0 on Longhorn Server, just as in Vista, you must have administrator rights to the system. In this example we will install the same features as the last procedure for Vista but using Longhorn Server's Server Manager:

1. Click the **Start** button and go to **Administrative Tools | Server Manager**, as shown in Figure 13.7.

Figure 13.7 Selecting Server Manager

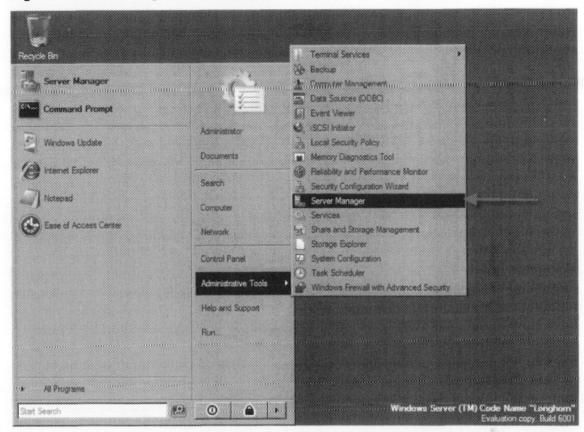

2. While in Server Manager, select **Roles** in the left window pane. Afterward the Roles view is displayed, similar to Figure 13.8. As you see, we have no roles installed on our server.

Figure 13.8 Roles View in Server Manager

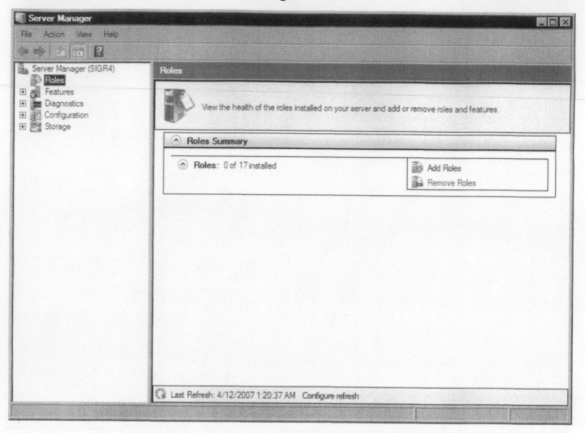

3. Now let's add the Web Server role for Longhorn Server. As shown in Figure 13.9, select **Add Roles**.

Figure 13.9 Selecting Add Roles in Server Manager

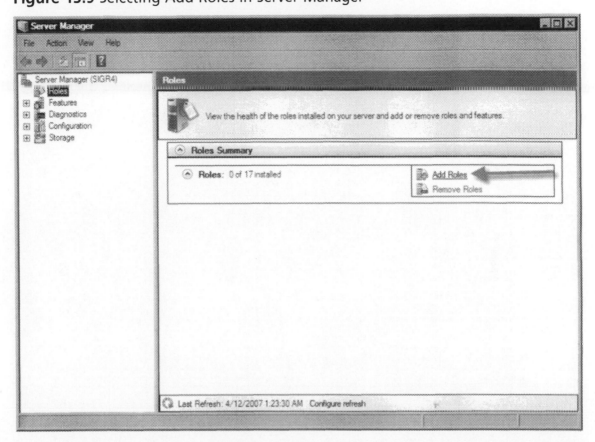

4. Now you should see the **Add Roles Wizard** in Figure 13.10. Click **Next**.

Figure 13.10 Add Roles Wizard in Longhorn Server

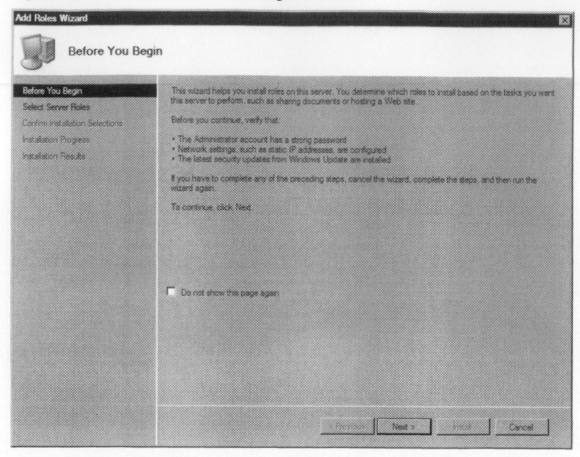

5.   The **Select Server Roles** screen appears as shown in Figure 13.11. Choose
     Web Server (IIS).

Figure 13.11 Selecting the Web Server Role

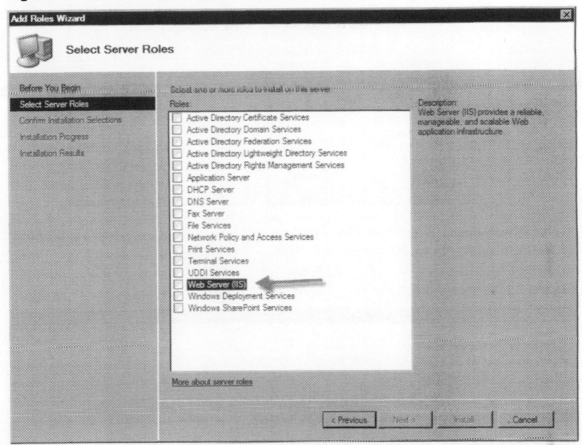

6. After you select Web Server (IIS), a popup screen like the one shown in Figure 13.12 will inform you that this role cannot be installed unless the Windows Process Activation Service is also installed. If you need to know why these features are required, simply click the **Why are these features required** link at the bottom of the dialog box. Now click **Add Required Features**. Once that's done, click **Next** back on the Select Server Roles screen.

Figure 13.12 The Features Required for Web Server (IIS) Screen

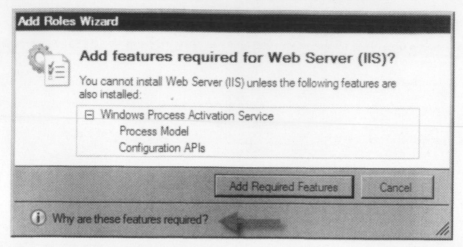

7. Now you will see the **Web Server (IIS)** screen shown in Figure 13.13, providing an introduction to the Web Server. Click **Next**.

Figure 13.13 Introduction to Web Server Wizard Screen

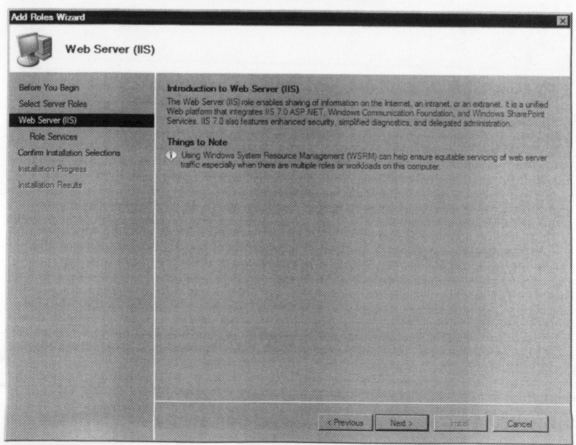

8. You will be allowed to select the features you want enabled in IIS 7.0, as shown in Figure 13.14. Since we are just taking the defaults, we won't be adding or deleting any features, so we can now click **Next**. Remember that with IIS 7.0, only the modules from the features you choose load, so the more you add, the larger the footprint becomes.

Figure 13.14 Selecting IIS 7.0 Features

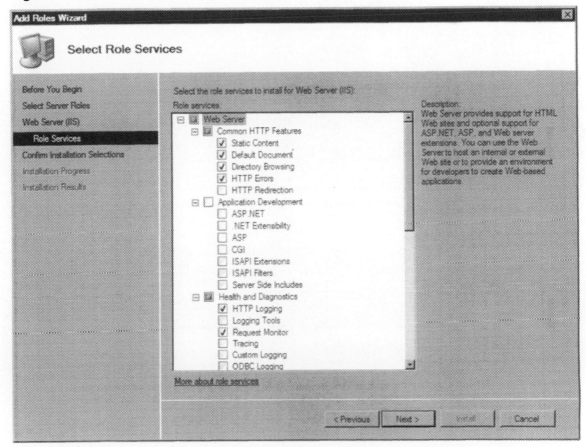

9. After selecting the features you require, the installation wizard provides you a breakdown of the roles, services, and features you are about to install, as shown in Figure 13.15. If you are sure of what you want to install, click **Install**. If not, click **Previous** and select the features you want.

Figure 13.15 List of Features to Be Installed

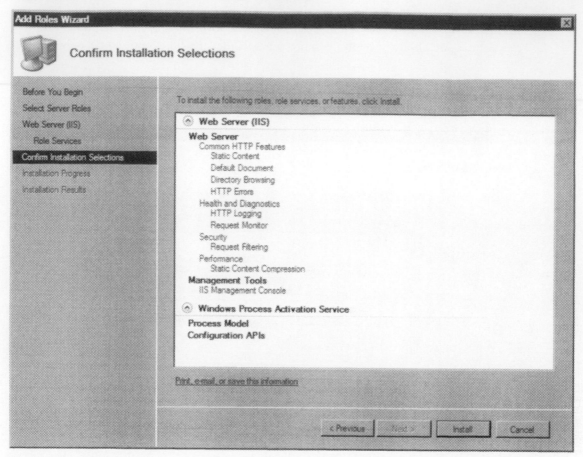

10. You will now see the **Installation Progress** screen, similar to the one shown in Figure 13.16.

Figure 13.16 Installation Progress

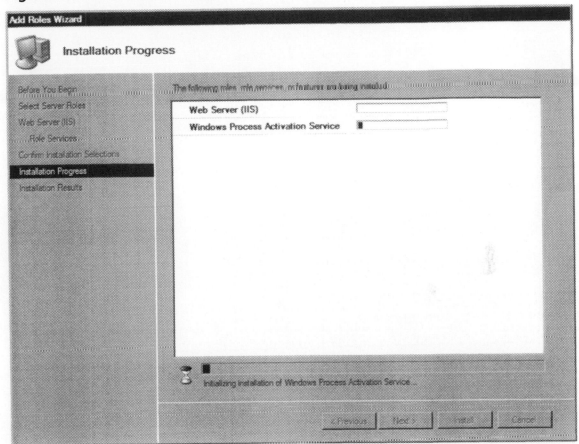

11. When the installation is complete, you will see the **Installation Results** shown in Figure 13.17. After viewing the installation results, click **Close**.

Figure 13.17 Installation Results

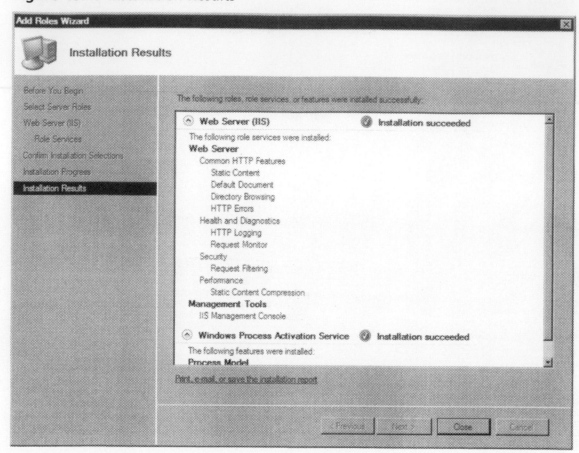

12. Now you should see Server Manager, showing that you have one role installed, that being **Web Server (IIS)**, as shown in Figure 13.18.

Figure 13.18 Web Server (IIS) Installed

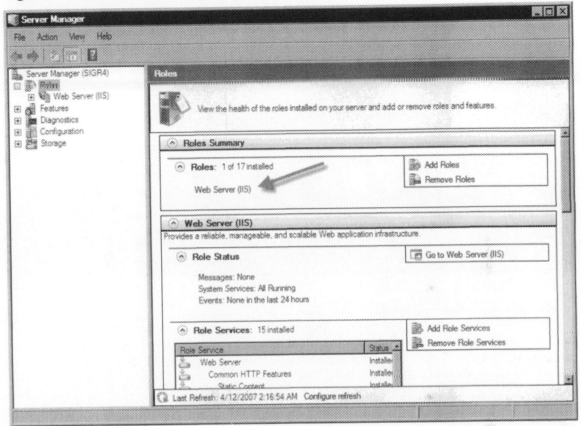

13. To verify that the installation was a success, just as in Vista, you can test using http://localhost. You should see the same screen as previously shown in Figure 13.6.

Just as in previous versions of IIS, we can install the server via the user interface, whether through Vista's Programs and Features or Longhorn Server's Server Manager. These methods are probably the easiest forms of installation. Now we will examine installing IIS 7.0 via the command line using PKGMGR.EXE.

Installing with PKGMGR.EXE

Since Windows 2000, administrators have been able to install optional features via sysocmgr.exe. Now, with both Windows Vista and Longhorn Server, command-line installation is done using pkgmgr.exe. This tool can install features directly from the command prompt or even from an XML file, which we will cover in unattended installations.

PKGMGR.EXE works with Windows Vista Home Premium, Business, Ultimate, and Longhorn Server editions. Here is the syntax for pkgmgr.exe:

```
Start /w pkgmgr.exe /iu:update1, update2…
```

And these are the commands for pkgmgr.exe:

- **/iu:{update name};** Specifies updates to install.

- **/uu:{update name};** Specifies updates to uninstall.

- **/n:{unattended XML};** Specifies the filename of the unattended XML file.

Using *start /w*

Running pkgmgr.exe without the *start /w* prefix will cause pkgmgr to return without the administrator knowing when the optional feature(s) installation has completed.

Now we will install IIS 7.0 with the default features using pkgmgr.exe. Just as before, you must have administrator rights or access to the local administrator's password while using the *runas* command:

1. In Windows, open a command window as shown in Figure 13.19.

Figure 13.19 A Command Window in Vista

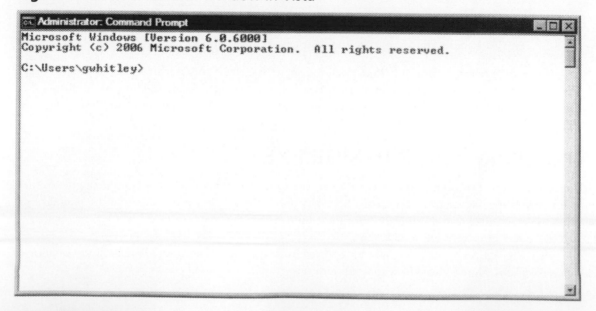

```
Administrator: Command Prompt

Microsoft Windows [Version 6.0.6000]
Copyright (c) 2006 Microsoft Corporation.  All rights reserved.

C:\Users\gwhitley>
```

2. Now type the following command in the command window:

```
start /w pkgmgr /iu:IIS-WebServerRole;WAS-WindowsActivationService;
WAS-ProcessModel;WAS-NetFxEnvironment;WAS-ConfigurationAPI
```

Note that the command must be typed as one line and it will scroll in the command window as needed, as shown in Figure 13.20.

Figure 13.20 Pkgmgr Command

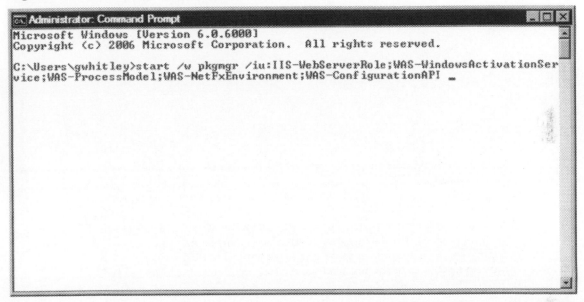

3. Press **Enter** to install IIS 7.0 with the default features. The installation can take between 1 and 5 minutes. Once it's complete, you will see a blinking cursor, as shown in Figure 13.21.

Figure 13.21 Pkgmgr.exe Installation Complete

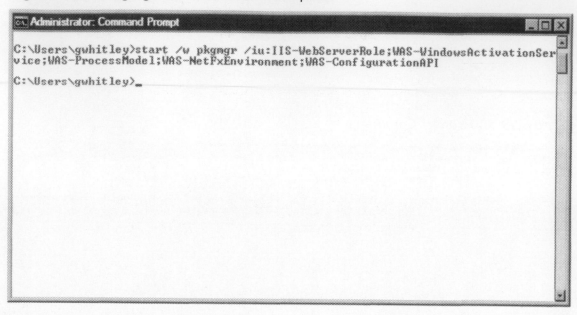

4. After you've completed the installation, you can test it by going to http://localhost, where you should see the IIS welcome screen that we saw in Figure 13.6.

Now that we know how to use the pkgmgr.exe command, let's put it in practice with an unattended XML file using Longhorn Server.

Unattended Installation

As we mentioned earlier, you can do an unattended installation for IIS 7.0 using an XML file. To do this, you will use the pkgmgr.exe command along with your XML file for the unattended installation. We won't go over how to create the XML file, but before creating it, you must obtain the build number of the operating system you are installing to:

1. Locate the **regedit.exe** file in the C:\Windows directory (assuming that you installed Windows in C:\Windows).

2. Right-click **regedit.exe** and click **Properties**.

3. Once the regedit properties come up, go to the **Details** tab and you will see the **Product version**, as shown in Figure 13.22. In our case the product version is 6.0.6001.16497. This number is used in the *<assemblyIdentity>* section of our unattend.xml file.

Figure 13.22 Obtaining the Build Number

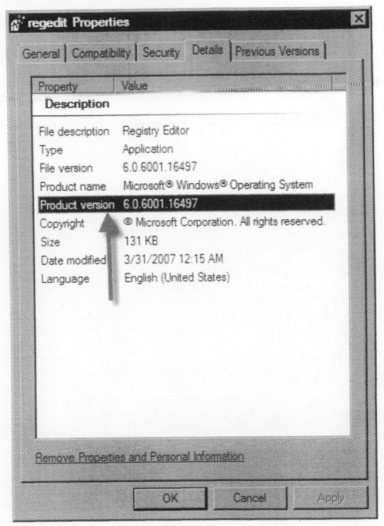

In this example, we will install all the features available for IIS 7.0 in Longhorn Server using the unattended installation method. In a situation where as the administrator you have to deploy numerous servers with multiple if not all features for IIS 7.0, using the unattended method will likely be your best bet:

1. Create a file named unattend.xml using a text editor like Notepad or a tool such as Visual Studio, as we have in Figure 13.23.

Figure 13.23 Unattend.xml file

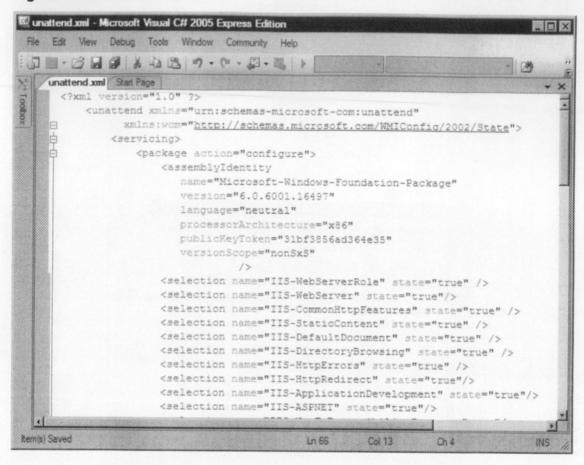

2. Now we will open a command window and install IIS 7.0 using pkgmgr as we did previously, but this time we'll call the unattend.xml file we created. So in the command window, type **start /w pkgmgr /n:C:\unattend.xml** as shown in Figure 13.24.

Figure 13.24 Starting Unattended Installation of IIS 7.0

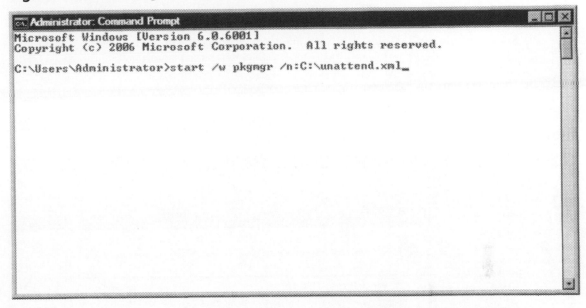

3. Once IIS 7.0 is installed, you will come to a blinking cursor (see Figure 13.25).

Figure 13.25 Unattended Installation Complete

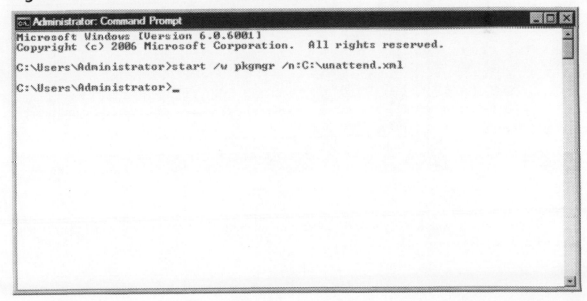

4. After installation is complete, go to http://localhost to test whether IIS is installed. If it's installed, you will see the IIS welcome screen shown in Figure 13.6, just as you've seen in the other examples. You can also verify the installation of the features by opening **Server Manager | Roles**, then scrolling down to **Role Services** and verifying that the appropriate services and features have been installed. Figure 13.26 shows Server Manager and the role services installed.

Figure 13.26 Server Manager and Role Services Installed

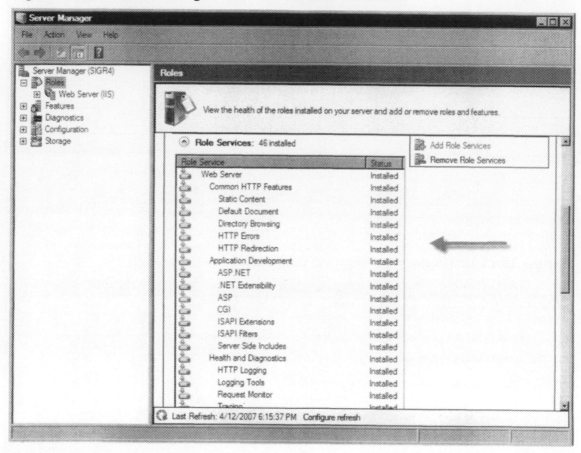

Now that we've gone over each of the installation methods, let's look at some major feature sets and what they offer users.

BEST PRACTICES ACCORDING TO MICROSOFT

Microsoft recommends using the unattended installation method for administrators deploying numerous Web servers that share the same features and modules, thereby creating installations that are consistent and quicker to complete.

SOME INDEPENDENT ADVICE

Always test your unattended installation in a lab or some sort of controlled environment. Now that administrators have the responsibility of understanding setup modules in greater detail, the chances of mistakes increase. In addition, since the unattended files are XML based, the syntax becomes tighter and less forgiving.

Installation Feature Sets

Unlike any other version of IIS, IIS 7.0 is broken down into the smallest possible installable components. In IIS 7.0, these components are called *modules* and are standalone in functionality or are grouped into a larger "feature set" to help install like modules. This section discusses the major feature sets and what they offer users:

- FTP Publishing Service
- Web Management Tools
  - IIS 6.0 Management Capability
- World Wide Web Services
  - Application Development Features
  - Common HTTP Features
  - Health and Diagnostics
  - Performance Features
  - Security

It is important to understand what each feature set installs and further realize what potential risks (such as open ports) come with each feature set.

As we stated earlier in this chapter, IIS 7.0 has a modular setup allowing administrators control of what modules are installed without concern of having non-installed modules residing in memory. Modules in IIS 7.0 can be standalone or grouped into larger feature sets, helping install similar modules. For administrators who will be installing IIS via a command line or script, it is especially important that they understand the details of each feature set. In this section we cover the following feature sets:

- FTP Publishing Service
- Web Management Tools
- World Wide Web Services

The FTP Publishing Service

The FTP Publishing Service provides FTP connectivity through IIS 7.0. It is available to Windows Vista Business, Enterprise, Ultimate, and Longhorn Server. It has not changed since IIS 6.0 in that it relies on the metabase, and therefore inetinfo.exe will reside in memory if installed. The FTP Publishing Service is not installed by default and is made up of two components, FTP Server and FTP Management Console. Their modules are listed in Table 13.1 along with their descriptions.

Table 13.1 FTP Publishing Modules

Module	Description
FTPServer	Installs the FTP Service
FTPManagement	Installs the FTP Management Console for administrators

FTP Server provides support for uploading and downloading files from systems using the File Transfer Protocol. The FTP Server in IIS 7.0 is simply the same one that shipped with IIS 6.0.

The FTP Management Console is used by administrators to manage FTP servers locally and remotely. It is located in the IIS 6.0 Manager, as shown in Figure 13.27.

Figure 13.27 The FTP Management Console

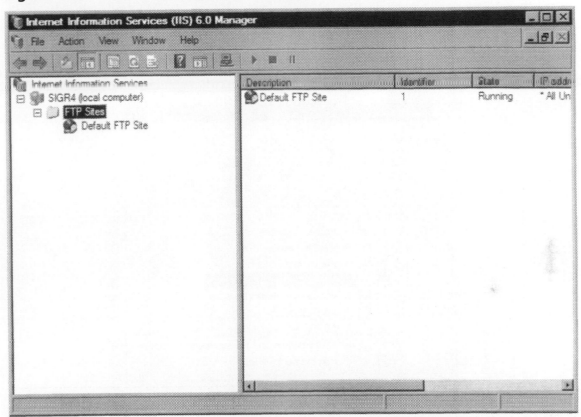

Web Management Tools

The Web Management Tools not only install IIS Manager, WMI, and Remote Management Service, but they are also responsible for loading IIS 6.0 Management Compatibility, which is not installed by default. This is important because if you or your developers have older applications that cannot be modified to take advantage of the new architecture, such as those that use Admin Base Objects (ABO) or Active Directory Service Interface (ADSI), you must install IIS 6.0 Management Compatibility so that these applications can be provided with the forward compatibility that they require to run on IIS 7.0. Figure 13.28 shows us installing Web Management Tools along with IIS 6 Management Compatibility with the IIS 6 Management Console and IIS Metabase and IIS 6 configuration compatibility in Windows Vista. Table 13.2 is a listing of the modules that make up the Web Management Tools feature set, along with their descriptions and dependencies.

Figure 13.28 Web Management Tools

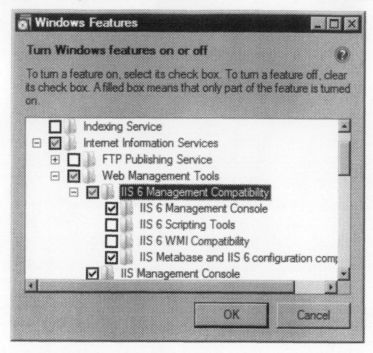

Table 13.2 Web Management Tools Modules

Module	Description	Depends On
ManagementConsole	Web server management console supporting management of local and remote Web servers	ConfigurationAPI
ManagementScripting	Provides the ability to manage a Web server with IIS configuration scripts	ConfigurationAPI
ManagementService	Allows the Web server to be managed remotely via the Web server management console	ManagementConsole

Table 13.2 Continued

Module	Description	Depends On
NetFxEnvironment		
ConfigurationAPI		
Metabase	Installs the IIS metabase and compatibility layer	—
WMICompatibility	Installs IIS 6.0 SMI scripting interface	—
LegacyScripts	Installs IIS 6.0 configuration scripts	Metabase
WMICompatibility		
LegacySnap-in	Installs IIS 6.0 management console	—

World Wide Web Services

The World Wide Web Services in Windows Vista and the Web Server role in Longhorn Server provide support for Web sites using HTML and optional support for ASP.NET, ASP, and other Web server extensions. This service gives servers running IIS 7.0 the ability to host Web sites and support Web-based applications. Unlike previous versions of IIS, administrators need to make informed decisions about what functionality is required for their servers.

Installation of World Wide Web Services is relatively easy using either the Programs and Features method for Windows Vista or Server Manager for Longhorn Server in that you don't have to know what dependencies are required. That is not the case for those using the command-line installation methods. When using those methods, you must know the features you want to install and their dependencies or your installations will fail.

World Wide Web Services depend on the existence of the Windows Process Activation Service (WAS). Earlier we walked through setting up IIS via Server Manager in Longhorn Server. When we went through the installation we were prompted that the features we were installing required WAS, as shown in Figure 13.12. WAS provides all necessary infrastructure for a base level of process activation and management as well as an HTTP processing infrastructure.

The World Wide Web Services feature is made up of five sections with various modules underneath each one:

- Application Development Features
- Common HTTP Features
- Health and Diagnostics
- Performance Features
- Security

The next section covers these features and their modules in more detail.

BEST PRACTICES ACCORDING TO MICROSOFT

Microsoft highly recommends learning each and every feature set, its modules, and any dependencies. This reduces the risk of mistakes that can cause instability and poor performance on Web servers.

SOME INDEPENDENT ADVICE

Examine the feature sets and modules we've listed in this chapter. Also check out Microsoft's article "IIS Setup Overview" at www.iis.net/default.aspx?tabid=2& subtabid=25&i=955 on Microsoft's IIS Web site; it provides a great deal of information on IIS 7.0 setup in general.

IIS 7.0 Modules

It is no secret that IIS 6.0 installs with a large set of components, or *dynamic linked libraries* (DLLs.) The fashion of security offered in IIS 6.0 is to not enable features that the administrator doesn't desire on a per-DLL basis. However, IIS 6.0 doesn't offer the opportunity to fully remove the unused DLL but instead just the ability to ensure it doesn't execute. This is important for administrators because they are the ones responsible for ensuring that Windows workstations and servers are patched appropriately. There is nothing more frustrating than installing patches for features not even used, yet the DLL still was installed. When you're installing IIS 7.0, selecting no feature installs the appropriate DLLs for that feature, creating an environment where administrators need not patch features not installed.

IIS 7.0 is based on more than 40 modules that cover the wide range of features offered by the Web server out of the box. In this section, we outline each module's name, purpose, and dependencies to ensure that only the correct pieces are installed.

IIS 6.0 was solid, secure, and powerful, but it wasn't modular in design. Components that were not enabled still had their DLLs loaded in memory. This increased the size of the footprint and created headaches for administrators having to patch features they weren't even using. Microsoft improved on this by loading only those modules in memory that were selected by the administrator, making them responsible for patching those specific modules only. Modules perform specific functions; they can stand alone or be part of a feature set. The onus is now on the administrator to understand the 40-plus modules offered in IIS 7.0 and correctly choosing the ones he or she needs. Although running setup through the user interface doesn't require the knowledge of the modules and their dependencies, installing IIS via scripts and the command line does. Here we cover the most important ones and their dependencies.

The Runtime Core "Bits"

Administrators installing IIS 7.0 via the command line and through scripts must understand in detail what feature sets include what modules and their dependencies. Simply forgetting a dependent module for a feature set you require can mean the difference between a smooth installation and a nightmare implementation, especially if it is on a grand scale. On the other hand, if administrators install more than they need, they have needlessly increased their security footprint, causing additional maintenance through unneeded patching and decreasing performance. In IIS 7.0, you get what you install—it's as simple as that. As the administrator, you have the control and, more important, the responsibility to install and maintain what is needed.

Figure 13.29 lists all the setup features and their associated modules in IIS 7.0. We will discuss in detail the five sections of the World Wide Web Services. We will describe each module and list any and all its dependencies.

NOTE

All IIS features have an implicit dependency with their parent. For instance, FTP Server depends on the FTP Publishing Service being enabled. Some IIS features, though, do depend on other IIS features for their functionality, and those are referred to as *intra-dependencies*.

Figure 13.29 IIS 7 Setup Features and Modules

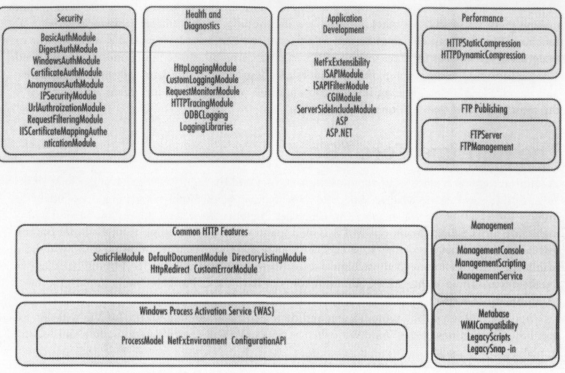

Application Development Features

The Application Development Features support the deployment of Web-based applications and dynamic content such as ASP.NET, ASP, ISAPI extensions, and filters. They also provide support for .NET extensibility, CGI executables, and files such as .stm, .shtm, and .shtml. The Application Development Features are made up of seven modules. Table 13.3 lists the modules available in the Application Development Features, with descriptions of each along with any dependencies required.

Table 13.3 Application Development Features Modules

Module	Description	Depends On
NetFxExtensibility	Enables Web servers to host .NET Framework managed module extensions	NetFxEnvironment

Table 13.3 Continued

Module	Description	Depends On
RequestFilteringModule		
ISAPIModule	Allows ISAPI extensions to handle client requests	—
ISAPIFilterModule	Allows ISAPI filters to modify Web server behavior	—
CGIModule	Enables support for CGI executables	—
ServerSideInclude Module	Provides support for .stm, .shtm, and .shtml include files	—
ASP	Enables Web servers to host classic ASP applications	ISAPIModule
RequestFilteringModule		
ASP.NET	Enables Web servers to host ASP.NET applications	NetFxExtensibility NetFxEnvironment ISAPIModule ISAPIFilterModule RequestFilteringModule

Common HTTP Features

Common HTTP Features install support for static Web server content such as HTML and image files, custom errors, and redirection. Default Document and Static Content are two of the more important modules supported here. Table 13.4 lists the modules available for the Common HTTP Features under IIS 7.0.

Table 13.4 Common HTTP Features Modules

Module	Description
StaticFileModule	Serves .htm, .html, and image files from a Web site
DefaultDocumentModule	Provides the ability to specify a default file to be loaded when users do not specify a file in a request URL

Continued

Table 13.4 Continued

Module	Description
DirectoryListingModule	Allows clients to see the contents of a directory on a Web server
CustomErrorModule	Installs HTTP error files; allows you to customize the error messages returned to clients
HttpRedirect	Provides support to redirect client requests to a specific destination

Health and Diagnostics

Highly invaluable in aiding debugging and resolving issues with IIS 7.0, the Health and Diagnostics feature allows administrators and developers to monitor and manage server, site, and applications. Many administrators might not want to load this module on production systems due to performance considerations. Instead, these features may be installed on test servers, therefore not affecting user access and performance. Table 13.5 lists the modules for Health and Diagnostics and a description of each.

Table 13.5 Health and Diagnostics Modules

Module	Description
HttpLoggingModule	Enables logging of Web site activity for a particular server
CustomLoggingModule	Enables support for custom logging for Web servers, sites, and applications
RequestMointorModule	Monitors server, site, and application health
HTTPTracingModule	Enables tracing for ASP.NET applications and failed requests
ODBCLogging	Enables support for logging to an ODBC-compliant database
LoggingLibraries	Installs IIS 7.0 logging tools and scripts

Performance Features

Performance features provide for output caching by integrating dynamic output-caching capabilities of ASP.NET with the static output-caching capabilities that were present in IIS 6.0. Administrators can more effectively and efficiently use networking bandwidth by using compression mechanisms such as Gzip and Deflate. Table 13.6 lists the Performance modules and their descriptions.

Table 13.6 Performance Modules

Module	Description
HTTPStaticCompression	Compresses static content before returning it to a client
HTTPDynamicCompression	Compresses dynamic content before returning it to a client

Security

Probably the most important of all feature sets, the Security feature requires administrators to install the right modules to be assured that security in their Web servers is effective and not compromised. The Security feature set secures the Web server from both users and requests. Here is where the authentication mechanisms such as Windows Authentication, Basic Authentication, and others for IIS 7.0 are supported. The ability to filter any incoming requests and reject them without ever processing them is supported. Table 13.7 lists the modules available under the Security feature set and their descriptions.

Table 13.7 Security Modules

Module	Description
BasicAuthModule	Requires a valid Windows username and password for connection
DigestAuthModule	Authenticates clients by sending a password hash to a Windows domain controller
WindowsAuthModule	Authenticates users by using NTLM or Kerberos
CertificateAuthModule	Authenticates client certificates with Active Directory accounts
AnonymousAuthModule	Performs Anonymous authentication when no other method succeeds
IPSecurityModule	Allows or denies content access based on IP address or domain name
UrlAuthorizationModule	Authorizes client access to the URLs that comprise a Web application
RequestFilteringModule	Configures rules to block selected client requests
IISCertificateMapping-AuthenticationModule	Performs Certificate Mapping authentication using IIS certificate configuration

Summary

IIS 7.0 is modular in design, allowing administrators to take more control over the features they require. This allows them to decrease the memory footprint that IIS 7.0 uses, improving security and performance while also minimizing the amount of patching required. Administrators can install IIS 7.0 using various methods. In Windows Vista they can use the user interface via Programs and Features. Longhorn Server's Server Manager serves the same purpose through Role Services. Both Windows Vista and Longhorn Server support the use of pkgmgr.exe, a command-line tool used for installing IIS 7.0 and its various features. Administrators looking to conduct mass IIS rollouts and deployments will want to take advantage of unattended installations. This method also uses pkgmgr. exe but streamlines the installation by using an unattended XML file.

It is important that administrators understand in detail the feature sets available in IIS 7.0, their modules, and any dependencies they require. Not doing so puts their installations at risk and can cause instability and a lack of functionality at the server. IIS 7.0 empowers administrators to make it what they want, but it also gives them a great deal of responsibility as well.

Solutions Fast Track

Installation Types Available in IIS 7.0

☑ In Windows Vista, IIS 7.0 can be installed using Programs and Features in Control Panel.

☑ Server Manager in Longhorn Server allows IIS 7.0 to be installed via its user interface.

☑ Pkgmgr.exe is a command-line tool that can be used for installing IIS 7.0 and can save time over using the user interface when kicked off from a script.

☑ Administrators deploying numerous servers should use unattended installations that employ an unattended XML file and pkgmgr.exe.

Installation Features

☑ FTP Publishing Service is the same as it was in IIS 6.0 in that it looks for the existence of the metabase.

☑ Web Management Tools installs the new IIS Manager, WMI support, remote management, and IIS 6.0 Management Compatibility.

☑ World Wide Web Services provides support for Web sites using HTML, ASP.NET, ASP, and other extensions. It is made up of five sections.

IIS 7.0 Modules

- ☑ Modules perform specific functions; they can stand alone or be part of a feature set.

- ☑ Modules allow the footprint of IIS 7.0 to be small while providing the required functionality.

- ☑ Administrators must understand each module in IIS 7.0's setup, along with its dependencies, before using pkgmgr.exe and unattended installations.

Frequently Asked Questions

Q: What is the best method of installation for IIS 7.0?

A: Depending on your situation, any one of the methods mentioned in this chapter could be the best. For large installations it is recommended that you use the unattended installation method. If you are installing one of two Web servers, it might be better to go through the user interface, such as Server Manager for Longhorn Server or Programs and Features for Windows Vista.

Q: Why should I learn each and every feature set, their modules, and their dependencies?

A: Administrators using pkgmgr.exe with or without an unattended XML file should know these components in great detail. Not knowing them puts at risk the stability of their servers and their performance.

Q: Why don't I simply install all the features? That way I won't miss anything.

A: You can do that, but you are putting at risk your IIS 7.0 installation by increasing the footprint in memory, possibly making it more vulnerable to attack. You are also degrading performance by loading unneeded modules and increasing the amount and frequency of patching.

Q: I thought the metabase was gone. Why does the FTP Publishing Service look for it?

A: The metabase is no longer the central repository for configuration in IIS. FTP Publishing is the same as it was in IIS 6.0, and in IIS 7.0 it believes that the metabase exists. IIS 7.0 actually translates the calls to the "old" metabase to the ApplicationHost.config file; therefore, the metabase doesn't actually exist—legacy applications and features only think it does.

Q: After I enabled IIS 6 Management Compatibility, I got the IIS 6 Management Console. Now I have two—one for IIS 7.0 and one for IIS 6.0. Why is that?

A: IIS 6.0 servers and their features must still be managed by the old IIS 6 Management Console, whereas IIS 7.0 servers can only be managed by the IIS 7 Management Console.

Chapter 14

The Extensible Core Server

Solutions in this chapter:

- **Understanding Development Advantages in IIS 7.0**

- **Extending IIS 7.0 with Native Modules**

- **Enabling Managed Code in IIS 7.0**

☑ **Summary**

☑ **Solutions Fast Track**

☑ **Frequently Asked Questions**

Introduction

There has never been so much excitement for a Microsoft Web server as there is for IIS 7.0. It is easy to understand why, when developers across all languages have the same freedoms. The parity stopped when a developer using ASP.NET attempted to garner full control of requests incoming to the Web server. This freedom wasn't allowed unless a developer knew C++ and was familiar with the complex Internet Server Application Programming Interfaces (ISAPIs) that were shipped with IIS 1.0 and later versions. These rules are changed with IIS 7.0, as developers can choose their languages of choice, and managed code developers have the same access to the same events as their C/C++ counterparts. The IIS 7.0 core server hasn't met a developer it doesn't like.

Understanding Development Advantages in IIS 7.0

We focus on administration more than development, but one cannot avoid the fact that the landscape for development on IIS has drastically increased with IIS 7.0. Administrators should know that IIS 6.0 and previous versions were in a semi-open system where developers were offered a complex mechanism to modify the behavior of the Web server via ISAPI filters. In IIS 7.0, that barrier has been broken down and is now open to developers who write both native (C/C++) and managed (VB.NET, C#) code.

It is important to understand how native code modules are implemented and installed in IIS 7.0. Beyond that, an administrator needs to understand the implications of introducing managed code into IIS 7.0 and furthermore, how to enable them.

Although most administrators typically do not create modules themselves, it is important that they understand from a high level what changes and improvements have been made in the architecture of IIS 7.0, in particular as it applies to developers and the improvements that they will experience.

As mentioned in Chapter 12, the core server in IIS 6.0 was monolithic with two request pipelines: one for native modules and another for managed modules. The previous platform didn't provide developers with the environment they desired. Developers who used managed code such as C# or VB.NET saw their requests treated as second-class citizens, thereby not having the same freedoms as those who wrote native code such as C/C++. All was not rosy for developers using low-level languages either; they experienced a difficult and cumbersome task in extending IIS 6.0 by creating complex ISAPI filters and extensions. All of this has changed in IIS 7.0.

Administrators and developers alike need to understand that IIS 7.0 resolves these issues with a more modular architecture and unified pipeline. Whether a developer uses native or managed code, they have full access to the same events. IIS 7.0 provides a friendlier place for developers of all types. Developers need to know what is involved in extending IIS 7.0 through building native and managed modules, and administrators need to understand the different methods that are available for deploying them.

IIS 7.0 supports two different environments brought under the concept of modes. Understanding how the two modes apply to application pools and when to use either is important for both administrators and developers. The following sections examine each of the concepts mentioned in this section and go through two demonstrations.

Inside the Unified Pipeline

In earlier versions of IIS (6.0 and earlier), the development of .NET application components was allowed through ASP.NET. This was integrated via ISAPI extensions; therefore, administrators ended up having two separate pipelines—one for native code (ISAPI filters and extensions) and a second for managed code (ASP.NET). Requests to non-ASP.NET content such as static files were not visible to ASP.NET under IIS 6.0 and earlier. When running in integrated mode, IIS 7.0 allows ASP.NET to integrate with the core server, thus providing a unified pipeline for both native and managed code and allowing ASP.NET modules to be used for requesting static files and other content. No longer do developers have to depend on an ISAPI intermediary, which is difficult to write and must be done in C or C++. Now managed code can control every request going to the application to which it is mapped. Figure 14.1 depicts the core server in IIS 7.0. Notice that both native and managed code have the same access to the same events.

BEST PRACTICES ACCORDING TO MICROSOFT

When you are examining the modules loaded in w3wp.exe, Microsoft recommends using the Windows Sysinternals process explorer. Opening up the worker process in process explorer, developers can examine their modules in action, whether they are loading or not, and determine the size of their footprint in memory.

SOME INDEPENDENT ADVICE

The tools provided at Windows Sysinternals are used by many at Microsoft and have been for years, so it made sense when Microsoft acquired the group headed by Windows guru Mark Russinovich. The tools created by this group are some of the best in the industry. What's even better is that they can be downloaded for free at www.microsoft.com/technet/sysinternals/default.mspx.

Through the use of the new native application programming interfaces (APIs) or ASP.NET, modules can be developed to extend IIS 7.0. Native code itself interacts with the IIS 7.0 request pipeline directly, without any intermediaries or shims. The advantage of this is speed and improved performance. Programmers who are used to writing ISAPI filters and extensions now have the option of using the new publicly available APIs for creating their new modules. These modules allow C and C++ programmers more freedom because they are not being bound by the tight restrictions in writing ISAPI code.

Figure 14.1 IIS 7.0 Core Server

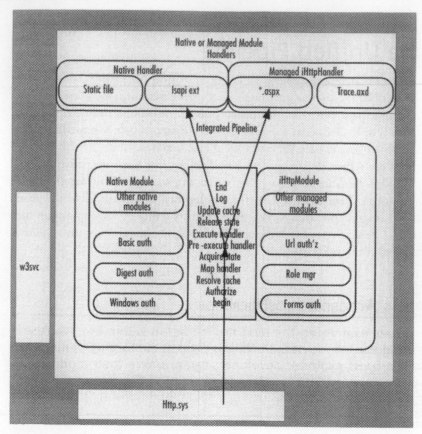

Extensibility in IIS 7.0 is also provided to manage code via webengine.dll. As we will see later, this native global module provides managed code direct access to the pipeline when running in integrated mode. Isapimodule.dll maps ISAPI calls as though modules were running in the older IIS 6.0 and earlier model in classic mode. There will be more about integrated mode versus classic mode later in this chapter.

Shortcut...

Modules and Kits

Microsoft provides sample modules and starter kits for both administrators and developers of IIS 7.0. Administrators can walk through adding and deleting modules, while developers can use the sample modules as examples for their own. These can be downloaded at www.iis.net.

Extending IIS 7.0 with Native (C\C++) Modules

Microsoft developers changed the way they developed the IIS Web server in IIS 7.0 by ensuring that they used the same APIs that were used by their customers. In IIS 7.0, the native APIs used to build features on top of the core server are the same as those used by developers. They are built and enabled the same way, and they are installed similarly.

It is important to know how a developer (or administrator) begins building a simple native module, but much more important to know how to install it correctly in IIS 7.0.

C and C++ developers do not have to deal with the difficulties of writing and debugging ISAPI filters and extensions anymore. Developers also do not need to create ISAPI code; anything they need can be accomplished by creating a module. As mentioned earlier, native code programmers can use the new server APIs that Microsoft developers used in developing IIS 7.0. Deployment is also much easier than in the past. It is important for administrators to understand how a developer goes through building native modules and what it takes to add them to IIS 7.0.

BEST PRACTICES ACCORDING TO MICROSOFT

Before modifying the applicationHost.config file, Microsoft recommends backing the file up. If after adding a native module IIS becomes unstable, it will be easier to restore to the previous file. Here is an example of performing such a backup using AppCmd.exe.

    Appcmd.exe add backup <name of backup>

SOME INDEPENDENT ADVICE

As an administrator, you may need to add modules on a regular basis. If this is the case, create a naming standard for your backups that makes sense to you. You may want to use a naming standard that mentions the module you are about to deploy. For instance, if you are about to deploy a module called MyModule, you can put it in the name of the backup. Below is an example of using the module's name, its version, and the date. This way you know that this backup was done before you added the module MyModule version 1.0.

    Appcmd.exe add backup MyModule-1.0-03-1007

Building Native Modules

Although server extensibility can now be done using managed code and the ASP.NET APIs, there still are reasons developers may want to create modules via native code. One of the biggest reasons is performance; native code runs faster than managed code. Although native and managed code strings have access to the same request pipeline, native code directly accesses it. Another reason you may want to create a native module is if you want to convert your ISAPI components into new native code modules.

A native code module contains the following:

- The RegisterModule function, which is responsible for creating a module factory and registering the module for server events.

- The implementation of the module class inheriting from the CHttpModule base class, which provides the main functionality for your created module.

- The implementation of the module factory class that implements the IHttpModuleFactory interface. It is responsible for creating instances of your newly created module.

The modules used in this example can be downloaded from Microsoft's *IIS.net* Web site at www.iis.net/downloads/default.aspx?tabid=34&g=6&i=1301. This module will be deployed as a global module in our demonstration, although any native module can be deployed at the application level just as managed modules are.

In developing a native module, the developer must implement the RegisterModule function that is started by the server when the module is loaded. In short, there are three tasks that are accomplished when implementing the RegisterModule function:

- **Saving the Global State**   This is done by saving the global server instance for future use.

- **Creating the Module Factory**   The module factory is responsible for creating instances of the native module for each request.

- **Registering for Server Events**   This registers the module factory for the desired request processing events.

The implementing of the RegisterModule and the three tasks that are required to do so are shown in Figure 14.2 through Visual Studio 2005.

Figure 14.2 Implementing RegisterModule

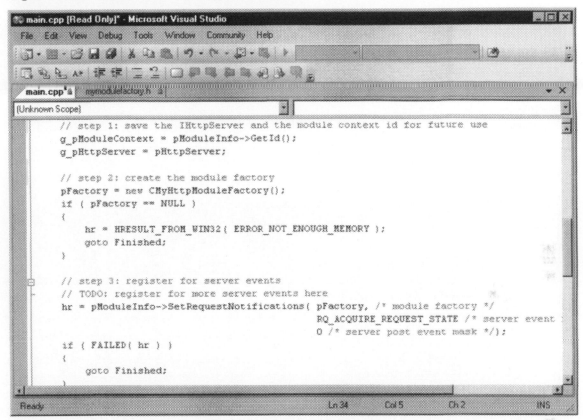

```
// step 1: save the IHttpServer and the module context id for future use
g_pModuleContext = pModuleInfo->GetId();
g_pHttpServer = pHttpServer;

// step 2: create the module factory
pFactory = new CMyHttpModuleFactory();
if ( pFactory == NULL )
{
    hr = HRESULT_FROM_WIN32( ERROR_NOT_ENOUGH_MEMORY );
    goto Finished;
}

// step 3: register for server events
// TODO: register for more server events here
hr = pModuleInfo->SetRequestNotifications( pFactory, /* module factory */
                            RQ_ACQUIRE_REQUEST_STATE /* server event
                            0 /* server post event mask */);

if ( FAILED( hr ) )
{
    goto Finished;
}
```

Registering a module factory is done through SetRequestNotifications. This tells the server to create the native module instance for each request using the module factory previously created, and to use the appropriate event handlers for each of the request processing stages. Once the developer has finished implementing the RegisterModule, he or she must export it to the server using a module definition file (.def). Afterward, the developer implements the module factory class. The module factory class implements the IHttpModuleFactory interface, which serves to create instances of the module on each request. Figure 14.3 shows the code for the module factory class.

Figure 14.3 Module Factory Class

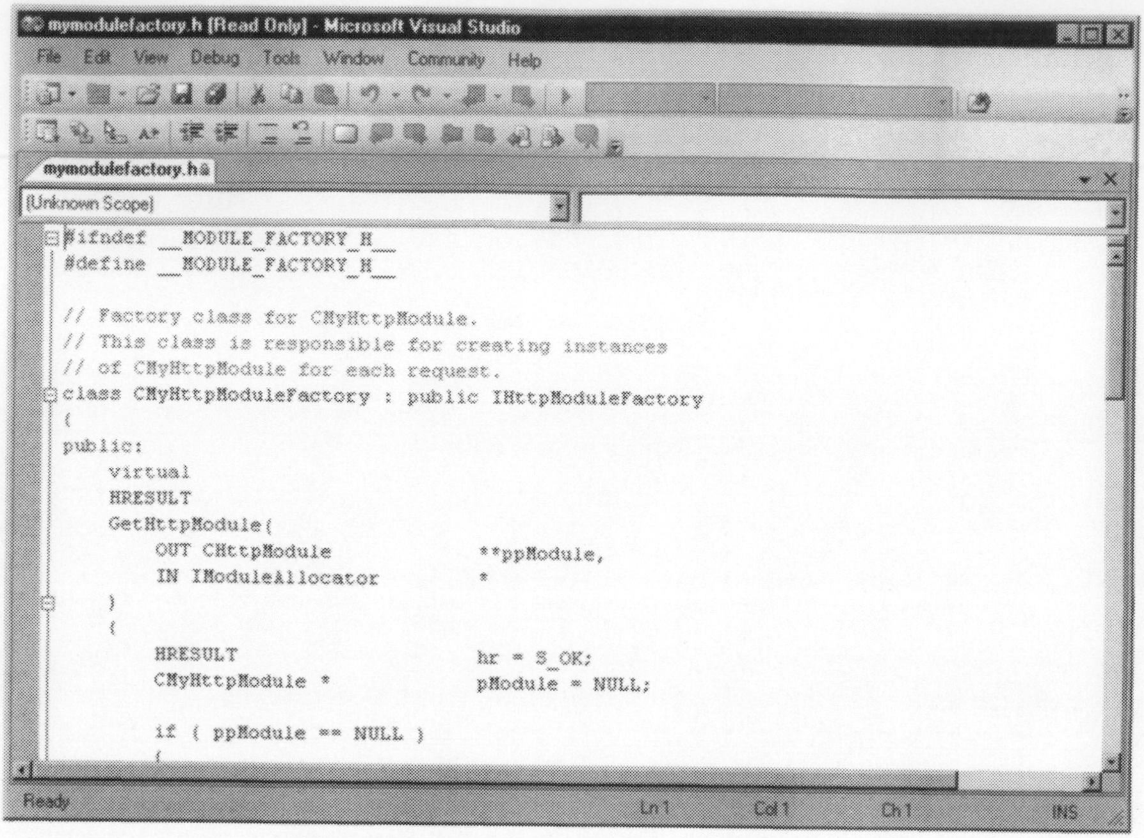

```
#ifndef __MODULE_FACTORY_H__
#define __MODULE_FACTORY_H__

// Factory class for CMyHttpModule.
// This class is responsible for creating instances
// of CMyHttpModule for each request.
class CMyHttpModuleFactory : public IHttpModuleFactory
{
public:
    virtual
    HRESULT
    GetHttpModule(
        OUT CHttpModule         **ppModule,
        IN IModuleAllocator     *
    )
    {
        HRESULT                 hr = S_OK;
        CMyHttpModule *         pModule = NULL;

        if ( ppModule == NULL )
        {
```

Once this code is complete, the developer implements the module class, which is responsible for the main functionality of the module during any server events. The code for the main module is shown in Figure 14.4. Once complete, the developer can compile the module. Managed code, however, does not have to be compiled (we discuss managed code later in this chapter).

Figure 14.4 Main Native Module

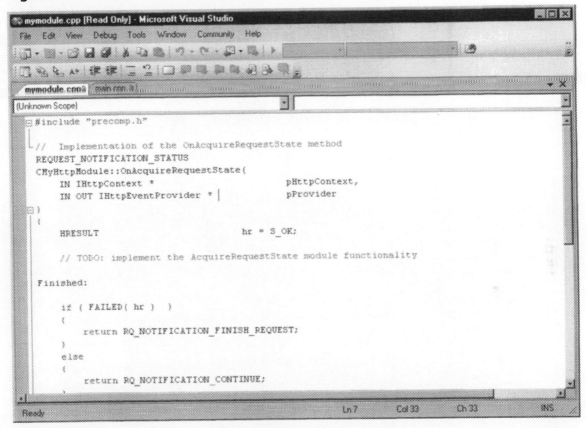

Adding Native Modules to IIS 7.0

In the previous section, we walked through what developers do to create a native module. In this section, we walk though what, as administrators, you will need to do to add these native modules to IIS 7.0. There are three ways to install a native module in IIS 7.0:

1. *APPCMD.exe*

2. IIS Manager

3. Manual Installation

Before adding the native module, you have to copy its .dll to the IIS server. There is no required location for the newly developed .dll, which in this case is called IIS7NativeModule.dll. Figure 14.5 shows that the new native module has been copied to the *C:\Native* directory, which was created on the IIS box. Now you need to deploy the module. First we will walk through using AppCmd, then IIS Manager, and finally manual deployment.

Figure 14.5 Location of the Native Module

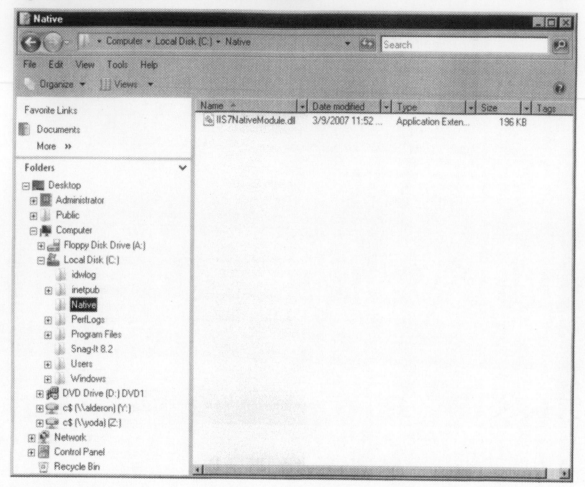

Using *APPCMD.exe* To Deploy Native Modules

As was introduced in Chapter 12, APPCMD.exe provides administrators with a new powerful command-line tool capable of managing IIS 7.0. To deploy a native module using APPCMD.exe, follow these steps:

1. Open a command prompt and go to the *%systemroot%\system32\inetsrv* directory.

2. As shown in Figure 14.6, type the command **appcmd.exe install module /name: MyModule /image:c:\Native\iis7nativemodule.dll**. Once the command has been executed, you should see a screen similar to that of Figure 14.7.

After adding the new module, you can verify that it has been added by examining the applicationHost.config file under the %systemroot%\system32\inetsrv\config folder. From the applicationHost.config file you can go to the <globalModules> section, as shown in Figure 14.8, and see that MyModule has been added.

Figure 14.6 Syntax for Using APPCMD.exe to Add a Native Module

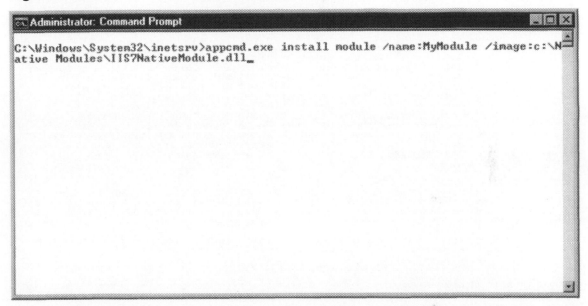

Figure 14.7 Results of Adding a Native Module with APPCMD.exe

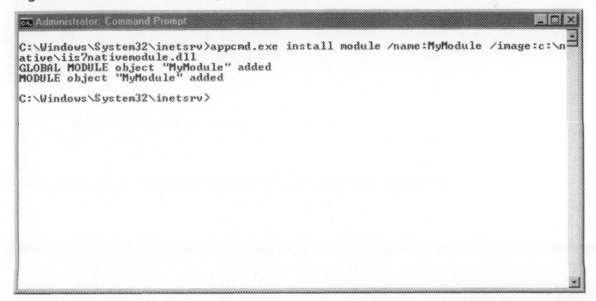

Figure 14.8 Deployed Native Module in applicationHost.config

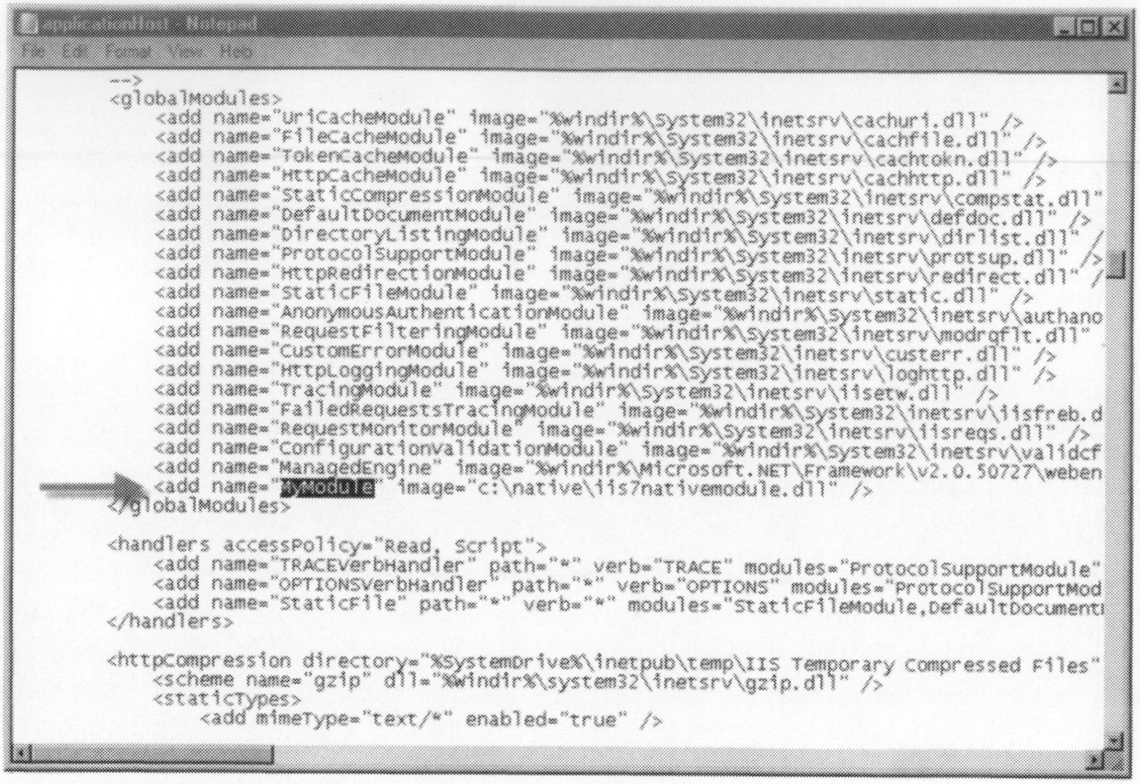

Deploying Native Modules with IIS Manager

As shown with the APPCMD.exe command, administrators and developers can deploy native modules at the command line. Another method in IIS 7.0 is using the user interface of IIS Manager. Here are the steps to follow when you are deploying a native module in IIS 7.0 with IIS Manager.

1. Open IIS Manager. From Windows Vista this can be accomplished by clicking **Start | Run**. Type **inetmgr** and press **Enter**. The same also works for Windows "Longhorn" Server as does clicking on **Start | Administrative Tools | Internet Information Services (IIS) Manager**. Do not choose the IIS 6.0 Manager if it is installed.

2. Once in IIS Manager, go to **IIS Category | Modules**, as shown in Figure 14.9.

Figure 14.9 Modules Section in IIS Manager

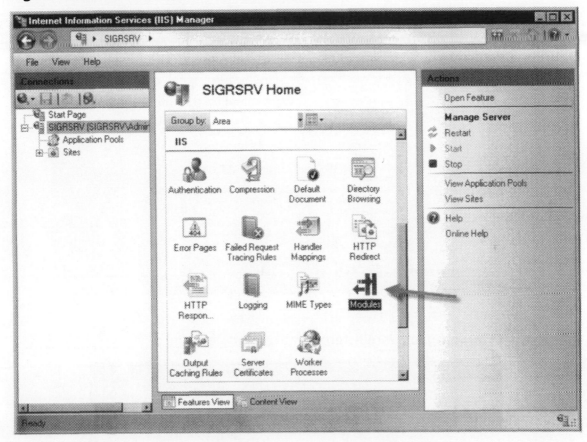

3. On the right side under **Actions** select **Add Native Module**, as shown in Figure 14.10.

4. Figure 14.11 shows the Add Native Module screen where you will see a list of registered modules. In this situation, the native module is not registered, so it must be registered first. On the right side of the dialog box select **Register**.

Figure 14.10 Add Native Module in IIS Manager

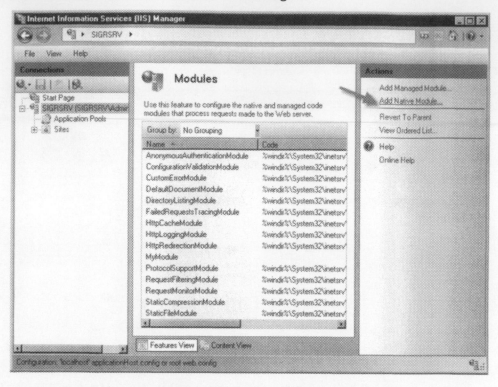

Figure 14.11 Adding an Unregistered Native Module

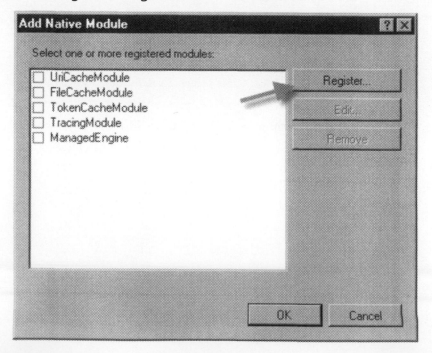

5. Under the Register Native Module dialog box (see Figure 14.12), enter the name of the module. For this instance the name is MyModule and the path is C:\Native\IIS7NativeModule.dll.

Figure 14.12 Register Native Module

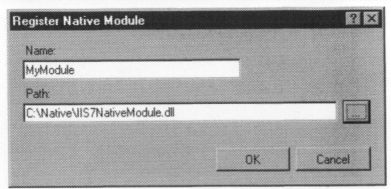

6. As shown in Figure 14.13, the native module (MyModule) is now selected from the list of registered native modules. Click **OK**.

Figure 14.13 Native Module Selected

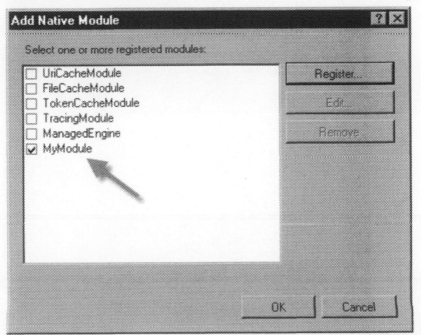

7.   Once finished you'll see the list of modules installed. You can change the view to the type of modules and then you will see that MyModule is installed as a native module, as shown in Figure 14.14.

Figure 14.14 Native Module Deployed From IIS Manager

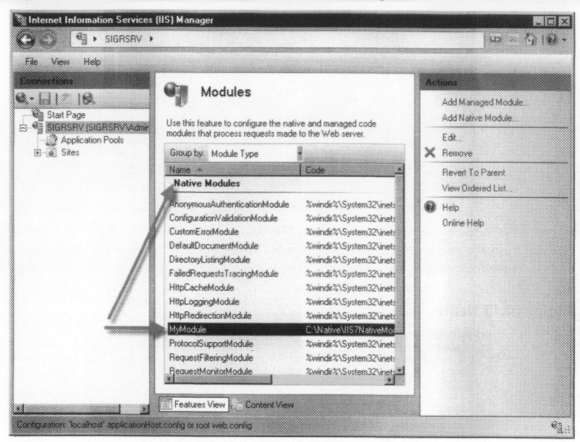

Manually Installing a Native Module

Manually deploying a native module is easier than it sounds. First, the .dll that accompanies the global module must be copied to the IIS server. After that, all it takes is editing the applicationHost. config file through any text editor such as Notepad, and entering the module information into the <globalModules> section.. The following example shows you how to install a newly created native module manually:

```
<add name="MyModule" image="c:\native\iis7nativemodule.dll"/>
```

As seen earlier, Figure 14.8 shows exactly how the aforementioned module would appear in the applicationHost.config file if it were a global module.

Enabling Managed Code (*ASP.NET*) in IIS 7.0

For the first time, managed code is a first-class citizen in IIS 7.0. In previous versions of IIS, managed code developers could not access data early in the request-processing cycle, because the IIS pipeline owned the area. Only when IIS sent the request (invoked) to ASP.NET could managed code act upon the request using a Hypertext Transfer Protocol (HTTP) module. In IIS 7.0, a managed module has the same level of access to the request processing events as a native module has, and gives developers greater access to events.

It is important to understand how to enable managed code (i.e., *webengine.dll*), how to access request processing events and the implications of doing so.

Previously, ASP.NET features could not be applied to IIS content types (e.g., forms authentication for static files).

In versions before 7.0, managed code could not access the pipeline directly. It depended on IIS sending the request to ASP.NET, and then the managed code could act upon the request. When combined with ASP.NET, the IIS 6.0 model produced a lot of duplication, such as Universal Resource Locator (URL) mapping, authentication, and handler mapping. This meant having to configure services in two different places.

In the previous sections, we talked about and demonstrated how to install native modules in IIS 7.0. The following sections talk about and demonstrate the same with managed code. If you enable managed code in IIS 7.0, you must understand the iHttpModule interface and how its behavior depends on what mode the application pool is running in. We briefly go over both Integrated Mode and Classic Mode and when to use them.

iHttpModule Interface Support

For those unfamiliar with ASP.NET, here is a brief overview. ASP.NET is a programming model from Microsoft used for developing dynamic Web sites and Web applications. It was first released in 2002 with Visual Studio.NET. As part of the .NET Framework, which succeeded the older Active Server Pages (ASP) technology, ASP.NET is built on the Common Language Runtime (CLR) and supports numerous programming languages such as, but not limited to, C#, VB.NET, and JScript.

ASP.NET provides an interface for developers in IIS called iHttpModule. In IIS 6.0, iHttpModule housed such events as URL mapping, authentication, and handler mapping, hence a separate pipeline that could be used only for files with .aspx and .asmx extensions, not for other content such as static files.

The good news for developers of managed code is that a second pipeline is not needed. IIS 7.0 supports the iHttpModule interface, but now features powered by managed modules can be applied to *all* requests to the server, and it is handled by a single request pipeline. Unlike native modules, managed modules can be deployed with content. In IIS 7.0, managed modules are loaded in two ways:

- via webengine.dll, which is supported in integrated mode
- via isapimodule.dll, which is supported in classic mode

We cover more about the supported modes of IIS 7.0 in the next two sections. Extensibility in IIS 7.0 is now available to developers writing managed code. Before deploying a managed module, ASP.NET must be installed on the IIS server. Figures 14.15 and 14.16 show where to enable ASP.NET on Microsoft "Longhorn" Server and Windows Vista, respectively. The sample code used for demonstration purposes is from the "IIS Managed Module Starter Kit," which is provided for free by the Microsoft IIS Team and can be downloaded from www.iis.net/downloads/default.aspx?tabid=34&i=1302&g=6

Figure 14.15 Adding ASP.NET to "Longhorn" Server

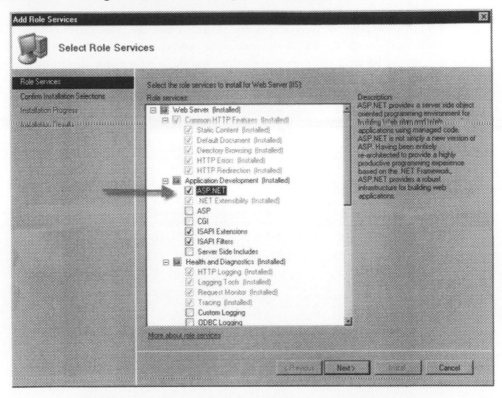

Figure 14.16 Adding ASP.NET to Windows Vista

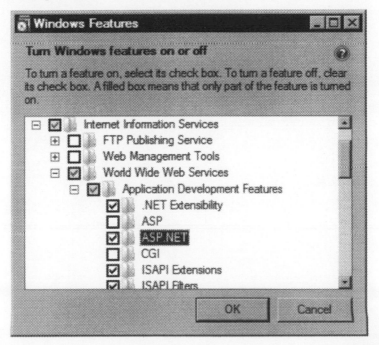

In Figure 14.17, you see some of the code for the managed module, which is written in C#. Notice IHttpModule in the code. Even if you weren't aware of the programming language used, this line shows that we are looking at a managed module and not a native one.

Although we will not go into the details of the code, it should be pointed out that the class MyModule's primary function is to register for event(s) that happen in the unified pipeline and then perform when IIS invokes the module's event handlers for its events. The Init statement sends up the module's event handler to the appropriate pipeline events. The Dispose line is used to clean up any resources after the module's instance is discarded.

Figure 14.17 Managed Code in C#

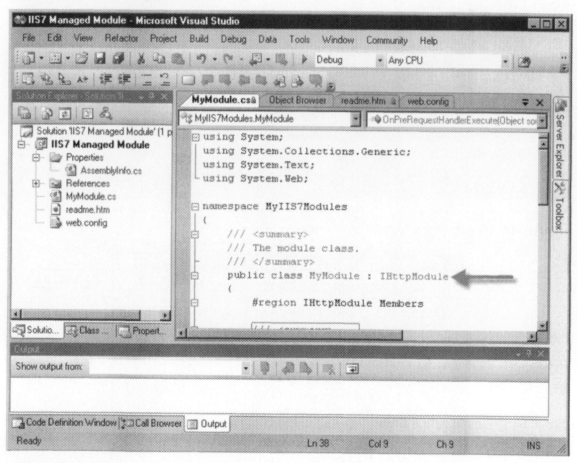

After the developer compiles his or her code, the module is stored in a .dll file. In this case, it is named MyIIS7Modules.dll. Figure 14.18 shows the web.config file for this application.

Figure 14.18 web.config

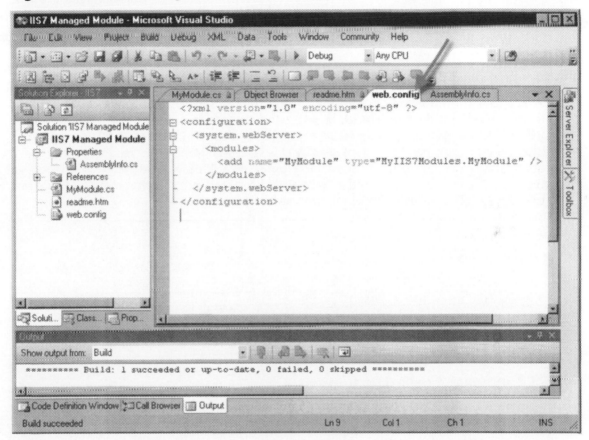

Once the code is compiled, you must deploy the module. Just as we did with the native module earlier in this chapter, copy the newly compiled .dll file somewhere on the IIS Server. In this example, we've copied it to the C:\Managed directory. Now copy the web.config file onto the server in the %systemroot%\inetpub\wwwroot directory. Open up IIS Manager (you can also deploy this with AppCmd.exe) and go to Modules. Under Actions, choose **Add Managed Module**, and then enter the information as shown in Figure 14.19.

NOTE

This application doesn't do anything, so for display purposes only, we chose **System.Web.Profile.ProfileModule**. After the module is added, it will appear in the list as a Managed Module under IIS Manager, as shown in Figure 14.20. You can also verify that it has been deployed by checking the <modules> section in the applicationHost.config file as shown in Figure 14.21. Please note that no managed modules will ever be added to the <globalModules> section, and that managed modules will always be loaded in the <modules> section.

Shortcut...

Managed Code Modules

Managed code modules don't have to be compiled by the developer. Simply take the application's logic in its file format (ex: .cs for C#) and drop it somewhere in the *app_code* directory on the server, and then ASP.NET will pick it up at runtime and compile it for you

Figure 14.19 Entering Managed Module Information

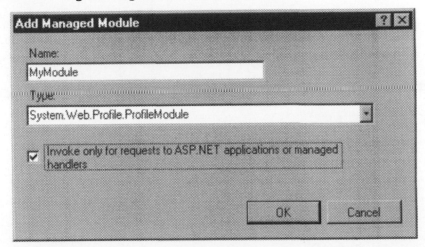

Figure 14.20 List of Managed Modules From IIS Manager

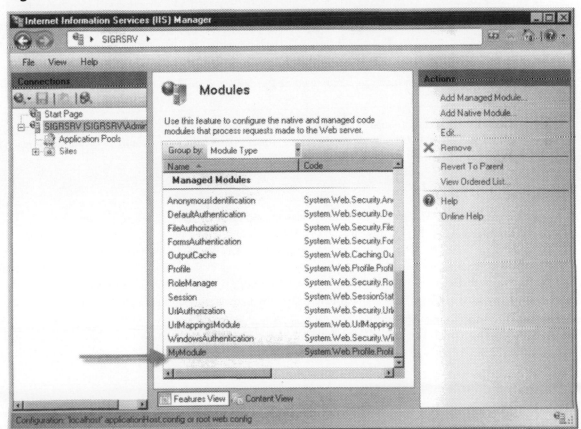

Figure 14.21 applicationHost.config File <modules> section

As we mentioned earlier, managed modules are loaded in IIS 7.0 in two ways and in two modes: integrated mode, which loads managed modules via webengine.dll, and classic mode, which loads via isapimodule.dll. Let's examine each.

Integrated Mode

Integrated mode in IIS 7.0 refers to the ability of managed code to have access to the unified pipeline. As mentioned earlier in this chapter, ASP.NET modules now have access to all content, not just from *.aspx* or *.asmx* files. So what actually creates the parity between managed code and native code in IIS 7.0? The answer is webengine.dll.

Webengine.dll is a native code module that resides under the <globalModules> section of the applicationHost.config file. It acts as a shim that allows managed code direct access to the fully integrated and unified pipeline. Developers using managed code still use the iHttpModule, but they are actually working with the shim. Webengine.dll allows managed code to be treated as a first-class citizen in IIS 7.0. To use it you must run in Integrated Mode.

Which mode you run in is determined at the application pool level. You can have some application pools running in integrated mode and others in classic. In Figure 14.22 we are creating a new application pool called MyTestApp. Notice that we can select which mode we want. In this example we've chosen **Integrated**.

Figure 14.22 MyTestApp

Classic Mode

Classic mode provides the same environment that we had in IIS 6.0. IIS 7.0 in classic mode installs both the ISAPI module and the ASPNET_ISAPI.dll ISAPI extension. In IIS 7.0 classic mode, managed modules are loaded using the isapimodule.dll file.

So, if we have this unified pipeline and the managed code is at the same parity as native code, why would we want to run in classic mode? The simple answer is if you have any custom modules defined they may not run in integrated mode. This environment is safe and robust for existing applications, and developers may see no need in converting existing applications.

- IIS 7.0 offers a new landscape for developers that was never available in IIS.

- In constructing IIS 7.0, Microsoft ensured that core processing of requests was removed from features that were implemented in individual modules.

- Access to early pipeline events, such as authenticating requests, were never possible for managed code developers until IIS 7.0.

Summary

IIS 7.0 now offers developers a better environment. It's easier than ever to extend IIS using either native or managed code. Access to a unified request pipeline now puts managed code in parity with its native brethren. IIS now ships with over 40 modules built-in for developers to take advantage of.

Extending IIS 7.0 with native modules is remarkably less stressful. No longer are native code developers dealing with the complexities of creating ISAPI filters and extensions. They now are able to make use of the same APIs that Microsoft used in creating IIS 7.0. Deployment of native modules is also easier. They can be placed anywhere on the server that they are running on. Developers and administrators also have the choice of how they want to deploy these modules. Deployments can be done from the AppCmd.exe command line utility, the IIS Manager, or by editing the applicationsHost.config file.

There are more options for developers using managed code. Managed modules can run in two different modes under IIS 7.0. Integrated mode provides the new features such as the unified request pipeline that both native and manage code share. Managed code has full access to all content not just that of ASP.NET. This available for managed modules through webengine.dll, a native global module that acts as a shim so that managed code can have direct access to the pipeline.

Developers who have applications that rely on the old IIS 6.0 architecture can do so by setting their application pools to run in classic mode. This provides the same pipeline behaviors and the limitations that come with IIS 6.0. It also provides a stable and secure environment to work in.

In IIS 7.0, Microsoft has created a much friendlier environment for developers and administrators alike.

Solutions Fast Track

Understanding Development Advantages in IIS 7.0

☑ IIS 7.0 offers a new landscape for developers never before available in IIS.

☑ In constructing IIS 7.0, Microsoft ensured that core processing of requests was removed from features that were implemented in individual modules.

☑ Access to early pipeline events, such as authenticating requests, were never possible for managed code developers until IIS 7.0.

☑ IIS 7.0 is easier to extend than ever before for developers.

☑ Because of the unified pipeline, managed code is no longer treated as a second-class citizen.

Extending IIS 7.0 with Native Modules

☑ Extending IIS with C or C++ no longer requires the creation of ISAPI extensions.

☑ Native code developers now have access to the same set of APIs that Microsoft used in developing IIS 7.0

☑ Deployment of native modules is easier because of tools such as AppCmd.exe and IIS Manager, or they can be done manually by editing the applicationHost.config file.

Enabling Managed Code in IIS 7.0

- ☑ ASP.NET has access to all content types.

- ☑ Application pools can run in one of two modes: Integrated or Classic.

- ☑ Integrated mode takes advantage of the new features and capabilities of IIS 7.0.

- ☑ Managed code running under integrated mode makes use of a native module called webengine.dll, which provides direct access to the unified pipeline.

- ☑ Classic mode provides the same environment of IIS 6.0 with all the stability and security that developers used for their legacy applications.

Frequently Asked Questions

Q: If managed code now has the same direct access to the request pipeline as native code, then why would you create native modules?

A: Performance for one. Native code will always run faster with less overhead than managed code. Second, managed modules are application-specific, where as if you need to create a global module, then you must do so in native code.

Q: Which method is best when deploying native modules (AppCmd.exe, IIS Manager, or manually)?

A: It depends. If you are deploying multiple native modules at one time, then creating a script that makes use of AppCmd.exe might be your best bet. IIS Manager is an excellent choice for those who prefer a more task-oriented way of doing things. A person might deploy a native module manually if they are comfortable editing configuration files and feel using either method mentioned earlier would slow them down.

Q: If I run my managed code module in classic mode, would I need to deploy webengine.dll in the applicationHost.config file?

A: No. Only if you choose to run your code in Integrated Mode would you need webengine.dll. It allows managed modules direct access to the request pipeline.

Q: I have some applications that must run in classic mode, but I want to create newer applications that take advantage of the changes in IIS 7.0. Can I have some application pools running in classic mode and others in integrated mode on the same box?

A: Yes. When you add your application pool, choose which mode you want. In IIS Manager you will see the coexistence of integrated and classic mode pools.

Q: Why can't I have a managed module in the <globalModules> section of the applicationHost. config file?

A: Only native modules can reside in the <globalModules> section. Managed modules can only be set at the application level, not the global level.

Chapter 15

Get Started with IIS 7.0's Configuration

Solutions in this chapter:

- Introducing ApplicationHost.config
- Enabling Delegated Administration in IIS 7.0

☑ Summary

☑ Solutions Fast Track

☑ Frequently Asked Questions

Introduction

Since IIS 4.0, administrators have grown to love the metabase, whereas developers did quite the opposite. The metabase offered a complex, ID-based system, with tight security. In fact, to have write access to the metabase required that a user account have administrative privileges on the Web server. In IIS 7.0, out with the old (metabase) and in with the new (applicationHost.config, web.config) was the order of the day. IIS 7.0 built on the successful and highly popular .config infrastructure ASP. NET used to build the next-generation Web server configuration. The major items introduced to this XML configuration were the System.WebServer and the System.ApplicationHost namespaces designed to give administrators and developers a multitude of access points to configuration. IIS 7.0 also enables system administrators (Windows administrators) to delegate sections of the configuration to nonadministrators easing the burden of management on themselves. Beyond that, Web farm synchronization has never been easier than it is with IIS 7.0's distributed configuration capabilities.

Introducing ApplicationHost.config

The metabase lived a long, strong, and good life. It wasn't until security, and developer productivity, came to the forefront that the metabase's shortcomings were exposed. The metabase was not architected in a manner that offered an easy, yet productive mechanism to delegate write capabilities to nonadministrator users. Furthermore, it offered undesirable child behavior not enabled at the parent level by copying the entire parent metadata to the child—potentially doubling the size of the metabase. With the new configuration, called ApplicationHost.config, IIS 7.0 natively supports the IIS 6.0 configuration while also supporting these new robust features such as distributed configuration, as well as delegated configuration.

It is important that we outline in this section the prevalent pieces of the new configuration, including System.WebServer and System.ApplicationHost. The latter is unable to be edited by anyone other than system administrators (Windows), whereas the former can be unlocked and edited as part of the application deployment process. We will focus on offering good clarification between <sites>, <globalModules>, and other ApplicationHost-enabled features.

For years the metabase has served the world of IIS well, but as the saying goes, "the only constant in life is change," and change is exactly what IIS 7.0 offers. The old metabase was not designed in a way that was easy to read, and it did not provided a mechanism for delegating control to nonadministrators. The ApplicationHost.config file has now replaced the metabase as the primary store for IIS configuration and settings. It has definitions for locking down most IIS sections to the global level so that by default they are not overridden by lower level web.config files. The ApplicationHost.config file is an XML file that resides in the *%windir%\system32\inetsrv\config directory*. It stores lists of sites, applications, virtual directories, logging, caching, and so on. It also can be viewed or modified in any text editor.

The ApplicationHost.config file contains many sections. The first section you come to in the ApplicationHost.config file and one of the most important is *<configSections>*. This section registers all IIS and Windows Activation System (WAS) sections. It contains a list of all other sections in the file. Figure 15.1 shows the *<configSections>* section and the section groups of *<system.applicationHost>* and *<system.webServer>* of the ApplicationHost.config file. Other sections to note from the ApplicationHost.config file are:

- **<globalModules>**   This section contains the collection of global modules on the server. All global modules are written in native code, such as C\C++.

- **<modules>**   This section contains the collection of modules that are written in a supported .NET language such as C# or VB.NET. Native modules written in C\C++ can also reside here as well.

- **<sites>**   This section contains the collection of site definitions. The ApplicationHost. config file has two main section groups:

- **system.applicationHost**   This group contains all settings for activation, such as the list of application pools, logging settings, listeners, and sites. It can be defined only at the global level, and only Windows systems administrators can edit it.

- **system.webServer**   This group contains sections for the Web server—for example, a list of modules and ISAPI filters, ASP, CGI, and others. Most of the sections in the ApplicationHost.config file are under this section group. Settings in this section group can also be set in individual web.config files. Two notable sections within the system.webServer section group of the ApplicationHost.config file are <globalModules> and <modules>.

Figure 15.1 applicationHost.config

XML 101: The Basics of Configuration in IIS 7.0

There are some fundamental things that everyone needs to understand to succeed in using IIS 7.0. The IIS 7.0 configuration offers a great number of ways to edit configuration, none more useful yet unforgiving than your favorite text editor. In this section, we will spend a little time helping you become familiar with how the XML structure works in IIS 7.0. We will also discuss how to configure each of the different types of data.

For those familiar with the .NET config files and how they are laid out, some of this will be a review. The .config files used with IIS 7.0 are text files using the XML structure. Any of the .config files can be edited using any text editor such as Notepad in Windows. XML is easy to read but case sensitive, making it very strict and easy to make mistakes when you are making changes. You must keep this in mind when working with .config files. While discussing the XML structure in IIS 7.0, we'll examine the ApplicationHost.config file.

An understanding of section groups, sections, and location tags is vital to correctly edit the ApplicationHost.config file. First a *section* is a basic unit of deployment, registration, locking, searching and containment of configuration settings. Every section belongs to one section group, known as the *immediate parent*. The section group contains related sections and is used solely for the purpose of a structured hierarchy. No operations can be done on section groups. They cannot have direct configuration settings. You cannot create a section group and then begin putting configuration settings directly underneath them without the use of sections. Also, section groups can be nested, whereas sections cannot.

Because most sections are locked down by default, the recommended way to unlock them is by using tags. In IIS 7.0, you use a *location tag*. A location tag unlocks the section for the location that it specifies. In Figure 15.2 we see an example of a location tag, multiple section groups, and sections from the ApplicationHost.config file. As we just mentioned location tags can be used to unlock sections; in Figure 15.2 the location tag has unlocked all sections under the *<system.webServer>* section group; therefore, the settings under the *<security>* section group, such as the "access" section can be modified.

Figure 15.2 ApplicationHost.config Hierarchy

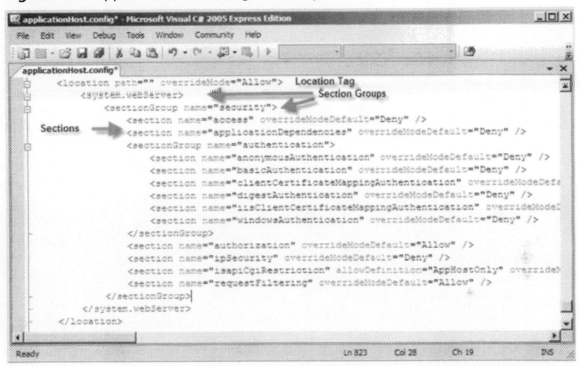

IIS 7.0 supports *distributed configuration*, which creates a unified hierarchy merged from multiple sources. Here is how it works: Values contained in the ApplicationHost.config and web.config files are merged into an effective result for each possible URL. Those familiar with the security in NTFS can think of files inheriting rights from their parent directory and any directory above that establishing effective rights. The same principle applies to distributed configuration in IIS 7.0. Figure 15.3 is a graphical representation of the distributed configuration and hierarchy in IIS 7.0.

Figure 15.3 Distributed Configuration and Hierarchy

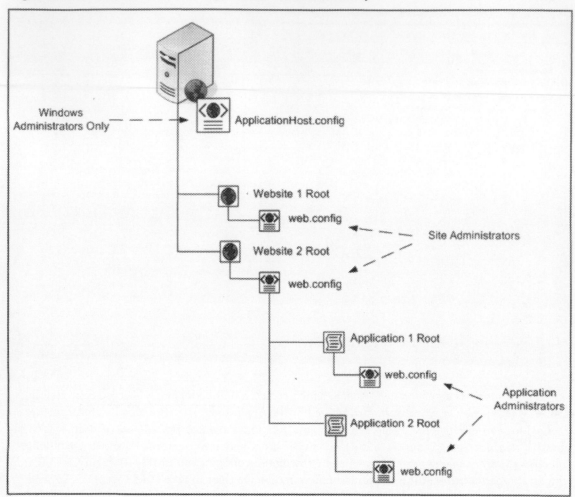

For instance, let's say that you are the site administrator (not the Windows administrator) for Web site 2. Your site has a link to a directory full of old Excel spreadsheets. People who use your site simply click this link on the Web page, and then the directory with all the Excel spreadsheets comes up. To allow this action, you must change the behavior of IIS 7.0. As the site administrator you can do this by creating your own web.config file that enables directory browsing, as shown in Figure 15.4. After you've deployed the new web.config file, users can now see the directory with all the Excel spreadsheets.

Figure 15.4 Sample web.config File

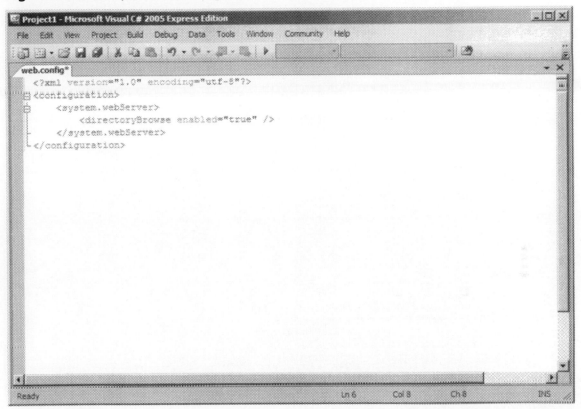

How is this possible? As the site administrator you can do this because the *overrideModeDefault* for the *directoryBrowse* setting in the ApplicationHost.config file is set to *Allow* (see Figure 15.5). This setting enables this feature to be delegated to developers or lower level administrators and allows them to change the behavior of IIS 7.0 without having to be system administrators. Reexamining Figure 15.3 shows us again how the new hierarchy in IIS 7.0 works. Notice that changes can be made at all levels, but changes can also be blocked at certain points, or for that matter, all levels in the case of denying a feature in the ApplicationHost.config file.

Figure 15.5 *directoryBrowse* Allowed in ApplicationHost.config

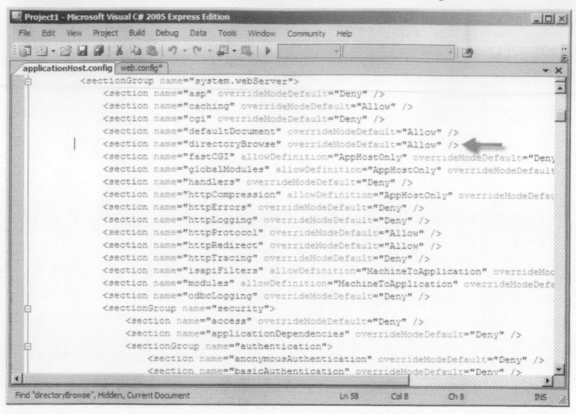

In our example, we stated that you were the site administrator for Web site 2. Now let's say you are the application administrator for Application 1 (refer back to Figure 15.3). Could you have accomplished the same thing? The answer is yes. As long as *directoryBrowse* was unlocked at the ApplicationHost.config file, which in our example it is, and the new site administrator for Web site 2 didn't disable it at the Web site level.

If the site administrator decided that he or she did not want the ability to browse directories available for any applications on his or her site, the administrator would simply set *<directoryBrowse enabled="false" />* in his or her web.config file (see Figure 15.6). Now no one below the site administrator for Web site 2 can use directory browsing in his or her applications. Remember that the ApplicationHost.config file unlocked the *directoryBrowse* feature, and that allowed it to be delegated to administrators and developers below the system administrator. If an administrator above you disables a feature that has been unlocked from the ApplicationHost.config file, then even if you set the feature to true in your web.config file, he or she will override you if he or she has set that same feature set to *false*.

Figure 15.6 Disabling a Feature in web.config

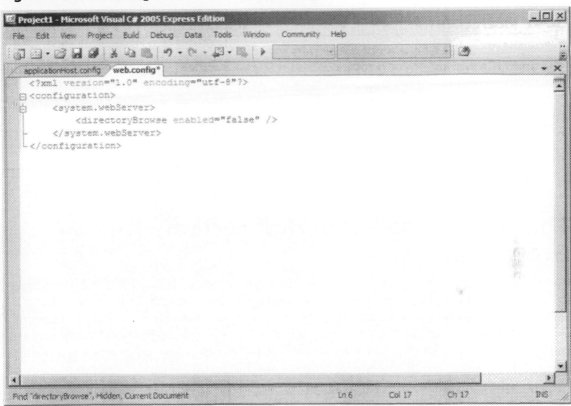

BEST PRACTICES ACCORDING TO MICROSOFT

Even though XML files can be edited via any text editor such as Notepad, Microsoft doesn't actually recommend that you use it. The reason is the strict nature of XML. XML is case sensitive and has a tight structure. Editing these files in Notepad would make it very easy to make syntax errors and difficult to find them. Microsoft recommends using a tool such as Visual Studio 2005. It makes reading XML easier. It color codes specific areas of a line and allows you to find the number of a line that might be causing a problem. Visual Studio also guides you through creating XML files such as web.config in avoiding syntax errors, making it easier on you when you are working with these files.

SOME INDEPENDENT ADVICE

Administrators who are not developers may have a tough time talking IT managers and CIOs into purchasing copies of Visual Studio for them so that they can easily edit .config files. Microsoft makes this easy for you. You can download express editions of Visual Studio for free at www.msdn.microsoft.com/vstudio/express. These are not full-blown editions of Visual Studio, but they will suffice in helping administrators who are not developers to work with these files—and at a cost any IT Manager or CIO can handle...free!

The System.ApplicationHost Section Group Purpose

We've learned what section groups and sections are in the ApplicationHost.config file. Now it's time to discuss one of the most important section groups there is: the system.ApplicationHost section group. Microsoft meticulously went through each part of the old metabase, broke it down into small pieces, and analyzed each piece from there. After the analysis, these pieces, based on functionality and purpose, were put into one of two locations: system.ApplicationHost or system.webServer section groups.

The system.ApplicationHost section group includes sections that define key parameters for a Web server. It holds sections that are used by the WAS service and are therefore defined globally. These sections include sites, application pools, applications, and virtual directories. They also contain some default settings for logging and application pools. Because it is a globally defined section group, it is protected from being delegated to nonadministrators. Figure 15.7 shows the actual system.ApplicationHost section group from the ApplicationHost.config file for IIS 7.0. Table 15.1 lists the sections and a brief explanation of each.

Figure 15.7 System.ApplicationHost

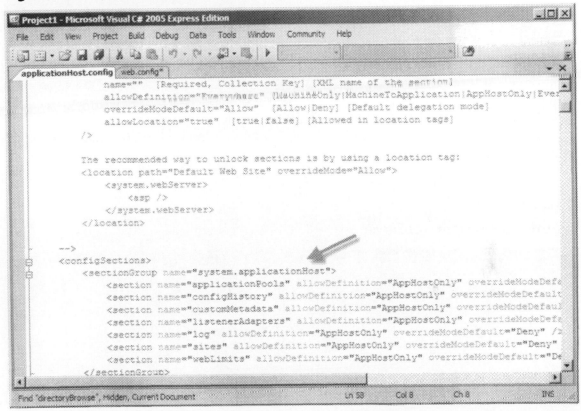

Table 15.1 Sections in system.ApplicationHost

Section Name	Description
applicationPools	Contains a collection of application pools.
customeMetadata	Used by the metabase compatibility component and should not be modified.
listenerAdapters	A collection of protocol adapters. Default protocol to serve is HTTP.
log	Contains global logging settings used by the WAS service.
sites	Contains the collection of site definitions.
webLimits	Contains some time-outs and limits used by the WAS service. By default this section is empty, and the defaults are taken from the schema.

Understanding system.webserver

Considered the most powerful section group in the ApplicationHost.config file, the system.webServer section group is where the power and magic of IIS 7.0 really take place. Gone is the monolithic Web server of the past; in comes a configuration that fully supports IIS 7.0. This section group contains all the default settings for most of the more familiar metabase properties. It's also where you will see new features, such as IIS 7.0's failed request tracing. Figure 15.8 shows some of the system.webServer section group. Table 15.2 lists each of the sections in the system.webServer, and Table 15.3 lists the nested section groups and their individual sections. As we mentioned earlier, section groups can be nested within section groups; the system.webServer is a prime example of this. By default it nests three section groups with their own sections.

Figure 15.8 system.webServer

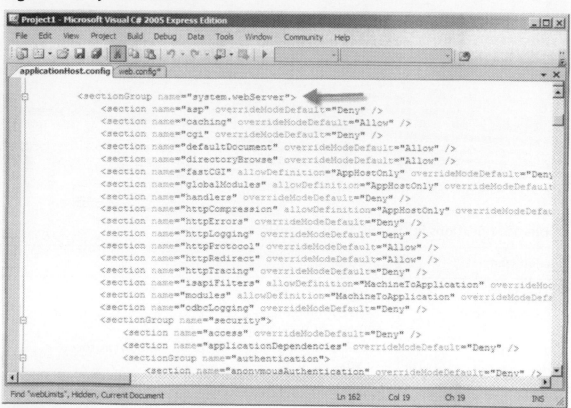

Table 15.2 system.webServer Sections

Section Name	Description
asp	Contains global defaults for ASP. By default its content is empty, and the defaults are taken from the schema.
caching	Contains cache-related configuration.
cgi	Contains the configuration for CGI.
defaultDocument	Contains the configuration for the default document functionality and the collection of files that can be served by default.
directoryBrowse	Contains the configuration for the directory listing functionality.
globalModules	Contains the collection of global native modules on the server.
handlers	Contains the collection of handlers: both native-code ISAPI extensions and managed-code HTTP handlers.
httpCompression	Contains configuration settings for both static and dynamic compression.
httpErrors	Contains the collection custom errors.
httpLoggins	Contains global defaults for the per-URL logging configuration.
httpProtocol	Contains the collection of HTTP custom and redirect headers.
httpRedirect	Contains the configuration settings for the client redirect functionality.
httpTracing	Contains trace-related configuration settings. By default its content is empty, and the values are taken from the schema.
isapiFilters	Contains the collection of ISAPI filters, both global filters and site filters.
modules	Contains the collection of modules, some native code and all managed code modules reside here. Can be customized per application.
odbcLogging	Contains configuration for the ODBC logging functionality. By default its content is empty, and the values are taken from the schema.
serverRuntime	Contains performance-related configuration settings that affect the runtime behavior. By default its content is empty, and values are taken from the schema.
serverSideInclude	Contains settings for the server side including functionality By default its content is empty, and values are taken from the schema.
staticContent	Contains configuration that controls static content serving, including the collection of MIME maps.

Continued

Table 15.2 Continued

Section Name	Description
urlCompression	Used to enable or disable per-URL and dynamic compression. By default its content is empty, and values are taken from the schema.
validation	Used to configure the validation module. It is responsible for detecting the existence of .NET Framework configuration that will be ignored by the Web server while integrated mode.

Now we will examine the security section group which is nested within the system. webServer section group in Table 15.3. The security section group contains sections related to web server security.

Table 15.3 Security Section Group

Section	Description
access	Contains global defaults for access flags.
applicationDependencies	Contains dependencies between applications or ISAPI filters for the purpose of security lockdown. By default its content is empty and is modified as applications are installed.
authorization	Contains configuration for authorizing users and roles optionally depending on whether HTTP is being used in the request.
ipSecurity	Contains the collection of IP addresses to block from accessing the server.
isapiCgiRestriction	Contains the extension restriction list configuration to control which functionality is enabled or disabled on the server.
requestFiltering	Contains configuration for restricting requests. It contains a collection of physical directories to hide from the Web space.

We've already shown that the security section group is nested in the system.webServer. Within the security section group is another section group called authentication. This section group contains several sections for authentication. Each section corresponds to a specific authentication schema. Table 15.4 displays its sections with some description and the default setting.

Table 15.4 Authentication Section Group

Section	Description
anonymousAuthentication	Contains configuration for anonymous authentication.
basicAuthentication	Contains configuration for basic authentication.
clientCertificateMappingAuthentication	Contains configuration for client certificate mapping authentication.
digestAuthentication	Contains configuration for digest authentication.
iisClientCertificateMapping Authentication	Contains configuration for IIS client certificate mapping authentication.
windowsAuthentication	Contains the configuration for Windows authentication.

Another section group is nested directly underneath the system.webServer section group: the tracing section group. The tracing section group contains sections for failed requests tracing. Table 15.5 lists its sections a description.

Table 15.5 Tracing Section Group

Section	Description
traceFailedRequests	Contains configuration for failed requests tracing. By default its content is empty.
traceProviderDefinitions	Contains the definitions for trace providers.

The IIS Schema: Your Cheat Sheet for Success

New users to IIS 7.0 are often caught off guard by errors, painful research, and unanswered questions. It isn't as though IIS 7.0 provides a cheat sheet or anything. Little do many users know that IIS 7.0's configuration is an open-book test with the answers living right inside the IIS schema. Many members of Microsoft's IIS team learned IIS 7.0 step by step using this schema as their guiding light. You should do the same thing if you want to understand the underlying configuration and how you work with it.

In this section, we will familiarize you with what the IIS schema looks like and show you how to understand what it is you are looking at.

What Is a Schema?

Before we can read the schema or extend it, we must first define is the term. A *schema* is an abstract representation of an object's characteristics and its relationship to other objects. An XML schema, such as the one in IIS 7.0, represents the interrelationship between the attributes and elements of an XML object. In IIS 7.0 the schema is declarative. In IIS 7.0, the schema is extensible in that all that needs to be done is add declarations to the system. Just like the ApplicationHost.config file, the schema is hierarchical and easy to read. The IIS 7.0 schema is located in the *%windir%\system32\inetsrv\configs\chema*. Those looking to extend the schema simply need to create their own schema files and drop them into the schema directory. You do not extend the schema by modifying any of the default schema files.

How to Read the Schema

Each configuration section in the schema is read as an XML element. Section groups found in the schema have no schema definition. The schema is read as follows:

```
<attribute-name>="<default-value>" [<metadata>] [<description>]
```

- **<attribute-name>** The name of the configuration attribute. Every attribute must have a name.

- **<default-value>** Value used if no other value is specified. Not all attributes have default values.

- **<metadata>** Contains several items such as the runtime type of the attribute. For example: *bool, enum, flags, int, int64, String, timeSpan*.

- **<description>** A short description of the attribute.

Section Schema

The *<sectionSchema>* is an XML element that represents the base unit of schema information. All schema information is specified underneath it. It has one direct attribute, which is *name*, and no others. The remaining parts of the schema are in subelements within the *<sectionSchema>*. Figure 15.9 shows the IIS_schema.xml file, notice the *<sectionSchema>* elements and the schema information in each.

Attribute Schema

All attributes are defined in corresponding *<attribute>* XML elements in the schema. The *<attribute>* element can be in the *<sectionSchema>*, in the element (if in a sub-element within the section), or in the *<collection>* element. The attribute schema has to specify a name and a runtime type for the attribute. It can also mark the attribute as required. For example, looking at Figure 15.9 you will find the following attribute under *<sectionSchema name="system.webServer/security/authorization">*:

```
<attribute name="accessType" type="enum" required="true">
```

Figure 15.9 IIS_schema.xml

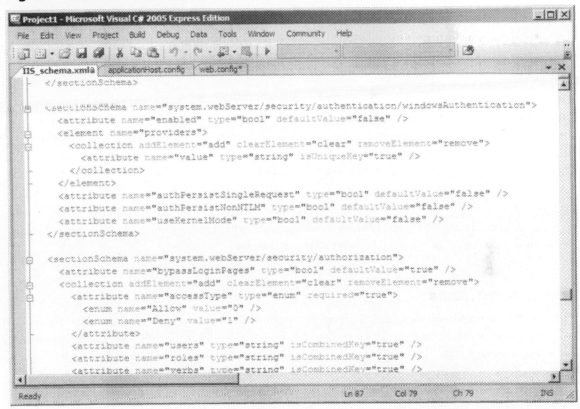

Obviously, the attribute name is *accessType*, the runtime type is *enum*, and that it is marked as required. *Enum* is a set of possible values, where only one of them can be set for the attribute. Below *accessType* you see the possible values for this attribute. We'll go over *Enum Schema* a little later. The attribute schema may also specify any of the following:

- Whether the attribute is required.

- Whether the attribute is a unique key or as part of a collection key along with other attributes.

- Whether the attribute has a default value.

- Whether the attribute is marked for automatic encryption on a disk.

- Whether the word *infinite* is allowed as a value for the attribute.

- Timespan format in seconds, minutes, or even a formatted string for timespan attributes.

- Validation rules for attributes.

Element Schema

All elements are defined in a corresponding *<element>* in the schema. The nesting of elements is supported. Simply put, an element is a container for other attributes or subelements. It is required to have a name, and it may even serve as a container of default values for collection elements. Figure 15.9 shows the *providers* element and its attributes. The syntax for the element schema is:

```
<element name="" [String, Required] [XML name of the element]
isCollectionDefault= [bool]>
```

Note, however, that *isCollectionDefault* would indicate whether the element schema has collection element default values, and not all element schemas have this.

Collection Schema

The *<collection>* XML element defines every corresponding collection in the schema. This element contains multiple elements that can be used and removed individually. Usually, its directive names are *addElement*, *removeElement*, and *clearElement*. You can see this by examining Figure 15.9 and noticing after the element *providers* is created below it, the collection schema is defined.

Enum Schema

Enum attributes must define their values to a corresponding *<enum>* XML element in the schema. Each value must have a friendly name and a numerical value. Remember our earlier example with the attribute *accessType*, the runtime type was listed as *enum*. After *accessType* was defined, we needed to define the *enum* values, which in Figure 15.9 show as:

```
<enum name="Allow" value="0" />
<enum name="Deny" value="1" />
```

Flags Schema

Every attribute of the *flags* type defines its values in corresponding *<flags>* XML element schema. They are required to have a friendly name and a numerical value. Figure 15.10 shows an example of the *flags* schema within the IIS_schema.xml file.

Figure 15.10 Example of Flags Schema

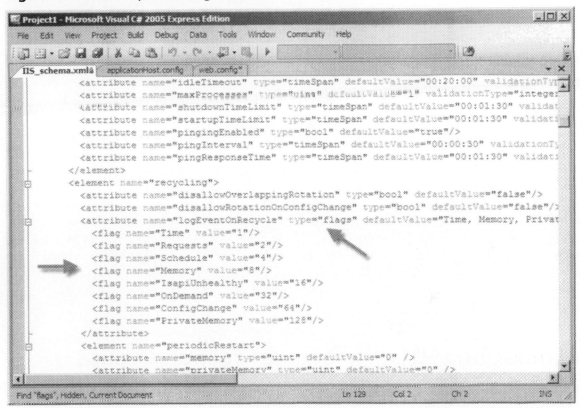

Enabling Delegated Administration in IIS 7.0

A fundamental security philosophy in the software world is to grant only what is needed, give what is necessary, and disable the rest. In IIS 7.0, the new configuration allows administrators control of features they never had before. An administrator of an IIS 7.0 server can leave the server as is and know that it is securely protected; meanwhile, another administrator has quick access to *unlock* feature by feature those that they deem necessary for nonadministrators.

It is important to understand which features are able to be delegated by default, but we should further outline how an administrator can enable delegation on a per-feature level in the configuration. It should be clearly outlined that this functionality is performed at the file level, but is also capable of being accomplished using the new IIS Manager (covered later).

Delegation Basics

You might have heard a bit about delegation prior to getting started with IIS 7.0. Delegation is a powerful feature in IIS 7.0 and one for which usage is likely in most organizations deploying IIS servers. However, you need careful planning to start to unlock feature by feature based on your environment requirements and Web application needs.

In this section, we will describe the overarching design of configuration delegation in IIS 7.0. Furthermore, we spend a great deal of time ensuring that you understand how to unlock the various pieces of configuration, such as section groups, sections, and attributes.

How It Works

As we've already discussed, IIS 7.0 supports delegation. For delegation to take place the system administrator must define the application or virtual directory from which to unlock features within the ApplicationHost.config file. Once this is done, developers or other administrators alike, then have the ability to alter the configuration of IIS for their Web sites and applications.

Figure 15.3 shows us how the hierarchy works. The system administrator creates Web sites and virtual directories, and then unlocks section groups, sections, and attributes. Site administrators can then distribute web.config files with whatever features they want to make available to developers of applications. Developers can also create their own web.config files to manipulate the configuration of IIS 7.0 to meet their needs. For IIS 7.0 to be altered by site administrators or application developers, the system administrator must unlock certain attributes and sections within the ApplicationHost.config file.

Unlocking system.webServer Section Groups

In vastly disconnected Web environments, it might be useful to completely delegate entire section groups such as security and other groups. This is useful to allow delegated management in enterprises or shared hosting environments where system administrators prefer to stay hands-off. The best way to do this is through the use of *location tags*.

Location tags specify path specific configurations and are used for locking and unlocking sections. The location tag for a path is set in a parent level in the configuration hierarchy, and considered to be at that parent level. This becomes important when it comes to locking semantics and what level can specify what sections. Unlocking can be done only at the level where the lock was defined.

If we wanted to unlock the *<security>* section group, we could place underneath a location tag similar to Figure 15.11. Just cut it from its current location in the ApplicationHost.config file and paste it to a location tag you create and a path you specify.

> **BEST PRACTICES ACCORDING TO MICROSOFT**
>
> Microsoft highly recommends creating a backup of the ApplicationHost.config file before you modify it. This can be done via the APPCMD command-line feature or simply by going to *%windir%\system32\inetsrv\config* and copying the file to another location.

SOME INDEPENDENT ADVICE

Encourage the system administrator to enable VSS (volume shadowing) if they haven't already done so, just in case they forget to manually backup the ApplicationHost.config file before modifying it. That way, if problems occur they can recover quickly to a working ApplicationHost.config file by choosing the last one that worked.

Figure 15.11 <security> and Location Tag

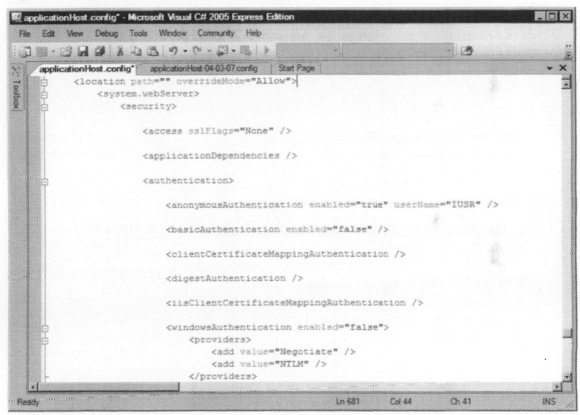

Section and Attribute locking in IIS 7.0

In more microscopic environments where system administrators desire some level of granular control, IIS' configuration offers section and attribute locking. For example, it might be necessary to allow developers to control just a simple section rather than an entire section group. Furthermore, system administrators might wish to keep control of the actual section while allowing application owners more control over particular settings for a section, in our case their attributes.

Unlocking Configuration Sections

As the system administrator you can unlock configuration sections for numerous situations. Here we will go through step by step where we need to add an application to our existing Default Web Site in IIS 7.0, and by unlocking configuration sections for delegation, we will be able to control certain settings via a web.config file. Before you start, do the following:

1. Back up the ApplicationHost.config file sitting in the *%windir%\system32\inetsrv\config* directory.

2. Create a directory to hold our web.config file that we will create later. In this example we are storing it in the C:\Test directory.

> **NOTE**
>
> For the purposes of this exercise we disabled directoryBrowse in our ApplicationHost.config file.

Now we will demonstrate how to unlock configuration sections in IIS 7.0.

1. First, you will add an application called *app* to your Default Web Site. To do this pull up IIS Manager; do not use the IIS 6.0 Manager. Open the site and highlight **Default Web Site**, as shown in Figure 15.12.

Figure 15.12 Default Web Site in IIS Manager

2. Right click **Default Web Site** and choose **Add Application**.

3. In the Add Application dialog box, enter the information as shown in Figure 15.13, then click **OK**.

Figure 15.13 Add Application Information

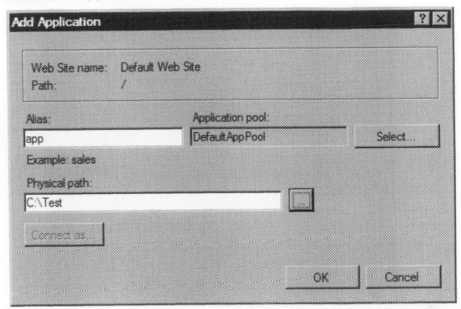

4. You should now see your application listed below Default Web Site in IIS Manager (see Figure 15.14).

Figure 15.14 Application app in IIS Manager

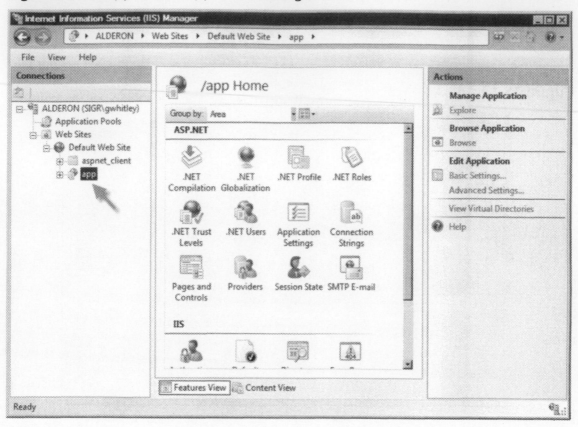

5. Now click on the server's name in the far left pane. In our example the server's name is **ALDERON**.

6. In the middle pane of IIS Manager, scroll down to the IIS Group and double-click **Directory Browsing**. After doing so you should see a screen similar to the one shown in Figure 15.15.

7. On the right side under **Actions**, select **Enable**. This will now allow directory browsing to be available to site administrators and application developers.

Figure 15.15 Authentication Section Group

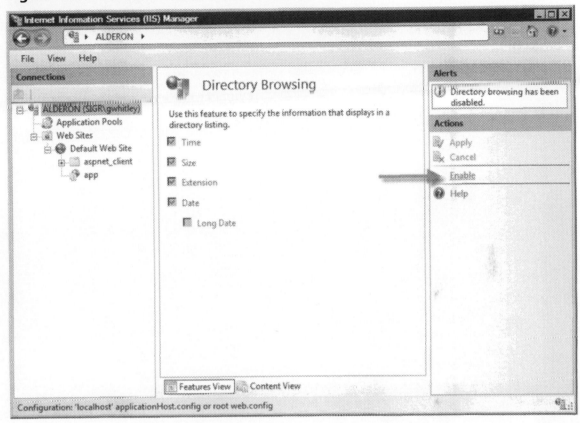

8. Open a text editor or Visual Studio and create a web.config file similar to the one in Figure 15.16. Save it in the C:\Test directory. Notice that in the web.config file has *directoryBrowse* enabled.

Figure 15.16 New Location Tag in ApplicationHost.config

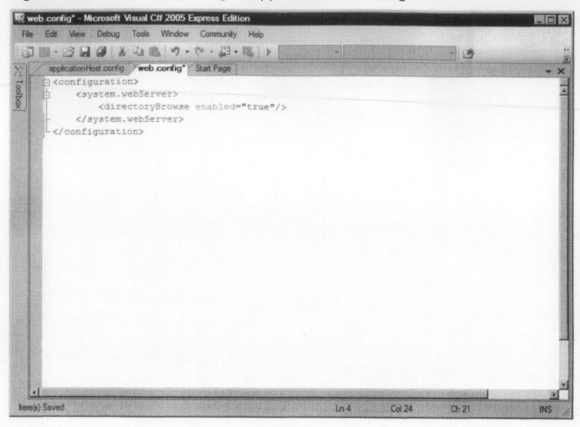

9. Now open Internet Explorer to the following URL: http://localhost/app.

10. You should now see the C:\Test directory with your web.config file in it (see Figure 15.17).

Figure 15.17 Results of Unlocking Configuration Sections

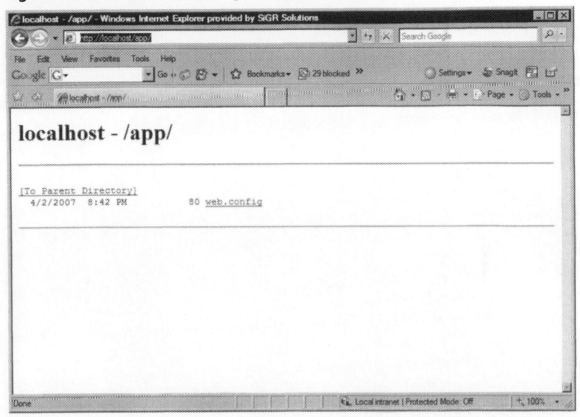

11. To disable it in your web.config change *<directoryBrowse enabled="false" />*, as you did in Figure 15.18.

Figure 15.18 Disabling Directory Browsing in Web.config

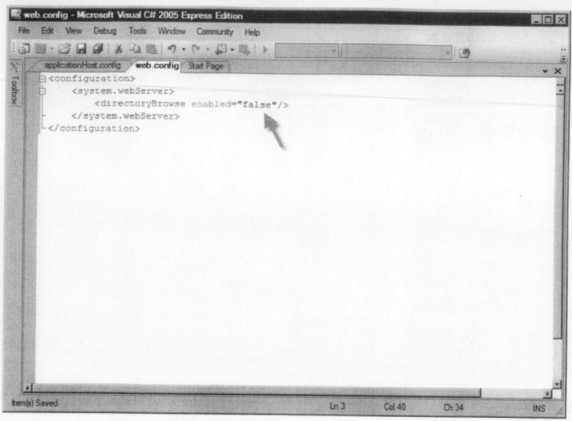

12. After disabling **<directoryBrowse>** refresh Internet Explorer, and you should see a screen similar to the one shown in Figure 15.19.

Figure 15.19 Testing Directory Browsing Disabled

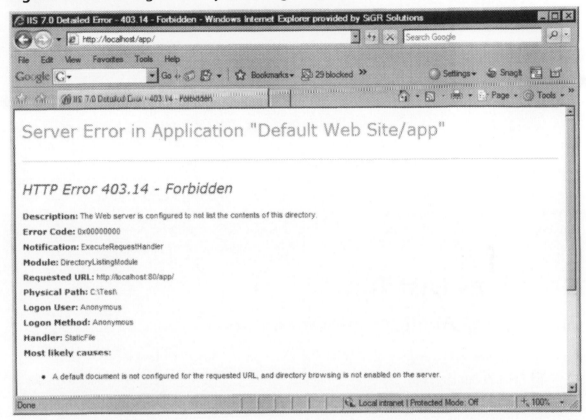

So why is delegation so important in IIS 7.0? First, IIS 7.0 configurations may now exist side by side with ASP.NET configurations. This means that Web server and application configurations can be deployed along with content. Another reason that delegation is so important is that security is not compromised. Administrators can pick and choose the features they make available for modification without having to provide system administrator rights to developers or lower level administrators; thus, everyone is more productive and efficient.

Summary

The old metabase was loved by some but hated by most because it was difficult to read and provided no mechanism for delegating to nonadministrators. It has been replaced by the XML configuration file ApplicationHost.config, which is easier to read and to configure. Within the ApplicationHost.config file are two important section groups: system.ApplicationHost and system.webServer. The system.ApplicationHost section group includes sections that define key parameters for a Web server. It holds sections that are used by the WAS service and are therefore defined globally. The system.webServer section group is where all the action is. It contains all the default settings and new features for IIS 7.0.

The schema in IIS 7.0 represents the interrelationship between the attributes and elements of each object. In IIS 7.0 the schema is hierarchical and easy to read, just as the ApplicationHost.config file is. A major improvement in IIS 7.0 over previous versions is delegation. Developers no longer need to have full administrative rights on the server to customize the behavior of IIS for their sites and applications. System administrators can simply delegate section groups or sections to developers, and then they are able to do the rest, easing the burden on administrators.

Solutions Fast Track

Introducing ApplicationHost.config

☑ ApplicationHost.config offers a level of configuration never before available in IIS

☑ Understanding who (security) can modify which configuration section, ApplicationHost versus WebServer is imperative to deploying a secure IIS 7.0

☑ Replaces the old hard-to-read metabase.

☑ It is the main configuration file in IIS 7.0.

☑ From within the file, administrators are able to delegate to non-administrators.

Enabling Delegated Administration in IIS 7.0

☑ Delegation is a powerful management tool and a much-needed feature in IIS 7.0.

☑ Able to unlock section groups, sections, and attributes.

☑ In xcopy scenarios, delegation is important where administrators simplify global configurations, allowing distributed and delegated configurations to exist on a per-site basis, thereby simplifying centralized management.

☑ Delegating administrative capabilities is accomplished in ApplicationHost.config, and yet some features are already enabled for delegation.

Frequently Asked Questions

Q: What is the difference between ApplicationHost.config file and a web.config file?

A: The ApplicationHost.config file is the main configuration file for IIS 7.0. It holds global information about the server. The web.config file is used mostly by developers for applications that need to alter some specific behavior of IIS.

Q: Can anyone change the ApplicationHost.config file?

A: No. Only Windows system administrators (server administrators) can.

Q: What exactly is a section group?

A: A section group contains related sections and is used solely for the purpose of a structured hierarchy in a .config file.

Q: Can you explain what a location tag is?

A: Location tags specify path-specific configurations and are used for locking and unlocking sections. They are used at various levels of the configuration stack, such as: ApplicationHost.config, site, virtual directories, physical directories, and file level.

Chapter 16

Administration
of an IIS 7.0
Web Server

Solutions in this chapter:

- **Accomplishing Tasks Using IIS Manager**

- **Accessing Information Using AppCmd.exe**

- **Configuring and Using Trace Log Data with AppCmd**

- **Writing Scripts Using the New WMI Provider**

- **Managed Code Administration: Inside Microsoft.Web.Administration**

☑ **Summary**

☑ **Solutions Fast Track**

☑ **Frequently Asked Questions**

Introduction

The IIS Manager of the past, albeit familiar by now, was clunky and difficult to familiarize yourself with. The goals of the IIS 7.0 user interface took the strong points of the old MMC-based user interface and added intuitive, useful scenario-based usage patterns. So out came the all-new IIS Manager, built to be task-based and extensible in order to ensure that Web administrators could tackle the most common tasks with little effort.

For many, IIS Manager simply doesn't scale since it isn't capable of managing large Web farms where a multitude of Web servers exist for a single site or application. The environments need more automated ways of making changes, and to do so as quickly, and with as few errors, as possible. IIS 7.0 offers users a plethora of options in this space with AppCmd.exe, WMI, and Microsoft's Web.Administration API for managed code.

Accomplishing Tasks Using IIS Manager

With a rewritten user interface, the first question that arises is how one can accomplish the same tasks using this new IIS Manager. The IIS Manager included with IIS 7.0 gets away from tabs (like IIS 6.0's IIS Manager) and uses feature-based access for its configuration. To configure the most popular features, a wizard will walk you through step-by-step instructions to fully enable the feature.

It is important to understand how to do the most important tasks, such as creating new Web sites, application pools, and applications. Beyond that, the most common task is to change the security settings and diagnostics settings using the IIS Manager.

BEST PRACTICES ACCORDING TO MICROSOFT

The all-new IIS Manager is available for Windows XP, Windows 2003, Windows Vista, and also for Windows Server "Codenamed" Longhorn. To use IIS Manager on Windows XP and Windows 2003, download the IIS Manager from www.iis.net/downloads/default.aspx&tabid=3.

IIS Manager: Getting Started

IIS Manager in IIS 7.0 gets away from the Microsoft Management Console (MMC) and instead was built using .NET's Windows Form technology. It offers most of the features available in the IIS 6.0 Manager, yet accessing these features is drastically different. Based on categories, the features are easily exposed at different levels of IIS Manager, such as the server, site, or application level.

Beyond that, IIS Manager fully supports IIS 7.0's delegation features at the various levels. A typical example of the delegation is allowing the server administrator to delegate administration to other users such as modifying authentication, default document settings, and much, much more.

Lastly, IIS Manager is built using managed code and is constructed on a nicely formed Web services architecture that allows developers to build custom modules and add them to IIS Manager to help you better manage their custom features. This is very useful for administrators since you can do tasks in IIS Manager for built-in IIS features and also for custom applications added later that are not part of IIS.

The one downside to the new IIS Manager is that it only supports administering IIS 7.0 servers. It doesn't support connecting to previous versions of IIS and making configuration changes. For customers needing this functionality, you should install the IIS 6.0 Management Tools. The end result is that you can have both IIS Manager for IIS 6.0 as well as the new IIS Manager.

The IIS Manager Overview

IIS Manager will always provide you with a view of only the objects you have permission to access. These permissions, though, do not change the primary view you will always see when using IIS Manager. The user interface is divided into three columns, with a left, center, and right column. In the left column, you will always be presented with a tree hierarchy, as shown in Figure 16.1. Based on your selection in the left column, the appropriate screen will appear in the center column (Figure 16.2), often referred to as the home page. The right column (Figure 16.3) is your task pane, offering you options based on your selection as well as helpful alerts, such as warning and informational text.

Figure 16.1 IIS Manager

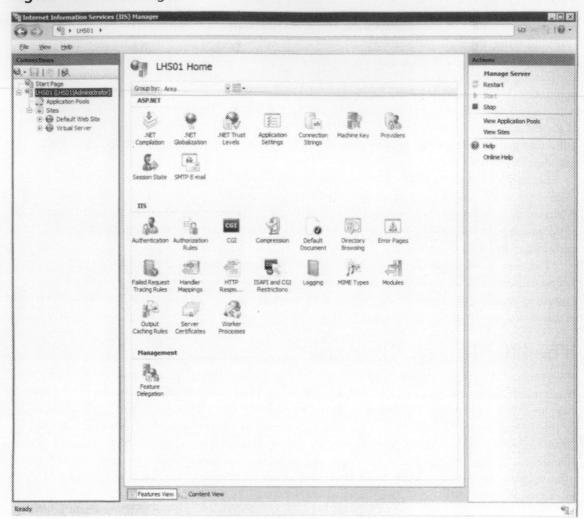

Figure 16.2 IIS Manager Center Column (e.g., Home Page)

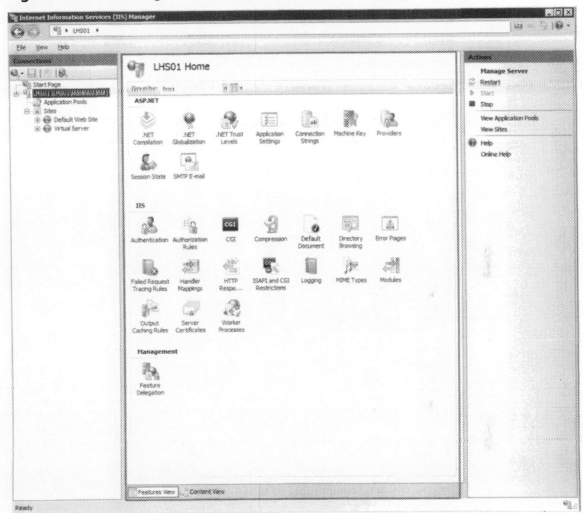

Figure 16.3 IIS Manager's Task Pane

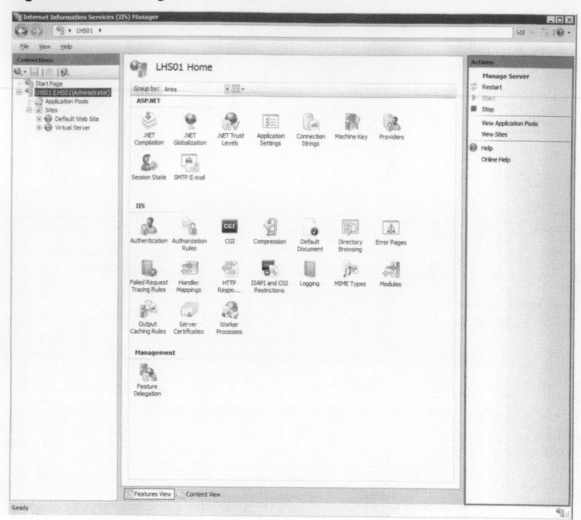

Adding Connections

In IIS 7.0, you can emulate the MMC behavior of having a single IIS Manager with multiple connections to servers. Beyond that, you can have connections directly to sites or applications all contained within the same IIS Manager. These connections, along with other preferences you select, are maintained even after shutting down the user interface.

The preferences, as well as modules and other relevant information, are stored in IIS Manager's configuration file named administration.config. This file is located in the %windir%\system32\ inetsrv\config directory like other key IIS 7.0 files such as applicationhost.config.

NOTE

In Windows Vista, IIS Manager doesn't support connections to sites and applications. This is by design because IIS 7.0 in Windows Vista was tuned to developers, and the connection functionality is built for administrators and delegated administration. Instead, Windows Vista's IIS 7.0 IIS Manager supports server-level connections only.

In Windows Server "Codenamed" Longhorn, the connections user interface is available to allow users to connect to sites and applications specifically.

To add connections to a site or application in IIS Manager on Windows Server "Codenamed" Longhorn:

1. Right-click **Start Page**.

2. Click the option based on your selection (e.g., Server, Site, or Application). See Figure 16.4.

3. Enter the server, site name, and\or application in the **Add...Wizard**.

4. Click **OK**.

Figure 16.4 The IIS Manager Connection Manager in Windows Server "Codenamed" Longhorn

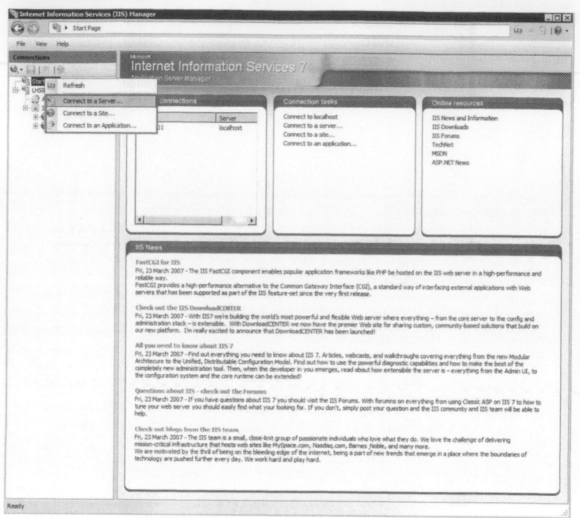

Sorting IIS Manager

IIS Manager in IIS 6.0 was heavily limited because of its hosted nature in the MMC. On the other hand, IIS Manager in IIS 7.0 offers you the ability to sort (group) the center column based on your preference. There are two sort-types and they are by area or category.

The area type will sort the features based on what that feature relates too, such as IIS or ASP.NET. Unlike any previous versions of IIS, IIS Manager is a consolidated user interface for both IIS and ASP.NET. Hence, this sorting will put IIS features under a heading called IIS, while ASP.NET is under a heading called ASP.NET, as shown in Figure 16.5.

In some cases, you are only interested in seeing them sorted, not based on technology, but rather by category. The category sorting will sort by the area per feature, such as application development, health and diagnostics, and so forth.

Lastly, you can choose to use No Sorting, which will present each feature as shown in Figure 16.4.

Figure 16.5 Selecting IIS Manager Sorting and Group By

Accomplishing the Most Common Tasks Using IIS Manager

It isn't very helpful to just look at IIS Manager. Rather, it is more important to know how to use IIS Manager. It is fairly intuitive to accomplish the high-level tasks you will often use IIS Manager for, such as creating Web sites, virtual directories, application pools, and applications. However, if you are new to IIS, then these tasks might not be as trivial as a veteran user so we will make sure you know how to easily accomplish these tasks so you can get started hosting your sites immediately.

Beyond that, you will need to manage your server's Secure Socket Layer (SSL) certificates and other settings. You will need to know how to enable these features in IIS Manager after you have created your sites or applications and we will show you how to do this.

Creating Web Sites

This is the most fundamental piece of the entire IIS 7.0 product. Without Web sites, you will not be interested in anything further about IIS 7.0. Web sites are simply containers for content such as application code, images, and style sheets. By default, IIS 7.0 provides you with a Web site called the Default Web Site. This site's default content path is located on %systemdrive%\inetpub\wwwroot.

To create a new Web site, do the following:

1. Right-click the server and select **Add Web Site**.

2. In the **Add Web Site Wizard**, enter the appropriate site name, content path, and binding information.

3. Click **OK**.

SOME INDEPENDENT ADVICE

When creating sites, you have three options of bindings. In IIS 7.0, you will need to ensure that the Ip:Port:HostHeader combination must be unique for both HTTP and HTTPS. You can select to bind a Web site to a single IP address, an IP address using a unique port, or using an IP address with a unique host header.

For SSL-enabled Web sites, you will need to ensure they are uniquely bound as well to a specific IP:Port unless you are using Wildcard SSL certificates.

Creating Virtual Directories

Virtual directories traditionally were created in IIS's Web sites to add content that lives outside the Web sites' root path. For example, if you are interested in adding content to your Default Web Site called app2 that exists in d:\MySecondApp, then you would create a virtual directory and point it to this path. Then, your Web clients can access this content using the Web sites URL plus /app2.

In IIS 7.0, virtual directories also define applications. For example, when you create a new virtual directory in IIS Manager, you will create a new application root for that directory. This behavior is slightly different than in previous versions of IIS. The important change is that virtual directories in IIS 6.0 were typically assigned to the application of their parent, where IIS 7.0 creates a new root application.

To create a new virtual directory, you do the following:

1. In the left column, select the Web site where you would like to create a virtual directory.
2. Right-click the Web site—for example, Default Web Site.
3. Click **Add Virtual Directory...**
4. In the **Add Virtual Directory Wizard**, type **alias** and enter the path.
5. Click **OK**.

Creating Applications

Many veteran IIS administrators were very familiar with the concepts sites and virtual directories, though, not nearly as familiar with applications. On the other hand, Web developers typically are the opposite and are focused on applications. IIS 7.0 brings the concept of applications to the forefront and makes applications first-class citizens. This isn't to say they haven't been important in the past, just that they typically weren't the focal point—something that is certainly different in IIS 7.0.

The key concept to grasp about applications is that applications are the fundamental building blocks of your Web sites. They are where your developers or Web business-logic is executed and where applications are assigned to a specific application pool. To isolate them fully, you would have one application per application pool, though you can certainly have many applications all participating in the same application pool.

To create a new application, do the following:

1. In the left column, select the Web site where you would like to create a virtual directory.
2. Right-click the Web site—for example, Default Web Site.
3. Click **Add Application...**
4. In the **Add Application Wizard**, type **alias**, select an application pool, and enter the path.
5. Click **OK**.

Creating Application Pools

Application pools is a concept that was added in IIS 6.0. In IIS 7.0, it changed very little and is basically the same and defines what applications run within what worker process. This is IIS's isolation functionality and is where you can recycle, change process identity security, and view health and diagnostics information. By default, IIS 7.0 provides you with a single application pool called DefaultAppPool.

> **SOME INDEPENDENT ADVICE**
>
> The default behavior for adding new Web sites in Windows Vista is to add it to the DefaultAppPool. This behavior is by design since Windows Vista is a client environment and isolating each Web site and its root application into its own application pool would hinder the performance of the client.
>
> In Windows Server "Codenamed" Longhorn, though, each time you create a new Web site using IIS Manager it will create a new application pool. This behavior is expected and creates maximum isolation of your Web applications and is a good security practice.

To create an application pool, do the following:

1. In the IIS Manager **Connections** pane, expand the server node and click **Application Pools**.

2. On the **Application Pools** node, right-click and choose **Add Application Pool...**

3. In the **Add Application Pool** dialog, provide a name for the application pool in the **Name** field.

4. From the **.NET Framework version** list, select the version required by your managed applications. Otherwise, choose **No Managed Code** if the applications in this pool don't require the .NET Framework.

5. From the **Managed pipeline mode** list, select the ASP request processing mode.

6. Select the **Start application pool immediately** check box to start the pool when the WWW service is started.

7. Click **OK** to create the new Application Pool.

> **NOTE**
>
> The Actions pane provides the same "right click" functionality for the Application Pools.

Changing Authentication Settings

You can take several actions in the security space, such as changing the authentication type for your Web site or application. The needs of your Web applications often differ even though they are running on the same server and it is important to understand how to change authentication settings.

Authentication in IIS 7.0

IIS 7.0 offers several options like previous versions of IIS for authenticating to your Web server. The default behavior for a typical installation of IIS 7.0 is to have all authentication types disabled except anonymous authentication.

Enabling Basic Authentication

Basic authentication is a standards-based authentication for HTTP clients. It is a popular authentication when protected by SSL, but should not be used on the Internet without protecting the authentication with SSL since it will expose your user's credentials, given it is an insecure protocol.

To enable Basic authentication, click the left column of your Web site, then follow these steps:

1. On the Web site home page, double-click **Authentication**.

2. Select **Basic Authentication** by clicking it.

3. In the right-column, click **Enable** in the Actions.

Enabling Windows Authentication

In Intranet environments, it is common to disable anonymous authentication and enable Windows authentication. In IIS 6.0, Windows authentication was enabled by default but this isn't the case in IIS 7.0. There is often a lot of confusion around Windows authentication because it has a couple of authentication protocols in it, namely NT Challenge\Response (NTLM) and Kerberos. The default setting is to allow both in IIS 7.0 and let the client select the protocol to use.

To enable Windows authentication:

1. Click your **Web site** in the left column.

2. On the Web site home page, double-click **Authentication**.

3. Select **Windows Authentication** by clicking it.

4. In the right-column, click **Enable** in the Actions.

SOME INDEPENDENT ADVICE

It is possible that when viewing Authentication in IIS Manager you will not see all the supported IIS 7.0 authentications in the list. This is what happens when you have chosen not to install the authentication during setup. If you do not see the authentication type you want, use setup to add the features binaries and then restart IIS Manager.

Enabling Digest Authentication

Digest authentication is a standards-based authentication protocol defined in RFC 2617 (www.ietf.org/rfc/rfc2617.txt). In IIS 7.0, there is only one version of digest authentication, unlike in IIS 6.0. For more information on digest authentication, see the following Microsoft Webcast www.iis.net/default.aspx?tabid=2&subtabid=26&i=67.

To enable Digest authentication:

1. Click the left column of your Web site.

2. On the Web site home page, double-click **Authentication**.

3. Select **Digest Authentication** by clicking it.

4. In the right-column, click **Enable** in the Actions pane.

Enabling Forms Authentication

The integration between IIS and ASP.NET is unprecedented in IIS 7.0. This integration lets you protect all your content using ASP.NET's forms-based authentication. This cookie or cookie-less-based authentication allows Web applications to be authenticated using credentials other than Windows. For more information on forms authentication, see the following http://msdn2.microsoft.com/en-us/library/aa480476.aspx.

To enable forms authentication:

1. Click the left column of your Web site.

2. On the Web site home page, double-click **Authentication**.

3. Select **Forms Authentication** by clicking it.

4. In the right-column, click **Enable** in the Actions pane.

SOME INDEPENDENT ADVICE

When using Forms Authentication, you will need to do a bit more work than just enabling it in IIS. You are required to create a default login page using ASP.NET's login control and save that page. The default settings for Forms Authentication are available in IIS Manager by clicking Edit after selecting Forms Authentication.

Viewing Worker Process Details

IIS 7.0 gives administrators some incredible information about what is occurring in IIS's worker processes. This includes giving you the ability to see what requests are currently executing within a worker process and other details, like how long it has been executing. This is all available by viewing worker process details in IIS Manager.

To view currently executing requests within a worker process:

1. Click the left column of the server.
2. Select **Worker Processes** on the home page.
3. Click **DefaultAppPool**.
4. In the **Actions** pane, click **View Current Requests**.

Changing Diagnostic Settings

IIS 7.0 offers some powerful diagnostics capabilities, in particular the all-new Failed Request Tracing. You will learn more about failed request tracing in Chapter 17, but for our purposes here we will show you how to enable failed request tracing to assist you in troubleshooting your Web applications.

Failed request tracing is a two-step process when using IIS Manager. The first step is to enable tracing for the server, and then configure your rule for tracing to capture the data.

Do the following to enable Failed Request Tracing:

1. Click the left column of your Web site.
2. In the right column, click **Failed Request Tracing** under Configure.
3. In the **Edit Web Site Failed Request Tracing Settings**, check **Enable** and choose a path for your log files.
4. Choose the number of log files to maintain in the Maximum number of trace files.
5. Click **OK**.

Best Practices from Microsoft

For Web sites that are heavily used with hundreds of requests per second, it is recommended you set the Maximum number of trace files much higher than the default of 50. This will aid you in ensuring that when your problem occurs you will not have lost the data because of the busy nature of the site.

Selecting Rules for Failed Request Tracing

The key step to ensuring you capture the right data is to set up the right rule. You will learn later that you can set up multiple rules for your server, site, or application to assist you in troubleshooting your problem. The key step to understand is how to narrow your rule to capture only the data you need, nothing more.

In our example, we will show how to use a simple rule for capturing data when a HTTP 500 error occurs. HTTP 500 errors are defined as server failures and come in various flavors.

To create an HTTP 500 Error for All ASP.NET Pages:

1. Click the server in IIS Manager.

2. On the IIS Manager server home page, double-click **Failed Request Tracing**, as shown in Figure 16.6.

Figure 16.6 IIS Manager Failed Request Tracing

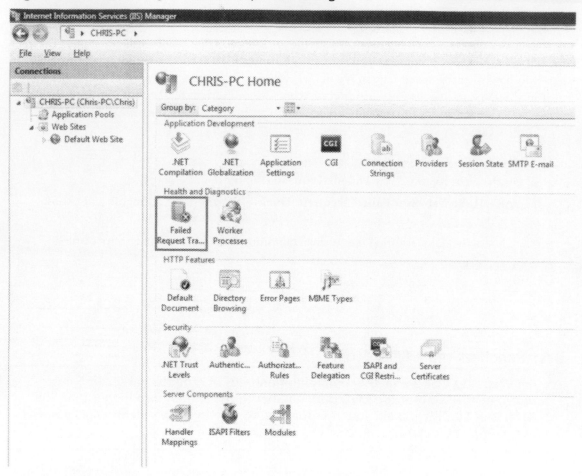

3. Click **Add** under **Actions** to start the Add Rule Wizard.

4. Select the content you would like traced—for example, ASPX pages (e.g., ASP.NET requests).

5. Choose what criteria, either HTTP status code or time-taken, to trace requests. Select **500** and click **Next**.

6. Select what providers to choose from—in your case, pick all providers, including ASP, ISAPI Extension, and WWW Server, as shown in Figure 16.7.

7. Click **Finish**.

Figure 16.7

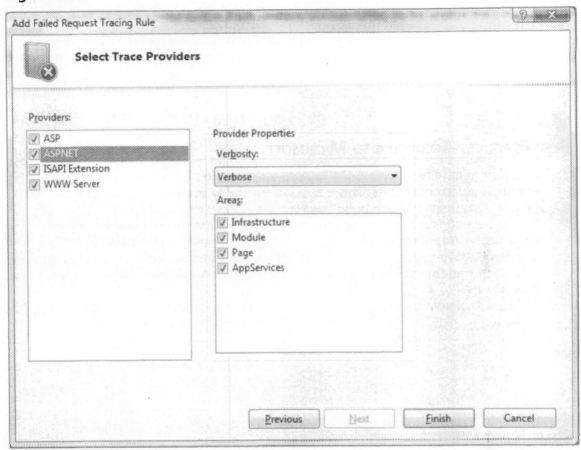

Accessing Information Using AppCmd.exe

AppCmd.exe is a convenient utility offered as an alternative to using IIS Manager, writing code, or building a script. Sometimes, you may be interested in making one or two changes to IIS's configuration but don't want to click this or that in IIS Manager. Or maybe the actual configuration isn't even available in IIS Manager, leaving you with no other choice. AppCmd solves this problem by using a familiar approach that employs verbs and objects. It combines much of the past power of the Visual Basic scripts (.vbs) shipped with IIS while providing a much more powerful functionality than ever offered by these scripts. Understanding how to use it will prove a strong and useful tool in managing your IIS servers.

BEST PRACTICES ACCORDING TO MICROSOFT

IIS 7.0 supports direct editing of the configuration files, including applicationHost. config and web.config files. This is a powerful ability considering that you can use your favorite text editor to build your custom server's configuration.

However, it is not recommended you directly edit the configuration using tools such as Notepad without first testing that your configuration is valid on your Web server. When using the text editor, there is no validation that your configuration is correct, something which can possibly render your Web server, sites, or applications unavailable.

This is where administration tools such as AppCmd.exe come in handy. They will not write invalid configurations but instead will return an error.

SOME INDEPENDENT ADVICE

AppCmd.exe does not work remotely. In order to successfully use AppCmd.exe, you must connect directly to your IIS 7.0 server. This is capable of being done using Terminal Services, such as using the command *mstsc /console /v:yourIIS7Server*, where *yourIIS7Server* is the name of your Web server.

An Introduction to AppCmd.exe

In IIS 6.0, you had a large list of toolsets available to you to make changes at the command line to the configuration. These were included in various Visual Basic scripts (.vbs) located in %windir%\system32 or in %systemdriver%\inetpub\adminscripts. The downside, though, was that they were specialized and each had different verb syntaxes and object manipulation styles. In IIS 7.0, your command-line experience is combined to a single application called AppCmd.exe. In this section, you are introduced to this powerful command-line tool aimed at simplifying your experience.

Server Management Objects and Commands

AppCmd allows you to create/configure Web sites, applications, application pools, and virtual directories. You can start and stop sites, recycle application pools, list worker processes, and examine currently executing requests. You can also search, manipulate, import, and export IIS and ASP.NET configuration data.

SOME INDEPENDENT ADVICE

AppCmd.exe is not located in the system path, but instead in %windir%\system32\inetsrv. If you want quick access to the IIS 7.0 configuration runtime information, add inetsrv to the system path.

To use AppCmd in changing directories, type:

set path=%path%;%windir%\system32\inetsrv

If you're not logged on as a member of the Administrator group, run this command in an elevated cmd window from Start | All Programs | Accessories | Command Prompt. Right-click and choose **Run as administrator**.

Command syntax is based on server management objects that expose methods to perform actions and properties that reflect the current state. Most objects provide list, add, and delete methods. Site objects have start/stop methods and properties that can be read, written, or searched. All commands provide a list of object instances and property values.

You execute AppCmd commands on server management objects with parameters to control command behavior, such as the following:

```
APPCMD <COMMAND> <OBJECT> <ID> [/parameter:value]
```

<COMMAND> specifies a command supported by the object.

The following basic commands are supported by most objects:

LIST	Displays all objects on the machine. Optional <ID> specifies a unique object.
ADD	Creates a new object with specified property values.
DELETE	Deletes specified objects by <ID>.
SET	Sets parameters specified by <ID>.

The *Site* object supports *START* and *STOP* commands.

<OBJECT> specifies a server management object:

SITE	Administration of virtual sites
APP	Administration of applications
VDIR	Administration of virtual directories
APPPOOL	Administration of application pools
CONFIG	Administration of general configuration sections
BACKUP	Management of server configuration backups
WP	Administration of worker processes
REQUEST	Display of active HTTP requests
MODULE	Administration of server modules
TRACE	Management of server trace logs

<ID> is the identifier for the object. The format is specific to each object.

[/parameter:value] specifies optional parameter(s) that depend on the object. Usually, commands that search objects or manipulate properties allow properties specified as a parameter.

Creating Web Sites

As we showed earlier, you can use IIS Manager to create Web sites. However, in some cases you might want an easier way to do this other than using a user interface. AppCmd.exe fills this void nicely and you can quickly get a site up and running using AppCmd.exe.

Before starting, you must have the name, path, and bindings to successfully create a new Web site with a root Web application using AppCmd.

To create a new Web site using AppCmd.exe, type the following:

```
AppCmd add site /name:"My First AppCmd Website"
/bindings:http/':80:www.myfirstsite.com
```

Creating Virtual Directories

As we said earlier, virtual directories are an important concept in IIS 7.0 because they are the definition of a root application. Thus, although we have created a new site in the preceding example, we haven't defined a new root application. We will do so in this example. If you do not define an application, or virtual directory physical path, then the site will run as part of IIS 7.0's default application pool.

```
AppCmd add site /name:"My First AppCmd Website"
/bindings:http/':80:www.myfirstsite.com
/physicalPath:"c:\inetpub\myfirstsite"
```

Creating Application Pools

The important step in creating an application pool is having applications read to define or run within your newly created application pool. Thus, after creating an application pool, you will want to assign your application to that application pool.

The syntax for creating a new application pool is the following:

```
appcmd add apppool /name:appPoolName
```

In the preceding case, *appPoolName* specifies the name of your new application pool.

By default, IIS adds application pools that run integrated managed pipeline mode and use .NET Framework version 2.0 for managed code execution. Otherwise, you can specify the .NET Framework version and managed code request processing mode.

To add an application pool to a Web server with different settings, use the following:

```
appcmd add apppool /name:appPoolName
/managedRuntimeVersion:dotNetVersion
/managedPipelineMode:pipelineMode
```

In this example, *dotNetVersion* equals the .NET Framework version the application pool runs. The possible options are v1.0, v1.1, v2.0, or blank for no managed code support.

Lastly, we set the application pool to run in either IIS 7.0's new *pipelineMode* as *Integrated* or the IIS 6.0 with ASP.NET mode called *Classic*.

Enter the following command to create an application pool that does not run managed code and uses classic mode:

```
appcmd add apppool /name:ClassicASPApp /managedRuntimeVersion:
/managedPipelineMode:Classic
```

Notice */managedRuntimeVersion:* is followed by a blank (space).

Managing Backups

IIS 7.0 configuration data stored in the administration.config, applicationHost.config, metabase.xml, and mbschema.xml files should be routinely backed up to provide quick and simple recovery to a known state or to recover from an unexpected loss. The metabase.xml and mbschema.xml files support IIS 6.0 compatibility and/or the FTP service and exist if one or both of these IIS features are selected.

While the Web application and web.config files are normally under version control, the IIS 7.0 configuration backup files could also be version controlled to aid deployment and to track changes.

The AppCmd's *BACKUP* statement allows you to easily manage server configuration data by copying the current configuration files to the specified backup folder.

To view *BACKUP* command syntax, execute:

```
C:\Windows\System32\inetsrv>AppCmd Backup /?
```

The syntax when using AppCmd and using the object *Backup* is the following:

```
APPCMD (command) BACKUP <identifier> <-parameter1:value1...>
```

The supported verbs (or commands) include the following:

List	Lists existing configuration backups
Add	Creates a configuration backup
Delete	Deletes a configuration backup
Restore	Restores a configuration backup

Creating a Backup

To create an IIS configuration backup in a subfolder named MyFirstBackup, execute the following:

```
AppCmd Add Backup "MyFirstBackup"
```

To create a backup folder named according to the current date and time, execute:

```
AppCmd Add Backup
```

This creates the folder, C:\Windows\System32\inetsrv\backup\20070325T191919\ into which the configuration files are copied.

Managing Existing Backups

To List existing backups, execute:

```
AppCmd List Backup
```

To delete a backup named, MyFirstBackup, execute:

```
AppCmd Delete Backup "MyFirstBackup"
```

To restore a backup named, 20070325T191919, execute:

```
AppCmd Restore Backup "20070325T191919"
```

By default, *Restore Backup* stops IIS, overwrites the configuration files, and completes by restarting IIS services. You can prevent the restart by adding */stop:false* to the *Restore Backup* command. Otherwise, other IIS components will detect configuration changes automatically without a restart.

Making Configuration Changes with AppCmd.exe

AppCmd can quickly list your current, or default, configuration for sections or section groups. It can find unique information in the configuration or go further, such as to modify the configuration setting for a particular, granular setting. Furthermore, it can help migrating customers solve problems with their ASP.NET applications by migrating their applications over to IIS 7.0 for use in the new integrated mode. As you can see, the list is long but powerful and this section will demystify much of that by opening your world to all new horizons.

Modifying Sections Using AppCmd.exe

Sections and section groups play an important role in the IIS 7.0 configuration as we have already learned. If you need to modify these configuration settings you can easily do so using AppCmd. As with any usage of AppCmd.exe, you can view the syntax for modifying configuration using AppCmd's help for configuration. To view configuration object help, do the following:

```
Appcmd config /?
```

The configuration stack in IIS 7.0 is complex and because of this, AppCmd has an extensive list of verbs to support this complexity. AppCmd.exe is the Swiss army knife for the configuration allowing just about any action capable of being performed against the configuration stack. This is why it is important to quickly reference all of the verbs to familiarize you with them and their function. The following table will show the verbs and their description:

Verb	Description
List	Lists the current configuration sections
Set	Writes the configuration to the appropriate section
Search	Finds the configuration paths where setting(s) are defined
Lock	Locks the configuration section
Unlock	Unlocks the configuration section
Clear	Clears the configuration section
Reset	Clears the current configuration and set to default values
Migrate	Migrates a legacy configuration to IIS 7.0

In our case, we will start simply by listing configuration sections' settings and then follow up by modifying this same section to another value.

SOME INDEPENDENT ADVICE

The configuration in IIS 7.0 is tightly tied to the IIS 7.0 schema. If you are unfamiliar with the configuration section or attributes you desire to change, start with the IIS schema file. The IIS schema provides not only the element names but also their possible settings, such as strings, dwords, and so on. The IIS schema file is located in %windir%\system32\inetsrv\config\schema.

To list the current settings for the configuration section authentication, input the following:

```
Appcmd list config /section:windowsAuthentication
```

This will return you to the XML section information for the section you asked for based on its location. In our example, it will return the status for the section *windowsAuthentication*, as shown next:

```
<system.webServer>
  <security>
    <authentication>
      <windowsAuthentication enabled="false">
        <providers>
          <add value="Negotiate" />
          <add value="NTLM" />
        </providers>
      </windowsAuthentication>
    </authentication>
  </security>
</system.webServer>
```

In our case, we would like to enable Windows Authentication for the Default Web Site to support our Web application. Using AppCmd.exe, simply issue the following command:

```
Appcmd set config "Default Web Site/"
/section:windowsAuthentication /enabled:true
```

This would effectively enable Windows Authentication for the Default Web Site.

SOME INDEPENDENT ADVICE

To successfully set section values, such as *windowsAuthentication* at a specific path like "Default Web Site/" requires delegation for that section to be enabled. By default, only four sections are unlocked on Windows Vista and they do not include the authentication section group. To unlock the entire group, or just the individual section (such as *windowsAuthentication*), you must change the *allowOverride* value in the configuration. You can do this using any of the administration tools.

To allow this example given, unlock this section using IIS Manager. You can do this by opening the **Feature Delegation** area at the server level and changing *windowsAuthentication* to *Read\Write* in the **Actions** pane.

After your testing is done, it is suggested you then re-lock the section unless you have a specific business need justifying it to be open. To do so, simply change the feature to read-only and it will be locked again.

Modifying Attributes Using AppCmd.exe

It becomes necessary to sometimes go lower than within a section and set a particular attribute. This is a low-level configuration setting defining a particular section, such as *authPersistSingleRequest* for the *windowsAuthentication* section. Using AppCmd.exe, you can modify this value using the following syntax:

```
Appcmd set config
```

Moving ASP.NET 2.0 Applications to IIS 7.0 Using AppCmd

As mentioned earlier, AppCmd.exe provides a convenient method for helping users move to IIS 7.0's new integrated mode. By default, ASP.NET configuration typically had configuration sections called httpModules and httpHandlers, while IIS used ScriptMaps and Isapi filters. The new integrated nature of IIS 7.0 with ASP.NET 2.0 combines these similar functioning features into a consolidated list called modules and handlers.

In some situations, a developer might deploy their custom module or handler in their web.config in IIS 6.0 using the old section name (e.g., httpModules or httpHandlers). This will cause a failure when using IIS 7.0 if the application pool is running in integrated mode. To correct this, AppCmd.exe can find use of these old section names and make the correct modifications to integrate them with IIS 7.0's modules and handlers sections.

To correct a problem with the ASP.NET configuration for use in IIS 7.0 using AppCmd, do the following:

```
Appcmd migrate config "Default Web Site/" /section:httpModules
```

In this example, we would migrate for the root application for the Default Web Site any configuration defined for *httpModules* to the IIS 7.0 configuration section modules. This would allow an application to run in Integrated mode; otherwise, the configuration itself would fail and require Classic mode.

Viewing IIS 7.0 Runtime Data Using AppCmd

Particular pieces of data aren't stored, or persisted, in a file, yet are still very important to many system administrators. This data comes as part of IIS 7.0's runtime information as well as the controls. You might, for example, be looking for the currently running sites on a particular server—no problem. On the other hand, you could be interested in shutting down a site for maintenance, yet not forcefully do so, and need to pause it. This data isn't stored in a single file somewhere; nevertheless, it is there and very much real. In this section, we will help you understand how to effectively view, set, or change this volatile data stored in the W3SVC service.

Viewing Currently Executing Requests with AppCmd

As we learned earlier, IIS 7.0 comes with some powerful diagnostics features that the administration tools can take advantage. The first nice functionality is the ability to review the currently executing requests occurring in an IIS worker process.

This is exposed using the *request* object and has the following syntax:

```
APPCMD list REQUESTS <identifier> <-parameter1:value1...>
```

The identifier and parameter values will help you narrow down the command to locate the specific type of requests you want to see.

To see all currently executing requests in all IIS application pools, enter the following:

```
Appcmd list requests
```

This command, though, isn't as useful on busy servers since it will return large amounts of data in which it is difficult to find what you are looking for. AppCmd.exe will make this easier by allowing you to narrow down the scope of your search by providing a site name or application pool.

To see all currently executing requests in the *DefaultAppPool*, enter the following:

```
Appcmd list requests /apppool.name:DefaultAppPool
```

To further narrow your search, you can use a parameter that allows you to ask only for show requests that match the following criteria (such as to request executing elapsed time) and AppCmd. exe will return this information to you. In the following example, we will attempt to locate requests that are currently executing in the *DefaultAppPool*, but that are still executing after 10 milliseconds.

To see all requests executing in *DefaultAppPool* that have elapsed for greater than 10 milliseconds, enter:

```
AppCmd list requests /apppool.name:DefaultAppPool /elapsed:10
```

As you have hopefully seen, AppCmd.exe provides you with some powerful command-line capabilities and insight into the Web server runtime. If you use this wisely, you will be well ahead in the troubleshooting and diagnostics in IIS 7.0.

Configuring and Using Trace Log Data with AppCmd

IIS 7.0 introduces Failed Request Tracing to help administrators and developers locate failures. As we mentioned earlier, setting up tracing requires you to enable this for the server, site, or application and then define a tracing rule. You can use AppCmd's *Trace* object to help you enable log files, set up rules, and even inspect your trace log files.

Enabling or Disabling Failed Request Tracing

Compared to IIS Manager, AppCmd is unique in allowing you to either enable or disable tracing with or without defining a tracing rule. This is nice because you can predefine rules and have them ready should they be needed. In this case, you would simply enable tracing and the existing rules will be used.

However, you might need to enable tracing for the URL but also define new rules at the same time. In IIS Manager, you had to take two separate actions, but with AppCmd.exe you can define all within a single command.

To enable tracing and define a rule, enter the following:

```
appcmd configure trace "Default Web Site/" /enable /path:*.aspx
```

To disable tracing for a URL, type:

```
appcmd configure trace "Default Web Site/" /disable /path:*.aspx
```

Viewing Trace Log Files Using AppCmd

As we mentioned earlier, you can also use AppCmd.exe to inspect previously created trace log files. This is a nice, handy feature but requires some insight into how tracing is designed and works. You will learn more about how tracing works in the next chapter, but for our purposes here let's define how you would view a trace log file. It is important to note that it is much easier to use Internet Explorer to view trace log files since it assists you in viewing the various errors, warnings, or informational data stored in the log files.

To view a trace log file using AppCmd, use the following syntax:

```
appcmd inspect trace "Default Web Site/fr000001.xml"
```

Writing Scripts Using the New WMI Provider

The first question asked by many when they hear there is a completely rewritten WMI provider in IIS 7.0 is why. You are surely asking the same if you are familiar with IIS 6.0's WMI provider. The reason is fundamental and centered on the IIS 6.0 provider more than anything else. The resources and work it would take to rewrite the IIS 6.0 provider to understand the brand-new configuration in IIS 7.0 was terribly expensive and potentially risky. Beyond that, the WMI provider in IIS 6.0 wasn't built with extensibility in mind, and building in extensibility after the fact is difficult.

The current provider in IIS 6.0 as well would be difficult to keep it compatible if you embarked on re-architecting it to support IIS 7.0.

Instead, Microsoft built a new WMI provider from the ground up that supported the new configuration as well as extensibility. Let's learn more about this new WMI provider.

Getting Started with WMI

Let's get started by familiarizing you with the objects available in the WMI provider, and then apply that learning to accomplish common tasks using that provider. WMI scripts start with a specific creation process where objects, methods, and wisdom come together.

The power of WMI is the fact that it has remoting built in to allow you to connect directly to a remote computer and manipulate its configuration. This is the downside to AppCmd.exe because it can't work remotely.

Starting Fresh with WMI in IIS 7.0

IIS 6.0 shipped with a WMI provider, and in fact, most of the command-line scripts were built using this provider. We mentioned though that the new provider in IIS 7.0 is completely new and provides a new object model to simplify the usage of WMI.

To learn WMI, you should start with simple, straightforward tasks and build upon them until you have a fully functional script to accomplish your Web deployment.

In our example, we will use similar heuristics as we did for IIS Manager and AppCmd.exe, where we do the following:

1. Create Web sites.

2. Add Virtual Directories to our Web sites.

3. Create an application pool.

4. Enable an authentication type for our Web site.

5. Set up tracing for our new Web site.

Creating Web Sites Using WMI

You might typically not work with single Web sites and need to manage or create multiple sites on your IIS 7.0 server. This administration task can be accomplished using IIS Manager, or AppCmd.exe, yet they require a little more work than one might want. Beyond that, they aren't reusable in the future. This is possible using WMI.

In this case, you can easily adapt using WMI, and with simple steps can start building your deployment automation.

To create a Web site using WMI, type this code and save it as **CreateWebsite.vbs:**

```
Set oIIS = GetObject("winmgmts:rootWebAdministration")
' Create a binding for the site
Set oBinding = oIIS.Get("BindingElement").SpawnInstance_
oBinding.BindingInformation = "`:80:www.myFirstWMISite.com"
oBinding.Protocol = "http"
' These are the parameters we will pass to the Create method
name = "My First WMI Site"
physicalPath = "C:\inetpub\wwwroot"
arrBindings = array(oBinding)
' Get the Site object definition
Set oSiteDefn = oIIS.Get("Site")
' Create site!!
oSiteDefn.Create name, arrBindings, physicalPath
```

Creating Virtual Directories Using WMI

To take the next step, you should now define your first virtual directory using WMI to allow you to further expand your arsenal of tools. In this example, you will add to your script the ability to create a virtual directory and define your first root application using WMI.

Add the following WMI script to your *CreateWebsite.vbs* to add a virtual directory:

```
Set oIIS = GetObject("winmgmts:rootWebAdministration")
' Define the Path, SiteName, and PhysicalPath for the new application.
strApplicationPath = "/NewApp"
strSiteName = "My First WMI Site"
strPhysicalPath = "D:\inetpub\NewApp"
' Create the new application
oIIS.Get("Application").Create strApplicationPath, strSiteName,_ strPhysicalPath
```

Using WMI to Create Application Pools

The goal is to step up your script to allow it to isolate your Web applications in IIS 7.0. In this next step, we will add script to allow you to create a new application pool and assign your root application for your new site to this application pool.

To create your application pool and assign an application to it, copy the following and save it as **CreateAppPool.vbs:**

```
Set oIIS = GetObject("winmgmts:root\WebAdministration")
oIIS.Get("ApplicationPool").Create("MyAppPool")
```

To assign your application, /NewApp, to your application pool, add this to CreateAppPool.vbs:

```
' Retrieve the NewApp application.
Set oApp = oWebAdmin.Get("Application.SiteName='My First WMI Site',
Path='/NewApp' ")
' Specify the new application pool name.
oApp.ApplicationPool = "MyAppPool"
' Save the change.
oApp.Put_
' Display the new application pool name.
WScript.Echo
WScript.Echo 'New application pool: " & oApp.ApplicationPool
```

Setting Authentication Using WMI

After you have created your Web site, root application, and virtual directory, the next major step is to modify the default configuration settings for your Web site. This sample could reach very, very far and is usable for many different properties or attributes in your Web site. In your case, you will start by modifying the default settings of your new Web site's authentication to support Windows authentication.

To change "My First WMI Site" authentication using WMI, copy the following and save it as **SetWindowsAuthentication.vbs:**

```
siteName = "Default Web Site"
Set oWmiProvider = GetObject("winmgmts:root\WebAdministration")
Set oAnonAuth = oWmiProvider.Get("AnonymousAuthenticationSection.Path='MACHINE/
WEBROOT/APPHOST',Location='" + siteName + "'")
Set oWinAuth = oWmiProvider.Get("WindowsAuthenticationSection.Path='MACHINE/
WEBROOT/APPHOST',Location='" + siteName + "'")
oAnonAuth.Enabled = false
oAnonAuth.Put_
oAnonAuth.Refresh_
oWinAuth.Enabled = true
oWinAuth.Put_
oAnonAuth.Refresh_
```

Enabling Failed Request Tracing Using WMI

Last, it is important to prepare yourself for any potential diagnostics you might need to do for your new Web site and application. The last step to perform will set up Failed Request Tracing for your new Web site.

To enable Failed Request Tracing using WMI, copy the following and save it as **EnableFREB.vbs**:

```
siteName = "Default Web Site"
myFrebDirectory = "%SystemDrive%\MyFrebDir"
Set oWmiProvider = GetObject("winmgmts:root\WebAdministration")
Set oSite = oWmiProvider.Get("Site.Name='" + siteName + "'")
oSite.TraceFailedRequestsLogging.Enabled = true
oSite.TraceFailedRequestsLogging.Directory = myFrebDirectory
oSite.Put_
oSite.Refresh_
```

Managed Code Administration: Inside Microsoft.Web.Administration

Microsoft's .NET Framework and its supporting development platforms offered yet another opportunity to manage your IIS Web servers. IIS 7.0 offers a new, robust, managed-code API aimed at empowering the manage code community of developers with the ability to not only build Web applications but also configure their IIS 7.0 servers.

Using your language of choice, you can quickly add the Microsoft.Web.Administration (MWA) binary to your Visual Studio project and modify your IIS 7.0 configuration. In this section, we will help you understand how MWA interacts with IIS 7.0 and give you a starter course on using it.

The Microsoft.Web.Administration Object Model

In this section, we will familiarize users with the object model that is available using MWA. It is also important to understand how to build scripts using MWA and we will help you get started with the most common tasks highlighted thus far in this chapter. The beauty of this administration stack is its powerful capabilities supporting all the .NET Framework languages. If you prefer VB.NET over C# then just set up the project and off you go using MWA—with your favorite development language.

In our examples, we will use C# to manipulate the IIS 7.0 configuration and also access runtime information all from within a console application. This makes the code reusable since it will be compiled to an EXE that can be reused on all your IIS 7.0 Web servers.

MWA, like all of our other toolsets, can only work against an IIS 7.0 server, thus causing you to use other administration tools to administer previous versions of IIS.

Getting Started with MWA

Using Microsoft.Web.Administration isn't necessarily the most convenient methodology for many administrators. However, there are a great deal of developers who would like to set up packages for their Web applications using Visual Studio, and MWA makes this extremely simple. Imagine you are a developer for your company and you have an HR application you have built and would like to create the setup so that all administrators are required to do is click setup.exe. With your project in Visual Studio, you can easily add a reference in your setup project to MWA and add logic to execute configuration changes to IIS 7.0.

You also can build console applications that would allow you to interface with the various server objects to give you quick access to executing requests, site status, or ASP.NET application domains.

In our example, we will take you through doing some simple administration using a compiled executable that is reusable throughout your Web infrastructure.

Using C# Express to Create a Console Application

The first step is to download a flavor of Visual Studio 2005 that works for you. For many, you already have Visual Studio 2005 and can't skip this step. However, if you do not have access to Visual Studio, you can download one of the Visual Studio Express Editions, such as Visual C# Express (available for download at http://msdn.microsoft.com/vstudio/express/visualcsharp/).

To create a console application project in C# express, add a reference to the Microsoft.Web. Administration library. To do this, perform the following steps:

1. Open Visual Studio 2005 or Visual C# Express Edition.
2. Enter your project name and select your save location.
3. Click **Project** and Select **Add Reference**.
4. Click the **Browse** tab.
5. Browse to **%windir%\system32\inetsrv**.
6. Select **Microsoft.Web.Administration.dll**.
7. Click **OK**.

Some Independent Advice

Microsoft.Web.Administration shipped as part of Windows Vista. The entire API documentation is available on Microsoft's MSDN Web site at http://msdn2.microsoft.com/en-us/library/microsoft.web.administration.

Figure 16.8 Create Your MWA Project

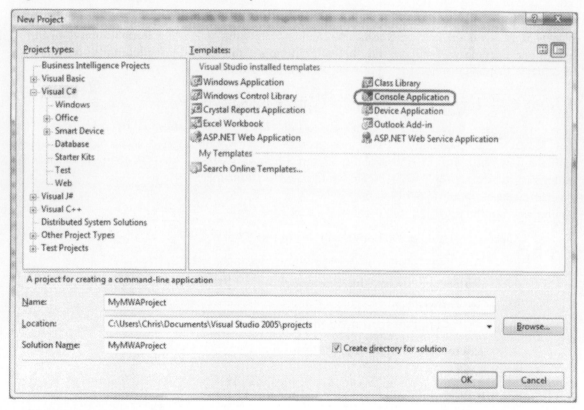

Figure 16.9 Add an MWA Reference on Windows Vista

Accessing Runtime Information with MWA

As you have learned, MWA is simple and easy to use to create Web sites, application pools, and applications. It can also be used easily access configuration attributes and properties on those Web sites such as authentication, default documents, and much more.

IIS 7.0 offers more than just configuration data—server objects and runtime data are also accessible using MWA. This includes server objects such as site status, application pool status, and ASP.NET application domains. These state objects are not represented in any configuration file and instead are stored within the worker process or Web Application Services (WAS) process.

Creating a Web Site Using MWA

It is a fundamental first step as we have seen when doing administration to create a Web site. You will need to understand how to instantiate the MWA objects and create the new site. Lastly, you will call the commit method to ensure that the new changes are committed to file.

```csharp
using System;
using System.Collections.Generic;
using System.Text;
using Microsoft.Web.Administration;
namespace MSWebAdmin_Application
{
  private static void CreateSite()
    {
      using (ServerManager serverManager = new ServerManager())
      {
        Site site = serverManager.Sites.Add("My First MWA Site", @"%SystemDrive%\
        inetpub\wwwroot", 8080);
        site.ServerAutoStart = true;
        serverManager.CommitChanges();
      }
    }
}
```

In this sample, we grabbed the *ServerManager* object and created a new instance. After that, we simply set the variable (*myFirstMWASite*) so we can use it later while also creating the new site using the *Add* method. Lastly, we set the site auto start status to True so that after creating the site it will automatically be started.

Shortcut...

Setting the Auto Start Status

This is often a confusing concept for IIS veterans. What exactly does the term site status mean? It is important to understand that it is possible to have a site created though not running. This is often the case in staging or development environments. When *ServerAutoStart* is set to false, you cannot access the Web site using the bindings (e.g., URL) until the administrator or site administrator enables it.

This step isn't required since the site will auto-start when you create it unless you explicitly set it to false. It should be noted that if you are creating a site without providing bindings that are unique, you should set *ServerAutoStart* to false until you set the bindings to be unique.

Creating Virtual Directories Using MWA

```
using System;
using System.Collections.Generic;
using System.Text;
using Microsoft.Web.Administration;
namespace MSWebAdmin_Application
{
  Class CreateVirtualDirectory("My First MWA Site","/", "/VDir", "C:\\temp");
  private static void CreateVirtualDirectory(string siteName, string
  applicationPath, string virtualDirectoryPath, string physicalPath)
  {
    using (ServerManager serverManager = new ServerManager())
    {
      Site site = serverManager.Sites[siteName];
      Application app = site.Applications[applicationPath];
      app.VirtualDirectories.Add(virtualDirectoryPath, physicalPath);
      serverManager.CommitChanges();
    }
  }
}
```

In this example, we create a virtual directory called for the site My First MWA site with the one single application. In this case, we point the root application and virtual directory content path to c:\temp.

Adding Application Pools Using MWA

In order to set My First MWA Site to run as isolated and in its own application pool, you must create the application pool and then assign the site's root application to run in this newly created application pool.

In this example, we will accomplish two goals:

1. Create a new application pool.

2. Assign the path My First MWA Site/ (root application) to your new application pool.

To create a new application pool, use the following:

```
using System;
using System.Collections.Generic;
using System.Text;
using Microsoft.Web.Administration;
namespace MSWebAdmin_Application
{
  class CreateApplicationPool()
  {
    private static void CreateApplicationPool()
    {
      using (ServerManager serverManager = new ServerManager())
      {
        ApplicationPool appPool = serverManager.ApplicationPools.Add("My First
        MWA AppPool");
        appPool.ProcessModel.UserName = "<User>";
        appPool.ProcessModel.Password = "<Password>";
      }
    }
  }
}
```

Assign My First MWA Site to the new application pool:

```
using System;
using System.Collections.Generic;
using System.Text;
using Microsoft.Web.Administration;
namespace MSWebAdmin_Application
{
  class AssignApplicatonPoolToSite("My First MWA Site", "/", "My First
  MWA AppPool");
    private static void AssignApplicationPoolToSite(string siteName, string
    applicationPath, string applicationPoolName)
  {
    using (ServerManager serverManager = new ServerManager())
    {
    serverManager.Sites[siteName].Applications[applicationPath].ApplicationPoolName =
    applicationPoolName;
      serverManager.CommitChanges();
    }
  }
}
```

Changing the Authentication Type for a Web Site Using MWA

Multiple properties are customizable for your Web sites, yet many times you will not touch them. The principles often are the thing to grasp, and in this illustration we will touch on one of those often changed settings: authentication. The goal though is to get away from creating sites or virtual directories and modifying actual site settings. This could stretch to things like adding modules, handlers, default documents, and much, much more.

In this example, you will enable Windows authentication for our newly created Web site.

```
using System;
using System.Collections.Generic;
using System.Text;
using Microsoft.Web.Administration;
namespace MSWebAdmin_Application
{
  class EnableWindowsAuthentication ("My First MWA Site")
  private static void EnableWindowsAuthentication(string siteName)
    {
      using (ServerManager serverManager = new ServerManager())
      {
        Configuration appHostConfig = serverManager.GetApplicationHostConfiguration();
        // Enable Windows Authentication
        ConfigurationSection windowsAuthentication =

        appHostConfig.GetSection ("system.webServer/security/authentication/
        windowsAuthentication", siteName);
        windowsAuthentication.SetAttributeValue ("enabled", true);
        // Disable Anonymous Authentication
        ConfigurationSection anonymousAuthentication =
        appHostConfig.GetSection ("system.webServer/security/authentication/
        anonymousAuthentication", siteName);
        anonymousAuthentication.SetAttributeValue ("enabled", false);
        serverManager.CommitChanges ();
      }
    }
}
```

Viewing Currently Executing Requests Using MWA

To access currently executing requests in IIS 7.0 using MWA, you do much of what you did earlier except you change the object you are using so it points to IIS 7.0 runtime objects. In this example, you will need to ensure you have executing requests running to ensure that data is returned.

In this example, you will view any currently executing requests occurring in IIS 7.0:

```
using System;
using System.Collections.Generic;
using System.Text;
using Microsoft.Web.Administration;
namespace MSWebAdmin_Application
{
  class DisplayRequests ()
    private static void DisplayRequests()
    {
      using (ServerManager serverManager = new ServerManager())
      {
        foreach (WorkerProcess workerProcess in serverManager.WorkerProcesses)
        {
          Console.WriteLine(workerProcess.ProcessId);
          foreach (Request request in workerProcess.GetRequests(0))
          {
            Console.WriteLine("{0} - {1} - {2}", request.Url, request.PipelineState,
            request.TimeElapsed);
          }
        }
      }
    }
}
```

Summary

Like Baskin Robbins' 31 flavors, IIS 7.0 has a talented array of administration features. Whether you subscribe to the user interface flavor, command line, or writing scripts or code, there is a flavor for everyone. Unlike previous IIS versions, there has never been such a powerful lineup of configuration opportunities for Microsoft's Web platform. As an administrator or developer, you must pick the tool that is right for your environment. You can select IIS Manager for a user interface experience, AppCmd.exe when using the command line, or use WMI or *Microsoft.Web.Administration* for scripting changes in IIS 7.0's configuration and to access runtime data.

In this chapter, you have gained insight into the powerful stack of administration capabilities built directly into IIS 7.0. There is a method for manipulating the IIS 7.0 configuration that fits any flavor of administrator from the user interface to the managed-code administrator. This isn't to say that IIS 7.0 has everything in-between.

It was important to start with the most common toolset used for day-to-day administration: IIS Manager. IIS Manager, re-built from the ground up, provides a new look and feel while maintaining most of the necessary tools to completely manage IIS. It offers you the ability to manage both IIS and ASP.NET settings in a consolidated, grouped, approach as well as provide you with delegated administration.

IIS Manager supports both previous clients such as Windows XP and Windows 2003 Server, along with Windows Vista and Windows Server "Codenamed" Longhorn. You can download IIS Manager from the IIS.NET DownloadCENTER at www.iis.net/downloads/default.aspx?tabid=3.

For some, the experience of learning IIS Manager is tedious and not what they desire to do. They prefer to use the command line to improve their experience with IIS 7.0's configuration. IIS 7.0 offers a powerful desktop command-line interface called AppCmd.exe that offers access using simple syntax and strong object support. From creating Web sites to viewing currently executed requests or migrating legacy configuration, AppCmd.exe offers a Swiss-army-knife-like experience for those desiring command-line support.

The reality in the Web server world is in deployments, not in doing individual tasks that IIS Manager and AppCmd.exe specialize in. For those desiring automated, deployable, and maintainable scripts, IIS 7.0 offers you the ability to use WMI and MWA.

In the end, IIS 7.0 provides a complete end-to-end story in the administration space, offering the best lineup of toolsets ever shipped with IIS.

Solutions Fast Track

Accomplishing Tasks Using IIS Manager

- ☑ IIS Manager offers easy access to all relevant features in an excellent three-column view.

- ☑ Creating Web sites, virtual directories, and much more is simple and intuitive with the redesign of IIS Manager.

- ☑ IIS Manager in IIS 7.0 offers a consolidated interface for managing IIS and ASP.NET settings.

Accessing Information Using AppCmd.exe

☑ AppCmd.exe offers command-line access to IIS 7.0 configuration, server objects, and runtime data, such as requests executing.

☑ AppCmd.exe offers powerful object access, including creating and managing configuration backups for applicationhost.config.

☑ AppCmd.exe is available in %windir%\system32\inetsrv, but is easily addable to the system path for quick access.

Writing Scripts Using the New WMI Provider

☑ WMI is rewritten in IIS 7.0 to support IIS's new configuration as well as extensibility.

☑ WMI is a nice means of automating tasks that are repetitive and usable across many machines.

☑ WMI can perform all the same tasks as IIS Manager and AppCmd.exe, all from a scripting, remotable interface.

Managed Code Administration: Inside Microsoft.Web.Administration

☑ Microsoft.Web.Administration (MWA) offers managed-code users the ability to manage IIS 7.0 configuration and other data.

☑ MWA supports all the .NET Framework languages and is easy to add as a reference in Visual Studio.

☑ MWA, like all other toolsets, is capable of creating Web sites, virtual directories, applications, and much, much more.

Frequently Asked Questions

Q: There seem to be differences in several tools when comparing the version that is part of Windows Vista versus the one that is part of Windows Server Codenamed "Longhorn". How does one determine how to choose?

A: This is a common question and it's easy to address. Microsoft released Windows Vista and IIS 7.0 as a ready product for the developer audience and optimized for that scenario. The features built for administration in production environments will be part of "Longhorn" Server and Windows Vista Service Pack 1. The nice thing is that Microsoft is building the products simultaneously and will release them at identical points, thus bringing Windows Vista RTM users up to the IIS 7.0 server level.

Q: Can remote administration in IIS Manager be used in Windows Vista?

A: No. Unfortunately, it can't and is only supported in "Longhorn" Server and Windows Vista Service Pack 1.

Q: Can AppCmd.exe be used from client workstations connecting to IIS 7.0 servers?

A: No, unfortunately it does not have any remote capabilities and is only available on the server you want to manage. To provide remote support, use WMI or MWA.

Q: Why did Microsoft rebuild the WMI provider when they had one in IIS 6.0?

A: The new provider provided users the ability to manage IIS 7.0 in a familiar environment (WMI) while not interfering with current scripts aimed at managing IIS 6.0. In fact, the WMI provider that is part of IIS 6.0 is completely available to be used in IIS 7.0 alongside the new provider.

Q: If I am not familiar with managed code development is there any reason to learn MWA?

A: No. IIS 7.0 offers a plethora of options for managing its configuration, server objects, and runtime data for this very reason. The toolsets as a whole should have very close feature capabilities, minus IIS Manager, which obviously can't expose everything to users and still maintain usability.

Chapter 17

Troubleshooting 101: Diagnostics in IIS 7.0

Solutions in this chapter:

- **Using IIS 7.0's Custom Detailed Errors**
- **Inside IIS 7.0's Failed Request Tracing**
- **Breakpoints: Extending IIS 7.0's Tracing**
- **Reality: Inside What Tracing Can't Do in IIS 7.0**

☑ **Summary**

☑ **Solutions Fast Track**

☑ **Frequently Asked Questions**

Introduction

No area in IIS 6.0 is more in need of improvement than diagnostics. Many users referred to IIS as a "black box" into which requests went, yet never came out. To complicate the matter further, administrators and developers were often left without any avenue to reproduce and hence correct IIS because there were no means to access request-based information at the point of failure.

In contrast, it has never been so easy to detect and isolate an error than in IIS 7.0, which offers detailed error messages that outline step-by-step instructions on what to try if a request fails. In the event that the error messages don't help, you can use IIS 7.0's new Failed Request Tracing. This new instrumentation offers a step-by-step output as requests, one by one, enter and exit the IIS request pipeline. This detailed tracing can be enabled based on HTTP error messages or by time taken, two of the most common troubleshooting starting points. Beyond that, developers can build on IIS 7.0's tracing to include their individual code "eventing" that allows administrators to see their status alongside IIS 7.0's status. This makes debugging failures of IIS and custom code a reality without attaching a debugger.

As great as IIS 7.0's diagnostics are, there are still areas where it can't help. It is important to understand these areas and ensure that you tackle them with the right tools to succeed.

Using IIS 7.0's Custom Detailed Errors

IIS 6.0 and previous versions included custom yet not very detailed errors. Unlike previous versions, IIS 7.0 includes Custom Detailed Errors that offer administrators console access to the most detailed error messages, such as the module processor and request state, and some steps to resolve the problems.

It is important to understand the default behavior to show only custom detailed errors for console (127.0.0.1) requests. However, it is possible to enable detailed error messages for nonconsole requests; we will outline how to accomplish this goal effectively.

Configuring Custom Error Messages

Custom errors are a powerful method for creating customized, styled, yet useful error messages for your users. HTTP errors are a rather unpleasant side effect of the Web experience, but custom error messages can improve this typically unpleasant experience. There is a wide array of configurable settings for custom errors, such as using a specific file, redirection to another URL, or executing another URL. We will help simplify how each works and furthermore tell you how you can configure IIS7.0 to use custom error pages other than the default shipped by Microsoft.

First, let's start by taking a look at a custom error message. As you can see in Figure 17.1, the custom error message is pretty simple.

Figure 17.1 IIS 7.0 Standard HTTP Custom Error Message

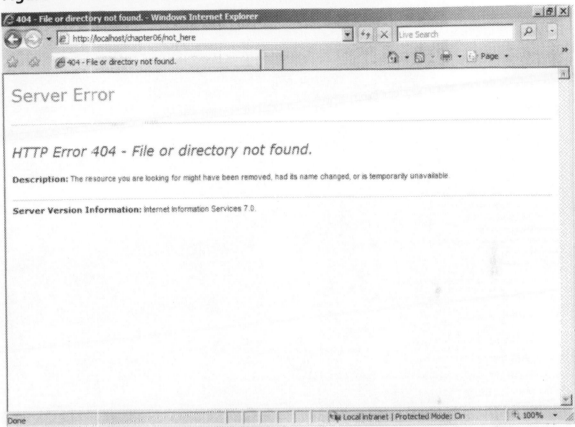

The custom error page is pretty basic and really only a placeholder until a developer can create an error page, or better yet handle the errors, that fits with the user experience and navigation that fits the rest of their application.

Now let's take a look at a detailed error message based on navigating to the same page from the IIS7 server console (see Figure 17.2).

As you can see, there is quite a bit of information available that can help a developer or administrator work toward finding the root issue. As interesting as this information is for a developer or administrator, it's equally interesting for a malicious user or hacker. As a best practice, you should not expose this information to end users unless you are in a development and testing phase.

There are a number of options to suppress this generic custom error and provide our own custom error page. As an administrator or developer, you'll have the ability to override the default error handling in IIS 7.0 using a redirection to a URL, custom static error page, or custom dynamic error page. The following section will explain how to define these by server, site, and/or application.

Figure 17.2 IIS 7.0 Detailed HTTP Error Message

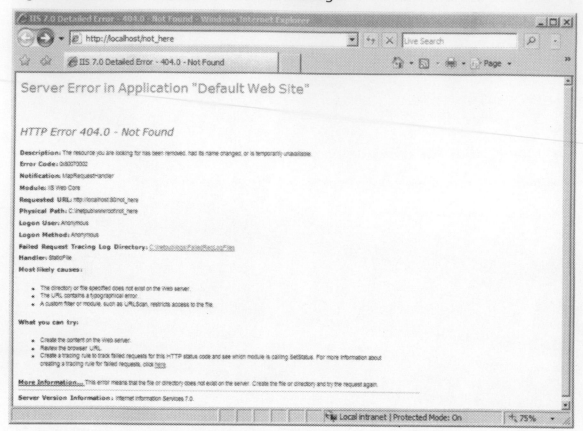

Configuring Custom Error Messages Using IIS Manager

Let's first take a look at viewing and updating the Custom Errors pages using IIS Manager.

After opening and connecting to an IIS 7 server, click the **Error Pages** icon in the IIS section and then click **Open Feature** from the Actions pane (or simply double-click the **Error Pages** icon), as shown in Figure 17.3. These are the default Error Pages defined for the entire Web server. Any changes done at this level will impact the error pages settings for all the sites supported on that IIS 7 server, except where a site or application overrides those values.

There are a number of options available at this point from a Status Code perspective. You can add a Status Code by clicking **Add. . .** in the Actions pane (see Figure 17.4).

The Add Custom Error Page dialog box will allow you to provide a Status Code (e.g., 404) or a Substatus Code (e.g., 404.14). The Path Type field allows you to define the kind of action to take based on the value in the path (see Figure 17.4). Table 17.1 provides details on the available path types.

Figure 17.3 The IIS Manager

Figure 17.4 The Add Custom Error Page

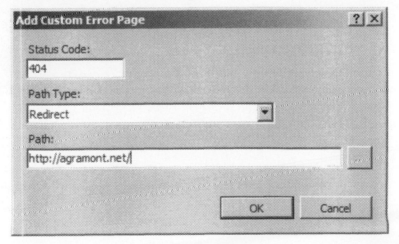

Table 17.1 Available Path Types

Path Type	Description	Path Examples
File	Points to a static file	404.htm
Execute URL	Points to a dynamic file	Error.aspx
Redirect	Redirects the client browser to a different URL	http://<URL>

Controlling the custom errors can be done at a variety of locations within IIS 7, and thus it's important to understand where these settings are actually being stored. For the entire Web server, those changes are done in the applicationHost.config file, which is located in the \Windows \System32\Inetsrv\Config folder. Additionally, when you're managing a given Web site, those changes can also be stored in the applicationHost.config file, or they can be managed within the web.config for the site.

HTTP error responses can be defined for the following IIS levels:

- Web server
- Web site
- Web application
- Physical directory
- Virtual directory
- File (URL)

These settings were previously available in IIS 6.0 but were not widely known and utilized. In IIS 6.0, this was done by setting a number of properties (HTTPErrorCode, HTTPErrorSubcode, URL, HandlerURL, FILE, or Filename) and using the proper combination, depending on the type of redirection you where going to use. With IIS 7.0, this is much easier to implement in the User Interface and via XML configuration.

<httpErrors> Configuration

With the rich integration between ASP.NET and IIS 7.0, a developer or administrator can define the httpError configuration at the server, Web site, or virtual directory level. This provides a greater amount of control versus what was previously available in IIS. The default *<httpErrors>* section is defined in the applicationHost.config file. (More information on the location and use of the applicationHost.config file can be found in Chapter 15).

```
<httpErrors>
  <error statusCode="401" prefixLanguageFilePath="%SystemDrive%\inetpub\custerr"
path="401.htn" />
  <error statusCode="403" prefixLanguageFilePath="%SystemDrive%\inetpub\custerr"
path="403.htn" />
  <error statusCode="404" prefixLanguageFilePath="%SystemDrive%\inetpub\custerr"
path="404.htn" />
  <error statusCode="405" prefixLanguageFilePath="%SystemDrive%\inetpub\custerr"
path="405.htn" />
  <error statusCode="406" prefixLanguageFilePath="%SystemDrive%\inetpub\custerr"
path="406.htn" />
  <error statusCode="412" prefixLanguageFilePath="%SystemDrive%\inetpub\custerr"
path="412.htn" />
  <error statusCode="500" prefixLanguageFilePath="%SystemDrive%\inetpub\custerr"
path="500.htn" />
  <error statusCode="501" prefixLanguageFilePath="%SystemDrive%\inetpub\custerr"
path="501.htn" />
  <error statusCode="502" prefixLanguageFilePath="%SystemDrive%\inetpub\custerr"
path="502.htn" />
</httpErrors>
```

The default location for the custom error pages is %SystemDrive%\inetpub\custerr. Within that folder will be additional folders that map to a localized code. For U.S. English, that subfolder is labeled "en-US." The localized version that will be used for the response will be defined by the actual browser setting that is set by the end user.

Table 17.2 Child <error> Node Attributes and Values

Attribute Name	Value
defaultPath	Default path to the HTTP error file or URL that will be used within the child *<error>* node.
detailedMoreInformationLink	At the bottom of a Detailed error page, a "More Information" link redirects the user to a Microsoft Support article. Setting the DetailedMoreInformationLink property can override the base URL for this link. This can be extremely useful if you want to capture these errors, even for internal testing, to store in a database or provide a response using an internal Knowledge Base article that directly references a particular product or module (Default="http://go.microsoft.com/fwlink/?LinkID=62293").
defaultResponseMode	Used to define the default Response Mode that will be used within the child *<error>* node (Default=File): **File** Static file will be used.

Continued

Table 17.2 Continued

Attribute Name	Value
	ExecuteURL Points to a URL within the same server. For this to work, it must be a URL that points to a dynamic page (e.g., ASPX page) that resides within the same application pool that generated the error. Needless to say, you might not want to set this at the server level if you host a number of sites with more than one application pool. By default, you will receive an error if you attempt to do this to a location outside the appPool. However, you can actually get around this and allow it to happen with an appropriate registry key. Read the "Some Independent Advice" sidebar for more details.
	Redirect Redirects to a specific URL. The URL can be on the same server or a completely different server or site.
errorMode	Defines whether a Custom Error page or Detailed Error page is used upon a given error being generated (Default=DetailedLocalOnly).
	DetailedLocalOnly A detailed error will only be displayed when the request comes from the local machine.
	Custom Custom pages will be used upon an error.
	Detailed A detailed error response will be provided regardless of a custom page being assigned or outside the local machine.
existingResponse	ASP.NET and IIS 7 are not integrated when it comes to error responses. Thus this value allows you to control the way you want to handle error responses (Default=Auto):
	Auto IIS 7.0 will go through a series of checks to decide which error response will be used:
	1. If the IHttpResponse::SetStatus method was called with the fTrySkipCustomErrors flag, the existing response is passed through, and no detailed or custom error is shown.
	2. If the ErrorMode property is set to Custom, the response is replaced.
	3. If ErrorMode is set to Detailed and there is an existing response, the response is passed through.
	4. If ErrorMode is set to Detailed and there is no existing response, the response is replaced with a detailed error message.

Table 17.2 Continued

Attribute Name	Value
	Replace When an error message is generated (e.g., 404, File not Found), IIS will take over the error and call the appropriate custom error page or URL.
	PassThrough When an error message is generated (e.g., 404, File not Found), IIS will not call out to the custom page but will allow the error to be handled by a module. For example, when calling a page that doesn't exist *and* has an extension of .aspx, which results in a 404 File not Found error, the error response will be created by ASP.NET and *not* IIS. So in this case, the custom page or detailed page, as defined in the web.config, will not be generated.

SOME INDEPENDENT ADVICE

For a site or application to leverage an error page that's in a different application pool than its own, the following registry change will need to be made. Keep in mind that this is a serverwide change and could open the attack surface on a Web server that is "hosting" a number of different Web sites.

Note: It is recommended that you back up your registry before modifying the registry with the new data. If you use Registry Editor (Regedit.exe) incorrectly, you could cause serious problems that might require you to reinstall your operating system.

1. Open Regedit.exe (you can quickly find this using Windows Vista search by clicking the **Windows** button and typing in **RegEdit**).

2. Navigate to the following key:
   HKEY_LOCAL_MACHINE\SYSTEM\CurrentControlSet\Services\W3SVC.

3. Within the W3SVC key, create a new DWORD called **IgnoreAppPoolForCustomErrors** and with a value of **1**.

4. For this change to take effect, you'll need to restart IIS 7.0.

The *<httpErrors>* node defines the base values for all the child *<error>* nodes (see Table 17.2).

The child nodes for *<httpErrors>* are *<error>*, *<remove>*, and *<clear>*. The *<error>* node defines a set of properties for a given error code. As you can see, each error code is then mapped to a specific file, which then provides appropriate error response. A number of options are available by error code, including handling suberror codes.

Table 17.3 provides details on the available attributes that can be used as part of the *<error>* XML node.

Table 17.3 <error> XML Node Attributes and Values

Attribute Name	Value Type	Value
statusCode	String	Primary status code for a given error.
subStatusCode	Integer	Substatus code for a given error that is a "child" of a high-level code.
prefixLanguageFilePath	String	Location of language-specific error code folders.
Path	String	Actual filename for the given page that will be used to provide the error message to the user.
responseMode	String	Defines the type of response that will be given. This will also treat the value in *Path* a bit differently. This is the same as Path Type as defined in the IIS Manager.

Within a given error code, additional suberror codes provide an even greater amount of detail. The following XML node can be added to the *<httpErrors>* node to handle a suberror code:

```
<error statusCode="404" subStatusCode=14 prefixLanguageFilePath="%SystemDrive%\
inetpub\custerr" path="404-14.htm" />
```

This XML looks much like the previous XML, except it uses a new XML attribute, subStatusCode, which takes an integer and is the suberror code. Thus, the preceding XML is capturing the 404.14 statusCode and is then being redirected to the 404-14.htm file. If an error code is raised and it's actually a suberror code, but no subStatusCode is defined in the *<httpErrors>* XML, the "parent" statusCode will be used.

The following URL points to a Microsoft Support page that provides a general list and description of Error Codes used by IIS 6.0 and 7.0: http://support.microsoft.com/kb/318380

The prefixLanguageFilePath attribute provides a pointer to a folder that holds additional folders with the language-specific error pages. For example, the default error code pages are located at ="%SystemDrive%\inetpub\custerr and contain a child folder named en-US. The en-US folder contains all of the individual error pages, such as 404-14.htm. The syntax (folder name) and acceptable languages that can be used here are defined in RFC 1766 (www.ietf.org/rfc/rfc1766.txt).

Overriding for a Site

Until now, we've focused mainly on configuring the errors page and behavior at the server level. As stated earlier, error configuration can be delegated down to the site and application/virtual directory level. This gives a Web site administrator and Web developer a greater amount of control than in the past, to define and manage how errors are handled for their site.

The following is a simple web.config file that overrides the default behavior when a file isn't found (404 error):

```
<configuration>
  <system.webServer>
  <httpErrors errorMode="Custom">
      <remove statusCode="404" subStatusCode="-1" />
      <error statusCode="404" prefixLanguageFilePath="" path="http://agramont.net/"
responseMode="Redirect" />
   </httpErrors>
  </system.webServer>
</configuration>
```

You'll notice that there are two XML nodes within the *<httpErrors>* node. Before you can add an error node that overrides a previously defined node, such as the default error nodes, you must first remove it using the *<remove>* node. Only then can you add the *<remove>* node that redefines that setting. When the preceding XML code is defined in the web.config, you'll see the information shown in Figure 17.5 represented in the IIS Manager.

Figure 17.5 HTTP Errors

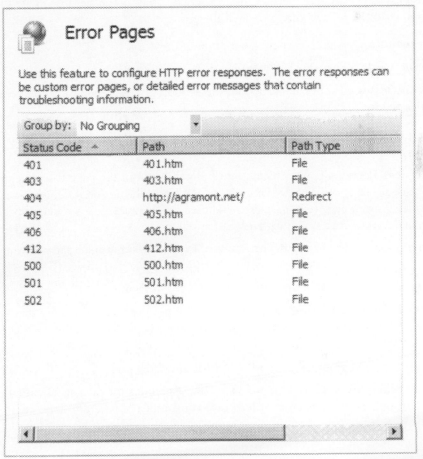

The IIS Manager provides a list of all the error pages defined for this given site. This also includes an aggregated view of the inherited and explicit (defined as "Local" in the Entry Type column) error pages and their associated values.

Understanding and Reading Custom Error Messages in IIS 7.0

In IIS 7.0, the data shared in custom errors is more robust than ever. IIS 7.0 offers detailed information about the request information itself as well as reasons that the failure might have occurred. In an unprecedented feature never available in custom errors in previous versions, step-by-step instructions provide information on how to further troubleshoot or fix the error. It is important to understand how to read the information IIS provides as well as how to further your research if the recommended steps don't resolve your problem.

The detailed error provides a wealth of information that can help a Web administrator or developer quickly narrow down the root cause of a given error. There are a number of helpful pieces of information on the Detailed Error page. Although the Error Code value provides the actual error code that was raised, it's only one piece of the puzzle. The other properties listed here provide additional context to the request that generated the error:

- **Description**   A user-friendly description of the error.
- **Error Code**   The actual error code.
- **Notification**   Event handler within the Module (see next bullet) that generated the error.
- **Module**   A pointer to the module that generated the error.
- **Requested URL**   The URL that was used by the end user. This will also include any information in the query string as well.
- **Physical Path**   A pointer to the actual physical path of the page that generated the error. This could be an ASP, ASPX, or even HTML page. This is useful if a user was trying to browse a given page (e.g., cart.aspx) and then was redirected to a different page that generated the actual error (e.g., newcart.aspx).
- **Logon User**   The username that was used by IIS 7.0 and Windows in performing the request.
- **Logon Method**   Defines the type of authentication method that was used as part of this request. For most public sites, this will be set to Anonymous.
- **Failed Request Tracing Log Directory**   A pointer to the directory that will hold the trace file for this error. This doesn't tell you the actual filename, which is a good thing from a security perspective.
- **Handler**   The Handler within IIS 7.0 that raised the error.
- **Most likely causes**   IIS 7.0 provides a list of pointers for each status code that can help you troubleshoot the issue or at least give you an idea of where to look next.
- **What you can try**   This field provides some helpful troubleshooting tasks that the developer or administrator can perform.

- **More Information**   This field provides yet another set of ideas on what the issue might be and how you could resolve it. What's interesting is that by clicking the "More Information" link, you'll be routed to a Microsoft support article that will provide—yes, you guessed it—more information.

Delegating Custom Errors

This detailed error data doesn't have security in mind, hence they aren't sent to any clients other than requests started at the IIS server console. However, in some situations, it is useful to have some of the custom errors delegated to clients other than the just the console. This section outlines ways you can carefully delegate custom errors and the security risks associated with doing so.

Controlling custom errors is, by default, a server-specific setting and can only be controlled by the Web server administrator. The great thing about IIS 7 is that it provides the ability to allow a Web site administrator or developer to control their own custom errors. To do this, you first must allow the ability to "override" the default settings that are defined in the applicationHost.config XML file.

Within the applicationHost.config file, you must make a change to the following XML node and change the overrideModeDefault from Deny to Allow:

```
<section name="httpErrors" overrideModeDefault="Deny" />
```

NOTE

Although shown here directly changing the XML configuration files, you can also do this in IIS Manager by clicking **Feature Delegation (Under Management Area) | Error Pages** and changing to **Read\Write**.

If you neglect to make this change before proceeding to the next set of steps, you'll get an "HTTP Error 500.19—Internal Server Error" error message from IIS that proceeds to tell you that overrideModeDefault needs to be changed.

Making a change to the Custom Errors properties using IIS Manager for a virtual directory named Chapter06 within the Default Web Site will result in the following XML being stored within the applicationHost.config file:

```
<location path="Default Web Site/Chapter06">
  <system.webServer>
    <httpErrors>
      <remove statusCode="500" subStatusCode="-1" />
      <error statusCode="500" prefixLanguageFilePath="" path="D:\\ web\Chapter06\
Error.aspx" responseMode="File" />
    </httpErrors>
  </system.webServer>
</location>
```

Let's say that we don't want to host this particular information within the applicationHost.config file, but we want the Web site developer/administrator to control it from their end. To do this, we could easily remove this XML from the applicationHost.config file and move it into the web.config file, which should be at the root folder for that application. The web.config should now look like the following XML:

```
<configuration>
  <system.webServer>
    <httpErrors>
      <remove statusCode="500" subStatusCode="-1" />
      <error statusCode="500" prefixLanguageFilePath="" path="D:\\web\Chapter06\
Error.aspx" responseMode="File" />
    </httpErrors>
  </system.webServer>
</configuration>
```

Custom Error Module

What drives the custom errors is the CustomErrorModule module, which is defined as a default module in the applicationHost.config file.

The following is a snapshot of a simple web.config file that will override the applicationHost.config file setting by removing the CustomErrorModule from the list of modules that will be used per request:

```
<configuration>
  <system.webServer>
    <modules>
      <remove name="CustomErrorModule" />
    </modules>
  </system.webServer>
</configuration>
```

If you now navigate to a file or folder that doesn't exist at http://*<site with above web.config>*/ file_not_here, you'll get a blank page. This is because the web.config removed the only module that would capture the error and provide a response.

If you remove the CustomErrorModule at a Web site or application level using IIS Manager, you'll end up with the following web.config (assuming that no other changes were made to the Web application):

```
<configuration>
  <system.webServer>
    <modules>
      <clear />
      <add name="HttpCacheModule" type="" preCondition="" />
      <add name="StaticCompressionModule" type="" preCondition="" />
```

```xml
    <add name="DefaultDocumentModule" type="" preCondition="" />
    <add name="DirectoryListingModule" type="" preCondition="" />
    <add name="ProtocolSupportModule" type="" preCondition="" />
    <add name="StaticFileModule" type="" preCondition="" />
    <add name="AnonymousAuthenticationModule" type="" preCondition="" />
    <add name="RequestFilteringModule" type="" preCondition="" />
    <add name="CustomErrorModule" type="" preCondition="" />
    <add name="IsapiModule" type="" preCondition="" />
    <add name="BasicAuthenticationModule" type="" preCondition="" />
    <add name="HttpLoggingModule" type="" preCondition="" />
    <add name="RequestMonitorModule" type="" preCondition="" />
    <add name="IsapiFilterModule" type="" preCondition="" />
    <add name="ConfigurationValidationModule" type="" preCondition="" />
    <add name="OutputCache" type="System.Web.Caching.OutputCacheModule"
preCondition="managedHandler" />
    <add name="Session" type="System.Web.SessionState.SessionStateModule"
preCondition="managedHandler" />
    <add name="WindowsAuthentication" type="System.Web.Security.
WindowsAuthenticationModule" preCondition="managedHandler" />
    <add name="FormsAuthentication" type="System.Web.Security.
FormsAuthenticationModule" preCondition="managedHandler" />
    <add name="DefaultAuthentication" type="System.Web.Security.
DefaultAuthenticationModule" preCondition="managedHandler" />
    <add name="RoleManager" type="System.Web.Security.RoleManagerModule"
preCondition="managedHandler" />
    <add name="UrlAuthorization" type="System.Web.Security.UrlAuthorizationModule"
preCondition="managedHandler" />
    <add name="FileAuthorization" type="System.Web.Security.
FileAuthorizationModule" preCondition="managedHandler" />
    <add name="AnonymousIdentification" type="System.Web.Security.
AnonymousIdentificationModule" preCondition="managedHandler" />
    <add name="Profile" type="System.Web.Profile.ProfileModule"
preCondition="managedHandler" />
    <add name="UrlMappingsModule" type="System.Web.UrlMappingsModule"
preCondition="managedHandler" />
    <add name="WindowsAuthenticationModule" type="" preCondition="" />
    <add name="IpRestrictionModule" type="" preCondition="" />
    <add name="CustomLoggingModule" type="" preCondition="" />
    <add name="FailedRequestsTracingModule" type="" preCondition="" />
  </modules>
 </system.webServer>
</configuration>
```

This web.config starts off by clearing all previously defined modules that would have be inherited by the web.config of the Default Web Site (because this application is within that particular site) and the applicationHost.config file. The IIS Manager then explicitly defines each additional module for us but does not add in the one module we wanted to remove.

Let's say we use the same web.config and now navigate to http://*<site with above web.config>*/file_not_here.aspx (see Figure 17.6).

Figure 17.6 A Server Error

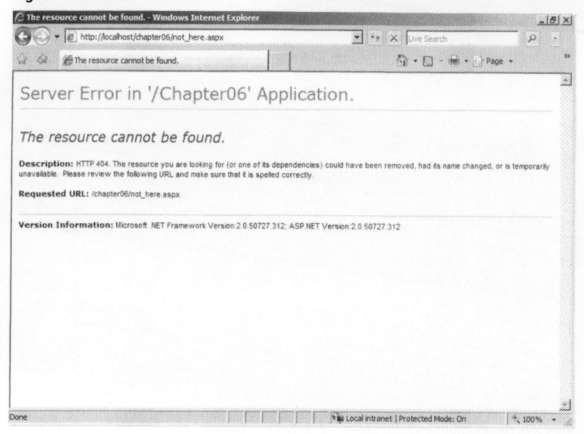

You now see that you'll get an error response from ASP.NET. Even if you set existingResponse to a value of Replace, which would normally have IIS do the error response instead of ASP.NET when an error is generated by ASP.NET, the response will still be handled by ASP.NET. This is because the previous web.config setting removed the module that would have handled the error. Thus, ASP.NET will continue to generate the error.

Inside IIS 7.0's Failed Request Tracing

Getting the current state of a request made to an IIS 7.0 server is easier than ever before when we use IIS 7.0's Failed Request Tracing. This feature allows an inside view to particular requests that are currently in process and how long they have been executing.

IIS's failed request tracing was designed in such a way that you shouldn't need to be present when a problem occurs; rather, you should simply be prepared for the problem if it arises. The success of this new feature depends solely on your ability to configure the appropriate rules for your Web applications prior to failures.

Failed Request Tracing Architecture

Although the underlying feature behind failed request tracing was introduced in Windows Server 2003 (Enterprise Tracing for Windows), its awareness and usability didn't become first class for IIS customers until IIS 7.0. The key to using this new feature is to understand how IIS 7.0's modularized core server emits events that are captured and stored for later retrieval.

At the heart of what allows Failed Request Tracing (FRT) is Enterprise Tracing for Windows (ETW), a platform component of the Windows Operation System. ETW was first leveraged by IIS with IIS 6.0 Service Pack 1. ETW is a kernel mode component that will keep track of all tracing events within nonpaged memory and will flush out the events to disk in a nonsequential order (important to note for navigating the trace files later). ETW provides a mechanism for applications to plug into the tracing infrastructure via a provider model. Each provider will have the opportunity to write relevant data per session or page requests as it relates to IIS 7.0.

With IIS 6.0/Service Pack 1, administrators had to interact directly with ETW via the command line to use ETW tracing with IIS. In addition, the ETL log file was difficult to use and often needed tools such as Log Parser (part of the IIS Diagnostics Toolkit at www.iisdiagnostics.com) to get to the relevant tracing information. Furthermore, a limited set of providers were available for tracing in IIS 6 and there was no "easy" way to add additional providers into the tracing pipeline from an ASP.NET/IIS application.

IIS 7.0 reduces the complexity in enabling and managing tracing data. Administrators can enable tracing from within the new IIS 7.0 administration console. Web developers can quickly and efficiently plug into the IIS 7.0 tracing pipeline (which uses ETW as the platform) with a few lines of additional code in their application.

For more information on Enterprise Tracing for Windows and the improvements to ETW in Windows Vista, you'll find a great article on the Microsoft Developer Network (MSDN) at http://msdn.microsoft.com/msdnmag/issues/07/04/ETW/.

Configuring IIS 7.0's Failed Request Tracing

By default, IIS 7.0's tracing isn't enabled on Windows Vista. It is available, though, if it's installed during the setup process. It is important to understand how to enable tracing and create rules to capture the events you are looking for.

A key aspect of failed request tracing is the understanding of how to scope rules to remove noise from the log files and help narrow down the problem. In such cases, you might only want to establish rules for a particular error or condition. Here we will walk you through how to best use this feature of tracing.

Enable Tracing for IIS 7.0

To use tracing in IIS 7.0, we first must add that in Windows Vista:

1. Click the **Windows** button and navigate to **Control Panel**.

2. From Control Panel Home (not Classic View, although you could take that route as well), click **Programs | Turn Windows features on or off**.

3. From within the Windows Features window, expand **Internet Information Services | World Wide Web Services | Health and Diagnostics**.

4. Check the **Tracing** check box and then click the **OK** button (see Figure 17.7).

Figure 17.7 Turning Windows Features on and off

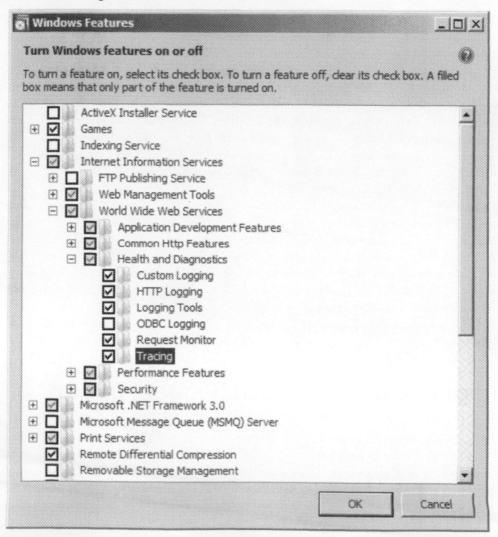

Using IIS Manager

To start the configuration Failed Request Tracing Rules, you use IIS Manager to enable Failed Request Tracing for a given Web application. Although you can define rules by virtual directory or by Web application level, the failed request tracing feature must be enabled at the site level first:

1. Using IIS Manager, navigate down to your target Web site.

2. Click **Failed Request Tracing Rules** and then click the **Open Feature** in the Actions pane.

3. Click **Edit Site Tracing ...** from the Actions pane.

4. Check the **Enable** check box.

5. Define the directory location where all failed request files will be stored and the maximum number of log files you'd like maintained.

6. Click the **OK** button.

Centralized Tracing for ASP.NET and IIS 7.0

Following the theme of integrating ASP.NET and IIS 7.0, tracing information is now aggregated into the same pipeline. In addition to the integration is the theme of extensibility, which allows Web developers to add their own tracing information into that same pipeline. This gives administrators and developers a single file that defines all the tracing information for all components that interact within a given request. This capability is not only great for testing purposes during a development phase, but it also provides a wealth of information while you're working on issues in production.

Let's first take a look at a simple scenario where an ASP.NET developer can plug into the IIS 7.0 tracing infrastructure. Create a simple .aspx page with the following code and save it as simpletrace.aspx:

```
<%@ Page language="C#" trace="true" %>
<%
  Trace.Write("HowToCheatIIS7- Chapter 6: Interesting Info");
  Trace.Warn("HowToCheatIIS7- Chapter 6: Issue");
  Response.Write("hello, world");
%>
```

If you now browse to this page, you'll see a wealth of information at the bottom of the page (see Figures 17.8 and 17.9). It also includes the tracing information we defined within the Tracing Information section.

Figure 17.8 Hello, World's Trace Information

hello, world			
Request Details			
Session Id:	ubnkajfcjk2wgqfblqxeer55	Request Type:	GET
Time of Request:	3/28/2007 9:36:07 PM	Status Code:	200
Request Encoding:	Unicode (UTF-8)	Response Encoding:	Unicode (UTF-8)

Trace Information

Category	Message	From First(s)	From Last(s)
aspx.page	Begin PreInit		
aspx.page	End PreInit	0.000107555569213406	0.000108
aspx.page	Begin Init	0.000269307970705774	0.000162
aspx.page	End Init	0.000392787351465061	0.000123
aspx.page	Begin InitComplete	0.000427707990820062	0.000035
aspx.page	End InitComplete	0.000463466725519584	0.000036
aspx.page	Begin PreLoad	0.000496990539300386	0.000034
aspx.page	End PreLoad	0.000529955622851508	0.000033
aspx.page	Begin Load	0.000562641341287789	0.000033
aspx.page	End Load	0.000626615952586153	0.000064
aspx.page	Begin LoadComplete	0.000660698496596635	0.000034
aspx.page	End LoadComplete	0.000697295326640676	0.000037
aspx.page	Begin PreRender	0.000731098505536318	0.000034
aspx.page	End PreRender	0.000775796923910721	0.000045
aspx.page	Begin PreRenderComplete	0.000809041372576682	0.000033
aspx.page	End PreRenderComplete	0.000842285821242644	0.000033
aspx.page	Begin SaveState	0.00110349220361806	0.000261
aspx.page	End SaveState	0.0011694223707203	0.000066

Figure 17.9 Hello Word Information

aspx.page	Begin PreRenderComplete	0.000809041372576682	0.000033
aspx.page	End PreRenderComplete	0.000842285821242644	0.000033
aspx.page	Begin SaveState	0.00110349220361806	0.000261
aspx.page	End SaveState	0.0011694223707203	0.000066
aspx.page	Begin SaveStateComplete	0.0012043430100753	0.000035
aspx.page	End SaveStateComplete	0.00123814618897094	0.000034
aspx.page	Begin Render	0.00127083190740723	0.000033
	HowToCheatIIS7- Chapter 6: Interesting Info	0.003860825887089	0.002590
	HowToCheatIIS7- Chapter 6: Issue	0.00394798780291909	0.000087
aspx.page	End Render	0.00419075608771506	0.000243

Control Tree

Control UniqueID	Type	Render Size Bytes (including children)	ViewState Size Bytes (excluding children)	ControlState Size Bytes (excluding children)
__Page	ASP.simpletrace_aspx	12	0	0

Session State

Session Key		Type	Value

Application State

Application Key		Type	Value

Request Cookies Collection

Name	Value	Size

There is nothing new here to experienced ASP.NET developers. That's actually the cool part! Although this tool was available in ASP.NET before IIS 7.0, it only maintained information from ASP.NET. With the @Page declaration having the trace attribute set to *true*, we will still only see ASP.NET-based information on this page.

Now it's time to see the centralized view of ASP.NET and IIS information in action. To do this, you must define the kind of information you want the Failed Request Tracing Rules to capture and store for you:

1. Using IIS Manager, navigate down to your target Web application.

2. Click **Failed Request Tracing Rules** and then click the **Open Feature** in the Actions pane.

3. From the Actions pane, click the **Add...**link.

4. From the Specify Content to Trace page, select **ASP.NET (*.aspx)** and click **Next**.

5. From the Define Trace Conditions page, check the **Status Codes** check box and enter **200** as the status code.

6. From the Select Trace Providers page, select only the following options:

   ■ Providers: ASPNET

   ■ Verbosity: Verbose

   ■ Areas: Page

7. Click **Finish**.

You'll now see the rule shown in Figure 17.10 in the Failed Request Tracing Rules page.

Figure 17.10 A Failed Request Rule

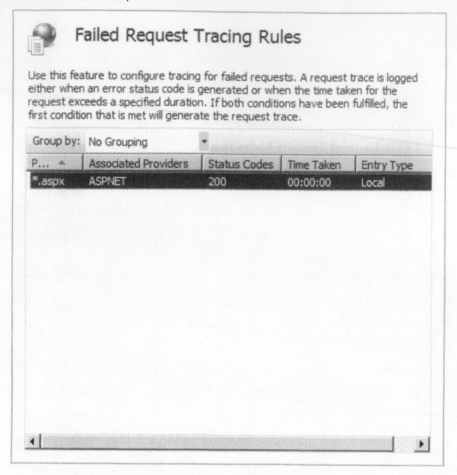

Using your browser, navigate back to the simpletrace.aspx page. You should see the same result. But now we need to look at the trace file that was produced by IIS 7.0:

1. Click the **Windows** button and click **Computer**.

2. Navigate to the folder where the defined Failed Tracing Rules should be stored. The default location is %SystemDrive%\inetpub\logs\FailedReqLogFiles\W3SVC1\.

Here you should see all the failed request files for this site. The format is in FR######.xml, where ###### is a number which increments with each new failed request being created. If you use a program like Notepad to open the contents of one of the failed request files, you'll notice that the file is actually just XML (the file extension points that out as well). By having the results stored in an XML format, Microsoft has opened up the possibilities of what can be done with this data—including pulling the data periodically from the local folder and storing it in a rich database such as SQL Server 2005!

There is also a file named freb.xsl that is an XML style sheet used to give the failed requests a nice look and feel when you open a failed request file using Internet Explorer. In fact, Figure 17.11 shows the failed request file for our previous request using Internet Explorer.

NOTE

Microsoft is continuing to invest in the IIS 7.0 platform and embedding those changes in the server version of IIS 7.0, which will ship as part of Windows Server 2008. One such improvement is an updated style sheet for the Failed Request Tracing files.

The past style sheet (Windows Vista) was great in terms of providing a more pleasant viewing experience of the FRT file versus a straight Notepad view of the XML, but it still required the user to hunt through the entire contents to find any warnings or failures. The new version of the style sheet (Windows Server 2008) will provide a simplified view of the trace file and focus on the warnings and failures within the contents. However, the user can still expand the views to see the entire contents. The goal was to reduce the amount of data users have to sift through each time they look at a Failed Request Trace.

As with the version of IIS 7.0 that ships with Windows Vista, the Windows Server 2008 version of IIS 7.0 will continue to provide all the rich tracing information in the same XML format.

With the release of Windows Server 2008, administrators will be able to store the FRT files on a remote share via a UNC path. At the time of this writing, Windows Server 2008 has yet to ship, so these features could change or could be cut in the final release of the product.

Figure 17.11 A Failed Request File

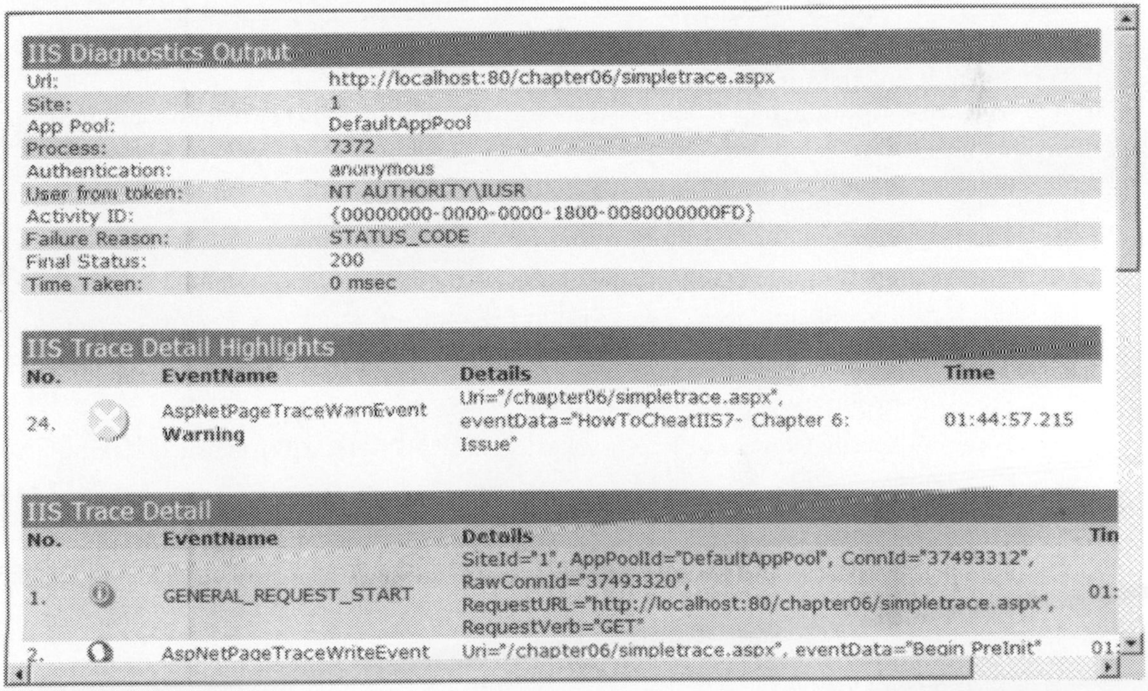

Toward the bottom of this Web page, you'll find the trace information as defined within the ASP.NET page (see Figure 17.12).

Figure 17.12 ASP.NET Trace Information

Now you're seeing the same basic results in this trace file as you saw on the actual page for ASP.NET. But what about the integration between ASP.NET and IIS 7.0? For that, we need to open up the scope of the information that we want to see in the failed request. To do that, we'll create a new rule and select all tracing providers:

1. Using IIS Manager, navigate down to your target Web application.

2. Click **Failed Request Tracing Rules** and then click **Open Feature** in the Actions pane.

3. First, select the *previous rule* and then click the **Remove** link in the Actions pane. We'll do this to keep things simple.

4. From the Actions pane, click the **Add…**link.

5. From the Specify Content to Trace page, select **ASP.NET (*.aspx)** and click **Next**.

6. From the Define Trace Conditions page, check the **Status Codes** check box and enter **200** as the status code.

7. From the Select Trace Providers page, we won't deselect anything. Thus, we'll watch for everything.

8. Click **Finish**.

9. Using a browser, navigate back to the **simpletrace.aspx** page and then open the latest failed request log file.

You should see an increase in the amount of information within the trace file. Although this is a bit "noisy," you get a good idea of the amount of information found within the trace, and you see how the ASP.NET, IIS 7.0, and developer-defined tracing information is centralized into a single file.

There is a known issue when trying to use the ASP.NET trace provider: It won't show up in the list of trace providers when you create a new rule.

Open %windir%\system32\inetsrv\config\applicationHost.config using Notepad and add the following to *<traceProviderDefinitions>*:

```
<traceProviderDefinitions>
  ...other providers defined...
    <add name="ASPNET" guid="{AFF081FE-0247-4275-9C4E-021F3DC1DA35}">
      <areas>
        <add name="Infrastructure" value="1" />
        <add name="Module" value="2" />
        <add name="Page" value="4" />
        <add name="AppServices" value="8" />
      </areas>
    </add>
  </traceProviderDefinitions>
```

The issue noted previously is relevant to the initial version of Windows Vista. This issue will be resolved in the final version of Windows Server 2008 and Windows Vista Service Pack 1 and the workaround will no longer be needed.

Modify the XML

The following XML is taken from the applicationHost.config file. It encapsulates all the changes we previously made. The *path* attribute in the *<location>* node points to the application path within the Default Web Site:

```
<location path="Default Web Site/Chapter06">
  <system.webServer>
    <tracing>
      <traceFailedRequests>
        <add path="*">
          <traceAreas>
            <add provider="ASP" verbosity="Verbose" />
            <add provider="ASPNET" areas="Infrastructure,Module,Page,AppServices"
verbosity="Verbose" />
            <add provider="ISAPI Extension" verbosity="Verbose" />
            <add provider="WWW Server" areas="Authentication,Security,Filter,
StaticFile,CGI,Compression,Cache,RequestNotifications" verbosity="Verbose" />
          </traceAreas>
          <failureDefinitions statusCodes="200" />
```

```
        </add>
      </traceFailedRequests>
    </tracing>
  </system.webServer>
</location>
```

The default Failed Request Tracing setting in IIS 7.0 is to not allow the trace Failed Request settings to be configured beyond the server level. To change this, you'll need to modify the section found within the applicationHost.config file and change the overrideModeDefault setting from Deny to Allow:

```
<sectionGroup name="tracing">
    <section name="traceFailedRequests" overrideModeDefault="Deny" />
    <section name="traceProviderDefinitions" overrideModeDefault="Deny" />
</sectionGroup>
```

Breakpoints: Extending IIS 7.0's Tracing

The theme of extensibility continues even into IIS 7.0's failed request tracing. The ability for a developer who develops custom modules using IIS 7.0's APIs to also push his or her module's errors into the same error log used by IIS is arguably the most powerful feature in all of IIS 7.0. A developer who raises events through the life of a module can emit these events in IIS 7.0's failed request logs in sequence with all other IIS events.

It is important for system administrators and developers alike is to understand how these custom events will be persisted to the log file. Beyond that, they need to know how to easily distinguish between these custom events and those emitted by the core IIS server.

How Developers Extend Their Module to Support Failed Request Tracing

A potential topic in and of itself, we can't turn a deaf ear to understanding how developers will take advantage of this feature. It is more important, though, to know how to find the custom events than to help narrow the problem to custom code rather than in IIS's core server. In this section, we will provide a sample of a module with events that are emitted to the trace log files in error conditions with the goal of showing how they live side by side with IIS's core server events. The core principles in this sample will show you how any Web application on IIS 7.0 can interject its own application information into the combined trace file generated by IIS 7.0.

Using Visual Studio C# Express Edition (which is a free download), let's develop a Custom Error Module that we'll use to override the default Error Module that ships with IIS 7.0. To develop an IIS 7 module or handler, we'll need to install all the required components for VS C# Express or VB.NET to work on Microsoft Windows Vista:

- Microsoft Visual Studio Express Editions (C#, VB.NET, J#)
- Visual Studio 2005 Service Pack 2
- Visual Studio 2005 Update for Windows Vista

You can download and install these components (and it should be done in the order defined previously) from http://msdn.microsoft.com/vstudio/express/downloads/.

Visual Studio C# Express Edition (VSCSE) provides the ability to compile in both Release and Debug modes. The main difference between the two when compiling your code base is that the Debug version of the DLL is a bit larger and includes the symbols (.pdb) file.

VSCSE has a default setting of building (aka compiling) in the Release format. To enable Debug mode building, we'll need first expose the ability to make this change with Visual Studio:

1. With VSCSE running, click **Tools | Options** from the menu bar.

2. At the bottom-left corner of the Options window, check the **Show all settings** check box.

3. Expand **Projects and Solutions** and then click the **General node**.

4. Check the **Show advanced build configurations** check box.

5. Click the **OK** button (see Figure 17.13).

Figure 17.13 VSCSE Options

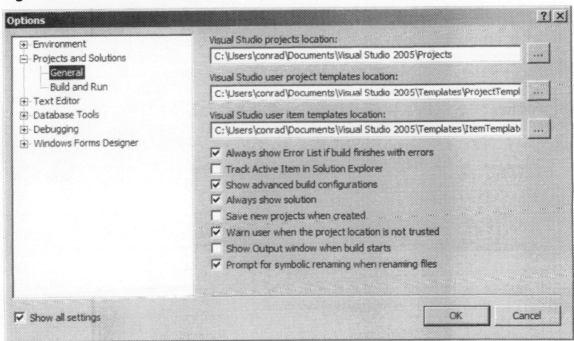

Now that we have this configured, we can select the build type we'd like to use in compiling our application or class.

Create and Compile

To get started, let's start the Microsoft Visual C# 2005 Express Edition development environment and create a new project:

1. Click the **Windows** button | **All Programs** | **Microsoft Visual C# 2005 Express Edition**.

2. From the top menu bar, click **File** | **New Project**.

3. Select **Class Library** and set the Name to **HowToCheatIIS7**.

4. Click **OK** (see Figure 17.14).

Figure 17.14 Creating a New Project with Visual C# 2005 Express Edition

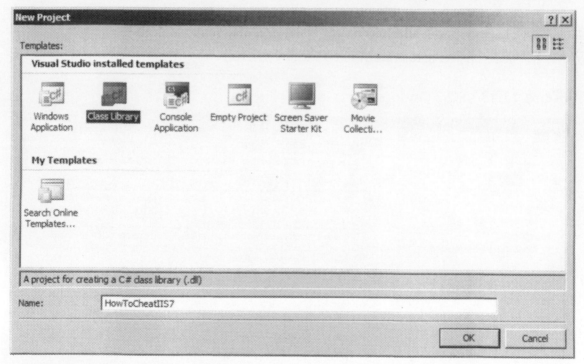

To leverage the Microsoft.Web.Administration object model and to connect into the IIS pipeline, we'll need to create a couple of references to our project:

1. Right-click the **References** folder and select **Add References...** from the context menu.

2. Within the **Browse** tab, navigate to the **%WINDIR%\System32\InetSrv** folder and select **Microsoft.Web.Administration.dll**, and then click the **OK** button.

Follow the same basic instructions, but this time we'll add the **System.Web** assembly from the **.NET** tab.

Ensure that the build is set to **Debug** by selecting it from the build drop-down menu (see Figure 17.15).

Figure 17.15 Setting the Build to Debug

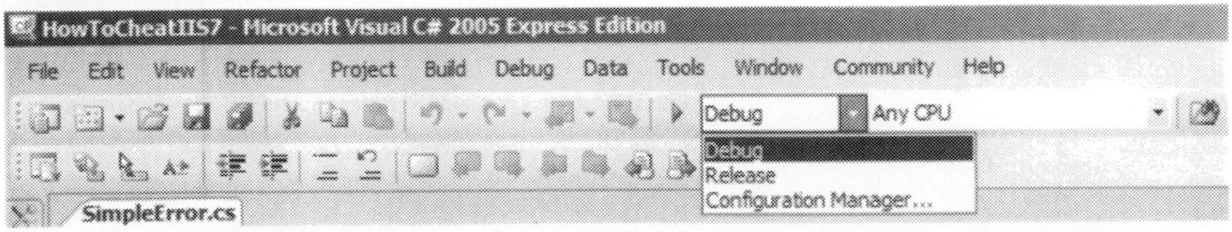

```csharp
using System;
using System.Web;
using System.Collections;
using System.Diagnostics;
namespace HowToCheatIIS7
{
  public class TraceModule : IHttpModule
  {
    TraceSource tsStatus;
    // register callbacks as well as the trace source.
    public void Init(HttpApplication application)
    {
      application.EndRequest += (new EventHandler(this.Application_EndRequest));
      tsStatus = new TraceSource("tsStatus");
    }
    private void Application_EndRequest(Object source, EventArgs e)
    {
      tsStatus.TraceEvent(TraceEventType.Start, 0, "[TraceModule] Start");
      tsStatus.TraceEvent(TraceEventType.Warning, 0, "[TraceModule] Warning");
      tsStatus.TraceEvent(TraceEventType.Stop, 0, "[TraceModule] Stop");
    }
    public void Dispose()
    {
    }
  }
}
```

Compile the application by clicking the **Build | Build Solution** menu. Once our code has been compiled, we can find the HowToCheatIIS7.dll and HowToCheatIIS7.dll.

Add Managed Module to IIS 7.0

With our new module compiled, we'll now add it to IIS 7.0. Before we can add our new module into IIS, we'll need to copy our compiled components to the /bin directory of our Web application.

Using IIS Manager, we'll now add our new module into the IIS 7 pipeline. In this example, we're going to add our module to a specific application within the Default Web Site:

1. Click **Modules** and then click the **Open Feature** from within the Actions pane. Or you can simply double-click the **Modules** icon (see Figure 17.16).

Figure 17.16 Adding a New Module to IIS 7

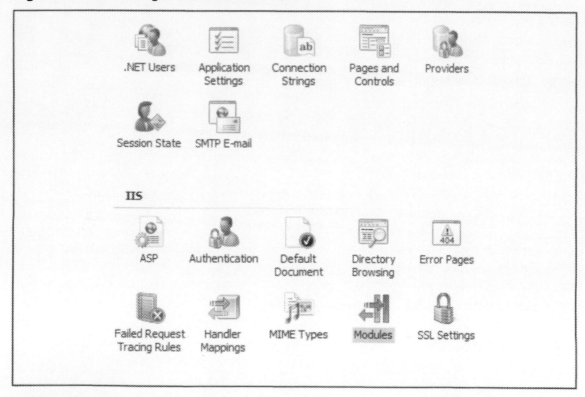

2. From the Actions pane, click **Add Managed Module**…(see Figure 17.17).

Figure 17.17 The Add Managed Module

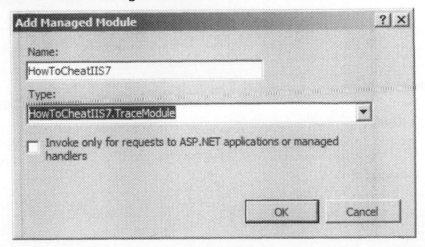

3. In the Add Managed Module window, provide the following information and then click the **OK** button:

    ■ Name: HowToCheatIIS7

    ■ Type: HowToCheatIIS7.TraceModule

This also could be done by directly updating the web.config file for the application. The following would be added within the <modules> XML node.

```
<add name="HowToChcatIIS7" type="HowToCheatIIS7.TraceModule" preCondition="" />
```

You'll now see HowToCheatIIS7 added to the list of modules. Clicking the **View Ordered List...**link in the Actions pane, you'll see the actual order in which IIS7 will process each module as a request is submitted to this application. Our new module will be at the bottom of this list. By moving it up in the list, you'll be able to capture and potentially modify data and actions before later modules. This is extremely useful when you want to trace certain types of information before another module handles the request.

Enabling Trace

Our module has now been developed, compiled, and configured in IIS 7, but we have to tell IIS 7 to listen for tracing information from our new component. The following web.config file defines the three configuration settings that need to be defined for our tracing information within our module to be captured and included in a Failed Request Tracing Log file:

```
<configuration>
  <system.webServer>
    <modules>
      <add name="TraceModule" type="HowToCheatIIS7.TraceModule" />
    </modules>
  </system.webServer>
  <system.diagnostics>
    <sharedListeners>
      <add name="IisTraceListener" type="System.Web.IisTraceListener, System.Web,
Version=2.0.0.0, Culture=neutral, PublicKeyToken=b03f5f7f11d50a3a" />
    </sharedListeners>
    <switches>
      <add name="DefaultSwitch" value="All" />
    </switches>
    <sources>
      <source name="tsStatus" switchName="DefaultSwitch">
        <listeners>
          <add name="IisTraceListener" type="System.Web.IisTraceListener, System.Web,
Version=2.0.0.0, Culture=neutral, PublicKeyToken=b03f5f7f11d50a3a" />
        </listeners>
      </source>
    </sources>
  </system.diagnostics>
</configuration>
```

Now that all of the pieces are in place, navigate your browser back to the simpletrace.aspx page. Once that page has completed rendering, open the latest FR######.xml file using your browser (see Figure 17.18).

Any Web developer who is building either a Web application or IIS 7.0 modules can now plug into the Failed Request Trace pipeline. This will result in less time and code the Web developer must focus on creating a tracing mechanism for the application. It will also reduce the number of trace files that a Web administrator must use to triage and resolve a given issue relating to a Web application.

Although our example explains how to override the tracing mechanism that ships with IIS 7.0, the same type of logic and code could be leveraged within a custom application or another module that is not specifically focused on tracing. Take, for example, a developer who is creating a customer authentication module that will replace how IIS 7.0 does authentication. The developer can plug her tracing details within the same tracing pipeline as IIS 7.0. By doing so, the operations team or Web server administrator can get a single trace file with all applications participating within a troubled or failed request on a production machine.

Figure 17.18 IIS Diagnostics Output and Trace Details

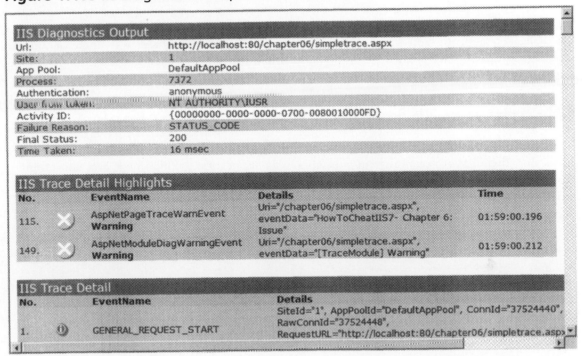

Due to the ability to have a single trace file for all components to plug into for a given request, Web server administrators and IT operations managers will be demanding that Web developers and ISVs plug into that infrastructure. In the long term, this will result in faster turnaround in resolving production issues and reduced overhead on server resources.

Reality: Inside What Tracing Can't Do in IIS 7.0

There is one undeniable truth in technology: There is no "magic pixie dust." The same goes for this powerful feature in IIS 7.0; there are simply some things that it can't do, and this section exists for this very reason. In some situations, failures exist outside the boundaries of the runtime engine, such as service failures or bad configurations. For these cases, most will find the Event Viewer is their best friend, whereas some errors might occur in Web applications during runtime that tracing simply can't help. In these cases, it is important to understand how to effectively tackle these issues.

For example, a difficult yet realistic reality in Web applications is the deployment of code that presents memory leaks. Tracing doesn't offer any functionality to ascertain the currently used memory of your Web application. How does one tackle this difficult problem? There are several different paths of attack, but the first action is to determine that you have a true leak, as well as to figure out how to attack the problem once it exists. At this point, we will discuss the tools available for closing in on this problem in Debug Diagnostics.

Identifying That You Have a Memory Leak

The unfortunate truth is that many times you anticipate a memory leak when you actually don't have one. Instead, you have different behaviors of an application, such as long-term allocations for performance or short-term allocations that cause spikes. You should understand how to use the Event viewer to best understand whether you have a memory leak; only then do you take action.

When researching a potential memory leak, you must first understand that there is a difference between objects hanging around longer than you expected and losing the handle on an object, which actually constitutes a leak.

The .NET Framework provides a rich and extensible object-oriented programming platform that also removes the developer from having to handle his or her own memory management. Although this does make developers more productive, it can become a bit frustrating when scaling your application for production use and seeing the memory allocations run wild. There is no actual "fix" to resolve this issue, but it requires that a developer understand how memory management in the .NET Framework works.

It is not the intended scope of this chapter to provide the definitive resource for memory management and performance for the .NET Framework, ASP.NET, or IIS 7.0, but it would be a bit neglectful to not at least mention a few guidelines to get you going.

The Garbage Collector (GC) is responsible for managing the memory allocation for all objects used within a .NET application. The GC will maintain the state of an object in memory and will remove it from physical memory when it needs to make more space using a finalizing process, or it will keep an object around due to a parent object keeping a reference to it. A common issue in memory management for ASP.NET is unknowingly maintaining an object or even a collection of objects. A good example of this is when you bind to an event handler to a static or cached object.

Here is an example of a simple event handler within ASP.NET:

```
private void InitializeComponent()
  {
    this.Load += new System.EventHandler(this.Page_Load);
    staticObject.myEvent += new myEventEventHandler(this.staticObject_myEvent);
  }
```

Each time the ASP.NET page that has this code in it is called, a new event handler and listeners will be created for it. The base object that the event handler is referencing is a static object and will live until it is explicitly finalized and destroyed or until the application is unloaded from the host application (i.e., restarting the IIS application pool). With the static object as an anchor, all the event handlers that were created per page request will continue to live on within the GC because there is a parent object that is still alive. One way to help clear this up is to manually unhook the event handler when it's no longer needed.

When using a COM object within your .NET code base, you'll have to ensure that you properly release the object and not simply set the object to null or *nothing*. The following method will instruct the .NET Framework to release a COM object. If you don't do this, the object may reside in memory for much longer that you expect:

```
System.Runtime.InteropServices.Marshal.ReleaseComObject(comObj)
```

Shortcut...

Native Code and Managed Code Is All the Same in IIS 7.0

In previous versions of IIS, the ability to control and override IIS functionality was limited to those that could code in native code (C and C++). With IIS 7.0, the playing field is a bit more level, although there are still areas where native code is the only option.

IIS 7.0 also provides a new native core server API for C++ developers that replaces ISAPI filters. To compile an IIS 7.0 module using native code, you'll need to use the latest Windows Vista Platform SDK, which contains the IIS header file (httpserv.h).

Microsoft provides a starter kit for IIS 7.0 module development for C++: www.iis.net/default.aspx?tabid=3&subtabid=31&g=5&i=1062.

Downloading Debug Diagnostics and Enable Leak Tracker

This section outlines how to obtain the download for Debug Diagnostics and enable a memory leak rule to track down a problem with memory allocation.

With all the great built-in tools and platform components for diagnostics that ship as part of IIS 7, Microsoft also provides some additional tools. One such tool is the IIS Debug Diagnostics Tool,

which is available as a free download from www.microsoft.com/downloads/
details.aspx?FamilyID=28bd5941-c458-46f1-b24d-f60151d875a3&DisplayLang=en.

Capturing Memory Links

With the Debug Diagnostics Tool (DDT) installed, do the following:

1. Open the tool by navigating to the **Windows** button | **All Programs | Debug
   Diagnostics Tool 1.1 | DebugDiag 1.1 (x86)**.

2. From within the Rules tab, click the **Add Rule30...**button (see Figure 17.19).

Figure 17.19 The Rules Tab

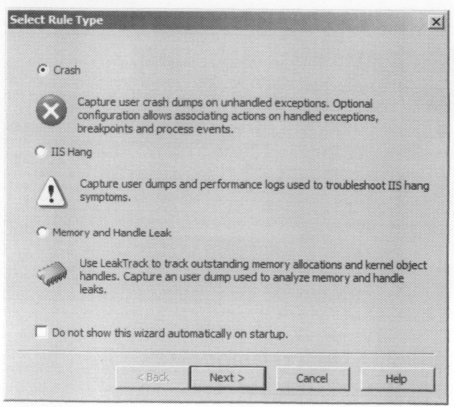

3. The Select Rule Type page provides three options:

- Crash

- IIS Hang

- Memory and Handle Leak

For the purpose of this exercise, select the **Memory and Handle Leak** option and click **Next**. From the Select Target page, find the IIS process (**w3wp.exe**) and click **Next** (see Figure 17.20).

Figure 17.20 The Select Target Page

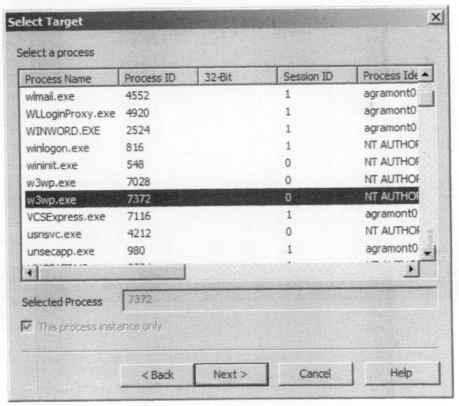

4. From the Configure Leak Rule page (see Figure 17.21), there are a number of options allow you to control the behavior of the new rule.

Figure 17.21 The Configure Leak Rule Page

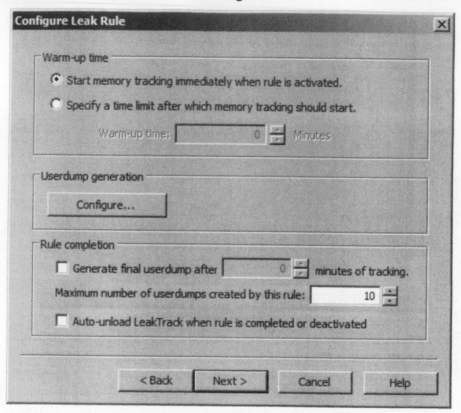

5. From the Select Dump Location and Rule Name (Optional) page (see Figure 17.22), this is where you give the rule a friendly name and a location where all the user dump information will be stored.

Figure 17.22 The Select Dump Location and Rule Name (Optional) Page

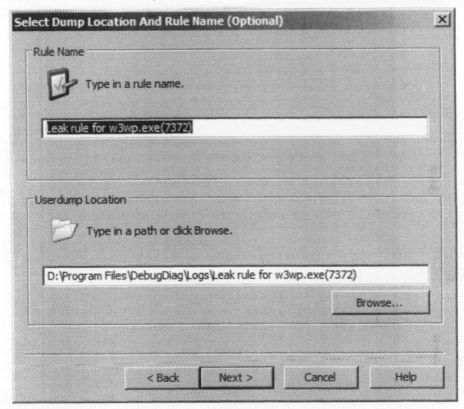

6. Finally, the Rule Completed page allows you to activate the rule for immediate use (see Figure 17.23).

Figure 17.23 The Rule Completed Page

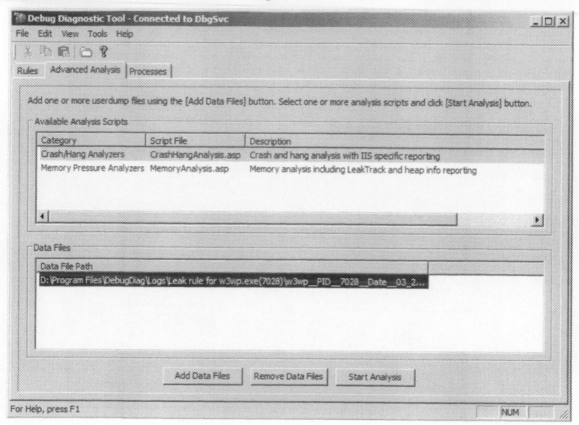

Summary

Unlike past IIS versions, the ability to troubleshoot your Web server and applications is a focal point for Microsoft. IIS 7.0 offers a strong troubleshooting approach using failed request tracing that is powerful and developer extensible and that easily pinpoints most of the common failures that occur in IIS 7.0. For the other lower percentage of problems, you can effectively understand the toolsets available to troubleshoot these problems when they occur. Finally, the key is to understand what failed request tracing can do for you—and what it can't.

Solutions Fast Track

Custom Error Messages

- ☑ Error messages can be configured by server, site, or application.

- ☑ Error messages are defined within the applicationHost.config file for the server or the web.config file for a given site or application/virtual directory.

- ☑ Error messages can be a static or dynamic file. You can also redirect to an external site when a specific error or status code is reached.

- ☑ Detailed error messages provide a rich set of details about a specific error that assist in troubleshooting the issue.

- ☑ ASP.NET and IIS 7 are not integrated when it comes to error responses. The default setting is for IIS 7 to automatically decide how to handle errors.

Failed Request Tracing

- ☑ Failed Request Tracing can capture more than just errors. Tracing can be done on a given set of HTTP status codes or an amount of time.

- ☑ Developers should incorporate tracing details into their Web applications and components. This will help Web server administrators troubleshoot issues in a production environment.

Writing Tracing Information

- ☑ Tracing information from ASP.NET, IIS, and custom modules can be written to a single XML file.

- ☑ Tracing information can be done within ASP.NET:

  ```
  Trace.Warn("HowToCheatIIS7- Chapter 6: Issue");
  ```

- ☑ Tracing information can be done within a .NET Module

  ```
  tsStatus.TraceEvent(TraceEventType.Warning, 0, "[TraceModule] Warning");
  ```

Frequently Asked Questions

Q: I'm a Web host and would like to be able to allow my customers to define their own tracing settings. Is this possible?

A: Yes, but doing so does require some thoughtful configuration. First, you'll need to change the <section name="traceFailedRequests" overrideModeDefault="Deny" /> in the applicationHost. config file and change the overrideModeDefault setting to Allow, but be careful because this will impact all the sites and applications on that server.

Q: Can I completely replace the ErrorModule that ships with IIS 7.0 with my own .NET code?

A: Absolutely! This is one of the great benefits of IIS 7.0 and the integration with ASP.NET. With some simple coding, a developer can create his or her own module that handles errors. Best of all, this can be done on a per-site level, so you don't have to impact the way all errors are going to be handled for other sites that want to use the default components.

Q: Can I use the Failed Request Tracing on production servers even if there aren't issues?

A: Sure, but there is always the I/O overhead when the log files are written to disk. Beyond that, you could have all File not Found (404) errors written out so you can see which URLs people are trying to navigate to and perhaps reroute those future requests. With the configuration setting that provides a maximum number of log files, you can be sure that you won't fill up your disk with log files.

Q: Can I enable/disable an existing Failed Request Tracing Rule?

A: No. At the moment, you have to delete a rule when you don't want it to "run" and then recreate it when you want those log files generated again.

Chapter 18

Putting It All Together

Solutions in this chapter:

- **Migrating to IIS 7.0**
- **Fitting and Finishing Work with IIS 7.0**
- **The Developer's Call-To-Arms**

☑ **Summary**

☑ **Solutions Fast Track**

☑ **Frequently Asked Questions**

Introduction

It has been said time and time again, there is no perfection in software. The entire planning process is focused on mitigating risks, avoiding pitfalls, and succeeding at all costs. In short, there is no "perfect" plan for moving from IIS 6.0 to 7.0. Guaranteed successes or failures in your planning or risk assessments just don't exist. At the end of the day, your success will be measured by how effective you leverage what is offered *in the box* for IIS 7.0. So study your current environment, understand your present dependencies on IIS features, and those non-IIS features your developer knows about. Using these as your building blocks, develop a step-by-step plan that takes the shortest yet most concise route to IIS 7.0. With the knowledge gained in this book, you will be well on your way to effectively deploying the most secure, powerful, and manageable Web server ever released by Microsoft.

BEST PRACTICES ACCORDING TO MICROSOFT

At the time of this writing, Microsoft was still actively working on IIS 7.0. The release of Windows Vista with IIS 7.0 offers a full Web server, though one that will change. It is because of this that Microsoft recommends IIS 7.0 on Windows Vista for development and learning purposes only—not for any true deployment scenarios. The release of Windows Server 2008 Beta 3 had primary changes in IIS 7.0 directed towards deployment. You should evaluate this version of IIS 7.0 to understand migrating to IIS 7.0 from IIS 6.0.

Migrating to IIS 7.0

The primary reason to migrate to IIS 7.0 is simple: flexibility. In previous chapters, you learned all the various moving parts that make up this profound release of IIS. Your migration strategy greatly depends on your ability to evaluate your IIS 6.0 environment, build a blueprint for your system on IIS 6.0, and cross-reference as you migrate to IIS 7.0. The end goal is to cause as little disruption as possible to your services, yet ensure you take advantage of the benefits IIS 7.0 has to offer.

Migration Considerations

Successful migrations to and from any platform are the end result of careful consideration, planning, and execution. Before you start upgrading servers willy-nilly, there are some questions you should ask to help identify how much of your network is eligible for the transition.

- Are any Web servers just serving up static content? For example, are you running several FTP servers, or sites that only store resources like images and JavaScript for other Web sites? If so, these are prime candidates for migration, and will probably provide the smoothest upgrade path. If these resource sites are spread out across your server farm, you should consider consolidating them onto one box.

- Are any of your sites using URLScan to filter requests? If yes, you'll need to consider moving to IIS 7.0's Request Filtering instead.

- Are you running ASP.NET 1.0, 1.1, or FPSE applications? If so, there will be additional configuration issues. You should consider the ramifications of converting your ASP.NET applications to ASP.NET 2.0 before undertaking the server migration.

- Are you running ISAPI filters from IIS 5.1 or earlier? You may have to check with the vendor for a newer version. There is a good possibility one might not be available, in which case a replacement must be built.

- Are you only running IIS on the boxes you're upgrading? Consider installing the Server Core version of Windows Server 2008 instead of a full-fledged version. Server Core is a command-line only flavor of Windows, a la Unix, that doesn't contain any GUI code. No shell means a smaller surface area than even the Web Edition. How can your Web server fall victim to an animated cursor flaw when the server is incapable of using animated cursors?

Upgrading Paths by OS Version

As I mentioned at the beginning of the chapter, if you're running anything older than Windows Server 2003 in a production environment, your migration experience will be slightly more complicated than if you had just bit the bullet and upgraded with the rest of the world.

The following direct upgrade paths are supported:

- IIS 6 | Windows Server 2003 => IIS 7 | Windows Server 2008
- IIS 5.1 | Windows XP => IIS 7 | Windows Vista

There are no guarantees that migration tools will be offered by Microsoft. As such, you will be tasked with building your own migration strategy. It goes without saying that if you are running previous versions of IIS before IIS 6.0, you should seriously consider moving to IIS 6.0 prior to jumping to IIS 7.0. The IIS 7.0 process model for the most part stole much of its design from the IIS 6.0 process model, so most applications running on IIS 6.0 will likely run fine on version 7. If you do choose to directly jump from IIS 4.0 or 5.0 to IIS 7.0, you should understand your migration strategy and how to execute it.

For example, in IIS 5.0 your process isolation was very different than in IIS 6. The process model in IIS 5.0 made assumptions that your ISAPI filters were always running as a local system, and in Inetinfo.exe, and that they had access to the raw HTTP request information. This isn't the case in IIS 6, nor is that changing in IIS 7.0. So the questions you should ask yourself include the following:

- How do you isolate your site and applications into application pools?
- Will your ISAPI filters work when used in multiple processes?
- Can your applications run with limited privileges such as Network Service?

This is the tip of the iceberg, but it gives you an idea of what to crunch when planning a migration from IIS 5 to 7.0. Nonetheless, it is completely possible to go from version 5 to version 7 of IIS.

Upgrade versus Clean Install

The time-tested rule-of-thumb regarding Windows is that it is always better to do a clean installation on existing hardware than it is to perform an in-place upgrade. That's because, in the past, Windows tried to install the newer version over the top of the older one, and it didn't always do the best job. Often, old files and settings were left behind, cluttering up the hard drive and making troubleshooting the system difficult. For some administrators, a new deployment of Windows provides a fresh start for servers that seem to get slower as time goes on.

But all that changed with Vista and Windows Server 2008. The new installer is image-based, not file-based. So during an upgrade, all the systems' programs and settings are backed up, a clean image is copied to the hard drive and expanded, and then the programs and settings are migrated to the new image. Thus, installations are just as painless as with a fresh partition.

That being said, a clean installation may still be the way to go for system administrators who need a cathartic release every five years or so. It also may be easier (and sometimes cheaper) for sysadmins to only deploy new OS releases on new hardware, in the same way they manage their desktops.

Upgrade Steps

As I mentioned earlier in the chapter, the installation process on Windows Vista and Windows Server 2008 is image-based, instead of file-based as in previous versions. This means upgrades are also handled differently than in earlier versions. Currently, the upgrade process happens in three stages:

- Detect and gather
- Image copy and unpacking
- Restore settings

Let's take a closer look at what occurs in these phases.

Detect and Gather

During an upgrade to Windows Vista or Windows Server 2008, the installer looks for all features and settings in the previous operating system. If IIS is detected on the existing Windows installation, all metabase and IIS state information will be gathered and persisted to a hidden folder on the main partition. Any file system content not created or owned by Windows will remain intact through the upgrade, so all Web content you have on the hard drive will still be there after first boot.

Image Copy and Unpacking

The installation phase consists of copying the installation image to the hard drive, and then activating optional features, such as IIS, if they were detected on the original OS. The IIS features activated are based on the IIS state information gathered from the original OS. Because IIS 6 was nowhere near as modular as IIS7, the installer will err on the side of caution when configuring IIS 7's new features. You won't be able to specify which features you want. Instead, if any of the main IIS-related Windows services are installed on the old OS, all of the related IIS 7 features will be installed for maximum compatibility.

The following series of tables illustrates the IIS 6 services that will be detected, and the IIS 7 features that will be installed as a result:

If World Wide Web Service (W3SVC) Is Installed

IIS-ASP	IIS-ISAPIFilter
IIS-BasicAuthentication	IIS-LegacyScripts
IIS-CGI	IIS-LoggingLibraries
IIS-ClientCertificateMappingAuthentication	IIS-ManagementScriptingTools
IIS-CustomLogging	IIS-ManagementService
IIS-DefaultDocument	IIS-ODBCLogging
IIS-DigestAuthentication	IIS-RequestFiltering
IIS-DirectoryBrowsing	IIS-RequestMonitor
IIS-HttpCompressionDynamic	IIS-ServerSideIncludes
IIS-HttpCompressionStatic	IIS-StaticContent
IIS-HttpErrors	IIS-URLAuthorization
IIS-HttpLogging	IIS-WindowsAuthentication
IIS-HttpRedirect	IIS-WMICompatibility
IIS-HttpTracing	WAS-ConfigurationAPI
IIS-IISCertificateMappingAuthentication	WAS-NetFxEnvironment
IIS-IPSecurity	WAS-ProcessModel
IIS-ISAPIExtensions	

If FTP Service (MSFTPSVC) Is Installed

IIS-FTPServer

If Internet Services Manager (INETMGR.EXE) Is Installed

IIS-FTPManagement
IIS-LegacySnapIn
IIS-ManagementConsole

If IIS Administrative Service (IISADMIN) Is Installed

IIS-Metabase

This strategy gives you the greatest chance of booting up with a Web server that is fully functional for your applications. Unfortunately, you won't have any control over which services are installed as a result of the service detection process. You will have an opportunity later to fine-tune your Web server footprint after the upgrade is complete.

Restore Settings

After the image is unpacked and the optional features like IIS are configured, the settings that were gathered and set aside during the first phase are reapplied. At this point, the metabase settings from the original IIS (5 or 6) are translated into the new XML format and applied to the ApplicationHost.config file.

SOME INDEPENDENT ADVICE

IIS 7.0 on Windows Vista or Windows Server 2008 is still in beta as of this writing. Currently, some known issues with upgrades will impact your sites upon completion. These will obviously be resolved prior to final release, despite their current presence, even with Microsoft offering you a Go Live license for IIS 7.0 customers.

After the Upgrade

The speed of your upgrade depends on a number of variables like hardware, the number of installed features, and so on. Afterwards, you're booted into Windows for the first time. Now what? Well, chances are that your server is probably not ready to start shelling out Web pages to the masses quite yet. So, let's look at some of the things you can do to optimize IIS 7.0.

Fitting and Finishing Work in IIS 7.0

No upgrade or clean install is complete without some action items. The first thing to understand is that often on clean installs many people will install the entire product. It is a well-known tactic that guarantees less troubleshooting since everyone knows they can always strip after the fact. This approach makes sense given that most administrators, like you, aren't deeply involved with just one technology or even a couple. Instead, you have to manage many servers, all running various applications from Microsoft and elsewhere. The least amount of toil entails making sure that with everything installed your Web applications actually do work. So cool, do that…When you're finished, then come back.

Afterward, you must diligently clean up to ensure you're running the most optimized, smallest footprint Web server possible. A great number of individuals doing server administration don't know what their Web applications are built on or what their dependencies are. Thus, the question is often asked, "How can I figure this out on my IIS 5.0 or 6.0 servers?"

This wasn't as easy on previous versions, but it certainly is on IIS 7.0. With the new tracing infrastructure in IIS 7.0, you can literally step through your Web applications and determine from the trace log what features are used.

Furthermore, you can spend much time and energy troubleshooting if you don't have the tools set up right off the bat. You can enable failed request tracing for only 500 errors to ensure that when they occur, you have access to the files. To strengthen that approach, set up a scheduled task to copy the old files to another location and increase the number of trace logs to keep.

The last step is to protect yourself in case of problems with your server. Unfortunately, IIS 7.0 does not make an initial configuration backup of applicationhost.config. Therefore, you need to. So let's make sure this is done.

Using Tracing to Isolate Your Server Features

In IIS 7.0, the Failed Request Tracing is misleading. Yes, it is used to locate potential failure points and causes but at the same time many don't realize it's just fine for requests that work like HTTP 200. It is so easy to learn what modules are used by your Web applications, yet it is so tricky to so many because they get caught up in the term "failed."

The first step is to build some sort of mechanism to allow you to emulate your client's use of your Web applications. This is often referred to as load testing, but in our case load isn't the goal of just using the application a good start? So many ways exist to do this that it is outside the scope of this chapter. However, let's assume you do have some sort of ability to make requests to your IIS 7.0 server.

Some Independent Advice

A number of solutions are available in the marketplace, varying from free to expensive, for automating requests to your Web server. In fact, if you are a developer, you can probably just build your own. If you struggle with not having a solution, take a look at tools like tinyget from Microsoft.

The second step is to enable tracing for all HTTP status codes equaling 200 and 300 for all content. This is important to ensure you grab all requests that do not equal an error—what many of us refer to as your application's "happy path." To set up this rule, do the following:

1. In IIS Manager, click the Web site name—for example, Default Web Site.

2. On the home page, click **Failed Request Tracing**.

3. In the task pane, click **Add**.

4. Select **All Content** when asked to select what to trace.

5. For conditions, check Status Codes and type **200, 301, 302**.

6. Click **Finish**.

To validate that your rule was successful, it should now appear in the list view on the failed request tracing page, as shown in Figure 18.1.

Figure 18.1 Failed Request Tracing Rule

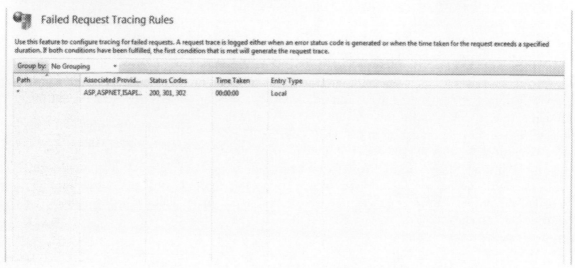

The next step is to enable tracing for the site and set the path. This will put the rule previously defined into action and start the tracing. This is an important concept covered in Chapter 17: that failed request tracing is always a two-step process. It requires that rules are defined and then tracing is enabled.

To enable tracing for your Web site, do the following:

1. In IIS Manager, click your Web site (for example, Default Web Site).

2. On the Default Web Site home, in the task pane click **Failed Request Tracing** under **Configure**.

3. Click **Enable** and set the path value and number of trace files to retain. Click **OK**.

Your rule is now enabled and new requests to the server that have the HTTP status 200, 301, 302 will have a trace file created.

Our last step is to create simulated requests that are similar to those sent to your production server. This, as mentioned earlier, is accomplished in a multitude of ways using load simulators or automated HTTP clients.

SOME INDEPENDENT ADVICE

This topic of simulating your client's usage is often confusing to many administrators. They are not aware that they have a blueprint of their clients' usage patterns for their Web applications in the IIS log files. The key goal is to extract those usage patterns out of the log files and put them into usage scenario scripts that will simulate the same traffic against your Web server.

Your IIS log files can be parsed in a multitude of ways, but we highly recommend using the Log Parser toolset. It can extract the necessary data from the log files and provide you with the HTTP requests to use in your automated HTTP scripts. For more information on Log Parser, see this online Webcast at http://www.iis.net/default.aspx?tabid=2&subtabid=26&i=36, as well as the Syngress book Log Parser Toolkit (ISBN: 1-932266-52-6).

After completing your simulated test, the evaluation stage takes place where you will analyze the failed request tracing logs. This is where the pattern of the requests will tell you what binaries are used.

For example, let's talk about those modules that are removable for a particular type of Web application. This includes sites and applications using static HTML requests, classic Active Server Pages (ASP), an ISAPI extension request, and, lastly, an ASP.NET request.

Static HTML Requests

These are fairly simple to recognize, but it's important you know what authentication types are used for the requests. This will tell you whether you need the static module (most will), as well as any authentication modules.

If you are using images, Cascading Style Sheets (CSS), or any text-based type of files on your server, you will likely need the default handler for static content. It is very unlikely you will need to remove this.

Module Name	Default IIS 7.0 Install Status
StaticFileModule	Default
AnonymousAuthenticationModule	Default
BasicAuthenticationModule	Not Installed
WindowsAuthenticationModule	Not Installed
DigestAuthenticationModule	Not Installed

As you can see, after upgrading from IIS 6.0 to IIS 7.0, the default state is to install all functionality IIS 7.0 offers. This could potentially result in having 1 to 4 modules installed that are not necessary, or installed by default on IIS 7.0 clean installs.

For example, using the preceding table, you could ascertain that after upgrading you do not need basic or digest authentication. To remove them, you can stop them from being loaded in any of the worker processes, as we showed in Chapter 14. To review, here is how you can remove modules easily from IIS 7.0.

You can use any one of the tools available, but for the sake of simplicity let's use the IIS Manager to remove the AuthDigest module since this is a seldom-used module. The same steps can be done to remove any of the preceding modules.

1. Go to **Start | Administrative Tools | Internet Information Services (IIS) Manager**.

2. At the server level, click **Modules**.

3. Click **DigestAuthenticationModule**. Then, in the **Actions** pane, click **Remove**.

4. Click **Yes** to confirm the removal.

Classic ASP Requests

ASP requests are slightly tricky in IIS 7.0 since they require two modules installed for one feature. However, if you aren't using ASP pages, you can remove at least one module, and possibly a second (IsapiModule). To determine if your Web application is using ASP, search your content directory (or directories) or use Failed Request Tracing to determine if you have files with the extension .asp. Also, if you have access to your IIS 6.0 server, you can view the ScriptMaps, as shown in Figure 18.2.

Figure 18.2 IIS 6.0 Default Install ScriptMaps

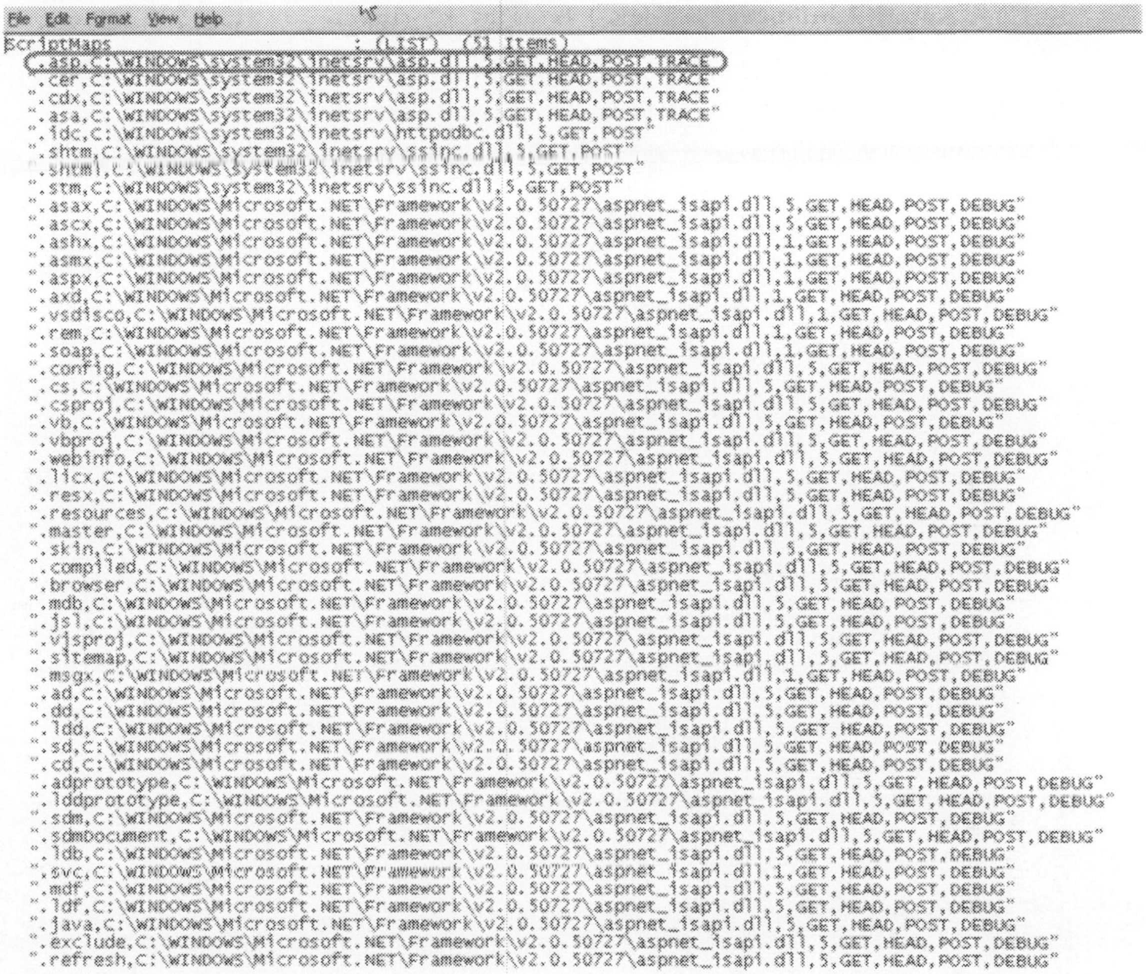

```
File  Edit  Format  View  Help
ScriptMaps                       : (LIST)  (51 Items)
".asp,C:\WINDOWS\system32\inetsrv\asp.dll,5,GET,HEAD,POST,TRACE"
".cer,C:\WINDOWS\system32\inetsrv\asp.dll,5,GET,HEAD,POST,TRACE"
".cdx,C:\WINDOWS\system32\inetsrv\asp.dll,5,GET,HEAD,POST,TRACE"
".asa,C:\WINDOWS\system32\inetsrv\asp.dll,5,GET,HEAD,POST,TRACE"
".idc,C:\WINDOWS\system32\inetsrv\httpodbc.dll,5,GET,POST"
".shtm,C:\WINDOWS\system32\inetsrv\ssinc.dll,5,GET,POST"
".shtml,C:\WINDOWS\system32\inetsrv\ssinc.dll,5,GET,POST"
".stm,C:\WINDOWS\system32\inetsrv\ssinc.dll,5,GET,POST"
".asax,C:\WINDOWS\Microsoft.NET\Framework\v2.0.50727\aspnet_isapi.dll,5,GET,HEAD,POST,DEBUG"
".ascx,C:\WINDOWS\Microsoft.NET\Framework\v2.0.50727\aspnet_isapi.dll,5,GET,HEAD,POST,DEBUG"
".ashx,C:\WINDOWS\Microsoft.NET\Framework\v2.0.50727\aspnet_isapi.dll,1,GET,HEAD,POST,DEBUG"
".asmx,C:\WINDOWS\Microsoft.NET\Framework\v2.0.50727\aspnet_isapi.dll,1,GET,HEAD,POST,DEBUG"
".aspx,C:\WINDOWS\Microsoft.NET\Framework\v2.0.50727\aspnet_isapi.dll,1,GET,HEAD,POST,DEBUG"
".axd,C:\WINDOWS\Microsoft.NET\Framework\v2.0.50727\aspnet_isapi.dll,1,GET,HEAD,POST,DEBUG"
".vsdisco,C:\WINDOWS\Microsoft.NET\Framework\v2.0.50727\aspnet_isapi.dll,1,GET,HEAD,POST,DEBUG"
".rem,C:\WINDOWS\Microsoft.NET\Framework\v2.0.50727\aspnet_isapi.dll,1,GET,HEAD,POST,DEBUG"
".soap,C:\WINDOWS\Microsoft.NET\Framework\v2.0.50727\aspnet_isapi.dll,1,GET,HEAD,POST,DEBUG"
".config,C:\WINDOWS\Microsoft.NET\Framework\v2.0.50727\aspnet_isapi.dll,5,GET,HEAD,POST,DEBUG"
".cs,C:\WINDOWS\Microsoft.NET\Framework\v2.0.50727\aspnet_isapi.dll,5,GET,HEAD,POST,DEBUG"
".csproj,C:\WINDOWS\Microsoft.NET\Framework\v2.0.50727\aspnet_isapi.dll,5,GET,HEAD,POST,DEBUG"
".vb,C:\WINDOWS\Microsoft.NET\Framework\v2.0.50727\aspnet_isapi.dll,5,GET,HEAD,POST,DEBUG"
".vbproj,C:\WINDOWS\Microsoft.NET\Framework\v2.0.50727\aspnet_isapi.dll,5,GET,HEAD,POST,DEBUG"
".webinfo,C:\WINDOWS\Microsoft.NET\Framework\v2.0.50727\aspnet_isapi.dll,5,GET,HEAD,POST,DEBUG"
".licx,C:\WINDOWS\Microsoft.NET\Framework\v2.0.50727\aspnet_isapi.dll,5,GET,HEAD,POST,DEBUG"
".resx,C:\WINDOWS\Microsoft.NET\Framework\v2.0.50727\aspnet_isapi.dll,5,GET,HEAD,POST,DEBUG"
".resources,C:\WINDOWS\Microsoft.NET\Framework\v2.0.50727\aspnet_isapi.dll,5,GET,HEAD,POST,DEBUG"
".master,C:\WINDOWS\Microsoft.NET\Framework\v2.0.50727\aspnet_isapi.dll,5,GET,HEAD,POST,DEBUG"
".skin,C:\WINDOWS\Microsoft.NET\Framework\v2.0.50727\aspnet_isapi.dll,5,GET,HEAD,POST,DEBUG"
".compiled,C:\WINDOWS\Microsoft.NET\Framework\v2.0.50727\aspnet_isapi.dll,5,GET,HEAD,POST,DEBUG"
".browser,C:\WINDOWS\Microsoft.NET\Framework\v2.0.50727\aspnet_isapi.dll,5,GET,HEAD,POST,DEBUG"
".mdb,C:\WINDOWS\Microsoft.NET\Framework\v2.0.50727\aspnet_isapi.dll,5,GET,HEAD,POST,DEBUG"
".jsl,C:\WINDOWS\Microsoft.NET\Framework\v2.0.50727\aspnet_isapi.dll,5,GET,HEAD,POST,DEBUG"
".vjsproj,C:\WINDOWS\Microsoft.NET\Framework\v2.0.50727\aspnet_isapi.dll,5,GET,HEAD,POST,DEBUG"
".sitemap,C:\WINDOWS\Microsoft.NET\Framework\v2.0.50727\aspnet_isapi.dll,5,GET,HEAD,POST,DEBUG"
".msgx,C:\WINDOWS\Microsoft.NET\Framework\v2.0.50727\aspnet_isapi.dll,1,GET,HEAD,POST,DEBUG"
".ad,C:\WINDOWS\Microsoft.NET\Framework\v2.0.50727\aspnet_isapi.dll,5,GET,HEAD,POST,DEBUG"
".dd,C:\WINDOWS\Microsoft.NET\Framework\v2.0.50727\aspnet_isapi.dll,5,GET,HEAD,POST,DEBUG"
".ldd,C:\WINDOWS\Microsoft.NET\Framework\v2.0.50727\aspnet_isapi.dll,5,GET,HEAD,POST,DEBUG"
".sd,C:\WINDOWS\Microsoft.NET\Framework\v2.0.50727\aspnet_isapi.dll,5,GET,HEAD,POST,DEBUG"
".cd,C:\WINDOWS\Microsoft.NET\Framework\v2.0.50727\aspnet_isapi.dll,5,GET,HEAD,POST,DEBUG"
".adprototype,C:\WINDOWS\Microsoft.NET\Framework\v2.0.50727\aspnet_isapi.dll,5,GET,HEAD,POST,DEBUG"
".lddprototype,C:\WINDOWS\Microsoft.NET\Framework\v2.0.50727\aspnet_isapi.dll,5,GET,HEAD,POST,DEBUG"
".sdm,C:\WINDOWS\Microsoft.NET\Framework\v2.0.50727\aspnet_isapi.dll,5,GET,HEAD,POST,DEBUG"
".sdmDocument,C:\WINDOWS\Microsoft.NET\Framework\v2.0.50727\aspnet_isapi.dll,5,GET,HEAD,POST,DEBUG"
".ldb,C:\WINDOWS\Microsoft.NET\Framework\v2.0.50727\aspnet_isapi.dll,5,GET,HEAD,POST,DEBUG"
".svc,C:\WINDOWS\Microsoft.NET\Framework\v2.0.50727\aspnet_isapi.dll,1,GET,HEAD,POST,DEBUG"
".mdf,C:\WINDOWS\Microsoft.NET\Framework\v2.0.50727\aspnet_isapi.dll,5,GET,HEAD,POST,DEBUG"
".ldf,C:\WINDOWS\Microsoft.NET\Framework\v2.0.50727\aspnet_isapi.dll,5,GET,HEAD,POST,DEBUG"
".java,C:\WINDOWS\Microsoft.NET\Framework\v2.0.50727\aspnet_isapi.dll,5,GET,HEAD,POST,DEBUG"
".exclude,C:\WINDOWS\Microsoft.NET\Framework\v2.0.50727\aspnet_isapi.dll,5,GET,HEAD,POST,DEBUG"
".refresh,C:\WINDOWS\Microsoft.NET\Framework\v2.0.50727\aspnet_isapi.dll,5,GET,HEAD,POST,DEBUG"
```

Unlike previous versions of IIS, IIS 7.0 exposes the ISAPI development platform in a single module. Any ISAPI extension built against the ISAPI platform will require that this module be installed to work. ASP.dll is an ISAPI extension that will take advantage of this module and, if not used, can safely remove the module.

Module Name	Handler Name	Default IIS 7.0 Install Status
IsapiModule	NA	Not Installed
	ASPClassic	Not Installed
	Isapi-dll	Not Installed

You can remove the Classic ASP module by doing the following:

1. Click **Start | Administrative Tools | Internet Information Services (IIS) Manager**.
2. At the server level, click **Handler Mappings**.
3. Click **ASPClassic**, and in the **Actions** pane, click **Remove**.
4. Click **Yes** to confirm the removal.

To remove IsapiModule as well, do the following:

1. Click **Start | Administrative Tools | Internet Information Services (IIS) Manager**.
2. At the server level, click **Modules**.
3. Click **IsapiModule**, then in the **Actions** pane, click **Remove**.
4. Click **Yes** to confirm the removal.

SOME INDEPENDENT ADVICE

You should cautiously move forward when deciding whether to remove IsapiModule from IIS 7.0. It is safer to understand the ISAPI extensions (for example, handler) that are safe to remove, rather than removing this module. If you choose to remove this module, keep in mind that doing so will disable any ISAPI extension on the system and cause a configuration error.

ISAPI-based Extension Requests

ISAPI-based extension requests are usually more difficult to ascertain since these requests are easily confused with ISAPI filters. It is important to understand how to locate these requests in trace files to ensure you understand how to effectively enable or disable this functionality on your IIS 7.0 server.

The easiest method prior to upgrading to IIS 7.0 is to use your IIS 6.0 system as a reference point. All ISAPI-based extensions are stored in the metabase and are available to you in one of two ways. The first is by reviewing the ISAPI\CGI restriction list, as shown in Figure 18.3. Otherwise, you can directly access the metabase and review your ScriptMaps to understand the ISAPIs currently installed. The safest method is to use the restriction list since it indicates which handler is actually installed and allowed to execute.

Figure 18.3 IIS 6.0 Web Service Extensions in IIS Manager

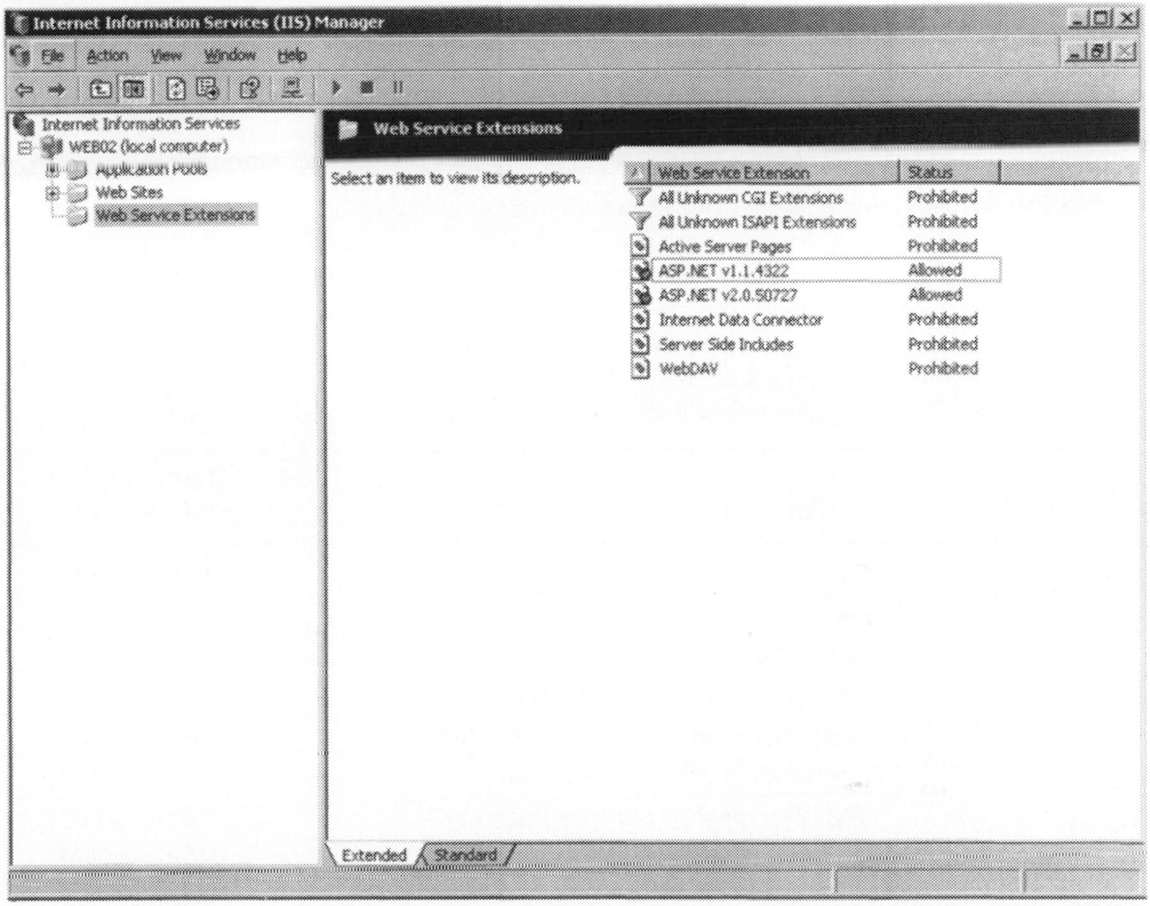

After already upgrading, you will need to use Failed Request Tracing or some other tool that will indicate what binaries are loaded in your worker process. A tool commonly used by many at Microsoft is Microsoft TechNet's SysInternals tool, Process Explorer. This tool (available for free from Microsoft at www.microsoft.com/technet/sysinternals/utilities/ProcessExplorer.mspx) gives you direct access to your worker process while executing to indicate what binaries are loaded in the worker process. It offers insight into the potential ISAPIs or CGIs loaded (if any) in your worker process.

To remove an ISAPI or CGI, perform the exact same steps used to remove ASP.dll earlier in this chapter.

ASP.NET Requests

ASP.NET requests are the more traditional type, such as ASPx pages. ASP.NET requests also are Web services, handlers, and so on, though the goal remains the same. The end plan is to determine whether ASP.NET is used, and furthermore, what version or versions are present.

ASP.NET is a platform-agnostic development platform that, as discussed earlier, is heavily used by many in the IIS community. Because it is agnostic, ASP.NET is made available for multiple platforms and originally started with ASP.NET 1.0 running on Windows 2000. The most common used today on IIS servers is ASP.NET 1.1 and 2.0.

ASP.NET 1.1 was released independently from IIS 6.0, yet it is available on the Windows Server 2003 CD-ROM. Furthermore, ASP.NET 1.1 and 2.0 are available on the disc starting with Windows Server 2003 R2. The goal of this exercise is to determine if you are in fact using ASP.NET 1.1 or 2.0 and ensuring you can enable, or better yet, disable the functionality on your server.

ASP.NET 1.1 in IIS 7.0 will require IsapiModule much like classic ASP (for example, asp.dll). To disable ASP.NET 1.1, simply remove the <handlers> section mapping for ASP.NET's ISAPI. Unlike ASP.NET 2.0, 1.1 does not participate nor support the new integrated pipeline.

For ASP.NET 2.0, it gets slightly trickier because of the new integrated pipeline. As we discussed in our core server chapter, IIS 7.0 supports two modes of operation for the application pool: Classic and Integrated. This makes it important to know what application versions your system needs in order to understand what is potentially removable.

For ASP.NET 2.0, the following table lists the modules or handlers used:

Module Name	Handler Name	Default IIS 7.0 Install Status
IsapiModule	N\A	Not Installed
WebEngine	N\A	Not Installed
	TraceHandler-Integrated	Not Installed
	WebAdminHandler-Integrated	Not Installed
	AssemblyResourceLoader-Integrated	Not Installed
	PageHandlerFactory-Integrated	Not Installed
	SimpleHandlerFactory-Integrated	Not Installed
	WebServiceHandlerFactory-Integrated	Not Installed
	HttpRemotingHandlerFactory-rem-Integrated	Not Installed
	HttpRemotingHandlerFactory-soap-Integrated	Not Installed
	AXD-ISAPI-2.0	Not Installed
	PageHandlerFactory-ISAPI-2.0	Not Installed
	SimpleHandlerFactory-ISAPI-2.0	Not Installed
	WebServiceHandlerFactory-ISAPI-2.0	Not Installed
	HttpRemotingHandlerFactory-rem-ISAPI-2.0	Not Installed
	HttpRemotingHandlerFactory-soap-ISAPI-2.0	Not Installed
	AXD-ISAPI-2.0-64	Not Installed
	PageHandlerFactory-ISAPI-2.0-64	Not Installed
	SimpleHandlerFactory-ISAPI-2.0-64	Not Installed
	WebServiceHandlerFactory-ISAPI-2.0-64	Not Installed
	HttpRemotingHandlerFactory-rem-ISAPI-2.0-64	Not Installed
	HttpRemotingHandlerFactory-soap-ISAPI-2.0-64	Not Installed
	ISAPI-dll	Not Installed

As you can see, there are many decisions to make when determining what is not needed. Keep in mind during the upgrade process that IIS 7.0 must be configured to ensure that Web applications still work. However, for compatibility reasons, the goal is to ensure that what was installed on previous versions is also installed and available. This makes for a happy cleanup for these upgrades, so enjoy it as you reduce your environment and management tasks.

Centralizing Your Log File to Reduce Clutter

Centralizing your log file isn't required, nor is it always the recommended approach for all environments. However, centralized logging (better known as server-wide logging) reduces disk clutter and simplifies access to log data. It also enhances performance by reducing the number of log file handles open on large servers. Obviously, on servers that host only one or two Web sites, centralized logging is potential overkill.

Centralized logging comes in two flavors—Centralized binary logging and Centralized W3C logging—and each has their upside. For 95 percent of the cases, Centralized W3C logging is the most effective and simplest approach.

Start off by ensuring you enable some extended properties so you can locate data for each individual site. This property, s-sitename, will log the site name the request is associated with, such as Default Web Site. For example, Default Web Site is logged as W3SVC1, indicating this request belongs to this site. It makes it easy to then extract it from the log files requests for the individual site.

BEST PRACTICES ACCORDING TO MICROSOFT

For more information on Centralized logging, Microsoft has a Webcast aimed at understanding each type, as well as discussions about how each works, their advantages and disadvantages, and lastly how to set them up on IIS 6.0. This Webcast will apply to IIS 7.0 for the most part, minus how to enable it. These log types were only enabled in the metabase in IIS 6.0 and had no IIS Manager–supported method. In IIS 7.0 on Windows Server 2008, logging changes are made in the IIS Manager, as well as directly in the configuration.

SOME INDEPENDENT ADVICE

In Windows Vista, there are no logging capabilities in the IIS Manager. The only way to change the logging type was directly through configuration or via one of the other administration tools discussed in Chapter 16. This was supplemented with community support on Microsoft's IIS.NET DownloadCENTER located at www.iis.net/downloads/default.aspx?tabid=34&g=6&i=1328 with a logging module.

Windows Server 2008 has full user interface support for logging.

To enable centralized W3C logging, do the following:

1. Open an elevated command-prompt.

2. Change to the **%windir%\system32\inetsrv** directory.

3. Using **Appcmd.exe**, issue the following command:

```
C:\Windows\System32\inetsrv>appcmd set config -section:log /
CentralLogFileMode:CentralW3C
```

After setting this value, you will must restart HTTP to have it change the logging type since HTTP.sys does all of the IIS logging. To do this, issue the following command:

```
Net stop http /y & net start w3svc
```

To view your consolidated log file, navigate to the %systemdrive%\inetpub\logs\w3svc directory.

Getting a Backup of Your Configuration

The last step is to ensure that you get a working, accurate backup of your primary configuration file. If you have enabled delegation allowing Web.config files to store IIS configuration then this is not a holistic backup, instead just the server configuration. It is, nonetheless, the most important aspect of IIS 7.0 so having a good backup is essential in case of a disaster or mistakes.

There are two methods to obtaining a backup of which you choose what you feel is most appropriate and comfortable for you. The first is to make a copy of the file and save it in another directory, such as appHostBackup directory. The second approach is to use appcmd.exe like we showed in Chapter 16.

To use AppCmd.exe, issue the following command:

```
Appcmd add backup MyFirstBackupInIIS7
```

In either case, it's paramount that you have a backup of applicationhost.config. As an administrator, you're doubtless aware that backups can rescue you from some very sticky situations.

The Developer's Call to Arms

IIS7 represents the most exciting developer opportunity since ASP.NET 1.0 was released five years ago. Never has Microsoft had an application platform so flexible. Plus, integrating the .NET Framework as a first-class citizen in the request pipeline opens the door to potentially fascinating new capabilities. Microsoft continues with the inclusion of FastCGI in IIS 7.0 to better support other languages such as PHP or Ruby on Rails delivered on top of this amazing platform.

If you are interested in understanding the multitude of ways to build custom functionality in IIS 7.0, start by understanding how to satisfy the business needs of the world. If they need caching servers, reverse proxies, or highly scalable front-end authentication servers, then IIS 7.0 is the Web platform to start with.

Downloading the Native C\C++ Starter Kit

If your responsibilities today include building ISAPI filters, you should start learning about the new, improved powers of the Native API for C\C++ developers. You can download this starter kit on www.iis.net (www.iis.net/downloads/default.aspx?tabid=34&g=6&i=1301) and learn how to get started building your first IIS 7.0 native module.

Downloading the Managed Code Starter Kit

With IIS 7.0's strong support for ASP.NET 2.0's managed interfaces, you can begin developing tomorrow's applications today. You can start converting your existing modules to IIS 7.0, or if new to the API, learn more by starting with the IIS 7.0 Managed Code starter kit at www.iis.net/ downloads/default.aspx?tabid=34&i=1302&g=6.

Building IIS Manager Extensions for Your Modules

You should no longer spend cycles building software for IIS that adds functionality but at the same time spend hundreds of design hours building user interfaces for that software. Instead, give the power to your customers by adding IIS Manager modules to your software package so your customers can configure your software using the same familiar tool they use for IIS 7.0: the IIS Manager.

SOME INDEPENDENT ADVICE

Microsoft has gone to great lengths to help developers get started building IIS Manager modules. Using managed code, you can quickly add functionality directly to the IIS Manager. To get started, use Microsoft's IIS.NET site at www.iis.net/devcenter.

Adding Tracing to Your Modules

In the software realm, a perfect world centers around shipping fascinating software to millions of users. In the not-so-perfect world, your software will have bugs and you have to support those millions of users, which gets very expensive. In this book, you are learning how powerful the diagnostics stack is in IIS 7.0, and as a developer you need to use it. You should add eventing to your modules to allow error conditions to get caught right alongside IIS 7.0's. With this powerful functionality, you can cut your time to resolution by almost 50 percent, if not more.

Get started learning about tracing your modules by using Microsoft's IIS.NET Developer Center at www.iis.net/devcenter.

Summary

Microsoft has given you a great deal of power with IIS 7.0. You are now tasked with harnessing that power and building a secure, robust, scalable Web solution. In this section, we provided you with the questions to ask yourself and strategies to consider. Beyond that, you learned about some of the changes that could potentially impact your environment that are considered one-off changes in IIS 7.0.

IIS 7.0 is as unique as the mathematical function pi (π) and offers numerous options. It is the LEGO Web server with enterprise-class features built in and developer-ready APIs to help make your mission possible. All you have to do is build it. With the guidance given in this book, administrators can effectively deploy Web servers that reap the rewards of building a highly secure, customized, performance-driven Web server.

As for you developers out there, don't miss the incredible opportunity to build what was never possible using IIS.

Solutions Fast Track

Migrating to IIS 7.0

☑ Upgrading to Windows Vista or Windows Server 2008 is nearly as clean as a fresh install with the new Image-based setup.

☑ Understanding how IIS 5.0, or IIS 6.0, features will be migrated to IIS 7.0 is the first step toward allowing you to be successful in your fit-n-finish work.

Fitting and Finishing Work with IIS 7.0

☑ Remove unnecessary components to avoid patching unnecessary binaries loaded in your IIS 7.0 worker process.

☑ Enable Centralized logging to reduce log file clutter.

☑ Create a configuration backup to ensure you're safe in case of catastrophic failures.

The Developer's Call to Arms

☑ Stop using the difficult ISAPI extension APIs and start using the APIs Microsoft used to build their 40+ modules.

☑ Start using the productivity given by manage code and apply it to the powerful IIS 7.0 Web request pipeline.

☑ Microsoft built it, so now all you have to do is add your modules to the IIS Manager and administration for your features to sit right with IIS's features.

☑ Reduce your support costs, add beneficial tracing to your modules and pages, and save countless support hours.

Frequently Asked Questions

Q: Are FrontPage Extensions (FPSE) supported on IIS 7.0?

A: Yes, but they aren't available as part of the IIS 7.0 installation. FPSE can be downloaded separately, with more information available at www.iis.net/downloads/default. aspx?tabid=34&g=6&i=1460.

Q: What will happen if FPSE is installed on the server before it is upgraded to Windows Server 2008?

A: None of your FPSE settings will be migrated, and the W3SVC service will be disabled after the upgrade has been completed. This is because Microsoft assumes that, since FPSE was required and in use, the server was insecure.

Q: Will I be able to upgrade from Windows 2000 Server to Windows Server 2008?

A: No, unfortunately not. If you're on anything other than Windows Server 2003, you will need to build a new IIS 7.0 box and manually migrate your sites.

Q: Will any IIS services be disabled after the upgrade?

A: Possibly, if the upgrade process detected settings that could make your server insecure. For example, if FPSE was installed on the server, the W3SVC service will be explicitly disabled.

Chapter 19

Introduction to SQL Server Security

Solutions in this chapter:

- Security: Why Worry About It?
- Installing SQL Server
- Building Security into Your Application
- Managed Code

☑ Summary

☑ Solutions Fast Track

☑ Frequently Asked Questions

Introduction

This chapter explains why you should be concerned with SQL Server security and introduces some of the more generic ideas, such as the principle of least access. It also covers the concept of planning for security in the design phase, building security into your application from the ground up, as opposed to "bolting it on" afterward, and installing and configuring SQL Server features. We also discuss the security risks associated with managed code in SQL server. CLR integration is the feature that allows managed code to be run in SQL server.

Multifaceted SQL Server Security

Security in SQL Server 2005 is multifaceted, and it can seem impossibly complicated. SQL Server 2005 security starts at the ground level and builds upon itself. This chapter discusses producing the foundations required to begin thinking in a natively secure manner, upon which the rest of the security principle in this book can be built. This chapter also starts you on the learning curve required to implement SQL Server 2005 security by providing a guide in your journey into SQL Server 2005 security.

Security: Why Worry About It?

In February 2000, the company RealNames informed its customers that its database had been broken into and that information including credit card numbers had been taken. The thought of being the person in charge of security on that database is enough to make anyone break into a cold sweat. How exactly do you go to your boss and tell him that the database that fuels your company and holds your customer's information has been broken into?

Then there were the W32.CBlade and W32.Digispid worms. These worms attacked SQL Servers using the SA account and a blank password. The fact that either of these two worms could get into systems spoke volumes about the security of the databases they were attacking. The one positive aspect was that when the SQL Slammer worm hit in 2003, IT security professionals had some knowledge of how databases are attacked by worms. Even more fortunate was that even though the Slammer worm was one of the most aggressive worms to date, it was dedicated to creating a denial-of-service (DoS) type attack where the goal was to flood the Internet with traffic, versus a database breach.

In 2001, the World Economic Forum had a database breach. Some of the information from this breach ended up on a Swiss newspaper's Web site. The data, including Bill Gate's e-mail address, PepsiCo Beverages CEO Peter Thompson's credit card number, and Jeff Bezos's home phone number were taken. Additionally, some 800,000 pages of data from people like Bill Clinton, Vladimir Putin, and Yassir Arafat were accessed using the passwords acquired when the database was breached.

Other companies whose databases were breached were PetCo.com and Guess, both of which fell victim to SQL Injection attacks on their Web sites. The attack on Guess netted the attackers an unknown quantity of credit card numbers. PetCo.com's Web site was later detected to have the same vulnerability. This vulnerability was detected by someone randomly checking sites for this issue, and would have provided about 500,000 credit card numbers to anyone less honest who discovered this vulnerability.

Information is money. Other than credit card numbers, there are people willing to pay for phone numbers, e-mail addresses, physical addresses, client information, social security information, and just about every other form of client or personal information available. With this as a driving force, people looking to make money, see databases as a bank vault full of money. Just as banks build their buildings with plans on how to secure their vault, you need to protect your information in your databases the same way.

Now that the Sarbanes Oxley (SOX), Gramm-Leach-Biley Act (GLBA), Health Insurance Portability and Privacy Act (HIPAA), Basel II, Code of Federal Regulation (CFR) Part 11, and the Japan Privacy Law (J-SOX) regulations are becoming the model for governments, private companies, and public companies across the globe, more and more companies are being affected even if these regulations do not apply directly to them. These regulations do not state what needs to be done in crystal clear terms. They hold you liable for the security of your information, but leave it up to you on how to interpret what they are saying.

It seems that in all of the preceding cases, there were security precautions that could have been taken to prevent the breaches. In most cases, applying the best practices of securing a SQL Server would prevent breaches from ever happening. It is just a matter of knowing what to secure, which is where this book comes in.

The Principle of Least Access

The principle of least access is a simple way to make databases more secure. Whenever you are presented with a choice of how to configure permissions, choose the method that provides the least access to the database. This goes for everything at every level. If you are asking yourself, "Do I need to install this feature?" the answer is either a definite yes or a definite no. If you are thinking maybe, possibly, "well, we might…", do not install it. If you think that this person might need access to a specific extended stored procedure, then they do get access. This also applies to the level of service accounts that run your SQL services. Start with the most secure setting, and only open it past that point of what you need it to do.

This is now a constant in the world of SQL Server 2005. By default, Microsoft has made things secure for when you start working in SQL Server 2005. But in order for it to work, it means resisting the urge to make sure everything works as it should by turning on everything and giving everyone owner permissions. Yes, it can be annoying when someone keeps coming back to your desk because they need more access to get their job done, but in order to offset this, keep in mind the person in charge of the RealNames database and how his day was when it was announced publicly that the database had been hacked.

Installing SQL Server

Let's start from the point of installing SQL Server 2005. From the time you put the disk into the machine, think security. At the beginning you will be asked what you want to install. There is the database engine itself, which is only installed when you are going to be immediately housing SQL Server 2005 databases on that server. Next there is the analysis services engine, which is the OLAP/data cubes portion of SQL Server 2005. This should only be installed if you are going to be immediately using OLAP cubes on the server. Additionally, there is Reporting Services, Integration Services, and Notification Services. Reporting Services is SQL Server 2005's Web-based reporting engine. Integration Services lets you design and deploy SSIS packages, the replacement for DTS. Notification Services provides the engine for keeping people notified. The same principle applies to these—install them only if you are going to use them immediately. Documents and samples is the last optional choice in installing SQL Server 2005, and is also the easiest to decide on whether to install or not. If you are installing on a development box, it is usually a good choice to choose to install both of these. For installation to any other server, never install the Documents and Samples. These are meant for learning, and although they have been reviewed to make sure that they follow Microsoft's best practices, they provide no benefits when installed to a production environment.

One note at this point has to do with the experience I had installing SQL Server. Many times I have installed SQL Server, adding in extra components because I was told that they would be needed next week, next month, or immediately. Although in every case the person who told me had the best of intentions, about 50 percent of the time they were never used. In the case where they have not been used, you end up having to make sure that they are configured correctly, are patched, and cause general overhead. During a security audit, they have been rightly referred to as a *security violation*. From this, a policy change has been made that states that no SQL Server 2005 components will be installed until they are required. Once they are no longer required, they are to be completely removed. Keep this in mind as you install components, and try to install them only when you know they will be used.

BEST PRACTICES ACCORDING TO MICROSOFT

- **Install only those components that you will use immediately.** Microsoft recommends that you create a list of components that you will be using, and only enable those. If the need arises, you can install the additional components at that time. The components in a SQL Server installation are the Database Engine, Analysis Services Engine, Reporting Services, Integration Services, Notification Services, and Documents and Samples.

- **Enable only the optional features you will use, and review optional feature usage before doing an in-place upgrade and disable unneeded features.** Microsoft recommends that you create a list of the optional features that you will use, and only turn those on. If this is an existing SQL Server that is being upgraded, they recommend creating the same list, and disabling any optional features not on the list. These optional features are CLR Integration, OLE Automation, remote use of a dedicated administrator connection, Database Mail and SQL Mail, OpenRowset and OpenDataSource functions, SQL Server Web Assistant, and xp_cmdshell availability.

- **Develop a policy with respect to permitted network connectivity choices and for the usage of optional features.** Microsoft recommends defining policies that would be company wide on Connectivity Choices and the use of optional features. They also recommend using SQL Server Surface Area Configuration to standardize this policy and documenting exceptions to the policy on a per-instance basis.

- **Turn off unneeded services by setting the service to either Manual startup or Disabled.** Microsoft recommends going into the service management area and setting all services that you will not be using to be disabled or manual. These services include SQL Server Active Directory Helper, SQL Server Agent, SQL Server FullText Search, SQL Server Browser, and SQL Server VSS Writer.

■ **Choose the service account with the last privilege possible.**   Microsoft recommends that the account you choose to run each of the SQL Services as should have the least possible level of privilege. You could use a domain user, local user, network service account, local system account, a local user that is an administrator, or a domain user who is a domain admin.

■ **Use a separate specific user account or domain account that has no special privileges for SQL Server Services.**   Microsoft recommends using a separate account for each SQL Service. This account should be a specific user or domain account rather than a shared account. It is also recommended that this account not be granted any special privileges, but if special privileges are required, manage those through the SQL Server-supplied group account.

■ **Always use Windows Authentication Mode if possible.**   Microsoft recommends using the Windows Authentication versus the Mixed Mode authentication. They recommend the mixed mode Authentication only for legacy application and non-Windows users.

■ **Do not expose a server that is running SQL Server to the public Internet.**   Microsoft recommends that any servers that are running SQL Server not be exposed to the Internet.

Some Independent Advice

Microsoft's best practices for SQL Server can often seem like a tangled web of rules that would be incredibly expensive and time consuming to follow. I have found that the best way to handle this is to create your own checklist for your company.

Mine started out as very basic, where the only thing being installed was the Database Engine, and all optional features were turned off. As time went by, my checklist has grown, but it is still fairly basic, because I follow one piece of logic: Nothing gets turned on unless there is a reason for it. If I have a good reason to use a feature, like it saves money and time or offers features that add value, then I'll take the time to look up what needs to be done to deploy that securely and add it to my checklist. In this manner, I am not attempting to secure everything at once, and my checklist is up-to-date at all times.

If migrating an existing system to SQL Server 2005 from a previous version for the first time, I tend to part ways with Microsoft. I have never successfully been able to create a list of used features for a previous SQL Server instance, without spending huge amounts of time reviewing each line of code in the database and every application that attaches to it to see what is being used. What I recommend is to again create a checklist like I did above, turn on only the very basic features, and create a checklist of what you are doing. Then TEST, TEST, TEST! If your older version of SQL had other things turned on or installed that you do not want, you can review whether it is an appropriate use as an additional step, or you can enable and secure them, documenting it in your checklist. When you are done, you will have the beginning of a policy, and your new server configured as you need it.

Features off by Default

In SQL Server 2005, optional features are turned off by default. These features include CLR Integration, OLE Automation system procedures, system procedures for Database Mail and SQL Mail, Ad Hoc Remote Queries, SQL Server Web Assistant, xp_cmdshell availability, and remote use of a dedicated administrator connection (see Figure 19.1).

Figure 19.1 The Surface Area Configuration for Features Screen

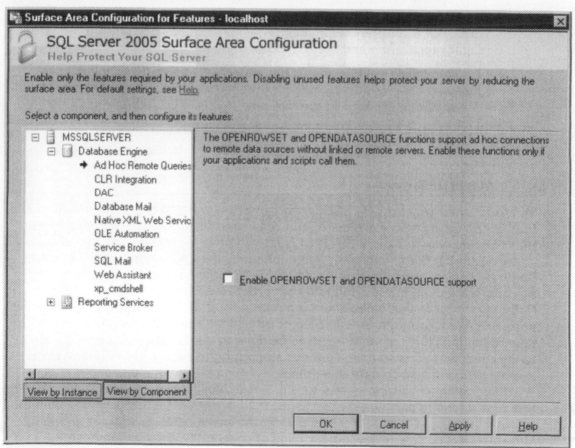

In order to enable these, you will need to use either the Surface Area Configuration for Features or the SQL Service Area Configuration command-line interface. However, before enabling any of these features, consider if using these features is the best way of achieving your goals. While each of these tools can be extremely useful, it comes at a cost of reduced security. For example, opening Database Mail or SQL Mail means you must configure not only SQL Server 2005 correctly, but also your e-mail server in order to remain secure. Otherwise, you could become responsible for a part of the SPAM e-mail flood that occurs on a daily basis. It also exposes both your SQL Server and e-mail server to possible attack.

Services off by Default

In SQL Server 2005, during installation, most services are turned off by default. You are provided with the option of turning each one on at installation. After installation, you can also choose to turn services on SQL Server on or off individually. The SQL Server 2005 services that can be turned off are the Database Engine, Analysis Services, Reporting Services, SQL Server Agent, FullText Search, Integration Services, and SQL Browser. It is highly recommended to turn off all of the services that you can. After installation, you can turn them off by going to the Surface Area Configuration Manager for Services and Connections (see Figure 19.2), while during the installation process, leaving the services you do not need unchecked will prevent them from being installed.

The best way to determine if you need to have each of these services running is to determine what each service does. If you do not use these features at the present time, it is safe to disable that service.

The database engine itself is the engine that stores SQL Server database files. In most installations this service is being used; however, if you were only using SQL Analysis Services on a server, it would then be safe to disable the Database Engine.

Analysis Services is the OLAP and data mining service used in cubes that make up the base for Business Intelligence applications. If you are not using OLAP cubes or data mining, you can safely disable these services.

Reporting Services is the Web-based application for creating and viewing reports. When using Reporting Services, it uses a SQL Server 2005 database to store its configuration, which requires that the Database Engine be enabled. If you are not utilizing Reporting Services 2005, it is best to disable this service.

The SQL Server agent is used to run jobs inside SQL Server. Two types of jobs are *maintenance jobs* and *custom jobs*. Maintenance jobs do things like back up your database at a particular time each day, whereas custom jobs can execute anything from T-SQL statements to things like SSIS packages. If you do not have reoccurring processes that you have scheduled through the SQL Agent, it is safe to disable this service.

The FullText Search service is disabled by default in most installations. The FullText Search is used when you need to go beyond the normal equal or like comparisons to things like finding two words near one another or some sort of fuzzy matching. If you currently do not use these features, FullText Search should be disabled.

Integration Services is the SQL Server 2005 upgrade to Data Transformation Services. It is a platform that allows ETL processes and other more complex processes to be stored as a process and scheduled in SQL Agent or executed manually. If you do not do any ETL processes, you most likely can disable this service.

For SQL Browser, this is required only when you are attempting to connect to named SQL Server instances that use dynamic port assignments. Named instances tend to be used only when you have more than one instance of SQL Server running on a server, or with things like clustering. If you are in charge of installing SQL Server and you have installed only one instance on each server, or if you have installed multiple instances but specified the Transmission Control Protocol/Internet Protocol (TCP/IP) port assignment, it is recommended that you disable the Browser Service.

As an additional note, if you are installing a named instance of SQL Server, it is definitely more secure to use a static TCP/IP port, as this will allow you to use the browser service. Earlier in the chapter, the SQL Slammer Worm was mentioned. The mechanism that was exploited was the SQL Server 2000 browser engine. Although the browser service has been updated for SQL Server 2005, this shows you how an apparently rather safe choice can be used in a malicious way to compromise security on your server.

Figure 19.2 The Surface Area Configuration Manager for Services and Connections Screen

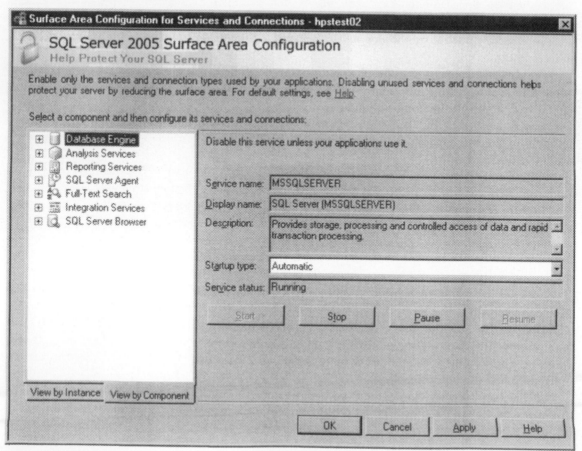

Additional services can also be turned off using the Service Manager in Windows (see Figure 19.3). These services are the Active Directory Helper and the VSS Writer.

Figure 19.3 The Windows Service Manager Screen

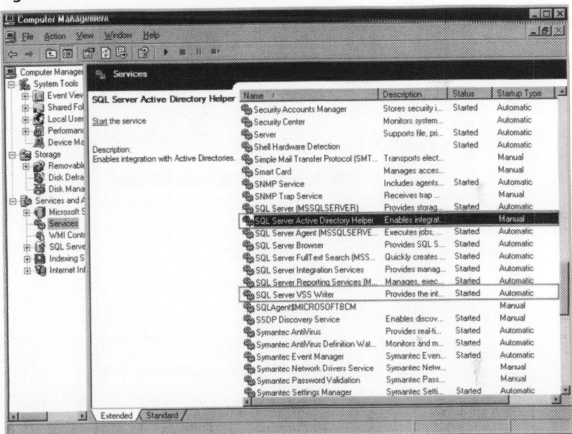

The VSS Writer provides integration into Visual Source safe and was introduced in SQL 2005. It is highly recommended to use the VSS Writer for source control integration; however, if you are not using this, you can safely shut down the service inside the Service Manager and set its startup type to Manual (see Figure 19.4).

Figure 19.4 The Windows Service Manager Service Property Screen

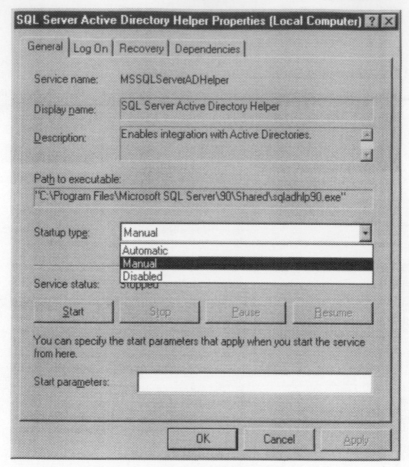

Another service that can be disabled in some companies is the Active Directory Helper. If your company does not use Active Directory, you can safely disable this service.

Once you have discovered what services can be disabled on your SQL Server 2005 instance, it is best to write it down and use it as the basis for the documentation for your SQL Server security protocols.

Microsoft's Baseline Security Analyzer

One you feel you have tightened up your SQL Server 2005 security at the application level, the next step is to rung Microsoft's free tool for checking your security setting, called Baseline Security Analyzer. Version 2.1 supports SQL Server 2005 installations. This tool will check for missing security updates, improperly set folder permissions, password policy, public access permissions, and other security issues for SQL Server 2005. It provides and icon-based scan result with icons representing whether the system passed the test, or if it failed, how critical of a failure it is. This tool is truly revealing in how well your server as a whole is set up while additionally scanning SQL Server 2005. It is also recommended that you run this tool every month to check for any new vulnerabilities.

When using Microsoft's Baseline Security Analyzer it is best to take a three-phased approach. The first phase is performing the scan. Here you select the computer or computers you want to scan. Next is analyzing the scan. The results set, as shown in Figure 19.5, is fairly intuitive, and provides you with links for results details and, if applicable, details on what was scanned. If the item failed the scan, there will also be a link for how to correct this. Following this link will provide you with details that you can use to correct the vulnerabilities. In the last phase, correcting the vulnerabilities, you will use the information provided by the link to decide how to correct the failure. However, please note that not all failures can, or should, be corrected. For instance, if you choose mixed authentication mode for SQL Server 2005, it will be listed as a scan failure. If you have mixed mode turned on, it is likely because legacy applications still access your database using SQL Server 2005 users rather than Windows Authentication. In this case, if you were to follow the recommendation, you would break the legacy application. So, consider the implications to all recommendations.

Figure 19.5 Microsoft's Baseline Security Analyzer

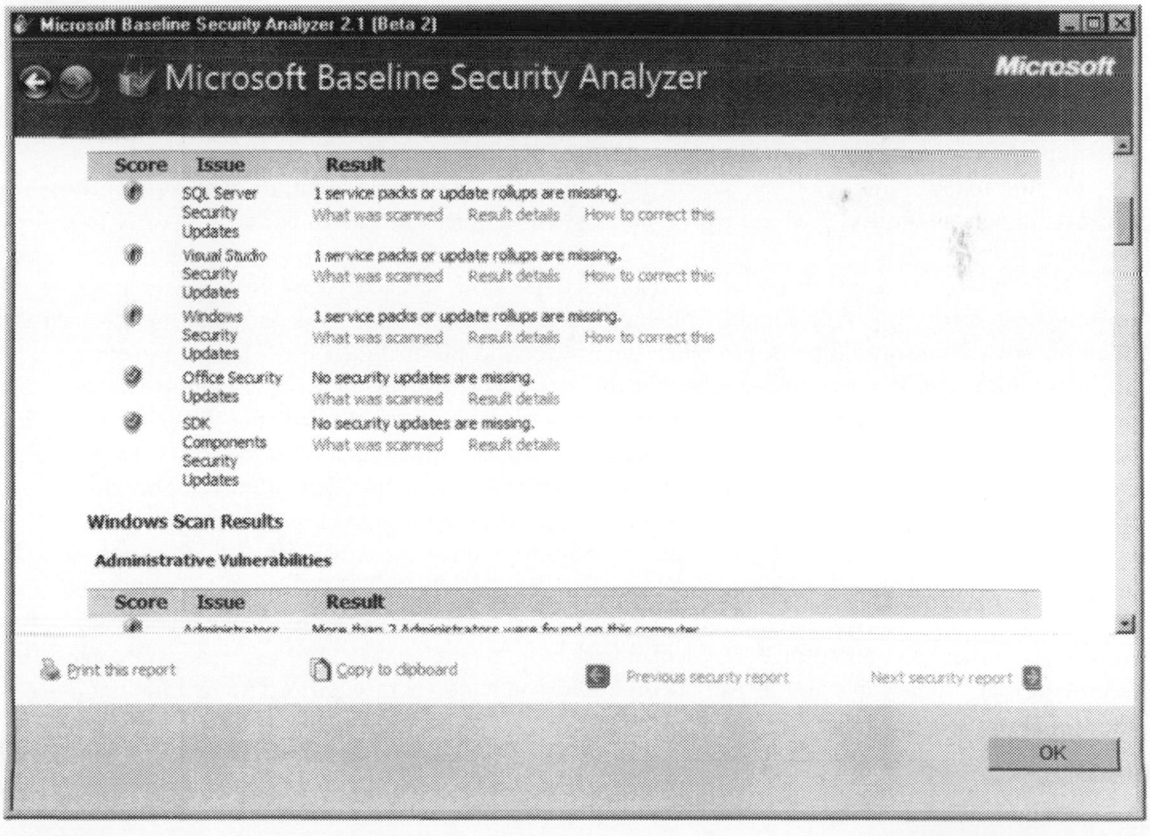

Building Security into Your Application

For the past couple of years, there has been a concerted effort by many companies to secure their databases. Many of these are taking years, are huge budget consumers, and could be destined for failure. The reasons for failure can be far ranging, from access from legacy systems that are too costly to modify to obey the new security standards to internal resistance from the crowd that always says, "but we've always done it this way." At some point, you need to step from the reactive to the proactive state in security design. Until you do, you will always be vulnerable to security breaches. There is always a chance that your applications that have never had security applied could be compromised, and each day that they run, increases the odds that this will happen. If in addition to those applications, you do not secure the new databases that are being created, every day the odds increase that you will need to have the dreaded "How could this happen?" discussion with your bosses.

How can you increase the odds that you never have to have that discussion with your boss? The answer is by designing security in from the very beginning. This means from day one, everything you do must be done with security in mind. The first steps of turning security from reactive to proactive is creating a Security Policy and a new SQL Server instance. The first version of the security policy was very limited in its scope, but due to the default secure stance that was taken, it was also very secure. All optional features were turned off, all unused services were set to disabled, and mixed security mode was disabled leaving the only connection method to be Windows Authentication. Next was the configuration of the model database on the server, changing the owner, the file locations and adding DDL triggers. Then Windows groups were set up and granted roles in SQL Server. Finally, the server was released for people to begin using.

For the next few weeks, a lot of time was spent answering everyone's questions. Many developers wanted to know "Why isn't this installed?," "How come we cannot use a SQL User?", and many other questions. Slowly things changed, and people began to consider security in their design, as the end goal was explained to them. People now had to consider security in their design.

Afterwards, it became obvious that a slight change in this initiative would have made it less troublesome, as the way it was implemented caused a lot of additional work for everyone involved. The biggest change would be not so much what was done, but bringing more people into the initiative. Although this was a team effort for the group in charge of the databases and database server, the developer team and the architects were not brought in to the initiative. The change would be to implement this more as a companywide team effort, as the biggest obstacles to the success of changing security from being reactive to being proactive is the people who are developing the applications that depend on the very databases you are attempting to secure.

The concept of designing security into databases and applications is becoming more and more mandatory as it reduces the likelihood of your database being breached. Microsoft has published a paper called "The Trustworthy Computing Security Development Lifecycle." The core concept of this paper is that in order to meet the demand for more secure applications, you need to implement a process that is repeatable and delivers a consistently higher level of security. This requires engineer education and accountability.

Managed Code

Managed code, often referred to as CLR, is a new feature in SQL Server 2005. This feature provides you with many benefits, including the ability to use anything as a data source, to creating your own built-in functions to do common operations like splitting strings on delimiters. There has been much back and forth on whether it is risky to enable CLR. In the end, it appears that the security risk is not so much in enabling CLR, but in having people not follow protocols when developing CLR components, called *assemblies*.

The first level of security in the CLR is whether it can be executed, which is turned off by default. You can use the SQL Server Surface Area Configuration Tool to allow CLR to be executed. If you decide to enable CLR, you will need to familiarize yourself with the security levels inside CLR itself.

The security layer inside CLR is very similar to T-SQL permissions on database objects. There is create assembly, execute, references, and select. Be judicious in granting the create assembly permission, as the person who has this permission can create CLR objects on your server.

The security inside the assembly is set by the person who is creating the assembly, and is aimed at protecting the database and assemblies. The levels are *safe*, *external_access*, and *unsafe*. Safe is the default security setting, and is highly restrictive. Safe limits your access to only local databases to perform data computations. external_access lets you access things outside of SQL Server, such as the file system, Windows event viewer, and Web services. The unsafe setting assumes full trust of the assembly and does not apply any access controls on it. There may be a situation where unsafe is required, but up to this point, I have yet to see one. In my protocol documentation, the developer of the CLR assembly has the choice of setting it to either safe or external_access, with safe being the preferred level, and external_access being used only when it is absolutely needed. CLR assemblies provide a good example of the teamwork required to institute security protocols on a SQL Server 2005 machine. Most CLR components are not going to be developed by database administrators, as the CLR components are written in your choice of .Net languages, not T-SQL. If your protocols are not established, it would be very easy to end up with an assembly set to unsafe that does nothing but data manipulation inside a local database. With established protocols set up that institute the concept of least access, this same component would be released with a setting of safe, and would again reduce the available surface area that can be used to attempt to breach your security.

Summary

At this point, you are beginning to understand the basics of security in SQL Server 2005. More details will be provided in the following chapters, letting you delve deeper into each section of security. What was not listed in this chapter is how the subjects we were talking about fit together in the bigger picture. Knowing how these relate will help you understand how these things work together to produce a more secure SQL Server 2005 installation.

It becomes more secure when the principle of least access is laid over the SQL Server 2005 features that are turned off. This prevents anybody but authorized people from going in and turning on features that you have deemed either unnecessary or dangerous. The same goes for SQL Server Services and the principle of least access, as you cannot use Analysis Services if it is not installed and you do not have permission to install this feature. The principle of least access and services and features that are turned off are all in turn used when designing an application residing on that server, resulting in an application that has security designed in from the beginning, and is more secure as a result.

Over time and with experience, these layers combine together to form the basis of a secure database framework without people even being conscious that they are, in fact, designing securely.

Solutions Fast Track

Security: Why Worry About It?

☑ User permissions should always be the least permission that users need to do their job.

☑ Services should run under accounts with the least possible permissions.

☑ Features and services installed should be limited to what needs to be used.

Installing SQL Server

☑ Install only the features and services that will be used immediately.

☑ Chose the services to run as account.

☑ Use Windows authentication mode whenever possible.

☑ Turn off all the following features if they are not being used, using the Surface Area Configuration for Features:

  ☑ CLR Integration

  ☑ OLE Automation system procedures

  ☑ Database Mail and SQL Mail

  ☑ Ad Hoc Remote Queries

  ☑ SQL Server Web Assistant

  ☑ xp_cmdshell availability

  ☑ Remote use of a dedicated administrator connection

☑ Turn off all the following services if they are not being used, using the Surface Area Configuration for Services and Connections:

☑ Database Engine

☑ Analysis Services

☑ Reporting Services

☑ SQL Server Agent

☑ FullText Search

☑ Integration Services

☑ SQL Browser

Building Security into Your Application

☑ Design databases with security in mind from the ground up.

☑ Implement a process that is repeatable and delivers a consistently higher level of security.

☑ Use Windows authentication mode whenever possible.

Managed Code

☑ Only use CLR components whenever it is the most efficient method.

☑ Design CLR with security in mind.

☑ Follow security protocols when developing CLR components.

Frequently Asked Questions

Q: What are the various methods of authentication inside SQL Server, and which is recommended?

A: There are two modes of authentication in SQL Server, *mixed mode* and *Windows only*. In mixed mode, both SQL level users and Windows level users are allowed. This mode of authentication is only recommended if it is absolutely required. Windows only allows users to authenticate into SQL Server.

Q: Why is it recommended not to use mixed-mode authentication?

A: Mixed-mode authentication means that SQL level users have to have their passwords maintained in SQL Server. Now consider the event of an employee leaving your company. If their Windows account is disabled, they can no longer access anything using that account. If they had the SA password, now not only do you have to disable the Windows user, but you also have to change the SA password on that SQL Server 2005 instance. This provides another level of possible breakdown in communications, where a former employee could gain access to data they should no longer have access to. There are additional reasons, but it is best to keep things in one location, especially information like passwords.

Q: Aren't Service Packs just updates to features? Why should we be concerned with them when it comes to security?

A: Service Packs often update both features and security concerns. It is necessary for keeping SQL Server 2005 up-to-date feature wise and security wise, to make sure you are up to date on both security patches and Service Packs.

Q: Is CLR bad for SQL Server 2005 security?

A: The answer to this is no, as long as the people writing the SQL Server 2005 CLR Code follow some basic security precautions. Treat CLR components like you would treat executables in Windows. If someone sent one through e-mail or you run across one on a site that you do not fully trust, that executable should never be run. If a trusted person or company provided the executable, then the executable could be run.

Q: Can the Surface Area Configuration tool be run from the command line?

A: There is a command-line interface for the Surface Area Configuration tool. It is called *sac* and is located in the *\90\shared* folder in the directory where you installed SQL Server. In a default installation, the path would be *C:\Program Files\Microsoft SQL Sever\90\shared\sace.exe*.

Q: Can you import settings from one SQL Server 2005 instance to another SQL Server 2005 instance?

A: Yes you can. You must use the *sac* command-line tool listed in the previous FAQ answer.

Q: Why is it necessary to run Microsoft Baseline Security Analyzer once a month?

A: Microsoft releases security patches and service packs for Microsoft SQL Server 2005 plus Windows and just about every other product. Running the Baseline Security Analyzer once a month keeps you informed of any patches or service packs you missed, and lets you know if any new vulnerabilities have been exposed on your server since the previous run.

Chapter 20

Surface Area Reduction

Solutions in this chapter:

- SQL Server Surface Area

☑ Summary

☑ Solutions Fast Track

☑ Frequently Asked Questions

Introduction

This chapter will help you gain a thorough understanding of what "surface area" is and why it's important when securing your server. After completing this chapter, you'll understand what the Surface Area Configuration tool is, and how to use the tool to help secure an SQL Server. You'll also learn why it's best to use the Surface Area Configuration tool as part of your SQL Server setup.

SQL Server Surface Area Configuration tool can also be used as an auditing tool to gauge the surface attack area on an existing SQL Server configuration.

Ideally, SQL Server surface area configuration tool should be run after installing or upgrading to SQL Server 2005. Take the time to verify which types of connections should be allowed, and which features should be enabled.

In addition to securing SQL Server, also secure the underlying operating system. The Microsoft Baseline Security Analyzer (MBSA) tool can help ensure the operating system is secure. Maintaining the operating system and installing service packs and patches will go a long way in helping to keep the data secure.

I'd also like to mention the fact there is also a Microsoft best practices analysis tool. Although this tool isn't focused strictly on security, it does have an impact on the overall security of the SQL Server's installation. I would highly recommend using the tool to ensure you are following the best practices recommended by Microsoft. There are a number of security related settings and features the Best Practices analyzer will check, including encryption settings, keys, system databases, authentication settings, and service accounts. Running the analyzer should be part of your regularly scheduled database administrator's activities.

SQL Server Surface Area

SQL Server is a feature-rich product, with many options when it comes to processing data. It is great having all these options available, but it can also mean vulnerability. Resist the urge to enable a service "just in case" you'll need it further down the road. Enable only services that are going to be used immediately, because each service and feature that is enabled increases the surface area available for an intruder to attack.

What Is Surface Area?

Surface area is defined as the parts of an application or server exposed to attack—some examples would be interfaces or enabled services. It can also be defined as everything that can be seen from the network on the SQL Server.

To help minimize the surface area exposed to attack, SQL Server 2005 now ships with many of its services and features disabled. As a rule of thumb, all services not being used should be disabled to reduce the server's vulnerability. This is not only true with SQL Server, but also with the operating system. Services that are not being used (Internet information Service, for example) should be disabled to minimize the risk of someone taking advantage and gaining control of the server.

Many of the features in SQL Server 2005 are disabled by default. This is part of Microsoft's new "trustworthy computing initiative." The idea is the installation is secure by default. It is still recommended to check a new installation and make sure all the services and features not being used are disabled.

It's much better to evaluate the security risk on the SQL Server installation than to respond to a security breach on the SQL Server. A security breach can result in the destruction of data, lost revenue, and information becoming public that shouldn't. If you security is compromised, and sensitive information is accessed by intruders, this could do irreparable harm to your business.

The Surface Area Configuration Tool

In the following section, we will discuss in detail each of the features of the Surface Area Configuration tool. Familiarize yourself with the features and options; they may come in handy when your boss or client asks you to perform a specific configuration task.

The Surface Area Configuration Tool GUI

SQL Server 2005 ships with a Surface Area Configuration tool. This tool allows the balance between enabled services and features to be controlled on the SQL Server installation. Administrative rights are needed in order to run the SQL Server Configuration tool.

The Surface Area Configuration tool can be used to start, stop, enable, and disable the various services and features associated with SQL Server. The SQL Configuration tool can be run against a local or remote machine.

In the following section, we'll walk through running the Surface Area Configuration tool step by step and examine some of the more common settings available within the tool.

To start things off, the tool needs to be run from the Start menu. To launch the SQL Server Surface Area Configuration tool on Windows "Longhorn" server, click **Start** then select all programs, then Microsoft SQL Server 2005, then Configuration Tools. Under Configuration Tools, the SQL Server Surface Area Configuration tool can be seen (see Figure 20.1).

It is not necessary to be logged into the machine being secured; it is possible to connect to an SQL Server remotely.

NOTE

On Microsoft Windows XP or Microsoft Windows 2003, the sequence for starting the tool may be slightly different; as the interfaces are slightly different in those operating systems. The SQL Server Surface Area Configuration tool is in the Configuration Tools subfolder of the SQL Server 2005 Start menu.

BEST PRACTICES ACCORDING TO MICROSOFT

The best practice is to reduce the surface area by enabling only services that are going to actually be used. For example, if xp_cmdshell is not used, disable it. That goes for services and applications within SQL Server, and the operating system as well. Enable only the protocols that will be used—this is another important (and usually forgotten) task. The idea is to reduce the attack surface for a hacker to compromise the system.

The SQL Server 2005 Surface Area Configuration tool is available on the Start menu under SQL Server 2005/configuration tools. See Figure 20.1 for more information.

Figure 20.1 The SQL Server 2005 Surface Area Configuration Tool

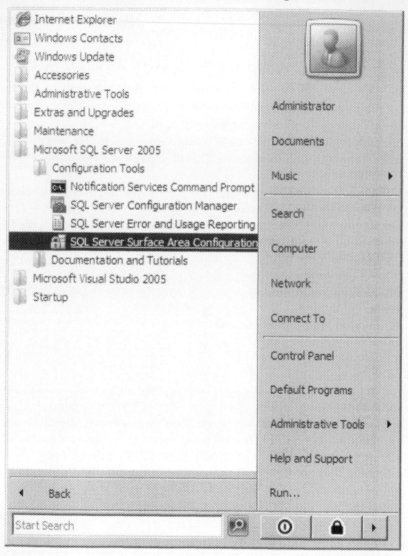

Selecting SQL Server Configuration tool will start the configuration process. Depending on the speed of the machine and system load, it may take a minute or two for the application to launch. Once the process is started, the screen shown in Figure 20.2 will be presented.

Figure 20.2 Launching the SQL Server Configuration Tool

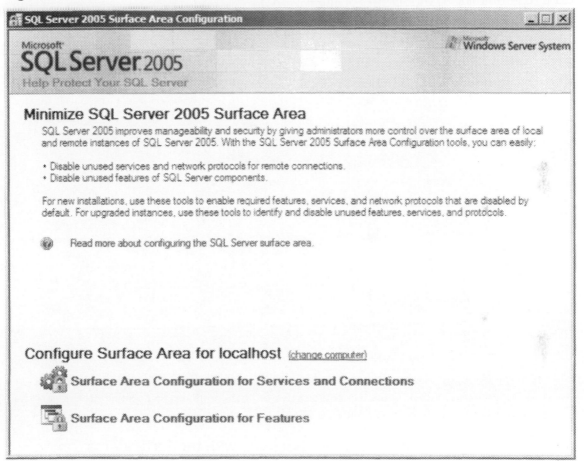

Once a selection is made, the Surface Area Configuration tool will load and display the settings (see Figure 20.3). The amount of time it takes to load the settings depends on the services installed on the system being managed, the speed of the connection, and server load.

Figure 20.3 Settings Displayed by the Surface Area Configuration Tool

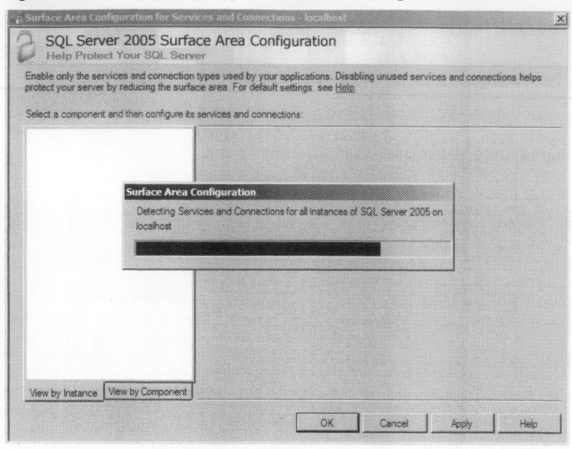

The Surface Area Configuration tool can be run on the host machine locally and be connected to a remote computer. When you select connect to a remote computer, you will be presented with a dialog similar to the one shown in Figure 20.4.

Figure 20.4 Connecting to a Remote Computer with the Surface Area Configuration Tool

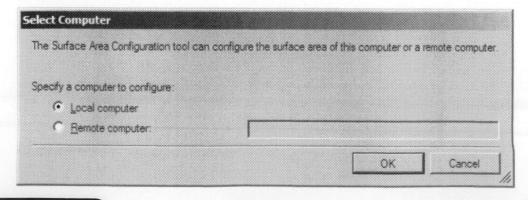

There are two main areas that can be configured using the Surface Area Configuration tool: Services and Connections and Features. Services and Connections controls more of the high-level features of SQL Server, whereas Features is much more granular. The following sections detail what may be controlled in each of the areas.

The Surface Area Configuration for Services and Connections

When selecting Surface Area Configuration for services and connections, a dialog similar to that shown in Figure 20.5 will be presented.

Figure 20.5 The Surface Area Configuration Tool's Services and Connections

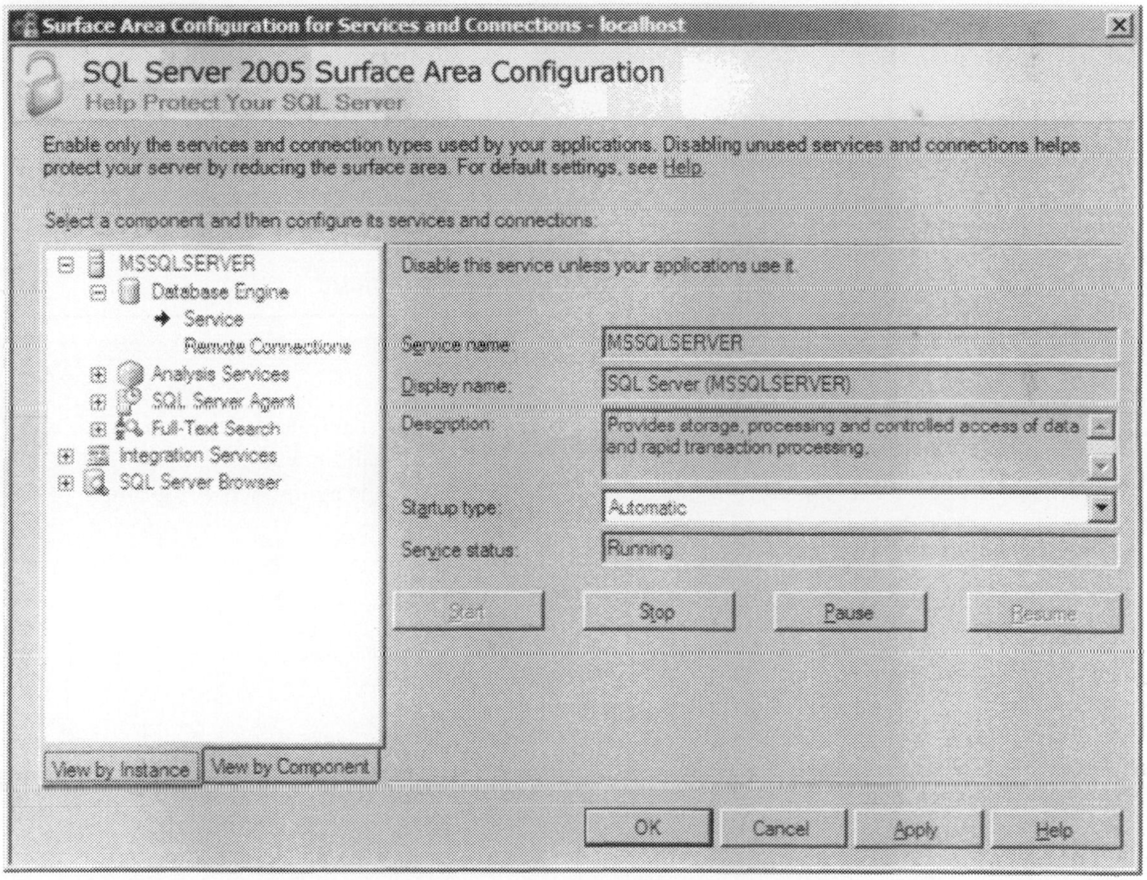

The Surface Area Configuration tool for services and connections includes such things as integration services, the SQL browser, as well as the SQL Server Agent Service. It provides a convenient place to manage most of the settings associated with surface area in one interface.

Table 20.1 shows the services associated with SQL Server, and the default startup configuration for each of the services. Make sure the overall impact is understood before disabling a service used by SQL Server, and be sure to test the changes on a nonproduction server first!

Table 20.1 Services Associated with SQL Server

Service	Default Startup
SQL Server	Automatic
Analysis Services	Automatic
SQL Server Agent	Manual
Integration Services	Automatic
Notification Services	Not Configured
Reporting Services	Automatic
SQL Browser	Disabled
SQL Server Active Directory Helper	Disabled
SQL Writer	Disabled
Full-Text Search	Automatic

In the case where there are multiple instances of SQL Server available, each of the instances will be displayed in the Surface Area Configuration tool. Each of the instances will have its own set of options associated with it, and each instance can have different options configured. An example of this is shown in Figure 20.6.

Figure 20.6 The Surface Area Configuration Tool's Options

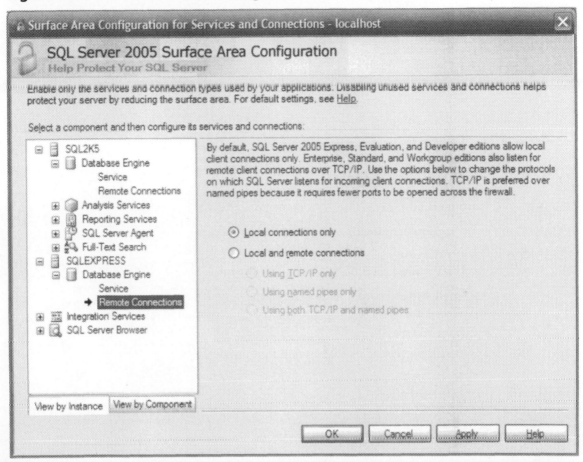

Shortcut...

Getting the Most Impact from Your Changes...

If a SQL Server instance is needed to be quickly secured, the services and protocols selection will allow the biggest impact on SQL Server security. It's usually best to start with the services and protocols tool when auditing or configuring a SQL Server instance.

For example, if Analysis Services is disabled, it won't matter how the Analysis Services features are configured.

The following section details the settings for each of the services available in the SQL Server Surface Area Configuration tool.

Database Engine Service

The Service name, Display name, and Service description are displayed on the screen for the service.

- **Startup type**.   Used to configure manual or automatic (or disabled) startup of the service.
- **Service status**.   Shows the current status of the service.

There are also buttons to stop, start, and pause the service.

Database Engine Remote Connections

- **Local connections only**.   Disables remote connections to the database.
- **Local and remote connections**.   Enables remote connections to the database.
- **Using TCP/IP protocol only**   (available only if local and remote connections are selected). Allows the connection protocol used for remote connections to be limited.
- **Using Named Pipes protocol only**   (available only if local and remote connections are selected). Allows the connection protocol used for remote connections to be limited.
- **Using both TCP/IP and Named Pipes protocols**   (available only if local and remote connections are selected). Allows the connection protocol used for remote connections to be limited.

Analysis Services Service

The Service name, Display name, and Service description are displayed on the screen for the service.

- **Startup type**.   Used to configure manual or automatic (or disabled) startup of the service.
- **Service status**.   Shows the current status of the service.

There is also a button to stop, start, and pause the service.

Analysis Services Remote Connections

- **Local connections only**.   Disables remote connections to the database.
- **Local and remote connections**.   Enables remote connections to the database.

Reporting Services Service

The Service name, Display name, and Service description are displayed on the screen for the service.

- **Startup type**.   Used to configure manual or automatic (or disabled) startup of the service.
- **Service status**.   Shows the current status of the service.

There are also buttons to stop, start, and pause the service.

SQL Server Agent Service

The Service name, Display name, and Service description are displayed on the screen for the service.

- **Startup type**.   Used to configure manual or automatic (or disabled) startup of the service.
- **Service status**.   Shows the current status of the service.

There are also buttons to stop, start, and pause the service.

Full-Text Search Service

The Service name, Display name, and Service description are displayed on the screen for the service.

- **Startup type**.   Used to configure manual or automatic (or disabled) startup of the service.
- **Service status**.   Shows the current status of the service.

There are also buttons to stop, start, and pause the service.

Notification Services Instance Services

The Service name, Display name, and Service description are displayed on the screen for the service.

- **Startup type**.   Used to configure manual or automatic (or disabled) startup of the service.
- **Service status**.   Shows the current status of the service.

There are also buttons to stop, start, and pause the service.

Integration Services Service

The Service name, Display name, and Service description are displayed on the screen for the service.

- **Startup type**.   Used to configure manual or automatic (or disabled) startup of the service.
- **Service status**.   Shows the current status of the service.

There are also buttons to stop, start, and pause the service.

SQL Server Browser Service

The Service name, Display name, and Service description are displayed on the screen for the service.

- **Startup type**.   Used to configure manual or automatic (or disabled) startup of the service.
- **Service status**.   Shows the current status of the service.

There are also buttons to stop, start, and pause the service.

SOME INDEPENDENT ADVICE

Make sure to document any changes made to the environment. If something goes wrong, it can aid in quickly diagnosing and fixing the problem.

It may be worthwhile keeping a "run book" for each of the servers with the configuration (and SQL Configuration) documented.

The Surface Area Configuration for Features

When selecting the surface area for features, a dialog similar to the one shown in Figure 20.7 will be presented.

Figure 20.7 The Surface Area Configuration Tool's Features

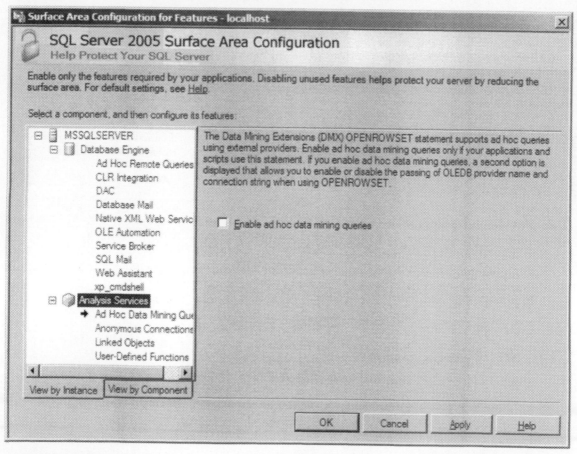

Within the Surface Area Configuration for features, as you click each of the features in the right tree view pane, the options will appear in the main window. Once the options are displayed, the configuration of the options may be completed.

Surface Area Configuration—Features

The following features can be configured using the Surface Area Configuration tool:

- Database Services
- Reporting Services
- Analysis Services

In the Database Services section, the following items can be configured:

- Ad hoc distributed queries
- Common language runtime (CLR) integration
- Database Mail
- Dedicated administrator connection (DAC)
- Native XML Web services
- OLE Automation stored procedures
- Service Broker
- SQL Mail
- Web Assistant stored procedures
- xp_cmdshell

In the Reporting Services section, the following items can be configured:

- Scheduled events and report delivery
- Web service requests and HTTP access
- Windows Integrated Security

In the Analysis Services section, the following items can be configured:

- Ad hoc data mining queries
- Anonymous connections
- Linked objects
- User-defined functions

In the left pane, each of the components and features can be selected and reviewed by clicking the feature to be examined.

The Surface Area Configuration Tool Command Line Utility

Along with the GUI version of the Surface Area Configuration tool, there is a command line version of the tool. The usefulness of this tool often is overlooked. The tool is invoked from the command prompt or can be called from a command batch file. This is ideal for automating installs and repeating the same configuration across many machines.

The command line version of the tool is installed by default in the "c:\program files\Microsoft SQL Server\90\shared" folder. Make sure that folder is in the path, or specify the full path to the file when executing it.

The syntax for the command line version of the tool is as follows:

```
sac {in | out} filename [-S computer_name] [-U SQL_login [-P SQL_ password]]
[-I instance_name ]
[-DE] [-AS] [-RS] [-IS] [-NS] [-AG] [-BS] [-FT] [-F] [-N] [-T] [-O] [-H | -?]
```

Table 20.2 explains the components of the syntax for the command line version.

Table 20.2 Syntax for the Command-Line Version of the Surface Area Configuration Tool

Syntax Component	Definition
in	Import the surface area settings from a file and configure the instance, specified by instance_name, using those settings.
out	Export the surface area configuration settings from an instance to the file specified by filename.
filename	The full path of the file used when importing or exporting the surface area settings.
-S computer_name	Specifies the name of a remote computer. If this argument is not specified, sac connects to the local computer.
-U SQL_login	Specifies the SQL Server Authentication login to use for the connection to the database engine. If not specified, sac uses Windows authentication to connect to the database engine.
-P SQL_password	Specifies the password for SQL_login. If this argument is not specified, sac prompts for a password. If -P is specified at the end of the command without a value, sac uses a null password.
-I instance_name	Specifies the SQL Server instance to run sac against. If this option is not specified, sac connects to all SQL Server instances. For the default instance, the instance name is MSSQLServer.
-DE	Import or export Database Engine settings.

Table 20.2 Continued

Syntax Component	Definition
-AS	Import or export Analysis Services settings.
-RS	Import or export Reporting Services settings.
-IS	Import or export Integration Services settings.
-NS	Import or export Notification Services settings.
-AG	Import or export SQL Server Agent settings.
-BS	Import or export the SQL Server Browser Service settings.
-FT	Import or export the Full-Text Search Service settings.
-F	Import or export the Features settings.
-N	Import or export the Network Protocols settings.
-T	Import or export the Windows Services settings.
-O	The output filename.
-H	Display the help text for the SAC command.

More details for the command line version of the of the Surface Area Configuration tool can be found in the SQL Server books online documentation.

Here is an example of using the command line utility to save the database engine settings on a computer:

```
Sac out c:\MySqlSettings.xml -DE
```

The preceding command will write out the settings to the file c:\MySqlSettings.xml for the data engine on the current SQL Server. Figure 20.8 shows the command being used to save the settings. The data actually is stored in a "standard XML format," which can be used by other third-party or custom written applications.

Once the information is saved to the file, copy it to another server and import the settings. The practical application of this would be if there are a lot of servers to customize, or a lot of servers from which to collect information.

The following example will export all the settings from the instance MSSQLSERVER:

```
sac out mysqlserver.xml -S mysqlserver1 -U sa -I MSSQLSERVER
```

The preceding example will export all the connection, feature, and service settings for the SQL Server MYSQLSERVER1 and store them in the file called mysqlserver.xml. In order to get the information, the tool will use the sa account. When the command is run, and no password is specified, it will prompt for the password of the sa account:

```
sac out mysqlserver.xml -S mysqlserver1 -U sa -I MSSQLSERVER
```

Figure 20.8 Saving Settings

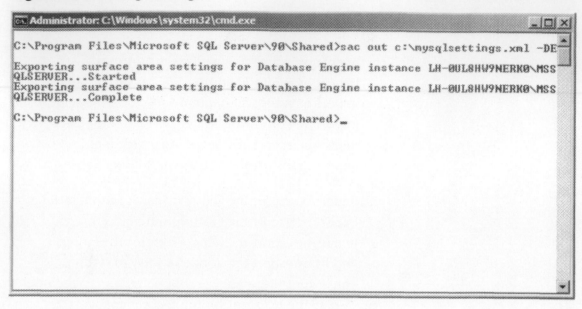

The following example will import all the settings contained in the file server1.xml and apply the settings to server2:

```
sac in server1.xml -S server2
```

In the preceding example, the settings contained in server1.xml are applied to server2. Since no username is specified, Windows authentication is used for security purposes.

Practical Applications for the Surface Area Configuration Tool

Now that we are familiar with the basic theory of operation behind the tool, let's discuss some practical applications of the tool, and which situations are called for.

Planning is important. Be sure not to turn services off that are needed on a particular server, and don't leave unneeded services on.

We would also caution against making changes to a live production environment before testing them thoroughly in a test environment. Ideally there should be an environment for testing that matches the production environment. Implementing changes without testing first could be a recipe for disaster.

Shortcut...

Saving Time When Configuring Multiple Servers

When there are a number of servers needed to configure, the command line version of the tool can save time. Use the GUI version of the Surface Area Configuration tool on one server and configure all the settings necessary for proper operation. Then, use the command line version of the tool to export the settings on that server.

If the settings file is copied to a disk, a network share, or some other portable media, the settings can then be imported on another server. By using the command line version of the Surface Area Configuration tool, configuring multiple servers can be done more accurately in less time.

Scenario 1

Company policy dictates no server may use xp_cmdshell system stored procedure. You are setting up a number of SQL Servers and quickly need to make sure xp_cmdshell is disabled.

Depending on the number of servers, it might make sense to create a batch file with the parameters in the batch file.

In the case where it's a smaller number of servers, it might make sense to use the GUI since it may take some time to create the batch file.

In our case, we'll assume the only customization we are making is to a few servers, and it's not necessary to change multiple settings on the server. In this example, we'd run the Surface Area Configuration tool after building the server.

First, select **Surface Area for Features**, then from the MSSQLServer list, select **XP_CMDSHELL**. We would verify the enable xpCmdshell checkbox is unchecked. If the checkbox is checked, uncheck it and click **Apply** (see Figure 20.9).

SOME INDEPENDENT ADVICE

Always test your changes first before implementing them in production! Be sure to test everything—even DTS and reporting services jobs that run only weekly. Having something break in production can be disastrous!

Figure 20.9 Disabling xp_cmdshell

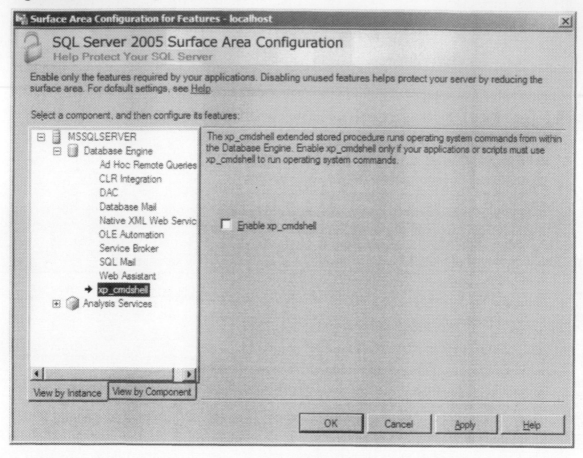

Scenario 2: Auditing an Existing Installation

You are asked to evaluate security on an existing SQL Server 2005 installation. There are three servers that need to be checked.

Solution: Use the Surface Area Configuration tool to examine each installation and each of the features the xp_cmdshell setting. Since remotely connecting to each of the servers without having to log in using terminal services is available, the Surface Area Configuration tool can save time. Examine each of the servers and document any settings that don't conform to company standards.

Scenario 3: Fixing an Issue

One of your developers has made some configuration changes to a server. There are a number of services (including CLR routines) that are no longer working. The developer has made the changes using a combination of registry key changes, enterprise manager, and SQL scripts.

Solution: Although not all problems are caused by services that are disabled, the tool can be used to check and see if there is a problem with security. Regardless of where the change was made, if the SQL Server Surface Area Configuration tool can manage the problem, it will.

When the instance is examined, it will be found that the CLR is disabled (see Figure 20.10).

Figure 20.10 Disabling CLR

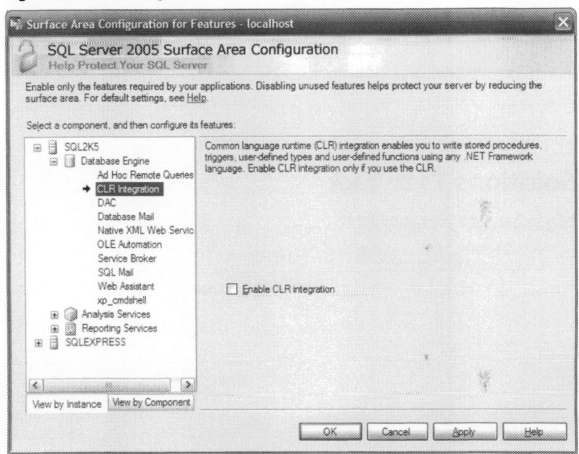

To resolve the problem, click the checkbox to turn on CLR integration, click **Apply**, and the problem with the CLR routines vanishes.

Although the SQL Server Surface Area Configuration tool isn't the only way to accomplish this, it's a handy solution.

BEST PRACTICES ACCORDING TO MICROSOFT

To ensure you're following the best practices according to Microsoft, you can use the Microsoft SQL Server Best Practices Analysis tool available as a free download from the Microsoft Web site. This tool is not only useful for security-related settings and configuration, but overall configuration of the SQL Server installation.

Summary

To recap what we've learned in this chapter, the SQL Server Surface Analysis tool gives us an easy way to manage security in SQL 2005. Surface area is a real concern.

The SQL Server Surface Area Configuration tool is a convenient way to manage surface area, connections and services on an SQL Server, or a group of SQL Servers.

We've also learned that it's important to disable services and features that are not being used. By disabling these services, it can go a long way to keep servers safe from intruders. It is one less potential path for an intruder to attack on the server.

It's important to remember to test any changes first before implementing them in a production environment. I can't stress testing enough; it would be a terrible thing to turn off a service that's being used (maybe once a week for a dataload) on a production server and break something.

Solutions Fast Track

SQL Server Surface Area

- ☑ The Surface Area Configuration tool can provide an easy centralized way to configure SQL Server security.

- ☑ The command-line version can help you quickly and easily configure multiple servers.

Frequently Asked Questions

Q: Can the SQL Server Surface Area Configuration tool be used on SQL 2000 or SQL 7.0?

A: No, the tool cannot be used to configure SQL 2000 or SQL 7.0.

Q: Can the SQL Server Surface Area Configuration tool be used with SQL Express?

A: Yes, it can be used to configure security settings in SQL Express.

Q: Can the SQL Server Surface Area Configuration tool be used to configure Security on a cluster? Are there any special requirements on a cluster?

A: The SQL Server Surface Area Configuration tool can be used with a cluster. You need to specify remote computer, and use the name of the failover instance for the computer.

Q: What rights are needed to run the SQL Server Surface Area Configuration tool?

A: Administrative rights are needed to use SQL Server Surface Area Configuration tool.

Q: Does the SQL Server Surface Area Configuration tool need to run on the server being worked on?

A: No, run the SQL Server Surface Area Configuration tool remotely. Click the change computer link on the main menu of the Surface Area Configuration tool and specify the remote computer that is presented, with the select computer dialog box.

Q: Can the SQL Server Surface Area Configuration tool be used to configure reporting services access?

A: Yes, the tool can be used to configure reporting services.

Q: Can the SQL Server Surface Area Configuration tool be used with integrated security?

A: Yes, the tool can be used with either integrated security or SQL Server security, provided the server is configured to support SQL Server and windows authentication.

Q: Can I use the SQL Server Surface Area Configuration tool with integrated security?

A: Yes, the tool can be used with either integrated security or SQL Server security, provided the server is configured to support SQL Server and Windows authentication.

Chapter 21

Roles

Solutions in this chapter:

■ Roles

☑ Summary

☑ Solutions Fast Track

☑ Frequently Asked Questions

Introduction

In this chapter, we'll introduce the concept of roles. By the end of the chapter, you should have a good understanding of how to use roles to grant access in SQL server. We'll cover how and when to use roles. We'll show you how to create a role and add users to the role via the GUI and via script.

Roles

Roles in SQL Server 2005 are a lot like groups in Windows. Their primary use is to allow an easy method of assigning permissions to a group of users. Roles can have built-in (predefined by SQL Server 2005) or user-defined permissions, and exist at both the server and database level. Most built-in roles cannot be modified, with the exception of the public role at the database level.

At the server level, roles are usually granted to give users some sort of SQL Server 2005 administration permissions. At the database level, roles have two purposes: to allow administration of the database, or to grant specific data or structure permissions inside that database. A role is used to grant certain permissions to SQL logins, SQL roles, Windows logins, or Windows groups. It's important to note that roles can be given other roles as well, making it possible to create roles which group other roles.

Using Roles

Roles can make your life easier when applying SQL Server 2005 security. Imagine you are told that eight logins are going to need select access to 133 tables, and write access to another 30 tables, and that they will need these first thing in the morning when the new project kicks off. You look in the database, searching for ways to make this task easier, only to find these tables are spread around and cover parts of many schemas. Sounds like you'll be working late, doesn't it? Well… maybe not. Rather than going through each of those eight logins and scrolling through the list clicking the 163 checkboxes necessary to give these users the permissions they require, you could create a user-defined role, click those checkboxes once rather than eight times, and give those eight users that role. With such simplicity, you might even get home in time to catch the end of the big game.

In addition to the role I talked about creating earlier, which would be a database-level user-defined role, there are a few other types of roles: application roles and server- and database-level predefined roles.

Shortcut...

Combining Roles and Windows Groups

Where the power of roles really starts to shine is when roles are used in conjunction with windows group permissions. Take setting up database permissions on a development server. You have several developers working on that server, and you need to give them the access they require. To do so, the first step is to have a windows group created and the developers for that project added to that group. The next step is to create a role called developer on that database and give the appropriate permissions to that role. Then, add that group to SQL Server 2005, give them the database role in your database, and everything is complete. If new people come onto the project, or people leave, you don't need to dig into your database and try to add new users or remove old ones. Why? Because when a user's Windows account is disabled, the user no longer has access to the database since the change is noted by SQL Server 20905, which is also using Windows security. If a new developer comes on board and is added to the group, that developer inherits the same permissions from the NT group that the rest of the developers have.

Role Types

Roles can exist at either the server level or the database level, and fall into a few different types. These role types are user-defined standard roles, user-defined application roles, and fixed server and fixed database roles. The fixed roles are normally used to give members administrative capabilities, and depending on the level, they either affect all databases for server-level roles, or just the single database for database-level roles. The fixed roles are called fixed because other than the public database-level role, they cannot have their rights modified.

User-Defined Standard Roles

User-defined standard roles are like the role that was added in the preceding example, called TheNewRole. These roles are used for grouping together permissions so each user does not have to be individually given permissions to the objects. These roles are created by the SQL Server 2005 administrator. The best way to think of these in categories is to imagine a company with a database. You have sales people, administrators, accounting folks, IT personnel, and all kinds of other groups. If I was administering SQL Server 2005 for this company, I would create a role for many of these groups. I would give the accounting people select, insert, and update on financial data. The personnel people would get select, insert, and update on the employee records. This is the typical use of user-defined standard roles.

In general, user-defined roles are typically underutilized. I can't even begin to count how many times I have come across SQL Server 2005 instances which were perfect opportunities for utilizing roles, yet all the permissions were set individually on the login and object level. By taking a few moments and classifying your objects with even a finer grain than I've just listed, you can begin to take advantage of the benefits of user-defined standard roles.

Let's take a look at a theoretical ordering system's database. Very typical classes of data exist in this theoretical ordering system, such as customers, orders, items, and inventory. You have set up a role called customer. Of course, the role grants access to the customer table, but also the pr_addnewcustomer user-defined stored procedure that adds new customers, along with the pr_getcustomerlist and the pr_getcustomerdetails procedures, and a couple customer-level views. This role is then given to the customer service people, customer service supervisors, and the quality control department, who all access the theoretical database's customer data. Now someone creates a new procedure called pr_getcustomerorders that all those same customer service people must be able to access. Because you granted each of these groups the role, you are only able to add execute permission to the new procedure to your customer role, and everyone in those groups inherits that new grant. Without utilizing roles, you must grant individual permission to this new procedure to the customer service employees, the customer service supervisors, and the quality control department individually. If you add this up each time this happens for each of the groups over each of the databases you run on SQL Server 2005, you're looking at a whole lot of work time.

User-Defined Application Roles

User-defined application roles are very similar to user-defined standard roles except that the roles are password protected and assigned to applications rather than users. Application roles can be used to allow access to specific data based on the application connecting to the database. Application roles cannot be granted to members, but are instead instantiated by the application that has connected to the database. The application inherits the role permissions by connecting to the database using standard Windows or SQL-level login credentials, and then executing the sp_setapprole stored procedure with a password known only to the application. The connection at this point gains its permissions from the application role. Because these are database-only permissions, any cross-database references will only work if objects that the application is attempting to access in the other database can be accessed using guest permissions. The sp_unsetapprole procedure is used by the application to deactivate the application role. When this procedure is executed, the application connection permissions revert to the previous security context.

Predefined Database Roles

SQL Server 2005 comes with certain predefined, or fixed, database-level roles. In general, these roles are used to define the administrative privilege of each user at the database level. Predefined roles cannot be changed with the exception of the public role. Predefined database roles also cannot be dropped and exist on every database in SQL Server 2005.

The public role is the default role for all database users. This role is inherited when the user is given permission to access the database. If you want to modify permissions to all users in a particular database, you can modify this role (see Figure 21.1).

Figure 21.1 The Public Role Securables List Showing Some of the Default Permissions

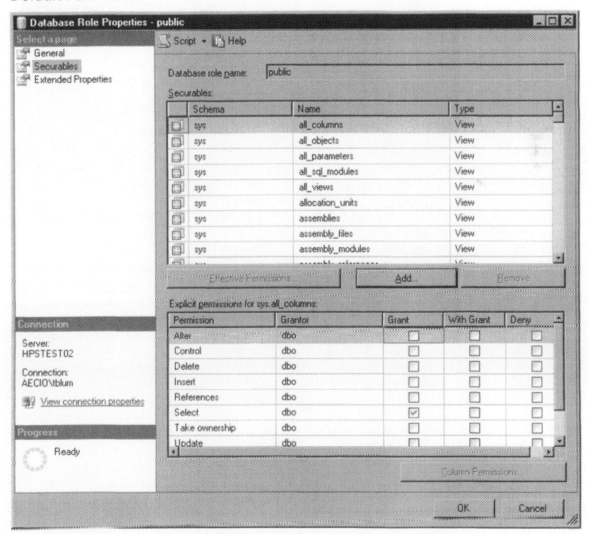

SOME INDEPENDENT ADVICE

The first step in checking the role security in SQL Server 2005 is to review all items in the public role and make sure they should truly have public permissions. For example, all items in the sys schema have select permission granted to the public by default. The question to ask is whether or not you really want everyone to see, edit, or delete a particular item. Many people will suggest that things like functions should be available in the public role. However, unless everyone truly needs access to something, it is best not to put that object in the public role, no matter whether it's a function, a view, a stored procedure, table, or anything else.

Two other fixed database roles are db_accessadmin, which gives its members the ability to add of remove logins in the database, and the db_backupoperator role, which gives its members the ability to back up a database. These roles are often given to the team or project leader in development projects. This allows them to add the users who need to perform the development, and perform backups at key intervals during development. Of course, the team leader does not have the same permissions on the production server. One rule I always follow is to have production servers tightly locked down, but have development servers remain secure, but not so locked down as to prevent users from doing what they need to on a day-to-day basis.

The next four roles all have to do with data access on the server. These roles are db_datareader, db_datawriter, db_denydatareader, and db_denydatawriter. These roles are the most often used roles in SQL Server 2005 installations. Their reader roles are fairly self-explanatory in that the data reader roles give their members the ability to read all data in user-defined tables for the database, whereas the db_denydatareader denies read access to all data in user-defined tables for the database. The write roles are fairly simple in that the db_datawrite role permits its members to perform inserts, updates, and deletes on any user-defined table in the database, while the db_denydatawriter role cannot perform any inserts, updates, or deletes on any user-defined table in the database.

The db_ddladmin role allows users to perform tasks related to the data definition language (DDL) in the current database. Members of this role are limited in that they cannot perform the grant, revoke, or deny data definition language commands, but they can execute all other DDL commands.

The db_securityadmin is for members who need to maintain all aspects of security on a particular database. This role allows its members to work with database roles, manager permissions, and object ownership. Finally, there is the db_owner role. This gives its members complete control over a database. They can perform maintenance, manage all aspects of the database's security, change settings for the database, and perform all administrative tasks on the database.

To grant the fixed database roles to a login, you would use the sp_addrolemember to grant SQL logins, SQL Roles, Windows users, or Windows groups membership. To check the membership of a fixed database role, use the sp_helprolemember system-stored procedure. Dropping members is done by utilizing the sp_droprolemember procedure (see Figure 21.2).

Figure 21.2 Script Code for Adding Members to Database-Level Fixed Roles

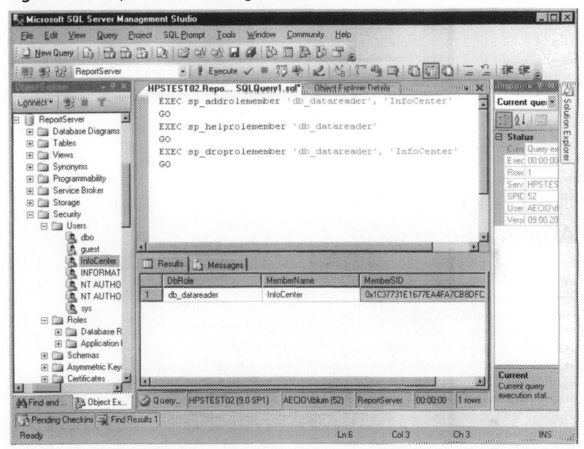

Fixed Server Roles

Fixed server roles cannot be dropped and so exist at the server level in SQL Server 2005. Fixed server roles include bulkadmin, dbcreator, diskadmin, porcessadmin, securityadmin, serveradmin, setupadmin, and sysadmin. Each of these roles has a specific purpose, but in general these tasks allow their members to perform administrative or maintenance duties at the server level.

Bulkadmin administers bulk copy and other bulk operations. dbcreator is a role that allows its members to create, alter, or drop databases. diskadmin allows its members to work with the actual files on the disk—for instance, it could manage filegroups. processadmins have the ability to manage SQL Server 2005 processes—for example, they can use the KILL command to terminate a session. Any members of the securityadmin role can alter, create, or delete any login. Serveradmin can change SQL Server 2005 settings, shut down SQL Server 2005, and alter the state, resources, or endpoint of SQL Server 2005. The setupadmin role allows members to add, change, or delete any linked server. The final role, sysadmin, can do anything on the server. These roles were listed in order of increasing power. Each should truly only be given to members of the database management team, with the possible exception of bulkadmin. If you have a particular group or individual (outside of the people who administer SQL Server 2005) whom you trust in performing bulkadmin duties, by all means add them as members of the bulkadmin role. Any other roles delegate a lot of power, and thus should be treated with caution.

Administering Roles

In SQL Server 2005, there are a couple of ways of administering roles. You can administer roles through SQL Server Management Studio by using the GUI, or through script. To modify server-level roles in the GUI, go to the security node in the server level of the treeview. If you select a server role, right-click, select Properties, and then enter the general page of the server role. On this page, you can add role members to the server role. This is the only modification you can make to server roles. Additionally, when you modify server roles via script, all you can do is grant users the role, or remove them from the role. To do this, use the system-stored procedure sp_addsrvrolemember to add a member to a role, or use sp_dropsrvrolemember to remove a member from the fixed server role. If you wanted to list all fixed server roles, use sp_helpsrvrole. This will list the fixed server roles, which would be the standard list. To list the members of one of these fixed server roles, use the sp_helpserverrolemember system-stored procedure. Be careful when attempting to list the permissions of a fixed server role using the sp_srvrolepermission system-stored procedure. The results from this procedure do not reflect changes to the permissions that have been made in SQL Server 2005.

To modify database-level roles in the GUI, expand the database you are working on in the treeview control in the object explorer. If you then expand the security section, the roles will appear as the second item down in the treeview. By right-clicking and selecting Properties on any existing roles, you can see the tabs for each role. If you selected a user-defined role, you will find three items listed in the top left section called Select A Page. These are General, Securables, and Extended Properties. In Figure 21.3, the General page for Role Properties has been selected.

The General page shows you the owner of the role, the schemas owned by this role, and the members of the role. This page is often used when you want to give the role ownership of an additional schema. Allowing schemas to be owned by a role is a feature introduced in SQL Server 2005. When you give a role ownership of a schema, anybody in the role can do any operation on any items in that schema. This means they cannot only delete data, but also objects themselves. I also commonly come to this page when I need to answer the question of what members belong to a role.

Figure 21.3 The General Page for Role Properties#

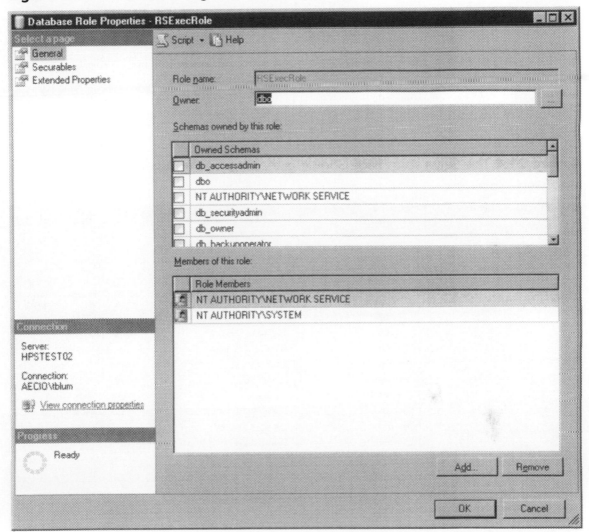

The Securables page lists the items the role has permission to at the top, and the explicit permission for the item selected at the top appears near the bottom of the page. This is the main section where role permissions are maintained. The bottom section changes to show the actual explicit permissions based on the type of item chosen in the top section. Figure 21.4 displays the list of explicit permissions for stored procedures. An understanding of available permissions and what they mean becomes valuable at this point. For example, while you most likely know that the alter permission on a stored procedure gives the permission to modify a stored procedures code, what is the difference between having Grant unchecked versus having Deny checked? It would seem to serve the same purpose, but in actuality there is a slight difference. This difference is that when Grant is not checked, it is possible it could be checked in another role. For example, let's consider a table named cardata, and two roles: one named role1 with select permission on the cardata table if no checkboxes are checked; and the other named role2, where select permission on the cardata table has only the Grant checkbox chosen. If a login was given both of these roles, the user would be able to gain access to the cardata table. However, if in the same example earlier, role1 has the Deny box checked on select for the cardata table, but everything else was the same, the user would not be able to gain access to the cardata table. This is the purpose of the Deny checkbox. Any time Deny is checked, it overrides any other setting that would attempt to grant permission to that object. The With Grant column gives the role permission to grant permissions on that object to others.

Figure 21.4 The Securables Page Showing the Explicit Permissions Available for a Stored Procedure

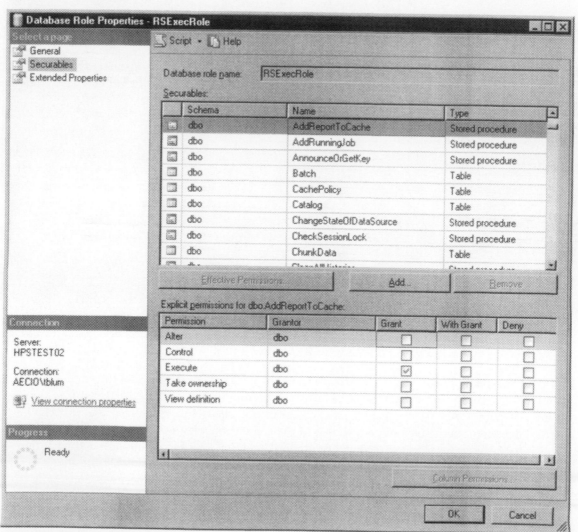

The Extended Properties window allows you to create extended properties where you can add text for such things as descriptive comments or instructional comments.

If the role you have selected is a fixed database role other than the public role, you will not be presented with the Securables tab since these roles are called fixed because they are not editable.

When using the scripts to administer roles, you can save an incredible amount of time. For example, refer to my earlier example where you were requested to give select permissions to 133 tables and insert permission to 30 more tables for eight logins. Let's reconsider this request. You need to add a role, the syntax for which is "CREATE ROLE [TheNewRole] AUTHORIZATION [dbo]". This will create a role named TheNewRole, which is owned by dbo. Now, if you use copy and paste, you can take the Grant statement and modify it for each of the 163 requests. If you are good at copy and paste, you can probably finish this in five minutes. Each one would look similar to this "GRANT SELECT ON [dbo].[DataTable] TO [TheNewRole]". Next, you would run the sp_addrolemember stored procedure once for each of the eight users. At this point, you execute and save the script with all 172 statements (the one create role, 163 grants, and eight add role members). And you still get home in time to catch the end of the big game. However, next week when you get asked to apply those same permissions to the acceptance server in addition to the server you just added all those users to last week, you can pull out your script, run it on acceptance, and be done in a matter of seconds. You can accomplish the same thing if you added all the permissions through the GUI by clicking the button to script all changes. However, you must remember to script out the changes, which is easy to forget, and not as flexible since you can only script out the changes you made that time.

To maintain database-level roles using script, you need to note a few things that have changed in SQL Server 2005 from pervious versions. The ability to create and drop user-defined standard roles using "Create Role [role_name]" and "Drop Role[role_name]" is the new syntax to handle creating or dropping user-defined standard roles (see Figure 21.5). The sp_addrole and sp_droprole are still included in SQL Server 2005, but only for backwards compatibility. They will be removed from a future version of SQL Server, so it would be a good time to get used to using the new syntax. Standard roles that have members cannot be dropped until the members have been removed.

The same new syntax applies to creating and dropping user defined application roles. You now will use "Create Application Role [role name]" or "Drop Application Role [role name]" as the sp_addapprole and sp_dropapprole system-stored procedures are being deprecated. Additionally, the sp_approlepassword procedure that changes the password of an application role in the current database is being replaced with the "Alter Application Role [role name]' syntax.

One particular system-stored procedure will list all of the database-level fixed roles. These roles do not change, so the data from this stored procedure will always provide you the list of public, db_accessadmin, db_backupoperator, db_datareader, db_datawriter, db_denydatareader, db_denydatawrite, db_ddladmin, db_securityadmin, and db_owner. The sp_helproles will list all roles in the current database, while the sp_helprolemember will provide you a list of members of a particular role.

In order to add a database user, database role, Windows login, or Windows group to a role in the current database, you should use the sp_addrolemember [@rolename =] 'role'. In order to delete a database user, database role, Windows login, or Windows group from a role in the current database, use the sp_droprolemember system-stored procedure.

Figure 21.5 Standard Users Roles Commonly Use Script Commands

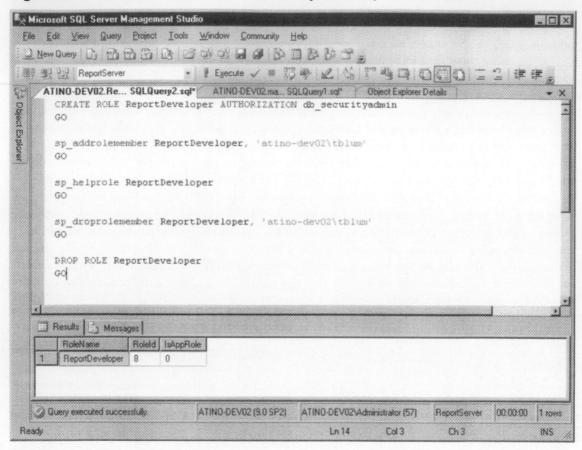

Situational Examples

Now let's look at a few situational examples and see how you would handle each. You need to grant access to 20 developers, who should only have the permission to create, delete, or modify objects in a database named ProductTest. How would you use roles to accomplish this?

The first thing you should consider is that the need is at the database level, so this will direct you to the database roles. Next, you need to look at who has the least permissions available to do what they need. In this case, there is the db_ddladmin role, which allows them to modify objects. Next, I would be considering how those users connect to my database. In the case of dealing with 20 people, I would create a Windows group and add each of them as members. I would then add the Windows group login permissions to my server, with the default database being ProductTest. I would then grant this group membership to the ddl_admin role in the ProductTest database. Now they are all set up, and they are not coming in as dbowner, which is so often the case in many development areas.

Okay, so how about the same situation, where they need to be able to create, modify, or delete objects, but in addition to this they also need to be able to back up and restore the database? Again, this can be done at the database level, letting you use the database roles. Next, you need to look at who has the least permissions available to do what they need. In this case, the db_ddladmin role allows them to modify objects, while the db_backupoperator role lets them back up the database. Again, I would consider how those users connect to my database. In the case of dealing with 20 people, I would create a Windows group and add each of them as members. I would then add the Windows group login permissions to my server, with the default database being ProductTest. I would then grant this group membership to the db_ddladmin and db_backupoperator roles in the ProductTest database. Again, they are not coming in as dbowner.

Let's change the scenario a bit. Let's say you get an assistant who is to help you maintain the server—in particular his first assignment will have him working with the filegroups. If you look at the scope (it is at the server level), you'll note that you'll be working with server roles. Looking at the server roles, you search for someone who can modify filegroups. That role is the diskadminrole. This is for one user, so the next step is to add his Windows login to SQL Server 2005, and then give them membership to the diskadmin role.

As you can see, deciding how and when to grant roles is all about understanding what power each role has, and granting the correct one. This keeps SQL Server 2005 as secure as possible, while allowing everyone to get their work done.

Summary

To recap what we have reviewed in this chapter, roles are easy ways to grant permissions to objects at the database and server level. Roles can be granted to SQL logins, SQL roles, Windows logins, or Windows groups. Both server-level and database-level roles exist; some of which are fixed, and some of which are user-defined. Certain application roles are used at the database level to grant permissions to applications without having to resort to using SQL logins. This eliminates an often forgotten hole in SQL Server 2005 security: the SQL login which former employees still remember.

You also learned that roles and memberships to roles can be maintained through the Microsoft SQL Server Management Studio interface or through script.

It is important to remember that using roles not only allows for easier permissions handling, but when used in conjunction with Windows authentication, they provide a greater measure of security for SQL Server 2005.

Solutions Fast Track

Roles

- ☑ Roles are a very simple method of making your life easier.

- ☑ The types of roles are user-defined roles, application roles, and server and database fixed roles.

- ☑ A role is used to grant certain permissions to SQL logins, SQL roles, Windows logins, or Windows groups.

- ☑ Administration can be done through the GUI SQL Server Management Studio interface or through script.

- ☑ The sp_createrole and sp_drop roles have been replaced by the Create Role and Drop role statements.

- ☑ Roles can exist on the server or database level and each of the role types has its own administration techniques.

- ☑ User-defined standard roles are created by the SQL Server 2005 administrator.

- ☑ User-defined standard roles are the most commonly underutilized type of role.

- ☑ User-defined standard roles group together permissions of like types.

- ☑ Application roles are assigned to applications rather than members, just like with standard roles.

- ☑ When application roles are assumed, all previous permissions are ignored and the permissions from the application role are inherited.

- ☑ When application roles are unset, the connection reverts back to its previous security context.

- ☑ Predefined database roles are used primarily to grant rights to specific duties.

☑ Predefined database roles apply only to the particular database.

☑ Public roles can be modified, whereas all other predefined database roles cannot be modified.

☑ Predefined database roles include public, db_accessAdmin, db_backupoperator, db_datareader, db_datawriter, db_ddladmin, db_denydatareader, db_denydatawriter, db_securityadmin, and db_owner.

☑ Fixed server roles are used primarily to grant rights to specific duties.

☑ Fixed server roles are applied at the server level.

☑ Fixed server roles include bulkadmin, dbcreator, diskadmin, processadmin, securityadmin, serveradmin, setupadmin, and sysadmin.

Frequently Asked Questions

Q: Can role membership be granted to other standard user-defined roles?

A: All types of database-level role membership can be granted to user-defined database roles or application roles. User-defined roles can be granted to the public fixed database role, but cannot be granted to any other fixed roles.

Q: What benefit is provided by using application roles instead of a SQL Server login when applications log in?

A: By eliminating the use of SQL Server logins inside of applications, and using application roles instead, you can change the SQL Server operation mode from mixed to Windows authentication only. This provides an even greater level of security for SQL Server 2005.

Q: Is there any difference regarding security levels in setting someone to Deny versus unchecking the Grant box?

A: Yes, there is. By setting the permissions on an object to Deny, this overrides all other permissions that may occur in other roles. If you just uncheck the Grant box, this is overridden by a grant on the object in another role.

Q: Can fixed server roles be overridden at the database level?

A: No. Fixed server roles override any permission set on the local database.

Q: Can fixed roles be edited or deleted?

A: No. Server fixed roles can be modified or deleted. At the database level, the public fixed role can be modified, but not deleted. No other database level fixed roles can be modified or deleted.

Chapter 22

Authentication and Granular Access

Solutions in this chapter:

- **Understanding the SQL Server Authentication Modes**

- **Endpoint Security**

- **Configuring Kerberos Support for Your SQL Server**

- **Auditing Authentication Attempts**

- **Understanding Granular Access**

☑ Summary

☑ Solutions Fast Track

☑ Frequently Asked Questions

Introduction

Authentication is a key concept in SQL Server. In this chapter we'll look at the two authentication modes SQL Server supports. In addition, we'll cover all the methods for authentication in this chapter. Finally, we'll take a look at granular access and how you can use this feature to further secure your SQL Server. By the end of this chapter, you will have a good understanding of the following concepts:

- SQL Server Authentication Modes
- Types of Endpoints
- Basic Authentication
- Digest Authentication
- NTLM Authentication
- Kerberos Authentication
- Integrated Authentication
- Certificate Authentication
- How to Configure Kerberos Authentication
- Fundamentals of Granular Access
- What Principals, Securables, and Permissions Are and How to Use Them

Understanding the SQL Server Authentication Modes

Before we look at the various ways SQL Server can authenticate, it's first best to look at what are known as the Authentication Modes. SQL Server is capable of validating two types of logins:

- Windows logins
- SQL Server logins

A Windows login can be a domain user account or a local user account on the computer on which SQL Server is running. SQL Server logins are those that exist only within SQL Server. SQL Server is responsible for keeping track of the login information, to include the password. The SQL Server login is a legacy holdover from earlier versions of SQL Server, as the preferred type of login is a Windows-based one. Windows logins generally are considered more secure. However, SQL Server logins aren't going away any time soon. They are used too extensively by third-party products and in situations where a client isn't on the same domain as the SQL Server being connected to (for instance, a web server that is set up to service the Internet).

In order to accommodate these two types of logins, SQL Server can be configured in one of two authentication modes. The first is Windows-only mode. When SQL Server is configured in this mode, it will only accept Windows-based logins. Even if SQL Server is aware of a SQL Server login, it will not accept the login. This goes for all SQL Server logins, to include the sa account. The second mode is what is commonly known as mixed mode. This is where SQL Server will accept both Windows logins and SQL Server logins. There is not a mode where only SQL Server logins are accepted. Although this could be accomplished by removing all Windows-based logins (both users and groups), this is not generally recommended.

Best Practices According to Microsoft

Microsoft's recommendations with respect to SQL Server Authentication Mode are:

- Use Windows-only authentication whenever possible.
- Only drop back to Mixed Mode due to applications that don't support Windows authentication or users coming from a non-Windows environment.
- Regardless of which authentication mode you select, secure the sa account with a strong password. Under *no* circumstances should you ever leave the SA password blank.
- If Mixed Mode is selected, use Windows logins to manage SQL Server.
- Rename the sa account so it cannot be targeted for a brute force password attack.

Some Independent Advice

Although I aim for Windows-only authentication as my authentication mode of choice on my SQL Servers, there are certain cases where I must plan for Mixed Mode. These usually involve what are known as untrusted clients. The term trust here refers to a Windows domain trust, either a transitive trust between Windows domains in the same forest (or domains in forests that have a forest-level trust) or two domains for which there is an external trust relationship. Therefore, a server sitting in a workgroup for security reasons would meet the criteria of an untrusted client. It has no way of connecting to SQL Server via an accepted Windows account. Examples of such servers might include:

- Web servers sitting in the Demilitarized Zone (DMZ) providing services to Internet-based users.
- Servers that contain potentially sensitive configuration information such as the router configurations for the network.
- Servers that run a building's access control system.

Ensure that you plan for these types of clients when selecting your authentication mode. Whenever possible, try to isolate applications requiring SQL Server logins to a particular set of SQL Servers running in Mixed Mode while configuring the remainder of your SQL Server for Windows-only authentication.

Changing the Authentication Mode

The authentication mode is read from the registry when SQL Server first starts up. Therefore, if you change the authentication mode, you must stop and restart the SQL Server service for it to take effect. Since this setting is stored in the registry, the only way to make the change using the SQL Server provided tools is through SQL Server Management Studio. In order to make this change, perform the following steps:

1. In *Object Explorer*, right-click on the SQL Server and choose **Properties** from the pop-up menu.
2. Click on the **Security** page under *Choose a Page* on the left side.
3. On the Security page, select the authentication mode under *Server authentication* (see Figure 22.1).
4. Click **OK** when you receive the message box indicating the setting won't take effect until SQL Server is restarted.

Figure 22.1 Security Page for SQL Server

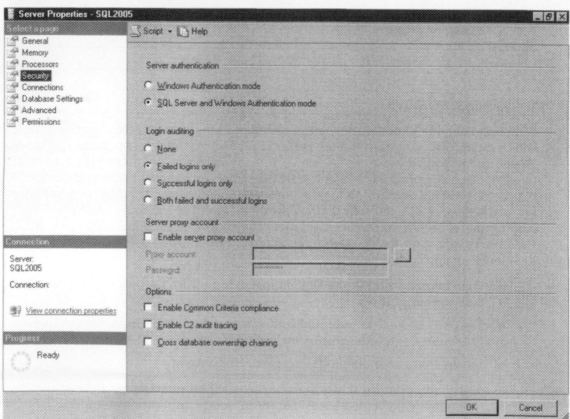

Finding the Authentication Mode by Using xp_loginconfig

SQL Server provides a system stored procedure that reveals the configuration details for SQL Server with respect to logins. It's appropriately named xp_loginconfig. To execute this stored procedure, you must have CONTROL permission on the master database. If you're not familiar with CONTROL, it's a new security permission in SQL Server 2005. We'll cover it a bit later in the chapter when we discuss granular access. By default, no login has this level of permission in SQL Server 2005. Therefore, only members of the sysadmin fixed server role can execute this stored procedure since that role bypasses all security permissions.

Used without any parameters, xp_loginconfig will return details on the security configuration such as the authentication mode, the default login if a connection's login cannot be validated (the guest login), the default domain (the domain which the SQL Server is a member of), and the audit level that SQL Server has configured for login attempts (none, success, failure, or both). However, if we're interested only in the authentication mode, we can pass the value 'login mode' as a parameter:

```
EXEC xp_loginconfig 'login mode';
GO
```

This will return a text string in the config_value column of either "Mixed" or "Windows Authentication" depending on how the SQL Server is configured.

Finding the Authentication Mode in the Registry

If you have more than a handful of SQL Servers in your environment, chances are you have some tools that have the ability to check the registry on multiple systems for particular values. An example of such a tool is Symantec's bv-Control product, which can be configured to run scans on certain registry settings and return the results into a report. Such tools allow you to quickly check all your SQL Servers to determine their authentication mode setting. The catch is to know where to look in the registry for this information. For an instance of SQL Server 2005, you can find the authentication mode in the following key:

```
HKEY_LOCAL_MACHINE\Software\Microsoft\Microsoft SQL Server\
MSSQL.x\MSSQLServer\LoginMode
```

The x is a positive integer value. With SQL Server 2005, each component of SQL Server, whether it be the database engine, Analysis Services, Integration Services, among others, has its registry settings under one of the MSSQL.x keys. As to which key is the right one, this typically depends on the order the components were installed. Therefore you may have to navigate all the various keys of MSSQL.x, especially if you have multiple instances installed. However, if you have installed just the default instance, you'll likely find the information in MSSQL.1. Once you've located the key, you can determine the authentication mode by examining the values shown in Table 22.1.

Table 22.1 Values for SQL Server Authentication Mode

Key Value	Meaning
0x00000001 (1)	Windows only authentication
0x00000002 (2)	SQL Server and Windows authentication

Endpoint Security

An endpoint is a new term in SQL Server 2005, but it's not a new concept. An endpoint is simply a means of connecting into the database engine. In SQL Server 2000 there were several endpoints that corresponded to the different enabled network libraries for SQL Server. For instance, on a given SQL Server 2000 it was possible to have the following endpoints:

- Shared Memory
- AppleTalk
- Banyan Vines
- Named Pipes
- NWLink IPX/SPX
- TCP/IP
- VIA

These endpoints provided T-SQL functionality and served as the basic connections for clients into SQL Server. You could configure SQL XML for Internet Information Server (IIS) in SQL Server 2000, which allowed for web access to SQL Server, but the truth of the matter is that behind the scenes, this still used an existing endpoint, providing an interface for HTTP access. SQL Server 2005 still maintains the following endpoints for T-SQL access:

- Shared Memory
- Named Pipes
- TCP/IP
- VIA

When SQL Server is first set up, it will have at least the Shared Memory endpoint configured. This allows connection attempts that originate from the server where SQL Server is installed to succeed. SQL Server Express and Developer Edition versions of SQL Server 2005 will not have any other type of endpoint enabled. Other editions of SQL Server 2005 will also have Named Pipes and TCP/IP endpoints enabled. This is the normal means for clients to connect in to SQL Server that has been present in previous versions. With these built-in endpoints, the only option we have available is to turn them on or off through the Surface Area Configuration utility or SQL Server Configuration Manager. These endpoints will provide T-SQL access to SQL Server and authenticate logins based on the authentication mode SQL Server is configured to run under.

However, in SQL Server 2005 we are not just limited to these default endpoints as we are in previous versions of SQL Server. SQL Server 2005 also gives us the capability to create new endpoints, including a new type of endpoint: HTTP. We have additional options for TCP endpoints in order to enable service broker and database mirroring connections. In addition, the endpoint doesn't just define the means of connection, it also defines the method of communication. The methods available to us are:

- Simple Object Access Protocol (SOAP)

- T-SQL

- Server Broker

- Databasve Mirroring

The latter two are not likely to used by most clients. However, with Service Oriented Architecture (SOA) becoming more and more the rage, an HTTP endpoint that communicates via SOAP can fit well with type of design. These customizable endpoints can increase the functionality of our SQL Servers. Along with the increased functionality, Microsoft has bundled additional authentication types. Let's take a look at what they are.

NOTE

Each endpoint represents a doorway into your SQL Server. This is why, by default, no endpoints for service broker or database mirroring are created for SQL Server when it is first installed. It is also the reason only the Shared Memory endpoint is enabled for SQL Server Express and SQL Server Developer Editions. Before creating a new endpoint for your SQL Server, ensure that there is a genuine requirement to have it. The fewer entry points into your SQL Server, the fewer options an attacker is going to have and the fewer places you'll have to watch for signs of intrusion.

Endpoint Authentication Types

There are several endpoint authentication types that you need to be aware of. Certain authentication types correspond to either the method of connection or the method of communication. Let's start with HTTP endpoints and discuss the authentication types available with them.

HTTP Endpoints

SQL Server 2005 uses http.sys, which is a native HTTP driver with Windows Server 2003. Because SQL Server 2005 implements this driver, SQL Server can now implement HTTP-based connections without the use of IIS. As a result, it must support the basic authentication types defined in the HTTP 1.1 specification in addition to more traditional Windows methods. One of these authentication types, basic authentication, is generally recommended against because it requires the transmission of the password across the network in a weakly encrypted manner. Others are simply stronger because of some of the features of the particular authentication protocol. Therefore, it is extremely important to make the correct choice with regard to how your HTTP endpoints authenticate, balancing functionality and security. The types of authentication with HTTP endpoints are:

- Basic Authentication
- Digest Authentication
- NTLM Authentication
- Kerberos Authentication
- Integrated Authentication

If you're familiar with the HTTP 1.1 specification or have experience administering IIS, you may be wondering why Anonymous "authentication" isn't on the list. SQL Server 2005 requires authentication; therefore, anonymous connections to SQL Server via HTTP are not supported.

Basic Authentication

Basic authentication is one of the authentication types specified in HTTP 1.1 that SQL Server 2005 does support. Basically the username and password are passed across the network in a base64-encoded format. This means of transmitting the username and password is not secure. As a result, SQL Server will not support creating an endpoint using basic authentication unless SSL is involved.

In order to use basic authentication, the login given must match a valid Windows login that has permission to log in to the SQL Server in question. SQL Server logins may not authenticate via basic authentication.

> **BEST PRACTICES ACCORDING TO MICROSOFT**
>
> Microsoft states that basic authentication should be used only as a last resort. Of the authentication methods available, basic authentication is the only one that requires the client to transmit the password across the network. As a result, you should choose basic authentication only when no other authentication type is possible.

Digest Authentication

Digest authentication is another authentication type specified in HTTP 1.1. Unlike basic authentication, digest authentication does not require the password to be transmitted. Rather, the client takes the username and password and uses the MD5 hashing algorithm to create a hash, which is then sent to the SQL Server.

If you are not familiar with hashing algorithms, they are one-way functions when you put in a stream of values (such as the username and password), and you get a stream of characters as a result. If the hashing algorithm is "reasonable secure," there is no way to take the output stream of characters from a hashing algorithm and get back to original stream. As a result, most of the research on hashing algorithms revolve around finding techniques to generate collisions. A collision is when two different input streams produce the exact same output stream. For instance, if "dog" and "cat" both produced "boy" when going through a hashing algorithm, we'd have a collision. Unfortunately, recent research against MD5 has found mechanisms for generating collisions rather quickly.

With respect to SQL Server 2005, digest authentication requires two key elements to work. First, the username must be a valid Windows domain login. A local Windows account on the server will not work. Neither will a SQL Server login. Second, the domain controllers for the domain must be at least Windows Server 2003. Windows 2000 domain controllers do not support digest authentication. There is a workaround to make digest authentication work with IIS 5.0, but it requires all user account passwords to be stored in a format where the encryption can easily be reversed (and the password revealed). This insecure method of supporting digest authentication is not utilized by SQL Server 2005. Therefore, if you have SQL Servers on a Windows 2000 domain, you likely won't be able to use digest authentication.

NTLM Authentication

NTLM stands for NT LAN Manager; it's the traditional authentication protocol for Windows NT-based kernels (to include Windows 2000, XP, and 2003). NTLM was the most secure protocol for NT 4.0 but it is considered a secondary means of authentication as of Windows 2000. Kerberos, which we'll discuss next, has taken its place as the primary security authentication protocol for Windows domains.

NTLM works on a challenge-response authentication mechanism. The authenticating mechanism, whether the local server or a domain controller, produces a challenge that the client must use to generate its response. The client takes the challenge and encrypts it with its password. It then sends the response back. The authenticating mechanism, which has the password, too, is able to validate whether or not the client knows the password. It does this by taking the challenge and encrypting it with the password it knows. If both are the same, the client has proven that it knows the password. Therefore, the authenticating mechanism recognizes the client. All this has taken place without a password being transmitted across the network.

Given this challenge response mechanism for authentication, NTLM is considered more secure than either basic or digest authentication. Whenever possible, it should be used rather than those two authentication types.

Kerberos Authentication

Kerberos was introduced as a security protocol starting with Windows 2000. Microsoft's implementation of this protocol is based off of Request for Comments (RFC) 1510, the RFC for Kerberos version 5 (since superseded by RFC 4120). Admittedly, though, Microsoft has "extended" the Kerberos implementation specified in this Internet "standard." One advantage Kerberos has over NTLM is that of mutual authentication. In NTLM, only the client is verified. The client must assume the server is legitimate. That is, no rogue server is pretending to be the server being connected to. Kerberos handles this issue by using a trusted third party (in an Active Directory implementation this trusted third party is a domain controller), the details of which are not germane to our discussion here.

However, in order to use Kerberos, the account being used to authenticate must be a domain account. In addition, there is likely some work that'll be required of a domain administrator in order to ensure the proper Service Principal Names (SPNs) are registered. How to do this will be covered later in this chapter.

Shortcut...

NTLM vs Kerberos

Given that Kerberos provides the same sorts of features as NTLM authentication plus the ability to mutually authenticate, is there a reason to use NTLM over Kerberos? Yes, as there are cases where Kerberos authentication cannot be used. In cases where the client and server are in different domains and those domains are not in the same forest or are not in forests where a forest-level trust has been established, there is no option to use Kerberos authentication. For instance, if domainA in forestA has an external trust with domainB in forestB, but no such forest level trust exists between forestA and forestB, Kerberos authentication cannot happen between domainA and domainB. In this case, only NTLM authentication is possible.

Integrated Authentication

Integrated authentication is actually NTLM and Kerberos Authentication rolled into one exchange. In order to understand what I mean by this, we have to take a look at how HTTP-based authentication normally happens. Let's take a closer look.

When a client wants to access a resource via HTTP, it first sends a request to the server identifying exactly what it wants. If the resource requires some sort of authentication (SQL Server does), the server will send back a response indicating that authentication is required. In that response the server will indicate to the client what methods of authentication are permitted. When an HTTP endpoint is configured to use Integrated authentication, the server will tell the client that it can choose either Kerberos or NTLM authentication. The client, if it chooses to continue, responds by following through with the appropriate form of authentication. In the case of integrated authentication, the client can either choose to authenticate via Kerberos or NTLM. If the authentication succeeds, the server then provides the resource as requested. However, if the authentication fails, SQL Server will not permit the client to try again with the second method without going through the whole connection process again.

Shortcut...

A Gotcha with HTTP Endpoints

SQL Server Management Studio doesn't provide a GUI interface to create an endpoint. The only means to do so is via the CREATE ENDPOINT T-SQL command. Working through the CREATE ENDPOINT syntax can be confusing, but when dealing with HTTP endpoints there can be another complication: the URL you want users to connect to may not be reserved for SQL Server use. For instance, if you want the users to connect to http://myserver.mydomain.com/sql, you need to reserve that namespace. The trick to doing so is another stored procedure, appropriately named *sp_reserve_http_namespace*. You'll have to execute this stored procedure first with the appropriate path (and port) before creating your HTTP endpoint.

TCP Endpoints

TCP endpoints have only a few authentication types, two of which we've talked about in the previous section. The types available to us are:

- NTLM Authentication
- Kerberos Authentication
- Negotiate Authentication
- Certificate Authentication

We've already covered NTLM and Kerberos authentication under HTTP endpoints. The authentication method doesn't differ except with respect to how the client is communicating with SQL Server. Otherwise, authentication is exactly the same. If we're setting up an endpoint for T-SQL traffic, we actually don't specify a means of authentication. SQL Server will use whatever the authentication mode is for the server. These authentication types only come into specific use when we're defining a service broker or database mirroring endpoint.

NOTE

Though it is possible in SQL Server to create more than one TCP endpoint for T-SQL, there's no point in doing so. One of the things I attempted when first experimenting with SQL Server 2005 endpoint security was trying to create a second TCP endpoint for T-SQL and locking down its access. The idea was to have one connection, from the internal network, with few restrictions, and a second connection, strictly locked down, for the web servers in the DMZ. Unfortunately, SQL Server 2005 treats all the T-SQL endpoints the same (with the exception of the Dedicated Administrator Connection). Therefore, there is no good reason to have more than one TCP endpoint for T-SQL.

Negotiate Authentication

Negotiate is like integrated authentication in that it's not an authentication mechanism unto itself. Rather, it combines both the NTLM and Kerberos protocols to offer the client a choice on how to authenticate. Unlike integrated authentication, however, both client and server use the Windows Negotiate protocol to determine which method to use.

Certificate Authentication

Because SQL Server 2005 has built-in encryption capabilities, it has the ability to generate certificates for use with authentication. While normal clients cannot connect using certificates, connections via service broker or database mirroring can be made using them. This permits SQL Servers from untrusted domains to connect to each other with hopefully better security than a username/password sent over the wire.

When a TCP endpoint is configured for either database mirroring or a service broker connection, the authentication of a particular certificate can be configured to be used. The certificate will need to be exported (using the BACKUP CERTIFICATE command) and securely copied to a SQL Server using that endpoint and then imported. In this case the certificate represents the shared secret. Therefore, it must be kept safe from compromise.

NOTE

When you are specifying the authentication type for a database mirroring or service broker TCP endpoint, both Windows methods of authentication (NTLM, Kerberos, or Negotiate) and certificate authentication can be combined. However, the order in which SQL Server attempts to authenticate must be set. Either certificate authenticate is attempted first or Windows authentication is. However, both types of authentication can be supported. This may be useful when you have trusted clients connecting to a service broker connection via Windows authentication and untrusted clients using a certificate.

Dedicated Administrator Connection

Though not an authentication type itself, the Dedicated Administrator Connection (DAC) does have authentication restrictions upon it, so I'll discuss it here. The DAC is a new feature of SQL Server 2005 that was created to address a serious problem in earlier versions of SQL Server: a query or process consuming all of the resources, thereby preventing a new connection from being established. In this situation a DBA would be unable to log on to SQL Server to determine what was the runaway query/process and be able to stop it. Enter the DAC.

The DAC is an administrator-only connection that SQL Server maintains for issues like the one just described. It is a TCP endpoint but with certain restrictions. First, only a member of the sysadmin fixed server role can use this connection. This connection was intended for administrator to be able to log in to SQL Server, attempt to diagnose the performance problem, and return SQL Server to a responsive state for other clients. Second, only one login at a time is allowed to use this connection. If someone were to attempt to make a second connection, they would receive an error. Third, what can be done through this connection is extremely limited. Parallel commands or queries are prohibited (queries that either have a high-enough cost for SQL Server to use parallelism or by their very nature are considered parallel such as BACKUP/RESTORE). Long running or memory intensive queries may fail because this connection doesn't have much memory assigned to it. And finally, by default the DAC only listens locally (meaning you'll need to log on to the server and establish a connection from that session), though it can be configured to listen remotely. You can do this either through the Surface Area Configuration Tool or the sp_configure stored procedure. In the latter case, use the remote admin connections option:

```
EXEC sp_configure 'remote admin connections', 1;
GO
RECONFIGURE
GO
```

To disable remote access to the DAC, execute the following:

```
EXEC sp_configure 'remote admin connections', 0;
GO
RECONFIGURE
GO
```

You can connect to the DAC either by using SQLCMD or another tool that supports and understands the DAC interface (such as SQL Server Management Studio). If you're using SQLCMD, you simply need to add the -A (Administrator) switch. For instance: SQLCMD -A. This attempts to use Windows Authentication to connect as the locally logged on user. For SQL Server Management Studio, before the server name, add ADMIN: to specify you want to make an administrator connection. For instance, use ADMIN:myserver.mydomain.com to log on to the DAC of myserver.mydomain.com (see Figure 22.2).

Figure 22.2 Establishing a DAC Using SQL Server Management Studio

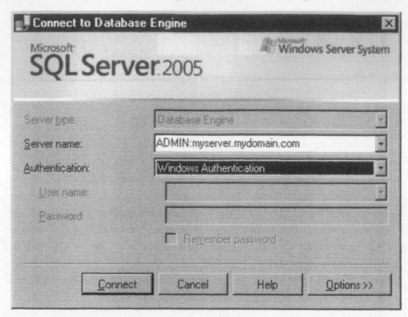

Shortcut…

DAC and SQL Server Express

SQL Server Express versions of SQL Server are designed to minimize the amount of resources they require. As a result, the DAC for a SQL Server Express instance will *not* be enabled unless you configure it to start with a specific trace flag, 7806.

Configuring Kerberos Support for Your SQL Server

Configuring Kerberos support for SQL Server is not as difficult as it might at first seem. In most cases SQL Server represents the last link in the Kerberos chain, meaning that as long as the Service Principal Names (SPNs) are set up correctly, your SQL Server will support Kerberos authentication. More detailed configuration steps are required in order to support Kerberos delegation, especially constrained delegation in Windows Server 2003 Active Directory. Kerberos delegation is usually an issue for web applications, such as the case with SQL Server Reporting Services when the web portion is installed on a different server than the database engine.

Basic Concepts of Kerberos Support

In order to configure Kerberos properly, you must first know a couple of things about your SQL Server configuration:

- The service account SQL Server is running under

- The TCP port SQL Server is listening on

- Whether or not your SQL Server is a clustered instance

NOTE

Kerberos works only with TCP. HTTP is built upon the TCP protocol, therefore, an HTTP endpoint can also use Kerberos authentication. However, the other built-in endpoints (Shared Memory, Named Pipes, and VIA) cannot use Kerberos. Therefore, if you need Kerberos authentication support, ensure your clients are connecting over TCP/IP.

SQL Server Service Account

The first thing to determine is the service account under which SQL Server is running. In order for Kerberos to be supported, SQL Server must either be running under a domain user account or the Local System or Network Service account. If a domain user account is being used, the SPNs must be configured under it. Otherwise, the SPNs must be configured under the computer account in the Active Directory domain. The easiest way to determine this is via SQL Server Configuration Manager:

1. In the left pane, expand SQL Server Configuration Manager (Local).

2. In the left pane, click **SQL Server 2005 Services**.

3. In the right pane, note the value for the *Log On As* column for the SQL Server instance.

BEST PRACTICES ACCORDING TO MICROSOFT

Microsoft recommends against the use of either the local System account or the Network Service account. In the case of the local System account, this account has more rights than SQL Server needs. As to the Network Service account, Microsoft doesn't give a specific recommendation as to why to avoid it, citing that local or domain user accounts are preferred. The most secure connection is to use a local user account that does not have administrative rights. However, doing so will prevent Kerberos authentication from working. In order for Kerberos authentication to function, SQL Server must be running under a domain account. That domain account can be the computer account (which is why the local System account would work).

SQL Server TCP Port

Second, if dealing with the database engine, you need to know on which TCP port SQL Server is listening. This can be determined using SQL Server Configuration Manager. The steps to determine what TCP port SQL Server is listening on are:

1. In the left pane, expand SQL Server Configuration Manager (Local).

2. In the left pane, click **Protocols for (Instance Name)**.

3. In the right pane, right-click **TCP/IP** and select **Properties** from the pop-up menu.

4. Click the **IP Addresses** tab.

5. Scroll to the bottom where you can see the *IPAll* settings.

6. Note the *TCP Dynamic Ports* and *TCP Port* settings (see Figure 22.3).

Figure 22.3 Determining SQL Server TCP Listening Port

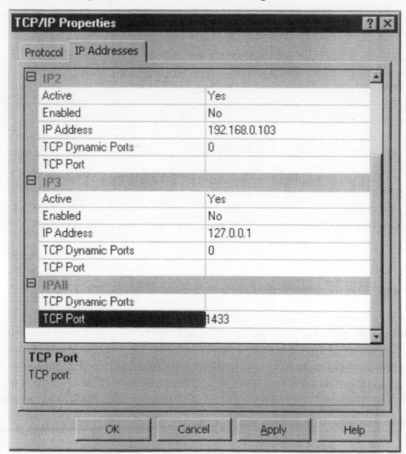

If the SQL Server is configured to listen on any dynamic ports, this has the potential to cause problems with Kerberos authentication. The reason for this is when configuring the SPNs for SQL Server, if SQL Server isn't listening on the default port of 1433, the port will need to be specified. If SQL Server is configured to use a dynamic port (which is the default setting for a named instance), SQL Server will attempt to listen on the port specified when it first starts up. However, if that port happens to be used by another process, SQL Server will change to a different port. If a client attempts to use Kerberos authentication, it's going to see the port mismatch and Kerberos authentication will fail. Therefore, it is best to ensure SQL Server is using static ports. If your SQL Server is using dynamic ports, here's how to change that (starting from the *IPAll* section).

To configure SQL Server to use a static TCP port, follow these steps:

1. Determine what port you want SQL Server to listen on. If SQL Server is using a dynamic port, you can choose to use that value.

2. Erase any entry for *TCP Dynamic Ports*.

3. Enter the appropriate port number for *TCP Port*.

4. Click **OK** to accept the settings.

5. Click **OK** to the message box indicating the settings won't take effect until SQL Server is restarted.

6. Stop and restart SQL Server.

The SETSPN.EXE Utility

The SETSPN.EXE utility first came with the Windows 2000 Server Resource Kit but is also found in the support tools for Windows Server 2003. If your SQL Server is using the local System account, you likely won't need the SETSPN.EXE utility except to verify the SPNs are set up correctly. In this particular case you should issue the following command to verify that is the case:

```
Setspn -L <server/user name>
```

You should get back something similar to:

```
Registered ServicePrincipalNames for <Distinguished Location of Server>:
MSSQLSvc/myserver.mydomain.com:1433
```

The Service Principal Name consists of two main parts separated by a /. The first part details what the service is. In this case the service is MSSQLSvc, which means Microsoft SQL Server. The second part of the Service Principal Name is how that service is named. In this case, the Microsoft SQL Server service is running on a server called myserver.mydomain.com, which listens on port 1433.

If SQL Server is not running as the local System account, the Service Principal Names will need to be set. In order to do so, a domain administrator must execute the appropriate command using the SETSPN utility. In the next couple of sessions I'll cover how to do so for both TCP and HTTP endpoints.

Configuring Kerberos for an HTTP Endpoint

When dealing with an HTTP endpoint, the service with respect to the SPN is naturally HTTP. If the service account for SQL Server is the local System account, the SPN should be registered automatically. However, if a domain user service account is used, a domain admin will need to set the SPN. Here's how:

```
Setspn -A HTTP/<Server Name> <Domain>\<Service Account>
Setspn -A HTTP/<Fully Qualified Domain Name>\<Domain><Service Account>
```

For instance, let's say we have a server called MyServer. SQL Server is running on this server and its service account is a domain user account: MyDomain\MyServiceAccount. The domain name (from a DNS perspective) is mydomain.com. The two SETSPN commands we'd execute to create the appropriate SPNs are:

```
Setspn -A HTTP/MyServer MyDomain\MyServiceAccount
Setspn -A HTTP/MyServer.MyDomain.com MyDomain\MyServiceAccount
```

It is important to add SPNs for both the server name (MyServer) as well as what is known as the Fully Qualified Domain Name (FQDN). The fully qualified domain name is the name of the server and the domain name together. The domain name is the domain name for Active Directory, and it was specified when the Active Directory domain was created. In this case the FQDN is myserver. mydomain.com because that's a combination of the server name (myserver) and the domain name (mydomain.com). The reason it's important to include both the server name by itself as well as the fully qualified domain name is to ensure that however the client trying to make the connection asks Active Directory about the server, the appropriate SPN can be found. If the client just checks using the server name, Active Directory can locate the SPN and answer the client that everything is okay. If the client contact Active Directory and is looking for the resource by the FQDN, we'd also be covered.

With respect to this specific example, we have created the SPNs for the HTTP endpoint, but we want to check to make sure we did things right. To verify that the SPNs are configured correctly, use the –L switch again, but specify the service account instead of the server name:

```
Setspn -L MyDomain\MyServiceAccount
```

Configuring Kerberos for a TCP Endpoint

Configuring Kerberos for a TCP endpoint is much the same as for an HTTP endpoint, except you must remember to specify the port as well. For instance, if SQL Server is listening on port 1433 (the default port for a default instance), that should be specified. Again, a domain admin will need to run the following commands:

```
Setspn -A MSSQLSvc/<ServerName>:<Port> <Domain>\<Service Account>
Setspn -A MSSQLSvc/<FQDN>:<Port> <Domain>\<Service Account>
```

As an example:

```
Setspn -A MSSQLSvc/MyServer:1433 MyDomain\MyServiceAccount
Setspn -A MSSQLSvc/MyServer.MyDomain.com:1433 MyDomain\MyServiceAccount
```

And to verify, execute the SETSPN command again with the –L switch:

```
Setspn -L MyDomain\MyServiceAccount
```

Extra Steps with Clustered Instances of SQL Server

When dealing with a clustered instance of SQL Server, there are a couple of more steps required. The first one ensures that the network name (or NetBIOS name) for the SQL Server virtual instance is registered with Active Directory. In order to do this, the administrator of the cluster should ensure the setting *Enable Kerberos Authentication* on the *Parameters* tab for the Network Name resource properties.

If you have a TCP endpoint, you'll need to make sure a couple of additional SPNs are set for the SQL Server. They are the same as before, except without the port specified. Therefore, you have:

```
Setspn -A MSSQLSvc/<ServerName> <Domain>\<Service Account>
Setspn -A MSSQLSvc/<FQDN> <Domain>\<Service Account>
```

As an example:

```
Setspn -A MSSQLSvc/MyServer MyDomain\MyServiceAccount
Setspn -A MSSQLSvc/MyServer.MyDomain.com MyDomain\MyServiceAccount
```

Verification is the same as before: use the SETSPN utility with the –L switch.

Shortcut...

Troubleshooting Kerberos Errors

Troubleshooting Kerberos setup issues can be a very complex topic. Microsoft has produced a very good whitepaper on how to go about this process. To locate this resource, search for *Troubleshooting Kerberos Errors* on the Microsoft.com Web site.

Auditing Authentication Attempts

It is always a good idea at least to audit failed authentication attempts against your SQL Server. However, when first configuring an endpoint, it's not a bad idea to authenticate both successes and failures. That can often reveal whether or not a client is connecting and if the issue is with the application. In situations like these, more information is always better than less. In order to configure your auditing to a particular level, follow these steps:

1. In *Object Explorer*, right-click the SQL Server and choose **Properties** from the pop-up menu.

2. Click the **Security** page under *Choose a Page* on the left side.

3. On the Security page, select the audit level under *Login auditing* (see Figure 22.1).

4. Click **OK** when you receive the message box indicating the setting won't take effect until SQL Server is restarted.

As you might guess, we can verify our server's auditing level by using xp_loginconfig. The parameter to use is 'audit level':

```
EXEC xp_loginconfig 'audit level';

GO
```

As with the Authentication Mode, you'll get back a text string in the config_value column. The possible values are none, success, failure, and all. If you're interested in determining this information via the registry, the information is found in the following key:

```
HKEY_LOCAL_MACHINE\Software\Microsoft\Microsoft SQL
Server\MSSQL.x\MSSQLServer\AuditLevel
```

Like the registry key for Authentication Mode, there are several values that are possible. Table 22.2 lists the values and their meanings.

Table 22.2 Values for SQL Server Login Auditing

Key Value	Meaning
0x00000000 (0)	None
0x00000001 (1)	Success
0x00000002 (2)	Failure
0x00000003 (3)	Both Success and Failure

Understanding Granular Access

In security there are the 3 A's: Authentication, Authorization, and Accounting (or Auditing). Thus far in this chapter, we've talked about the first A, Authentication. It naturally follows that we should now begin our discussion on the second A, Authorization. Once a login has been authenticated, SQL Server is not done. It must determine what rights that login has—that's authorization.

SQL Server 2005 has a robust security model that allows for very customizable rights, especially when compared to its predecessors. For instance, in SQL Server 2000, server administration type functionality was rolled up into predefined fixed server roles. If a particular fixed server role (let's use serveradmin) had the permission you wanted to assign someone (such as giving a junior DBA the ability to execute SHUTDOWN on the SQL Server) but the fixed server role had more permissions that what you wanted to give out, there was no recourse. Either you didn't assign the permission or you lived with the fact that the role gave more permission than you wanted to be given out. In SQL Server 2005 this is no longer an issue. The granularity of permissions has been greatly increased, leading to the concept called Granular Access. That means that if you want that junior DBA to have SHUTDOWN permissions but nothing else that a serveradmin role has, you can simply assign the SHUTDOWN permission. However, in order to understand Granular Access, we must first start with the concept of principals.

Principals

In SQL Server 2005, a principal is a server login, a database user, or a role. Server logins can be Windows users, Windows security groups, or SQL Server logins. In previous versions of SQL Server the terms logins and users were used, but users was used to mean domain user, database user, a user of the SQL Server, and so on, and this could lead to confusion, especially if the context wasn't clear. In order to try and remediate that issue, Microsoft introduced the terms server principals for logins and server-level roles and database principals for database users and database-level roles (including application roles).

Principals are the "who" when we grant access. For instance, if we're talking about granting execute rights against a particular stored procedure, we have to define who is getting those rights. That's what the principal is for. Now that we know the who, we have to understand what we are assigning rights to. Those are *securables*.

Securables

Securables are simply any resource within SQL Server, to include the server itself, which can be assigned access. Some of these securables are containers that can contain other securables. These container securables are called *scopes*. The entire set of securables is a hierarchical structure that allows us to assign permissions at the correct level to grant the access needed and no more, in keeping with the Principle of Least Privilege.

If you are familiar with Active Directory, think along the lines of organizational units (OUs). Domains contain OUs. OUs can be assigned permissions, and this is often a way to delegate certain administrative tasks within Active Directory (such as the ability to reset user passwords). OUs can also contain objects such as user, computer, and group accounts, each of which can have their own set of security permissions assigned. Unless inheritance is intentionally broken on these objects, the actual permissions on them are a superset combining the permissions assigned at the OU level as well as the permissions assigned directly against the object. Securables work in a similar fashion.

The scopes within SQL Server are:

- Server
- Database
- Schema

Each of these scopes has its own set of securables. The Server securables are small in number:

- Database
- Endpoint
- Login
- Remote Binding
- Route

Note that the Database securable, one of the three scopes, is in the list of the Server securables. Therefore, permissions assigned at the server level (which are applicable to databases) are applied to each database. If we look at the Database scope, we have quite a few more securables. Some of the securables of interest to the discussion at hand are:

- User
- Role
- Application Role
- Schema

This doesn't represent the whole list of the securables in the Database scope. However, it gives us the ability to see the effect permissions assigned at the Database scope level can have. Note that just as the Database scope is a securable in the Server scope, the Schema scope is a securable within the Database scope. As a result, we can clearly see a hierarchy, even among the scopes that go from Server to Database to Schema.

Permissions

The securables represent what resources we can assign access to within SQL Server. However, in order to understand granular access, we must understand what permissions we can assign and what those permissions do. With SQL Server 2005 we have the following new set of permissions:

- CONTROL
- ALTER
- ALTER ANY
- TAKE OWNERSHIP
- IMPERSONATE
- CREATE
- VIEW DEFINITION
- BACKUP (or DUMP)
- RESTORE (or LOAD)

If you aren't familiar with the permissions from earlier versions of SQL Server, they are:

- SELECT
- INSERT
- UPDATE
- DELETE
- REFERENCES
- EXECUTE

Let's take a look at the new permissions in more detail.

Notes from the Underground...

Compact Permissions

There are additional permissions, such as SHUTDOWN, that are very specific with respect to what they do. Although they technically apply to securables, they aren't as broad in scope or use as the ones listed in this section. In order to see all the permissions in SQL Server 2005 and what securables they apply to, use the sys.fn_builtin_permissions system function. For instance, the following query will return all possible permissions:

```
SELECT * FROM sys.fn_builtin_permissions(DEFAULT)
```

CONTROL

Control is a permission that conveys all the benefits of ownership over a securable without actually taking ownership of the object. SQL Server resources like databases and schemas can have only one owner, but there are situations where you want ownership like rights given to multiple users. In this case, CONTROL is the appropriate permission to use.

Having CONTROL permissions means having all permissions over a given securable. It also means having the ability to assign permissions against that securable. Not only that, but given the hierarchical structure of securables, having CONTROL on a particular scope means having CONTROL access on any securables that are below that scope. For instance, having CONTROL access over a database means having CONTROL access over all securables inside that database.

ALTER

Although ALTER has been around in previous versions of SQL Server, what it applies to has been greatly expanded. ALTER gives the ability to change the properties, with the exception of changing the securable's owner, on a securable. If assigned to a scope, such as ALTER SCHEMA, it gives the ability to CREATE, ALTER, or DROP any securables under that securable. In the case of ALTER SCHEMA, this would be any table, view, stored procedure, function, or other securables within the schema.

ALTER ANY

ALTER ANY can apply either to server- or database-level securable. It does not apply to schema-level securables because the ALTER (without the ANY) already conveys the same rights. For instance, giving a principal ALTER TABLE rights gives that principal the ability to alter any table. The ALTER ANY permissions gives the ability to alter the properties of any securable of that type within the scope. For instance, ALTER ANY DATABASE gives the ability to change the properties of any database on the server. This allows access to be given across a given securable type without having to worry about reassigning permissions every time a new securable of that type is added.

TAKE OWNERSHIP

This permission allows the principal to take ownership of the securable. This permission doesn't change the ownership; however, the principal will have the ability to take ownership so long as it has this permission.

IMPERSONATE

IMPERSONATE gives the ability to act as another login or user. If a principal is granted the right to impersonate another principal, it can switch its execution context to the other principal. This is similar to using Run As at the operating system level. Previous versions of SQL Server allowed a member of the sysadmin fixed server role change execution context using the SETUSER command. However, other principals were not capable of changing context. In SQL Server 2005 any principal has the ability, if granted IMPERSONATE permissions, to change execution context.

CREATE

Like ALTER, CREATE has been around in previous versions of SQL Server. Also like ALTER, what it applies to has been expanded to include server- and database-level securables. Previously it applied only to schema-level securables such as tables, views, and stored procedures. For instance, the ability to create an endpoint can be granted using this permission.

VIEW DEFINITION

The VIEW DEFINITION permission was added to SQL Server 2005 because the newest version of SQL Server locks down the definition of objects like stored procedures and views. Previous versions of SQL Server had an information disclosure issue where any user with access to a database had the ability to view the definitions of any of the database objects. Even though these definitions could be encrypted, the majority of the time they aren't. As a result, SQL Server 2005 solves this issue by not allowing a principal to see an object's definition unless explicitly granted otherwise.

Is this permission very useful given that database administrators should already have the ability to view the definitions anyway? Yes, because there are cases where non-DBAs need the ability to see the definitions. For instance, in the development environment, QA personnel may need the ability to see object definitions to ensure design patterns and best practices are being followed. In a production environment auditors may need to check definitions to ensure that no unauthorized changes have occurred.

BACKUP

This permission is self explanatory. It gives a principal the ability to back up a database or log (each is a different permission). The fixed database role db_backupoperator has the ability to do both. There may be cases where you want to grant access only to one and not both. This permission gives such a capability, but it is likely a rare situation that you would use it.

RESTORE

Like BACKUP, this grants specific access to restore databases. By default, none of the fixed database roles short of db_owner has the ability to execute a restore statement. Though the RESTORE command is something most DBAs hold close to the vest, like the BACKUP permission, there may be cases where you want to assign it without giving out db_owner. As a result, it has been added to the permissions list for SQL Server 2005.

Managing Granular Access

We've talked about principals, securables, and the permissions themselves. Now let's talk about some best practices with respect to managing them. First and foremost, never forget the Principle of Least Privilege. Because of the potential complexities with SQL Server 2005's granular access model, it's very easy to take shortcuts, like giving CONTROL over a schema when a principal only needs CREATE permissions for stored procedures. This is an exaggerated example, but it illustrates the point that it is very easy to grant more rights than is absolutely necessary. A small weakness in a security model is usually an audit point at best, an exploited vulnerability at worst. Therefore, honor the Principle of Least Privilege.

Second, try to avoid assigning permissions to individual users (people). Seek to use Windows groups and SQL Server roles as the principals. The reason for this is that you have to assign permissions only once. Consider if there are two auditors in your organization. You grant the VIEW DEFINITION permission to both of these auditors as individuals. As your company expands, two more auditors are hired. Because the permissions were granted to individuals, you're now faced with reassigning permissions for these new auditors. Another example is when a user changes roles in the organization. For instance, a user transfers from Accounts Payable to Capital Markets. The two departments share some of the same databases but the permissions are different. If permissions are done on a person-by-person basis, this will be a tedious change for the database administrator. If, however, permissions were assigned to user-defined database roles, it's a simple matter of taking the user's database principal out of the role for Accounts Payable and putting that principal in the role for Capital Markets.

Finally, develop a plan with it comes to managing permissions. When permissions are managed on an ad hoc basis, permissions tend to become duplicated and/or violations of the Principle of Least Privilege begin to occur. By developing a plan (and having it reviewed) you can think about the possible scenarios and insure you've covered them with your security plan. As a result, you can also minimize permission duplication and you can ensure that no person has more permissions than he or she should.

Understanding Implied Permissions

Given the hierarchical nature of the securables, it is very easy to forget what a particular permission at a particular scope gives access to down the hierarchy. For instance CONTROL DATABASE gives permission to do anything to any securable within the Database scope (and as a result, any Schema scope, too). These kinds of permissions are called implied permissions and they can lead to violations of the Principle of Least Privilege.

Microsoft has foreseen this issue and provided a function called *dbo.ImplyingPermissions* to be able to trace what higher level permissions grant an implied permission to perform that action. For instance, if we're interested in what permissions grant the equivalent of CREATE TABLE, we would use *dbo.ImplyingPermissions* to determine that. Unfortunately, *dbo.ImplyingPermissions* is not created automatically in SQL Server 2005. You'll have to copy the source code for it from the Books Online topic Covering/Implied Permissions. However, if you have any question about what permissions might imply a certain lower-level permission, it's a good idea to do so on a development or nonproduction SQL Server.

Assigning Permissions

When it comes to SQL Server, there are three actions with respect to permissions to understand:

- GRANT
- DENY
- REVOKE

Let's look at each one. To give a principal access, we GRANT the permission. GRANT is therefore a synonym for assign. To prevent a principal from having access, things are bit more complicated. This is because, by default, if no permissions are defined, no access is granted. Therefore, if there are no GRANT permissions, a principal will not have access. However, if a security principal has received access due to its membership in a role and that permission cannot be removed (for instance, there are other members of the role who should have that level of access), the only option is to use DENY. DENY blocks access. It'll trump any GRANTs that are in place. If you're familiar with NTFS file system security, it's the same idea. As with the file system, the use of DENY should be rare. It's a solution when nothing else works. Otherwise, seek to remove the GRANT. If GRANT permits access and DENY blocks access, what does REVOKE do? Quite simply, REVOKE removes whatever has been set, whether it be a GRANT or DENY. Think of REVOKE as undo. It undoes what has been done, regardless of what it is.

When it comes to assigning permissions, there are two more terms to become familiar with. They are *grantee* and *grantor*. The grantee is the security principal to which the permission is assigned. The grantor is the security principal assigning the access. The grantor is there for audit purposes. It allows us to see who assigned a permission. If the permission was set incorrectly, we know who to go speak with. This is great in theory, but falls short in practice. Unfortunately, when permissions are assigned, it is usually a DBA who is a member of the sysadmin fixed server role doing the task. In this case, server-level securables will show the grantor as sa and database or schema-level securables will show the grantor as dbo. The DBA's actual login won't be shown as the grantor.

Now that we've discussed the actions around assigning permissions and the concept of grantee vs. grantor, let's step through how to assign permissions using SQL Server Management Studio:

1. In *Object Explorer*, locate the object to assign permissions against in the hierarchy. Some objects may be under the *Programmability* or *Security* folders.

2. Right-click the object and choose **Properties** from the pop-up menu.

3. Click on the **Permissions** page under *Select a Page* (see Figure 22.4).

Figure 22.4 Assigning Permissions to an Object

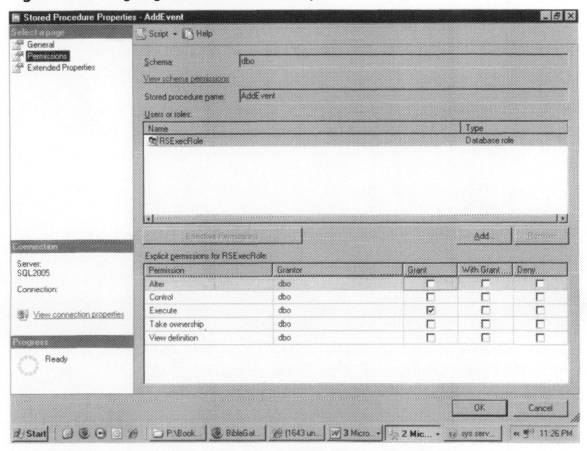

4. If the security principal isn't present in the list, click the **Add** button (otherwise go to step 6).

5. Enter the name of the security principal to manage permissions on in the **Enter the object names to select** text box for the *Select Logins/Users or Roles* dialog window and click **OK** (see Figure 22.5).

Figure 22.5 Select Logins/Users or Roles Dialog Windows

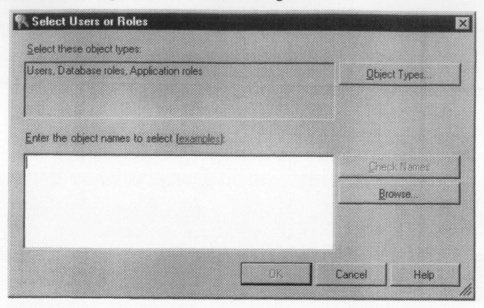

6. On the **Security** page, modify the permissions for that security principal as necessary and click **OK**.

Shortcut...

Managing Permissions through T-SQL

Permissions can be managed through T-SQL via the GRANT, REVOKE, and DENY statements. If you are quickly trying to lock down or manage access to your SQL Server, the GUI is probably the quickest way to do so. However, if you're managing source code, the permissions for objects should be included with the object definitions themselves. For instance, the code that defines a stored procedure should include the GRANT EXECUTE statements for the appropriate security principals. In this way, the proper permissions for the objects are maintained with the source code in your code repository system.

Summary

In this chapter we first looked at authentication in detail. We covered the two authentication modes for SQL Server, Windows-only, and Mixed, and how to configure SQL Server to use one or the author. We also looked at endpoints and the methods of authentication available to them. For HTTP endpoints we define, there is basic and digest authentication from the HTTP 1.1 specification as well as NTLM and Kerberos authentication. In addition, HTTP endpoints can use integrated authentication, which allows the client to choose between NTLM and Kerberos. We also looked at the authentication methods available for TCP endpoints we create for Service Broker and Database Mirroring Connections. We again saw NTLM and Kerberos authentication, but TCP endpoints can also use certificate-based authentication. We wrapped up authentication by covering how to configure Kerberos support for your SQL Server.

We also looked at the concept of granular access. In SQL Server 2005 many resources can have access assigned against them, more so than in predecessor versions. These resources are called securables. Logins and database users have been called principals and these principals can be assigned permissions against any of the securables. The securables model is hierarchical, with higher level permissions given implied access to lower level securables in the model. Several securables are containers containing other securables. We call these containers scopes and those scopes are Server, Database, and Schema. Because managing granular access can be a complex undertaking, it is best to develop a plan that tries to adhere to the Principle of Least Privilege and take advantage of assigning permissions against roles and Windows groups where possible.

Solutions Fast Track

Understanding the SQL Server Authentication Modes

- ☑ SQL Server has two authentication modes: Windows-only and Mixed.

- ☑ Windows-only, which does not permit SQL Server-based logins, is preferred.

- ☑ Third party and applications connecting from untrusted sources often force Mixed Mode.

- ☑ Try and consolidate applications that require SQL Server-based logins to be a subset of your SQL Servers and enforce Windows-only authentication on the rest.

Endpoint Security

- ☑ SQL Server 2005 has default endpoints installed for Shared Memory, Named Pipes, TCP/IP, and VIA. On a normal configuration, only Shared Memory and TCP/IP is enabled.

- ☑ SQL Server 2005 has the capability of creating HTTP endpoints for SOAP access and TCP endpoints for Service Broker and Database Mirroring Connections.

- ☑ HTTP endpoints can use Basic, Digest, NTLM, Kerberos, or Integrated Authentication.

- ☑ Created TCP endpoints for Service Broker or Database Mirroring can use NTLM, Kerberos, Negotiate, or Certificate Authentication.

Configuring Kerberos Support for Your SQL Server

☑ Kerberos authentication only works over TCP/IP and HTTP.

☑ You must know the service account and TCP listening port for your SQL Server.

☑ SQL Server should not be configured to use dynamic ports.

☑ A domain admin can use the SETSPN.EXE utility to set the needed Service Principal Names to enable Kerberos authentication.

Auditing Authentication Attempts

☑ SQL Server can audit successful logins, login failures, both, or neither.

☑ Changing what SQL Server audits for requires a restart of SQL Server to take effect.

☑ At a bare minimum, audit for login failures.

☑ Auditing successful logins can assist with troubleshooting as it will tell if the application is successfully connecting or not.

Granular Access

☑ SQL Server 2005 provides very fine-grained access over nearly every resource in SQL Server.

☑ Principals can be assigned permissions against securables, which are SQL Server objects and resources.

☑ The securable model is a hierarchical one with scopes at the server, database, and schema level.

☑ Granular access should be planned and should follow the Principle of Least Privilege.

Frequently Asked Questions

Q: Is it possible to switch authentication modes without restarting SQL Server?

A: No, unfortunately it is not. SQL Server reads the authentication only at start-up.

Q: How do I determine if my SQL Server is listening for (Shared Memory | Named Pipes | TCP)?

A: The best tools to use for this are the SQL Server Configuration Manager and the SQL Server Surface Area Configuration tool.

Q: I tried to configure my SQL Server for Kerberos using the SETSPN.EXE utility but keep getting a permissions error. What am I doing wrong?

A: Likely you are not executing the utility with an account that has domain admin privileges. If your organization does not permit you to have such privileges, check with someone who has such rights.

Q: Can permissions at the database or schema level carry down to individual objects such as tables and stored procedures?

A: Yes, they can. These are called implied or covered permissions. Please see the Permissions Hierarchy topic in Books Online. Also, you can use the ImplyingPermissions function, which is presented in the Covering/Implied Permissions topic in Books Online.

Chapter 23

Schemas

Solutions in this chapter:

- **Understanding Schemas**
- **Changes Due to the User-Schema Separation**
- **Designing Schemas**
- **Managing Schemas**

☑ **Summary**

☑ **Solutions Fast Track**

☑ **Frequently Asked Questions**

Introduction

Schemas are nothing more than containers with a fancy name. They are extremely important, though, because they are integral to the creation of object namespaces in SQL Server, as well as to the administration of ownership and privileges for those objects. Schemas are not new in SQL Server 2005. They did exist in previous versions as required by the SQL specification, but unfortunately they were implicitly tied together. In SQL Server 2005, the schemas and users have been separated. There are some very good reasons for this change including enhanced security and simplified administration. We will explore this change and its impact on security and administration throughout this chapter.

Understanding Schemas

The American National Standards Institute (ANSI) SQL specification requires implementing schemas in a database management system (DBMS) in order for that DBMS to be considered SQL compliant. Schemas are simply a collection of objects within a database. Throughout this section you will learn more about how and why schemas exist, how they have been implemented in previous versions of SQL Server, how this has changed in the latest version, and how the change will help administrators implement better security in databases.

The Schema as a Container

As I said before, schemas are nothing more than containers. Schemas exist in order to implement two rules of the SQL specification:

- All objects within a schema must have unique names. The schema forms part of that namespace.

- All objects within a schema must have the same owner. Objects in SQL Server can be a number of things, but the most common ones are tables, stored procedures, and views.

So, schemas contain objects and databases contain schemas. You can even go up another level, and note that a server instance contains databases. Together these containers create a namespace where the schema is one of the namespace boundaries. Table 23.1 shows the mapping between the SQL naming scheme, and SQL Server naming schemes.

Table 23.1 The ANSI SQL Specification and SQL Server Schemes for Creating an Object Namespace

SQL	SQL Server 2000 and Prior	SQL Server 2005
Catalog	Database	Database
Schema	Owner	Schema
Object	Object	Object

One way to conceptualize this is to think about a namespace as an address. If you want to access a specific database object, you need to know where that object is. How do you get there? The same is true for finding a house. You need to know that it is in a specific city, on a specific street, at a specific address. Similarly, you traverse the database namespace going from the large metropolis that is your database, to the street that is your schema, to the exact address, which is your object. Figure 23.1 shows us a map of a sample database.

Figure 23.1 A Namespace Map for a Sample Database

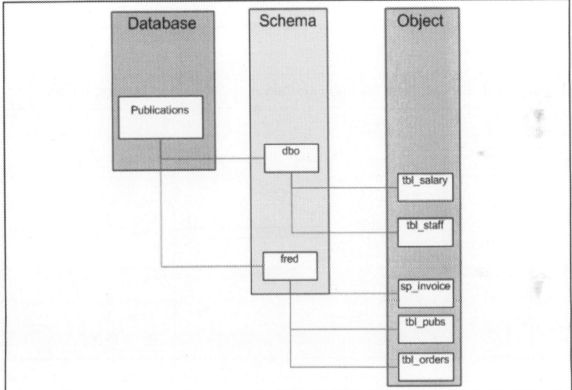

When you look at the namespace map in Figure 23.1 you can think of the table *tbl_orders* as being in the schema *fred*. In turn, the schema *fred* is within the database *Publications*. By extension, *tbl_orders* is in the *Publications* database. When you need to navigate to *tbl_orders* you would first need to go to *Publications*, then go to *fred*, and then head to *tbl_orders*. In order to reference this object, you can use the fully qualified name *Publications.fred.tbl_orders*. This is similar to saying that in order to get to Homer's house, you must first go to Springfield, then to Evergreen Terrace, and finally to #742.

It is important to remember that part of the namespace requirement is that all objects have unique names. When you look at the database you cannot have two discrete objects that both have the same fully qualified name. So, while it would be illegal to place two distinct objects named *tbl_orders* within the *fred* schema, you can indeed place both of these objects in two different schemas, as shown in Figure 23.1.

Schemas in Previous SQL Server Versions

In versions of SQL Server prior to SQL Server 2005, you were accustomed to an object's namespace containing the name of the object's owner. The general namespace syntax was *database.owner.object*, as noted in Table 23.1. The owner was used as the schema for an object. You might have seen an object named something like *Northwind.dbo.Orders* before. This object is in the sample database *Northwind*, with the default owner of *dbo*, and the object itself is the sample table named *Orders*. It is important to note that we referred to *dbo* as the owner of the *Orders* object, because in prior versions of SQL Server, the owner *was* the schema. Every time a new user was created in a database, a new schema was created as well. These entities were implicitly tied together. You can think of the schema as a shadow of the user. This concept is illustrated in Figure 23.2.

Figure 23.2 User and Schema Implementation in SQL Server 2000 and Prior

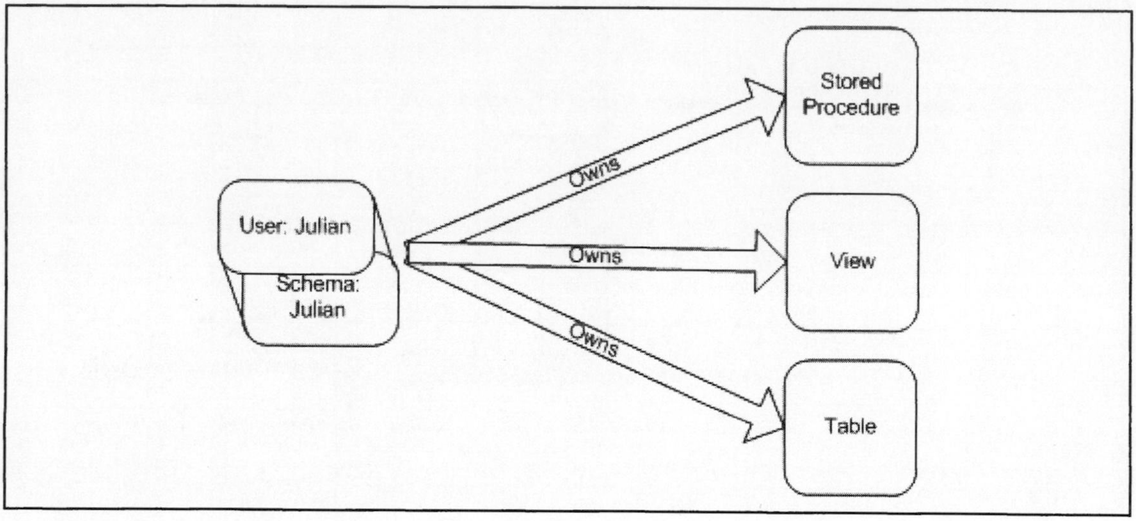

This implementation makes sense given the two aforementioned SQL specification rules. One says that an object must have a schema included as part of the namespace of the object. The other states that all objects within a schema must have the same owner. During the design of SQL Server, someone decided it made so much sense that they tied users and schemas together. If the schema is the owner, then you satisfy the rule that all objects within a schema have the same owner. As we shall see, though, while this idea seems logical, it can lead to problems with administration and security.

Generally, database administrators who were a part of the *sysadmin* role would create objects ensuring that they belonged to the *dbo* schema, so the line between the schema and the user was blurred. The SQL Server 2000 book that I have referred to while working with that version includes a table that maps the different parts of the SQL Server and SQL specification namespace, which shows that a SQL Server *owner* is simply a different name for what SQL refers to as a *schema.* In other words, the SQL specification called for schemas, which is the way it worked in SQL Server.

Again, schemas are required to have an owner. If you are familiar with the *CREATE SCHEMA* statement, then you know that the *AUTHORIZATION* attribute is a required parameter, and this parameter accepts a valid security account in the database as an argument. In the Books Online for SQL Server 2000 there is an entry under the Transact-SQL (T-SQL) Reference for *CREATE SCHEMA*, which lists the *AUTHORIZATION* parameter as the only one required. As we will see in the next section, the entry for this topic in the Books Online for SQL Server 2005 is different in that it no longer assumes that the creation of a schema is in any way associated with the user who creates it. Instead of naming a schema based on a user's name, you must specify what the name of the schema is in your *CREATE SCHEMA* statement.

Shortcut...

Shortcuts for Referencing Objects

Using the *Northwind* database example, SQL Server allowed for shortcuts in referencing objects in your applications and ad hoc queries. If you have already connected to the server and made *Northwind* the active database, then SQL Server allows you to simply call on *Orders* (without the prefix) in all your SQL statements. However, the fully qualified namespace to the *Orders* object is *Northwind.dbo.Orders*. This is true only when the object is owned by *dbo*, or when the user you are connected as owns the object. Again, your lives are simpler when *dbo* owns all the objects in a database in SQL Server 2000.

Problems That Arise

Now that you understand the implicit link between schemas and users, let's look at some of the problems that this link causes. The main problem is an administration and management problem. Let's say that you have a database set up to manage the sales team at a fictional real estate company, like the one shown in Figure 23.3. In this database, you have segmented off the client and sales data for each salesman into different schemas, because you wanted to maintain and manage the data per salesman. The sales team will use a single application to access the database and record/edit information, but the specific tables accessed will depend on the user that is logged into the application.

Figure 23.3 A Schema Diagram for the Mitch and Murray Realty Company Database

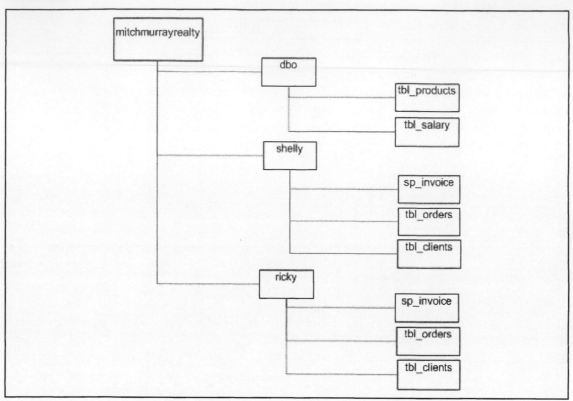

After some tough times, the user shelly is fired. The company would like to maintain this user's information, turning all of their clients and sales over to a new hire who will access the database as user dave. The problem is that the schema that this information is in is linked to a user that you need to delete. The result is that before you can delete the user account you have to add the new user to the database, and assign ownership of shelly's objects to dave. Then you can delete shelly. If you delete the user account first, then you will end up deleting all of the objects that shelly owns as well.

The problem does not end here, however. What if you have hard-coded into the application the fully qualified name for these objects? Once you have changed ownership of the objects, you have changed the schema and thus the namespace these objects are in. You now need to modify the application itself. Additionally, if you want to give ricky ownership of these objects, you will have a real problem. Recall that no two objects can have the same fully qualified name. That is exactly what will happen if you assign ownership of shelly's objects to ricky. You simply won't be able to do it, because SQL Server will not allow you to execute that transaction.

The way to avoid this situation was to adopt the best practice of having a System Administrator create all objects. Objects created by users in this role are placed into the *dbo* schema by default, and you can rest assured that you will never delete the built-in *dbo* schema. Obviously, the problem here is that you are encouraging the use of very powerful accounts or roles, when all you need to do is create a lowly object in a single database on a server. The principle of least privilege is out the window.

What about Your Security Perimeters?

Let's revisit the concept of a namespace and the schema as a container, which creates a boundary within that namespace. If you adopt the best practice of the day, and you've got all your database objects placed in the *dbo* schema, then you've basically rendered the schema useless for defining a namespace boundary. Since all objects are in the same schema, it really isn't much of a boundary is it? The boundary created by the schema is as large as the database itself. That second level in your *database.owner.object* namespace is meaningless. You may as well refer to all your objects as *database.object*.

However, the real problem is not one of naming conventions. This is a very serious security issue. In the field of information security you are all familiar with boundaries. You create boundaries, or security perimeters, around groups of entities that you need to apply equal levels of protection to. If you have a network that needs to be able to communicate securely, you place firewalls, proxies, routers, intrusion detection systems (IDSes), and other devices around it to segment it off from other networks. If you have a collection of files containing salary, performance review, and other sensitive information, you create a boundary around that by placing all of the files into a folder that you lock down. In the folder structure on the shared drive you create a security perimeter around the "HR" folder.

When you create these boundaries, you establish a place at which you can apply security controls that will protect everything inside of that boundary. You make your life simpler by avoiding having to apply those security measures to each single object within the boundary, and when you make your work simpler, you avoid mistakes that lead to compromise. In SQL Server versions prior to 2005, you were placing all of your objects into the *dbo* schema. The security perimeter around your database was the only one you could really establish with any effectiveness.

Schemas in SQL Server 2005

In SQL Server 2005, you have an entirely different scenario when it comes to schemas. Schemas are no longer linked to users. Instead, SQL Server 2005 provides a more pure implementation of the ANSI SQL concept of schemas, where the schema is nothing more than a container. It is not simultaneously a user, and it does not in any way imply ownership by any one principal. Figure 23.4 illustrates this separation of the user and schema entities in SQL Server 2005.

Figure 23.4 User and Schema Implementation in SQL Server 2005

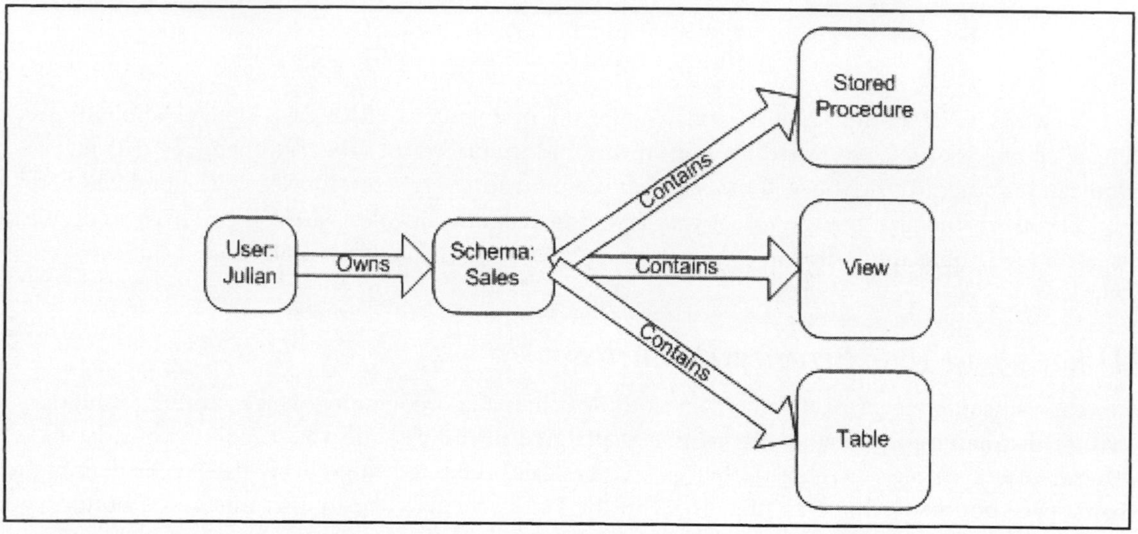

SQL Server 2005 gives youi the ability to get down to a more granular level with security implementations in your database. You can throw up walls around tables, views, and other objects so that you may apply uniform protections to the collections of these objects that require them. When you need to protect a set of objects within a database that contains sensitive information, you can place them into a schema and apply ownership properties and permissions to that schema that implement the security requirements that the set of data requires. You do not need to implement the security properties on each object in the set.

This brings the concept of scope within SQL Server to reality. We touched on scope when we discussed securables and principals in Chapter 22. We know that in SQL Server 2005 we have this hierarchy of securables that contains other securables that have a smaller scope. As you work your way down the hierarchy from server to database, you achieve a smaller scope, which provides a finer level of detail in implementing permissions. You no longer go from the broad, clumsy scope at the database level to the individual object level. The pure implementation of schemas in SQL Server 2005 is the mechanism by which you can achieve that interim layer of control over your databases that you need in order to produce an efficient, effective implementation of security controls.

Built-in Schemas

There are a number of built-in schemas included in SQL Server 2005, many of which correspond to built-in server roles. However, there are a few special purpose schemas. Table 23.2 shows the built-in schemas, a role that might be associated with them, the default owner of the schema, and any special notes.

Table 23.2 Built-in Schemas and Owners in SQL Server 2005

Schema Name	Default Owner	Notes
db_accessadmin	db_accessadmin	This role and its corresponding schema are a carry-over from SQL Server 2000 and earlier versions.
db_backupoperator	db_backupoperator	This role and its corresponding schema are a carry-over from SQL Server 2000 and earlier versions.
db_datareader	db_datareader	This role and its corresponding schema are a carry-over from SQL Server 2000 and earlier versions.
db_datawriter	db_datawriter	This role and its corresponding schema are a carry-over from SQL Server 2000 and earlier versions.
db_ddladmin	db_ddladmin	This role and its corresponding schema are a carry-over from SQL Server 2000 and earlier versions.
db_denydatareader	db_denydatareader	This role and its corresponding schema are a carry-over from SQL Server 2000 and earlier versions.
db_denydatawriter	db_denydatawriter	This role and its corresponding schema are a carry-over from SQL Server 2000 and earlier versions.
db_owner	db_owner	This role and its corresponding schema are a carry-over from SQL Server 2000 and earlier versions.
db_securityadmin	db_securityadmin	This role and its corresponding schema are a carry-over from SQL Server 2000 and earlier versions.
dbo	dbo	This is the default schema for all new users as well as for any principal belonging to the built-in server admin role.
guest	guest	This role and its corresponding schema is a carry-over from SQL Server 2000 and earlier versions.
INFORMATION_SCHEMA	INFORMATION_SCHEMA	This schema contains views that provide access to information from some of the system tables. This is useful;
sys	sys	This schema contains most of the default views and all of the default stored procedures in any new database you create. These objects are all system objects that allow you to access information about the structure of a database.

SOME INDEPENDENT ADVICE

Thorough testing is required. The migration to SQL Server 2005 will require some re-coding and testing specifically due to the change in how schemas have been implemented. Incorrect results may be returned if the application assumes that schemas and users are the same entity, but the schema may no longer be identical to the name of the user who owns it. Pay special attention to the way objects are referenced in your application when upgrading.

Changes Due to the User-Schema Separation

As we have seen, schemas are a foundational element of SQL Server. They play a part in the names of objects, they contain database objects, and they are securables. Due to the separation of users and schemas in SQL Server 2005, many functions, design rules, and other aspects of SQL Server that seem familiar have changed a great deal, and need to be re-learned. We cover several tripping points you might come across in this section.

New Flexibility with Ownership

For starters, while in previous versions a schema owner could not change since it was forever linked to a specific user, schema ownership can now change whenever necessary. That is not to say that object ownership could not change in prior versions, but it required the schema itself to change resulting in a change to the fully qualified name of any objects in the schema.

Also as a result of cutting the tie between users and schemas, a schema can contain objects owned by multiple users. Remember that in previous versions of SQL Server the object owner *was* the schema. Thus, you could not assign ownership to an object without inherently changing the schema. Now the schema is purely a container for objects, and it is a securable itself. So you can have three tables that are all owned by different users, and you can place all of them inside a single schema. You could assign ownership of the schema itself to yet a fourth user.

Additionally, schemas no longer need to be tied to users. Groups can be assigned ownership of schemas, meaning that ownership of the schema has even less impact on the objects within it. It is convenient to be able to drop the owner of a schema and add a new owner without impacting the namespace of the objects in the schema. It is even more convenient to be able to assign ownership of the schema to a group. Users can be added to and removed from the group as they come to or leave the company or as their roles in the company change, and schema ownership never has to be reassigned.

Using Default Schemas

Every time a user was created in prior versions of SQL Server, a corresponding schema was also created. Aside from being bonded to the user, it was also the default schema for the user. However, now that a new user does not result in a new schema, you must set a default schema for a user. Additionally, it is possible to set the same schema as the default for multiple users.

Changes to the Functionality of Familiar Concepts

In SQL Server 2000 and prior versions, the *CREATE SCHEMA* statement existed, but in reality it did not create a schema! Instead, it served as a method of creating objects that belonged to a specific user, and granting permissions on those objects all in a single T-SQL code block. In SQL Server 2005, you can create schemas in the pure sense of the word. You can still use the *CREATE SCHEMA* statement to simultaneously create objects in the schema and to grant permissions. The ability to execute the *CREATE SCHEMA* statement is still supported for now, but is deprecated and will not be supported in future releases.

Catalog views are different. The *sysobjects* system table was unaware of schemas, and thus incapable of supporting user-schema separation. Instead, you need to use the *sys.database_principals*, *sys.schemas*, and *sys.objects* system tables to query information about schemas, objects, and principals. Additionally, the old catalog views are now deprecated, and will be dropped entirely in a future release. Similar functionality with perhaps a little more ease of use can be gained from using the *INFORMATION_SCHEMA* views, so you will cover how to use these later in the chapter.

For applications that need to dynamically create objects, they can do so without needing to use *dbo* permissions so that the object would be added to the *dbo* schema. This allows us to more strictly implement the principle of least privilege.

SOME INDEPENDENT ADVICE

Do not unintentionally create new schemas. Do not use the *sp_adduser* stored procedure to create new users in SQL Server 2005. This stored procedure mimics the SQL Server concept of users and schemas by creating a new user according to your input, an identical schema, and assigning ownership of that schema to the new user. Instead, use the *CREATE USER* T-SQL statement. This statement creates *only* a new user, and nothing else.

Ownership Chaining

In some cases, a database object may access other objects sequentially in what is known as a *chain*. Think of each object as a link in the chain. When SQL Server traverses the links, it evaluates permissions differently than if it were accessing each object independently. These chains are not created as entities unto themselves, but instead arise from the way in which one object accesses another, which in turn accesses another.

Checking Permissions in an Ownership Chain

When checking the permissions through a chain of objects, the owner of each object becomes critically important. In fact, in some ways this is more important than who the user accessing the objects is. This is because when SQL Server evaluates permissions on a chain of objects, it begins checking each link on the chain by determining who the owner of that link is. If the owner of the object is the same as the owner of the first object in the chain who granted the user access, then that user's permissions on this object are not evaluated. SQL Server assumes that the owner of the initial object wanted to grant the same permissions on all objects he or she owns to that user. Obviously this can be an extremely dangerous assumption.

In Figure 23.5 you see an example of an ownership chain. Let's walk through the evaluation of permissions on the objects in this chain.

Figure 23.5 Traversing Ownership Chains

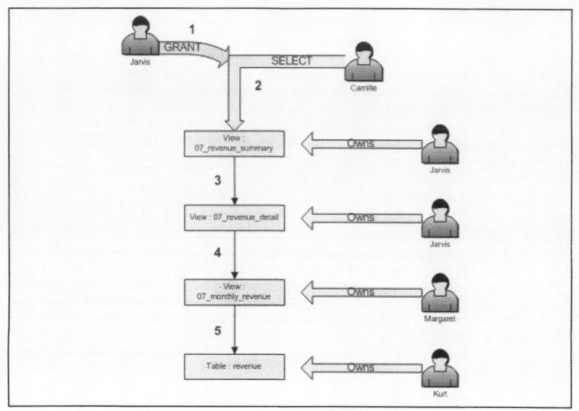

1. Jarvis grants *SELECT* permission on the *07_revenue_summary* view that he owns, to Camille.

2. Camille executes a *SELECT* statement on the view.

3. The *07_revenue_summary* view requires data in the *07_revenue_detail* view. SQL Server checks the ownership of this view, and since it has the same owner as the view that calls it, permissions on this view are not checked. The required data is passed up to the *07_revenue_summary* view.

4. The *07_revenue_detail* view requires data in the *07_monthly_revenue* view. SQL Server checks the ownership of this view, and the owner is different from the owner of the view that called it. Since Margaret owns this view, permissions on this view are checked fully. As long as the view has permissions that allow Camille to access it, the required data is passed up to the *07_revenue_detail* view.

5. The *07_monthly_revenue* view requires data in the revenue table. SQL Server checks the ownership of this view, and since Kurt owns this view, not Margaret, permissions on this view are checked fully. As long as the view has permissions that allow Camille to access it, the required data is passed up to the *07_monthly_revenue* view.

In SQL Server 2005, the process of evaluating ownership chains does not really change, but the process does become a little more complex due to the separation of users and schemas. In previous versions of SQL Server you could rely on the fact that all objects owned by user trogdor would reside in the trogdor schema. If a security administrator wanted to audit how ownership chaining would impact object access, they simply needed to look at which objects were in the trogdor schema.

In SQL Server 2005, however, you have the ability to change the owner of a schema. You also have the ability to change the owner of an object from a principal to SCHEMA OWNER. This means that the object belongs to whomever the schema it resides in belongs to, and this can change without anyone actually altering the object itself. Therefore, you must always be thorough when evaluating ownership chains.

Ownership Chains Gain Complexity in SQL Server 2005

In SQL Server 2005, however, the security administrator cannot assume that all objects owned by the user trogdor are contained within a single schema conveniently named trogdor. Instead, trogdor might own two schemas, neither of which matches the username. The security administrator now needs to track down which schemas trogdor owns, and might find the answer to be a schema named burninate and another schema named villagers. While trogdor may have granted the username bob access to an object contained in the burninate schema, bob could potentially access objects within the villager's schema as a result of an ownership chain.

It may seem as though SQL Server 2005 is providing a more dangerous and insecure platform than prior versions due to this added level of complexity with regards to ownership chains. However, let's return for a moment to our best practice from previous versions of SQL Server: make sure that all database objects are owned by *dbo*. Recall that there was generally no real boundary created by schemas in previous versions of SQL Server, because in most cases everything was owned by *dbo*. It quickly becomes clear that if *dbo* grants access to an object to a user, that the user can potentially access any object in the database through an ownership chain since every object is probably owned by *dbo*.

Obviously, it is critical to evaluate the impact of ownership chains when designing and building a database regardless of the version of SQL Server being used. In SQL Server 2005, evaluating ownership chains has become more complicated than in previous versions, but this complexity is due to an improved ability to create namespace boundaries through schemas.

Upgrading Existing Servers to SQL Server 2005

When you upgrade from prior versions of SQL Server, you need to consider how the new user-schema separation will impact the upgrade. Due to this fundamental change in how the ANSI SQL specification has been implemented, Microsoft designed a way to translate "owners" into the new pure schema implementation. As a result, when you upgrade from prior versions of SQL Server, all object owners from an existing database will be migrated to SQL 2005 as a user and as a schema with an identical name, and the user account will own the schema. For instance, the user Franklin will appear in your SQL Server 2005 instance as a user account, and a schema named Franklin will be owned by the user. Be sure to test your upgrade in a non-production environment prior to upgrading your production environment.

Designing Schemas

Now that you have a thorough understanding of what schemas are, how they function, and why you should care about them, it's time to take your knowledge from a conceptual level to the real world. When you begin building a database for an application, you always begin with the design. In previous versions of SQL Server, you may not have given a lot of thought to schemas when designing databases, since you didn't really have schemas. Now that you do, it's time to consider them during the design phase, and you must consider them from a naming perspective and a security perspective.

Best Practices According to Microsoft

Implement least privilege in your database. There are plenty of objects that should not be owned by *dbo*. By providing ownership to other principals, it reduces the need to give those principals access to the *dbo* schema and many of the objects they do not need access to.

Use logical groupings. If a collection of objects share similar properties, these objects should probably be placed into the same schema.

Designing the Namespace

The impact of schemas on an object namespace should be fairly obvious now that we have an understanding of how schemas are implemented in SQL. However, when designing databases, you should attempt to create naming standards for your schemas as you would implement naming standards for server names, database names, functions in your code, and most other technical implementations where you are naming entities. Just as it is helpful to know that deleting a user within any number of enterprise applications will always require us to call the *deluser* function, not the *deleteuser* function, you also should be able to rely on the fact that objects in your databases that contain employee salary information will be contained within the Human Resources schema as opposed to the HR schema. Standardization is a wonderful thing.

When designing the schema namespace, there are a few rules to keep in mind. The basic constraints on schema names are:

- Names can be up to 128 characters long

- They must begin with an alphabetic character

- Names can contain underscores (_), the at (@) symbol, the pound sign (#), and numerals

- They must be unique within a database

Designing Schemas for Security

More important for those of us concerned with securing SQL Server, is how to design schemas with an eye towards security. When you consider this facet of schema design, you should first look at the data. Data, especially the kind you'd want to store in a Relational Database Management System (RDBMS), has a natural hierarchy. It breaks down into different categories of data, and generally these different types of data need to be accessed by different groups of people.

When you consider the organic organization of the data that you are going to store, you should be able to see how permissions to the data should be applied. You should see that a subset of the data is highly sensitive and access must be restricted to specific privileged sets of people. In order to implement this access control, you need to create a principal for that group of people. You should also consider building a schema that will contain all of your database objects that store or process this sensitive data.

Considering Security throughout the System Development Life Cycle

To make this a serious discussion of security, we need to consider how schemas impact your ability to perform everyday management tasks such as assigning permissions. We also need to consider some of the concepts that come with a mature development process. A mature development process will have a robust System Development Life Cycle (SDLC) (sometimes referred to as Life Cycle Management [LCM]) structure in place. One piece that is often left out of the SDLC discussion is security, which is really unfortunate.

Security is not something that can be "bolted on" after the fact, if there is any hope for it to be done properly. Security must be considered at every phase of the SDLC, especially during the design phase. After all, why should you expect that everything except security needs some planning and forethought in order to work effectively. Security is no exception to this rule.

Are You Rewriting Your SDLC Due to This New SQL Server Release Then?

Why are we talking about the SDLC in a section on using SQL Server 2005 schemas to implement security? The answer is that most of the features we are discussing in this book are enhancements and improvements that administrators will be able to use in the operational phase of their SQL Server deployments.

Permissions, roles, and encryption are critical tools you will use to secure your SQL Server 2005 deployments, and all of these require planning to be implemented properly. The unique aspect of schemas is that they support many of these functions, and are intertwined with the actual applications developed on these SQL Server platforms. Schema design will have an impact on the object namespace, and in turn this will impact how developers code their applications. Schemas support the implementation of different permissions and ownership schemes. In other words, you have to make sure that you get the design of your database schemas right before you can ever hope to get the rest of the application right.

So, don't plan on rethinking whatever SDLC is in place in your environment. Simply consider bringing security considerations to the table as early as possible in the process, and make sure that the topic of schemas is on the agenda. Schemas are a foundational part of SQL Server-based application development and security.

Managing Schemas

Schema management consists of a few basic tasks. Generally these tasks can be accomplished using either the SQL Server Management Studio (SSMS) Graphical User Interface (GUI), or by executing a T-SQL statement. Your T-SQL statements can be run in SSMS; therefore, either way you wish to do something you'll probably want to have SSMS open. However, in the following sections when I provide instructions for doing something in SSMS, I am referring to accomplishing the task through the use of the GUI wizards and dialog boxes portion of SSMS, not using it to execute your T-SQL statements.

Best Practices According to Microsoft

Simplify the complex. Minimize the number of owners for schemas so that you do not lose track of individual users who have ownership due to their membership in a group that owns a schema. Many principals may need access to a group of objects that can be provided through granting permissions, without the need to assign them ownership.

Apply permissions as high up in the SQL Server scope as possible. You will rarely want to assign permissions or ownership at the database or object level. The database level is too broad, while the object level is to minute. Therefore, it is appropriate in most cases to manage object security at the schema level.

In the following sections we will cover the following schema-related tasks:

- Viewing schema information.
- Creating a schema.
- Moving objects from one schema to another.
- Dropping (also referred to as deleting) a schema.
- Changing schema ownership.
- Setting permissions on a schema.
- Setting the default schema for a user.
- Changing the default schema for any new user that is created.

Shortcut...

Become Familiar with Transact-SQL

Most experienced SQL Server database administrators do not need a lecture on Transact-SQL. However, I have seen a lot of smaller development groups that need a database backend for some application, but do not have a veteran SQL administrator on staff. I will be encouraging these SQL Server neophytes to learn and use Transact-SQL throughout the remainder of this chapter, because using it will simplify anything you are doing, make the performance of your tasks more scalable, and allow you to save scripts in case you need to perform the tasks again in the future. Although this may seem like common sense to the more experienced database administrators, many new SQL Server users do not understand that Transact-SQL is a shortcut that they need to know how to use.

Viewing Schema Information

SQL Server 2005 stores a great deal of information in the *INFORMATION_SCHEMA* views. These are nothing more than tables that contain some background information on various parts of a database, such as the names of schemas, who owns these schemas, and user-defined objects. There are several of these views, but for the purposes of this chapter we consider only a few. In order to keep track of your database, it is helpful to query these tables from time to time. The specific *INFORMATION_SCHEMA* views that are of interest to us in managing database schemas are:

- *INFORMATION_SCHEMA.ROUTINES* This view contains information on user-defined stored procedures and other functions. Basically, any user-defined entity you might find under the Programmability node in your database should have a record in this view.

- *INFORMATION_SCHEMA.TABLES* This view contains information on user-defined tables and views.

- *INFORMATION_SCHEMA.SCHEMATA* This view contains information on all the schemas in your database, including the ones that are built in by default.

These *INFORMATION _SCHEMA* views become important to schema management, because of the way that schemas relate to securables. Schemas contain securables as we know, and the

INFORMATION _SCHEMA.ROUTINES and *INFORMATION _SCHEMA.TABLES* views contain basic information about those securables such as:

- The schema the entity is contained in.

- The name of the entity.

- The type of entity it is.

When you combine this information about the entities with information about the schemas they are contained in, you can use simple queries to determine a good idea of what exists in your database. This can be effective for several purposes:

- You can build a list of information about database entities to include in formal documentation.

- You can run the same "data call" at regular intervals to get a picture of what is changing in the database. This can be used as a form of auditing either for security or performance purposes.

- You can gather information you may need before implementing a change to the design of the database. For instance, you may need to move all objects from one schema to a new one, and need a comprehensive list of those objects first.

Using SQL Server Management Studio

The T-SQL we are going to cover is basic, and you cannot effectively use the GUI for these tasks. Please get a good book on T-SQL if you are new to the language. When you need to know who the owner of each schema in your database is, are you going to go through and expand all the nodes in your database, traverse each listing of objects with your eyes, write down all the different schema names you see, and then separately go into the Schemas node and check who the owners of those are? It could take you hours on a sizable database, and you are bound to make mistakes. With T-SQL, however, you can execute very simple statements as we'll see shortly.

Using T-SQL

So, T-SQL is the tool for the job, right? Well, let's see how easy and effective it really is. First, one of the basic things you want to do is establish what schemas are in your database. To do this you need to select from a single *INFORMATION_SCHEMA* view, as shown in Figure 23.6. Pretty simple, right? What do you get in return? In my sample database I would see the output shown in Figure 23.7.

Figure 23.6 Viewing All Schemas in Your Database and Their Owners

```
USE <database_name>
GO
SELECT SCHEMA_OWNER, SCHEMA_NAME
FROM INFORMATION_SCHEMA.SCHEMATA
GO
```

Figure 23.7 Viewing All Schemas in Your Database and Their Owners

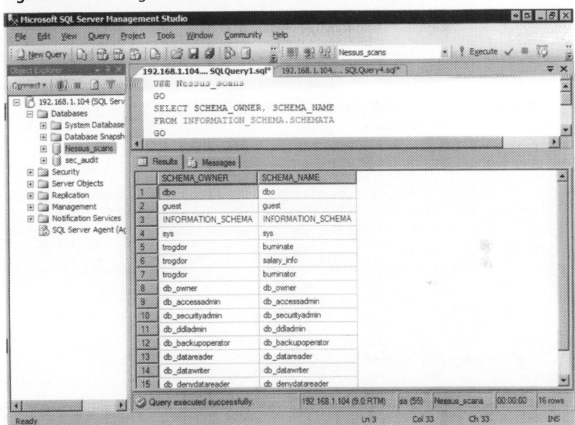

This might actually be too much information for us. Perhaps you only want to know about the schemas that are user defined. You know what the built-ins are so leave them out by using the query in Figure 23.8. This query assumes you haven't named any of your user-defined schemas starting with "db_." Your output would be shortened, so you would see only the user-defined schemas.

Figure 23.8 Viewing All User-Defined Schemas in Your Database and Their Owners

```
USE <database_name>
GO
SELECT SCHEMA_OWNER, SCHEMA_NAME
FROM INFORMATION_SCHEMA.SCHEMATA
WHERE SCHEMA_OWNER NOT LIKE 'dbo' AND
  SCHEMA_OWNER NOT LIKE 'guest' AND
  SCHEMA_OWNER NOT LIKE 'sys' AND
  SCHEMA_OWNER NOT LIKE 'INFORMATION_SCHEMA' AND
  SCHEMA_OWNER NOT LIKE 'db_%'
GO
```

Assume that you are not content knowing only what schemas exist and who owns them. You are tired of writing boring T-SQL statements that pull information from a single table. Well, you can view your user-defined schemas, their owners, and also check which objects exist inside of them. See Figure 23.9 and the resulting record set shown in Figure 23.10.

Figure 23.9 Viewing All User-Defined Schemas in Your Database, Their Owners, and the Objects They Contain

```
USE <database_name>
GO
SELECT s.SCHEMA_OWNER, t.TABLE_SCHEMA AS object_schema, t.TABLE_NAME AS obj_name,
t.TABLE_TYPE AS object_type
FROM INFORMATION_SCHEMA.SCHEMATA s
LEFT OUTER JOIN INFORMATION_SCHEMA.TABLES t
  ON s.SCHEMA_NAME = t.TABLE_SCHEMA
WHERE s.SCHEMA_OWNER NOT LIKE 'dbo' AND
  s.SCHEMA_OWNER NOT LIKE 'guest' AND
  s.SCHEMA_OWNER NOT LIKE 'sys' AND
  s.SCHEMA_OWNER NOT LIKE 'INFORMATION_SCHEMA' AND
  s.SCHEMA_OWNER NOT LIKE 'db_%'
UNION
SELECT s.SCHEMA_OWNER, r.ROUTINE_SCHEMA AS object_schema, r.ROUTINE_NAME AS obj_
name, r.ROUTINE_TYPE AS object_type
FROM INFORMATION_SCHEMA.SCHEMATA s
LEFT OUTER JOIN INFORMATION_SCHEMA.ROUTINES r
  ON s.SCHEMA_NAME = r.ROUTINE_SCHEMA
WHERE s.SCHEMA_OWNER NOT LIKE 'dbo' AND
  s.SCHEMA_OWNER NOT LIKE 'guest' AND
  s.SCHEMA_OWNER NOT LIKE 'sys' AND
  s.SCHEMA_OWNER NOT LIKE 'INFORMATION_SCHEMA' AND
  s.SCHEMA_OWNER NOT LIKE 'db_%'
GO
```

Figure 23.10 Viewing All User-Defined Schemas in Your Database, Their Owners, and the Objects They Contain

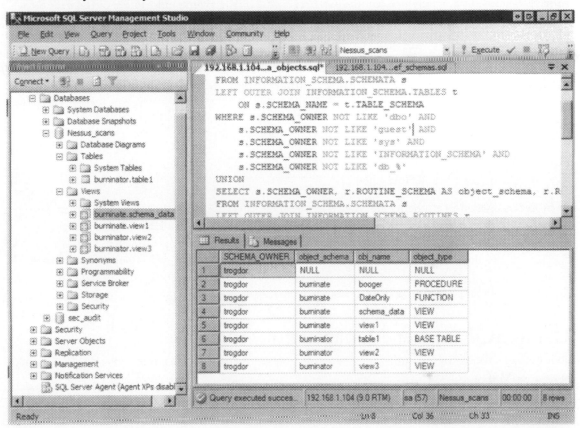

The first and second *SELECT* statements are identical aside from needing to switch out the word *TABLE* for *ROUTINE*. Also, if you like you can add a *CREATE VIEW view_name AS* statement above the first *SELECT* statement, and have a new view that just shows you what you want. Then, all you'd need to do is *SELECT ★ FROM view_name* to get the same output. In the end you'll avoid the mistakes of manually going through and attempting to catalog everything with your eyes and a GUI, and you can fairly easily combine data from different sources when necessary.

Creating a Schema

In SQL Server 2005, when you use the *CREATE SCHEMA* command, *AUTHORIZATION* is not the only required parameter. You should also specify the name of the schema you are creating. This is because the names of schemas are not assumed to be identical to user names. *CREATE SCHEMA* statements that do not provide the schema name are permitted for backward compatibility only.

Here are some ground rules for schema security:

- Each schema can have only one principal as the owner. Since a principal can be a group, you can assign multiple users as the owner using a group.

- A single user can own multiple schemas.

- Each user has a default schema.

Objects created in a schema are owned by the schema owner by default, not by the user who created the object. A user can create objects in a schema if they have the *ALTER SCHEMA* permission on the schema. They do not need to be assigned ownership of the schema to do so. Again, least privilege is possible here. You can allow users in the finance department to create tables in the *finance_dept* schema without giving them rights that should be reserved for the Director of the Office of Finance or for database administrators.

Using SQL Server Management Studio

The following directions include the basic navigation required to get to the SQL Server Management Studio (SSMS).

1. Open SSMS by clicking **Start | All Programs | Microsoft SQL Server 2005 | SQL Server Management Studio.**

2. Enter the appropriate credentials for the server you wish to connect to.

3. Expand the **Databases** node in the Object **Explorer** (this is the left pane in the default configuration of the SSMS).

4. Expand the ***database_name*** node where *database_name* is the name of the database you want to work in.

5. Expand the **Security** node under the database you want to create the new schema in.

6. Right-click the **Schemas** node, and you will see a **New Schema** option, as shown in Figure 23.11.

Figure 23.11 Navigating to the New Schema Command in SSMS

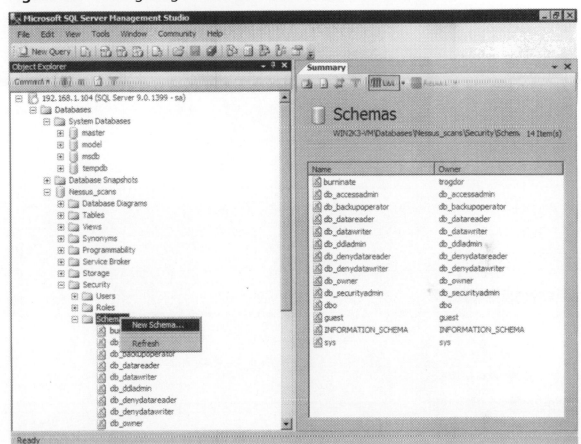

7. Click **New Schema** which will open the **Schema – New** dialog box, as shown in Figure 23.12.

8. Type a name for the schema in the **Schema name** field, and the account or role name of the owner in the **Schema owner** field. If you do not know the exact name of the principal you wish to assign ownership to, you can click the **Search** button to find the principal.

Figure 23.12 The New Schema Dialog Box

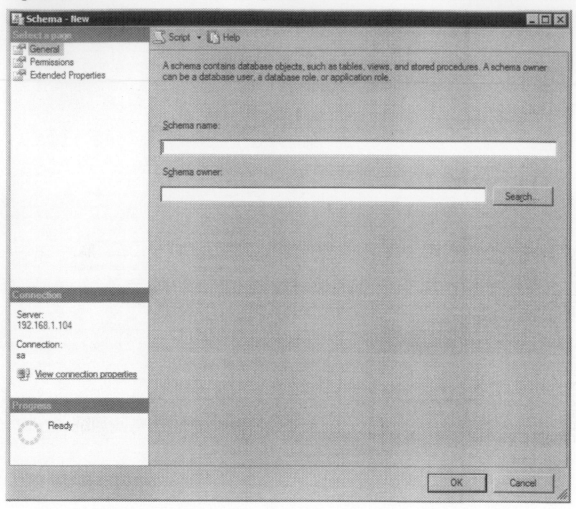

9. When you click **Search**, the **Search Roles and Users** dialog box will open.

10. Click the **Object Types** button to select the types of principals (Users, Database Roles, or Application Roles) you wish to search through, and then click **Browse** to open the **Browse for Objects** dialog box, as shown in Figure 23.13.

Figure 23.13 The Search Roles and Users Dialog Box

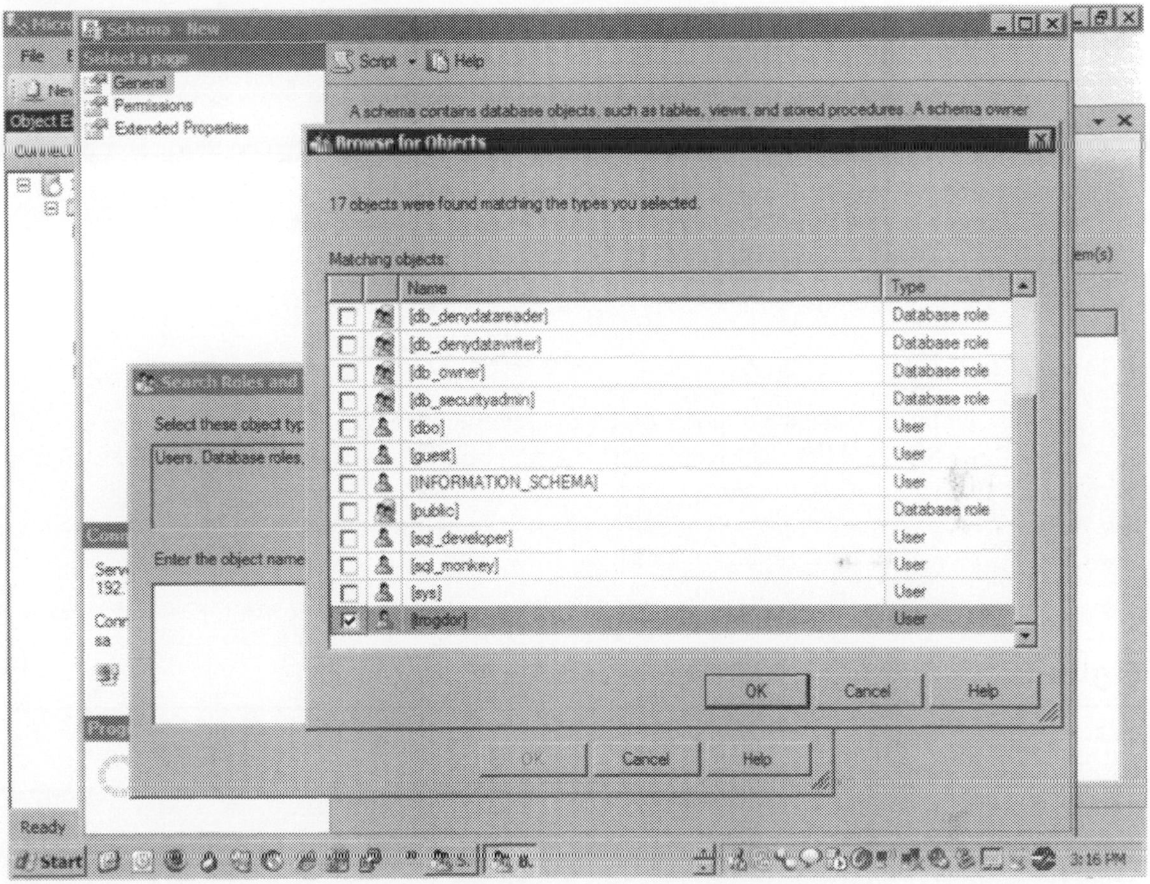

11. Select the principal you wish to assign ownership to and click **OK**.

12. Click **OK** again to return to the **Schema – New** dialog box where your principal selection will be shown in the **Schema owner** field.

13. On the left side of the dialog box you can select the **Permissions** page to modify the permissions on the new schema as you create it. More detail on using SSMS to modify permissions is provided in the "Alter Schema" section.

14. Click **OK** to create the schema. The new schema will appear under the **Schemas** node in your database.

> **SOME INDEPENDENT ADVICE**
>
> ___
>
> ***Each schema can have only one owner.*** You'll notice that the **Browse for Objects** dialog box allows you to select as many principals as you want. You can successfully add them all to the **Search Roles and Users** dialog box, and then click **OK** to set them as the owners without receiving an error message. However, only the first principal will appear in the **New Schema** dialog box in the **Schema owner** field.

Using T-SQL

For anyone accustomed/addicted to using a GUI to perform administrative tasks, I suggest you get a good book on T-SQL and become familiar with the language. There is very little you will do with SQL Server that you will want to use a GUI for. Creating a schema is a great example of this. All of the activity clicking, typing in names, and searching you did in the last section can be accomplished with the block of code shown in Figure 23.14.

Figure 23.14 Creating a New Schema with T-SQL

```
USE <database_name>
GO
CREATE SCHEMA schema_name AUTHORIZATION owner_name
GO
```

That's it. I couldn't make this any simpler. The funny thing is, the more you try to do when creating the schema, the easier it gets, and some things that are not possible in the GUI are quite easy in T-SQL. For example, while you can assign permissions to the schema at the time of creation using the GUI, you cannot simultaneously create objects within the schema. This requires a different dialog box to run. So you would have to run the new schema function and the new object function, and then run yet a third function to place the object into the schema. Lastly, you can even create multiple objects all at once in your *CREATE SCHEMA* statement. Figure 23.15 shows a block of code that will accomplish this:

1. Create a new schema named *burninator* with the owner *trogdor*.
2. Create a new table named *table1*.
3. Create a new view named *view1* based on *table1*.
4. Grant *SELECT* permissions on *view1* to the public database role.

Figure 23.15 Creating a New Schema, Two Objects, and Granting Permissions with T-SQL

```
USE <database_name>
GO
CREATE SCHEMA [burninator] AUTHORIZATION [trogdor]
GRANT SELECT on view1 TO public
CREATE VIEW view1(c1, c2) AS SELECT c1, c2 from table1
CREATE TABLE table1(c1 int, c2 varchar)
GO
```

Moving Objects

You may need to move objects from one schema to another at some point. We know that with the new user-schema separation of SQL Server 2005, that assigning a new owner and changing permissions are not valid reasons to move objects. More than likely, your need to move objects will be a result of either the need to accommodate some requirement from the development team, or because a subset of the objects in a schema needs to be segmented off into a new, more fine-grained security perimeter.

There are a few rules and caveats to consider when moving objects:

- You can move objects from one schema to another schema *within the same db*.

- When moving objects to a new schema, all permissions are dropped.

- If a specific user or role owns the object, this will be retained; if ownership is set to SCHEMA OWNER then the new schema owner applies.

- To move objects you must have CONTROL permission on the object and ALTER permission on the destination schema.

- If the object has *EXECUTE AS OWNER* specification, and the owner is set to *SCHEMA OWNER*, then you must also have *IMPERSONATION* permissions on the owner of the destination schema.

Using SQL Server Management Studio

1. Expand the **Databases** node in the Object **Explorer** (this is the left pane in the default configuration of the SSMS).

2. Expand the **database_name** node, where *database_name* is the name of the database you want to work in.

3. Expand the **object_type** node, where *object_type* is the type of object (table, view, function, stored procedure, and so on) you wish to move.

4. Right-click *object_name*, where *object_name* is the name of the object you want to move, and select **Modify**.

5. In the **Properties** pane on the right side of SSMS you will see a heading titled **Identity** with an entry underneath named **Schema**.

6. Click the drop-down list of existing schemas, and select the destination schema you want to send the object to, as shown in Figure 23.16.

Figure 23.16 Selecting the Destination Schema for an Object

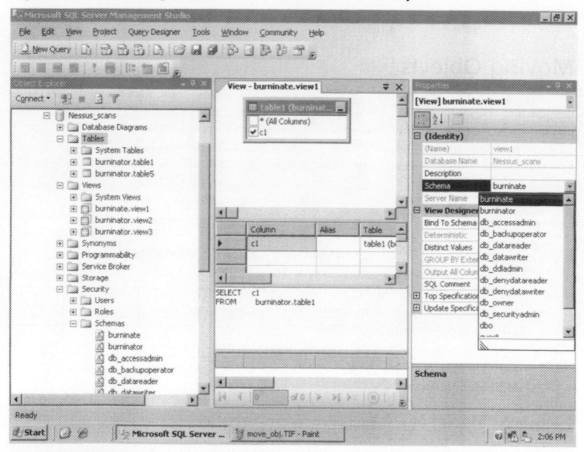

7. As soon as you select a destination schema for the object, SSMS will pop up a warning message notifying you that the permissions on the object will be dropped. Select **Yes** to continue.

8. Click **File | Save** *object_type – object_name* to execute the object move you just planned.

Using T-SQL

How many times do you need to see fewer than 10 words replace numerous button clicks, pop-up windows, dialog boxes, and screen navigation, before you get the idea that T-SQL is better for the job? *ALTER SCHEMA dest_schema TRANSFER src_schema.obj* will move a single object from one schema to another. When you need to move several objects, you may encounter some difficulty at first. *ALTER SCHEMA* does not seem to accept either wildcards or variables for the *src_schema.obj* parameter. I got around this by creating a bit of code that will move multiple objects by making the entire *ALTER TABLE* statement a variable and using the *EXEC* command to execute it. I simply loop through all the objects I want to move, creating a different *ALTER SCHEMA* statement for each (see Figure 23.17).

Figure 23.17 Moving Multiple Objects with ALTER SCHEMA

```
USE <database_name>
GO
DECLARE @objectName char(100),
  @SQL char(100)
SET @objectName = 'a'
WHILE NOT (@objectName = '')
BEGIN
  SET @objectName = (SELECT TOP 1 TABLE_NAME FROM INFORMATION_SCHEMA.TABLES WHERE
TABLE_SCHEMA = 'burninator')
  SET @SQL = 'ALTER SCHEMA burninator2 TRANSFER burninator.' + @objectName
  EXEC (@SQL)
END
GO
```

Dropping Schemas

A schema may need to be dropped for any number of reasons. You generally want to create boundaries around data using schemas, and those boundaries give us something you can apply security controls to in the form of permissions. Perhaps the roles and functions in an application your database is supporting have been reorganized. Or maybe the type of data you are storing has changed somewhat. These situations may require some modifications to be made to the schemas you're using.

Whatever the reason is, there are a few rules to keep in mind when dropping schemas. To drop a schema you must have *CONROL* permission on the schema. Also, you need to move all of the objects in the schema into a new schema. If the schema you are trying to drop contains any objects, then the drop operation will fail.

Using SQL Server Management Studio

1. Expand the **Databases** node in the Object **Explorer** (this is the left pane in the default configuration of the SSMS).

2. Expand the *database_name* node where *database_name* is the name of the database you want to work in.

3. Expand the **Security** node under the database containing the schema you wish to modify.

4. Expand the **Schemas** node, right-click *schema_name* where *schema_name* is the name of the schema you want to drop, and select **Delete**.

5. The **Delete Object** dialog box will open.

6. Click **OK** to drop the schema from the database.

7. If the schema you are attempting to drop still contains objects, you will see an error message similar to the one in Figure 23.18.

Figure 23.18 Error Message When Attempting to Drop a Schema That Is Not Empty

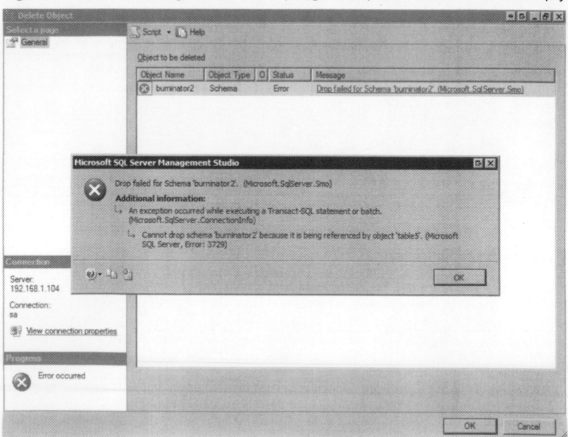

Using T-SQL

The T-SQL command is quick and dirty. Attaching to a database and executing a simple *DROP SCHEMA schema_name* where *schema_name* is the name of the schema you want to delete, will drop the schema from the database. Be careful when doing this, though, as it is an irreversible operation. Also, you may want to use some of the techniques we covered in the "Viewing Schema Information" section in order to be sure you are dropping the right schema.

You will encounter problems in trying to drop schemas that contain objects (see Figure 23.18). If you want to keep the objects but drop the database (as opposed to dropping everything), then you will need to move the objects first. We covered moving objects in the last section, and as you may have guessed you can crack this nut a lot easier with T-SQL than you can with mouse-clicking. If you want to move all the objects from the *burninator2* schema to the *burninator* schema so that you can then drop the *burninator2* schema, you can borrow the code from Figure 23.17 and just add a *DROP SCHEMA* statement at the end, as shown in Figure 23.19. Before you do anything like this, though, you need to be intensely aware of the following:

- When you move all these objects, the permissions will be dropped.

- When you drop the schema, you will not be able to execute any sort of Undo function.

Figure 23.19 Moving Objects Out of a Schema and Dropping the Schema

```
USE Nessus_scans
GO
DECLARE @objectName char(100),
  @SQL char(100)
SET @objectName = 'a'
WHILE NOT (@objectName = '')
BEGIN
  SET @objectName = (SELECT TOP 1 TABLE_NAME FROM INFORMATION_SCHEMA.TABLES WHERE
TABLE_SCHEMA = 'burninator2')
  SET @SQL = 'ALTER SCHEMA burninator TRANSFER burninator2.' + @objectName
  EXEC (@SQL)
END
DROP SCHEMA burninator2
GO
```

Changing Ownership

It is extremely likely that you will need to change the owner of a schema at some point. As we discussed earlier in this chapter, what was once an impossible task is now relatively easy. Whereas in previous versions of SQL Server you could only change ownership by actually moving the objects in a schema to a new schema, now you can reassign ownership of a schema without altering the object namespace. You may need to change the schema owner for any of the following reasons:

- The schema was owned by a user who has left the company.

- The schema was owned by a user who has changed roles within the company.

- The schema was owned by a group, but that group's role no longer requires them to have ownership of the schema.

- The schema owner cannot use the schema as their default schema.

Using SQL Server Management Studio

1. Expand the **Databases** node in the Object **Explorer** (this is the left pane in the default configuration of the SSMS).

2. Expand the *database_name* node where *database_name* is the name of the database you want to work in.

3. Expand the **Security** node under the database containing the schema you wish to modify.

4. Expand the **Schemas** node, right-click *schema_name* where *schema_name* is the name of the schema you want to reassign ownership of, and select **Properties**.

5. The **Schema Properties** dialog box will open.

6. Replace the name of the owner in the **Schema owner** field with the name of the new desired principal. If you do not know the exact name of the principal you wish to assign ownership to, you can click the **Search** button to find the principal.

7. When you click **Search**, the **Search Roles and Users** dialog box will open.

8. Click the **Object Types** button to select the types of principals (Users, Database Roles, or Application Roles) you wish to search through, and then click **Browse** to open the **Browse for Objects** dialog box open.

9. Select the principal you wish to assign ownership to, and click **OK**.

10. Click **OK** again to return to the **Schema Properties** dialog box, where your principal selection will be shown in the **Schema owner** field.

11. Click **OK** to save the change.

Using T-SQL

You can use the *ALTER AUTHORIZATION* statement to change the owner of a schema. The statement simply requires you to specify the name of the schema and the new owner as in: *ALTER AUTHORIZATION ON SCHEMA::burninator TO sql_monkey; GO*

Always remember that you can use this same statement to change the ownership of other objects such as tables and views. This can make the SQL statement from the last section more robust. When you move the objects to a new schema before dropping the old one, you want to make sure they are all changed to be owned by the user who owns the destination schema. You can add a line similar to *ALTER AUTHORIZATION ON OBJECT::<object_name> TO SCHEMA OWNER* to that same block of code to accomplish this.

Setting Permissions on Schemas

There is always a need to change permissions on objects throughout the enterprise. Schemas in SQL Server 2005 are no different. The applications your database supports will evolve along with the business requirements those applications support, and changes to the permissions required by different roles and groups in the application will need to be altered.

Whenever granting and revoking permissions, it is important to remember that permissions in SQL Server are hierarchical. As you move down the namespace from server to database to schema to objects, permissions granted at one level carry down to the levels below that. So, *CONTROL* permission granted at the database level gives the grantee *CONTROL* not only of the database, but also of the schemas and objects in the database. A listing of the permissions that may be granted on schemas is shown in Table 23.3.

Table 23.3 The Permissions That May Be Defined on Schemas

Permission	Description
ALTER	This permission allows the principal granted the permission to change the properties of a schema. When the *ALTER* permission is granted on a schema, it allows the principal to create, drop, and alter objects contained in the schema. This is similar to the *MODIFY NTFS* permission.
CONTROL	This gives the grantee ownership-like rights on the schema. The grantee effectively has all other definable permissions on the schema, making it unnecessary to grant any further permissions. The principal with *CONTROL* permission also has the ability to change permissions on the schema. This is similar to the *FULL CONTROL NTFS* permission.
DELETE	The grantee has the ability to drop objects contained in the schema. However, the principal with the *DELETE* permission cannot drop the schema itself.
EXECUTE	This allows the grantee to run *EXECUTE* statements on objects contained in the schema. For example, a principal with the *EXECUTE* permission could execute all the stored procedures contained in the schema.
INSERT	The grantee has the ability to insert content into objects contained in the schema. However, the principal with the *INSERT* permission cannot insert new objects into the schema.
REFERENCES	The grantee has the ability to reference the object using foreign keys.
SELECT	The grantee has the ability to view the contents of objects contained in the schema.

Continued

Table 23.3 Continued

Permission	Description
TAKE OWNERSHIP	This allows the grantee to assume ownership of the schema as well as any objects contained in the schema.
UPDATE	The grantee has the ability to update the contents of objects contained in the schema. The principal with the *UPDATE* permission cannot change the schema itself in any way though.
VIEW DEFINITION	The grantee can access metadata on the schema as well as any objects within the schema.

Permissions can be granted to any principal in the database. This includes any of the following:

- A database user who is mapped to a Windows login
- A database user who is mapped to a Windows group
- A database user who is mapped to a certificate
- A database user who is mapped to an asymmetric key
- A database user who is not mapped to a server principal
- A database role
- An application role

Permissions can be granted, revoked, or denied. When you deny permissions for a principal, you are explicitly prohibiting the principal from having that permission on the schema. Even if they should have the permission due to being granted the permission on an object higher up in scope, they will be prevented from exercising the permission on the schema which you are using the deny setting on, and the deny permission will filter down to lower objects.

On the other hand, revoking permissions simply removes either a granted or denied setting for the principal. Effectively, this allows all other inheritance rules to take effect without any intervening permission settings. When you revoke permissions, you will see any evidence of a permission setting disappear. The principal will have neither an explicitly granted or denied permission.

Using SQL Server Management Studio

1. Expand the **Databases** node in the Object **Explorer** (this is the left pane in the default configuration of the SSMS).

2. Expand the *database_name* node where *database_name* is the name of the database you want to work in.

3. Expand the **Security** node under the database containing the schema you wish to modify.

4. Expand the **Schemas** node, right-click *schema_name* where *schema_name* is the name of the schema you want to reassign ownership of, and select **Properties**.

5. The **Schema Properties** dialog box will open.

6. Select the **Permissions** page from the left-hand side of the window, and the **Permissions** page will open as shown in Figure 23.20.

To add a new principal with permissions, follow these steps:

1. Click the **Add** button.

2. Click the **Object Types** button to select the types of principals (Users, Database Roles, or Application Roles) you wish to search through, and then click **Browse** to open the Browse for Objects dialog box.

3. Select the principal you wish to assign permissions to, and click **OK** to return to the Permissions page. Now the principal name will appear in the Users or Roles field, and available permissions will appear in the Explicit permissions for <principal_name> field. This is shown in Figure 23.20.

Figure 23.20 Setting Permissions on a Schema

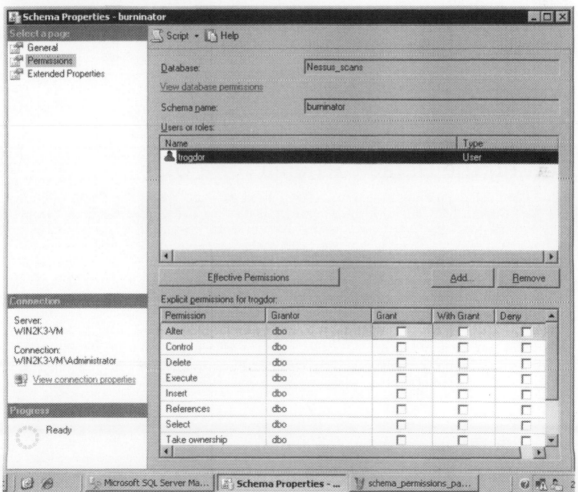

4. Click the checkbox for each permission you wish to set for the principal, and then click **OK** when you are done.

To remove an existing principal with permissions, follow these steps:

1. Select the principal name in the Users or Roles field

2. Click the **Remove** button.

3. Click **OK** when you are done.

To alter the permissions for an existing principal, follow these steps:

1. Select the principal name in the Users or Roles field.

2. Click the **checkbox** for each permission you wish to set or unset for the principal, and then click **OK** when you are done.

3. Click **OK** to save the change.

Using T-SQL

Setting permissions using T-SQL is a fairly simple operation. Permissions can be set either by granting them, revoking them, or denying them. Appropriately, there are three statements that may be executed when setting permissions:

- *GRANT <permission> ON SCHEMA::<schema_name> TO <principal>*

- *REVOKE <permission> ON SCHEMA::<schema_name> TO <principal>*

- *DENY <permission> ON SCHEMA::<schema_name> TO <principal>*

Setting the Default Schema for a User

As we discussed, in previous versions the default schema for a user was identical to the username, and there was no ability to change this. Objects created by the user were created in the schema bound to the user, unless they were a member of the *sysadmin* role, in which case the object was created in the *dbo* schema. In SQL Server 2005, you can change the default user schema to any schema in the database, and objects created by the user will be placed into this schema automatically. As with previous SQL Server versions, the default schema is also used as the default search context for objects that are referenced only using the object name as opposed to the fully qualified name.

For any new user, if no default schema is specified, then the user is created with *dbo* as the default schema. It is interesting to note that SQL Server will allow administrators to set the default schema for a user to a schema that has not even been created yet. Also, when creating a user mapped to a Windows group, a certificate, or an asymmetric key, you will need to remember that you cannot assign a default schema to these users.

Using SQL Server Management Studio

1. Expand the **Databases** node in the Object **Explorer** (this is the left pane in the default configuration of the SSMS).

2. Expand the **database_name** node where *database_name* is the name of the database you want to work in.

3. Expand the **Security** node under the database containing the schema you wish to modify.

4. Expand the **Users** node, right-click **user_name** where *user_name* is the name of the user you want to change the default schema for, and select **Properties**.

5. The **User Properties** dialog box will open.

6. Replace the name of the schema in the **Default schema** field with the name of the new schema you wish to set as the default. If you do not know the exact name of the schema you wish to designate as the default, you can click the **Ellipsis** button to find the schema.

7. When you click the **Ellipsis** button, the Select Schema dialog box will appear.

8. Click **Browse** to open the Browse for Objects dialog box open.

9. Select the schema you wish to set as the default, and click **OK**.

10. Click **OK** again to return to the User Properties dialog box where your schema selection will be shown in the Default schema field.

Using T-SQL

In order to set the default schema for a user, you will need to use the *DEFAULT_SCHEMA* argument. If you are creating a new user, you will set the parameter in your *CREATE USER* statement, and if you are changing the default schema of an existing user, you will set it in an *ALTER USER* statement. Figure 23.21 shows an example of both types of statements.

Figure 23.21 Setting the Default Schema for a New and an Existing User

```
USE <database_name>
CREATE USER bob_sacamano
FOR LOGIN bob_sacamano
WITH DEFAULT_SCHEMA = humanresources
GO
USE <database_name>
ALTER USER bob_sacamano
WITH DEFAULT_SCHEMA = executives
GO
```

Summary

At this point, you should be familiar with the concept of schemas, and how their implementation in SQL Server 2005 is significantly different from previous versions. We've covered not only the implications for security resulting from this change, but also the impact the change will have on application development. It is important to understand this when your organization begins to discuss the upgrade to SQL Server 2005, because ample time will be required to plan for the upgrade. You will need to understand fully how the design of your database and the application residing on it will need to be altered.

Additionally, you need to consider points where changes are not required, but are strongly recommended. It is very likely that many organizations will plan for and execute an upgrade to SQL Server 2005 that does not take advantage of the enhanced security features which user-schema separation allows, such as implementation of least privilege permissions, creation of secure boundaries below the database level, and so on.

Solutions Fast Track

Understanding Schemas

☑ Schemas are containers for objects that allow us to group like objects together, apply uniform security protections to those objects, and implement granular permissions on objects.

☑ Schema names form part of the fully qualified name of an object. The four-part name of an object is in the format server_name.database_name.schema_name.object_name.

☑ In SQL Server 2005, schema and object owners can now be changed without affecting the object namespace and requiring developers to alter application code.

Changes Due to the User-Schema Separation

☑ User are no longer bound to their schemas as if they are their shadows. You can set the default schema for a user to basically anything you want or need to, and this includes setting it to schemas that do not exist yet in the database.

☑ The *sysobjects* system table is no longer recommended as a source of information on SQL Server objects. The reason is that the structure of this table does not support the separation of schemas and users.

☑ Many Transact-SQL statements that you are familiar with may perform slightly different functions or require different parameters. Some examples of statements you should read up on in SQL Server Books Online are *CREATE SCHEMA*, and the *DEFAULT_SCHEMA* option for both the *CREATE USER* and *ALTER USER* statements.

Designing Schemas

☑ When designing the schemas for a database, it is important to consider the design from both a security and object naming perspective, as schemas necessarily impact both of these.

☑ Group similar objects together, and use a schema as a way to place a boundary around them.

☑ Consider schema design as early as possible in the System Development Life Cycle, as the final schema design will impact nearly everything else that is developed.

Managing Schemas

☑ Learn how to use T-SQL for any task you need to accomplish, as it will make your life simpler and you will accomplish repetitive administrative tasks faster.

☑ Include copies of all the scripts you use to create a database in your system design documentation. Detailed documentation of the procedures used to create the database, especially in the form of scripts, simplifies a primary security concern—the ability to reconstitute the system and fully recover in a timely fashion after a disaster.

☑ If ample consideration is given to schemas during the design phase, then managing schemas will be simpler with less fixing of design mistakes required.

Frequently Asked Questions

Q: What is a schema?

A: A schema is a container that objects such as tables, stored procedures, and views are placed into. In versions of SQL Server prior to 2005, schemas were the same things as users, and therefore, each time a user was added to a database a new schema was added as well. In SQL Server 2005, schemas and users have been separated.

Q: Why is the user-schema separation important from the perspective of security?

A: There are several reasons that this is important. First, it gives us an improved ability to group together objects that require similar permissions, creating a security boundary around those objects. It also provides clear separation between the ownership of objects and permissions on objects. You have a better ability to implement the principle of least privilege. Also, it reduces security holes that arise when administrators need to remove or alter the access level of a user in some way, but cannot do this immediately due to the need to change the namespace of the objects that user may own, as well as the application code that accesses those objects.

Q: Can a schema be owned by more than one entity?

A: In previous versions of SQL Server, the schema was the owner of an object. Therefore, it was impossible to separate these two concepts. By definition, the schema was owned by the user that was tied to the schema. The *dbo* schema must be owned only by *dbo*. In SQL Server 2005, schemas and users are no longer fused together. A schema is simply a container, and administrators can assign ownership of the container to multiple principals.

Q: How do schemas and ownership chains relate to each other?

A: Ownership chains have not changed. However, since "schema" is no longer just another word for the owner of an object, an object can be owned by a user, but be contained in a schema belonging to a different user. Taking it a step further, objects can have their owner property set to *SCHEMA OWNER* so that whoever owns the schema they belong in effectively owns the object. Thus, moving the object from one schema to another can change the owner.

Q: How does the separation of schemas and users impact T-SQL statements that I'm used to using to manage schemas?

A: Most importantly you will need to become accustomed to using the *CREATE SCHEMA* statement to actually create schemas. Previously, this statement was really only a method of creating objects within a schema attached to a user or role. Similarly, you will need to recognize that the *ALTER SCHEMA* statement provides the ability to change who the schema owner is. Additionally, some T-SQL statements relating to user creation or management (*CREATE USER* and *ALTER USER*) now provide the ability to change the default schema for the user.

Q: Why is SQL Server giving me errors when I try to delete a schema?

A: The most likely cause is that the schema still contains objects. You will need to drop or move the objects in the schema so that it is empty before SQL Server will allow you to drop the schema itself.

Q: I want to give a group of users the ability to create objects in a particular schema. Should I assign them ownership of the schema?

A: This answer has two parts. The first part is that you cannot assign ownership to multiple principals, so in order to give all of these users ownership you would need to assign ownership to a group that they were all members of. The second part of the answer is that you probably shouldn't make these people owners of the schema anyway. All they need to create objects in the schema is *ALTER* permissions on the schema. Following the principle of least privilege, I'd discourage you from making these users schema owners unless there is some other reason for doing so.

Q: I thought that schemas and users were separated in SQL Server 2005, but every time I add a user via the *sp_adduser* stored procedure, a new schema named after the user is created as well. Why?

A: Users and schemas are separate in SQL Server 2005. However, the *sp_adduser* stored procedure attempts to maintain functionality similar to its implementation in SQL Server 2000 and earlier versions. This means that it not only creates a user, but creates a schema with the same name as the user as well, and sets the new user as the schema owner. This feature will be removed in future SQL Server releases, and use of the stored procedure is discouraged. It is recommended that existing applications be altered so that they do not use this stored procedure.

Chapter 24

Password Policies

Solutions in this chapter:

- **Password Policies in SQL Server 2005**
- **SQL Server Scenarios**

☑ **Summary**

☑ **Solutions Fast Track**

☑ **Frequently Asked Questions**

Introduction

By the end of this chapter, you should have a good understanding of password policies and how they integrate with the underlying operating system. We'll cover not only how to set password policies in SQL server, but also why. You'll see by example how to create and administer password policies.

You'll also gain an understanding of how group policy works in Microsoft Windows, and the impact of changes you make to group policy on the underlying operating system.

Password Policies in SQL Server 2005

Password polices are a new feature in SQL Server 2005. So what are password policies? They are a series of rules enforced to ensure passwords in SQL server follow standards set forth in the operating system via group policy.

Password policies can be turned off and on in SQL server. There may be reasons for not using password policies overall, or just on specific accounts.

Password Policies Explained

Password polices force the account to adhere to a specific set of rules. The rules can be broken down into two distinct types, one set of rules related to password policies, and another related to account lockout policies. The following sections detail each of these policies.

SOME INDEPENDENT ADVICE

Since group policies are usually controlled by the network administration group in most organizations, be sure to communicate with the appropriate teams in your organization before making any changes.

Using the Group Policies Console

The easiest way to use the group policy console is to start the management console by typing "MMC" in the run box in Microsoft Windows. To access the run box, click the **Start** menu, and select the run box. The Microsoft management console has other functions besides controlling group policy.

Once the MMC is started, you need to click **Add/Remove Snap-in**. The "Add/Remove" snap-in dialog is available on the file menu (see Figure 24.1).

Figure 24.1 Adding the Snap-in (Part 1)

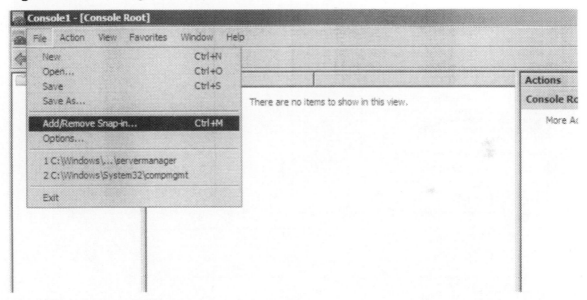

Click the **Add/Remove Snap-in** menu selection, and a dialog that allows selection of snap-ins to be added will be presented. It is recommended to only select the add-in for group policy; otherwise, the menu can get very cluttered very quickly.

Scroll down and select the **Local Group Policy Object**, and click the **Add** button (see Figure 24.2). Note that when using Microsoft Windows 2003 or Microsoft Windows XP, the dialog boxes may look slightly different.

Figure 24.2 Adding the Snap-in (Part 2)

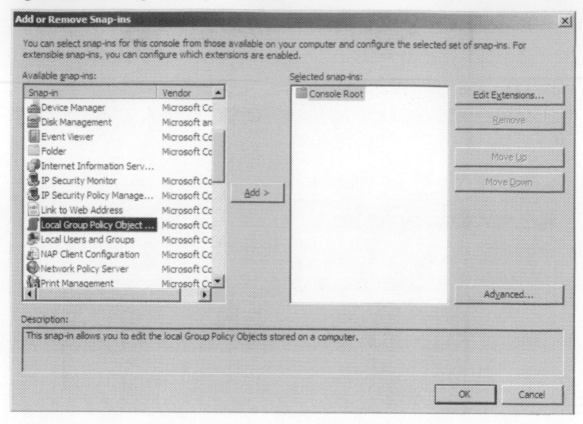

When you add the snap-in after selecting it and click **OK**, the selection of which computer you wish to manage dialog will be presented (see Figure 24.3). Note that it's not necessary to be logged into the computer to be managed, but the account used needs administrative rights on the computer to be managed.

Figure 24.3 Selecting the Computer

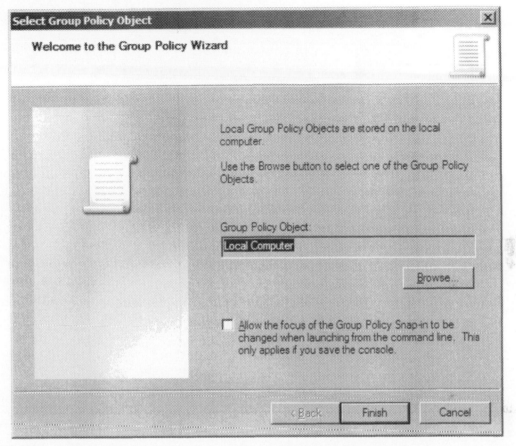

After you select the computer (in most cases it will be the local computer), the initial Group Policy Management console snap-in screen will be presented (see Figure 24.4).

As one can see in group policy, there are also a number of other items to be controlled. It is strongly suggested to refrain from changing anything, unless the impact is known, as there is no "undo" for the settings in group policy. Once a change is made, if the previous value is forgotten, there is no way to go back and see what it was.

In order to use the group policy snap-in to control the password policies, expand the tree under "console root" on the left-hand pane.

Expand each of the nodes under "Windows Settings" until Account Policies is shown.

Figure 24.4 The MMC Initial Screen

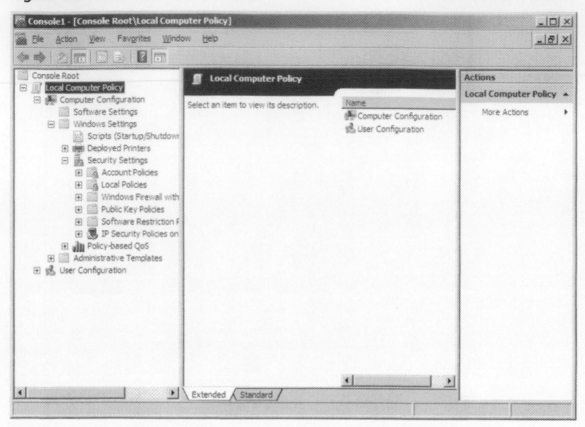

SOME INDEPENDENT ADVICE

Group policy is complex in the way it's applied. Group policy is applied at different points (at the domain or group level in Active Directory). One of the options when it's applied through Active Directory, is to disallow it to be overridden. In the event an option is configured to not be overridden at a higher level, even if it has been set at the local level, the setting won't take effect if it's set via Active Directory.

This is why it is important to involve the appropriate groups in your organization when working with group policy.

Password Policies

The following password policies can be enforced in SQL server 2005:

- Enforce password history
- Minimum password age
- Maximum password age
- Minimum password length

Password must meet complexity requirements

Figure 24.5 depicts the password settings in the management console for group policy.

Figure 24.5 Group Policy for Passwords

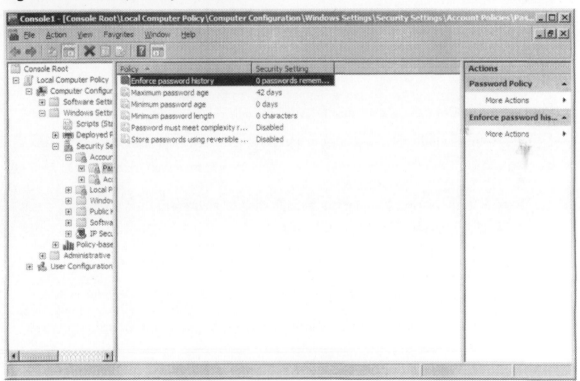

In the next section, we'll discuss each of these options in more detail.

The "Enforce password history" option is used to prevent users from reusing old passwords. This makes the system more secure; a user needs to use a new password (one that has never been used before) each time they change the password. Valid values for this are between 0 and 24. The default is 24 on domain controllers and 0 on standalone servers. It would be bad practice to install SQL server on a domain controller, so I would surmise that it will be 0 on your server. If this option is to be used, it is a good idea to also use the "Minimum password age" option as well.

The "Minimum password age" option is used to set the period of time in days that the password must be used before the user can change it. On the surface, you'd wonder why you'd want to use this setting, but it has an important use. It also prevents users from changing the password in order to defeat the "Enforce password history" option, by going through passwords until they get back to an old favorite. This also helps to discourage users from changing their passwords so frequently that they forget them. The default is 0, which allows the user to change the password at any time. Note that the "Minimum password age" must be less than the "Maximum password age."

The "Maximum password age" is used to set the period of time in days that a password may be used before requiring the user to change it. This can be set from 0 (never expire) to 999. Note that the "Minimum password age" must be less than the "Maximum password age."

The "Minimum Password Length" option is used to set the minimum password length for a password. This can be set from 0 to 14. When the "Minimum Password Length" is set to 0, it allows for any length password.

The "Password Must Meet Complexity Requirements" option is used to set complexity requirements, causing the password to be more secure and less apt to guessing.

The attributes of the password must be as follows when this is enabled:

- Not contain the user's account name or parts of the user's full name that exceed two consecutive characters

- Be at least six characters in length

- Contain characters from three of the following four categories:

- English uppercase characters (A through Z)

- English lowercase characters (a through z)

- Base 10 digits (0 through 9)

- Nonalphabetic characters (for example, !, $, #, %)

Complexity requirements are enforced when passwords are changed or created.

◤ **SOME INDEPENDENT ADVICE**

It's usually a good idea to enable the "Password Must Meet Complexity Requirements" option; however, it's also a good idea to communicate this to your users prior to enabling this, as it can lead to user confusion when they attempt to change their passwords, and may result in an increase in support calls to your helpdesk.

Using the Local group policy console to administer settings is easy. Double-click on the setting to be changed and a dialog box will be presented where changes will be made. The console checks the values to be sure they are within the proper range. Double-click on the option, and a dialog box similar to that in Figure 24.6 will be presented.

Figure 24.6 The UI for Administering Settings

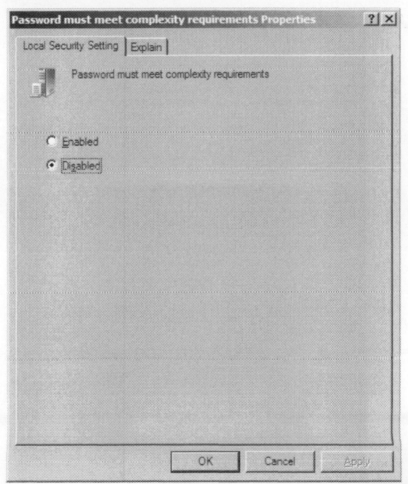

NOTE

If more information is needed about what a setting does, the Group Policy Snap-in provides an explanation for each of the settings. When an item is double-clicked, a tab to see a detailed explanation is available. Clicking the **Explain** tab will present the information (see Figure 24.7).

Figure 24.7 A Group Policy Setting Explanation

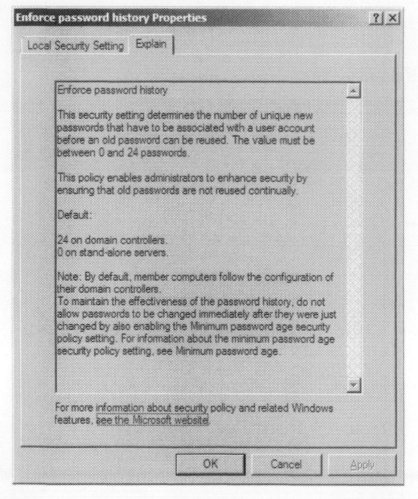

The explanations are very clear and concise, and they usually show the default values as well as ranges for the settings.

BEST PRACTICES ACCORDING TO MICROSOFT

According to Microsoft, these are some best practices to follow:

- Set the maximum password age for passwords to expire every 30 to 90 days
- If the "Enforce password history" selection is used, be sure to set a minimum password age.

Account Lockout Policies

The account lockout policies are as follows:

- Account lockout threshold option (number of invalid logins before lockout)
- Account lockout duration (amount of time locked out)
- Reset lockout counter after n minutes

Figure 24.8 depicts the Account lockout settings in the management console for group policy.

Figure 24.8 The Account Lockout Group Policy

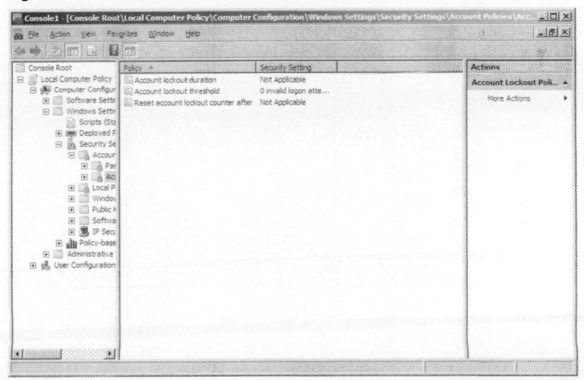

In the next section, we'll discuss each of these options in more detail.

The "Account lockout threshold" option is used to set the number of invalid logins before the account is locked out. Valid settings are 0 (which is never lock out an account) to 999. Once an account is locked out, it needs to be unlocked by an administrator, or the "Account lockout duration" time needs to expire. The default is 0.

The "Account lockout duration" option is used to automatically unlock the account after a period of time. The time is in minutes. Valid settings are 0 (which is never unlock an account until an administrator resets it) to 99,999. This is especially useful for organizations that have busy administrators or no off-hours support.

The "Reset lockout counter after n minutes" option is used to determine how many minutes need to elapse before the failed logon attempt counter is reset. The range is 1 to 99,999. In order to use this setting, the "Account lockout threshold" must be set. The reset time must be less than or equal to the "Account lockout duration" (if the account lockout duration is set).

Why Use Password Policies?

Using password policies in SQL Server 2005 will help to ensure that uniform security is enforced across all SQL logins. Password policies can be enforced at the domain level, the container level, or at the local machine level via group policy. Password polices are not a "silver bullet," but in today's society, any help keeping SQL server installation more secure is a good thing.

When establishing password polices in the organization, they will most likely be across all systems, including SQL server and the Microsoft windows logins. Group policy can help ensure uniform application across systems.

Shortcut...

Using Group Policy

It may be more efficient to implement group policy at the Active Directory level. It makes sense to create a container in Active Directory for all of the SQL servers if there are a number of them in your organization, and apply the group policy at that level. While this is outside the scope of this discussion, it would be beneficial to learn more about Windows Group policy and Active Directory so the strategy can be implemented in the most efficient manner.

Operating System Requirements

In order to use password policies, SQL server 2005 needs to be running on Windows Server 2003 or later. SQL 2005 password policy functionality depends on the NetValidatePasswordPolicy application program interface (API), which is only available in Windows Server 2003 and later versions. Also, password policies need to be enabled for that machine via group policy. Password policies are part of Windows group policies. Group policies can be applied to different containers in Active Directory, as well as locally on the machine.

SOME INDEPENDENT ADVICE

Since group policies can affect other Windows services such as windows user passwords and passwords used by service accounts, be sure to completely test your changes in a test environment before making any changes to your production environment. It's very important to understand the impact of any changes you are going to make before making them.

Using Password Policies

First, to use password policies in SQL server 2005, password policies need to be enabled. This is accomplished by turning on password policies in SQL server when creating a login.

Here is an example of creating a login for SQL server using T-SQL, which will use the policies defined in the operating system:

```
CREATE LOGIN Robby with
  password='Test$12345',
  CHECK_POLICY = ON,
  CHECK_EXPIRATION = ON
```

Figure 24.9 is an example of creating a login for SQL Server using SQL Server Management Studio, which will use the policies defined in the operating system.

When you are creating a login, be sure to check the "enforce password policy" checkbox so the login will adhere to the password policy rules defined in the operating system. This is a good idea unless there is a compelling reason not to. The same holds true with password expiration.

It's possible to enable one or both of the settings, because they function independently of each other.

Figure 24.9 Creating a Login That Uses Password Policy

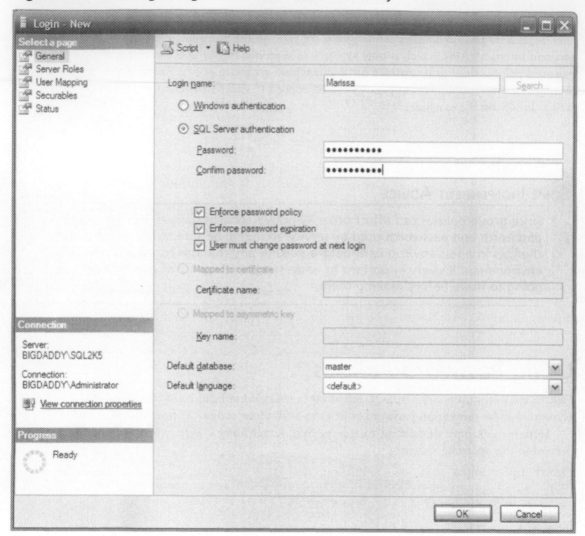

BEST PRACTICES ACCORDING TO MICROSOFT

- Mandate a strong password policy, including expiration and a complexity policy for the organization.

- If SQL logins are required, ensure that SQL Server 2005 runs on the Windows Server 2003 operating system and use password policies.

- Outfit the applications with a mechanism to change SQL login passwords. This includes application logins.

- Set *MUST_CHANGE* for new logins where practical.

Some Independent Advice

While group policy can make your environment more secure when it comes to using SQL logins, it's still a better practice to use Windows logins wherever possible.

SQL Server Scenarios

In this section we present three scenarios related to securing SQL Server 2005 and provide solutions for each of these problems. These scenarios represent real-world tasks that IT administrators are bound to end up doing at some point.

Scenario 1

You've been given the task of creating a login for an application. The password cannot be changed within the application. The application uses a database called CaddyShack.

Group policy is enabled on your domain for all computers and requires the password to be changed every 30 days. Since this application has no facility for changing passwords, you obtain agreement and authorization from all appropriate stakeholders to create a login that doesn't need to be changed at regular intervals. The application is designed so it must use an SQL server login. What are the possible solutions?

The Solution

There are a number of possible solutions to this scenario. First off, you want the system to be as secure as possible, so you should use a complex login and password.

An Example

MyCoolApp$RT1Kj8 for the login and *PogDog87!ReadTh3maNual* for a password. This incorporates letters and numbers and is pretty hard to guess.

To create the login through T-SQL you'd execute:

```
CREATE LOGIN [MyCoolApp$RT1Kj8]
WITH PASSWORD=N'Pog$Dog$87!ReadTh3maNual',
DEFAULT_DATABASE=[caddyshack],
CHECK_EXPIRATION=OFF,
CHECK_POLICY=OFF
```

Figure 24.10 shows how to create the login using the SQL Server Management Studio. Be sure not to check the "Enforce password policy" checkbox, as policy would require the password to be changed at regular intervals.

Figure 24.10 Creating a Login

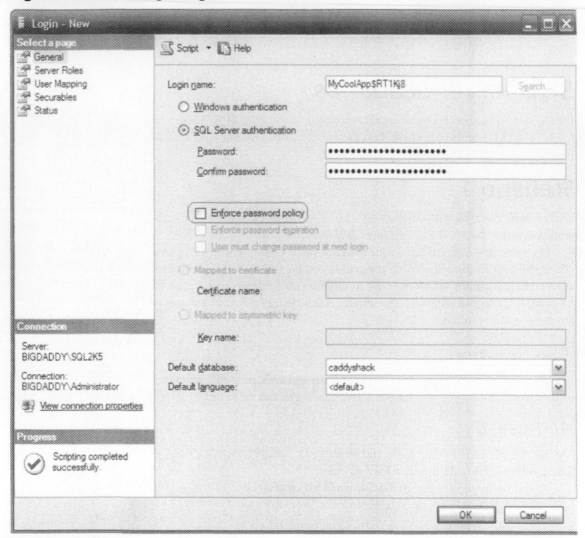

Creating the login via the graphical user interface (GUI) or via script produces the same result; however, by using script to create your login, you have an "audit trail" of what you actually did to create the login. If a question should arise later and you've saved the script, you can refer back to your script to see what was actually executed.

Completion of the steps outlined in this section should yield the appropriate results. Remember to test each login and make sure it works as expected.

Scenario 2

You've been given the task of creating three logins for users who will be using an application for Ad-hoc querying via Query analyzer and other similar applications. Group policy is enabled on your domain for all computers, and requires the password to be changed every 30 days, as well as password complexity rules. The users need access to a database called CaddyShack. Logins must be reset by the users at first login.

It's not practical to use Windows logins in this situation, as not all users will be using Windows-based machines.

The Solution

In this situation, it's more practical to create the logins using T-SQL as opposed to the user interface, since we are creating multiple logins; however, we will show both methods.

First, here is how to create the logins using T-SQL.

```
CREATE LOGIN [User1]
WITH PASSWORD=N'ChangeMeNow$1234'
MUST_CHANGE,
DEFAULT_DATABASE=[caddyshack],
CHECK_EXPIRATION=ON,
CHECK_POLICY=ON
GO
CREATE LOGIN [User2]
WITH PASSWORD=N'ChangeMeNow$1234'
MUST_CHANGE,
DEFAULT_DATABASE=[caddyshack],
CHECK_EXPIRATION=ON,
CHECK_POLICY=ON
GO
CREATE LOGIN [User3]
WITH PASSWORD=N'ChangeMeNow$1234'
MUST_CHANGE,
DEFAULT_DATABASE=[caddyshack],
CHECK_EXPIRATION=ON,
CHECK_POLICY=ON
```

As you can see in this situation, if a quantity of users needs to be created, it will be much easier to do so using cut-and-paste techniques.

SOME INDEPENDENT ADVICE

Using scripts to create logins as opposed to using the GUI can make testing easier, because it is fast and easy to delete and recreate logins quickly.

To produce the same result using the SQL Server Management server GUI, you would have to add each user individually (see Figure 24.11).

Figure 24.11 Creating a User with the GUI

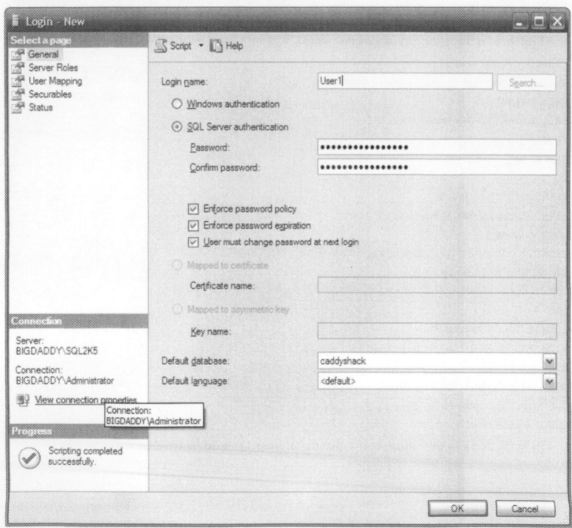

Completion of the steps outlined in this section should yield the appropriate results. Remember to test each login and make sure it works as expected.

Scenario 3

You've been given the task of creating the logins on an SQL server to be used for an Internet application. Three logins for users who will be using the database for ad-hoc querying via Query analyzer and other similar applications need to be created, as well as an application login.

Group policy is not enabled on your domain; however, management would like you to configure group policy on the server such that the configuration in Table 24.1 is met.

The users need access to a database called CaddyShack. Logins must be reset by the users at first login. The application has no facility for changing the password used to connect to the database, so the password for the application login should not expire. Management recommends that this login not use group policy, but that the login is secure. Using Windows trusted logins in this scenario is not possible.

Table 24.1 lists the settings for the user accounts.

Table 24.1 Settings for User Accounts

Item	Configuration
Password expiration	30 days
Password complexity	Yes
Minimum password age	5 days
Account lockout after X logins	4
Reset lockout counter after X minutes	30
Enforce password history	10
Password length	8
Password must meet complexity requirements	yes

The Solution

Initially, we should create the local policy on the machine. Each of the settings outlined in Table 24.1 are configurable through group policy.

First, with the Local group policy Microsoft Management Console (MMC) snap-in, create a local policy that meets the aforementioned criteria. For information about how to start the console, refer to the section titled "Using the Group Policies Console" earlier in this chapter. Figure 24.12 shows how to select the password policy section.

Figure 24.12 The Password Policy Section

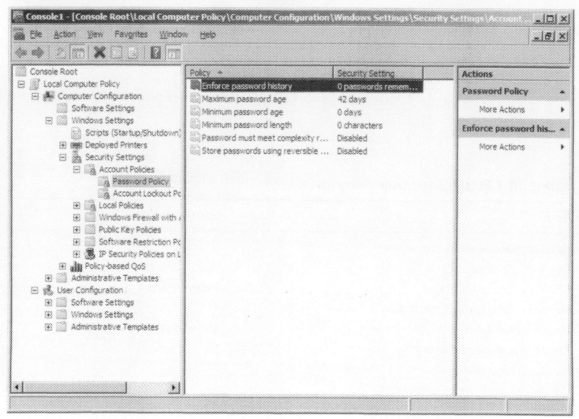

For each of the requirements outlined in Table 24.1, make the appropriate changes to the group policy using the group policy console. By double-clicking on a setting, a dialog box will be presented that will allow the setting to be changed (see Figure 24.13).

Figure 24.13 Setting the Password History Parameter

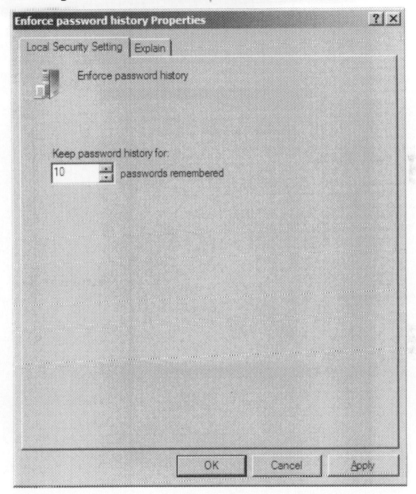

Once each of the settings outlined in the table is changed in the local policy MMC snap-in, the Password Policies screen should look like Figure 24.14.

Figure 24.14 Password Policies Settings

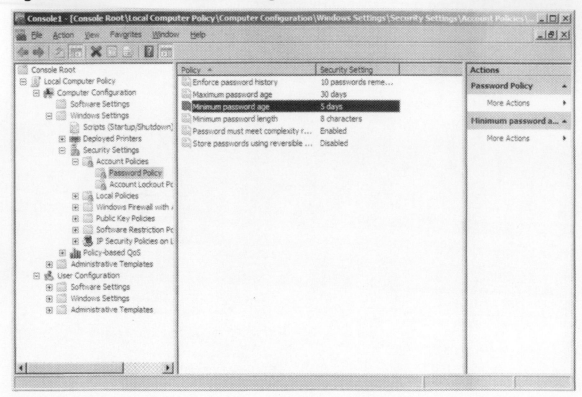

Since the settings in the table also affect the account lockout policies, they will need to be changed as well. Once the changes are completed, the Account Lockout Policies screen should look like Figure 24.15.

Figure 24.15 Account Lockout Policies Settings

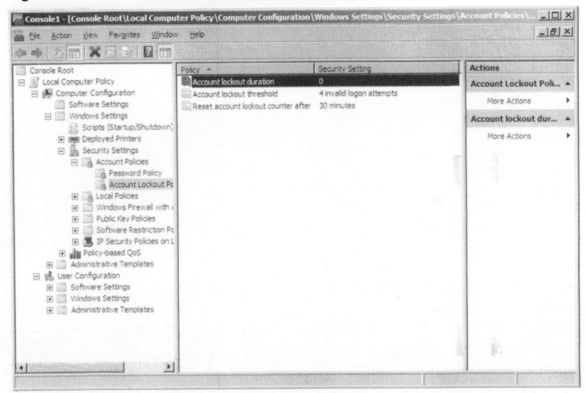

Next, the logins need to be created. The logins may be created using T-SQL or with the user interface. We will show both methods.

First, here is the syntax for creating logins using T-SQL:

```
CREATE LOGIN [Mark]
WITH PASSWORD=N'ChangeMeNow$1234'
MUST_CHANGE,
DEFAULT_DATABASE=[caddyshack],
CHECK_EXPIRATION=ON,
CHECK_POLICY=ON
GO
CREATE LOGIN [Robby]
WITH PASSWORD=N'ChangeMeNow$5678'
MUST_CHANGE,
DEFAULT_DATABASE=[caddyshack],
CHECK_EXPIRATION=ON,
CHECK_POLICY=ON
GO
CREATE LOGIN [Debbie]
WITH PASSWORD=N'ChangeMeNow$3322'
MUST_CHANGE,
DEFAULT_DATABASE=[caddyshack],
CHECK_EXPIRATION=ON,
CHECK_POLICY=ON
```

Creating the logins with the aforementioned configuration options should meet the requirements for creating the user logins. To create the application login, the following SQL could be used:

```
CREATE LOGIN [MyCoolAppLogin]
WITH PASSWORD=N'ThisIsaC0mpl3x$PassW3rd$0987'
DEFAULT_DATABASE=[caddyshack],
CHECK_EXPIRATION=OFF,
CHECK_POLICY=OFF
```

To produce the same result using the SQL Server Management server GUI, it will be necessary to add each user individually (see Figure 24.16).

Figure 24.16 Adding Users

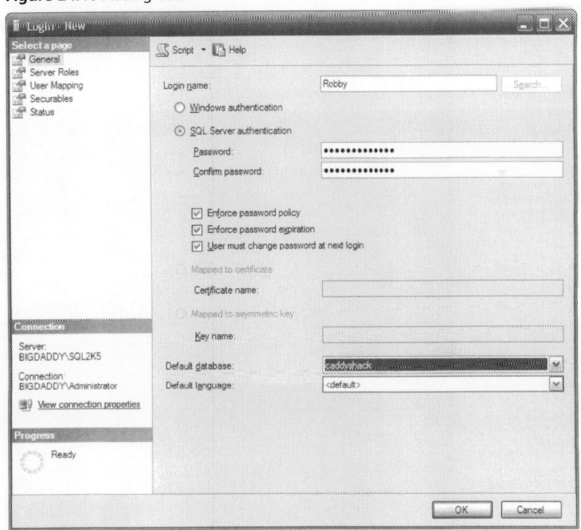

Note that in Figure 24.16, the "Enforce password policy," "Enforce password expiration," and "User must change password at next login" are all checked. This is necessary to meet the requirements outlined in the requirements table.

For the login used by the application, the settings are slightly different (see Figure 24.17).

Notice that in Figure 24.17, the "Enforce password policy," "Enforce password expiration," and "User must change password at next login" are all checked. This is necessary to meet the requirements outlined in the requirements table. Once again, be sure to test everything first in a development environment.

Figure 24.17 Application Login Account Creation

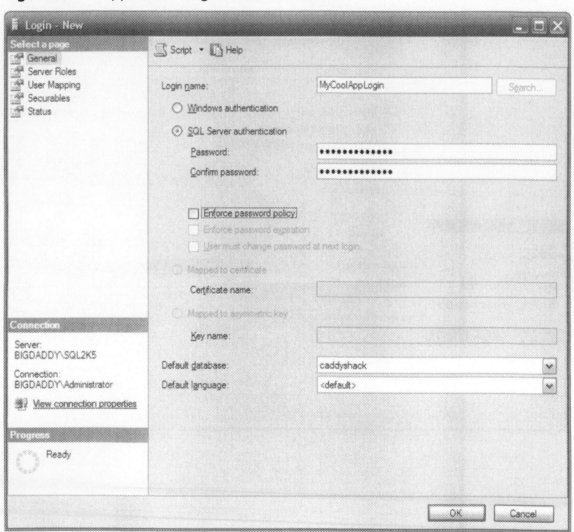

Summary

In this chapter, we covered the how's and why's of group policy. We've shown how to use group policy to make our passwords more secure.

Group policy can be overridden at the domain level, which means that changes on the local machine may not take effect. This is why it's important to talk with the appropriate department (usually network engineering, but it depends on the organization) and involve them in any group policy changes that are made.

It's important to remember that when it comes to security, there is no silver bullet. No system is truly secure unless it's disconnected, turned off, and locked in a secure room, which is impractical in most cases. That being said, we should take any steps we can to make our data more secure.

Solutions Fast Track

Password Policies in SQL Server 2005

☑ Group policy helps ensure uniformity in the way passwords are enforced.

☑ Be sure to test any proposed changes before moving them into production.

☑ By requiring your passwords to be more secure, it will make it harder for hackers to guess a password.

☑ Group policy is configured via the operating system, using the Microsoft management console and the local group policy snap-in.

☑ In order for SQL 2005 to use group policy, SQL 2005 needs to be installed on Microsoft Windows 2003 or later.

☑ As each login is created in SQL Server 2005, it is possible to enable or disable the enforcement of Windows group policy.

☑ Group policy can be overridden at the domain level, which means that changes on the local machine may not take effect.

SQL Server Scenarios

☑ In scenario 1, use a complex login and password to maximize security of a system.

☑ In scenario 2, using T-SQL is more practical for creating multiple logins, but you can also use the GUI method.

☑ In scenario 3, each of the settings outlined in Table 24.1 is configurable through group policy.

Frequently Asked Questions

Q: Can I use password polices on an SQL Server 2005 installation running on Windows Server 2000?

A: No. In order to use password policies, SQL Server 2005 needs to be running on Windows Server 2003 or later. SQL 2005 password policy functionality depends on the NetValidatePasswordPolicy API, which is only available in Windows Server 2003 and later versions.

Q: I can't find any way to set group policies in SQL Server Management Studio. Am I missing something?

A: No. Password policies are set via group policy at the operating system level. The group policy snap-in for the Microsoft management console is used.

Q: Can I define different policies in SQL Server for different logins? I want the password history to be 10 for one set of logins and 20 for another.

A: No. The password policies are defined at the operating system level, and are applied (or not applied) to each of the logins. You can have the policy active for some logins and not others, but you cannot have different policies applied.

Q: Can I apply the same group policy to all 100 SQL servers we have in place easily?

A: Yes. It's best to work with the team responsible for managing Active Directory and domain group policy to accomplish this. In fact, this is the kind of scenario domain group policy is meant for.

Q: I made changes to my local group policy but they don't seem to be working. What's wrong?

A: The most likely problem is that the policy is defined at the domain level, and cannot be overridden.

Chapter 25

DDL Triggers

Solutions in this chapter:

- DDL Triggers Explained
- Implementing DDL Triggers
- Managing DDL Triggers
- Scenarios for Deploying DDL Triggers

☑ Summary

☑ Solutions Fast Track

☑ Frequently Asked Questions

Introduction

This chapter introduces DDL triggers. It explains what they are, demonstrates how to implement them, and shows you when to implement them. It also provides real-world examples of how and when DDL triggers can be used to help secure an SQL Server.

DDL Triggers Explained

Data Definition Language (DDL) is the subset of T-SQL instructions and statements that define structure, whether that structure is objects like tables and views, schemas, or security principals like server logins and database users. Although triggers have been a part of the SQL Server product, they only applied to certain Data Manipulation Language (DML) instructions, including *INSERT*, *UPDATE*, and *DELETE*. Until this latest version of SQL Server, there was no capability to fire a trigger on a DDL statement (such as *DROP TABLE*).

Since SQL Server 2000, triggers can fire either before a statement executes, intercepting that statement, or afterwards. Triggers that fire before a statement executes are called *INSTEAD OF* triggers, because they execute "instead of" the statement itself. Triggers that fire after the statement executes (but before the transaction or batch process completes) are called *AFTER* triggers. *AFTER* triggers were available prior to SQL Server 2000, and as a result, represent the default trigger behavior. DDL triggers can only be defined as *AFTER* triggers. They do not intercept the DDL statement before it executes. However, triggers, including DDL triggers, do provide the capability of rolling back the statement. We can't stop a DDL statement from executing, but we can quickly undo its effects before they become permanent.

If we have the ability to undo a potentially damaging or simply unapproved structural change using a trigger, that means we can prevent situations like someone mistakenly dropping or altering a table, a SQL Server login without authority, or some other structural change that would break an application, compromise an audit requirement, or both. I say mistakenly, because normally most security-related events are not incidents. The difference between an event and an incident usually involves malicious intent. An event is something that would cause a security system to fire, for instance, someone typing in the wrong password. An incident is where someone is actively trying to hack passwords. When it comes to structural changes in SQL Server, most security events are the result of a mistake.

A classic example is when a DBA is logged on to a production server, but thinks he or she is logged on to a development server instead. There is a change that needs to be made in development, so he or she executes it, not realizing that they are logged on to a production server, thereby changing the structure of a key table. The production application hasn't been updated to handle this change, rendering a key piece of functionality unavailable. Only when the phone starts ringing on the DBA's desk does he or she realize what has happened. Prior to SQL Server 2005, there would be no way to prevent that change. In SQL Server 2005, a DDL trigger can fire and roll back the change before it can affect the application. Depending on the application, that DDL trigger on the production server could mean the difference between being employed the next day or scanning job sites for a new position.

SOME INDEPENDENT ADVICE

One way to attempt to avoid this sort of issue is to use two tiers of accounts, one "normal" and one "privileged." The normal account would have *SELECT* and *VIEW DEFINITION* rights only. Therefore, if the DBA did execute code in production (where he or she should only be logged into the normal account on a regular basis), he or she would get an error indicating the DDL command couldn't be executed. Couple this with using *RunAs* to start a second tool with the privileged set of credentials, the DBA could be logged on to production with the normal account and development with the privileged account at the same time, on the same computer, and with less risk of an unwanted change occurring in this manner.

Techniques in Older Versions of SQL Server

Given that we didn't have DDL triggers available in older versions of SQL Server, there are techniques that have been implemented, with varying degrees of success. Quite simply, without DDL triggers, each of these techniques were either based on a workaround that permitted a preventative control (a security control that prevents certain actions from occurring), or were a detective control, which could report the issue but which in and of itself couldn't prevent or correct the issue. Let's look at one of these methods, which uses the *SCHEMABINDING* attribute for views.

Using SCHEMABINDING

The SCHEMABINDING option for views and functions locks in objects that are referred to by the respective view or function, to prevent it from being dropped or altered in such a way that would cause the view or function to "break." For instance, take the following table definition:

```
CREATE TABLE dbo.SchemaBindingEx
(
  SchemaBindingInt int,
  SchemaBindingChar char(5)
)
GO
```

We can create a view that would prevent the table from being dropped if we use the SCHEMABINDING option:

```
CREATE VIEW dbo.SchemaBindingView
WITH SCHEMABINDING
AS
SELECT SchemaBindingInt, SchemaBindingChar
FROM dbo.SchemaBindingEx
GO
```

Since the view refers to the table *dbo.SchemaBindingEx*, any attempts to drop the table will fail with an error indicating it is being referenced by the view dbo.*SchemaBindingView*. However, if someone makes an alteration not related to what columns the view covers, such as adding a column, the base table can be changed:

```
ALTER TABLE dbo.SchemaBindingEx
ADD SchemaBindingVarChar varchar(25)
GO
```

Executing this *ALTER TABLE* statement does not return an error. Instead, SQL Server permits the execution to happen, because the view isn't affected. The columns it depends on haven't changed. Because of situations like these, *SCHEMABINDING* is only of limited effectiveness in preventing unexpected changes.

DDL Trigger Scope and Permissions

DDL Triggers have two levels for scope: server and database. It isn't possible to monitor just one schema or a particular database table. DDL triggers weren't intended to protect specific named resources such as a particular login, but rather all of the instances of a SQL Server resource. As a result, DDL triggers fire on specific events for all objects of a given type. For instance, a DDL trigger defined to fire on *DROP LOGIN* will fire on all *DROP LOGIN* events. You cannot define it to fire only if someone attempts to drop the login *YouCannotDropMe*. With that said, a DDL trigger is similar to a stored procedure, meaning you could check for a particular login name within the trigger itself and take action accordingly. We will look to do just that in one of the DDL triggers that define a maintenance window for database work.

The scope of the DDL trigger also determines what permissions are necessary to create, alter, or drop the DDL trigger. For DDL triggers firing on events of server scope, only logins with *CONTROL* permissions can create, change, or delete the DDL trigger. By default, no login is explicitly assigned this level of permissions. Members of the *sysadmin* role have this permission implicitly, because they bypass all security checks. For triggers with database events, the *ALTER ANY DATABASE DDL TRIGGER* permission is required for the database where the trigger is being created. By default, only the database owner (who bypasses all security on the database), members of the *db_owner* fixed database role (implied permission because of *CONTROL* permission on the database), and members of the *db_ddladmin* fixed database role have permissions to work with database-level DDL triggers.

Events and Event Groups

While DDL triggers can be deployed against individual events such as for *CREATE TABLE* calls, they can also be set up to fire on event groups. For instance, *CREATE TABLE's* event with respect to DDL triggers is *CREATE_TABLE*. *CREATE_TABLE* as an event is in the *DDL_TABLE_EVENTS* group. This group also comprises *ALTER TABLE* and *DROP TABLE* commands. The *DDL_TABLE_EVENTS* group is part of the larger *DDL_TABLE_VIEW_EVENTS* group, which is part of the top-level database event group, *DDL_DATABASE_LEVEL_EVENTS*. There is a definite hierarchy to the events and event groups. Here is part of that hierarchy showing *CREATE_TABLE* to give you a visual idea of how the event groups work:

- *DDL_DATABASE_LEVEL_EVENTS*
  1. *DDL_TABLE_VIEW_EVENTS*
     - *DDL_TABLE_EVENTS*
     - ***CREATE_TABLE***
     - *ALTER_TABLE*
     - *DROP_TABLE*
     - *DDL_VIEW_EVENTS*
     - *DDL_INDEX_EVENTS*
     - ...
  2. *DDL_TRIGGER_EVENTS*
  3. ...

If you're looking to audit all of a group of events, you can specify the appropriate event group instead of specifying each individual event.

DDL Triggers and Temporary Objects

DDL statements executing against temporary objects, such as temporary tables and temporary stored procedures, do not cause DDL triggers to fire, even if the DDL trigger is set for the particular event being generated by a statement (such as *CREATE_TABLE*). SQL Server 2005 simply handles the creation of temporary objects differently.

Those familiar with *TempDB* may recall that temporary objects are actually created in *TempDB*. However, if the appropriate DDL trigger is placed on *TempDB* events for "permanent" objects, it can certainly cause the trigger to fire, but temporary objects still will not. Therefore, a DDL trigger cannot be used to intercept a temporary object. This means that even if the appropriate DDL triggers are in place to prevent schema changes for permanent objects, the permanent objects like stored procedures and functions can continue to make use of temporary objects such as temporary tables, without concern.

Multiple DDL Triggers

It is possible to have multiple DDL triggers defined for the same event. As long as there are no more than three DDL triggers defined, it is possible to specify trigger order using *sp_settriggerorder*, because this stored procedure can designate which trigger fires first and which trigger fires last. After that, you cannot predict the order triggers will fire in. If you've not used *sp_settriggerorder*, do not assume the triggers fire in any particular order. In general, it is best to limit the number of triggers for a particular event or object (if a DML trigger).

A situation where multiple triggers can fire even though you don't have multiple triggers explicitly defined for a single event, is if you have DDL triggers defined at multiple levels of the hierarchy. For instance, there is a trigger defined for *CREATE_TABLE* and another trigger defined for *DDL_TABLE_EVENTS*. Because the triggers are not at the same level of the hierarchy, it's possible to indicate which one fires before another. Be careful to avoid situations like these, as there is no guarantee of firing order.

Differences from DML Triggers

We've already talked about one key difference between DDL and DML triggers and that is the *INSTEAD OF* trigger. DML triggers can be defined as *INSTEAD OF* triggers, firing before statement execution. However, DDL triggers are only *AFTER* triggers, meaning the statement executes first. Another key difference we've discussed is scope. DML triggers apply to specific database objects such as tables and views. DDL triggers fire all objects of a given type if the trigger conditions are met (the event the DDL trigger is supposed to fire on occurs).

Another difference is the lack of the *inserted* and *deleted* tables, as with DML triggers. These two special tables provide the rows affected by the DML operation. For *INSERT* statements, the added rows are in the inserted table. For *UPDATE* statements, the rows as they will appear when the transaction is complete appear in the inserted table, and the rows as they were originally are in the deleted table. For *DELETE* operations, the rows deleted are in the deleted table. They are appropriate for DML triggers, but they don't fit DDL triggers. DDL triggers should capture the event and the query that caused the event. That doesn't fit with either the inserted or deleted tables. As a result, SQL Server 2005 implements the *EVENTDATA* function to capture information of pertinent interest for a DDL trigger. We'll look at *EVENTDATA* more in the next section.

Using CLR for DDL Triggers

Like DML triggers, DDL triggers can be Common Language Runtime (CLR) code. This requires the SQL Server to be configured to support the CLR. By default, CLR support is turned off. While there are particular situations where a CLR trigger may be more useful than a T-SQL trigger, we will concentrate on T-SQL triggers in this chapter.

Implementing DDL Triggers

Now that we've looked at what DDL triggers are, let's look at what it takes to implement them on our SQL Server 2005 instances. Implementing DDL triggers properly involves more than just knowing the basic syntax, which is our starting point. We'll also look at how to capture the event information that caused a DDL trigger to fire. In addition, we'll look at the basic techniques we'll use with DDL triggers, such as rolling back to DDL statements. We'll also cover how to manage DDL triggers, such as how to disable them so we can implement changes when appropriate.

Basic Syntax

The basic syntax for creating a DDL trigger is:

```
CREATE TRIGGER <trigger name>
ON { ALL SERVER / DATABASE }
[ WITH <DDL trigger option> [, … n]]
{ FOR | AFTER } {<event type> | <event group> } [, … n]
```

```
AS
{ <trigger body in T-SQL> |
  EXTERNAL NAME <assembly name>.<class name>.<method name> [;] }
```

The first option we have is the choice between *ALL SERVER* and *DATABASE*. This determines the scope of the trigger. If we want a DDL trigger firing on server-level objects and actions, we want to use *ALL SERVER*. If it's something in the database we're looking to watch for, *DATABASE* is our scope. The second option is the *WITH* clause and the DDL trigger options *ENCRYPTION* and *EXECUTE AS*. We'll discuss them shortly.

Next is the *FOR* or *AFTER* choice. This is a semantic choice and both words have the same meaning with respect to syntax; they specify the trigger fires after the statement. The reason for both words is that in versions prior to SQL Server 2000, the syntax used the word *FOR*, because there were only triggers that fired after the statement executed. In SQL Server 2000, the *AFTER* was added as valid syntax, because it makes clear the trigger fires are the statement executes just as *INSTEAD OF* makes it clear the trigger fires before the statement is allowed to execute. *FOR* was retained and kept the meaning of *AFTER*. DDL triggers can only fire *AFTER* a statement has executed, so use *FOR* or *AFTER* as is your preference.

The next choice is where we specify the event types or event groups. Multiple event types and/or groups can be specified for a single DDL trigger. Finally, we specify either the T-SQL statements the trigger should execute or point SQL Server to CLR code. Let's look at a basic example of a DDL trigger firing on a *CREATE_TABLE* event:

```
CREATE TRIGGER trigDDL_CreateTable
ON DATABASE
FOR CREATE_TABLE
AS
BEGIN
  -- T-SQL Code
END;
GO
```

With respect to dropping (deleting) a trigger, the format is similar to dropping a DML trigger. However, instead of specifying the object on which the trigger fires, we must specify the scope. The basic syntax for dropping a DDL trigger is:

```
DROP TRIGGER <trigger name>
ON { ALL SERVER | DATABASE }
```

If you fail to specify the scope, SQL Server will return an error indicating it could not find the trigger or that you don't have permissions to complete the *DROP*. Therefore, the scope is essential. For instance, if we wanted to drop the example DDL trigger created previously, we would execute:

```
DROP TRIGGER trigDDL_CreateTable
ON DATABASE;
GO
```

Shortcut...

SQL Server Management Studio (SSMS) and Trigger Support

SQL Server Management Studio's (SSMS) Object Explorer has limited support for triggers. Basically, you can script or delete existing triggers, but it doesn't do anything else, such as assisting with the creation of a trigger. Therefore, it is extremely important to understand the T-SQL syntax if you want to use DDL triggers (or DML triggers, for that matter), because the only way to create and manage triggers is by using a Query Window and T-SQL.

DDL Trigger Options

Because triggers are similar to stored procedures, they share two options with stored procedures:

- ENCRYPTION
- EXECUTE AS

Specified using the *WITH* clause, both of these trigger options are just that: options. They are not required when you are creating a trigger (this includes DML trigger). Each option serves a specific purpose, so let's look at what they do.

ENCRYPTION

This database option hides the trigger definition from prying eyes. SQL Server uses a symmetric encryption algorithm to encrypt the trigger code should someone want to view the definition of it (and has permission to do so). When SQL Server needs to execute the trigger, it'll decrypt it and execute the code accordingly.

This option wasn't very effective in previous versions of SQL Server. Scripts and products that could decrypt encrypted definitions were and are freely available. However, in SQL Server 2005, decrypting is a bit harder, with all the techniques I've seen to date requiring a connection using the Dedicated Administrator Connection (DAC). If DAC hasn't been enabled for remote connections, such an attempt must come from the server itself. Someone with console or Remote Desktop access and membership in the *sysadmin* fixed server role could certainly decrypt a trigger that was encrypted using this option, but it'll keep the generally curious out. However, this also might mean it would keep legitimate users from viewing the trigger definition, such as auditors.

EXECUTE AS

EXECUTE AS is another new feature in SQL Server 2005, which allows for a security context switch. The EXECUTE AS option for triggers follows all the requirements of the EXECUTE AS clause for stored procedures. When included in the trigger definition, the trigger will run under the security context specified. This may be useful in a situation we'll examine a bit later, where a DDL trigger executes in one database but inserts information about the event that triggered it into a table in another database.

Getting Event Information

The event information for a DDL trigger is stored in the *EVENTDATA* function. This is a new feature in SQL Server 2005, specifically for DDL triggers. The *EVENTDATA* function does not return a traditional recordset (it is not a table variable), but rather an XML value. For instance, here is what it might return for a *CREATE TABLE* statement:

```
<EVENT_INSTANCE>
  <EventType>CREATE_TABLE</EventType>
  <PostTime>2007-07-06T01:10:26.470</PostTime>
  <SPID>52</SPID>
  <ServerName>TESTSQL</ServerName>
  <LoginName>TESTINGDBA</LoginName>
  <UserName>dbo</UserName>
  <DatabaseName>DDL_Test</DatabaseName>
  <SchemaName>dbo</SchemaName>
  <ObjectName>foo</ObjectName>
  <ObjectType>TABLE</ObjectType>
  <TSQLCommand>
    <SetOptions ANSI_NULLS="ON" ANSI_NULL_DEFAULT="ON"
      ANSI_PADDING="ON" QUOTED_IDENTIFIER="ON" ENCRYPTED="FALSE"/>
    <CommandText>CREATE TABLE foo&#x0D;
    (&#x0D;
    foo1 int&#x0D;
    )&#x0D;
    </CommandText>
  </TSQLCommand>
</EVENT_INSTANCE>
```

The XML has basic information that's of use to us, but chances are we don't want the *<ObjectName> </ObjectName>* tags if we can do without them and we may not be interested in the Options the client connection had set. Rather than dealing with everything as one big XML stream, we want certain properties such as the *EventType*, the *LoginName*, the *ObjectName*, the *PostTime*, and the actual *TSQLCommand* which was issued. This is where we can use *XQuery*.

Using *XQuery*

XQuery is a language used for querying an XML data type. SQL Server 2005 implements part of the language in T-SQL, enough to be of use to us. *XQuery* is still under development by the World Wide Web Consortium (W3C), so the methods for *XQuery* in SQL Server 2005 may change in future versions. However, we can use the implemented part of the language today to help us parse *EVENTDATA()*. For instance:

```
CREATE TRIGGER trigDDLExample_XQuery
ON DATABASE
FOR CREATE_TABLE
AS
BEGIN
  SELECT
    EVENTDATA().value('(/EVENT_INSTANCE/EventType)[1]','nvarchar(max)'),
    EVENTDATA().value('(/EVENT_INSTANCE/LoginName)[1]','nvarchar(max)'),
    EVENTDATA().value('(/EVENT_INSTANCE/ObjectName)[1]','nvarchar(max)'),
    EVENTDATA().value('(/EVENT_INSTANCE/PostTime)[1]','nvarchar(max)'),
    EVENTDATA().value('(/EVENT_INSTANCE/TSQLCommand/CommandText)[1]',
    'nvarchar(max)');
END;
GO
```

The use of the *value()* method allows us to take out the pieces of the XML stream that we want. In this case, I've isolated the fields mentioned above. When it comes to dealing with DDL triggers, using *XQuery* is a good way to strip out the information from *EVENTDATA()* you don't need.

> **SOME INDEPENDENT ADVICE**
>
> While the example shown here for a DDL trigger simply used a *SELECT* statement to return parts of the *EVENTDATA()* XML that we were interested in, in reality, triggers should not return result sets like this. Should a trigger return a result set, it could result in unexpected behavior on the client. You can prevent triggers from returning result sets by setting a server configuration option "disallow results from triggers" for *sp_configure*, though an error will be generated if a trigger attempts to return a result set.

Important Techniques for DDL Triggers

There are certain techniques we'll use again and again in our DDL triggers, such as rolling back the statement that was executed, capturing the information about the statement, and firing off an e-mail alert (assuming database mail is enabled). Let's look at each of these techniques against the *CREATE_TABLE* event.

Rolling Back a DDL Statement

While DDL triggers do not fire prior to the statement executing, they do provide the capability to undo the statement that caused the trigger to fire by using the *ROLLBACK* command. As long as the command is issued within the body of the trigger, the statement will be forced to rollback. The user will receive an error indicating the transaction ended within the trigger. Given that this is not a particularly informative error message, a *PRINT* statement can be used to explain what the real issue is. Here's an example:

```
CREATE TRIGGER trigDDL_CreateTable
ON DATABASE
FOR CREATE_TABLE
AS
BEGIN
  -- Rollback the CREATE TABLE statement
  ROLLBACK;
  -- Warn the user that table creation isn't allowed.
  PRINT 'Table Creation not permitted.';
END;
GO
```

Auditing DDL Statements

If we want to keep a log of what DDL statements are being executed, the best way is to create an audit or change log table in a work database. Here is a sample table that can record DDL events:

```
CREATE TABLE dbo.ChangeLog
(
  DBName sysname,
  EventTime datetime,
  ServerLogin nvarchar(100),
  DBUser nvarchar(100),
  [Event] nvarchar(100),
  ObjectName nvarchar(255),
  [TSQL] nvarchar(2000)
);
GO
```

Once the change log table has been built, the DDL trigger can insert the event details into this table. However, if *ROLLBACK* is being utilized, it is important to observe the order of the particular steps. They are:

1. Parse the event details from *EVENTDATA()* into the appropriate variables.

2. Issue the *ROLLBACK* statement.

3. *INSERT* into the change log table.

If the *ROLLBACK* is issued before *EVENTDATA()* is parsed, the details will have been lost. Likewise, if the *INSERT* is issued before the *ROLLBACK*, it too will be rolled back, again losing the details. Here is the trigger with the steps in the proper order:

```
CREATE TRIGGER trigDDL_CreateTable
ON DATABASE
FOR CREATE_TABLE
AS
BEGIN
  -- Capture the pertinent event information prior to the ROLLBACK
  -- statement, otherwise it'll be lost.
  DECLARE @ServerLogin nvarchar(100);
  DECLARE @EventType nvarchar(100);
  DECLARE @PostTime datetime;
  DECLARE @TSQL nvarchar(2000);
  -- Use XQuery()'s value() method to extract the relevant
  -- event information.
  SET @ServerLogin = EVENTDATA().value(
    '(/EVENT_INSTANCE/LoginName)[1]',
    'nvarchar(100)');
  SET @EventType = EVENTDATA().value(
    '(/EVENT_INSTANCE/EventType)[1]',
    'nvarchar(100)');
  SET @PostTime = EVENTDATA().value(
    '(/EVENT_INSTANCE/PostTime)[1]',
    'datetime');
  SET @ObjectName = EVENTDATA().value(
    '(/EVENT_INSTANCE/ObjectName)[1]',
    'nvarchar(255)');
  SET @TSQL = EVENTDATA().value(
    '(/EVENT_INSTANCE/TSQLCommand/CommandText)[1]',
    'nvarchar(2000)');
  -- Rollback the CREATE TABLE statement
  ROLLBACK;
  -- Audit the attempt
  INSERT INTO DBWork.dbo.ChangeLog
  (DBName, EventTime, ServerLogin, DBUser, [Event], ObjectName, [TSQL])
```

```
    VALUES
    (DB_NAME(), @PostTime, @ServerLogin, CONVERT(nvarchar(100),
        CURRENT_USER), @EventType, @ObjectName, @TSQL)
END;
GO
```

Sending an E-mail Alert

If we want to send an e-mail alert, Database Mail must be enabled. If it is, we can use the *sp_send_dbmail* stored procedure within our DDL trigger to fire an e-mail alert. We can also use this in conjunction with the other techniques, such as rolling back the statement. Here is an example that captures the relevant event information (i.e., what server, what database, who did it, and what they did) and both rolls back the statement and sends an e-mail to the database group:

```
CREATE TRIGGER trigDDL_CreateTable
ON DATABASE
FOR CREATE_TABLE
AS
BEGIN
    -- Capture the pertinent event information prior to the ROLLBACK
    -- statement, otherwise it'll be lost.
    DECLARE @LoginName nvarchar(MAX);
    DECLARE @TSQLCommandText nvarchar(MAX);
    DECLARE @message_text nvarchar(MAX);
    -- Use XQuery()'s value() method to extract the relevant
    -- event information.
    SET @LoginName = EVENTDATA().value(
        '(/EVENT_INSTANCE/LoginName)[1]',
        'nvarchar(MAX)');
    SET @TSQLCommandtext = EVENTDATA().value(
        '(/EVENT_INSTANCE/TSQLCommand/CommandText)[1]',
        'nvarchar(MAX)');
    -- Create the body of the email with the pertinent details.
    SET @message_text = '
Server: ' +@@SERVERNAME + '
Database: ' + DB_NAME() + '
Login: ' + @LoginName + '
DDL Statement:
' + @TSQLCommandText;
    -- Rollback the CREATE TABLE statement
    ROLLBACK;
```

```
-- Send the email alert
EXEC msdb.dbo.sp_send_dbmail
  @recipients = 'AllDBAs@mycompany.com',
  @body = @message_text,
  @importance = 'High',
  @subject = 'CREATE TABLE Attempt';
END;
GO
```

This trigger fires whenever someone tries to create a table in the database. The first major step I performed was the rollback. Then I sent the e-mail. With respect to the e-mail, I've specified the recipient (assume ALLDBAs@mycompany.com is a distribution list for all the DBAs), I've created a body that provides the relevant details, I've marked the importance of the message so it flags everyone's attention, and I've given it a suitable title. SQL Server will take this message and hand it over to Database Mail, which will queue it up and send it off as soon as it can.

BEST PRACTICES ACCORDING TO MICROSOFT

Database Mail is not enabled when you first install SQL Server. As with any component of SQL Server, ensure you have a need for it before enabling it. Certainly if you have a requirement for mail, plan to use Database Mail if at all possible. SQL Mail is still supported in SQL Server 2005, but only for backward compatibility. SQL Mail depends on MAPI, which has proven problematic in past versions of SQL Server. Because of this, Microsoft recommends converting anything that depends on SQL Mail to use Database Mail and refrain from building new solutions using SQL Mail.

SOME INDEPENDENT ADVICE

Another way to handle e-mail alerts is to write the pertinent information to a table (such as an audit table). Let a SQL Server Agent job query the table and generate the e-mails accordingly. If e-mail alerts are embedded into the trigger, the whole transaction is delayed until Database Mail or SQL Mail receives the e-mail and completes its actions on them. This can cause a user to sit and wait, not knowing why the system appears to be hung up. By writing to a table that a SQL Server Agent is looking at, the transaction can complete quickly, whether it is rolled back or allowed to continue through.

Managing DDL Triggers

Part of implementing DDL triggers is understanding how to manage them. In this section we'll look at how DDL triggers can impact certain system-stored procedures. We'll also cover how to disable and re-enable DDL triggers for when you do want changes to occur. Finally, we'll look at querying the metadata on DDL triggers by utilizing some of the views provided in SQL Server 2005.

Impact of DDL Triggers on System Stored Procedures and SSMS

DDL triggers can affect certain system-stored procedures if the system-stored procedure performs an action that the DDL trigger would normally intercept as a T-SQL statement. For instance, an *ALTER AUTHORIZATION* on a particular database changes the database's owner. Therefore, a DDL trigger designed to fire on an *ALTER AUTHORIZATION* event will also catch the system-stored procedure *sp_changedbowner*. There are several system-stored procedures that will cause DDL events to fire. As a result, when you're designing your DDL triggers, plan to look at the "DDL Events for Use with DDL Triggers" topic in books online. It presents all of the events for both database and server scope in a tabular format. The information on the events also include what system-stored procedures are affected. For instance, the *CREATE_SCHEMA* event will trigger any time a schema is created, meaning the following system stored procedures will cause it to fire: *sp_addrole*, *sp_adduser*, *sp_addgroup*, and *sp_ grantdbaccess*.

The same issue exists for SQL Server Management Studio and any applications that use the SQL Management Objects (SMO) interface. For instance, if a DDL trigger is defined which prevents logins from being dropped, SSMS will be unable to drop it through the GUI interface, just as a *DROP LOGIN* statement or *sp_droplogin* stored procedure would fail.

SOME INDEPENDENT ADVICE

Many of these system-stored procedures are considered deprecated as of SQL Server 2005, and may not be supported in previous versions. For instance, *sp_addrole* has a successor in the *CREATE ROLE* DDL statement. While it may be easy to use the old familiar methods such as *sp_addrole*, in order to prepare for when those system-stored procedures are no longer available, it's best to require the use of the new statements when deploying and managing SQL Server 2005.

Enabling and Disabling DDL Triggers

At some point, you'll likely want to make changes, but the DDL trigger is enabled and therefore you aren't permitted to make any. Rather than dropping the DDL triggers and then having to recreate them, a better option is to simply disable them, perform the work, and re-enable them when you're done. SQL Server event provides an option to enable and disable all of the events at a given scope.

But before we look at the blanket enable/disable statements, let's look at how to disable and enable individual DDL triggers. The syntax for disabling a trigger is:

```
DISABLE TRIGGER <trigger name>
ON { ALL SERVER | DATABASE };
```

As always, specifying the correct scope is required. An example of disabling the DDL trigger we defined earlier is:

```
DISABLE TRIGGER trigDDL_CreateTable
ON DATABASE;
GO
```

To enable a trigger, the format is similar to:

```
ENABLE TRIGGER <trigger name>
ON { ALL SERVER | DATABASE };
```

Enabling and Disabling All the DDL Triggers of a Given Scope

If you've put in place multiple DDL triggers (e.g., specific triggers for tables, views, stored procedures, and so on), you may want to disable all of them at one time. The syntax for enabling all the triggers of a given scope is:

```
ENABLE TRIGGER ALL
ON { ALL SERVER | DATABASE };
```

For example, to enable all the DDL triggers on a particular database:

```
ENABLE TRIGGER ALL ON DATABASE;
GO
```

Disabling all triggers follows a similar syntax:

```
DISABLE TRIGGER ALL
ON { ALL SERVER | DATABASE };
```

And to disable all the DDL triggers on a particular database:

```
DISABLE TRIGGER ALL ON DATABASE;
GO
```

SOME INDEPENDENT ADVICE

If your solution implements independent triggers for each type of DDL event, it is probably best to disable all of the triggers at a database level using the one statement and then re-enabling likewise. Otherwise, certain triggers might be skipped either during the disable or re-enable process. The greater risk is during re-enabling. Missing a trigger could mean unwanted changes.

Getting Metadata on DDL Triggers

In SQL Server 2005, Microsoft added catalog views to reveal more metadata than what is available in the *INFORMATION_SCHEMA* views. DBAs and developers have made it a habit of querying against system tables, which Microsoft has always reserved the right to change between versions or even between service packs. The catalog views were introduced to provide the same type of information that could be obtained from the system tables, but with an interface that should not change over time. With respect to triggers, there are several catalog views we're interested in. A list of them is presented in Table 25.1.

Table 25.1 DDL Trigger Catalog Views

Catalog View	Scope	Purpose
sys.triggers	Database	Provides general information on all triggers.
sys.trigger_events	Database	Reports what events various triggers fire on.
sys.sql_modules	Database	Contains the trigger definitions (if T-SQL-based).
sys.assembly_modules	Database	Contains the reference to the CLR assembly (if CLR-based).
sys.server_triggers	Server	Provides general information on all triggers.
sys.server_trigger_events	Server	Reports what events various triggers fire on.
sys.server_sql_modules	Server	Contains the trigger definitions (if T-SQL-based).
sys.server_assembly_modules	Servers	Contains the reference to the CLR assembly (if CLR-based).

Since they are views, they can be queried just as with any other view. For instance, the following query returns all the server-level triggers, what they fire on, and what the definition of those triggers are:

```
SELECT st.name, ste.type_desc, ssm.definition
FROM sys.server_triggers st
  JOIN sys.server_trigger_events ste
    ON st.object_id = ste.object_id
  JOIN sys.server_sql_modules ssm
    ON ssm.object_id = st.object_id
ORDER by st.name;
GO
```

Scenarios for Deploying DDL Triggers

We've covered how DDL triggers work and how to implement and manage them. Now let's look at some common scenarios where we'd consider using DDL triggers to prevent or audit changes. In scenarios labeled "preventing," the DDL trigger rolls back the change (if necessary) and provides a suitable warning to the user if a rollback occurred. These D"DL triggers could easily be modified to include auditing or to fire off e-mails utilizing the techniques described in "Important Techniques for DDL Triggers." For scenarios labeled "auditing," the DDL trigger writes to the Change Log table described in the same section.

SOME INDEPENDENT ADVICE

As with any security solution, carefully plan on how you want to implement DDL triggers in your environment and first test on a non-production environment. A poorly planned and implemented DDL trigger "solution" can wreak havoc on a production system, especially if DDL triggers are preventing needed security updates, timely changes to schema, and so on. Also, if you're putting DDL triggers in place due to the Sarbanes-Oxley Act of 2000 (SOX), Basel II, the Health Insurance Portability and Accountability Act of 1996 (HIPAA), or any of the other compliance standards or legislation, you also will want to check with your auditors to verify that the measures you are implementing are considered satisfactory controls.

Preventing Endpoint Creation

Endpoints represent new entry points into SQL Server. Therefore, an endpoint should never be created arbitrarily. Because of this, preventing endpoint creation is a good first scenario for a DDL trigger. Remember, if at some point an endpoint is needed, the trigger can be disabled, the endpoint created, and then the DDL trigger re-enabled. Since we're preventing a new endpoint, we'll need to fire on the *CREATE_ENDPOINT* event and force a rollback.

One other point to make is with regards to the scope. The examples thus far in this chapter have been database-level DDL triggers. As a result, the *ON* clause always had *DATABASE*. For a server-level DDL trigger, the *ON* clause must have *ALL SERVER*. Just *SERVER* isn't correct syntax and will return an error if you attempt to create a DDL trigger without the *ALL*.

```
CREATE TRIGGER trigDDL_CreateEndpoint
ON ALL SERVER
FOR CREATE_ENDPOINT
AS
BEGIN
  -- Prevent the endpoint creation
  ROLLBACK;
```

```
-- Notify the user that the operation was blocked
PRINT 'New endpoints are not authorized.';
END;
GO
```

Preventing Database Ownership Changes

Changing the database owner can have a serious impact on security, if a particular SQL Server login is the database owner and ownership is suddenly changed. The login that was previously the database owner may no longer have rights to perform actions against the database, and a new login might suddenly have such rights. In addition, if cross-database ownership chaining was being used, this may now be broken since the security principal for the database owner, which means the owner of the *dbo* schema, has now changed. Here's how to prevent database ownership changes on a particular database:

```
CREATE TRIGGER trigDDL_AlterAuthDB
ON DATABASE
FOR ALTER_AUTHORIZATION_DATABASE
AS
BEGIN
  -- Prevent the ownership change
  ROLLBACK;
  -- Notify the user that the operation was blocked
  PRINT 'Changing the owner of the database is not permitted.';
END;
GO
```

This DDL trigger will also affect the *sp_changedbowner* system stored procedure.

Preventing DDL Changes to Objects

You've got a database in production, and normally no changes should occur to the traditional objects such as tables, views, and stored procedures. However, security changes should still occur granting login access as users to the database. If this describes your scenario, the following script details how to fire on the related object events, but not fire on any security events such as *CREATE USER*. As you can see by the code, there are eight different event groups specified. If, however, you want to audit any object changes to include security surrounding database users, you can replace the eight separate event groups with *DDL_DATABASE_LEVEL_EVENTS*.

```
CREATE TRIGGER trigDDL_ObjectChanges
ON DATABASE
FOR DDL_TABLE_VIEW_EVENTS, DDL_SYNONYM_EVENTS,
    DDL_FUNCTION_EVENTS, DDL_PROCEDURE_EVENTS,
    DDL_TRIGGER_EVENTS, DDL_EVENT_NOTIFICATION_EVENTS,
```

```
        DDL_ASSEMBLY_EVENTS, DDL_TYPE_EVENTS
AS
BEGIN
  -- Prevent the DDL change
  ROLLBACK;
  -- Notify the user that the operation was blocked
  PRINT 'No DDL changes on database objects may be performed.';
END;
GO
```

Preventing DDL Changes Except During a Maintenance Window

A possible scenario is that the DBAs are allowed to make changes during a certain maintenance window after hours. For instance, 7:00 P.M. through 7:00 A.M. the DBAs can make the changes they want. However, during the workday, no one is allowed to make changes. This DDL trigger prevents a method for doing this. Otherwise, it's the same as the previous scenario.

```
CREATE TRIGGER trigDDL_ObjectChangesMainWindow
ON DATABASE
FOR DDL_TABLE_VIEW_EVENTS, DDL_SYNONYM_EVENTS,
    DDL_FUNCTION_EVENTS, DDL_PROCEDURE_EVENTS,
    DDL_TRIGGER_EVENTS, DDL_EVENT_NOTIFICATION_EVENTS,
    DDL_ASSEMBLY_EVENTS, DDL_TYPE_EVENTS
AS
BEGIN
  -- Get the current time in order to check the window.
  DECLARE @current_time smalldatetime;
  SET @current_time = GETDATE();
  -- Maintenance window is from 7 PM to 7 AM. Prevent any
  -- changes outside of this block of time.
  IF (DATEPART(hh, @current_time) > 6) OR
     (DATEPART(hh, @current_time) < 19)
  BEGIN
    -- Prevent the DDL change
    ROLLBACK;
    -- Notify the user that the operation was blocked
    PRINT 'The maintenance window for database changes is 7 PM - 7 AM.';
  END;
END;
GO
```

Videos of SQL Server Tasks

I first got the idea of building a DDL trigger around a maintenance window from noted SQL Server expert Brian Knight. Brian used the maintenance window as one of his examples of DDL triggers in a video on JumpStart TV. While Jumpstart TV has videos on a number of subject areas, there are quite a few short videos on SQL Server-related tasks. You can access this resource at www.jumpstarttv.com/.

Auditing Login Creation/Deletion

Auditing login creation and deletion, at first glance, seems fairly easy. However, upon a second look, there are cases where we are not able to capture the audit information we want to see, like the command that was used. We can still capture the object (login) being referenced. That gives us some of the information. Why can't we capture the T-SQL command? In the case of *CREATE LOGIN* or *sp_addlogin*, there's a password that needs to be specified. If SQL Server allowed us to see the T-SQL text as is, we'd see the username and password. Since our DDL trigger example takes information like the T-SQL text and inserts it into a table, that would mean anyone with access to that table would also know it. As a result, SQL Server blocks the T-SQL text when it comes to security-sensitive commands like *CREATE LOGIN*. Here is the auditing example. Note that if the T-SQL text is not present, the trigger notes it and provides an explanation as to why (in case your auditor asks):

```
CREATE TRIGGER trigDDL_AuditCreateDropLogin
ON ALL SERVER
FOR CREATE_LOGIN, DROP_LOGIN
AS
BEGIN
  -- Capture the pertinent event information.
  DECLARE @ServerLogin nvarchar(100);
  DECLARE @EventType nvarchar(100);
  DECLARE @PostTime datetime;
  DECLARE @ObjectName nvarchar(255);
  DECLARE @TSQL nvarchar(2000);
  -- Use XQuery()'s value() method to extract the relevant
  -- event information.
```

```
SET @ServerLogin = EVENTDATA().value(
    '(/EVENT_INSTANCE/LoginName)[1]',
    'nvarchar(100)');
SET @EventType = EVENTDATA().value(
    '(/EVENT_INSTANCE/EventType)[1]',
    'nvarchar(100)');
SET @PostTime = EVENTDATA().value(
    '(/EVENT_INSTANCE/PostTime)[1]',
    'datetime');
SET @ObjectName = EVENTDATA().value(
    '(/EVENT_INSTANCE/ObjectName)[1]',
  'nvarchar(255)');
SET @TSQL = EVENTDATA().value(
    '(/EVENT_INSTANCE/TSQLCommand/CommandText)[1]',
    'nvarchar(2000)');
-- Note a T-SQL statement, SMO call, or system stored procedure
-- was used which could potentially contain a password. In these
-- cases, The CommandText element will not be populated. If that's
-- the case, test for it and make a note in the change log.
IF (@TSQL IS NULL)
BEGIN
    -- Set the @TSQL to indicate it was a blocked operation.
  SET @TSQL = 'Unknown: Blocked for security reasons.'
END;
-- Audit the attempt
INSERT INTO DBWork.dbo.ChangeLog
(DBName, EventTime, ServerLogin, DBUser, [Event], ObjectName, [TSQL])
VALUES
(DB_NAME(), @PostTime, @ServerLogin, CONVERT(nvarchar(100),
    CURRENT_USER), @EventType, @ObjectName, @TSQL)
END;
GO
```

On a related note, if you use SQL Server Profiler, you'll see the same sort of behavior with respect to hiding the exact T-SQL statement if a password is involved. Therefore, in these cases, we can audit the object being touched and follow the back up to try and determine what changes actually took place.

Auditing Changes to Specific Logins

If we want to audit changes to specific logins, we'll first need a source that holds the list of logins to monitor. Here is a simple table in the *DBWork* database, which contains a single column with the login name. We'll use it to match up against the *ObjectName* element from *EVENTDATA()*:

```
CREATE TABLE dbo.SensitiveLogin
(
  LoginName nvarchar(255)
)
GO
```

Now for the audit trigger. If we already have the DDL trigger in place to monitor for all login creations and deletions, the only thing we need to audit for is *ALTER LOGIN* attempts. I'll assume this is the case with the example. If it is not, you can use the *DDL_LOGIN_EVENTS* event group in place of the *ALTER_LOGIN* event. Speaking of other login events, *ALTER LOGIN* suffers from the same issue that *CREATE LOGIN* does: the T-SQL will be hidden by the SQL Server. As a result, we will know a change has happened and who did it, but we won't know exactly what was done. But at least we have an audit trail to investigate in case something breaks:

```
CREATE TRIGGER trigDDL_AuditAlterLogin
ON ALL SERVER
FOR ALTER_LOGIN
AS
BEGIN
  -- Capture the pertinent event information.
  DECLARE @ServerLogin nvarchar(100);
  DECLARE @EventType nvarchar(100);
  DECLARE @PostTime datetime;
  DECLARE @ObjectName nvarchar(255);
  DECLARE @TSQL nvarchar(2000);
  -- Use XQuery()'s value() method to extract the relevant
  -- event information.
  SET @ServerLogin = EVENTDATA().value(
      '(/EVENT_INSTANCE/LoginName)[1]',
      'nvarchar(100)');
  SET @EventType = EVENTDATA().value(
      '(/EVENT_INSTANCE/EventType)[1]',
      'nvarchar(100)');
```

```
SET @PostTime = EVENTDATA().value(
    '(/EVENT_INSTANCE/PostTime)[1]',
    'datetime');
SET @ObjectName = EVENTDATA().value(
    '(/EVENT_INSTANCE/ObjectName)[1]',
    'nvarchar(255)');
SET @TSQL = EVENTDATA().value(
    '(/EVENT_INSTANCE/TSQLCommand/CommandText)[1]',
    'nvarchar(2000)');
IF EXISTS (SELECT LoginName FROM DBWork.dbo.SensitiveLogin
    WHERE LoginName = @ObjectName)
BEGIN
  -- Note a T-SQL statement, SMO call, or system stored procedure
  -- was used which could potentially contain a password. In these
  -- cases, The CommandText element will not be populated. If that's
  -- the case, test for it and make a note in the change log.
  IF (@TSQL IS NULL)
  BEGIN
    -- Set the @TSQL to indicate it was a blocked operation.
    SET @TSQL = 'Unknown: Blocked for security reasons.'
  END;
-- Audit the attempt
  INSERT INTO DBWork.dbo.ChangeLog
  (DBName, EventTime, ServerLogin, DBUser, [Event], ObjectName, [TSQL])
  VALUES
  (DB_NAME(), @PostTime, @ServerLogin, CONVERT(nvarchar(100),
    CURRENT_USER), @EventType, @ObjectName, @TSQL)
  END;
END;
GO
```

Auditing User Creation/Deletion

The lat scenario we'll look at is auditing user creation/deletion within the database. Unlike with the logins, we don't have to deal with the SQL Server hiding the T-SQL. As a result, there is no *IF* clause to determine whether or not the *CommandText* element was populated. Given that, auditing user creation/deletion is an easy endeavor:

```
CREATE TRIGGER trigDDL_AuditCreateDropUser
ON DATABASE
FOR CREATE_USER, DROP_USER
AS
BEGIN
  -- Capture the pertinent event information.
  DECLARE @ServerLogin nvarchar(100);
  DECLARE @EventType nvarchar(100);
  DECLARE @PostTime datetime;
  DECLARE @ObjectName nvarchar(255);
  DECLARE @TSQL nvarchar(2000);
  -- Use XQuery()'s value() method to extract the relevant
  -- event information.
  SET @ServerLogin = EVENTDATA().value(
    '(/EVENT_INSTANCE/LoginName)[1]',
    'nvarchar(100)');
  SET @EventType = EVENTDATA().value(
    '(/EVENT_INSTANCE/EventType)[1]',
    'nvarchar(100)');
  SET @PostTime = EVENTDATA().value(
    '(/EVENT_INSTANCE/PostTime)[1]',
    'datetime');
  SET @ObjectName = EVENTDATA().value(
    '(/EVENT_INSTANCE/ObjectName)[1]',
    'nvarchar(255)');
  SET @TSQL = EVENTDATA().value(
    '(/EVENT_INSTANCE/TSQLCommand/CommandText)[1]',
    'nvarchar(2000)');
  -- Audit the attempt
  INSERT INTO DBWork.dbo.ChangeLog
  (DBName, EventTime, ServerLogin, DBUser, [Event], ObjectName, [TSQL])
  VALUES
  (DB_NAME(), @PostTime, @ServerLogin, CONVERT(nvarchar(100),
    CURRENT_USER), @EventType, @ObjectName, @TSQL);
END;
GO
```

Summary

In this chapter, we looked at DDL triggers in detail. We first covered what they were and why they came about: to prevent or intercept unwanted or unexpected DDL changes in SQL Server. SQL Server 2005 is the first version of SQL Server to implement this technology. DDL triggers can be at the server or the database level, meaning they can protect our server configuration in addition to database objects like tables and views.

We then investigated how to implement DDL triggers on our SQL Servers. Because SQL Server Management Studio doesn't provide much GUI support for triggers, we looked at the T-SQL syntax for creating and dropping triggers. We also covered how to get the event information for what caused the trigger to fire. This involved using the *EVENTDATA()* function and *XQuery()* methods to isolate key elements we are interested in. Finally, we talked about several key techniques for use with DDL triggers, including rolling back the firing statement, writing the details to an audit table, and sending an e-mail alert should a DDL trigger fire.

After discussing how to implement DDL triggers, we dove into how to maintain them. DDL triggers can have an effect on SMO calls as well as system-stored procedures. It's important to note that when you're designing your DDL triggers. Finally, we looked at the T-SQL commands to disable and enable triggers as needed. These commands give us the ability to turn off the triggers long enough to make planned changes to a monitored database and then reactivate the triggers. We also covered what catalog views are provided in SQL Server 2005 for us to query against to get metadata on our triggers.

The final section presented several scenarios where DDL triggers should be considered. From preventing a new endpoint from being created, to auditing the user creation/deletions on a given database, we investigated potential issues with the auditing and presented T-SQL code to give you a starting point.

Solutions Fast Track

DDL Triggers Explained

☑ DDL triggers fire on DDL statements such as *CREATE*.

☑ Events or event groups specified in the DDL trigger definition, determine what a particular DDL trigger will fire on.

☑ DDL triggers can be of server or database scope.

☑ DDL triggers always fire after the statement is executed, and they provide rollback capabilities.

Implementing DDL Triggers

☑ DDL triggers follow a syntax similar to DML triggers.

☑ When dropping a DDL trigger, specifying the scope is required.

☑ Event information is stored in the *EVENTDATA()* function, which returns an *xml* type. Use *XQuery()* methods within SQL Server 2005 to parse the XML.

Managing DDL Triggers

☑ DDL triggers can affect particular system-stored procedures.

☑ Like DML triggers, DDL triggers can be disabled and enabled as needed to perform database work.

☑ SQL Server 2005 provides catalog views we can query for the metadata of DDL triggers.

Scenarios for Deploying DDL Triggers

☑ DDL triggers can be used to prevent unwanted changes to the server configuration, such as the creation of new endpoints.

☑ DDL triggers can be used to audit changes to sensitive server logins.

☑ DDL triggers can be used to prevent unwanted schema changes within a database.

Frequently Asked Questions

Q: Aren't triggers nothing more than stored procedures attached to events or objects?

A: Not exactly. DML triggers have access to two special result sets, *inserted* and *deleted*. DDL triggers have access to the *EVENTDATA()* function. These are not available to normal stored procedures.

Q: I want to determine the order in which my triggers fire. Can I do this?

A: Using *sp_settriggerorder* you can set what triggers fire first and last on a given object or a given event. However, if you have more than three triggers, only the trigger that fires first and the trigger that fires last can be set. The others will fire in whatever order SQL Server executes them, and there is no guarantee that SQL Server will be consistent every time. When dealing with DDL triggers, triggers at multiple levels of the event group hierarchy cannot be set to fire in a particular order. Therefore, the order in which they fire cannot be guaranteed.

Q: I want to put DDL triggers in place to keep my DBAs from making changes in production. Will they be effective?

A: To a point, yes. DDL triggers, when enabled, will fire on the appropriate DDL event and can undo a change. However, if a DBA wants to get around a DDL trigger, all a person has to do is disable it. If he or she has the rights to do so, you cannot stop a person with malicious intent and with that level of access from making changes.

Q: Can DDL triggers affect system-stored procedures?

A: Yes, they can. See the "DDL Events for Use with DDL Triggers" section in Books Online for a chart that shows what DDL event corresponds to what stored procedures.

Q: If I want to e-mail an alert when a DDL trigger is fired, can I do so?

A: Yes, but it will require either Database Mail or SQL Mail to be configured and enabled on your SQL Server. If you have a choice, use Database Mail, as SQL Mail has been a problem child in previous versions of SQL Server.

Q: Can I use a DDL trigger to prevent a particular table from being changed?

A: While you cannot assign a DDL trigger against a particular table, you can have a DDL trigger fire on all *DDL_TABLE_EVENTS* for that database. Within the trigger definition itself you can look to see what table is being affected. Then you can take action if it's the table you want to protect.

Q: In SQL Server 2000 we used *SCHEMABINDING* to protect key tables and views. However, it only protected against some of the changes. Are DDL triggers any better?

A: Yes, they are. A DDL trigger will fire on an event as a whole, such as an *ALTER TABLE* statement. Within the definition of the DDL trigger you determine what action you're going to take. Therefore, a change like adding a column to a table, which wouldn't have been stopped by *SCHEMABINDING*, can be prevented using a DDL trigger.

Q: I've put in place a DDL trigger that prevents against DDL changes. However, I have changes I need to implement. Do I need to drop the trigger, perform my work, and then recreate it?

A: No you do not. You have the capability of disabling the trigger and then re-enabling it again when you are done.

Chapter 26

Data Encryption

Solution in this chapter:

- **Data Encryption Explained**

☑ **Summary**

☑ **Solutions Fast Track**

☑ **Frequently Asked Questions**

Introduction

In this chapter, we take a detailed look at data encryption and how it can be applied to protect SQL Server 2005 data. Currently, large data security breaches are occurring at an alarming rate. There has been a notable shift in cyber crime from intrusive denial of service (DoS) attacks to covert attacks targeting sensitive financial and personal data, often stored within databases. In response, several legislations/regulations have been released mandating that organizations implement adequate security controls that protect sensitive data. Some of these legislations dictate that security breaches involving sensitive information must be reported to impacted individuals.

Although other chapters in this book cover multiple effective and practical methods to secure your SQL Server 2005 database server, data encryption covered in this chapter is the last line of defense which, when implemented correctly, can provide an excellent layer of security. We will discuss side effects associated with database data encryption and the pitfalls that you should be aware of before implementing it within your environment.

Regardless of whether you are considering database data encryption as a means of satisfying regulatory compliance requirements, trying to safeguard your organization's sensitive data, or you would simply like to learn more about the encryption capabilities of SQL Server 2005, this chapter is a must read and will provide you a clear end-to-end view into the data encryption and decryption processes that can be used to protect SQL Server 2005 data.

Data Encryption Explained

Data encryption can be defined as the translation of plain text into a format that cannot be easily understood. This is referred to as *cipher text*. A mathematical procedure called an algorithm is used in combination with a string of data, known as a *key*, to translate plain text data into cipher text. As a rule of thumb, the longer the key, the greater the protection it provides. Cipher text can only be reversed by an individual who possesses the appropriate key to reverse the encryption. Data encryption can be performed on data stored locally, called data "at-rest," or while the data is being transmitted over the network, referred to as data "in-flight."

BEST PRACTICES ACCORDING TO MICROSOFT

Symmetric keys should be used to encrypt database data. The speed of symmetric encryption keys make them a good choice for routine data encryption and decryption functions.

Asymmetric keys should be used to encrypt symmetric keys. Leveraging the strength of asymmetric key encryption is an ideal means of securing symmetric keys.

To prevent data loss, create and securely store backups of all of your keys. You should make copies of your encryption keys and store them at a secure off-site location.

Ensure only strong passwords are used in conjunction with securing keys. The passwords used to protect encryption keys are prone to password-guessing attacks. Successful attacks can lead to the disclosure of your encrypted data. Using strong passwords will help maintain the confidentially of your keys and associated data.

Encrypt only the sensitive data that is critical to your organization. Data encryption affects performance; therefores encryption should be restricted to only the required data elements.

RC4 and RC2 algorithms are weak and should not be used to encrypt sensitive data. The RC2 and RC4 algorithms are extremely quick and use minimal system resources; however, the underlying encryption is relatively weak. Sensitive information should be encrypted by stronger algorithms such as Triple Data Encryption Standard (3DES) and Advanced Encryption Standard (AES).

SOME INDEPENDENT ADVICE

This chapter will cover a plethora of database encryption methods, which you may be anxious to apply on your database servers. However, before implementing database encryption, you should ensure that you have developed a data encryption and key management strategy that meets the requirements of your organization. Rushing into data encryption without the proper planning can give you a false sense of security and result in immediate disk space and performance issues or worse case, cause you to lock yourself out of your data. Performing the following steps will help you identify your organization's data encryption requirements:

- *Classify your data.* Review your database and ensure you have identified the sensitive information that needs to be encrypted.

- *Determine whom you are trying to protect the data from.* This may be remote attackers, a local sysadmin, or unauthorized individuals who may come into possession of lost or stolen database media.

- *Pinpoint where the data is at risk.* Identify application data flows and determine where the greatest risk lies. This may be when the data is transferred over an un-trusted network, when the data is locally stored and processed, or a mixture of both.

- *Determine the level of encryption required.* The strength of the encryption algorithm you select should match the data in which it is protecting. In most cases, if you are protecting highly sensitive information, you should ensure that a strong encryption algorithm and key-bit are used. Alternatively, you may decide to encrypt information that your organization deems less valuable with an algorithm that is weaker, but has better performance.

Completion of the aforementioned points should provide you with the information you need to develop the correct encryption strategy for your organization. The encryption aspect is only half of the solution. In addition, you must also develop a key management strategy, which factors in where the keys will be stored, who has access to them, and if or when they are recycled. Focusing on both encryption and key management will ensure that the implementation of database encryption into your environments is as seamless as possible.

Why Secure Data?

Databases often contain sensitive financial, healthcare, and corporate data. As mentioned earlier, data security breaches are occurring at an alarming rate and international legislations have been passed, which set regulations on how organizations must protect this sensitive data. The Payment Card Industry (PCI), Health Insurance Portability and Accountability Act (HIPAA), Personal Information Protection and Electronic Documents Act (PIPEDA), Gramm-Leach-Bliley Act (GLBA), and the UK Data Protection Act are just a few of these regulations. Several regulations require that sensitive data be encrypted and that organization's must identify and report data disclosure or misuse. If these regulations are not followed, organizations can face serious repercussions, ranging from financial penalties to imprisonment of responsible parties. Depending on the nature of your business, the above regulations may not apply, but before you discount the need to encrypt data consider that sensitive information can also include corporate information including confidential HR data, trade secrets, patents, designs, or client listings, which, if disclosed to unauthorized individuals, could have a grave impact on your organization.

At this point you may be wondering, "why not just encrypt all data using a secure algorithm?" instead of determining specifically what data elements require encryption. The answer is that there is a significant performance impact when encrypting data, as SQL Server must perform authentication, encryption, and decryption functions seamlessly to encrypt and decrypt the data. In addition, there are several other side effects associated with data encryption, which we will touch on later in this chapter. For these reasons, you should use data encryption only when required and only on the required data elements.

Shortcut...

The Risk Associated with Unencrypted Backup Tapes

Most organizations invest substantial resources into physical and technological security controls in an effort to protect data. However, some of these organizations store and transport this data on unencrypted backup tapes, which significantly increases the risk of disclosure. Several organizations have reported data security breaches resulting from misplaced backup tapes, that contained unencrypted data. Some regulations specifically require that sensitive data backups be encrypted. Encrypting backups can mitigate the security risk posed by misplaced backup tapes and possibly prevent your organization from publicly reporting a data security breach.

Performing Encryption

SQL Server 2005 data encryption can be performed using native SQL Server functionality, file-system-based Encryption File System (EFS), or third-party encryption tools. These encryption methods use one or a combination of symmetric and asymmetric encryption methods. Symmetric encryption uses one key to both encrypt and decrypt data, whereas asymmetric encryption can use two keys, one to encrypt and the other to decrypt. Each encryption method contains advantages and disadvantages, both of which are detailed later in this chapter.

EFS Encryption

EFS can be used to encrypt SQL Server 2005 data files and folders. EFS is supported on Windows 2000 and later operating systems with New Technology File Systems (NTFS) formatted drives. EFS uses a combination of symmetric and asymmetric methods to provide transparent SQL Server 2005 data encryption. On Windows 2003 Server and newer operating systems, EFS by default creates a random File Encryption Key, which is a 256-bit AES key to perform data encryption. The File Encryption Key is then itself encrypted with the user's public key and stored within the encrypted file or folder.

To encrypt SQL Server 2005 data files and folders using EFS, follow these steps:

1. Stop the SQL Server service.

2. Log out and log in using the SQL Server service account credentials.

3. Right-click on the file or folder to be encrypted and select **Properties | General Tab | Advanced**.

4. Within the Advanced attributes window, select **Encrypt contents to secure data**.

5. Within the Advanced attributes window, press **OK**.

6. Within the Properties tab, press **OK**.

7. If you are encrypting a folder containing subfolders, you will be presented with another window asking if you would like to encrypt them as well. Press **OK**.

8. EFS encrypted files and folder names should now appear in green within any Windows file explorer window.

9. Re-start the SQL Server services.

If errors are generated, you may have encrypted the SQL Server data files using an account that is not linked to the SQL Server service account. You can decrypt the data folders by reversing the steps above and trying again. When encrypting individual database files, EFS first creates a plain text copy of the file to be encrypted, encrypts the target file, and then deletes the temporary file. This temporary file is not securely deleted and can be recovered using common data recovery tools. To prevent local file disclosure, you should use a secure data deletion tool to overwrite the areas of disk containing the temporary file. Alternatively, you can simply encrypt the parent folder that contains the database files to ensure any temporary files are also encrypted.

EFS encryption is beneficial if the database media is stolen or misplaced. When transferring EFS encrypted files over the network, Windows first decrypts the file and then transfers the plain text equivalent. Some administrators perform manual backups of database files prior to implementing changes on the database server. If this backup involves copying data files from one server to another, you will effectively be storing an unencrypted copy of your database on the destination server.

Shortcut...

Encryption File System Contains Inherit Flaws

On Windows Server 2003, EFS uses a strong 256-bit AES key to encrypt data. Under most circumstances, this would be an effective method of encryption; however, this AES key is protected by the user's public key, which is based on the user's Windows login password. This ultimately reduces EFS protection to the strength of the user's Windows password. There are publicly available tools that can successfully decrypt EFS encrypted data by exploiting this flaw. Because of this, EFS should not be used to encrypt sensitive database data.

Working with EFS Encrypted Data

EFS encryption is managed by the operating system, and seamlessly provides file and folder encryption to SQL Server 2005. All SQL Server functions and operations remain unchanged when using this encryption method. Because EFS is handled outside of SQL Server 2005, encryption keys must be backed up separately in addition to your database backups.

Hierarchal Encryption

SQL Server 2005 uses a hierarchal encryption and key management model. Each level in the hierarchy encrypts the layer underneath. The foundation of the SQL Server 2005 encryption hierarchy depends on Data Protection API (DAPI), which is native in all Windows 2000 and newer operating systems. SQL Server 2005 relies on DAPI to create the SQL Server Service Master and Database Master Keys. Once these keys have been created, you can create database encryption keys, certificates, and pass-phrases, and use them to encrypt database data. An illustration of the hierarchal encryption model can be found in Figure 26.1.

Figure 26.1 The Hierarchal Encryption Model

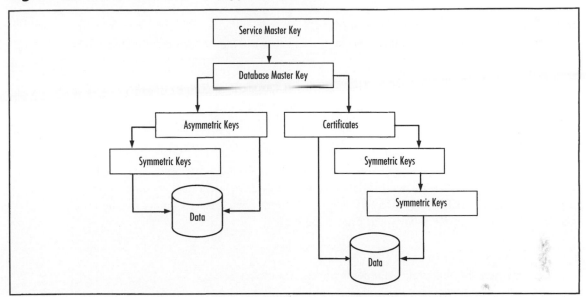

Native SQL Server 2005 data encryption is restricted to the encryption and decryption of the varbinary data type. This encryption can be performed down to the cell level, meaning that the contents of each column within each row can be encrypted using different encryption keys, certificates, and pass-phrases. Depending on the data types currently used within your database, implementing native data encryption may require schema changes and/or data type conversions to the varbinary data type.

When a SQL Server 2005 instance is started for the first time, a 128-bit 3DES symmetric Service Master Key is automatically created and encrypted, using both the active SQL Server service account credentials and the machine credentials. This way, if one becomes corrupt, SQL Server 2005 can still access the key using the other method. This Service Master Key is the single most important key within your SQL Server instance, because it is ultimately used to encrypt all other keys within the database instance. Additionally, the key is used to encrypt SQL Server-linked server passwords, connection strings, and account credentials.

Immediately after starting SQL Server 2005 for the first time, you should backup the Service Master Key. To protect the Service Master Key backup file, it is encrypted using a user-supplied password. You should make sure that this password is securely stored within a password management solution and readily available, as you will not be able to restore the Service Master Key backup without it. The syntax for the *BACKUP SERVICE MASTER KEY* statement is as follows:

```
BACKUP SERVICE MASTER KEY TO FILE = 'FILE'
  ENCRYPTION BY PASSWORD = 'PASSWORD'
```

Here are definitions of two arguments of this syntax:

- ***FILE***   Specifies the directory path and the filename in which to create the key backup file.
- ***PASSWORD***   The password used to encrypt the Service Master Key backup file.

You will need the *CONTROL SERVER* permission on the database server to run the *BACKUP SERVICE MASTER KEY* statement. The following syntax uses the *BACKUP SERVER MASTER KEY* statement to back up the Service Master Key, and encrypts the backup file with the user-supplied password:

```
BACKUP SERVICE MASTER KEY TO FILE = 'C:\backup\keys\Service_Master.key'
  ENCRYPTION BY PASSWORD = '$ytRi@8&XeEl67'
```

It is possible that the Service Master Key may be accidentally disclosed, corrupted, or will need to be proactively recycled for security reasons. You can regenerate a new random Service Master Key using the *ALTER SERVICE MASTER KEY* statement. The common syntax for the *ALTER SERVICE MASTER KEY* statement is as follows:

```
ALTER SERVICE MASTER KEY [FORCE] REGENERATE
```

Let's analyze the following arguments of this syntax:

- ***FORCE***   Regenerates the Service Master Key regardless of encountered errors.
- ***REGENERATE***   Regenerates the Service Master Key.

For a listing of additional statement arguments, please see SQL Server 2005 Books Online. To execute the *ALTER SERVICE MASTER KEY* statement, you will need the *CONTROL SERVER* permission within the database server. The following syntax regenerates a new random Service Master Key:

```
ALTER SERVICE MASTER KEY REGENERATE
```

You can use the *RESTORE SERVICE MASTER KEY* statement to restore a previously backed up Service Master Key. The syntax for the *RESTORE SERVICE MASTER KEY* statement is as follows:

```
RESTORE SERVICE MASTER KEY FROM FILE = 'FILE'
  DECYRPTION BY PASSWORD = 'PASSWORD' [FORCE]
```

Now let's analyze some of the arguments of this syntax:

- ***FILE***   Specifies the directory path and filename of the key to be backed up.
- ***PASSWORD***   Indicates the password used to encrypt the Service Master Key backup file.
- ***FORCE***   Replaces the Service Master Key regardless of encountered errors.

You will need the *CONTROL SERVER* permission on the database server to run the *RESTORE SERVICE MASTER KEY* statement. The following syntax restores our previously backed up Service Master Key using the *RESTORE SERVICE MASTER KEY* statement:

```
RESTORE SERVICE MASTER KEY FROM FILE = 'C:\backup\keys\Service_Master.key'
  DECRYPTION BY PASSWORD = '$ytRi@8&XeEl67'
```

Underneath the Service Master Key in the hierarchal encryption model is the Database Master Key. A Database Master Key is a 128-bit 3DES symmetric key, which is encrypted using a user-supplied password and stored within the database. Each database can have only one Database Master Key, and this key is used exclusively by SQL Server for the management of other keys. Database Master Keys are not created by default, and must be manually created in a database. To create a Database Master Key, you can use the *CREATE MASTER KEY* statement, which has the following syntax:

```
CREATE MASTER KEY ENCRYPTION BY PASSWORD = 'PASSWORD'
```

In this statement, *PASSWORD* specifies the password used to encrypt and protect the database master key.

You will need the *CONTROL* permission within the database in order to run the *CREATE MASTER KEY* statement. The following syntax creates a Database Master Key and encrypts it with the user-supplied password:

```
CREATE MASTER KEY ENCRYPTION BY PASSWORD = '@iLz&7%DyUio16'
```

When a Database Master Key is created, a backup is also performed, and is encrypted using the Service Master Key and stored within the Master database. This feature is referred to as *Auto Key Management* and ensures that there is a Database Master Key backup and that SQL Server can decrypt and use the Database Master Key as required, without knowing the user-supplied password. A downside to *Auto Key Management* is that users with sysadmin privileges can use the Service Master Key to gain access to the Database Master Key. To alter the properties of the Database Master Key, including disabling the *Auto Key Management* feature, you can use the *ALTER MASTER KEY* statement:

```
ALTER MASTER KEY
  [FORCE] [REGENERATE WITH ENCRYPTION BY PASSWORD = 'PASSWORD'|
  ADD ENCRYPTION BY [PASSWORD = 'PASSWORD' | SERVICE MASTER KEY] |
  DROP ENCRYPTION BY [PASSWORD = 'PASSWORD' | SERVICE MASTER KEY]
```

Here are explanations of some of the arguments of this syntax:

- **FORCE** Regenerates the Database Master Key regardless of encountered errors.

- **REGENERATE WITH ENCRYPTION BY PASSWORD** Regenerates the Database Master Key and all keys that it protects.

- **PASSWORD** Specifies the password in which to encrypt or decrypt the Database Master Key.

- **ADD ENCRYPTION BY** Encrypts the Database Master Key with a user-supplied password or the Service Master Key.

- **DROP ENCRYPTION BY** Removes password or Service Master Key encryption applied to the Database Master Key.

To execute the *ALTER MASTER KEY* statement you will need the *CONTROL* permission within the database. The following syntax regenerates a Database Master Key:

```
ALTER MASTER KEY REGENERATE WITH ENCRYPTION BY PASSWORD = '9m87hU&X^6Z6%R'
```

Shortcut...

Disabling Master Key Encryption

Turning off Master Key encryption prevents sysadmins from having global access to the keys required to decrypt data. However, SQL Server decrypts encrypted data before processing, and stores this data in memory. This data can be retrieved from memory by a system admin as required. Once encryption by Master Key is disabled, anyone needing to access the Database Master Key will need to know the password that was used to encrypt it. This includes SQL Server, which will no longer be able to load the Database Master Key at server start-up. Therefore, each time you need to use the Database Master Key, you will need to manually open and close it using the *OPEN MASTER KEY* and *CLOSE MASTER KEY* statements. You should weigh the pros and cons with disabling the Master Key encryption when determining what works best for your database systems.

Even if Auto Key Management is enabled, the backup Database Master Key still resides on the server and should be backed up and stored at a secure off-site location. You can use the *BACKUP MASTER KEY* statement to perform a manual backup of the Database Master Key. The syntax of this statement is as follows:

```
BACKUP MASTER KEY TO FILE = 'FILE'
  ENCRYPTION BY PASSWORD = 'PASSWORD'
```

Here are definitions of the arguments of this syntax:

- **FILE**   Specifies the directory path and the filename in which to create the backup file.

- **PASSWORD**   Specifies the password used to encrypt the Database Master Key backup file.

To execute the *BACKUP MASTER KEY* statement, you will need the *CONTROL* permission within the database. The following syntax uses the *BACKUP MASTER KEY* statement to back up the Database Master Key, and encrypts it with the supplied password:

```
BACKUP MASTER KEY TO FILE = 'C:\backup\keys\Database_Master.key'
  ENCRYPTION BY PASSWORD = '9m87hU&X^6Z6%R'
```

Similar to the Service Master Key, the password used to protect the Database Master Key backup will be needed again to restore the key, so you should be sure to keep it safe. To restore your Database Master Key from backup, you can use the *RESTORE MASTER KEY* statement:

```
RESTORE MASTER KEY FROM FILE = 'FILE'
  DECRYPTION BY PASSWORD = 'PASSWORD'
  ENCRYPTION BY PASSWORD = 'PASSWORD'
  [FORCE]
```

Here are definitions of the arguments of this syntax:

- **FILE**   Specifies the directory path and the filename in which to create the backup file.
- **DECRYPTION BY PASSWORD**   Specifies the password required to decrypt the Database Master Key backup file.
- **ENCRYPTION BY PASSWORD**   Specifies the password used to encrypt the imported Database Master Key.
- **FORCE**   Replaces the Database Master Key regardless of encountered errors.

You will need the *CONTROL* permission with the database to run the *RESTORE MASTER KEY* statement. When a Database Master Key is restored, SQL Server first decrypts all encrypted keys and then encrypts the keys with the newly created Database Master Key. If errors are encountered at any point during the associated decryption process, the entire restore process will fail. However, you can use the *FORCE* argument to perform the restore regardless of any encountered errors. Please note that this can result in the loss of encryption keys and associated data, so use this option with caution.

The following syntax uses the *RESTORE MASTER KEY* statement to restore our previously backed up Database Master Key, and encrypts it with the supplied password:

```
RESTORE MASTER KEY FROM FILE = 'C:\backup\keys\Database_Master.key'
  DECRYPTION BY PASSWORD = '9m87hU&X^6Z6%R'
  ENCRYPTION BY PASSWORD = 'J#yAsdl8z)f3tq'
```

SQL Server is intelligent and will not unnecessarily decrypt and re-encrypt data. In the preceding syntax, we restored the same Database Master Key that was present within the database. SQL Server should have returned a message stating that the old and new master keys were identical, therefore decrypting data and re-encrypting with the same Database Master Key was not required.

Using Keys to Encrypt Data

Encryption keys are the next level within the encryption hierarchy. As covered earlier, keys are used in conjunction with an algorithm to convert plain text into cipher text. There are two types of encryption keys within SQL Server 2005, *symmetric* and *asymmetric*.

Symmetric Key Encryption

Symmetric encryption uses a single key, which is distributed to all individuals who need to either encrypt or decrypt data. Symmetric keys are often used for data encryption, due to their speed and flexibility. An illustration of the symmetric key encryption and decryption process can be found in Figure 26.2.

Figure 26.2 Symmetric Key Encryption and Decryption

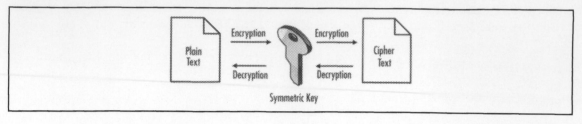

SQL Server 2005 supports the following symmetric encryption algorithms:

- Rivest Cipher 2 (RC2)

- Rivest Cipher 4 (RC4)

- Rivest Cipher 4 (RC4) – 128-bit

- Data Encryption Standard XORed (DESX)

- AES - 128-bit

- AES - 192-bit

- AES - 256-bit

- DES

- 3DES

You can use the *CREATE SYMMETRIC KEY* statement to create the encryption key:

```
CREATE SYMMETRIC KEY KEYNAME [AUTHORIZATION OWNERNAME]
WITH [KEY_SOURCE = 'PASS_PHRASE' |
ALGORITHM = <ALGORITHM> |
IDENTITY_VALUE = 'IDENTITY_PHRASE']
ENCRYPTION BY [CERTIFICATE CERTIFICATE_NAME |
PASSWORD = 'PASSWORD' |
SYMMETRIC KEY SYMMETRIC_KEY_NAME |
ASYMMETRIC KEY ASY_KEY_NAME]
```

Here are definitions of the arguments of this syntax:

- *AUTHORIZATION OWNERNAME* Specifies the user who will own the key.

- *KEY_SOURCE = PASS_PHRASE* Specifies the pass phrase used to build the key.

- *ALGORITHM = <ALGORITHM>* Specifies the encryption algorithm that the key will use. The available algorithms are DES, TRIPLE_DES, RC2, RC4, RC4_128, DESX, AES_128, AES_192, and AES_256.

- *IDENTITY_VALUE = IDENTITY_PHRASE* Specifies a phrase to be used to create a Globally Unique Identifier (GUID) for use in data encryption with a temporary key.

- **CERTIFICATE_NAME**   Specifies the name of the certificate that will be used to encrypt the created key.

- **PASSWORD**   Specifies the password that will be used to encrypt the created key.

- **SYMMETRIC_KEY**   Specifies the name of the symmetric key that will encrypt the created key.

- **ASY_KEY_NAME**   Specifies the name of the asymmetric key that will encrypt the created key.

You will need the *ALTER ANY SYMMETRIC KEY* permission within the database to run the *CREATE SYMMETRIC KEY* statement. When a symmetric key is created, it is encrypted using a password, certificate, or another encryption key, and stored locally within the database. It is also possible to use several of these encryption methods on the same symmetric key. Depending on the options specified, additional permissions may be required on the key and associated objects.

For example, if you are protecting the symmetric key with a certificate, users will need privileges on the symmetric key as well as the associated certificate used to encrypt it. For a full list of permission requirements, please refer to SQL Server 2005 Books Online. The following syntax uses the *CREATE SYMMETRIC KEY* statement to create a symmetric key and encrypts it using the supplied password:

```
CREATE SYMMETRIC KEY SymmetricKey01
  WITH ALGORITHM = TRIPLE_DES
  ENCRYPTION BY PASSWORD = 'UsQ5z&Sa@dwThX'
```

Shortcut...

Carefully Choose How to Protect Your Encryption Keys

When passwords are used to encrypt your symmetric keys, the 3DES algorithm is used. If you are using a strong encryption algorithm such as AES, it is possible that your encryption key will be secured by the weaker 3DES algorithm. For database systems storing highly sensitive information, you should use key encryption of equal to or higher protection than that of the underlying encryption key.

When using symmetric key encryption, you will most likely create more than one symmetric encryption key to encrypt data. To help keep track of the symmetric keys that have been created on your database server, you can query the *sys.symmetric_key* view. This view returns a listing of all symmetric keys created on a given SQL Server. The following syntax queries the *sys.symmetric_key* view and returns a listing of all symmetric keys on a database server:

```
Select * from sys.symmetric_keys
```

Within SQL Server 2005, there is no direct way to back up a symmetric key. Symmetric keys are created and stored within the user databases; therefore, to back up symmetric encryption keys you must back up the entire user database. An encryption key must be decrypted and opened prior to use. To open an encryption key, you can use the *OPEN SYMMETRIC KEY* statement:

```
OPEN SYMMETRIC KEY [KEY_NAME]
  DECYRPTION BY
    [CERTIFICATE CERTIFICATE_NAME {WITH PASSWORD = 'PASSWORD'} |
    ASYMMETRIC KEY ASYM_KEY_NAME {WITH PASSWORD = 'PASSWORD'} |
    SYMMETRIC KEY DECRYPTING_KEY_NAME |
    PASSWORD = 'PASSWORD']
```

Here are definitions of the arguments of this syntax:

- **KEY_NAME**   Specifies the name of the key to be opened.
- **CERTIFICATE_NAME**   Specifies the name of the certificate that will be used to decrypt the symmetric key.
- **ASYMMETRIC KEY ASYM_KEY_NAME**   Specifies the name of the asymmetric key that will be used to decrypt the symmetric key.
- **SYMMETRIC KEY DECRYPTING_KEY_NAME**   Specifies the name of the symmetric key that will be used to decrypt the symmetric key to be opened.
- **PASSWORD = 'PASSWORD'**   Specifies the password to be used to encrypt the symmetric key.

The permissions required to execute the *OPEN SYMMETRIC KEY* statement vary, depending on the symmetric key encryption methods in place. In order to execute the statement, you will need access to both the symmetric key to be opened and the associated protection method. For a full list of permission requirements, please refer to SQL Server 2005 Books Online. The following syntax uses the *OPEN SYMMETRIC KEY* statement to decrypt and open our previously created symmetric key using the supplied password:

```
OPEN SYMMETRIC KEY SymmetricKey01
  DECRYPTION BY PASSWORD = 'UsQ5z&Sa@dwThX'
```

You can use the *sys.openkeys* view to obtain a listing of all keys open within your database session. The following syntax queries this view to generate a listing of open keys:

```
Select * from sys.openkeys
```

You can add or remove encryption methods by using the *ALTER SYMMETRIC KEY* statement:

```
ALTER SYMMETRIC KEY KEY_NAME
  [{ADD | DROP} ENCRYPTION BY {CERTIFICATE CERTIFICATE_NAME |
                             PASSWORD = 'PASSWORD' |
    SYMMETRIC KEY KEY_NAME |
    ASYMMETRIC KEY KEY_NAME}]
```

Here are definitions of the arguments of this syntax:

- **ADD ENCRYPTION BY**   Adds a symmetric key encryption method.
- **DROP ENCRYPTION BY**   Removes a symmetric key encryption method.
- **CERTIFICATE_NAME**   Specifies the certificate that will encrypt the symmetric key.
- **PASSWORD**   Specifies the password that will encrypt the symmetric key.
- **SYMMETRIC KEY KEY_NAME**   Specifies the symmetric key that will encrypt the symmetric key being altered.
- **ASYMMETRIC KEY KEY_**   Specifies the asymmetric key used to encrypt the symmetric key.

To use the *ALTER SYMMETRIC KEY* statement, you will need the *ALTER* permission on the symmetric key being altered. When adding encryption methods, you will need the *VIEW DEFINITION* permission on the certificate or asymmetric key being added, and when dropping encryption methods you will need the *CONTROL* permission on the associated certificate or asymmetric key. The following code uses the *ALTER SYMMETRIC KEY* statement to add another password encryption method to our symmetric key:

```
ALTER SYMMETRIC KEY SymmetricKey01
  ADD ENCRYPTION BY PASSWORD = '78u!A%s@iOlpP)'
```

You can use the *ENCRYPTBYKEY* statement to perform the actual data encryption. This statement requires the GUID of the key to be used for data encryption. The *KEY_GUID* statement can be used to obtain the GUID of the key:

```
KEY_GUID ('KEYNAME')
```

In this statement, *KEYNAME* specifies the name of the symmetric key to be used.

You will need the *VIEW* permission on the key to obtain the GUID. The following syntax obtains the key GUID from our previously created symmetric key:

```
select Key_GUID ( 'SymmetricKey01' )
```

Results:

```
79541500-4642-41D5-8006-6B4FA86F114F
```

Note that the key GUID on your database server will differ, as SQL Server uses some random variables when creating the GUID. Now that we have the key GUID, we can use the *ENCRYPTBYKEY* statement to encrypt data. The common syntax for the *ENCRYPTBYKEY* is as follows:

```
ENCRYPTBYKEY (KEY_GUID, 'PLAINTEXT')
```

KEY_GUID specifies the GUID of the key to be used for encryption. *PLAINTEXT* is the data string to be encrypted.

For a full list of statement arguments, please see SQL Server 2005 Books Online. No additional permissions are required to use the *ENCRYPTBYKEY* statement; however, you will need the appropriate permissions to decrypt and open the symmetric key to be used for encryption.

For convenience, the syntax below shows how to combine the *KEY_GUID* and *ENCRYPTBYKEY* statements together into a single line statement:

```
ENCRYPTBYKEY (KEY_GUID('KEYNAME'), 'PLAINTEXT')
```

The following syntax uses this statement with our previously created symmetric key to encrypt the supplied string:

```
SELECT ENCRYPTBYKEY(KEY_GUID('SymmetricKey01'), 'symmetric encryption test')
```

Results:

```
0x00AD3385CCE4774A89719A0A429E5067010000005BB250C2665E9F3B94CDFC87B8FDD67A6880CD51E
DD361AFF8E85786B1357E3196640C4E69D8030331BD879B91C693F28DC37D9E078623E2ABFDD5651D2F
B9B5A37B4E30112D31D6
```

The preceding statement results illustrate that the plain text string was successfully encrypted using our symmetric key. SQL Server 2005 uses a random value during the encryption process, which results in unique cipher text each time a value is encrypted. This means that the results above will be different than what you will see on your database server. Notice that the length of the cipher text is substantially longer than that of its plain text equivalent. Encryption using strong algorithms and keys can result in data padding of over 2,000 times its plain text equivalent, so you should encrypt with caution.

To decrypt data, you can use the *DECRYPTBYKEY* statement. The common syntax for the *DECRYPTBYKEY* statement is as follows:

```
DECRYPTBYKEY ('CIPHERTEXT')
```

In this statement, *CIPHERTEXT* is the data string to be decrypted.

For a full list of statement arguments, please see SQL Server 2005 Books Online. No additional permissions are required to use the *DECRYPTBYKEY* statement, but you will need the appropriate permissions on the key or certificate encryption methods used to protect the symmetric key. The following syntax decrypts the cipher text and converts the varbinary data type to the human readable varchar data type:

```
SELECT CAST(DECRYPTBYKEY (0x00AD3385CCE4774A89719A0A429E5067010000005BB250C2665E9F3
B94CDFC87B8FDD67A6880CD51EDD361AFF8E85786B1357E3196640C4E69D8030331BD879B91C693F28D
C37D9E078623E2ABFDD5651D2FB9B5A37B4E30112D31D6)AS varchar)
```

Note that you should substitute the cipher text in the preceding statement with the cipher text that you obtained from the earlier *ENCRYPTBYKEY* statement. Here is what the results of running the preceding statement will look like:

```
symmetric encryption test
```

After you use an encryption key, it will remain open unless you explicitly close it. To close a symmetric key, you can use the *CLOSE* statement.

```
CLOSE [SYMMETRIC KEY KEY_NAME | ALL SYMMETRIC KEYS]
```

In this statement, *SYMMETRIC KEY KEY_NAME* specifies the name of the single symmetric key to be closed. *ALL SYMMETRIC KEYS* closes all open symmetric keys tied to the active session and the open database master key.

No additional permissions are required to execute the *CLOSE* statement. The following syntax closes our open symmetric key:

```
CLOSE SYMMETRIC KEY SymmetricKey01
```

When the symmetric key is no longer needed, it can be deleted using the *DROP SYMMETRIC KEY* statement.

```
DROP SYMMETRIC KEY [KEY_NAME]
```

In this statement *KEY_NAME* specifies the name of the symmetric key to be removed from the database.

To execute the *DROP SYMMETRIC KEY* statement, you will need the *CONTROL* permission on the symmetric key to be dropped. The following syntax drops our previously created symmetric key:

```
DROP SYMMETRIC KEY SymmetricKey01
```

SQL Server 2005 contains safeguards to prevent the accidental deletion of encryption keys, and will not allow you to drop keys if they are in use or have been used to encrypt data currently encrypted within the database. The following syntax walks you through the end-to-end symmetric encryption and decryption process of table data:

```
-- Demonstration of symmetric key encryption
-- Create Database
CREATE Database SymKeyEncryptDemo
GO
USE SymKeyEncryptDemo
--
-- Switch to database context
--
-- Create table for data to be encrypted
CREATE Table Customers(
FirstName varchar(30),
LastName varchar(30),
CreditCardNum varbinary(300))
--
--** Remember to backup this key immediately on your database server! **
--
-- Create Database Master Key
CREATE MASTER KEY ENCRYPTION BY PASSWORD = '0%q9y7@D!@FE87'
--
-- Create symmetric key
CREATE SYMMETRIC KEY SymmetricKey02
WITH ALGORITHM = TRIPLE_DES
```

```
ENCRYPTION BY PASSWORD = 'St(N'&G67yY&'Q5'
--

--Open the symmetric key
OPEN SYMMETRIC KEY SymmetricKey02 DECRYPTION BY PASSWORD = 'St(N'&G67yY&'Q5'
-- Populate table with data included encrypted credit card numbers
INSERT INTO Customers Values('Michael', 'Smith',
EncryptByKey(Key_GUID('SymmetricKey02'), '45187328943209423'))
INSERT INTO Customers Values('Sean', 'Malone',
EncryptByKey(Key_GUID('SymmetricKey02'), '31238977673292340'))
INSERT INTO Customers Values('Mikaela', 'Morris',
EncryptByKey(Key_GUID('SymmetricKey02'), '63457324982847293'))
--

--View the contents of the table
Select * from Customers
--

--View table data including the decrypted plain text credit card numbers
--

SELECT Firstname,LastName, CAST(decryptbykey(CreditCardNum) AS varchar)
as 'CreditCardNum' from customers
--

--Clean-up objects
CLOSE SYMMETRIC KEY SymmetricKey02;
DROP SYMMETRIC KEY SymmetricKey02;
DROP MASTER KEY;
USE TEMPDB
DROP DATABASE SymKeyEncryptDemo;
-- END
```

Asymmetric Encryption

Asymmetric encryption uses two keys: one is referred to as a *public key* that encrypts data, and the other is known as a *private key* that decrypts data. These keys together form a *key pair*. Due to this key pair, you can freely share the public key, which allows individuals to encrypt data, but ensure only the authorized individual who possesses the private key can decrypt it. Asymmetric encryption provides superior encryption when compared to symmetric encryption; however, it is also significantly slower and more resource-intensive. As a result, asymmetric encryption is normally reserved for the encryption of symmetric keys or data that is infrequently encrypted or decrypted. An illustration of the asymmetric key encryption and decryption process can be found in Figure 26.3.

Figure 26.3 Asymmetric Key Encryption and Decryption

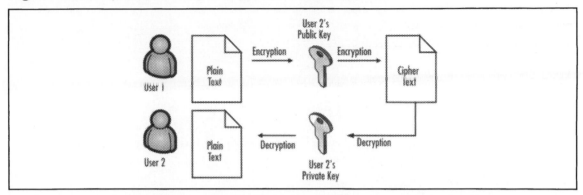

SQL Server 2005 supports the following asymmetric encryption algorithms:

- Rivest, Shamir and Adleman (RSA) 512-bit

- RSA 1024-bit

- RSA 2048-bit

To create an Asymmetric key pair, you can use the *CREATE ASYMMETRIC KEY* statement:

```
CREATE ASYMMETRIC KEY ASYM_KEY_NAME
  [AUTHORIZATION DATABASE_PRINCIPAL_NAME]
  [FROM FILE = 'PATH_TO_STRONG_NAME_FILE' |
             EXECUTABLE FILE = 'PATH_TO_EXECUTEABLE_FILE' |
             ASSEMBLY ASSEMBLY_NAME]
  WITH ALGORITHM = {RSA_512 | RSA_1024 | RSA_2048}
  [ENCRYPTION BY PASSWORD = 'PASSWORD']
```

Here are explanations of the arguments of this syntax:

- *AUTHORIZATION DATABASE_PRINCIPAL_NAME*   Specifies the user who will own the asymmetric key.

- *FILE = PATH_TO_STRONG_NAME_FILE*   Specifies the path of a strong-name file in which to load an existing key pair.

- *EXECUTABLE FILE = PATH_TO_EXECUTABLE_FILE*   Specifies the assembly from which the public key will be loaded.

- *ASSEMBLY ASSEMBLY_NAME*   Specifies the assembly name from which to load the public key.

- *ALGORITHM*   Specifies the bit-length of the private key.

- *PASSWORD*   Specifies the password that will be used to encrypt the private key.

To execute the *CREATE ASYMMETRIC KEY* statement, you will need the *CREATE ASYMMETRIC KEY* permission within the database. The following syntax creates an asymmetric key pair and encrypts the private key with a user-supplied password:

```
CREATE ASYMMETRIC KEY ASymmetricKey01
WITH ALGORITHM = RSA_1024
ENCRYPTION BY PASSWORD = '7q^3USu#6Ts@70'
```

Because the private key was protected with a user-supplied password, the 3DES algorithm was used. You can query the *sys.asymmetric_keys* view to obtain a listing of all asymmetric keys on your database server. The following syntax queries selected fields within this view, to obtain specific information about our previously created asymmetric key:

```
select name, pvt_key_encryption_type_desc, algorithm_desc from sys.asymmetric_keys
where name = 'AsymmetricKey01'
```

Results:

```
Name                 pvt_key_encryption_type_desc   algorhithm
---------------      ----------------------------   ----------

ASymmetricKey01      ENCRYPTED_BY_PASSWORD          RSA_512
```

Similar to symmetric keys, there is no direct way to back up individual asymmetric keys, and you will need to back them up via a full database backup. If you need to change the properties of an asymmetric private key by resetting the password used to encrypt it or adding or removing protection mechanisms, you can use the *ALTER ASYMMETRIC KEY* statement:

```
ALTER ASYMMETRIC KEY ASYM_KEY_NAME
    [REMOVE PRIVATE KEY |
    WITH PRIVATE KEY {ENCRYPTION BY PASSWORD = 'PASSWORD' |
    DECRYPTION BY PASSWORD = 'OLD_PASSWORD'}]
```

Here are the definitions for the arguments of this syntax:

- **ASYM_KEY_NAME**   The name of the asymmetric key to be altered.

- **REMOVE PRIVATE KEY**   Removes the private key associated with the asymmetric key.

- **WITH PRIVATE KEY**   Modifies the protection of the private key.

- **ENCRYPTION BY PASSWORD = 'PASSWORD'**   Specifies the new password in which to encrypt the private key.

- **DECRYPTION BY PASSWORD = 'OLD_PASSWORD'**   Specifies the old password required to decrypt the private key.

To execute the *ALTER SYMMETRIC KEY* statement, you will need the *CONTROL* permission within the database. As mentioned earlier, strong keys protected by passwords are ultimately protected using weaker encryption. The following syntax replaces the password–based private key encryption with encryption provided by the Database Master Key:

```
ALTER ASYMMETRIC KEY ASymmetricKey01
WITH PRIVATE KEY (DECRYPTION BY PASSWORD = '7q^3USu#6Ts@70' )
```

If we query the *sys.asymmetric_keys* view again, we receive the following results, which show that the encryption method has changed from *"ENCRYPTED_BY_PASSWORD"* to *"ENCRYPTED_BY_MASTER_KEY"*:

```
select name, pvt_key_encryption_type_desc, algorithm_desc from
sys.asymmetric_keys where name = 'AsymmetricKey01'
```

Results:

```
Name              pvt_key_encryption_type_desc    algorhithm
---------------   ----------------------------    ----------
ASymmetricKey01   ENCRYPTED_BY_MASTER_KEY         RSA_512
```

To encrypt data using asymmetric keys, you can use the *ENCRYPTBYASYMKEY* statement.

```
ENCRYPTBYASYMKEY (ASYM_KEY_ID, 'PLAINTEXT')
```

In this statement, *ASYM_KEY_ID* refers to the ID of the asymmetric key to be used for encryption. *PLAINTEXT* specifies the data string to be encrypted.

To execute the *ENCRYPTBYASYMKEY* statement, you will need the *VIEW DEFINITION* permissions on the asymmetric key. The following syntax encrypts the supplied string using our asymmetric key:

```
SELECT ENCRYPTBYASYMKEY(AsymKey_ID('ASymmetricKey01'),
'asymmetric encryption test')
```

Results:

```
0x8188A9FF913A7821CCE127E93903E738C1DD0BA8B95E2D17C689F3012441AE7FF2EBF12836B4AE8
4F0CE2B5252E05B020DC4BDDE5863D134D7872B1E49B83B1201C9A540EC9A428BA337381646816F783F
226F788C81DA3D9956FB8C817BA3996DEC00BCCFCF37E3A2127F3331FB76E8B9CC57323F16F1F873CFC
936650079B3
```

As mentioned earlier, the results above will differ than what you receive on your SQL Server. Once data has been encrypted, it can be reversed using the *DECRYPTBYASYMKEY* statement:

```
DECRYPTBYASYMKEY (ASYM_KEY_ID, 'CIPHERTEXT', 'ASYM_KEY_PASSWORD')
```

Here are definitions of the arguments of this syntax:

- **ASYM_KEY_ID** The ID of the key to be used for data decryption.
- **CIPHERTEXT** The text to be decrypted.
- **ASYM_KEY_PASSWORD** The password originally used to encrypt the asymmetric key.

To execute the *ENCRYPTBYASYMKEY* statement, you will need the *VIEW DEFINITION* permission on the asymmetric key. The following syntax decrypts the cipher text and converts the varbinary data type to the human readable varchar data type:

```
SELECT CAST (DECRYPTBYASYMKEY (AsymKey_ID('ASymmetricKey01'), 0xD02E38FFAA7F03C013B
84FAD4F8179E656E6248F587E4B06F13ECD7FB09C5FA51AAF80D5B6168BE02EF76D815E05930965F9EB6
3319797AB3058AF771A2C947B89A4D2EC0BF560E36D38F4520D81BF82C08167A69539B40EE2AF7ECD1C0
89368709DEAFAA1FB5C5AF200B2BAD6A7BC75B193FE3B5030478876EC6CB7B554295A) AS varchar)
```

Note that you should substitute the cipher text in the above statement with the cipher text that you obtained from the earlier *ENCRYPTBYASYMKEY* statement. Here is what the results of running the preceding statement will look like:

```
asymmetric encryption test
```

The performance impact of encrypting data using asymmetric encryption is even larger than that of symmetric encryption, so encrypt with caution. When the asymmetric keys are no longer needed, the *DROP ASYMMETRIC KEY* statement can be used to remove the key from the database:

```
DROP ASYMMETRIC KEY KEY_NAME
```

In this statement, *KEY_NAME* is the name of the asymmetric key to be removed from the database.

To execute the *DROP ASYMMETRIC KEY* statement, you will need the *CONTROL* permission on the key. The following syntax removes our asymmetric key from the database:

```
DROP ASYMMETRIC KEY ASymmetricKey01
```

The following script outlines the asymmetric encryption process from end-to-end:

```
-- Demonstration of symmetric key encryption
-- Create Database
CREATE Database ASymKeyEncryptDemo
GO
USE ASymKeyEncryptDemo
--
-- Switch to database context
--
-- Create table for data to be encrypted
CREATE Table Customers(
FirstName varchar(30),
LastName varchar(30),
CreditCardNum varbinary(300))
--
--** Remember to backup this key immediately on your database server! **
-- Create Database Master Key
CREATE MASTER KEY ENCRYPTION BY PASSWORD = '8%q$y7@D!@FE87'
--
```

```
--Create asymmetric key and use the databse master key to encrypt the private key
CREATE ASYMMETRIC KEY ASymmetricKey02
WITH ALGORITHM = RSA_1024
--
-- Populate table with data included encrypted credit card numbers
INSERT INTO Customers Values('Mark', 'Sloan', EncryptByAsymKey
(AsymKey_ID('ASymmetricKey02'), '4556456812426280'))
INSERT INTO Customers Values('Addison', 'Dodge', EncryptByAsymKey
(AsymKey_ID('ASymmetricKey02'), '38696177059004'))
INSERT INTO Customers Values('Rebecca', 'Jones', EncryptByAsymKey
(AsymKey_ID('ASymmetricKey02'), '628262815022262'))
--
--View the contents of the table
Select * from Customers
--
--View table data including the decrypted plain text credit card numbers
--
SELECT Firstname,LastName, CAST(DecryptByAsymKey(AsymKey_ID('ASymmetricKey02'),
CreditCardNum) AS varchar) as 'CreditCardNum' from customers
--
--Clean-up demo
DROP ASYMMETRIC KEY ASymmetricKey02;
DROP MASTER KEY;
USE TEMPDB
DROP DATABASE ASymKeyEncryptDemo;
-- END
```

Using Certificates to Encrypt Data

Certificates are parallel with asymmetric keys in the SQL Server 2005 encryption hierarchy. A certificate is simply a method of using asymmetric encryption. Certificates bind public keys to individuals who hold the associated private key. Certificates use the same RSA algorithm as asymmetric keys; therefore, they are resource-intensive and their use is normally restricted to encrypting other keys. SQL Server contains an integrated certificate authority, which it uses to issue its own self-signed, and industry standard X.509 certificates. Alternatively, you can import certificates from an external certificate authority. The use of external certificates allows you to use a wider range of key lengths, which can provide enhanced security. Certificates are the most secure way in which to encrypt data natively within SQL Server 2005. You can use the *CREATE CERTIFICATE* statement to create a certificate within SQL Server 2005. The common syntax of the *CREATE CERTIFICATE* statement is as follows:

```
CREATE CERTIFICATE CERTIFICATE_NAME [AUTHORIZATION USER_NAME]
  {FROM FILE = 'PATH_TO_PRIVATE_KEY'
  WITH PRIVATEKEY [, ENCRYPTION BY PASSWORD = 'PASSWORD' |
                  , DECRYPTION BY PASSWORD = 'PASSWORD']}
```

```
WITH SUBJECT = CERTIFICATE_SUBJECT_NAME, |
[START_DATE = MM/DD/YYYY
END_DATE = MM/DD/YYYY]
```

Here are definitions of the arguments in this syntax:

- **FILE = PATH_TO_PRIVATE_KEY**   Specifies the directory and the file name to the private key.

- **ENCRYPTION BY PASSWORD = 'PASSWORD'**   Specifies the password that will be used to encrypt the certificate private key.

- **DECRYPTION BY PASSWORD = 'PASSWORD'**   Specifies the password originally used to encrypt the private key.

- **CERTIFICATE_SUBJECT_NAME**   A descriptive string that will be embedded into the certificate metadata.

- **START_DATE**   Specifies the date in which the certificate becomes valid.

- **END_DATE**   Specifies the date in which the certificate expires.

For a full listing of all statement arguments, please refer to SQL Server 2005 Books Online. You will need the *CREATE CERTIFICATE* permission within the database to create a certificate. The following syntax creates a certificate and encrypts the certificate private key with the supplied password:

```
CREATE CERTIFICATE Certificate01
ENCRYPTION BY PASSWORD = '&7YuKj%4@)aSZ@'
WITH SUBJECT = 'Certificate to test encryption',
START_DATE = '8/13/2007',
EXPIRY_DATE = '8/13/2011'
```

Unlike symmetric and asymmetric keys, certificates can be backed up individually. To back up a certificate, you can use the *BACKUP CERTIFICATE* statement:

```
BACKUP CERTIFICATE CERT_NAME TO FILE = 'PATH_TO_FILE'
  [WITH PRIVATE KEY
    (FILE = 'PATH_TO_PRIVATE_KEY_FILE',
     ENCRYPTION BY PASSWORD = 'ENCRYPTION_PASSWORD',
     DECRYPTION BY PASSWORD = 'DECRYPTION_PASSWORD')]
```

Here are definitions of the arguments of this syntax:

- **CERT_NAME**   Specifies the name of the certificate to be backed up.

- **PATH_TO_FILE**   Specifies the directory path and the filename that will be used for the certificate public key backup.

- **PATH_TO_PRIVATE_KEY_FILE**   Specifies the directory path and the filename that will be used for the certificate private key backup.

- **ENCRYPTION_PASSWORD**   Specifies the password that will be used to encrypt the certificate private key backup.

- **DECRYPTION_PASSWORD**   Specifies the password that will be used to decrypt the certificate private key within the database.

To execute the *BACKUP CERTIFICATE* you will need the *CONTROL* permission on the certificate and the *VIEW DEFINITION* permission on the database. The following syntax uses the *BACKUP CERTIFICATE* statement to back up both the public and private key of our previously create certificate, and encrypts the private key backup file with a user-supplied password:

```
BACKUP CERTIFICATE Certificate01 TO FILE = 'C:\backup\certificates\Certificate01.pub'
  WITH PRIVATE KEY
  (DECRYPTION BY PASSWORD = '&7YuKj%4@)aSZ@',
  ENCRYPTION BY PASSWORD = '9UyZ%E!b8%7Ly#',
  FILE = 'C:\backup\certificates\Certificate01.prv')
```

For a complete listing of statement arguments and permission requirements, please see SQL Server 2005 Books Online. To restore a certificate from a backup file, you can use the *FROM FILE* argument within the *CREATE CERTIFICATE* statement, which we covered earlier. The following syntax restores our previously backed up public and private key:

```
CREATE CERTIFICATE Certificate01 FROM FILE = 'C:\backup\certificates\Certificate01.pub'
  WITH PRIVATE KEY (FILE = 'C:\backup\certificates\Certificate01.prv',
  DECRYPTION BY PASSWORD = '9UyZ%E!b8%7Ly#',
  ENCRYPTION BY PASSWORD = '&7YuKj%4@)aSZ@')
```

Note that if you created *Certificate01* previously, you will need to drop the certificate prior to running the above syntax. You can obtain a listing of all certificates present in your database by using the *sys.certificates* view:

```
Select ' from sys.certificates
```

To change the properties of a certificate you can use the *ALTER CERTIFICATE* statement:

```
ALTER CERTIFICATE CERTIFICATE_NAME
  REMOVE PRIVATE KEY |
  WITH PRIVATE KEY (FILE = 'PATH_TO_PRIVATE_KEY' |
                    DECRYPTION BY PASSWORD = 'PASSWORD' |
                    ENCRYPTION BY PASSWORD = 'PASSWORD')
  WITH ACTIVE FOR BEGIN_DIALOG = [ON | OFF]
```

Here are definitions of the arguments of this syntax:

- **CERTIFICATE_NAME**   The name of the certificate to be altered.

- **REMOVE PRIVATE KEY**   Removes the private key from the certificate.

- **FILE = 'PATH_TO_PRIVATE_KEY'**   Specifies the directory and the file name to the pHrivate key.

- **DECRYPTION BY PASSWORD = PASSWORD**   Specifies the password in which to decrypt the private key.

- **ENCRYPTION BY PASSWORD = PASSWORD**   Specifies the password in which to encrypt the private key.

- **ACTIVE FOR BEGIN_DIALOG**   Enables or disables a certificate for use with Service Broker.

To run the *ALTER CERTIFICATE* command you will need the *ALTER* permission on the certificate. The following syntax changes our certificate private key protection method from user-supplied password to database master key:

```
ALTER CERTIFICATE Certificate01
WITH PRIVATE KEY (
DECRYPTION BY PASSWORD = '&7YuKj%4@)aSZ@')
```

To encrypt data using the certificate public key, we can use the *ENCRYPTBYCERT* statement:

```
ENCRYPTBYCERT (CERTIFICATE_ID, 'PLAINTEXT')
```

In this statement, *CERTIFICATE_ID* specifies the ID of the certificate to be used for encryption. *PLAINTEXT* is the data string you wish to encrypt.

You will need the *VIEW DEFINITION* permission on the certificate to execute the *ENCRYPTBYCERT* statement. The following syntax uses the *ENCRYPTBYCERT* statement to encrypt the supplied string using our certificate:

```
SELECT ENCRYPTBYCERT(Cert_ID('Certificate01'), 'certificate encryption test')
```

Results:

```
6999578923DAEC2B3EE96E69174429EBF54C392A532919679624097CD050110CEEF4DDB3BF22656549
268848C2F6E6BA70C0E543DFB411B654302AB9582A525DB835940FB76F9AAC501BBC5E3D689FB0431B
A7AF3C51A4DCDC5BCB7D101324E466A23447DF916E80D026E2A2E6D5A433E75804ADF8E9B75BF0E097
```

As we mentioned earlier, the results above will differ from what you receive on your SQL Server. To decrypt the cipher text, we can use the *DECRYPTBYCERT* statement:

```
DECRYPTBYCERT (CERTIFICATE_ID, 'CIPHERTEXT', CERT_PASSWORD)
```

Here are the definitions of the arguments of this syntax:

- **CERTIFICATE_ID**   The ID of the certificate to be used for encryption.

- **CIPHERTEXT**   The string that was previously encrypted with the certificate public key.

- **CERT_PASSWORD**   The password that encrypts the certificate private key.

To execute the *DECRYPTBYCERT* statement, you will need the *VIEW DEFINITION* permission on the certificate. The following syntax uses the *DECRYPTBYCERT* statement to decrypt the cipher text and convert the results into the human readable varchar data type:

```
SELECT CAST (DECRYPTBYCERT(Cert_ID('Certificate01'),
0x50BCA9702D6999578923DAEC2B3EE96E69174429EBF54C392A532919679624097CD050110CEEF4DDB
3BF22656549268848C2F6E6BA70C0E543DFB411B654302AB9582A525DB835940FB76F9AAC501BBC5E3D
689FB0431BA7AF3C51A4DCDC5BCB7D101324E466A23447DF916E80D026E2A2E6D5A433E75804ADF8E9B75BF0E097)
AS varchar)
```

Note that you should substitute the cipher text in the above statement with the cipher text that you obtained from the earlier *ENCRYPTBYCERT* statement. Here is what the results of running the preceding statement will look like:

```
certificate encryption test
```

When you no longer need a certificate, it can be removed from the database using the *DROP CERTIFICATE* statement:

```
DROP CERTIFICATE CERTIFICATE_NAME
```

In this statement, *CERTIFICATE_NAME* specifies the name of the certificate to be removed.

To execute the *DROP CERTIFICATE* statement, you will need the *CONTROL* permission on the certificate. The following syntax drops our previously created certificate.

```
DROP CERTIFICATE Certificate01
```

The following script outlines the certificate encryption process from end-to-end:

```
-- Demonstration of certiifcate encryption
-- Create Database
CREATE Database CertEncryptDemo
GO
USE CertEncryptDemo
--
-- Switch to database context
--
-- Create table for data to be encrypted
CREATE Table Customers(
FirstName varchar(30),
LastName varchar(30),
CreditCardNum varbinary(300))
--
-- Create Database Master Key
CREATE MASTER KEY ENCRYPTION BY PASSWORD = '5YtF4$aQ#W4d^W'
--
--** You should backup the Database Master Key immediately after creation! **
--
-- Create certificate and use the database master key to encrypt the
private key
CREATE CERTIFICATE Certificate02
  WITH SUBJECT = 'Test certificate for encryption',
  START_DATE = '1/1/2007',
  EXPIRY_DATE = '1/1/2012';
```

```
--
-- Populate table with data included encrypted credit card numbers
INSERT INTO Customers Values('Blake', 'Cabbage',
EncryptByCert(Cert_ID('Certificate02'), '342724356361631'))

INSERT INTO Customers Values('Colin', 'Edwareds',
EncryptByCert(Cert_ID('Certificate02'), '4516525615214110'))

INSERT INTO Customers Values('Anoson', 'Monroe',
EncryptByCert(Cert_ID('Certificate02'), '5582858885802510'))

--
--View the contents of the table
Select ` from Customers

--
--View table data including the decrypted plain text credit card numbers
--
SELECT Firstname,LastName, CAST(DecryptByCert(Cert_ID('Certificate02'),
CreditCardNum) AS varchar) as 'CreditCardNum' from customers

--
--Clean-up demo
DROP CERTIFICATE Certificate02;

DROP MASTER KEY;

USE TEMPDB

DROP DATABASE CertEncryptDemo;

--END
```

Using Pass Phrases to Encrypt Data

A password that allows for spaces can be referred to as a *pass phrase*. The benefit of pass phrases is that you can make them meaningful and easy to remember. Instead of creating and managing encryption keys or certificates in your database server, you can encrypt data using only a pass phrase. The *ENCRYPTBYPASSPHRASE* statement uses the supplied pass phrase to generate a symmetric key, which is used to perform the actual data encryption. No key management is required, as the key will be recreated each time the same pass phrase is supplied. The common syntax of the *ENCRYPTBYPASSPHRASE* statement is as follows:

```
ENCRYPTBYPASSPHRASE ('PASSPHRASE', 'PLAINTEXT')
```

In this statement, *PASSPHRASE* specifies the data string to be used to derive an encryption key. *PLAINTEXT* specifies the data to be encrypted.

No permissions are required to run the *ENCRYPTBYPASSPHRASE* statement. The following syntax encrypts the string using the supplied pass phrase:

```
SELECT ENCRYPTBYPASSPHRASE('SQL Server 2005 Pass Phrase Encryption', 'pass phrase
encryption test')
```

Results:

```
0x01000000B0FA66E0152FB0B655B23439904E36F3ED5B758618BEED0F2A2BF918C6CF9DF685BC2A60A
AD5E81D660BA5A396D1CA89
```

As mentioned earlier, the results above will differ than what you receive on your SQL Server. To decrypt data, you can use the *DECRYPTBYPASSPHRASE* statement. The general syntax of this statement is as follows:

```
DECRYPTBYPASSPHRASE ('PASSPHRASE', 'CIPHERTEXT')
```

In this statement, *PASSPHRASE* specifies the data string to be used to derive a decryption key. *CIPHERTEXT* specifies the data to be decrypted.

Similar to the *ENCRYPTBYPASSPHRASE* statement, no permissions are required to execute the *DECRYPTBYPASSPHRASE* statement. The following syntax uses the *DECRYPTBYPASSPHRASE* statement to decrypt the previously encrypted data, and converts it into the human readable varchar format:

```
SELECT CAST (DECRYPTBYPASSPHRASE('SQL Server 2005 Pass Phrase Encryption', 0x01000
000B0FA66E0152FB0B655B23439904E36F3ED5B758618BEED0F2A2BF918C6CF9DF685BC2A60AAD5E81D
660BA5A396D1CA89) AS varchar)
```

Note that you should substitute the cipher text in the above statement with the cipher text that you obtained from the earlier *ENCRYPTBYPASSPHRASE* statement. Here is what the results of running the preceding statement will look like:

```
pass phrase encryption test
```

The encryption algorithm and key length used by pass phrase encryption has not been formally documented by Microsoft. Because of this, it is recommended that you do not use this encryption mechanism to encrypt sensitive data.

Encrypting Stored Procedures, Functions, Views, and Triggers

SQL Server 2005 allows users to obfuscate the contents of a stored procedure, view, function, or trigger using the *WITH ENCRYPTION* argument within the object *CREATE* or *ALTER* statement. Once a stored procedure, function, view, or trigger has been encrypted, you will not be able to decrypt it to alter or view the contents. Therefore, before applying this encryption, ensure that you have a good plain text copy of all object source code in a secure code management solution. The below syntax creates a plain text stored procedure, which we will later encrypt:

```
CREATE PROCEDURE sp_encryptedobjects
  AS
  PRINT 'Plain Text Contents'
```

We will now use the *sp_helptext* procedure to view the contents of our stored procedure:

```
sp_helptext sp_encryptedobjects
```

Results:

```
Text
--------------

CREATE PROCEDURE sp_encryptedobjects
AS
PRINT 'Plain Text Contents (1)'
```

The results show that the contents of the procedure are plain text and easily obtainable. Now, using the *ALTER PROCEDURE* statement and specifying the *WITH ENCRYPTION* argument, we will encrypt our previously created stored procedure:

```
ALTER PROCEDURE sp_encryptedobjects
  WITH ENCRYPTION
  AS
  PRINT 'Plain Text Contents (1)'
```

Now when we attempt to look at the contents again using *sp_helptext*, the following message is displayed:

```
The text for object 'sp_encrytpedobjects' is encrypted.
```

This shows that we could not obtain the logic contained within the encrypted stored procedure. If you navigate to the stored procedure within SQL Server Management Studio, the procedure contains a lock beside it and you will not be allowed to view the procedure contents. This feature was integrated into Microsoft SQL Server to help protect sensitive information and code logic contained within stored procedures, views, functions, and triggers from disclosure.

Shortcut...

Flaws within Microsoft Object Encryption

The object encryption used by Microsoft is weak, and there are publicly available scripts that can successfully decrypt the objects. Further, at run-time, SQL Server internally decrypts the object and SQL Profiler can be used to capture object logic in plain text form. Due to this, object encryption should not be used to encrypt sensitive information, and you should not embed key or certificate passwords or pass phrases in SQL Server objects encrypted using object-based encryption.

Working with Data Encrypted by Native SQL Server 2005 Encryption

When SQL Server 2005 data is encrypted using keys, certificates, and pass phrases, the database changes the way this data is handled and processed.

Indexing Encrypted Data

SQL Server uses a random vector during the encryption process, to help protect the cipher text from pattern detection attacks. However, this protection also means that encrypting the same data twice will produce different cipher text. This side effect prevents you from efficiently using an index created on an encrypted data column. Although it is possible to build and use an index on encrypted data, in the background, SQL Server 2005 decrypts each encrypted cell within the column, and then attempts to satisfy the associated query. This is extremely time consuming and resource-intensive. Additionally, the index will not be used as SQL Server will not know what the actual decrypted cell values will be until the data is actually decrypted. If the data you will encrypt presently contains an index, you should seriously consider the performance impact associated with encrypting it.

Replicating Encrypted Data

SQL Server 2005 replication will replicate encrypted data but not the associated encryption keys. This can result in replicated data being unusable on the various replication partners. To correct this, you will need to create the encryption key on the publisher database using the *KEY_SOURCE* and *IDENTITY* arguments of the *CREATE* or *ALTER SYMMETRIC KEY* statements. These arguments will ensure that you can manually create an identical key on the other servers, which will need to decrypt the data. For further details on this, please refer to SQL Server 2005 Books Online.

Symmetric Key Usage Tracking

SQL Server 2005 symmetric keys can encrypt data at a cell level, meaning different columns and rows can be encrypted using different keys. Although this adds flexibility, it can make it difficult for you to keep track of which keys were used to encrypt table cells and identify the appropriate key required to decrypt them. SQL Server 2005 internally tracks this by prefixing the GUID of the encryption key used to encrypt a cell to the actual cipher text stored within it. Therefore, examining the cipher text will allow you to retrieve the GUID and determine which key was used to encrypt the data. The following syntax can perform the translation for you:

```
SELECT NAME FROM SYS.SYMMETRIC_KEYS
WHERE KEY_GUID = CAST ([CIPHERTEXT] AS uniqueidentifier)
```

In this statement, *CIPHERTEXT* specifies the encrypted data in which to identify the key used to encrypt it.

Replicating Encrypted Stored Procedures, Views, Functions and Triggers

Once stored, procedures, views, functions, or triggers are encrypted and will no longer be published as part of SQL Server replication. Therefore, you must manually replicate any new versions of encrypted objects to your SQL Server replication partners.

Using Endpoint Encryption

SQL Server endpoints are communication channels used to transfer data to and from a SQL Server instance. This data can be prone to eavesdropping, interception, and manipulation attacks, which can result in data disclosure or modification. To prevent this, SQL Server 2005 has encryption features integrated into database endpoints, which can protect data sent over the network. Database endpoints can be configured for Service Broker, Database Mirroring, and Hypertext Transfer Protocol (HTTP) payloads, which each provide unique functionality.

Service Broker

Service Broker is a message-queuing system that manages the messages sent between two SQL Server 2005 endpoints. Within Service Broker, encryption can be applied at both the transport level (network connection) and at the dialog (message/conversation) level.

Transport Level Encryption

When a Service Broker endpoint is created, the encryption option is set at REQUIRED by default. This means that the endpoint will only send encrypted messages, and will refuse all unencrypted network connections. RC4 is the default Service Broker encryption algorithm, and has little performance impact; however, it is a fairly weak algorithm. Alternatively, you can manually configure Service Broker to use the stronger AES algorithm.

The *ENCRYPTION* and *ALGORITHM* arguments can be added to the *CREATE ENDPOINT* and *ALTER ENDPOINT* statements to apply encryption to a Service Broker endpoint. The syntax of the *ENCRYPTION* and *ALGORITHM* arguments is as follows:

```
...
ENCRYPTION = {DISABLED | REQUIRED | SUPPORTED}
ALGORITHM = {RC4 | AES | AES RC4 | RC4 AES}
...
```

Here are definitions of the arguments of this syntax:

- **ENCRYPTION = DISABLED** Specifies that no encryption will be applied to data sent over the network.

- **ENCRYPTION = REQUIRED** Specifies connections to the endpoint must be encrypted and use a supported algorithm.

- **ENCRYPTION = SUPPORTED** Specifies encrypted connections will be used only if supported by the connecting endpoint.

- *ALGORITHM = RC4*   Specifies that endpoint encryption will use the RC4 algorithm.

- *ALGORITHM = AES*   Specifies that endpoint encryption will use the AES algorithm .

- *ALGORITHM = AES RC4*   Specifies that the endpoint will give preference to the AES algorithm during endpoint negotiation; however, RC4-encrypted connections are accepted.

- *ALGORITHM = RC4 AES*   Specifies that the endpoint will give preference to the RC4 algorithm during endpoint negotiation; however, AES encrypted connections are accepted.

You will need the respective *CREATE ENDPOINT* and *ALTER ANY ENDPOINT* permissions to use the *ENCRYPTION* and *ALGORITHM* arguments. The following syntax creates a Service Broker endpoint, which exclusively accepts encrypted RC4 connections:

```
CREATE ENDPOINT SB_EndPoint
  STATE = STARTED
  AS TCP ( LISTENER_PORT = 9999 )
  FOR SERVICE_BROKER
  (AUTHENTICATION = WINDOWS,
  ENCRYPTION = REQUIRED ALGORITHM RC4)
```

To change the encryption properties of an endpoint, you can use the same *ENCRYPTION* and *ALGORITHM* arguments of the *ALTER ENDPOINT* statement. The following syntax replaces the RC4 encryption on our endpoint to the stronger AES algorithm:

```
ALTER ENDPOINT SB_ENDPOINT
  FOR SERVICE_BROKER
  (ENCRYPTION = REQUIRED ALGORITHM AES)
```

Dialog Encryption

The second level of encryption within Service broker encrypts the individual messages sent between service broker endpoints. For any dialog that uses security, *SERVICE_BROKER* encrypts all messages that are sent outside of a SQL Server instance. SQL Server 2005 creates a symmetric session key, which is used to encrypt the contents of the messages sent through *SERVICE_BROKER*. This key remains in the database for the duration of the conversation, and is encrypted using the Database Master Key to protect it from disclosure. Both databases that participate in the service broker communication, are required to have a Database Master Key in order to encrypt the session key. However, *SERVICE_BROKER* conversations that remain within a single database can still successfully occur without having a Database Master Key to encrypt the session key. The *ENCRYPTION* argument of the *BEGIN DIALOG CONVERSATION* statement can be used to add encryption to a dialog conversation:

```
...
ENCRYPTION = {ON | OFF}
...
ENCRYPTION = {ON | OFF}
```

Specifies whether encryption will be applied to messages sent outside of the SQL Server 2005 instance. The following syntax adds encryption to a Service Broker dialog:

```
DECLARE @ConversationHandle UNIQUEIDENTIFIER;
  BEGIN DIALOG CONVERSATION @ConversationHandle
  FROM SERVICE SBEncryptionSVC1
  TO SERVICE 'SBEncryptionSVC2'
  ON CONTRACT SBEncryptionCNT
  WITH ENCRYPTION = ON
```

Mirroring

Encryption can be applied to database mirroring endpoints in the same manner as it is applied to Service Broker endpoints, using the *ENCRYPTION* and *ALGORITHM* arguments of the *CREATE ENDPOINT* and *ALTER ENDPOINT* statements. Database mirroring endpoints support the same encryption algorithms and encryption options as Service Broker endpoints. The following syntax creates a Database Mirroring endpoint, which accepts only encrypted connections using the AES algorithm:

```
CREATE ENDPOINT MR_EndPOINT
  STATE=STARTED
  AS TCP ( LISTENER_PORT = 8888 )
  FOR DATABASE_MIRRORING
    (ROLE = PARTNER,
  AUTHENTICATION = WINDOWS,
  ENCRYPTION = REQUIRED ALGORITHM AES)
```

Setting the encryption requirement of Mirroring Endpoints can be completed no more than one level at a time, meaning, if you are required to change a mirroring endpoint from *DISABLED* to *REQUIRED*, you will need to break this up into two steps. The first step is to set all endpoints from *DISABLED* to *SUPPORTED*, and the second step is changing all endpoints from *SUPPORTED* to *REQUIRED*.

HTTP

Within SQL Server 2005, HTTP endpoints can be encrypted using Secure Socket Layer (SSL) certificates. You can either create a new certificate from the integrated SQL Server certificate authority, or import a certificate from an external certificate authority. To enable encryption on a HTTP endpoint, you can use the *PORTS* argument of the *CREATE ENDPOINT* or *ALTER ENDPOINT* statements:

```
...
PORTS = {CLEAR | SSL}
...
```

In this statement, PORTS = CLEAR specifies that the request should use the HTTP protocol. PORTS = SSL specifies that request should use the HTTPS protocol.

The following syntax creates a new HTTP endpoint which is encrypted by SSL:

```
CREATE ENDPOINT HTTP_EndPOINT
  STATE = STARTED
  AS HTTP (
  AUTHENTICATION = (INTEGRATED),
  PATH = '/sql/httpendpoint',
  PORTS = (SSL))
  FOR SOAP (
  BATCHES = ENABLED,
  WSDL = DEFAULT)
```

If you would like to import a certificate from another CA for use in encryption, the certificate must adhere to strict rules. Please consult SQL Server 2005 Books Online for additional information.

Third-Party Encryption

There are several third-party database encryption applications on the market that can be used to encrypt SQL Server 2005 database data "at rest" and "in flight". A few popular products are DbEncrypt, SecureDB, Defiance DPS, and SQL Shield. Any data encryption products you are considering should use secure algorithms and keys in accordance to industry standards such as the Federal Information Processing Standards (FIPS).

Summary

In this chapter, we've covered the numerous SQL Server 2005 data encryption methods used to encrypt database data both "at-rest" and "in-flight." These encryption methods are often used in combination to develop a sound data encryption strategy. A common approach is to use the speed of symmetric key encryption to encrypt database data, and the strength of asymmetric keys or certificates to protect the symmetric key. The keys, certificates, and pass phrases that you will use to encrypt your data will require careful attention, maintenance, and support in addition to what you normally do to maintain the SQL Server.

Implementing database encryption is a large exercise and can require data type conversions, table schema changes, and/or hardware upgrades. Each encryption method you implement will increase your data protection, but detract from the performance and usability of your database server. The information obtained in this chapter, combined with proper planning, will help you develop and implement the data encryption and key management strategy that provides the correct balance of security, performance, and usability for your organization.

Solutions Fast Track

Data Encryption Explained

- ☑ EFS can be used to provide SQL Server 2005 database wide encryption.

- ☑ Data encryption and decryption can be performed natively within SQL Server 2005, using encryption keys, certificates, and pass phrases.

- ☑ Stored procedures, views, functions, and triggers can be encrypted to protect internal logic from disclosure.

- ☑ Endpoint encryption can encrypt data both at the network level and within a specific dialog conversation.

Frequently Asked Questions

Q: How can you restrict access to encryption keys and certificates?

A: Keys and certificates can be referred to as *cryptographic objects*. Access to these objects can be controlled using SQL Server-based roles and permissions. For further details, please see the SQL Server 2005 Books Online.

Q: How can you size your database to allow for the storage of encrypted data?

A: Depending on the algorithm and key strength used to encrypt data, the cipher text can range from 43 percent to 2,460 percent larger than its plain text equivalent. To size your table columns, you will also need to factor in the length of the plain text column data to be encrypted. Microsoft has developed a script that can calculate the exact length of cipher text based on the plain text values within your database. This script can be downloaded from www.microsoft.com.

Q: Is there a limit on the size of string that can be encrypted?

A: Native SQL Server 2005 encryption supports the encryption of the varbinary data type only. This data type can support a maximum of 8,000 bytes. Even if the cipher text will not be stored in a column, the associated buffer enforces the 8,000-byte limitation. Looking at the average data bloat associated with the 3DES algorithm, you can encrypt a value of roughly 45 bytes before hitting the limit. Cipher text that exceeds 8,000 bytes will need to be split into multiple columns and encryption, and decryption and concatenation functions will need to be handled by application logic.

Q: What's the difference between encryption certificates and asymmetric keys?

A: Both certificates and asymmetric keys encapsulate RSA keys and support identical native key bits. There is no difference in strength of encryption between the two. While certificates were introduced initially, asymmetric keys were later released to allow for the import of cryptographic keys from strong name files and assemblies. An advantage of certificates is that they can be backed up individually where asymmetric keys can only be backed up as part of the full database backup.

Chapter 27

Reporting Services, Analysis Services, and Integration Services

Solutions in this chapter:

- **General SQL Server Best Security Practices**

- **Securing Reporting Services**

- **Securing Analysis Services**

- **Securing Integration Services**

☑ **Summary**

☑ **Solutions Fast Track**

☑ **Frequently Asked Questions**

Introduction

Security must be maintained at every level in an enterprise solution. Each of these three major SQL Server 2005 services (Reporting, Analysis, and Integration) handles security differently in terms of authenticating user accounts, authorizing access to various processing and rendering components, and connecting to the underlying data store. After reading this chapter, you will have gained the essential knowledge to protect your systems and data from unauthorized access.

For Reporting Services, we'll cover role-based security and how to secure reporting resources and define tasks that a user may perform. We'll also cover other techniques for securing reports, including data filtering and data hiding.

For Analysis Services, we'll review how Analysis Services applications are secured. For Integration Services, we'll review how Integration Services "packages" are secured using package-level properties, database roles, operating system permissions, and digital signatures.

You'll also learn that the default security settings can work well under certain circumstances, but there's never one single "best way" for all situations and that understanding the fundamentals is critical to designing a customized solution for your specific environment.

General SQL Server Best Security Practices

Properly securing Reporting, Analysis, and Integration Services requires careful attention to all of the SQL Server security best practices (as described in this book), in addition to standard information technology systems' best practice.

Keep in mind the great importance and legal obligation of strong security. Whether it's intellectual property, personal financial data, or protected health information, there is no "second chance" to make it right *after* the breach has occurred. Furthermore, Federal regulations, such as the Health Insurance Portability and Accountability Act of 1996 (HIPAA) Privacy and Security rules and the Sarbanes-Oxley Act (SOX), which mandates, "Chief information officers are responsible for the security, accuracy, and the reliability of the systems that manage and report the financial data," have introduced a legal aspect into Information Technology (IT) security in addition to just being good common sense.

Best Practices According to Microsoft

- Review the physical and logical isolation, which are at the core of all secure systems.
- The server should be in a physically protected room accessible *only* to authorized personal.
- A locked and monitored computer room with fire/flood detection is typically used.

- Back up all data regularly and store in a secure off-site location.

- Locate a firewall between the server and the Internet.

- Block all traffic, and selectively allow only what is required.

- In a multitier environment, use multiple firewalls to create screened subnets.

- In a Windows domain, configure inside firewalls for Windows Authentication.

- In a Windows domain where all clients are Windows XP and servers are Windows Server 2003, disable NTLM Authentication.

- Do not install SQL Server on a domain controller.

- Run SQL Server services under separate Windows accounts created with least privileges.

- When modifying Windows services, grant only the required permissions.

- Isolating services minimizes the risk that a compromised service could compromise another.

- In a multitier environment, run Web sites and business logic on separate servers.

SOME INDEPENDENT ADVICE

- Only enable services that are being used. Do not enable services "just in case" or "for future use."

- Be sure to test any changes in a non-production environment before moving to production.

Securing Reporting Services

Report security is serious business as reports often expose sensitive data that must be protected. The Reporting Services role-based security model restricts user access based on the user's credentials. By default, Windows Integrated Security (NTLM) is used to identify users, although this is not practical for Internet-based solutions.

SQL Server 2005 Reporting Services (SSRS) is secured by ASP.NET, Internet Information Services (IIS), Windows authentication, and built-in role-based authorization. In a role-based security infrastructure, policies define the tasks each user or group is permitted to perform on a specific item.

Architecture

It's important to understand the Reporting Services architecture of SQL Server 2005 (see Figure 27.1). Application-level security is provided by ASP.NET. Access to the Report Server virtual directory (Web service) and Report Manager Web tool is secured by IIS, which authenticates users to the reporting server. By default, the Reporting Services virtual directories are configured to use Windows Integrated Security (NTLM or Kerberos).

Figure 27.1 SQL Server 2005 Reporting Services Architecture

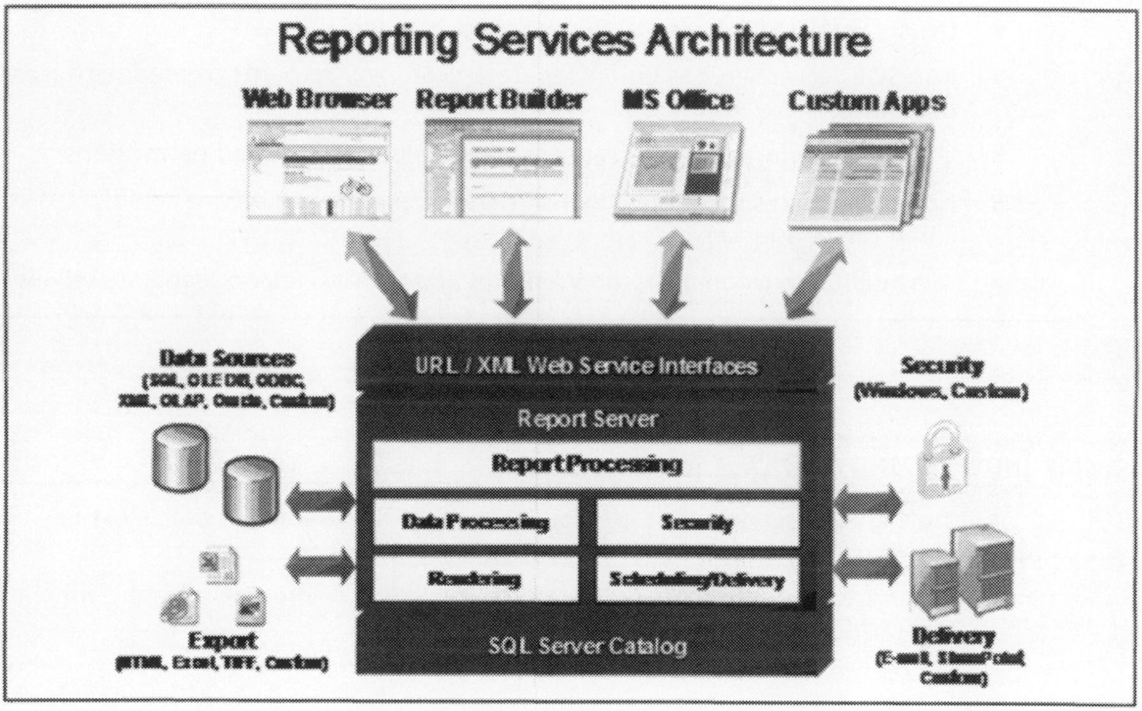

Role-Based Security

Role-based security provides:

- **Authentication**   Authentication establishes a user's identity based on a trusted authority.
- **Authorization**   Authorization determines which tasks the user is permitted to perform.

Reporting Services has a role-based security model that provides authorization for authenticated users. User connections exist in the context of a role that maps user accounts to permitted tasks. During authorization, the Report Server verifies user permissions to run reports based on a security policy established for the user (see Figure 27.2).

Figure 27.2 Role-Based Security Model

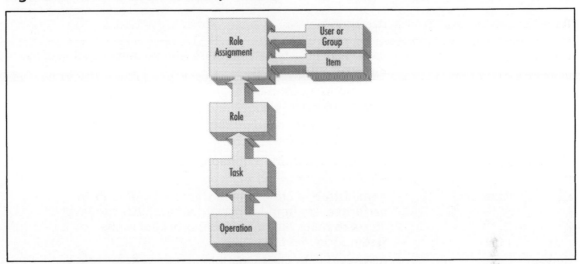

Once a user is authenticated, the user can execute tasks according to authorization rules defined by role membership, which grants or denies access to tasks or resources.

In the role-based security model, tasks are:

- Sets of low-level operations
- Item-level (create report) or system-level (manage jobs) resources
- Not customizable

Roles are:

- Named sets of tasks
- Default roles installed by default (browser, publisher)
- Default roles can be customized, new ones created
- Roles identified by name, localized

Groups/users are:

- Windows/Active Directory or custom authentication users

Role assignments are:

- Associates groups/users with roles
- Inherited from parent in namespace

A SharePoint Integrated Mode maps to WSS Permissions (SP2). The default security roles are described in Table 27.1.

Table 27.1 Reporting Services Default Security Roles

Role	Description
Browser	Users may view reports, folders, and resources and manage their own subscriptions.
My Reports	Automatically creates individually administered report folders for each user.
Publisher	For report authors publishing reports and data sources with Report Designer.
Report Builder	Edit report definitions in Report Builder, view and navigate folders.
Content Manager	Administrators are assigned this role by default to perform every item-level task, but excludes site-level access to items and operations provided in the System Administrator role.
System User	Allows users to view schedule and basic Report Server information.
System Administrator	Provides site-level access to configure features and security, define roles, set defaults, and manage reporting jobs, but excludes item-level tasks provided in the Content Manager role.

Report Management

Report Manager is a Web-based management tool installed and configured by the default SQL Server 2005 installation to provide a simple and secure method to manage reports, data sources, and security (see Figure 27.3).

Figure 27.3 Reporting Services Report Manager

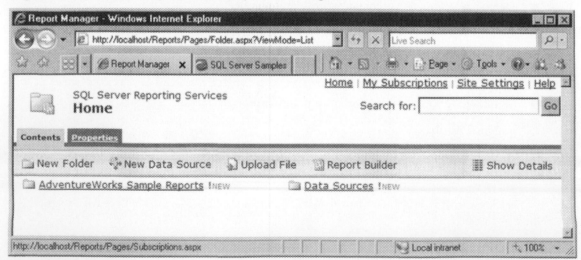

The Report Manager and Report Server Web Service application program interface (API) provide support for the following three common Web authentication methods: Windows Integrated (possibly with delegated or impersonated credentials), Basic, and Anonymous. Note that Anonymous access is generally not recommended, and should only be used along with custom application security to provide authentication to support secure remote administration and other role-based features.

Roles are defined by the tasks for which they provide permission to assigned users or groups. Roles may be created or modified according to the tasks they contain (see Figure 27.4).

Figure 27.4 Report Manager Editing a Role Definition

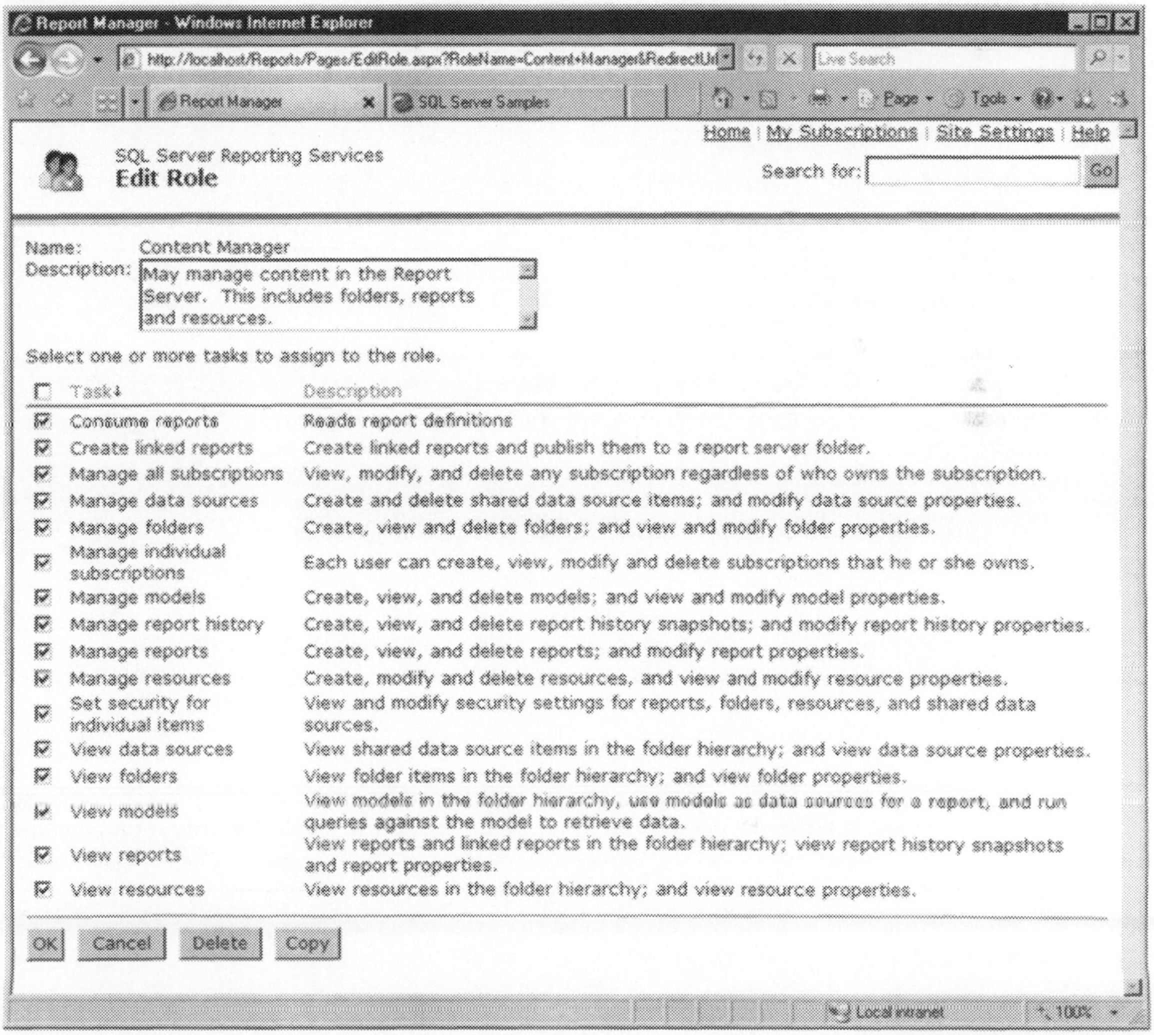

Role assignments determine the set of tasks a user or group is permitted to perform. Users can have membership in multiple roles (see Figure 27.5).

Figure 27.5 Report Manager Editing a Role Assignment for Administrators

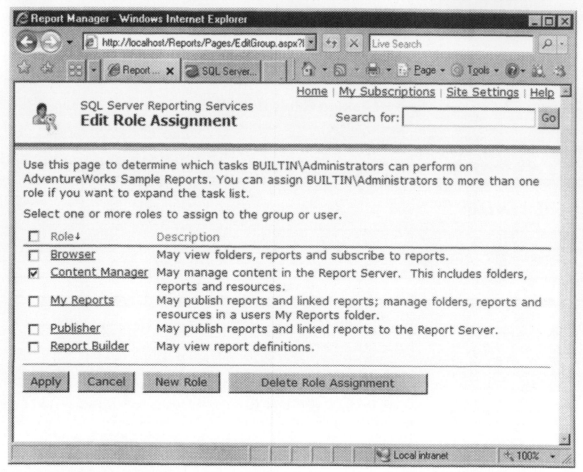

Reporting Services is secure by default and initially "locked down," such that only local machine administrators are permitted to manage the report environment and view reports. This security policy cannot be changed and will, therefore, always allow local administrators to view items and change security policy, even if they're not explicitly defined in a role-based security policy. Naturally, additional roles and policies can be defined.

SSL Data Encryption

Regardless of the authentication and authorization methods used, all data can be secured using Secure Sockets Layer (SSL) encryption of the communication channel. SSL is highly recommended to protect sensitive data transported by Hypertext Transfer Protocol (HTTP). An SSL connection can be selected using the Reporting Services Configuration Manager, or through the configuration setting, SecureConnectionLevel in the *RSReportServer.config* file (located in /Program Files/Microsoft SQL Server/MSSQL.x/Reporting Services/ReportServer).

The range of values are:

- **3** Use SSL for all data
- **2** Use SSL for rendering, but not for all Web Service calls
- **1** Allows non–SSL calls, but requires SSL for calls that are passing credentials
- **0** No SSL

Continued

> Typically, a trusted certificate authority issues digital certificates to identify the data s ource. Digital certificates are most commonly used by Web servers to support SSL, which depend on a "hierarchy of trust" to authenticate the server to the client based on locally stored trusted "root" certificates of the issuing authorities (VeriSign, Thawte, and so on). The server's certificate also provides the keys for encryption of data in the channel after the client accepts the authenticity of the server.

Administration

The Reporting Services installation includes server-side components that must be managed:

- Report Server Windows service to handle scheduling and delivery of reports.
- Report Server Web service providing the main interface for report management and execution.
- Report Server database containing report definitions and security configuration.

To fully administer a Reporting Services installation, you must have the following permissions:

- Membership in the local Administrator group on the report server computer.
- If the installation includes server components running on remote computers, you must also have administrator permissions on those computers to manage by remote connection.
- Database administrator permissions for the SQL Server instance hosting the database.

Managing Service Accounts

Reporting Services is based on a Windows service and Web service for server operations. Like any other service, each run under specific user accounts.

Default Accounts and Initial Configuration

The Report Server Windows service can run under a built-in account or domain user account. The Windows service account is always configured during Setup. SQL Server Setup's Service Account page provides options for selecting a domain user account or the built-in Local System account.

Setup does not allow the Network Service to be specified. To choose the Network Service account, use the Reporting Services Configuration Management tool to modify the service account properties after setup is finished.

Be aware that changing the Report Server Windows service account can affect report server operations. Always use the Reporting Services Configuration Management tool to change a service account. The Configuration tool performs the following three critical steps, ensuring the report server continues to operate:

1. Updates the encryption key to include profile information of the new account.
2. Updates login permissions on the SQL Server Database Engine instance hosting the report server database. If the service accounts are used to connect to the database, SQL Server

login permissions granted to the service accounts require connection information to be updated.

3. Adds new accounts to the report server group created locally, which is specified in the access control lists (ACLs) securing the Reporting Services files.

BEST PRACTICES ACCORDING TO MICROSOFT

Be aware that integrated security may introduce a security threat through an elevation-of-privileges attack if a report that was published contains malicious SQL statements, and is executed under administrator credentials, and the data source is using integrated security or if the user provides administrator credentials.

To mitigate the elevation-of-privileges attack, apply one or more of these security practices:

- Configure report data sources using stored credentials of a least-privilege account for external data.

- Use shared data sources with role assignments to control access to the settings (e.g., connection string, and so on).

- Ensure only trustworthy reports are published to a report server through role assignments restricting publication to specific folders, and require final approval of the newly published report.

- Using the Reporting Services section of the Surface Area Configuration for Features, disable integrated security as a report data source credential option by clearing the Enable Windows integrated security for report data sources check box.

Understand that Reporting Services does not enforce workflow procedures such as report approval prior to publication. This would have to be enforced through other means, policy, or procedure.

SOME INDEPENDENT ADVICE

- Your standard operating procedures must always include security.
- Only enable required services to minimize the attach surface.
- Know the business rules that form the basis of security roles.
- The principle of least privilege always applies.
- Layered security is a key to good defense against attacks.
- User education is an essential component of system security.
- Security configuration settings should be periodically reviewed.

Setting Up Data Sources

Reports, report models, and data-driven subscriptions read data from external sources. Connecting to an external source requires connection information from the report, model, or subscription. The data source properties include the following:

- Data source type
- Connection string
- Credentials

Data source properties may be set at design time or after the report or model is published. Data sources can be managed independently in that they are stand-alone items. While reports, models, and subscriptions specify data source connection information when defined, any user with permission to manage these can modify the data source configuration after being published.

You can use SQL Server Management Studio or Report Manager to modify data source settings on a properties page as follows:

- Configure reports to use shared or report-specific data sources. Report models always use shared data sources.
- Change how credentials are obtained or select a different authentication mode.
- Scheduled reports must use stored credentials, which are used by all users accessing a report. Avoid using accounts that have more permissions than required.
- Modify connection strings.
- Make a data source unavailable for shared data sources.

Providing Credentials for Data Sources

Credentials are used to connect to external data sources providing content to reports. Credentials can use Windows, database, custom, or no authentication. A report server connection request either impersonates a user account or uses the unattended execution account. In addition, credentials may also be used to authenticate users accessing the report server.

A report server connects to the database server to retrieve data for a report using credentials provided at report design time or obtained at run time (see Figure 27.6). The data source credentials can be specified by:

- Stored credentials
- Using Windows integrated security
- Prompting the user for credentials
- Using no credentials

Figure 27.6 Report Manager Editing a Data Source

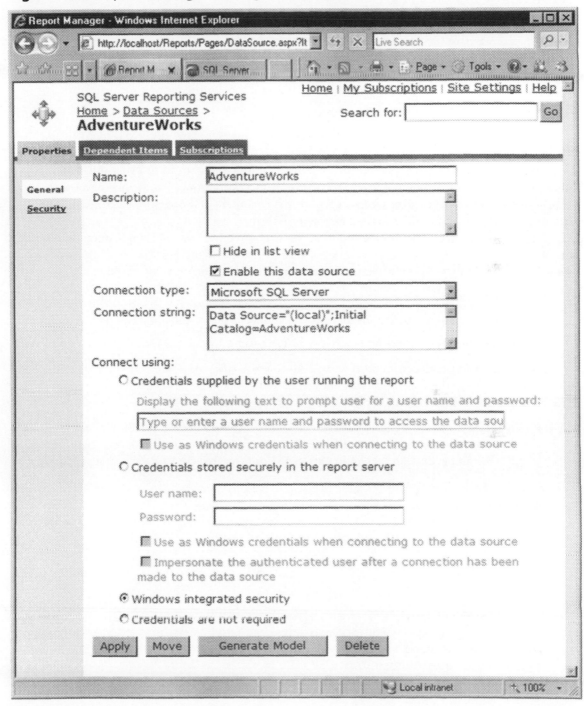

Making Connections

There are three main connections that can be made whenever a user runs a report or a tool that connects to a report server:

- A connection using the user's own Windows domain credentials
- A connection to the report server database
- A connection to other servers

Users typically connect to a report server using their own Windows domain credentials and integrated security.

Forms authentication is supported by creating a custom authentication extension. Basic authentication can also be used if the report server is in a Workgroup. The report server then checks permissions to authorize access to report server content and operations defined in role assignments that describe which tasks a user can perform.

The report server connects to the report server database to retrieve and store content, metadata, and server state. The report server is based on a Web service and Windows service where each service connects to the database. The following account types may be chosen for this purpose:

- Service accounts where each service may run using its own service account.
- Domain account where both services can connect using a single domain user account.
- SQL server login where both services connect using a single database login.

The report server connects to other servers hosting external data. Connections to these data sources are initially defined in the report, but can be independently managed after publishing. The report server gets credentials in one of the following ways:

- Impersonate or use delegated credentials of the user running the report. This requires the report server also be configured for the Windows security extension. If forms authentication or basic authentication is used, impersonated or delegated credentials are not supported.
- Prompt the user to type credentials.
- Retrieve stored credentials from the report server database.
- Use no credentials.

NOTE

SQL Server 2005 Express Edition with Advanced Services requires that report data sources must be SQL Server relational data sources running on the local SQL Server Express Database Engine instance.

Installing Reporting Services

A brief review of installation is useful to ensure understanding of how Reporting Services is installed by default and to consider the security options available during installation.

Typically, enterprise solutions have a distributed architecture over multiple servers. This necessitates creation of multiple domain user accounts to allow SQL Server 2005 to connect with other clients and servers.

Please refer to ReadmeSQL2005.htm and other appropriate documentation about your installation of SQL Server 2005 for specific information to prior to installation. It is very important to carefully review the SQL Server 2005 Books Online topics, "Preparing to Install SQL Server 2005" and "Setting Up Windows Service Accounts" *before* installation.

Our focus here is on the Reporting Services security-related aspects. This procedure assumes attended installation using the setup wizard.

Procedure to Install and Configure Reporting Services Using Default Security

Remote setup is not supported using the *TARGETCOMPUTER* parameter. You must install reporting services using a remote connection running in user interface mode or from the command prompt. IIS must be installed and running prior to installing Reporting Services. Simple Mail Transfer Protocol (SMTP) and File Transfer Protocol (FTP) services are not required; otherwise, use the default IIS configuration.

During installation, the wizard presents this list of components to choose from (see Figure 27.7).

Shortcut...

If ASP.NET was Installed Before IIS

If. Net Framework 2.0 was installed before IIS, you must fix the IIS mappings for ASP.NET. Follow this Microsoft Knowledgebase article (306005), "How to repair IIS mapping after you remove and reinstall IIS" http://support.microsoft.com/default.aspx?scid=kb;en-us;q306005 or uninstall the. Net Framework(s) and simply run the SQL Server 2005 installation. In other words, *always* install IIS before the. Net Framework!

Figure 27.7 SQL Server 2005 Setup Components Selection

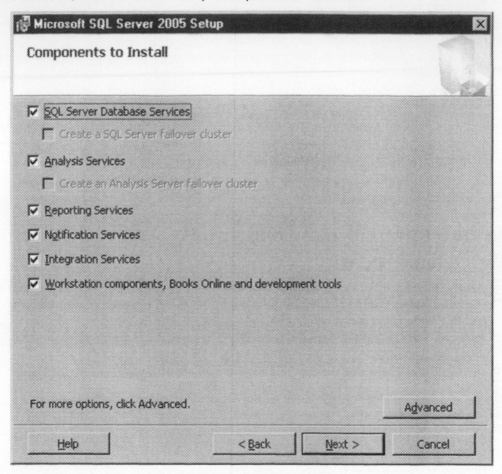

The Advanced button displays the following (see Figure 27.8). Install the default configuration is the default selection to automatically create and configure the Report Manager Web tool and Report Server Web Service.

This default selection generally prevents you from having to run the Reporting Services Configuration Manager after installation is complete, except for backup of encryption keys and some other settings.

Figure 27.8 SQL Server 2005 Setup Report Server Configuration Settings

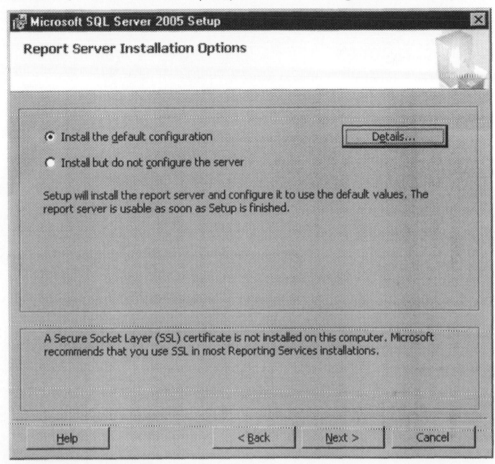

Once complete, reboot to initialize Reporting Services. Initialization creates and stores a symmetric key used for encryption. To test the installation, run Reporting Services Configuration Tool (see Figure 27.9).

From the Start menu, run **All Programs | Microsoft SQL Server 2005 | Configuration Tools | Reporting Services Configuration** or run **C:/Program Files/Microsoft SQL Server/90/Tools/Binn/RSConfigTool.exe**. Configuration should have the following Green Checked status indicators:

1. Server Status (initialized and running)

2. Report Server Virtual Directory

3. Report Manger Virtual Directory

4.   Windows Service Identity

5.   Web Service Identity

6.   Database Setup

7.   Initialization (grayed out)

Figure 27.9 Reporting Services Configuration Manager

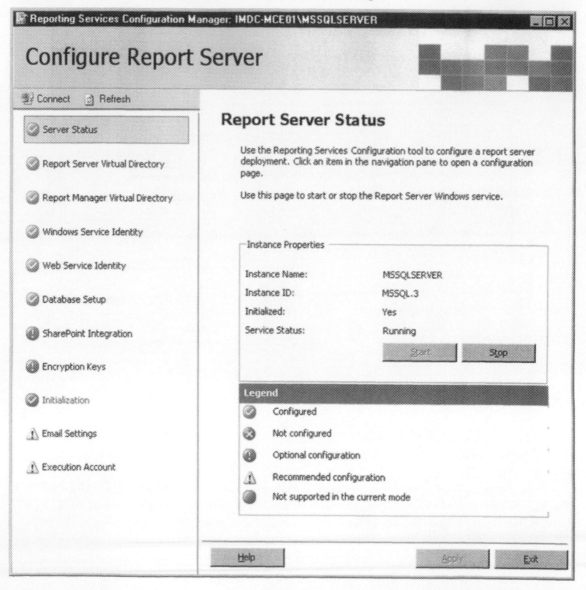

To verify Reporting Services is installed and configured properly, use Web browser and go to http://localhost/Reports. The Report Manager home page should load without error.

Using SQL Server 2005 Management Studio

The view of Management Studio has the default instance of SQL Server connected (which is collapsed) and an instance of Reporting Server in an expanded view with the Adventure Works sample reports deployed. The Adventure Works and Data Sources folders are created when the SQL Server 2005 samples are installed (see Figure 27.10).

Figure 27.10 Management Studio View of Reporting Services

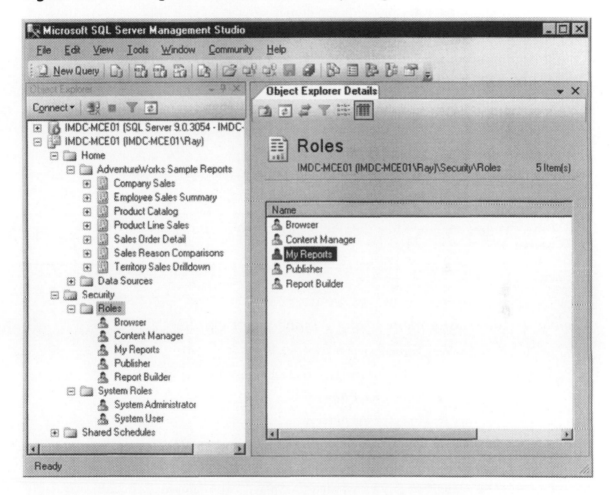

Performing Common Tasks Using SQL Server 2005 Management Studio

Management Studio provides a convenient and familiar way to manage Reporting Services as an alternate to using the Report Manager Web tool, depending on your enterprise security configuration and personal preferences.

Create a Role Assignment Using Management Studio

Follow these steps to create a role assignment using Management Studio:

1. In Object Explorer, expand a report server node.

2. Expand the Home folder, and navigate to the item to set security.

3. Right-click the item, and click **Properties**.

4. From the page selector, click **Permissions**.

5. Select **Use these roles** for each group or user account.

6. Click the **Add Group or User...** button.

7. Type the **account name** of the group or user to create a role assignment.

8. Click **OK**.

9. Select one or more roles for the user or group on the item.

10. Click **OK**.

> **NOTE**
>
> Once changes are made to a child, security settings are no longer inherited from the parent.

Delete a Role Assignment Using Management Studio

1. In Object Explorer, expand a report server node.

2. Expand the Home folder, and navigate to the item to set security.

3. Right-click the item, and click **Properties**.

4. From the page selector, click **Permissions**.

5. Click the group or user whose role assignment is to be deleted.

6. Clear all roles that are currently enabled for the group or user.

7. Click **OK** and **OK** again (after warning) to remove user or group.

Modify a Role Assignment Using Management Studio

1. In Object Explorer, expand a report server node.

2. Expand the Home folder, and navigate to the item to set security.

3. From the page selector, click **Properties**.

4. From the page selector, click **Permissions**.

5. Click the **role assignment** that you want to modify.

6. Select one or more roles for the user or group on the item.

7. Click **OK**.

Shortcut...

Be Sure to Always Reference the Latest SQL Server 2005 Documentation

Microsoft is constantly improving the quality of their documentation. Follow the link to "Technical Reference", then to "SQL Server 2005 Books Online" for the most up to date, detailed reference information.
http://technet.microsoft.com/en-us/sqlserver/default.aspx

If updated, the date of your local Books Online appears in the Help Viewer's title bar, but only when opened from Management Studio, the SQL Server group in the Start menu, or a desktop shortcut. Otherwise, no date is displayed on the original version or if opened from Business Intelligence Development Studio.
http://technet.microsoft.com/en-us/sqlserver/bb428874.aspx

The latest release of SQL Server 2005 Books Online is May 2007 as of the writing of this book.

Using the Report Server Web Service

The Report Server Web Service exposes the full functionality of the report server objects to create custom tools for report management and execution. This provides an API to integrate custom applications and provides functionality extension.

If a deeper level of control is required, several built-in techniques exist for filtering data, querying dynamically, hiding data, and so on. Beyond that, customized security techniques may be employed by leveraging the highly extensible Reporting Services security model.

For complete documentation see Microsoft SQL Server 2005 Books Online and search the index for "ReportingService2005 class".

Example Code: Programmatic Report Deployment and Setting Policies

These code fragments comprise a C# Windows console application using the ReportingService2005 API provided by the Report Server Web Service, and they deploy a report into a newly created folder adding the Browser role for the Users Group. The entire project will be made available to registered book owners at www.syngress.com.

```
internal static ReportingService2005 rs = rsProxy();
internal static ReportingService2005 rsProxy()
{
  ReportingService2005 rsProxy = new ReportingService2005();
  rsProxy.Credentials = System.Net.CredentialCache.DefaultCredentials;
  rsProxy.Url = "http://localhost/ReportServer" + "/ReportService2005.asmx";
  return rsProxy;
}

// Delete Report Folder
rs.DeleteItem(reportFolderPath);

// create application's report folder, set role assignment
rs.CreateFolder(txtFolderPath, "/", null);

// get Browser role object, create new role assignment
Role[] roles = rs.ListRoles(SecurityScopeEnum.Catalog);
Role[] policyRoles = new Role[1];
foreach (Role r in roles)
{
  if (r.Name == "Browser")
  {
    policyRoles[0] = r;
    break;
  }
}

// get current policies of folder
bool inheritParent = false; // read only output, unused
Policy[] currentPolicies = rs.GetPolicies(reportFolderPath,
Out inheritParent);

// create new policy array, add new user
ArrayList arrPolicies = new ArrayList(currentPolicies);
Policy p = new Policy();
p.GroupUserName = groupUserName;
p.Roles = policyRoles;
arrPolicies.Add(p);
// set policies
rs.SetPolicies(
reportFolderPath,(Policy[])arrPolicies.ToArray(typeof(Policy)));
```

```
// CREATE REPORTS
foreach (FileInfo tempfileInfo in fileInfo)
{
  txtReportFileName = tempfileInfo.Name;
  txtReportName = txtReportFileName.Split(new char[] { '.' }, 2)[0];
  // Read the RDL file and convert to byte array
  FileStream stream = tempfileInfo.OpenRead();
  definition = new Byte[stream.Length];
  stream.Read(definition, 0, (int)stream.Length);
  stream.Close();
  // Upload report which uses a "private" (embedded) data source
  warnings = rs.CreateReport(txtReportName, reportFolderPath, true, definition, null);
  // check warnings
  if (warnings == null)
  {
    Console.WriteLine(String.Format("Report: {0} created successfully with no
warnings.", txtReportName));
  }
}
```

Impersonating Users

To impersonate a user, the *web.config* file requires the following elements, attributes, and values:

```
<authentication mode="Windows"></authentication>
<identity impersonate="true"/>
```

The user's identity or a Windows account can then be impersonated. If the trusted subsystem and the Report Server are on separate machines, Kerberos authentication must be enabled to pass the user identity between the machines because NTLM does not support delegation.

Filtering Data

Sensitive data can be filtered at the data source by a parameterized query that matches user or role name based on the built-in User.UserID parameter, which returns the Windows login ID if Windows authentication was used.

Hiding Data

To leverage role-based security to protect sensitive data, use an expression for the Bonus column or chart's Hidden property to hide it if the user is not an authorized Vice President's role member.

```
Hidden = Not Code.IsInRole("VP")
```

This function would be implemented as embedded code in the report.

```
Function IsInRole(ByVal role as String) As Boolean
  Dim winPrincipal As WindowsPrincipal = _
    New WindowsPrincipal(WindowsIdentity.GetCurrent())
  Return winPrincipal.IsInRole(role)
End Function
```

Securing Reporting Services in SharePoint Integrated Mode

When the report server is configured for SharePoint integrated mode, the authentication provider and permissions assigned in the SharePoint Web application control report server access (see Figure 27.11).

Permissions are granted by SharePoint security, which maps accounts to permission levels. The concept is identical to role assignments in Reporting Services, where role assignment maps accounts to permitted tasks performed upon a specific item. As expected, permission inheritance simplifies maintenance.

Figure 27.11 Security in SharePoint Integrated Mode

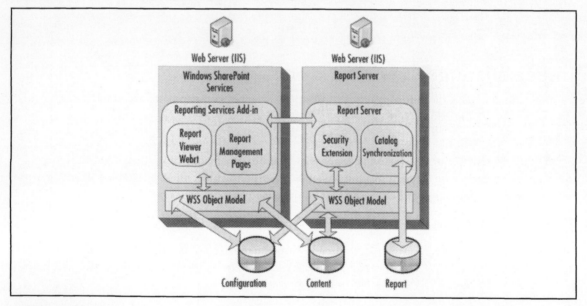

SSL Requirements

Running a report server that is SSL-enabled in SharePoint integrated mode requires that the SharePoint Web application also be configured to use SSL.

SSL on SharePoint is necessary because all report server requests originating from SharePoint are sent through a Reporting Services Uniform Resource Locator (URL) proxy endpoint running within SharePoint, which obtains encryption requirements from the report server. By configuring the SharePoint Web application to use SSL, the endpoint uses SSL.

Install and configure the server certificates on both servers. Using IIS Manager, assign ports and select the **Require secure channel (SSL)** check box on the Web sites accessing the SharePoint Web application and the report server. Assign a unique port if the default port, 443, is used elsewhere on the server.

To configure report server integration in SharePoint Central Administration, specify the report server URL as: httpoi//MyServerName:443/MyReportServerName.

Securing Analysis Services

Securing SQL Server 2005 Analysis Services (SSAS) is a multilevel process. Each instance of Analysis Services and the data sources must be secured to ensure only authorized users have permissions on cubes, dimensions, data sources, and so on. It is essential to prevent unauthorized users from accessing information. Securing Analysis Services is described in the following sections.

Architecture

SQL Server 2005 Analysis Services (SSAS) relies on Windows to authenticate users (see Figure 27.12).

Figure 27.12 Analysis Services Architecture

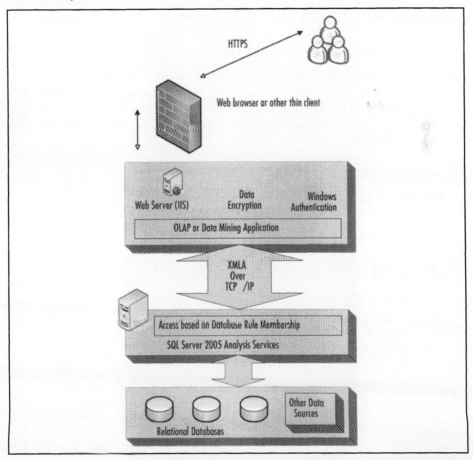

Understanding the Security Architecture of Analysis Services

By default, only authenticated users having SSAS rights can connect. After connection, permissions that users have in SSAS are determined by rights assigned to SSAS roles of which that user has membership, directly or through a Windows role membership.

SSAS contains a fixed server role, which grants permission to members to perform tasks. Users who are not server role members can be made members of a database role. Each database role has a customized permission set allowing user access to data and to perform tasks on that database.

Database role members that have administrator permissions can view or update all data in the database. Other database role members can only view or update data objects to which they have been specifically granted permissions.

SSAS permissions are initially granted at the database level. The role must then be granted specific permissions for each object in the database, such as cube dimensions, dimension members, cubes, cells within a cube, mining structures and models, data sources, and stored procedures.

SSAS encrypts all communication to protect sensitive information from unauthorized use. SSAS features that might possibly compromise security if inappropriately configured or used are disabled by default. Users could be permitted to connect without authentication or submit credentials in clear text, but these features require modification of default settings.

Supporting Unauthenticated Clients

If data security is not a concern, SSAS can allow unauthenticated clients to connect. Using SQL Server 2005 Management Studio, make a connection to an instance of Analysis Services. In the Object Explorer, right-click the SSAS instance and click Properties. On the General page, change the **Security | RequireClientAuthentication** property from a default of true to false to allow unauthenticated clients.

Modifying Encryption Settings

If Internet Information Services (IIS) is used to access SSAS data from the Internet, SSL should be required to protect data. If using a secure intranet connection, encryption may be disabled to increase performance. Please consult the latest Microsoft documentation for this procedure.

Configuring the Logon Account

An appropriate logon account for SSAS and permissions for this account must be specified. Make sure the SSAS logon only has those permissions necessary to perform required tasks. This includes appropriate permissions to the data sources.

SSAS executes some tasks in the security context of the Windows logon account that starts Analysis Services and other tasks under the user who requested the task. Regardless of the security context, SSAS verifies permissions of the user issuing the request, prior to running it.

For tasks that SSAS performs in the context of its logon account, the account must have adequate permissions and rights to perform the tasks. The logon account should not, however, be granted rights not required to perform the expected tasks, as granting excessive rights may pose a potential security threat.

Selecting an Appropriate Logon Account

SSAS may run in the security context of different accounts. However, it is recommended that a domain or local user account be used as the logon account for SSAS. Using a domain or local user account depends on the need to connect to network resources.

- If SSAS needs to connect to network resources using its logon account, SSAS should run under a dedicated domain user account.
- If SSAS does not need to connect to network resources using its logon account, SSAS can run under a local user account or a domain user account.
- Do not use the SSAS logon account for other purposes to protect connection string and password encryption.
- Ensure the logon account has minimal permissions to perform necessary tasks and data source access.

Securing an Instance of Analysis Services

Secure the physical server, operating system, SSAS itself, and the data sources.

The most direct way to access data in SSAS is through the physical computer. If an unauthorized individual obtains physical access to the computer, that individual can potentially access any data stored, regardless of other security measures to secure the data. To prevent this scenario, follow these practices:

- Ensure only authorized individuals have physical access to the computer.
- Disable the floppy-based boot option or remove the floppy disk drive.
- Disable the CD-ROM-based boot option.
- Use a power-on password, and protect the Basic Input Output System (BIOS) settings by using password.
- Use a computer case that locks with a key and provides intrusion detection.
- Store the key safely away from the computer.

The next most effective security measure is securing the operating system and network access:

- Restrict which users have interactive logon access to the computer. SSAS users and administrators don't need local logon to access data or manage SSAS. These users can connect remotely, and therefore require only network access rights.
- Use the Local Security Policy tool to prevent the Domain Users global group from being added to the Users local group when a computer joins a domain, because those domain users have permission to log on interactively to the SSAS computer.

- Rename the default Windows Administrator account and make sure it has a strong password, or allow the Administrator account to exist and remove all access rights, but create a new account to act as administrator to frustrate would-be hackers.
- Make sure that the Windows Guest account is disabled, which is the default.
- Enable strong password policies for the Windows operating system using the Local Security Policy tool. Strong password policy is enabled by default in Windows Server 2003.

Last, but not least, controlling access to the underlying data source is your last line of defense.

SSAS connects to the underlying data through a DataSource object. The security account used is either the user's own security credentials or the user name and password in the connection string stored in the DataSource object.

If unauthorized users access the SSAS data sources, those users can access the same information stored in SSAS. Limit access to these data sources. SSAS users browsing cubes and dimensions do not need permissions on the data sources.

> **WARNING**
>
> If SSAS connects to its data sources using the logon account, members of a database role having Full Control permissions gain access to the data source, regardless of whether that data source is used within that database.

Configuring Access

Set up and define authorized users. Determine which users have administration permissions on database objects, to view definitions, and access to data sources.

In addition to securing the SSAS computer, you must secure SSAS itself, which only permits connections by users who have been authenticated by Windows, unless anonymous connections have been enabled, and who have specifically been granted permissions within SSAS

Be aware that SSAS does not perform its own authentication of users. Analysis Services relies entirely on Windows to authenticate users before authorizing access to SSAS data or allowing users to perform administrative tasks.

By default, the only users who have permissions within Analysis Services are those who are members of the Server role, which has server-level privileges and can perform any SSAS task.

By default, the local Administrators group, including the local Administrator user and all Domain Administrators, become Server role members, and have Full Control permissions on every SSAS instance.

While members of the local Administrators group are members of the Server role, their membership in the Server role is not visible in the user interface.

Securing Integration Services

SSIS security consists of several layers. SSIS security uses package-level properties, database roles, digital signatures, and operating system permissions (see Figure 27.13).

Figure 27.13 Integration Services Architecture

Architecture

SSIS enforces security on the client and server through the following methods:

- The ProtectionLevel of the package specifies if all or part of the package data should either be encrypted using passwords or keys, or removed before saving to protect sensitive data.
- Controlling access to packages using SQL Server database-level roles.
- Protecting file locations and limit package access to secure the operational environment.
- Guarantee the integrity of packages by signing packages with digital certificates.

Protecting Packages

Set the protection level of packages to protect their property values. For example, a package can be encrypted using a password.

An SSIS package protection level can be set in Business Intelligence Development Studio. The package protection level is then updateable in SQL Server Management Studio, or when exported from Business Intelligence Studio (see Table 27.2).

Table 27.2 Integration Services Package Protection Levels

Protection Level	Description
DontSaveSensitive	Sensitive information is not saved in the package, but is replaced with blanks.
EncryptAllWithPassword	Entire package is encrypted using a password.
EncryptAllWithUserKey	Entire package is encrypted using keys from the user profile, where only the same user/profile can load the package
EncryptSensitiveWithPassword	Only sensitive information contained in the package is password-encrypted using Data Protection Application Programming Interface (DPAPI).
EncryptSensitiveWithUserKey	Entire package is encrypted using the current user's keys, where only the same user/profile can load the package. While a different user may open the package, sensitive information is replaced with blanks. DPAPI is used for this encryption.
ServerStorage	Package is encrypted within a SQL Server **msdb** database. Supported only when package is stored in SQL Server. Access is controlled by SQL Server database roles.

Database Roles

There are three fixed database-level roles for SSIS: *db_dtsadmin*, *db_dtsltduser*, and *db_dtsoperator* for access control on packages. Each package can have a reader and a writer role. Custom database-level roles can be defined for SSIS packages. Note that only packages saved to the msdb database in SQL Server can have roles. SQL Server Management Studio allows you to assign roles to a package, which are saved to the msdb database. If user-defined roles are not assigned to packages, access is controlled by the fixed database-level roles.

Storing Packages

SSIS packages can be stored in the file system as XML, with the DTSX file extension, or to the msdb database.

Storing packages to msdb provides server, database, and table-level security. SSIS packages that are saved to the *sysdtspackages90* and *sysdtspackages* tables are backed up when msdb is backed up. If packages are not stored in msdb, be sure to secure the file system folders that contain the package files.

Package Configurations

Package configurations can be stored in the file system or a table in any SQL Server 2005 database as a repository of package configurations. SSIS automatically creates the table with the correct structure for the table that will contain the package configurations. Storing configurations to a table provides server, database, and table-level security.

Packages can be stored in the *sysdtspackages90* table in msdb or in a file on the disk. The package store is monitored and managed by SSIS, and includes the msdb database and file system folders specified in the SSIS configuration file.

SSIS provides the ability to import and export packages, change the storage format and location, and update the protection level to add packages to the file system, package store, or msdb database, and copy from one format to another.

Using SQL Server Management Studio, you can move packages among the following storage types using Import or Export Package commands:

- File system folders located anywhere
- SSIS Package Store folders
- SQL Server msdb database

Shortcut...

DTutil.exe Command Prompt Utility

The *dtutil* utility copies packages to different locations and formats.

Dtutil can also move, delete, or check for existence of packages in any one of the three locations.

Sign a package stored in SQL Server on a local instance using Windows Authentication

dtutil /FILE srcPackage.dtsx /SIGN FILE;destpkg.dtsx;1767832648954389fc9fds819 873a91f919

Encrypt *MyPackage.dtsx* to *MyEncryptedPackage.dts* using full package encryption, with a password, MyPwd,

dtutil /FILE MyPackage.dtsx /ENCRYPT file; MyEncryptedPackage.dtsx;3;MyPwd

Integration Services Folders

Management Studio uses the SQL Server service to enumerate running packages. You must restrict access to computers running a SQL Server service, to prevent unauthorized users from viewing sensitive information.

Package Files

Packages that have been using configurations, checkpoints, and logging, produce information stored outside the package that may be sensitive and should be protected. Checkpoint files can only be stored to the file system, but configurations and logs can be stored in a file or in SQL Server database tables. Configurations and logs stored in SQL Server are protected by SQL Server security, but information contained in files require additional security measures.

Digital Signatures

Packages can be signed with a certificate (digital signature). The package can verify the signature when loaded, issuing a warning if alteration has occurred. Set the Package's CheckSignatureOnLoad property to **True**, which requires the certificate is verified on every load.

Signing a Package with a Digital Signature

Signing prevents loading and running of altered packages. A trusted certificate authority must issue the certificate, which must be specifically created for code signing.

1. In Business Intelligence Development Studio, open an SSIS project.

2. In Solution Explorer, open the package by double-clicking.

3. In SSIS Designer, on the SSIS menu, click Digital Signing.

4. In the Digital Signing dialog box, click Sign.

5. In the Select Certificate dialog box, select a certificate.

6. Click OK to close Select a Certificate.

7. Click OK to close Digital Signing.

8. Save the updated package by clicking Save Selected Items in the File menu.

Summary

SQL Server security can be very complex, requiring various security enforcement techniques on multiple layers of an application. Fortunately, SQL Server 2005 provides many new security features to support robust application design, by reducing the attack surface and supporting security at every layer in today's modern enterprise solutions. This very rich security feature set is designed to be versatile such that applications can be secure by default without great effort, yet scale to support a multiplicity of authentication and authorization techniques based on familiar and proven underlying technologies.

Make no mistake, security is never easy and cannot be left to chance. Entire books have been written on Reporting Services, Analysis Services, and Integration Services, where complete chapters address the topic of security. This book provides a great jumping off point and useful reference, but we encourage you to drill into these topics as necessary, taking advantage of all the great resources available on the Web and in print.

Solutions Fast Track

General SQL Server Best Security Practices

☑ Security requires careful attention to all the SQL Server security best practices, in addition to standard IT systems best practices.

☑ There is a great importance and legal obligation in maintaining strong security. There is no "second chance" to make it right *after* the breach has occurred.

☑ Federal regulations, such as HIPAA and SOX, have introduced a legal aspect into IT security in addition to just being good common sense.

Securing Reporting Services

☑ Application-level security is provided by ASP.NET. Access to the Report Server is secured by IIS.

☑ Reporting Services has a role-based security model that provides authorization for authenticated users.

☑ Roles are defined by the tasks for which they provide permission to assigned users or groups.

☑ Reporting Services is secure by default such that only local machine administrators are permitted to manage the report environment and view reports.

☑ Report Manager is a Web-based management tool installed and configured to provide a simple and secure method to manage reports, data sources, and security.

☑ Management Studio provides a convenient and familiar way to manage Reporting Services.

☑ The Report Server Web Service exposes the full functionality of the report server objects, to create custom tools for report management and execution.

Securing Analysis Services

☑ SSAS is a multilevel process. Each instance of Analysis Services and the data sources must be secured to ensure only authorized users have permissions on cubes, dimensions, data sources, and so on.

☑ SSAS relies on Windows to authenticate users. By default, only authenticated users having SSAS rights can connect.

☑ SSAS contains a fixed server role, which grants permission to members. Users who are not server role members can be made members of a database role.

☑ An appropriate logon account for SSAS and permissions for this account must be specified. Make sure the SSAS logon only has the necessary permissions.

☑ SSAS encrypts all communication to protect sensitive information from unauthorized use.

Securing Integration Services

☑ SSIS security is comprised of package-level properties, database roles, digital signatures, and operating system permissions.

☑ The ProtectionLevel of the package specifies if the package data should either be encrypted using passwords or keys, or removed before saving.

☑ SSIS provides the ability to import and export packages, change the storage format and location, and update the protection level.

Frequently Asked Questions

Q: How does Reporting Services security work?

A: Reporting Services has a role-based security model that provides authorization for authenticated users. User connections exist in the context of a role that maps user accounts to permitted tasks. During authorization, the Report Server verifies user permissions to run reports based on a security policy established for the user.

Q: Which accounts have access to Reporting Services after a default installation?

A: Reporting Services is secure by default, and initially "locked down" such that only local machine administrators are permitted to manage the report environment and view reports. This is to prevent the administrator from being locked out.

Q: For Reporting Services, is Windows Integrated security always the most secure?

A: Generally yes, but integrated security may introduce a security threat through an elevation-of-privileges attack if a report that was published contains malicious SQL statements and is executed under administrator credentials, and the data source is using integrated security or if the user provides administrator credentials.

Q: How does Analysis Services use Windows Authentication to authenticate users?

A: Analysis Services (SSAS) relies on Windows to authenticate users. By default, only authenticated users having SSAS rights can connect. After connection, permissions that users have in SSAS are determined by rights assigned to SSAS roles of which that user has membership, directly or through a Windows role membership.

Q: Doesn't Analysis Services have its own method of authenticating users?

A: SSAS does not perform its own authentication of users. Analysis Services relies entirely on Windows to authenticate users before authorizing access to SSAS data or allowing users to perform administrative tasks.

Q: How does Integration Services handle security?

A: SSIS security uses package-level properties, database roles, digital signatures, and operating system permissions. SSIS enforces security on the client and server through the ProtectionLevel of the package, controlling access to packages using SQL Server database-level roles, protecting file locations and limiting package access to secure the operational environment, and guarantees the integrity of packages by signing packages with digital certificates.

Q: Isn't security difficult and boring?

A: Security can certainly be very difficult, but it's like anything else in terms of learning something new. While it may take some time, the pay off is well worth it. As far as boring, it's much better to avoid the "excitement" of dealing with unauthorized access than having to explain the security breach. Remember, an ounce of prevention is worth a pound of cure!

Index

Printed and bound by CPI Group (UK) Ltd, Croydon, CR0 4YY

07/10/2024

01041741-0001